SQL Server 2012 Data Integration Recipes

Adam Aspin

SQL Server 2012 Data Integration Recipes

ISBN-13 (pbk): 978-1-4302-4791-3

ISBN-13 (electronic): 978-1-4302-4792-0

President and Publisher: Paul Manning
Lead Editor: Jonathan Gennick
Technical Reviewers: Ben Eaton, Robin Dewson and Jason Brimhall
Editorial Board: Steve Anglin, Mark Beckner, Ewan Buckingham, Gary Cornell, Morgan Ertel,
    Jonathan Gennick, Jonathan Hassell, Robert Hutchinson, Michelle Lowman, James Markham,
    Matthew Moodie, Jeff Olson, Jeffrey Pepper, Douglas Pundick, Ben Renow-Clarke,
    Dominic Shakeshaft, Gwenan Spearing, Matt Wade, Tom Welsh
Coordinating Editor: Brigid Duffy
Copy Editor: Kimberly Burton
Compositor: SPi Global
Indexer: SPi Global
Cover Designer: Anna Ishchenko

Distributed to the book trade worldwide by Springer Science+Business Media, LLC., 233 Spring Street, 6th Floor, New York, NY 10013. Phone 1-800-SPRINGER, fax (201) 348-4505, e-mail orders-ny@springer-sbm.com, or visit www.springeronline.com.

For information on translations, please e-mail rights@apress.com, or visit www.apress.com.

Apress and friends of ED books may be purchased in bulk for academic, corporate, or promotional use. eBook versions and licenses are also available for most titles. For more information, reference our Special Bulk Sales–eBook Licensing web page at http://www.apress.com/bulk-sales.

Any source code or other supplementary materials referenced by the author in this text is available to readers at www.apress.com. For detailed information about how to locate your book's source code, go to www.apress.com/source-code.

To the memories of Georges and Colette Mallet.
They taught me more about life than anyone—either before or since, and they showed me
how truly wonderful people can be.

Contents at a Glance

Contents

About the Author

Adam Aspin is an independent Business Intelligence consultant based in the United Kingdom. He has worked with SQL Server for seventeen years. During this time, he has developed several dozen reporting and analytical systems based on the Microsoft BI product suite.

A graduate of Oxford University, Adam began his career in publishing before moving into IT. Databases soon became a passion, and his experience in this arena ranges from dBase to Oracle, and Access to MySQL, with occasional sorties into the world of DB2. He is, however, most at home in the Microsoft universe when using SQL Server Analysis Services, SQL Server Reporting Services, and above all, SQL Server Integration Services.

Business Intelligence has been his principal focus for the last ten years. He has applied his skills for a range of clients, including J.P. Morgan, The Organisation for Economic Co-operation and Development (OECD), Tesco, Centrica, Harrods, Vodafone, Crédit Agricole, Cartier, and EMC Conchango.

Adam has been a frequent contributor to SQLServerCentral.com for several years. He has written numerous articles for various French IT publications. A fluent French speaker, Adam has worked in France and Switzerland for many years.

Contact him at adam@calidra.co.uk.

About the Technical Reviewers

Ben Eaton is an independent consultant based in the Midland counties of England, specialising in business intelligence, software architecture, and application development with the Microsoft stack. Ben began professional development with Microsoft Access in the late 1990s, until he discovered that providing the same end-to-end data management features on an enterprise level required a whole new toolset. Access databases with SQL Server back ends were soon followed by .NET SOA applications and early adoption of Reporting Services. Apart from the odd dabble in SharePoint, he now works with the SQL Server stack (SSIS, SSAS, SSRS) and most of the .NET framework (WCF, WPF, ASP.NET) for a broad range of private and public sector clients.

Jason Brimhall is first and foremost a family man. He has 15+ yrs experience in IT and has worked with SQL Server starting with SQL Server 6.5. He has worked for both large and small companies in varied industries. He has experience in performance tuning, high transaction environments, large environments, and VLDBs. He is currently a DB Architect and an MCITP for SQL 2008. Jason regularly volunteers for PASS and is the VP of the Las Vegas User Group (SSSOLV). You can read more more from Jason on his blog at: `http://jasonbrimhall.info`.

Acknowledgments

Writing a technical book can be a lonely occupation. So I am all the more grateful for the help and encouragement that I have received from so many fabulous friends and colleagues.

Firstly, my considerable thanks go to Jonathan Gennick, the commissioning editor of this book. From my initial contact with Apress through to final publication, Jonathan has been both a tower of strength and an exemplary mentor. He shared his vast experience selflessly and courteously. It is thanks to him that this book has seen the light of day.

Heartfelt thanks goes to Brigid Duffy, the Apress coordinating editor, for managing this book through the publication process. She succeeded in the near-impossible task of making a potentially stress-filled agenda into a journey filled with light and humor. Her team also deserve much praise for their calm under pressure. So thanks to Kimberly Burton for her tireless and subtle work editing and polishing the prose, and also to Dhaneesh Kumar for the hours spent formatting—and reformatting—the text.

When lost in the depths of technical questions, it is easy to lose sight of what should be one's main objectives. Fortunately, the team of technical reviewers—Robin Dewson, Ben Eaton, and Jason Brimhall—have all worked unstintingly to remind me of where the focus should be. All three have placed their considerable experience at my disposal and have enriched the subject matter enormously with their suggestions and comments. Always patient and endlessly helpful, I owe them a deep debt of gratitude. Thank guys!

A penultimate thanks goes to my old friend and colleague Steven Wilbur for his helpful comments on the initial manuscript and his encouragement to persevere in the path to publication when this book was in its initial phase of gestation. Thanks also to Steve Jones at SQLServerCentral.com for encouraging me to write over the years—and for publishing my articles.

However, my deepest gratitude must be reserved for the two people who have given the most to this book. They are my wife and son. Timothy has put up with a mentally absent father for months, while providing continual encouragement to persevere. Karine has given me not only the support and encouragement to continue, but also the love without which nothing would be worth it. I am a very lucky man to have both of them.

Introduction

Microsoft SQL Server 2012 is a vast subject. One part of the ecosystem of this powerful and comprehensive database which has evolved considerably over many years is data integration – or ETL if you want to use another virtually synonymous term. Long gone are the days when BCP was the only available tool to load or export data. Even DTS is now a distant memory. Today the user is spoilt for choice when it comes to the plethora of tools and options available to get data into and out of the Microsoft RDBMS. This book is an attempt to shed some light on many of the ways in which data can be both loaded into SQL Server and sent from it into the outside world. I also try to give some ideas as to which techniques are the most appropriate to use when faced with various different challenges and situations.

This book is not, however, just an SSIS manual. I have a profound respect for this excellent product, but do not believe that it is the "one stop shop" which some developers take it to be. I wanted to show readers that there are frequently alternative technologies which can be applied fruitfully in many ETL scenarios. Indeed my philosophy is that when dealing with data you should always apply the right solution, and never believe that there is only one answer. Consequently this book includes recipes on many of the other tools in the SQL Server universe. Sometimes I have deliberately shown varied ways of dealing with essentially the same challenge. I hope by doing this to arouse your curiosity and also to provide some practical examples of ways to get data from myriad sources into SQL Server databases cleanly and efficiently.

Although this book specifically targets users of SQL Server 2012 I try, wherever feasible, to say if a recipe can be applied to previous versions of the database. I also try and highlight any new features and differences between SQL Server 2012 and older versions. This is because it is unlikely that users will only ever deal with the latest version of this RDBMS, and are likely to have multiple versions in production on most sites. I only ever go back to SQL Server 2005 when pointing out how the database has evolved, as this was the version which introduced SSIS - which was the major turning point in SQL Server-based ETL.

As the book is focused on SQL Server nearly all the code used is T-SQL. Some of the samples given are extremely simple, others are more complex. All of it is concentrated on ETL requirements. Consequently you will find no OLTP or DBA-based examples in this book. You will find a few touches of MDX where handling Analysis Services data is concerned and some VB.Net where SSIS script tasks are used. I have chosen to use VB.Net in nearly all the SSIS script tasks described in this book as it is, in my experience, the .Net language that many T-SQL programmers are most familiar with. Nonetheless I have added one or two snippets of C# (particularly where CLR assemblies are used) to avoid accusations of neglecting this particular language.

Data integration is a vast subject. Consequently, in an attempt to apply a little structure to a potentially enormous and disparate domain, this book is divided into two main parts.

The *first part*—Chapters 1 through 7—deals with the mechanics of getting data into and out of SQL Server. Here you will find the essential details of how to connect to various data sources, and then ingurgitate the data. As many potential pitfalls and traps as possible are brought to your attention for each data source.

The *second part*—Chapters 8 through 15—deal with the wider ETL environment. Here we progress from the nuts and bolts to the coordinated whole of extracting, transforming, and (efficiently) loading data. These chapters take the reader on a trip through the process of metadata analysis, data transformation, profiling source data, logging data processes, and some of the ways of optimizing data loads.

For this book I decided to avoid the ubiquitous AdventureWorks, and use my own sample database. There are a few reasons for this. Firstly, I thought that AdventureWorks was so large and complex that it could divert attention from some of the techniques which I wanted to explain. I prefer to use an extremely simplistic data structure so that the reader is free to focus on the essence of what is being explained, and not the data itself. Secondly I wished to avoid the added complexity of the multiple interrelated tables and foreign keys present in AdventureWorks. Finally I did not want to be using data which took time to load. This way, once again, you can concentrate on process and principle, and not develop "ETL-stare" while you watch a clock ticking as thousands of records churn into a table, accompanied by whirling on-screen images or the blinking of a bleary-eyed hard disk indicator. Consequently I have preferred to use an extremely uncluttered set of source data. A full description of the source database(s) is given in Appendix B.

Please also note that this book is not destined to be a progressive self-tuition manual. You are strongly advised to drop and recreate the sample databases between recipes to ensure a clean environment to test the examples that are given. Indeed the whole philosophy of the recipe-based approach is that you can dip in anywhere to find help, except in the rare cases where there are specific indications that a recipe requires prior reading or builds on a previous explanation.

The recipes in this book cover a wide variety of needs, from the extremely simple to the relatively complex. This is in an attempt to cover as wide a range of subjects as possible. The consequence is that some recipes may seem far too simplistic for certain readers, while others may wonder if the more advanced solutions are relevant to their work. I can only hope that SQL Server beginners will find easy answers and that advanced users will nonetheless find tweaks and suggestions which add to their knowledge. In all cases I sincerely hope that you will find this book useful.

Inevitably, not every question can be answered and not every issue resolved in one book. I truly hope that I have covered many of the essential ETL tasks that you will face, and have provided ways of solving a reasonable number of the problems that you may encounter. My apologies, then, to any reader who does not find the answer to their specific issue, but writing an encyclopaedia was not an option. In any case, I can only encourage you to read recipes other than those that cover the precise subject that interests you, as you may find potential solutions elsewhere in this book.

I wish you good luck in using SQL Server to extract, transform, and load data. And I sincerely hope that you have as much fun with it as I had writing this book.

—Adam Aspin

■ ■ ■

CHAPTER 1

Sourcing Data from MS Office Applications

I suspect that many industrial-strength SQL Server applications have begun life as a much smaller MS Office-based idea, which has then grown and been extended until it has finished as a robust SQL Server application. In any case, two Microsoft Office programs—Excel and Access—are among the most frequently used sources of data for eventual loading into SQL Server. There are many reasons for this, from their sheer ubiquity to the ease with which users can enter data into Access databases and Excel spreadsheets. So it is no wonder that we developers and DBAs spend so much of our time loading data from these sources into SQL Server.

There are a number of ways in which data can be pushed or pulled from MS Office sources into SQL Server. These include:

- Using T-SQL (OPENDATASOURCE and OPENROWSET)

- Linked Servers (yes, an Access database or even an Excel spreadsheet can be a linked server)

- SSIS

- The SQL Server Import Wizard

- The SQL Server Migration Assistant for Access

This chapter examines all these techniques and tries to give you some guidelines on their optimal uses (and inevitable limitations).

Any sample files used in this chapter are found in the C:\SQL2012DIRecipes\CH01 directory—assuming that you have downloaded the samples from the book's companion web site and installed them as described in Appendix B.

1-1. Ensuring Connectivity to Access and Excel
Problem

You want to be able to import data from all versions of Excel and Access (including the latest file formats) in both 32-bit and 64-bit environments.

Solution

You need to install the Microsoft Access Connectivity Engine (ACE) driver. Here are the steps to follow:

1. Click Download on the requisite web page. This will download the executable file to your selected directory.

> ■ **Note** The ACE driver can be found at www.microsoft.com/en-us/download/details.aspx?id=13255. This location could change over time—but a quick Internet search should point you to the current source fast enough.

2. Double-click the AccessDatabaseEngine.exe file that you have downloaded. This will be AccessDatabaseEngine_x64.exe for the 64-bit version.

3. Follow the instructions.

4. In SSMS, expand Server Objects ➤ Linked Servers ➤ Providers.

5. Assuming that the driver installation was successful, you should see the Microsoft.ACE.OLEDB.12.0 provider.

6. Double-click the provider and check Allow InProcess and Dynamic Parameter.

As an alternative to steps 4-6, if you prefer a command-line approach, run the following T-SQL snippet (C:\SQL2012DIRecipes\CH01\SetACEProperties.Sql in the samples for this book):

```
EXECUTE master.dbo.sp_MSset_oledb_prop N'Microsoft.ACE.OLEDB.12.0' , N'AllowInProcess' , 1;
GO
EXECUTE master.dbo.sp_MSset_oledb_prop N'Microsoft.ACE.OLEDB.12.0' , N'DynamicParameters' , 1;
GO
```

You now have the driver installed and ready to use.

How It Works

Before attempting to read data from Excel or Access, it is vital to ensure that the drivers that allow the files to be read are installed on your server. Only the "old" 32-bit Jet driver is currently installed with an SQL Server installation, and that driver has severe limitations. These are principally that it cannot read the latest versions of Access and Excel, and that it will not function in a 64-bit environment.

Using the latest ACE driver generally makes your life much easier, as the newest versions have all the capabilities of the older versions as well as adding extra functionality. Despite being called the "AccessDatabaseEngine," this driver also reads and writes data to Excel files, as well as to text files.

Confusingly, the 2007 Office System Driver and the Microsoft Access Engine 2010 redistributable are both found as "Microsoft.ACE.OLEDB.12.0" in the list of linked server providers in SSMS. The 64-bit SQL Server applications can access to 32-bit Jet and 2007 Office System files by using 32-bit SQL Server Integration Services (SSIS) on 64-bit Windows.

The versions of the Office drivers currently available are listed in Table 1-1.

Table 1-1. *MS Office Drivers*

Driver Title	Driver Name	Source	Comments
OLEDB Provider for Microsoft Jet	Microsoft.Jet. OLEDB.4.0	SQL Server Installation (installed with the client tools)	32-bit only
			Reads and writes Excel & Access 97-2003
			Accepts .xls and .mdb formats
2007 Office System Driver	Microsoft. ACE. OLEDB.12.0	www.microsoft.com/downloads/ thankyou.aspx?familyId= 7554f536-8c28-4598-9b72- ef94e038c891&displayLang=en	32-bit only
			Reads and writes Excel & Access 97-2007
			Accepts .xls/.xlsx/.xslm/.xlsx/ .xlsb and .mdb/.accdb formats
Microsoft Access Engine 2010 redistributable	Microsoft. ACE. OLEDB.12.0	www.microsoft.com/downloads/en/ details.aspx?familyid=C06B8369-60DD- 4B64-A44B-84B371EDE16D&displaylang =en#Instructions	32-bit or 64-bit versions available
			Reads and writes Excel & Access 97-2010
			Accepts .xls/.xlsx/.xslm/.xlsx/. xlsb and .mdb/.accdb formats

Hints, Tips, and Traps

- If you still want to use the old 32-bit Jet driver, then you can do so provided that you save the Excel source in Excel 97–2003 format and are working in a 32-bit environment.

- The ACE drivers are supported by Windows 7; Windows Server 2003 R2, 32-bit x86; Windows Server 2003 R2, x64 editions; Windows Server 2008 R2; Windows Server 2008 with Service Pack 2; Windows Vista with Service Pack 1; and Windows XP with Service Pack 3.

- You can only install **either** the 64-bit version of the ACE driver **or** the 32-bit version on the same server. This means that you cannot develop in Business Intelligence development Studio (BIDS) or SQL Server Development Tools (SSDT) with the 64-bit ACE driver installed—as BIDS/SSDT is a 32-bit environment. However, if you install the 32-bit ACE driver instead, then you cannot run a 64-bit package, and have to use one of the 32-bit workarounds. Ideally, you should develop in a 32-bit environment with the 32-bit ACE driver installed (or on a 64-bit machine, but do not expect to run the package normally), and deploy to a 64-bit environment where the 64-bit driver is ready and waiting.

1-2. Importing Data from Excel
Problem

You want to import data from an Excel spreadsheet as fast and as simply as possible.

Solution

Run the SQL Server Import and Export Wizard and use it to guide you through the import process. Here is the process to follow:

1. In SQL Server Management Studio, right-click a database (preferably the one into which you want the data imported), click Tasks ➤ Import Data (see Figure 1-1).

Figure 1-1. *Launching the Import/Export Wizard from SSMS*

2. Skip the splash screen. The Choose a Data Source screen appears.

3. Select Microsoft Excel as the data Source, and enter or browse for the file to import. Be sure to select the Excel version that corresponds to the type of source file from the pop-up list, and specify if your data includes headers (see Figure 1-2).

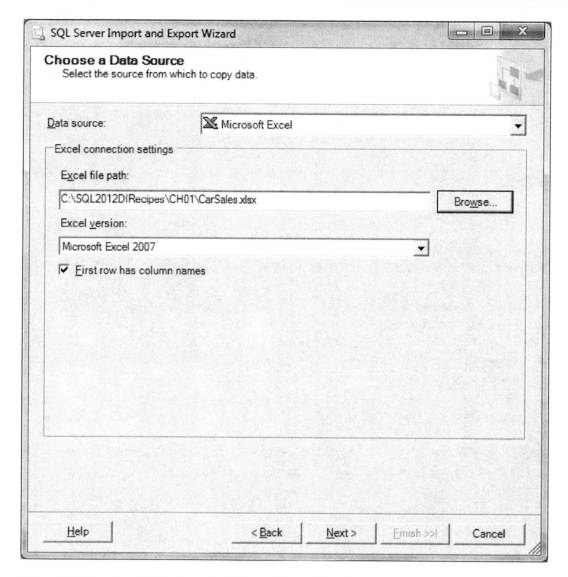

Figure 1-2. *Choosing a Data Source in the Import/Export Wizard*

    4.   Click Next. The Choose a Destination dialog box appears (see Figure 1-3).

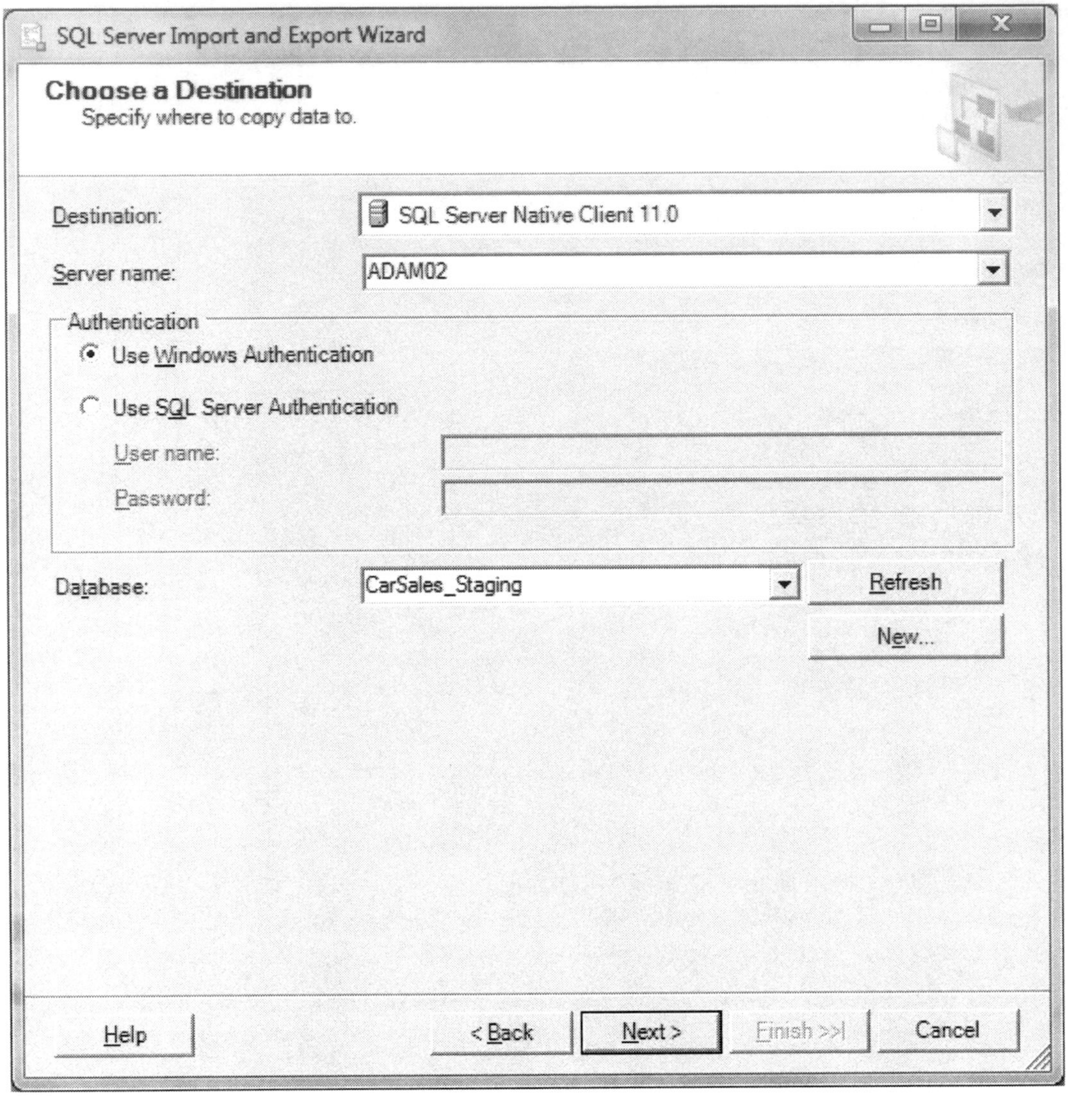

Figure 1-3. Choosing a Destination in the Import/Export Wizard

5. Ensure that the destination is SQL Server Native Client, that the server name is correct, and that you have selected the right destination database (CarSales_Staging in this example) and the authentication mode which you are using (with the appropriate username and password for SQL Server authentication).

6. Click Next. The Specify Table Copy or Query dialog box appears (see Figure 1-4).

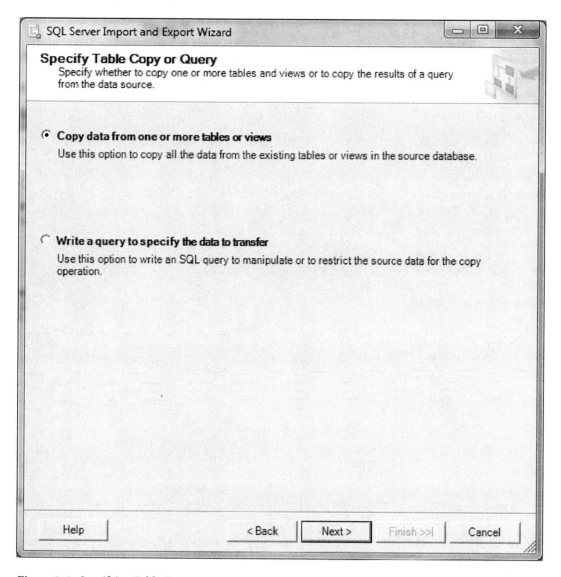

Figure 1-4. *Specifying Table Copy or Query in the Import/Export Wizard*

7. Accept the default "Copy data from one or more tables or views".

8. Click Next. The Select Source Tables or Views dialog box appears (see Figure 1-5).

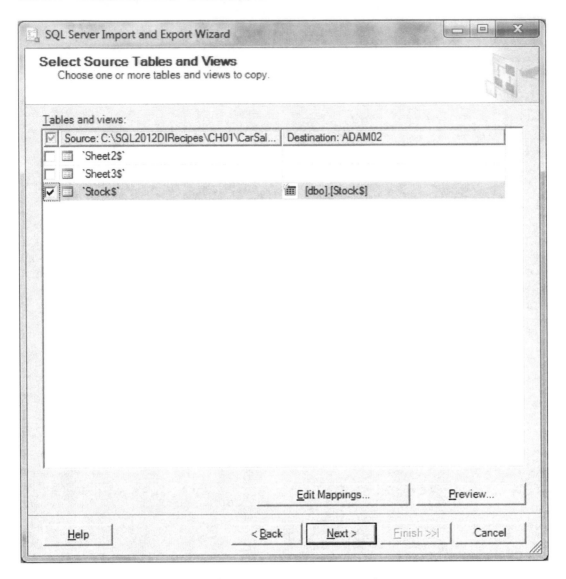

Figure 1-5. *Choosing the Source Table(s) in the Import/Export Wizard*

9. Select the worksheet(s) to import.

10. Click Next. The Save and Run Package dialog box appears (see Figure 1-6).

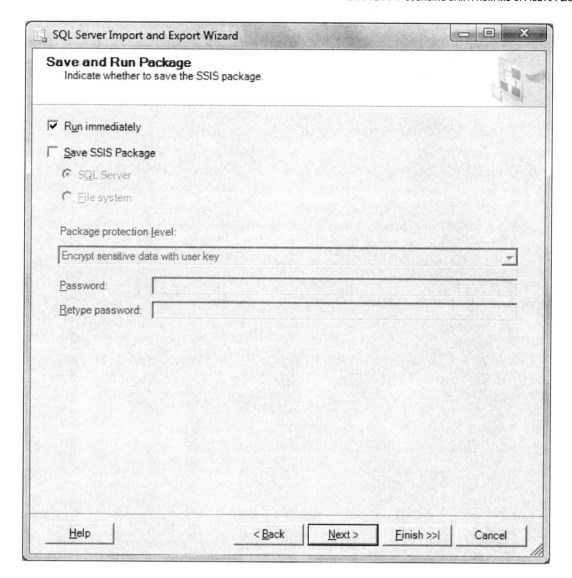

Figure 1-6. *Running the Import/Export Wizard package*

11. Ensure that Run Immediately is checked and that Save SSIS Package is not checked.

12. Click Next. The Complete the Wizard dialog box appears (see Figure 1-7).

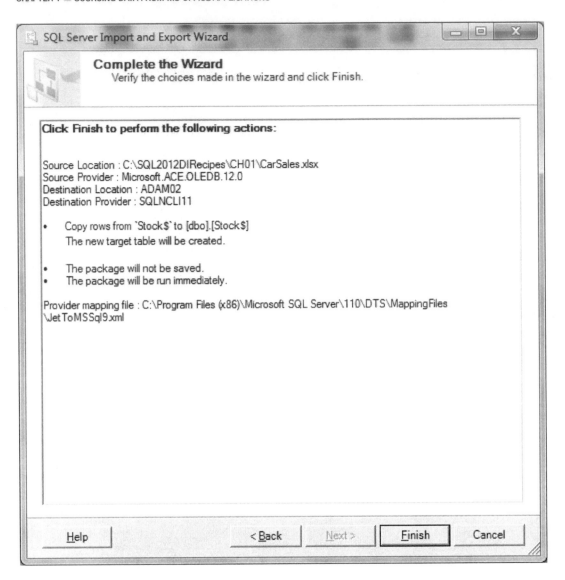

Figure 1-7. *Completing the Import/Export Wizard*

13. Click Finish. The Execution Results dialog box appears. Assuming that all went well, the data has loaded successfully (see Figure 1-8).

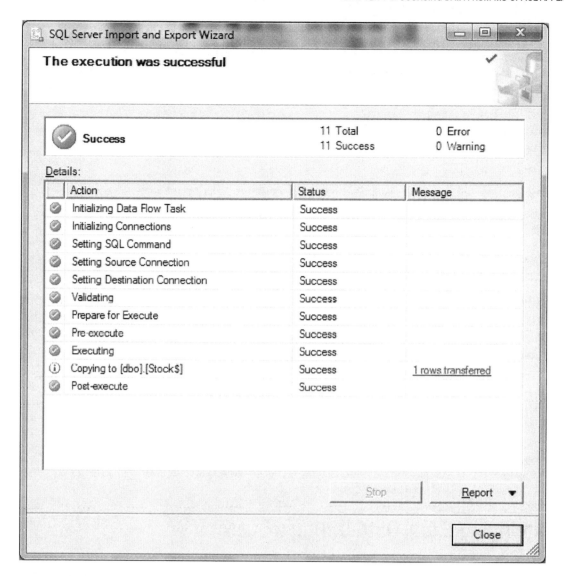

Figure 1-8. *Successful execution using the Import/Export Wizard*

14. Click Close to end the process.

How It Works

There will probably be times when your sole aim is to get a load of data from an Excel spreadsheet into an SQL Server table as fast as possible. Now, when I say "fast," I do not only mean that the time to load is very short, but that the time spent setting up the load process is minimal and that the job gets done without going to the bother of setting up an SSIS package, defining a linked server, or writing T-SQL using OPENROWSET to do the job. This is where the SQL Server Import and Export Wizard (DtsWizard for short) comes into its own. An extra inducement is that the guidance provided by the DtsWizard application can be invaluable if you only import spreadsheet data infrequently.

As this is the first time that the Import and Export Wizard is explained in this book, I have tried to make the explanation as complete as possible. The advantage is that you will find many of the techniques explained here useable for other types of source data, too.

You should use the SQL Server Import and Export Wizard:

- When you need to import data from an Excel spreadsheet into an SQL Server table just once.

- When you do not intend to perform the action regularly or frequently.

- When you rarely import Excel data, you don't want to get lost in the arcane world of SSIS and/or rarely used SQL commands. You want the data imported fast.

- When you want to import data from multiple worksheets or ranges in the same workbook.

Assuming that your Excel data is clean and structured like a data table, then the data will load. It can either be transferred to a new table (or new tables), which are created in the destination database with the same name(s) as the source worksheets, or into existing SQL Server tables. You can decide which of these alternatives you prefer in step 8.

Hints, Tips, and Traps

- If you are working in a 64-bit environment, the 32-bit version of the Import/Export Wizard runs from SSMS. To force the 64-bit version to run, choose Start ➤ All Programs ➤ Microsoft SQL Server 2012 ➤ Import and Export Data (64 bit). Should you need to install the 32-bit version of the wizard, select either Client Tools or SQL Server Data Tools (SSDT) during setup.

- If you plan on using the DtsWizard.exe frequently, add the path to the executable to your system path variable—unless it has already been added.

- You can also launch the SQL Server Import and Export Wizard executable by entering Start ➤ Run ➤ DtsWizard.exe (normally found in C:\Program Files\Microsoft SQL Server\110\DTS\Binn), or by double-clicking on the executable in a Windows Explorer window (or even a command window).

1-3. Modifying Excel Data During a Load

Problem

You want to import data from an Excel spreadsheet, but need to perform a few basic modifications during the import. These could include altering column mapping, changing data types, or choosing the destination table(s), among other things.

Solution

Apply some of the available options of the SQL Server Import and Export Wizard. As we are looking at options for the SQL Server Import and Export Wizard, I will describe them as a series of "mini-recipes," which extend the previous recipe.

■ **Note** Step numbers in the sections to follow refer to the process in Recipe 1-2.

Querying the Source Data

To filter the source data, at step 6, choose the "Write a query to specify the data to transfer"option. You see the dialog box in Figure 1-9.

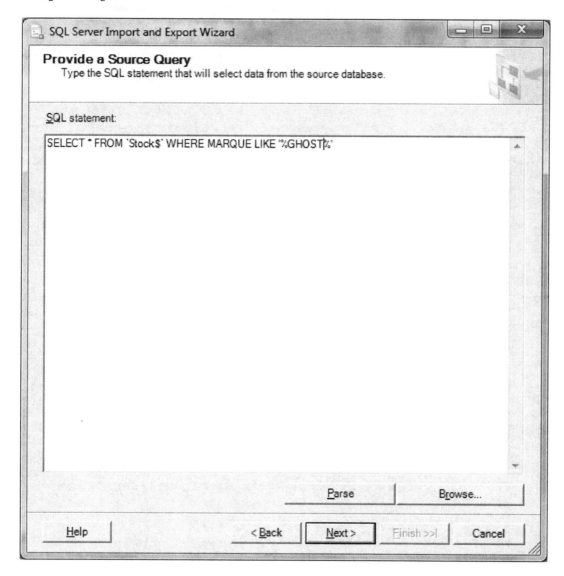

Figure 1-9. *Specifying a source query to select Excel data*

Here you can enter an SQL query to select the source data. If you have a saved an SQL query, you can browse to load it. Note that you use the same kind of syntax as when using OPENROWSET, as described in Recipe 1-4. When writing queries, note that worksheet data sources have a "$" postfix, but ranges do not.

Altering the Destination Table Name

In step 8, you can change the destination table name to override the default worksheet or range name.

Replacing the Data in the Destination Table

Another available option is to replace all the data in the destination table. Of course, this will only affect an existing table—if the table does not exist, then DTSWiz creates one whichever option is selected.

To do this, at step 8 from earlier, click Edit Mappings. The Column Mappings dialog box appears (see Figure 1-10).

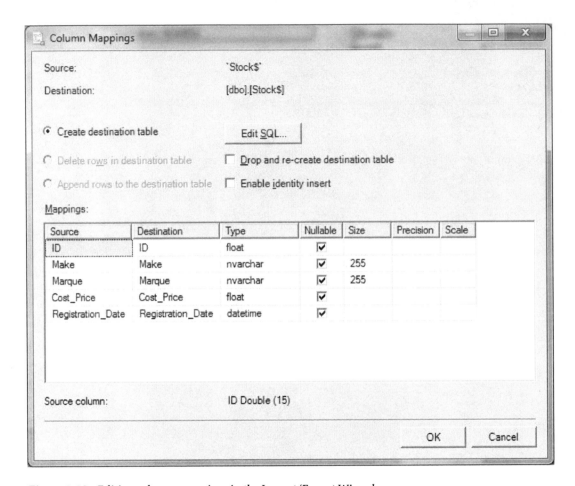

Figure 1-10. *Editing column mappings in the Import/Export Wizard*

Selecting Delete Rows in Destination Table truncates the destination table before inserting the new data. This option is only available if the file exists already.

Enabling Identity Insert

The Column Mappings dialog box (see Figure 1-10) also lets you enable identity insert, and insert values into an SQL Server Identity column. Simply check the "Enable identity insert" check box.

Adjusting Column Mappings

The Column Mappings dialog box also lets you specify which source column maps to which specific destination column. Simply select the required destination column from the pop-up list—or <Ignore> if you do not wish to import the data for a specific column.

Changing Field Types for New Tables

You can—within the permissible limits of data type mappings—change both field types and lengths/sizes. Altering the size of a text field avoids the default 255-character import text field length. Changing the field type modifies the field type during the data load.

If you are creating a new table, then the new table is created with the newly defined field types and sizes. However, be warned, altering data types will not alter the data, and any types or data lengths that you choose must be compatible with the source data, or the load will fail.

Creating an SQL Server Integration Services (SSIS) Package from the Import/Export Wizard

An extremely useful feature of the Import/Export Wizard is the ability to create a fully-fledged SSIS package from the parameters that you have set when configuring your import. This is probably no surprise, as the Import/Export Wizard is, essentially, an SSIS package generator. While the packages that it generates are not perfect, they are a good—and fast—start to an ETL creation process.

To generate the SSIS package, simply check the Save SSIS Package box in the Save and Execute Package dialog box (see step 9, Figure 1-6). You are prompted for a file location. The package is created when you click Finish.

How It Works

Having stressed (I hope) that DtsWizard is a fabulous tool for rapid, simple data imports, I wanted to extend your understanding by showing how versatile a tool the DtsWizard can prove to be in more complex import scenarios. This is due to the wide range of options and parameters that are available to help you to fine-tune Excel imports.

Hints, Tips, and Traps

- If you are using SQL Server 2005, then you will find a couple of minor differences in the Choose a Data Source dialog box shown in Figure 1-2.

- Clicking on any messages in the message column of the final dialog box (see Figure 1-8) is invaluable for getting error messages should there be any problems.

1-4. Specifying the Excel Data to Load During an Ad-Hoc Import

Problem

You want to import only a specific subset of data from an Excel spreadsheet by defining the rows to load or filtering the source data.

Solution

Use SQL Server's OPENROWSET command as part of a SELECT statement. This lets you use standard T-SQL to subset the source data. For example, you can run the following code snippets:

1. In the CarSales_Staging database, create a destination table named LuxuryCars defined as follows (C:\SQL2012DIRecipes\CH01\tblLuxuryCars.Sql):

    ```
    CREATE TABLE dbo.LuxuryCars
    (
        InventoryNumber int NULL,
        VehicleType nvarchar(50) NULL
    ) ;
    GO
    ```

2. Enable remote queries, either by running the Facets/Surface Area Configuration tool (or the Surface Area Configuration tool directly in SQL Server 2005), or running the T-SQL given in the following (C:\SQL2012DIRecipes\CH01\AllowDistributedQueries.Sql):

    ```
    EXECUTE master.dbo.sp_configure 'show advanced options', 1;
    GO
    reconfigure ;
    GO
    EXECUTE master.dbo.sp_configure 'ad hoc distributed queries', 1 ;
    GO
    reconfigure;
    GO
    ```

3. Run the following SQL snippet (C:\SQL2012DIRecipes\CH01\OpendatasourceInsertACE.Sql):

    ```
    INSERT INTO CarSales_Staging.dbo.LuxuryCars (InventoryNumber, VehicleType)
    SELECT CAST(ID AS INT) AS InventoryNumber, LEFT(Marque, 50) AS VehicleType
    FROM OPENDATASOURCE(
    'Microsoft.ACE.OLEDB.12.0',
    'Data Source=C:\SQL2012DIRecipes\CH01\CarSales.xls;Extended Properties=Excel 12.0')...
    Stock$
    WHERE MAKE LIKE '%royce%'
    ORDER BY Marque;
    ```

How It Works

There are times when quick access to the data in an Excel worksheet is all you need. This could be because you need to perform a quick SELECT...INTO or INSERT INTO...SELECT using Excel as the data source. In this case, firing up SSIS—or even running the Import Wizard (see Recipe 1-2)—to load data can seem like overkill. This is where judicious application of SQL Server's OPENDATASOURCE and OPENROWSET commands as part of a SELECT statement can be extremely useful.

Indeed, as you will see shortly, once you know how to connect to the source file, even quite complex T-SQL SELECT statements can be used on Excel source data. And, as you are writing standard SQL commands, they can be run from a query window or as part of a stored procedure. This is particularly useful when:

- You want to read the contents of an Excel worksheet, but don't want to clutter up your database with extra tables of information.

- The data will be read infrequently.

- You know the file (workbook) and worksheet names, and have a good idea of the data structures—in other words, you can open the file to read it.

- When you want to perform ad hoc querying, and choose the columns and filter the data using standard SQL commands.

Without attempting to be exhaustive, there are some variations on this theme. I use either the Jet driver or the ACE driver indiscriminately. I use Excel worksheets in both 97–2003 and 2007–2010 formats because the techniques described works with all these formats. I am not adding INSERT INTO or SELECT ... INTO Code here, but presume that you will be selecting one or the other in a real-world scenario,

---

■ **Note** As this is, after all, an ad-hoc scenario, you could well have to run SSMS in "Administrator" mode – by right-clicking on SQL Server Management Studio from the start menu and selecting "Run as Administrator". This is because the user running SSMS must have read and Write permissions on the TEMP directory used by the SQL Server Startup account.

Assuming that you have a named range (TinyRange in the sample file), then you can return the data in the range using T-SQL like this:

```
SELECT ID, Marque FROM OPENROWSET('Microsoft.Jet.OLEDB.4.0',
   'Excel 8.0;Database=C:\SQL2012DIRecipes\CH01\CarSales.xls', TinyRange);
```

If the range does not contain column headers, then you will need to add the HDR=NO property to the T-SQL, as follows. Otherwise, the first row is presumed to be column headers.

```
SELECT ID, Marque FROM OPENROWSET('Microsoft.Jet.OLEDB.4.0',
   'Excel 8.0;HDR=NO;Database=C:\SQL2012DIRecipes\CH01\CarSales.xls', TinyRange);
```

If you know the Excel range references corresponding to the data that you want to return, then you can use an SQL snippet like this:

```
SELECT ID, Marque FROM OPENROWSET('Microsoft.ACE.OLEDB.12.0',
   'Excel 12.0;Database=C:\SQL2012DIRecipes\CH01\CarSales.xlsx',
 'SELECT * FROM [Stock$A2:B3]');
```

You must remember to provide the worksheet as well as the range, as no default worksheet is presumed. Similarly, remember to add HDR=NO if the range does not contain column headers.

As the previous snippet showed, you can pass an entire SELECT statement via the OLEDB driver to Excel. This presents a whole range of possibilities, such as choosing individual columns. For example:

```
SELECT ID, Marque FROM OPENROWSET('Microsoft.ACE.OLEDB.12.0',
   'Excel 12.0;Database=C:\SQL2012DIRecipes\CH01\CarSales.xlsx',
 'SELECT ID, Marque FROM [Stock$A1:C3]');
```

Just as in a standard T-SQL statement, you can alias the columns returned. For example:

```
SELECT InventoryNumber,VehicleType FROM OPENROWSET('Microsoft.ACE.OLEDB.12.0',
    'Excel 12.0;Database=C:\SQL2012DIRecipes\CH01\CarSales.xlsx',
 'SELECT ID AS InventoryNumber, Marque AS VehicleType FROM [Stock$A2:C3]');
```

The "pass-through" query that you send to Excel can also sort the data that is returned. The following example sorts by Marque:

```
SELECT ID, Marque FROM OPENROWSET('Microsoft.ACE.OLEDB.12.0',
    'Excel 12.0;Database=C:\SQL2012DIRecipes\CH01\CarSales.xlsx',
 'SELECT ID, Marque FROM [Stock$A2:C3] ORDER BY Marque');
```

Finally, if you want to add a WHERE clause, you can do so:

```
SELECT InventoryNumber,VehicleType FROM OPENROWSET('Microsoft.ACE.OLEDB.12.0',
    'Excel 12.0;Database=C:\SQL2012DIRecipes\CH01\CarSales.xlsx',
 'SELECT ID AS InventoryNumber, Marque AS VehicleType
FROM Stock$ WHERE MAKE LIKE ''%royce%'' ORDER BY Marque');
```

In the provider options, you need to check Supports 'Like' Operator for such a sort to work. Note also that you will need to duplicate the single quotes if you are using the LIKE operator.

You might have a source file without headers for the data. In this case, all you need to do is add HDR=NO; to the syntax. In these circumstances, it is probably best to use column aliases to give the output data greater readability, or the OLEDB provider will merely rename all the columns F1, F2, and so forth. For example:

```
SELECT InventoryNumber,VehicleType FROM OPENROWSET('Microsoft.ACE.OLEDB.12.0',
    'Excel 12.0;HDR=NO;Database=C:\SQL2012DIRecipes\CH01\CarSales.xlsx',
 'SELECT F1 AS InventoryNumber, F2 AS VehicleType FROM [Stock$A2:C3] WHERE MAKE LIKE
''%royce%'' ORDER BY Marque');
```

HDR is not the only property that you might need to know about when importing Excel data. Table 1-2 describes your options. Understanding the IMEX (mixed data types) property is also useful in some cases.

Table 1-2. *Jet and ACE Extended Properties*

Property Name	Description	Examples
HDR	Specifies if the first row returned contains headers.	HDR = NO
IMEX	Allows for mixed data types to be imported inside a single column.	IMEX = 1

Extended properties do require further explanation. Here, HDR merely indicates to the driver whether your source data contains header rows. As the presumption (at least using the Jet and ACE drivers) is that there are header rows, setting this property to NO when there are no headers avoids not only having the first record appear as the column names, but also a potential mismatch of data types. It is worth noting that you do not need to specify the Excel file type (.xls/.xlsx/.xslm/.xlsx/.xlsb) as the ACE driver will recognize the file type automatically.

IMEX is marginally trickier. It does not force the data in a column to be imported as text—it forces the mixed data type defined in the registry for this OLEDB driver to be used. As this registry entry is text by default, it nearly always forces the data in as text. It will not convert the data to text. Depending on the driver (that is, when using the Jet driver in most cases), not setting IMEX = 1 can cause a load failure or return NULLs instead of numeric values in a column containing text and numbers.

1-5. Planning for Future Use of a Linked Server

Problem

You want to import only a subset of data from an Excel spreadsheet, but you suspect that you will need to carry out this operation repeatedly, and eventually migrate it to a linked server solution. You do not want to have to rewrite everything further down the line.

Solution

Use SQL Server's OPENDATASOURCE command as part of a SELECT statement. For example, (C:\SQL2012DIRecipes\CH01\OpendatasourceSelect.Sql):

```
SELECT ID AS InventoryNumber, LEFT(Marque,20) AS VehicleType
INTO RollsRoyce
FROM OPENDATASOURCE(
'Microsoft.ACE.OLEDB.12.0',
'Data Source=C:\SQL2012DIRecipes\CH01\CarSales.xls;Extended Properties=Excel 8.0')...Stock$
WHERE MAKE LIKE '%royce%'
ORDER BY Marque;
```

How It Works

The OPENROWSET command is suited to ad hoc querying. However, you may be evaluating data connection possibilities with a view to eventually using a linked server. In this case, you may prefer to use the OPENDATASOURCE command as a kind of "halfway house" to linked servers (described in the next recipe). This sets the scene for you to update your code to replace OPENDATASOURCE with a four-part linked server reference.

Inevitably, there are many variations on this particular theme (which only selects all the data from a source worksheet and uses only the ACE driver), so here are a few of them. As the objective is to import data into SQL Server, I will let you choose whether to include this code in either a SELECT..INTO or an INSERT INTO ...SELECT clause. Of course, you can use the Jet driver if you prefer. If you are using Excel 2007/2010, you must set the extended properties in the T-SQL to Excel 12.0.

```
SELECT ID, Marque FROM OPENDATASOURCE(
'Microsoft.ACE.OLEDB.12.0',
'Data Source=C:\SQL2012DIRecipes\CH01\CarSales.xlsx;Extended Properties=Excel 12.0')...Stock$;
```

To select all the data in a named range, use the following T-SQL:

```
SELECT ID, Marque
FROM OPENDATASOURCE(
'Microsoft.ACE.OLEDB.12.0',
'Data Source=C:\SQL2012DIRecipes\CH01\CarSales.xls;Extended Properties=Excel 8.0')... TinyRange;
```

To select—and if you wish alias—columns in the Excel source data, use T-SQL like in the following. Note that this is applied to the T-SQL, and is not part of a pass-through query.

```
SELECT ID AS InventoryNumber, Marque AS VehicleType
FROM OPENDATASOURCE(
'Microsoft.ACE.OLEDB.12.0',
'Data Source=C:\SQL2012DIRecipes\CH01\CarSales.xls;Extended Properties=Excel 8.0')...Stock$;
```

Finally, to use WHERE and ORDER BY when returning Excel data, merely extend the T-SQL like this:

```
SELECT ID AS InventoryNumber, Marque AS VehicleType
FROM OPENDATASOURCE(
'Microsoft.ACE.OLEDB.12.0',
'Data Source=C:\SQL2012DIRecipes\CH01\CarSales.xls;Extended Properties=Excel 8.0')...Stock$
WHERE MAKE LIKE '%royce%'
ORDER BY Marque;
```

In this case, the Excel file must not be password-protected. It is worth noting that OPENDATASOURCE only works when the DisallowAdhocAccess registry option is explicitly set to 0 for the specified provider, and the Ad Hoc Distributed Queries advanced configuration option is enabled as described in Recipe 1-3. OPENDATASOURCE also expects the source data to resemble a table complete with header rows, so ensure that any named ranges have a header row.

Whether using ACE for Office 2007 or for Office 2010, you must set the Excel version to 12.0—not 14.0 as the download page suggests. Also, if you are using the Jet driver when connecting to Excel (and Access), these approaches will not work in a 64- bit environment in SQL Server (2005-2012), even if the Excel format is 97–2003. If you have to use a driver that causes problems when there are mixed data types in a column, then you can force the driver to scan a larger number of rows (the default is 8)—or indeed the entire worksheet—to test for mixed data types. To do this, edit the following registry setting:

```
HKEY_LOCAL_MACHINE\Software\Microsoft\Jet\4.0\Engines\Excel\TypeGuessRows
```

Setting this value to a figure other than 8 scans that number of rows. Setting it to 0 scans the entire sheet. This, however, inevitably causes a severe performance hit.

Should you wish to alter the mixed data setting, it is in the following registry hive for Office 2010:

```
HKEY_LOCAL_MACHINE\Software\Microsoft\Office\14.0\Access Connectivity Engine\Engines\Excel\
ImportMixedTypes
```

The usual caveats apply to changing registry settings: back up your registry first, and be very careful!

Hints, Tips, and Traps

- An error message along the lines of *"Msg 7314, Level 16, State 1, Line 2 The OLE DB provider "Microsoft.Jet.OLEDB.4.0" for linked server "(null)" does not contain the table "Sheet1$".* "Either the table does not exist or the current user does not have permissions on that file or folder. It could also mean that you have not specified the right file and/or path.

- An error message such as *"Msg 7399, Level 16, State 1, Line 4 The OLE DB provider "Microsoft.Jet.OLEDB.4.0" for linked server "(null)" reported an error. The provider did not give any information about the error. Msg 7303, Level 16, State 1, Line 4 Cannot initialize the data source object of OLE DB provider "Microsoft.Jet.OLEDB.4.0" for linked server "(null)".* " This could very well mean that the Excel workbook file is open, thus it cannot be opened by SQL Server. All you have to do is close the Excel Workbook. Alternatively there could be a permissions problem - are you running SSMS as an Administrator?

- The Excel file must not be password-protected.

- If all you get back is a NULL value (with a column header of F1), then you probably have not specified the correct worksheet name.

- You cannot use UNC paths in ad hoc queries.

- For permissions on folders used by Jet, see http://support.microsoft.com/kb/296711/EN-US

1-6. Reading Data Automatically from an Excel Worksheet

Problem

You need to be able to query or import data directly from an Excel spreadsheet without (re)loading data every time.

Solution

Configure the Excel spreadsheet as a linked server. This is how to do it:

1. Define the linked server using the following code snippet
   (C:\SQL2012DIRecipes\CH01\AddExcelLinkedServer.Sql):

   ```
   EXECUTEmaster.dbo.sp_addlinkedserver
   @SERVER = 'Excel'
   ,@SRVPRODUCT = 'ACE 12.0'
   ,@PROVIDER = 'Microsoft.ACE.OLEDB.12.0'
   ,@DATASRC = 'C:\SQL2012DIRecipes\CH01\CarSales.xlsx'
   ,@PROVSTR = 'Excel 12.0';
   ```

2. Query the source data, only using the linked server name and worksheet (or range)
   name in four-part notation using a T-SQL snippet like
   (C:\SQL2012DIRecipes\CH01\SelectEXcelLinkedServer.Sql):

   ```
   SELECT ID, Marque
   INTO XLLinkedLoad
   FROM Excel...Stock$;
   ```

How It Works

There are occasions when data in an Excel worksheet is used as a quasi-permanent source of data, yet you do not want to import the data, but prefer to leave it in Excel. To handle this you might need to set up a linked server to an Excel spreadsheet. The advantage to this approach is that the syntax used to query the data is the standard four-part notation used with any linked server (Server.Database.Schema.Table), and that all the configuration information is defined once for the linked server itself, and not every time that a query is used, as is the case with OPENROWSET and OPENDATASOURCE. This is particularly useful in the following situations:

- When you need to return data from an Excel spreadsheet on a regular basis.

- When you feel that spreadsheet data is sufficiently trusted to be a reliable source for your application.

The risk with this approach is the same that you face with all spreadsheet data— it is all too frequently incoherent, erroneous, or just plain wrong because human error introduced the wrong data into the wrong cells. Because no automated process can obviate such errors, there is no process that can alleviate the problem. If the Excel file can be trusted to be sufficiently accurate, then this technique can be a great way to allow SQL Server to read Excel data without having to reload the file every time that it is modified, because all that has to be done is to drop the Excel workbook into the required directory. Moreover, there are a few tricks that you might find useful when dealing with Excel linked servers.

Before using a linked server, you can test the server to see if it works using the following system-stored procedure:

```
EXECUTE master.dbo.sp_testlinkedserver Excel2
```

This returns a "Command completed successfully" if all works—and an error message if there is a problem. Unfortunately, the error messages can be somewhat cryptic, so be prepared to be patient when deciphering them.

To alter the connection to an Excel linked server, you are, in most cases, better off dropping the old linked server and re-creating. The following is the code to drop the linked server:

```
IF EXISTS (SELECT name FROM sys.servers
WHERE server_id != 0 AND name = 'Excel')
EXECUTE master.dbo.sp_dropserver @server='Excel';
```

To list the available worksheets and named ranges for an Excel linked server, use the following system-stored procedure:

```
EXECUTE master.dbo.sp_tables_ex EXCEL;
```

For a more visual representation of the data ranges available via your linked server, you can use SQL Server Management studio. All you have to do is expand Server Objects ➤ Linked Servers ➤ (Server Name) ➤ Catalogs ➤ Default ➤ Tables, as shown in Figure 1-11.

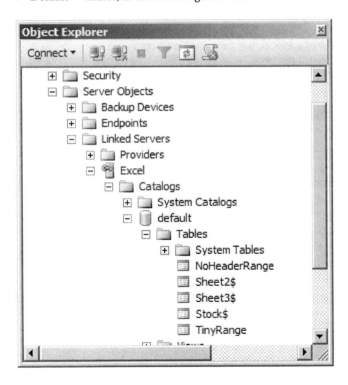

Figure 1-11. *Excel linked server tables*

To load data into a destination table, you can use both INSERT INTO...SELECT and SELECT...INTO—as you would expect for what is, after all, standard T-SQL.

A linked server assumes that the dataset contains a header row. However, an Excellinked server (unlike OPENDATASOURCE) accepts named ranges without a header row. Should this be the case in your data set, then be sure to add HDR=NO in the @PROVSTR argument of the sp_addlinkedserver command. This sets the column names to F1, F2, and so forth. So if some of your source ranges have header rows and others do not, you will have to set up two linked servers, one with HDR = NO and the other with HDR = YES. Also, you need to be aware that a linked server to an Excel spreadsheet is extremely slow, and that if you are reusing the data in your ETL process, then loading it into a staging table is probably a lot faster overall.

Querying the data uses a standard T-SQL SELECT query, and you can restrict the selection using specified column names (or F1, F2, and so forth, if there is no header row), a WHERE clause, ORDER BY, and so on. This means that you can also use CAST and CONVERT to change data types, and all the usual text functions (LTRIM, RTRIM, and LEFT spring to mind) to apply elementary data manipulation to text fields. As I gave plenty of examples of this in Recipes 1-4 and 1-5, I refer you back to those recipes for more details on this.

Hints, Tips, and Traps

- Be sure to set the provider to the ACE or Jet connection string. You also have to set the @PROVSTR argument to Excel 8.0 (for Jet) or Excel 12.0 (for ACE).

- The @SRVPRODUCT argument is purely decorative.

- The Excel file need not exist when the linked server is defined.

- You can see the linked server by expanding Server Objects/Linked Servers in SSMS. Double-click the linked server name in SSMS to view the properties which you set using the sp_addlinkedserver command.

- You can also define a linked server using SSMS. This is described (for Access) in Recipe 1-13. The principles are virtually identical, however.

- The Excel source file must not be password-protected.

- Note that you do not need either a schema or a database reference in the four-part notation. Just type in the three periods.

- If the Excel workbook contains multiple data sets (either as separate worksheets or named ranges), then you, in effect, only have to configure the connection once (by setting up the linked server. You can then query the various source data sets merely by altering the worksheet/range name that is the final part of the four-part notation in the SELECT query (Stock$ in this example).

1-7. Loading Excel Data as Part of a Structured ETL Process

Problem

You want to perform industrial-strength data loads from an Excel workbook. This will be performed regularly as part of a controlled ETL process.

Solution

Create an SSIS package to load the Excel source data. This opens all the power and flexibility of Microsoft's principal ETL tool to manage your data loads.

If you are a seasoned SSIS professional, you may well be used to the process described in this recipe, and indeed may have your own ways of carrying out the package creation process. In which case, feel free to jump ahead because this recipe targets readers who may not be fully conversant with SSIS.

1.   Create a new SSIS package.

2.   Add a Data Flow task onto the Control Flow area.

3.   Double-click the Data Flow task to jump to the Data Flow pane.

4.   Add an Excel Source onto the Data Flow area.

5.   Double-click the Excel Source task to open the Excel Source Editor. Click New to open the Excel Connection Manager dialog box.

6.   Click Browse and select your Excel source file.

7.   Select the Excel version corresponding to the version of the Excel workbook (.xls for Excel 97–2003, .xlsx for Excel 2007/2010). You should see something similar to Figure 1-12.

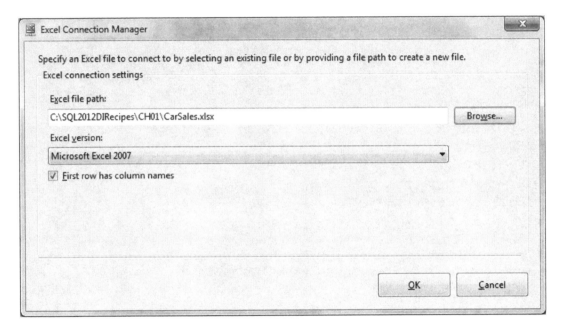

Figure 1-12. *Excel Connection Manager*

8.   Click OK. You return to the Excel Source Editor dialog box.

9.   Select the Excel worksheet or range containing the data that you wish to import from the "Name of the Excel sheet:" pop-up, as shown in Figure 1-13.

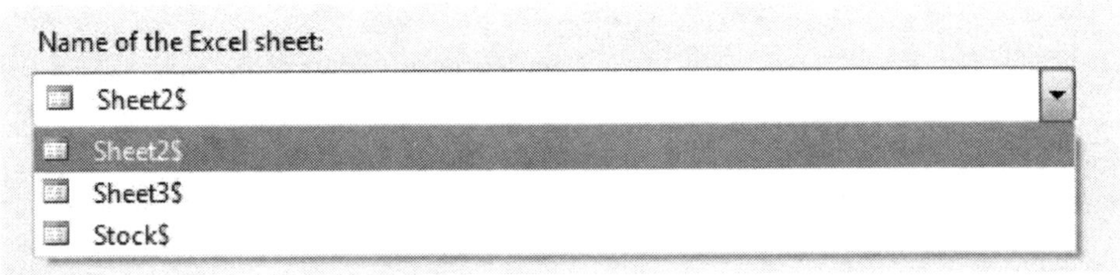

Figure 1-13. *Selecting the Excel worksheet to load in SSIS*

10. Click OK to return to the Data Flow pane.

11. Add an OLEDB destination task to the Data Flow pane, preferably under the Excel source task.

12. Drag the green connection (or Precedence Constraint as it is called) from the Excel Source task to the OLEDB destination task.

13. Double-click the OLEDB destination task to open the OLEDB Destination Editor. Click New to create a new OLEDB Connection, and then click New again to specify the connection manager.

14. Select or enter the server name, and then select or type the database name. I am using CarSales_Staging in this example. You should see a dialog box as shown in Figure 1-14.

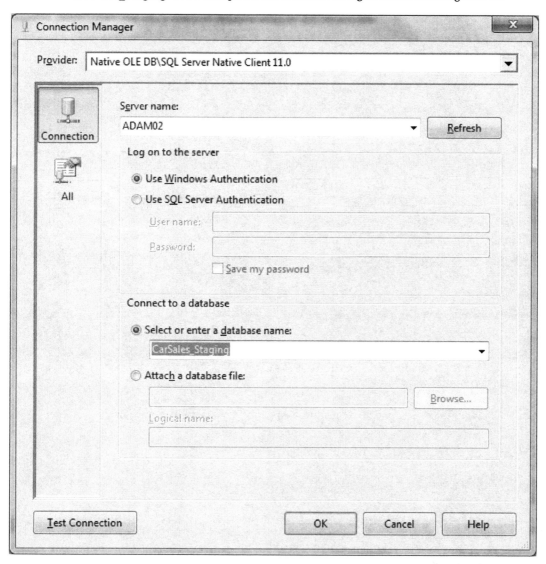

Figure 1-14. *Destination connection manager in SSIS*

15.   Click OK twice to return to the OLEDB Destination Editor. Then select the name of an existing destination table, or click New to create a new table. You can change the table name (if you so wish). If you have created a new table, click OK to finish this step. You should see something like Figure 1-15.

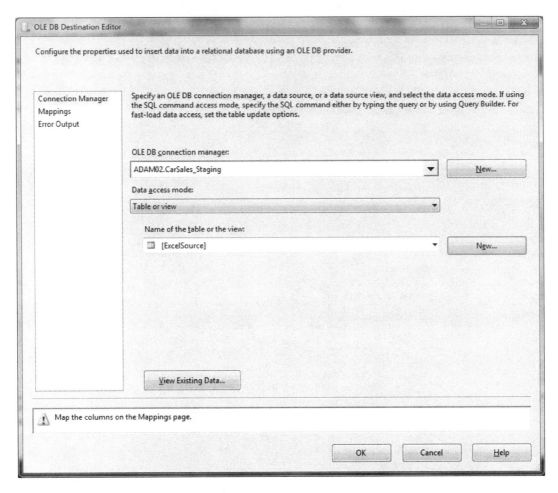

Figure 1-15. *SSIS destination task for Excel import*

16.   Click Mappings to create the input to output mappings. Drag columns from left to right to map. Click Delete to remove mappings.

17.   Click OK to finish configuring the OLEDB destination.

18.   Run the package by either pressing F5 or clicking the green Start Debugging triangle in the Standard toolbar. Or, select Debug ➤ Start Debugging from the menu.

How It Works

For regular imports or when you need the full power of an ETL tool to schedule and process data into SQL Server, SSIS is the tool to use. This recipe uses the SSIS Excel source to connect to an Excel workbook. It then loads the data from the selected worksheet into an SQL Server destination table using the OLEDB destination component.

Hints, Tips, and Traps

- If you prefer, you can create the OLEDB destination connection manager before adding the OLEDB destination. Then all you have to do is to select it from the list of available connection managers in theOLEDB Destination Editor dialog box. In SSIS 2012, this could be a package-level connection manager.

- If your destination table exists, you can select it from the list of those appearing in the Name of the Table or View.

- If you prefer, you can create the Excel connection manager before adding the data Flow task. You can even create package-level connection managers (in SSIS 2012). However in my experience, this is rarely useful for the essentially "single use" connection managers that are used with spreadsheet sources.

- If the Excel worksheet is filtered, then SSIS will only import the filtered data, not the entire range or worksheet.

1-8. Importing Excel 2007/2010 Data Using SSIS 2005

Problem

You want to import Excel data from an Excel 2007 or 2010 workbook, which cannot be read natively by SQL Server 2005.

Solution

Use the ACE driver and tweak the connection manager extended properties to allow it to read the more modern format.

Importing Excel 2007 worksheets using SSIS 2005 is very similar to the process described in Recipe 1-7. You need to be aware of a couple of tweaks, however, which are required to make it work properly. So here they are:

1. As for ad hoc queries or linked servers using Excel 2007 or above, you must first download the 2007/2010 Office System driver (the ACE driver described at the start of the chapter).

2. In step 4, use an OLEDB data flow source, not an Excel source.

3. Configure the Microsoft.ACE.OLEDB.12 as the data source (provider: Microsoft Office 12.0 Access Database Engine). The Connection Manager dialog box should look something like Figure 1-16.

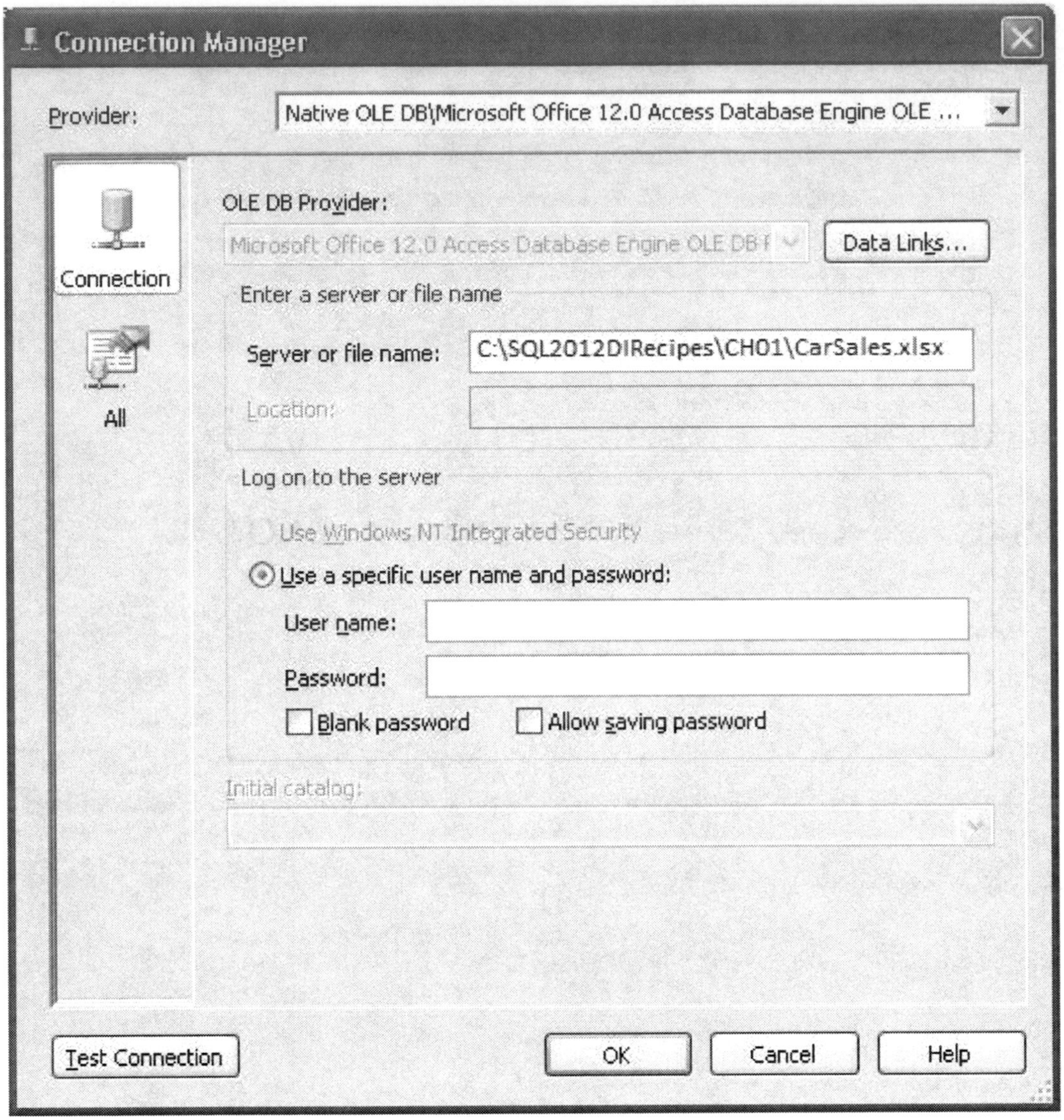

Figure 1-16. *Excel 2007/2010 data source in SSIS 2005*

    4.   Click All in the left pane. Enter **Excel 12.0** for the Extended Properties, as shown in Figure 1-17.

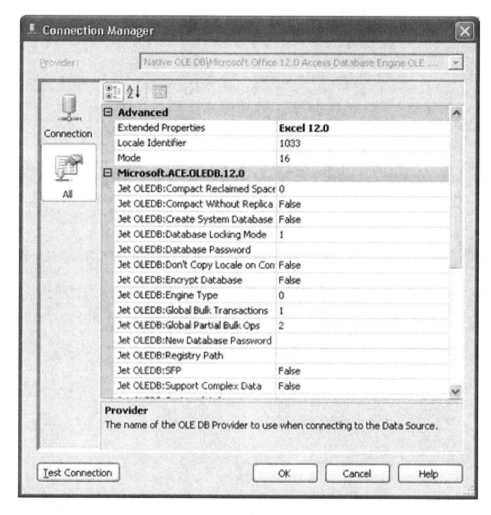

Figure 1-17. Extended Properties for Importing Excel 2007/2010 in SSIS 2005

You can now run the package and import the spreadsheet data.

How It Works

Instead of using the Excel data source in SSIS, you choose the OLEDB source. This is then configured to use the ACE provider.

Hints, Tips, and Traps

- Excel 2007 is not limited to 65,536 rows, as is the case with earlier versions, so you can import correspondingly larger amounts of data. However, the time taken by SSIS to validate this data can be prohibitive when designing a package in BIDS/SSDT—unless you display the properties for the OLEDB data flow source and then set ValidateExternalMetadata to False, as shown in Figure 1-18.

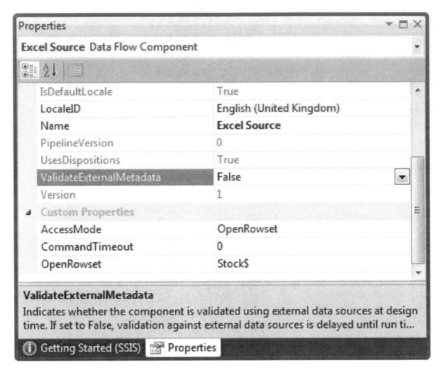

Figure 1-18. *Delayed validation*

- You can alter the registry entry that SSIS uses to guess the data type of an Excel 2007 column using the following registry key:

  `HKEY_LOCAL_MACHINE\Software\Microsoft\Office\12.0\Access Connectivity Engine\Engines\Excel\TypeGuessRows.`

Setting this to 0 forces SSIS to read every row for each column; otherwise, you can alter the default of 8 to strike a happy medium between incorrectly guessing the data type and long minutes spent waiting for SSIS to finish parsing the spreadsheet.

1-9. Handling Source Data Issues When Importing Excel Worksheets Using SSIS

Problem

You have data in Excel files that are failing to load due to truncation errors or that cannot be mapped to destination columns due to data type errors.

Solution

Tweak the standard SSIS Excel source properties to handle tricky source data issues. Here are some techniques that you can use:

1. In the Data Flow pane of SSIS, right-click the Excel source task and select Show Advanced Editor.

2. Select the Input and Output Parameters tab, and expand Output Columns. Then click the column whose column length you wish to change. This is shown in Figure 1-19.

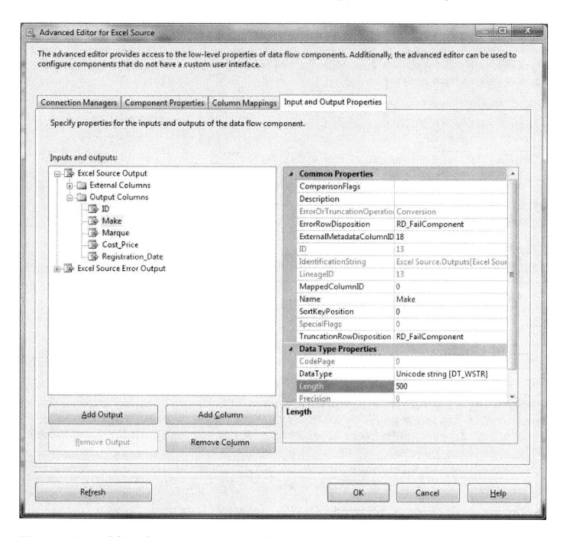

Figure 1-19. *Modifying datasource types in Excel*

3. Select Unicode String [DT_WSTR] and enter a length (500 in this example). Of course, the columns will be those of your source data.

4. Confirm by clicking OK.

5. Add a Data Conversion task to the Data Flow pane and connect the Excel Source task to it. Then double-click the Data Conversion task to edit it.

6. Select the output column that you modified in step 3, and specify that the output data type is String [DT_STR], with the length you require.

How It Works

When the Excel worksheet is simple, you probably do not need to make many tweaks to an SSIS import package. However, there could be times when you need to "coerce" SSIS to import the source data correctly. Specifically, you mayoccasionally need to specify the length of the data in a column imported from Excel. This is because the old Excel 255-character limit on the amount of data that a cell could hold has been lifted for some time now. Indeed, SSIS detects cells containing more than this character amount (if they are in the first "n" rows specified using the TypeGuessRows Registry setting).

There are occasions when you will have to adjust some of the standard settings in order to:

- Import text longer than 255 characters by selecting Unicode Text Stream [DT_NTEXT] to specify text more than 255 characters in the Input and Output properties of the Excel Source.

- Specify a different source data type.

- Convert Excel Unicode data into non-Unicode text data using a Data Conversion task.

Should you wish, you could override Excel's choice of source data to force a data type conversion. The available conversions are shown in Table 1-3.

Table 1-3. *Excel to SSIS Data Type Mapping*

Excel Data Type	SSIS Type Name	SSIS Data Type
Date:	Date	[DT_DATE]
Short Text:	Unicode String	[DT_WSTR]
Number:	Double precision float	[DTR8]
Long Text:	Unicode Text Stream	[DT_NTEXT]

In step 3 of this recipe, select any of these data types from the Input and Output Properties tab for the field you wish to change. Excel data is read as Unicode, and try as you might, you cannot specify that it is otherwise (for instance, by changing the source data type). So you have to convert the data from Unicode to a non-Unicode string using the SSIS Data Conversion task. You can do this as follows

1. Add a Data Conversion task to the Data Flow pane and connect the Excel Source task to it. Then double-click the Data Conversion task to edit it.

2. Select the input column that you modified in step 3, and specify that the output data type is String [DT_STR] with the length you require.

3. Confirm with OK.

Hints, Tips, and Traps

- You will need to handle Unicode character conversion errors by configuring the error output. At the very least, set the Data Conversion to ignore errors.

- It is not possible to select any other source types, and attempting to do so results in a variety of errors.

- As Excel source data (at least when generated by end-users) can be full of errors, it is a good idea to include some error handling. There is an introduction to this in Chapter 15.

- You cannot specify a Unicode string and merely change the length parameter; SSIS will revert to text stream.

1-10. Pushing Access Data into SQL Server

Problem

You want to transfer some or all the tables in an Access database into SQL Server directly from Access itself.

Solution

Use the Access Upsizing Wizard, which you can run from inside Access as follows:

1. From Access 2007/2010/2013 Activate the Database Tools ribbon, click SQL Server. (From Access 2000 or Access XP, click Tools ➤ Database Utilities ➤ Upsizing Wizard).

2. Click Use Existing Database, and then Next.

3. Select an ODBC driver that you have created, or configure a new one at this point as described in Recipe 6-12, and then click OK.

4. Select the table(s) you wish to import, add them to the Export to SQL Server pane using the Chevron buttons, and then click Next.

5. Uncheck all the table attributes to upsize, and "No, never" for the "Add timestamp fields to tables" pop-up. Then click Next.

6. Select "No application changes". Click Next and then Finish.

7. Close the upgrade report.

8. If you now switch to SSMS, you can see the results of the upsizing process—and the real work refactoring the database can begin!

How It Works

The Access Upsizing Wizard is a venerable tool that has been around for at least 15 years to my knowledge (possibly more, but I cannot remember exactly). Despite its simplicity and extreme slowness, it is a tried and trusted solution that works well for small data loads and RAD development where small to medium-sized data transfers from Access into SQL Server are all that is required.

Here, I am *only* considering using this tool to transfer into SQL Server. I am *not* looking at application conversion because this area is a matter of considerable divergence of opinion. Fortunately, many products and books and papers exist on this subject, so I will leave you to consult them while I avoid the field completely, and stick to this book's subject matter—data ingestion into SQL Server.

That said, in my experience with upsizing Access databases, the real problem is not anything technical at all, but is all too often the lack of proper database design in the source Access database. All too frequently, third normal form is a distant dream in databases drawn up over time by end users and/or enthusiastic amateurs. This can be accompanied by the total lack of a coherent naming convention for source tables and fields, and redundant, duplicated, or superfluous data. In other words, you can be dealing with vast amounts of rubbish masquerading as a database. So attempting to re-create the same mess only bigger and faster is to miss the point, which is that you should perhaps be seizing the opportunity to redesign the database and clean up the data. However, even if this is the case, at some point you will have to transfer data from Access to SQL Server. So, to remain resolutely positive, the Upsizing Wizard can most likely help you in the following situations:

- When the source data is simple and without complex data structures.

- When the source data is not extensive.

- When you want a quick transfer of most—or all—of an Access database into SQL Server to handle the data structures and the data itself.

The Access Upsizing Wizard can fail. The keys to a successful upsizing process are to do the following:

- Work on a copy of the source database.

- Alter all table and field names in the copy of the source database to conform to SQL standards (remember to remove any special characters and possibly apostrophes)—and use your SQL Server naming convention.

- Do not transfer indexes, validation rules, defaults, and referential integrity—re-create these in SQL Server. At the very least, you will be able to define constraint names using your own naming convention. These areas seem to cause the Upsizing Wizard to fail most often, in my experience. This mostly seems due to missing defaults or foreign key relationships.

The Upsizing Wizard converts Microsoft Access primary keys to Microsoft SQL Server nonclustered, unique indexes and sets them as primary keys in SQL Server. Removing primary keys from Access tables lets you specify the index type (clustered, for instance, sorts in TempDB and other SQL Server index settings) and a Primary Key constraint.

Hints, Tips, and Traps

- You can create a new database during the process; but for greater control over where the database files are created, and to define database properties precisely, it is probably wiser to create the destination database first.

- To upgrade data from a view, run a "create table" query in Access to create a table based on the view first, and then upsize the resulting table.

- Note that you can use the Upsizing Wizard to create table structures, and transfer the data once you have tweaked and perfected the tables using SSIS. This approach also lets you move tables to a schema other than dbo—the default for the Upsizing Wizard.

- Autoincrement fields are not transferred as IDENTITY fields in SQL Server, but as INTs, so you have to modify your SQL Server table structure to specify identity fields.

- Upsizing the OLE object keeps OLE image data as an OLE object—remember, this is not the binary image data!

- Hyperlink fields are transferred as text fields.

- To avoid date overflow errors with SQL Server 2008 and above, ensure that you are using DATETIME2 fields.

- When upsizing data to SQL Server 2005, you frequently see overflow errors. In this case, query the source data in Access to ensure that any Access date fields do not contain data outside the SQL Server date ranges (January 1, 1753, through December 31, 9999). A good initial workaround is to set all dates greater than the upper limit (31 Dec 9999) and dates less than the lower limit (1 Jan 1753) using an Access query before attempting the conversion.

- When importing large data sets, you can get timeouts. To resolve this, use the Registry editor to set HKEY_LOCAL_MACHINE\Software\Microsoft\Jet\4.0\Engines\ ODBC\QueryTimeout to 0 (for Access 97 to 2003) and HKEY_LOCAL_MACHINE\Software\Microsoft\Office\12.0\Access Connectivity Engine\Engines\ODBC QueryTimeout for Access 2007–2010.

- If you have databases from earlier versions of Access, open and save the databases in Access 97 or a later version. See the Office Online web site for information about converting Access databases.

1-11. Importing Multiple Access Tables

Problem

You want to import as quickly and easily one or more tables from an Access database. This is destined to be a one-off operation.

Solution

Use the SQL Server Import Wizard. Here is how:

1. In SQL Server Management Studio, right-click a database (preferably the one into which you want the data imported). Click Tasks ➤ Import Data. Alternatively, you can run this from Start-All programs ➤ Microsoft SQL Server 2012 ➤ Import and Export Data (32-bit or 64-bit). The Choose a Data Source window appears.

2. Select Microsoft Access (Microsoft Access Database Engine).

3. Browse to the source file, and click OK.

4. Select the destination server and database, and the authentication type, specifying the user and password if you are not using Windows authentication. Click Next. The Specify Table Copy or Query window appears.

5. Accept the default Copy Data from one or more tables or views. Click Next. The Select Source Tables or Views dialog box appears.

6. Select the tables and/or views to import. Click Next. The Save and Execute Package dialog box appears.

7. Click Next. The Complete the Wizard dialog box appears.

8. Click Finish. The Execution results dialog box appears.

How It Works

For Access (as was the case with Excel), there are occasions when you want to import data from an Access database into SQL Server table(s) quickly and efficiently, without setting up an SSIS package to do the job. Here too, the Data Import Wizard is one of the best tools for the job. Be warned that importing data and metadata will probably not avoid a lot of refactoring work. This approach is probably most practicable when you need to import data from Access into SQL Server only occasionally, or when the objective is an initial analysis of the data.

As the screenshots for an Access import are virtually identical to those given in Recipe 1-2 for importing Excel data using the SQL Server Import Wizard, I have not reproduced the same ones here. Also, as when importing data from Excel, you can specify a range of parameters and options to fine-tune the import process. To recapitulate, these include:

- Enabling identity insert
- Replacing the data in the destination table

- Specifying data types
- Column mapping

A couple techniques were not outlined previously that you may find interesting,however. These are:

- Creating a new database
- Querying the source data

Creating a new database while importing Access data is as easy as clicking the New button in the Choose a Destination dialog box, and then entering a database name. You get some choice of database properties that you can define, as shown in Figure 1-20.

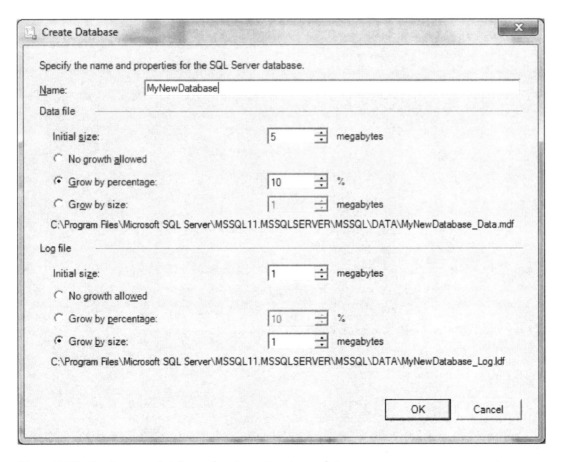

Figure 1-20. *Create a new database when importing Access data*

Querying the source data lets you write SQL to select the data from a table (or a series of joined tables) and filter the source data using a WHERE clause if you so desire. Unfortunately, you need to write the query in full to do this because there is no query generator built into the Import Wizard. Fortunately, there is a handy workaround for this:

1. At step 4, select "Write a query to specify the data transfer".

2. In the source Access database, create a new Access query. Join the tables you wish to query. Add your source columns and any criteria, sorting, and column aliases.

3. Click View/SQL View from the Design ribbon in Access 2007/2010 to display the SQL for the query.

4. Copy and paste the SQL into the Provide a Source Query dialog box of the SQL Server Import Wizard.

Hints, Tips, and Traps

- The Parse button of the "Provide a source query" dialog box validates your Access-based SQL.

- As was the case with Excel, you can define column properties when creating a new table as part of the import. This can be useful to get round defaults such as the 255-character specification for all text fields.

- If you need to specify datafile names or disk locations, you are better off creating the database manually first.

- As is the case with the Upsizing Wizard, dates outside the SQL Server 2005 date data type range can cause problems, so it is advised to use a query to set all dates greater than the upper limit to 31 Dec 9999 and dates less than the lower limit to 1 Jan 1753 before attempting the conversion. Or use the DATETIME2 data type in SQL Server 2008 and above.

- An old alternative technique when faced with troublesome dates in the source data is to map Access date data types to VARCHAR(30) SQL Server data types, and convert the data in SQL Server.

1-12. Ad Hoc Imports of Access Data
Problem

You want to import Access databases using T-SQL. This will probably only be carried out occasionally.

Solution

Use OPENROWSET to query the Access database in T-SQL.

The following query selects all the rows from the "stock" table in the Access database (C:\SQL2012DIRecipes\CH01\AccessACEOpenrowset.Sql):

```
SELECT ID, Marque
INTO MyAccessTempTable
FROM OPENROWSET('Microsoft.ACE.OLEDB.12.0',
    'C:\SQL2012DIRecipes\CH01\CarSales.accdb';'admin';'', stock);
```

How It Works

This is very similar to reading—or importing—data from Excel, as described in Recipe 1-4. Indeed, it is so similar that most of the comments stated for Excel will apply here, so I refer you to that recipe for the full details. Here, I will only draw your attention to a subset of important points.

First, you are better off (in most cases), downloading and installing the latest ACE driver because it can read all versions of Access from 97 upward. The old Jet driver cannot read Access 2007/2010 and the Jet driver exists only as a 32-bit version. Also note the following:

- If you are using Access 2007/2010/2013, then first download the 2007 ACE driver, as described in Recipe 1-1.

- Ad hoc queries must be enabled, as described in Recipe 1-4.

Second, I find that OPENROWSET is best when you will not be querying the database regularly, but just want to see the data from inside SQL Server or perform an ad hoc load, and when you know the table names that you will be querying. Note that you are sending the five parameters described in Table 1-4 to the OPENROWSET command.

Thirdly – you could need to be running SSMS as an Administrator.

Table 1-4. *OPENROWSET Parameters*

Parameter	Example	Comments
Driver	`'Microsoft.ACE.OLEDB.12.0'`	The Jet driver can be used.
Source path and database	`'C:\SQL2012DIRecipes\CH01\↵CarSales.accdb'`	You need the full path.
User	`'admin'`	The Access database user.
Password	`' '`	Use an empty string if there is no password.
Table, query (view) or pass-through query	stock	Can be a single Access table or saved query or an Access SQL string.

It is also worth paying attention to the use of semicolons to separate the three "subelements" composing the Access database parameters, and commas to separate the driver and source data from these.

Finally, you can refine your query in several ways. In the following code snippets I will not be adding the INSERT INTO ... SELECT or SELECT ... INTO code which you will doubtless be using. To start, you could send an Access pass-through query, like this:

```
SELECT ID, Marque
FROM OPENROWSET('Microsoft.ACE.OLEDB.12.0',
    'C:\SQL2012DIRecipes\CH01\CarSales.accdb';'admin';'',
    'SELECT ID, Marque FROM stock WHERE ID=5');
```

Or, if the WHERE clause is slightly more complex and involves quotes, you could try this:

```
SELECT ID, Marque
FROM OPENROWSET('Microsoft.ACE.OLEDB.12.0',
    'C:\SQL2012DIRecipes\CH01\CarSales.accdb';'admin';'',
    'SELECT ID, Marque FROM stock WHERE MAKE LIKE ''Tr%'' ');
```

You can also be selective in the data that is returned by tuning the SQL Server SELECT statement, in this way:

```
SELECT MAKE, MARQUE as CarType
FROM OPENROWSET('Microsoft.ACE.OLEDB.12.0',
    'C:\SQL2012DIRecipes\CH01\CarSales.accdb';'admin';'', stock)
WHERE ID = 5;
```

And of course, the OPENDATASOURCE syntax works just as well, and of course, it allows you to alias columns and apply a WHERE clause (here using the Jet driver, for a bit of variety):

```
SELECT MAKE, MARQUE as CarType FROM OPENDATASOURCE(
'Microsoft.Jet.OLEDB.4.0',
'Data Source=C:\SQL2012DIRecipes\CH01\CarSales.mdb;')...stock
WHERE ID = 5;
```

Although the title of this recipe states that this technique is for occasional data loads, there is nothing to prevent you from using it as part of a regular T-SQL-based ETL process. However, SSIS does provide more enhanced logging and error-trapping capacity – as well as none of the permissions issues which you can experience with SSMS – which is why it is preferable in many cases.

Hints, Tips, and Traps

- Remember that here you are writing T-SQL, not Access SQL. So, for instance, you cannot use the IIF function with older versions of SQL Server and must use % instead of * in WHERE clauses, as well as many other Access-specific SQL tricks!

- You can use double-quotes ("") instead of doubled single quotes (" ") in LIKE clauses in the pass-through query.

- If the Access database file is password-protected, then you need to add the password to the OPENROWSET parameters, for instance:

  ```
  SELECT MAKE, MARQUE as CarType
  FROM OPENDATASOURCE(
  'Microsoft.ACE.OLEDB.12.0',
  'Data Source=C:\SQL2012DIRecipes\CH01\CarSales.accdb;User
  Id=Admin;Password=MyPassword')...stock;
  ```

- If OPENDATASOURCE and OPENROWSET are using the Jet driver, they will not work in a 64-bit environment in SQL Server (2005 and 2008). Remember that later versions of Access and/or 64-bit environments necessitate the ACE driver. Consequently, the connection parameter will be 'Microsoft.ACE.OLEDB.12.0'.

- Unlike Excel worksheets—or Access files when using the SQL Server Import Wizard— Access files and tables can be open when being queried with OPENROWSET and OPENDATASOURCE.

- It is a good idea to compact and repair Access files before attempting to read data from them; corrupt data can cause problems that are best avoided.

- If you are using Access workgroup security (by definition on an Access 97–2003 database) you need to add: `'Jet OLEDB:System database=C:\Windows\System.mdw'`—or the path to the workgroup security file.

1-13. Obtaining Access Data Without Regular Imports

Problem

You need to read data in an Access database on a regular basis, without importing the data every time.

Solution

Set up a linked server to Access. This is one way to do it:

1. In SQL Server Management Studio, expand Server Objects. Right-click Linked Servers and fill in the New Linked Server dialog box using the following parameters:

Linked Server	AccessACE
Provider	Microsoft Office 12.0 Access Database Engine OLEDB Provider
Product Name	Access
Data Source	C:\SQL2012DIRecipes\CH01\CarSales.accdb

The dialog box should look something like Figure 1-21.

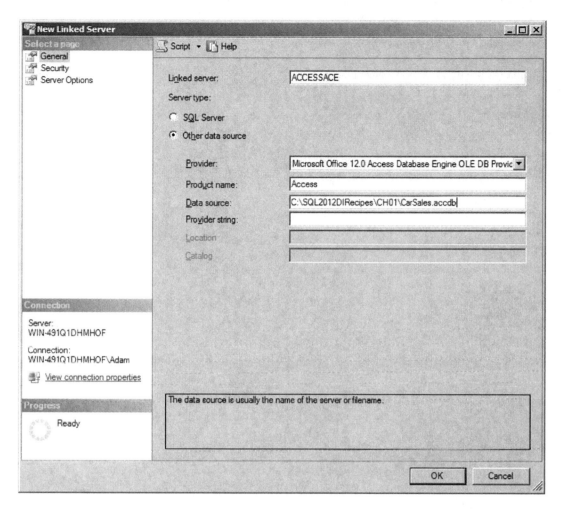

Figure 1-21. Creating an Access linked server in SSMS

2. Click OK. You then see a linked server named Access2010 in the list of linked servers. Of course, you have to enter your own Access data file and path in the Data Source field.

3. To read the data from a linked Access database, use the following four-part T-SQL syntax:

```
SELECT ID, Marque from ACCESSACE...Stock WHERE ID IN(1,3) ORDER BY ID;
```

How It Works

This approach works best:

- When you are querying the Access data regularly, but do not want to load the data into SQL Server.

- When the Access data is reliable and no data types in the tables that you query map incorrectly to SQL Server data types. Specifically, dates outside SQL data ranges (especially in SQL Server 2005).

This is standard T-SQL, so column aliases and complex WHERE clauses—indeed almost all T-SQL—are at your disposal. Alternatively, you can use the OPENQUERY syntax, as was described for Excel:

```
SELECT ID, Marque
FROM OPENQUERY(ACCESSACE, 'SELECT * FROM Stock WHERE ID = 1 ORDER BY ID');
```

One thing that you probably want to do is see the available tables and views. Run the following T-SQL (where 'AccessACE' is the linked server name) to list all the tables and queries (views) in a linked server:

```
EXECUTE master.dbo.sp_tables_ex 'ACCESSACE';
```

Alternatively, if you expand the relevant Linked server object in SSMS, you can display the tables in the linked Access database, as shown in Figure 1-22.

Figure 1-22. *Viewing Access linked servers in SSMS*

As was described earlier for Excel, you can use SELECT...INTO as well as INSERT INTO...SELECT statements, which refer to the table in a linked Access server.

To link to an Access 2007/2010/2013 file, you have to use the Microsoft Office 12.0 Access Database Engine OLEDB provider. For an Access 97–2003 database, you can use the Jet provider—if you must. You cannot add a linked server if a linked server with the same name already exists. In this case, first delete the existing linked server (by right-clicking the linked server name, selecting Delete from the shortcut menu, followed by OK).

The risk here is that as you are linking to a file, this object can easily be moved, renamed, or deleted; so render useless any processing that depends on the data it contains. If this approach is used in any production system, you should consider applying relevant directory security to the folder where the Access file resides.

If the Access data cannot be converted to SQL Server data types, then you will get an error. If you experience these types of problems, then consider creating queries in Access that use IIF functions to set high and low boundaries for dates (for example), or functions to set N/A for invalid data. Then link to these queries rather than to the source data tables.

Hints, Tips, and Traps

- It is a good idea to compact and repairAccess files before linking—corrupt data can cause problems.

- You can use T-SQL to create the linked server extremely easily. The following code snippet will do it (C:\SQL2012DIRecipes\CH01\CreateAccessLinkedServer.Sql):

```
EXECUTE master.dbo.sp_addlinkedserver
@SERVER = 'ACCESSACE'
,@SRVPRODUCT = 'ACE 12.0'
,@PROVIDER = 'Microsoft.ACE.OLEDB.12.0'
,@DATASRC = 'C:\SQL2012DIRecipes\CH01\CarSales.accdb';
```

- If you have expanded the list of tables in the linked server (as illustrated earlier), you can drag these to the query pane in SSMS, just as you would with SQL Server tables.

1-14. Importing Access Data as Part of a Regular ETL Process

Problem

You are importing Access data into SQL Server regularly, or as part of a repeatable process. Moreover, you need to transform data as part of the load process.

Solution

Use SSIS to import and transform Access data. It can be done in the following way:

1. Install the latest ACE driver, if this is not already done.

2. Create a new SSIS package.

3. Create an OLEDB destination Configuration Manager, named CarSales_OLEDB, which you configure to point to your chosen destination database.

4. Add a Data Flow task to the Control Flow pane, and double-click to edit it.

5. Add an OLEDB Source component, and double-click to edit.

6. Click New to create a new Connection Manager.

7. Click New to add a new Data Connection.

8. Select the Microsoft Office 12.0 Access Database Engine OLEDB Provider from the pop-up list of installed drivers.

9. Click in the Server field or file name and enter the full path to the Access file (mdb or accdb).

10. Enter the username and password (if there is one)—or check the Blank Password box. The dialog box should look like Figure 1-23.

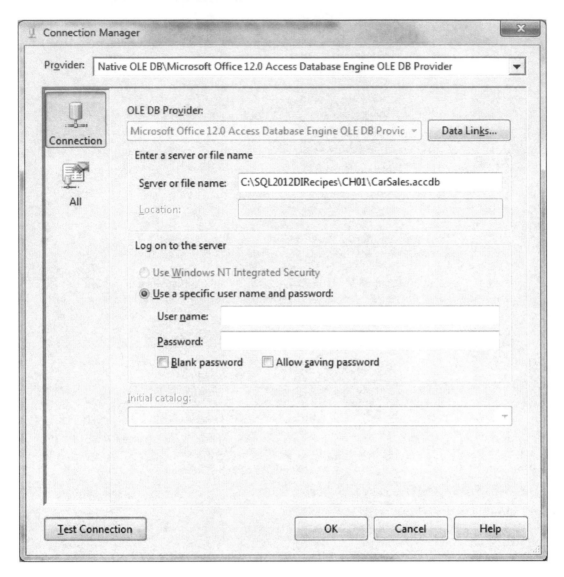

Figure 1-23. *An SSIS Connection Manager for Access*

11. Click OK to return to the OLEDB Source Editor.

12. Select Table or View as the data access mode.

13. Select the Access table from which you wish to import data.

14. Click OK to return to the Data Flow pane.

15. Add an OLEDB destination component to the Data Flow pane, and connect the source component to it. Double-click the destination component to edit it.

16. Select the OLEDB connection manager named CarSales_OLEDB, which you created in step 2 as the OLEDB connection manager to use.

17. Click New to create a new destination table. Change its name to suit your requirements.

18. Click Mappings on the left of the dialog box, and ensure that all fields are mapped, either by dragging them from the available source columns to the available destination columns, or by right-clicking Name in the available source columns, followed by "Map items by matching names".

19. Click OK to finish.

You can now run your import process and load the data.

How It Works

Here I am presuming that you are probably using SSIS to handle most of your industrial-strength ETL requirements. After all, this product was developed precisely to satisfy such requirements. As is the case with other methods of performing data import from Access sources, the choice of driver is important. Consequently, I can only recommend always using the latest ACE driver, as it will handle all versions of Access from '97 upward.

ACE is not the only game in town, and I have worked in many environments where Access 97–2003 was the preferred Access file format for reasons of standardization and portability. So it is worth learning how to use the Jet driver to read these files—if only because it is so simple to do.

- Essentially, you follow steps 1–7, and then select the Native OLEDB Microsoft Jet 4.0 OLEDB Provider.

- Click Browse to select the path and file name of the Access source database.

Then continue with steps 10–19.

There are several potential hurdles to overcome when you are using SSIS with the (32-bit) Jet driver in a 64-bit environment. As previously mentioned, when you install Integration Services on a 64-bit Windows Operating System, it normally installs both the 32-bit and the 64-bit versions of the DTExec.exe executable, which is used to execute SSIS packages. The problem is that SSIS may use the wrong one—especially when developing and debugging SSIS packages with BIDS/SSDT. This is because BIDS/SSDT is a 32-bit development environment, so if your SSIS package is referencing any 32-bit DLL or 32-bit drivers, then you must use the 32-bit executable—and BIDS/SSDT tries to use the 64-bit version. To get around this, carry out the following steps:

1. Click Project ➤ (Your Project Name) Properties.

2. Select Debugging from the configuration properties.

3. Change Run64BitRuntime to False. The dialog should look something like Figure 1-24.

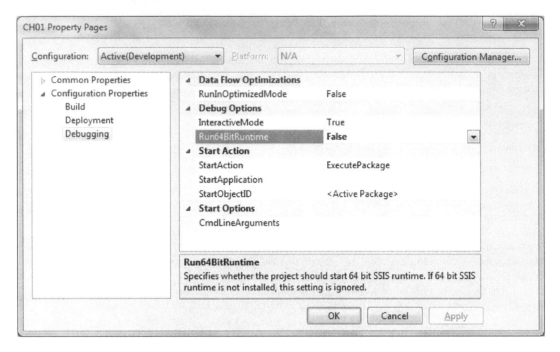

Figure 1-24. *Setting the 64-bit runtime in SSIS*

A classic problem, once our package is built tested and deployed on a 64-bit server, is to have an Access (or Excel) data load fail in production. This failure is accompanied by a host of error messages that give no indication of the real problem, which is that SSIS is (naturally) running the 64-bit DTExec.exe—which cannot use a 32-bit Jet driver.

There are a couple of classic solutions to this.

1. Separate out the Access data load part of your project into a separate SSIS package (if this is not already done).

2. Call it from the main SSIS package, not by using an Execute Package task, but rather by using an Execute Process task.

3. In the Execute Process Task, click Process in the left pane.

4. Click Executable and enter (in double quotes) the path to the 32-bit DTExec.

5. Follow this with a space, then the path to the SSIS package to run.

If you are using an Access 97–2003 database that has workgroup protection, and you cannot use a unprotected database, then there are a couple of solutions. The first approach is as follows:

1. When defining the connection manager for Access at step 10 in the main recipe, use the workgroup login/password as the username and password.

2. Click All in the left of the dialog box and enter or copy the full path and filename of the workgroup file for the Jet OLEDB:System Database parameter.

The second possibility is more of a workaround. You have to link, import, or export the table data to a new Access database and point SSIS to that.

Of course, you can use an existing destination table if one exists. Equally, you may prefer to create the destination connection manager while configuring the OLEDB destination component. This may well be a package-level connection manager (with the .conmgr extension) in SQL Server 2012.

As you have probably seen, SSIS names the source component with the full path and file name, followed by the username. You may prefer to rename this to something more palatable. Should you need to alter any aspect of the source connection manager, just double-click it in the lower pane, and edit the connection manager. For a package-level connection manager, you have to edit it in the Connection Managers folder of the Solution Explorer window. Finally, it can be worth clicking the Test Connection button at step 10—if only to get early warning of a connection problem.

Hints, Tips, and Traps

- Yes, it is a real pain that you have to copy and paste (or worse, type in) the path and file name of the Access source database when using the ACE driver.

- In a real-world scenario, it is advisable to select SQL Command as the data access mode in step 11, and enter or build a query in step 12 (using the aptly-named Build Query button) to select only the columns that you need, as well as filtering out any unwanted records, aliasing column names, converting data types, and so forth.

- Should you be writing a query to select the source data, then note that you must use T-SQL, not Access SQL.

- Should you need to massage your data as it flows from source to destination, then myriad techniques to do this are described in Chapter 9.

- The 32-bitDTExec is found in `C:\Program Files (x86)\Microsoft SQL Server\110\ DTS\Binn` for SQL Server 2012. Replace 110 with 90 for SQL Server 2005, and with 100 for SQL Server 2008.

- Calling a 32-bit executable from SQL Server agent is easy; just check the check box on the Job Step page to run the package in 32-bit mode.

1-15. Convert a Complex Access Database to SQL Server
Problem

You have a complex Access database that cannot be imported quickly or easily and which may potentially require considerable repurposing and refactoring.

Solution

Use the SQL Server Migration Assistant for Access (SSMA).

1. Install SSMA (described in detail shortly).

2. Launch SSMA from the Start menu.

3. Click Close to exit the Migration Wizard. The four empty panes of the SSMA interface appear.

4. Click File ➤ New Project (or the button on the toolbar), enter the project's name, and enter or browse for a directory where the project (and all the metadata for the source and destination objects) will be stored. Choose a destination SQL Server database version (this even works with SQL Server Azure). The dialog box looks like Figure 1-25.

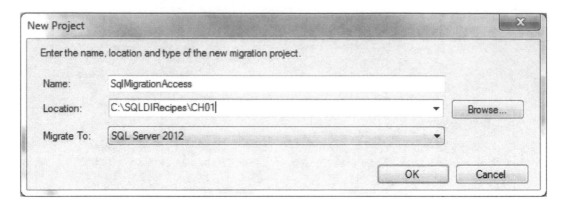

Figure 1-25. Creating a new SSMA project

5.   Click OK.

6.   Click File ➤ Add Databases (or the toolbar button), and select the Access database(s) you wish to migrate. Repeat this step for each database to add. The database(s) appear in the top-left pane, Access Metadata Explorer.

7.   Expand the databases and select the table(s) you wish to migrate. The table structure appears in the top-right pane, something like Figure 1-26.

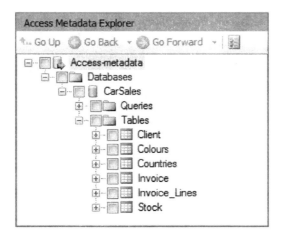

Figure 1-26. Source metadata in SSMA

8.   Click File ➤ Connect to SQL Server (or the button in the toolbar) and enter the details of the server to connect to, and then click OK. The list of all the available databases on the destination server appear in the bottom left pane, SQL Server Metadata Explorer.

9.   Expand the destination database, and select the destination schema (see Figure 1-27).

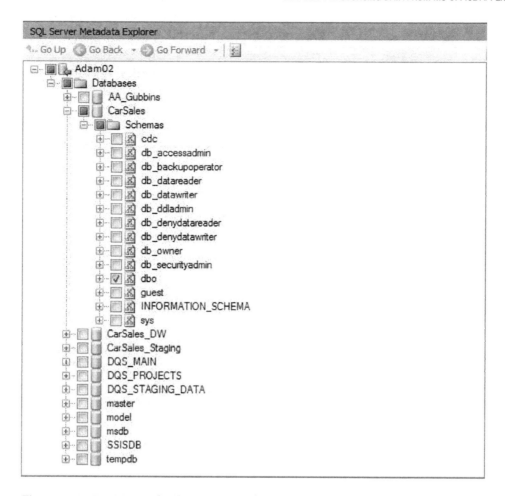

Figure 1-27. *Destination database metadata in SSMA*

10. In the Access Metadata Explorer window, select the databases. Click Tools ➤ Convert Schema (or the Convert Schema button) to have SSMA create the proposed schema of the table(s) to be converted. The proposed schema appears in the bottom-right pane, and the output window appears. The screen should look something like Figure 1-28.

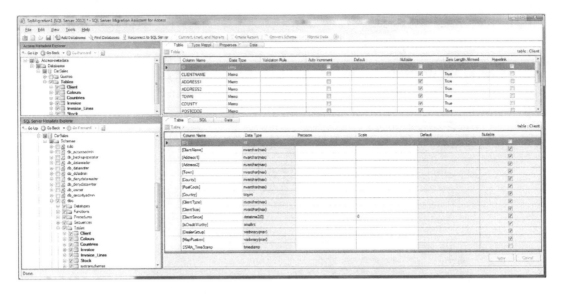

Figure 1-28. *SSMA data conversion*

11. Clicking on any table name in the Access Metadata Explorer window displays the source and destination metadata for the selected object. Note that the objects have not yet been created in SQL Server.

12. In the SQL Server Metadata window, check all the tables you wish to create in SQL Server.

13. In the SQL Server Metadata window, right-click Tables in the hierarchy above the tables that you have checked. Select Synchronize with Database, and then click OK if a detail window is displayed. This creates the objects in SQL Server.

14. Click Tools ➤ Migrate Data (or click the Migrate Data button) to transfer the data from all the source objects into the destination tables.

How It Works

The SQL Server Migration Assistant for Access (SSMA) has evolved steadily over the last few years into a powerful tool that attempts to migrate all the "back-end" aspects of an Access database to SQL Server. That is, it attempts to convert metadata (table structures), data, some programming code, but not forms and reports, into their SQL Server equivalents.

This recipe has only looked at how this fabulous utility can help you migrate data into SQL Server and create the requisite accompanying table definitions. Any other uses for SSMA are outside the scope of the book.

I am not saying that you should prefer SSMA to SSIS or to any of the other methods of getting data into SQL Server; however, for data migration, where you are working toward a "big bang" single data transfer that must be made to work, it has the following things going for it:

- It can help you to produce a detailed and customized database structure in SQL Server from one or several Access databases.

- It scripts out your database structure in T-SQL from Access.

- It allows you work on a conversion project over time, saving and opening the project as it develops, and making frequent changes as the project evolves.

- It helps to achieve reliable conversions, and offers extensive informational and warning messages.

- It maintains metadata from both the source and the destination databases.

- It can convert Access databases in all formats from 97 to 2013— and can even convert multiple database formats in parallel.

Yet we have to be clear. This is not an ETL tool that loads data on a regular basis. It expects all destination tables to be empty before beginning a load, and truncates destination tables if they contain data.

Also, this utility can do much, much more than create tables and upload data. It converts Access queries into SQL Server views, adds indexes and constraints, and so forth. However, as all this is outside the scope of this book, I am afraid that I have to let you discover these aspects of SSMA on your own.

It is easy to be enthusiastic about SSMA, but I have to be truthful and admit that even this silver lining has its cloud. The data migration is somewhat slow. So you could, in the real world, only be using SSMA as a metadata definition utility, and then use SSIS or the Data Import Wizard to load the actual data.

Requirements for the SSMA for Access are:

- Windows XP or 2003, at the least.

- Microsoft Windows Installer 3.1 or a later version.

- The Microsoft .NET Framework 2.0 or a later version.

- The ACE OLEDB driver.

- Microsoft SQL Server Native Client (SNAC) version 10.5 and above for migrating to SQL Azure. A lot of people install this as part of an SQL Server installation. Otherwise, you can find the latest link to it via your favorite search engine or by finding the `sqlncli.msi` file that is on your Microsoft SQL Server installation media.

- Access to the computer that hosts the target instance of SQL Server.

- 1 GB RAM (minimum).

- A reasonable amount of disk space to store the metadata about the source and destination databases.

I suggest that you always download and install the latest version of SSMA because it is constantly evolving, and because (now) the latest versions can open migration projects created with earlier versions. The latest version (5.2 at the time of writing) contains the following enhancements:

- Support for migration to SQL Server 2012.

- Multithread data migration for improved scale and performance.

- Globalization support for migrating nonEnglish databases to SQL Server.

Earlier I said that I would explain how to install SSMA, so here is the way to do this:

1. Extract all files from the zip file that you downloaded.

2. Extract the installation file SSMA for Access 5.2.exe using a suitable utility.

3. Double-click SSMA for Access 5.2.exe.

4. On the Welcome page, click Next.

5. If you do not have the prerequisites installed, a message will appear that indicates that you must first install required components. Make sure that you have installed all prerequisites (see earlier list), and then run the installation program again.

6. Select the "I accept the agreement" option to agree to the terms.

7. Click Next.

8. Select or clear the feature reporting box.

9. Click Next.

10. On the Choose Setup Type page, click Typical (or another type, Custom or Complete, if you wish).

11. Click Install.

12. Click Finish.

When running SSMA for the first time, you have to register for a license and download a free license key. This requires a Windows Live ID. Once you have done this, point to the directory containing the downloaded license key and click Refresh License to apply the license and start SSMA.

■ **Note**   The URL for SSMA is currently www.microsoft.com/en-us/download/details.aspx?id=28763.

Hints, Tips, and Traps

- If you suspect that your migration will be fairly simple, then it may be easier to use the Migration Wizard.

- SSMA will not let you select only some fields from a source table, it is an all-or-nothing process. If you only want to load a subset of a table, then the fastest solution is to run an Access Make Table query first to define the data subset as a new table.

- When creating the destination metadata (by selecting Convert Schema), you can choose a level in the hierarchy of databases and tables in the Access Metadata Explorer window to have the schema created for all objects below the selected level.

- Selecting Tools ➤ Convert, Load, and Migrate, create the table in the destination database metadata, and transfer the data in one fell swoop.

- SSMA does not test the schema it produces using SQL Server; it simply shows what the schema could be.

- Access queries are converted into SQL Server views—not data tables. To have SSMA create tables, use an Access Make Table query first to create the table to export.

- To preview the source data in an Access table, click the Data tab in the top-right pane. You can then visualize the source data without opening Access.

- An SSMA project can be saved at any time—just click File ➤ Save (or the Save toolbar button). Of course, you can reopen a previously saved project to continue working on it.

- If any of your Access databases are modified, then this will not be reflected automatically in the Access Metadata window of SSMA. To update the metadata, right-click Databases(to update all metadata) or a database name (to update the metadata for a single database) and select "Refresh from database".

1-16. Resolving Complex Data Migration Problems During an Access to SQL Server Upgrade

Problem

You have a complex Access database transformation and data load that needs a lot of work. This project may take place over an extended time and require considerable development effort.

Solution

Use the extended functions of SSMA to change data types, apply custom type mappings, and generate custom scripts—among other possibilities.

As we are looking at a range of options for SSMA, this will not be a single recipe—it would be too difficult to follow. I prefer to explain the available options as a series of "mini-recipes" where you can look at the options that interest you.

Use SSMA to Alter Data Types

Altering data types in SSMA is as simple as doing the following:

1. In either of the Metadata Explorer windows on the left, click the table name whose metadata you wish to alter.

2. In the SQL Server metadata for the table (lower-right side), alter the data type, precision, scale, nullability, or default.

3. Click Apply.

4. Right-click the table name in the SQL Server Metadata Explorer window on the left and select "Synchronize with database".

5. Click OK for any message box that appears.

Use SSMA to Migrate Data for a Single Table

This is how to migrate data for a single table in SSMA:

1. Right-click the table to migrate into either of the Metadata Explorer windows on the left.

2. Select Migrate Data.

Use SSMA to Create a Report on a Table or Tables

SSMA can also create reports on Access objects in this way:

1. Click the object (or hierarchical level) in the Access Metadata Window.

2. Click Tools ➤ Create Report (or click the Create Report button). A report is created and displayed, as shown in Figure 1-29.

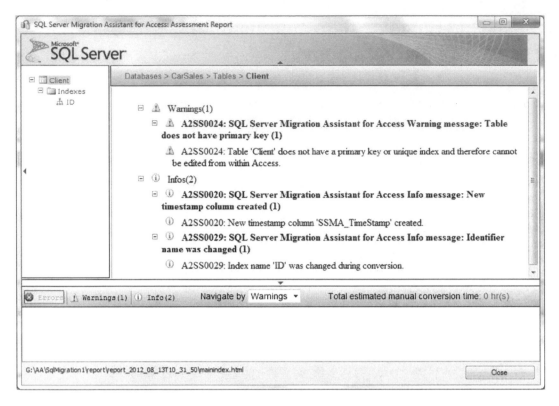

Figure 1-29. *SSMA report creation*

Use SSMA to Apply Custom Data Type Mapping for a Project

Creating custom data type mapping in SSMA is also extremely easy, and can be done as follows:

1. Click Tools ➤ Project Settings.

2. In the Project Settings dialog box, click Type Mapping in the lower-left corner. The dialog box will look like Figure 1-30.

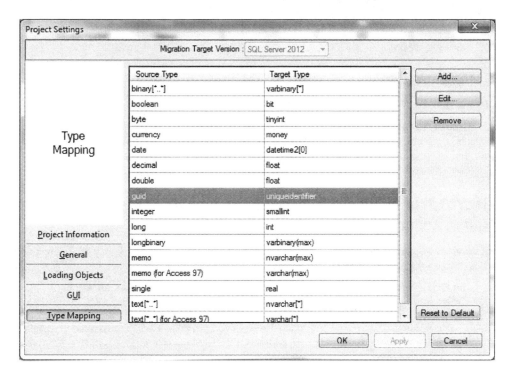

Figure 1-30. Source and target data type mappings

3. Click the type mapping pair that you wish to modify.

4. Click Edit. The dialog box shown in Figure 1-31 appears.

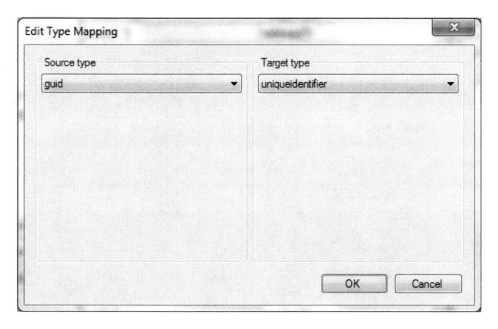

Figure 1-31. SSMA type mapping

5.   Select a different target type and, if necessary, any other attributes.

6.   Click OK twice.

Use SSMA to Create T-SQL Scripts of Destination Tables

If you need the DDL for destination tables, SSMA can create them for you, as follow:

1.   Clicking Create Schema creates the T-SQL necessary to create a table. To use this
     code, click the SQL tab in the bottom -right pane. Scroll down to the bottom of the
     SQL code, and you find the both the table DROP and CREATE scripts. These can be
     copied into SQL Server Management Studio and tweaked to suit your requirements.

Use SSMA to Find All the Access Databases on Any Drives to Which Your Computer is Connected

SSMA can trawl through all the disks to which your computer is connected and display all the Access databases it
finds. This is done in the following way:

1.   Click File ➤ Find databases, the Find Databases dialog box appears, as shown in
     Figure 1-32.

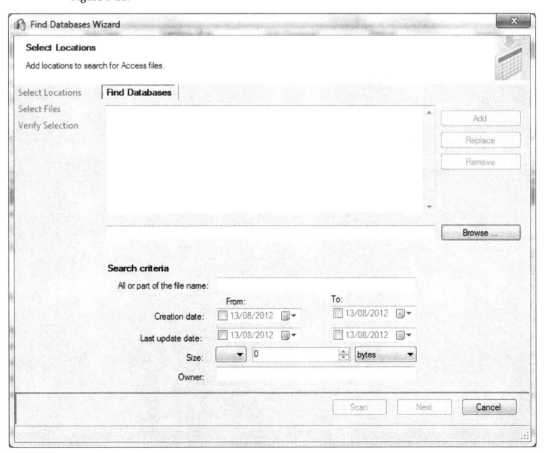

Figure 1-32. *SSMA Find Database Wizard*

2. Browse for the drive and/or directory you wish to search. Click Add. Repeat this step as many times as there are paths you wish to search.

3. Add all or part of the file name to search for (if required).

4. Select data ranges and file sizes (if required).

5. Click Scan. SSMA finds all Access files corresponding to your search criteria. They will appear in the dialog box, where you can select files to add by Control-clicking.

6. Click Next to display the list of files to verify, and then click Finish to add the selected files to the Access Metadata Explorer pane.

How It Works

SSMA is a very powerful tool, but also very flexible in the many ways it can help you upgrade your Access databases to SQL Server. As we have seen in the mini-recipes, these include modifying SQL Server tables based on the metadata in SSMA, migrating data for a single table, creating a report on a table or tables, applying custom data type mapping for a project, using SSMS for T-SQL scripting of destination tables, and finding Access databases.

As you have seen, SSMA creates SQL Server tables that are, in essence, the source Access tables that have been adapted to SQL Server data types. However, you are not obliged to accept the data types or field lengths proposed by SSMA, and you can modify them to your heart's content. Be warned that doing this causes the old version of the table to be dropped and re-created, and any data will have to be reloaded. SSMA converts Access data according to a tried and tested mapping scheme. However, if you prefer, you can alter this mapping for an entire project.

One of SSMA's most valuable functions is its ability to forewarn you of impending problems. You are free to heed or ignore—or even doubt the sagacity of—the report, but it can be useful to know, in advance, where the data migration might fail.

There are several known migration issues; however, most of these do not apply to simple data migration, and are only a problem in the case of a full-blown upgrade to an SQL Server back-end with an Access front-end.

Interestingly, many of the potential problems are the same as those encountered when using the Access Upsizing Wizard, so first I suggest that you look at the hints given earlier in Recipe 1-10—specifically those concerning effective ways to prepare an Access database for a trouble-free upgrade.

You can also save yourself time and trouble by looking into a few classic problem areas—shown in Table 1-5.

Table 1-5. SSMA Problem Areas

Problem	Solution
Access object names can beSQL Server keywords.	Access and SQL Server have different reserved keywords, so you need to double-check that Access is not using a reserved word that causes SQL Server to throw a fit.
Field and Table Names	Access field and table names can contain characters not generally considered acceptable for SQL Server. You should modify the T-SQL generated by SSMA and then use it instead to create the destination tables.
Dates	The SQL Server DATETIME type accepts dates in the range of 1 Jan 1753 to 31 Dec 9999 only. However, Access accepts dates in the range of 1 Jan 1000 to 31 Dec 9999. Map Access data fields to DATETIME2 fields in SQL Server 2012.

Remember that if you are faced with a potentially tricky Access database to load into SQL Server, you might find it easier to create a copy of the database, and then look at ironing out any problems in the copied Access database—this could include removing indexes and constraints, renaming tables and fields etc. In my experience, this is often the fastest way to get your source data into SQL Server quickly.

Hints, Tips, and Traps

- You cannot alter the field names, as one important function of SSMS is to migrate data and metadata to SQL Server, while leaving Access as a data interface. Altering field names would make an interface unworkable, and so—no altering field names.

- If you really have to alter field names, and wish to use SSMA as a metadata scripting tool, then you have to use the T-SQL scripts generated by SSMA, and tweak them before running them in SSMS. Yes, you have to copy and paste each one, individually, into SSMS.

- Although you must remember to click Apply to complete all the modifications for a table, you can synchronize with the database just once. Only remember to right-click the database name in the SQL Server metadata window to do this.

- You see a warning dialog box if the table into which you are copying data is not empty. If you continue, the table will be truncated.

- Each report is saved to disk in a subdirectory named "report" on the project directory.

- You can also add and remove type mappings—but I would not advise this in a real-world scenario.

- Doing this for the Default Project Settings alters the data type mappings for all future SSMA projects.

- To create tables without indexes or primary keys, only select the code for the CREATE statement, and do not copy the ALTER TABLE statement.

- SSMA cannot migrate databases that use workgroup protection. You have to remove Workgroup protection before using SSMS. I suggest that you consult the Microsoft web site for the best way of doing this.

Summary

This chapter has contained many ways of getting Office data into SQL Server. Some of them may seem to be similar, duplicate methods, or simply plain abstruse. So to give you a clearer overview, Table 1-6 shows my take on the various methods, and their advantages and disadvantages.

Table 1-6. *Techniques Suggested in This Chapter*

Technique	Advantages	Disadvantages
OPENROWSET	Uses pass-through queries.	Can be tricky to set up.
OPENDATASOURCE	Allows source data to be manipulated using T-SQL.	Can be tricky to set up.
Linked Server	Allows source data to be manipulated using T-SQL.	Can be difficult to set up. Frequently very slow in practice.
Import and Export Wizard	Easy to use. Can generate SSIS package.	Limited conversion options.
SSIS	Full data conversion, modification, and manipulation. Incremental data loads.	Longer to implement. Cannot create all destination objects at once.
SSMA	Iterative development. Extensive options. Can create all destination objects at once.	Limited conversion options. No incremental data loads. No partial data selection.
Access Upgrade Wizard	Easy to use. Can create all destination objects at once.	Very slow. Limited conversion options. No incremental data loads.

Now, which solution is best suited to a particular challenge depends on many factors, such as the time you have available to develop a solution, the need for resilience and logging—or quite simply the nature of the requirement. You will probably not try to develop an earth-shattering SSIS package when your requirement is to carry out a one-off load of a few records from Excel. Conversely, automating the Import/Export Wizard is impossible, so you will not want to use it for daily data loads.

When you have a regular data load to perform, the choice of data load technique can get trickier. One of the T-SQL-based solutions (OPENROWSET, OPENDATASOURCE, or a linked server) can simplify deployment considerably. In these circumstances, you will, in all probability, merely copy a stored procedure over to a production server and/or execute some simple T-SQL snippets. If, however, you want to be able to track all the details of a data load, then SSIS with its myriad logging possibilities (explained in the final chapter of this book) is doubtless the tool to choose.

So "it depends" is probably the answer to the question "which approach should I take?". The main thing to remember from this chapter is that there are a variety of tools available and you need to be aware of their possibilities and limitations. This way, you can choose and apply the most appropriate technique in your specific circumstances to obtain the best solution to your specific challenge.

CHAPTER 2

Flat File Data Sources

For more years than most of us care to remember, the single most common source of external data facing an SQL Server developer or DBA was a text file. The inevitable consequence of the near ubiquity of the "flat" file is the minor ecosystem of tools and techniques that has grown over time to help us all load text file data sources into SQL Server.

Faced with such a plethora of solutions, the main approaches that I examine in this chapter are the following:

- The Import/Export Wizard

- SSIS

- OPENROWSET and OPENDATASOURCE

- BULK INSERT

- Linked servers

- BCP

All have their advantages and drawbacks, as you would expect. The aim of this chapter is to introduce you to the uses and usefulness of each, and hopefully to explain how and when each can and probably should be used. Then, as text files are often not as simple as they could be, I will outline a few techniques to handle some of the trickier problems that they can pose.

However, before getting into the nitty-gritty of importing data from text files (or flat files—I use the terms interchangeably), we need to clarify a few basic concepts. First among these: are you dealing with a real CSV file, and does it matter? It is important to clear this up, as many text files are described as CSV files when this is simply not the case.

Assuming that the text file that you are receiving does not contain multiple, differing types of records in a single file, you are probably looking at a delimited file, where the data is "tabular" but the "columns" are separated by a specific character and the "rows" by another (nonprinting) character. Depending on how such a file is laid out, it may be considered to be a CSV file.

There is much discussion as to when a text file is a CSV (comma-separated values) file or not. Thanks to some sterling work a few years ago, there is now a specification, in the form of an RFC (Request For Comment), of what a CSV file is (see http://tools.ietf.org/html/rfc4180 for details). I suggest considering CSV as a subset specification of what most flat files are, which is a delimited data format using column separators and record separators. The RFC specification essentially boils down to the following:

- Each record is located on a separate line, delimited by a line break (CR/LF).

- The last record in the file may or may not have a final line break.

- There may be an optional header line appearing as the first line of the file with the same format as normal record lines. This header contains names corresponding to the fields in the file and should contain the same number of fields as the records in the rest of the file.

- Within the header and each record, there may be one or more fields separated by commas.

- Each line should contain the same number of fields throughout the file.

- Spaces are considered part of a field and should not be ignored.

- The last field in the record must not be followed by a comma.

- Each field may or may not be enclosed in double quotes. If fields are not enclosed in double quotes, then no double quotes may appear inside the fields.

- Fields containing double quotes, commas and line breaks (CR/LF), should be enclosed in double quotes.

- If double quotes are used to enclose fields, then a double quote appearing inside a field must be "escaped" by preceding it with another double quote.

What precedes is the theory. Practice—as you have probably discovered—can be quite another kettle of fish. As the RFC states, there are "considerable differences among implementations." Indeed, many flat-file transfers are called CSV when they are TSV (tab separated), PSV (pipe separated)—or indeed anything-under-the-sun separated. So my take is that what matters above all else in real-world data transfer scenarios for delimited data transfer is consistency. It is simply not important whether the file matches the RFC specification or not. Just about all the tools that SQL Server offers for flat file loads can handle (or be tweaked to handle) a consistent delimited file format. So in essence, if you are requesting a CSV, TSV, PSV, or indeed any other form of essentially tabular data file, you need to ask the following:

- Which character is used as a field separator in the source data?

- How is the end of a record indicated?

- Should the first two characters escaped in the file be used inside a field?

- Are quotes used consistently (that is, either for all data in each file "column")—or not at all?

Once you know these things, then you can attempt to load a file, and try and deal with any difficulties that it may present. In most cases, if you receive a CSV file that does respect the standard, then you could consider yourself fortunate. If you are really lucky, you can specify the format. Should this be the case, then the four questions that I just listed should serve as your basic guideline for specifying the source format.

The "classic" field separator is the comma (the "C" in CSV). However, you may frequently find tab separated, pipe separated, and many other characters—even small strings of characters—used as field separators. If you are dealing with data from continental Europe (not to mention other areas of the globe), you may need to use a semicolon as the separator in order to allow the comma to remain as the decimal separator.

The CSV specification defines the end of record indicator as the CR/LF character. You could also find either the carriage return (CR) or the line feed (LF) is being used.

This is where, in practice, things can get sticky. You might find that a field separator is escaped by a backslash (\) or that the whole field is enclosed in quotes, with all quotes in the body of a field doubled. This is often the single trickiest aspect of flat-file loads. Various techniques to deal with this are described in this chapter.

Sometimes you might have to deal with text files that contain more than one type of record, and are not as simply tabular as is a "classic" CSV file. These will inevitably require some custom processing, and are examined at the end of this chapter. Fortunately, SQL Server 2012 has made considerable progress in handling text files containing varying columns (or multiple column delimiters if you prefer to think of it that way). We will also see this at the end of the chapter.

To follow the examples given in this chapter, you need to create the sample CarSales and CarSales_Staging databases that are described in Appendix B. You will also need to download the sample files from the book's companion web site and place them in the C:\SQL2012DIRecipes\CH02\ directory on your SQL Server. I advise you to drop and re-create the destination tables (if they exist already) between recipes to ensure a clean destination structure.

2-1. Importing Data From a Text File

Problem

You want to import a flat file as fast and as easily as possible

Solution

Run the Import/Export Wizard.

When faced with a delimited text or CSV file, the classic way to begin is to try and import it using the Import/Export Wizard. Since this wizard was covered in Chapter 1, I will be more succinct here. For a more detailed description, please refer to Recipe 1-2.

1. Ensure that the correct table structure has been created in the destination database. In this example, it is the dbo.Invoices table in CarSales_Staging. See Appendix B for details.

2. In SSMS, right-click the destination database (CarSales_Staging in this example) and select Tasks ➤ Import Data. If the Welcome screen appears, click Next.

3. Select Flat File Source as the Data Source. The dialog box switches to offer all the flat file options. Browse to your source file or enter the full path and file name (C:\SQL2012DIRecipes\CH02\Invoices.Txt).

4. Specify that the column names are in the first row, and that the text qualifier is <none>. Define the Header Row Delimiter as <CR><LF> and select the format as delimited. You should end up with a dialog box like Figure 2-1.

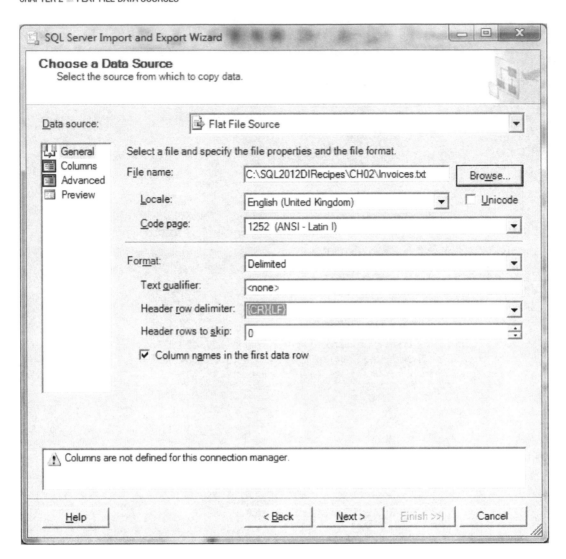

Figure 2-1. *Flat file sources in the Import/Export Wizard*

5. Click Columns, which shows you the list of available columns. Here you can change specific column delimiters if you need to.

6. Click Advanced. This lets you define the data type for each column. You can also set the length, precision, or scale (depending on the data type)—or leave the defaults, as shown in Figure 2-2.

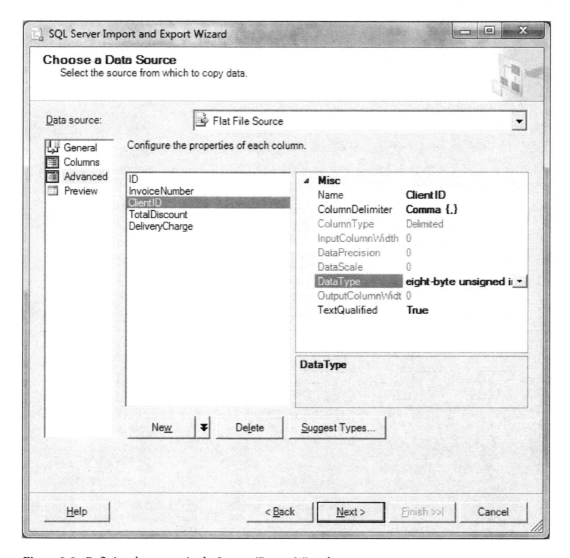

Figure 2-2. *Defining data types in the Import/Export Wizard*

7. Click Next. Check that the destination server, database, and authentication are correct.

8. Click Next. Ensure that the requisite destination table is selected.

9. Click Next. Verify that Run Immediately is selected.

10. Click Next, followed by Finish, then Finish again, and Close. Your data should be correctly imported.

How It Works

The Import/Export Wizard takes your flat file and assists you in defining its principal characteristics. You then specify any more-advanced properties at the column level. If required, you can get this wizard to guess the characteristics of the metadata in the source file.

Hints, Tips, and Traps

- For the other ways of launching the Import/Export Wizard, see the Recipe 1-2.

- You can ask the Import/Export Wizard to suggest data types for each column of data by clicking the Suggest Types button. This is explained in more detail in Recipe 2-3.

2-2. Importing a Delimited Text File

Problem

You want to import a flat file on a regular basis and/or apply data transformation as part of a structured ETL process.

Solution

Create an SSIS package to import the file. This is how you do it:

1. Create a new SSIS project, or open an existing project, and add a new package.

2. Add a Data Flow task onto the Control Flow pane. Edit this task by doing any of the following:

    - Double-click.

    - Right-click and select Edit.

    - Click the Data Flow tab.

3. Add a Flat File source from the Data Flow sources in the toolbox. Double-click the Flat File source to edit it. You should see the dialog box shown in Figure 2-3.

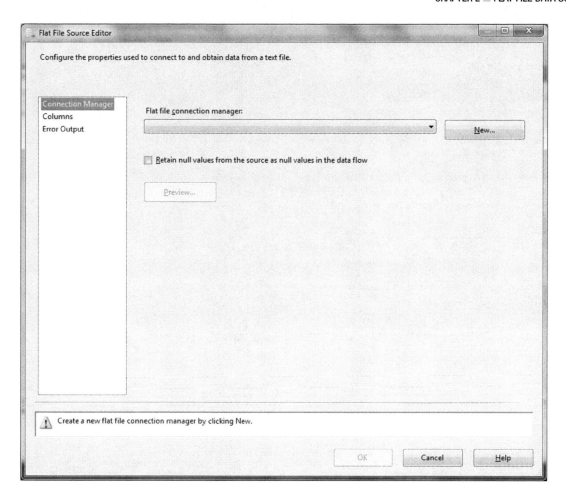

Figure 2-3. *Flat File Source Editor in SSIS*

4. Click New to specify the file connection, which opens the File Connection Manager Editor. Browse to select the source file (or type it in if you prefer). In this example, it is C:\SQL2012DIRecipes\CH02\Invoices.Txt. Specify whether column names are in the first row, enter the text qualifier, and select the row delimiter (or leave the defaults). You should end up with something like what you see in Figure 2-4.

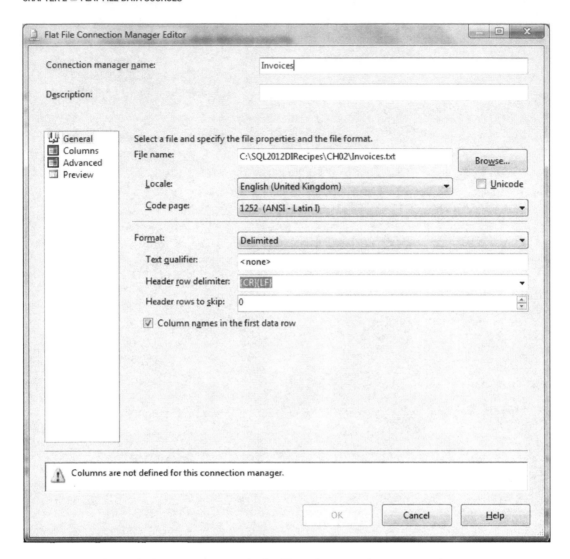

Figure 2-4. Defining the basic parameters of a flat file in the Import/Export Wizard

5. Click Advanced. For each output column, define the data type and length. The dialog box should look like that in Figure 2-5.

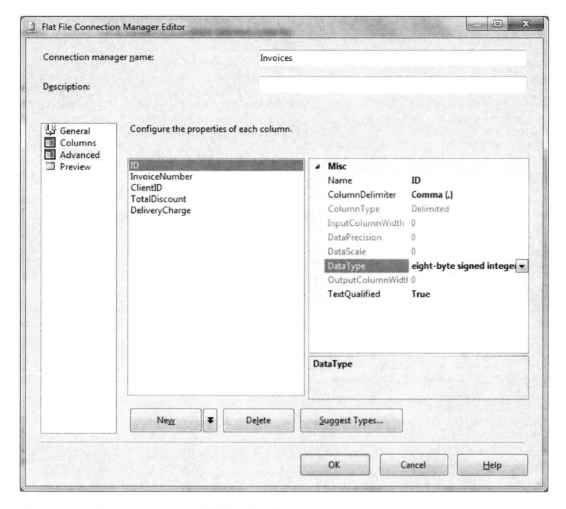

Figure 2-5. *Defining data types in SSIS for a flat file*

6. Click OK twice to confirm and return to the Data Flow pane.

7. Add an OLEDB destination from the toolbox to the Data Flow pane, and connect the output (the green arrow) from the text source to the OLEDB destination.

8. Double-click the OLEDB destination to edit it. Click New to add an OLEDB connection manager that you configure to connect to the destination database (CarSales_Staging in this example.) As an alternative, you can select an existing connection manager.

9. Select the destination table (dbo.Invoice in this example). Alternatively click New to create a new table, which is designed automatically to map to the perceived source structure. You can change the destination table name from the name suggested by SSIS if you prefer. Confirm with OK.

10. Click Mappings in the list on the left side of the OLEDB Connection Manager dialog box. Ensure that the source data maps to the destination columns.

11. Click OK.

12. Click Debug ➤ Start Debugging to import the data from the text file.

SSIS will now import your data.

How It Works

In the real-world of data import, SSIS is probably the tool that you will use the most. Nonetheless, it always helps if you can open the source file to get a look at its contents, or have been informed about its contents enough to know

- Whether it contains column headers or not.

- What the data types and lengths are for each column of data.

- That the file always contains the same number of column delimiters.

If you do not have the core information about the data in the text file available, however, then you can glean metadata for the source file from SSIS by previewing the data and getting SSIS to guess the data types—as you will discover in Recipe 2-3. Assuming that you have this information, SSIS will help you through the process of importing a text file. In the case of flat files that are not too huge, you can open the source in a text editor and attempt to deduce the metadata directly.

■ **Note** If you do not specify any data types when setting up the Data Flow task, SSIS presumes that every column is VARCHAR(50).

Defining and adjusting the data types as the pass-through SSIS can mean a lot of work. Fortunately, SSIS has ways to help you in this, as you will see in Recipe 2-3. Interestingly, the real work is done in the Flat File connection manager, not the Data Source task.

Should you encounter difficulties, the first thing to look at is probably the basic text file specifications. If you look at the Flat File Connection Manager dialog box, shown in step 5 of this recipe, you will see the items listed in Table 2-1 in the General pane.

Table 2-1. *Flat File Connection Manager General Pane Options*

Pane	Element	Comments
General	Locale	Allows you to select a locale for the source data. This is used when importing and sorting date and time data types.
General	Code Page	Gives the code page of the source data file. You can select from one of the available source code pages—if you are certain about the correct one to use.
General	Unicode	Specifies that the source file is in Unicode, which makes specifying a code page superfluous.
General	Text Qualifier	You can enter the text qualifier here if the source data encloses text data in double quotes (or single quotes). Column delimiters can be set globally at the file (general) level and then overwritten for each individual column, if required.
General	Header row delimiter	Allows you to select the delimiter for the header row.
General	Header rows to skip	Defines the number of rows at the start of the file to skip (including the header row).
General	Column names in the first data row	Allows you to specify that the source file's first row of data contain column headings. These will then be used by SSIS in the data flow.
Columns	Reset Columns	Resets all column definitions to the SSIS standard (VARCHAR(50)).

So how are you likely to use these elements? In my experience, the following are the ones that you are most likely to need:

> **Text qualifier**. Indicates that the data (of whatever type) is enclosed in quotes. This could be, for instance, because the textual data contains the column delimiter (frequently a comma). This way, such characters are handled gracefully. In any case, the quotes are removed during the import process, obviating the need to remove them after import.

> **Column names in the first data row**. Indicates that the first row consists of column headings. As the name implies, the first row of the data is taken to be the column names, and, consequently, is not imported.

2-3. Automatically Determining Data Types
Problem

You want to deduce the structure of the data in a source flat file.

Solution

Use the SSIS Suggest Types option in the Flat File connection manager.

I will explain the simple approach to getting a reasonable approximation of the real data types and lengths in a source text file. This too is done using the advanced pane of the Flat File Connection Manager Editor. As this recipe builds on Recipe 2-2, to avoid repetition, you need to have read the preceding recipe before using this one.

1. Follow steps 1 to 4 in Recipe 2-2.

2. Click Advanced.

3. Click Suggest Types. The Suggest Column Types dialog box appears, as shown in Figure 2-6.

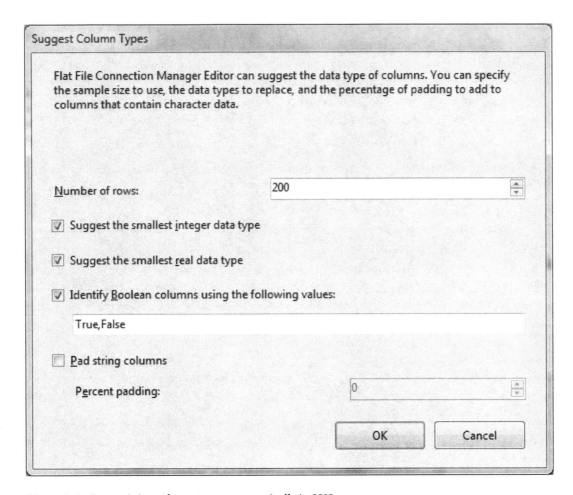

Figure 2-6. Determining column types automatically in SSIS

4. Alter any options you wish to tweak (for instance, the number of rows may be far too small for an accurate sample of a large file). Click OK.

You will see that all the data types (and lengths, where appropriate) have been sampled and adjusted in the advanced pane of the dialog box (Figure 2-5).

How It Works

You probably noticed that when importing text files, the Flat File connection manager assumes that all source columns in a delimited text file are strings with a length of 50 characters. This can be too restrictive for several reasons:

- Many fields are not strings and consequently require data type conversion as part of the SSIS package.

- The suggested length of 50 characters is insufficient for many string fields, and can cause package errors at runtime.

- Even if all the source columns can fit into 50 characters, this is frequently too wide, as it reduces the number of records that can fit into the SSIS pipeline buffer, and consequently, slows down the load process.

Frequently, of course, the problem is solved by the people who provide the source files, who will have thoughtfully handed over a complete data type description of the file contents. However, there just may be times when this is not the case, and you have to deduce, discover, or guess the field (or column if you prefer) types and lengths in a source file. This can be a painful process, especially if it means a trial-and-error-based cycle of loading and reloading a text file until you have finally found, for each source column, an acceptable data type. Consequently, a much simpler solution is to ask SSIS to guess the data types and lengths for you. Admittedly, you can open some files to look at the source data. A quick glance is rarely an accurate analytical sample, however. What is more, there will be some source flat files that are so large that they either take forever to open or simply crash your favorite text editor.

It helps to understand your options when determining the data types in the source file, as provided in Table 2-2.

Table 2-2. *Suggested Column Type Options*

Option	Description
Number of rows	The number of rows to sample. There seems to be no upper limit in SQL Server 2012. Up to SSIS 2008, it was limited to 1000 records.
Suggest the smallest integer data type	For columns that contain integers only, suggest the smallest integer type that can accommodate the data without overflowing.
Suggest the smallest real data type	For columns that contain real (numeric data type) numbers, suggest the smallest numeric type that can accommodate the data without overflowing.
Identify Boolean columns using the following values	Indicates that values can be interpreted as Boolean
Pad string columns / Percent Padding	Takes the length of the longest string ([n]varchar, [n]char) element and extends the length by the percentage you specify to anticipate longer strings in future source files.

Assuming that you know which column needs to be set to which data type, as well as setting a specific column delimiter for one or more columns, you might wish to fine-tune the data types using the Advanced pane. Table 2-3 describes the available options.

Table 2-3. *Flat File Connection Manager Advanced Pane Options*

Option	Description
Name	The column name can be set or overridden here. This is the name that is used from this point on in the SSIS data flow.
Column delimiter	The specific column delimiter for one or more columns. You can select from the list, or enter or paste the column delimiter used in the source data.
Data Type	Select the data type from the list of SSIS data types.
Output Column width	The width of the output column. This is for single-byte characters.
Text Qualified	Allows you to specify if the text in this column is qualified by using the text qualifier set in the General pane.

For example, if you wish to override the current settings for a column's data type, you could set the data type, as shown in Figure 2-5.

Should your source data change, you do not have to redo the entire column mapping structure from scratch, as SSIS lets you add or remove columns to adjust the package to changes in the source data structure.

To add a column, do the following:

1. Click the column that precedes (or follows) the column to insert.

2. Click the arrow on the right of the New button. Select Insert Before (or after). A new column is added to the mapping structure.

Clicking New or Add Column inserts a new column after the existing columns.
Removing a column is as simple as the following:

1. Select the column to remove.

2. Click Delete.

The Advanced pane of the Flat File connection manager also lets you specify, for each column, whether the column is enclosed in quotes. All you have to do is set TextQualified to True, if this is the case, and False if there are no quotes.

Hints, Tips, and Traps

- The details of OLEDB Connections in SSIS are explained in Recipe 1-7.

- You can use a .NET destination from SQL Server 2008. From SQL Server 2008 R2 and up you have the "Use Bulk Insert whenever possible" option for this destination component to accelerate the data load.

- To have SSIS handle varying numbers of column delimiters, see Recipe 2-16.

- Adjusting the data types for an existing package generates a warning triangle on the Flat File source task. To have the warning disappear, just double-click this task and confirm that you wish for SSIS to resynchronize the metadata.

- If you are not using SSIS 2012, then the maximum number of rows to sample is 1000; in some cases, this is not a representative sample. If you are experiencing problems, then it is probably best to set large data types (I8 for integers, large lengths for character fields), and then check the maximum real data lengths in the table into which the data is imported. Data length analysis like this is described in Chapter 8.

- Personally, I find it unlikely that you will ever define Flat File connection managers at package level in SQL Server 2012 (remember this is done in the Connection Managers folder of the Solution Explorer). This is because they are essentially "one-off" connections. A destination connection is another matter entirely; it would probably benefit from being defined at package level.

- If the source file is not Unicode, then do not attempt to set it to Unicode, or you risk losing all your existing column type definitions.

- SSIS will not verify that your modifications map to the source file's structure—so you need to know what you are doing.

- The ways to handle column truncation and data type transformation are given in Chapter 9.

- SSIS data types are described in Appendix A.

- You might have to copy and paste unusual column separators into the Flat File Connection Manager Editor, one row at a time, because multiple pasting is not offered.

2-4. Importing Fixed-Width Text Files
Problem
You want to import a fixed-width text file into SQL Server.

Solution
Create an SSIS package and define a Data Flow using a Flat File connection manager set to accept fixed-width files. The following explains how you can do this.

1. Create an SSIS package as described in Recipe 2-2, preparing a Flat File source and an OLEDB destination.

2. Create an OLEDB connection manager connecting to CarSales_Staging named **CarSales_Staging_OLEDB**.

3. Create a connection manager for the flat file, either as described earlier in Recipe 2-2 step 3, or by right-clicking the Connection Managers tab and selecting New Flat File Connection, as shown in Figure 2-3.

4. Once you have specified the connection name and the source file (`C:\SQL2012DIRecipes\CH02\StockFixedWidth.Txt`), specify that the format be fixed width, as shown in Figure 2-7.

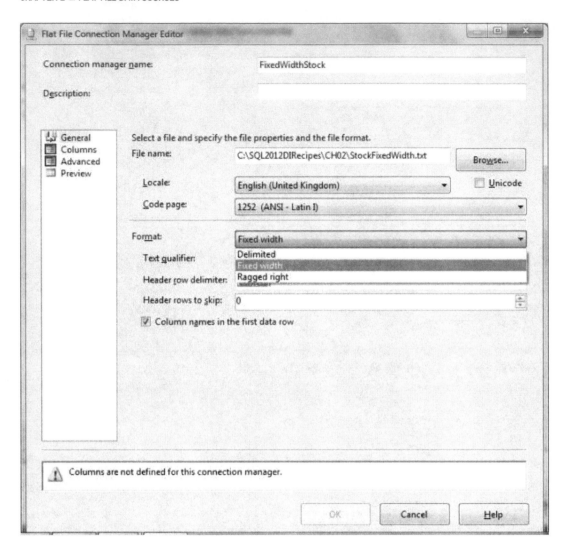

Figure 2-7. *Defining a fixed-width data source*

    5.   Display the Columns pane by clicking Columns in the left of the dialog box. You should see something like Figure 2-8.

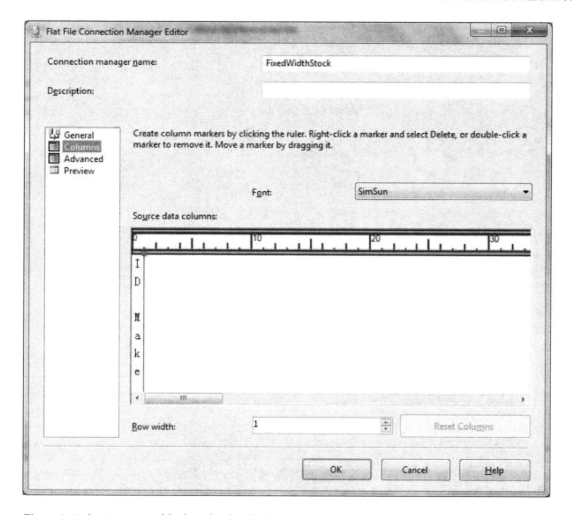

Figure 2-8. *Setting row widths for a fixed-width flat file*

6. Enter the row width. If you do not know it, try a large number! The red row marker will jump to the position you entered. You can always fine-tune the length based on the data you can see previewed in the Source Data Columns grid of the Columns pane of the Flat File Connection Manager Editor.

7. Scroll left and right through the data. Add any column delimiters that you need by clicking on the Ruler. You should end up with something like Figure 2-9.

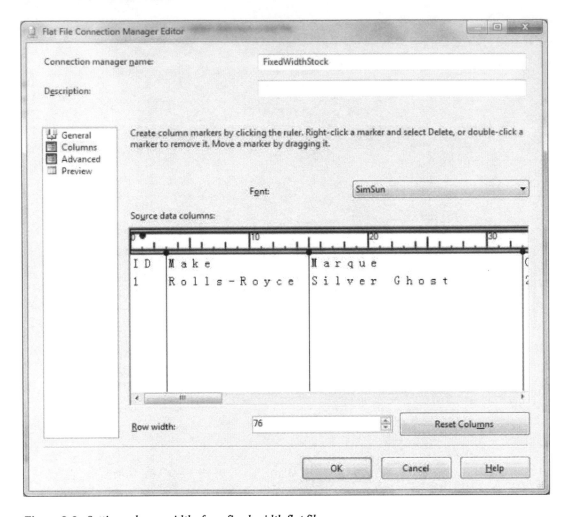

Figure 2-9. *Setting column widths for a fixed-width flat file*

8. Click OK to confirm the Connection Manager settings. You can now add the connection manager to the Flat File source (unless you are creating it as part of the Flat File source definition).

9. Connect the Flat File source to the OLEDB output.

10. Configure the OLEDB output to use the connection manager CarSales_Staging_OLEDB.

11. Add the column mappings and select or create a data table and run the import package as described in Recipe 2-2, steps 7 to 12.

How It Works

Occasionally, you may have to deal with a fixed-width file that requires importing into SQL Server. This is very similar to a delimited file, except that you have to tell SSIS where the column breaks are. All you know is that the source file is completely fixed width—that is, it has the following characteristics:

- All rows are the same width.

- All columns are of a fixed width (which can vary for each column, of course).

- There is **no** Carriage Return / Line Feed (CR/LF) at the end of each row.

This is very similar to importing a delimited file as described in the Recipe 2-2. As is the case with delimited files, you can set the following:

- Whether or not the first row contains column names

- The header rows to skip

- The text delimiter

- The names of columns

- The data types of columns

- Output column widths

All these are done as described in Recipe 2-2.

░ **Note** There may be times when you need to import a flat file where all the columns are fixed width except for the last one, which can be of variable length **or** where each row ends with a CR/LF. This is also known as a *ragged right* text file. This makes a ragged right file essentially a fixed-width text file with one major—and fundamental—difference. Each row has a CR/LF at the end. In all other respects, the Import process is the same as that for fixed-width sources.

2-5. Importing Text Files Using T-SQL
Problem

You want to import a text file using T-SQL as you are building a scripted ETL solution.

Solution

Use OPENROWSET to import text files.

In the following examples, I will use the C:\SQL2012DIRecipes\CH02\Invoices.Txt file as the source data. You can use the following code snippet(s) to load data using only T-SQL (the entire code is at C:\SQL2012DIRecipes\CH02\OpenrowsetLoad.sql):

```
SELECT    CAST(BILLNO AS VARCHAR(5)) AS BILLNO
INTO      MyTextImport
FROM      OPENROWSET('MSDASQL', 'Driver={Microsoft Text Driver (*.txt; *.csv)}; ↵
                DefaultDir=C:\SQL 2012 DI Recipes\CH02;', ↵
                'SELECT INVOICENUMBER AS BILLNO FROM INVOICES.TXT WHERE CLIENTID=1');
```

If you have spaces in the path, then you need to use the DefaultDir parameter to separate the path from the actual file name, as follows:

```
SELECT    InvoiceNumber
INTO      MyTextImport2
FROM      OPENROWSET('MSDASQL', 'Driver={Microsoft Text Driver (*.txt; *.csv)}; ↵
                DefaultDir=C:\SQL2012DIRecipes\CH02;','select * from Invoices.txt');
```

Whereas spaces in the file name require that the file name be enclosed in square brackets to allow things to work:

```
SELECT     InvoiceNumber
INTO       MyTextImport3
FROM       OPENROWSET('MSDASQL', 'Driver={Microsoft Text Driver (*.txt; *.csv)}; ↩
               DefaultDir=C:\SQL2012DIRecipes\CH02;','SELECT * FROM [In voices.txt]');
```

Should you prefer (which is another way of saying, "if you hit problems with the Microsoft text driver, try this as a first fallback position"), then you can use MSDASQL and the Jet text driver, like this:

```
SELECT     InvoiceNumber
INTO       MyTextImport4
FROM       OPENROWSET('MSDASQL', 'Driver={Microsoft Access Text Driver (*.txt, *.csv)};', ↩
               'SELECT * FROM C:\SQL2012DIRecipes\CH02\Invoices.txt');
```

Note that (*.txt, *.csv) are separated by a comma in this case. It is also worth noting that you can use the ACE OLEDB driver (described in Recipe 1-1) directly (without needing to run ODBC over OLEDB, as is the case with the MSDASQL driver), as follows:

```
SELECT     InvoiceNumber
INTO       MyTextImport5
FROM       OPENROWSET('Microsoft.ACE.OLEDB.12.0', ↩
               'Text;Database=C:\SQL2012DIRecipes\CH02;HDR=Yes','SELECT * FROM Invoices.txt');
```

How It Works

Sometimes SSIS is either overkill or simply not your preferred solution when you want to import a text file. This is where OPENROWSET comes in. It both allows you to query the source data file and returns a rowset that can then be used to insert data, as part of a subquery, in a JOIN statement or in a Common Table Expression (CTE).

You should use this approach in the following circumstances:

- When you have a consistently-structured delimited CSV or text file.

- When the source data file is not overly large—otherwise, you are better off using BULKINSERT, as explained in Recipe 2-10.

- When ad hoc querying has been enabled (see Recipe 1-4).

- When the source file is structured coherently (all columns have comma-separated headers), then you should be able to return your source data to SQL Server using a code snippet like the one shown.

Because OPENROWSET is designed to be used as an integral part of T-SQL programming to read—and load—delimited data files into SQL Server, you would expect it to allow T-SQL variables to be used to define its various parameters. Unfortunately, this is not the case. The only way to use T-SQL variables is to use dynamic SQL with OPENROWSET. This means that the command in its entirety will be a string variable with other T-SQL variables inserted where required. This can rapidly become extremely clunky and difficult to debug (remember all those quoted strings). However, if you remember that OPENROWSET is designed essentially for ad hoc data requests, you could consider this limitation to be a nudge in the direction of good programming practice. In these examples, I used SELECT...INTO. There is nothing to prevent you from using INSERT INTO...SELECT instead.

Hints, Tips, and Traps

- The source data file must be flawless (or at least perceived as error-free by the Microsoft text driver) for this to work.

- Column names can be aliased, and data subsetted, using T-SQL as described in Recipe 1-4.

- If you are using a WHERE clause involving a text value, you will need to enclose the text in double quotes.

- Column headers in the first row are optional, but if there are no column names then the text driver will use the first row as column headers. To get around this see how to use a Schema.ini file as described in Recipe 2-6.

- The SELECT statement can contain an ORDER BY if you wish.

- Ad hoc queries must be enabled, as described in Recipe 1-4.

- The ADODB provider MSDASQL reads CSV files correctly, unlike the BCP utility described in Recipe 2-9.

- For complex source data files where you need to specify delimiters and separators, you need to use BULK INSERT, as described in Recipe 2-10.

- If there are any NULL fields in the first row, you will get the following error message:

  Msg 492, Level 16, State 1, Line 1 (more information ommitted)

- Duplicate column names are not allowed in result sets obtained through OPENQUERY and OPENROWSET. In this case, you either have to add column names manually to the source text file (which can be difficult to impossible for files that are gigabytes in size), or use a schema information file, as described in Recipe 2-6.

- Because both the MSDASQL driver and the ACE driver are available in 64-bit versions, either will work in a 64-bit environment.

- I presume that you will run this type of import on an OS server—possibly using a Remote Destktop connection. In my experience, Vista causes permissions problems with MSDASQL. The quick solution to these problems is to run SSMS as an Administrator.

2-6. Mapping a Source File

Problem

You need to apply complex mapping to a source file to import it correctly and avoid errors due to duplicate column names or data type issues.

Solution

Create a schema information file that you place in the same directory as the source data file.

A simple schema information file designed to handle the C:\SQL2012DIRecipes\CH02\Invoices2.Txt sample file—that unfortunately does not have column names—could look like this (C:\SQL2012DIRecipes\CH02\Schema.ini):

```
[Invoices2.txt]
Format = CSVDelimited
CharacterSet = OEM
ColNameHeader = False
Col1 = ID Integer
Col2 = InvoiceNumber Char Width 255
Col3 = ClientID Integer
Col4 = TotalDiscount Currency
Col5 = DeliveryCharge Currency
```

How It Works

If the source data, does not have a header record, or if you wish to provide data type information to the text driver, then you may need to provide a schema information file to indicate to the Microsoft text driver how best to deal with the source data structure. A schema information file is a text file, always named Schema.ini, and **always** kept in the same directory as the text data source files. It can contain schema information for multiple source files, because each file name must be given.

A schema information file can specify the following:

- The text file name (as there is only one possible Schema.ini file, this can contain information for multiple source files, each identified by the source file name in square brackets)

- The file format

- The character set

- Special data type conversions

- Column header indicators

- The field names, widths, and types

However, a Schema.ini file does not exist only to add column names. You can use it to override the existing column names and alter data types when reading the source data, as shown in the following part of a schema information file. This snippet of the C:\SQL2012DIRecipes\CH02\Schema.Ini Schema.ini file overrides the data types and column names of the text file (C:\SQL2012DIRecipes\CH02\Invoices.Txt) that we used in Recipe 2-5.

```
[Invoices.txt]
Format = CSVDelimited
CharacterSet = OEM
ColNameHeader = True
Col1 = ID Integer
Col2 = BillNumber Char Width 255
Col3 = IDClient Integer
Col4 = TotalDiscount Integer
Col5 = DeliveryCharge Currency
```

These examples only show a few of a schema information file's possibilities. Table 2-4 provides a fuller description of many of the available parameters.

Table 2-4. *Schema.ini File Options*

Specifier	Comments
Format = CSVDelimited	Indicates to the driver that it is processing a CSV file.
Format = TabDelimited	Indicates to the driver that the records are in a tab-delimited format.
Format = Delimited(delimiter)	Lets you to specify a custom delimiter.
Format = FixedLength	Indicates to the driver that this is a fixed-length data file.
CharacterSet = ANSI	Tells the driver that the file consists of ANSI characters.
CharacterSet = OEM	Tells the driver that the file consists of non-ANSI characters.
ColNameHeader = True	Tells the driver that the first row contains column headers.

There are further options available, but in my experience, they are rarely used. Should you need this information, you can find it at http://msdn.microsoft.com/en-us/library/windows/desktop/ms709353(v=vs.85).aspx.

In this example, I named the schema information file C:\SQL2012DIRecipes\CH02\Schema.Ini. OPENROWSET automatically uses the information in the schema information file for each source file that is referenced.

Rather than handcraft a schema information file, you can create one a using the ODBC Administrator to save time and minimize the potential for error. This can be done at the same time you create a System DSN, like this:

1. Open the ODBC Data Source Administrator (Control Panel ➤ Administrative Tools ➤ DataSources). Click System DSN. The dialog box looks like that shown in Figure 2-10.

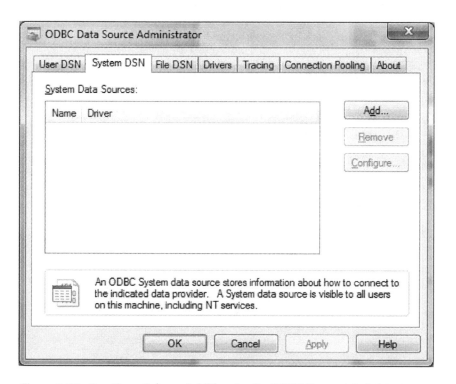

Figure 2-10. *Creating a Schema.ini File using the ODBC Source Administrator*

2. Click Add. Select Microsoft Text Driver (as shown in Figure 2-11).

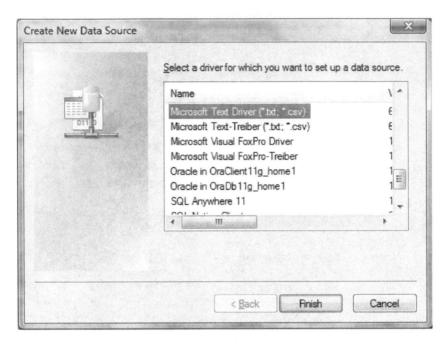

Figure 2-11. *Selecting the Microsoft text driver*

3. Click Finish, then Options in the ODBC Text setup dialog box.

4. Enter a data source name.

5. Uncheck Use Current Directory. Click Select Directory to browse to the directory where the source text files are located.

6. Uncheck Default and select or enter the required file extension if it is not in the existing list. The dialog box should look something like Figure 2-12.

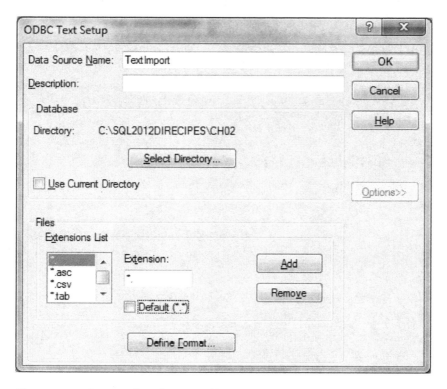

Figure 2-12. *Creating the Schema.ini file*

7. Click Define Format. Then click each file you wish to create full schema information for, followed by Guess.

8. Click OK. Confirm any error message. Cancel out of the ODBC Data Source Administrator.

■ **Note** On 64-bit machines where you are running the 32-bit version of the Microsoft text driver, you must run the 32-bit version of Odbcad32.exe (located in %systemdrive%\Windows\SysWoW64) for this recipe's solution to work. Otherwise, you will not see the (32-bit) Microsoft text driver.

You will find a Schema.ini file containing base elements for all the files of the selected type—and full column specifications for all files where you requested the ODBC Data Source Administrator to guess the data structures. You may now modify this file to suit your precise requirements. The resulting file is very dense and generally difficult to read. You may want to consider editing it to remove any unwanted file specifications, and to generally clean it up.

Hints, Tips, and Traps

- Whether the column headers exist in the first row or not, you must refer to the columns as Col1, Col2...Col'n', and so forth in the Schema.Ini file.

- I have read on various web postings that there is a limit of 255 columns in a Schema.ini file. Although as I have not had to import files this wide using OPENROWSET, I cannot say that it has ever been a problem for me.

2-7. Importing Data Using T-SQL in Anticipation of Using a Linked Server

Problem

You want to—eventually—use a linked server to import a text file. Until this is set up, you want to code your T-SQL for an (eventual) linked server so that you don't have to rewrite too much code when the linked server is set up.

Solution

Use OPENDATASOURCE. The following shows the code to do it (C:\SQL2012DIRecipes\CH02\OpendatasourceAndDestinationTable.sql).

1. Create a suitably structured destination table:

```
CREATE TABLE Text_OpenrowsetInsert
(
 ID
 ,InvoiceNumber INT
 ,ClientID INT
 ,TotalDiscount NUMERIC (18,2)
 ,DeliveryCharge NUMERIC (18,2)
);
GO
```

2. Run the following code snippet, which loads the C:\SQL2012DIRecipes\CH02\Invoices.Txt source file:

```
INSERT INTO    Text_OpenrowsetInsert (ID, InvoiceNumber, ClientID, TotalDiscount,
                                      DeliveryCharge)
SELECT         F1,F2,F3,F4,F5
FROM           OpenDataSource('Microsoft.ACE.OLEDB.12.0',
                      'Data Source = C:\SQL2012DIRecipes\CH02;
                       Extended Properties = "Text;HDR=NO;"'
                   )... Invoices#txt;
```

How It Works

Should you consider using a linked server to connect to your text file, but want to "test the waters" first, then you might want to use OPENDATASOURCE to read your flat file.

You might want to use OPENDATASOURCE in the following circumstances:

- When you have a consistently-structured delimited CSV or text file.

- When you wish to specify parameters such as the header rows, or specify columns to select even if there are no column names.

- When the source data file is reliably and consistently structured (or at least perceived as error-free by the Microsoft text driver).

I use the ACE driver with OPENDATASOURCE whenever possible. There are a couple of good reasons for this:

- It gracefully handles the absence of column headers in the first row by naming the columns F1, F2...F'n', and so forth.

- There are generally few 32-bit/64-bit issues.

For the Jet driver (and so by definition in a 32-bit environment), the code is

```
INSERT INTO      Text_OpenrowsetInsert (ID, InvoiceNumber, ClientID,
                                        TotalDiscount, DeliveryCharge)
SELECT           F1,F2,F3,F4,F5
FROM             OPENDATASOURCE( 'Microsoft.Jet.OLEDB.4.0',
                                 'Data Source = C:\SQL2012DIRecipes\CH02;
                                 Extended Properties = "Text;HDR=YES;"'
                                 )...Invoices#txt;
```

You can easily specify if there are header rows by setting the extended property flag to either "Text;HDR=YES;" or "Text;HDR=NO;".

▓ **Note**   You have to use a hash/pound sign (#) in the file name instead of a dot/period.

If there are no column names in the first row, the ACE driver will name the columns F1, F2... and so forth. These names can then be used to query the data, as shown in the following. In this case, NULLS are accepted in the first row.

```
SELECT           F1
FROM             OPENDATASOURCE(
                                 'Microsoft.Jet.OLEDB.4.0',
                                 'Data Source = C:\SQL2012DIRecipes\CH02;
                                 Extended Properties = "Text;HDR=NO;"'
                                 )...Invoices#txt
```

If you have created a System DSN (described in Recipe 4-8), then you can use this with OPENDATASOURCE, as follows:

```
SELECT           ID, InvoiceNumber, ClientID, TotalDiscount, DeliveryCharge
FROM             OPENDATASOURCE('SQLOLEDB', 'DSN=MyDSN;')...Invoices#txt
```

Hints, Tips, and Traps

- In a 32-bit environment, you can use the MS Jet driver instead of the ACE driver.

- You need a Schema.ini file (described in Recipe 2-6) if using a text driver over MSDASQL if the text file does not contain column headers. This is because OPENDATASOURCE expects a tabular structure with headers, and the MSDASQL driver will not (unlike Jet and ACE) provide "dummy" column headers.

- It is worth noting that if you are using MSDASQL to access the venerable text file driver you can now download a 64-bit version for older versions of 64-bit Windows computers. This driver is included in Windows Server 2008 through Vista SP1. You can find it at www.microsoft.com/en-gb/download/details.aspx?id=20065.

- If you do create a schema information file, then the column names that you specify there will be used by the Jet driver instead of the F1, F2, and so forth—and even to override the column headers if the file contains them.

- The T-SQL used with OPENDATASOURCE and the ACE driver can be extended using WHERE, ORDER BY, CAST, CONVERT. You can also alias column names.

2-8. Accessing a Text File As a Linked Server Table
Problem

You want to avoid importing data from a text file, yet be able to use it in T-SQL queries.

Solution

Access the text file as a Linked Server table. The following explains how, using the C:\SQL2012DIRecipes\CH02\Invoices.Txt file as the data source.

1. Run the following T-SQL snippet (which, along with all the T-SQL in this recipe, can be found in C:\SQL2012DIRecipes\CH02\FlatFileLinkedServer.sql):

    ```
    EXECUTE master.dbo.sp_addlinkedserver TXT_INVOICES, ' ', 'Microsoft.ACE.OLEDB.12.0', ↵
                        'C:\SQL2012DIRecipes\CH02', NULL, 'Text';
    ```

2. Define security—or rather its absence:

    ```
    EXECUTE master.dbo.sp_addlinkedsrvlogin 'TXT_INVOICES', false, NULL, 'admin';
    ```

3. Create a Schema.ini file, using either a text editor or the ODBC Administrator, as described in the last recipe.

4. If you have a System DSN set up, you can use this in the linked server configuration. In this example, I have set up a System DSN using the Microsoft text driver. I called it MSTEXT:

    ```
    EXECUTE master.dbo.sp_addlinkedserver 'TXT_INVOICES', ↵
                        ' ', 'MSDASQL', 'MSTEXT';
    ```

5. You can then use the linked server in a standard four-part SQL query, which can become part of a more complex T-SQL command, such as:

```
INSERT INTO Text_OpenrowsetInsert (ID, InvoiceNumber, ClientID, TotalDiscount,
                                   DeliveryCharge) ;
SELECT ID, InvoiceNumber, ClientID, TotalDiscount, DeliveryCharge
FROM TXT_INVOICES...Invoices#txt;
```

or:

```
INSERT INTO Text_OpenrowsetInsert (ID, InvoiceNumber, ClientID, TotalDiscount,
                                   DeliveryCharge)
SELECT ID, InvoiceNumber, ClientID, TotalDiscount, DeliveryCharge
FROM OPENQUERY(TXT_INVOICES,'SELECT * FROM Invoices#txt');
```

How It Works

As is the case with Excel, Access, and most relational data sources, you can use a delimited flat file data source as a linked server. As linked servers require OLEDB, you have either to use ODBC over OLEDB, or use an OLEDB provider. Be warned, however, that this will run extremely slowly on any driver that you use—and some drivers (Jet, for instance) are limited to 32-bit environments. Also be aware that a Schema.ini file is required. This is best used in the following circumstances:

- When you have a consistently-structured delimited CSV or text file.

- When you wish to use ad hoc queries frequently to load flat-file data in your T-SQL code, but do not wish to import the data using SSIS.

- When the source data can change frequently, and so requires immediate access without any form of data import.

- When the source data is not too voluminous, and quick querying is not essential.

I prefer to use the ACE driver to set up a linked server to a text file, because it is available for 32- and 64-bit environments, and has always worked for me.

If you wish to avoid T-SQL to set up a linked server, you can use SSMS to carry out the task. This is explained in Recipe 1-13. Linked server security is irrelevant for a flat file—so at least there are no extra complications at this level as long as the SQL account using the linked server can access the folder where the flat file is stored.

Hints, Tips, and Traps

See Recipe 2-6 for details on how to set up an ODBC DSN.

- A linked server will use a Schema.ini file if you have created one.

- The last example deliberately uses SELECT * in the pass-through query to show that the pass-through query and the T-SQL can be slightly different.

- If you wish to create a linked server using slightly longer-winded (but easier to debug) code, you can try something like this—for Jet, here—using a fully parameterized statement:

```
EXECUTE master.dbo.sp_addlinkedserver
 @SERVER = 'TXTACCESS',
 @PROVIDER = 'Microsoft.Jet.OLEDB.4.0',
 @SRVPRODUCT = 'Jet',
 @DATASRC = 'C:\SQL2012DIRecipes\CH02\',
 @PROVSTR = 'Text'
```

2-9. Importing Flat Files from the Command Line

Problem

You want to load flat files from the command line as fast as possible.

Solution

Load the data using BCP. It can be done like this:

1. Ensure that a destination table whose structure maps to the source file exists. In this example, it is CarSales_Staging.dbo.Invoice.

2. Open a command prompt.

3. Enter the following:

    ```
    BCP CarSales_Staging.dbo.Invoices IN C:\SQL2012DIRecipes\CH02\Invoices.txt ↵
    -T -SADAM02
    ```

4. Press Enter to run the BCP command from the command prompt.

5. Confirm the data type, prefix length, and field terminator for each field in the data source when prompted.

How It Works

BCP (Bulk Copy Program) has been around since SQL Server first appeared. While nobody would describe it as "user-friendly," it certainly does what its name suggests. That is, it copies bulk data into—and also out of—SQL Server with outstanding efficiency. BCP is not just designed to copy text data (as you will see in Chapter 5). It also has a large number of switches that can make it seem daunting at first. However, it is a tool that repays many times over the effort involved in mastering it, despite the seemingly arduous learning curve.

I am assuming that there may be times when you wish to import text files from outside SQL Server, either interactively from the command line or from a command (.cmd) file. Whatever your reasons, it will certainly do the same job as BULK INSERT (as explained in Recipe 2-10)—only from a command prompt. Should you choose this path, then you can use the same format files as BULK INSERT, and essentially, you will be using the same options, only as command line flags. BCP is best used

- When you wish to load data without invoking T-SQL (though this is possible - if your SQL Server security considerations allow it, then you can also use xp_cmdshell to run BCP from a T-SQL script).

- When you want to use a batch file or a non-SQL Server–based process to load data.

- When the source flat file is rigorously uniform and error-free.

At its most streamlined, BCP requires four parameters:

- The fully-qualified three-part table name for the destination table (database.schema.table).

- The keyword "IN" to tell BCP that data is being imported into SQL Server.

- The full path to the source data file. The full path must be enclosed in double quotes if it contains spaces.

- Any required switches—specifically the SQL Server security being used (integrated security or user and password) and the SQL Server instance name.

■ **Note** If there is only one active SQL Server instance on the server, you do not need to specify the destination server. Otherwise, you must specify the SQL Server instance to use. It is always good practice to specify the server and the database.

A format file is optional, but without one, BCP will ask for confirmation of the data type, prefix length, and field terminator for each field in the data source. This is something that you may already have discovered, and I find that it can rapidly become extremely wearing. Admittedly, if you do this once, then BCP asks at the end of the process if you want to create a format file to reuse. My advice is to always say Yes. This will be an older, text-type format file because you have to create XML format files using the -x switch, as described in Recipe 2-11.

So, assuming that you have created a format file as defined in Recipe 2-11, or asked BCP to create one when running an initial import, this is how to use it:

```
BCP CarSales_Staging.dbo.Invoices IN C:\SQL2012DIRecipes\CH02\Invoices.txt -T -f ↲
C:\SQL2012DIRecipes\CH02\Invoices.Fmt
```

For BCP to stand any chance at all of working properly, you need to be able to connect to the server. There are two options:

- Integrated security

- SQL Server authentication

For the former, simply add the -I switch to any BCP switches used.

To use SQL Server authentication, add -UyourUserName -PyourPassword to any BCP switches used. For instance:

```
BCP CarSales_Staging.dbo.Invoices IN C:\SQL2012DIRecipes\CH02\Invoices.txt -UAdam -PMe4Boss
```

These three switches must be in UPPERCASE. You can add a space between the switch and the name or password if you wish.

If you are not connecting to a single instance of SQL Server on the server itself, you need to specify the server and/or instance. This is done using the -S switch. For instance:

```
BCP CarSales_Staging.dbo.Invoices IN C:\SQL2012DIRecipes\CH02\Invoices.txt ↲
-T -SmyServer\FirstInstance
```

This switch must be in UPPERCASE too.

As BCP has a plethora of command line parameters, Table 2-5 is a résumé of the major parameters (also called flags) that you may find useful.

Table 2-5. *BCP Command-Line Parameters*

BCP Flag	Description	Comments
-m	Max errors	This flag specifies the maximum number of errors you want BCP to allow before the process is halted and an error raised.
-f	Format file	This flag specifies the format file to be used (in either the "old" text-based format or the "new" XML format).
-e	Err file	This flag specifies the error file and path where error file is created.
-F	First row	This flag specifies the first row to import.
-L	Last row	This flag specifies the last row to import.
-b	Batch size	This flag specifies the number of rows from the source file that are committed per batch. They can be rolled back in the event of failure.
-c	Character file	Using this flag ensures that BCP will not prompt for data types. It presumes that all fields are text fields. It also presupposes a tab character as the field terminator and the newline character (CHAR(10)) as the row terminator.
-w	Unicode file	Using this flag ensures that BCP will not prompt for data types. It presumes that all fields are Unicode. It also presupposes a tab character as the field terminator and the newline character (CHAR(10)) as the row terminator.
-q	Quoted Identifiers	This flag must be used if you have spaces or quotes in the names of the database and/or file(s).
-t	Field terminator	Use this flag if you need to override the default (\t tab character) field separator.
-r	Row terminator	Use this flag if you need to override the default (\n newline character) row terminator.
-T	Trusted connection	This flag specifies that integrated security will be used to connect to SQL Server.
-U	Username	This flag gives the user login to connect to SQL Server if integrated security is not used.
-P	Password	This flag gives the user password to connect to SQL Server if integrated security is not used.
-S	Server name	This flag gives the name of the server you want to connect to.
-k	Keep NULLS	Use this flag to keep NULLS from the source data, rather than using default values specified in the table definition.
-E	Keep IDENTITY values	This flag tells BCP to use the values in the source data for the IDENTITY column, and not continue the existing sequence in the destination table.
-h	Hints	Allows you to specify that CHECK_CONSTRAINTS, TABLOCK, and ORDER will be used.

Running BCP from T-SQL is devastatingly simple. The following code snippet also loads the data in the previous example from the same source file into the same destination table:

```
DECLARE @BCPVARIABLE VARCHAR(500) = 'BCP CarSales_Staging.dbo.Invoices ↵
IN C:\SQL2012DIRecipes\CH02\Invoices.txt -T -SADAMO2 -f C:\SQL2012DIRecipes\CH02\Invoices.Fmt';
EXECUTE master.dbo.xp_cmdshell @BCPVARIABLE;
```

You will need to allow the use of xp_cmdshell, from either Facets ➤ Surface Area Configuration (obtained by right-clicking the server/instance in SSMS) or the Surface Area Configuration utility (if you are using an older version of SQL Server). Of course, I am presuming that the DBA will allow this, which might not be the case. You can also run the following T-SQL to enable xp_cmdshell:

```
EXECUTE sp_configure 'show advanced options', 1;
GO
RECONFIGURE;
GO
EXECUTE sp_configure 'xp_cmdshell', 1;
GO
RECONFIGURE;
GO.
```

Hints, Tips, and Traps

- BCP displays the message "1000 rows sent to SQL Server" after every 1000 rows. This message is informational only. It occurs whatever the batch size.

- You can save the BCP text in a command file (.cmd) and execute that if you prefer.

- BCP options are case sensitive, so be careful when entering them.

- If the source data file contains column headers, remember to set the -F (first data row) flag to 2.

- BCP can also export flat files, but this is handled in Recipe 7-4. It is particularly efficient at transferring data between SQL Servers, as you will see in Chapter 4.

2-10. Importing Large Text Files Using T-SQL and Putting the Emphasis on Speed
Problem

You want to import a large text file as fast as possible using a T-SQL-based approach.

Solution

Load the file using T-SQL's BULK INSERT Command. I'll explain how.

1. Create a destination table to hold the data that you will be importing. For this example the DDL is (C:\SQL2012DIRecipes\CH02\tblInvoiceBulkLoad.Sql):

```
CREATE TABLE CarSales_Staging.dbo.InvoiceBulkLoad
(
 ID int IDENTITY(1,1) NOT NULL,
 InvoiceNumber VARCHAR(50) NULL,
 ClientID INT NULL,
 TotalDiscount numeric(18, 2) NULL,
 DeliveryCharge numeric(18, 2) NULL
) ;
GO
```

2. Run the following code to load the C:\SQL2012DIRecipes\CH02\InvoiceBulkLoad. Txt text file into the dbo.InvoiceBulkLoad table (which was created before beginning the load process).

```
BULK INSERT CarSales_Staging.dbo.InvoiceBulkLoad
    FROM 'C:\SQL2012DIRecipes\CH02\InvoiceBulkLoad.Txt'
    WITH
       (
          FIELDTERMINATOR = ',',
          ROWTERMINATOR = '\n',
          FIRSTROW = 2
       );
```

How It Works

When faced with large and complex source text files, then there is only one real answer for developing a T-SQL-based solution: use BULK INSERT to do the heavy lifting. Before starting, you would do well to forget some of the myths that surround this particular data integration option. Contrary to popular opinion, it need not be complex, and it has the following advantages:

- It is one of the fastest available solutions.
- It can be parameterized to handle complex data sources, including only loading certain parts of the source data.
- It can be tweaked to process very large loads in an optimal manner.

Most of the power of the BULK INSERT command comes from the following:

- The multiple parameters you can set.
- The control that is provided by the format files that you create to control data mapping during the load process.

Format files have received bad press over the years; they are perceived as unduly complex since they appeared with the venerable BCP program (to which BULK INSERT is a dignified successor). However, you will see in Recipe 2-11 that in their second incarnation as XML files, there is nothing difficult about them, and the possibilities they bring to the potentially arduous task of loading large amounts of data from text files makes them well worth mastering.

BULK INSERT is best used in the following circumstances:

- When the destination table structure exists
- When you need to specify global and/or specific column and row delimiters
- When speed is of the essence
- For large loads
- When you need the greatest possible control over the load process

In this example, the source file contains header information, so the BULK INSERT begins at the second row in order to load the data only—and to avoid type conflicts when loading numeric data as a field name is nearly always character data.

Now that you have seen how simple BULK INSERT can be, let's look at the options it provides, as shown in Table 2-6.

Table 2-6. *BULK INSERT Options*

Option	Comments
BATCHSIZE	Specifies the number of rows from the source file that will be loaded (committed) or rolled back in the event of a load failure.
CHECK_CONSTRAINTS	Causes user-defined check constraints to be applied. Note that UNIQUE, PRIMARY KEY, FOREIGN KEY, or NOT NULL constraints are always enforced.
CODEPAGE	This option specifies the code page of the data in the data file. This is only of use if the data contains char, varchar, or text using extended characters.
DATAFILETYPE	Specifies the type of data file.
ERRORFILE	Gives the path and name of the error file in which errors will be logged.
FIELDTERMINATOR	Specifies the character(s) used to end a field (column) when using char and widechar source data files. The default field terminator is the tab character (\t).
FIRE_TRIGGERS	Indicates that triggers must fire for each row imported.
FIRSTROW	Gives the row at which the import will begin.
KILOBYTES_PER_BATCH	Specifies the number of kilobytes per batch.
KEEPIDENTITY	Indicates that the values in the source data for the IDENTITY column must be used, rather than continuing with the destination table's IDENTITY sequencing.
KEEPNULLS	Keeps NULLS—rather than loading any default values that are specified in the destination table.
LASTROW	The final row to load from the source file.
MAXERRORS	The maximum number of rows that fail during a load before a BULK INSERT fails. The default is 10.
ORDER	Specifies the sort order of the source data. The source file must be presorted if this is defined.
TABLOCK	Locks the destination table to speed up data load by preventing lock escalation.
ROWTERMINATOR	Defines the character that ends each row. The standard is '\n'—the new line character.

More practically, how can you use these options? The next few paragraphs will give some examples. This is not intended to be exhaustive, but to give you some ideas for your own data-loading solutions.

Selecting a number of records allows you to import the source data in smaller chunks. There could be several possible reasons for needing to do this, including:

- You need to debug the process and have to "close in on" an error in a very large source file.

- You are required to insert batches into multiple tables.

The following code snippet selects a subset of rows (C:\SQL2012DIRecipes\CH02\BulkInsertSubset.sql):

```
BULK INSERT dbo.InvoiceBulkLoad
    FROM 'C:\SQL2012DIRecipes\CH02\InvoiceBulkLoad.Txt'
    WITH
        (
            FIELDTERMINATOR = ',',
            ROWTERMINATOR = '\n',
            FIRSTROW = 2,
            LASTROW = 5
        );
```

Setting the batch size ensures that the entire load will not fail once the minimum number of errors has been reached. The following code snippet shows how to do this. It also creates the error files InvoicesErr and InvoicesErr.Error.Txt. The first allows you to see any errors created during the load; the second contains any error messages and row number(s) and offsets to help you track the error down. Setting MAXERRORS-0 will cause failure on the first error encountered during the data load (C:\SQL2012DIRecipes\CH02\BulkInsertFailOnError.sql).

```
BULK INSERT dbo.InvoiceBulkLoad
    FROM 'C:\SQL2012DIRecipes\CH02\InvoiceBulkLoad.Txt'
    WITH
        (
            FIELDTERMINATOR = ',',
            ROWTERMINATOR = '\n',
            FIRSTROW = 2,
            BATCHSIZE = 5,
            MAXERRORS = 0,
            ERRORFILE = 'C:\SQL2012DIRecipes\CH02\InvoicesErr'
        );
```

So, if the following text file is used (note the alphabetical character as an ID in the last line):

```
ID,InvoiceNumber,ClientID,TotalDiscount,DeliveryCharge
1,a5,1,500.00,250.00
2,a6,2,50.00,150.00
3,a5,1,500.00,250.00
4,a6,2,50.00,150.00
5,a5,1,500.00,250.00
6,a6,2,50.00,150.00
7,a5,1,500.00,250.00
Z,a6,2,50.00,150.00
```

Then the load will fail—but the first four records (the header row is counted toward the batch size of five) are loaded successfully. The InvoicesErr file will look something like Figure 2-13.

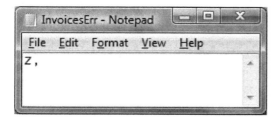

Figure 2-13. *A bulk load error file*

And the InvoicesErr.Error.Txt file is as follows:

```
Row 9 File Offset 207 ErrorFile Offset 0 - HRESULT 0x80020005
```

All of which helps you to locate the error very quickly.

The following code snippet will keep NULL values in the source data (instead of using default values), apply all constraints, fire triggers, and use the IDENTITY values in the source data (C:\SQL2012DIRecipes\CH02\BulkInsertKeepIdentity.sql).

```
BULK INSERT dbo.InvoiceBulkLoad
    FROM 'C:\SQL2012DIRecipes\CH02\InvoiceBulkLoad.Txt'
    WITH
        (
            FIELDTERMINATOR = ',',
            ROWTERMINATOR = '\n',
            FIRSTROW = 2,
            KEEPNULLS,
            KEEPIDENTITY,
            FIRE_TRIGGERS,
            CHECK_CONSTRAINTS
        ) ;
```

If you want the import to perform as fast as possible, then you need to ensure the following:

- That minimal logging is used. This is described in Chapter 14.

- That there are no indexes on the table.

- That the table has a clustered index, that the ORDER hint tells BULK INSERT that the column in the source data is the requisite column—and the source data is already sorted by this key.

- That the table can be locked (that is, there are no locks already on it when running the BULK INSERT).

- That the data is imported in a single batch.

- That triggers and constraints are not applied.

- That NULLS are kept instead of default values being applied.

The following code snippet uses these hints to maximize import speed, and assumes that there is a clustered index on the ID column of the destination table (C:\SQL2012DIRecipes\CH02\BulkInsertOrderedSource.sql):

```
BULK INSERT dbo.Invoice
    FROM 'C:\SQL2012DIRecipes\CH02\Invoices.Txt'
    WITH
        (
            FIELDTERMINATOR = ',',
            ROWTERMINATOR = '\n',
            FIRSTROW = 2,
            TABLOCK,
            KEEPNULLS,
            ORDER (ID ASC)
        ) ;
```

While the many options available using BULK INSERT can handle many of the tweaks required to guarantee a successful import, they cannot handle column mapping. That is, the source file must, for a "plain vanilla" BULK INSERT, contain the same number of columns as the destination table, and the columns must be in the same order in both the source file and the destination table. So, before we see how to handle column mapping using format files, you might want to consider a fairly simple alternative that will allow you to load text files—use a view as the destination. This approach lets you avoid mapping columns using a format file. It is most effective when

- There are fewer columns in the source than in the destination.

- The source and destination columns are in differing order.

- There are no NOT NULL columns in the destination table that do not have corresponding source data in the source text file.

- You do not have insert privileges on certain of columns in the destination table.

You will require a view based on the destination table containing the columns found in the source file. A sample that will load data into the same destination table used in the preceding examples, but from a source file with only three columns of data (Invoices2.Txt) is as follows (C:\SQL2012DIRecipes\CH02\BulkInsertView.sql contains both the view and the BULK INSERT command):

```
CREATE VIEW dbo.vw_Invoice2
AS
SELECT     ID, InvoiceNumber, ClientID
FROM       dbo.Invoice;
GO
```

Once the view has been created, it can be used for a BULK INSERT, like this:

```
BULK INSERT dbo.vw_Invoice2
    FROM 'C:\SQL2012DIRecipes\CH02\Invoices2.Txt'
    WITH
        (
            FIELDTERMINATOR = ',',
            ROWTERMINATOR = '\n'
        );
```

You can also use the view to change the column order if you need to. This can be an extremely useful technique when the source file changes structure (with or without warning) and you need a quick fix to allow the data to be loaded. The view used as a data load destination must be updatable, however. Moreover, the modifications made by the INSERT statement cannot affect more than one of the base tables referenced in the FROM clause of the view. For example, an INSERT into a multitable view must use a column_list that references only columns from one base table. Remember also that a view is not allowed if there is a self-join with the same view or with any of the member tables in the statement. Finally, to update a partitioned view, the user must have INSERT, UPDATE, and DELETE permissions on the member tables. There are other restrictions that apply when updating partitioned views, for which I advise you to consult Books OnLine (BOL).

If you have to load a file where all the fields are enclosed in quotes, this can be handled using code as follows (C:\SQL2012DIRecipes\CH02\BulkInsertQuotedFields.sql):

```
BULK INSERT dbo.Invoice
    FROM 'C:\SQL2012DIRecipes\CH02\Invoices.Txt'
    WITH
      (
          FIELDTERMINATOR = '","',
          ROWTERMINATOR = '"\n',
          FIRSTROW = 2
      );
```

All the fields must be quoted for this approach to work.

Hints, Tips, and Traps

- Data type conversions mean that you must use a format file. These are described in Recipe 2-11.

- The source data file can be locally connected or specified using the Universal Naming Convention.

- The standard row terminators are '\r' for a line feed and '\n' for a carriage return, or '\r\n' for both (CR/LF).

- The field and row terminators used in the source text file can be any printable character (control characters are not printable—except null, tab, newline, and carriage return)—or a string of up to 10 printable characters, including some or all of the terminators listed earlier.

- Specifying the ORDER hint if there is no clustered index will cause the hint to be ignored.

- Once the data is imported, you can (re)apply indexes. If there is no clustered index, then remember to create the clustered index first, and nonclustered indexes afterward.

- The InvoicesErr error file is particularly useful because it gives the data causing the error. The InvoicesErr.error error file provides the row number causing the error. This can be extremely useful when you wish to continue a load, rather than restart.

- Always delete the error files before rerunning the process, or you will get an error.

- BULK INSERTS can be run in parallel—see Recipe 13-10 for more details on possible parallel load patterns.

2-11. Creating a Format File for Complex Flat File Loads Using Bulk Insert or BCP

Problem

You want to perform column-mapping as well as other tweaks between the source and destination tables, and yet still use a BULK INSERT to take advantage of the speed it offers.

Solution

Create a format file to handle the column mapping—and more. I'll explain how.

1. To create a format file, run the following at the command prompt:

```
bcp CarSales_Staging.dbo.Invoice  format nul -c -x -f ↵
C:\SQL2012DIRecipes\CH02\Invoicebulkload.Xml -T -SADAMO2
```

2. This should create the following XML format file (C:\SQL2012DIRecipes\CH02\Invoicebulkload.Xml):

```xml
<?xml version="1.0"?>
<BCPFORMAT xmlns="http://schemas.microsoft.com/sqlserver/2004/bulkload/format" ↵
           xmlns:xsi="http://www.w3.org/2001/XMLSchema-instance">
 <RECORD>
  <FIELD ID="1" xsi:type="CharTerm" TERMINATOR="\t" MAX_LENGTH="12"/>
  <FIELD ID="2" xsi:type="CharTerm" TERMINATOR="\t" MAX_LENGTH="50"
         COLLATION="Latin1_General_CI_AS"/>
  <FIELD ID="3" xsi:type="CharTerm" TERMINATOR="\t" MAX_LENGTH="12"/>
  <FIELD ID="4" xsi:type="CharTerm" TERMINATOR="\t" MAX_LENGTH="41"/>
  <FIELD ID="5" xsi:type="CharTerm" TERMINATOR="\r\n" MAX_LENGTH="41"/>
 </RECORD>
 <ROW>
  <COLUMN SOURCE="1" NAME="ID" xsi:type="SQLINT"/>
  <COLUMN SOURCE="2" NAME="InvoiceNumber" xsi:type="SQLVARYCHAR"/>
  <COLUMN SOURCE="3" NAME="ClientID" xsi:type="SQLINT"/>
  <COLUMN SOURCE="4" NAME="TotalDiscount" xsi:type="SQLNUMERIC" PRECISION="18"
         SCALE="2"/>
  <COLUMN SOURCE="5" NAME="DeliveryCharge" xsi:type="SQLNUMERIC" PRECISION="18"
         SCALE="2"/>
 </ROW>
</BCPFORMAT>
```

How It Works

If the source data file is of any complexity, then you will probably need to apply a format file. These are relatively straightforward—especially since the new XML format files were introduced in SQL Server 2005. Given that the XML style is the way forward, we will not here be looking at the "old" non-XML versions. They are best used in the following circumstances:

- When the data file has a different number of columns than the target table.

- When the data file has columns in a different order than the target table.

- When the data elements in the data file have different column terminators.

- When you need to remove quotes from certain fields.

- When the same data file is used as a source for multiple tables with differing schemas.

- When a user does not have INSERT privileges on some columns of the target table.

A format file is an XML document that follows a simple and well-defined structure—but the best thing of all is that you do not need to create the XML from scratch. You can get SQL Server to do most of the work using the BCP utility, and then merely tweak the results to get exactly what you need.

I realize that the structure of an XML format file may look a little complex at first sight, but it is relatively simple to understand and use. Let us start by looking at the structure of a format file. It is divided into three parts:

The **XML declaration**

The **RECORD** element, which describes the source data

The **ROW** element, which describes the destination table

As the XML declaration is essentially static, let's examine the other two parts of the file.

First, we have the ROW element. This contains the FIELD elements that can contain the following attributes provided in Table 2-7.

Table 2-7. *Field Elements in a BCP XML Format File*

Field Element	Description
ID	Gives the sequential field number in the source file.
TYPE	Any data types. See http://msdn.microsoft.com/en-us/library/ms187833.aspx for the available data types.
TERMINATOR	The field terminator for each field. In the final field in the row, the record terminator is specified.
MAX_LENGTH	Use this to specify the maximum possible length of a field. If you have generated a format file, this is derived from the metadata in a corresponding field for destination table.
COLLATION	When dealing with character fields, you can specify the collation that must be used.
PREFIX_LENGTH	Use this to define the prefix length for a binary data representation. If used, it must be either 1, 2, 4, or 8.
LENGTH	The data length for fixed-width elements.

Second, you have the RECORD elements that describe the destination table.

Hints, Tips, and Traps

- Of course, you can replace the Database.Schema.Table parameter (CarSales_Staging.dbo.Invoice) with your own object reference, just as you can replace the resulting file path and name it with your own file to create.

- You will need to specify the SQL Server instance if there is more than one instance running on your server.

- You will also need to specify the user and password if you are not using integrated security. All these BCP options are described fully in Recipe 2-9.

- BULK INSERT will carry out suitable type conversions based on the column types specified under < ROW > and the corresponding column in the target table. This can slow down the import process, so it is best to define the most appropriate data type in the format file.

- Setting the MAX_LENGTH parameter to a value shorter than the length of the longest element of data in the corresponding column will not truncate the data—it will cause the load to fail at that point.

- A format file can be used with either BCP or BULK INSERT. An example of BCP using a format file is given in Recipe 2-9.

2-12. Performing a BULK INSERT with a Format File

Problem

You want to use a format file (such as the one that you created in Recipe 2-11) to ensure a smooth and efficient Bulk Load process.

Solution

Add the FORMATFILE parameter to a BULK INSERT statement.

The following code snippet shows how to do this using the same source file and destination table that you used in Recipe 2-10 (C:\SQL2012DIRecipes\CH02\BulkInsertWithFormatFile.sql):

```
BULK INSERT CarSales_Staging.dbo.Invoice
    FROM 'C:\SQL2012DIRecipes\CH02\Invoices.Txt'
    WITH
        (
            FIRSTROW = 2,
            FORMATFILE = 'C:\SQL2012DIRecipes\CH02\Invoicebulkload.Xml'
        )
```

How It Works

If we take the BULK INSERT process just given, we can now indicate that a format file must be used to fine-tune the data load. Running this T-SQL fragment will load the source data file and apply the parameters and mappings in the format file.

To understand the power of format files, it is probably best to see a few examples that suit everyday data import needs where format files are required. In all the examples, we will take the preceding format file and tweak it to show how useful format files can be.

First, if your source file is comma-delimited (as the example used here is), you need to perform a minor tweak to the format file by replacing TERMINATOR = "\t" with TERMINATOR = "," in the < RECORD > section. Fortunately, a global replace using a text editor will take care of this. What you are doing is telling BULK INSERT that the field separator is the comma, not the default tab character.

Suppose that a new version of the source data inverses the column order for the final two columns. The following format file will handle this (C:\SQL2012DIRecipes\CH02\InvoiceNewColumnOrder.Xml):

```xml
<?xml version = "1.0"?>
<BCPFORMAT xmlns=http://schemas.microsoft.com/sqlserver/2004/bulkload/format ↵
           xmlns:xsi = "http://www.w3.org/2001/XMLSchema-instance">
 <RECORD>
  <FIELD ID = "1" xsi:type = "CharTerm" TERMINATOR = "," MAX_LENGTH = "12"/>
  <FIELD ID = "2" xsi:type = "CharTerm" TERMINATOR = "," MAX_LENGTH = "50"
         COLLATION = "Latin1_General_CI_AS"/>
  <FIELD ID = "3" xsi:type = "CharTerm" TERMINATOR = "," MAX_LENGTH = "12"/>
  <FIELD ID = "4" xsi:type = "CharTerm" TERMINATOR = "," MAX_LENGTH = "41"/>
  <FIELD ID = "5" xsi:type = "CharTerm" TERMINATOR = "\r\n" MAX_LENGTH = "41"/>
 </RECORD>
 <ROW>
  <COLUMN SOURCE = "1" NAME = "ID" xsi:type = "SQLINT"/>
  <COLUMN SOURCE = "2" NAME = "InvoiceNumber" xsi:type = "SQLVARYCHAR"/>
  <COLUMN SOURCE = "3" NAME = "ClientID" xsi:type = "SQLINT"/>
  <COLUMN SOURCE = "5" NAME = "DeliveryCharge" xsi:type = "SQLNUMERIC" PRECISION = "18" SCALE = "2"/>
  <COLUMN SOURCE = "4" NAME = "TotalDiscount" xsi:type = "SQLNUMERIC" PRECISION = "18" SCALE = "2"/>
 </ROW>
</BCPFORMAT>
```

The following format file will only load the first field in the source file, and will ignore the others. Essentially, this technique allows you to subset source data vertically, and only loads the columns that interest you (C:\SQL2012DIRecipes\CH02\InvoiceSubset.Xml).

```xml
<?xml version = "1.0"?>
<BCPFORMAT xmlns = "http://schemas.microsoft.com/sqlserver/2004/bulkload/format" ↵
           xmlns:xsi = "http://www.w3.org/2001/XMLSchema-instance">
 <RECORD>
  <FIELD ID = "1" xsi:type = "CharTerm" TERMINATOR = "," MAX_LENGTH = "12"/>
  <FIELD ID = "2" xsi:type = "CharTerm" TERMINATOR = "," MAX_LENGTH = "50" ↵
         COLLATION = "Latin1_General_CI_AS"/>
  <FIELD ID = "3" xsi:type = "CharTerm" TERMINATOR = "," MAX_LENGTH = "12"/>
  <FIELD ID = "4" xsi:type = "CharTerm" TERMINATOR = "," MAX_LENGTH = "41"/>
  <FIELD ID = "5" xsi:type = "CharTerm" TERMINATOR = "\r\n" MAX_LENGTH = "41"/>
 </RECORD>
 <ROW>
  <COLUMN SOURCE = "1" NAME = "ID" xsi:type = "SQLINT"/>
 </ROW>
</BCPFORMAT>
```

Even if you are only loading a single field from the source file, all the source fields have to be described in the < RECORD /> section.

Should you need to do the opposite of what was described previously, then you can load all (or a selection) of fields from a source file where the destination table contains many more fields. For this, we will use the Invoices2.txt source file, which only has three fields. The format file to use looks like this (C:\SQL2012DIRecipes\CH02\Invoices2.Xml):

```xml
<?xml version = "1.0"?>
<BCPFORMAT xmlns = "http://schemas.microsoft.com/sqlserver/2004/bulkload/format" ↵
           xmlns:xsi = "http://www.w3.org/2001/XMLSchema-instance">
 <RECORD>
  <FIELD ID = "1" xsi:type = "CharTerm" TERMINATOR = "," MAX_LENGTH = "12"/>
```

```
  <FIELD ID="2" xsi:type="CharTerm" TERMINATOR="," MAX_LENGTH="50" ⏎
       COLLATION="Latin1_General_CI_AS"/>
  <FIELD ID="3" xsi:type="CharTerm" TERMINATOR="\r\n" MAX_LENGTH="12"/>
 </RECORD>
 <ROW>
  <COLUMN SOURCE="1" NAME="ID" xsi:type="SQLINT"/>
  <COLUMN SOURCE="2" NAME="InvoiceNumber" xsi:type="SQLVARCHAR"/>
  <COLUMN SOURCE="3" NAME="TotalDiscount" xsi:type="SQLNUMERIC" PRECISION="18" SCALE="2"/>
 </ROW>
</BCPFORMAT>
```

It is worth noting that the source column fields are still numbered sequentially, but that the mapping to the destination table columns has changed. As the source file only contains three columns, but the destination table has five columns, the format file indicates to BCP that columns to use and maps them to the destination using the "NAME" attribute. Of course, you could always restructure the destination table, but this is frowned upon by SQL purists, and in any case, should your existing destination table contain hundreds of millions of records (or more) then tweaking the format file is by far the easier option.

As the source file does not contain column headers, the BULK INSERT command looks like this (C:\SQL2012DIRecipes\CH02\BulkInsertNoColHeaders.Sql):

```
BULK INSERT dbo.Invoice
   FROM 'C:\SQL2012DIRecipes\CH02\Invoices2.Txt'
   WITH (FORMATFILE='C:\SQL2012DIRecipes\CH02\Invoices2.Xml');
```

Note that you can map the source field to any existing destination field, whatever the field order in the destination table, providing that the data types are compatible. You will not need to specify the field and row terminators as BULK INSERT parameters, as these options are defined in the format file.

Not all source files use the same separator for each field. This too can be handled by a format file. The C:\SQL2012DIRecipes\CH02\Invoices5 sample file contains a comma for the first field separator; @#@ for the second; a pipe character (|) for the third; and a tab for the fourth. The following shows the format file to handle this. You can even use multiple characters as a field separator if you really need to (C:\SQL2012DIRecipes\CH02\BulkLoadZanySeparators.Xml).

```
<?xml version="1.0"?>
<BCPFORMAT xmlns="http://schemas.microsoft.com/sqlserver/2004/bulkload/format" ⏎
           xmlns:xsi="http://www.w3.org/2001/XMLSchema-instance">
 <RECORD>
  <FIELD ID="1" xsi:type="CharTerm" TERMINATOR="," MAX_LENGTH="12"/>
  <FIELD ID="2" xsi:type="CharTerm" TERMINATOR="@#@" MAX_LENGTH="50" ⏎
       COLLATION="Latin1_General_CI_AS"/>
  <FIELD ID="3" xsi:type="CharTerm" TERMINATOR="|" MAX_LENGTH="12"/>
  <FIELD ID="4" xsi:type="CharTerm" TERMINATOR="\t" MAX_LENGTH="41"/>
  <FIELD ID="5" xsi:type="CharTerm" TERMINATOR="\r\n" MAX_LENGTH="41"/>
 </RECORD>
 <ROW>
  <COLUMN SOURCE="1" NAME="ID" xsi:type="SQLINT"/>
  <COLUMN SOURCE="2" NAME="InvoiceNumber" xsi:type="SQLVARCHAR"/>
  <COLUMN SOURCE="3" NAME="ClientID" xsi:type="SQLINT"/>
  <COLUMN SOURCE="4" NAME="TotalDiscount" xsi:type="SQLNUMERIC" PRECISION="18" SCALE="2"/>
  <COLUMN SOURCE="5" NAME="DeliveryCharge" xsi:type="SQLNUMERIC" PRECISION="18" SCALE="2"/>
 </ROW>
</BCPFORMAT>
```

If ever you are (un)fortunate enough to receive a source file that encloses one or more fields in quotes, then you will have noticed that the quotes are loaded into the destination table. Assuming that this is not what you want (and that you do not want to have to pre-process the data, as described Recipe 2-21), then you can tweak a format file to strip out the quotes during the data load. For example, I have a file, C:\SQL2012DIRecipes\CH02\Invoices4.Txt, where the second field is enclosed in quotes. The following is the format file that will remove the quotes (C:\SQL2012DIRecipes\CH02\QuotedSecondField.Xml):

```xml
<?xml version="1.0"?>
<BCPFORMAT xmlns="http://schemas.microsoft.com/sqlserver/2004/bulkload/format" ↵
           xmlns:xsi="http://www.w3.org/2001/XMLSchema-instance">
 <RECORD>
  <FIELD ID="1" xsi:type="CharTerm" TERMINATOR=",&quot;" MAX_LENGTH="12"/>
  <FIELD ID="2" xsi:type="CharTerm" TERMINATOR="&quot;," MAX_LENGTH="50" ↵
         COLLATION="Latin1_General_CI_AS"/>
  <FIELD ID="3" xsi:type="CharTerm" TERMINATOR="," MAX_LENGTH="12"/>
  <FIELD ID="4" xsi:type="CharTerm" TERMINATOR="," MAX_LENGTH="41"/>
  <FIELD ID="5" xsi:type="CharTerm" TERMINATOR="\r\n" MAX_LENGTH="41"/>
 </RECORD>
 <ROW>
  <COLUMN SOURCE="1" NAME="ID" xsi:type="SQLINT"/>
  <COLUMN SOURCE="2" NAME="InvoiceNumber" xsi:type="SQLVARCHAR"/>
  <COLUMN SOURCE="3" NAME="ClientID" xsi:type="SQLINT"/>
  <COLUMN SOURCE="4" NAME="TotalDiscount" xsi:type="SQLNUMERIC" PRECISION="18" SCALE="2"/>
  <COLUMN SOURCE="5" NAME="DeliveryCharge" xsi:type="SQLNUMERIC" PRECISION="18" SCALE="2"/>
 </ROW>
</BCPFORMAT>
```

You will need to add the " (the HTML entity for double quotes) for every single occurrence of an opening or a closing double quote around a field. This respects the CSV standard and allows you to load quoted fields containing commas (or any other character used as the column separator) contained in the quoted field.

If a field in one record is enclosed in quotes, the same field in all the records of the source file must also be quoted, or the load will fail.

Hints, Tips, and Traps

- Remember to use FIRSTROW = 2 if the source data file contains a header row.

2-13. Loading a Text File Fast Using T-SQL
Problem

You want to perform a fast data load from a text file.

Solution

Use OPENROWSET (BULK) from T-SQL. The following is a code snippet to do this (C:\SQL2012DIRecipes\CH02\BulkInsertWithOpenrowset.sql):

```
INSERT INTO    CarSales_Staging.dbo.Invoices
SELECT         ID, InvoiceNumber, ClientID
FROM           OPENROWSET(BULK 'C:\SQL2012DIRecipes\CH02\Invoices.Txt', ↵
               FORMATFILE='C:\SQL2012DIRecipes\CH02\Invoicebulkload.Xml') AS MyDATA;
```

How It Works

Assuming that you master the basics of format files, you can now proceed to use the OPENROWSET (BULK) T-SQL command, for which a format file is compulsory. The preceding code snippet loads a text file using a predefined format file.

Hints, Tips, and Traps

- The alias (MyDATA in this example) must be provided, or you will get an error message.

- The T-SQL used with OPENROWSET (BULK) can be extended using WHERE, ORDER BY, CAST, CONVERT, and aliases. This gives you great flexibility when loading the data.

2-14. Executing BULK INSERT from SSIS

Problem

You want to get the extra speed that BULK INSERT provides, but from inside an SSIS process.

Solution

Use the SSIS BULK INSERT task to import data as part of an SSIS process. What follows is the method to do this.

1. In an SSIS package, add a BULK INSERT task to the Control Flow pane. Double-click to edit the task.

2. Click the Connections option on the left to display the Connections pane on the right.

3. Select or create a destination connection. In this example it will be to the CarSales_Staging database. Once the connection is established, select the destination table (dbo.Invoices). Defining a destination connection is described in detail in Recipe 2-2.

4. Select the connection to the source file—or create it if it does not exist.

5. If you are using a format file, create or select the connection to the format file. You should end up with something like Figure 2-14.

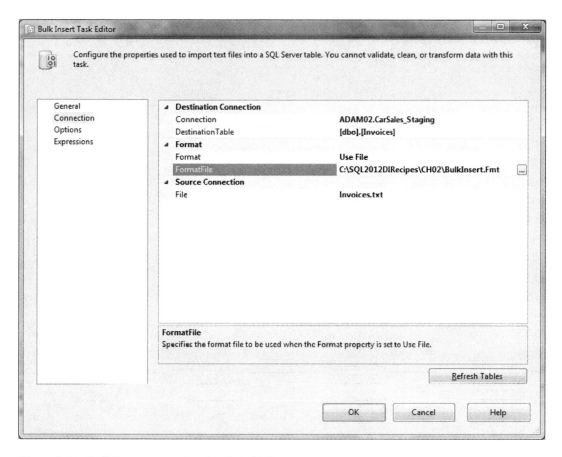

Figure 2-14. *Bulk Insert connection details in SSIS*

    6.   Select Options in the left list to display the Options pane, as shown in Figure 2-15.

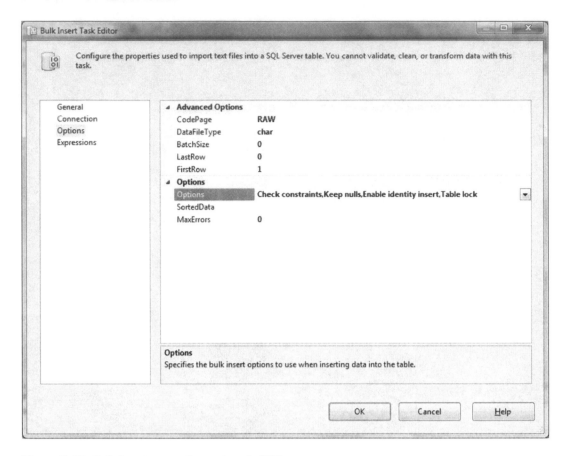

Figure 2-15. Bulk Insert connection options in SSIS

7. Here you can set the BULK INSERT options, as described in Recipe 2-12 for T-SQL-based BULK INSERT.

8. Click OK to return to the Control Flow pane.

9. Run the import.

How It Works

Using the SSIS Bulk Insert Task allows you to insert text data extremely fast into SQL Server, using most of the options described in Recipe 2-12. Here you are essentially using SSIS as a "wrapper" for the T-SQL BULK INSERT task. As with T-SQL BULK INSERT, a format file is not necessary—unless column mappings, skipping columns, stripping out quotes, and so forth, is required.

In this recipe, I am presuming that you know how to create SSIS connection managers. If this is not the case, then refer to other recipes on this book. You will need a destination table and a format file (if you need one, and/or are using one).

The following BULK INSERT options can be selected from the Options drop-down menu:

- Keep Nulls

- Identity Insert

- Table Lock
- Fire Triggers
- Check Constraints

The Sorted option allows you to specify which source column(s) the source data is sorted on. This speeds up the import if there is a clustered index on the sorted column(s) in the destination table.

Hints, Tips, and Traps

- If you are not using a format file, select Specify, and then select the row and column delimiters for a simple source file in the Connections pane.

- To see how to use the Batch Size, First Row, and Last Row options, see Recipe 2-9.

- As this is nothing more than an interface to the BULK INSERT command, the format file creation and specification is identical to that described in Recipe 2-11.

2-15. Handling Complex Flat File Formats with a Row Prefix in SSIS

Problem

You have a flat file that is not a simple set of pseudo-columns, but contains multiple row structures, each type prefixed with a specific indicator. You need to load this file into SQL Server.

Solution

Use SSIS to identify and separate the record types into individual data flows. You then load each row structure into appropriately structured separate destination tables.

I am assuming that you have a text file delivered with what are essentially multiple types of rows in it.

For this example, I will limit the extent of the file's complexity to two different row types. We can consider them as header rows and child rows. Here is a (very tiny) example (C:\SQL2012DIRecipes\CH02\MultipleSubsets.Txt):

```
HDR:-3,3A9271EA-FC76-4281-A1ED-714060ADBA30,3,2011-04-01 00:00:00.000,500.00,250.00
LNE:-1,3,1,5000.00,0x00000000000007DB,,1
LNE:-2,3,2,12500.00,0x00000000000007DC,,2
HDR:-4,C9018CC1-AE67-483B-B1B7-CF404C296F0B,4,2011-09-01 00:00:00.000,0.00,500.00
LNE:-3,4,3,17250.00,0x00000000000007DD,,1
LNE:-4,4,4,52000.00,0x00000000000007DE,,2
LNE:-5,4,5,71000.00,0x00000000000007DF,,3
```

As you can see, each row begins with either HDR:- or LNE:-, which allows you (and SSIS) to determine which type of record the row contains. The following explains how to handle this.

1. Create the two destination tables corresponding to the two types of records set in the source file (C:\SQL2012DIRecipes\CH02\tblMultipleSubsets.sql):

    ```
    CREATE TABLE InvoiceHeader
    (
     ID INT
     ,InvoiceNumber VARCHAR(50)
     ,ClientID INT
     ,InvoiceDate DATETIME
     ,TotalDiscount NUMERIC(18,2)
     ,DeliveryCharge
    ) ;
    GO
    CREATE TABLE InvoiceLine
    (
     ID INT
     InvoiceID INT
     StockID INT
     SalePrice NUMERIC(18,2)
     Timestamp BIGINT
     DateUpdated DATETIME
     LineItem INT
    ) ;
    GO
    ```

2. Create a new SSIS package and add an OLEDB connection manager named **CarSales_Staging** to connect to the CarSales_Staging database. You may reuse an existing package-level connection if you are using SQL Server 2012.

3. Add a Flat File connection manager that you configure to connect to the source file (C:\SQL2012DIRecipes\CH02\MultipleSubsets.Txt). While editing the connection manager, and assuming that the row prefix is of fixed length, set the file format to Ragged Right. In the Columns pane, set the column marker to divide the data into two columns. The first will contain the row prefix, while the second will contain the row data. This should look like what's shown in Figure 2-16.

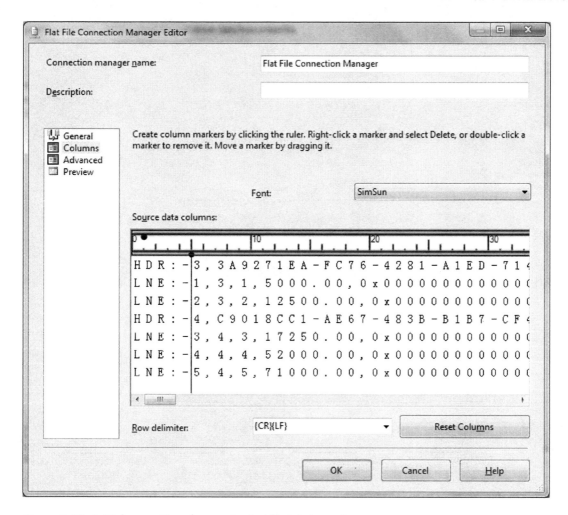

Figure 2-16. *Initial separation of a complex text file into two columns*

4. In the Advanced pane, give the two columns more user-friendly names (ColIdentifier and ColData, in this example), and set the OutputColumnWidth for the column that will hold the data to a large value. An example is given in Figure 2-17.

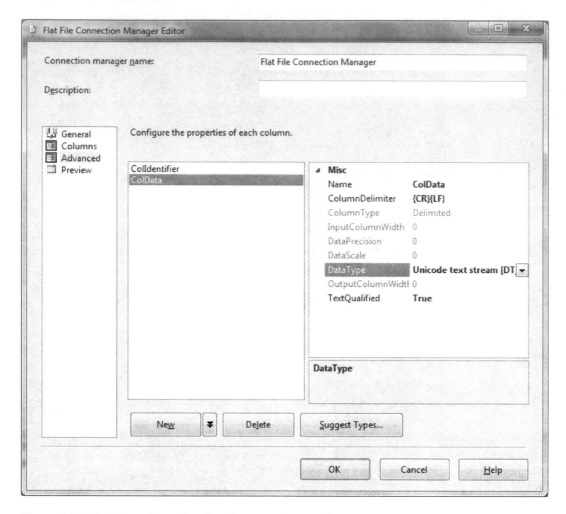

Figure 2-17. Defining column identifiers for a complex text file

5. Confirm your modifications with OK.

6. Add a Data Flow task. Double-click to edit it.

7. Add a Flat File data source. Configure it to use the Flat File connection manager that you just created.

8. Add a Conditional Split transform to the Data Flow pane. Connect the Flat File data source to it. Double-click to edit. Create two new outputs, configured like this:

OutputName	Condition
InvoiceHeader	ColIdentifier == "HDR:-"
InvoiceLine	ColIdentifier == "LNE:-"

9. Add a Derived Column transformation to the Data Flow pane and connect the Conditional Split to it. Select InvoiceHeader as the output to use. Double-click to edit. Add the following derived columns (the Expressions code used here and in step 11 is in `C:\SQL2012DIRecipes\CH02\ExpressionCode.Txt`):

Derived Column Name	Expression	Data Type	Length
ID	`(DT_I4)SUBSTRING(ColData,1,` ↵ `FINDSTRING(ColData,",",1) - 1)`	4-byte signed integer	
InvoiceNumber	`SUBSTRING(ColData,` ↵ `FINDSTRING(ColData,",",1)` ↵ `+ 1,FINDSTRING(ColData,",",2)` ↵ `- FINDSTRING(ColData,",",1) - 1)`	Unicode string	25
ClientID	`(DT_I4)SUBSTRING(ColData,` ↵ `FINDSTRING(ColData,",",2)` ↵ `+ 1,FINDSTRING(ColData,",",3)` ↵ `- FINDSTRING(ColData,",",2) - 1)`	4-byte signed integer	
InvoiceDate	`(DT_DBDATE)SUBSTRING(ColData,` ↵ `FINDSTRING(ColData,",",3)` ↵ `+ 1,FINDSTRING(ColData,",",4)` ↵ `- FINDSTRING(ColData,",",3) - 1)`	Database date	
TotalDiscount	`(DT_DECIMAL,2)` ↵ `SUBSTRING(ColData,` ↵ `FINDSTRING(ColData,",",4)+1,` ↵ `FINDSTRING(ColData,",",5)` ↵ `- FINDSTRING(ColData,",",4) - 1)`	Decimal	
DeliveryCharge	`(DT_DECIMAL,2)` ↵ `RIGHT(ColData,LEN(ColData)` ↵ `- FINDSTRING(ColData,",",5))`	Decimal	

10. Add an OLEDB destination. Connect the Derived Column transformation that you just created to it. Name it **Invoice Header**. Configure the destination task to use the CarSales_Staging connection manager and point to the InvoiceHeader destination table. Map the derived columns (that is, not the two initial ColIdentifier and ColData columns) to the destination table.

11. Repeat steps 7 and 8, only using InvoiceLine as the output from the Conditional Split transformation, and pointing to the InvoiceLine table. The derived columns to create are:

Derived Column Name	Expression	Data Type	Length
ID	`LEFT(ColData,FINDSTRING(ColData,",",1) - 1)`	4-byte signed integer	
InvoiceID	`SUBSTRING(ColData,FINDSTRING(ColData,",",1)` ↵ `+ 1,FINDSTRING(ColData,",",2)` ↵ `- FINDSTRING(ColData,",",1) - 1)`	4-byte signed integer	
StockID	`SUBSTRING(ColData,FINDSTRING(ColData,",",2)` ↵ `+ 1,FINDSTRING(ColData,",",3)` ↵ `- FINDSTRING(ColData,",",2) - 1)`	4-byte signed integer	
SalePrice	`SUBSTRING(ColData,FINDSTRING(ColData,",",3)` ↵ `+ 1,FINDSTRING(ColData,",",4)` ↵ `- FINDSTRING(ColData,",",3) - 1)`	Decimal	
Timestamp	`SUBSTRING(ColData,FINDSTRING(ColData,",",4)` ↵ `+ 1,FINDSTRING(ColData,",",5)` ↵ `- FINDSTRING(ColData,",",4) - 1)`	8- byte signed integer	
DateUpdated	`SUBSTRING(ColData,FINDSTRING(ColData,",",5)` ↵ `+ 1,FINDSTRING(ColData,",",6)` ↵ `- FINDSTRING(ColData,",",5) - 1)`	Database Date	
LineItem	`RIGHT(ColData,LEN(ColData)` ↵ `- FINDSTRING(ColData,",",6))`	4-byte signed integer	

The package should look something like Figure 2-18.

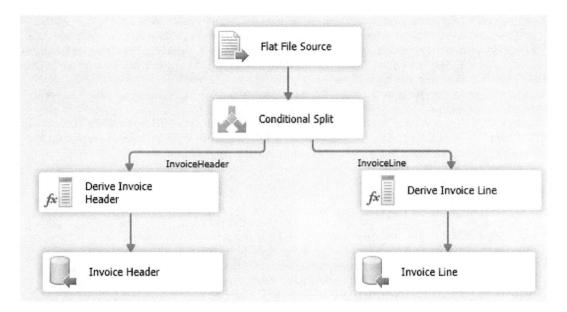

Figure 2-18. *SSIS data flow to handle a complex flat file*

> **12.** Run the package.

Your complex source file will be imported into the two destination tables.

How It Works

You may meet text files that contain two or more very different types of record. In many cases, you could regard them as being a way of sending "normalized" data in a single file, as opposed to the single table per file approach of a standard CSV file. I have seen files like these produced by mainframes and by ERP systems, for instance. In these cases, I am presuming that each row for these "multiformat" text files has a row prefix to allow you to identify the type of data contained in each row.

This more convoluted approach is necessary, as just about all the techniques described so far in this chapter will work fine with standard text files, but not with more complex formats. Now, by "standard" I mean files that have an identical row structure from top to bottom and that can consequently be painlessly loaded into a tabular structure because there are the same number of column separators in each text row. The reality is that all too often a minor variation in the format of a text file—or a deliberate design decision—can make a text file difficult to load. Or at the very least, further processing steps will be required to manage the original structure features of the source data file, as is the case here.

■ **Note** This example only shows two record types. It can easily be extended to accommodate multiple record types.

Here we are using a two-phased approach.

> **First:** Split each row into two columns, one containing the row prefix, the other the actual data.

> **Second:** Parse each record according to the type of data it contains.

Parsing data using a Derived Column transformation looks more complex than it really is. The last column uses the RIGHT function in SSIS to get the rightmost column. All other columns use SUBSTRING to isolate the data and FINDSTRING to identify the separator characters. This is where SSIS has a wonderful advantage over T-SQL, as FINDSTRING can indicate from which occurrence of the character that it is looking for to begin the search. Also in SSIS 2012, the 4000-character limit no longer applies, and so you can handle much longer source records. Note that it is important to set the data types in the Derived Column transformation for the data ingestion process to run efficiently and without error.

If you are using SQL Server 2005 or 2008, then the first column must be isolated using SUBSTRING(ColData, 1,FINDSTRING(ColData,",",1) - 1). This is because the LEFT function is not available in these versions of SSIS. Essentially, the first column has to use the SUBSTRING function to imitate the LEFT function.

Hints, Tips, and Traps

- If the row prefix is not a fixed length, then you can set the file format as "delimited" and specify the delimiter to be whatever character ends the row prefix—in this example a hyphen (-). Then in the Advanced pane of the Flat File connection manager, ensure that there are only two columns (this normally means deleting any other columns) and specify the column delimiter for the second column to be the row delimiter (most times this will be {CR}{LF}). This is described in more detail in Recipe 2-16.

- It is nearly always preferable to remove any referential integrity constraints on the destination tables before running the import process, as you cannot be sure that a header record will be imported before a line record. You can always reapply them after the import process.

- In SSIS 2005 and 2008, this approach is limited to records with a maximum length of 4000 characters. Unfortunately, trying to get around this limit by using parsing a text stream is not possible because SUBSTRING will not work with this data type.

- Any records in the source file that do not begin with the row prefix(es) are ignored.

2-16. Pre-Parsing and Staging File Subsets in SSIS
Problem

You want to load a complex text file consisting of two or more different record types. You want to separate the constituent elements first so that you can load the constituent tables in a specific order.

Solution

Use SSIS to parse the source file and stage it on disk as subfiles as part of the process. Then load the two tables while respecting relational integrity constraints.

This recipe handles the problem of a flat "mainframe-style" text file that contains multiple record types, but in a different way than the method used in the Recipe 2-15. It will use the same source file, however, and consequently, I suggest that you refer to Recipe 2-15 before proceeding with the process that follows. This could help in your understanding of the solution. The following explains how you can subset the source file into separate staging files before carrying out the final data load.

1. Create a new SSIS package, and add a Flat File connection manager named **MainFrame**, which you configure to connect to the source file.
   (C:\SQL2012DIRecipes\CH02\MultiFormatSource.Txt in this example)

2. In the Flat File Configuration Manager Editor, set the format to Delimited.

3. Click the Advanced tab. Remove all but two columns (or add columns until you have two columns). Name the first one **ColIdentifier** and the second one **ColData**. Set the DataType for the first column (ColIdentifier) to String, and the ColumnDelimiter to hyphen (-). (This is what we are using in this example; you have to use whatever separator is used in your source file). Set the DataType for the second (ColData) column to Unicode text stream. The dialog box should look like Figure 2-17 in Recipe 2-15.

4. Confirm your configuration changes.

5. Create two new Flat File connection managers, named **InvoiceHeader** and **InvoiceLine**, respectively. Configure each to point to a text file (I have imaginatively named mine InvoiceHeader.Txt and InvoiceLine.Txt). For each, click the Advanced pane and add a new column, which you set to the Unicode Text stream data type (or the Text stream data type). Name the column **Coldata**. The Advanced pane will look like Figure 2-19.

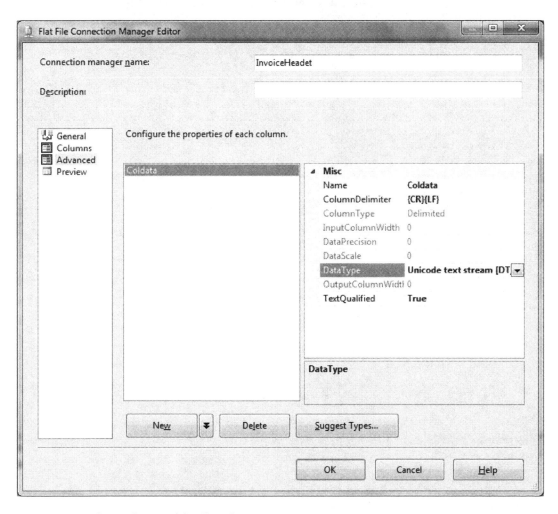

Figure 2-19. Advanced pane of the Flat File connection manager

6. Confirm your configuration changes.

7. Add a Data Flow task. Double-click to edit.

8. Add a Flat File source. Configure it to use the MainFrame configuration manager. It should only have two columns—ColIdentifier and ColData.

9. Add a Conditional Split task. Configure it exactly as described in the previous recipe.

10. Add a Flat File destination to the Data Flow window. Connect the Conditional Split task to it. Use the output named InvoiceHeader. Configure this destination to use the Flat File connection manager named InvoiceHeader—and check the Overwrite Data in the file box.

11. Click Mappings. Map the Coldata column between the available input and available destination columns.

12. Repeat steps 10 and 11 for the invoiceLine output and Flat File connection manager.

13. Return to the Control Flow window. Add a Data Flow task named Import Headers. Connect this to the previous Data Flow task.

14. Add a Data Flow task named Import Lines. Connect this to the previous Data Flow task (Import Headers). The whole data flow should look like Figure 2-20.

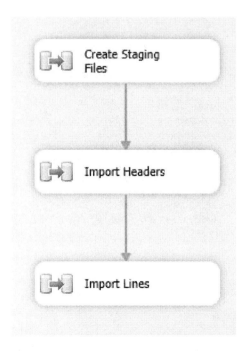

Figure 2-20. *Importing a complex source text file while staging the data*

15. Set up the two data flow tasks that you just created to import the InvoiceHeader.Txt and InvoiceLines.Txt delimited files. This was described in detail in Recipe 2-2. The script to create the two destination tables is
C:\SQL2012DIRecipes\CH02\tblMultipleSubsets.sql.

How It Works

There may be times when you wish to process, for example, a file sourced from a mainframe, or certain enterprise resource planning software solutions. These files can contain multiple row formats. However, you want—or need—to store the data in temporary text files as the first stage in the process. By this I mean that each record type (header and line in this example) will first be separated from the single source file into a separate staging file; each will then be loaded from the resulting staging file. There are several reasons why such an approach may be preferable or even necessary. Among these are the following:

- The record length exceeds 4000 characters, and so the method described in the previous recipe cannot be used.

- Relational integrity is in place on the destination files, and so they have to be loaded in the correct (parent followed by child) order.

- Writing extended parsing code using derived column transformations is impractical.

- You want to examine, debug, profile, or pre-process the separate source files before loading them.

These constraints mean that you need to use the approach given in this recipe. Essentially, it uses the row prefix to separate each type of record and sends it to a staging file on disk. Each of the resulting files is then loaded as a separate Data Flow task.

Hints, Tips, and Traps

- You can set the data types (in the Flat File connection managers for both the input and output files) to string or widestring data types if you are certain that no record is longer than the 4000-character maximum.

- As this approach writes text files to disk (and then reads them back in again afterward), it will be quite a bit slower than a "pure" SSIS in-memory approach.

- If you are loading multiple source files, then do not check the "Overwrite Data in the file" box, but use an initial File System task to delete the contents of the staging files at the start of this process.

- Any records in the source file that do not begin with the row prefix(es) are ignored.

2-17. Handling Irregular Numbers of Columns in the Source File Using SQL Server 2012

Problem

You want to load a source file that has irregular numbers of columns.

Solution

Use SSIS in SQL Server 2012.

You have nothing particular to configure when importing text files that have varying numbers of columns, as it is the default as of SQL Server 2012. Merely create a Flat File connection manager and configure it to use the relevant source file.

How It Works

Fortunately, SQL Server 2012 has come to the rescue of data integration developers everywhere by including in SSIS the ability to handle flat files with multiple column separators. It is worth noting that this behavior is completely different to that of previous versions. Before, if SSIS met with different numbers of column separators in a source file, the row terminator would not be handled "correctly" and data would snake round into the next record, more often causing the data load to fail. As of SQL Server 2012, record terminators will always force a new record to begin.

Hints, Tips, and Traps

- To prevent SSIS from handling disparate numbers of columns in a source file, you can set the property AlwaysCheckForRowDelimiters to false. This will cause SSIS to behave as it did for previous versions.

- The maximum number of column delimiters in a record can be in any row in the source file. SSIS will guess the requisite number of columns and apply this to the entire data load.

- The record terminator (or row delimiter if you prefer) must not be enclosed in quotes for it to be recognized by SSIS.

2-18. Handling Embedded Qualifiers in SQL Server 2012

Problem

You want to load data from a text file that has embedded qualifiers.

Solution

Use SSIS in SQL Server 2012. That version of SSIS handles embedded qualifiers automatically, with no effort needed on your part.

How It Works

Once again, SQL Server 2012 has ridden to the rescue of data integration developers by extending SSIS so that it can handle embedded text qualifiers. This means that if a character (for instance, a single quote or a double quote) is used for qualifying a column, the character must be escaped if it is to be used as a literal. This is done by doubling up the qualifier character. So a quote (") in a flat file must be a double set of quotes ("") to be imported correctly. Put another way, a double instance of that text qualifier, inside a field enclosed in the qualifier, is interpreted as a literal single instance of that string.

Hints, Tips, and Traps

- This behavior of handling embedded qualifiers is always active for text qualified columns/files and cannot be disabled.

- This behavior means that the number of qualifiers must conform to expectations. For instance, if you have a field—"Adam "Aspin"—then the field cannot be loaded, as an escaped double quote inside the qualified field is expected. If this is a problem, then the best solution is not to use the field qualifier and to use a script component (extending the techniques described earlier) to handle the qualifier.

2-19. Handling Irregular Numbers of Columns in the Source File in SQL Server 2005 and 2008

Problem

You want to load a source file that has irregular numbers of columns, but you are using SQL Server 2005 or 2008.

Solution

Use an SSIS custom script to parse the source file.

1. Create a destination table containing the required number of columns—that is, having at least as many columns as the row with the greatest number of delimiters. In this example it will be (C:\SQL2012DIRecipes\CH02\tblInvoiceLines_Multifield.sql):

    ```
    CREATE TABLE CarSales_Staging.dbo.InvoiceLines_Multifield
    (
     ID INT NULL,
     InvoiceID VARCHAR(25) NULL,
     StockID INT NULL,
     Quantity INT NULL,
     SalePrice MONEY NULL,
     Comment1 VARCHAR(150) NULL,
     Comment2 VARCHAR(500) NULL
    ) ;
    GO
    ```

2. Create a new SSIS package, add a Flat File connection manager, and configure it to connect to the source file (C:\SQL2012DIRecipes\CH02\InvoicesMultifield.Txt) using the ragged right format. Do not set any fixed-width column limits in the Columns pane. Name the single source column **SourceData** in the Advanced pane. While in this pane, set the data type to Text Stream. Ensure that the Unicode check box in the General pane is not checked (keep reading to see how to handle Unicode sources).

3. Add an OLEDB destination connection manager. Configure it to connect to the destination database and table (CarSales_Staging and InvoiceLines_Multifield, respectively, in this example).

4. Add a Data Flow task. Double-click to edit.

5. In the Data Flow pane, add a Flat File source. Double-click to edit. Set the connection manager as the one that you created in step 1. Check that SourceData, the single source column, is available. Confirm your modifications.

6. Add a Script component and set it to be a Transform. Connect the Flat File source to it. Double-click to edit.

7. Click Inputs and Outputs. In the pane, add as many output columns as there are source columns (to do this expand Output 0, then Output Columns, and click Add Columns). Set the column data types and lengths to correspond to the source data. In this example that will be:

Column Name	Data Type	Length
ID	4-byte signed integer	
InvoiceID	4-byte signed integer	
StockID	String	50
Quantity	4-byte signed integer	
SalePrice	Currency	
Comment1	String	150
Comment2	String	500

The Inputs and Outputs pane will look like the one shown in Figure 2-21.

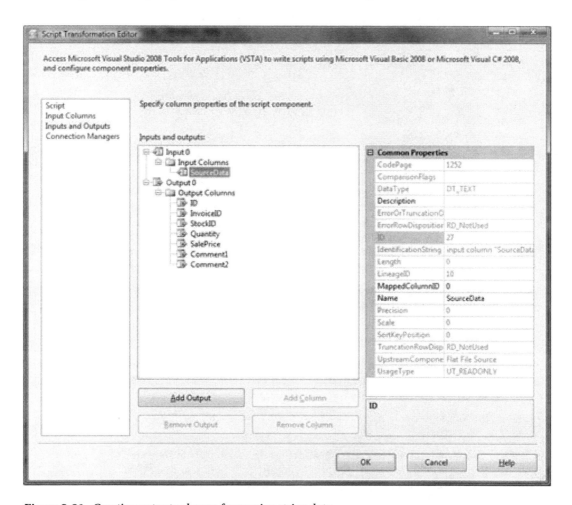

Figure 2-21. *Creating output columns for parsing string data*

8. Click Script to activate the Script pane. Set the ScriptLanguage to Microsoft Visual Basic 2010. Click Edit Script.

9. In the Script editor, type or copy the following script for the Input0_ProcessInputRow method:

```vb
Public Overrides Sub Input0_ProcessInputRow(ByVal Row As Input0Buffer)

        Dim NbCols As Integer
        Dim Delimiter As String = ","
        Dim StartPosition As Integer = 0
        Dim EndPosition As Integer = 0
        Dim RowContents As String = System.Text.Encoding.UTF8.GetString( ↵
                            Row.SourceData.GetBlobData ↵
                            (0, Convert.ToInt32(Row.SourceData.Length)))

        ' Count the number of delimiters - and so the No of columns
        NbCols = (RowContents.Length - RowContents.Replace(Delimiter, "").Length)

        ' Set the output array as a function of the number of columns
        Dim OutputCols(NbCols) As String

        ' Parse the data
        For Ctr = 0 To NbCols + 1
            If Ctr = 0 Then
                If NbCols = 0 Then
                    OutputCols(Ctr) = RowContents
                    Exit For
                Else
                    StartPosition = 0
                    EndPosition = RowContents.IndexOf(",", StartPosition)
                    OutputCols(Ctr) = Left(RowContents, EndPosition)
                End If
            Else
                StartPosition = RowContents.IndexOf(",", StartPosition)
                EndPosition = RowContents.IndexOf(",", StartPosition+1)
                If EndPosition = -1 Then
                    OutputCols(Ctr) = RowContents.Substring(StartPosition+1)
                    Exit For
                Else
                    OutputCols(Ctr) = RowContents.Substring(StartPosition+1, ↵
                                            (EndPosition - StartPosition) - 1)
                End If
            End If
            StartPosition = EndPosition
        Next

        ' Send parsed data to the appropriate output column
        For ColIDOut As Integer = 0 To NbCols
            If ColIDOut = 0 Then
                Row.ID = OutputCols(0)
            End If
```

123

```
            If ColIDOut = 1 Then
                Row.InvoiceID = OutputCols(1)
            End If
            If ColIDOut = 2 Then
                Row.StockID = OutputCols(2)
            End If
            If ColIDOut = 3 Then
                Row.Quantity = OutputCols(3)
            End If
            If ColIDOut  = 4 Then
                Row.SalePrice = OutputCols(4)
            End If
            If ColIDOut = 5 Then
                Row.Comment1 = OutputCols(5)
            End If
            If ColIDOut = 6 Then
                Row.Comment2 = OutputCols(6)
            End If

        Next

    End Sub
```

10. Close the Script window. Confirm your changes to the Script component.

11. Add an OLEDB destination and connect the Script transform to it. Select the OLEDB connection manager that you defined in step 2. Select the destination table. Click Mappings. Ensure that all the fields except SourceData are mapped.

You can now run the process and import the data.

How It Works

One eventuality that you may have to face is a source text file that has a variable number of delimiters—and consequently a varying number of columns—per row. As this is not something that SSIS handled very well until SQL Server 2012 appeared, you have to use an SSIS script component to parse rows containing a variable number of columns if you are using older versions of the Microsoft flagship database.

The script that parses each row works like this:

- First, the text stream is converted to text—otherwise .NET string functions such as Replace will not work.

- Then, the number of columns is determined by comparing the original row length to the length of the input text once all separators have been removed.

- Next, the leftmost column is handled (or the entire record if there are no other columns) and placed in an array.

- Then, all other columns except the right-hand column are determined (using the start and end positions between separators) and placed in an array.

- Next, the rightmost column is handled and placed in an array.

- Finally, all the contents of the array are mapped to the SSIS output columns.

This technique will nonetheless require you to define the maximum number of possible columns in the source file, and will only map the columns on a simple left-to-right basis. It cannot guess that source column should map to that output column if column separators are missing. It is possible to hard-code the input parsing to the output columns (which you have to do for SSIS output), but that would be less elegant. Of course, you can change the delimiter character used by the Delimiter variable.

If you are using an Unicode text source, you will need to do the following:

- In the General pane of the Flat File Connection Manager Editor, check the Unicode box.

- In the Advanced pane of the Flat File Connection Manager Editor, set the DataType for the SourceData column to Unicode String (DT_WSTR).

- In the SSIS Script task, replace the line that handles UTF8 encoding to the following:

```
ColText = System.Text.Encoding.Unicode.GetString(Row.SingleCol.GetBlobData ↵
          (0, Convert.ToInt32(Row.SingleCol.Length)))
```

Hints, Tips, and Traps

- Remember that (in versions 2005 and 2008) you can copy connection managers between packages to save redefining them.

- If your source file has very short records, you can avoid text streams entirely by setting the DataType for the SourceData column (in the Advanced pane of the Flat File Connection Manager Editor) to String, with a length of 8000, or Unicode string, with a length of 4000. You can then either set the ColText variable simply to the source column (ColText = Row.SingleCol.ToString)—or avoid using a variable at all, and refer in the script to the source column directly.

2-20. Determining the Number of Columns in a Source File
Problem

You want to determine the number of columns in a flat file.

Solution

Use a custom SSIS script to analyze the source file. The following explains how to do this.

1. Set up an SSIS package with the Flat File connection manager, as described in Recipe 2-2.

2. Add a Data Flow task and a Flat File source, also as described in Recipe 2-2.

3. Add a Script task connected to the Flat File source using the techniques described in Recipe 2-19. Do not create any output columns. Add the following script:

```
Public Class ScriptMain
    Inherits UserComponent
    Dim MaxNbCols As Integer = 0

    Public Overrides Sub PreExecute()
        MyBase.PreExecute()

    End Sub
```

```
        Public Overrides Sub PostExecute()
            MyBase.PostExecute()

            MsgBox(MaxNbCols)

        End Sub

        Public Overrides Sub Input0_ProcessInputRow(ByVal Row As Input0Buffer)

            Dim NbCols As Integer = 0
            Dim Delimiter As String = ","
            Dim ColText As String = ""

            'ANSI text
            ColText = System.Text.Encoding.UTF8.GetString(Row.SingleCol.GetBlobData ↵
                            (0, Convert.ToInt32(Row.SingleCol.Length)))

            NbCols = (ColText.Length - ColText.Replace(Delimiter, "").Length) + 1

            If NbCols > MaxNbCols Then
                MaxNbCols = NbCols
            End If

        End Sub

    End Class
```

4. Close the Script task. Confirm with OK.

How It Works

This simple script counts the number of delimiters (set using the Delimiter variable) in each record in the data flow. When you run the package, a message box displays the maximum number of columns in the source file. Clearly this approach is very "quick and dirty" because it uses a MessageBox to return the column count. So it is more a development technique than anything else, but nonetheless a useful tool.

■ **Note** You will not ever use SSIS packages with MessageBoxes in a production environment.

Hints, Tips, and Traps

- Alternatively, you can use LogParser to do this, as described in the next recipe.

- For more advanced techniques on profiling source files, see Chapter 10.

- To be somewhat purist, you should also create an integer variable and then add a Row Count task that uses this variable as a destination transform by connecting the Script task to the new Row Count task.

2-21. Preparing CSV Files for Import

Problem

You have a tricky flat file that you need to tweak so it can be imported easily.

Solution

Use LogParser to prepare flat files for import.

In reality, this recipe is a series of mini-recipes that give you a few examples of what LogParser can do. As LogParser operates outside of SQL Server, all the following code snippets must be run from a Command window. All the code in this recipe is in a single file (C:\SQL2012DIRecipes\CH02\LogParserScripts.Txt).

Let's start by converting a CSV file to a tab-separated file. You can do this by running:

```
LogParser "SELECT ID,InvoiceNumber,ClientID,TotalDiscount,DeliveryCharge INTO ↵
C:\SQL2012DIRecipes\CH02\AA1.TSV FROM C:\SQL2012DIRecipes\CH02\Invoices.Txt" -i:CSV -o:TSV
```

It is every bit as easy to convert a file to XML using LogParser. The command line is

```
LogParser "SELECT ID,InvoiceNumber,ClientID,TotalDiscount,DeliveryCharge INTO ↵
C:\SQL2012DIRecipes\CH02\AA1.Xml FROM C:\SQL2012DIRecipes\CH02\Invoices.Txt" -i:CSV -o:XML
```

You can then use some of the techniques described in Chapter 3 to load the file that LogParser has created.

LogParser can also add a row number to the output file. This can help when tracking down load errors. You do this by adding the keyword Rownumber to the SELECT statement, as follows:

```
LogParser "SELECT Rownumber,ID,InvoiceNumber,ClientID,TotalDiscount,DeliveryCharge INTO ↵
C:\SQL2012DIRecipes\CH02\AA1.TSV FROM C:\SQL2012DIRecipes\CH02\Invoices.Txt" -i:CSV -o:TSV
```

If speed is not essential, then you can use LogParser to load a text file into SQL Server directly. This is using 32-bit ODBC, however—with all the caveats that that implies.

```
LogParser "SELECT * INTO AA1 FROM C:\SQL2012DIRecipes\CH02\Invoices.Txt" ↵
-i:CSV -headerRow:OFF -o:SQL -dsn:SQLServer -username:Adam -password:Me4Boss
```

The SQL-like approach that LogParser takes makes it easy to load subsets of data either by creating an intermediate, pre-processed file in CSV, TSV, or XML format or by loading directly into SQL Server over ODBC. The following are a few examples of how the SELECT statement can work to subset data:

- You can select the columns to load or transform—and the order in which they will appear in an output file—just as you would in T-SQL:

```
SELECT InvoiceNumber, ID DeliveryCharge INTO C:\SQL2012DIRecipes\CH02\AA1.TSV FROM ↵
C:\SQL2012DIRecipes\CH02\Invoices.Txt" -i:CSV -o:TSV
```

- You can filter rows to be loaded or output using a WHERE clause (just like in T-SQL):

```
SELECT InvoiceNumber, ID DeliveryCharge INTO C:\SQL2012DIRecipes\CH02\AA1.TSV FROM ↵
C:\SQL2012DIRecipes\CH02\Invoices.Txt WHERE ID>4" -i:CSV -o:TSV
```

- Or even

```
SELECT InvoiceNumber, ID DeliveryCharge INTO C:\SQL2012DIRecipes\CH02\AA1.TSV FROM ⮐
C:\SQL2012DIRecipes\CH02\Invoices.Txt WHERE ID BETWEEN 4 AND 6" -i:CSV -o:TSV
```

- And also

```
SELECT InvoiceNumber, ID DeliveryCharge INTO C:\SQL2012DIRecipes\CH02\AA1.TSV FROM ⮐
C:\SQL2012DIRecipes\CH02\Invoices.Txt WHERE InvoiceNumber LIKE '%A%'" -i:CSV -o:TSV
```

There is nothing to prevent you from writing quite complex WHERE clauses, using <, >, <=, >=, and parentheses to ensure that the logic that you require is applied.

LogParser can return row counts from source files without having to load the file—a very quick and simple method to verify that a data load has handled all the rows in a source file—using the following command-line syntax:

```
LogParser "SELECT COUNT(*) INTO C:\SQL2012DIRecipes\CH02\AA1.CSV FROM ⮐
C:\SQL2012DIRecipes\CH02\Invoices.Txt" -i:CSV -o:CSV
```

You can use an Execute Process task to run LogParser as a "pre-processing" task (to convert a CSV file to a tab-delimited file, for instance). You first have to place the "SQL" that LogParser uses into a file, however, and refer to this as one of the arguments that are used when calling LogParser.

1. Create a file named **AnETLQuery.Txt** that contains the following SQL-Like command:

   ```
   SELECT ID,InvoiceNumber,ClientID INT O C:\SQL2012DIRecipes\CH02\AA1.Txt ⮐
   FROM C:\SQL2012DIRecipes\CH02\Invoices.Txt
   ```

2. Create a new SSIS package. Add an Execute Process task. Double-click to edit.

3. Click the Process pane. Enter the following executable: **C:\Program Files\Log Parser 2.2\LogParser.Exe** (or the correct path to LogParser on your machine).

4. Enter the following arguments file:
   C:\SQL2012DIRecipes\CH02\AnETLQuery.Txt -o:TSV -i:CSV

You can now run the package, which will convert a (presumable recalcitrant) CSV file into a suave tab-delimited file ready for SSIS to load as the next step in the package.

How It Works

There may well be times when you have little choice but to "pre-parse" a text/CSV file in order to get it into a state where it can be loaded gracefully using one of the standard tools examined earlier in this chapter. It is not my intention to explain all the ways in that various programming languages can prepare text files, as that could be the subject of a separate book. Instead, I want to focus on a stable and efficient Microsoft utility called LogParser, and show you how it can be used to rejig text files to make them digestible by SSIS, BCP, and BULK INSERT. LogParser is a command-line tool that uses an SQL-like syntax and a series of parameters (not unlike a BCP QUERYOUT command) to achieve its ends.

The examples given in this recipe only scratch the surface of this wonderful tool but, I hope, provide some solutions to common problems, and act as an introduction to basic pre-processing.

▓ **Note** LogParser is available for download at www.microsoft.com/en-us/download/details.aspx?id=24659.

If you are faced with SSIS choking on a file where the separator exists inside a quoted field, then LogParser can help by transforming the file into a tab-separated file. You will find LogParser in the Start menu once you have installed it.

So, what does LogParser bring to the party? Well, among other things, it can:

- Select subsets of data from large source files (by column and row), and create smaller staging files that can then be loaded.

- Ignore delimiters in quoted fields in text files and convert to TSV (tab separated) or XML that can then be loaded.

There is much more that it can do, but these are, for starters, a couple of useful additions to your ETL armory when faced with recalcitrant text files.

The command line that invokes LogParser gives the following information:

- The source file: FROM C:\SQL2012DIRecipes\CH02\Invoices.Txt

- The destination file: INTO C:\SQL2012DIRecipes\CH02\AA1.TSV

- The source format: -i:CSV

- The destination format: -o:TSV

There are many LogParser parameters that you may find useful. Table 2-8 provides a succinct overview of a selection that you may find helpful when parsing text files.

Table 2-8. *LogParser Parameters*

Parameter	Example	Comments
headerRow	-headerRow:OFF	This flag says whether or not the file contains row headers. You can set it to OFF or ON.
iDQuotes	-iDQuotes:Ignore	If you set this flag to Ignore, it tells LogParser to take no notice of double quotes surrounding columns, and output the column with the quotes. If you set this flag to Auto it tells LogParser to remove the quotes.
nSkipLines	-nSkipLines:5	This flag indicates to LogParser the number of header rows to skip before importing data.
I	-i:CSV	This flag indicates to LogParser that the input format is TSV (tab separated), CSV (comma separated), or XML (well, XML!).
o	-o:TSV	This flag indicates to LogParser that the output format is TSV (tab separated), CSV (comma separated), or XML.
iSeparator	-iSeparator:space	This flag tells LogParser—when reading tab-separated source files—that a separator (space or tab) will be used.
iHeaderFile	-iHeaderFile:" C:\ ↵ SQL2012DIRecipes\CH02\ ↵ header.csv"	If you have a source file without row headers, then this flag indicates a second file containing **only** row headers.

(continued)

129

Table 2-8. (*continued*)

Parameter	Example	Comments
fixedFields	-fixedFields:OFF	This flag states whether every row in the data file has the same number of columns (i.e., set to ON) or not (set to OFF).
nFields	-nFields:3	If the source file has a variable number of fields, this flag states the number of rows to scan in the source file to determine the correct number of columns. The more you specify, the longer it will take.
dtLines	-dtLines:50	This flag indicates the number of rows to scan in the source file to discover the column data types and lengths. The more you specify, the longer it will take.
file	file:AnETLQuery.Sql	This flag lets you to store the SQL-like query in a file rather than run it directly from the command line.

Note that the hyphen is not required before a file name. Also note that even if a source column is enclosed in quotes and contains a comma, that column will be gracefully handled as a whole field, and not split unnecessarily. The quotes will be stripped out automatically.

Hints, Tips, and Traps

- Inevitably, any co nversion of large files will add extra time to the ETL process. Only you can decide if this time is the best price to pay, or if you need to look at developing a custom method of parsing a "difficult" file in an SSIS Script task, for instance.

- While it is possible to use LogParser to load data directly into SQL Server, this is likely to be incredibly slow because it will only use 32-bit ODBC. You might find it faster to use it as a pre-parser to sort out any anomalies in your source file, and load the file that results from the LogParser conversion into SQL Server using BULK INSERT or SSIS.

- To create a System DSN, see Recipe 6-12.

- If you prefer, you can open a command window, navigate to the LogParser directory (currently C:\Program Files\Log Parser 2.2), and run LogParser from there.

- You can also call LogParser from XP_CmdShell or the SSIS Execute Process task.

Summary

This chapter illustrated many ways of importing text files into SQL Server. The technique that you will use inevitably depends on the precise challenges that you face. These include the structure of the source file(s) that you have to process, the time available to complete the job, and the SLA (Service Level Agreement) you have to meet, which best translates as "how fast can I load the data I have without wasting hours writing code?". The variety of available options need not cause confusion, however. If you work on the principle that you should use the Import and Export Wizard for unforeseen exports, T-SQL solutions for ad hoc challenges, and SSIS for structured ETL processes, then you have a baseline from which to work. Clearly, each situation will be different, and each set of circumstances will have its own specific obstacles. Yet with persistence and forethought, you should be able to load most, if not all, text files successfully into SQL Server.

To give you a simpler overview, Table 2-9 presents my take on the various methods, and their advantages and disadvantages.

Table 2-9. *Advantages and Disadvantages of the Approaches Used in This Chapter*

Technique	Advantages	Disadvantages
OPENROWSET	Uses pass-through queries.	Can be tricky to set up.
OPENDATASOURCE	Allows source data to be manipulated using T-SQL.	Can be tricky to set up.
BULK INSERT	Possibly the fastest solution.	Requires correct parameterization. Can necessitate format files.
SSIS BULK INSERT TASK	Very fast.	Requires correct parameterization. Can necessitate format files.
LINKED SERVER	Allows source data to be manipulated using T-SQL.	Unsuitable for large files.
Import and Export Wizard	Easy to use. Can generate an SSIS package.	Limited conversion options.
SSIS	Full data conversion, modification, and manipulation. Incremental data loads.	Longer to implement. Cannot create all destination objects at once.
BCP	Fast and efficient.	Complex parameters.

CHAPTER 3

XML Data Sources

It has become a truism, but XML is now the lingua franca of data exchange. Where, four or five years ago, delimited text files would have been the norm, XML files are now being used in their place. Certainly XML has its faults—and file size is not the least of them, especially when compared to text file source data. But for sheer reliability and ease of debugging XML-based data loads, I prefer to use XML files as source data over flat files any time.

So this chapter will lead you through the classic ways of getting XML data into SQL Server. However, before beginning, a few words of warning. XML is horrendously complex, the subject of countless tomes—that will doubtless become the subject matter for endless others. This chapter is not going to introduce XML and all its subtleties in any way. Instead, it will lead you through the standard ways of loading this type of source data into SQL Server.

3-1. Loading XML Files for Storage in SQL Server
Problem

You want to load an XML document—or multiple XML fragments—into an SQL Server table, where they will be stored "as is."

Solution

Use OPENROWSET (BULK) from T-SQL to push XML files into SQL Server without being "shredded" into multiple columns.

1. Create a destination table using the following code (C:\SQL2012DIRecipes\CH03\tblXmlImportTest.Sql):

   ```
   CREATE TABLE XmlImportTest
   (
    Keyword NVARCHAR(50),
    XMLDataStore XML
   );
   GO
   ```

2. Locate an XML source file, like the following simple example (C:\SQL2012DIRecipes\CH03\Clients.Xml):

   ```
   <?xml version = "1.0" encoding = "UTF-8"?>
   <CarSales>
     <Client>
       <ID>3</ID>
   ```

```
      <ClientName>John Smith</ClientName>
      <Address1>4, Grove Drive</Address1>
      <Town>Uttoxeter</Town>
      <County>Staffs</County>
      <Country>1</Country>
   </Client>
```

. . . many other elements were omitted here to save space . . .

```
   <Client>
      <ID>7</ID>
      <ClientName>Slow Sid</ClientName>
      <Address1>2, Rue des Bleues</Address1>
      <Town>Avignon</Town>
      <County>Vaucluse</County>
      <Country>3</Country>
   </Client>
</CarSales>
```

3. Run the following T-SQL code to import the contents of the XML file that is referenced, as well as any other data you wish to store in the table (C:\SQL2012DIRecipes\CH03\XmlImportTestInsert.Sql).

```
INSERT INTO XmlImportTest(XMLDataStore, Keyword);

SELECT XMLDATAToStore, 'Attribute-Centric' AS ColType
FROM
(
   SELECT    CONVERT(XML, XMLCol, 0)
   FROM      OPENROWSET (BULK 'C:\SQL2012DIRecipes\CH03\Clients_Simple.Xml' ,
                          SINGLE_BLOB) AS XMLSource (XMLCol)
                          ) AS XMLFileToImport (XMLDATAToStore);
```

How It Works

XML files can be loaded directly into an SQL Server table as pure XML data—that is, they are not "shredded" (or broken down) into rows and columns. This is done using OPENROWSET (BULK), which essentially reads the source file into a T-SQL process. The same file can be either an XML "fragment"—that is, not forced to conform to an XML schema, or a "well-formed" XML document, which conforms to an XML schema definition. This technique is useful in the following circumstances:

- When you wish to store XML documents or fragments in the database, rather than in the file system.

- When you do not wish to shred the XML data into a fully-relational SQL Server table structure.

Such a data load could be an end in itself, where, once loaded into the database, you query this XML data using the subset of the XQuery language that SQL Server uses to query the XML data type. Alternatively, it could be part of a data-staging process, where you want to store the XML fragments in SQL Server before other processing takes place.

This technique can be extended to update (or rather replace) an XML fragment or document equally easily. The code required is (C:\SQL2012DIRecipes\CH03\LoadXMLToUpdateInTable.sql):

```
UPDATE XmlImportTest

SET XMLDataStore =
                    (
                     SELECT XMLDATAToStore
                     FROM
                        (
                         SELECT    CONVERT(XML, XMLCol, 0)
                         FROM   OPENROWSET (BULK
                                              'C:\SQL2012DIRecipes\CH03\Clients_Simple.Xml',
                                              SINGLE_BLOB) AS XMLSource (XMLCol)
                        ) AS XMLFileToImport (XMLDATAToStore)
                    )
WHERE Keyword = 'Attribute-Centric'
```

It could be that you have many XML fragments or documents to load, and do not want to develop an SSIS package to perform such a task. Fortunately, with a little ingenuity (and some dynamic SQL), the script used in the current recipe can be extended to load multiple XML fragments or documents. The script to load a series of files is (C:\SQL2012DIRecipes\CH03\LoadMultiplexmlFiles.sql):

```
-- Used for dynamic SQL
DECLARE @SQL VARCHAR(8000) ;
-- Table variable to hold file names
DECLARE @FileList TABLE (XMLFile VARCHAR(150))  ;
-- Table variable to capture "raw" file listing
DECLARE @DirList TABLE (List VARCHAR(250))  ;

-- Load the output from the DIR command into the @DirList
-- Table variable
INSERT INTO @DirList
EXEC master.dbo.xp_cmdshell 'Dir D:\BIProject\*.Xml';

-- Parse out the file names - caveats, no spaces in file names,
-- All files have the correct and identical structure...
INSERT INTO   @FileList
SELECT        REVERSE(LEFT(REVERSE(List), CHARINDEX(' ', REVERSE(List))))
FROM          @DirList
WHERE         List LIKE '%.Xml%';

-- Cursor to loop through file names and load xml files
DECLARE @FileName VARCHAR(150);

DECLARE  FileLoad_CUR CURSOR
FOR
SELECT XMLFile FROM @FileList

OPEN FileLoad_CUR
```

```
FETCH NEXT FROM FileLoad_CUR INTO @FileName

WHILE @@FETCH_STATUS <> -1
BEGIN

-- The XML load process
SET @SQL = 'INSERT INTO AA1 (XMLData) SELECT CAST(XMLSource AS XML) AS XMLSource
            FROM OPENROWSET(BULK ''' + @FileName + ''', SINGLE_BLOB)  AS X (XMLSource)'

EXEC (@SQL)

FETCH NEXT FROM FileLoad_CUR INTO @FileName

END;

CLOSE FileLoad_CUR;
DEALLOCATE FileLoad_CUR;
```

The T-SQL, which loads multiple files, works this way:

- First, the list of files to be processed is defined using xp_cmdshell to call a Dir (directory listing) command.

- This list is then parsed to get useable file names.

- A cursor loops through the list of files and loads them.

The dynamic SQL used here makes certain presumptions:

- The files have the .Xml extension.

- There are no spaces in the file names.

The script can be extended, if required, to accept multiple extensions or file names with spaces. Please note that this recipe only purports to help you load XML data as XML into an SQL Server table. The many and varied ways of extracting and querying the data are, unfortunately, beyond the scope of this book. However, if you store XML data as an XML data type, do remember that SQL Server allows you to index XML columns for faster querying with the subset of the XQuery language that SQL Server uses.

The "keyword" use here is, of course, optional, and I have left it there to show how XML and "normal" data can be imported together. It is important to use the SINGLE_BLOB parameter, so the entire file is handled as the contents of one column. Also, no XML document can be greater than 2 gigabytes in size. Note also that the CONVERT parameter 0 used here discards insignificant white space and does not allow for an internal DTD (Document Type Definition) subset. I am going to presume that DTDs are not going to be used.

To query the contents of the XML column, you can use the following T-SQL syntax, for example:

```
SELECT XMLDataStore.query('(/ROOT/Customer/CustomerID)') FROM XmlImport
```

Hints, Tips, and Traps

- The dynamic SQL is predicated on having the rights to use xp_cmdshell. There are many DBAs who will not countenance this, and so you need to discover vast reserves of charm—or irrefutable technical arguments—to get this allowed. Alternatively, you can write a CLR (Common Language Runtime) routine to list the files in a directory and persuade the DBA that this approach is safer.

- By using SINGLE_BLOB (as opposed to SINGLE_CLOB or SINGLE_NCLOB), you avoid a potential mismatch between the encoding of the XML document (as given in the XML encoding declaration) and the code page of the server.

- Recipes 3-2 and 3-3 show how to take the data from an XML column and shred it into separate columns of a destination table.

- Shock and horror—a *cursor*! Well, as I say elsewhere in this book, cursors are not inevitably wrong, and there are occasions when they are the easiest solution to use and debug—and where the resource hit is negligible. This whole approach is predicated on the fact that you are probably only loading a few dozen XML files at most. If you will be loading many more files than this, then a cursor-free recipe (Recipe 6-7) can be adapted to your needs.

3-2. Loading XML Data into Rows and Columns
Problem

You want to load data from small- to medium-sized XML files into an SQL Server table, correctly "shredded" into rows and columns.

Solution

Use OPENXML to load and shred both element-centric and attribute-centric XML files into an SQL Server table.

1. Place your (in this case, element-centric) XML file in the requisite source directory. The file looks like this (C:\SQL2012DIRecipes\CH03\ClientLite.Xml):

```
<CarSales>
  <Client>
    <ID>3</ID>
    <ClientName>John Smith</ClientName>
    <Country>1</Country>
  </Client>
```

Data omitted to save space . . .

```
  <Client>
    <ID>7</ID>
    <ClientName>Slow Sid</ClientName>
    <Country>3</Country>
  </Client>
</CarSales>
```

2. Load the XML file using the following T-SQL code (C:\SQL2012DIRecipes\CH03\ShredClientLite.Sql):

```
DECLARE @DocID INT;
DECLARE @DocXML VARCHAR(MAX);

SELECT @DocXML = CAST(XMLSource AS VARCHAR(MAX))
FROM OPENROWSET(BULK 'C:\SQL2012DIRecipes\CH03\ClientLite.xml', SINGLE_BLOB)
            AS X (XMLSource);
```

```
        EXECUTE master.dbo.sp_xml_preparedocument @DocID OUTPUT, @DocXML;

        SELECT      ID, ClientName, Country
        INTO        XmlTable
        FROM        OPENXML(@DocID, 'CarSales/Client', 2)
                        WITH (
                                ID VARCHAR(50)
                                ,ClientName VARCHAR(50)
                                ,Country VARCHAR(10)
                             );

        EXECUTE master.dbo.sp_xml_removedocument @DocID;
```

3. Query the XmlTable table and you should see something like the following result:

    ```
    ID   ClientName           Country
    3    John Smith           1
    4    Bauhaus Motors       2
    5    Honest Fred          3
    6    Fast Eddie           2
    7    Slow Sid             3
    ```

How It Works

Ever since SQL Server 2000 was released, OPENXML has been helping developers and DBAs load (or "shred" as it is known) XML data into relational tables. This technology is still supported in the current version of SQL Server, and is easy and efficient to use. The result is totally different from that obtained in Recipe 3-1, as this time the source file is broken down into its constituent data fragments and each element or attribute loaded into a separate column in one or more tables.

First, the source file is loaded into the @DocXML variable. Then, the sp_xml_preparedocument stored procedure is run against this variable to prepare the XML and return a handle, in this case, @DocID. The handle is passed to the OPENXML command, which reads the XML data and shreds it into rows and columns in the destination table. Then, in the OPENXML statement, the row pattern ('CarSales/Client') identifies which <Client> nodes to process.

The WITH clause is the ColPattern, which allows you to traverse the hierarchy of the XML and select any element you choose. For attributes, you can merely use a ColPattern like Invoice/@InvoiceNumber. You can traverse the XML up beyond the initial node specified using the RowPattern, by using (for example) ../Invoice—assuming that the row pattern was 'CarSales/Client'/Invoice. If a ColPattern is not specified, the default mapping (attribute-centric or element-centric mapping, as specified) will take place.

Be warned, however, that although simple, OPENXML is very memory-intensive. Also OPENXML uses XPath (not XQuery). Taken together, this signifies that OPENXML is best used in the following situations:

- When you do not wish to import the XML data into SQL Server before using it in a T-SQL query.

- When you have a properly formed XML document.

- When the XML document is less that 2 gigabytes in size.

To extend this example slightly, let us assume that you have an (admittedly fairly simple) attribute-centric XML file, something like this (C:\SQL2012DIRecipes\CH03\ClientLiteAttributeCentric.Xml):

```
<CarSales>
  <Client ID="3" ClientName="John Smith" Country="1" />
  <Client ID="4" ClientName="Bauhaus Motors" Country="2" />
```

```
  <Client ID="5" ClientName="Honest Fred" Country="3" />
  <Client ID="6" ClientName="Fast Eddie" Country="2" />
  <Client ID="7" ClientName="Slow Sid" Country="3" />
</CarSales>
```

To load this file, simply change the OPENXML flags parameter to 1, as in the following example (C:\SQL2012DIRecipes\CH03\ShredClientLiteAttributeCentric.Sql):

```
DECLARE @DocID INT;
DECLARE @DocXML VARCHAR(MAX);

SELECT @DocXML = CAST(XMLSource AS VARCHAR(MAX))
FROM OPENROWSET(BULK 'C:\SQL2012DIRecipes\CH03\ClientLite.xml', SINGLE_BLOB)  AS X (XMLSource);

EXECUTE master.dbo.sp_xml_preparedocument @DocID OUTPUT, @DocXML;
SELECT      ID, ClientName, Country
FROM        OPENXML(@DocID, 'CarSales/Client', 1)
                    WITH (
                            ID VARCHAR(50)
                            ,ClientName VARCHAR(50)
                            ,Country VARCHAR(10)
                            );

EXECUTE master.dbo.sp_xml_removedocument @DocID;
```

Obviously, it is impossible to predict the multiple permutations of an XML data source. However, it is probably fair to say that not all source files will be as simple as the one we used here. Fortunately, OPENXML can handle more complex data sources. The art and science of OPENXML is in the two elements that make up an OPENXML command. These are:

- The *row pattern*, which identifies the nodes to process ('/CarSales/Client' in the examples given in this recipe).

- The *schema declaration*, which is the WITH clause that specifies the column output.

As a more complex example, here is an XML fragment with nested elements (C:\SQL2012DIRecipes\CH03\NestedClients.Xml):

```
<CarSales>
  <Client>
    <ID>3</ID>
    <ClientName>John Smith</ClientName>
    <Country>1</Country>
    <Town>Uttoxeter</Town>
    <Invoice>
      <InvoiceNumber>3A9271EA-FC76-4281-A1ED-714060ADBA30</InvoiceNumber>
      <TotalDiscount>500.00</TotalDiscount>
    </Invoice>
  </Client>
  <Client>
    <ID>4</ID>
    <ClientName>Bauhaus Motors</ClientName>
    <Country>2</Country>
    <Town>Oxford</Town>
```

```
    <Invoice>
      <InvoiceNumber>C9018CC1-AE67-483B-B1B7-CF404C296F0B</InvoiceNumber>
      <TotalDiscount>0.00</TotalDiscount>
    </Invoice>
  </Client>
</CarSales>
```

And here is the code to read it using OPENXML (you will need, of course, to wrap it in the preceding code to load, prepare, and remove the XML document from memory—omitted here to save space) (C:\SQL2012DIRecipes\CH03\ShredNestedClients.Sql):

```
SELECT  ID, ClientName, Country, TotalDiscount
FROM    OPENXML(@DocID, 'CarSales/Client', 2)
                WITH (
                       ID VARCHAR(50) 'ID'
                      ,ClientName VARCHAR(50) 'ClientName'
                      ,Country VARCHAR(10)'Country'
                      ,TotalDiscount NUMERIC(18,2) 'Invoice/TotalDiscount'
                     )
```

One final thing to take away is that whether you are using attribute- or element-centric XML, you are still using T-SQL. This means that you can use WHERE to filter output and ORDER BY to sort it. The snippet given at the top of this recipe could be extended like this (C:\SQL2012DIRecipes\CH03\ShredNestedClientsFilterAndSort.Sql):

```
DECLARE @DocID INT;
DECLARE @DocXML VARCHAR(MAX);

SELECT @DocXML = CAST(XMLSource AS VARCHAR(MAX))
FROM OPENROWSET(BULK 'C:\SQL2012DIRecipes\CH03\ClientLite.xml', SINGLE_BLOB)  AS X ↵
                (XMLSource);

EXECUTE master.dbo.sp_xml_preparedocument @DocID OUTPUT, @DocXML;

SELECT       ID, ClientName, Country
INTO         XmlTable
FROM         OPENXML(@DocID, 'CarSales/Client', 2)
                 WITH (
                        ID VARCHAR(50)
                       ,ClientName VARCHAR(50)
                       ,Country VARCHAR(10)
                      )
WHERE        Country = 3
ORDER BY  ID

EXECUTE master.dbo.sp_xml_removedocument @DocID;
```

Hints, Tips, and Traps

- The XML document must be well-formed—and specifically only have one top-level (root) element.

- Despite being an older technology, OPENXML is reputed to be the fastest solution when it comes to loading XML data into a relational structure from T-SQL.

3-3. Shredding an XML File into an SQL Server Table

Problem

You want to load XML data into SQL Server tables and columns without the overhead of
sp_xml_preparedocument.

Solution

Use OPENROWSET (BULK) and SQL Server's XQuery support to shred and load the source file.

1. Create a destination table using the following code
    (C:\SQL2012DIRecipes\CH03\tblXMLImport_Clients.Sql):

    ```
    CREATE TABLE dbo.XmlImport_Clients
    (
     ID int NULL,
     ClientName varchar(50) NULL,
     Town varchar(50) NULL,
     County varchar(50) NULL,
     Country int NULL
    ) ;
    GO
    ```

2. Locate an XML source file—I will use C:\SQL2012DIRecipes\CH03\ClientLite.Xml,
    as used in Recipe 3-2.

3. Load the file using the following code snippet
    (C:\SQL2012DIRecipes\CH03\ShredXMLUsingOPENROWSETBulk.Sql):

    ```
    DECLARE @XMLSource XML;

    SELECT   @XMLSource = CAST(XMLSource AS XML) ;
    FROM     OPENROWSET(BULK 'C:\SQL2012DIRecipes\CH03\ClientLite.xml', SINGLE_BLOB) ↵
                        AS X (XMLSource);

    INSERT INTO XmlImport_Clients (ID, ClientName, Town, County, Country)

    SELECT
    SRC.Client.value('ID[1]', 'INT') AS ID
    ,SRC.Client.value('ClientName[1]', 'VARCHAR(50)') AS ClientName
    ,SRC.Client.value('Town[1]', 'VARCHAR(50)') AS Town
    ,SRC.Client.value('County[1]', 'VARCHAR(50)') AS County
    ,SRC.Client.value('Country[1]', 'INT') AS Country

    FROM @XMLSource.nodes('CarSales/Client') AS SRC (Client);
    ```

How It Works

OPENXML is a venerable approach that still works well, but since SQL Server 2005, there have been other
solutions to getting XML data into SQL Server using SQL Server's support for XML and XQuery. Though a little
disconcerting at first (perhaps because it is less "T-SQL" and more XQuery), using an XML data type can be both
an efficient and a powerful way to load XML source data into a database structure. Unlike OPENXML, loading XML

data using the .nodes() method will not require sp_xml_preparedocument to instantiate an XML object. This technique is best used in the following situations:

- When you want to load all or part of the contents of the source document into table columns.

- When setting up an SSIS package to shred the data is overkill.

In this recipe, we loaded the source file into a variable, from which it is shredded into a table using the .nodes() method of an XML data type. The .value() method extracted values from the XML instance stored as an XML type.

The "staging variable" approach used here requires lots of memory for large files. So, if you find that using a staging variable seems somewhat old-fashioned, then there is a solution to avoid the staging variable—with a judicious application of CROSS APPLY. So, using the same XML source file as earlier in this recipe, the code for this approach is as follows
(C:\SQL2012DIRecipes\CH03\ShredXMLUsingOPENROWSETBulkAndCrossApply.Sql):

```
INSERT INTO XmlImport_Clients (ID, ClientName, Town, County, Country)

SELECT
SRC.Client.value('ID[1]', 'INT') AS ID
,SRC.Client.value('ClientName[1]', 'VARCHAR(50)') AS ClientName
,SRC.Client.value('Town[1]', 'VARCHAR(50)') AS Town
,SRC.Client.value('County[1]', 'VARCHAR(50)') AS County
,SRC.Client.value('Country[1]', 'INT') AS Country

FROM
    (
      SELECT  CAST(XMLSource AS XML)
      FROM     OPENROWSET(BULK 'C:\SQL2012DIRecipes\CH03\Clients_Simple.xml', SINGLE_BLOB) ↵
                    AS X (XMLSource)
    ) AS X (XMLSource)
CROSS APPLY XMLSource.nodes('CarSales/Client') AS SRC (Client);
```

This second CROSS APPLY approach is slightly more complex, but shreds the data directly into the destination table.

Once again, as we are in the world of T-SQL, the code we have used so far can be extended to filter and sort the data that you are loading. So, if we take the preceding example and decide only to load the records where the country is "3"—and also to order by the Town element, the following is the code to use
(C:\SQL2012DIRecipes\CH03\ShredXMLUsingOPENROWSETBulkAndCrossApplyWithFilter.Sql):

```
INSERT INTO XmlImport_Clients (ID, ClientName, Town, County, Country)
SELECT
SRC.Client.value('ID[1]', 'INT') AS ID
,SRC.Client.value('ClientName[1]', 'VARCHAR(50)') AS ClientName
,SRC.Client.value('Town[1]', 'VARCHAR(50)') AS Town
,SRC.Client.value('County[1]', 'VARCHAR(50)') AS County
,SRC.Client.value('Country[1]', 'INT') AS Country
FROM
        (
          SELECT CAST(XMLSource AS XML)
          FROM OPENROWSET(BULK 'C:\SQL2012DIRecipes\CH03\Clients_Simple.xml', SINGLE_BLOB) ↵
          AS X (XMLSource)
        ) AS X (XMLSource)
```

```
CROSS APPLY XMLSource.nodes('CarSales/Client') AS SRC (Client)
WHERE SRC.Client.value('Country[1]', 'INT') = 3
ORDER BY SRC.Client.value('Town[1]', 'VARCHAR(50)');
```

This technique may be familiar, but it can rapidly become unusably slow for large files. Of course, this depends on each person's definition of "large," but if you are waiting for several minutes—or even hours—for SQL Server to finish the process, then perhaps you might be willing to consider another approach. So should you be faced with XML data loads that are taking hours, there is one solution, which requires a little upfront work, but can reduce hours of processing to seconds, and apparently will reduce memory pressure too. The trick is to use a typed XML column in a staging table to hold the source file (or files), and then apply XML indexes to this. You will also have to add a primary key first, or you will not be able to add the XML indexes.

■ **Note**   Thanks to Dan on Stack Overflow (http://stackoverflow.com) for describing how to use XML indexes to accelerate XML loads this way.

In this example, I have added secondary XML indexes too. These may not be completely necessary in many cases, but as they only take a short time to generate, even for large files, I would suggest applying them in any case. Once the XML data is loaded into the staging table and has been indexed, you use the indexed table as the source for the XQuery and use CROSS APPLY to shred the data (C:\SQL2012DIRecipes\CH03\ShredXMLWithIndexes.Sql):

```
-- Apply an XSD
DECLARE @XSD XML;
SELECT @XSD=CONVERT(XML, XSDDef) FROM OPENROWSET ↵
 (BULK 'C:\SQL2012DIRecipes\CH03\Clients_Simple.xsd', SINGLE_BLOB) AS XSD (XSDDef)

CREATE XML SCHEMA COLLECTION XML_XSD AS @XSD;
GO

-- Staging table to hold XML data

CREATE TABLE dbo.Tmp_XMLLoad(
ID int IDENTITY(1,1) NOT NULL,
XMLData xml(CONTENT dbo.XML_XSD) NULL,
 CONSTRAINT PK_Tmp_XMLLoad PRIMARY KEY CLUSTERED
(
ID ASC
)WITH (PAD_INDEX = OFF, STATISTICS_NORECOMPUTE = OFF, IGNORE_DUP_KEY = OFF, ALLOW_ROW_LOCKS  = ON,
ALLOW_PAGE_LOCKS = ON)
);
GO

-- XML index
CREATE PRIMARY XML INDEX XX_XMLData ON Tmp_XMLLoad (XMLData)
CREATE XML INDEX SX_XMLData_Property ON Tmp_XMLLoad (XMLData) ↵
USING XML INDEX XX_XMLData FOR PROPERTY
CREATE XML INDEX SX_XMLData_Value ON Tmp_XMLLoad (XMLData) ↵
USING XML INDEX XX_XMLData FOR VALUE
CREATE XML INDEX SX_XMLData_Path ON Tmp_XMLLoad (XMLData) ↵
USING XML INDEX XX_XMLData FOR PATH
```

```
-- Load data into table
INSERT INTO Tmp_XMLLoad (XMLData)

SELECT CAST(XMLSource AS XML) AS XMLSource
FROM OPENROWSET(BULK 'C:\SQL2012DIRecipes\CH03\Clients_Simple.xml', SINGLE_BLOB) ↵
                AS X (XMLSource)

-- and to output:
INSERT INTO XmlImport_Clients (ID, ClientName, Town,  Country)
SELECT
SRC.Client.value('ID[1]', 'INT') AS ID
,SRC.Client.value('ClientName[1]', 'VARCHAR(50)') AS ClientName
,SRC.Client.value('Town[1]', 'VARCHAR(50)') AS Town
,SRC.Client.value('Country[1]', 'INT') AS Country
FROM Tmp_XMLLoad
CROSS APPLY XMLData.nodes('CarSales/Client') AS SRC (Client) ;
```

Just to finish—and hopefully to start you on the road to XQuery—the following is an example of how you can avoid T-SQL to filter data without the T-SQL WHERE clause used previously:

```
CROSS APPLY XMLSource.nodes('CarSales/Client[ID=3]') AS SRC (Client);
```

Yes, if you know XQuery, you can use it instead to filter the data. Now, this is not the time or place for an intensive XQuery course—but at least you know that it can be done.

Hints, Tips, and Traps

- I am presuming that you have an XSD file to work with—if not, then you can use SSIS to create one from the data, as described in Recipe 3-4.

- Also, if you are testing the @XMLSource variable used in the examples, do not worry if it only appears in a truncated form—if you use the PRINT statement, for instance. T-SQL will only display the first 8000 characters of the 2 billion that it can handle. To reassure yourself, you can always output a DATALENGTH(@XMLSource) to confirm that all the data is in the variable. Incidentally, if you do wish to print the @XMLSource variable from T-SQL, you will need to cast it back to a VARCHAR or NVARCHAR.

3-4. Importing XML Data as Part of an ETL Process
Problem

You want to import (and shred) XML data as part of a structured and controlled ETL process.

Solution

Use SSIS and the XML Source task as the data source.

1. Open SSIS, create a new package and add a Data Flow task onto the Data Flow pane.

2. Double-click the Data Flow task to open it. Add an XML source task onto the Data Flow pane. Double-click the XML source task to open it.

3. Leaving the data access mode as XML File Location, browse to the XML source file (C:\SQL2012DIRecipes\CH03\ComplexNested.XML in this recipe), then click Generate XSD. Either keep the proposed file name (which will be the same as the XML file, but with an XSD extension) or enter the name you require (C:\SQL2012DIRecipes\CH03\ComplexNested.Xsd here). Click Save. The dialog box should look something like Figure 3-1 (except with your file names if you are not using the examples from this book).

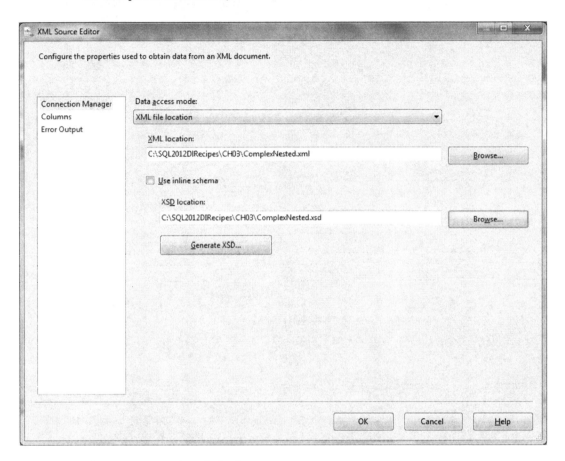

Figure 3-1. *The XML Source Editor dialog box*

4. Click Columns. You see a table represented for each node in the XML hierarchy, something like Figure 3-2.

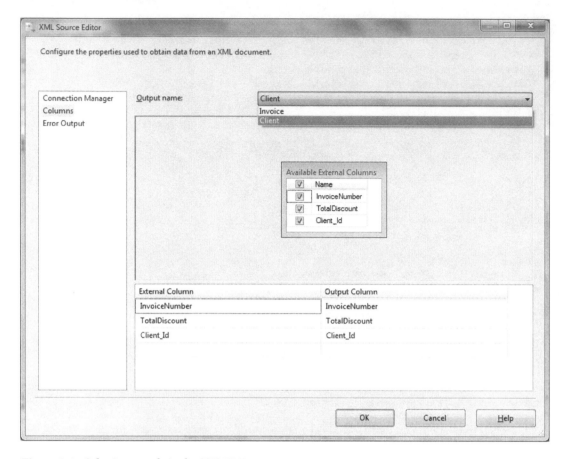

Figure 3-2. *Selecting a node in the SSIS XML source*

5. Click OK to confirm the source file selection. Return to the Data Flow pane.

6. Add an OLEDB destination task to the Data Flow pane. Drag the green output connection to link the XML source to the OLEDB output. Unless there is only one XML node, or this is the last node, the Input Output Selection dialog box will appear, allowing you to select the XML node to output—as in Figure 3-3.

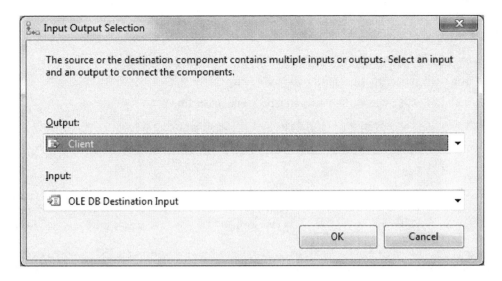

Figure 3-3. *Selecting the XML node to process in an SSIS data flow*

7. Somewhat confusingly, the output is the XML source and the input is the OLEDB destination! Click OK to return to the Data Flow pane.

8. Double-click the OLEDB destination task. Select an existing OLEDB connection manager (or create a new one, as described in Recipe 1-2, among others). Select an existing table or click the New button to create a new one. Click OK to return to the Data Flow pane. This step must now be repeated for every node in the XML hierarchy.

9. Run the SSIS package (right-click the package in Solution Explorer and select Execute Package).

How It Works

For a regular data import, once again SSIS is probably the best tool to use. It will not only import the XML source structure into appropriate SQL Server tables, but will also create the XSD file required to perform the import.

Having said that, it is worth noting that a complex XML source file will leave SSIS suggesting the creation of very many shred tables in SQL Server, and will leave you with a complex (not to say convoluted) hierarchy of tables, mapping to the hierarchy of nodes in the XML document. So for a complex source file, be prepared to spend time refactoring the extremely verbose XSD file generated by SSIS to

- Reduce the complexity of the XSD file.

- Reduce the complexity of the shred tables in SQL Server.

- Flatten the XML hierarchy.

- Import only the parts of the XML hierarchy that interest you.

Another thing to note is that once all the data is imported into the shred tables, you will probably have to create either T-SQL code or views to join the shred tables in order to extract the salient data resulting from the import. For a complex XML source, this can be challenging, to say the least. It does, however leave you, the data person, facing your data in relational form, which is probably more intuitive for database developers and DBAs alike. This is best when

- You will be shredding the source data into SQL Server on a regular basis.

- You wish to import either all or part of the source file.

- You want SSIS to create all the shred tables semiautomatically.

- You wish to access all the XML data in a relational structure.

- You want to select part of the XML data using SQL to define the selection.

- The data files are not too large.

This recipe, of course, has described only the "core" XML part of an SSIS import package. You may well want to precede the XML import with an SQL task to truncate destination tables and drop any indexes on the destination tables, and then follow the Data Flow task with an SQL task to re-create indexes on all fields used in joins on the shred tables.

Another point to note is that when confirming the source file—and unless the XSD file defines data lengths—you could well see the alert shown in Figure 3-4.

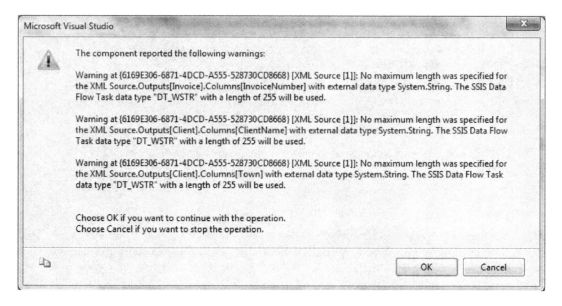

Figure 3-4. XML data type warning

Clicking OK removes the alert, and you can then, if you wish, tweak the data types on the output by right-clicking the XML source task and selecting Show Advanced Editor. Next, click the Input and Output Properties tab, and select a different data type or data length. The dialog box shown in Figure 3-5 gives one example.

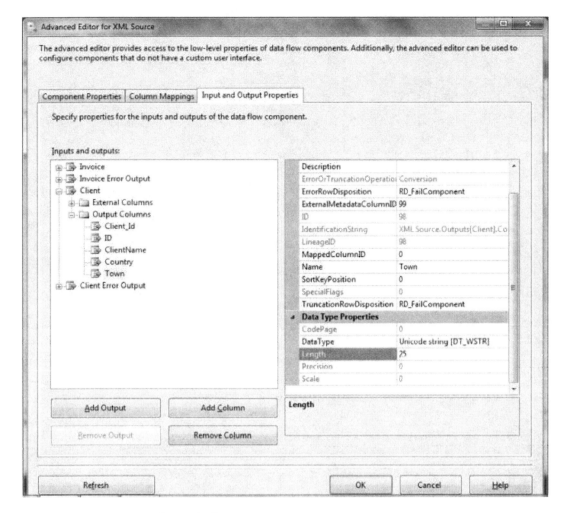

Figure 3-5. *XML Source Advanced Editor*

This allows you to extend the length of character columns over the default 255, or to avoid truncation when mapping to VARCHAR(MAX) columns by setting the output type to Unicode text stream [DT_NTEXT].

Consider creating keys and indexes on the key and foreign key fields of all the shred tables to accelerate querying or re-assembling the data. This may take some time (as could setting up the process to drop all indexes before importing data, at least if you are using the package on a regular basis), but you could find that the performance gains are well worth this extra effort if you are importing large amounts of XML source data.

Hints, Tips, and Traps

- Do not forget that in a production environment, you need to set the Error handling of the XML source task. This will allow you, at the very least, to specify how the task is to handle errors for each column of each XML node. An extremely simple approach is given in Figure 3-6.

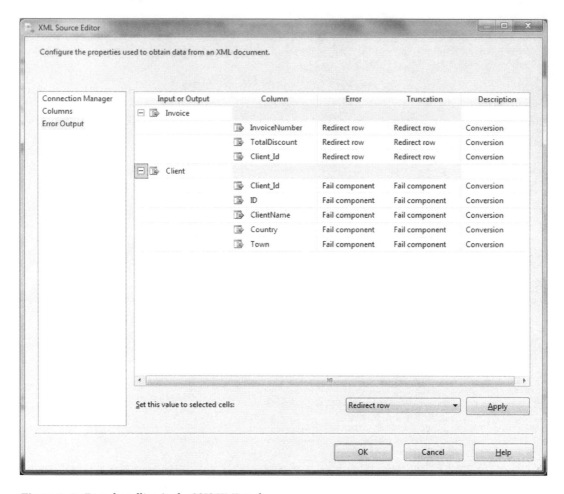

Figure 3-6. Error handling in the SSIS XML task

- You could face a situation where a source file is too large to be processed—because there is not enough available memory for SSIS to load the Document Object Model for the source. In this case, you would have to use an XSLT transform to break down the source file into smaller files (as in Recipe 3-7), or use SQLXML Bulk Load (as described in Recipe 3-8).

- As I pointed out in previous chapters (but it bears repeating), if you use the same destination connection manager, then it is worth defining it at package-level (in the Connection Managers folder of the Solution Explorer) if you are using SQL Server 2012. For earlier versions of SQL Server, simply copy a working connection manager between packages.

3-5. Importing Complex XML Files
Problem

You want to import data from a complex source XML file.

Solution

Use SSIS and shred the data into staging tables, which you then overlay with views to extract the normalized records.

Figure 3-7 shows an example of a view overlaid across five tables that resulted from a complex XML import using SSIS.

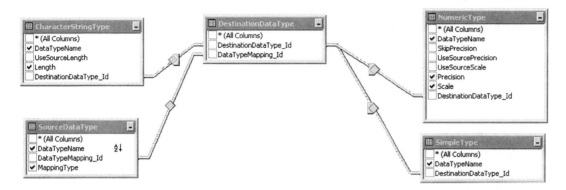

Figure 3-7. *Using views to flatten a complex XML import file structure*

This view, in effect, "denormalizes" the multiple hierarchical tables from XML into a form that is more suited to the subsequent data load.

How It Works

As mentioned in Recipe 3-4, if you have a complex source file—which implies a complex schema file—then you need to extend your package in the following ways:

- Create multiple OLEDB destination tasks, one for each output that SSIS has detected.

- Use the initial output from SSIS as staging tables.

- Decipher the interconnections between the staging tables in your destination database, and define views or stored procedures to join the data—probably flattening it into a more useable form, which is then output into more simplified final tables.

- Index larger staging tables before denormalizing them into the final tables.

This can be more time-consuming than setting up the actual SSIS task, but is frequently a necessary phase of the import process.

3-6. Importing Multiple XML Files into SQL Server
Problem

You want to import multiple XML files into SQL Server in a single structured and controlled ETL process.

Solution

Use SSIS and a Foreach Loop container to loop through the source directory by setting the data access mode to XML File from Variable.

1. Create an XML data flow, as described in Recipe 3-4.

2. Add a Foreach Loop container and place the Data Flow task inside it. Configure the task to iterate over a set of files in a specified directory. Load the path to each one into a suitable variable (user::FileName in this example). This technique is described in detail in Recipe 13-1.

3. Double-click the XML source task and define the data access mode as XML File from Variable. Select the variable that you used in the Foreach Loop container to hold the file name, as shown in Figure 3-8.

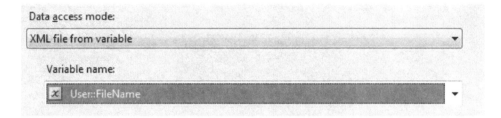

Figure 3-8. *Selecting the XML source file from a variable*

4. Click OK to confirm your changes.

5. Switching to a variable for the file name invalidates all the destination tasks, so double-click each one, followed by OK to remove the error indicators.

How It Works

Clearly, there will be times when you will be faced with not one, but several XML files to import at a time. Providing that they are all identically structured, then the standard way to do this is to use a Foreach Loop container. The trick here is to set up the process the first time using a direct path to a data source file, and only once the package has run successfully do you switch to using a variable for the file name.

■ **Note**   Any modifications to the XML structures will probably involve resetting the data access mode to XML File Location, revalidating all the destination tasks, retesting the data load for a single-source file, and then switching back to the file variable—and once again revalidating all the destination tasks!

3-7. Flattening an XML File to Prepare It for Import
Problem

You want to restructure a source XML file to "flatten" it – that is make it less complex - in order to simplify an XML import process.

Solution

Use the SSIS and the XML task to process the source file before importing it. The following explains how to apply an XSLT transform to a source XML file.

1. Copy a source XML file to a source directory. In this example it is
    `C:\SQL2012DIRecipes\CH03\XMLToFlatten.Xml`, and looks like this:

```
<Clients>
  <Client>
    <ClientName>John Smith</ClientName>
    <ID>3</ID>
    <Details Town="Uttoxeter">
      <County>Staffs</County>
      <Address1>4, Grove Drive</Address1>
    </Details>
  </Client>

... Data omitted to save space ...

  <Client>
    <ClientName>Slow Sid</ClientName>
    <ID>7</ID>
    <Details Town="Avignon">
      <County>Vaucluse</County>
      <Address1>2, Rue des Bleues</Address1>
    </Details>
  </Client>
</Clients>
```

2. Prepare an XSLT file, which transforms the XML file. In this example, it is named
    `C:\SQL2012DIRecipes\CH03\FlattenedOutput.Xlt`, and looks like this:

```
<xsl:stylesheet version="1.0" xmlns:xsl="http://www.w3.org/1999/XSL/Transform"
                              xmlns="http://www.w3.org/TR/xhtml1/strict">
  <xsl:output method="xml" indent="yes"/>
  <xsl:template match="/">

  <Clients>

    <xsl:for-each select="Clients/Client">

     <Client>

        <xsl:element name="ID">
          <xsl:value-of select="ID"/>
        </xsl:element>
        <xsl:element name="Name">
          <xsl:value-of select="ClientName"/>
        </xsl:element>
        <xsl:element name="Town">
          <xsl:value-of select="Details/@Town"/>
        </xsl:element>
```

```
      <xsl:element name="County">
        <xsl:value-of select="Details/County"/>
      </xsl:element>
      <xsl:element name="Address">
        <xsl:value-of select="Details/Address1"/>
      </xsl:element>

    </Client>

  </xsl:for-each>

  </Clients>
  </xsl:template>

</xsl:stylesheet>
```

3. Open or create an SSIS package. Add an XML task onto the Control Flow pane.

4. Double-click the XML task to open it. Change the Operation Type to XSLT (which change the General pane significantly).

5. For the Input section, set the SourceType to File Connection. Create a new connection manager for the Source, which points to your XML data file.

6. For the Second Operand section, set the SecondOperandType to File connection. Create a new connection manager for the Source that points to your XSD schema file.

7. In the Outputsection, set SaveOperationResult to True.

8. In the OperationResult section, set the DestinationType to File Connection. Create a new connection manager for the Destination, which creates your resulting flattened XML document. Be sure to select Create File when defining the connection manager. Be sure to set OverwriteDestination to True. The dialog box should look something like Figure 3-9.

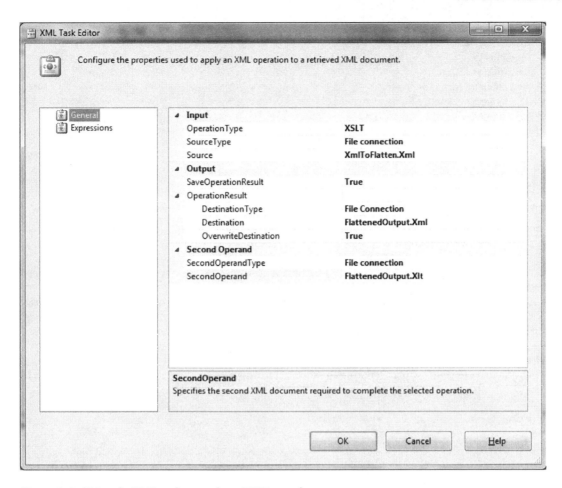

Figure 3-9. Using the XML task to apply an XSLT transform

9. Confirm your changes with OK.

10. Run the SSIS package, and if all goes well, a new destination XML file is created,
    named C:\SQL2012DIRecipes\CH03\FlattenedOutput.Xml. It should look like this:

```
<?xml version="1.0" encoding="utf-8"?>
<Clients xmlns="http://www.w3.org/TR/xhtml1/strict">
  <Client>
    <ID>3</ID>
    <Name>John Smith</Name>
    <Town>Uttoxeter</Town>
    <County>Staffs</County>
    <Address>4, Grove Drive</Address>
  </Client>
```

... Data omitted to save space ...

```
<Client>
  <ID>7</ID>
  <Name>Slow Sid</Name>
  <Town>Avignon</Town>
  <County>Vaucluse</County>
  <Address>2, Rue des Bleues</Address>
</Client>
</Clients>
```

How It Works

Another weapon in the SSIS armory to help you deal with XML data is the XML task. This task has several uses, but the one that we start with is using it to apply an XSLT transform to an XML document. There are many—very many—possible reasons to apply an XSLT transform, but here we only look at "flattening" an XML document. This means reducing the complexity of the source file to make it easier to load. As you can see, the XML produced is much simpler, thanks to the work performed by an XML style sheet.

Of necessity, applying such transforms requires reasonable knowledge of XML and XSLT, or the willingness to learn how XSLT functions. As the aim here is not to provide a crash-course on the subject of XSLT, the example is very simple. Armed with the principle, you can then apply it to your own specific business requirements. There are, however, many excellent books and articles on this subject for you to consult should you need to pursue the subject further.

Other frequent uses for XSLT when preparing source files include:

- Slicing large source files into smaller, more manageable files.

- Removing data.

- Deleting references to schemas.

Hints, Tips, and Traps

- As was the case with flat files and spreadsheets, I suggest that it is probably not worth defining package-level connection managers for such single-use connections as XML files.

3-8. Importing XML Data from Very Large Files, Putting a Priority on Speed

Problem

You want to import large XML data files as fast as possible because you have challenging SLAs (service-level agreements) that you have to meet.

Solution

Use the SQLXML Bulk Load executable to load the data, as it is nearly always the fastest available option. The following explains how you use it.

1. Download and install SQLXML 4.0, unless it is already installed (see the upcoming note on this).

2. Locate an XML source data file. In this example, it is the C:\SQL2012DIRecipes\CH03\Clients_Simple.Xml file.

3. Create a destination table. The following is the one to use in this example (C:\SQL2012DIRecipes\CH03\tbl Client_XMLBulkLoad.Sql):

```
CREATE TABLE CarSales_Staging.dbo.Client_XMLBulkLoad
(
 ID int NULL,
 ClientName NVARCHAR(1000) NULL,
 Address1 NVARCHAR(1000) NULL,
 Town NVARCHAR(1000) NULL,
 County NVARCHAR(1000) NULL,
 Country NUMERIC(18, 0) NULL
);
GO
```

4. Create an XML schema file. Note the extensions that are part of the Microsoft mapping schema (C:\SQL2012DIRecipes\CH03\SQLXMLBulkLoadImport_Simple.Xsd):

```
<xsd:schema xmlns:xsd=http://www.w3.org/2001/XMLSchema ↵
            xmlns:sql="urn:schemas-microsoft-com:mapping-schema">

    <xsd:element name="CarSales" sql:is-constant="1" >
      <xsd:complexType>
        <xsd:sequence>

<xsd:element name="Client" sql:relation="Client_XMLBulkLoad"  maxOccurs="unbounded">
      <xsd:complexType>
        <xsd:sequence>
          <xsd:element name="ID"         type="xsd:integer" sql:field="ID" />
          <xsd:element name="ClientName" type="xsd:string"  sql:field="ClientName" />
          <xsd:element name="Address1"   type="xsd:string"  sql:field="Address1" />
          <xsd:element name="Town"       type="xsd:string"  sql:field="Town" />
          <xsd:element name="County"     type="xsd:string"  sql:field="County" />
          <xsd:element name="Country"    type="xsd:decimal" sql:field="Country" />
        </xsd:sequence>
      </xsd:complexType>
</xsd:element>
        </xsd:sequence>
      </xsd:complexType>
    </xsd:element>
</xsd:schema>
```

5. Create the VBScript used to invoke SQLXML Bulk Load and load the data, as follows
    (name this file **C:\SQL2012DIRecipes\CH03\SQLXMLBulkload.vbs**):

```
Set objBL = CreateObject("SQLXMLBulkLoad.SQLXMLBulkload.4.0")
objBL.ConnectionString = "provider=SQLOLEDB;data
source=MySQLServer;database=CarSales_Staging; ↵
integrated security=SSPI"
objBL.ErrorLogFile = "C:\SQL2012DIRecipes\CH03\SQLXMLBulkLoadImporterror.log"
objBL.Execute "C:\SQL2012DIRecipes\CH03\SQLXMLBulkLoadImport_Simple.xsd", ↵
"C:\SQL2012DIRecipes\CH03\Clients_Simple.xml"
Set objBL = Nothing
```

6. Double-click the C:\SQL2012DIRecipes\CH03\SQLXMLBulkload.vbs file to run the
    bulk load. If all goes well, you should be able to open the Client_XMLBulkLoad table
    and see the data from the XML source file correctly loaded.

How It Works

Although perhaps not a standard part of the XML toolkit when using SQL Server, SQLXML Bulk Load is a hidden gem among the resources for the developer. Quite simply, it allows you to import extremely large data files into SQL Server as multiple tables, preserving referential integrity if this is required—and at amazing speed. It is, quite simply a COM (Component Object Model) object that allows you to load semistructured XML data into SQL Server tables.

■ **Note**   While SQLXML 4.0 is installed by default in editions of SQL Server up to and including 2005, for SQL editions from 2008 onward, it needs to be downloaded and installed separately
(www.microsoft.com/en-us/download/details.aspx?id=3522).

Despite these advantages, many SQL Server developers either ignore the existence of this superb tool, or fail to implement it because it is poorly explained in the SQL Server documentation. Perhaps as a consequence, it is unfairly perceived as hard to implement. From SQL Server 2008, it even ceased to be part of the standard installation, and has to be installed as part of the Feature Pack.

So this recipe attempts to put the record straight. This tool is best used in the following situations:

- When the source XML file is large. What is large? Well, if you were planning on using
  OPENXML, then that means over 2 gigabytes. The same upper limit is true of XML loaded
  into a variable and shredded using XQuery. With SSIS, it depends on the memory
  available. I have loaded XML files of tens of gigabytes using SQLXML Bulk Load.

- When the XML source is relatively simple XML (essentially tables and fields, but nothing
  too complex). The source data cannot be too complex (in XML terms), or it will not load.
  It is not for nothing that this is called "semistructured" XML data.

- When you wish to load multiple tables from the same source file.

- When speed loading the data is important. In my tests, SQLXML Bulk Loadloaded data
  at about 90 percent of (native) BCP speeds for separate tables without relational links—
  which is fast by any standards!

The core part of getting SQLXML to load data is in the XSD file. As you can see, it contains (apart from the Microsoft mapping schema) a few extra tidbits that allow it to perform its job so efficiently. The main mapping elements are shown in Table 3-1.

Table 3-1. *SQLXML Mapping Attributes*

XML Attribute	Explanation	Use
Sql:relation	The table into which the data is loaded.	Table-level
sql:field	The field in the destination table into which the data is loaded.	Field-level

Essentially, you have to extend the schema (suitably hand-crafted or initially created using one of the methods described in Recipe 7-12) with the attributes that allow SQLXML to channel the source data into the correct table(s) and fields. This is the hard part of this XML loading technique, and will probably be where you spend the most time, so it is worth ensuring that you have understood the XSD extensions before attempting a complex data load. You may even find that practicing on a simple XML file to start with can reap dividends.

The .vbs file that invokes SQLXML Bulk Loader can be extremely simple, and needs at a minimum, the following.

- The object creation statement—to invoke the SQLXML Bulk Load COM object.

- A connection string, containing, at a minimum:

    - The server and, if required, instance name (Data Source).

    - The destination database name (CarSales_Staging in this example).

- The SQL Server security information (Windows integrated security or SQL Server security).

- The Execute command, which provides paths to the XSD and XML files.

- A SET command to dispose of the COM object.

- An ErrorLog file. While this is not strictly essential, it is more than useful.

You will know if it has worked if there is no ErrorLog file—or if the old ErrorLog file is removed (assuming that you have requested a log file). Oh, and the fact that the data loaded correctly.

Should the data not load, then your first port of call is the ErrorLog file that SQLXML Bulk Load created (assuming that you used the objBL.ErrorLogFile = "Log File and path" parameter). So, while creating this file is not compulsory, it is a practical necessity if you want to debug a data load operation using SQLXML Bulk Load. Fortunately, these files are very explicit, and will doubtless prove to be an invaluable source of debugging information. The ErrorLog file is optional—but it is invaluable for debugging the process (unless everything works perfectly first time, and every time).

There are, however, some classic things to watch out for when creating the XSD file if you want to avoid errors. In my experience, it is the schema file that is the most common source of problems, because it involves a certain amount of hand-crafting. Potential problems include:

- Making sure that there are no spaces immediately inside all the double-quotes that are used in the xsd:element definition.

- Ensuring that you do not inadvertently close elements such as xsd:sequence and xsd:complextype—or even some of the xsd:element definitions.

- Respecting case-sensitivity. So in the preceding example, having an element called "Country", and a schema mapping element named "country" would cause the process to fail.

This simple script assumes that the destination table already exists (you can, however, create the table as part of the load shown in the next recipe). It also presumes integrated security. It is interesting that, somewhat counter-intuitively, the XML schema (.xsd) file is passed as the first parameter to the XML Bulk Loader. The XML file itself is passed in as the second parameter.

Hints, Tips, and Traps

- This example uses XML elements, but attribute-centric XML source data can also be loaded with SQLXML Bulk Loader.

- A complex XML source file can be "flattened" using XSLT to produce a file amenable to processing by SQLXML. The XML task to execute the XSLT could precede the Bulk Load itself in SSIS.

- Inline schemas are not supported. Indeed, if you have an inline schema in the source XML document, XML Bulk Load will ignore the inline schema.

- An XML document is checked for being well-formed, but it is not validated. If the XML document is not well-formed, processing is cancelled.

3-9. Loading Multiple Tables at Once from a Single XML Source File

Problem

You want to load data from an XML source file that contains data for multiple unrelated tables.

Solution

Use the SQLXML Bulk Load executable and a suitably-crafted XSD file.

You can load multiple tables from a single XML file as follows.

1. Locate your XML file, which contains data from multiple tables. This recipe's example uses C:\SQL2012DIRecipes\CH03\SQLXMLSourceDataMultipleTables.xml, which holds data for Invoice and Invoice_Lines tables. The contents look like this:

```xml
<?xml version="1.0" encoding="UTF-8" ?>
<ROOT>
<Invoice>
    <ID>3</ID>
    <InvoiceNumber>AA/1/2014-07-25</InvoiceNumber>
    <DeliveryCharge>250</DeliveryCharge->
</Invoice>
<Invoice_Lines>
    <InvoiceID>3</InvoiceID>
    <SalePrice>5000</SalePrice>
</Invoice_Lines>
<Invoice_Lines>
    <InvoiceID>3</InvoiceID>
    <SalePrice>12500</SalePrice>
</Invoice_Lines>
</ROOT>
```

2. Create the tables required to hold the data in SQL Server
    C:\SQL2012DIRecipes\CH03\tblInvoiceMulti.Sql:

```sql
CREATE TABLE CarSales_Staging.dbo.Invoice_XML_Multi
(
 ID INT NULL,
 InvoiceNumber VARCHAR (50) NULL,
 DeliveryCharge SMALLMONEY NULL
) ;
GO

CREATE TABLE CarSales_Staging. dbo.Invoice_Lines_XML_Multi
(
 InvoiceID INT NULL,
 SalePrice MONEYNULL,
) ;
GO
```

3. Create an XSD file (stored as
    C:\SQL2012DIRecipes\CH03\SQLXMLBulkLoadImportMultipleTables.xsd):

```xml
<xsd:schema xmlns:xsd = "http://www.w3.org/2001/XMLSchema"
            xmlns:sql = "urn:schemas-microsoft-com:mapping-schema">

  <xsd:element name="ROOT" sql:is-constant="1" >
   <xsd:complexType>
    <xsd:sequence>

<!-- Invoice -->
     <xsd:element name="Invoice" sql:relation="Invoice_XML_Multi" >
      <xsd:complexType>
       <xsd:sequence>
        <xsd:element name="ID"               type="xsd:integer"
                                             sql:field="ID" />
        <xsd:element name="InvoiceNumber"    type="xsd:string"
                                             sql:field="InvoiceNumber" />
        <xsd:element name="DeliveryCharge"   type="xsd:decimal"
                                             sql:field="DeliveryCharge" />
       </xsd:sequence>
      </xsd:complexType>
     </xsd:element>

<!-- Invoice Lines -->
     <xsd:element name="Invoice_Lines" sql:relation="Invoice_Lines_XML_Multi" >
      <xsd:complexType>
       <xsd:sequence>
        <xsd:element name="InvoiceID"  type="xsd:integer" sql:field="InvoiceID" />
        <xsd:element name="SalePrice"  type="xsd:string"  sql:field="SalePrice" />
       </xsd:sequence>
      </xsd:complexType>
     </xsd:element>
```

```
        </xsd:sequence>
      </xsd:complexType>
    </xsd:element>
  </xsd:schema>
```

4. Create a .vbs script that refers to the appropriate .XML and .XSD files, as follows:

```
Set objBL = CreateObject("SQLXMLBulkLoad.SQLXMLBulkload.4.0")
objBL.ConnectionString = "provider=SQLOLEDB;data source=ADAM02; ↵
database=CarSales_Staging; integrated security=SSPI"
objBL.ErrorLogFile = "C:\SQL2012DIRecipes\CH03\SQLXMLBulkLoadImporterror.log"
objBL.Execute "C:\SQL2012DIRecipes\CH03\SQLXMLBulkLoadImportMultipleTables.xsd", ↵
"C:\SQL2012DIRecipes\CH03\SQLXMLSourceDataMultipleTables.xml"
Set objBL = Nothing
```

5. Double-click the .vbs file to run SQLXML Bulk Load and import the source data.

How It Works

One advantage that an XML file can have over a CSV—or other flat—file is the capacity to store multiple unrelated tables in a single source file. This allows you, in effect, to transfer an entire subset of data in a single file, ready to be loaded into multiple tables in a destination database—simultaneously. If you are using SQLXML Bulk Load to carry out this process the data load can be blindingly fast.

This technique is predicated on the fact that the source XML is very simple in layout. It presumes that you are essentially loading data from a "table dump" in an XML file, where each table is stored in the file sequentially. To emulate such a scenario, the data file used here contains two tables in XML format. These tables are Invoice and Invoice_Lines. This example file only has one record for Invoice and two for Invoice_Lines, but clearly in reality there could be dozens of tables, each containing millions of records. Note that there is no presumption in the XML of any relational link between the Invoice and Invoice_Lines.

The only potential issue with this approach is that the XSD file, which you have to define, can become extremely complex. However, it is not necessarily difficult to create, just arduous. So arm yourself with patience, and be prepared for some repetitive testing.

As you can see, each XML element that maps to a table is a separate XML node, and the order of the elements is unimportant. What is important, however, is to have a single root node—unless the XMLFragment SQLXML parameter is set to true (the default is False), as described in Recipe 3-11.

Hints, Tips, and Traps

- There is nothing to stop you from enforcing referential integrity through the addition of primary and foreign key constraints once the load has finished. In practice, this is likely to be much faster than loading data from a "hierarchical" XML source, as described in the next recipe.

- This example presumes that the destination tables do not have IDENTITY fields. As with most forms of bulk load, this eventuality can be handled, too (as explained shortly).

- It is worth noting that the XML file (the data file) can contain more "tables" and "records" than are defined in the schema (.xsd) file. However, only those that are specified in the XSD file will be loaded.

3-10. Loading and Shredding Relational Tables from an XML Source File

Problem

You want to load a source XML file that contains XML data described as relational tables.

Solution

Use the SQLXML Bulk Load executable and a suitably-crafted XSD file to maintain the foreign key relationships assumed or defined in the source file.

You can load relational tables stored in an XML file using the SQLXML Bulk Load executable.

1. Drop the two tables used in the previous recipe. Re-create them with a foreign key constraint. This action requires the following DDL (C:\SQL2012DIRecipes\CH03\LoadRelationalXML.Sql):

```sql
DROP TABLE CarSales_Staging.dbo.Invoice_XML_Multi;
DROP TABLE CarSales_Staging.dbo.Invoice_Lines_XML_Multi;
CREATE TABLE CarSales_Staging.dbo.Invoice_XML_Multi
(
 ID INT NOT NULL PRIMARY KEY,
 InvoiceNumber VARCHAR (50) NULL,
 DeliveryCharge SMALLMONEY NULL
) ;
GO

CREATE TABLE CarSales_Staging.dbo.Invoice_Lines_XML_Multi
(
 ID INT NOT NULL PRIMARY KEY,
 InvoiceID INT NOT NULL FOREIGN KEY REFERENCES Invoice_XML_Multi (ID),
 SalePrice MONEYNULL,
) ;
GO
```

2. Create an appropriate XML schema (the following is stored as C:\SQL2012DIRecipes\CH03\SQLXMLBulkLoadImportReferential.xsd):

```xml
<xsd:schema xmlns:xsd = "http://www.w3.org/2001/XMLSchema"
            xmlns:sql = "urn:schemas-microsoft-com:mapping-schema">

<xsd:annotation>
  <xsd:appinfo>
    <sql:relationship name = "InvoiceToLine"
          parent=      "Invoice_XML_Multi"
          parent-key = "ID"
          child=       "Invoice_Lines_XML_Multi"
          child-key=   "InvoiceID" />
  </xsd:appinfo>
</xsd:annotation>
```

```xsd
<xsd:element name="Invoice" sql:relation="Invoice_XML_Multi" >
  <xsd:complexType>
    <xsd:sequence>
            <xsd:element name="ID"                type="xsd:integer" sql:field="ID" />
            <xsd:element name="InvoiceNumber"    type="xsd:string"
                                                  sql:field="InvoiceNumber" />
            <xsd:element name="DeliveryCharge"   type="xsd:decimal"
                                                  sql:field="DeliveryCharge" />
      <xsd:element name="Invoice_Lines"
                        sql:relation="Invoice_Lines_XML_Multi"
                        sql:relationship="InvoiceToLine" >
            <xsd:complexType>
            <xsd:sequence>
                <xsd:element name="ID" type="xsd:integer" sql:field="ID" />
                <xsd:element name="InvoiceID" type="xsd:integer"
                                              sql:field="InvoiceID" />
                <xsd:element name="SalePrice" type="xsd:string"
                                              sql:field="SalePrice" />
            </xsd:sequence>
            </xsd:complexType>
      </xsd:element>
    </xsd:sequence>
  </xsd:complexType>
</xsd:element>
</xsd:schema>
```

3. Locate your data file (stored here as
    C:\SQL2012DIRecipes\CH03\SQLXMLSourceDataRelatedTables.xml):

    ```xml
    <?xml version="1.0" encoding="UTF-8" ?>
    <ROOT>
    <Invoice>
        <ID>3</ID>
        <InvoiceNumber>3A9271EA-FC76-4281-A1ED-714060ADBA30</InvoiceNumber>
        <DeliveryCharge>250</DeliveryCharge>
                    <Invoice_Lines>
                        <ID>1</ID>
                        <InvoiceID>3</InvoiceID>
                        <SalePrice>5000</SalePrice>
                    </Invoice_Lines>
                    <Invoice_Lines>
                        <ID>2</ID>
                        <InvoiceID>5</InvoiceID>
                        <SalePrice>12500</SalePrice>
                    </Invoice_Lines>
    </Invoice>
    </ROOT>
    ```

4. Run this example after you have altered the vbs script to refer to the new .XML and
    .XSD files by modifying the objBL.Execute statement, as follows:

    ```
    objBL.Execute "C:\SQL2012DIRecipes\CH03\SQLXMLBulkLoadImportReferential.xsd", ↵
    "C:\SQL2012DIRecipes\CH03\SQLXMLSourceDataRelatedTables.xml"
    ```

How It Works

This recipe's example builds on the approach from the previous recipe. However, it does presume the following prerequisites:

- Destination tables with primary key to foreign key relationships. This is why we have to re-create the destination tables.

- Source data where the "parent-child" data relationship is directly expressed in the XML structure. This is the case in the source data where the `<Invoice>` element contains one or more `<Invoice_Lines>` elements.

More generally, if the source XML is hierarchically structured to map to a relational source, then SQLXML Bulk Load can shred the data into SQL Server tables while maintaining foreign key relationships. Here, as was the case in the previous recipe, any potential difficulty lies in the definition and creation of the XSD file. Indeed, everything that is important is in the schema file. I'll explain the salient points.

First, note the `<xsd:annotation>` and `<xsd:appinfo>` elements at the start of the schema file. The foreign key mapping is specified inside these elements. It must be present—and correctly defined—for the load to work.

Then, inside these elements, you have the `sql:relationship name = "InvoiceToLine"` element. This names, or identifies if you will, each relationship between tables as part of the appinfo, as it will then be used as part of the `sql:element` definition for a "table" in the schema file. The relationship definitions are as follows:

`parent = "Invoice_XML_Multi"`: The "parent" table.

`parent-key = "ID"`: The primary key column of the "parent" table.

`child = "Invoice_Lines_XML_Multi"`: The "child" table.

`child-key = " InvoiceID "`: The foreign key column of the "child" table.

`sql:relationship = "InvoiceToLine"`: Inside the XML element, which contains the child elements, this attribute specifies the relationship to use.

As you can see from this information, the ID field is now considered as a primary key in the Invoice_XML_Multi table, and the InvoiceID is taken to be the foreign key in the Invoice_Lines_XML_Multi table. Executing the `.vbs` script loads the data into the two tables, while maintaining the ID as the foreign key constraint for the Invoice_Lines_XML_Multi.

If you have a mapping schema that defines a primary key/foreign key relationship between two tables (such as between Invoice and Invoice_Lines), the table with the primary key **must** be described first in the schema. The table with the foreign key column must appear later in the schema.

You also need to know that SQLXML Bulk Load generates records as their nodes enter into scope, and sends those records to SQL Server as their nodes exit scope. This means that the data for the record must be present within the scope of the node. Consequently, the data for the "child" table cannot follow the data for the "parent" table, as was the case for loading multiple (independent) tables.

In all the SQLXML Bulk Load examples used so far, we have used element-centric XML in the source data. As I do not want to give the impression that this is the only option available to you, I would like to make it clear that you can, of course, use attribute-centric XML as well—or indeed a mixture of the two.

So, to resume, where so far you have seen:

```
<xsd:element name = "InvoiceID" type = "xsd:integer" sql:field = "InvoiceID" />
```

It could just as easily have been:

```
<xsd:attribute name = "InvoiceID" type = "xsd:integer" sql:field = "InvoiceID" />
```

165

I have not given a complete example using just XML attributes, but the schema file given here should be enough to allow you to create a schema file where the source data is all attribute-based. In any case, as long as the mapping is accurate, your data will load.

Indeed, you are not limited to using just XML elements or attributes, but can mix the two in an XML Bulk load, as shown in the following example:

The XML schema is the following (stored as C:\SQL2012DIRecipes\CH03\SQLXMLBulkLoadImportElementAndAttribute.xsd). The destination table is one we have used before—Client_XMLBulkLoad:

```
<xsd:schema xmlns:xsd="http://www.w3.org/2001/XMLSchema"
            xmlns:sql="urn:schemas-microsoft-com:mapping-schema">
<xsd:element name="Invoice" sql:relation="Client_XMLBulkLoad" >
    <xsd:complexType>
        <xsd:sequence>
            <xsd:element name="ClientName" type="xsd:integer" sql:field="ClientName"/>
            <xsd:element name="County" type="xsd:integer " sql:field="County"/>
        </xsd:sequence>
            <xsd:attribute name="ID" type="xsd:integer" />
    </xsd:complexType>
</xsd:element>
</xsd:schema>
```

The following is the data (stored as C:\SQL2012DIRecipes\CH03\SQLXMLSourceDataElementAndAttribute.xml):

```
<?xml version="1.0" encoding="UTF-8" ?>
<Invoice ID="3">
    <ClientName>John Smith</ClientName>
    <County>Staffs</County>
</Invoice>
```

To run this example, you need to alter the .vbs script to refer to the new .xml and .xsd files (objBL.Execute "C:\SQL2012DIRecipes\CH03\SQLXMLBulkLoadImportElementAndAttribute.xsd", "C:\SQL2012DIRecipes\CH03\SQLXMLSourceDataElementAndAttribute.xml"). Running the script will load the data into the destination tables while maintaining relational integrity.

■ **Note**   Loading tables while maintaining referential integrity can be considerably slower than a multiple table load where there is no referential integrity.

3-11. Overcoming Bulk Loading Challenges for XML Files
Problem

You want to use all the power of SQLXML Bulk Load to ensure a fast and trouble-free bulk XML data load.

Solution

Apply the relevant SQLXML Bulk Load options to accelerate the load and/or resolve potential load issues.

The available options are shown in Table 3-2.

Table 3-2. *SQLXML Bulk Load Options*

Parameter	Explanation	Example
BulkLoad	No data will be loaded—however, the table structure will be generated (assuming that SchemaGen is specified).	=False
CheckConstraints	Ensures that the data being inserted into the tables applies all constraints that have been specified on the tables (primary and foreign key constraints, for example). The process fails if this parameter is set to True, and constraints are violated.	=False
ForceTableLock	This property applies a table lock, which reduces load time. However, if a table lock cannot be obtained, the process will fail.	=True
IgnoreDuplicateKeys	Issues a COMMIT for every row inserted (requiring the Transaction property to be set to False). Be warned, this is very slow!	=False
KeepIdentity	Specifies that IDENTITY values from the source XML be used. SQL Server will not generate IDENTITY values during the load process.	=True
KeepNulls	Any NULLS in the source data will be inserted into the destination table(s).	=True
SchemaGen	Setting this property to True will create the destination table(s). The mapping defined in the XML schema file will serve as the basis for the table structure. The table must not already exist, or the whole process will fail.	=True
SGDropTables	Setting this property to True will drop any existing destination table(s)—provided that there are no foreign key constraints, for instance.	=False
TempFilePath	Specifies the path to the temp file that is used if the process is in a transaction. This allows you to specify a different disk array for increased speed.	="\\TheServer\TheShare"
Transaction	Guarantees that the operation is a transaction—that is, loads or fails entirely.	=True
XMLFragment	This property specifies that the XML data file is an XML fragment (has no single top-level node). This must be set for XML fragments, or the whole process will fail.	=True

How It Works

SQLXML Bulk Loader can go far beyond the examples given in the previous recipes. It seems a shame not to take advantage of its immense power, including the ability to

- Mix XML attributes and elements in the source data.
- Use the available XML data types.
- Create and drop the destination table automatically (as well as enable or disable constraints and transactions).

- Use overflow columns to trap unmapped data.

- Apply various schema tweaks when mapping data.

These options can be added to the .vbs file, which invokes SQLXML Bulk Loader. Used appropriately, they can considerably enhance the effectiveness of this utility.

It is important to remember that SQLXML Bulk Loader is a bulk load mechanism—and is optimized for speed, and that speed implies simplicity—hence the parameters that are very similar to those that you may already know from BCP or BULK INSERT (or, if you do not yet know them, they are explained in Chapter 2).

All parameters are used in the way that you saw in the .vbs files we have seen so far in this chapter; that is:

```
Object.Parameter = attribute
```

So to force a table lock, the command would be objBL.ForceTableLock = True.

All the examples used so far have presumed that you use Windows integrated security. Given that this may not always be the case, you need to know that the alternatives are (in the ConnectionString parameter):

```
Uid = UserName; Pwd = ThePasswordTouse
```

or

```
integrated security = SSPI
```

You can use SQLXML to create any required destination tables, and then either load the data or not. So, for example, in the VBScript file we have been using so far, add the following lines to create the tables, but not load the data:

```
objBL.SchemaGen = True
objBL.BulkLoad = False
```

Using SQLXML Bulk Loader to create tables is a bit of a blunt instrument, but it can save a lot of time when starting out on an XML Bulk Load process. You can always fine-tune the tables later. In fact, this is what many pundits suggest that you do.

Although it will perform more slowly, SQLXML can use a transaction when loading to ensure rollback in case it fails. This will require you to add the following lines to a VBScript file:

```
objBL.Transaction = True
objBL.TempFilePath = \\Server\Share
```

Bulk loading data within a transaction is much slower—and for large imports, you have to ensure that there is enough disk space on the drive where you specify the temporary file. This requires the TempFilePath parameter. As far as the TempFilePath parameter is concerned, remember that the temporary file path must be a shared location that is accessible to the service account of the target instance of SQL Server, and also to the account that is running the bulk load application. This means that, unless you are bulk loading on a local server, the temporary file path must be a UNC path (such as \\servername\sharename). If speed is of the essence, then loading a file into an empty table or partition (which can be truncated if an error is thrown) can be a faster solution.

Another eventuality to consider is what will happen if there is more data than you expected in the source XML, and this data is not mapped? Unless SQLXML Bulk Loader is told what to do with such "overflow" data, then it quietly and simply ignores it. As this can be dangerous in practice, here is the simple technique to catch overflow data, which you can then handle separately—or use as an indicator that some more work needs to be done on the schema file.

1. For each table mapping in the schema file, specify which column will handle any (and all) overflow. The example from the preceding recipe would read:

```
<xsd:element name = "Invoice" sql:relation = "Invoice"
sql:overflow-field = "DataOverflowColumn">
```

2. Add a column to the destination table using the name you specified in the schema file. Again, to use the example from the preceding recipe:

```
ALTER TABLE Invoice ADD DataOverflowColumn NVARCHAR(MAX)
```

Of course, you can set the type and length of the overflow column to whatever you feel appropriate. Now when you run the SQLXML import, any data not mapped in the XML schema file will be inserted into the overflow column, for each row. If the schema does not specify overflow columns by using the sql:overflow-field annotation, XML Bulk Load ignores any data that is in the XML document but that is not in the mapping schema.

As with most bulk load tools, SQLXML allows you to keep identity column information from the source file. This is done using the following extra parameter in the VBScript file:

```
objBL.KeepIdentity = True
```

The data types that you can use are not limited the (nearly) ubiquitous int and string types. The XML schema definition allows the following—given with their SQL Server counterparts in Table 3-3.

Table 3-3. *SQLXML Bulk Load Data Types*

SQL Server Data Type	XSD Data Type
bigint	long
binary	base64Binary
bit	boolean
char	string
datetime	dateTime
decimal	decimal
float	double
image	base64Binary
int	int
money	decimal
nchar	string
ntext	string
nvarchar	string
numeric	decimal
real	float
smalldatetime	dateTime
smallint	short
smallmoney	decimal

(*continued*)

Table 3-3. (*continued*)

SQL Server Data Type	XSD Data Type
sql_variant	string
sysname	string
text	string
timestamp	dateTime
tinyint	unsignedByte
varbinary	base64Binary
varchar	string
uniqueidentifier	string

However, SQLXML ignores the type specified in the schema file (except in a couple of cases given shortly). So you may be asking, "What is the purpose of this, then?" I can see two uses:

- To force the developer to keep track of the external data types.

- To generate tables (using the SchemaGen option) that map as closely as possible to the source data.

Therefore, when you are crafting the schema file, you can even specify the exact SQL Server data type and length to be used. This could be, for instance:

```
xsd:element name="Name" type="xsd:string" sql:field="FieldName" sql:datatype="NVARCHAR(15)"/>
```

However, this parameter is ignored during an import operation, and is only used to create the table.

If the type is dateTime or time, you must specify the sql:datatype because SQLXML Bulk Load converts the data before sending the data to SQL Server. Alternatively, map to a VARCHAR field, and CAST or CONVERT to a date/time type after import (which also allows you to ensure that SQL Server date ranges are respected).

Remember that when you are bulk loading into a column of uniqueidentifier type in SQL Server and the XSD value is a GUID that includes braces ({ and }), you must specify sql:datatype="uniqueidentifier" so that SQLXML Bulk Loader will remove the braces before the value is inserted into the destination column. If you do not specify the data type, then the value is sent with the braces and the load will fail. You can set defaults using the following syntax: < xsd:element name="Comments" default="N/A" />. If the mapping schema specifies the default value for an attribute and the XML source data does not contain that attribute, XML Bulk Load will use the default value.

You can skip an element (other than by simply omitting the element from the schema file) by adding sql:mapped="false" to the element description. This is useful for "commenting out" an element temporarily.

Up until now you have been running SQLXML Bulk Load by executing a VBScript file. You can also do this from T-SQL as part of a wider automation process. To load the initial XML file used in Recipe 3-9, the T-SQL will be (C:\SQL2012DIRecipes\CH03\LoadXMLFromTSQLWithvbs.Sql):

```
DECLARE   @handle INT;
DECLARE   @VBSobject INT;

EXECUTE   @handle = sp_OACreate 'SQLXMLBulkLoad.SQLXMLBulkLoad.4.0', @VBSobject OUT;
EXECUTE   @handle = sp_OASetProperty @VBSobject, 'ConnectionString', ↵
                    'provider=SQLOLEDB;data
```

```
source=ADAM02;database=CarSales_Staging;Uid=Adam;Pwd=Me4BOss;
EXECUTE   @handle = sp_OASetProperty @VBSobject, 'ErrorLogFile', ↵
                     'C:\SQL2012DIRecipes\CH03\SQLXMLBulkLoadImporterror.log';
EXECUTE   @handle = sp_OAMethod @VBSobject, 'Execute', NULL, ↵
                      'C:\SQL2012DIRecipes\CH03\SQLXMLBulkLoadImport_Simple.xsd', ↵
                      'C:\SQL2012DIRecipes\CH03\Clients_Simple.xml';
EXECUTE   @handle = sp_OADestroy @VBSobject;
```

This requires OA_Automation to be enabled, either by using Facets/Surface Area Configuration tool (or just Surface Area Configuration in SQL Server 2005), or by running:

```
EXECUTE master.dbo.sp_configure 'Ole Automation Procedures', 1;
GO
reconfigure;
GO
```

Of course, You may use T-SQL variables instead of hard-coding the files, paths, server, database, and connection string elements when invoking SQLXML Bulk Load.

3-12. Running SQLXML Bulk Loader As Part of a Regular ETL Process

Problem

You want to invoke SQLXML Bulk Loader as part of a regular ETL process.

Solution

Call a .vbs file from SSIS to invoke the SQLXML Bulk Loader.

1. Create a .vbs file, altered to accept input parameters (and named **C:\SQL2012DIRecipes\CH03\SQLXMLBulkloadSSIS.vbs**) as follows:

    ```
    Set InputVars = Wscript.Arguments
    XMLSource = InputVars.Item(0)

    Set objBL = CreateObject("SQLXMLBulkLoad.SQLXMLBulkload.4.0")
    objBL.ConnectionString = "provider=SQLOLEDB;data ↵
    source=ADAM02;database=CarSales_Staging;Uid=Adam;Pwd=Me4BOss"
    objBL.ErrorLogFile="C:\SQL2012DIRecipes\CH03\SQLXMLBulkLoadImporterror.log"
    objBL.Execute "C:\SQL2012DIRecipes\CH03\SQLXMLBulkLoadImportElementAndAttribute.xsd", ↵
    XMLSource
    Set objBL = Nothing
    ```

2. Create a new SSIS package and add the following variable:

Variable	Scope	Type	Value
SourceFile	Package	String	C:\SQL2012DIRecipes\CH03\ ↵ SQLXMLSourceDataElementAndAttribute.Xml

3.   Add an Execute Process task. Double-click to edit.

4.   Click Process on the left.

5.   Set the Executable as C:\Windows\System32\WScript.exe.

6.   Set the Arguments as C:\SQL2012DIRecipes\CH03\SQLXMLBulkloadSSIS.vbs.

7.   Set the WindowStyle as Hidden.

8.   Click Expressions on the left. Browse the Property Expressions Editor. Select Arguments. Browse to the Expression Builder.

9.   Expand Variables and drag the [User::SourceFile] variable into the Expression field. The Expression Builder should look like Figure 3-10.

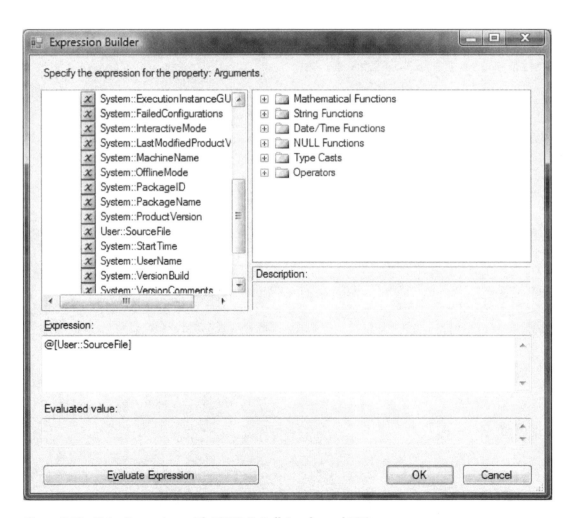

Figure 3-10. *Using Expressions with SQLXML Bulk Loader and SSIS*

10. Confirm the expression selection with OK, twice.

11. Click OK to confirm your modifications.

12. Run the package will invoke SQLXML Bulk Load and import the XML file.

How It Works

So far, we have looked at SQLXML Bulk Loader independently of SSIS, as if the two were destined to live separate existences. This, fortunately, need not be the case, and the two can work together as part of an ETL process. My preference—for the sake of simplicity—is to run SQLXML Bulk Loader using an Execute Process task. This may seem overtly simplistic, but with a little tweaking, it can be made to work extremely smoothly. Indeed, what this recipe does is to pass the name of the file to import to the .vbs (VBscript) file as the parameter XMLSource—which then allows you to use this approach as part of a multiple-file load using a Foreach container.

Adding the new top line to the .vbs script allows you to pass variables into the script. There can be as many of these as you wish, but you must capture them all in the script—and pass them in the correct order. This means that you can pass in multiple parameters (a schema file for instance). Merely add another line to the top of the .vbs file, like this:

```
SchemaFile = InputVars.Item(1)
```

You then use this variable as part of the "Execute" command instead of the hard-coded XSD file and path.

If you prefer not to use a variable, then you can place the file name in the arguments field. This will be passed to the .vbs VBscript file. If you do this, then creating the variable (and using it in an expression) are superfluous.

Hints, Tips, and Traps

- If you place this task in a Foreach Loop container (with the collection set to Foreach File Enumerator and the variable mapping set to output to the User::SourceFile SSIS variable), you can load multiple files from a directory.

- If you browse for the .vbs file, remember to set the file type to All Files.

3-13. Validating an XML Document Against a Schema File As Part of a Scripted Solution

Problem

You want to validate an XML data file against an XSD file.

Solution

Create a .vbs file and use the Microsoft MSXML2 XML Parser. This is how it is done:

1. Create a .vbs file named **C:\SQL2012DIRecipes\CH03\Validate.vbs**, like this:

```
Dim SchemaCache
Set SchemaCache = CreateObject("MSXML2.XMLSchemaCache.6.0")
```

```
SchemaCache.Add "", "C:\SQL2012DIRecipes\CH03\FlattenedOutput.Xsd"

Dim XMLDoc
Set XMLDoc = CreateObject("MSXML2.DOMDocument.6.0")

Set XMLDoc.schemas = SchemaCache

XMLDoc.async = False
XMLDoc.Load "C:\SQL2012DIRecipes\CH03\FlattenedOutput.xml"

If XMLDoc.parseError.errorCode <> 0 Then
wscript.quit 1
end if
```

2. Run the file by double-clicking it in Windows Explorer.

How It Works

If you are faced with a truly large XML file source, then nothing is worse than having a load fail after many minutes of processing. So it can be a lot faster to be forewarned of potential errors by verifying that the XML data source file is properly constructed first. This is not an instantaneous process for large files—but it can be a much faster way of discovering errors than having a load fail. One way of verifying an XML document against the schema file is to use VBScript. This can then be run from a Command window, from T-SQL, or from SSIS. This recipe shows how to create a generic validation routine. It simply determines if a file can be validated—it does not attempt to log the errors.

First, the schema file is added to a schema cache. This is then set as the schema for an XML document, which is finally loaded. If there are no errors, the script returns 0, if there are errors it returns 1.

You can run this script from an Execute Process task in SSIS just like you run an SQLXML Bulk Load task. Just remember to check that the SuccessValue field is set to 0. In fact, you can pass in the XML and XSD files as parameters in exactly the same way as described previously. Indeed, as the task will succeed or fail like any other SSIS task, you can then branch the processing according to the result, similar to the way described in Recipe 3-14. You might need to adjust the FailParentOnFailure and FailPackageOnFailure properties, depending on how your package is constructed.

Hints, Tips, and Traps

- If you are running the script file from a Command window or by double-clicking, you may want to add

  ```
  MsgBox("Errors encountered")
  ```

  or something similar before the wscript.quit 1 line. Of course, you should not use a message box if the script is to run as part of an automated process.

- If you want the bulk load process to run if the validation is successful, you can add an Else to the XMLDoc.parseError.errorCode, and then add the code (used earlier in this chapter) that invokes SQLXMLBulkLoad, and loads the data.

3-14. Validating an XML Document Against a Schema File in SSIS

Problem

You want to validate a source XML file against an XSD schema as part of an SSIS process.

Solution

Use an SSIS script task to perform XML validation using the .NET XML.Schema class.

1. Create a new SSIS package and add the following variables:

Variable	Scope	Type	Value
XSDFile	Package	String	C:\SQL2012DIRecipes\CH03\Clients_Simple.xsd
XMLFile	Package	String	C:\SQL2012DIRecipes\CH03\Clients_Simple.xml
LogFile	Package	String	C:\SQL2012DIRecipes\CH03\ValidationLog.txt
IsValidateFailure	Package	Boolean	False

2. Add a Script task. Double-click to edit. Set the Script Language to Microsoft Visual Basic 2010. Set the variables LogFile, XMLFile, and XSDFile as read-only variables. Set IsValidateFailure as a read-write variable.

3. Click Edit Script.

4. Add the following directives to the Import region:

```
Imports System.IO
Imports System.Xml
Imports System.Xml.Schema
Imports System.Xml.XPath
```

5. Replace the Main method with the following (C:\SQL2012DIRecipes\CH03\ValidateXML.vbs):

```
Dim SW As StringWriter = New StringWriter
Dim IsValidateFailure As Boolean = False

   Public Sub Main()

     Dim XSDFile As String = Dts.Variables("XSDFile").Value.ToString
     Dim XMLFile As String = Dts.Variables("XMLFile").Value.ToString
     Dim LogFile As String = Dts.Variables("LogFile").Value.ToString
     Dim XMLDoc As New XmlDocument

     XMLDoc.Load(XMLFile)
     XMLDoc.Schemas.Add("", XSDFile)

     Dim EvtHdl As ValidationEventHandler = ↵
         New ValidationEventHandler(AddressOf ValidationEventHandler)
```

```
            XMLDoc.Validate(EvtHdl)

            If IsValidateFailure Then

                If File.Exists(LogFile) Then
                    File.Delete(LogFile)
                End If

                Dim FlOut As New System.IO.StreamWriter(LogFile)
                FlOut.Write(SW.ToString)

            End If

            Dts.Variables("IsValidateFailure").Value = IsValidateFailure
            Dts.TaskResult = ScriptResults.Success

        End Sub

        Private Sub ValidationEventHandler(ByVal sender As Object, ↵
                                        ByVal e As ValidationEventArgs)

            SW.WriteLine(e.Message.ToString)
            IsValidateFailure = True

        End Sub
```

6. Close the Script window and confirm your changes with OK.

7. Add a Data Flow task (if you are loading the XML file using SSIS) or an Execute Process task (if you are loading the XML file using SQLXML Bulk Load) to the Data Flow pane, and connect the Script task to it.

8. Double-click the constraint (the connector) and set it to

    Evaluation Operation: Expression And Constraint
    Value: Success
    Expression: @IsValidateFailure == False

9. Configure the XML load as described earlier in this chapter in Recipe 3-4.

10. Add a Send Mail task to the Data Flow pane, and connect the Script task to it.

11. Double-click the constraint (the connector) and set it to

    Evaluation Operation: Expression And Constraint
    Expression: @IsValidateFailure == True

12. Configure the Send Mail task to alert you to the good news that the XML cannot be validated. The package should look like Figure 3-11.

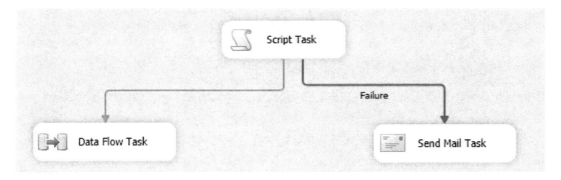

Figure 3-11. *XML validation in SSIS*

How It Works

This fairly simple SSIS Script task verifies an XML document against a schema file, and (in this example) directs the process flow according to the result of the validation. That is, the data will load if validation is successful, and will stop (and send an e-mail) if it is not. Moreover, a log file of all errors encountered will be created should validation fail. It works in this way:

- First, references are set to the XML and System.IO libraries.

- Then the files to be processed (XML and XSD) are attributed to variables in the Script task.

- The source file is read and validated. Any errors are detected by the ValidationEventHandler, and each error written to a StringWriter. The error flag is set.

- Finally, the error flag is returned to SSIS, and the list of errors written to a file (which is deleted first—if it already exists).

Hints, Tips, and Traps

- Clearly, if the XML file and the schema file are massively out of sync, then the log file will be not only very large, but also extremely repetitive.

- Of course, you do not need to use a Send Mail task—indeed you can do nothing whatsoever to indicate failure to validate the XML source data.

Summary

As this chapter has tried to demonstrate, there are a wide variety of methods available to take XML source files and load them into SQL Server. In some cases, the choice will depend on what your objectives are—if you want to load the file "as is" without shredding the data into its component parts, then clearly OPENROWSET (BULK) could be the best solution. If, however, the source file is being used as a medium for data transfer, then you have a wider set of options available. If you are basing your ETL process around T-SQL, you could find that using SQL Server's XQuery support is the way to go. If, on the other hand, you are more "SSIS-centric," then the SSIS XML task can be an excellent solution in many cases. For really large source files—or where speed is of the essence—then SQLXML Bulk Loader is possibly the only viable option.

All these techniques have their drawbacks as well as their positive points, however. So here, then, in Table 3-4 is a concise overview of these various methods, along with their advantages and disadvantages.

Table 3-4. *Advantages and Disadvantages of Approaches Used in This Chapter*

Technique	Advantages	Disadvantages
Store XML files directly into SQL Server tables	Fast and easy. XML can be queried using XQuery in SQL Server.	Only LOB storage—not shredded.
OPENXML	Fast to use and easy to set up. Handles complex XML shredding.	Memory-intensive. 2GB file size limit.
SQL Server XQuery	Efficient and can handle even the most complex XML. No memory limitations when using `OPENROWSET` `(BULK)`.	More XQuery than T-SQL.
SSIS XML Task	Easy for less complex files.	Can get complex. Requires normalization.
SQLXML Bulk Load	Extremely fast. Multiple parallel table loads. Built-in XML verification.	Complex XSD definition.

CHAPTER 4

■ ■ ■

SQL Databases

An awful lot of the data that you will be called upon to load into SQL Server is probably already stored in a relational database. While you can certainly export from most of the currently available commercial SQL-based databases into a text or XML file, and from there into SQL Server, there are also standard ways of connecting directly to most RDBMSs (relational database management systems) and then extracting data from them into the Microsoft RDBMS. In this chapter, therefore, we will be looking at some of the available ways of ingesting and linking to data from the following:

- Oracle
- DB2
- MySQL
- Sybase
- Teradata
- PostgreSQL

As you will see, the techniques used to ingest data are very similar for all the databases that we will cover. They include (depending on the source database):

- SSIS
- Ad hoc connections
- Linked servers

The one thing that they all have in common is that you need to get a provider for the source database installed and working on the SQL Server destination. In most cases, you can use either an OLEDB or an ODBC provider (or for SSIS in some cases, a .NET provider). From then on, the differences are essentially minor. So we will look at each database, and show you how to connect to the source database and to load data from there into SQL Server.

Once we have established these basic approaches, there are a few other interesting things to look at, notably, how to use the SQL Server Migration Assistant (SSMA) for Oracle, MySQL, and Sybase.

As you are probably aware, the real world of interdatabase data connectivity has its fair share of challenges, and you will have to deal with some or all of the following:

- Installing and configuring OLEDB and ODBC providers
- Network and firewall issues
- Database security
- Data type mapping

In an ideal universe, these elements are clear and well-documented. In the reality that most of us inhabit, things are somewhat murkier, and you could end up requiring knowledge of multiple IT systems, or at least a precise knowledge of certain extremely focused aspects of several systems. This is always a challenge, and can require much delving into various sets of documentation.

Preamble: Installing and Configuring OLEDB and ODBC Providers

If you are going to import data directly from another relational database, the essential thing is to have a working and proven provider in place. This is easy to say, but by far can be the hardest part of the data load for several reasons. Consider the following questions that you will have to answer:

- Which type of provider do you install, and from which vendor?

- What level of database compatibility does it provide?

- Is it 64- and 32-bit?

- What level of support is available?

Now, which provider you use, which type (OLEDB, ODBC, or .NET) and which supplier you prefer, is entirely up to you. SQL Server comes with the following OLEDB providers to facilitate connection to certain other relational databases:

- The Microsoft OLEDB provider for Oracle (MSDAORA.1), which is part of an SQL Server installation.

- The Microsoft OLEDB provider for DB2 (provided with the Feature Pack, but requires the Enterprise edition of SQL Server).

- The Attunity OLEDB provider for Oracle (requires the Enterprise edition of SQL Server).

- The Attunity OLEDB provider for Teradata (requires the Enterprise edition of SQL Server).

Then, of course, you have the OLEDB and .NET providers from the database vendors themselves. At the time of writing—and for the data sources referred to in this chapter—these are some of the available providers:

- The Oracle Provider for OLE DB 11.2.0.3.0 from Oracle Corporation.

- The Oracle Data Provider for .NET 4 11.2.0.3.0 from Oracle Corporation.

- IBM DB2 for I5/OS IBMDA400 OLEDB Provider

- IBM DB2 for I5/OS IBMDARLA OLEDB Provider

- IBM DB2 for I5/OS IBMDASQL OLEDB Provider

- The IBM OLEDB Provider (IBMDADB2)

- The IBM OLE DB .NET 7 Data Provider

- The Sybase ASE OLEDB Provider

- The Sybase ASE ODBC Provider

- The Sybase ASE .NET Provider

- The MySQL ODBC Provider

- The PostgreSQL Native OLEDB Provider (PGNP)

Given the constant evolution in this area, I will not specify which version you should be using. Clearly, the latest version is preferable in virtually all cases. Also, it is up to you to ensure that you have complied with any licensing requirements if you are using these drivers in a production environment.

Of course, there are many other commercially-available providers, and I can only advise you to search the Web for others. There are many that are available from many different sources. Equally varied are the claims to purported superiority for each provider. I will certainly not be emitting any judgments here. I will only here be explaining those available from either Microsoft or the suppliers themselves of the RDBMSs that we are looking at in this chapter. This is in no way a criticism or a judgment, merely a voluntary limitation on the scope of this chapter. Once downloaded and installed, these providers should be visible both in the SSIS connection manager list of OLEDB sources, and also in SQL Server Management Studio when you expand Server Objects ➤ Linked Servers ➤ Providers.

Network and Firewall issues

It is imperative to ensure that you make friends with the network architects in your organization, as you will need their help. Either that, or obtain full documentation about the network architecture. On reading that last sentence, I imagine that most developers and DBAs will emit a hollow laugh, and come to the conclusion that charm will be needed to ensure that their SQL Server can at least see the other database hosts, as this is the starting point for establishing server-to-server database connectivity.

Database Security

Once you have made friends with the infrastructure people, the next charm offensive will doubtless concern the source system DBAs. You will need logon and SELECT permissions (at a bare minimum) for the source databases—and more wide-ranging permissions will be necessary if you are to examine the source database metadata. Indeed, this is a prerequisite for using SSMA, as you will see.

Data Type Mapping

Fortunately, the SQL Server development team has, over the years, defined a robust set of data type correlations for the major competitor databases. Many of these are given in Appendix A. SSMA also has predefined (and configurable) data type mapping schemata that you can not only use when loading data with this tool, but also as a reference for suggested mappings. Fortunately, in my experience, these suggestions are very robust and make difficulties in this area the exception rather than the rule. When a problem does occur, you will probably have little choice but to refer to the documentation of the source system.

Before starting on the recipes in this chapter, there is one thing that I have to make clear immediately. I realize that talking about half a dozen major databases and ways of connecting them to SQL Server has the potential to be a vast subject. Consequently, I am going to be extremely selective about which products and which connection methods I discuss. As it is impossible to discuss all aspects of all the ways of loading data from all the relational databases in the known universe, I have chosen to be deliberately succinct in this chapter, and concentrate on the major players in the RDBMS market whose products I have had the pleasure of grappling with over the years. Inevitably, much will not be covered, but I am afraid that a line has to be drawn somewhere.

Moreover, I will always use the sample databases supplied with each of the RDBMSs that we are looking at. If there is no standard sample database for a data source, I will use INFORMATION_SCHEMA data, or any tables found as standard in the source database.

> ■ **Note** The difficulty with importing data from other SQL RDBMSs is that in some situations you need to have a certain level of basic knowledge about the database from which you are sourcing data. In other cases, SQL knowledge is sufficient. In this chapter, therefore, I am presuming basic familiarity with the external database—or at least a level of initial understanding that can be acquired fairly rapidly.

I will presume that you have downloaded the example files for this chapter from the book's companion web site, and installed them in the `C:\SQL2012DIRecipes\CH02\` directory. Similarly, if you are following the examples, you will need to have created the `CarSales` and `CarSales_Staging` databases as described in Appendix B.

4-1. Configuring Your Server to Connect to Oracle

Problem

You want to be certain that the SQL Server into which you will be importing Oracle data is correctly configured and able to connect to an Oracle database.

Solution

Install either the 32-bit Oracle client on a 32-bit SQL Server, or a 64-bit Oracle client on a 64-bit SQL Server. This is how to do it:

1. Download the Oracle 11G full client. Install it by following Oracle guidelines. Make sure that you install the Oracle OLEDB, .NET, and ODBC providers.

2. Configure Oracle access by editing the `TNSNames.ora` file. I explain this in the "How it Works" section.

3. Reboot the SQL Server on which the Oracle drivers are installed.

How It Works

As it is the database with the largest market share on the planet, we will begin by looking at how to connect to Oracle databases. Despite the fact that the instructions given in this recipe presume only a very basic knowledge of Oracle, you might need input from an Oracle DBA when it comes to establishing connectivity to an Oracle server. This is simply due to the wide range of potential scenarios that you could face when connecting to Oracle databases. The subject is so vast, it precludes a detailed description here, so I am only showing how to use TNS (Transparent Network Substrate) connectivity.

Note that in the `TNSNames.ora` file, the Address is the top element for a connection. You will need it when connecting later. So, using a purely hypothetical example, the Address name for the following `TNSNAMES` entry is `MyOracle`:

```
MyOracle =
  (DESCRIPTION =
    (ADDRESS_LIST =
      (ADDRESS = (PROTOCOL = TCP)(HOST = aa.calidra.co.uk)(PORT = 1521))
    )
```

```
 (CONNECT_DATA =
   (SERVER = DEDICATED)
   (SERVICE_NAME = MyOracleReally)
 )
)
```

However, I can only advise you to consider installing both the 32-bit client and the 64-bit client on a 64-bit server, as this will allow you not only to connect to Oracle (in a 64-bit environment) but also to develop, tweak, finalize, and test in SSDT (SQL Server Data Tools)/BIDS (Business Intelligence Development Studio)—both of which, remember, run as a 32-bit application. The steps to do this are as follows:

1. Remove any existing Oracle clients. Reboot.

2. Download the Oracle 11G full client. Install the 32-bit client by following Oracle guidelines. Make sure that you install the Oracle OLEDB, .NET, and ODBC providers. Carefully define which Oracle home and directory path it is using. It could be something like C:\Oracle\product\11.2.0\Client32.

3. Select the Oracle Windows Interfaces 11.x.x component for OLEDB in Available Product Components. You can add the .NET provider too, if you wish.

4. Reboot the server.

5. Download the Oracle 11G full client. Install the 64-bit client by following Oracle guidelines. Make sure that you install the Oracle OLEDB, .NET, and ODBC providers. Define which Oracle home it is using. The directory path could be something like C:\Oracle\product\11.2.0\Client64.

6. Select the Oracle Windows Interfaces 11.x.x component for OLEDB in Available Product Components. You can add the .NET provider too, if you wish.

7. Reboot the server.

8. Configure Oracle access by editing TNSNames.ora for both the 32-bit and 64-bit environments. This means the TNSNames.ora file in both the C:\Oracle\product\11.2.0\Client32\Network\Admin and C:\Oracle\product\11.2.0\Client64\Network\Admin directories.

Hints, Tips, and Traps

- When removing any old Oracle clients, you can only delete the old directory once the server has been rebooted.

- The simplest way to test client connectivity is to run SQL+ (Start ➤ All programs ➤ Your Oracle Home ➤ Application Development ➤ SQL Plus) and enter the Oracle username and password, possibly like this: TheUserName@TheDatabase/PasswordHere.

4-2. Importing Data from Oracle As a Regular Process
Problem

You want to import Oracle data on a regular basis and can connect to the Oracle source database over your network.

Solution

Implement an SSIS package to load the data. Follow these steps to do it:

1. Open or create an SSIS package. Add a Data Flow task to the Control Flow pane.

2. Double-click the Data Flow task to edit it. Add an OLEDB source and an OLEDB destination task.

3. Create an OLEDB Connection Manager named **CarSales_Staging_OLEDB** which establishes a connection to the CarSales_Staging database.

4. Right-click the Connection Managers tab at the bottom of the screen and select New OLEDB Connection. Click New. In the list of providers, select the Oracle Provider for OLEDB. You should see something like Figure 4-1.

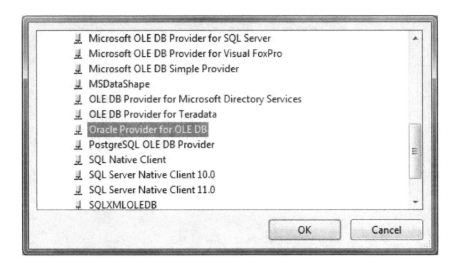

Figure 4-1. *Selecting the Oracle Provider for OLEDB*

5. Click OK to confirm the provider.

6. Enter the Address name from the TNSNames.ora file as the Server or File Name in the Connection Manager dialog box.

7. Enter the Oracle logon information in the Connection Manager dialog box (see Figure 4-2).

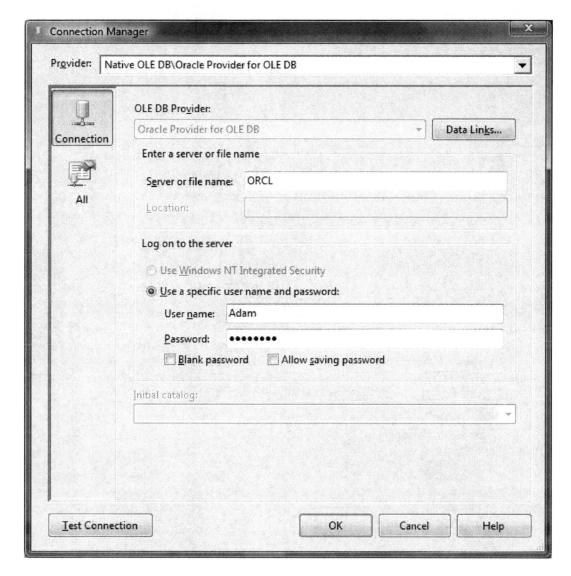

Figure 4-2. The SSIS connection manager for Oracle

8. Test the connection. If the message indicating a successful connection is confirmed, click OK to finish creating the connection manager. Rename it **ORCLAdam**—or a name that suits your requirements.

9. Double-click the OLEDB source task. Select the connection manager you just defined (see Figure 4-3).

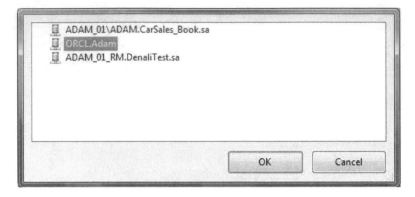

Figure 4-3. *Selecting an Oracle connection manager*

10. Select the table or view in the source database that you wish to use. Alternatively, set the data access mode to SQL command and write the SQL to select the data. The source dialog box should look like Figure 4-4.

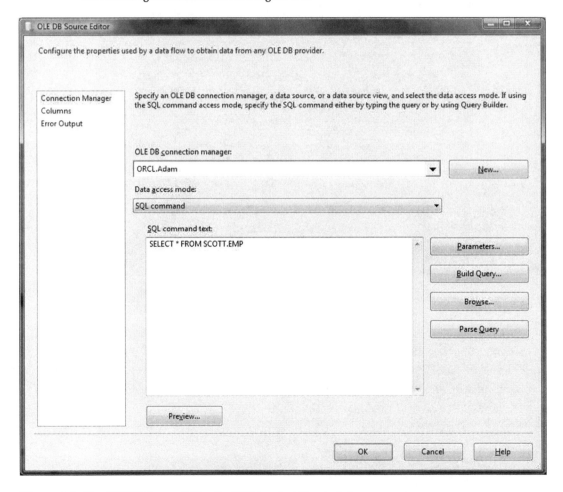

Figure 4-4. *The OLEDB Source Editor for SSIS to select Oracle data*

11. Confirm your configuration with OK.

12. Link the OLEDB source task to the destination task. Configure it to use the CarSales_
    Staging_OLEDB connection manager.

13. Click "New" to create a new table. Click "OK" to confirm.

14. Map the columns in the destination task. Confirm that the destination task is correct.
    The full details of this are described in Recipe 1-7, among many others.

You can now run the SSIS package and import the source data.

How It Works

Fortunately, importing external data using SSIS is extremely simple. I will presume here that you know basic SSIS because there are many examples of SSIS data import in this book, so I have not explained every detail. The point here is to concentrate on the OLEDB link to the Oracle database. Once this is working, the rest should be easy. However, as described in the Recipe 4-1, Oracle has a clear set of prerequisites:

- You need the Oracle client to be installed on the SQL Server.

- You must ensure a working network connection to the Oracle server.

- You need an Oracle user logon and password with rights to the data you wish to retrieve.

Hints, Tips, and Traps

- In a large, "real-world" Oracle data load situation, you are probably better advised to create the connection manager at package level (in the Connection Managers folder of the Solution Explorer) if you are using SQL Server 2012. This is because you are likely to be using it many times across multiple packages to source many (many) tables.

- You could get a Column Code Page warning at step 11. To avoid it, remember that you can use the Advanced Editor to set the AlwaysUseTheDefaultCodePage property of the Component Properties tab to True. The DefaultCodePage can be set to 1252, which is fine for most Western languages. If Oracle is using another character set, you will need to determine which one and select an equivalent in SSIS.

- As BIDS/SSDT is (still) a 32-bit tool, you will only see the Oracle OLEDB provider on a 64-bit computer if both 32-bit and 64-bit Oracle providers have been installed, as described in Recipe 4-1.

- Some Oracle source tables do not use a precision with the NUMBER data type. This can cause an issue with SSIS, and you may need to add the precision. The simplest way to carry this out is to use the Oracle CAST or CONVERT functions in the SQL used to extract the source data in step 9.

- When configured for an Oracle provider, the Connection Manager dialog box will not list all available catalogs.

- In a production environment, presumably, you store the password as part of a package configuration.

- Data type mapping is discussed in Appendix A.

4-3. Accelerating Oracle Data Import

Problem

You have to load a quantity of Oracle data that will take longer to load than you have time available.

Solution

To accelerate the data load, use the Attunity SSIS Connectors for Oracle, which are available with the SQL Server Enterprise edition. The following explains how you can do this:

1. Download the Attunity SSIS Connector for Oracle that corresponds to your environment (32-bit or 64-bit). They are currently available at www.microsoft.com/en-gb/download/details.aspx?id=29284.

2. Double-click the .msi file and install the connector. You can modify some of the installation parameters, but accepting the defaults is nearly always easier.

3. In an SSIS package, right-click inside the Connection Managers tab and select MSORA in the Add SSIS Connection Manager dialog box. The dialog box should look like Figure 4-5.

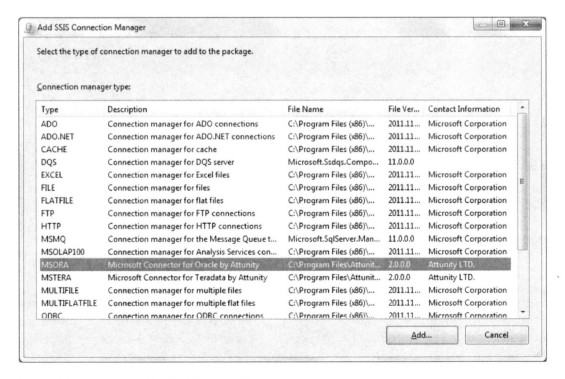

Figure 4-5. *Adding an Attunity SSIS connection manager*

4. Click OK and add all the required connection parameters. These are essentially the same ones described in step 6 of Recipe 4-2. The dialog box should look like Figure 4-6.

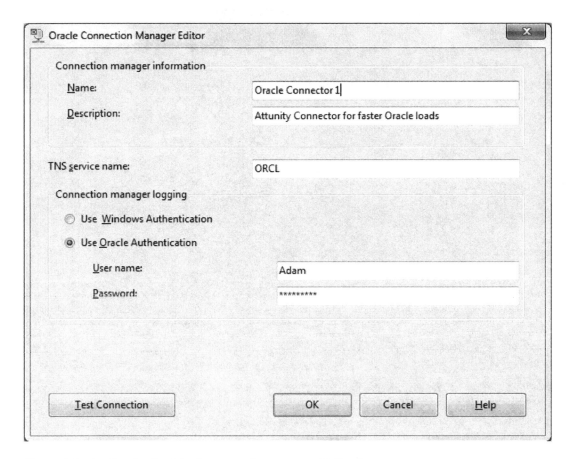

Figure 4-6. *Configuring the Attunity connection manager for Oracle*

5. Add a Data Flow task to the SSIS package. Double-click to edit.

6. Double-click Source Assistant in the SSIS Toolbox.

7. Select Oracle as the source type in the left pane. Select the connection manager that you just created in the right pane. The dialog box should look like Figure 4-7.

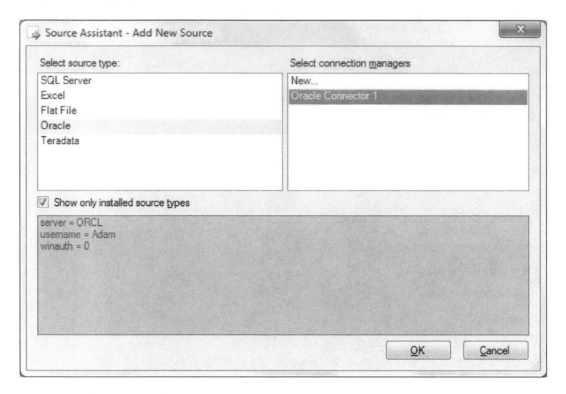

Figure 4-7. *The SSIS Data Flow Source Assistant*

8. Click OK. An Attunity Oracle source component is added to the Data Flow pane. Double-click to edit.

9. Ensure that the required connection manager is selected. Then, select the required data access mode (Table or SQL command).

10. Select the table or view—or enter the appropriate SQL SELECT statement. Click OK.

11. Add a destination component, connect the source to it, and map the columns. The Data Flow pane should look something like Figure 4-8.

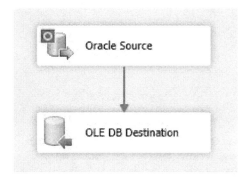

Figure 4-8. *The completed SSIS Data Flow using an Attunity Oracle source*

You can now run your Oracle data import.

How It Works

If you are using the Enterprise edition of SQL Server, you can download the Attunity connectors for Oracle, and use SSIS to achieve much faster data loads than those that are possible using the Oracle connector. You will have to install an Oracle client on the SQL Server. Use the TNS service name that you configured when setting up the Oracle client. Otherwise, if anything, the Attunity connector is simpler than the Microsoft or Oracle providers; and in the tests that I carried out, it is several times faster at loading Oracle data. One interesting aspect is that you have to use the SSIS Data Flow Source Assistant to create the Attunity data source, and not drag a source task directly from the SSIS toolbox. Here again (essentially to avoid pointless repetition), I have not gone into the minutiae of configuring an OLEDB destination. Recipe 1-7 contains an example of an OLEDB destination in greater detail, should you need it.

Hints, Tips, and Traps

- Unlike with SQL Server 2008, you apparently cannot add the Attunity connector to the SSIS toolbox.

- When migrating entire databases, you may find the following resources useful:
  www.microsoft.com/sqlserver/en/us/product-info/migration-tool.aspx#Oracle.

4-4. Importing Oracle Data on an "Ad Hoc" Basis
Problem

You want to import data into SQL Server from Oracle over your network without going to the trouble of developing an SSIS-based solution.

Solution

Use T-SQL and `OPENROWSET`—or set up a linked server.

The following code will insert data from Oracle into an SQL Server table using `OPENROWSET` (`C:\SQL2012DIRecipes\CH02\OpenRowsetOracle.sql`):

```
SELECT *
INTO MyOracleTable
FROM OPENROWSET ('OraOLEDB.Oracle', 'MyOracle';'SCOTT';'Tiger',
'select * from SCOTT.EMP');
```

How It Works

As with the Microsoft Office products described in Chapter 1 (or indeed when accessing data from other SQL Server instances), you can read and write data on an "ad hoc" basis from Oracle as a data source. To begin, let's see how to use OPENROWSET to run an "ad hoc" query. This can be somewhat slow, however, depending on your environment. So I advise you to test this approach thoroughly to ensure that you can meet your SLAs if you choose to implement it.

At a minimum, you will need the following:

- The Oracle client installed on the SQL Server.

- A network connection to the Oracle server (no Firewall issues!).

- An Oracle user logon and password with rights to the data you wish to retrieve.

- Ad hoc queries enabled on the SQL Server (as described in Recipe 1-4).

There are three elements that make up the OPENROWSET function:

- The OLEDB provider (OraOLEDB.Oracle). I am using the Oracle provider.

- The connection string ('MyOracle';'SCOTT';'Tiger').

- The query ('select * from SCOTT.EMP').

The main thing to note is that the connection string contains (in this order):

- The Oracle instance (MyOracle in the example given earlier).

- The user ID (SCOTT).

- The password (Tiger).

Note that all of these are separated by a semicolon, and the connection string is separated from the query by a comma.

For more permanent two-way connections to an external database (using OLEDB), a linked server can frequently be the best answer. To add an Oracle linked server, execute the following code snippet in SQL Server Management Studio. I have placed all the code that follows this recipe in a single sample file (C:\SQL2012DIRecipes\CH02\OracleLinkedServer.sql):

```
EXECUTE master.dbo.sp_addlinkedserver
    @server = 'MyOracleDatabase',
    @srvproduct = 'Oracle',
    @provider = 'OraOLEDB.Oracle',
    @datasrc = 'MyOracle';

EXECUTE master.dbo. sp_addlinkedsvrlogin
    @rmtsrvname = 'MyOracleDatabase',
    @useself = 'false',
    @locallogin = NULL,
    @rmtuser = 'SCOTT',   -- The Oracle User name
    @rmtpassword = 'Tiger'; -- The Oracle User password
```

You can then use the standard four-part convention to read data from (or write to) tables and views in the linked server.

Execute the following code snippet in SQL Server Management Studio to read the contents of an Oracle table and import them into an SQL Server table:

```
SELECT *
INTO dbo.MyOracleTable
FROM MyOracleDatabase..SCOTT.EMP;
```

If you only want to import the table structure (or a the structure of a source view), then you can use the following snippet:

```
SELECT *
INTO dbo.MyOracleTable
FROM MyOracleDatabase.. SCOTT.EMP
WHERE 1=0;
```

This will show you how SQL Server is mapping data types, which can be extremely useful.

Alternatively, you can use the OPENQUERY syntax to import data, like this:

```
SELECT *
INTO dbo.MyOracleTable
FROM OPENQUERY(MyOracleDatabase,'select * from SCOTT.EMP');
```

Another method of extracting data is to use the SQL Server 2005 (and up) feature EXEC...AT. At its most simple, it uses a linked server to execute a command, like this:

```
EXEC ('SELECT * FROM SCOTT.EMP') AT MyOracleDatabase;
```

So, assuming that you have a destination table structure, you can import data like this:

```
INSERT INTO dbo.MyOracleTable
EXEC ('SELECT * FROM SCOTT.EMP') AT MyOracleDatabase;
```

This can then be tweaked very easily to accept parameters as part of the T-SQL, which allows you to fine-tune the data selection:

```
DECLARE @EMPNO INT = 7369;

INSERT INTO dbo.MyOracleTable
EXEC ('SELECT * FROM SCOTT.EMP WHERE EMPNO = ' + @EMPNO ) AT MyOracleDatabase
```

Finally, if the Oracle DBA has set up a PL/SQL stored procedure to return a dataset, you can run:

```
INSERT INTO dbo.SCOTT_EMP
EXEC (BEGIN SCOTT.MyPLSQLProcedurehere; END) AT MyOracleDatabase;
```

The external server could be case sensitive—indeed most Oracle implementations that I have seen have been. So, to avoid potential problems, it is advisable to use the same case that the objects require when using linked objects. More precisely, Microsoft Books Online (BOL) says that if the table and column names were created in Oracle without quoted identifiers, use all uppercase names; otherwise, use the exact same case.

Hints, Tips, and Traps

- The `AllowInProcess` property must be set to 1 for the `'OraOLEDB.Oracle'` provider (right-click the provider in Server Objects ➤ Linked Servers ➤ Providers in SSMS to change this).

- You will need to set the `Set RPC OUT` server option for the linked server that you are using for `EXEC...AT` to work. In SSMS right-click the linked server and select "Properties" to modify this option.

- The SQL Server Data Import Wizard can also import Oracle data. Since this tool was described fairly exhaustively in Recipes 1-2 and 2-1, I will refer you to Chapters 1 and 2. When using it for Oracle source data, you need to specify that you will use an OLEDB driver for Oracle (provided by either Microsoft or -preferably- Oracle).

- To list all the available tables in the linked server, see Chapter 8.

■ **Note** I am aware that using `SELECT *` in this recipe is bad programming practice. My reason for this approach is that, in practice, you do not always have the details of the source data when connecting to external databases. By returning all the available fields, you can at least get an initial idea of what the source data is like, and take a closer look at the fields and data itself. When defining the definitive code for production, you should, of course, `SELECT` only the fields that you want to import into SQL Server.

4-5. Migrating Multiple Oracle Tables and Views
Problem

You have tens—or hundreds—of Oracle source tables and/or views that need loading into SQL Server as part of a migration.

Solution

Use SSMA (SQL Server Migration Assistant) for Oracle. The following explains how to prepare the SQL Server objects and load data from an Oracle schema:

1. Download and install SSMS for Oracle. It is currently at www.microsoft.com/en-us/download/confirmation.aspx?id=28766.

2. Run SSMA for Oracle (Start ➤ All Programs ➤ SQL Server Migration Assistant 2012 for Oracle).

3. Click File ➤ New Project. Enter a name. Then, either enter or browse to find the directory where the project will be stored.

4. Click the Connect to Oracle toolbar button. Enter the Oracle connection information. You should see something like Figure 4-9.

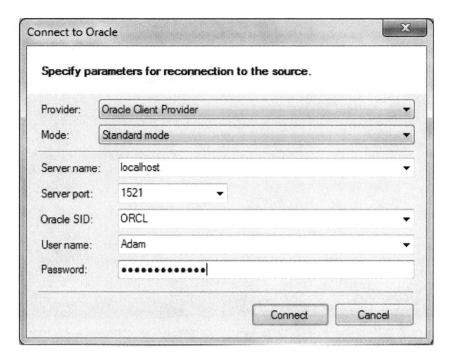

Figure 4-9. *Oracle connection for SSMA*

5. In the Oracle Metadata Explorer pane, expand the schemas and then expand the schema—or schemas—containing the tables you wish to migrate. Check the Tables check box to select all the tables in the schema (or select the tables you wish to migrate).

6. Click Connect to SQL Server. Enter your SQL Server connection parameters. In the SQL Server Metadata Explorer pane, select the destination database. You should see a screen that is something like Figure 4-10.

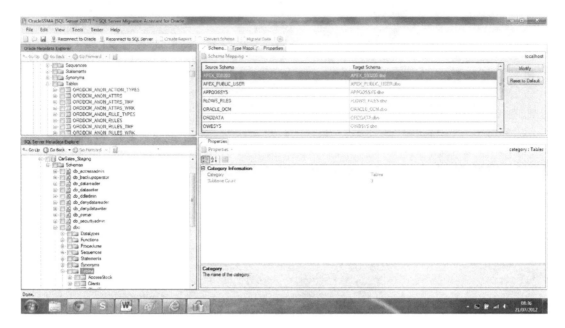

Figure 4-10. *SSMA for Oracle*

7. Click Tables in the Oracle Metadata Explorer pane. Click the Convert Schema button. SSMA creates the T-SQL to define the selected Oracle tables Then it displays the number of objects for which it has produced the metadata in the Properties tab in the pane to the right of the SQL Server Metadata Explorer pane.

8. In the SQL Server Metadata Explorer pane, right-click Tables. Select Synchronize. SSMA creates the selected tables in the SQL Server database.

9. Click Tables in the Oracle Metadata Explorer pane. Then click the Migrate Data button. SSMA will ask for a new connection to Oracle. Enter and/or confirm the connection parameters. Click OK. SSMA loads the data and opens a dialog box containing the conversion report.

10. Save the SSMA project.

How It Works

If you are only importing a few tables or views from one of the databases that we are looking at, then the SSIS approach outlined in Recipe 4-2 is probably sufficient. However, when you have one or more schemas full of tables (and, of course, their corresponding data) that you need to ingest into SQL Server, you probably need a tool capable of some extremely heavy lifting. Fortunately, SSMA (SQL Server Migration Assistant) for Oracle can come to your aid. It can help you analyze the source metadata and create the destination tables in SQL Server. It will also script out the SQL Server objects. An added advantage is that with SSMA, you can pause and restart—and above all, tweak—your work, which allows you to perform multiple iterations on the data migration.

SSMA can also migrate the data. In its latest iteration, it can perform client-side migration, where the migrated data does not flow through SSMA, but directly from the Oracle database to SQL Server. This is explained in more detail in Recipe 4-13, and it requires that the SSMS extension pack be installed. For more detail on downloading and installing SSMS and the extension pack, please see Recipe 4-13. Installing the extension pack will create a database on SQL Server to store metadata about the data load. Using the extension pack to carry out a data migration requires the SQL Server agent to be running.

I will not explain how SSMA can convert other database objects; instead, I will confine the discussion to obtaining metadata and importing the data.

There are a few things to note before starting the world of SSMA:

- An Oracle schema corresponds to an SQL Server database.

- When SSMA creates the SQL Server database schema, this is only a metadata view. You can see what the SQL Server schema will be, but nothing is written to the destination SQL Server until Synchronize is selected in the SQL Server Metadata Explorer pane.

- You can only import data from entire tables (and not views). You cannot filter source records or carry out column selection.

There are prerequisites that are important to note:

> **Firstly**, you must download and install SSMA for Oracle. To find it, just enter **SSMA for Oracle (Sybase or MySQL)** in your favorite search engine (if the address provided earlier is no longer valid). You have to get a (free) `oracle-ssma.license` file as part of the installation. Be sure to download the latest version.

> **Secondly**, CLR must be enabled in the SQL Server database. Use Facets ➤ Surface Area Configuration or the T-SQL snippet shown in Recipe 10-21 to enable CLR if it is not already enabled.

You are best creating database(s) in SQL Server ready to hold the objects and data from the Oracle source schema(s) before running SSMS. Although you can do this while using SSMA, separate database creation gives you greater control over the database configuration.

Unfortunately, the myriad subtleties of SSMA will only become apparent with use, but I hope to have given you an idea of just how useful it can be. SSMA really is a fabulous tool. In my opinion, it repays—many times over—the (admittedly short) time spent on the initial learning curve.

Hints, Tips, and Traps

- If the Oracle user you are using to connect has extended privileges (such as DBA or rights over many schemas), then SSMA may take time to load all the objects in the database. As this could include many thousands of tables in a large production database, you may be better-off connecting as a user with rights only to the objects that you wish to migrate.

- When importing schema information into a project that already contains the selected schema object(s), you get a warning that the existing metadata will be overwritten. SSMA cannot append metadata into existing schema information.

- When importing data into a database that contains data, you get a warning that the existing data will be overwritten.

- You do not have to convert and load an entire Oracle schema, of course. You may wish only to select a subset of the available tables by selecting the check boxes to the left of only those objects you wish to migrate.

- SSMA can generate the scripts for to the object(s) that you wish to migrate. You do this by right-clicking the element to script out and selecting Save As Script. So to script a single table, right-click it in the SQL Server Metadata Explorer pane. To script a set of selected tables, select the check boxes for the tables. Then, right-click Tables in the SQL Server Metadata Explorer pane and select Save As Script. Of course, you have to enter or browse to the requisite directory. These scripts can then be loaded into SQL Server Management Studio and adjusted as you see fit.

- For a complex conversion project, you may prefer to first generate an Assessment Report. To do this, in the Oracle Metadata Explorer pane, right-click the schema name and select Create Report. This report can then be saved. It may contain valuable information about potential problems.

- SSMA has many other features that reward the voyage of discovery required to find them. Many of these are described in Chapter 1, where SSMA for Microsoft Access is described, and are either totally or virtually identical across all the versions of SSMA.

- SSMA allows you to alter the data type mapping for either the whole project, or for a specific object. To alter the type mapping for a specific object, first click the object in the Oracle Metadata Explorer pane. Then click the Type Mapping tab on the right of this pane. Select a type and click Edit/ You can then tweak the data type mapping in the dialog box that is displayed—something like Figure 4-11.

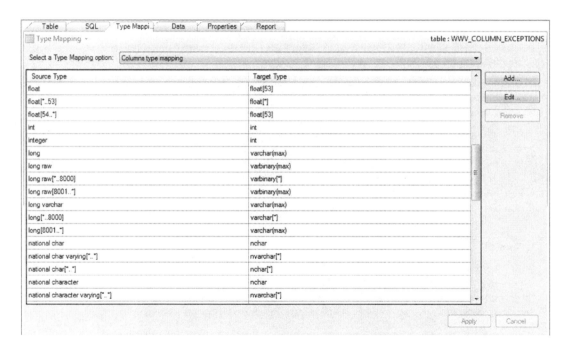

Figure 4-11. *Data type mapping in SSMA*

4-6. Loading DB2 Data on a Regular Basis

Problem

You have a DB2 database on an IBM AS400 server and can connect to this over your corporate network. Consequently, you want to extract data from the DB2 source and load it into SQL Server.

Solution

Use SSIS to load the data using an OLEDB connection to DB2. Here is one way of doing this:

1. Install the appropriate DB2 provider from your IBM source media. In this recipe, I will use the IBM DB2 for I5/OS IBMDA400 OLEDB Provider.

2. Create an SSIS package. Add a new connection manager.

3. Choose the IBM DB2 for I5/OS IBMDA400 OLEDB Provider.

4. Enter the fully qualified server name in the Server or File Name field.

5. Enter the DB2 logon information in the Connection Manager dialog box (see Figure 4-12).

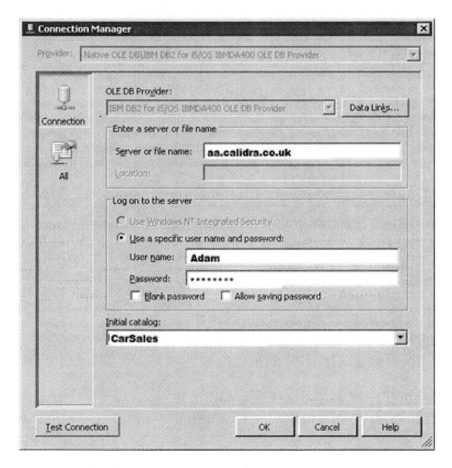

Figure 4-12. *Configuring an OLEDB source for DB2 in SSIS*

6. Select the initial catalog from the list of those available.

7. When defining an OLEDB source using this connection manager, set the data access mode as SQL command, and write a select statement to select data, using the appropriate schema.

8. Add an OLEDB destination, connect the source to it, and edit the destination.

9. Define the destination database and table, and map the columns.

199

How It Works

In this recipe I am assuming that you already know SSIS fairly well, and am concentrating on the interesting new aspect—the DB2 connection. In reality, linking to a DB2 database is essentially a question of choosing the correct OLEDB provider and drilling through via the catalog (the database in DB2-speak) to the schema and table. The good news with DB2 is that it makes connectivity easier in at least two respects:

- There is no full-fledged client software to install, only the DB2 provider.

- There is no connectivity information to configure in external files (as is the case with TNSNames.ora in Oracle).

However, DB2 compensates for this level of simplicity with the choice of available OLEDB providers (depending on which environment you are connecting to), and the mind-numbing complexity of the connection strings when using T-SQL connectivity. And this is without looking at DB2 Connect (for mainframes), as the subject is simply too vast. So the hard part when faced with DB2 data sources is probably choosing the appropriate provider. In this recipe, I am presuming that you are connecting to DB2 on an AS400, using a correctly installed IBM DB2 for I5/OS IBMDA400 OLEDB Provider. As was the case with an Oracle connection, you could well find that a helpful and dynamic DB2 DBA can be of invaluable assistance and guide you in the choice of the appropriate driver.

■ **Note** Many – if not all – the DB2 OLEDB providers do not allow the use of parameterized queries. One solution to this conumdrum is to build the SQL with a Script task, and then pass the SQL out to an SSIS variable which is used in an OLEDB source.

Should you choose to use the Microsoft OLEDB provider for DB2 with SSIS, then you will find that things are nearly the same as those described previously using the IBM OLEDB provider for DB2. This means that at step 4, you will see the Connection Manager dialog box shown in Figure 4-13, and not the IBM dialog box.

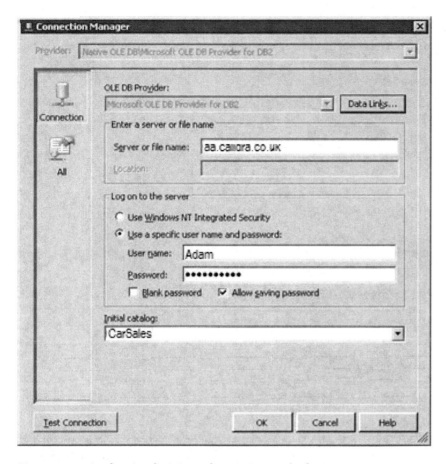

Figure 4-13. *Configuring the Microsoft OLEDB Provider for DB2*

If you click the "Data Links" button you can define extended data link properties, such as the initial catalog (database) and schema, as shown in Figure 4-14.

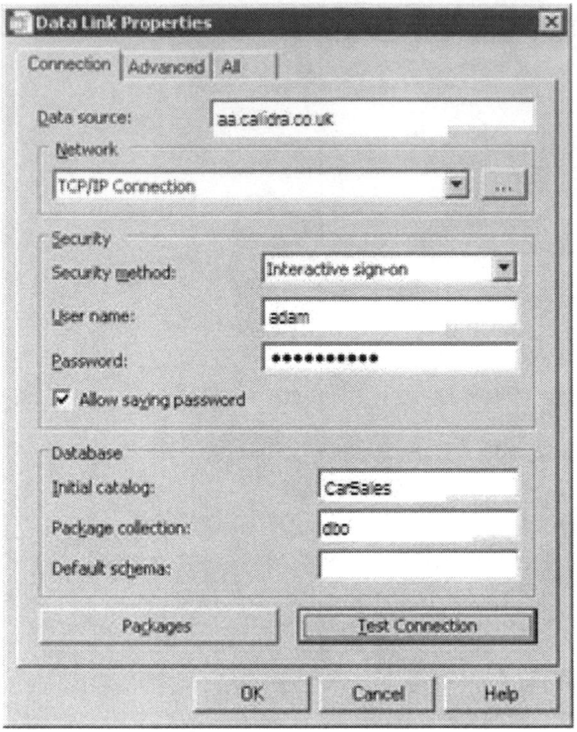

Figure 4-14. Configuring the Data Link Properties of the MS OLEDB Provider for DB2

If you will be using the IBM OLEDB provider, then you may well end up needing to use ODBC, and so to set up an ODBC System DSN (data source name). Creating a DSN is discussed in Recipe 4-10, so Figure 4-15 shows only the configuration panel for the IBM DB2 ODBC provider.

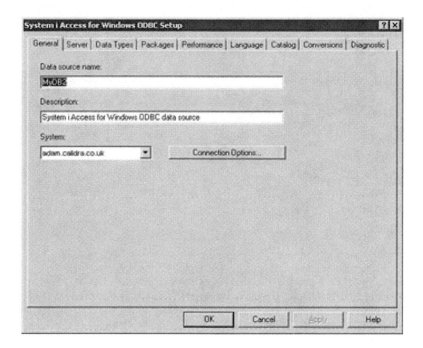

Figure 4-15. *The configuration panel for the IBM DB2 ODBC provider*

Hints, Tips, and Traps

- When adding the DB2 SQL SELECT statement, you might want to use the DB2 statement FOR READ ONLY—it is roughly equivalent to T-SQL's WITH (NOLOCK).

- Just as was stated previously for Oracle data sources, you are probably better-off defining the Connection Managers for both source and destination at package-level when using SQL Server 2012.

4-7. Importing DB2 Data Without SSIS
Problem

You want to import DB2 data without the challenge of creating an SSIS package.

Solution

Set up a linked server connection to DB2. This is the code to do it
(C:\SQL2012DIRecipes\CH02\MSDB2LinkedServer.sql):

```
USE master;
GO
EXECUTE master.dbo.sp_MSset_oledb_prop N'IBMDA400', N'AllowInProcess', 1 ;
GO
EXECUTE master.dbo.sp_MSset_oledb_prop N'IBMDA400', N'DynamicParameters', 1 ;
GO
```

```
EXECUTE master.dbo.sp_addlinkedserver
@server = 'MyDB2Server'
,@srvproduct = 'IBMDA400'
,@provider = 'MSDASQL'
,@datasrc = 'MyDB2'  -- DSN, previously defined
,@catalog = 'CALIDRA02'
,@provstr = 'CMT = 0;SYSTEM = adam.calidra.co.uk' ;

EXECUTE master.dbo.sp_addlinkedsrvlogin
@rmtsrvname = N'MyDB2Server'
,@locallogin = NULL
,@useself = N'False'
,@rmtuser = N'Adam'
,@rmtpassword = N'Me4B0ss';
```

How It Works

Assuming that you will use one of the available OLEDB providers that has been correctly installed, you can set up a linked server to import data from DB2 using a fairly "classic" script, as provided in this recipe (for the IBM DB2 provider and a previously-defined ODBC DSN).

For the IBM DB2 OLEDB provider, the T-SQL will look something like this (C:\SQL2012DIRecipes\CH02\IBMDB2LinkedServer.sql):

```
EXECUTE master.dbo.sp_addlinkedserver
    @server = N'DB2',
    @srvproduct = N'Microsoft OLE DB Provider for DB2',
    @catalog = N'DB2',
    @provider = N'DB2OLEDB',
    @provstr = N'Initial Catalog = CarSales;
        Data Source = DB2;
        HostCCSID = 1275;
        Network Address = 257.257.257.257;
        Network Port = 50000;
        Package Collection = admin;
        Default Schema = admin;
```

Hints, Tips, and Traps

- See Recipe 4-10 for details about how to set up an ODBC DSN.

4-8. Sourcing Data from MySQL on a Regular Basis
Problem

You have a MySQL database on your network, and you want to carry out regularly scheduled data loads from this database.

Solution

Use SSIS and use the MySQL ODBC driver to connect to the source database. The following describes how it is done.

1. Launch the ODBC Data Source Administrator (odbcad32.exe or Control Panel ➤ System and Security ➤ Administrative Tools ➤ Data Sources ODBC). Click the System DSN tab. You should see the dialog box shown in Figure 4-16.

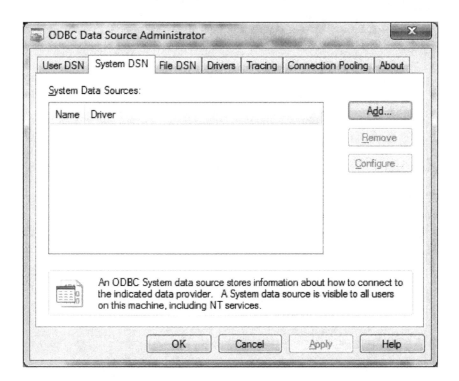

Figure 4-16. *The ODBC Data Source Administrator*

2. Click Add. Select the MySQL ODBC 3.51 driver (see Figure 4-17).

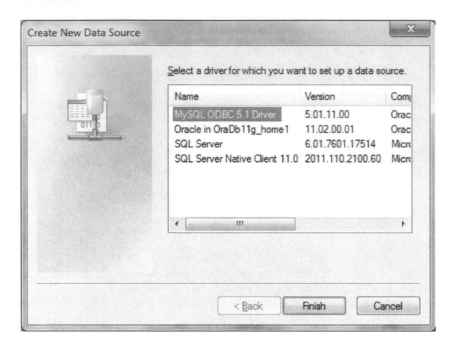

Figure 4-17. *Adding a new System DSN using the ODBC Data Source Administrator*

3.   Click Finish. The ODBC Connector dialog box will appear. Enter the following information:

- A data source name of your choosing. I am using MySQLAdam.

- A description (if you want to add one)

- The server name (or localhost)

- The user you will be connecting as. I am using the *root* user.

- The relevant password

- The database to connect to

You should see something like Figure 4-18.

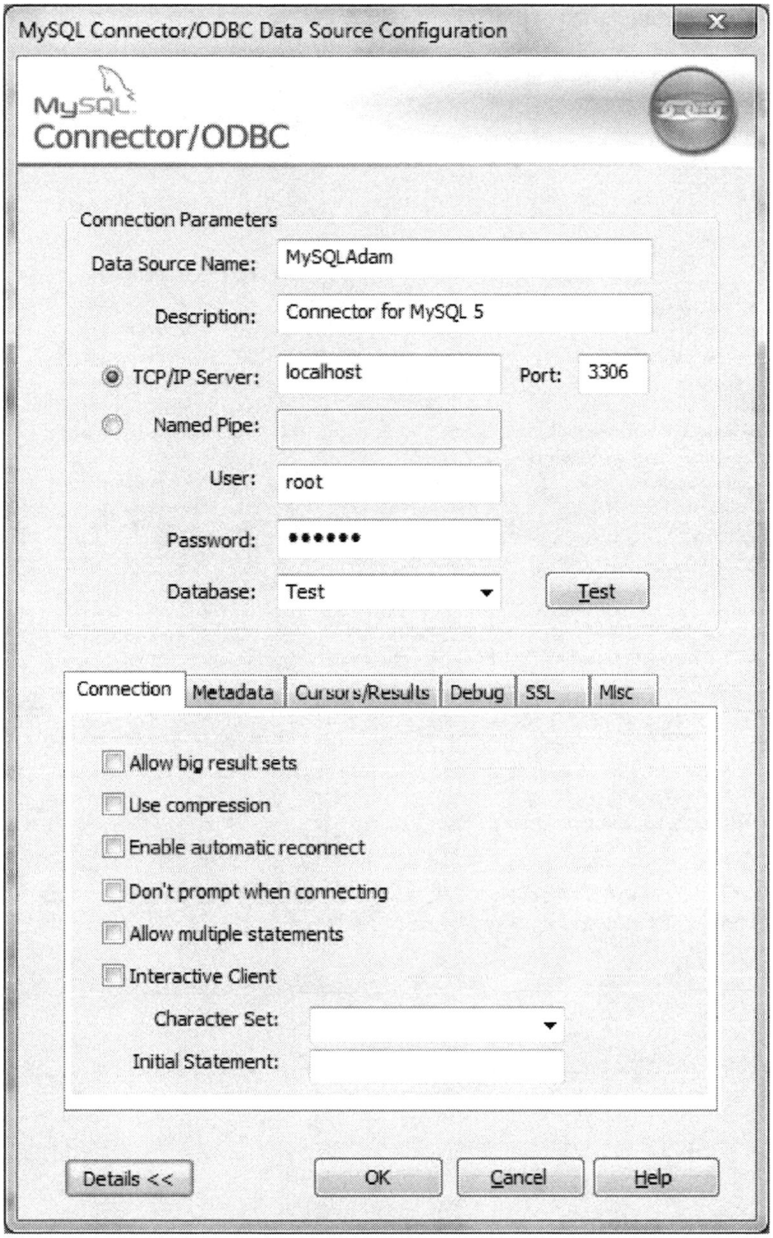

Figure 4-18. *Configuring a MySQL ODBC DSN*

4. Click Test to test the connection. Assuming that you receive confirmation that the connection has been made, click OK twice to complete the DSN creation.

5. In a new or existing SSIS package, right-click in the Connection Managers tab and select New Connection. . . (or right-click Connection Managers in the Solution Explorer and select New Connection Manager).

6.   Select the ODBC type from the list of providers, as shown in Figure 4-19.

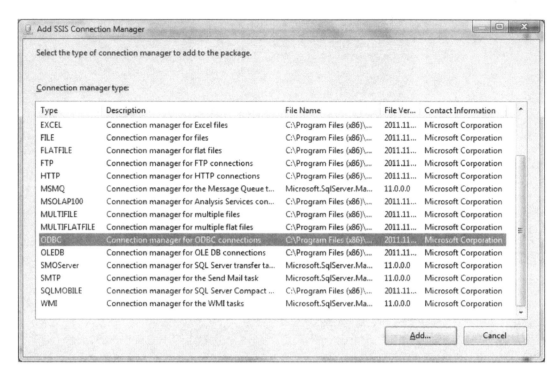

Figure 4-19. *Adding an ODBC connection manager in SSIS*

7.   Click Add. Select the System (or User) DSN that you just created (MySQLAdam in this example). The dialog box should look like Figure 4-20.

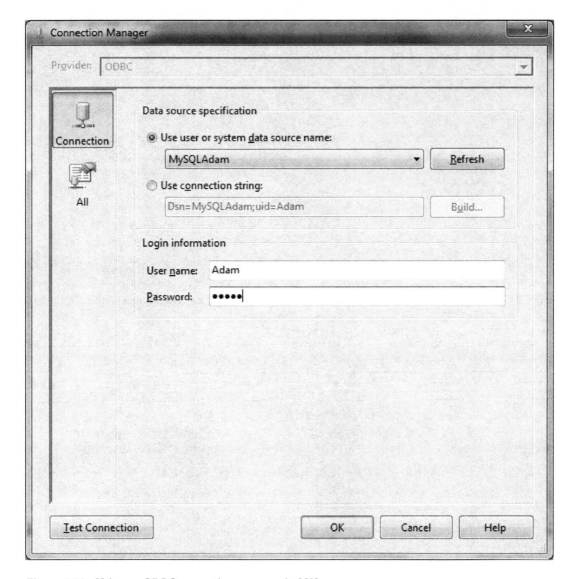

Figure 4-20. *Using an ODBC connection manager in SSIS*

8. Click OK to complete the creation of the MySQL connection manager. Rename the connection manager.

9. Add a Data Flow task. Double-click to edit.

10. Add an ODBC data source. Double-click to edit.

11. Set the ODBC connection manager to the name that you created in step 8.

12. Set the data access mode to SQL command. Enter the SQL to determine the source data. In this example, I suggest **SELECT * FROM INFORMATION_SCHEMA.TABLES**.

13. Click OK to confirm. Continue with your package creation, as described in Recipes 4-2 and 1-7, among others.

How It Works

There is not, at the time of writing, a MySQL-supported OLEDB provider. So the only solution is to import data using ODBC. Obviously this is not ideal, but sometimes you have no choice. The disadvantages to this approach are

- ODBC using the MySQL provider can be very slow.

- Configuring the Microsoft OLEDB provider for ODBC drivers can be finicky.

The latest version of the MyODBC driver from the MySQL web site must be installed. Currently, it is 5.1.1, and exists in both 32- and 64-bit versions. Enter **MySQL ODBC** in your favorite search engine. You should find the relevant page on the MySQL site to download it.

One of the new features in SSIS 2012 is ODBC connection managers (thanks to Microsoft's partnering with Attunity), and this certainly makes life a little simpler as far as using ODBC is concerned. Once you have configured the ODBC DSN, you can use it as the System DSN in the ODBC connection manager. The various elements of the DSN are explained in Table 4-1.

Table 4-1. *The MySQL ODBC DSN*

Parameter	Description
A data source name	You can choose any name you like, but obviously the simpler and more memorable it is, the better.
A description	This is not compulsory, but can prove useful when returning to DSNs months later when you have forgotten all about what it does.
The server name	This must be the exact name of the MySQL server.
The user you are connecting as	This user must have all the necessary rights to the source data.
The corresponding password	
The database to connect to	

Hints, Tips, and Traps

- The DSN is limited to the selected database, so you will need to set up multiple DSNs for ODBC connections to multiple databases.

- To save a System DSN, you need to be running the ODBC Data Source Administration Tool as a local system administrator (right-click the odbcad32.exe and select Run as Administrator).

- The current version of the MySQL ODBC driver will not list the available tables, so you have to know the tables that you are looking for. If you do not have this information on hand, then you can use the techniques given in Chapter 8 to discover it. Getting source metadata can, however, be a lengthy process. So, once again, obtaining any documentation about the source can save a lot of valuable time—your own!

- If the DSN contains the logon and password, you do not need to repeat them in SSIS.

- If you cannot see the DSN in the list in the Connection Manager dialog box, then select Use Connection String, and enter something like:

  `DRIVER={MySQL ODBC 5.1 Driver};SERVER=localhost;DATABASE=AdamTest;UID=root`

- If you are working in a 64-bit environment with only the 32-bit driver installed, you will need to set the Run64BitRuntime setting to False before running the package.

- Once again, consider defining the connection managers at package level.

4-9. Importing MySQL Data on an "Ad Hoc" Basis
Problem

You want to import data from MySQL without the hassle of using SSIS.

Solution

Configure a linked server to link to a MySQL database. I'll explain how it is done.

1. In SSMS, expand Server Objects. Then right-click Linked Servers and select New Linked Server.

2. Enter a linked server name of your choosing. I am using MySQLLink here.

3. Click the Other Data Source radio button. Select "Microsoft OLEDB provider for ODBC drivers" as the provider.

4. Enter a product name of your choosing.

5. Enter the System DSN that you created in the Recipe 4-8 (MySQLAdam) as the Data Source.

You should see something like what's shown in Figure 4-21.

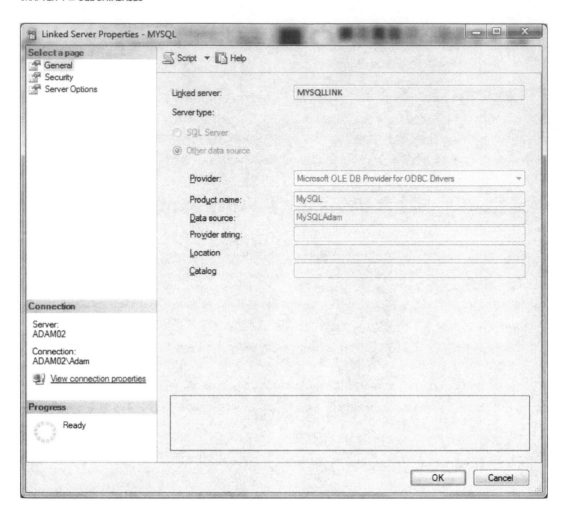

Figure 4-21. *Configuring a MySQL linked server*

6. Click Security in the list on the left. Select the "Be made without using a Security Context" radio button. The logon defined in the DSN provides the user ID and password (see Figure 4-22).

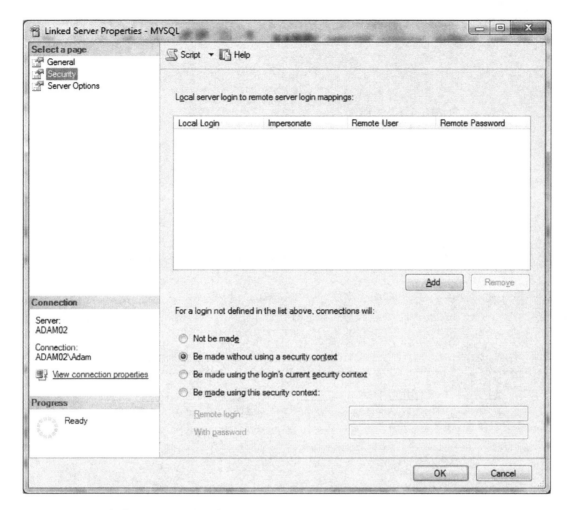

Figure 4-22. *Linked server properties for MySQL*

      7.   Click OK.

You can now select data from the linked server using a standard four-part `SELECT` statement, like this:
`SELECT * FROM MYSQLLINK...INFORMATION_SCHEMA.TABLES`.

How It Works

By using ODBC, you can create a linked server to a MySQL database. In my opinion, while it is easier to define a DSN first and use this as the data source, you can create a "DSN-less" linked server by supplying a full provider string if you so prefer.

    If you are having difficulties with certain data types, you might need to tweak the MSDASQL (Microsoft OLEDB provider for ODBC drivers) properties. To do this, do the following:

      1.   Expand Server Objects ➤ Linked Servers ➤ Providers. Then, right-click MSDASQL and select properties. You will see a dialog box like the one shown in Figure 4-23.

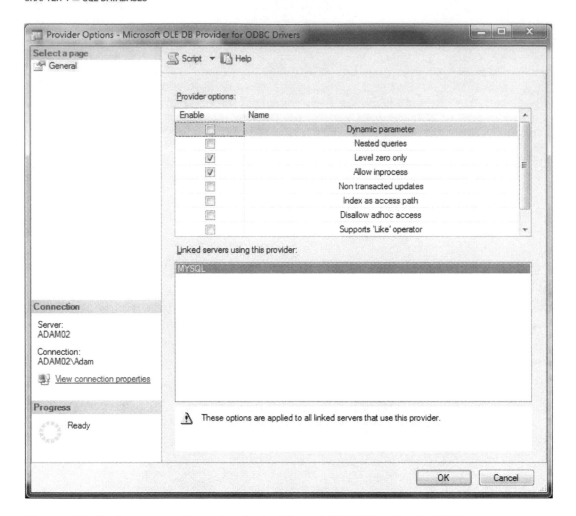

Figure 4-23. *Configuring provider options for the Microsoft OLEDB Provider for ODBC*

 2. Check Zero Level Only and/or Allow Inprocess. Click OK.

■ **Note** Remember that you are altering MSDASQL for all ODBC over OLEDB connections—so be careful that you do not prevent another connection from working by modifying the Provider properties!

Now that the linked server is set up, it makes using OPENQUERY to send pass-through queries a breeze. Use a simple code snippet like (C:\SQL2012DIRecipes\CH02\MySQLOpenQuery.sql):

```
SELECT * FROM OPENQUERY(MYSQLLINK, 'SELECT * FROM INFORMATION_SCHEMA.TABLES');
```

You can also use this DSN with ad hoc (OPENROWSET) queries—assuming that ad hoc queries have been enabled as described in Recipe 1-4. This is one example: (C:\SQL2012DIRecipes\CH02\MySQLOpenRowset.sql):

```
SELECT * FROM OPENROWSET(N'MSDASQL', 'DSN=MySQLAdam',
                         'SELECT * FROM INFORMATION_SCHEMA.TABLES) AS A
```

Hints, Tips, and Traps

- OK, so I was playing fast and loose with database security. For greater security on the Security pane, select the Not Be Made radio button and then click Add. Set up a login mapping between an SQL Server login and the MySQL user. The dialog box should look like Figure 4-24.

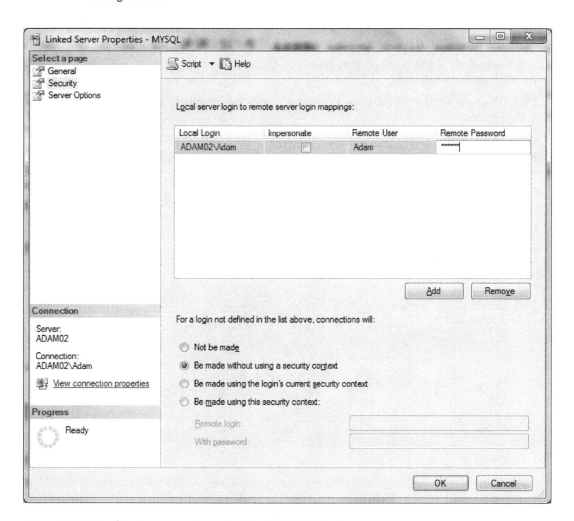

Figure 4-24. *Configuring a security context for a MySQL linked server*

> ■ **Note** Once again, using SELECT * is not for production environments. It can be very useful when getting an initial idea of the source data, however.

4-10. Importing MySQL Data Using SSIS 2005 and 2008

Problem

You are still using SQL Server 2008 (or even 2005) and need to import MySQL data.

Solution

Use ODBC over ADO.NET instead of using the Attunity ODBC connection manager, which only became available as standard in SQL Server 2012. The following explains how to configure it.

1. In a new or existing SSIS package, right-click in the Connection Managers tab. Select New ADO.NET connection.

2. Click New. Select the ODBC Data Provider from the pop-up list of providers, as shown in Figure 4-25.

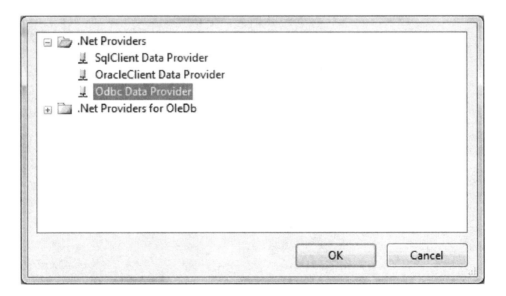

Figure 4-25. *Using an ODBC provider with an ADO.NET connection*

3. Click OK. Select the System (or User) DSN that you created previously (see Recipe 4-8).

4. Click OK twice to complete the creation of the MySQL Connection Manager.

5. Add a Data Flow task. Double-click to edit.

6. Add an ADO.NET data source. Double-click to edit.

7. Set the ADO.NET connection manager to the name that you created previously.

8. Set the data access mode to SQL command. Enter the SQL to determine the source data.

9. Click OK to confirm. Continue with your package creation.

How It Works

Should you be using SQL Server 2005 or 2008, then the approach to using the DSN is very slightly different, since you have to use ODBC over ADO.NET. You will still have to configure a DSN, but fortunately this is the same using any version of SQL Server because it depends on the MySQL ODBC driver.

Hints, Tips, and Traps

- The same hints apply to using previous versions of SSIS as those given for SSIS 2012. This is because they all concern the ODBC driver, and not SSIS.

4-11. Migrating Complete Tables from MySQL

Problem

You want to migrate multiple complete tables from several MySQL databases in a single, simple operation.

Solution

Use SSMA for MySQL to migrate tables from multiple tables and/or databases at once.

1. Download the latest version of the SQL Server Migration Assistant for Sybase. It is currently version 5.2, available at www.microsoft.com/en-us/download/details.aspx?id=28764.

2. Install SSMA and the SSMA extension pack. This is described in Recipes 4-5 and 4-13.

3. Install the latest version of the MySQL ODBC driver.

4. Run SSMS. Download and refresh the (free) license key.

You can now carry out a data migration exactly as described in Recipes 4-5 and 4-13. Without all the detail (and to save you jumping from recipe to recipe), this means you need to do the following:

1. Create a new project and save it.

2. Connect to MySQL. Drill down to the databases and table(s) that you wish to transfer.

3. Connect to SQL Server.

4. Convert the source schema.

5. Synchronize the schema with that of the destination database (this will create any required tables, if they do not already exist).

6. Migrate the data.

How It Works

There are so few differences with SSMA for Oracle and Sybase that I cannot really describe it once more without shameless repetition. So, provided that you have installed the MySQL ODBC driver to handle the connection to MySQL, you can use SSMA to migrate multiple tables to SQL Server quickly and easily. The only caveat is that the throughput of the migration over ODBC can be somewhat slow compared to text export and import, in my experience.

One of the few, rare differences between SSMA for Oracle/Sybase and MySQL is the MySQL Connection dialog box, which looks like Figure 4-26.

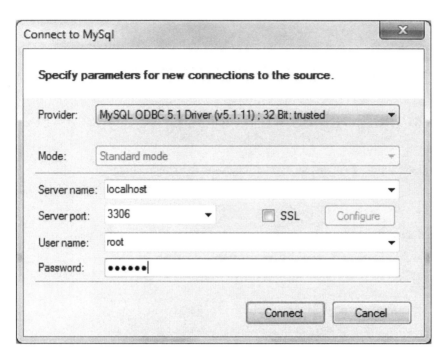

Figure 4-26. *The SSMA for MySQL Connection dialog box*

Hints, Tips, and Traps

- You may find useful resources for migrating whole databases at
  www.microsoft.com/sqlserver/en/us/product-info/migration-tool.aspx#MySQL.

4-12. Loading Data from Sybase Adaptive Server Enterprise (ASE)

Problem

You have Sybase databases on the corporate network from which you have to extract data to load into SQL Server.

Solution

Use SSMA for Sybase to transfer the data. Take the following steps:

1. Download the latest version of the SQL Server Migration Assistant for Sybase. It is currently version 5.2, available at www.microsoft.com/en-us/download/details.aspx?id=28765.

2. Install SSMA and the SSMA for Sybase 5.2 extension pack. The latter will ask you for a server to connect to, as shown in Figure 4-27.

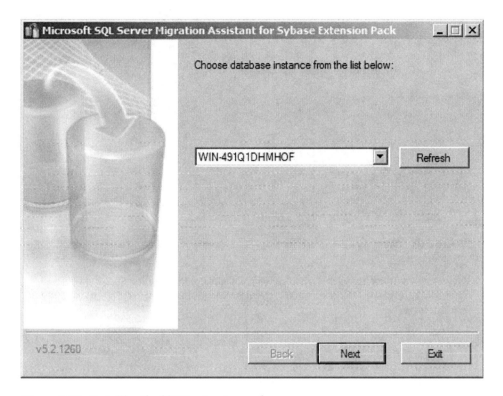

Figure 4-27. *Installing the SSMA extension pack*

3. You will also be asked for a password for the extension pack database master key, as seen in Figure 4-28.

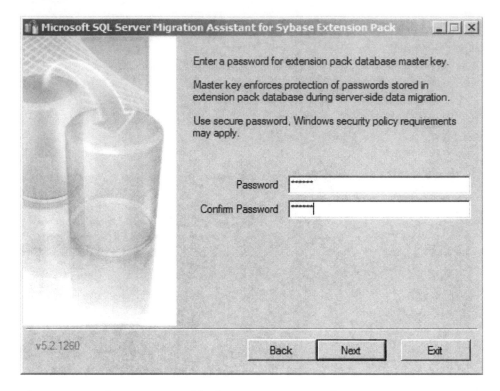

Figure 4-28. *Defining a password for the SSMA extension pack*

4. The extension pack installation routine will also ask if you want to install the tester database. I advise you to accept this suggestion, shown in Figure 4-29, if you have the required privileges.

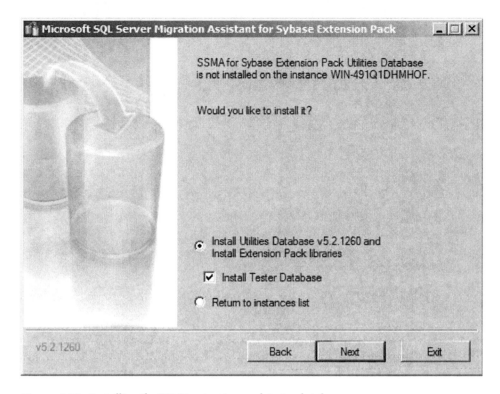

Figure 4-29. Installing the SSMA extension pack tester database

5.   Once SSMA and the extension pack are successfully installed, the Installation package will ask you if you want to install the products on another instance. Unless you do, click No and Exit. If you examine the databases on the SQL Server instance that you chose you will see the sysdb database.

6.   Create a new SQL Server database in SSMS named **SybaseImport**.

7.   Click Start ➤ All Programs ➤ Microsoft SQL Server Migration Assistant for Sybase ➤ Microsoft SQL Server Migration Assistant for Sybase. SSMA will open.

8.   Click File ➤ New Project. Enter the directory where the project will be stored. The dialog box should look like Figure 4-30.

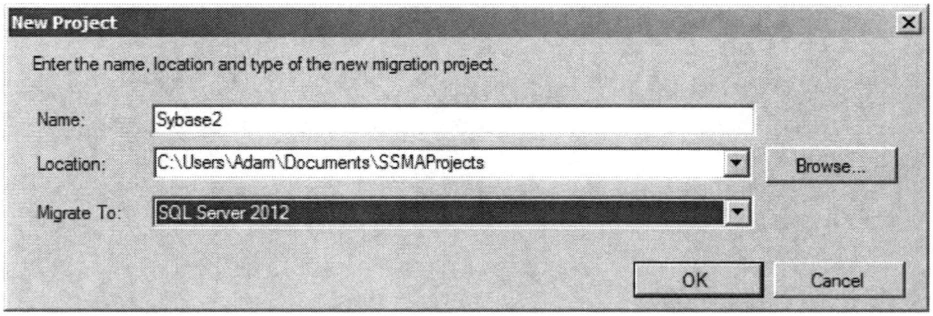

Figure 4-30. Creating a new SSMA project

9. Click the Connect to Sybase button and enter all the required connection parameters in the dialog box, which should look something like Figure 4-31.

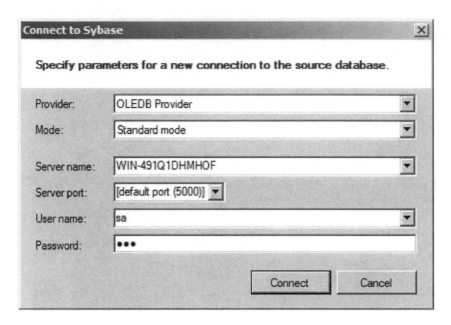

Figure 4-31. *Connecting to Sybase ASE from SSMA*

10. Expand the database that has now appeared in the Sybase Metadata Explorer pane. Drill down to select the database(s), schema(s), and table(s) whose data you wish to migrate. With a hint of nostalgia, I am using the pubs2 database. The panel should look like Figure 4-32.

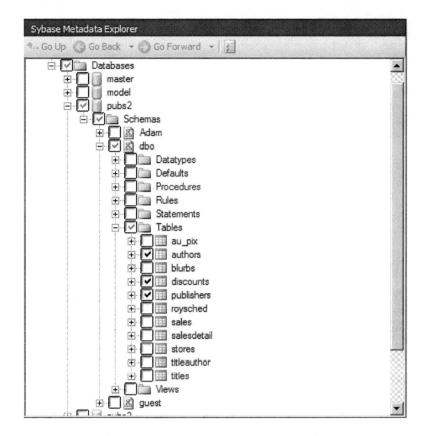

***Figure 4-32.** Selecting Sybase ASE source tables in SSMA for Sybase*

11. Click the Connect to SQL Server button and enter all the required connection parameters.

12. Click Databases in the Sybase Metadata Explorer pane. Then click the Convert Schema button. Note any warning messages.

13. As we will be transferring data to a database with a different name in SQL Server, click the Schema (dbo) source in the Sybase Metadata Explorer pane.

14. In the Sybase Metadata Details pane, ensure that the Schema pane is active. Click the dbo schema.

15. Click Modify. The Choose Target Schema dialog box will appear.

16. Click the Ellipses button. Select the destination database and schema. An example is shown in Figure 4-33.

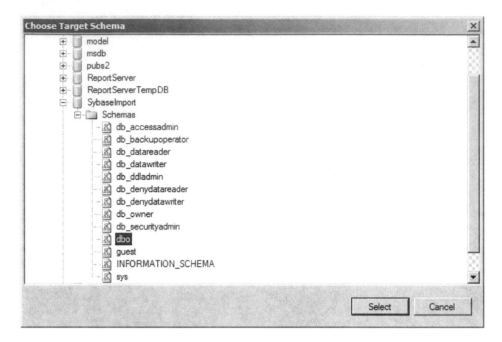

Figure 4-33. Choosing an SQL Server schema in SSMA

17. Click Select. The Choose Target Schema dialog box will reappear, looking something like Figure 4-34.

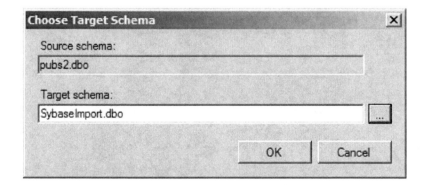

Figure 4-34. The Choose Target Schema dialog box in SSMA with a new target schema selected

18. Click OK. The Sybase Metadata Details pane will look something like Figure 4-35.

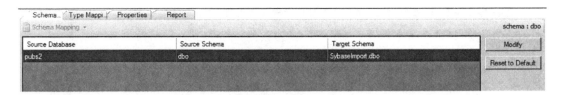

Figure 4-35. The SSMA Sybase Schema Metadata pane

19. Right-click the destination database in the SQL Server Metadata Explorer pane. Select Synchronize with Database. A dialog box will appear, where you see the objects that will be created and/or modified in SQL Server (see Figure 4-36).

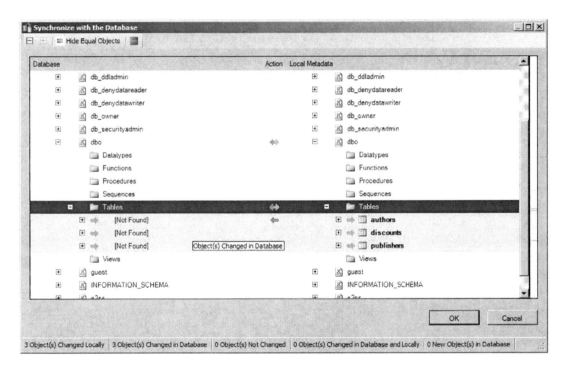

Figure 4-36. The SSMA database synchronization dialog box

20. Click OK.

21. Select Tools ➤ Project Settings. Then Click General on the bottom left, followed by Migration. Select Server Side Migration Engine as the migration engine. The dialog box should look like Figure 4-37.

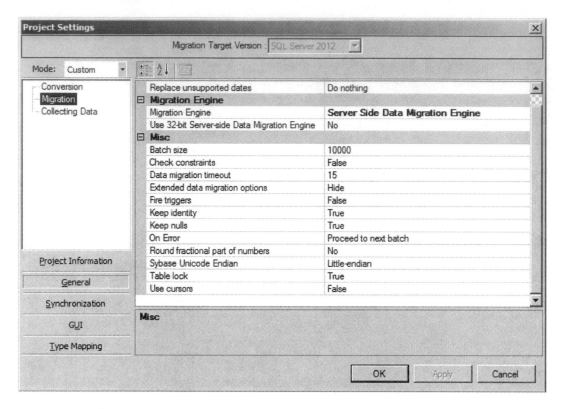

Figure 4-37. *Selecting server-side migration in SSMA*

22. Click OK to confirm your changes.

23. Click Migrate Data. The data will be migrated. Then the Data Migration Report dialog box will appear (see Figure 4-38).

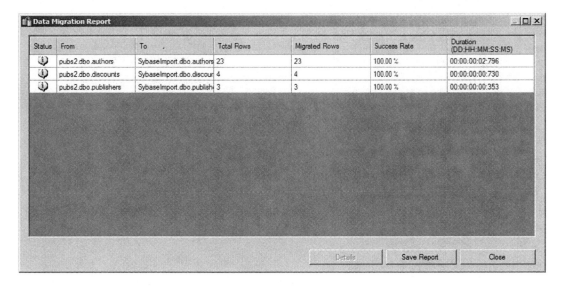

Figure 4-38. *The Data Migration Report dialog box in SSMA*

That is it. You have transferred the data from the selected tables into SQL Server from Sybase.

How It Works

As this process can seem rather complex, the following is a high-level overview of what was carried out:

- Download and install SSMA for Sybase and the extension pack.

- Install the Sybase OLEDB, ODBC, and ADO.NET drivers.

- Create an SSMS project and connect to Sybase.

- Select the source tables and/or views to migrate.

- Convert the schema.

- Synchronize with the destination database. This will create any required tables, if they do not already exist.

- Convert the data.

If you have used SSMA for (say) Oracle, then you may feel a certain sense of déjà vu. I nonetheless prefer to give those readers who are importing data from Sybase a complete import process to follow without presuming that they have already done this for an Oracle source. Of course, there are many, many variations on the theme that can be performed when using SSMA. As many of the available possibilities have been described in Recipe 4-5 (with regards to Oracle) or in Recipe 1-15 (concerning Access), I will not rehash them here, but refer you to those recipes to complete your knowledge of this product.

We have seen one important new feature of SSMA in this recipe: server-side migration. It is the reason why the extension pack was installed. It generally makes the transfer of large amounts of data faster because the data does not go through SSMA, but directly from the Sybase source server to the SQL Server destination. This also requires that the SQL Server agent be running on the SQL Server destination. You can stick to client-side processing if you prefer, but you may find it slower.

SSMA can also import data directly to Windows Azure SQL Database, and not just into "classic" SQL Server databases. All you have to do, when defining the SQL Server connection in step 11, is to supply the correct Azure database name (for example, recipes.database.windows.net) and the username (for example, meforprimeminister@recipebook).

The account that is used to connect to ASE must have at least public access to the master database and any source databases to be migrated to SQL Server or Windows Azure SQL Database. In addition, to select permissions on tables that are being migrated, the user must have SELECT permissions on the following system tables:

- [source_database].databaseo.sysobjects

- [source_database].databaseo.syscolumns

- [source_database].databaseo.sysusers

- [source_database].databaseo.systypes

- [source_database].databaseo.sysconstraints

- [source_database].databaseo.syscomments

- [source_database].databaseo.sysindexes

- [source_database].databaseo.sysreferences

- master.databaseo.sysdatabases

Hints, Tips, and Traps

- There are other versions of Sybase apart from ASE (SQL Anywhere springs to mind), but in my experience, ASE is the principal source of industrial-strength data that an SQL Server person may be called to extract data from, so I have only shown this product as a Sybase data source.

- If you need to, you can run the 32-bit version of SSMA, which is available from Start ➤ All Programs ➤ Microsoft SQL Server Migration Assistant for Sybase ➤ Microsoft SQL Server Migration Assistant for Sybase (32-bit).

- The first time that SSMA runs, it asks for the (free) license key that you must download to an appropriate directory.

- When you save the SSMA project, you will be asked which schemas on the source database you want to save the metadata for. Choose wisely, or you could be faced with a very long-lasting process while SSMA gathers all the metadata from the source.

- For a list of resources useful in migrating entire databases, take a look at www.microsoft.com/sqlserver/en/us/product-info/migration-tool.aspx#Sybase.

4-14. Importing Sybase ASE Data on an "Ad Hoc" Basis
Problem

You want to import data into SQL Server from Sybase ASE over your network without developing an SSIS-based solution.

Solution

Use T-SQL and OPENROWSET—or set up a linked server.

The following code inserts data from Sybase ASE into an SQL Server table using OPENROWSET (C:\SQL2012DIRecipes\CH02\SybaseOpenRowset.sql):

```
SELECT *
INTO MySybaseASETable
FROM OPENROWSET ('ASEOLEDB', 'WIN-491Q1DHMHOF:5000';'Adam';'Me4B0ss',
'select au_lname from dbo.authors');
```

How It Works

The Sybase ASE OLEDB provider is very well-behaved and allows you to import data using OLEDB into SQL Server using T-SQL. At a minimum, you will need the following:

- A functioning network connection to the Sybase ASE server.

- The ASEOLEDB provider installed on the SQL Server.

- A Sybase ASE user logon and password with rights to the data you wish to retrieve.

- Ad hoc queries enabled on the SQL Server, as described in Recipe 1-4.

There are three elements that make up the OPENROWSET function:

- The OLEDB provider (ASEOLEDB).

- The connection string ('WIN-491Q1DHMHOF:5000';'Adam';'Me4B0ss'). You have to use your own connection parameters, of course.

- The Query ('select au_lname from dbo.authors'). Here I am using a standard Sybase ASE sample database. You can use any database to which you have the appropriate rights.

The main thing to note is that the connection string contains (in this order):

- The Sybase ASE instance (WIN-491Q1DHMHOF:5000 in the example provided). Note that this is the server name (or the Sybase ASE Server name if one was given at installation) and the port (which you can roughly think of as an SQL Server instance), which was configured at installation for Sybase ASE.

- The user ID (Adam). You will use an appropriate user, of course.

- The password (Me4B0ss).

Note that all of these are separated by a semicolon, and the connection string is separated from the SQL query by a comma. Inevitably, you can use INSERT INTO ... SELECT if you prefer, rather than create a table using SELECT...INTO as I did here.

There are several valid reasons for using OPENROWSET to import data. In no particular order, and without any pretentions to completeness, they are as follows:

- You can use all the power of the SELECT clause to choose the columns to import.

- You can filter imported data using a WHERE clause.

- You can sort the imported data using an ORDER BY clause.

You can also set up a linked server to Sybase ASE if you want. I'll explain the easiest way to do this.

1. Create an ODBC System DSN using the Adaptive Server Enterprise ODBC driver, configured as shown in Figure 4-39.

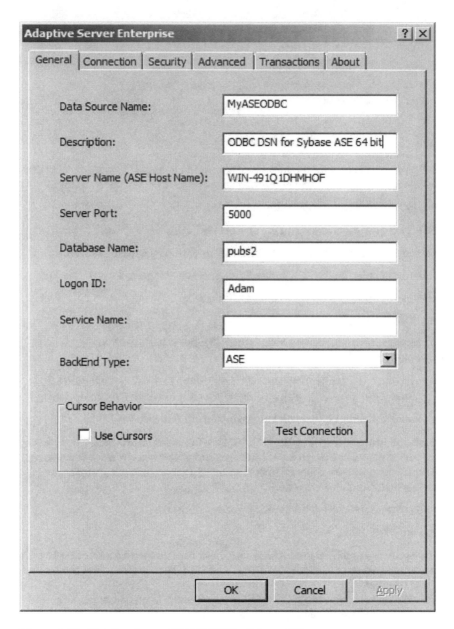

Figure 4-39. Configuring an ODBC DSN for Sybase ASE

2. Run the following T-SQL to create a linked server using the MyASEODBC System DSN as the data source (all three following snippets are in C:\SQL2012DIRecipes\CH02\SybaseLinkedServer.sql):

```
EXECUTE master.dbo.sp_addlinkedserver
    @server = 'MySybaseASEDatabase',
    @srvproduct = 'Sybase ASE',
    @provider = 'MSDASQL',
    @datasrc = 'MyASEODBC' ;
```

3. Run the following T-SQL snippet to define security for ASE access:

```
EXECUTE  master.dbo.sp_addlinkedsrvloginSP_ADDLINKEDSRVLOGIN Ã
    @rmtsrvname = 'MySybaseASEDatabase',
    @useself = 'false',
    @locallogin = NULL,
    @rmtuser = 'Adam',   -- The Sybase ASE User name
    @rmtpassword = 'Me4BOss' ; -- The Sybase ASE User password
```

You can then use four-part notation to import data from the Sybase ASE server, like this:

```
SELECT *
INTO SybaseTable
FROM MySybaseASEDatabase.pubs2.dbo.authors;
```

Hints, Tips, and Traps

- It is very probable (though not inevitable) that Sybase ASE will be case sensitive. So if you get an error message with an OPENROWSET query, you can always start by verifying that you are using the correct case for all objects to which you are referring.

- When defining a Sybase ASE ODBC System DSN, be sure to use the 64-bit ODBC administrator if you are in a 64-bit environment. Otherwise, you will create a DSN that you can see and test—but not use for a linked server connection.

- Yes, you are right, SELECT * is very bad practice. My excuse here is that when faced with third-party databases, you may want to use this in order to return all the columns if you do not have the metadata available.

4-15. Importing Sybase ASE Data on a Regular Basis
Problem
You want to import data into SQL Server from Sybase ASE over your network on a regular basis.

Solution
Use SSIS and the Sybase ASE OLEDB provider. The following explains how.

1. In an SSIS package, right-click in the Connection Managers pane. Select New OLEDB Connection.

2. Click New.

3. Select the Sybase OLEDB Provider from the pop-up list of installed providers.

4. Enter the server name, followed by a colon and the port number.

5. Enter the username and password.

6. Select the database (Initial Catalog) you wish to connect to.

7. Click OK.

8. Extend and finish the SSIS package with an appropriate destination.

You can then import data from Sybase ASE into SQL Server.

How It Works

Once again, the art here is to ensure that the Sybase OLEDB provider is installed and functioning correctly. With the provider up and running, connecting to Sybase ASE and selecting data for import is easy. Virtually the only trick to know is that you must add a colon (:) and the Sybase ASE port number to the server name for the connection manager to work properly.

Hints, Tips, and Traps

- You can also use the Sybase ODBC provider (assuming that it is installed on the SQL Server). You will have to create a DSN first, and then use this with the ODBC source in a Data Flow task.

4-16. Loading Teradata Data
Problem

You have data stored in a Teradata database that you need to load into SQL Server Enterprise edition.

Solution

Download and install the Attunity SSIS Connector for Teradata. Then load the data using an SSIS Data Flow task.

1. Download the Attunity SSIS Connector for Teradata that corresponds to your environment (32-bit or 64-bit). They are currently available from www.microsoft.com/en-gb/download/details.aspx?id=29284.

2. Double-click the .msi file and install the connector. You can modify some of the installation parameters, but accepting the defaults is nearly always easier.

3. In an SSIS package, right-click inside the Connection Managers tab. Select MSTERA in the Add SSIS Connection Manager dialog box. The dialog box should look like Figure 4-40.

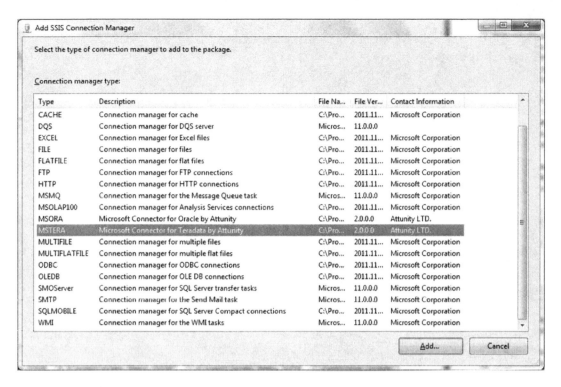

Figure 4-40. *Adding an Attunity SSIS connection manager for Teradata*

4. Click OK. Add all the required connection parameters. The dialog box should look like Figure 4-41—but with your specific connection parameters, of course.

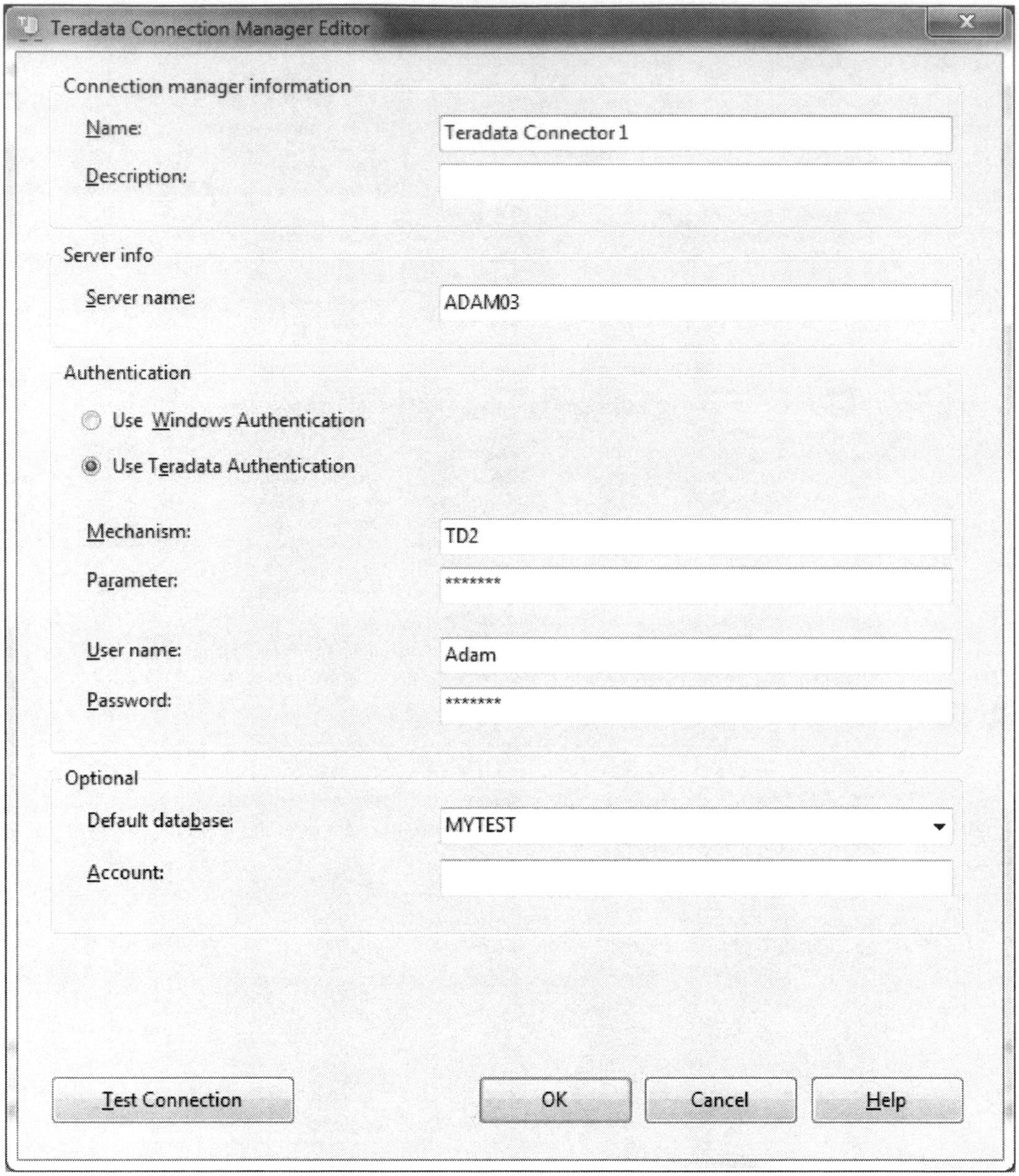

Figure 4-41. *Configuring the Attunity SSIS connection manager for Teradata*

5. Add a Data Flow task to the SSIS package. Double-click to edit.

6. Double-click Source Assistant in the SSIS toolbox.

7. Select Teradata as the source type in the left pane. Select the Teradata connection manager that you just created in the right pane. The dialog box should look like Figure 4-42.

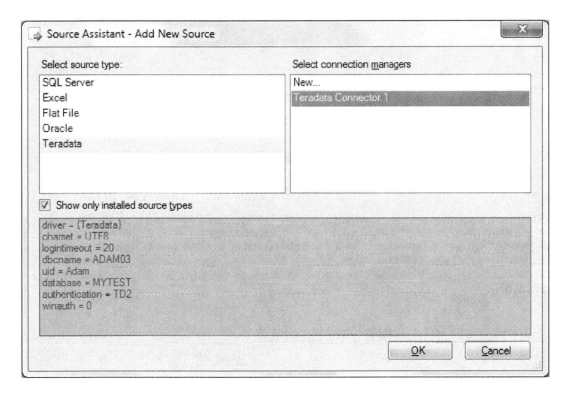

Figure 4-42. *Adding a Teradata Source using the Attunity Teradata provider for SSIS*

8. Click OK. An Attunity Teradata source component is added to the Data Flow pane. Double-click to edit.

9. Ensure that the required connection manager is selected. Then select the required data access mode (Table or SQL command).

10. Select the table or view—or enter the SQL SELECT statement, and click OK.

11. Add a destination component, connect the source to it, and map the columns. Since this aspect of SSIS is handled in other recipes (1-7, for instance), I will not explain all the details. The Data Flow pane should look something like Figure 4-43.

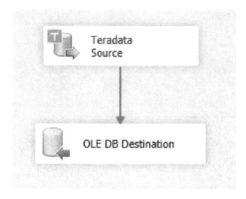

Figure 4-43. *The complete Teradata data flow*

You can now run your Teradata data import.

How It Works

While it is possible to use the Teradata ODBC driver to connect to Teradata and load data into SQL Server, in my opinion, it is much easier to use the Attunity-developed Teradata Connector, which can be used with the Enterprise edition of SQL Server. Once downloaded and installed, it makes connection to Teradata extremely simple. You could need the help of a Teradata DBA, however, when it comes to configuring the connection correctly, because a discussion of the available connection mechanisms and other Teradata subtleties are beyond the scope of this book.

4-17. Sourcing Data from PostgreSQL
Problem

You want to load data that is currently in a PostgreSQL database into SQL Server.

Solution

Install and configure the PostgreSQL ODBC driver. Use this with an SSIS or T-SQL-based solution.

1. Install the PostgreSQL ODBC driver from the PgFoundry.org web site.

2. Launch the ODBC Data Source Administrator (odbcad32.exe in %SystemRoot%\
    system32\ or Control Panel ➤ Administrative Tools ➤ Data Sources ODBC). Click the
    System DSN tab. You should see the dialog box shown in Figure 4-44.

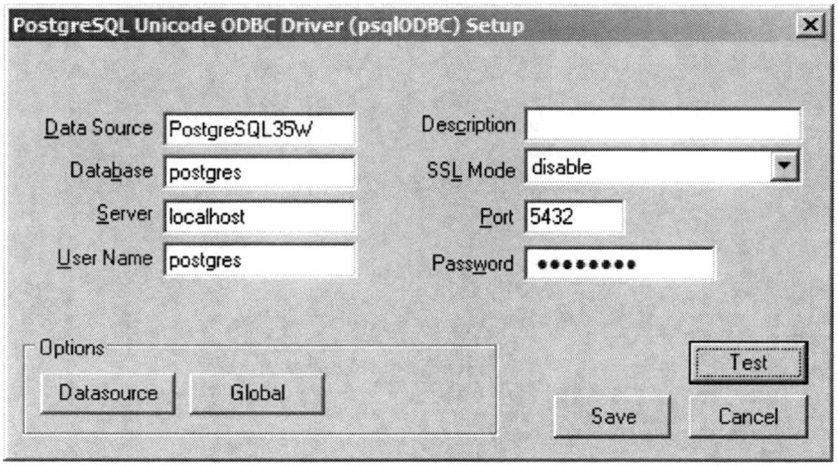

Figure 4-44. *Configuring a PostgreSQL ODBC driver*

3. Click Add. Select the PostgreSQL ODBC driver.

4. Click Finish. The ODBC Connector dialog box will appear. Configure the PostgreSQL ODBC driver so that it contains the elements shown in Figure 4-44. You will use your own specific parameters, of course.

5. Save your changes.

How It Works

There is an excellent and functional ODBC driver available to download from the PostgreSQL web site (www. postgresql.org), which, once configured, allows you to use SSIS, linked servers, OPENROWSET, and OPENQUERY without any difficulties. As was the case with DB2 and MySQL, no client software is required, which certainly simplifies matters.

So, to avoid fruitless repetition, and assuming that you have downloaded the latest version of this driver, all you have to do is to create a DSN as described for MySQL—only configured as in Figure 4-44 (step 4 for DSN setup).

The configuration elements are largely self-explanatory, but nonetheless a concise description is given in Table 4-2.

Table 4-2. PostgreSQL ODBC Configuration

Configuration Element	Description
DataSource	The name you choose to identify the ODBC DSN.
Database	The database you are connecting to.
Server	The server hosting the database.
Username	The user with the required access rights to the data source.
Description	An optional description of the DSN.
SSL mode	The SSL mode used. SSL disabled works perfectly fine.
Port	The PostgreSQL port (here, the default is used).
Password	The user password.

Once you have configured the DSN, you can use SSIS, linked servers, OPENROWSET, or OPENQUERY to import data from PostgreSQL. This can be done exactly as described for MySQL—only using the DSN name that you gave to the PostgreSQL driver, of course; so I will not repeat it all here, but refer you back to Recipe 4-9 for the details.

Summary

This chapter demonstrated many ways of importing source data from SQL databases. The subject is broad, and—as I wrote initially—not everything can be covered given the enormous scope of the subject. However, in this chapter you saw how to download data from many of the major relational databases that are currently available. Specifically, you saw examples involving the following:

- Oracle
- DB2
- MySQL
- Sybase
- Teradata
- PostgreSQL

Table 4-3 gives you my take on the various methods outlined in this chapter, listing their advantages and disadvantages.

Table 4-3. *Comparison of the Methods Used in This Chapter*

Technique	Advantages	Disadvantages
OLEDB providers	Generally faster.	More complex to install and configure.
ODBC providers	Easier to install and configure.	Generally slower.
SSIS	Fast data load.	Longer time to set up a package.
Linked servers	Easy to use for querying external databases.	Can be complex to configure.
		Requires greater permissions.
SQL Server Migration Assistant	Rapid acquisition of source metadata. Can build up a data load project over time.	Can only open entire tables and datasets.

I have to be fair, and warn you that cross-database data migration can truly be a minefield. All too often it can be a "minor" detail about the source database that can hold you up for hours until the issue is resolved. Even more frequently the source database DBA can prove reluctant to share their knowledge. Nevertheless, if you are patient, and above all do not rush things, then there is nothing to stop you migrating source data from the databases that we have looked at, and/or connecting to them to define and create a truly heterogeneous data extraction and load process. All I am trying to say is that a little calm and some charm can be your greatest allies in this particular corner of the ETL battlefield.

You will notice that I have not discussed the SQL Server Import Wizard in this chapter. Quite simply, if you have configured the provider and/or client for an external database, then using the SQL Server Import Wizard is exactly as described in Recipe 1-2 (among others). All you have to do is use an OLEDB or ODBC connection (depending on the source database and your specific preferences) as the data source. So I will not waste time here on pointless repetition, and let you use the SQL Server Import Wizard if you so desire.

CHAPTER 5

▓ ▓ ▓

SQL Server Sources

In this book, we look at importing data from several relational databases, and some of the ways in which they can be used as data sources for SQL Server. Yet there is one relational database we have not talked about, and that is SQL Server itself. So to continue our "data source tour," let's examine at some of the ways in which you can transfer data between SQL Server databases.

This overview includes:

- Ad hoc querying external SQL Server instances

- SQL Server linked servers

- Bulk loading of data from one SQL Server database to another SQL Server database

- Loading data from older versions of SQL Server into SQL Server 2005, 2008, and 2012

- Backup using COPY_ONLY

- Snapshot replication

- Copying and pasting tiny amounts of data between databases

- Loading data into SQL Server Azure

The choice of SQL Server as a data source may seem surprising, but in many enterprises, there are dozens—if not hundreds—of SQL Servers, often running different versions of the Microsoft RDBMS. So you may well need to know what your options are as far as getting data between versions of SQL Server is concerned.

It is not possible to discuss every aspect of data transfer between SQL Server versions, and there are inevitably certain technologies that fall outside the scope of this book. As my focus is on data integration with a strong focus on ETL, I will not be examining any of the many High Availability options for SQL Server, nor anything touching on Service Broker. Neither will I mention the Import/Export Wizard, as this has been covered extensively in Chapters 1, 2 and 4.

I will look at migrating data to SQL Server Azure in this chapter, however. While the Microsoft database "in the cloud" will doubtless replace onsite databases from many vendors, it seems most fruitful and comprehensible to discuss it as a logical destination for data from Microsoft databases.

There are a few points to note as far as following the example given in this chapter is concerned. First, you will need another SQL Server 2012 instance for many of the examples. This can be either a separate networked server or a second installation of SQL Server with a defined instance name. I am using the ADAMO2\AdamRemote instance in the examples. You will need to replace this with the server and possibly instance that you are using. You will also need to deploy the CarSales example database onto this second instance. All examples presume that you are using the CarSales database unless another database is indicated. Any sample files used in this chapter are found in the C:\SQL2012DIRecipes\CH05 directory—assuming that you have downloaded the samples from the book's companion web site and installed them as described in Appendix B.

5-1. Loading Ad Hoc Data from Other SQL Server Instances

Problem

You want to load data on an ad hoc basis from another SQL Server instance quickly and easily.

Solution

Use OPENROWSET and OPENDATASOURCE. This allows you to connect quickly to the source data and select any data subsets using T-SQL.

This is the code to use for using OPENROWSET (C:\SQL2012DIRecipes\CH05\OpenRowset.Sql):

```
SELECT Lnk.ClientName
INTO MyTable
FROM OPENROWSET('SQLNCLI', 'Server=ADAM02;Trusted_Connection=yes;',
    'SELECT          ClientName
     FROM            CarSales.dbo.Client
     ORDER BY        ClientName') AS Lnk;
```

You can use OPENDATASOURCE like this (C:\SQL2012DIRecipes\CH05\OpenDataSource.Sql):

```
SELECT ID, ClientName, Town
INTO MyTable
FROM OPENDATASOURCE('SQLNCLI', 'Data Source=ADAM02\AdamRemote;
                     Integrated Security=SSPI').CarSales.dbo.Client
```

The source data is loaded into the destination table in both cases.

How It Works

Should you want to import data as a "one-off," then a quick connection to another SQL server instance is, fortunately, extremely easy. There are, as for most external relational sources, two ways of establishing the connection. They are

> OPENROWSET: for occasional queries.

> OPENDATASOURCE: for occasional queries that could evolve into linked servers one day.

The following are the relevant prerequisites.

- An OLEDB provider must be installed on every external SQL Server instance. Admittedly, this is normally part of an SQL Server installation, but I prefer to state the obvious.

- An OLEDB provider must be installed on every SQL Server that is part of a cluster.

- Ad hoc distributed queries must be enabled on the server from which you are running the query. This is done using the following T-SQL snippet (C:\SQL2012DIRecipes\CH05\ConfigureDistributedQueries.Sql):

```
EXECUTE master.dbo.sp_configure 'show advanced options', 1;
GO
RECONFIGURE;
GO
EXECUTE master.dbo.sp_configure 'ad hoc distributed queries', 1;
GO
RECONFIGURE;
GO
```

For an occasional ad hoc query, you may find that OPENROWSET is the easiest solution. To clarify, the parameters for OPENROWSET are essentially in three parts:

- The OLEDB provider

- A provider string, containing server and security parameters

- A T-SQL query to retrieve the data

As the provider string only specifies the server, you are probably best advised to use three-part notation to specify the database, schema, and table or view from which you wish to source data. If the login defaults to that database and schema, then of course, you will have no problems; but I advise this as a best practice habit. If you wish to use SQL Server security rather than a trusted connection, then replace Trusted_Connection=yes with logon and password details like this:

```
'datasource=ADAM02\AdamRemote;user_id=AdamRemote;password=AdamRemPwd'
```

Note that the security information is all part of the second parameter, and the parameter elements are separated by a semicolon. Also, at the risk of stating the obvious, leaving security information in clear text like this is extremely risky. If you have no other choices, then you should consider wrapping the SELECT statement in a stored procedure created using the WITH ENCRYPTION option, which hides the text of the stored procedure from many—but not all—prying eyes. Alternatively, the stored procedure could reside on the remote server. In this case, it would need to be created by the team that administers that server. A stored procedure is generally the better option for security because you would not be passing details of your schema over the network.

Remember that you are using pure T-SQL, and so can extend the SELECT clauses (both that passed to the external server and the code wrapping the OPENROWSET command) to include a WHERE, ORDER BY, and GROUP BY clauses, as well as column aliases. These techniques are described in greater detail in Recipes 1-4 and 1-5.

If you are using OPENDATASOURCE, you can use SQL Server security, with all the caveats that leaving passwords in clear text imply. Here is a snippet to show it:

```
SELECT   ClientID
FROM     OPENDATASOURCE('SQLNCLI',
             'Data Source=ADAM02\ AdamRemote;User ID Adampassword=
             AdamRemPwd';').CarSales.dbo.Client'
```

Hints, Tips, and Traps

- If you suspect that an ad hoc query may have to become part of something more permanent one day, then setting it up using OPENDATASOURCE allows you to make the change to a linked server more easily. Its use of the SQL Server four-part notation allows you to replace the SQL snippet with a linked server reference at a later date.

- You cannot use CLR-based data types with distributed queries. In practice, this means not reading (or converting the data types of) GEOGRAPHY, GEOMETRY, or HIERARCHYID data types. However, these data types can be used in pass-through queries—so you can use them in Linked server queries that use OPENQUERY (as opposed to four-part notation) or OPENROWSET.

5-2. Reading Data from Another SQL Server Instance over a Permanent Connection

Problem

You want to read data from another SQL Server instance over a permanent connection using simple T-SQL.

Solution

Configure a linked server to connect to the source data and use four-part notation in your T-SQL.

The way to carry this out is as follows:

1. Run the following T-SQL (C:\SQL2012DIRecipes\CH05\AddLinkedServer.Sql):

    ```
    EXECUTE master.dbo sp_addlinkedserver
        @server = N'SQLLinkedServer',
        @srvproduct = N' ',
        @provider = N'SQLNCLI',
        @datasrc = N'ADAMO2\AdamRemote',
        @catalog = N'CarSales';
    ```

2. The linked server can then be easily queried using four-part notation, as the following example shows:

    ```
    SELECT
    ClientName, Town
    INTO  dbo.CarSales
    FROM  SQLLinkedServer.CarSales.dbo.Client;
    ```

How It Works

For a more permanent way of reading data from another SQL Server instance, it is probably preferable to think in terms of setting up a linked server. The advantages of linked servers were described in Chapters 1–4, so I refer you there for reasons behind this choice.

The sp_addlinkedserver stored procedure requires you to supply:

- A linked server name
- The SQL Server provider (SQLNCLI)
- The source server
- A source database

Adding a linked server requires the `ALTER ANY LINKED SERVER` permission. The grantor (or the principal specified with the AS option) must have either the permission itself with `GRANT OPTION` or a higher permission. Then, they can run the following code snippet:

```
GRANT ALTER ANY LINKED SERVER TO Adam;
```

If you prefer, you can also specify a linked server using Management Studio, as follows.

1. In the Object Explorer pane, expand Server Objects, and then right-click Linked Servers and choose New Linked Server. Enter the name of the SQL Server (or the instance name) in the New Linked Server dialog box and select the SQL Server radio button, as shown in Figure 5-1.

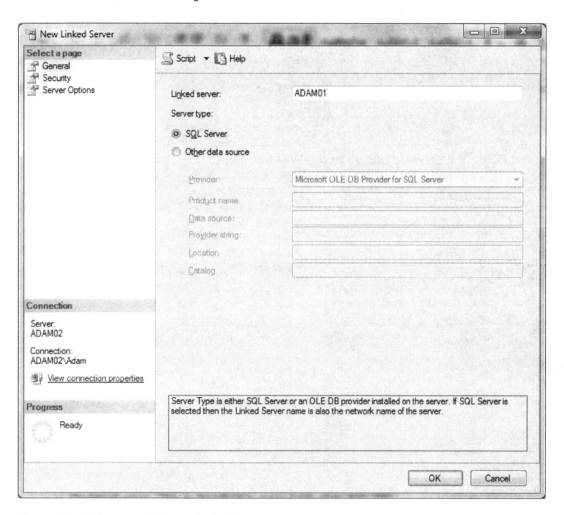

Figure 5-1. *Adding a linked server in SSMS*

2. Click Security in the left pane. Specify the security context of any connections using the linked server (this is described in Recipe 4-9). Then click OK.

Security is a major consideration when using linked servers. Unfortunately, it is a vast subject with myriad ramifications. So all I can offer are a few simple guidelines; a complete analysis of this area is beyond the scope of this book.

When connecting to a linked server, inevitably there will be a security context under which the remote login operates. By default (and assuming that security account delegation is available), the remote server uses the security credentials of the current login from the calling server. Given this potential simplicity, Windows authentication is the way to go, if you can. The account that you are using has to have SELECT permissions on the tables that you are reading on the remote server.

If you are not using Windows Authentication, or if Delegation is not configured, you need to add a linked server login. You could use code like the following:

```
EXECUTE master.dbo.sp_addlinkedsrvlogin @rmtsrvname = N'SQLLinkedServer', @locallogin = NULL,
                    @useself = N'False', @rmtuser = N'Adam', @rmtpassword = N'Me4BOss';
```

If there is no security account delegation, then you have to map the account on the local server to a remote login using SQL Server authentication on the remote machine.

When querying a linked server, there are other approaches that you may choose to use to return data using a linked server connection. For instance, you can also use EXEC...AT in this way, if you desire. First, you need to enable RPC OUT, as follows:

```
EXECUTE sp_serveroption @server='SQLLinkedServer', @optname='rpc out', @optvalue='TRUE';
```

Then you can run an EXECUTE...AT command, like this:

```
INSERT INTO dbo.Client (ClientName, Town )
EXEC ('SELECT ClientName, Town FROM CarSales.dbo.Client') AT SQLLinkedServer;
```

If you need to parameterize a query, it can be done like this:

```
DECLARE @ID INT = 2
INSERT INTO dbo.Client (ClientName, Town)
EXEC ('SELECT ClientName, Town FROM CarSales.dbo.Client WHERE ID=' + @ID) AT SQLLinkedServer;
```

Rather than sending SELECT queries, you can use a stored procedure to load data. As an example of this, first create the following two stored procedures on the remote server using the following code (C:\SQL2012DIRecipes\CH05\ pr_GetETLData.Sql and C:\SQL2012DIRecipes\CH05\pr_GetETLDataWithParameter.Sql):

```
CREATE PROCEDURE CarSales.dbo.pr_GetETLData
AS
SELECT
ClientName, Town

FROM    dbo.Client
;
GO

CREATE PROCEDURE CarSales.dbo.pr_GetETLDataWithParameter
(
@ID INT
)
```

```
AS
SELECT
ClientName, Town

FROM    dbo.Client
WHERE   ID = @ID
;
GO
```

You can now call a stored procedure on the linked server using the following code snippet:

```
INSERT INTO dbo.Client (ClientName, Town)
EXECUTE ('EXECUTE CarSales.dbo.pr_GetETLData') AT SQLLinkedServer
```

Finally, your remote stored procedure can have parameters. I find the following the easiest way to call it:

```
INSERT INTO dbo.Client (ClientName, Town)
EXECUTE SQLLinkedServer.CarSales.dbo.pr_GetETLDataWithParameter 1
```

Here, the "1" is the ID parameter expected by the pr_GetETLDataWithParameter stored procedure.

There are a few linked server options that you may find useful and that can be set using EXECUTE sp_serveroption. These linked server options are listed in Table 5-1.

Table 5-1. *Linked Server Options*

Option	Description
RPC	Enables RPC **from** the given server. A stored procedure can be executed on the server.
RPC Out	Enables RPC **to** the given server. A stored procedure on the remote server can be executed.
Collation Compatible	Affects Distributed Query execution against linked servers. If this option is set to true, SQL Server assumes that all characters in the linked server are compatible with the local server, with regard to character set and collation sequence (or sort order). This enables SQL Server to send comparisons on character columns to the provider. If this option is not set, SQL Server always evaluates comparisons on character columns locally. Essentially this allows optimal query plans on remote server to be used.
Connect Timeout	Time-out value in seconds for connecting to a linked server.
Query Timeout	Time-out value for queries against a linked server.
Enable Promotion of Distributed Transactions	Use this option to protect the actions of a server-to-server procedure through a Microsoft Distributed Transaction Coordinator (MS DTC) transaction. When this option is True, calling a remote stored procedure starts a distributed transaction and enlists the transaction with MS DTC. If set to False, the remotely stored procedure can still work. MS DTC must be enabled on all servers for this to work. Unfortunately, a discussion of MTC is outside the scope of this book.

Hints, Tips, and Traps

- Use the Network name of SQL Server (for the default instance on a server) or use the servername\instancename (for a specific instance).

- To drop a linked server, right-click the linked server name in the list of linked servers, click Delete, and confirm; or use the following T-SQL snippet:

```
EXECUTE master.dbo.sp_dropserver SQLLinkedServer, 'droplogins';
```

- You cannot use CLR-based data types with linked servers either. This means not sourcing GEOGRAPHY, GEOMETRY, or HIERARCHYID data types unless you use CAST or CONVERT on these types—or OPENQUERY.

- At the risk of stating the obvious, you need a destination table to run EXEC...AT, whose DDL matches the source data.

5-3. Loading Large Data Sets Using T-SQL
Problem

You want to load large data sets from one SQL Server instance to another using T-SQL. You want to perform the load as efficiently as possible.

Solution

Export the source data using BCP in native format and use the T-SQL BULK INSERT command to load the file.
The simple and fast way to load data between SQL Server instances is to do it like this:

1. Create a destination table. The following is the one that I use in these examples (C:\SQL2012DIRecipes\CH05\TblClient_BCP.Sql):

```
USE CarSales_Staging
GO
CREATE TABLE dbo.Client_BCP
(
ID int NOT NULL,
ClientName nvarchar(150) NULL,
Town varchar(50) NULL,
County varchar(50) NULL,
ClientSize varchar(10) NULL,
ClientSince smalldatetime NULL
) ;
GO
```

2. Run the following T-SQL snippet to import the native BCP file
    (C:\SQL2012DIRecipes\CH05\Clients.bcp in the accompanying examples):

```
BULK INSERT CarSales_Staging.dbo.Client_BCP
FROM 'C:\SQL2012DIRecipes\CH05\Clients.bcp'
WITH
        (
         DATAFILETYPE = 'widenative'
        ) ;
```

How It Works

When a direct connection to another SQL Server instance is not possible, you may have to resort to "indirect" means. In essence, you have to export the data as a file, copy the file onto the destination server, and re-import it into another instance. Now, you can export data as a flat file or as XML; these subjects are handled in Chapter 7. Equally, importing them in these formats is the subject of Chapters 2 and 3. However, if you are sending data between SQL Server databases, instances, and even versions, then the venerable yet magisterial BCP utility (and with it the BCP native file format) really comes into its own. Consequently, I wish to concentrate here on ways of loading BCP files. The reasons for choosing this method are fairly simple:

- *reliability*—BCP has been around since the very beginnings of SQL Server, and is remarkably robust, as is its descendant, BULK INSERT.

- *speed*—nothing loads as fast as a native BCP file, in my experience.

This does not mean that it is a perfect solution. The following are a few minor quibbles.

- You always need to know the details of a BCP file and to have knowledge about the DDL defining the table whose data it contains separately.

- You cannot just open a native BCP file and reverse-engineer its structure.

- If you are not loading *all* the columns in the source file into the destination table, or if the source file columns are *not* in the same order as those of the destination table, you need a format file to perform column mapping.

- This approach is built for bulk loading—not selecting and/or transforming data en route.

There are several advantages to using BULK INSERT for the import phase of this process.

- As it is nothing but T-SQL, it can be run from a query window, a stored procedure, or even using SQLCMD.

- BULK INSERT runs in-process; this makes it the fastest option.

- You do not need xp_cmdshell and the requisite permissions as you do with BCP when run from T-SQL.

- It is arguably less clunky to use than the BCP command-line executable and all its flags.

- BULK INSERT accepts parallel loads, as described in Chapter 13.

The main thing to ensure with BULK INSERT is that the DATAFILETYPE parameter matches the flag used when exporting the data. Essentially, -n maps to native and -N maps to widenative.

The BULK INSERT snippet in step 2 of this recipe used only one of the available options. As you may surmise, there are many others. Table 5-2 provides a succinct overview.

Table 5-2. BULK INSERT Options

Parameter	Definition	Comments
DATAFILETYPE='native'	The native (database) data type	SQL Server data types are used, and all character fields are non-Unicode.
DATAFILETYPE='widenative'	The native (database) data types and Unicode data type for character data	SQL Server data types are used, and all character fields are Unicode.
ERRORFILE='pathandfile'	The error file	The file name and full path for the error file used to log errors.
KEEPNULLS	Null value handling	Any empty columns keep NULLs rather than inserting default values if these are specified.
KEEPIDENTITY	Keep Identity hint	This keeps IDENTITY data during an import.
CHECK_CONSTRAINTS	Check and foreign key constraints are applied during the load	The default is that no check constraints or foreign key constraints are applied.
FIRETRIGGERS	Triggers fire during the load	The default is not to fire triggers during a data load
FIRSTROW=n	The first row to be loaded	The default is the first row of the file.
LASTROW=n	The last row to be loaded	The default is the is last row of the file.
ROWS_PER_BATCH=n	The number of rows per batch of imported data	Each batch is imported and logged in a separate transaction. The whole batch must be successfully imported before any records are committed.
KILOBYTES_PER_BATCH=n	The batch size hint	Approximate number of kilobytes of data per batch.
MAXERRORS=n	The maximum number of errors before the load fails	Default = 10
ORDER	Sort hint	Tells BULK IMPORT the sort order of the source data. The source data **must** be sorted if this is used.
TABLOCK	Table locking hint	A table-level lock are applied during the load to minimize resources used on lock escalation

To see how you can use multiple load options, consider the following snippet, which takes the original BULK INSERT command and extends it to specify a number of options (C:\SQL2012DIRecipes\CH05\BulkInsertWithOptions.Sql):

```
BULK INSERT CarSales_Staging.dbo.Client_BCP
FROM 'C:\SQL2012DIRecipes\CH05\Clients.bcp'
WITH
        (
          DATAFILETYPE = 'widenative'
         ,KEEPIDENTITY
         ,TABLOCK
```

```
        ,KEEPNULLS
        ,ERRORFILE='C:\SQL2012DIRecipes\CH05\BulkInsertErrors.txt'
        ,MAXERRORS=50
)
```

Hints, Tips, and Traps

- One final point to note is that, in my experience, you should always export data onto a local disk and load data from a local disk unless you have absolutely no alternative. Using data stored locally usually makes for shorter load times and offers less risk of load failure due to a timeout caused by network latency.

- You are probably best advised to drop all indexes on the destination table (in most cases) and re-create them afterward.

- The version of BCP utility used to read a format file must be the same as, or a later than the version of the format file. For example, SQL Server 2012 BCP can read a version 10.0 format file, which is generated by SQL Server 2008 BCP; but SQL Server 2008 BCP cannot read a version 11.0 format file, which is generated by SQL Server 2012 BCP.

- If you want to create the BCP export file, then you can use the following code:

```
C:\>BCP "SELECT ID, ClientName, Town, County, ClientSize, ClientSince FROM CarSalesdbo.Client ↵
ORDER BY ID" queryout C:\SQL2012DIRecipes\CH05\Clients.bcp -N -SADAMO2\AdamRemote ↵
-UAdam -PMe1BOss
```

5-4. Load Data Exported from SQL Server from the Command Line

Problem

You want to load data exported from SQL Server using the command line, without using SSMS or SQLCMD.

Solution

Run BCP.exe to load the data—previously exported as a native BCP file—from a Command window.

Loading data from a native BCP file can be as simple as (C:\SQL2012DIRecipes\CH05\BCPLoad.cmd):

```
BCP CarSales_Staging.dbo.Client_BCP IN C:\SQL2012DIRecipes\CH05\Clients.bcp -N -T -SADAMO2
```

How It Works

Should you prefer the time-honored way of importing data, then the venerable BCP can import it for you. The code in this recipe, run from a command prompt, imports the file used in Recipe 5-3 into the destination table whose DDL is in that same recipe. In fact, it is essentially identical to the BULK INSERT command used earlier. One major difference is that you can run it without SSMS or SQLCMD.

As you can see, this is very close to the T-SQL used for a BULK INSERT. The major difference is that you needed to add security information; in this case, -T for integrated security.

The following are things to note from the start:

- The destination table must exist in the destination database.

- It is normally best to drop any indexes before the data load and re-create them afterward.

- You can use a URL (\\server\share) rather than a drive letter to reference the source data file. Nonetheless, I suggest that you consider copying the data to a local disk before loading it for the reasons given in the previous recipe.

- Any of the options described in Table 5-3 can be used when running BCP.

- If tweaking all these case-sensitive flags in a command window is less than unhallowed pleasure for you, then you can always write the BCP command as a script (.cmd) file and run it by double-clicking.

There are many options that you may be required to use when loading data using BCP. Table 5-3 lists the key flags which you might need one day.

Table 5-3. *BCP Options*

Argument	Definition	Comments
-m	Maximum number of errors	Default = 10.
-n	The native (database) data types	SQL Server data types are used, and all character fields are non-Unicode.
–N	The native (database) data types and Unicode data type for character data	SQL Server data types are used, and all character fields are Unicode.
-S	The server or server\instance name	If no server is specified, BCP connects to the default instance of SQL Server on the local computer.
-U	User	The login ID used to connect to SQL Server.
-P	Password	The user password.
-T	Integrated security	If used, then no –P and –U flags can be used.
-e	An (optional) error file	The file name and full path for the error file used to log errors – if needed.
-F	The first row to be loaded	The default is the first row.
-L	The last row to be loaded	The default is the last row.
-b	The number of rows per batch of imported data	Each batch is imported and logged in a separate transaction. The whole batch must be successfully imported before anything is committed.
-V	Version	See Table 5-6.
-q	Quoted identifiers	This is used to specify a database, owner, table, or view name that contains a space or a single quotation mark. You must enclose the entire three-part table or view name in quotation marks.

(continued)

Table 5-3. (*continued*)

Argument	Definition	Comments
-a	Packet size	PacketSize can be from 4096 to 65535 bytes; the default is 4096. Increasing this can make a difference to throughput. You should, however, always test any changes you make to PacketSize to ensure that you are truly accelerating the load.
-k	Null value handling	Specifies that empty columns should retain a null value during the operation, rather than have any default values for the columns inserted.
-E	Keep Identity	Keeps IDENTITY data during an import.
-h "ORDER Colname1 ASC, Colname2 DESC"	Sort hint	Tells BCP what the sort order of the source file is.
-h "ROWS_PER_BATCH=n"	Batch size hint	The number of rows committed in a transaction.
-h "KILOBYTES_PER_BATCH=n"	Batch size hint	Approximate number of kilobytes of data per batch (can be used to generate a more efficient query plan that accelerates the load).
-h "TABLOCK"	Tablock hint	A table-level lock is applied during the load.
-h "CHECK_CONSTRAINTS"	Check and foreign key constraints are applied during the load	Default is not check constraints or foreign key constraints applied during data load.
-h "FIRE_TRIGGERS"	Triggers fire during the load	Triggers not fired during data load.

Hints, Tips, and Traps

- Remember that these arguments are case-sensitive!

- When loading BCP files in an SQL Server native (–n or -N) format, you will *not* need to use a format file. These are described in the next recipe.

- BCP can load a single table in parallel. This is explained in Chapter 13.

- Multiple hints can be used; an example is –h"TABLOCK,ORDER Col1 DESC".

- Unlike a QueryOut, there is no concept of a QueryIn with BCP. You have to load the entire table structure contained in the BCP file unless you use a format file. Of course, once loaded into a staging table, you can then transfer data into a final table, but this is clearly going to be very costly in terms of server resources.

- You cannot use the –b (batch size) and the ROWS_PER_BATCH or KILOBYTES_PER_BATCH hints together.

- Since SQL Server 2005, BCP.exe no longer performs implicit data type conversion.

- When data types do not match between the file and the target table, BCP.exe raises an error if there is any data that would have to be truncated to fit into the target table.

5-5. Loading SQL Server Data from a Native SQL Server File
Problem

You want to load SQL Server data from another SQL Server; however, you want to SELECT the records in the BCP file, change the column order, sort the data, and use standard T-SQL commands to shape the data.

Solution

Use OPENROWSET (BULK) and a format file to apply column mapping.

The following process not only loads data from an SQL Server native file, it also tweaks it on its way into the destination table.

1. Prepare the following format file (C:\SQL2012DIRecipes\CH05\Clients.fmt in the sample files), which corresponds to the BCP output file, in the old "classic" format:

```
11.0
6
1                0    4      " "   1   ID                " "
2   SQLNC        2    300    " "   2   ClientName        Latin1_General_CI_AS
3   SQLN         2    100    " "   3   Town              Latin1_General_CI_AS
4   SQLNCHAR     2    100    " "   4   County            Latin1_General_CI_AS
5   SQLNCHAR     2    20     " "   5   ClientSize        Latin1_General_CI_AS
6   SQLDATETIM4  1    4      " "   6   ClientSince       " "
```

2. Run the following T-SQL (C:\SQL2012DIRecipes\CH05\OpenRowsetShaped.Sql):

```
USE DATABASE CarSales;
GO

SELECT  CAST(ID AS VARCHAR(5)) AS IdentityNumber, LEFT(Town, 25) AS Town
INTO    MyTableForShapedBulkInserts
FROM    OPENROWSET(
                BULK 'C:\SQL2012DIRecipes\CH05\Clients.bcp'
                ,FORMATFILE='C:\SQL2012DIRecipes\CH05\Clients.fmt'
                ) as Cl
WHERE ClientSize = 'M'
ORDER BY County DESC;
```

This loads the source data into the MyTableForShapedBulkInserts table with slightly modified column order and data types.

How It Works

One of the four ways we look at in this chapter to load a BCP file (and the second which is T-SQL-based) is to use the OPENROWSET (BULK) command. The major difference between this approach and BCP is that here you can use T-SQL to sort and shape the data as it flows through a perfectly standard T-SQL-based Data Flow on its way to the destination table. However, a format file is absolutely indispensable in this case, and without it, the source file cannot be loaded. This is why the only two fundamental parameters that must be passed to OPENROWSET (BULK) are the source data file and the format file. Creating a format file is explained in Recipe 5-6.

OPENROWSET (BULK) has a more limited set of options than the two other techniques discussed previously. Table 5-4 presents the list of available possibilities.

Table 5-4. *OPENROWSET (BULK) Options*

Argument	Definition	Comments
FORMATFILE	A (compulsory) format file	The file name and full path of any format file used.
ERRORFILE	An (optional) error file	The file name and full path of any error log file used.
FIRSTROW	The first row to be loaded	The default is the first row.
LASTROW	The last row to be loaded	The default is the last row.
MAXERRORS	The maximum permissible number of errors	The maximum permissible number of errors before the load fails.
ORDER	Sort hint	Indicates the sort order of the source file.
ROWS_PER_BATCH	Batch size hint	Specifies the number of rows per transaction to be committed.
CODEPAGE	The codepage to be used	'ACP', 'OEM', 'RAW', or the 'code_page' itself.

The hints provided in Table 5-5 may also be used.

Table 5-5. *OPENROWSET (BULK) Hints*

Hint	Comments
TABLOCK	Apply a table lock.
IGNORE_CONSTRAINTS	Do not apply table constraints.
IGNORE_TRIGGERS	Do not apply table triggers.
KEEPDEFAULTS	Apply defaults to NULL columns.
KEEPIDENTITY	Keep IDENTITY data from the source file.

Hints, Tips, and Traps

- As mentioned, you must supply a valid format file (in the classic or newer XML format).

- The OPENROWSET dataset must be aliased.

- OPENROWSET (BULK) logs the data insert if the recovery model is "FULL". To ensure a non-logged operation, switch to a BULK LOGGED recovery model first. This means ensuring that you make a full backup immediately after the data load, and revert to the LOGGED recovery mode.

- Specifying column aliases in the rowset alias overrides the column names in the format file.

- One major parameter to note and potentially apply is ROWS_PER_BATCH. For large data loads, setting a suitable figure for this parameter can optimize load times. The required number of rows for a batch depends on your environment, so it can only be arrived at by experimentation. The risk of using the default is that a large load could require full table scans in memory that can slow down the load. Equally, setting a suitable figure for ROWS_PER_BATCH can mean not losing data already loaded in the case of a failure, and a restart from the FIRSTROW corresponding to the row immediately following the last successful batch.

- If you want to get the benefits of optimized loads with a suitable ROWS_PER_BATCH defined, but require no data to be loaded in the case of a failure, then you can enclose the T-SQL given in step 2 in a transaction to ensure a complete rollback in the event of a failure.

5-6. Transferring Data Between SQL Server Databases Regularly

Problem

You want to load data (exported as BCP native format) using SSIS as part of a regular ETL process.

Solution

Use the SSIS BULK INSERT task. The following steps describe how to do it.

1. Create (or have the people providing the source data deliver) a BCP data file (in widenative format, using the default column and row delimiters) from the source data table, or view using code similar to the following on a command line:

    ```
    bcp CarSales_Staging.dbo.Client OUT C:\SQL2012DIRecipes\CH05\ClientForBulkInsert.bcp ↩
     -T -SADAM02 -N
    ```

2. Create a new SSIS package.

3. Add an OLEDB connection manager to the destination database named **CarSales_Staging_OLEDB**. Configure it to connect to the CarSales_Staging database.

4. Add a Flat File connection manager and configure it to connect to the BCP file created in step 1. Name it **BCPConnection**.

5. Add a BULK INSERT task onto the Control Flow pane. Double-click this task to edit it.

6. Click Connections in the list on the left and select the CarSales_Staging_OLEDB destination connection.

7. Select the dbo.Client destination table.

8. In the Source Connection File field, select the BCPConnection defined in step 4. Once complete, the dialog box should look like Figure 5-2.

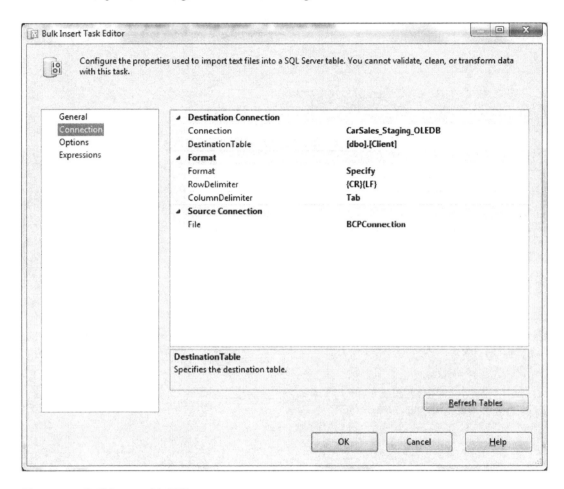

Figure 5-2. *Bulk Insert with SSIS*

9. Click Options in the pane on the left. Ensure that the data file type is set to widenative (as this was the BCP export option chosen).

10. Select the Keep Nulls and Table Lock options. You should see a dialog box like Figure 5-3.

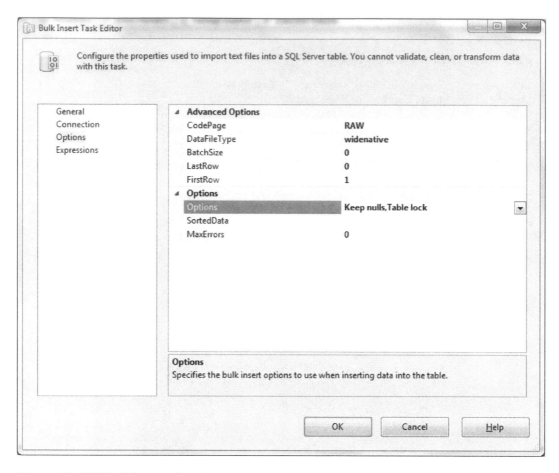

Figure 5-3. SSIS Bulk Insert task options

      11.   Click OK to confirm your selections.

You can now run the SSIS package and load the data into SQL Server.

How It Works

SSIS can also perform BULK INSERTs of SQL Server source data in native format. A BULK INSERT task cannot perform any data cleansing or data modification during the data load, however. Also, you must ensure that you are using the type of native format (character or Unicode) that you specified when exporting the data itself. Moreover, the destination table must exist before you can set up this package. This technique is quite possibly the fastest load option available in SSIS.

This example used the default column and row terminators (tab and CR/LF). If these are set to anything different as part of the BCP export command, then you need to ensure that the corresponding terminators are chosen in the Connection pane of the BULK INSERT task editor. Similarly, if you have chosen—or been given—a different data file type (native, character, or widechar) in the source file, you need to ensure that this maps to the character type chosen in the BULK INSERT task.

Hints, Tips, and Traps

- If the source data is already sorted, then you can enter the column(s) composing the sort keys at step 10 in the SortedData field.

- If the destination table does not map exactly to the source table structure, or if you wish to load only a subset of columns, then you have to define and use a format file.

- There are many ways in which bulk loads of data using BCP, BULK INSERT, and OPENROWSET (BULK) can be optimized. Please see Chapter 14 for details on bulk load optimization.

- BULK INSERT treats scientific-notation float data as invalid and gives conversion errors. You must use a format file if faced with this problem.

5-7. Porting a Tiny Amount of Data Between SQL Server Databases

Problem

You want to transfer a small amount of data between SQL Server databases quickly and easily without any complex T-SQL or using SSIS.

Solution

Script out the data from SSMS as INSERT statements.

The following steps detail how you can carry out this operation.

1. Right-click the database name. Select Tasks ➤ Generate scripts.

2. Click Next if the introduction dialog box is displayed.

3. Click Select Specific Objects. Expand Tables and check the table(s) whose data you wish to script out. The dialog box should look something like Figure 5-4.

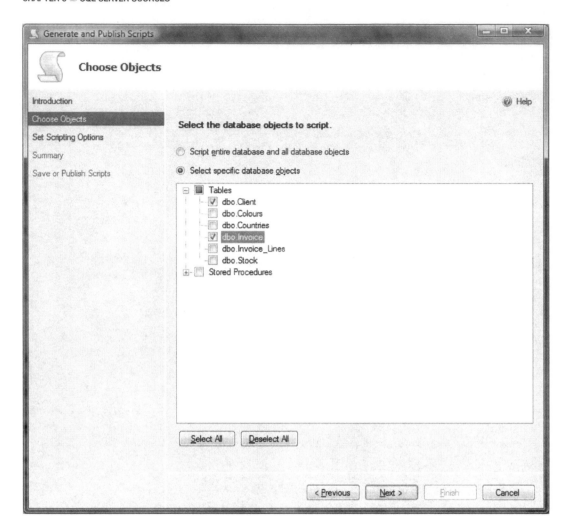

Figure 5-4. *Scripting data from SSMS*

4. Click Next, and then click Advanced. Find the Types of Data to Script option. Select Data Only, as shown in Figure 5-5.

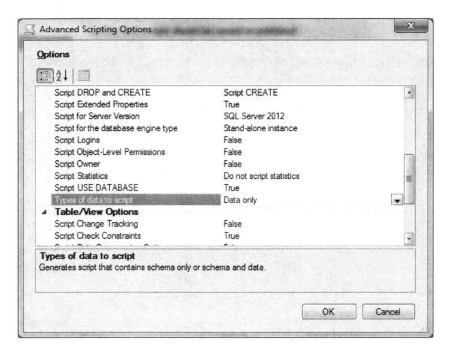

Figure 5-5. *Data scripting options in SSMS*

5. Click OK. Define a file in which to save the script. Then click through Next, Next, and Finish.

If you open the file you defined in step 5, you see a (very long-winded) series of insert statements, like the following shortened version of an output file.

```
SET IDENTITY_INSERT [dbo].[Client] ON
INSERT [dbo].[Client] ([ID], [ClientName], [Address1], [Address2], [Town], [County],
[PostCode], [Country], [ClientType], [ClientSize], [ClientSince], [IsCreditWorthy],
[DealerGroup], [MapPosition])
VALUES (3, N'John Smith', N'4, Grove Drive', NULL, N'Uttoxeter', N'Staffs', NULL, 1,
N'Private', N'M', NULL, 1, NULL, NULL)
INSERT [dbo].[Client] ([ID], [ClientName], [Address1], [Address2], [Town], [County],
[PostCode], [Country], [ClientType], [ClientSize], [ClientSince], [IsCreditWorthy],
[DealerGroup], [MapPosition])
VALUES (7, N'Slow Sid', N'2, Rue des Bleues', NULL, N'Avignon', N'Vaucluse', NULL, 3,
N'Private', N'M', NULL, 1, NULL, NULL)
SET IDENTITY_INSERT [dbo].[Client] OFF
```

261

How It Works

If you have only (relatively) small amounts of data to transfer between SQL Server, then you can always use SSMS to script out the data from one or more tables. This creates a series of INSERT ... VALUES statements—one for each record in the data source.

Hopefully you can see why this is not recommended for large quantities of data. However, for small reference tables that have to be inserted into database creation scripts, it is an incredibly useful technique to know and use.

Hints, Tips, and Traps

- You might be tempted to use the "script for server version" to try and copy data over to an older version of SQL Server. If the current version of SQL Server contains data types (such as GEOGRAPHY, GEOMETRY, or HIERARCHYID) that are incompatible with the chosen SQL Server version, then the script creation fails.

- There is no option to choose the columns to script out. Equally unfortunately, you cannot script the data from a view. So if you want to subset a table's data vertically, you have to perform a SELECT...INTO to export the data into a new table, script out the data from this "staging" table, and then delete it.

5-8. Copying and Pasting Between Tables

Problem

You want to copy a tiny amount of data between a couple of tables without any hassle or time spent on the process.

Solution

Copy and paste the data.

Incredible as it may sound, this can be done as follows:

1. In SSMS, expand the database containing the source table, expand Tables, right-click the table whose data (all or in part) you want to copy, and select Edit Top 200 Rows.

2. Click inside the data table that is displayed and select Query Designer ➤ Pane ➤ SQL (or click the Show SQL toolbar button).

3. Add a suitable WHERE clause to the SQL SELECT statement to display the data you wish to copy, and alter TOP (200) to match the approximate number of records that you plan to copy.

4. Click the Execute toolbar button or select Query ExecuteSQL.

5. Select all the output data (by clicking in the gray square to the left of the first column header in the grid). You should see something like Figure 5-6.

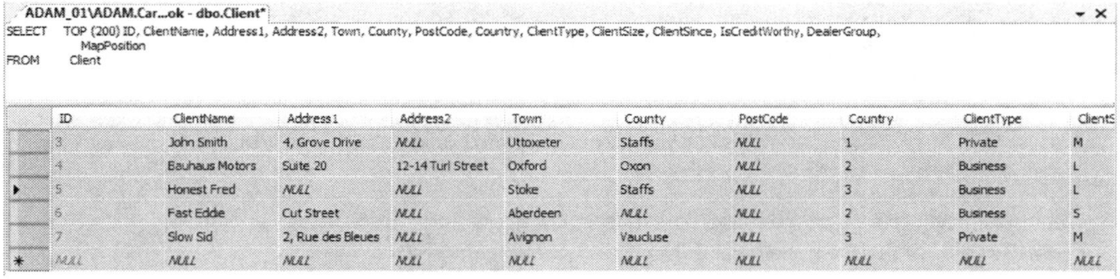

Figure 5-6. *Copying and pasting data in SSMS*

6. Copy the data (I will not insult your intelligence by saying how).

7. Right-click the destination table. Select Edit Top 200 Rows.

8. Select a blank record (for instance, at the bottom of the record set) and paste the data.

How It Works

I imagine that the thought of simply copying and pasting hundreds or thousands of rows of data into an SQL Server table has most developers' eyebrows raised. Well, it is possible—and it can be a valuable time-saving technique when deploying databases and synchronizing development environments. You will note that I am not suggesting this as a production technique. It is nonetheless worth looking at, as you can do in SQL Server what Access developers have been doing for 20 years.

You need a destination table identical in structure to the source data—right down to column order. This destination table must not contain any duplicate key data.

Hints, Tips, and Traps

- You can define a view as the data source, and copy from this. Your destination table must be identical in structure to the view, however.

- This is not (really, truly not) recommended for large amounts of data.

- I doubt that you would want to use this in a mission-critical environment.

5-9. Loading Data as Fast as Possible in an ETL Process
Problem

You want to load data as fast as possible on a regular basis as part of an ETL process.

Solution

Use the SSIS SQL Server Destination as part of an SSIS project. This requires you to do the following:

1. Create a new SSIS package.

2. Add an OLEDB source connection manager. Configure it to use the ADAM02\Remote server and the CarSales database.

3. Click the Data Flow tab. As no Data Flow task has been added yet, click "No Data Flow tasks have been added to this package. Click here to add a new Data Flow task".

4. Add a new OLEDB source task, and configure it to use the Client table as the data source.

5. Add an SQL Server destination task to the Data Flow, and connect the source task to it. Double-click to edit the SQL Server destination task.

6. Click New and create a new OLEDB connection manager using the SQL Server Native Client 11.0. Configure it to point to the CarSales_Staging database.

7. Select Client as the destination table.

8. Click Mappings on the left. Map the available columns.

9. Click Advanced on the left to display the Advanced tab.

10. Check Keep Identity, Table Lock, and Keep Nulls. The dialog box should look like Figure 5-7.

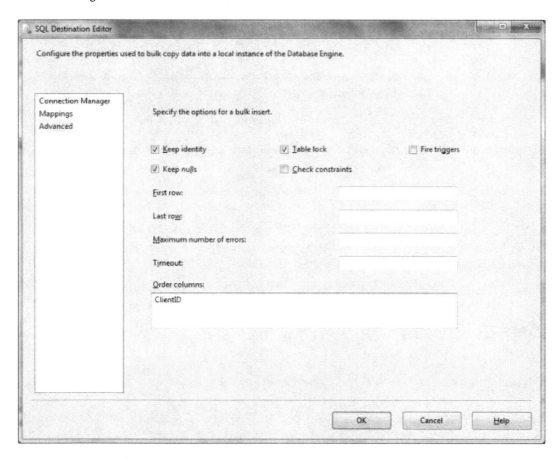

Figure 5-7. *Specifying the advanced options for the SSIS Bulk Insert task*

11. Click OK.

You can now run the package and insert the source data into the destination database.

How It Works

So far in this book, we have only used OLEDB destinations in SSIS packages. Yet there is another destination option, which is the SQL Server Destination. You do not have to be loading data from another SQL Server to use the SQL Server destination—I simply chose to discuss it in this chapter. The SQL Server destination can be used to load data from any data source, and has been the subject of much debate given its presumed advantages and drawbacks. Quite simply—and providing that you are running SSIS on the server where the destination SQL server instance is running—you can use it instead of an OLEDB destination. Essentially, the core options are those that are available when using BULK INSERT, which are described in Recipe 5-3.

So there you have the SQL Server destination. But why does it arouse such discussion? After all, all that happens is that the SQL Server destination provides high-speed data insertion into SQL Server as does the BULK INSERT task. The difference is that by using the SQL Server destination, you can apply transformations to column data during the load process. The big problem seems to be that any speed gain (itself somewhat disputed, but tangible in most cases due to the shared memory used to connect to the SQL server database) is mitigated by these facts:

- This is a non-scalable solution because you cannot move the package to another machine without replacing the SQL Server destination with an OLEDB destination.

- You have to edit the package on the server on which it will be running.

Since SQL Server 2012 appeared, there has been much discussion in the blogosphere as to whether the SQL Server destination even provides a speed advantage anymore. All I can suggest is that you test it in your environment if you want to try to achieve a small decrease in load times. Anyway, now that you know the advantages and limitations, you can choose to use it or not. I suspect that this decision depends on the restrictions of your environment and potential speed gain when loading data.

5-10. Importing and Exporting All the Tables in a Database
Problem

You want to export and import the tables in one SQL Server database to another SQL Server instance.

Solution

Use T-SQL and the database metadata to create BCP import and export scripts for a subset of tables. You can then run the scripts to (first) export and then import the data.

1. Run the following script with the @InOut variable set to 1 on the source SQL Server to get a list of the BCP commands (one per table) that exports the data on the source SQL Server database. This script is C:\SQL2012DIRecipes\CH05\BCPAllTablesOutAndIn.Sql in the samples.

```
DECLARE @InOut BIT = 0;
DECLARE @BCPDatabaseName  VARCHAR(128)      = 'CarSales';
DECLARE @BCPDirectoryName VARCHAR(128)      = 'C:\SQL2012DIRecipes\CH05\';
DECLARE @BCPParameters    VARCHAR(100)      = '-T';
DECLARE @BCPOutServer     VARCHAR(50)       = 'ADAM02';
DECLARE @SQLTextBI        NVARCHAR(4000)    = '';
DECLARE @SQLTextBCP       NVARCHAR(4000)    = '';
DECLARE @SQLParametersBulkInsert NVARCHAR(4000)  =
                                    N'@BCPDatabaseNameIN VARCHAR(128)
                                    ,@BCPDirectoryNameIN   VARCHAR(128)';
```

```
DECLARE @SQLParametersBCPOUT NVARCHAR(4000) =
                                           N'@BCPDatabaseNameIN VARCHAR(128)
                                           ,@BCPDirectoryNameIN VARCHAR(128)
                                           ,@BCPOutServerIN VARCHAR(128)
                                           ,@BCPParametersIN VARCHAR(128)';
DECLARE @BCPSchemaName VARCHAR(128);
DECLARE @BCPTableName VARCHAR(128);


IF @InOut = 1

BEGIN
SET @SQLTextBCP = 'SELECT ''BCP '' + @BCPDatabaseNameIN + ''.'' + TABLE_SCHEMA + ''.''
+ TABLE_NAME + '' OUT '' + @BCPDirectoryNameIN + TABLE_SCHEMA + ''_'' + TABLE_NAME
+ ''.bcp'' + '' -N '' + ''-S'' + @BCPOutServerIN + '' '' + @BCPParametersIN '

SET @SQLTextBCP = @SQLTextBCP + ' FROM ' + @BCPDatabaseName + '.INFORMATION_SCHEMA.TABLES'
SET @SQLTextBCP = @SQLTextBCP + ' WHERE TABLE_TYPE = ''BASE TABLE''';

EXECUTE master.dbo.sp_executesql @SQLTextBCP
                            ,@SQLParametersBCPOUT
                            ,@BCPDatabaseNameIN = @BCPDatabaseName
                            ,@BCPDirectoryNameIN = @BCPDirectoryName
                            ,@BCPOutServerIN = @BCPOutServer
                            ,@BCPParametersIN = @BCPParameters;

END

ELSE

BEGIN
SET @SQLTextBI = 'SELECT ''BULK INSERT '' + @BCPDatabaseNameIN + ''.'' + TABLE_SCHEMA
+ ''.'' + TABLE_NAME + '' FROM '''''' + @BCPDirectoryNameIN + TABLE_SCHEMA + ''_''
+ TABLE_NAME + ''.bcp'''' WITH (DATAFILETYPE='''''widenative''''')'''

SET @SQLTextBI = @SQLTextBI + ' FROM ' + @BCPDatabaseName + '.INFORMATION_SCHEMA.TABLES'
SET @SQLTextBI = @SQLTextBI + ' WHERE TABLE_TYPE = ''BASE TABLE''';

EXECUTE master.dbo.sp_executesql @SQLTextBI
                            ,@SQLParametersBulkInsert
                            ,@BCPDatabaseNameIN = @BCPDatabaseName
                            ,@BCPDirectoryNameIN = @BCPDirectoryName;
END
```

2. Execute the output from the script on the source server to create the BCP native files.

3. Copy the BCP files to the destination server.

4. Run the script with the @InOut variable set to 0 to get the script that loads the BCP files.

5. Run the output of the script—the BULK INSERT commands that reloads the data.

How It Works

Transferring data from SQL Server can sometimes involve an entire database or a large subset. In the best of all possible worlds, of course, you just use backup and restore. Fortunately, SQL Server lets you backup and restore between 64-bit and 32-bit environments, as the SQL Server on-disk storage format is the same in the 64-bit and 32-bit environments. Consequently, a backup created on a server instance running in one environment can be restored on a server instance that runs in the other environment. However, as I am sure you have found, backup and restore will not work at all in some cases—such as (sometimes) from a more recent version of SQL Server to an older version.

In these cases, one solution is to export the selected tables as BCP files, and then to reload them with BULK INSERT. I am not suggesting that this is an optimal solution; only that it has always worked for me when other solutions were overly complex or unfeasible.

This snippet uses the database metadata to select all the tables and create the corresponding BCP .. OUT and BULK INSERT scripts for all the tables. All you have to do is set the @InOut parameter in this snippet to 1 to obtain a script that you can then run to export one BCP file per database table. Inversely, setting the @InOut parameter to 0 outputs a script that imports the same tables on a destination server. Of course, you must set the @BCPDirectoryName parameter to the directory where you want to store the BCP files in each case, just as you have to set your own server (@BCPOutServer), staging directory (@BCPOutServer), and database (@BCPDatabaseName).

This script makes no bones about being simple and efficient—that is, it will not handle many levels of complexity such as foreign key dependencies, primary keys, and identity insert, to name but a few. It will help you to transfer data remarkably quickly and easily, however.

Hints, Tips, and Traps

- This snippet can be tweaked to select (or exclude) tables through judicious use of the WHERE clause used to return data from the INFORMATION_SCHEMA tables.

- You can parallelize the process by running separate BCP and BULK INSERT commands simultaneously—for different tables and files, of course.

5-11. Loading Data from Different Versions of SQL Server
Problem

You want to load data from older versions of SQL Server into SQL Server 2005, 2008, and 2012 using a native format.

Solution

Use BCP to export, and then import, the data in native format to ensure that the tables are loaded quickly and flawlessly.

The following code snippet imports a BCP file exported from a previous version of SQL Server (C:\SQL2012DIRecipes\CH05\BCPNative.cmd) in the sample files:

```
BCP CarSales_Staging.dbo.Client_BCP IN C:\SQL2012DIRecipes\CH05\Clients.bcp -N -T -V 70 -SADAMO2
```

How It Works

Sometimes you may have a series of tables to export from an older version of SQL Server that you want to re-import into SQL Server 2005 or 2008. To do this, you must import the tables from the older version of SQL Server using the BCP version for that server. When importing with BCP, add the −v NN flag, where NN is the version number. The BCP version options are provided in Table 5-6.

Table 5-6. *BCP Version Options*

Flag	Description
-V 70	SQL Server version 7.0
-V 80	SQL Server 2000
-V 90	SQL Server 2005
-V 100	SQL Server 2008
-V 110	SQL Server 2012

In SQL Server 2012, the BCP utility only supports native data files compatible with SQL Server 7.0, SQL Server 2000, SQL Server 2005, and SQL Server 2008. SQL Server 6.0 and SQL Server 6.5 native data files are not supported by SQL Server 2012.

Hints, Tips, and Traps

- Be sure to use the flag corresponding to the data type that was used for the export.
- The destination table structure must exist in the destination database.
- Remember, it is normally best to drop any indexes and re-create them.
- The BCP options described in Recipe 5-4 can also be used.
- If you are importing data from SQL Server 6.0 or 6.5, then your best option is to export as text (-c or -w) and create a format file. Then you can load the text file as if it came from any source system.

5-12. Copying Entire Databases
Problem

You want to copy all the data in a database between SQL Server instances as simply as possible.

Solution

Use a COPY_ONLY backup to transfer all the database objects—and the data—to a new database without disrupting any backup sequencing.

This simple but effective technique requires you to do to the following.

1. Use the following code snippet to create a COPY_ONLY backup (this cannot be done using the SSMS GUI) and must be done using a T-SQL script in a query window:

```
BACKUP DATABASE CarSales TO DISK=' C:\SQL2012DIRecipes\CH05\CopyOnlyDatabase.bak'
WITH INIT, COPY_ONLY
```

2. Then, to restore the database on another SQL Server, use T-SQL along these lines:

```
RESTORE DATABASE CopyOnlyDatabase
FROM  DISK = N' C:\SQL2012DIRecipes\CH05\CopyOnlyDatabase.bak'
WITH  REPLACE,
MOVE 'CarSales' TO ' C:\SQL2012DIRecipes\CH05\CopiedDatabase.Mdf',
MOVE 'CarSales_log' TO ' C:\SQL2012DIRecipes\CH05\CopiedDatabase.ldf'
```

These scripts are in C:\SQL2012DIRecipes\CH05\CopyOnlyBackup.Sql in the sample files.

How It Works

Should you need all the data in an SQL Server database, then you can copy the entire database and restore it on the destination server. There is a trick to ensure that this simple operation does not cause problems with your backup strategy, however. You must use the COPY_ONLY parameter of the BACKUP command to ensure that the LSNs in your differential and log backups are not altered by a backup that is used as a data transfer technique, and not as part of a recovery strategy. If you are looking at performing a partial transfer of a database, you have to DROP unwanted tables and any other objects in the restored copy of the source database.

Hints, Tips, and Traps

- A backup copy using COPY_ONLY preserves the existing log archive point and, therefore, does not have any effect on the sequencing of regular log backups.

- You cannot use the Management Studio GUI to restore the database because you will not be able to display the backup file in the list of backup sets to restore. You have to use a script to perform the restore.

5-13. Transferring a Complex Subset of Data Between Databases

Problem

You want to transfer a complex, but clearly defined, subset of data from multiple tables between databases.

Solution

Apply snapshot replication between databases.

The following is an overview of how to set up snapshot replication.

1. Set up a distributor on the SQL Server instance that will be the replication subscriber by right-clicking Replication and selecting Configure Distribution (if distribution already exists for this instance, you need to select Distributor Properties). Skip the Configure Distribution Wizard splash screen by clicking Next. The Distributor dialog box appears.

2.   Since in this example the subscriber is the distributor, the wizard has correctly inferred the instance to use it. Confirm with Next. The Snapshot Folder dialog box appears.

3.   Enter a new network path for the snapshots if you are not willing to use the standard SQL Server path. Click Next. The Distribution Database dialog box appears.

4.   Change any paths that you find unacceptable, and then change the Distribution Database name if you prefer another name. Then click Next to display the Publishers dialog box. This will have selected the current instance as a Publisher, so uncheck this instance name. Next, click Add, and then select the instance that is publishing its data.

5.   Click Next to display the Distributor Password dialog box. Enter the Distributor Password. Make sure that you note this!

6.   Click Next twice, and then click Finish to configure the Publisher. Hopefully, you see the final dialog box confirming that the distribution has been configured successfully.

7.   You now need to configure the publication—the source data, in effect. In the SQL Server instance that supplies the data, expand Replication, right-click Local Publications, and select New Publication. Click Next to bypass the splash screen. The Distributor dialog box appears.

8.   Select the Use the Following Server as the Distributor radio button. Click Add to Select the Distributor. Confirm your choice. Click Next.

9.   Enter the Administrative password that you set (and noted) earlier. Click Next.

10. Select the database containing the object(s) that you want to replicate. The Publication Database dialog box lists all available databases. Click Next.

11. Select Snapshot Replication from the Publication Type dialog box. Click Next.

12. Select the Table(s) to publish.

13. Click Next to display the Filter Table Rows dialog box.

14. Click Next to display the Snapshot Agent dialog box. Check the Create a Snapshot Immediately check box and the Schedule the Snapshot Agent check box (also configure the schedule you require) if you wish for replication to be carried out on a regular basis.

15. Click Next. Select the security settings for the SQL Server Agent that the replication will run.

16. Click Next to display the Wizard Actions dialog box. Choose to create the publication immediately, script the creation, or both!

17. Click Next to display the final dialog box. Enter a name for the Publication.

18. Click Finish to complete the process. If you have selected immediate creation of the publication, the snapshot is created. A final dialog box shows you the status of the process.

19. You now need to set up the subscriber. Expand Replication, right-click Local Subscriptions, and select New Subscription. Click Next to bypass the splash screen. The Publication dialog box then allows you to select a publication. Select the SQL Server instance that is publishing the data (you can browse for it if necessary). Click Next.

20.   Select Run All Agents at the Distributor. Click Next.

21.   Select the database (you can create it from this dialog box if it does not already exist). Click Next.

22.   Select the account under which Distribution will run. Click Next.

23.   Select a synchronization schedule. Click Next.

24.   Ensure that the Initialize check box is ticked so that the replication is initialized. Click Next.

25.   Choose to create the subscription immediately, or to script the creation, or both. Click Next.

26.   Verify that you have chosen all the options that you wanted. Click Finish.

27.   The subscription is created and the data is loaded into the subscriber database. You should see the final dialog box confirming that all has run smoothly.

How It Works

The solution is an extremely succinct overview of snapshot replication. You did the following:

1.   Set up an SQL Server distributor on the source server.

2.   Defined the publisher (source) database and the source data (the publication).

3.   Ran the initial process to create a snapshot of the source data.

4.   Set up the destination (subscriber) database.

5.   Loaded the snapshot data into the destination.

One method of transferring data from one SQL Server instance to another that cannot be left out of the data integration toolkit of any SQL developer or DBA is replication. As this is a vast subject with multiple ramifications, I will not go into the full details of all the types of replication, and specifically all the management issues that can arise. I can only refer you to *Pro SQL Server 2005 Replication* by Sujoy Paul (Apress, 2006), which covers the ground in detail and with clarity. However, as an effective way of importing and updating data tables (and of course subsets of data tables), replication is an efficient technology. If snapshot replication works, then it can be a lifesaving technology. If it doesn't, then it can consume hours or days of your life as you try to make it work. However, that is another story.

I only covered snapshot replication because it can be claimed to be a data integration technique. For details on transactional and merge replication, peer-to-peer replication, and managing replication, I suggest that you consult some of the excellent material already written on the subject.

As far as terminology is concerned, mapping replication to data integration is not difficult. Essentially, the data source is the replication publisher, and the data destination is the replication subscriber. The distributor can be considered a part of the subscriber in this example, merely because I am presuming that this is a more "local" instance. Of course, you can set up the distributor on the publisher, subscriber, or on a separate SQL Server instance.

Assuming that you want to use this technique, just make sure that you are aware of the potential drawbacks. Specifically, that locks are held during the replication process and all destination data is completely overwritten.

5-14. Loading Data into SQL Server Azure Interactively

Problem

You want to load data directly into an SQL Azure database interactively.

Solution

Use SSMS and write a SELECT...INTO or INSERT INTO...SELECT query.

You can script data into an Azure table using SSMS just as you can into a traditional SQL Server table. All you have to do is the following.

1. Connect to the cloud-based database, as shown in Figure 5-8.

Figure 5-8. *Connecting to SQL Server Azure*

2. You can then run a standard INSERT INTO...VALUES statement to insert data in a query window.

How It Works

As we are living in interesting times, we are facing interesting new challenges, and using cloud-hosted databases is one of the most exciting new things to happen in quite a while. So how does SQL Server manage this new opportunity?

The answer is "with considerable ease"—providing that you are using SQL Server 2008 R2 or later. If you are using SQL Server 2008, then you can use only SSIS.

Describing how to set up an SQL Server Azure database is beyond the scope of this book; but presuming that you have an Azure database subscription, and that you have defined the required firewall rules to allow your workstation to communicate with SQL Server Azure, then you can load data into a cloud-hosted database almost as if it were on your local server.

Because you will meet them frequently in these recipes, I prefer to explain the connection string parameters of the SQL Server Azure database. This helps you understand the various code snippets and screen captures that you encounter. The SQL Azure connection parameters are provided in Table 5-7.

Table 5-7. *SQL Azure Connection Parameters*

Parameter	Element
User	MeForPrimeMinister
Server	recipes.database.windows.net
Password	Gubbins
Database	CarSales

Hints, Tips, and Traps

- SQL Server Azure only supports SQL Server authentication.

- You must use the fully qualified DNS name as it is given in the Azure Management Portal.

5-15. Loading Data into SQL Server Azure as Part of a Regular ETL Process

Problem

You want to load data SQL Server Azure as part of a regular ETL process.

Solution

Use SSIS to load data into Azure. This is done as follows:

1. Create a new SSIS package, name it appropriately, and add a new OLEDB connection manager to your source database (CarSales in this recipe). Name it **Source_OLEDB**.

2. Add a new ADO.NET connection manager named **Azure_ADONET**. Configure it to connect to your SQL Server Azure database, as shown in Figure 5-9.

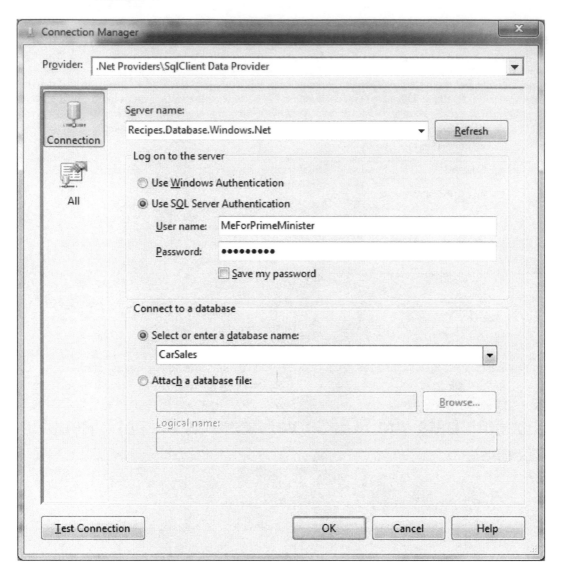

Figure 5-9. SSIS and .NET connection to SQL Server Azure

3. Add a new Data Flow task to the Control Flow pane. Double-click to edit.

4. Add an OLEDB Data Flow source, double-click to edit, and configure as follows:

OLEDB Connection Manager:	Source_OLEDB
Data Access Mode:	SQL Command
SQL Text:	SELECT ClientName, Country, Town, County,
	Address1, Address2, ClientType, ClientSize
	FROM dbo.Client

5. Add an ADO.NET destination. Connect the OLEDB source.

Connection Manager:	Azure_ADONET
Use a table or view:	"dbo"."Client"

6. Click Mappings and map all the columns between the source and the destination.
   Click OK to confirm your modifications.

How It Works

This process is virtually identical to a "standard" SSIS package used to load data into SQL Server. This is because SSIS SQL Server Azure is a (largely) normal data source or destination. Indeed, Azure supports both ADO.NET and OLEDB connection managers. However, the only slight difference is that you cannot select the database name, but must enter it in the database name pop-up list. In a real-world scenario, you will inevitably need an SSIS configuration file (or another configuration method) to store the password used to connect to the SQL Server Azure database.

Hints, Tips, and Traps

- You can also use an OLEDB destination if you prefer. This means configuring an OLEDB connection manager for the Azure database. It is identical to the ADO.NET connection manager except in one respect—the username must also have @ServerName appended, as shown in Figure 5-10.

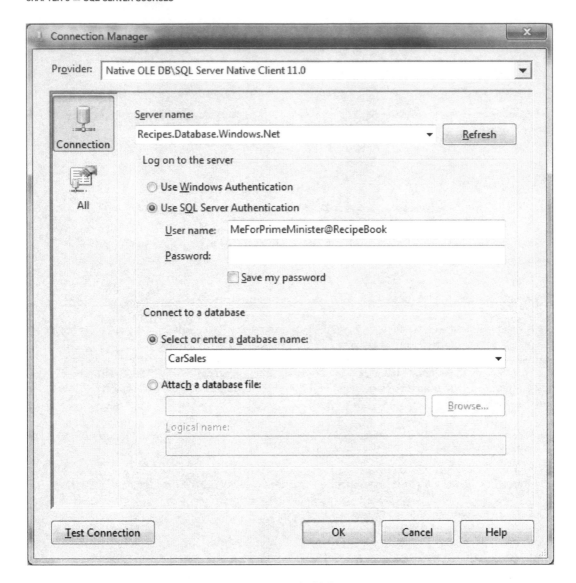

Figure 5-10. *OLEDB connection to SQL Server Azure in SSIS*

- While it is possible to use SSIS to create the destination tables, I recommend scripting and creating the requisite DDL using SSMS, as it helps to avoid the pitfalls that can trip up the unwary developer when moving to SQL Server Azure. One such trap is the absolute requirement for a clustered index, which SSIS does not add for you and then causes the data load to fail. Otherwise, remember to create a clustered index after you have created the table using SSIS.

- You can use any data source that you would use normally to load data into SQL Server Azure. You can use SSIS to its full potential to transform the data.

- An Azure connection manager can be defined at package level if you are using SQL Server 2012. Also available, since SSIS for SQL Server 2008 R2, is the "Use bulk insert when possible" option, which speeds up larger data loads.

5-16. Loading Data into SQL Server Azure from the Command Line

Problem

You want to load data into SQL Azure quickly and easily from the command line.

Solution

Load data into SQL Server Azure using BCP.

Providing that you have the version of BCP starting with SQL Server 2008 R2, you can load data into SQL Server Azure.

1. Create a BCP export file, preferably in SQL Server native or widenative format, as this removes the need for format files.

2. Run the following BCP command:

```
C:\Users\Adam>BCP Carsales.dbo.client IN C:\SQL2012DIRecipes\CH05\Azure.BCP -U ↵
MeForPrimeMinister@recipebook -PGubbins -Srecipes.database.windows.net -N -E
```

How It Works

Should you prefer (or need) to load data the good old-fashioned way, you can use BCP to do it. You must use SQL Server authentication. It is essential to add @ServerName to the username in the BCP string. Of course, you can use your own user/server/password. As I wish to override the IDENTITY setting of the destination table, I am using the -E parameter here.

Hints, Tips, and Traps

- All other BCP elements are those described in Recipe 5-4.

- You must use the fully qualified DNS name as it is given in the Azure Management Portal as the server name.

5-17. Loading Ad Hoc Data into SQL Server Azure

Problem

You want a quick and user-friendly way to load ad hoc data into SQL Server Azure.

Solution

Use the Import/Export Wizard that can connect to SQL Server Azure, and load the data. This is easy to do.

1. Launch the Import/Export Wizard. Define your source database (SQL Server or other). Click Next to move the Choose a Destination page.

2. Select .Net Framework Data Provider for SQL Server.

3. Specify the following:

Parameter	Element
Data Source:	recipes.database.windows.net (your Azure Server)
UserID:	MeForPrimeMinister (your Azure user)
Password:	Gubbins (your Azure password)
Initial Catalog:	CarSales (your Azure database)
Trust Server Certificate:	True
Encrypt:	True

The dialog box should look something like Figure 5-11.

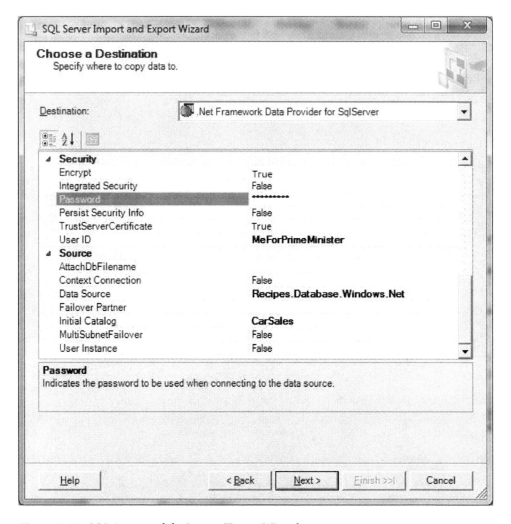

Figure 5-11. *SQL Azure and the Import/Export Wizard*

4. Continue as you would for any other SSIS load operation.

How It Works

Another valid option for importing data into SQL Server Azure is to use the Import/Export Wizard. As this has been amply described in Recipes 1-2 and 1-11, I will only point out the differences when using SQL Server Azure as a destination here. The database and tables must already exist in SQL Azure, however. It is worth noting that at the time of writing, SQL Server Azure does not support linked servers.

5-18. Transferring Tables Between Databases

Problem

You want to copy multiple tables and their data between SQL Server instances over a network connection, replacing any existing objects in the destination database.

Solution

Use SSIS and the Transfer Database Objects Task to copy selected tables, data, and potentially indexes, primary and foreign keys, and extended properties. The following steps describe the way to do it.

1. Create a new SSIS package.

2. Right-click in the Connection Managers tab and select Add Connection.

3. Select the SMOServer connection manager type. The dialog box should look like Figure 5-12.

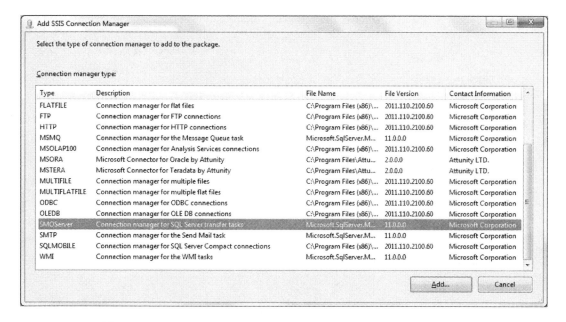

Figure 5-12. *Adding an SMOServer connection manager*

4. Click Add. Enter or browse for the source server. The dialog box should look like Figure 5-13.

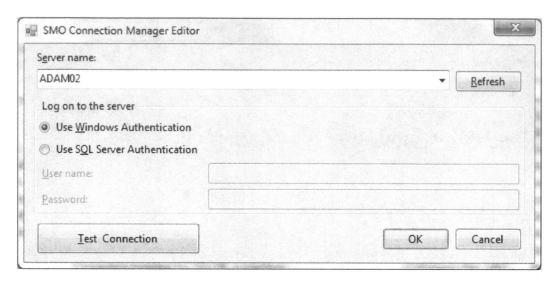

Figure 5-13. Configuring an SMOServer connection manager

5. Click Test Connection.

6. Click OK to confirm your modifications.

7. Right-click the connection manager in the Connection Managers tab and click Rename. Rename the connection manager **CarSales_OLEDB**.

8. Repeat Steps 4–6 for the destination server (Adam02\AdamRemote in this example). Name the connection manager **CarSales_Staging_OLEDB**.

9. Add a Transfer Database Objects Task to the Control Flow pane.

10. Double-click to edit the Transfer Database Objects Task.

11. Click Objects on the left.

12. Select CarSales_OLEDB as the source connection.

13. Select CarSales_Staging_OLEDB as the destination connection.

14. Select CarSales as the source database.

15. Select CarSales_Staging as the destination database.

16. Set the following properties:

DropObjectsFirst:	False
IncludeExtendedProperties:	True
CopySchema:	True
CopyData:	True
CopyAllObjects:	False
CopyPrimaryKeys:	False
CopyForeignKeys:	False

17. Expand ObjectsToCopy. Click the Ellipses button to the right.

18. Select the tables that you wish to copy. The dialog box should look like Figure 5-14.

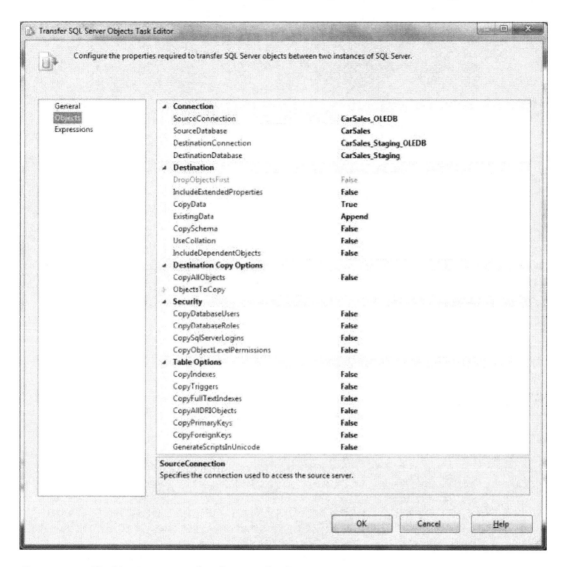

Figure 5-14. The SQL Server transfer Objects Task Editor

19. Click OK to confirm. You return to the Transfer SQL Server Objects Task Editor, which should look like Figure 5-15.

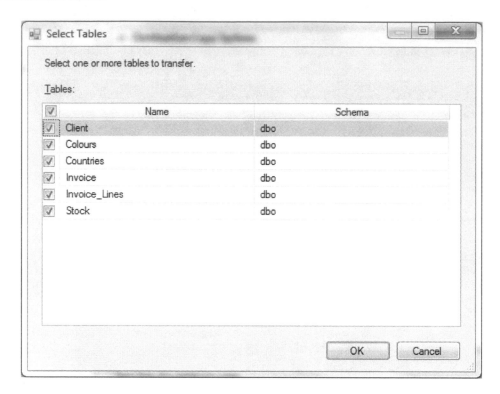

Figure 5-15. *Selecting the tables to transfer using the SSIS Transfer SQL Server Objects Task*

20.   Click OK to confirm.

You can now run the package. All the selected tables will have transferred.

How It Works

The Transfer SQL Server Objects Task is, in essence, a GUI to SQL Server Management Objects (SMO). This, as you probably know, is a collection of objects designed to make programming the management of SQL Server more accessible. One of the things that SMO can do (among so many others) is to drop and create tables, and to transfer data between tables. In this recipe, we are using the Transfer SQL Server Objects Task to carry out this operation. As you can see, it allows you to not only select the table(s) to be copied, but can also extend this operation by copying other elements such as indexes and primary/foreign keys.

You need to be warned that the Transfer SQL Server Objects Task is relatively simplistic in its approach, and is best suited to transferring tables and data that have few or no dependencies. However, as a tool for copying entire tables between SQL Server instances, it is unrivalled in its simplicity. A prerequisite for running this task is to use identical table structures in both the source and destination databases.

When using the Transfer SQL Server Objects Task to load data, you can also request that the task generate any required tables before it migrates the data. This is as simple as setting the CopySchema option to True. Be warned, however, that if the tables exist and you set CopySchema to True, then you will get an error when running the package, as the tables exist already. If you wish, you can set the option DropObjectsFirst to True, as well as CopySchema to True to replace the structure and data of the existing tables. If the tables already exist in the destination database and CopySchema is set to False, you will have the option to append—rather than replace—data by setting ExistingData to Replace.

The Transfer SQL Server Objects Task is an "all or nothing" solution as far as data migration is concerned. It will not allow you to subset source data, use source queries, or select only a partial column set. These limitations can be overcome by using workarounds such as running SELECT...INTO clauses to create temporary tables to serve as the data source; but then if you are going to do this, you may as well use other solutions to transfer the data, in my opinion. This task can—as you can see from the available options—do much more than just transfer data, but a complete analysis of these possibilities is outside the scope of this book.

Summary

This chapter contained many ways of getting data from SQL Server sources into SQL Server destinations. Some of them may seem similar, or to duplicate methods, or simply plain abstruse. To give you a clearer overview, Table 5-8 shows my take on the various methods, and their advantages and disadvantages.

Table 5-8. *Advantages and Disadvantages of the Methods Used in This Chapter*

Technique	Advantages	Disadvantages
OPENROWSET	Easy to use.	Slow (OLEDB).
OPENDATASOURCE	Easy to use.	Slow (OLEDB).
LINKED SERVER	Easy to use, secure.	Slow (OLEDB).
BULK INSERT	Incredibly fast.	Needs table metadata.
BCP	Extremely fast, fairly cryptic.	Needs to run outside SQL Server—or required xp_cmdshell rights. Needs table metadata.
OPENROWSET (BULK)	Fast.	File-based only. Requires format file. Needs table metadata.
SSIS (OLEDB)	Intuitive.	Not the fastest method.
SSIS BULK INSERT TASK	Incredibly fast.	File-based only, requires format file.
REPLICATION	Fast and automatic.	Complex to debug and troubleshoot.
Scripting out data	Incredibly easy.	Not for large amounts of data.
Backup copy	Incredibly easy.	The whole database or nothing.
Copy and paste	Unbelievably simple.	Only for miniscule amounts of data. Not suited to a production environment.

When you have to transfer data from one SQL Server instance to another, the only real difficulty is knowing which of the abundant available options to choose. At least that is how it may seem at first. As I have tried to show in this chapter, each of the available techniques has its advantages and disadvantages, with some being better suited to certain circumstances than others are.

So if you are only loading a few records of reference data, then a copy-and-paste may suffice. If you are moving a few hundred thousand records across a fast network, a linked server might a good solution. If you have to load many millions of records between servers, then you are probably best advised to think in terms of using BCP and BULK INSERT. However, it is not for me to mandate solutions. My goal for this chapter was to make you aware of the many available techniques, along with their salient features. You can choose the most appropriate technique for your specific requirements and environment.

CHAPTER 6

■ ■ ■

Miscellaneous Data Sources

To conclude our tour of source data, we need to look at a handful of data repositories that do not fall under the more clearly-defined categories of the first five chapters. I suppose that this is another way of saying that the current chapter is something of a ragbag of diverse data sources, so please accept the rather disjointed nature of them as we proceed. This does not mean that any of these data sources are unlikely to be used or are not potentially useful. I am merely stating that they are somewhat more "exotic" and therefore rarer—at least in my experience.

In this chapter, we will look at the following:

- Loading data from Analysis Services sources

- Storing image and document files in SQL Server

- Loading data from Visual FoxPro files

- Loading data from dBase files

- Returning data from Web Services

- Capturing WMI data

- Using ODBC connections to connect to miscellaneous data sources

I know that there are many sources of data not included in this book. Perhaps one day you will need to import Paradox data files or access the wealth of information available in Directory Services, for instance. Unfortunately, there is simply not space available to cover every possible source of data that can be loaded into SQL Server, so I selected a core group of sources that I had to handle over the years, and left the others out of the book.

Sample files used in this chapter are found in the `C:\SQL2012DIRecipes\CH06` directory—assuming that you have downloaded the samples from the book's companion web site and installed them as described in Appendix B. This includes a sample SSAS cube that you can load into Analysis Services.

6-1. Importing Data from SQL Server Analysis Services
Problem

You want to import data from an SQL Server Analysis Services (SSAS) cube into an SQL Server relational table on a regular basis.

Solution

Use SQL Server Integration Services (SSIS) and the Microsoft OLEDB provider to connect to Analysis Services and import the data in tabular format. This is done as follows:

1. Create a new Integration Services package. Add a Data Flow task to the Control Flow pane. Double-click to switch to the Data Flow pane—or click the Data Flow tab, if you prefer.

2. Right-click in the Connection Managers tab at the bottom of the screen. Select New OLEDB Connection. Click New.

3. Select Native OLEDB\Microsoft OLEDB Provider for Analysis Services 11.0. Enter the Analysis Services server name — localhost in this example. Choose Integrated Security. You can then select the cube to which you wish to connect from the Initial Catalog drop-down list. You should see something like Figure 6-1.

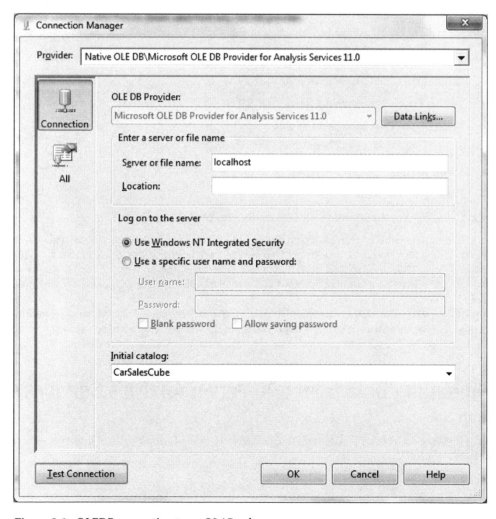

Figure 6-1. *OLEDB connection to an OLAP cube*

4. Test the connection. Click OK twice to finish creating it.

5. Add an OLEDB source task to the Data Flow pane. Select the OLEDB connection manager that you just created. Select SQL Command as the Data Access Mode, and enter the MDX (MultiDimensional eXpression) code required to select the data you wish to import. An example is follows (C:\SQL2012DIRecipes\CH06\ProductsAndClients.Mdx in the sample files):

```
SELECT
NON EMPTY([Dim Clients].[Client Name].[Client Name]) ON COLUMNS
,EXCEPT([Dim Products].[Make].[Make], [Dim Products].[Make].UNKNOWNMEMBER) ON ROWS
FROM [Car Sales DW]
WHERE [Measures].[Cost Price]
```

The dialog box should look something like Figure 6-2.

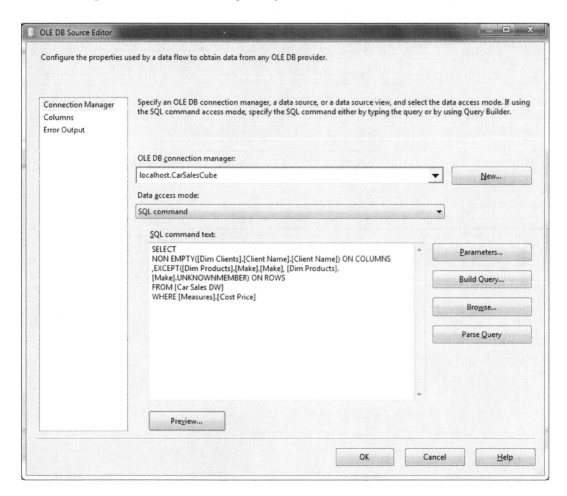

Figure 6-2. *An MDX query in an OLEDB source*

6. Click Preview to see if the connection and MDX selection work. You could get the following alert (see Figure 6-3), which need not worry you.

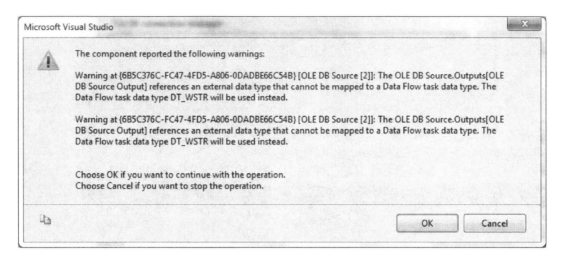

Microsoft Visual Studio

The component reported the following warnings:

Warning at {6B5C376C-FC47-4FD5-A806-0DADBE66C54B} [OLE DB Source [2]]: The OLE DB Source.Outputs[OLE DB Source Output] references an external data type that cannot be mapped to a Data Flow task data type. The Data Flow task data type DT_WSTR will be used instead.

Warning at {6B5C376C-FC47-4FD5-A806-0DADBE66C54B} [OLE DB Source [2]]: The OLE DB Source.Outputs[OLE DB Source Output] references an external data type that cannot be mapped to a Data Flow task data type. The Data Flow task data type DT_WSTR will be used instead.

Choose OK if you want to continue with the operation.
Choose Cancel if you want to stop the operation.

OK   Cancel

Figure 6-3. *OLAP warning*

7. Click OK, and you should see your sample data.

8. Click OK to confirm the data source creation. SSIS once again complains and displays the warning dialog box. Click OK to close it.

9. Add a Data Conversion task onto the Data Flow pane, and join the OLEDB source task to it. You now need to convert all numeric data from DT_WSTR (Unicode string) to the required data type in your ultimate SQL Server table. So double-click the Data Conversion task to open it. Select the input columns that you wish to modify, and then map them to the required output data types. This simple example looks like Figure 6-4.

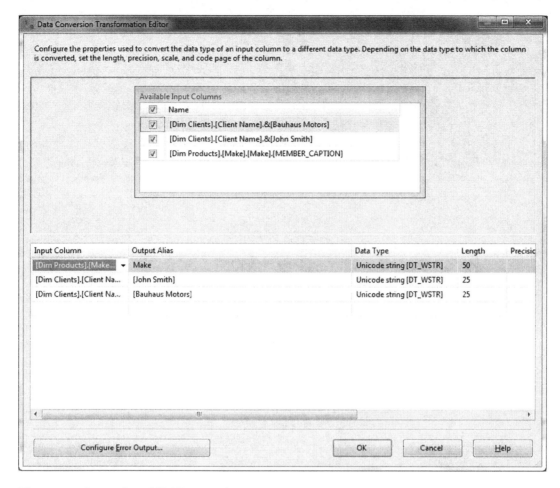

Figure 6-4. *Conversion of OLAP source data*

10. Click OK to confirm the data conversion.

11. Add an OLEDB destination to the Data Flow pane, connect the Data Conversion task to it, and double-click the OLEDB destination. Select or create an OLEDB connection manager, and then click New to create a destination table. Accept the table specification, but change the name to a name which you prefer. Click OK to confirm the table creation.

12. Click Mappings. Ensure that the source and destination data columns are connected. Click OK to close the dialog box.

You can now execute the package and import the data from Analysis Services.

How It Works

Counterintuitive as it may sound, there are occasions when you may need to import data from an SQL Server Analysis Services database back into an SQL Server relational table. This could be because

- You prefer to use the aggregations that already exist in an OLAP cube rather than re-create parallel queries in T-SQL that are not only more complex to write, but can also take longer to return results.

- The OLAP cube contains data from sources to which you do not have access—and it is faster and easier to source this data from Analysis Services.

- The SSAS cube is the enterprise's "single version of the truth" and you are obliged to use the data that it contains.

The hard work is done by the OLEDB provider for Analysis Services, based on the MDX that you must write. The MDX can be as simple—or as complex—as you wish. However, you might prefer to write and test the MDX query in SQL Server Management Studio, as the OLEDB Source query builder will not let you build MDX. It will parse the query, however.

Otherwise, this is a fairly standard SSIS Data Flow task. You will need, at a minimum, connection rights to the OLAP data source. The warning dialog box appears if you try to see the source data columns, or indeed every time that you do almost anything in the data source task. Just take no notice. Interestingly, SSAS returns everything as text—so you need to convert all numeric data to an appropriate numeric data type.

You need to ensure that the MDX you use returns two-dimensional tabular data, with only single columns and row headings. After all, you are importing multidimensional data into a "two-dimensional" SQL database. You can also alias columns using MDX, as shown in a Recipe 6-3, which can be worth the extra effort.

Hints, Tips, and Traps

- If you are using a previous version of SQL Server instead of the Native OLEDB\Microsoft OLEDB Provider for Analysis Services 11.0, choose the provider version 10.0 for SQL Server 2008 and version 9.0 for SQL Server 2005.

- If you get an error when testing the connection in older versions of Analysis Services, click All in step 4 and add **Format = Tabular** to the Extended Properties.

- It is worth noting that where the OLEDB source task says SQL Command Text, it in fact means "pass-through query." You can send through any query that is in a dialect that the source server expects and can handle. Here it *must* be MDX.

6-2. Importing Data from an Analysis Services Cube on a Regular Basis
Problem

You want to import data from an Analysis Services database on a regular basis using a T-SQL command, but without developing a structured ETL process.

Solution

Set up a linked server to connect to an Analysis Services database and import the data in tabular format. You can do it as follows.

1. Configure the MSOLAP provider to allow in-process connections, as described in the Recipe 4-7.

2. Expand Server Objects, followed by Linked Servers, and then Providers. Right-click MSOLAP.

3. Select Properties, and then select Allow Inprocess, as shown in Figure 6-5.

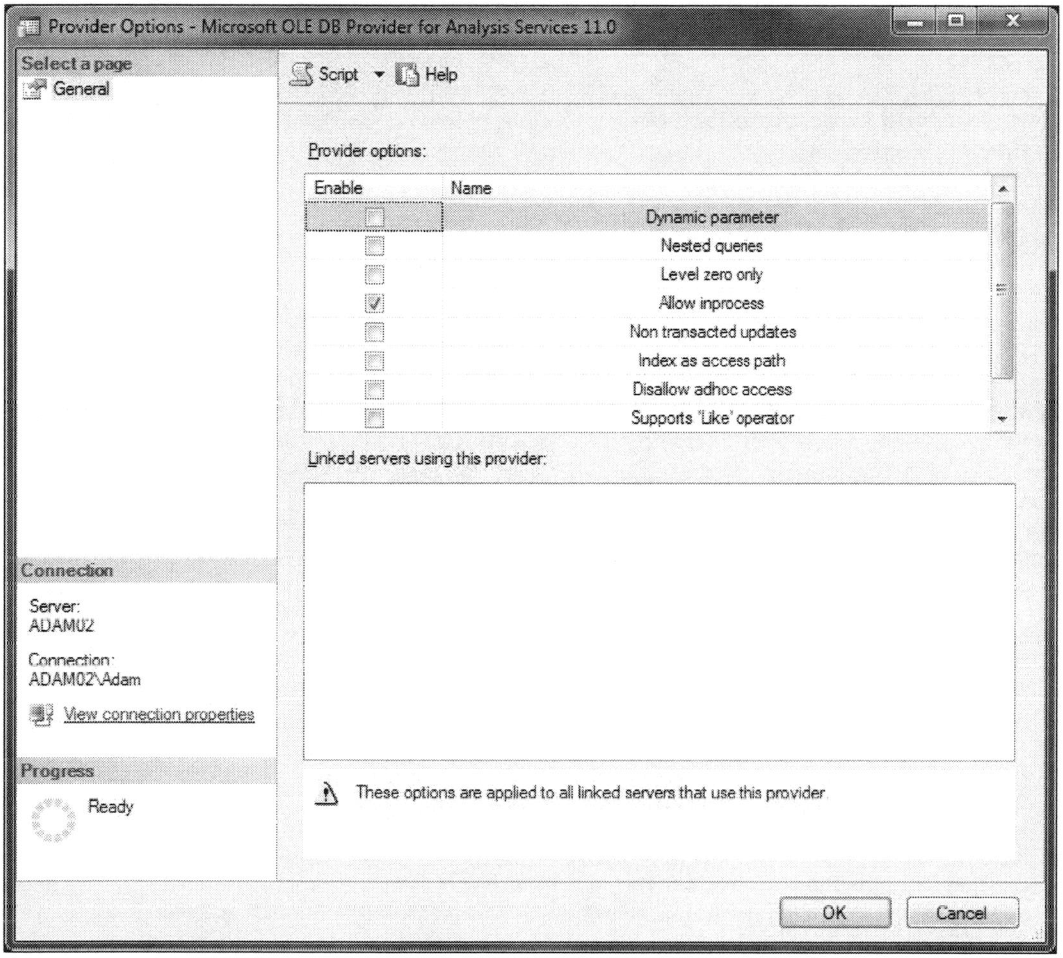

Figure 6-5. OLAP linked server provider

4. Click OK.

5. From SQL Server Management Studio, run the following T-SQL snippet to create a linked server (C:\SQL2012DIRecipes\CH06\OLAPLinkedServer.Sql). You will need to specify your own Analysis Services server for the @datasrc parameter:

```
EXEC master.dbo.sp_addlinkedserver
@server = N'CarSales',
@srvproduct=N'MSOLAP',
@provider=N'MSOLAP',
@datasrc=N'ADAM02',
@catalog=N'CarSales_OLAP';
```

6. Run an OPENQUERY query to extract the data
(C:\SQL2012DIRecipes\CH06\OLAPOpenQuery.Sql):

```
SELECT * FROM OPENQUERY(CarSales,
'SELECT
NON EMPTY([Dim Clients].[Client Name].[Client Name]) ON COLUMNS
,EXCEPT([Dim Products].[Make].[Make], [Dim Products].[Make].UNKNOWNMEMBER) ON ROWS
FROM [Car Sales DW]
WHERE [Measures].[Cost Price]' );
```

You should see a tabular representation of the data you selected from SSAS. You can use this as part of an INSERT INTO or a SELECT ... INTO statement to load the data into SQL Server.

How It Works

Should you wish to access data from an Analysis Services database on demand, instead of having to run an SSIS package, you can also set up a linked server connection to SSAS. This linked server can then be queried from T-SQL by sending a pass-through query in MDX using OPENQUERY. You must use MDX because a standard four-part T-SQL notation query will not work.

You can both rename the output columns and convert data types using T-SQL. The trick is to note the exact column name returned by the MDX query, and enclose it in double-quotes, as shown in the Recipe 6-3.

Hints, Tips, and Traps

- Note that the name that you give to the linked server (OLAP, in this example) will be used in the OPENQUERY command. When defining the linked server, the provider must be MSOLAP, the data source is your Analysis Services server, and the catalog is the database that you wish to query.

- If the login is made to SQL Server using SQL Server security (login name and password), SQL Server sends the credentials of the SQL Server services startup account to OLAP services for authentication. If SQL Server authentication is used, then configure SQL Server services to run under either a local or domain user account rather than using a SYSTEM account.

- If the login is made to SQL Server using Windows authentication, then SQL Server hands the credentials of this Microsoft Windows NT account to OLAP services.

6-3. Querying an OLAP Source on an Ad Hoc Basis
Problem

You want to query an OLAP source to carry out an ad hoc data load of SSAS data into SQL Server.

Solution

Use the OPENROWSET command from T-SQL to send a pass-through query to an Analysis Services cube and return the data that you then insert into SQL Server.

1. Create a destination table using the following DDL
   (C:\SQL2012DIRecipes\CH06\tblSsalesAnalysis.Sql):

```sql
CREATE TABLE dbo.SalesAnalysis
(
MakeOfCar NVARCHAR(150)
,BauhausMotors NVARCHAR(150)
,JohnSmith NVARCHAR(150)
);
GO
```

2. Use T-SQL like the following to query an OLAP cube using MDX as the pass-through
   query (C:\SQL2012DIRecipes\CH06\PassthroughOLAP.Sql):

```sql
INSERT INTO dbo.SalesAnalysis (MakeOfCar, BauhausMotors, JohnSmith)

SELECT OLP."[Dim Products].[Make].[Make].[MEMBER_CAPTION]" AS MakeOfCar
,"[Dim Clients].[Client Name].&[Bauhaus Motors]" AS [Bauhaus Motors]
,"[Dim Clients].[Client Name].&[John Smith]" AS [John Smith]

FROM OPENROWSET('MSOLAP','DATASOURCE=ADAM02; Initial Catalog=CarSalesCube;',
'SELECT NONEMPTY([Dim Clients].[Client Name].Children) ON COLUMNS
,NONEMPTY([Dim Products].[Make].children) ON ROWS
FROM [Car Sales DW]
WHERE [Measures].[Cost Price]') AS OLP;
```

How It Works

Should your needs be merely a passing requirement for data from an Analysis Services cube and you do not want the hassle of setting up a linked server, then you can query an OLAP source using the OPENROWSET command as shown. Once again, you must use MDX because this is a pass-through query. Be warned that the MDX can give results that may surprise you when used inside T-SQL. For instance, if you have hierarchies, then you will get an extra column for every hierarchy level. You can both rename the output columns and convert data types as described in the previous recipe. You will need to specify your own Analysis Services server for the DATASOURCE in the provider connection string.

6-4. Loading Images and Documents into an SQL Server Table
Problem

You want to import images and documents to store them in an SQL Server table using T-SQL.

Solution

Use OPENROWSET(BULK) from T-SQL. This takes image and document files from the file system and stores them as binary objects in an SQL Server table.

Loading files into SQL Server tables requires you to do the following.

1. Create the following table structure(C:\SQL2012DIRecipes\CH06\tblDocuBlobs.Sql):

```sql
CREATE TABLE CarSales_Staging.dbo.DocuBlobs
(
 ID int IDENTITY(1,1) NOT NULL,
 ExternalFileName nvarchar(255) NULL,
```

```
FileData varbinary(max) NULL,
FileType char(10) NULL,
ExternalFileDirectory nvarchar(255) NULL
) ;
GO
```

2. Run the following T-SQL (C:\SQL2012DIRecipes\CH06\InsertDocuBlobs.Sql):

```
INSERT INTO CarSales_Staging.dbo.DocuBlobs
(
ExternalFileName,
ExternalFileDirectory,
FileData,
FileType
)
SELECT
'MyWordDocument.doc',
'C:\SQL2012DIRecipes\CH06\',
(SELECT * FROM OPENROWSET(BULK 'C:\SQL2012DIRecipes\CH06\MyWordDocument.doc',
SINGLE_BLOB) AS MyDoc ),
'Doc' ;
```

How It Works

There are occasions when you may wish to import documents as Binary Large Objects (BLOBS) into SQL Server and store them inside the database. This also covers cases where you have created FILESTREAM or FILETABLE columns to store the BLOBs in the file system, while maintaining the transactional control provided by SQL Server. To do this, the SQL snippet in this recipe inserts a BLOB into a VARBINARY(MAX) column.

For this recipe to work, the destination table must have the following:

- A VARBINARY(MAX) column to store the document

- A unique ID column (a prerequisite for full-text indexing)

- A document type column (a necessity for full-text indexing BLOBs)

- The column (FileData, in this example) that stores the binary file can be a FILESTREAM or FILETABLE column, as these are handled transparently by SQL Server

So why would you need to store documents or images in SQL Server? A few ideas include:

- To store a canonical version of a document, possibly locked away from user intervention (accidental deletion, for instance)

- The ability to use full-text search to find data in certain file formats (Word, Excel, PowerPoint, HTML, PDF, etc.)

- The ability to maintain multiple versions of files

Hints, Tips, and Traps

- You can insert only the BLOB itself—the directory, file name, and document type are not required. I am merely assuming that you are storing documents in SQL Server.

- Of course, there are ways of importing BLOBs via a front-end using ADO.NET. These methods are outside the scope of this book, however.

- If you are importing a file into a FILESTREAM or a FILETABLE column, then OPENROWSET (BULK) has no problem loading files more than 2 gigabytes in size—providing that you are not passing them to a VARBINARY(MAX) variable in your T-SQL.

6-5. Importing Multiple Files into an SQL Server Table

Problem

You want to import multiple files into SQL Server from the file system and store them in a database.

Solution

Use dynamic SQL to process a list of files and load them into an SQL Server table. The following shows one way of doing it for tens, hundreds, or thousands of files.

1. Create a table of source document references, like this (C:\SQL2012DIRecipes\CH06\tblDocumentList.Sql):

```
CREATE TABLE CarSales_Staging.dbo.DocumentList
(
 ID int IDENTITY(1,1) NOT NULL,
 ExternalFileName nvarchar(255) NULL,
 FileType char(10) NULL,
 ExternalFileDirectory nvarchar(255) NULL
);
GO
```

2. Add the list of files to load into the table that you just created. This must include the file name, extension, and full path to the file.

3. Use the following T-SQL to take this list of documents and load them into an SQL Server table (C:\SQL2012DIRecipes\CH06\DocumentLoad.Sql):

```
DECLARE @DocName              NVARCHAR(255)
DECLARE @DocFullName          NVARCHAR(255)
DECLARE @DocPath              NVARCHAR(255)
DECLARE @DocType              CHAR(10)

DECLARE @SQL                  NVARCHAR(4000)
DECLARE @SQLPARAMETERS        NVARCHAR(4000)

DECLARE DOCLOAD_CUR CURSOR

FOR
SELECT  ExternalFileName, ExternalFileDirectory, FileType
FROM CarSales_Staging.dbo.DocumentList

OPEN DOCLOAD_CUR

FETCH NEXT FROM DOCLOAD_CUR INTO @DocName, @DocPath, @DocType

WHILE @@FETCH_STATUS = 0
BEGIN
```

```
SET @DocFullName = @DocPath + '\' + @DocName

SET @SQL =
'
INSERT INTO dbo.DocuBlobs
(
ExternalFileName,
ExternalFileDirectory,
FileData,
FileType
)

SELECT '
+ '''' + @DocName + ''','
+ '''' + @DocPath + ''','
+ '(SELECT * FROM OPENROWSET(BULK ''' + @DocFullName + ''', SINGLE_BLOB) AS MyDoc ),'
+ '''' + @DocType + ''''

EXEC (@SQL)
FETCH NEXT FROM DOCLOAD_CUR INTO @DocName, @DocPath, @DocType

END

CLOSE DOCLOAD_CUR
DEALLOCATE DOCLOAD_CUR
```

How It Works

This recipe takes a table with the file names, directories, and file types that you have (laboriously) assembled, to use as the source of the data required to load hundreds of files. A cursor iterates through every record in this table, and passes the file name, file type, and path into variables, which are then used by OPENROWSET to load each file. So, with my apologies to all the SQL purists out there for my daring to use a cursor, here is the code to get a few hundred documents into SQL Server quite fast—and very easily!

The code is predicated on the fact that OPENROWSET cannot take a variable as the file reference—so the whole snippet must be made into dynamic SQL. There seems to be no way to use sp_executesql to run OPENROWSET, as this command will not accept variables as the document parameter. So you have to use ad hoc dynamic SQL—and beware of all the quoted elements in the SQL string.

I found that a cursor is the easiest way to process hundreds of documents. Yes, I know, this is supposedly bad programming practice—but in this particular case, it is the exception that proves the rule. It really shines for its simplicity. And I must admit, I have never seen a requirement for loading more than a few hundred documents at a time, which is not going to take that long in any case, so the undeniable slowness of a cursor is unlikely to be a problem.

Hints, Tips, and Traps

- I have not added error-trapping code to this snippet. You might need to trap errors such as missing documents.

- No document can be more than 2 gigabytes in size, unless you are using FILESTREAM or FILETABLE. For more information on configuring these, please consult Books On Line.

6-6. Importing Files into SQL Server on a Regular Basis

Problem

You want to import document or image files into SQL Server regularly as part of a structured ETL process.

Solution

Use SSIS to load the files from the file system into an SQL Server table as binary objects.

1. Create the table described in step 1 in the previous recipe if you have not already done so (CarSales_Staging.dbo.DocumentList).

2. Create a stored procedure called pr_LoadBLOBsFromSSIS using the following T-SQL (C:\SQL2012DIRecipes\CH06\pr_LoadBlobsFromSSIS.Sql):

```
CREATE PROCEDURE CarSales_Staging.dbo.pr_LoadBLOBsFromSSIS
(
@DocName NVARCHAR(255),
@DocPath NVARCHAR(255),
@DocFullName NVARCHAR(255),
@DocType CHAR(3)
)

AS

DECLARE @SQL NVARCHAR(4000)
DECLARE @SQLPARAMETERS VARCHAR(8000)

SET @SQL =
'
INSERT INTO dbo.DocumentList
(
ExternalFileName,
ExternalFileDirectory,
FileData,
FileType
)

SELECT '
+ '''' + @DocName + ''','
+ '''' + @DocPath + ''','
+ '(SELECT * FROM OPENROWSET(BULK ''' + @DocFullName + ''', SINGLE_BLOB) AS MyDoc ),'
+ '''' + @DocType + ''''

EXEC (@SQL)
```

3. Create a new SSIS package.

4. Add the following variables to your package:

Variable	Type
DocName	String
DocFullName	String
DocPath	String
DocType	String

5. Add a Foreach Loop container to the Control Flow pane. Name it **Collect All Documents in Directory**. Double-click to edit it. Click Collection on the left.

6. Select the Foreach File Enumerator as the Foreach Loop Editor type. Browse to or enter the folder containing the documents that you wish to load, as well as the file filter (*.Docx in this example). Ensure that you select Fully Qualified as the file type. You should end up with a dialog box that looks like Figure 6-6.

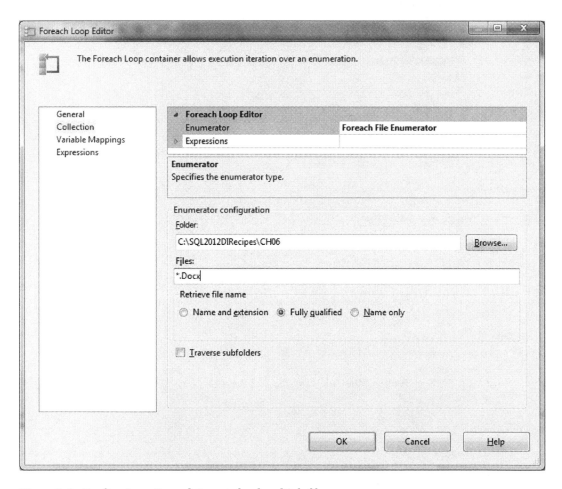

Figure 6-6. *Configuring a Foreach Loop to load multiple files*

7. Click Variable Mappings on the left, and select the User::DocFullName variable as the variable that SSIS will use to hold the file name when loading the file into SQL Server. The dialog box should look like Figure 6-7.

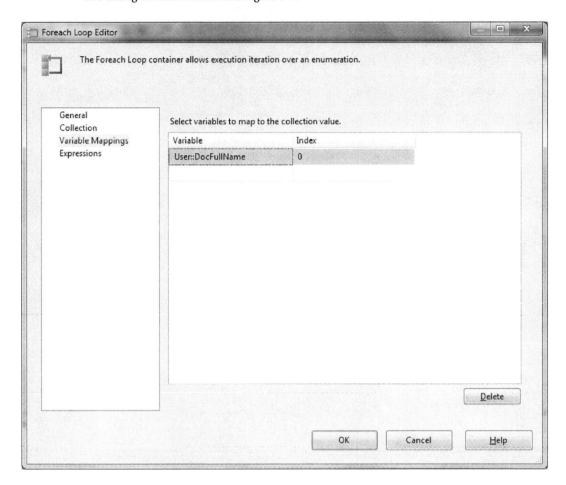

Figure 6-7. Setting the variable for multiple file loads

8. Click OK to confirm the parameters of the Foreach Loop container.

9. Add a Script task inside the Foreach Loop container. Name the Script task **Get File and Path Elements**. Double-click to edit and click Script on the left. In the pane on the right, enter the following:

Variable Type	Variable
ReadOnlyVariables	DocFullName
ReadWriteVariables	DocName
ReadWriteVariables	DocPath
ReadWriteVariables	DocType

You should see something like Figure 6-8.

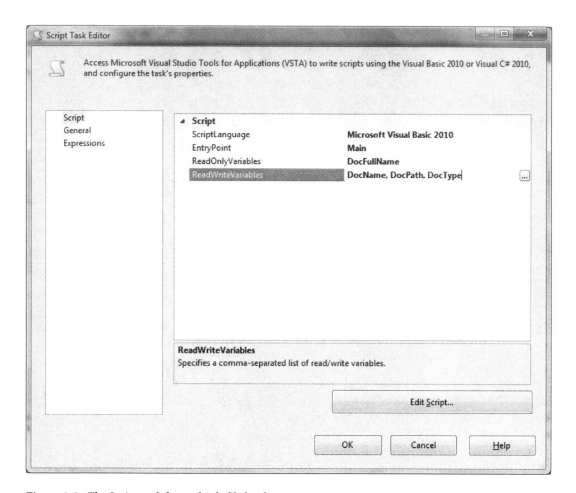

Figure 6-8. *The Script task for multiple file loads*

10. Select Microsoft Visual Basic 2010 as the Script Language. Click Edit Script.

11. Add the following line to the Imports region:

```
Imports System.IO
```

12. Replace the Main method with the following code
     (C:\SQL2012DIRecipes\CH06\DocuBlobs.vb):

```
Public Sub Main()

        Dim sDocName As String

        sDocName = Dts.Variables("DocFullName").Value.ToString
```

```
            Dts.Variables("DocType").Value = Right(Path.GetExtension(sDocName), 3)
            Dts.Variables("DocPath").Value = Path.GetDirectoryName(sDocName)
            Dts.Variables("DocName").Value = Path.GetFileName(sDocName)

            Dts.TaskResult = ScriptResults.Success

        End Sub
```

13. Close the Script editor. Click OK to close the Script task.

14. Add an Execute SQL task inside the Foreach Loop container, under the Script task, and connect the Script task to the SQL task.

15. Double-click the SQL task to edit it. Select ADO.NET as the connection type. Create or select a .NET connection to the database where you have created the stored procedure (CarSales_Staging) and select dbo.DocumentList as the destination table.

16. Click Parameter Mapping on the left. Add four parameters, configured as follows:

VariableName	Direction	DataType	ParameterName
User::DocFullName	Input	String	@DocFullName
User::DocType	Input	String	@DocType
User::DocPath	Input	String	@DocPath
User::DocName	Input	String	@DocName

This will give you the dialog box shown in Figure 6-9.

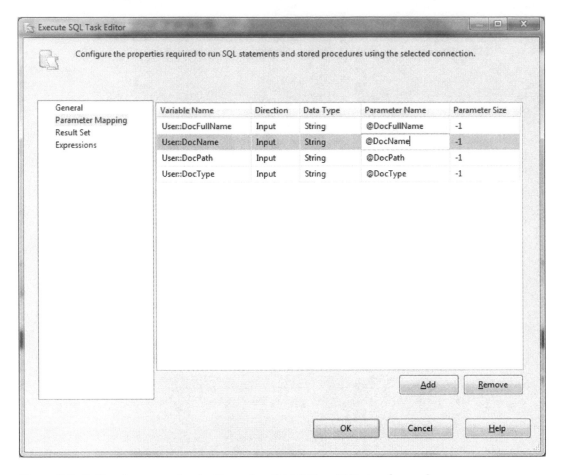

Figure 6-9. *Setting the parameters for the pr_LoadBLOBsFromSSIS stored procedure*

17. Set IsQueryStoredProcedure to True.

18. Add the following to the SQLStatement: **pr_LoadBLOBsFromSSIS**. Click OK to
     confirm. The resulting SSIS package should look more or less like in Figure 6-10.

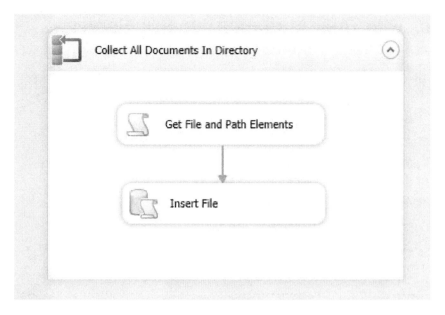

Figure 6-10. *The completed SSIS package*

You can now run the SSIS package, which will import all the files of the specified type into the SQL Server table.

How It Works

Using SSIS as part of a structured ETL process to load files into a database can bring several useful features to the party, including:

- Cycling through directories to find files

- File name manipulation (if required) using .NET string functions

Given the requirement to use dynamic SQL and the multiple variables that are needed, I find it easier to present the T-SQL to SSIS as a stored procedure, and call the stored procedure from SSIS that passes in the required variables (the document name, type, path, and file to be loaded). This is an extension of the code used in the previous recipe.

The Script task harnesses the power of the System.IO class in .NET to separate out the file name, extension, and path, which are then passed to the stored procedure. They are also stored in the destination table. Admittedly, this path parsing could be done using T-SQL—but it is so much easier using a script component and the ready-made .Net IO class. The stored procedure pr_LoadBLOBsFromSSIS then performs the actual load as many times as required by the iterations in the Foreach Loop container. This approach can be extended very easily to handle multiple source directories or file types—but I will leave that up to you.

Hints, Tips, and Traps

- Creating the variables before adding any other objects to the SSIS package avoids potential scope bugs. You can create the variables at any time, of course.

- Remember to use Imports System.IO in the script, or you will not have access to the extremely useful built-in .NET functions for parsing the file and path data.

- Don't forget that SSIS variables are case-sensitive!

6-7. Importing Files with Their Attributes into SQL Server
Problem

You want to import files for storage in SQL Server tables using SSIS along with their attributes as a step toward efficient file management.

Solution

Use SSIS to load the files by configuring an Import Column task to do this, and then add a Script task to add the required file metadata. You can do it as follows.

1. Create the following destination table (C:\SQL2012DIRecipes\CH06\tblCarPhotos.Sql):

   ```
   CREATE TABLE CarSales_Staging.dbo.CarPhotos
   (
    ID int IDENTITY(1,1) NOT NULL,
    FileName varchar(50) NULL,
    FileExtension varchar(10) NULL,
    DirectoryName varchar(150) NULL,
    FileSize bigint NULL,
    DateFileCreated datetime2(7) NULL,
    DateFileModified datetime2(7) NULL,
    ItemImage varbinary(max) NULL,
    UNIQUE NONCLUSTERED (ID ASC )
   );
   GO
   ```

2. Create a new SSIS package, and add a new Data Flow task. Click the Data Flow tab to edit the Data Flow task.

3. Add a new OLEDB connection manager for the destination database (CarSales_Staging), name it **CarSales_Staging_OLEDB**.

4. Add a Script Component to the Data Flow pane. When prompted, set it to be a "source". Name it **Script Component to collect source files**.

5. Double-click the Script Component to edit it. Set the Script Language to Microsoft Visual Basic 2010.

6. Click Inputs and Outputs on the left. Select Output 0 in the Input Output columns list view and rename it to **SourceOutput**.

7. Expand SourceOutput in the Input Output columns list view and expand OutputColumns. Add the following columns:

Column Name	Column Type
FileExtension	String - 10
FileName	String - 50
DirectoryName	String - 150
FileSize	8-byte signed integer
DateModified	Date
DateCreated	Date
FullPath	String - 150

The result should look something like Figure 6-11.

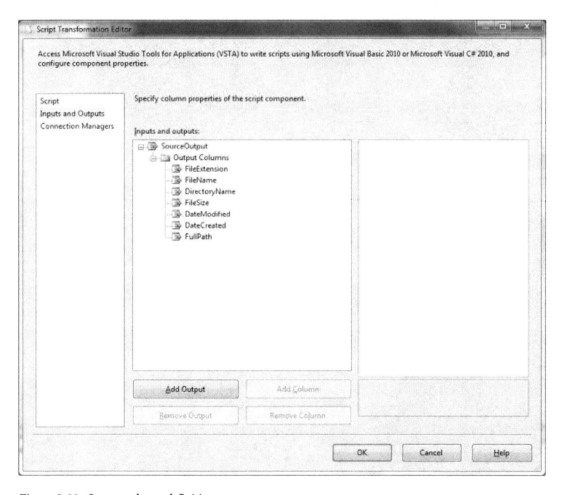

Figure 6-11. *Source column definition*

8. Add the following line to the Imports region:

```
Imports System.IO
```

9. Click Script on the left, and Edit Script. Replace the method CreateNewOutputRows with the following (C:\SQL2012DIRecipes\CH06\FileAttributes.vb):

```
Public Overrides Sub CreateNewOutputRows()

        Dim DrInfo As New IO.DirectoryInfo("C:\SQL2012DIRecipes\CH06")
        Dim fInfo As IO.FileInfo() =DrInfo.GetFiles("*.jpg")

        For Each FI In fInfo
            SourceOutputBuffer.AddRow()
            SourceOutputBuffer.FullPath = FI.FullName
            SourceOutputBuffer.FileName =FI.Name
            SourceOutputBuffer.FileExtension = FI.Extension
            SourceOutputBuffer.DirectoryName = FI.DirectoryName
            SourceOutputBuffer.FileSize = FI.Length
            SourceOutputBuffer.DateCreated = File.GetCreationTime(FI.FullName)
            SourceOutputBuffer.DateModified = File.GetLastWriteTime(FI.FullName)
        Next
    End Sub
```

10. Close the Script window. Click OK.

11. Add an Import Column task to the Data Flow pane, and connect the Script task to it. Name it **Import Files** and double-click to edit.

12. Select the Input Columns tab and select FullPath. This will indicate to SSIS the column indicating where the file is found. The dialog box should look something like Figure 6-12.

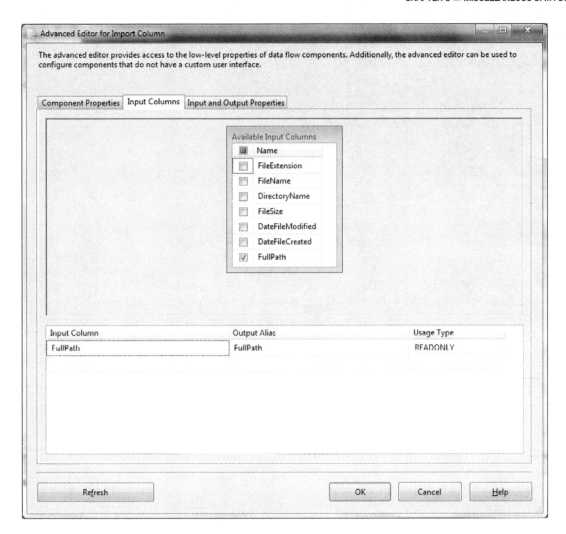

Figure 6-12. *Specifying the column to hold the file path*

13. Select the Import and Output properties tab. Expand the Input Column Output node and click Add Column. Rename the new column **ImageColumn**.

14. Select ImageColumn. Note the ID of the column (this is the internal lineage ID). The dialog box should look something like Figure 6-13.

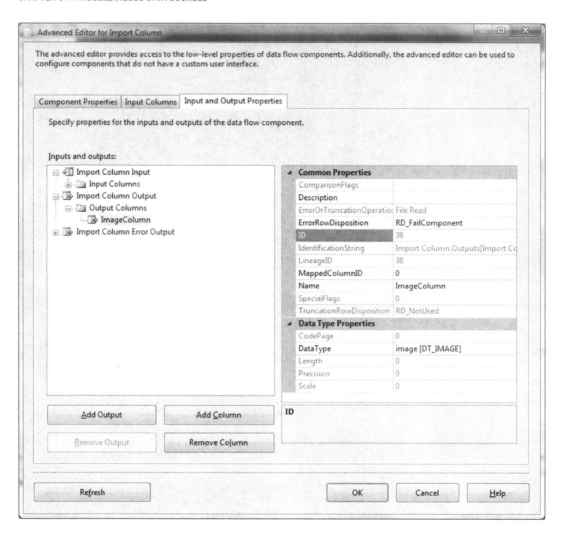

Figure 6-13. *The Output column for files*

15. Expand the Import Column Input node and expand Input Columns. Click Full Path. Enter the ID you just noted for the FileDataColumnID. The dialog box should resemble Figure 6-14.

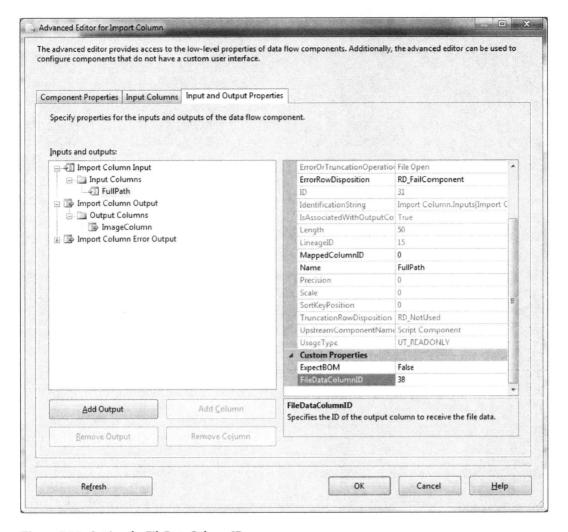

Figure 6-14. *Setting the FileDataColumnID*

16. Confirm with OK.

17. Add an OLEDB destination to the Data Flow pane. Name it **Load files and attributes**. Connect the Import Column task to it. Double-click to configure. Select the OLEDB connection manager that you configured in step 3 (CarSales_Staging_OLEDB). Select Table or View as the Data Access mode, and then select the table you created (dbo.CarPhotos, in this example).

18. Map the columns, as follows:

Source Column	Destination Column
FileName	FileName
FileExtension	FileExtension
DirectoryName	DirectoryName
FileSize	FileSize
FileCreated	DateFileCreated
FileModified	DateFileModified
ImageColumn	ItemImage

19. Confirm with OK. The final package will look like Figure 6-15.

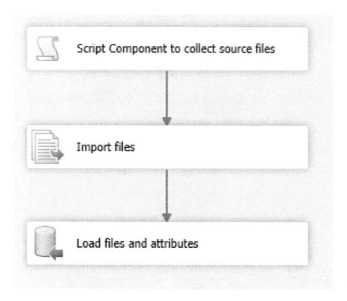

Figure 6-15. *The completed SSIS package to import multiple files with attributes*

You can now run the package. All the files in the source directory that have the chosen extension will be loaded into SQL Server.

How It Works

SSIS also has a "native" way of importing files (as text or binary files) into SQL Server. This method avoids you having to use a stored procedure and to pass variables to it. It uses an SSIS transformation called the Import Column task. The process used here loads every file in a specified directory, and gathers and writes various attributes into the same table.

However, in my opinion it is too much hard work to use it to import one or two files, and this is an approach that comes into its own when used to process hundreds, or even thousands of files. So I have shown you one approach to loading an entire directory of binary files using the Import Column task. It shows you how to use an SSIS Script task not only as a data source, but also as a way of leveraging the .NET IO class to get all the relevant file attributes for each source file, which can then be stored in an SQL Server table alongside the binary data.

It is worth noting that this approach is not without its drawbacks, which are, principally, as follows:

- It is slow—many orders of magnitude slower than the T-SQL approaches described previously.

- It requires considerable server resources— specifically memory—and can produce memory-based errors.

- It is limited to a maximum of 2 gigabytes per file. This is because it uses the DT_IMAGE SSIS data type, which is a binary value with a maximum size of 2^{31-1} (2,147,483,647) bytes.

Hints, Tips, and Traps

- You can also define the ItemImage column as a FILESTREAM column—if your database is FILESTREAM-enabled because SSIS will just as easily load the file into a FILESTREAM column as a VARBINARY(MAX) column. In this case, the DDL for the table would be (assuming that you have created a file group named CarSalesFS) (C:\SQL2012DIRecipes\CH06\CarPhotosFilestream.Sql):

```
CREATE TABLE dbo.CarPhotosFS
(
 ID int IDENTITY(1,1) NOT NULL,
 ItemID uniqueidentifier ROWGUIDCOL  NOT NULL,
 FileName varchar(50) NULL,
 FileExtension varchar(10) NULL,
 DirectoryName varchar(150) NULL,
 FileSize bigint NULL,
 DateFileCreated datetime2(7) NULL,
 DateFileModified datetime2(7) NULL,
 ItemImage varbinary(max) FILESTREAM  NULL,
UNIQUE NONCLUSTERED
(
ItemID ASC
)WITH (PAD_INDEX  = OFF, STATISTICS_NORECOMPUTE  = OFF, IGNORE_DUP_KEY=OFF,
ALLOW_ROW_LOCKS  = ON, ALLOW_PAGE_LOCKS  = ON) ON PRIMARY
) ON PRIMARY FILESTREAM_ON CarSalesFS
```

- Of course, you can set the directory and the file filter to be SSIS variables, and thus make this package more user-friendly.

6-8. Loading Visual FoxPro Files
Problem

You want to load data from Visual FoxPro files into SQL Server.

Solution

Use SSIS and the OLEDB provider for Visual FoxPro to load the data as part of a Data Flow task. This is how to do it:

1. First, if you have not done it already, you need to download the Visual FoxPro OLEDB driver from the Microsoft web site (it is currently at www.microsoft.com/en-us/download/details.aspx?id=14839). Once downloaded, you need to install it. Then you will be able to use the VFPOLEDB.1 provider to connect to FoxPro database files and databases.

2. Create a new SSIS package and add a Data Flow task onto the Control Flow pane. Double-click to edit the task.

3. Right-click in the Connection Manager tab and add a new OLEDB connection. Make sure that you select the Microsoft OLEDB Provider for Visual FoxPro. Enter (or copy and paste) the path to the FoxPro file containing the tables you wish to import. You should end up with something like Figure 6-16.

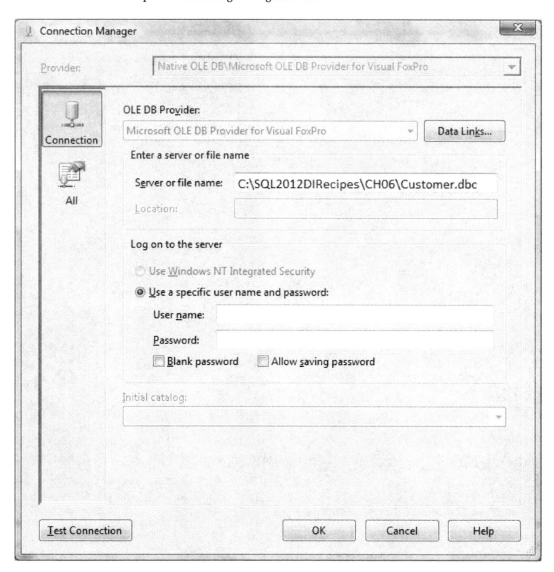

Figure 6-16. *Importing Visual FoxPro data*

4. Confirm the connection manager. Add a new OLEDB source to the Data Flow pane and edit it. Select the connection manager that you just created. Select the required table from the list of available data tables—or enter the SQL to select the subset of data that you require.

5. Confirm, add an OLEDB destination, connect the two tasks, and map the columns to the destination table (or create it if necessary).

6. You can now run the package and import your data.

How It Works

Yes, there are still a great many Visual FoxPro applications out there—it is, after all a Microsoft product. Indeed, some commercial data providers still use it as a standard data format. So, assuming that you need to get data from Visual FoxPro into SQL server, there are potentially four ways (at least that I know of) to do it, including:

- OLEDB linked server

- SSIS over OLEDB

- SSIS using ODBC

- The Visual FoxPro upgrade wizard

Let's be clear. I am not going to be exhaustive here and review all these methods. For me, the best and simplest way of getting data from Visual FoxPro into SQL Server is to use OLEDB and SSIS. So this is the only method that I have shown in this recipe. My reasoning is that once you have installed the Visual FoxPro provider, the whole process is a fairly standard SSIS import process.

You can, if you prefer, use ODBC and the .NET provider (as described in Recipe 6-12), but this is considerably slower and more cumbersome to set up than the OLEDB provider is. It might be necessary to use it in some cases, however, if you meet otherwise insurmountable difficulties using OLEDB.

Hints, Tips, and Traps

- The upsizing wizard can be found on CodePlex at http://vfpx.codeplex.com/releases/view/10224, if you wish to use it.

- Interestingly, installing the VFPOLEDB.1 provider will not register it (at least to allow SQL Server to create a linked server). There are (unsupported) workarounds on the Web, but if you need a linked server, then ODBC over OLEDB could be the safest solution—if the slowest.

6-9. Importing Data from dBase
Problem

You want to load legacy data from dBase files into SQL Server.

Solution

Use SSIS and a suitably configured OLEDB connection manager to load the dBase file as part of an SSIS Data Flow.

dBase files can be loaded like this:

1. Rename any dBase data files that are longer than eight characters to the old DOS 8.3 format.

2. Create a new SSIS package. Add a Data Flow task.

3. Add an OLEDB connection manager. Configure it to connect to the destination database.

4. For the dBase source file, add an OLEDB connection manager. Set the provider as Microsoft Office 12.0 Access Database Engine OLEDB Provider.

5. Set the database file name as the path (only) to the source file(s). In this example, it is C:\SQL2012DIRecipes\CH06\.

6. Click All on the left. Set Extended properties to dBase III, dBase IV, or dBase 5.0 as appropriate for the version of the dBase file that you are using.

7. Confirm with OK, twice.

8. Add a Data Flow task. Double-click to edit.

9. Add an OLEDB source. Double-click to edit. Select the OLEDB connection manager corresponding to the OLEDB connection manager defined in step 3.

10. Set the data access mode as Table or View.

11. Select the dBase file from the list of tables. Confirm with OK.

12. Add a destination OLEDB task. Configure with the OLEDB connection manager defined in step 2. Connect the source task to it. Run the package.

How It Works

Probably the most venerable data file format of them all, dBase, is still to be found in many organizations. Considering it has been around for some thirty-odd years, that is quite something. So, in case you ever need to load dBase data files, I wanted to show you how. I feel that the recipe is self-explanatory because it is essentially a standard data load process—except for one interesting point: the source database file name is the directory where the dBase files are stored.

Hints, Tips, and Traps

- To work, this recipe presumes that you have installed the ACE (Access Database Engine) driver as described in Recipe 1-1. If you are in a 32-bit environment then you can use the Jet provider instead of the ACE provider if you prefer. In a 64-bit environment only the ACE provider will work unless you run the package in 32-bit mode.

- Be sure to name files in the venerable 8.3 format without spaces.

6-10. Loading Data from Web Services
Problem

You want to access reference data available from a web services provider as part of an ETL process.

Solution

Use the SSIS Web Services task to source the data that you need to use as part of your ETL process. The following tells how to look up currency conversion data and apply it to data in the SSIS pipeline.

1. Create a blank file into which you will later download the WSDL (Web Services Description Language). In this example, it is called C:\SQL2012DIRecipes\CH06\CurrencyConversion.wsdl.

2. Create the following table in the CarSales_Staging database (C:\SQL2012DIRecipes\CH06\tblStockInDollars.Sql):

```
CREATE TABLE CarSales_Staging.dbo.StockInDollars
(
 ID bigint NULL,
 Make varchar(50) NULL,
 Marque nvarchar(50) NULL,
 Mileage numeric(32, 4) NULL,
 Cost_PriceGBP numeric(18, 2) NULL,
 Cost_PriceUSD numeric(18, 2) NULL,
 ExchangeRate float NULL
) ;

GO
```

3. Create a new SSIS package.

4. Add the two following OLEDB connection managers to the SSIS package:

    CarSales_OLEDB, which you configure to connect to the CarSales database.

    CarSales_Staging_OLEDB, which you configure to connect to the CarSales_Staging database.

5. Right-click the Control Flow pane and add the following variables to the SSIS package:

Name	Scope	DataType	Value
ConversionCurrency	Package	String	USD
ConversionRate	Package	Double	
XMLOutput	Package	String	

The Variables pane should look like Figure 6-17.

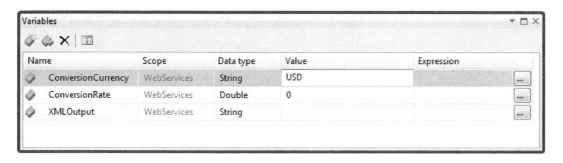

Figure 6-17. *The Variables pane for a Web Services task*

6.	Right-click in the Connection Managers tab. Select New Connection. You should see the dialog box in Figure 6-18.

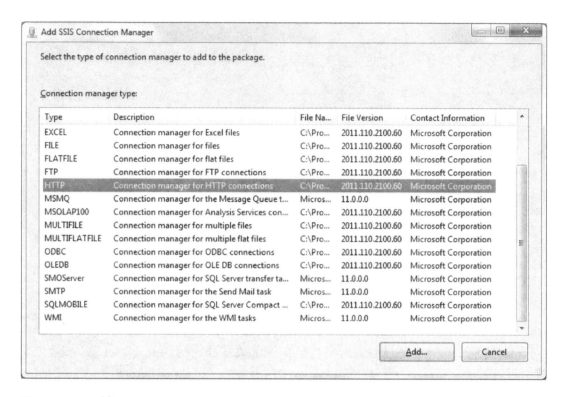

Figure 6-18. *Adding an HTTP connection manager*

7.	Select HTTP. Click Add.

8.	Right-click the connection manager. Select Rename and name it **WebServicesConnection**.

9.	Double-click the WebServicesConnection connection manager. Configure the HTTP connection manager to connect to the web service you will be using by entering the required URL in the Server URL field. In this example, it is `http://www.webservicex. net/CurrencyConvertor.asmx?WSDL`, which is a free web service to obtain currency conversion information. You should see a dialog box like Figure 6-19.

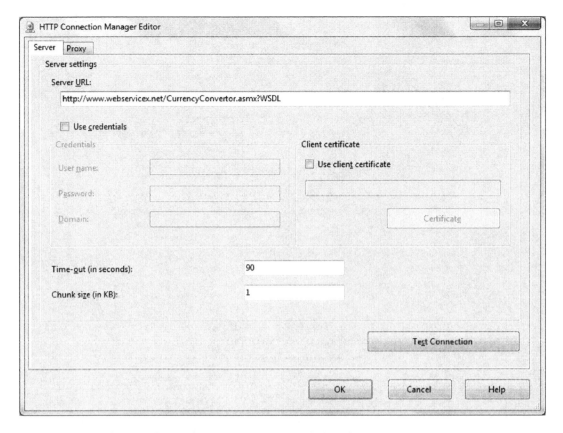

Figure 6-19. Configuring the HTTP connection manager for a web service

10. Confirm your configuration with OK.

11. Add a Web Services task on to the Control Flow pane. Name it **Lookup Dollar to GBP Exchange rate** and double-click to edit.

12. Ensure that the HTTP connection is set to WebServicesConnection, which you created previously.

13. Connect the WSDL file to the empty file that you created in step 1. In this example, it is C:\SQL2012DIRecipes\CH06\CurrencyConversion.wsdl. Ensure that Overwrite WSDL File is set to True. The result should be close to that shown in Figure 6-20.

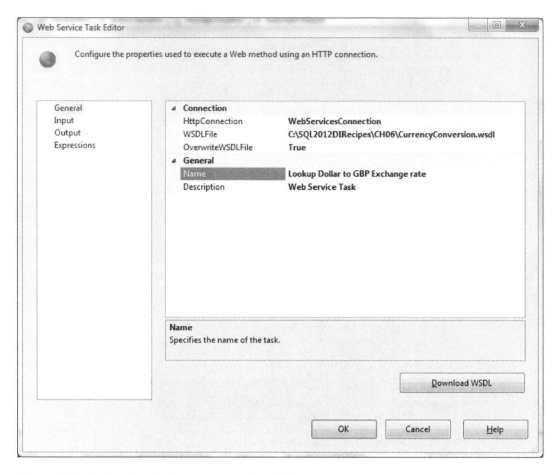

Figure 6-20. *Configuring the General pane of the Web Services task*

14. Click Download WSDL to obtain the WSDL file, which allows the Web Services task to use the Web Service.

15. Click Input to view the Input pane. Select the service that you will use (CurrencyConvertor in this example) and the method that you will apply (ConversionRate in this example).

16. Check the variable for the ToCurrency element, and select the User::ConversionCurrency variable as its value. The dialog box should look like Figure 6-21.

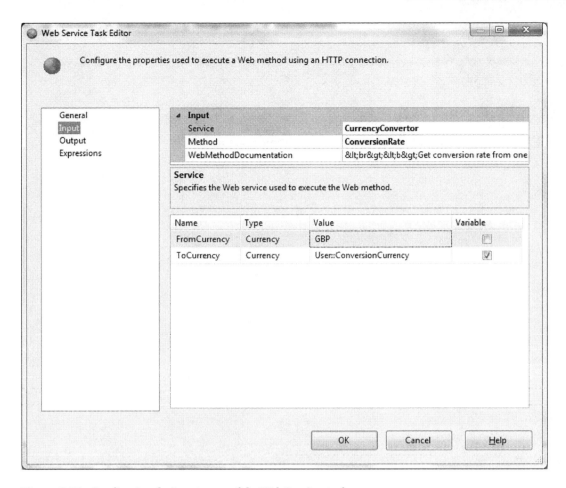

Figure 6-21. *Configuring the Input pane of the Web Services task*

> 17. Click Output to view the Output pane. Select Variable as the OutputType and choose the variable XMLOutput. The dialog box should look like Figure 6-22.

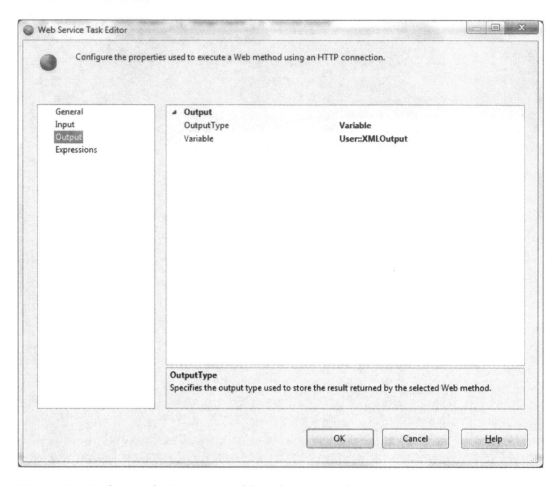

Figure 6-22. *Configuring the Output pane of the Web Services task*

18. Click OK to confirm your modifications. Return to the Control Flow pane.

19. In the Control Flow pane, add a Script task. Connect the Web Services task to it. Name it **Isolate Value Returned**. Double-click to edit. Add the XMLOutput variable as a read-only variable and the ConversionRate variable as a read-write variable. The dialog box should look like Figure 6-23.

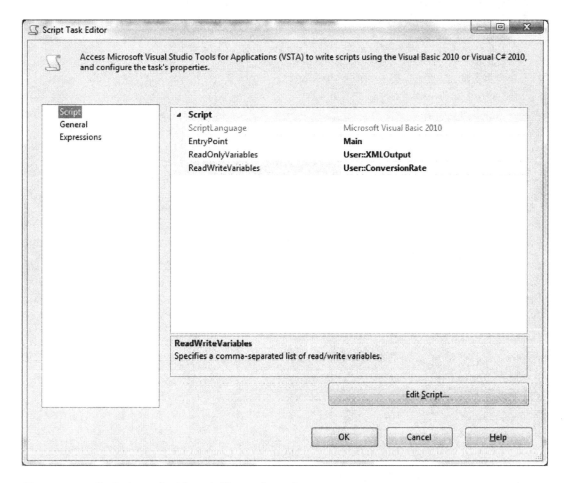

Figure 6-23. *The Script task with variables configured*

20. Click EditScript.

21. In the Imports region, add the following:

```
Imports System.Xml        'Added as not part of the basic SSIS task
```

22. Replace the Main method with the following
     (C:\SQL2012DIRecipes\CH06\WebServices.vb):

```
Public Sub Main()

    Dim xDdoc As New Xml.XmlDocument

    xDdoc.LoadXml(Dts.Variables("XMLOutput").Value.ToString)
```

```
        Dts.Variables("ConversionRate").Value = ↵
            CDbl(xDdoc.SelectSingleNode("double[1]").InnerText)

        Dts.TaskResult = ScriptResults.Success

    End Sub
```

23. Close the Script window.

24. Click OK to close the Script task editor.

25. Add a Data Flow task to the Data Flow pane and name it **Load data and convert prices**. Connect the Script task to it. The Control Flow pane should look like Figure 6-24.

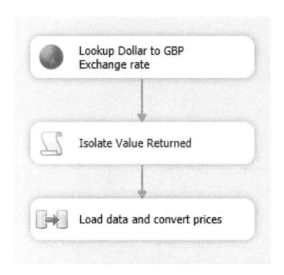

Figure 6-24. *The overall process flow using Web Services*

26. Double-click to edit the Data Flow task.

27. In the Data Flow pane, add an OLEDB source task. Configure it as follows:

Configuration Manager:	CarSales_OLEDB
Data Access Mode:	SQL Command
SQL Command Text:	`SELECT   ID, Make, Marque, Mileage`
	`FROM     Stock`

28. Add a Derived Column task and connect the OLEDB source task to it. Add two new derived columns named **Cost_PriceUSD** and **ExchangeRate**. Set the expression for Cost_PriceUSD to **Cost_Price * @[User::ConversionRate]**, and the expression for ExchangeRate to **@[User::ConversionRate]**. The dialog box should look like Figure 6-25.

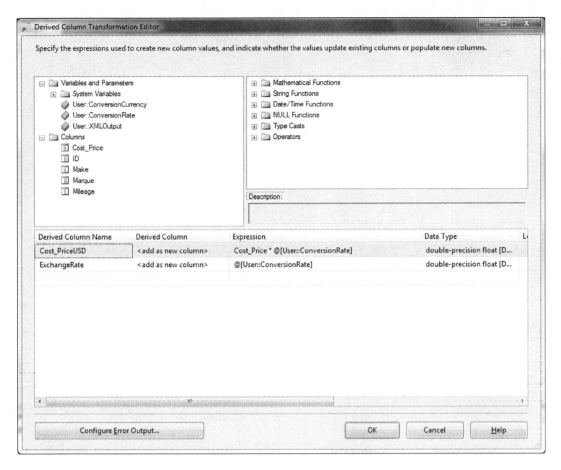

Figure 6-25. *The Derived Column transformation using a variable to calculate a derived column*

29. Click OK to confirm your modifications and return to the Data Flow pane.

30. Add an OLEDB destination task. Connect the Derived Column task to it and configure it as follows:

OLEDB Connection Manager:	CarSales_Staging_OLEDB
Data Access Mode:	Table or View—Fast Load
Name of the Table or View:	Dbo.StockInDollars

31. Click Mappings. Ensure that the source columns are mapped to the destination columns.

32. Click OK. The Data Flow should look like Figure 6-26.

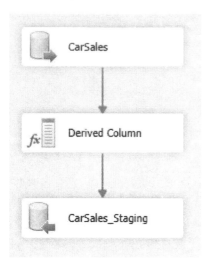

Figure 6-26. *The final Data Flow*

How It Works

Should you ever need to, then it is possible to insert data into an SSIS package using the SSIS Web Services task. This requires two things:

- Access to a web services provider
- The Web Services description file that allows the web service to be understood

Both of these are available from many free web services providers. I chose to use www.webservicex.net. You can use any web service that is available to you, of course.

■ **Note**   As this example is using a free third-party web service, there can be no guarantee that the web service will be available or that its methods will not change in the future.

First, we defined which web service you will be calling and established a connection to it using an HTTP connection manager. We then downloaded into an existing empty file the Web Services Description Language file that describes the web service to the Web Services task. With these elements in place, we were then able to configure the Web Services task to call the ConversionRate method of the web service we are using. Of course, in your own environment, you will probably use a different web service, and so will see different available web services and methods. Then, we set the output—that is, the XML returned from the web service—to a variable. (This could be written to a file on disk.) We defined the choice of a destination currency as a variable to make the task more easily reusable. This and the destination currency are elements required by the specific web service.

With the web service task configured, we can then use its output. The XML returned from each web service varies, so exactly how you process the output will vary in your real-world environment. In this example, we used a Script task to take the "raw" XML snippet returned from the call to the web service and used the power of the .NET System.XML class to read the value inside the XML. This value was then passed out from the Script task to an SSIS variable (ConversionRate) that was used to convert the source data that was loaded from CarSales.Stock into CarSales_Staging.StockInDollars. This was done using a Derived Column transformation to add not only the new cost in dollars, but also the exchange rate. You can use the output from the web service to call in any way that suits your needs, of course.

Hints, Tips, and Traps

- You can set the output to a variable, if you prefer.

- When using variables and columns in a Derived Column transformation, you can drag the variables and columns into the Expression area from the top-left pane of the dialog box.

6-11. Importing Windows Management Instrumentation Data
Problem

You want to import Windows Management Instrumentation (WMI) data into SQL Server.

Solution

Use the SSIS WMI Data Reader task as a data source in a standard data flow. The following tells how you can do this.

1. Create a new SSIS package (in a new SSIS project if you wish to isolate the package). Right-click the Task pane. Select Variables and add a variable (I will call it oWMI), which you set to data type "object". Ensure that the scope is package level.

2. Right-click the Connection Managers tab. Select New Connection and then select WMI, as shown in Figure 6-27.

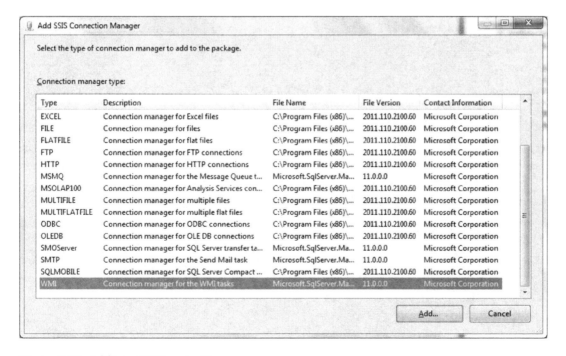

Figure 6-27. Adding a WMI connection manager

3. Click Add. Enter a name for the connection manager, enter a server name (unless the default localhost is what you wish to query), and check Use Windows Authentication (again, unless you need to log on as a specific user). You should have a dialog box that looks something like Figure 6-28.

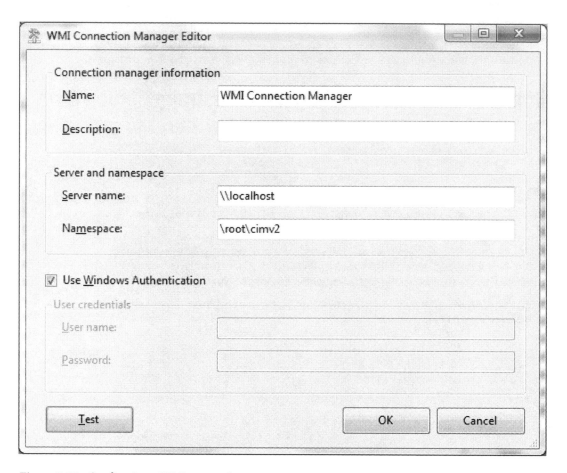

Figure 6-28. *Configuring a WMI connection manager*

4. Click Test to test the connection. Click OK to confirm. Close the dialog box.

5. Add a WMI Data Reader task onto the Control Flow pane. Double-click to edit it.

6. Set the following options:

Option	Value
WMIConnection	WMI Connection Manager
WQLQuerySourceType	Direct Input
OutputType	DataTable
OverwriteDestination	Overwrite destination
Destinationtype	Variable
Destination	oWMI (or the variable name that you chose)

7. In the WQLQuerySource, enter the following code (C:\SQL2012DIRecipes\CH06\Wmi.wmi):

```
SELECT      EventCode, EventIdentifier, EventType, Message, TimeGenerated
FROM        Win32_NTLogEvent
WHERE       Category = 2
```

You should have a dialog box that looks something like Figure 6-29.

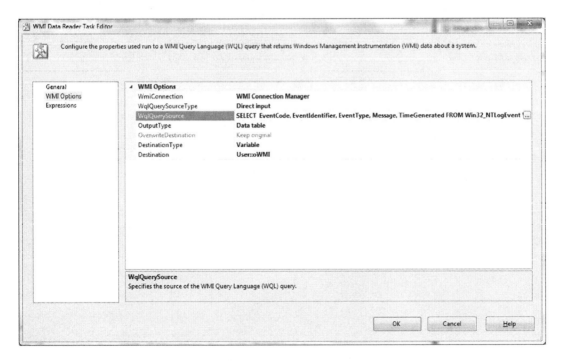

Figure 6-29. *Configuring the WMI Data Reader Task*

8. Click OK to confirm the WMI task creation.

9. Add a Data Flow task onto the Task pane and double-click to edit it. In the Data Flow pane, add a Script Component to the workspace. Click Source when the Select Script Component Type dialog box appears.

10. Click OK. Double-click the Script Component to edit it. Click inputs and outputs. Then expand Output0.

11. Click Output Columns, and click Add Column.

12. Give the column a name (the first one will be **EventCode**), and set its data type (8-byte unsigned integer in this case).

13. Repeat steps 17 and 18 for every output column that exists in the WQL query.

14. This should give you the dialog box shown in Figure 6-30.

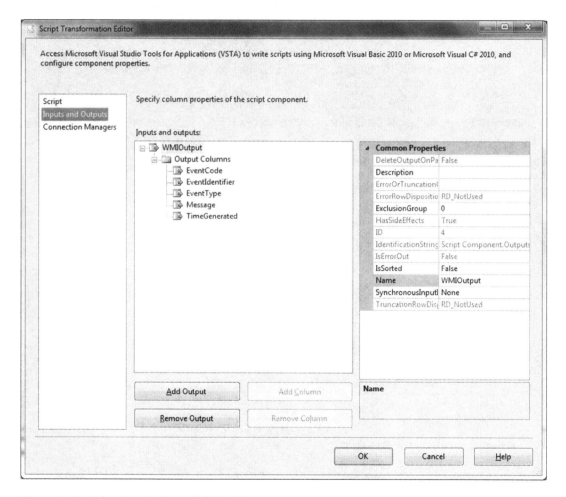

Figure 6-30. *Adapting a Script task for WMI sources*

15. Click Script on the left, and then enter the variable name you used earlier—Destination—as the WMIDestination in the ReadOnlyVariables.

16. Click Edit Script.

17. Add the Imports System.Xml directive to the Imports region.

18. Add the following code snippet in place of the CreateNewOutputRows method
(C:\SQL2012DIRecipes\CH06\Wmi.vb):

```vb
Public Overrides Sub CreateNewOutputRows()

        Dim WMIdataTable As System.Data.DataTable
        Dim WMIdataRow As System.Data.DataRow

        WMIdataTable = CType(Me.Variables.oWMI, Data.DataTable)

        For Each WMIdataRow In WMIdataTable.Rows

            OutputOBuffer.AddRow()

            OutputOBuffer.EventIdentifier = CULng(WMIdataRow.Item("EventIdentifier"))
            OutputOBuffer.EventCode = CInt(WMIdataRow.Item("EventCode"))
            OutputOBuffer.EventType = CInt(WMIdataRow.Item("EventType"))
            OutputOBuffer.Message = WMIdataRow.Item("Message").ToString
            OutputOBuffer.TimeGenerated = WMIdataRow.Item("TimeGenerated").ToString

        Next

        OutputOBuffer.SetEndOfRowset()

End Sub
```

19. Close the Script editor, and click OK to close the Script task.

20. Add an OLEDB destination to the Data Flow pane, connect the Script task to it, and
double-click to edit.

21. Select or create an OLEDB connection manager. Select Table or View as the Data
Access Mode. Click New to have SSIS define a new table. Change the table name from
OLE DB Destination to something more appropriate to your project and click OK.
Click Mappings. Ensure that the source and destination mappings are correct.

22. Click OK to close the OLEDB destination task.

You can now run the process, which will import the selected WMI data into SQL Server.

How It Works

Every Windows PC or server contains a vast amount of management data that can be queried for the information
that it contains. A huge subject in its own right, WMI can help manage Windows computers and many of the
applications (IIS and SQL Server for starters) that run under Windows. Here I wanted to show how you could
gather data using WMI and place it in SQL Server tables for analysis.

This process uses SSIS, but you need to configure the SSIS WMI task to send the output data to an ADO
record set. In turn, this becomes the data source used in a Data Flow task, accessed via a script component.

To keep the WMI part of this process simple, we queried the Windows Event Log to find certain categories of
events and the associated message. With WMI, you can do so much more than this, of course; but the subject is
vast—so a good reference book on WMI queries, or a trawl through the Web, should help give you some ideas as
to how WMI can help you.

Source-to-destination mapping is a little arduous for WMI. It follows that you have to be prepared to note down the source columns that you use, as you will have to define them as the Script Task Output columns, and as the outputbuffer in the script code, as was done here in the Script task.

Hints, Tips, and Traps

- You need to have a firm grasp of the column types because you have to convert all DataRow.Items to the requisite output type. This may involve some trial and error! Of course, you could go for the easy option and define them all as large VARCHAR types—at least to begin with.

- Until you know WMI (and WQL) well, you might find it faster to create a simple WMI task first (using a text file destination), which allows you to see the results of the WQL query and to tweak it to get what you want (as well as getting a better idea of the required data types).

6-12. Importing Data over ODBC

Problem

You want to import data but there is no OLEDB provider available for you to connect to a data source.

Solution

Create and use an ODBC data source using an available ODBC driver, assuming that one is available.

As ODBC is not a subject that can be handled in a purely linear fashion, I find it easier to look at some of the characteristics of how to use ODBC as a series of mini-recipes that explain how to configure and use ODBC drivers with SQL Server. I always assume that prior to using these recipes you have downloaded and installed the driver that is required for your specific data source.

ODBC in SSIS 2012

SSIS 2012 makes things slightly easier than previous versions, as you can use the ODBC connection manager directly rather than have to use an ADO.NET connection. The following explains how you use it.

1. In a new or existing SSIS package, right-click Connection Managers in the Solution Explorer. Select New Connection Manager.

2. Select ODBC from the list of available connection managers. The list should look something like Figure 6-31.

Figure 6-31. *Adding an ODBC connection manager*

3. Click Add.

4. Click New. You then must either select an existing DSN from those available (as described in the following mini-recipe) or select Use Connection String and enter the appropriate ODBC connection string for DSN-less connectivity.

5. Click OK to complete the configuration.

Generating an ODBC connection string is described in the last of the mini-recipes in this recipe.

Configuring an ODBC DSN

The standard way to configure an ODBC DSN is like this:

1. Click Start menu ➤ Control Panel ➤ Administrative Tools ➤ Data Sources (ODBC). You might need to give Windows permission to run it!

2. Select System DSN. The ODBC Data Source Administrator dialog box should look like Figure 6-32.

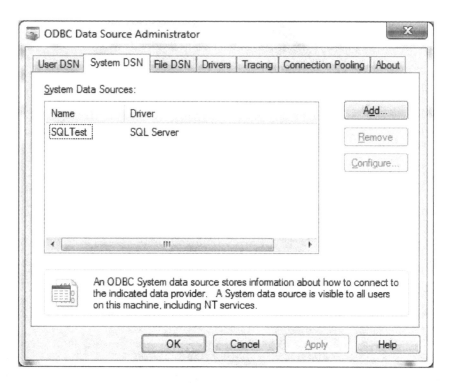

***Figure 6-32.** The ODBC Data Source Administrator*

3. Click Add. Select the data source to which you want to connect from those available (and by definition installed on your server). You should see the Create New Data Source dialog box, as shown in Figure 6-33.

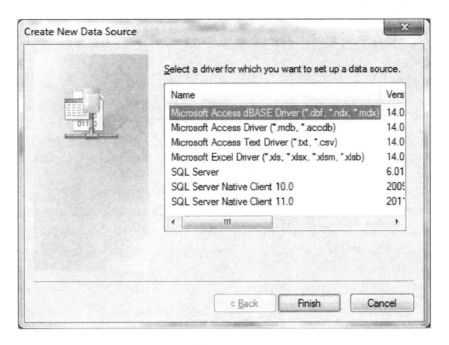

Figure 6-33. *Creating a new ODBC data source*

4. Select the driver and click Finish. You should then see the dialog box specific to the ODBC driver that you have selected, which you must now configure.

5. Create or open an SSIS package.

6. Add a new connection manager (at package level, if you prefer—and if you are using SSIS 2012).

7. For SSIS 2012, select the ODBC Connection Manager and select the DSN that you created. (For SSIS 2005 and 2008, select an ADO.NET connection and use the ODBC data provider. Then select the DSN that you created.)

You can then use the ODBC source in an SSIS Data Flow process, or when using OPENROWSET, or in a linked server connection. I cannot give examples of these because I am trying to remain as resolutely generic as possible. So you have to consult the documentation for your specific ODBC driver for examples of how to use these connectivity methods.

File DSNs

You can also use the ODBC Administrator tool to create file DSNs. The technique is virtually identical to that just described, except that after selecting the ODBC driver, you have to click Next and enter a file name for the DSN (and potentially choose a destination directory) before clicking Finish.

A file DSN is simply a text file that could be something like the following (C:\SQL2012DIRecipes\CH06\File.dsn):

```
[ODBC]
DRIVER=SQL Server Native Client 10.0
UID=Adam
```

```
DATABASE = CarSales
WSID = ADAM02
APP = Microsoft® Windows® Operating System
Trusted_Connection = Yes
SERVER = ADAM02
```

File DSNs can be used by SSIS to create connection strings for ODBC connection managers (in SSIS 2012) or for ODBC over ADO.NET connection managers (in SSIS 2005/2008), as is shown next.

File DSNs in SSIS 2012

File DSNs can also be used to configure the connection string for ODBC connections in SSIS 2012.

1. Follow steps 1 to 3 in the ODBC in SSIS 2012 mini-recipe above.

2. Click New.

3. Click Use Connection String.

4. Click Build.

5. Browse to the directory where you saved the file DSN.

6. Click OK.

7. Finalize any parameters that are required but not supplied by the DSN.

8. Click OK twice.

The connection string will be added to the dialog box.

ODBC and SSIS 2005/2008

The "older" versions of SSIS require you to use ODBC over ADO.NET as your System and User DSNs.

1. In a new or existing SSIS package, right-click in the Connection Managers tab and select New ADO.NET Connection.

2. Click New.

3. Click the pop-up list of providers. You should see something like Figure 6-34.

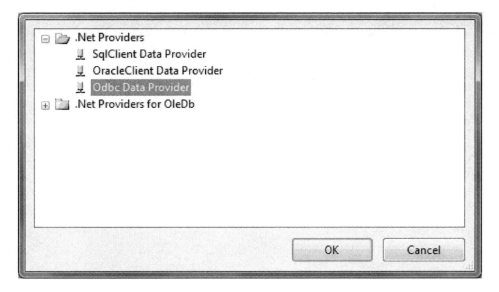

Figure 6-34. *.NET data providers*

4. Select the ODBC data provider.

5. Click OK.

6. Ensure that the "Use user or system data source name" radio button is selected. Choose an existing DSN from those available when you expand the list of DSNs. You should see a dialog box like Figure 6-35.

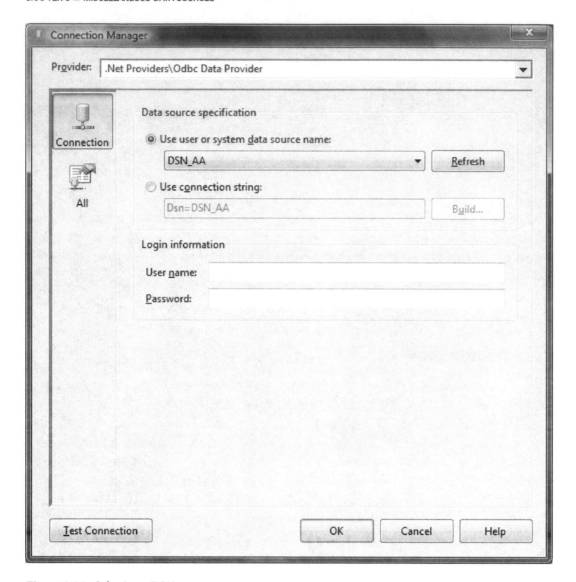

Figure 6-35. *Selecting a DSN*

7. Enter the username and password, if required.

8. Click OK.

File DSNs in SSIS 2005/2008

File DSNs can also be used to configure SSIS ODBC connection managers. It is worth noting nonetheless that the configuration information in the file DSN is used as a source, and that no link to the file is maintained, as all the configuration information is stored in SSIS.

1. Follow steps 1 to 5 in the "ODBC in SSIS 2005/2008" mini-recipe.

2. Ensure that the Use Connection String radio button is selected. Click Build.

3. Browse to the file DSN that you created—or were given.

4. Once the file DSN is selected, click OK.

5. Provide any required security/logon information. The dialog box should look like Figure 6-31.

6. Test the connection. Click OK.

"DSN-less" ODBC Connections

You can make SSIS use an ODBC driver without needing an existing DSN. This works for all versions of SSIS. It creates a .dsn file on disk in any case.

1. Using the preceding recipe(s) for file DSNs, display the Connection Manager dialog box shown in Figure 6-36.

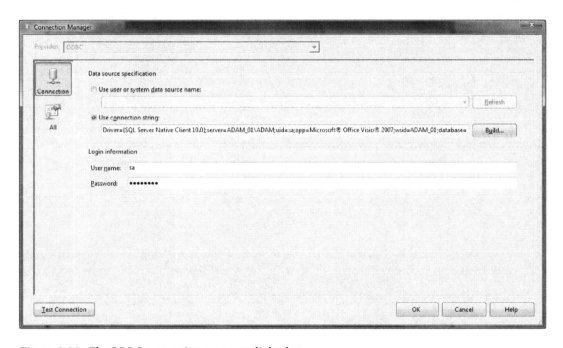

Figure 6-36. *The ODBC connection manager dialog box*

2. Ensure that the Use Connection String radio button is selected. Click Build.

3. Click New. Select the ODBC driver corresponding to the data source that you wish to use.

4. Click Next.

5. Save the File DSN. You may decide on the file name and directory—but the .dsn extension is added automatically.

6. Click Next.

7. Click Finish.

8. Configure the ODBC driver.

9. Click OK.

Exporting and Importing System and User DSNs

System and User DSNs are stored in the registry. While this makes them easy to tweak using the ODBC Administrator tool, it makes deployment a little more complex.

There is a particular registry entry:—HKEY_LOCAL_MACHINE\SOFTWARE\ODBC\ODBC.INI—that contains a complete list of the System DSN sources defined on your machine. You can use regedit (or a similar utility) to export your registry entries, which can then be copied as required. This avoids regenerating DSNs manually. It can be done as follows:

1. Open the registry editor.

2. Navigate to the ODBC folder (under HKEY_LOCAL_MACHINE > SOFTWARE).

3. Export a .reg file with a suitable name.

4. Import the .reg file into the registry of a destination server using regedit.exe—or by double-clicking the .reg file.

5. Reboot the destination server.

User DSNs are found in HKEY_CURRENT_USER\Software\ODBC\ODBC.INI.

Assuming that you have created a System or User DSN, it is worth looking at how these may be used by SSIS.

▪ **Note** Be extremely careful when using a Registry editor and ensure that you do not make any unwanted or dangerous changes to the registry.

How It Works

Well, finally, you have tried everything else every other way, and you have come to the conclusion that ODBC is the only remaining solution. Yes, it can be slow (at least when run over an ADO.NET provider), and, yes, it can be clumsy with some data types, but when all is said and done, it may be the only way to go. Intriguingly, Microsoft has indicated that ODBC is the future, so the time when this type of connection was to be relegated to "outsider" status is clearly past.

As specific ODBC connections are described in detail for MySQL and other relational sources, this recipe is a succinct generic overview of how to create and use ODBC connection managers. As each ODBC driver has its own specific configuration options, you have to know how to set up each one; so be prepared to dive into the source documentation and any other useful reference information that you can find. This means that out of necessity I must remain very generic when explaining the configuration techniques for ODBC drivers.

I imagine that most times you will create a DSN using the ODBC Administrator tool. On a 32-bit or a 64-bit system, this is found in %SystemRoot%\system32\odbcad32.exe. Admittedly, this is a surprising naming convention. Should you need the 32-bit version on a 64-bit machine, you need to look for %SystemRoot%\Windows\SysWOW64\odbcad32.exe.

I have a weakness for creating System DSNs rather than User DSNs. The reasons for this are as follows:

- Because they are not specific to the user who is running the process, it is one less potential source of failure.

- Possibly more important, because there is no registry redirection for User DSNs, and the ODBC Administrator tool displays both 32-bit and 64-bit DSNs, you can end up attempting to use a DSN that cannot function in the environment that you are using.

It is also worth noting that a 64-bit server running `odbcad32.exe` from the Control Panel will run the 64-bit version of the ODBC connection manager.

Hints, Tips, and Traps

- If you create a connection string–based DSN in SSIS, the ODBC Administrator will create a `.dsn` file on disk in any case. You have to delete this file manually if you do not want it stored on disk.

- The ODBC Administrator displays User DSNs for both 32- and 64-bit drivers. This does not mean that a 64-bit application uses the 32-bit driver, however, because registry redirection is not available for User DSNs.

- Redirection is available for System DSNs. Consequently, System DSNs for 32-bit drivers and 64-bit drivers are kept separate. The 64-bit ODBC Administrator does not display System DSNs that are created by the 32-bit ODBC Administrator. Similarly, the 32-bit ODBC Administrator does not display System DSNs that are created by the 64-bit ODBC Administrator.

- Consequently, on 64-bit systems, you are best advised to install both 32-bit and 64-bit versions of drivers where these are available.

- In SSIS 2005 and 2008, don't try to set up an ODBC connection manager by right-clicking in the Connection Manager pane, and then selecting New Connection, followed by ODBC. This will not work because it is not a "managed" connection!

6-13. Linking to 32-bit data sources from a 64-bit SQL Server
Problem

You are working in a 64-bit environment and need to implement a linked server to data for which only a 32-bit provider is available.

Solution

Install a second 32-bit instance of SQL Server and set up a (32-bit) linked server to your source data. You can then link the 64-bit version of SQL Server to this. Although painful to carry out and slow to load data, this is how it can be done (here using Access as a sample 32-bit data source).

1. Install a second 32-bit instance of SQL Server.

2. Configure both servers to allow ad hoc distributed queries. This is described in Recipe 1-4.

3.   Select—or better still, create—a database on the 32-bit SQL Server instance that will be used to route the queries from the linked Access database to the 64-bit instance. I will name the database CarSales32.

4.   On the 32-bit SQL Server instance, create a linked server to connect to the Access database. The following code snippet can do this. Of course, this is where you will have to configure the source data which you are using to be as a linked server:

```
EXECUTE master.dbo.sp_addlinkedserver @server = N'Access', @srvproduct = N'Access',
@provider=N'Microsoft.Jet.OLEDB.4.0', @datasrc = C:\SQL2012DIRecipes\CH01\CarSales.mdb';
```

5.   On the 32-bit SQL Server instance, in the database that you created in step 3, create a view to query the source data database. This could be as simple as (C:\SQL2012DIRecipes\CH01\vw_SQL32.Sql):

```
CREATE VIEW vw_SQL32
AS
SELECT theText from Access...Client;
GO
```

6.   On the SQL Server 64-bit instance, create a linked server to the 32-bit SQL Server instance.

```
EXECUTE master.dbo.sp_addlinkedserver @server = 'ADAM32', @srvproduct = '', ↵
@provider = 'SQLNCLI', @datasrc = 'ADAM02\SQL32Bit';
```

7.   From the 64-bit instance, read the data from the 32-bit linked server:

```
SELECT ID, Marque FROM ADAM32.CarSales32.dbo.vw_SQL32;
```

How It Works

So, what can you do if you are working in a 64-bit environment and need to implement a 32-bit linked server when only a 32-bit driver (OLEDB or ODBC) exists? The approach described here is a possible workaround, although it is a lot of initial effort.

What you did was:

- Install a second 32-bit SQL Server instance.

- Link the source data to the 32-bit SQL Server instance.

- Link this second instance to your 64-bit instance.

I agree that this is a lot of effort to achieve something that should be simple; but in some cases, you may find that you have no alternative.

Hints, Tips, and Traps

- You can also link to 32-bit Excel in a 64-bit environment this way.

- I am assuming that you have full admin rights to both servers. If this is not the case, you have to map local and remote logins appropriately.

- Views are not the only way of returning the data from the source; you can use OPENROWSET As well.

- For an ODBC source you will probably have to define a DSN and use MSDASQL as the OLEDB provider.

▪ **Note**   You will have to comply with any licensing requirements if you set up a second SQL Server instance. Remember that SQL Server express can handle databases of up to 10 GB and can use 1 GB of memory – so it could be a solution to this kind of problem.

Summary

In this chapter, you have seen some data sources that you will probably encounter less often. However, just because a data format is older—think dBase or Visual FoxPro—doesn't mean that you won't need to load the information it contains into SQL Server one day.

On a slightly different plane, loading data into SSAS from SQL Server doesn't mean that you won't want Analysis Services to allow you to return data from a cube into a relational table; so, we saw how to do this too. Should you be using the Microsoft RDBMS as a repository for files, you have seen how to load files—individually and en masse—into data tables. And, of course, you have discovered how to use Web Services as a source of data.

Then there are the myriad sources that have ODBC drivers, which you must use to access the data that they contain. Every one is different, but this chapter tried to show you how to use ODBC in SQL Server 2012 to allow you a gateway into many, many other data repositories.

All in all, this chapter has taken you on a tour of the farther shores of data integration. The techniques that were used may be employed more rarely, but they can be vital when faced with an ETL challenge involving one of the less traditional sources of data.

CHAPTER 7

Exporting Data from SQL Server

Getting data into SQL Server can be a major challenge faced by a developer or a DBA. Yet there are frequent occasions when data needs to be pushed in the other direction—out of SQL Server and into another program or system. This aspect of data integration also has its tricks (which you need to know) and pitfalls (which you need to know how to avoid). This chapter looks at some of the main methods of sending data from SQL Server into other environments. Fortunately, you have are two main advantages when exporting data from SQL Server as compared to importing it:

- You possess complete knowledge and control of the data and its structures.

- You can use the core language that you are intimately familiar with (T-SQL) to handle how the data is transformed for the destination system.

Indeed, many of the techniques that are used in exporting data in this chapter are similar to those that you have already seen in previous chapters. So we will only need a single chapter to look at the ways of exporting data:

- As text (delimited and fixed-width) files.

- As XML files.

- Into Access and Excel.

- As SQL Server–native BCP files.

- Into other SQL Server databases.

- Into other SQL databases.

There are many other export destinations that I will not be covering, even if they were discussed as possible sources of data in other chapters. This is because it is clearly impossible to describe every eventuality, and because I consider some data sources to be in either a "legacy" or an "extremely rare" category, where they are unlikely to be required as data output destinations.

If you have downloaded the sample files from the book's companion web site, you will find them in `C:\SQL2012DIRecipes\CH07`.

7-1. Exporting Data Occasionally in Various Formats
Problem

You want to export SQL Server data from time to time to one of the many available formats—possibly to satisfy an unexpected request.

Solution

Use the Import/Export Wizard and select one of its many destination formats to output the data.

As the SQL Server Import/Export Wizard can export data in many formats I will show you here how to export data to another SQL Server database, and give comments on other possible destinations at the end of the recipe. To do this, follow these steps:

1. In SSMS, right-click the database from which you want to export data (CarSales in this example) and select Tasks ➤ Export Data. If the Welcome pane shows, click Next.

2. In the Choose a Datasource pane, check that the source database (CarSales) and authentication mode/credentials are correct. Click Next.

3. In the Choose a Destination pane, select the required destination. In the Destination pop-up, you see a list of all installed drivers. If you cannot see the destination you require here, then you need to halt the process and install the required driver. In this example, select SQL Server Native Client 11.0. Enter any authentication required, and then the destination database. The dialog box should look something like Figure 7-1.

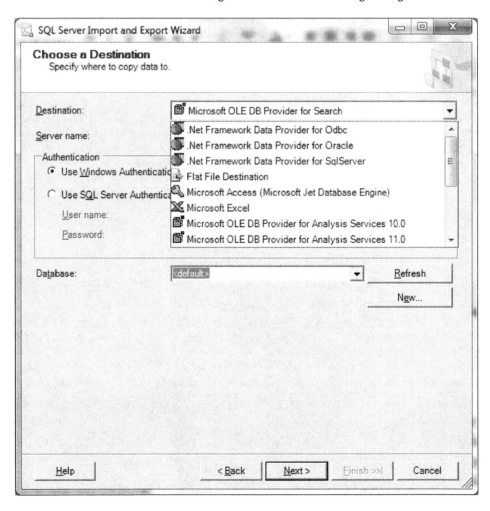

Figure 7-1. *SQL Server Import/Export Wizard*

4. Click Next.

5. In the Specify Table Copy or Query pane, choose whether to select multiple tables or views (by clicking Copy Data from one or more tables or views) or to export a single table resulting from an ad hoc query or stored procedure (Write a Query to Specify the Data to Transfer). In this case, select Copy Data from one or more tables or views, and then click Next.

6. In the Select Source Tables and Views pane, select all the tables and views that you wish to export, and then click Next.

7. In the Review Data Type Mapping pane, review all the data type mappings. You will need to do this for every table by clicking the table name in the upper part of the dialog box, and then examining (and possibly changing) the data type mappings in the lower part of the dialog box. Fortunately, the wizard will alert you to possible anomalies using the yellow triangle, as seen in Figure 7-2.

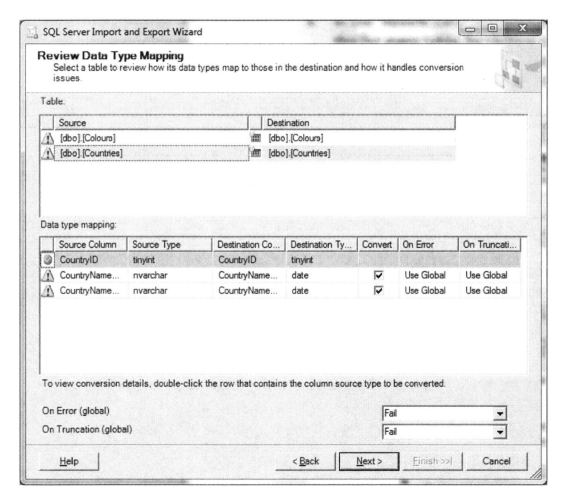

Figure 7-2. Data type mapping in the SQL Server Import/Export Wizard

8. Once you are happy with this, click Next.

9. In the Save and Run Package pane, choose whether to save the export process as an SSIS package or not—and if so, where to save it. Then click Next.

10. You now have a final chance to review all your options. Assuming that everything seems in order, click Finish.

Assuming that all has gone well, the data will have been exported.

How It Works

For quick and simple data export to a wide variety of classic formats, few approaches are as easy as the Export Wizard. In a few clicks, you can export SQL Server tables or views to

- Flat files (fixed-width and delimited).
- Excel.
- Access.
- SQL Server.
- Other relational databases.

Indeed, you can export SQL Server data to almost any data recipient for which an OLEDB or .NET provider is correctly installed. When exporting, you can choose

- Multiple tables or views.
- A single ad hoc SQL query.
- To create (and define data types for) a new destination table or file.
- To add data to an existing destination.
- To replace data in an existing destination.
- To save the export definition as an SSIS package.

Exactly what the Export Wizard can do depends largely on the export format. To give you an idea, Table 7-1 presents a succinct overview of the possibilities. In all cases, you can only define destination data types if you are creating a new destination object (flat file, Excel sheet, or relational database table) and cannot modify the existing object.

Table 7-1. Import/Export Wizard Options

Destination	Multiple Source Tables or Views	Create Destination Table/File/Worksheet	Define Destination Data Types
Flat file	No	Yes	Yes
Excel	Yes	File and Worksheet(s)	Yes
Access	Yes	Yes	Yes
SQL Server	Yes	Yes	Yes
Other Relational Databases	Yes	Yes	Yes

The main limitation of the Export Wizard is that it is for exporting data "as is" in your SQL Server database only. That is, you will not be able to carry out the following:

- Data transformation
- Data flow logic
- Aggregations
- Logging

The Export Wizard can also be invaluable as an "SSIS package generator" that can create starter packages for you. You can then extend them further to your heart's content in SSIS, where you can add any process control logic and other more complex data flow elements that you require. Moreover, it is worth noting that complex data sources with aggregations and data conversions can be prepared as Views, scripts or stored procedures that can be used as data sources.

I will not be looking at any data destinations other than those listed, since my experience leads me to believe that this will cover a considerable range of simple data export requirements. After all, that is what the wizard was designed for!

This recipe only shows one possible path through all the alternatives that the Export Wizard offers—copying all the data from one or more tables to any of the destinations for which an appropriate driver has been configured on the source server. While showing every possible combination would be a Herculean task (and completely superfluous), there are a few variations on the export process. The prerequisites for a successful export are as follows:

- All OLEDB and .NET drivers must be installed for the destinations to which you wish to export data.
- You need all the relevant permissions for your user account on all the destination files, folders, and databases to which you wish to export data.

A Few Variations on the Theme of the Export Wizard

Now for a few variations on the theme explained in this recipe. The only basic assumption that I can make in this chapter is that the data source will be SQL Server. You can choose from many other options as you proceed through the Export Wizard. These include:

- The choice of destination.
- The selection of source data—both with objects and subsetting the source data.
- Data transformation and column mappings during the export process.

While I do not want to attempt to cover all available options, what follows are some of the core elements that you may be called to use as you export data using this utility.

SQL Statement

If you select Write a Query to Specify the Data to Transfer at step 4, you get the option to type or insert from file an SQL query in the Provide a Source Query pane. What is worth noting here is that . . .

- If you are exporting data using a stored procedure, then enter **EXECUTE ProcName** in the SQL Statement pane.
- If your data source is a stored procedure or complex query, then you cannot return data from a session-scoped temporary table. You can, however, use CTEs to circumvent this limitation in many cases.

- Clicking the Browse button allows you to select a source SQL script file.

- This path only allows a single set of data to be exported.

Flat File

If you select a Flat File destination, then you will have to decide from the following options in the Choose a Destination pane:

- A file name and path

- Unicode or a code page

- Delimited, fixed-width, or ragged right

- A text qualifier

- Whether you want column names in the first row

In the Configure Flat File Destination pane, you can select the row and column delimiter—and the source table or view.

Excel

There are a few interesting points to note when exporting to Excel:

- The Export wizard can create an Excel file for you. It can use existing files and worksheets.

- You must use the ACE driver for Excel version 2007 or later, and the 64-bit ACE driver in 64-bit systems.

Access

There are a couple of interesting points when exporting data to Access:

- The Export Wizard will not create an Access database—you must create it first.

- Use the ACE driver for Access version 2007 or newer, and the 64-bit ACE driver in 64-bit systems.

Relational Databases

For all relational database exports (including SQL Server), you need the following:

- Client software correctly set up on the SQL Server, if client software is required (Oracle springs to mind).

- All necessary providers (OLEDB or ODBC) correctly installed on the SQL Server.

- Write permission to the destination server and database, and DDL permissions if you will be creating destination tables.

Column Mappings

When you are selecting source tables and views, you can select column mappings for each table. This gives you the option to fine-tune the output by the following:

- Specifying which column is the destination (for an existing destination table).

- Altering the column name and data type/size (when creating a new table).

- Deciding whether to drop and re-create the destination table.

- Appending or replacing data in the destination table.

- Allowing IDENTITY insert (for SQL Server destinations).

All this is carried out in the Column Mappings dialog box (see Figure 7-3), which appears when you click Edit Mappings.

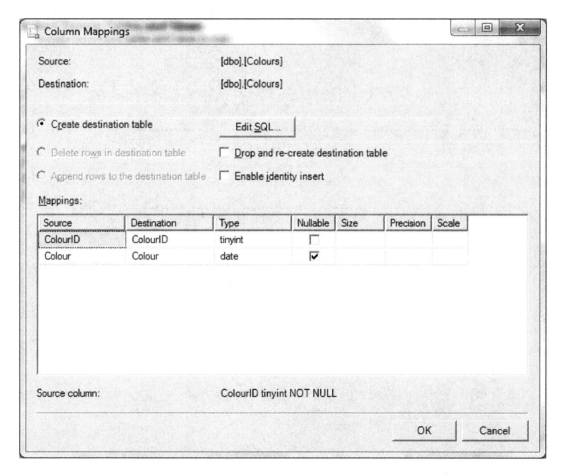

Figure 7-3. *Column mappings*

Also, if you click the Edit SQL button, the Export Wizard will return the CREATE TABLE statement that it will use on the destination server. You may edit this if you wish (see Figure 7-4).

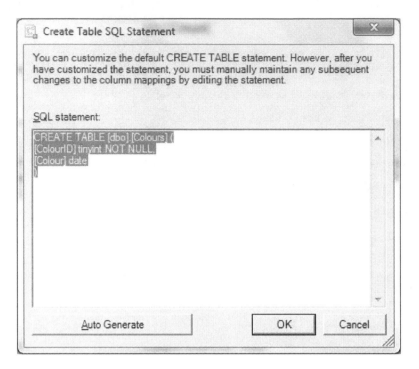

Figure 7-4. *Create Table DDL in the SQL Server Import/Export Wizard*

Hints, Tips, and Traps

- When saving the work you did using the Export Wizard as an SSIS package, you can choose to save the SSIS package the way you would any other SSIS package—that is in SQL Server or as a file.

- If you are exporting multiple tables, then the actual export process will group them into sets of four tables. If your system has additional available processors and the dataset is large, you may find it more efficient to save the package and tweak it to run more than four exports in parallel.

- There are several other ways to run the data Export Wizard. These include:

  - On the Start menu, select All Programs, then Microsoft SQL Server 2012, followed by Import and Export Data.

  - In SQL Server Data Tools (SSDT—or Business Intelligence Development Studio if you are using an older version of SQL Server) right-click the SSIS Packages folder, and then select SSIS Import and Export Wizard.

  - In BIDS/SSDT, click SSIS Import and Export Wizard on the Project menu.

  - From a Command window, type **DTSWizard.exe**.

7-2. Exporting Data As a Delimited Text File

Problem

You want to export data as a delimited text file—and you need to understand the various subtleties of flat file output.

Solution

Use SQL Server Integration Services (SSIS) and the Flat File destination to send data from a table, view, or query to a text file.

The following steps explain how to export a delimited text file from an SQL Server table.

1. Create a new SSIS package and add an OLEDB connection manager named **CarSales**, which connects to your source database (CarSales in this example).

2. Add a Data Flow task. Double-click to edit.

3. Add an OLEDB source, and configure as follows:

Connection Manager:	CarSales
Data Access Mode:	SQL Text
SQL Command Text:	SELECT ID, ClientName, Country, Town, County, Address1, Address2, ClientType, ClientSize
	FROM dbo.Client

4. Confirm your modifications.

5. Add a Flat File destination to the Data Flow pane, and connect the OLEDB source to it. Double-click to edit. Click New to create a new Flat File connection manager. Select Delimited from the Flat File Format dialog box, and click OK, as shown in Figure 7-5.

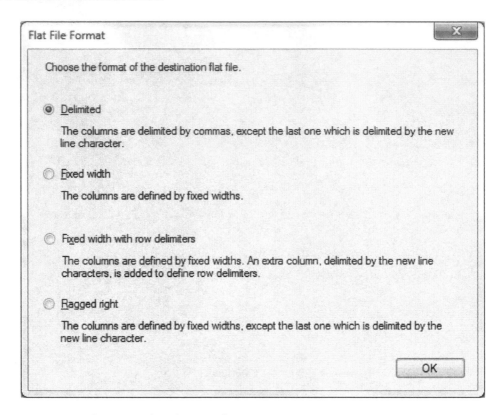

Figure 7-5. *Choosing a Flat File export format*

6. Configure the Flat File Connection Manager Editor as follows (assuming that you are using the examples for this book—otherwise, use your own file path):

Name:	Delimited_Unicode
File Name:	`C:\SQL2012DIRecipes\CH07\ClientsDelimited.txt`
Unicode:	Ticked
Column Names in First Data Row	Ticked
Text Qualifier	<none>
Header rows to skip	0
Header Row delimiter	<CR><LF>

The dialog box should look like Figure 7-6.

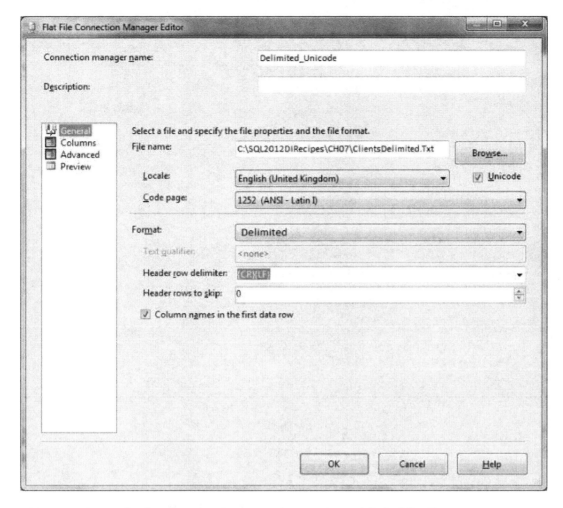

Figure 7-6. *Setting the Flat File connection manager to export to a delimited flat file*

      7.   Click OK to confirm your changes.

      8.   Click Mappings and ensure that all the output columns are mapped to the source columns.

And that, fairly simply, is that. You can now export your data.

How It Works

Quite possibly the most frequently used export type (in my experience) is text. This is probably because most database or spreadsheet programs can accept external delimited text files. At risk of stating the obvious, a text file will have the characteristics shown in Table 7-2.

Table 7-2. *Text File Characteristics*

Option	Definition
Character type	ASCII or Unicode. For ASCII export, the code page can be defined.
Column separator	Chosen by the user. The default is comma (,).
Row Delimiter	Chosen by the user. The default is Carriage Return + Line Feed (CR/LF).
Text Qualifier	Optional. Can be defined for each column.

You can choose to add data to an existing text file, or delete the contents of an existing file. To replace the file contents, check "Overwrite data in the file" in the Flat File Destination Editor. It is worth noting that you can create a Flat File connection manager before creating the Flat File destination and connecting it to the OLEDB source, but this will not automatically generate the destination column structure for you. This means that you will have to create all the columns manually, which is laborious, to say the least. A consequence of this is that if the source data changes radically, you may find it easier to delete the existing Flat File connection manager and replace it with a new one, rather than attempt to reconfigure the destination. This is compounded by the fact that the only way to reorder columns, unfortunately, is to delete and re-insert them.

When tweaking (as opposed to re-creating) a Flat File destination, you can add or delete columns using the New and Delete buttons. When adjusting column specifications in the Advanced pane, you can select multiple columns with the Ctrl key and sets of columns using the Shift key.

There are a series of useful options for exporting text files (delimited or fixed-width). Table 7-3 provides a brief explanation of the principal variations on this particular theme.

Table 7-3. *SSIS Text Destination Options*

Option	Dialog Box Page	Comments
Locale	General page	Currency settings and so forth.
Unicode	General page	Checking this will export the file using Unicode.
Code Page	General page	If your destination file must use a specific code page (and therefore is non-Unicode)
Header Row Delimiter	Columns page	Specifies the header row delimiter. This can be different from the delimiter for data rows.
Header Rows to Skip	General page	Entering a figure here will cause the output to skip the first "n" records.
Text Qualifier	General page	The character—usually doublequotes (")—that will be used to encapsulate text fields that contain extra occurrences of the column separator character(s).
Column Names in the First Data Row	General page	Adds the column names as the first row in the output file.
Row Delimiter	Columns page	Specifies the default row delimiter.
Column Delimiter	Columns page	Specifies the default column delimiter. This can be specified individually for each column in the Advanced page. Equally, if you want to use a delimiter that is not in the pop-up list, use the Advanced page.

(continued)

Table 7-3. (*continued*)

Option	Dialog Box Page	Comments
Name	Advanced page	Allows you to rename a column. The name that will be used if you choose to add the column names as the first row in the output file.
Column Delimiter	Advanced page	Allows you to specify the column delimiter for this column, and override the default. You can also enter a character (or several characters) if the one(s) you require are not in the list.
Text Qualified	Advanced page	You can specify if this column is enclosed in the text qualifier.

Hints, Tips, and Traps

- Exporting a text file as Unicode will double its size—as each character will be two bytes instead of one. For extremely large files, the simplicity of avoiding the hassle of code pages can come at a considerable cost in disk space and network transfer times.

- You may prefer to alias columns in the T-SQL SELECT statement at source rather than rename them in the Advanced page of the Flat File destination adapter.

- Of course, you can select a table as the source for the data, but this is only good practice if you are using all the source columns. SSIS will export the data faster if you choose only the required columns as part of the SELECT statement, rather than choosing a table or view source and subsequently deselecting the columns that you do not require in the data flow.

- Adding a text qualifier will also encapsulate the column title in quotes for each column where the TextQualified advanced column property is set to True. If you find this annoying or unusable, then consider outputting the column headers as part of the SELECT statement using a UNION clause, as shown in Recipe 7-4.

- You are free to choose the file name and extension that you prefer, but it makes it easier for those who receive your files if you respect the (fairly) standard conventions of .CSV for comma-separated values, .PSV for pipe-separated values, and so forth.

- If you are trying to adhere to the CSV specification (of course, I am using the term somewhat loosely) and wish to escape double quotes inside field data, then the easiest—if not the only—way to do this is to extend the SQL SELECT clause to include a REPLACE function. To give an example, your code could be:

```
SELECT      ID, ClientName, Country, Town, County,
            REPLACE(Address1,'"','"""'), Address2,
            ClientType, ClientSize
FROM        dbo.Client;
```

This will replace every double quote in the Address1 field with two double quotes.

- The Flat File destination does not have to be simply connected to a single OLEDB source; it can be the result of a complex SSIS data transformation process from multiple data sources.

7-3. Exporting Data to a Fixed-Width Text File

Problem

You want to export data to a text file, but the recipient of the data wants it to be in fixed-width format, not the usual delimited type.

Solution

Use SSIS and the Flat File destination, but specify a fixed-width file format. You export data in this format in the following way.

1. Perform steps 1 to 4 from Recipe 7-2, but specify Fixed Width as the Flat File format. Configure the new Flat File connection manager that you create so that it looks like Figure 7-7.

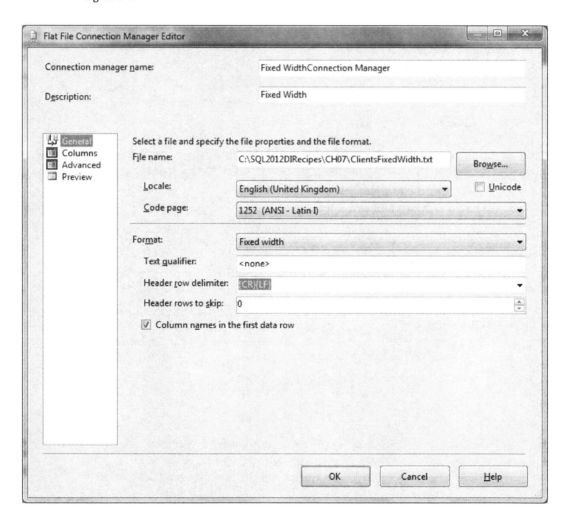

Figure 7-7. *Fixed-width flat file output*

2. Check the Advanced page, where you should see that the column widths have been calculated for you, with the maximum text width for each text column, and the widest necessary column for each numeric or date/time field type.

How It Works

Exporting a fixed-width file is largely similar to the process described in Recipe 7-2. It is, if anything, even simpler than exporting a delimited file. One thing that makes it easier is that you do not need to worry about column separators since columns are "delimited" according to the number of characters from the start of the row. Another thing that makes it easier is that since there are no column delimiters, there is no requirement to escape any character.

Hints, Tips, and Traps

- A ragged-right export includes a CR/LF at the end of every row; a fixed-width export will not.

7-4. Exporting Text Files from the Command Line
Problem

You want to export text files without using SSIS, T-SQL, or the Import/Export Wizard, possibly as part of a script.

Solution

Use BCP to export data from a Command window or a Command (.cmd) file as a text file.

To export data as a text file from a table, use the following code snippet in a Command window. (Note that all the following code extracts are in the file C:\SQL2012DIRecipes\CH07\BCPOut1.cmd):

```
bcp CarSales.dbo.Client OUT C:\SQL2012DIRecipes\CH07\aa1.txt -SAdam_01\Adam –c -T
```

Something similar, but using a SELECT, statement would be:

```
bcp "SELECT ID,ClientName FROM CarSales.dbo.Client" ↵
QUERYOUT C:\SQL2012DIRecipes\CH07\aa1.txt -SAdam_01\Adam –c -T
```

This command uses a stored procedure to return data (assuming that I had previously created one called pr_OutputClients containing a query such as SELECT ID,ClientName FROM CarSales.dbo.Client):

```
bcp "EXECUTE CarSales.dbo.pr_OutputClients" ↵
QUERYOUT C:\SQL2012DIRecipes\CH07\aa1.txt -SAdam_01\Adam –c -T
```

The easiest way to encapsulate column data in quotes is to include it in the source T-SQL:

```
SELECT  ID, + '"' + ClientName + '"', Country
FROM    CarSales.dbo.Client;
```

BCP does not have an option to include column headers. Should you need them, then you need to tweak the SQL to include column headers, possibly using a UNION clause in your T-SQL along these lines (C:\SQL2012DIRecipes\CH07\IncludeHeadersInTextFile.sql):

```
SELECT ID, ClientName, Country
FROM (
      SELECT 'ID' AS ID, 'ClientName' AS ClientName, 'Country' AS Country, 0 AS RowOrder
      UNION
      SELECT CAST(ID AS VARCHAR(11)), ClientName, Country, 1 AS RowOrder
      FROM CarSales.dbo.Client
      ) A
ORDER BY RowOrder,ID;
```

Should the destination database require different field delimiters (a rare occurrence admittedly), then it is probably easier also to generate these as part of the source SQL.

```
SELECT   CAST(ID AS VARCHAR(11)) + '/' + ClientName + ';' + Country
FROM     CarSales.dbo.Client;
```

■ **Note**   In all these examples, I am presuming that you will use the CarSales sample database and the directory structure of the book samples. Should this not be the case, then you have to substitute the table and field names as well as the file path with those that you are using.

How It Works

When you think BCP, you probably think "import." Well, the venerable Bulk Copy program can also be remarkably efficient when you need to export data as text files from SQL Server. No, the command-line interface is not the most user-friendly—and indeed, it has been criticized as being clunky, but this utility can nonetheless help you in many circumstances.

As most of the intricacies of BCP were explained in Chapters 2 and 5, I will only focus on the things that you need to know to extract data from SQL Server using this tool. To start with, when exporting text data, BCP needs to know a minimum of six things. These are outlined in Table 7-4. However, the first three elements must be provided in the order shown in this table, the others can be added in any order.

Table 7-4. Required BCP Parameters

Element	Comments
The source data	This can be a table, a stored procedure call, a view, or a query. If using a table, view or stored procedure you should apply three-part notation to include the database name.
The extract type	OUT for a table or view, QUERYOUT for a query (either a select statement or a stored procedure).
The file path	The complete path and file name, including the extension. Remember to enclose in double quotes if it contains spaces.
The character type	-c for ASCII, -w for Unicode.
The server name	-S for servername.
The connection type	-T for a trusted connection, -U for username, -P for password for an SQL Server connection.

When using BCP, there are a few things to consider. First, BCP will always overwrite the contents of a destination file. Moreover, BCP can only export one table or view at a time—though you can use queries to create denormalized export tables. Also, if you suspect that a delimiter will be found anywhere inside a data field (a comma inside an address for instance), then you are strongly advised to use a custom delimiter. Just remember to tell the person to whom you are sending the data what you have used. Finally, when using a query or executing a stored procedure with BCP, always enclose it in quotes in the BCP command line.

You may have to escape (or remove) certain characters to ensure that your destination database can load the text file that you are outputting. For example, if you (or a colleague or client) will later be using MySQL's LOAD DATA INFILE to bulk load a text file that you have exported, you should use a backslash (\) to escape instances of tab, newline, or backslashes that occur within field values. This is most easily done by using T-SQL's REPLACE function—although this will slow down the export process a little.

BCP has a few options that are important for you to understand. For instance, by default, BCP uses the tab character as a column separator, and the newline character as the row terminator. You may need to use other characters to act as separators, in which case a few well-used variations include

Comma separator: -t,

Pipe separator: -t¦

Tab separator: -t\t

Custom delimiter: -t@@#@@

Newline: -r\n

Carriage Return/Line Feed (CR/LF): -r\r

■ **Note** Exporting a text file as Unicode doubles its size since each character will be two bytes instead of one. To avoid this, you may prefer to specify a code page for large files, and if the data that you are exporting lends itself to this treatment. For example, you can use Code Page -C nnnn (where nnnn is the four-digit reference of the code page).

Hints, Tips, and Traps

- To export data as BCP files, you must remember that you cannot use BULK INSERT to output data, and so will have to resort to command-line BCP.exe, and this means knowing a few of its many parameters. As we will see, you can also run BCP using xp_cmdshell.

- You will need read and write permissions on the path used for the output file.

- You will have to CAST or CONVERT any noncharacter values to a VARCHAR of a suitable length if you are using a UNION query to include column headers.

- Remember to handle NULL values if concatenating source fields, or you will lose entire records from the output should any fields contain NULLs.

- If you need to transfer binary and/or CLOB (**C**haracter **L**arge **OB**ject) values between databases, then you are probably best to use the techniques described in Recipes 7-24 and 7-25.

- In particularly complex output selection (perhaps involving quoted fields, column headers, etc.), consider creating the definition of the output as a view or as a stored procedure, which will then be output as a text file using BCP.

7-5. Exporting Data Using BCP Without Recourse to the Command Line

Problem

You want to exploit all the power of BCP to export data, but do not want to be restricted to using it from the command line because you wish this to be part of a wider scripted process.

Solution

Run BCP from T-SQL, SSIS, or SQL Server agent.

Running BCP from SSIS

From SSIS, BCP is run like any other operating system executable—using an Execute Process task, which you would configure as shown in Figure 7-8 (to use the code that is given in Recipe 7-4).

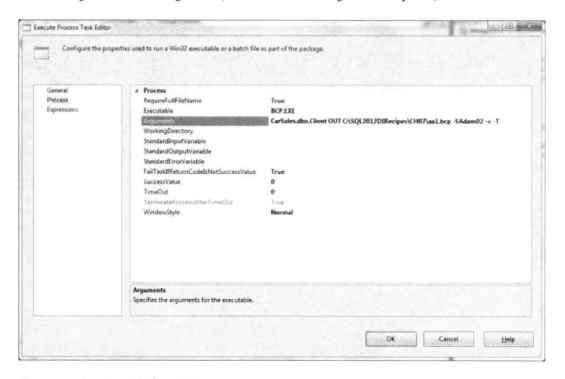

Figure 7-8. *Running BCP from SSIS*

Running BCP from SQL Server Agent

To run a BCP export from SQL Server agent, define the job step as:

Type:	Operating System (CmdExec)
Command:	Any valid BCP command—such as:

```
bcp CarSales.dbo.Client OUT ↵
C:\SQL2012DIRecipes\CH07\aa1.txt ↵
 -SAdam_01\Adam -c -T
```

A valid SQL Agent task to run a BCP command should look something like that shown in Figure 7-9.

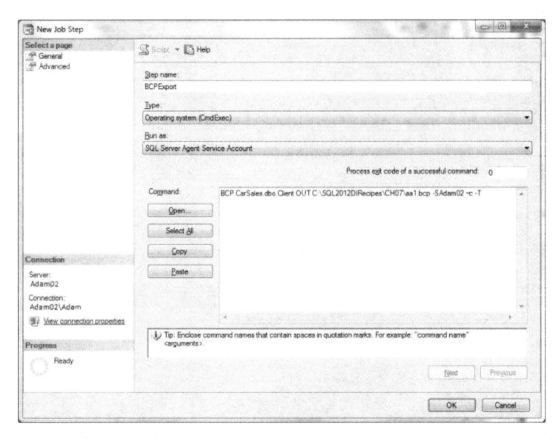

Figure 7-9. *Running BCP from SQL Server Agent*

How It Works

There are essentially five main ways of running a BCP export, so it is worth knowing all of them, along with their uses and any possible limitations. They are shown in Table 7-5.

Table 7-5. *Methods of Running a BCP Export*

InvocationMethod	Comments
Command prompt	Great for ad hoc exports.
T-SQL	If (and this can be a big if) xp_cmdshell is authorized on your server, then you can run BCP from SSMS or a stored procedure.
SSIS	You can run BCP exports using an Execute Process task.
SQL Agent	Ideal for scheduled tasks.
Batch files	A reliable way to run a sequential process. Can be run from an OS scheduler using xp_cmdshell or from SSIS using an Execute Process task.

This recipe looked at the middle three of these in more detail, since we have used the command prompt in the examples in the preceding recipe, and batch files are little more than a string of BCP commands. The advantage of BCP exports from T-SQL are that you can use dynamic SQL and cursors (whose overhead is normally minimal in this context) to export multiple tables, views, or the output from stored procedures.

Hints, Tips, and Traps

- To run BCP.exe from T-SQL, you will need to enable xp_cmdshell using Policy-Based Management, sp_configure, or Facets/Surface Area configuration. Be aware that it is considered a potential security loophole and should only be used with caution.

- When running BCP from SSIS, you will need to enclose the path and any query in double quotes, as you would when using BCP interactively.

7-6. Exporting Data As Text Files from T-SQL
Problem

You want to export data as text files simply and easily, without the complexity of developing an SSIS package to export data as text files from T-SQL.

Solution

Use T-SQL's OPENROWSET or OPENDATASOURCE functions.

You can populate a delimited text file using a script similar to this (C:\SQL2012DIRecipes\CH07\ExportDelimitedTextWithOpenRowset.sql):

```
INSERT INTO OPENROWSET('Microsoft.Jet.OLEDB.4.0','Text;Database=C:\SQL2012DIRecipes\CH07\;',
                  'SELECT ID, ClientName FROM InsertFile.txt')
SELECT     ID, ClientName FROM dbo.Client;
```

For OPENDATASOURCE use the following
(C:\SQL2012DIRecipes\CH07\ExportDelimitedTextWithOpendatasource.sql):

```
INSERT INTO
OPENDATASOURCE('Microsoft.Jet.OLEDB.4.0',
'Data Source=C:\SQL2012DIRecipes\CH07\;Text; FMT=Delimited')...[InsertFile#Txt]
SELECT ID, ClientName  FROM dbo.Client;
```

How It Works

Should you prefer to run text exports from inside T-SQL—and avoid having to use BCP and xp_cmdshell—then you can use OPENROWSET and OPENDATASOURCE. This is the very quick and easy way to export text files from T-SQL without undue hassle. There are several limitations, however.

- The destination file must be created before you run the command.

- This process will only append data to the file.

- The column headers must exist in the destination file—even if you use the HDR = YES extended property.

- By default, this procedure automatically adds double quotes to the data in every column.

- By default, commas are used as the delimiter.

- Ad hoc distributed queries must be enabled. This can be considered a security weakness by some DBAs.

As you can see, there is nothing unusual about using OPENROWSET and OPENDATASOURCE to export data. They are used virtually as you saw them used for importing data in Chapter 2. It is worth noting, nonetheless, that it is the MS.Jet OLEDB driver that allows you to do this—not the MSDASQL driver. However, if you want a quick way to output data without the time and effort of SSIS or BCP, and if you can live with the limitations, this can be very useful. To add column headers, you will need a destination text file containing a comma-delimited set of column headers. If there are too many to copy and paste, consider using the INFORMATION_SCHEMA system views to gather the list of column headers. The column headers in the text file do not have to correspond to those in the source table. However, if you are using OPENROWSET, the column headers in the text file must be identical to those in the SELECT clause of the OPENROWSET command. If you are using OPENDATASOURCE, then the exact column headers in the text file do not have to map to those in the SELECT clause—but their order and number must correspond exactly.

Hints, Tips, and Traps

- Don't bother trying to use MSDASQL (which you would expect to use for text export) because it can only read, but not write, text files.

- While simple and easy for small- to medium-sized datasets, this approach will probably prove significantly slower than BCP or SSIS for larger datasets.

- In a 64-bit environment, and assuming that you have installed the 64-bit driver, use Microsoft.ACE.OLEDB.12.0 instead of Microsoft.Jet.OLEDB.4.0. Indeed, even in a 32-bit environment, you can use the ACE driver if you prefer.

- If you wish to use nondefault delimiters and to specify the data types (thus avoiding quoted fields for nontext columns), you can create or extend a Schema.ini file. These are discussed in Recipe 2-6. If you need such a level of precision at this point, however, you could be better off using the data Export Wizard.

7-7. Exporting Data to Another SQL Server Database
Problem

You want to export data to another SQL Server database. You want to minimize the time spent developing, and transfer the data as fast as possible.

Solution

Use BCP to both export and import the data the SQL Server native format.

To export a full table—where the column structure is identical—the BCP command will look something like this:

```
BCP CarSales.dbo.Client OUT C:\SQL2012DIRecipes\CH07\SQL2000.bcp -N -SADAM02 -T
```

How It Works

This is essentially "classic" BCP, with a source table (though it could be a query as shown in Recipe 7-4) and a destination file. The big difference is that you are specifying the -N flag to tell BCP to use native format. A consequence of this is that you will not have to confirm column lengths and data types.

Native format export is for those occasions when the destination database is not a different system, but another SQL Server database. In these cases, you may find it easier to use the BCP/SQL Server native format to export and import between SQL Server instances. I realize that this may seem like a complicated route to take, but there are times when this is the only practical solution. Some of the situations when this could be necessary—among the many possible cases—include:

- When you need to transfer a subset of tables between databases.

- When your databases are using different versions of SQL Server (even SQL Server 2008 and SQL Server 2008 R2 are considered different versions), and so backup and restore will not work.

- Linked servers contravene corporate security requirements.

- Only file transfer is permissible or practical.

When having to map, exclude, and add fields, you have three choices:

> **Add the whole SELECT statement to the BCP command**, in quotes, and use QUERYOUT. This can be difficult to get right the first time, so I always advise perfecting the SELECT statement in SSMS and then copying and pasting into the Command window.

> **Wrap the SELECT statement in a view**, and call the view from BCP. This is worth the effort for tables that will be frequently exported, or when denormalizing data.

> **Wrap the SELECT statement in a stored procedure**, and call the stored procedure from BCP using EXECUTE .. QUERYOUT. Remember that session-scoped temporary tables cannot be used.

The advantages and disadvantages of the native format are detailed in Table 7-6.

Table 7-6. *Advantages and Disadvantages of BCP Native Format*

Advantages	Disadvantages
Speed	Cannot use format files—so column structures need to be identical in the output file and the destination table.
No need for format files	

There are a few SQL Server to SQL Server export options—shown in Table 7-7—that are also well worth knowing.

Table 7-7. *SQL Server to SQL Server Export Options*

Option	Comments
Native format (–n)	Can only be used for data that does not contain any extended/double-byte character set (DBCS) characters. To keep any extended characters you must specify a code page that supports the characters you wish to transfer.
Unicode native format (–N)	Prevents the loss of any extended characters during bulk transfer of data between servers using different code pages. This will apply to all char, nchar, varchar, NVARCHAR, text, varchar(max), and NVARCHAR(max) fields.
-V70	SQL Server version 7
-V80	SQL Server 2000
-V90	SQL Server 2005
-V100	SQL Server 2008/2008 R2

The only real hiccup when exporting a table to a previous version of SQL Server is that mapping fields will probably be required in some form. I advise shaping and mapping data at the output stage, using T-SQL, and ensuring that the data sent to a BCP file will map automatically to the destination table. This avoids the use of format files and ensures that any newer data types—as well as fields not present in the destination server—are omitted from the file.

Put simply, you need to

- Remove fields by not adding them to the SELECT statement.

- Add fields by inserting CAST(NULL AS data type) AS FieldName into the SELECT statement.

CONVERT any data types that you can convert from the later version for fields that exist in another data type in the older, destination version. This is not always possible, however, so you might have to skip some fields.

If you do all these, and export in SQL Server native or wide-native format (using the -n or -N flags), as well as specifying the SQL Server version using the -Vnn flag, then your output file should load fluidly into the destination server.

To export a full table—where there are no data types that are too new to be converted, and the column structure is identical—the BCP command will look something like this:

```
BCP CarSales.dbo.Client OUT C:\SQL2012DIRecipes\CH07\SQL2000.bcp -N -SADAM02 -T -V80
```

7-8. Exporting Text Files Regularly from T-SQL

Problem

You want to export text files on a regular basis, but want to use T-SQL rather than any other means.

Solution

Set up a linked server to the destination text file and then use T-SQL INSERT to export data to the file.

1. Begin by defining a linked server for the directory. Issue T-SQL like the following
   C:\SQL2012DIRecipes\CH07\TextFileLinkedServer.sql:

   ```
   EXECUTE Master.dbo.sp_addlinkedserver
   srv_Text                           -- The Linked Server name
   ,'ACE'                             -- The product name
   ,'Microsoft.ACE.OLEDB.12.0'        -- The provider name
   ,'C:\SQL2012DIRecipes\CH02'        -- The data source
   ,NULL                              -- The location
   ,'Text';                           -- The provider string
   GO
   ```

2. Set the security context for accessing the data directory by expanding Server Objects
   ➤ Linked Servers in SSMS by right-clicking the server name and selecting properties.
   Click Security and select "Be made without using a security context".

3. Append data to the file using T-SQL something like this:

   ```
   INSERT INTO srv_Text...InsertFile#txt (IDNo,ClientNameHere)
   SELECT     ID,ClientName FROM dbo.Client;
   ```

How It Works

For more regular text exports—but with limitations to all intents and purposes identical to those outlined for ad hoc exports using OPENROWSET—you can set up a linked server to a text file. This is done using the sp_addlinkedserver stored procedure.

Hints, Tips, and Traps

- It is certainly worth the effort, if you are setting up a linked server, to configure a Schema. ini file. These are described in Recipe 2-6.

- You cannot delete rows in the linked text file.

- All the hints that are specified for OPENROWSET apply to linked server exports.

- The destination file must be created before you run the command.

- This process will only append data to the file.

- The column headers must exist in the destination file.

7-9. Exporting and Compressing Multiple Tables
Problem

You want to export several tables from SQL Server and compress them as part of the output process.

Solution

Use SSIS to call BCP and export the tables as files. Then use a Script task to compress the output files. What follows is one way of exporting and compressing tables.

1. Use the following DDL to create a table to hold the list of tables in the database that you wish to process:

```
CREATE TABLE CarSales_Staging.dbo.TableList
(
 ID int IDENTITY(1,1) NOT NULL,
 TableName NVARCHAR(50) NULL
) ;
GO
```

2. Add the names of all tables that you wish to export in this table.

3. Create a new SSIS package. Right-click the Connection Managers tab and select New OLEDB Connection. If you have an existing connection to your database, select it; otherwise, click New and select the server, security mode, and database. Click OK twice to finish creating the connection.

4. Add the following three new variables:

Variable	Type	Comments
oTblList	Object	Used to hold the ADO recordset of table names.
sTableName	String	Used in the script task to process each table individually.
FilePath	String	Used in the script task to specify the path where the BCP and .gz (compressed) files will reside.

5. You should also specify the path as the value of the FilePath variable - C:\SQL2012DIRecipes\CH07 in this example.

6. Add an OLEDB data source onto the Control Flow pane, and double-click to edit it.

7. In the Data Flow pane, add an OLEDB data source task onto the pane, and double-click to edit. Select the OLEDB Connection manager that you just created, and choose SQL Command as the data access mode. Enter the following SQL as the SQL Command Text:

```
SELECT TableName FROM TableList
```

8. Add a Recordset destination onto the Task pane, and double-click to edit it. Select User::oTblList in the VariableName pop-up as the variable that will be populated by the Data Flow process. You should see a dialog box like the one shown in Figure 7-10.

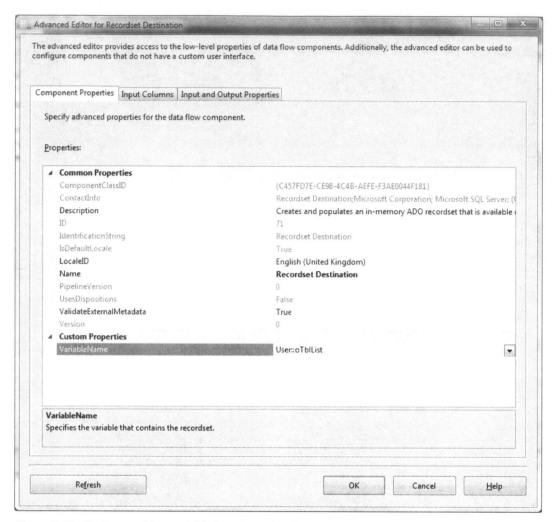

Figure 7-10. *Setting an object variable for a Recordset destination*

9.   Click OK, and then click the Control Flow tab.

10.   Add a Foreach Loop container onto the Control Flow area under the Data Flow task. Connect the latter to the Foreach Loop container.

11.   Add an Execute Process task into the Foreach Loop container. Double-click to edit it.

12. Click Process (on the left) and enter the following:

Process	Parameter	Comments
Executable	`C:\Program Files\Microsoft SQL Server\110\Tools\Binn\ bcp.exe`	The SQL Server BCP Executable. This will be C:\Program Files\Microsoft SQL Server\110\Tools\Binn\bcp.exe for SQL Server 2012. This will be 90 for SQL Server 2005 and 100 for SQL Server 2008.
Arguments	`CarSales.dbo. OUT .bcp -N -T`	The core BCP command (minus the table and file names).
WorkingDirectory	`\\Server\Path`	The directory that the BCP files will be exported to.

13. You should see something like what's shown in Figure 7-11.

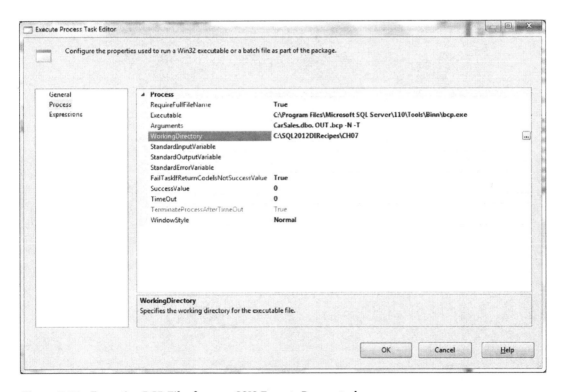

Figure 7-11. *Exporting BCP Files from an SSIS Execute Process task*

14. Click Expressions, and then click to display the property Expressions Editor. Select Arguments, as shown in Figure 7-12.

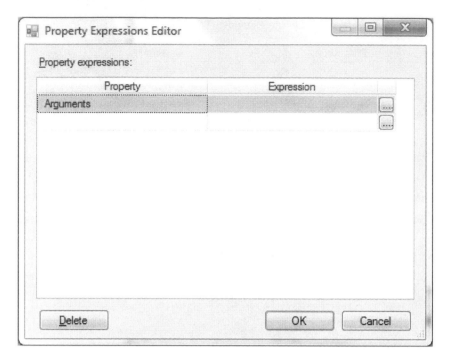

Figure 7-12. *Defining an expression in SSIS*

15. Click to display the Expression Builder. Enter the following expression:

```
"Book_TestData.dbo." + @[User::sTableName]  + " OUT " + @[User::sTableName]
+ ".bcp -N -T"
```

16. You should see a dialog box like the one shown in Figure 7-13.

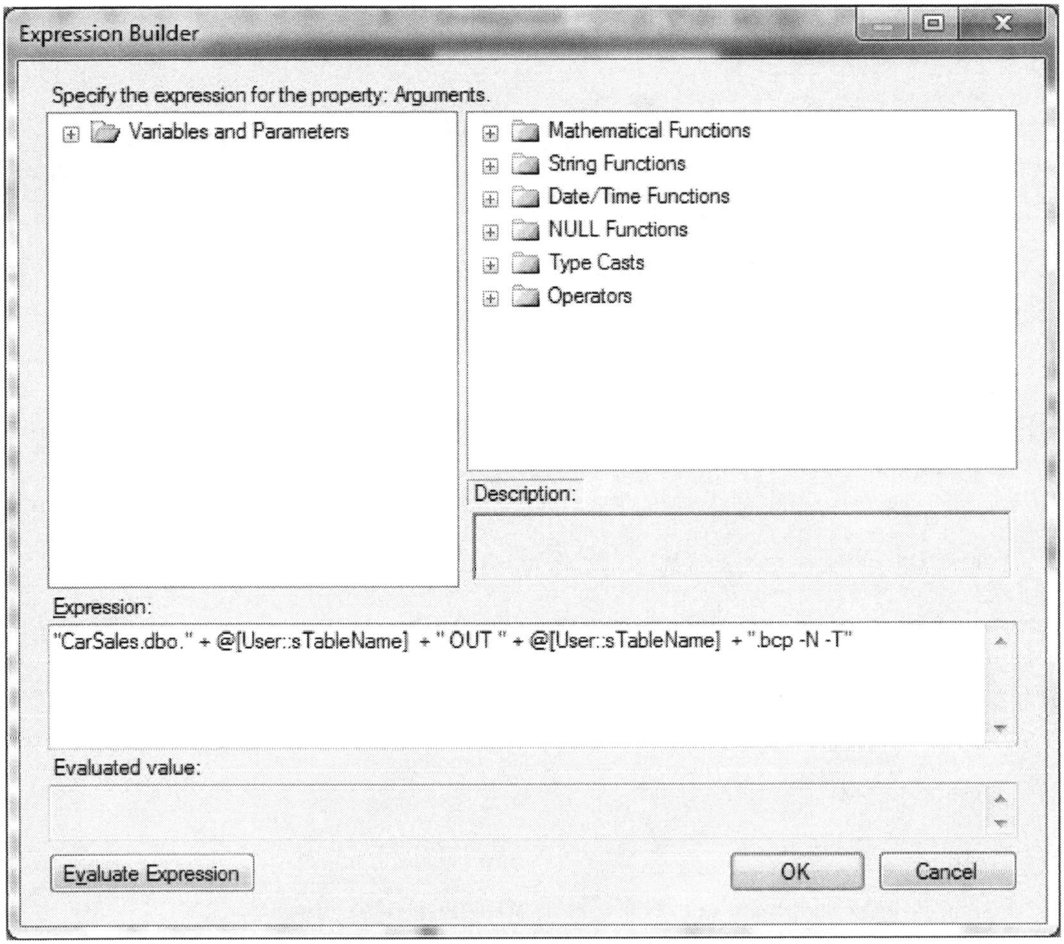

Figure 7-13. *Building an expression to run BCP*

17. Test the expression (by clicking Evaluate Expression). Then click OK three times to confirm the Execute Process task and return to the Data Flow pane.

18. Add a Script task to the Data Flow pane—inside the Foreach Loop container and under the Execute Process task. Link the latter to the former.

19. Double-click the Script task to edit it, and click Script on the left. In the Script pane on the right, enter **sTableName** as a read-only variable.

20. Click Design Script. Replace the Main method with the following code (C:\SQL2012DIRecipes\CH07\CompressFiles.vb):

```vb
Public Sub Main()

    Dim fileName As String
    Dim filePath As String
    Dim streamWriter As StreamWriter
    Dim fileData As String
```

```
        Dim WriteBuffer As Byte()
        Dim GZStream As GZipStream

        fileName = Dts.Variables("sTableName").Value.ToString
        filePath = Dts.Variables("FilePath").Value.ToString

        Dim fileStream As New FileStream(↩
            filePath & fileName, FileMode.Open, FileAccess.Read)

        WriteBuffer = New Byte(CInt(fileStream.Length)) {}

        fileStream.Read(WriteBuffer, 0, WriteBuffer.Length)

        Dim strDestinationFileName As String
        strDestinationFileName = filePath & fileName & ".gz"

        Dim fileStreamDestination As New FileStream(↩
            strDestinationFileName, FileMode.OpenOrCreate, FileAccess.Write)

        GZStream = New GZipStream(fileStreamDestination, CompressionMode.Compress, True)

        GZStream.Write(WriteBuffer, 0, WriteBuffer.Length)

        fileStream.Close()
        GZStream.Close()
        fileStreamDestination.Close()

        Dts.TaskResult = Dts.Results.Success

    End Sub
```

21. Save and close the Script editor. Click OK to close the Script task.

You can now run the process, which will export all tables defined in the TableList table to both BCP and compressed (.gz) files.

How It Works

BCP export is a valid way of transferring multiple tables—assuming that your database's design and constraints allow you to re-import data in this way. This recipe shows how SSIS can really shine by not only selecting the tables to export from a list, but also compressing the exported files.

The set of tables to be exported is held in an SQL Server table named TableList. Of course, this could be an Excel spreadsheet or a text file. This table is read using an Execute SQL task, which loads the table data into an SSIS object variable. This variable is then iterated over by an SSIS Foreach Loop container, and each individual table is exported using a BCP command. The point to note here is that the BCP parameters are defined as part of an SSIS expression.

Once each table is exported as a BCP file, an SSIS Script task is used to call the GZipStream class to compress the file.

> ■ **Note** The interesting thing about this recipe is that it requires no third-party software to compress the files. Instead, the .NET GZIPStream class is used to compress the files. They can later be decompressed by the most currently available compression utilities, or by an SSIS Script task that uses the GZIPStream class to decompress the files.

Hints, Tips, and Traps

- The path to the BCP executable is normally added to the PATH system variable during installation. If this has not been done, you might find it worth your while to add it manually.

- A simple script like this can be enhanced by the use of variables to hold the table name and so forth. I will leave you to extend it if you so wish.

- This approach is no replacement for a valid backup strategy.

7-10. Exporting a Tiny Dataset As XML

Problem

You want to export a very small dataset from an SQL Server table as an XML file, probably in response to a completely "ad hoc" request from a user.

Solution

Manually craft the XML as part of a T-SQL SELECT clause, and then copy the output to a text editor and save it.

1. Use the following code snippet to add beautifully-formed XML containing the data from the Client table in the sample CarSales database to an XML file (C:\SQL2012DIRecipes\CH07\SimpleXMLExport.sql):

```
CREATE VIEW CarSales.dbo.vw_XMLTest
AS

SELECT XMLCol, SortKey FROM
(
SELECT '<Root>' AS XMLCol, 0 AS SortKey

UNION

SELECT
'<Client>'
+ '<ID>' + ISNULL(CAST(ID AS VARCHAR(12)),'') + '</ID>'
+ '<ClientName>' + ISNULL(ClientName,'') + '</ ClientName>'
+ '</Client>' AS XMLCol
,1 AS SortKey

FROM dbo.Client
```

```
        UNION

        SELECT '</ROOT>' AS XMLCol, 2 AS SortKey
        ) MainXML ;
        GO
```

2. In an SSMS query window run the following code:

```
SELECT * FROM CarSales.dbo.vw_XMLTest;
```

3. Copy and paste the output into a text file

4. Save the text file.

How It Works

It is possible to export simple XML in the simplest way possible—by hand-crafting the XML, as shown in this recipe. This will only be of any use if the XML that you are exporting is really uncomplicated—by that I mean, essentially, that you are exporting a table or view as "flattened" XML, with no hierarchies. However, if this is the case—then it is your lucky day, as breaking down the output into chunks is not required, and you can output your XML quickly and easily, as each database record becomes an output record. In a production environment you are probably going to use FOR XML, so I have to admit, this is a largely theoretical example. Here I have wrapped the XML in a view that may not be necessary in all circumstances. The reason to wrap this in a view is to include the <Root> element to form valid XML. The correct order of the output is forced by using a hard-coded SortKey column. If you need to sort the XML records, use a secondary sort key. You may prefer to wrap the XML SELECT clauses in a stored procedure—this can also be run from BCP.

This recipe, begs the question "what is a tiny dataset?" Unfortunately, the answer can only be "it depends." For me the technique used here is only suitable when exporting a handful of columns (given the fact that hand-crafting XML is laborious) in a simple XML format where the rowset is small enough to be copied and pasted. However, you can decide when—or when not—to use it according to your requirements. Since this approach is really only designed for more ad hoc XML exports, I am presuming that a simple cut-and-paste will suffice to save the output as a file. For a more fully automated approach to exporting XML data, please see Recipe 7-11.

7-11. Exporting a Larger Dataset As XML
Problem

You want to export a medium-sized dataset from an SQL Server table as an XML file in a single process. You want to use T-SQL if possible.

Solution

Create a BCP format file that you then use with BCP to export the XML file. The following code snippet will add beautifully-formed XML containing the data from the Client table to an XML file.

1. Create the following BCP format file (C:\SQL2012DIRecipes\CH07\XmlExport.Fmt):

```
11.0
1
1       SQLBINARY    0       0       ""    1    XmlData          ""
```

2. Use the following T-SQL to output the XML into a table
(`C:\SQL2012DIRecipes\CH07\ExportXMLFromTSQL.sql`):

```
IF OBJECT_ID('dbo.XMLOutput') IS NOT NULL DROP TABLE XMLOutput;

CREATE TABLE XMLOutput (XMLCol XML);

INSERT INTO XMLOutput (XMLCol)

SELECT XMLOut FROM
(
 SELECT  C.ID, ClientName, Country, Town
 FROM    CarSales.dbo.Client C
 FOR XML PATH('Client'), ROOT('RootElement')
) A (XMLOut);

EXEC Master.dbo.xp_cmdshell
'BCP CarSales.dbo.XMLOutput OUT C:\SQL2012DIRecipes\CH07\XMLOut.xml -w -SADAMO2 -T'
```

3. Run the following command from a Command window to export the table that you
created in the preceding code snippet:

```
BCP XMLOutput OUT C:\SQL2012DIRecipes\CH07\Clients.Xml -T -N -f ↵
C:\SQL2012DIRecipes\CH07\XmlFormat.Fmt
```

4. Drop the table that contains the XML using the following line of code:

```
DROP TABLE XMLOutput;
```

How It Works

Since SQL Server 2005 appeared on the scene, XML has been integral to Microsoft's flagship DBMS, and consequently, exporting data from an SQL Server database as XML is relatively easy. However, XML is a vast concept, and the ways in which the exported data is shaped can get fairly complex. So in the recipes relating to XML output, I keep to simple XML output examples, since the topic of forming complex XML is, in itself, sufficiently vast as to merit entire chapters—or even books.

Because XML is really only text, you will see that there are essentially two main difficulties when exporting anything but the simplest XML:

- Defining (shaping) the XML

- Exporting what is generally only one large record into a text file

As far as defining XML is concerned, I use the FOR XML clause in most cases since it is infinitely preferable to attempting to handcraft all but the simplest XML. I suggest reading Recipe 7-14 for a short introduction to basic FOR XML.

This technique uses FOR XML PATH to create the XML from a source table, and then exports this using BCP. Points of note are, first, the destination file does not need to exist—and will be overwritten if it does. Second, xp_CmdShell must be enabled to invoke BCP from T-SQL. Finally, you cannot use a temporary table, and so must use a "real" table when using BCP. This is because a temporary table is not visible to BCP—even if you wrap this code in a stored procedure and call it from BCP.

When it comes to outputting the results to disk, things are generally easy if the XML output is small. Life can get more complicated when the XML is larger, given that SSIS and BCP will choke on the single-record output generated by FOR XML. However, almost all problems can be solved by using various "chunking" routines, which allow you to break down the monolithic, single-record XML output that FOR XML produces into multiple records. This added requirement for XML output may seem complex, but it is fundamental for large XML files. There is more on this in the next recipe.

Hints, Tips, and Traps

- You can avoid unjustified annoyance with BCP if you test your query in SSMS before copying it into the BCP command line.

- The destination file does not need to exist—and will be overwritten if it does.

- You can always create the BCP command as a .cmd text file, and then run it by double-clicking, rather than work in a Command window.

- If you prefer to use a CLR-stored procedure to write to disk, then see Recipe 10-15.

- As for the technique described in the previous recipe, only you can decide as a function of your environment and requirements if this technique suits the size of the XML dataset to be exported.

7-12. Exporting Large Datasets As XML
Problem

You want to export a large dataset as an XML file.

Solution

Use BCP and T-SQL, and export the file as multiple batches to avoid creating a single massive XML output record.

The way to do this is to run the following T-SQL snippet to export XML in batches, which ensures that large datasets are handled (C:\SQL2012DIRecipes\CH07\LargeXMLOutput.sql):

```
-- Instantiate temp table of sequential IDS mapping to unique keys in data source
IF OBJECT_ID('Tempdb..#IDSet') IS NOT NULL DROP TABLE #IDSet;

SELECT ID, ROW_NUMBER() OVER (ORDER BY ID) AS ROWNO
INTO #IDSet
FROM dbo.Client;

-- Create temp table to hold XML output and ordering info
IF OBJECT_ID('dbo.XMLOutput') IS NOT NULL DROP TABLE XMLOutput;

CREATE TABLE XMLOutput (XMLCol NVARCHAR(MAX), SortID INT);

-- Iteration variables
DECLARE @LowerThreshold INT = 0
DECLARE @UpperThreshold INT
DECLARE @Range INT = 20000

SELECT @UpperThreshold = MAX(ROWNO) FROM #IDSet;
```

```
-- Add root element
INSERT INTO XMLOutput (XMLCol, SortID)
VALUES ('<Root>', 0);

-- Loop through data and output XML
WHILE @LowerThreshold <= @UpperThreshold
BEGIN

INSERT INTO XMLOutput (XMLCol, SortID)

SELECT A.ClientXML, @LowerThreshold
FROM
(
SELECT          C.ID, ClientName, Country, Town
FROM            CarSales.dbo.Client C
                INNER JOIN #IDSet S
                ON C.ID = S.ID
WHERE           ROWNO > @LowerThreshold AND ROWNO <= @LowerThreshold + @Range
FOR XML PATH('Client')
) A (ClientXML);

SET @LowerThreshold = @LowerThreshold + @Range

END;

-- Add closing root element
INSERT INTO XMLOutput (XMLCol, SortID)
VALUES ('</ROOT>', @LowerThreshold + 1);

-- Export the data
EXEC Master..xp_cmdshell 'BCP "SELECT XMLCol  FROM CarSales.dbo.XMLOutput" QUERYOUT
C:\SQL2012DIRecipes\CH07\XMLOut.xml -w -SADAM_01\Adam -T'

-- Clean up the table
DROP TABLE XMLOutput
```

How It Works

If you execute the SELECT query with a FOR XML statement, you will see that a single record is output. Outputting one—and only one—record can be a problem with larger datasets because they can cause problems when the dataset is written to disk using BCP or SSIS. So we also need to look at a method of breaking down a query into multiple records, and then exporting each record using BCP, as described in the previous recipe.

The code in this recipe worked like this:

- First, it created the XML for a series of subsets of the source data.

- Then, it added this data to a staging table in the database.

- Next, it added the opening and closing ROOT elements separately

- Finally, it outputted the contents of the staging table ordered correctly to enclose the XML in the ROOT elements.

377

The #IDSet temporary table is used to map source IDs to a contiguous set if IDs used to chunk the data. It might not be strictly necessary in all cases, but generally ensures that the extraction subsets are nearly the same size, and avoids the overhead of processing nearly empty subsets should there be many missing IDs in the source data when using source IDs to break down the data into chunks. It is also essential when the source data does not have monotonically increasing IDs, and/or multi-column unique IDs, as it then can map more complex source IDs to a simple numeric ID.

I advise you to set the @Range variable to a figure that gives you the best trade-off between speed (that is the fewest SELECT calls to the database) and efficiency (i.e., BCP failing as it chokes on the output). Only trial and error will allow you to find an optimal number of records that can create an XML fragment that BCP can export without failing. The smaller the recordset, the slower the process (as multiple SELECT...FOR XML routines are called). This will depend on the size of the XML fragments, so be prepared for some iterative testing until you attain an optimized process.

If you want to tweak this code to break down the output into multiple XML files, you need to

- Set an SQL variable as a counter that is incremented with each cursor iteration.

- Set the BCP output script as an SQL variable—and use the previously created variable as part of the file name.

- Add the header and footer < Root > elements inside the cursor, and execute the BCP output as part of each cursor iteration.

Hints, Tips, and Traps

- When testing and debugging, it is probably best to comment-out the final DROP TABLE XMLOutput statement and check that the output table contains the data that you expect to find.

- As I can almost hear the gasps of horror from T-SQL purists at the use of a cursor in production code, I would like to add a few words in mitigation. First, cursors are not always evil—they can be a simple solution, so using them occasionally is not necessarily a reason for instant revulsion. Second, in my experience, when exporting XML like this, the cursors only loop a few times, even for fairly large datasets, and so the performance hit is negligible.

7-13. Creating an XML Schema
Problem
You want to create an XML schema file from XML data in an SQL Server table and save it for later use.

Solution
Use T-SQL and FOR XML AUTO, XMLSCHEMA.

1. Create an XML schema file from XML data in an SQL Server table to accompany the data itself using the following code snippet (C:\SQL2012DIRecipes\CH07\CreateXMLSchema.sql):

```
SELECT
[ID]
,[ClientName]
```

```
,[Address1]
,[Address2]
,[Town]
,[County]
,[PostCode]
,[Country]
FROM [CarSales].[dbo].[Client]
WHERE 1=0
FOR XML AUTO, XMLSCHEMA;
```

2. Once you have output the schema to a rowset, simply click it to have it appear in a new query window, which you then can save as an XSD file.

How It Works

XMLSCHEMA used with FOR XML AUTO generates an XML Schema (.xsd) automatically. The WHERE 1=0 clause is to prevent the actual XML data and the schema from being output. Of course, you can omit this if you want both the schema and the data.

7-14. Shaping XML Export Data
Problem

You want to export data as XML while shaping the XML to your requirements, rather than have SQL Server decide the XML output.

Solution

Learn to use the subtleties of FOR XML PATH and use it to shape the XML as part of the SELECT clause.

This recipe really lends itself to being several mini-recipes, so I will show you a few XML output techniques independently.

No Highest-Level Element Name

Merely adding FOR XML PATH will add a <ROW> element to each record that is created. To test this, run the following T-SQL snippet (C:\SQL2012DIRecipes\CH07\TopLevelElementXML.sql):

```
SELECT
C.ID
,C.ClientName
,C.Country
FROM dbo.Client C
FOR XML PATH ;
```

This should produce the following output from the sample data (shortened for publishing purposes):

```
<row>
<ID>3</ID>
<ClientName>John Smith</ClientName>
<Country>1</Country>
</row>
<row>
<ID>4</ID>
<ClientName>Bauhaus Motors</ClientName>
<Country>2</Country>
</row>
```

Defining the Highest-Level Element Name

Adding the name of the element to use—instead of <ROW> —is done like this
(C:\SQL2012DIRecipes\CH07\TopLevelElementName.sql):

```
SELECT
C.ID
,C.ClientName
,C.Country
FROM dbo.Client C
FOR XML PATH('Client');
```

And it gives (again, much shortened):

```
<Client>
<ID>3</ID>
<ClientName>John Smith</ClientName>
<Country>1</Country>
</Client>
<Client>
<ID>4</ID>
<ClientName>Bauhaus Motors</ClientName>
<Country>2</Country>
</Client>
```

Adding a ROOT Element

To progress to better formed XML, you can add a root element as follows
(C:\SQL2012DIRecipes\CH07\RootElementXML.sql):

```
SELECT
C.ID
,C.ClientName
,C.Country
FROM dbo.Client C
FOR XML PATH('Client'), ROOT('CarSales');
```

The result will be:

```
<CarSales>
<Client>
<ID>3</ID>
<ClientName>John Smith</ClientName>
<Country>1</Country>
</Client>
```

(Records ommitted to save space)

```
<Client>
<ID>7</ID>
<ClientName>Slow Sid</ClientName>
<Country>3</Country>
</Client>
</CarSales>
```

Defining Attributes

If you prefer attribute-centric XML, then you can shape it using aliases in this way
(C:\SQL2012DIRecipes\CH07\AttributeCentricXML.sql):

```
SELECT
C.ID '@ID'
,C.ClientName '@ClientName'
,C.Country '@Country'
FROM dbo.Client C
FOR XML PATH('Client'), ROOT('CarSales');
```

You should get back:

```
<CarSales>
<Client ID="3" ClientName="John Smith" Country="1" />
<Client ID="4" ClientName="Bauhaus Motors" Country="2" />
<Client ID="5" ClientName="Honest Fred" Country="3" />
<Client ID="6" ClientName="Fast Eddie" Country="2" />
<Client ID="7" ClientName="Slow Sid" Country="3" />
</CarSales>
```

Outputting More Complex Nested XML

Finally, to set you on the path to more complex output, you can create nested XML by aliasing fields using code
like the following (C:\SQL2012DIRecipes\CH07\ComplexNestedXML.sql):

```
SELECT
C.ID
,C.ClientName
,C.Country
,C.Town
```

```
,I.TotalDiscount AS 'Invoice/@TotalDiscount'
,I.InvoiceNumber AS 'Invoice/InvoiceNumber'
FROM dbo.Client C
INNER JOIN dbo.Invoice I
ON C.ID = I.ClientID
FOR XML PATH('Client'), ROOT('CarSales');
```

The output from this will be

```
<CarSales>
<Client>
<ID>3</ID>
<ClientName>John Smith</ClientName>
<Country>1</Country>
<Town>Uttoxeter</Town>
<Invoice TotalDiscount="500.00">
<InvoiceNumber>3A9271EA-FC76-4281-A1ED-714060ADBA30</InvoiceNumber>
</Invoice>
</Client>
<Client>
<ID>4</ID>
<ClientName>Bauhaus Motors</ClientName>
<Country>2</Country>
<Town>Oxford</Town>
<Invoice TotalDiscount="100.00">
<InvoiceNumber>C9018CC1-AE67-483B-B1B7-CF404C296F0B</InvoiceNumber>
</Invoice>
</Client>
</CarSales>
```

Obviously, the output shown is only a small part of the final result.

How It Works

In some of the preceding recipes, I used FOR XML PATH to "shape" the XML that is output. Now, without any attempt at being exhaustive, here is a crash-course on using FOR XML PATH to deliver the XML that you want to export.

The main keyword to note is AUTO, which is used to create XML hierarchies using the source tables to define the XML hierarchy. You need to remember that the order of the columns in the SELECT clause is important because this will influence the nesting of XML elements.

Hopefully, this shows that

- You define nested elements by aliasing them with the full path through the XML Node tree from the top-level element.

- You create attributes rather than elements by prefixing the attribute name with an at symbol (@), and use the full path through the XML Node tree from the top-level element.

- You must define attributes for a node before defining any lower-level elements.

You will need to watch out for typos when defining complex, multilevel XML schemas. It is all too easy to create parallel levels. Also remember that the schema is casesensitive. While we are discussing this, it is worth noting that

- It is vital in the SELECT clause to choose fields from the Client table before fields from the Invoice table to obtain the hierarchy that was produced in the XML, where invoice elements were nested inside Client data.

- Aliasing table names provide element names.

- Aliasing column names provide element names.

The options shown in Table 7-8 can be used when outputting XML.

Table 7-8. *FOR XML PATH Options*

Option	Description
TYPE	Outputs the result as SQL Server's XML datatype, and not as a NVARCHAR(MAX).
ELEMENTS	Ensures that XML elements, and not attributes (the default), are used.
XSINIL	Forces empty elements to be output, rather than skipped entirely.
ROOT	Adds a root element of your choice.

There is also the somewhat feared FOR XML EXPLICIT command, which you can use when the XML you need to output cannot be created using PATH or AUTO XML Explicit is outside the scope of these recipes. I leave it to you to research that option from other sources, such as Books Online and the Internet.

7-15. Exporting XML Data on a Regular Basis
Problem
You want to export data as XML as part of a structured ETL package.

Solution
Use SSIS to export XML data. I'll explain one way to do this.

1. Create a new SSIS package and add three connection managers, configured as follows:

Name	Connection	Comments
CarSales_OLEDB	OLEDB	Connect to the source database (CarSales here). Set the property RetainSameConnection to True.
CarSales_ADONET	ADO.NET	Connect to the source database (CarSales here).
XMLOut	flat file	The file must be Unicode and have one destination column (added using the Advancedpane) named **XMLOut**. This column must be a Unicode text stream.

2. Add the following five SSIS package-scoped variables. Their usage will become apparent as the package is created:

Name	DataType	Value	Description
ChunkRecordNo	Int	350000	The number of records to be processed for each SSIS buffer.
Chunks	Int	30	The number of chunks that will be processed.
CurrentChunk	Int	30	The current chunk to process.
LoadProcedure	String	dbo.pr_GetChunkedXML	The stored procedure that creates the XML, chunk by chunk.
OutputFile	String	C:\SQL2012DIRecipes\ ↵ CH07\Massive.xml	The destination file.
SQLProc	String	EXECUTE dbo.pr_GetChunkedXML	The stored procedure to run.

3. Create the following SQL stored procedure in the source database. It will be used to create the XML, chunk by chunk (C:\SQL2012DIRecipes\CH07\pr_GetChunkedXML.sql):

```
CREATE PROCEDURE CarSales.dbo.pr_GetChunkedXML
(
 @ChunkID INT
)

AS

SELECT A.XmlOut
FROM
(
SELECT
S.ID
,InvoiceID
,StockID
,SalePrice
,DateUpdated

FROM dbo.Invoice_Lines S
INNER JOIN ##Tmp_ChunkDef Tmp -- This table is defined in step 6
ON S.ID = Tmp.ID

WHERE Tmp.ChunkID = @ChunkID

FOR XML PATH ('Invoice_Lines'), TYPE
) A (XmlOut);
```

4. Add an initial Execute SQL task. Name it **Get Number of Chunk Iterations**. Double-click to edit and configure as follows:

Connection Type: ADO.NET

Connection: CarSales_ADONET

SQL Statement:
```
SELECT @Chunks = CAST(COUNT(*) /
@ChunkRecordNo AS INT)
FROM dbo.Invoice_Lines.
```

5. Define the following parameters in the Parameter Mapping pane of the Get Number of Chunk Iterations task:

Variable Name	Direction	Data Type	Parameter Name
User::Chunks	Output	Int	@Chunks
User::ChunkRecordNo	Input	Int	@ChunkRecordNo

6. Confirm your modifications to the Get Number of Chunk Iterations task with OK.

7. Add an Execute SQL task. Name it **Prepare temp table of chunk segmentation**. Connect the Get Number of Chunk Iterationstask to it. Double-click to edit and configure as follows:

Connection Type: OLEDB.NET

Connection: CarSales_OLEDB

SQL Statement:
```
IF OBJECT_ID('TempDB..##Tmp_ChunkDef') IS NOT NULL

DROP TABLE TempDB..##Tmp_ChunkDef

SELECT NTILE(?) OVER (ORDER BY AccountID) AS ChunkID,
CAST(AccountID AS BIGINT) AS AccountID

INTO ##Tmp_ChunkDef

FROM dbo.Invoice_Lines
```

8. Define the following parameter in the Parameter Mapping pane of the "Prepare temp table of chunk segmentation"task:

Variable Name	Direction	Data Type	Parameter Name
User::Chunks	Input	LARGE_INTEGER	@Chunks

9. Confirm your modifications to the "Prepare temp table of chunk segmentation"task with OK.

10. Add a Data Flow task to the Control Flow pane, connect the previous task (Prepare temp table of chunk segmentation) to it, and name it **Add Opening Root Element**. Double-click to edit.

11. Add an OLEDB Source task to the Data Flow pane. Configure it as follows:

OLEDB Connection Manager: CarSales_OLEDB

Data Access Mode: SQL Command

SQL Command Text:
```
DECLARE @RootOpen VARCHAR(50) = '<Root>'
SELECT @RootOpen AS XmlOut
```

12. Add a Flat File destination task to the Control Flow pane. Connect the OLEDB Source task to it and double-click to edit. Set the Flat File connection manager to XMLOut and check "Overwrite Data in the file". Click Mappings and ensure that the single column XMLOut is mapped between source and destination. The Data Flow pane should look like Figure 7-14.

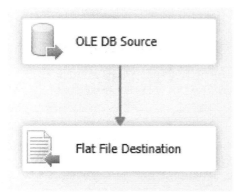

Figure 7-14. *Data Flow task to add initial XML elements for chunked export*

13. Return to the Control Flow tab and add a Foreach Loop container. Name it **Loop through chunk counter** and connect the preceding "Add Opening Root Element" Data Flow task to it. Configure it as follows:

InitExpression: @CurrentChunk = 1

EvalExpression: @CurrentChunk <= @Chunks

AssignExpression: @CurrentChunk = @CurrentChunk + 1

14. Inside the Foreach Loop container, add a Script task named **Define executable variable**. Add the following variables:

ReadOnlyVariables: User::CurrentChunk,User::LoadProcedure

ReadWriteVariables: User::SQLProc

15. Set the ScriptLanguage to Microsoft Visual Basic 2010 and click the Edit Script button to display the Script editor. Add the following method:

```
Public Sub Main()
Dts.Variables("SQLProc").Value = ↵
"EXECUTE " & Dts.Variables("LoadProcedure").Value.ToString & " " & ↵
Dts.Variables("CurrentChunk").Value.ToString
Dts.TaskResult = ScriptResults.Success
End Sub
```

16. Close the Script window and click OK to finish editing the Script task.

17. Add a Data Flow task inside the Foreach Loop container. Connect the Script task to it. Name it **Output XML** and double-click to edit.

18. In the Data Flow pane, add an OLEDB source and configure as follows:

    OLEDB Connection Manager: CarSales_OLEDB

    Data Access Mode: SQL Command from Variable

    Variable Name: User::SQLProc

19. Click OK to finish editing the OLEDB source.

20. Add a Flat File destination task to the Control Flow pane. Connect the OLEDB source task to it and double-click to edit. Set the Flat File connection manager to XMLOut. Make sure that Overwrite Data in the File is **not** checked. Click Mappings and ensure that the XMLOut single column is mapped between source and destination.

21. Return to the Control Flow pane. The Foreach Loop task should look like Figure 7-15.

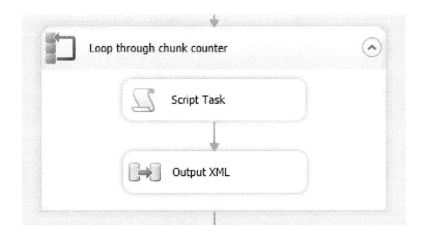

Figure 7-15. *Looping through XML chunks output to a file*

22. In the Control Flow pane, add a Data Flow task to the Control Flow pane. Connect the Foreach Loop container to it and name it **Add Closing Root Element**. Set this up exactly like the "Add Opening Root Element"Data Flow task, as described earlier, except that the SQL reads:

```
DECLARE @RootClose VARCHAR(50) = '</ROOT>'
SELECT @RootClose AS XmlOut
```

23. Ensure that "Overwrite Data in the file" is not checked as the script destination.

The package is now complete. You can test large XML exports. The completed package should look like Figure 7-16.

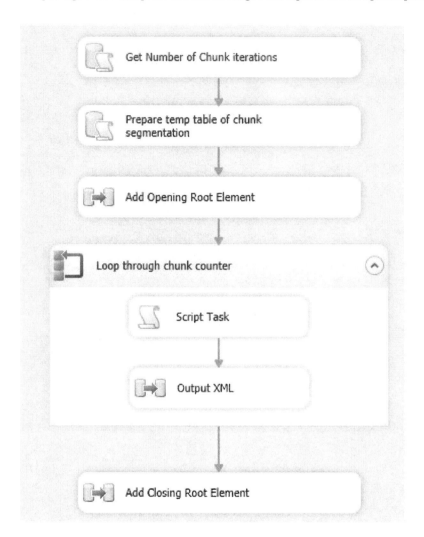

Figure 7-16. *The complete SSIS package to export large XML datasets*

How It Works

Even if SSIS has no XML Destination component, you can (fairly) easily output XML from SQL Server. Once again, the only problem will be the size of the output. If it is too big to fit into an SSIS buffer, then the process will fail. So once again, the real art is finding an efficient chunking mechanism for large datasets to handle bulk XML export.

Unfortunately, not all XML export files will be small enough to fit into an SSIS buffer, and so again, it was necessary to define a subsetting process to output the core data as chunks small enough to be processed by SSIS and then add the XML ROOT elements to the top and bottom of the output file.

The SSIS package described here broke source data down into "chunks," and then exported the output as a single XML file. More precisely, the first "Get Number of Chunk iterations" Execute SQL task described in step 4 calculated the number of chunks that will need to be processed based on the chunk size that you have specified in the @ChunkRecordNovariable, and will set the SSIS variable accordingly. The second Execute SQL task, "Prepare temp table of chunk segmentation," populates a global temporary table with the IDs of all records to be processed. This task—described in step 7—also attributes a ChunkID to each recordID so that each record will be output as part of a specified chunk. The question mark in the T-SQL NTILE(?) will be replaced with the @Chunks parameter (which contains the calculated number of chunks according to the record size that you specified) at execution time. The "Loop through chunk counter" Foreach Loop task ensures that the XML export process processes every chunk previously defined. The Script task guaranteed that the SQL that will run for each set of records in a chunk has the appropriate input parameters passed to it. Finally, the XML <ROOT>...</ROOT> elements are added to the data output from the core process.

This process is rather intricate and contains several dependencies. The pr_GetChunkedXML stored procedure can be created before the global temporary table (##tmp_ChunkDef) that it uses is created, but you cannot run the stored procedure outside the context of the package that creates this table.

Hints, Tips, and Traps

- You can use only one connection manager (OLEDB or ADO.NET) for the package if you prefer. I tend to use ADO.NET connection managers when passing variables to stored procedures, as I find them easier to debug and maintain, whereas for pure data transfer, OLEDB seems a little faster. So *my* habit is to use two connection managers, where one suffices purely to ease writing and debugging Execute SQL tasks that need input and output variables for the T-SQL that they contain.

- Rather than checking "Overwrite Data in the file" for the Flat File destination task in step 8, you can add an initial File System task to delete the file if you prefer.

- It is possible to set the "SQLProc" SSIS variable at step 11 without using a Script task—but again, as a question of clarity and maintainability; I prefer to add a task component to do this.

- Some trial and error will be required to ascertain the optimal number of source records that make for efficient processing.

- There are many, many ways of chunking datasets. This is one more to add to those described elsewhere in the book. Of course, you are free to choose the method most suited to your specific data structures.

7-16. Routinely Exporting Small XML Datasets
Problem

You want to export small XML datasets on a regular basis.

Solution

Use SSIS to export XML data. The following shows a specific way to handle small datasets.

1. Create a new SSIS package and add an OLEDB connection manager. Connect to the source database (CarSales in this example) and name it **CarSales_OLEDB**.

2. Add a Data Flow task. Double-click to edit it.

3. Add an OLEDB source and double-click to edit. Configure as follows:

OLEDB Connection Manager:	CarSales_OLEDB
Data Access Mode:	SQL Command
SQL Command text:	SELECT XMLCol

```
SELECT XMLCol
FROM (
        SELECT  ID, ClientName, Country, Town
        FROM    CarSales.dbo.Client
        FOR XML PATH('Client'), ROOT('RootElement')
) A (XMLCol)
```

4. The dialog box should look something like what's shown in Figure 7-17.

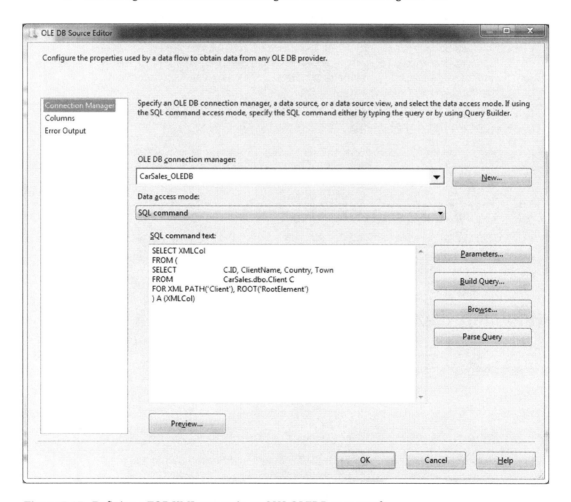

Figure 7-17. *Defining a FOR XML output in an SSIS OLEDB source task*

5. Add a Flat File destination to the Data Flow pane. Connect the OLEDB source component to it. Double-click to edit.

6. Click New to add a new Flat File connection manager. Give it a name and define an output file (C:\SQL2012DIRecipes\CH07\ClientExport.Xml in this example). Make sure that "Column names in first data row" is not checked, but that Unicode is checked. The dialog box should look like Figure 7-18.

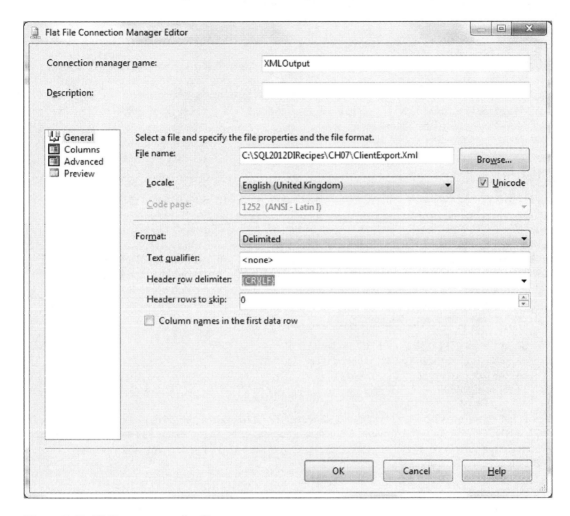

Figure 7-18. *XML output as a flat file*

7. Click OK to confirm.

8. In the Flat File Destination Editor, click Mappings. Make sure that it is only the XMLColcolumn and that it is mapped between source and destination.

And that is it! Executing this package will export an XML file.

How It Works

All this recipe does is create XML from the data source using FOR XML PATH as a single record. This record is then written to disk as a text file. The dataset *must* be small enough to fit into the SSIS buffer.

7-17. Exporting Data to Excel Using T-SQL
Problem

You want to export data from SQL Server to Excel or Access using T-SQL.

Solution

Use OPENROWSET and OPENDATASOURCE. This is how you do it (C:\SQL2012DIRecipes\CH07\ExcelExport.sql):

```
INSERT INTO OPENROWSET('Microsoft.ACE.OLEDB.12.0','Excel 12.0;
Database=C:\SQL2012DIRecipes\CH07\InsertFile.xlsx;', 'SELECT ID, ClientName FROM [Clients$]')
SELECT ID, ClientName FROM dbo.Client;
```

How It Works

If you wish to export a set of data from SQL Server into Excel with minimal fuss, then using OPENROWSET or OPENDATASOURCE is a clean and simple solution. All you have to do is run the T-SQL snippet shown earlier.

Exporting to the MS Office suite—by which I mean essentially Access and Excel, but also occasionally Word—has become a fundamental requirement for all those who develop and manage SQL Server databases. Ad hoc exports are best handled using OPENROWSET and OPENDATASOURCE. For this to work you must have set up an Excel worksheet containing the column names in the first row, starting in cell A1, and no data under the column headers. Also, Ad hoc queries must be enabled on the server—as has been explained previously. Once these preconditions are met, the rest is a fairly simple piece of T-SQL.

To use OPENDATASOURCE, try the following:

```
INSERT INTO OPENDATASOURCE('Microsoft.ACE.OLEDB.12.0',
'Data Source=C:\SQL2012DIRecipes\CH07\InsertFile.xls;
Extended Properties=Excel 12.0')...[Clients$]
SELECT ID, ClientName  FROM dbo.Client
```

Instead of placing the column headers at the top-left of an Excel worksheet, you can place them anywhere in any worksheet, and name the range comprising the headers. You can then export using this name instead of the worksheet names. An example could be—assuming that you have named the headers DestinationRange (C:\SQL2012DIRecipes\CH07\ExcelRangeExport.sql):

```
INSERT INTO OPENROWSET(
'Microsoft.ACE.OLEDB.12.0','Excel 12.0; Database=C:\SQL2012DIRecipes\CH07\InsertFile.xlsx;'
, 'SELECT ID, ClientName FROM DestinationRange')
SELECT ID, ClientName FROM dbo.Client
```

Hints, Tips, and Traps

- See Recipe 1-1 for information on how to find and install the OLEDB ACE driver. Remember to use the 64-bit version in a 64-bit environment.

- The column names used in the SELECT clause of the OPENROWSET pass-through query must match the column names in the spreadsheet.

- Data will be appended to any existing rows.

- You can also use the Microsoft.Jet.OLEDB.4.0 driver, but I advise installing the more recent ACE driver, even when exporting to older Excel versions. This avoids unexpected surprises when accidentally using a version of Excel that the older (Jet) driver does not support. An added advantage is that you do not even have to specify which version of Excel (8.0, 12.0) you are using, or whether you are using the Office XML-based file format or the older binary format.

- Remember to close the destination file before exporting data.

- Note that Excel has a limit on the number of rows that you can export. This was 65,536 up to the 2003 version and 1,048,576 thereafter.

7-18. Exporting Data to Access Using T-SQL

Problem

You want to export data from SQL Server to Access using T-SQL.

Solution

Use OPENROWSET and OPENDATASOURCE.

To export SQL Server data to Access, run the following T-SQL snippet (C:\SQL2012DIRecipes\CH07\AccessExportOPENROWSET.sql):

```
INSERT INTO OPENROWSET('Microsoft.ACE.OLEDB.12.0',C:\SQL2012DIRecipes\CH07\TestAccess.mdb';
'admin';'',ClientExport)
SELECT ID, ClientName FROM dbo.Client
```

How It Works

As was the case for Access, OPENROWSET and OPENDATASOURCE allow you to export a subset of data quickly and easily as part of a T-SQL statement. You need to have created an Access database containing a destination table ready to receive the data. Ad hoc queries must also be enabled on the server. This snippet inserted rows into the ClientExport table in the TestAccess.mdb database. Data is appended to any existing rows in the destination table.

To use OPENDATASOURCE, try the following (C:\SQL2012DIRecipes\CH07\AccessExportOpendatasource.sql):

```
INSERT INTO OPENDATASOURCE('Microsoft.ACE.OLEDB.12.0',
'Data Source=C:\SQL2012DIRecipes\CH07\TestAccess.mdb;')...ClientExport
SELECT ID, ClientName  FROM dbo.Client;
```

Hints, Tips, and Traps

- You will need to replace 'admin'; and ''; in the OPENROWSET command with a valid username and password if your Access database is protected.

- You can replace the table name with a SELECT query (in single quotes, as with Excel) to specify the columns in the destination table. Here, too, the column names do not have to be identical in source and destination, but the column order must match.

- See Chapter 1 for details on how to use a database protected with an Access Workgroup (.mdw) file.

7-19. Exporting Data Securely to Excel from T-SQL
Problem

You want to export data into Excel securely—that is, without exposing security information in T-SQL code.

Solution

Create a linked server to an Excel workbook.

To export data using a linked server to Excel, perform the following steps.

1. Set up a linked server. The code will be something like this:

```
EXECUTE sp_addlinkedserver
EXCEL_SQL,                                    -- The Linked Sever name
'Jet 4.0',                                    -- The (purely decorative) product name
'Microsoft.Jet.OLEDB.4.0',                    -- The installed driver
'C:\SQL2012DIRecipes\CH07\InsertFile.xls',    -- The destination file and path
NULL,                                         -- The location - not used
'Excel 8.0';                                  -- The provider string, specifying the
                                                 Excel version

GO
```

2. Set up a login for the linked server, like this:

```
EXECUTE sp_addlinkedsrvlogin
EXCEL_SQL,      -- The name of the linked Server
false,          -- UseSelf - overrides the default
NULL,           -- Local user
NULL,           -- Remote user
NULL;           -- Remote login
GO
```

3. Finally, you can use the linked server to insert data into Excel:

```
INSERT INTO     EXCEL_SQL...[Clients$]
SELECT          ID, ClientName from dbo.Client;
```

How It Works

Excel can be set up as a linked server from SQL Server's perspective. As with all linked server connections, you will have to be careful to set all the configuration information properly. I can only stress that it is worth taking the time to do this correctly, as the error messages (should anything not work) are extremely cryptic and can be hard to decipher, which makes debugging difficult. However, once done, all security information is hidden from any prying eyes. You have not only to set up the linked server, but also configure a login for the linked server using sp_addlinkedsrvlogin.

The Excel file does not have to be created before adding the linked server and defining access permissions. However the Excel worksheet must have the correct column names defined before inserting data. Also, Instead of a worksheet (which presumes that the column names are in place beginning in cell A1) you can use a named range for the export. This means using T-SQL like the following:

```
INSERT INTO   EXCEL_SQL...DestinationRange
SELECT        ID, ClientName from dbo.Client
```

Of course, using a named range presumes that the column headers are in place, and that the range (covering just the cells containing the column headers) has been created in the Excel workbook.

Hints, Tips, and Traps

- The Excel workbook cannot be password protected.

- It is good idea to format the columns before inserting the data.

- I used the (older) Jet driver here. As I explain in Recipe 7-17, using the ACE driver will ensure that you can export to a greater range of Excel versions.

7-20. Exporting Data Securely to Access from T-SQL
Problem

You want to export data into Access securely—that is, without exposing security information in T-SQL code.

Solution

Create a linked server to an Access database and export the data from T-SQL.

The following steps explain how to export data using a linked server to Excel.

1. Add a linked server:

   ```
   EXECUTE master.dbo.sp_addlinkedserver
   @server = N'Access'
   ,@srvproduct=N'Access'
   ,@provider=N'Microsoft.ACE.OLEDB.12.0'
   ,@datasrc=NC:\SQL2012DIRecipes\CH07\TestAccess.mdb'
   ```

2. Set data access without a security context:

   ```
   EXECUTE master.dbo.sp_addlinkedsrvlogin
   @rmtsrvname=N'Access', @useself=N'False', @locallogin=NULL, @rmtuser=NULL,
   @rmtpassword=NULL
   ```

3. Export data using four-part notation, as follows:

   ```
   INSERT INTO   Access...ClientExport (ID, ClientName)
   SELECT        ID,  ClientName FROM dbo.Client
   ```

Hints, Tips, and Traps

- The Access database does not have to be closed to export data. In fact, the table itself can be open.

- Access will enforce any constraints (such as a unique primary key) that have been applied to the destination table.

- The Access table data types must be able to store the exported data types.

- If the Access database is password protected, then you will need to set the linked server login, using something like this:

  ```
  EXECUTE master.dbo.sp_addlinkedsrvlogin @rmtsrvname = N'Access', @locallogin = NULL ,
  @useself = N'False', @rmtuser = N'YourAccessUserName', @rmtpassword = N'AccessPassword'
  ```

▪ **Note**   You need to replace the username and password shown here with your username and password.

7-21. Exporting Data to Excel Using SSIS
Problem

You want to export data to Excel on a regular basis.

Solution

Use the Excel destination as part of an SSIS Data Flow task.

To export data to Excel from SSIS, perform the following steps.

1. Create a new SSIS package and add an OLEDB connection manager. Name it **CarSales_OLEDB** and configure it to connect to your source server. Add a Data Flow task and double-click to edit.

2. Add a new OLEDB source component, and configure it to use the CarSales_OLEDB connection manager that you added. Select a source table or enter an SQL query to define the source columns.

3. Add a new Excel destination task. Connect the source task to it. Double-click to edit.

4. Click Browse to create a new Excel file (or select an existing Excel file)—or even type the path to the file, be it new or existing. Select the version of Excel to export to, and then click OK.

5. If you are creating an Excel file—or if you want to add a new worksheet to an existing file—click New, followed by OK, to create the worksheet.

6. If you have created a new worksheet, click OK at the following message (see Figure 7-19).

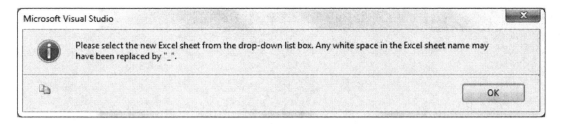

Figure 7-19. *New worksheet warning*

7. Select the worksheet that you want to use as an Excel destination from the Name of the Excel Sheet drop-down list.

8. Click Mappings and map all source to all destination columns.

9. Click OK.

Your SQL Server data will be exported into the Excel workbook.

How It Works

As probably one of the most-used export processes, outputting data to Excel using SSIS is mercifully simple. You do not even have to create the destination file first, just be sure to use the Excel destination task. You may prefer—or need—to use the ACE provider to export data successfully. If this is the case, when creating the destination OLEDB provider (in step 2) select Microsoft Office 12.0 Access Database Engine OLEDB Provider from the pop-up list. You will then have to type or paste in the full path to the Access database as the Server or File name.

You will notice that if your source data contains any non-Unicode (that is to say VARCHAR) columns, then the destination task will indicate a problem. There are two solutions to this:

- Use an SQL statement to select the source data, and use CAST or CONVERT to alter the source data types to NVARCHAR.

- Add a Data Conversion task between the source and the destination, and convert all non-Unicode columns to Unicode String [DT_WSTR]. It will probably make life easier if you set the output alias to the original, column name, as well—something like in Figure 7-20.

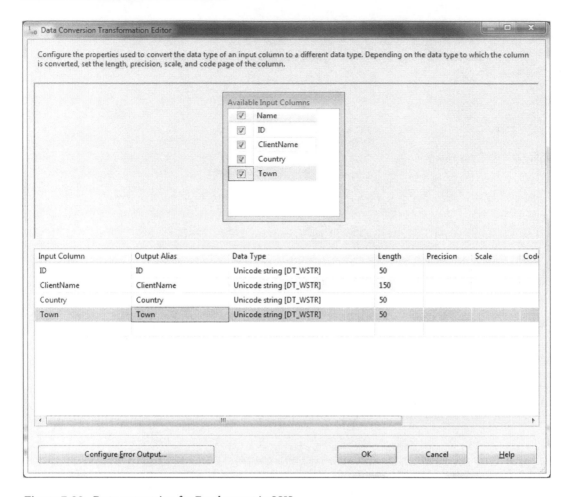

Figure 7-20. *Data conversion for Excel export in SSIS*

When mapping the columns, ensure that you are mapping the **converted** columns—named Copy of ColumnName or DataConversion.ColumnName. If you add the data conversion task before adding the destination task, then mapping will be a little more complex because both the source and the destination columns will appear in the Create Table dialog box—and you will have to remove the duplicate (non-Unicode) columns. Also, this makes it harder for SSIS to map to the correct output data types.

Hints, Tips, and Traps

- As with exporting to Office applications, the question of whether you are in a 32-bit or 64-bit environment can have wide-ranging ramifications. These are the same as those explained in Recipe 1-1.

- You can rename the Excel worksheet from OLEDB Destination when you create a new worksheet, if you prefer.

- The intricacies of Excel data type mapping are explained in Recipe 1-3.

7-22. Exporting Data to Access Using SSIS

Problem

You want to export data to Access as part of an SSIS package.

Solution

Use an OLEDB destination task as part of an SSIS data flow, as follows:

1. Create a new SSIS package and add an OLEDB connection manager. Name it **CarSales_OLEDB** and configure it to connect to your source server.

2. Add a second OLEDB connection manager. Click New and select Microsoft Jet 4.0 OLEDB Provider from the pop-up list of Providers at the top of the dialog box. Browse to or type in the path to an existing Access database. Confirm with OK, twice. Name the second connection manager **Access_OLEDB**.

3. Add a Data Flow task and double-click to edit.

4. Add a new OLEDB source component, and configure it to use the CarSales_OLEDB connection manager that you added. Select a source table or enter an SQL query to define the source columns.

5. Add a new OLEDB destination component. Select the Access_OLEDB connection manager and either select an existing table as a destination, or click New to create a new table.

6. Click Mappings and map the source columns to the destination columns.

7. Click OK.

You can now run the package.

How It Works

You may prefer—or need—to use the ACE provider to export to Access—specifically if exporting in a 64-bit environment. When creating the destination OLEDB provider (step 2) in this case, select Microsoft Office 12.0 Access Database Engine OLEDB Provider from the pop-up list. You will then have to type or paste in the full path to the Access database as the Server or File name. If you are using the ACE provider, you could get a message warning you about data type problems when creating a new table. In most cases, this can be ignored. What it means is that the specific Access limited data types will not be used to create the table, but more generic OLEDB data types. Of course, you can rename any new destination table from OLEDB Destination to a name of your choice when you create it.

Hints, Tips, and Traps

- As with exporting to Office applications, the question of whether you are in a 32-bit or 64-bit environment can have wide-ranging ramifications. This is the same as explained in Recipe 1-1.

- If your Access database is password protected, you will need to enter connection details as part of the OLEDB connection manager configuration.

- If your source data contains any non-Unicode (that is to say, VARCHAR) columns, then the destination task will indicate a problem. There are two solutions to this:

- Use an SQL statement to select the source data and use CAST or CONVERT to alter the source data types to NVARCHAR.

- Add a Data Conversion task between the source and the destination, and convert all non-Unicode columns to Unicode String [DT_WSTR].

7-23. Pulling Data from Office Applications

Problem

You want to "pull" SQL Server data into Access, Excel, or Word.

Solution

Use the link and/or import options in Access, Excel, and Word.

As there are several ways of pulling data from MS Office applications, I will handle the various scenarios as individual mini-recipes.

Linking Excel to SQL Server Databases

To link Excel to an SQL Server database:

1. Click Data to activate the Data ribbon. Select From Other Sources ➤ From SQL Server (see Figure 7-21).

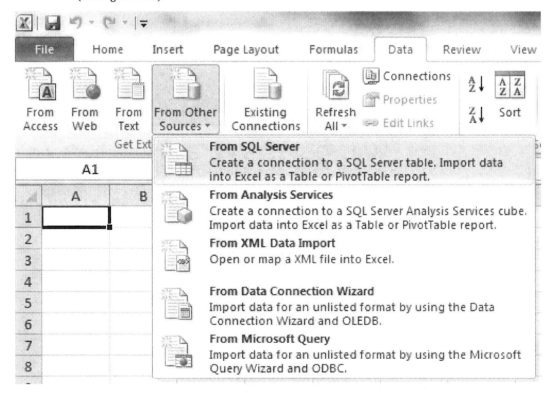

Figure 7-21. Linking Excel to an SQL Server database

2. Enter the server name and credentials (if you are not using a trusted connection). Click Next.

3. Select the database you wish to connect to. Choose a table or view. Click Next.

4. Enter a Data Connection file (and path, if necessary). This will allow you to reuse the connection. Tweak the parameters if you need to. Click Finish.

5. Select or confirm the top-left destination cell for the data, and click OK. Re-enter the password if you are using an SQL Server connection, when prompted.

Clicking the Refresh button in the Data ribbon updates the Excel workbook with the latest version of the data in SQL Server.

Access Linked or Imported Tables

To link Access to an SQL Server data source:

1. Click External Data to activate the External Data ribbon. Click ODBC databases.

2. Choose from one of the following:

   • Import the Source data into a new table in the current database.

   • Link to the data source by creating a linked table.

3. Select—or create a DSN (described in Chapter 4 in Recipes 4-6 and 4-10).

4. Select all the tables you want to link to—or import. Check "Save password" if you are not using a trusted connection. Click OK.

The source data will be imported into Access.

Linking Word to SQL Server

To use SQL Server data in Word for mailings:

1. In Word, activate the Mailings ribbon. Click Start Mail Merge. Choose a mailing type, such as Letters.

2. Click Select Recipients, and then click Use Existing List, followed by New Source.

3. In the Data Connection Wizard, select Microsoft SQL Server as the data source, and then click Next.

4. Enter the Server and connection credentials (or confirm that integrated security will be used). Click Next.

5. Select the source table, and then click Finish.

The source data is now available to be used in Word Mailings.

Using PowerPivot

To import data from PowerPivot:

1. Activate the PowerPivot ribbon. Click PowerPivot Window. PowerPivot will open.

2. In the Home ribbon, click From Database ➤ From SQL Server. This is shown in Figure 7-22.

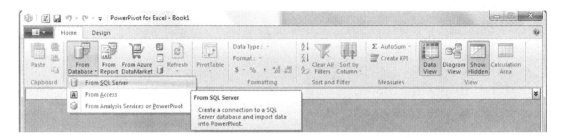

Figure 7-22. *Selecting an SQL Server data source from the PowerPivot Home ribbon*

3. Define all the connection options (server name, database, authentication mode at a minimum, plus any other available options that you wish) as in Figure 7-23.

Figure 7-23. Configuration information for a PowerPivot data import

4. Click Next.

5. Choose whether to select a table or set of tables (or views), or to write a specific query to output data, as shown in Figure 7-24.

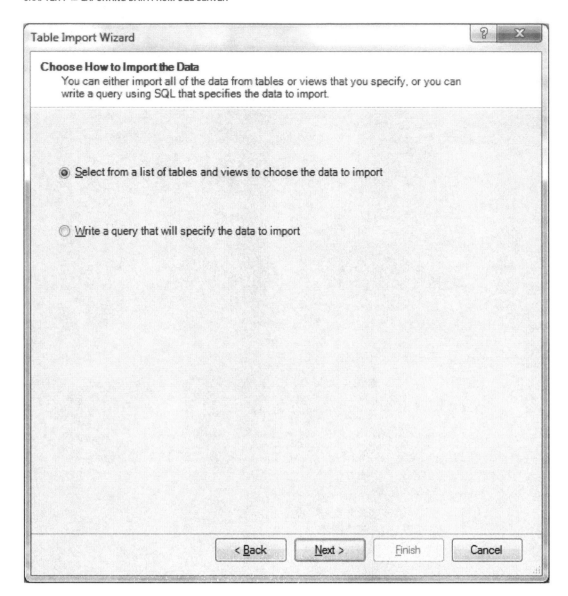

Figure 7-24. Choosing to import a list of tables or write a query to import data into PowerPivot

6. Click Next.

7. Select the table(s) or write the query. An example of this for the CarSales databaseis shown in Figure 7-25.

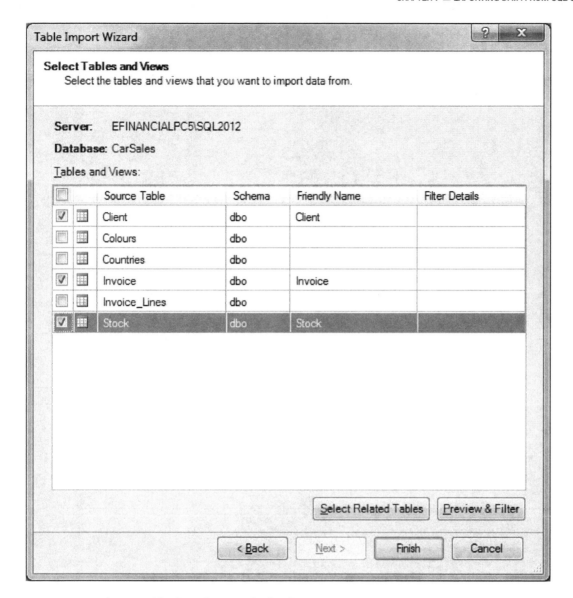

Figure 7-25. *Selecting tables from the CarSales database*

    8.   Click Finish. The final pane of the Table Import Wizard will appear, as in Figure 7-26.

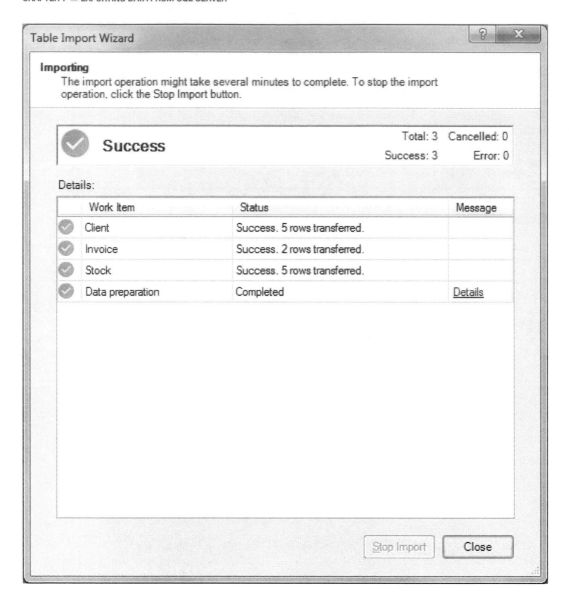

Figure 7-26. *Selecting tables from the CarSales database*

> 9. Click Close to close the dialog box once the data is transferred to PowerPivot.

How It Works

Although this chapter has so far dealt with pushing data from SQL server, there are times when you will need to pull data as well. Normally, I would claim that this is the responsibility of the person handling the destination application. However, in the case of MS Office products, I have made an exception, and explained some of the ways in which Excel, Access, and even Word can pull SQL Server data into their respective worksheets, databases, and documents. The reason that I do this is simple: when a DBA cannot import SQL Server data into his/her

MySQL server, it is their problem. When a Microsoft Office user (or even power user) cannot import SQL Server data into his/her application, it is frequently also a problem for the SQL Server developer or DBA.

To avoid blushing when faced with a user demanding that their data become immediately available, these are the classic ways to pull SQL Server data into Microsoft Office applications. In these recipes, I am using Office 2010. The techniques are virtually identical to those in Office 2007 or Office 2013. For older Office versions, I can only suggest that you use this as a template, since the principles are the same; it is only the interface that changes. Remember that Excel allows you to connect to an SQL Server over ODBC. It will store all workbook connections you make to a data source, and you can re-use them by clicking the Connections button in the Data ribbon. For an Analysis Services link, select From Analysis Services in the From Other Sources pop-up. Access also lets you link to SQL Server—or import data—over ODBC. The process for linking to SQL Server tables—or importing them—is virtually identical since Access 2007.

There are doubtless many reasons to want to link Microsoft Word to SQL Server databases. It could be because you have a report that needs data from SQL Server that has to be included and updated as the data changes, or it could be because you are using Word as a front-end for mailshots (frequently called mailings or mailmerge). Here again, I explained how to use Word 2007 and up, and leave you to adapt the process to earlier versions. Oh, and if you are wondering exactly what this has to do with an SQL Server developer, I can only suggest that you ask for a bottle of wine each time that an end-user wants to use corporate data for a mailshot. You will soon have a fabulous cellar! Since explaining all the subtleties of actually producing mailshots is outside the scope of this book, I suggest that you use some of the excellent resources available in book and Web form to help you from this point on.

Inevitably, PowerPivot, the new kid on the block, can import data from SQL Server and SQL Server Analysis Services. This can be done from the PowerPivot ribbon. It assumes that PowerPivot has been successfully installed and that Excel is open.

▓ **Note** The current version of PowerPivot can be found at www.microsoft.com/en-gb/download/ details.aspx?id=29074.

Hints, Tips, and Traps

- One of PowerPivot's clever options is that it automatically selects all tables (both immediately upstream and downstream, using foreign key constraints for all selected tables) if you click the Select Related Tables button at step 7.

- The Preview and Filter button allows you to apply data source filters and sorting.

- While the Microsoft Word Mailing connection does not allow you to write a custom query, you can always create a view in SQL server to join tables, aggregate, filter, and sort data ready for the mailmerge process.

- Clicking the Edit Recipient List button (in the Mailings ribbon) displays the Mail Merge Recipients dialog box that will let you

  - Filter the dataset.

  - Sort the source data.

  - Find duplicates and select the records to use.

  - Search the source data.

7-24. Exporting Files Stored in SQL Server Using T-SQL
Problem

You want to export binary files stored in an SQL Server table as part of a scripted T-SQL process.

Solution

Use BCP to export binary files with the help of a specific format to handle the export file. The following steps show how it can be done.

1. Create a format file exactly like the following (C:\SQL2012DIRecipes\CH07\ BinaryExport.fmt):

    ```
    11.0
    1
    1       SQLBINARY        0       0       ""   1    CarPhoto                ""
    ```

2. Use the following T-SQL to export all the binary files from a table (C:\SQL2012DIRecipes\CH07\BinaryExport.sql):

    ```
    DECLARE @SQLTEXT VARCHAR(8000);
    DECLARE @Make VARCHAR(50), @CarPhotoType VARCHAR(5);
    DECLARE @CarPhoto VARBINARY(MAX);
    DECLARE @ID INT;

    DECLARE BCPBinaryOUT_CUR CURSOR
    FOR
    SELECT  ID, Make, CarPhotoType, CarPhoto
    FROM    dbo.Stock
    WHERE   CarPhotoType IS NOT NULL;

    OPEN BCPBinaryOUT_CUR;

    FETCH NEXT FROM BCPBinaryOUT_CUR INTO @ID, @Make, @CarPhotoType, @CarPhoto

    WHILE @@FETCH_STATUS = 0
    BEGIN

    SET @SQLTEXT='BCP "SELECT CarPhoto FROM CarSales.dbo.Stock WHERE ID ='
    + CAST(@ID AS VARCHAR(11)) +  '" QUERYOUT C:\SQL2012DIRecipes\CH07\'+ @Make + '.'
    + @CarPhotoType + '-fC:\SQL2012DIRecipes\CH07\Binary.Fmt -SAdam02 -UAdam –PMe4B0ss';

    FETCH NEXT FROM BCPBinaryOUT_CUR INTO @ID, @Make, @CarPhotoType, @CarPhoto

    EXECUTE master.dbo.xp_cmdshell   @SQLTEXT
    END;

    CLOSE BCPBinaryOUT_CUR;
    DEALLOCATE BCPBinaryOUT_CUR;
    ```

How It Works

If you are using SQL Server to store **L**arge **OB**jects (LOBs), then there will be occasions when you need to export some, most, or all from a table.

If you are using T-SQL to export a BLOB (**B**inary **L**arge **OB**ject), then you will need a format file that contains a single column defining a VARBINARY data type. You then use this format file in a BCP export (BCP OUT). The SQL here loops through all the records in a table using a cursor, and exports all the BLOBs in the table.

Hints, Tips, and Traps

- Ensure that the file names that you create using the dynamic SQL are unique, or the process will cheerfully overwrite any existing file. Using the unique ID or a combination of fields that guarantee a unique file name is one method. Failing all else, use an SQL variable that you increment with each file exported.

- All the risks and possible refusals by the DBA as well as the caveats that were mentioned in Recipe 7-5 concerning xp_cmdshell, apply here, too.

- Unfortunately, it does not seem possible to use the newer XML format file to do this.

- This approach will only cope with "standard" VARBINARY(MAX) fields, and not FILESTREAM or FILETABLE files of more than 2 gigabytes in size.

- If you are using SQL Server 2008, the format file has to begin with 10.0; for SQL Server 2005, the format file has to begin with 9.0.

7-25. Exporting Files Stored in SQL Server on a Regular Basis

Problem

You want to export binary files stored in an SQL Server table as part of a controlled export process.

Solution

Use the SSIS Export Column task in a Data Flow to output binary files to disk, as described in the following steps.

1. Create a new SSIS package and add an OLEDB connection manager. Name this **CarSales_OLEDB** and connect to your source database (CarSales in this example).

2. Add a Data Flow task, double-click to edit, and add an OLEDB source component. Configure as follows:

OLEDB Connection Manager:	CarSales_OLEDB
Data Access Mode:	SQL Command
SQL Command Text:	SELECT CarPhoto, 'C:\SQL2012DIRecipes\CH07\'
	+ Make + '.'
	+ CarPhotoType AS FilePath
	FROM dbo.Stock
	WHERE CarPhotoType IS NOT NULL

3. Confirm your modifications with OK.

4. Add an Export Column task to the Data Flow pane. Connect the OLEDB source control to it. Double-click the Export Column task to edit it. Configure it as follows:

   Extract Column: CarPhoto

   File Path Column: FilePath

5. Confirm your modifications with OK. The Data Flow pane should look like Figure 7-27.

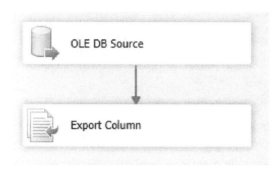

Figure 7-27. *Using SSIS to export files stored in SQL Server*

You can now execute the SSIS task. All the BLOBs will be extracted to the destination directory.

How It Works

Happily, exporting any large object (binary or text) from SSIS is extremely easy, since the SSIS development team has provided an SSIS Data Flow transformation to do just this—the Export Column task. As this is a data flow, you do not even need to use a Foreach Loop container to determine the files to copy to disk, merely concatenate a unique file name for each record in the source table. You must ensure that the file that you create has a unique name, or the process will cheerfully overwrite any existing file without giving any warnings. Use a unique ID or a combination of fields, which will guarantee a unique file name is one method to achieve this.

Hints, Tips, and Traps

- If you prefer, you can assemble the File Column Path as a derived column, and use SSIS variables and column data to define the output path.

- Files cannot exceed 2 gigabytes in size when using this technique.

- When exporting a BLOB (I will use this to cover Character Large Objects as well), the SQL will be something like this:

```
SELECT    CarDocumentation, CAST('C:\SQL2012DIRecipes\CH07\' + Make + '.txt'
          AS NVARCHAR(MAX))
          AS FilePath
FROM      dbo.Stock
WHERE     CarDocumentation IS NOT NULL;
```

7-26. Exporting Data from SSAS Using T-SQL on an Occasional Basis

Problem

You want to export tabular data from an SSAS cube on an occasional basis.

Solution

Use OPENROWSET to export the data in tabular format.

The code to do this is (C:\SQL2012DIRecipes\CH07\SSASExport.sql):

```
INSERT INTO OPENROWSET('Microsoft.ACE.OLEDB.12.0','Text;Database=C:\CookBook\;' ↵
,'SELECT Client_Name, Sale_Price, Cost_Price FROM InsertMDXFile.txt')

SELECT
CS.[[Dim Clients]].[Client Name]].[Client Name]].[MEMBER_CAPTION]]] AS Client_Name
,CS.[[Measures]].[Sale Price]]] AS Sale_Price
,CS.[[Measures]].[Cost Price]]] AS Cost_Price
FROM OPENROWSET
(
'MSOLAP','DATASOURCE=localhost; Initial Catalog=CarSales_OLAP;',
'SELECT
{[Measures].[Sale Price], [Measures].[Cost Price]} ON COLUMNS,
NONEMPTY(EXCEPT([Dim Clients].[Client Name].MEMBERS, [Dim Clients].[Client Name].[All])) ON ROWS
FROM [Car Sales DW]'
) AS CS;
```

How It Works

When discussing data export from SQL Server, it is too easy to forget that SQL Server also encompasses SQL Server Analysis Services (SSAS), and that there can be times when you need to export data from here, too. While not technically difficult, you will need to remember that a multidimensional data structure is fundamentally different from a relational structure, and that you will, of necessity, have to "flatten" the exported data to some extent.

OPENROWSET allows you to send pass-through queries to an OLAP data source, just as you can to any supported relational data source. When querying Analysis Services, this will mean ensuring that the MSOLAP provider is installed. Assuming that this is the case, you can write an MDX query as the query section of the OPENROWSET command, and return a dataset that you can then export as a text file, an Excel worksheet, an Access database, or a BCP file.

The interesting thing in this recipe is that you are using OPENROWSET not only to return data from SSAS, but also to output this dataset to disk as a text file.

The OPENROWSET command is aliased, which is not a problem. The difficulty lies in the way that the column headers are returned by the MDX query. Entering the column headers as they are returned by SQL Server gives you an error message like this:

```
Msg 207, Level 16, State 1, Line 3
Invalid column name 'Dim Clients'.
Msg 207, Level 16, State 1, Line 4
Invalid column name 'Measures'.
Msg 207, Level 16, State 1, Line 5
Invalid column name 'Measures'.
```

Encasing the whole column name in square brackets does not help matters. The trick is to understand that the right square bracket is an escape character. So what you have to do is

- Add an extra right square bracket for each existing square bracket.

- Encase the entire header text for each column in square brackets.

- Be sure not to double-up on the final right square bracket that encases the entire column title—then you will get a working and usable result set.

The hard part of exporting SSAS data is writing a correct and efficient MDX query to pass through to SSAS. I can only refer you to the many excellent books and many other resources on MDX that are available to help with this, since a discussion of MDX is outside the scope of this book.

Hints, Tips, and Traps

- As with all ad hoc exports using OPENROWSET, the destination file must exist and the column names must be present in the file.

- You will nonetheless need to remember that MDX queries and SQL queries are very different animals, and that not every MDX query that returns data will be able to return this data in the way you expect—if at all—to a T-SQL query.

- To export MDX data using BCP, I suggest first using the OPENROWSET command to insert the SSAS data into a database table, and then using BCP to export this table. You can then delete the table in the database.

- You will need more than just a passing familiarity with MDX to output data coherently, so be prepared for a steep learning curve if MDX is not yet part of your skill set.

7-27. Exporting Data from SSAS Using T-SQL on a More Regular Basis

Problem

You want to export tabular data from an SSAS cube using T-SQL on a regular basis.

Solution

Configure a linked server to connect to SSAS, and then export the data in tabular format over the linked server connection. I'll show you how to do this.

1. Create a destination table called **SSASData** already set up to hold the source data, created as follows (C:\SQL2012DIRecipes\CH07\tblSSASData.sql):

```
CREATE TABLE dbo.SSASData
(
 Client_Name NVARCHAR (250) NULL,
 Sale_Price INT NULL,
 Cost_Price INT NULL
) ;
```

2. Add a linked server called **OLAPSERVER**, using the following code snippet
(C:\SQL2012DIRecipes\CH07\SSASExportLinkedServer.sql):

```
EXEC master.dbo.sp_addlinkedserver @server = N'OLAPSERVER', @srvproduct=N'Analysis
Services', @provider=N'MSOLAP', @datasrc=N'localhost'
```

3. Run the following code snippet to extract SSAS data into an SQL Server table:
(C:\SQL2012DIRecipes\CH07\SSASToSQL.Sql)

```
INSERT INTO SSASData (Client_Name, Sale_Price, Cost_Price)
SELECT
CS.[[Dim Clients]].[Client Name]].[Client Name]].[MEMBER_CAPTION]]] AS Client_Name
,CS.[[Measures]].[Sale Price]]] AS Sale_Price
,CS.[[Measures]].[Cost Price]]] AS Cost_Price
FROM OPENQUERY(OLAPSERVER,
'SELECT
{[Measures].[Sale Price], [Measures].[Cost Price]} ON COLUMNS,
NONEMPTY(EXCEPT([Dim Clients].[Client Name].MEMBERS, [Dim Clients].[Client Name].
[All])) ON ROWS
FROM [Car Sales DW]
WHERE [Dim Products].[ProductVehicleHierarchy].[Product Type].&[Van]'
) AS CS;
```

IIow It Works

If you will be performing OLAP-to-SQL output on a regular basis, then you are probably better off setting up a linked server. The main reason for this is that you can define security as part of the linked server configuration, and avoid—potentially—leaving logins and passwords in clear text in a T-SQL script.

As is the case for all linked server data transfers, this is generally a more robust solution, and allows you to define the connection once and for all. In this case, I will assume that the export that we want to perform is from SSAS into SQL Server.

The T-SQL snippet that adds a linked server assumes that your local SQL Server is hosting both the database engine and Analysis Services. Please note that I am presuming that you are trying these commands on a machine where you have system admin rights, so as not to get diverted into questions of privileges. Should this not be the case, then you will have to establish security as part of the linked server setup.

Once a linked server is set up, you can query it using an MDX pass-through query, just as you did when using OPENROWSET. This time the data is exported into an SQL Server table.

Hints, Tips, and Traps

- A linked server source can pass data to an OPENROWSET query or another linked server—be it SQL Server, Access, Excel, flat file, or another relational database. These techniques are the ones described elsewhere in this chapter.

7-28. Exporting an SSAS Dimension Using SSIS
Problem

You want to export the data from an SSAS dimension as part of a regular and controlled export process.

Solution

Use SSIS to connect to an SSAS cube and export the data. I'll explain how.

1. Create a new SSIS package. Add an OLEDB connection manager named **OLAP_ Source**, configured as follows:

OLEDB Provider:	Microsoft OLEDB Provider for Analysis Services 11.0
Server or File Name:	localhost (or your SSAS instance, if on another box)
Initial Catalog:	CarSales_OLAP (for my examples—use your SSAS database for your data).

2. Add a new Flat file destination. Name it **SSASOutFlatFile** and specify the file location. Check the Unicode box and check "Column names in the first row".

3. Go to the Advanced pane and add four new columns. Define the types as follows:

Name	DataType	OutputColumnWidth
ID	Four byte signed integer	
ClientName	string [DT_STR]	50
ClientSize	Four byte signed integer	
WholesaleRetail	string [DT_STR]	20

4. Confirm your modifications with OK.

5. Add a Data Flow task. Double-click to edit.

6. In the Data Flow pane, add an OLEDB source. Configure as follows:

OLEDB Connection Manager:	OLAP_Source
Data Access Mode:	Table or View
Name of Table or View:	[Car Sales DW].[$Dim clients]

7. Click Columns and alias all the Output Columns to simpler names without square brackets or spaces, as shown in Figure 7-28.

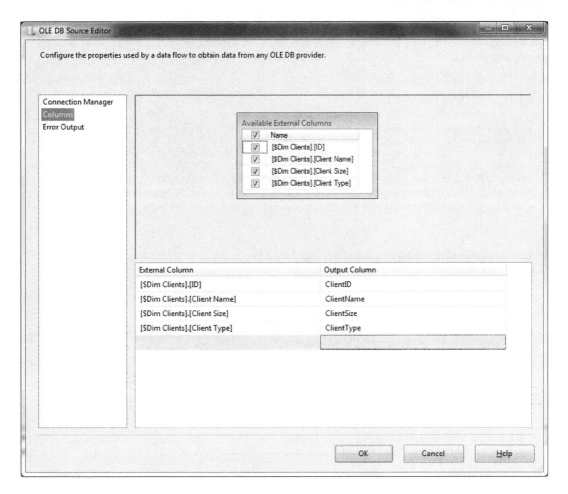

Figure 7-28. *Renaming the column output from SSAS*

8. Confirm your modifications with OK.

9. Add a Flat File destination. Connect the Copy Column task to it. It should default to using the SSASOutFlatFile connection manager —if not, select it. Click Mappings and ensure that the copied columns only are mapped to the destination columns.

10. Confirm your modifications with OK.

How It Works

As if to prove its credentials as an excellent all-round data transfer tool, SSIS can export data from Analysis Services too. What is more, it can export to any standard Data Flow destination. In fact, SSAS is so similar to any other OLEDB or ADO.NET data source that there is very little unusual to remark. The exceptions are that a dimensional data source is very different from a relational or flat file source, and that some careful MDX querying may be required to output the exact data you want in the form that SSIS can process.

As an introduction to SSIS for SSAS, it is probably easiest to start with a simple dimension extract. A dimension in SSAS, after all, closely resembles a relational table. Here we exported as a flat file—but you can export to any SSIS destination.

Hints, Tips, and Traps

- You should use the Analysis Services provider that is installed on your server. The version will correspond to the installed version(s) of SSAS.

- If you are using an older version of SSIS and exporting data to a relational table, you will have to take care in specifying the destination columns, and more particularly, the data types, since SSAS does not provide sufficient information to allow a destination component to create tables perfectly—which a warning dialog box will state (see Figure 7-29).

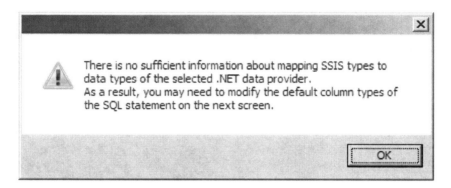

Figure 7-29. *Data type warning in SSAS 2005/2008*

- You will probably always be better off to think through the destination table first, and then create it in the destination server before creating the SSIS package. In this particular example, the DDL is:

```
CREATE TABLE SSASExport
(
 [ID] INT,
 [Client Name] NVARCHAR(50),
 [Client Size] INT,
 [Wholesale Retail] NVARCHAR(20)
);
GO
```

7-29. Exporting the Result of an MDX Query in SSIS
Problem

You want to transfer tabular SSAS data into an SQL Server table using a complex MDX query on a regular basis.

Solution

Use an SSIS data flow task to export the data. I'll show you how.

1. Create a destination table called **CubeOutput** already set up to hold the source data, created as follows (`C:\SQL2012DIRecipes\CH07\tblCubeOutput.sql`):

```
CREATE TABLE CarSales_Staging.dbo.CubeOutput
(
 ClientName NVARCHAR(250),
 SalePrice NVARCHAR (250),
 CostPrice NVARCHAR (250)
);
GO
```

2. Create a new SSIS package. Add an ADO.NET connection manager named **OLAP_Source**, configured as follows:

ADO.NET Provider:	.NET Providers for OLEDB \Microsoft OLEDB Provider for Analysis Services 11.0
Server or File Name:	localhost (or your SSAS instance, if on another box)
Initial Catalog:	CarSales_OLAP (for my examples—use your SSAS database for your data).

3. Click All on the left of the dialog box, scroll up to Extended Properties, and enter **FORMAT = TABULAR**.

4. Add an OLEDB connection manager named **OLEDB_Destination**, configured as follows:

OLEDB Provider:	SQL Server Native Client 11.0
Server or File Name:	ADAM02 (Substitute with your SQL Instance)
Initial Catalog:	CarSales (or your database)

5. Add a Data Flow task. Double-click to edit. In the Data Flow pane, add an ADO.NET source. Configure as follows:

ADO.NET Connection Manager:	OLAP_Source
Data Access Mode:	SQL Command
SQL Command Text:	WITH MEMBER

```
WITH MEMBER
[Measures].[SalePrice] AS CSTR([Measures].[Sale Price])
MEMBER [Measures].[CostPrice] AS CSTR([Measures].[Cost Price])
SELECT
{[Measures].[SalePrice], [Measures].[CostPrice]}
ON COLUMNS,
NONEMPTY(EXCEPT([Dim Clients].[Client Name].MEMBERS,
[Dim Clients].[Client Name].[All]))
ON ROWS
FROM [Car Sales DW]
```

6. Confirm your modifications with OK. Click OK to disregard the warning message.

7. Add an OLEDB destination task, and connect the source task to it. Configure as follows:

OLEDB Connection Manager:	OLEDB_Destination
Data Access Mode:	Table or View – Fast Load
Name of Table or View:	CubeOutput

8. Map the (peculiarly named) source columns to the destination columns, and click OK.

How It Works

Exporting the result of an MDX query is virtually identical to the process described in the previous recipe, so I will not re-explain the principles here. I accept that calling an MDX pass-through query an SQL Command is counter-intuitive, yet nonetheless it works—and so this is how you pass MDX to the SSAS cube. You need to remember that MDX can only export the data as a Unicode text stream, so you will then have to CAST or CONVERT all fields to other data types in your SQL, or use a view to overlay the output table and convert the field types to the appropriate data types. In my opinion, it is advisable to create the destination table with columns sufficiently large (at least the first time you export the data) to prevent the export from failing.

Hints, Tips, and Traps

- A warning triangle will remain in the source component. This is because the driver is having difficulties with the measures output from the MDX query. Nonetheless, it will work.

- If you do not use named members and convert the output to string, you will have difficulties (sometimes, but not always) when exporting the data.

- If you are exporting to a text file, then add the column headers manually to the destination file, and uncheck "Overwrite data in the file".

- If the complexity of the required data conversion annoys you too much, then you can always use OPENROWSET in an OLEDB source (using the code described previously) for an SQL Server source. The downside to this, in practice, is the complexity of permissions and the requirement for ad hoc queries to be enabled.

7-30. Exporting Data to Other Relational Databases Using T-SQL

Problem

You want to export data into a third-party RDBMS using T-SQL.

Solution

Use OPENROWSET, OPENDATASOURCE, or a linked server. The following steps show how to export data to Oracle using OPENROWSET.

1. Configure a linked server using the script given in Recipe 4-4.

2. Create a table called **Client_Dest** on the SCOTT schema of the destination Oracle database:

```
CREATE TABLE "SCOTT"."Client_Dest"
(
    "ID" INTEGER,
    "ClientName" VARCHAR2(150),
    "Country" VARCHAR2(50),
    "Town" VARCHAR2(50),
    "County" VARCHAR2(50),
    "Address1" VARCHAR2(50),
    "Address2" VARCHAR2(50),
    "ClientType" VARCHAR2(20),
    "ClientSize" VARCHAR2(10)
);
```

3. Use the following SQL snippet to insert data into the Client_Dest Oracle table:

```
INSERT INTO OPENROWSET('OraOLEDB.Oracle', 'ORCL';'SYSTEM';'Me4B0ss',
                  'select ID,ClientName,Country,Town from SCOTT.Client_Dest')
SELECT    ID,ClientName,Country,Town
FROM      dbo.Client;
```

How It Works

Thanks to the maturity of the OLEDB and .NET providers for a range of relational databases, exporting data to Oracle, DB2, Sybase, Informix, and PostgreSQL (to name but a few) is remarkably simple—providing that the required drivers, and where necessary, client software are correctly installed. I feel that it is difficult not to stress this point forcefully enough. In my experience, the vast majority of cross-database import and export problems boil down to these two basic elements. Once they are in place and tested, the rest is a piece of cake. So I encourage you to ensure that these fundamental aspects of the link are set up correctly before proceeding with any attempt at exporting data.

However, even establishing the linking infrastructure correctly is not always a guarantee of flawless execution. You need a sound knowledge of the data types of the destination tables and any limitations imposed by the relational structure—that is, any unique constraints, foreign keys, non-nullable fields, and so forth. This enables you to ensure that the data that you are exporting is suitable for the destination data structure and loads successfully.

The OPENROWSET command needs the parameters shown in Table 7-9.

Table 7-9. *OPENROWSET Parameters for Oracle Export*

Description	Example
Oracle OLEDB Provider	OraOLEDB.Oracle
Oracle Address in TNSNames.Ora file	ORCL
Oracle Logon	SYSTEM
OraclePassword	Me4BOss
Destination Fields	select ID,ClientName,Country,Town

I use Oracle as the external data destination for the examples in this recipe because as far as I can ascertain, it seems to be the most frequently used database for exporting data from SQL Server. The techniques described shortly will work with most other relational sources, and it is (with a few rare exceptions) only a case of altering the provider name for the destination database. Other database providers and some of their quirks are described in detail in Chapter 4.

Using OPENROWSET and OPENDATASOURCE is not difficult when using either the Microsoft or the Oracle providers. These examples use the more modern Oracle provider.

If you prefer to use OPENDATASOURCE, then the following SQL snippet will insert data into the Client_Dest Oracle table:

```
SELECT * FROM OPENDATASOURCE('OraOLEDB.Oracle', 'Data Source=ORCL;User
ID=SYSTEM;Password=Me4BOss')..SCOTT.EMP;
```

Assuming that you have a linked server named MyOracleDatabase already set up (as described in Recipe 4-4), then inserting data into a linked server is a standard INSERT...SELECT operation, only using four-part notation, something like this:

```
INSERT INTO MyOracleDatabase.CarSales.dbo.Client_Dest
(
ID
,ClientName
,Country
,Town
)

SELECT
ID
,ClientName
,Country
,Town
FROM dbo.Client;
```

Hints, Tips, and Traps

- It is up to you to ensure that data types (and field lengths) are compatible between the source and destination servers. This could mean using CAST and/or CONVERT to ensure data type compatibility, and LEFT to truncate character data.

- When exporting data, it will be up to you to ensure that data types and lengths allow you to complete an export process successfully. Chapter 8 contains information on obtaining linked server metadata. Appendix A has extensive information on data type mapping between databases.

7-31. Exporting Data to Other Relational Databases Using SSIS

Problem

You want to export data into an external RDBMS using SSIS.

Solution

Use an SSIS Data Flow with an OLEDB Destination component, using an OLEDB connection manager configured for the third-party database.

The following explains how you can export data from SQL Server to Oracle.

1. Create a new SSIS package. Add a new OLEDB connection manager, configured to connect to your SQL Server source. Name it **CarSales_OLEDB**.

2. Add a new OLEDB connection manager, name it **Oracle_OLEDB** and configure it as follows:

Provider:	Oracle Provider for OLEDB
Server or File Name:	Your Oracle instance
Username:	Your Oracle login
Password:	Your Oracle password

3. Add an OLEDB source component. Configure it to use the CarSales_OLEDB connection manager. Select a source table or enter an SQL query. In this example, I will use the Clients table.

4. Add an OLEDB Destination component. Configure it to use the Oracle_OLEDB connection manager. Set the AlwaysUseDefaultCodePage property to True. Set the data access mode to Table or View and click New to create a new table—or select an existing table. If you are creating a new table, you will see that SSIS attempts to translate SQL Server data types to the corresponding Oracle data types. In this example, I will set the destination table name to SCOTT.SQLSERVEREXPORT. Assuming that you are creating a table, click OK. The following dialog box will appear (see Figure 7-30).

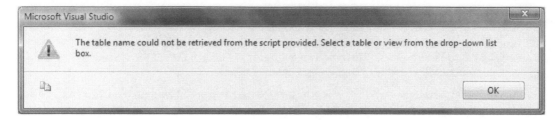

Figure 7-30. OLEDB warning when table metadata is unavailable

5. Click OK and select the destination table from the pop-up list of tables and views.

6. Click OK to confirm your modifications.

How It Works

This recipe is superficially simple. In the real world, there can be many tricky details to finalize before it works this simply. However, providing that the Oracle client software and the Oracle OLEDB driver are installed correctly—and you have a valid Oracle account to use—then there is no reason for this not to work. You must ensure the Oracle client software has been correctly installed and configured on the server where the SSIS package will run, along with either the Microsoft Oracle OLEDB driver—or preferably the Oracle OLEDB driver. Also, an Oracle account with sufficient privileges to write data to the Oracle destination schema and table is required along with table creation rights, if you are creating a new table via SSIS.

Hints, Tips, and Traps

- The reason to set the `AlwaysUseDefaultCodePage` property to True is that you will otherwise get an annoying—and pointless—code-page warning message. Also, the Oracle OLEDB destination will contain a (pointless) warning triangle.

- This example is extreme in its simplicity. Of course, you may perform a variety of SSIS data transformation processes on the data (including tweaking data types) before the final export to Oracle.

7-32. Exporting Data from SQL Server Azure

Problem

You want to export data from SQL Server Azure to a text file or third-party database.

Solution

Use SSIS, BCP, or the Import/Export Data Wizard and specify SQL Server Azure as the data source.

I will illustrate SQL Server Azure export with three mini-recipes since the Microsoft cloud-based RDBMS is essentially just another SQL Server database.

Using SSIS

When using SSIS to connect to an SQL Server Azure data source, you can use either an OLEDB or an ADO.NET data source. Just remember to use SQL Server authentication and to specify the fully qualified domain name of the SQL Server Azure database (and append @Database to the username if you are using the OLEDB data source).

Using BCP

Providing that you are using the version of BCP that comes with SQL Server 2008 R2 or above, then the following command will export data from SQL Server Azure:

```
C:\Users\Adam>BCP Carsales.dbo.client OUT C:\SQL2012DIRecipes\CH07\Azure.BCP -U ↲
MeForPrimeMinister@ETLCookbook -PGubbins -SETLCookbook.database.windows.net -N
```

Using the Import/Export Data Wizard

Merely use the .NET Framework data provider for SQL Server as the data source. Configure it as described in Chapter 5.

How It Works

For all intents and purposes, SQL Server Azure is just another SQL Server database. So as long as you are using SQL Server 2008 R2 and above, you can use all the tools that you are used to using to export data from Microsoft's cloud-based RDBMS. The essential thing to remember is that you must specify the fully qualified domain name of the SQL Server Azure database. If you are using the OLEDB data source, you must also append @Database to the username.

Hints, Tips, and Traps

- It is essential to add @ServerName to the usernamewhen using BCP.

- You must use SQL Server authenticationwhen using BCP.

- You must use the fully qualified DNS name (as it is given in the Azure Management Portal) as the server name.

- You do not have to use SQL native format with BCP. You can otherwise treat this as a standard BCP command.

- You can use SQL Select statements or stored procedures to select the data that is returned.

Summary

This chapter reviewed many ways of exporting data using SQL Server. To recap these methods, Table 7-10 summarizes my take on the various methods.

Table 7-10. Advantages and Disadvantages of Approaches Used in This Chapter

Technique	Advantages	Disadvantages
SSIS	Intuitive, efficient and powerful.	Something of a learning curve.
BCP	Ruthlessly efficient.	Clunky and definitely not intuitive.
OPENROWSET	Good for ad hoc exports.	Requires a destination file or table to exist.
OPENDATASOURCE	Good for ad hoc exports.	Requires a destination file or table to exist.
Linked Server	Once up and running is easy to use.	Can be tricky to configure, slow.
Import/Export Wizard	Easy to use.	Needs a little learning.
XML using SSIS	Quick to set up.	Requires lots of memory.
XML using BCP	Fast.	Can require source data to be "chunked."

Clearly, the technique that you decide to apply when exporting data will depend entirely on the requirements of your environment. The T-SQL-based solutions (OPENROWSET and OPENQUERY) are easy to deploy, but are limited when it comes to debugging and logging. Linked servers can be notoriously slow and tricky to set up, yet once in production tend to be very reliable. SSIS is the tool of choice for scheduled and regular export processes, despite the development (and deployment) efforts that it can require. BCP can leave you wondering why the command line was ever invented—except as a form of torture—until the sheer speed of data export using it begins to impress. But nothing beats the Export Wizard when you have the requirement to export a few tables, or even subsets of data from a few tables "off the cuff."

CHAPTER 8

■ ■ ■

Metadata

Metadata is data about data. Specifically, in the context of data ingestion processes, it means discovering and knowing all that is necessary to know about the structures of your source data. This means having, at a minimum, all the details of the following:

- Tables used

- Columns available

- Data types

- Length of data in columns

- Column nullability

For certain sources, you should also know:

- Primary and unique keys

- Indexes

- Triggers

Exactly how much of this information is essential to the process you are building will depend on each individual project. Some of it will be merely useful, but other aspects could be key to a successful data load process.

Now, while it is possible to create and operate highly successful ETL processes without knowing very much about the source metadata, having a clear definition of how your source data is structured and defined can be very useful for several reasons, including:

- When you are defining data flows, if you can specify the correct data types and lengths from the start, you will make your process more robust and avoid unexpected package failures when your code moves into production.

- When you are mapping a source data type to a destination data type, you can have greater confidence in their compatibility.

I am sure that you can find other reasons to complement this short list. So, having assumed that obtaining and understanding the metadata that underpins data flows is the key to creating and maintaining robust and efficient data ingestion processes, this chapter will show you how to

- Obtain metadata.

- Use metadata to debug data ingestion issues.

- Store metadata and use it to detect changes in source data structures, such as structural modifications (new or removed columns) and type changes.

We will look at the following primary ways that metadata can be obtained:

- Metadata from linked server connections.

- Metadata repositories—and the requisite techniques for accessing them—in the major relational databases that we have used for source data so far in this book.

- Using .NET and its GetSchema method, which can be used with database connection objects to get schema data for SQL Server, OLEDB, and ODBC connections.

Essentially, then, this chapter is all about becoming forearmed through being forewarned. You may be able to manage quite cheerfully without digging for source system metadata for years—or simply by using the metadata provided by SSIS or T-SQL when linking to source data tables. Yet there are bound to be occasions when digging into the source data to learn how it is defined is a prerequisite for a successful ETL process. The following recipes are designed to help you in this process of discovery.

If you have downloaded the accompanying files from the book's companion web site, you will find the examples for this chapter in C:\SQL2012DIRecipes\CH08\.

8-1. Listing Available Tables from a Linked Server
Problem

You want to discover the tables available over a linked server connection.

Solution

Use the sp_tables_ex system stored procedure to list all the tables that you can query using a linked server. This stored procedure is as easy as it is effective. At its simplest, it only requires the linked server name, as the following code snippet (using an Oracle linked server) shows:

```
EXECUTE master.dbo.sp_tables_ex 'MyOracleDatabase'
```

Running this code snippet will return the list of all tables that are visible to the user on the MyOracleDatabase linked server.

How It Works

If you have a linked server connection to an external database, then obtaining the metadata from these is really easy, as SQL Server provides the stored procedure sp_tables_ex, which returns a list of the tables that you can query across a linked server. The only required parameter is the linked server name. The linked server can be any correctly configured linked server, be it an Excel spreadsheet, an SQL Server database, or any data source that SQL Server allows to be defined as a linked server. Also, if you wish, you can restrict the data returned by this stored procedure by adding the schema and table type. Here again, I am showing how this can be done for an Oracle linked server—though this is common to all linked server sources (C:\SQL2012DIRecipes\CH08\LinkedServerTables.sql):

```
EXECUTE master.dbo.sp_tables_ex @table_server = 'MyOracleDatabase', @table_schema = 'HR',
@table_type = 'VIEW'
```

The data that is returned is given in Table 8-1.

Table 8-1. *Metadata Returned from the sp_tables_ex System Stored Procedure*

Column Name	Data Type	Description
TABLE_CAT	sysname	The database name.
TABLE_SCHEM	sysname	The table schema.
TABLE_NAME	sysname	The table name.
TABLE_TYPE	VARCHAR(32)	The table type—user table, system table, or view.
REMARKS	VARCHAR(254)	SQL Server leaves this blank.

The sp_tables_ex stored procedure uses the parameters shown in Table 8-2. These parameters allow you to filter the information returned by the stored procedure.

Table 8-2. *sp_tables_ex Parameters*

Parameter	Comments
@table_server	The linked server name.
@table_catalog	The database name.
@table_schema	The table schema name.
@table_name	The table name.
@table_type	The three really useful table types are SYSTEM TABLE, TABLE, and VIEW.

░ **Note** The sp_tables_ex stored procedure returns an empty result set if the OLEDB provider of the linked server does not support the TABLES rowset of the IDBSchemaRowset interface.

8-2. Listing the Columns Available When Using a Linked Server
Problem
You want to list all the columns that you can query using a linked server.

Solution
Use the sp_columns_ex system stored procedure to display the columns in the tables accessible over a linked server connection. Here is a code snippet to illustrate this:

```
EXECUTE master.dbo.sp_columns_ex @table_server = 'MyOracleDatabase'
```

How It Works

The approach described in the previous recipe can be extended to return data about the columns in the linked server, using the sp_columns_ex stored procedure as shown in this recipe. You can restrict the data returned by the stored procedure by adding the @table_name and @table_server optional parameters for an Oracle linked server, as follows (C:\SQL2012DIRecipes\CH08\LinkedServerColumns.sql):

```
EXEC sp_columns_ex @table_server = 'MyOracleDatabase', @table_name = 'Car_Sales'
```

The data that is returned is provided in Table 8-3.

Table 8-3. *Metadata Returned Using the sp_columns_ex System Stored Procedure*

Column Name	Data Type	Description
TABLE_CAT	sysname	The database name.
TABLE_SCHEM	sysname	The table schema.
TABLE_NAME	sysname	The table name.
COLUMN_NAME	sysname	The column name.
DATA_TYPE	smallint	The column data type ID.
TYPE_NAME	VARCHAR(13)	The friendly name of the column data type.
COLUMN_SIZE	int	The column size or length.
BUFFER_LENGTH	int	Data transfer size.
DECIMAL_DIGITS	smallint	The number of figures to the right of the decimal.
NUM_PREC_RADIX	smallint	The numeric base type.
NULLABLE	smallint	If 1, then the column can contain NULLs. Otherwise contains 0.
REMARKS	VARCHAR(254)	SQL Server leaves this blank.
COLUMN_DEF	VARCHAR(254)	Any default value.
SQL_DATA_TYPE	smallint	Essentially the same as the DATA_TYPE.
SQL_DATETIME_SUB	smallint	A subtype for the datetime and SQL-92 interval data types—else is NULL.
CHAR_OCTET_LENGTH	int	The maximum length of the data in bytes.
ORDINAL_POSITION	int	1-based position of the column in the table.
IS_NULLABLE	VARCHAR(254)	ISO nullability. If 1, then the column can contain NULLs. Otherwise, contains 0.
SS_DATA_TYPE	TINYINT	Extended stored procedure data type.

The sp_columns_ex stored procedure uses the parameters shown in Table 8-4. These parameters allow you to filter the information returned by the stored procedure.

Table 8-4. *The Possible Parameters for the sp_columns_ex System Stored Procedure*

Parameter	Comments
@table_server	The linked server name.
@table_name	The table name.
@table_schema	The table schema.
@table_catalog	The database name.
@column_name	The database column name.

Hints, Tips, and Traps

- The solution in this recipe will not work with an Excel or Access linked server.

8-3. Discovering Flat File Metadata

Problem

You want to obtain the column definitions for a flat file you need to import.

Solution

Use the Flat File connection manager in SSIS to guess the data types.

How It Works

If you are lucky, the supplier of the text (flat) file that you received will also have described the data it contains. If fortune has not smiled on you that particular day, you have only a couple of options available. The first is to use SSIS. In the Flat File Connection Manager Editor dialog box, you can evaluate the source data, and automatically guess and apply the length of columns in the flat file to prevent truncation of data or excess column width. This is described in Chapter 2's Recipe 2-1.

Another option—if your flat file is set up as a linked server—is to use sp_tables_ex to look at the data types. In my experience, the information returned from this procedure—when used on flat file linked servers—is often insufficient. So you are faced with a choice:

- Spend a potentially large amount of time pre-analyzing an entire source file (or multiple files if your source data is delivered this way).

- Estimate approximate data types and lengths, which means that

    - If they are too long, then the load will be slower than necessary.

    - If they are too short, then the load will fail.

    - If they are the wrong type, then the load will fail.

To obtain valid metadata for flat files, I advise loading a representative sample of data into an SQL Server table where the column widths are set to NVARCHAR type—and suitably wide. Then use the T-SQL in Recipe 8-6 to analyze the data.

8-4. Returning Simple SQL Server Metadata

Problem

You want to find basic metadata about SQL Server tables and columns simply and easily.

Solution

Query the INFORMATION_SCHEMA views to get a reasonable idea of the metadata describing your source database. The following describes a way to do this.

1. Expand Views ➤ System Views for the database that you wish to return metadata. You should see the screenshot shown in Figure 8-1.

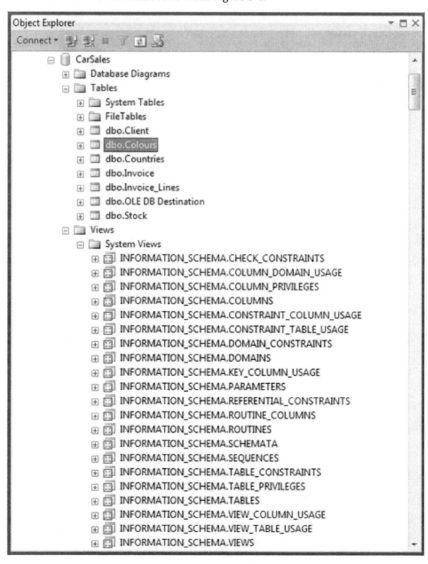

Figure 8-1. *INFORMATION_SCHEMA tables*

2. Right-click the view containing the metadata that interests you. Choose Select Top 1000 Rows.

The metadata that you selected will be displayed as the results of the SELECT query. You can then tweak the query to return a dataset suited to your exact needs.

How It Works

As you probably know, another way of getting a subset of essential metadata is through judicious use of the INFORMATION_SCHEMA views, which appeared with SQL Server 2005. This data can be found by querying the system views of any database. Fortunately, most of the views are self-explanatory and save memorizing the names of system-stored procedures, which you can also use to return metadata about tables, views, columns, and so forth. All you have to do is run a simple SELECT query.

The INFORMATION_SCHEMA views that I use most are provided in Table 8-5.

Table 8-5. *Frequently Used INFORMATION_SCHEMA Views*

INFORMATION_SCHEMA View	Useful Columns	Comments
COLUMNS	COLUMN_NAME	The exact column name.
	IS_NULLABLE	Indicates if the column can contain NULLs.
	DATA_TYPE	The column's data type.
	CHARACTER_MAXIMUM_LENGTH	The maximum number of characters in a column.
	CHARACTER_OCTET_LENGTH	The maximum size of a column in bytes.
	NUMERIC_PRECISION	A numeric column's precision.
	NUMERIC_PRECISION_RADIX	The numeric base type.
	NUMERIC_SCALE	A numeric column's scale.
	CHARACTER_SET_NAME	For a non-Unicode column, the character set used.
	DATETIME_PRECISION	The DATETIME precision.
	COLLATION	The column collation.
CONSTRAINTS	CONSTRAINT_NAME	The name of a constraint.
	CHECK_CLAUSE	The exact check code.
CONSTRAINT_COLUMN_USAGE	COLUMN_NAME	Lists all columns with constraints—and the name of the constraint.
	CONSTRAINT_NAME	This allows you to ensure that you are passing valid data through a data flow that will not be rejected by the destination table.

(continued)

431

Table 8-5. (*continued*)

INFORMATION_SCHEMA View	Useful Columns	Comments
CONSTRAINT_TABLE_USAGE	COLUMN_NAME	Lists all columns with constraints—and the name of the constraint.
	CONSTRAINT_NAME	The name of any constraint on a column.
KEY_COLUMN_USAGE	CONSTRAINT_NAME	The name of a key constraint.
	TABLE_NAME	The table to which the constraint applies.
	COLUMN_NAME	The column to which the constraint applies.
SCHEMATA	SCHEMA_NAME	The schema name.
TABLES		Tables and their schemata.
REFERENTIAL_CONSTRAINTS	CONSTRAINT_NAME	A list of all the foreign key constraints in a database.
	UNIQUE_CONSTRAINT_NAME	A list of all the unique key constraints in a database.
	SCHEMA_OWNER	The schema owner.
VIEWS		Views and their schemata.

Hints, Tips, and Traps

- There is much more information available from the INFORMATION_SCHEMA views, so have some fun delving into them. Taking the time to learn what is available can reap real rewards in time saved from having to later debug errors in data flows.

- There has been some discussion as to whether the INFORMATION_SCHEMA data is valid, and indeed if it can be trusted at all. I tend to regard it as accurate, but too minimalistic, and so prefer to base analysis on the information contained in the catalog views.

8-5. Gathering Tailored SQL Server Metadata
Problem

You need to obtain precise SQL Server table metadata to validate your ETL data type mappings.

Solution

Use the SQL Server INFORMATION_SCHEMA views to return selective table metadata about data types.

The following query will return somewhat essential metadata for data integration purposes from an SQL Server database using the INFORMATION_SCHEMA views (C:\SQL2012DIRecipes\CH08\EssentialSQLServerMetadata.sql):

```
SELECT
C.TABLE_CATALOG,
C.TABLE_SCHEMA,
```

```
C.TABLE_NAME,
C.COLUMN_NAME,
C.COLUMN_DEFAULT,
C.IS_NULLABLE,
C.DATA_TYPE,
C.CHARACTER_MAXIMUM_LENGTH,
C.CHARACTER_OCTET_LENGTH,
C.NUMERIC_PRECISION,
C.NUMERIC_SCALE,
A.CONSTRAINT_TYPE,
A.CHECK_CLAUSE

FROM         INFORMATION_SCHEMA.COLUMNS C LEFT OUTER JOIN

(
  SELECT
  CCU.TABLE_CATALOG,
  CCU.TABLE_SCHEMA,
  CCU.TABLE_NAME,
  CCU.COLUMN_NAME,
  CT.CONSTRAINT_TYPE,
  CHK.CHECK_CLAUSE
  FROM      INFORMATION_SCHEMA.CONSTRAINT_COLUMN_USAGE CCU
            INNER JOIN INFORMATION_SCHEMA.TABLE_CONSTRAINTS CT
            ON CCU.CONSTRAINT_NAME = CT.CONSTRAINT_NAME
            LEFT OUTER JOIN INFORMATION_SCHEMA.CHECK_CONSTRAINTS CHK
            ON CT.CONSTRAINT_NAME = CHK.CONSTRAINT_NAME
) A

ON A.COLUMN_NAME = C.COLUMN_NAME
AND A.TABLE_NAME  = C.TABLE_NAME
AND A.TABLE_SCHEMA = C.TABLE_SCHEMA;
```

A sample of the output that this script can produce is shown in Figure 8-2.

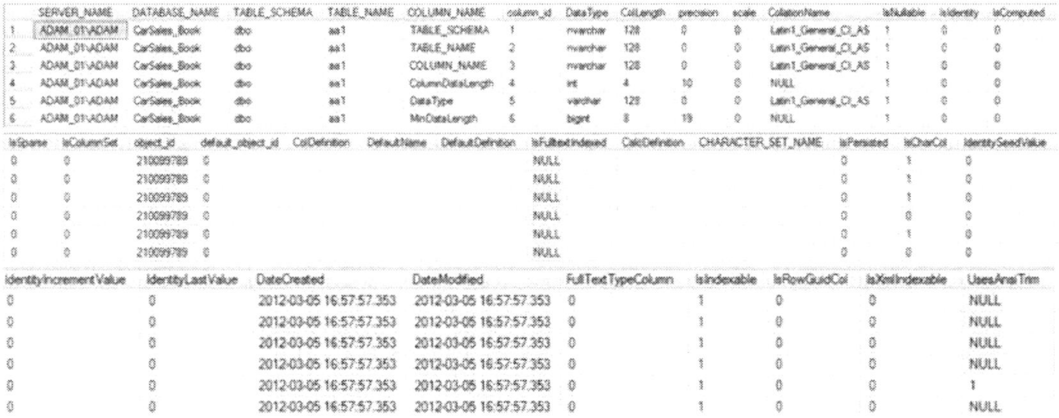

	SERVER_NAME	DATABASE_NAME	TABLE_SCHEMA	TABLE_NAME	COLUMN_NAME	column_id	DataType	ColLength	precision	scale	CollationName	IsNullable	IsIdentity	IsComputed
1	ADAM_01\ADAM	CarSales_Book	dbo	aa1	TABLE_SCHEMA	1	nvarchar	128	0	0	Latin1_General_CI_AS	1	0	0
2	ADAM_01\ADAM	CarSales_Book	dbo	aa1	TABLE_NAME	2	nvarchar	128	0	0	Latin1_General_CI_AS	1	0	0
3	ADAM_01\ADAM	CarSales_Book	dbo	aa1	COLUMN_NAME	3	nvarchar	128	0	0	Latin1_General_CI_AS	1	0	0
4	ADAM_01\ADAM	CarSales_Book	dbo	aa1	ColumnDataLength	4	int	4	10	0	NULL	1	0	0
5	ADAM_01\ADAM	CarSales_Book	dbo	aa1	DataType	5	varchar	128	0	0	Latin1_General_CI_AS	1	0	0
6	ADAM_01\ADAM	CarSales_Book	dbo	aa1	MinDataLength	6	bigint	8	19	0	NULL	1	0	0

IsSparse	IsColumnSet	object_id	default_object_id	ColDefinition	DefaultName	DefaultDefinition	IsFulltextIndexed	CalcDefinition	CHARACTER_SET_NAME	IsPersisted	IsCharCol	IdentitySeedValue
0	0	210099789	0				NULL			0	1	0
0	0	210099789	0				NULL			0	1	0
0	0	210099789	0				NULL			0	1	0
0	0	210099789	0				NULL			0	0	0
0	0	210099789	0				NULL			0	1	0
0	0	210099789	0				NULL			0	0	0

IdentityIncrementValue	IdentityLastValue	DateCreated	DateModified	FullTextTypeColumn	IsIndexable	IsRowGuidCol	IsXmlIndexable	UsesAnsiTrim
0	0	2012-03-05 16:57:57.353	2012-03-05 16:57:57.353	0	1	0	0	NULL
0	0	2012-03-05 16:57:57.353	2012-03-05 16:57:57.353	0	1	0	0	NULL
0	0	2012-03-05 16:57:57.353	2012-03-05 16:57:57.353	0	1	0	0	NULL
0	0	2012-03-05 16:57:57.353	2012-03-05 16:57:57.353	0	1	0	0	NULL
0	0	2012-03-05 16:57:57.353	2012-03-05 16:57:57.353	0	1	0	0	1
0	0	2012-03-05 16:57:57.353	2012-03-05 16:57:57.353	0	1	0	0	NULL

Figure 8-2. *Metadata output from INFORMATION_SCHEMA views*

How It Works

This script joins a set of tables (COLUMNS, CONSTRAINT_COLUMN_USAGE, and TABLE_CONSTRAINTS) to return a selected subset of metadata about the available tables. The output from the script can, if you so wish, be inserted into a table using SELECT...INTO. You can modify the elements that are returned to suit your own requirements.

Hints, Tips, and Traps

- You can add a WHERE clause to filter the table(s) that you want.

- The results that are returned can then be used to verify the state of—or changes in—the metadata.

- When querying the INFORMATION_SCHEMA views, always qualify the view name with INFORMATION_SCHEMA. For example:

```
SELECT    TABLE_CATALOG, TABLE_SCHEMA, TABLE_NAME
FROM      INFORMATION_SCHEMA.TABLES
WHERE     TABLE_TYPE = 'BASE TABLE'
```

- You can join INFORMATION_SCHEMA views to derive the information that you are looking for.

- You can use INFORMATION_SCHEMA views in an SSIS package to export data to Excel (for instance) to compare with the metadata you have produced for the source data—and produce a spreadsheet detailing how the data maps and what the potential problems are. To do this, all you have to do is to create an SSIS package with a data source that is an OLEDB or ADO.NET connection to your database using the preceding code as its SQL command text, and link this to an Excel destination.

8-6. Analyzing SQL Server Table Metadata

Problem

You need to obtain SQL Server table metadata for analysis.

Solution

Use the SQL Server system views to return full table metadata.

Running the following script will give you extensive information about all the SQL Server tables in a specified database.

```
DECLARE @SERVER_NAME NVARCHAR(128) = @@SERVERNAME
DECLARE @DATABASE_NAME NVARCHAR128) = DB_NAME()
-------------------------------------------
IF OBJECT_ID('tempdb..#MetaData_Tables') IS NOT NULL
DROP TABLE tempdb..#MetaData_Tables;
```

```
-- Table data

CREATE TABLE #MetaData_Tables
(
 SCHEMA_NAME SYSNAME NOT NULL,
 TABLE_NAME SYSNAME NOT NULL,
 object_id INT NOT NULL,
 TableType NVARCHAR(60) NULL,
 DateCreated DATETIME NOT NULL,
 DateModified DATETIME NOT NULL,
 uses_ansi_nulls BIT NULL,
 text_in_row_limit INT NULL,
 large_value_types_out_of_row BIT NULL,
 IsCDCTracked BIT NULL,
 lock_escalation_desc NVARCHAR(60) NULL,
 LobDataSpace SYSNAME NULL,
 FilestreamDataSpace SYSNAME NULL,
 DataSpace VARCHAR(250) NULL,
 DataSpaceType VARCHAR(250) NULL,
 NbrColumns  SMALLINT NULL,
 IsHeap BIT NULL,
 NoIndexes BIT NULL,
 NoRows BIGINT NULL,
 HasAfterTrigger  BIT NULL,
 HasDeleteTrigger BIT NULL,
 HasInsertTrigger BIT NULL,
 HasInsteadOfTrigger BIT NULL,
 HasUpdateTrigger BIT NULL,
 IsAnsiNullsOn BIT NULL,
 IsEncrypted BIT NULL,
 IsIndexed BIT NULL,
 IsIndexable BIT NULL,
 IsQuotedIdentOn BIT NULL,
 IsSystemTable BIT NULL,
 IsUserTable BIT NULL,
 DeleteTriggerCount SMALLINT NULL,
 FullTextBackgroundUpdateIndexOn BIT NULL,
 FulltextCatalogId SMALLINT NULL,
 FulltextChangeTrackingOn BIT NULL,
 FulltextKeyColumn SMALLINT NULL,
 HasActiveFulltextIndex BIT NULL,
 HasCheckCnst BIT NULL,
 HasClustIndex BIT NULL,
 HasDefaultCnst BIT NULL,
 HasForeignKey BIT NULL,
 HasForeignRef BIT NULL,
 HasIdentity BIT NULL,
 HasIndex BIT NULL,
 HasNonclustIndex BIT NULL,
 HasPrimaryKey BIT NULL,
 HasRowGuidCol BIT NULL,
 HasTextImage BIT NULL,
```

```
 HasTimestamp BIT NULL,
 HasUniqueCnst BIT NULL,
 HasVarDecimalStorageFormat BIT NULL,
 InsertTriggerCount SMALLINT NULL,
 TextInRowLimit SMALLINT NULL,
 UpdateTriggerCount SMALLINT NULL,
 HasColumnSet BIT NULL,
 DataCompression NVARCHAR(60)
)

INSERT INTO  #MetaData_Tables
(
SCHEMA_NAME
,TABLE_NAME
,object_id
,TableType
,DateCreated
,DAteModified
,uses_ansi_nulls
,text_in_row_limit
,large_value_types_out_of_row
,IsCDCTracked
,lock_escalation_desc
,LobDataSpace
,FilestreamDataSpace
,DataSpace
,DataSpaceType
,NbrColumns
,IsHeap
,NoIndexes
,NoRows
,HasAfterTrigger
,HasDeleteTrigger
,HasInsertTrigger
,HasInsteadOfTrigger
,HasUpdateTrigger
,IsAnsiNullsOn
,IsEncrypted
,IsIndexed
,IsIndexable
,IsQuotedIdentOn
,IsSystemTable
,IsUserTable
,DeleteTriggerCount
,FullTextBackgroundUpdateIndexOn
,FulltextCatalogId
,FulltextChangeTrackingOn
,FulltextKeyColumn
,HasActiveFulltextIndex
,HasCheckCnst
,HasClustIndex
,HasDefaultCnst
```

436

```
,HasForeignKey
,HasForeignRef
,HasIdentity
,HasIndex
,HasNonclustIndex
,HasPrimaryKey
,HasRowGuidCol
,HasTextImage
,HasTimestamp
,HasUniqueCnst
,HasVarDecimalStorageFormat
,InsertTriggerCount
,TextInRowLimit
,UpdateTriggerCount
,HasColumnSet
)

SELECT
SCH.name AS SCHEMA_NAME
,TBL.name AS TABLE_NAME
,TBL.object_id
,TBL.type_desc AS TableType
,TBL.create_date AS DateCreated
,TBL.modify_date AS DAteModified
,TBL.uses_ansi_nulls
,TBL.text_in_row_limit
,TBL.large_value_types_out_of_row
,TBL.is_tracked_by_cdc AS IsCDCTracked
,TBL.lock_escalation_desc
,DSP.name AS LobDataSpace
,DSP1.name AS FilestreamDataSpace
,CAST(NULL AS VARCHAR(250)) AS DataSpace
,CAST(NULL AS VARCHAR(250)) AS DataSpaceType
,CAST(NULL AS SMALLINT) AS NbrColumns
,CAST(NULL AS BIT) AS IsHeap
,CAST(NULL AS BIT) AS NoIndexes
,CAST(NULL AS BIGINT) AS NoRows
,OBJECTPROPERTY(TBL.object_id, 'HasAfterTrigger') AS HasAfterTrigger
,OBJECTPROPERTY(TBL.object_id, 'HasDeleteTrigger') AS HasDeleteTrigger
,OBJECTPROPERTY(TBL.object_id, 'HasInsertTrigger') AS HasInsertTrigger
,OBJECTPROPERTY(TBL.object_id, 'HasInsteadOfTrigger') AS HasInsteadOfTrigger
,OBJECTPROPERTY(TBL.object_id, 'HasUpdateTrigger') AS HasUpdateTrigger
,OBJECTPROPERTY(TBL.object_id, 'IsAnsiNullsOn') AS IsAnsiNullsOn
,OBJECTPROPERTY(TBL.object_id, 'IsEncrypted') AS IsEncrypted
,OBJECTPROPERTY(TBL.object_id, 'IsIndexed') AS IsIndexed
,OBJECTPROPERTY(TBL.object_id, 'IsIndexable') AS IsIndexable
,OBJECTPROPERTY(TBL.object_id, 'IsQuotedIdentOn') AS IsQuotedIdentOn
,OBJECTPROPERTY(TBL.object_id, 'IsSystemTable') AS IsSystemTable
,OBJECTPROPERTY(TBL.object_id, 'IsUserTable') AS IsUserTable
,OBJECTPROPERTY(TBL.object_id, 'DeleteTriggerCount') AS DeleteTriggerCount
,OBJECTPROPERTY(TBL.object_id, 'FullTextBackgroundUpdateIndexOn')
    AS FullTextBackgroundUpdateIndexOn
```

437

```
,OBJECTPROPERTY(TBL.object_id, 'FulltextCatalogId') AS FulltextCatalogId
,OBJECTPROPERTY(TBL.object_id, 'FulltextChangeTrackingOn') AS FulltextChangeTrackingOn
,OBJECTPROPERTY(TBL.object_id, 'FulltextKeyColumn') AS FulltextKeyColumn
,OBJECTPROPERTY(TBL.object_id, 'HasActiveFulltextIndex') AS HasActiveFulltextIndex
,OBJECTPROPERTY(TBL.object_id, 'HasCheckCnst') AS HasCheckCnst
,OBJECTPROPERTY(TBL.object_id, 'HasClustIndex') AS HasClustIndex
,OBJECTPROPERTY(TBL.object_id, 'HasDefaultCnst') AS HasDefaultCnst
,OBJECTPROPERTY(TBL.object_id, 'HasForeignKey') AS HasForeignKey
,OBJECTPROPERTY(TBL.object_id, 'HasForeignRef') AS HasForeignRef
,OBJECTPROPERTY(TBL.object_id, 'HasIdentity') AS HasIdentity
,OBJECTPROPERTY(TBL.object_id, 'HasIndex') AS HasIndex
,OBJECTPROPERTY(TBL.object_id, 'HasNonclustIndex') AS HasNonclustIndex
,OBJECTPROPERTY(TBL.object_id, 'HasPrimaryKey') AS HasPrimaryKey
,OBJECTPROPERTY(TBL.object_id, 'HasRowGuidCol') AS HasRowGuidCol
,OBJECTPROPERTY(TBL.object_id, 'HasTextImage') AS HasTextImage
,OBJECTPROPERTY(TBL.object_id, 'HasTimestamp') AS HasTimestamp
,OBJECTPROPERTY(TBL.object_id, 'HasUniqueCnst') AS HasUniqueCnst
,OBJECTPROPERTY(TBL.object_id, 'HasVarDecimalStorageFormat') AS HasVarDecimalStorageFormat
,OBJECTPROPERTY(TBL.object_id, 'InsertTriggerCount') AS InsertTriggerCount
,OBJECTPROPERTY(TBL.object_id, 'TextInRowLimit') AS TextInRowLimit
,OBJECTPROPERTY(TBL.object_id, 'UpdateTriggerCount') AS UpdateTriggerCount
,OBJECTPROPERTY(TBL.object_id, 'HasColumnSet') AS HasColumnSet

FROM        sys.schemas AS SCH
            INNER JOIN sys.tables AS TBL
            ON SCH.schema_id = TBL.schema_id
            LEFT OUTER JOIN sys.data_spaces DSP1
            ON TBL.filestream_data_space_id = DSP1.data_space_id
            LEFT OUTER JOIN sys.data_spaces DSP
            ON TBL.lob_data_space_id = DSP.data_space_id

WHERE TBL.is_ms_shipped = 0

--------------------------------------------------------------------------------
-- Get all secondary elements, process later
--------------------------------------------------------------------------------


-- FileGroup

IF OBJECT_ID('tempdb..#Tmp_FileGroupDetails') IS NOT NULL
DROP TABLE tempdb..#Tmp_FileGroupDetails;

SELECT DISTINCT

DSP.name AS DataSpace
,DSP.type_desc AS DataSpaceType
,TBL.name AS TABLE_NAME
,TBL.object_id AS TableObjectID

INTO    #Tmp_FileGroupDetails
```

```
FROM      sys.data_spaces DSP
          INNER JOIN sys.indexes SIX
          ON DSP.data_space_id = SIX.data_space_id
          INNER JOIN sys.tables TBL
          ON SIX.object_id = TBL.object_id
-------------------------------------------------------------------------------
-- Process all secondary elements
-------------------------------------------------------------------------------


-- FileGroup

UPDATE    D

SET       D.DataSpace = Tmp.DataSpace
          ,D.DataSpaceType = Tmp.DataSpaceType

FROM      #MetaData_Tables D
          INNER JOIN #Tmp_FileGroupDetails Tmp
          ON D.object_id = Tmp.TableObjectID

-- Column Counts

;
WITH NoCols_CTE (SCHEMA_NAME,TABLE_NAME,object_id, NoCols)
AS
(
SELECT    TOP (100) PERCENT
SCH.name AS SCHEMA_NAME
,TBL.name AS TABLE_NAME
,COL.object_id
,COUNT(COL.column_id) AS NoCols

FROM      sys.columns COL
          INNER JOIN sys.tables TBL
          ON COL.object_id = TBL.object_id
          INNER JOIN sys.schemas SCH
          ON TBL.schema_id = SCH.schema_id

GROUP BY COL.object_id, TBL.name, SCH.name
)

UPDATED
SET    D.NbrColumns = CTE.NoCols
FROM   #MetaData_Tables D
INNER JOIN NoCols_CTE CTE
ON D.object_id = CTE.object_id

-- Heaps

UPDATE #MetaData_Tables

SET IsHeap = 1
```

439

```
WHERE object_id IN(
                    SELECT DISTINCT TBL.object_id
                    FROM      sys.tables TBL
                              INNER JOIN sys.schemas SCH
                              ON TBL.schema_id = SCH.schema_id
                              INNER JOIN sys.indexes SIX
                              ON TBL.object_id = SIX.object_id

                    WHERE     SIX.type_desc = N'HEAP'
                )
-- Rows

;
WITH RowCount_CTE (SCHEMA_NAME, TABLE_NAME, object_id, NoRows)
AS
(
SELECT
SCH.name AS SCHEMA_NAME
,TBL.name AS TABLE_NAME
,TBL.object_id
,SSX.rows

FROM    sys.tables TBL
        INNER JOIN sys.schemas SCH
        ON TBL.schema_id = SCH.schema_id
        INNER JOIN sys.sysindexes SSX
        ON TBL.object_id = SSX.id
)

UPDATED

SETD.NoRows = CTE.NoRows

FROM      #MetaData_Tables D
          INNER JOIN RowCount_CTE CTE
          ON D.object_id = CTE.object_id

-- Indexes

;
WITH Indexes_CTE (SCHEMA_NAME, TABLE_NAME, object_id, NoIndexes)
AS
(
SELECT
SCH.name AS SCHEMA_NAME
,TBL.name AS TABLE_NAME
,TBL.object_id
,COUNT(SIX.index_id) AS NoIndexes

FROM      sys.tables TBL
          INNER JOIN sys.schemas SCH
          ON TBL.schema_id = SCH.schema_id
```

```
            INNER JOIN sys.indexes SIX
            ON TBL.object_id = SIX.object_id

GROUP BY    SCH.name, TBL.name, TBL.object_id
)

UPDATE      D

SET         D.NoIndexes = CTE.NoIndexes

FROM        #MetaData_Tables D
            INNER JOIN Indexes_CTE CTE
            ON D.object_id = CTE.object_id

-- Compression
;
WITH Compression_CTE
AS
(
SELECT
SCH.name AS SCHEMA_NAME
,TBL.name AS TABLE_NAME
,PRT.data_compression_desc
,TBL.object_id

FROM        sys.partitions PRT
            INNER JOIN sys.tables TBL
            ON PRT.object_id = TBL.object_id
            INNER JOIN sys.schemas SCH
            ON TBL.schema_id = SCH.schema_id

WHERE PRT.index_id = 0
OR PRT.index_id = 1
)

UPDATE      D

SET         D.DataCompression = CTE.data_compression_desc

FROM        #MetaData_Tables D
            INNER JOIN Compression_CTE CTE
            ON D.object_id = CTE.object_id

SELECT * from #MetaData_Tables; -- Yes SELECT * is bad—but here it saves space!
```

The output from this script (cut into several parts for easier viewing in a book format) looks like Figure 8-3.

	SCHEMA_NAME	TABLE_NAME	object_id	TableType	DateCreated	DateModified	uses_ansi_nulls	text_in_row_limit	large_value_types_out_of_row	IsCDCTracked
1	dbo	aa1	210099789	USER_TABLE	2012-03-05 16:57:57.353	2012-03-05 16:57:57.353	1	0	0	0
2	dbo	aa2	226099846	USER_TABLE	2012-03-05 16:57:57.447	2012-03-05 16:57:57.447	1	0	0	0
3	dbo	Invoice_Lines	325576198	USER_TABLE	2011-05-23 15:27:15.350	2011-09-21 09:05:25.960	1	0	0	0
4	dbo	sysdiagrams	885578193	USER_TABLE	2011-05-23 15:41:14.143	2011-05-23 15:41:14.160	1	0	0	0
5	dbo	Colours	1125575048	USER_TABLE	2011-05-23 15:42:34.840	2011-05-23 15:43:25.537	1	0	0	0
6	dbo	Stock	1173579219	USER_TABLE	2011-05-23 15:43:25.537	2011-05-23 15:58:51.203	1	0	0	0

lock_escalation_desc	LobDataSpace	FilestreamDataSpace	DataSpace	DataSpaceType	NoColumns	IsHeap	NoIndexes	NoRows	HasAfterTrigger	HasDeleteTrigger	HasInsertTrigger	HasInsteadOfTrigger
TABLE	NULL	NULL	PRIMARY	ROWS_FILEGROUP	22	1	1	3	0	0	0	0
TABLE	NULL	NULL	PRIMARY	ROWS_FILEGROUP	4	1	1	9	0	0	0	0
TABLE	NULL	NULL	PRIMARY	ROWS_FILEGROUP	7	NULL	1	5	0	0	0	0
TABLE	PRIMARY	NULL	PRIMARY	ROWS_FILEGROUP	5	NULL	1	1	0	0	0	0
TABLE	NULL	NULL	PRIMARY	ROWS_FILEGROUP	2	NULL	1	2	0	0	0	0
TABLE	PRIMARY	NULL	PRIMARY	ROWS_FILEGROUP	17	NULL	1	5	0	0	0	0

HasUpdateTrigger	IsAnsiNullsOn	IsEncrypted	IsIndexed	IsIndexable	IsQuotedIdentOn	IsSystemTable	IsUserTable	DeleteTriggerCount	FullTextBackgroundUpdateIndexOn	FulltextCatalogId	FulltextChangeTracking
0	1	NULL	0	1	1	0	1	NULL	NULL	NULL	NULL
0	1	NULL	0	1	1	0	1	NULL	NULL	NULL	NULL
0	1	NULL	1	1	1	0	1	NULL	NULL	NULL	NULL
0	1	NULL	1	1	1	0	1	NULL	NULL	NULL	NULL
0	1	NULL	1	1	1	0	1	NULL	NULL	NULL	NULL
0	1	NULL	1	1	1	0	1	NULL	NULL	NULL	NULL

FulltextKeyColumn	HasActiveFulltextIndex	HasCheckCnst	HasClustIndex	HasDefaultCnst	HasForeignKey	HasForeignRef	HasIdentity	HasIndex	HasNonclustIndex	HasPrimaryKey	HasRowGuidCol	HasTextImage
NULL	NULL	NULL	NULL	NULL	NULL	NULL	NULL	NULL	NULL	NULL	NULL	NULL
NULL	NULL	NULL	NULL	NULL	NULL	NULL	NULL	NULL	NULL	NULL	NULL	NULL
NULL	NULL	NULL	NULL	NULL	NULL	NULL	NULL	NULL	NULL	NULL	NULL	NULL
NULL	NULL	NULL	NULL	NULL	NULL	NULL	NULL	NULL	NULL	NULL	NULL	NULL
NULL	NULL	NULL	NULL	NULL	NULL	NULL	NULL	NULL	NULL	NULL	NULL	NULL
NULL	NULL	NULL	NULL	NULL	NULL	NULL	NULL	NULL	NULL	NULL	NULL	NULL

HasTimestamp	HasUniqueCnst	HasVarDecimalStorageFormat	InsertTriggerCount	TextInRowLimit	UpdateTriggerCount	HasColumnSet	DataCompression
NULL	NULL	NULL	NULL	NULL	NULL	NULL	NONE
NULL	NULL	NULL	NULL	NULL	NULL	NULL	NONE
NULL	NULL	NULL	NULL	NULL	NULL	NULL	NONE
NULL	NULL	NULL	NULL	NULL	NULL	NULL	NONE
NULL	NULL	NULL	NULL	NULL	NULL	NULL	NONE
NULL	NULL	NULL	NULL	NULL	NULL	NULL	NONE

Figure 8-3. *Metadata returned from the script in Recipe 8-6*

How It Works

It is important to cover the topic of SQL Server metadata for the following reasons:

- If you are dealing with SQL Server source data, then there is a tendency to think that this will be the easy part, and so to push ahead with the creation of a data flow, only to be tripped up later when a datatype limitation or a constraint causes unforeseen and unexpected problems. And, of course, these are always the ones you never expect, and so they take hours to debug.

- When dealing with SQL Server tables—be they staging tables or a final database (possibly one that you did not design), it is better to be forewarned about as much as possible.

- Isolating and analyzing the SQL Server destination metadata just as you would the source metadata allows you to compare the two cleanly and efficiently.

Let's be clear, there are a multitude of ways to query the metadata of an SQL Server database. In fact, you may wonder why you need to see so many ways of extracting the source metadata. The answer is—you never know when you will need each one, so it is better to be aware that they exist.

For in-depth detail of source metadata, nothing can beat the system views. As you have probably found out by now, using them properly requires a serious investment in understanding how they work. As this is not entirely easy, I am proposing two scripts (in this recipe and the following one) that can return a relatively in-depth analysis of SQL Server metadata for both tables (or views) and columns. If these scripts provide too much information, then you can always reduce their complexity and limit the metadata that they provide. The main thing is to have a tool to start your analysis. The script used in this recipe hopefully proves to be such a starting point, and returns the table metadata shown in Table 8-6.

Table 8-6. *Table Metdata Returned by the Script in Recipe 8-6*

Field Name	Description
SCHEMA_NAME	The schema of the table.
TABLE_NAME	The table name.
object_id	The internal object ID used by the system metadata.
TableType	The table type (table or view).
DateCreated	The date the table was created.
DateModified	The date the table was modified.
uses_ansi_nulls	The table uses ANSI NULLS.
text_in_row_limit	The upper limit (in bytes) for LOBs stored in-row.
large_value_types_out_of_row	Large values are stored out of row.
IsCDCTracked	The table has changes tracked using Change Data Capture.
lock_escalation_desc	The table's Lock Escalation threshold.
LobDataSpace	The LOB dataspace type for the table's LOB columns.
FilestreamDataSpace	The FILESTREAM dataspace type for the table's FILESTREAM column.
DataSpace	The table dataspace.
DataSpaceType	The table dataspace type.
NbrColumns	The number of columns in the table.
IsHeap	The table is a heap (no clustered index).
NoIndexes	The number of indexes on the table.
NoRows	The number of rows in the table.
HasAfterTrigger	The table has an After trigger.
HasDeleteTrigger	The table has a Delete trigger.
HasInsertTrigger	The table has an Insert trigger.
HasInsteadOfTrigger	The table has an Instead Of trigger.
HasUpdateTrigger	The table has an Update trigger.
IsAnsiNullsOn	ANSI NULLS are active for this table.
IsEncrypted	The table is encrypted.
IsIndexed	The table is indexed.
IsIndexable	The table can be indexed.
IsQuotedIdentOn	The table uses quoted identifiers.
IsSystemTable	The table is a system table.

(*continued*)

Table 8-6. (*continued*)

Field Name	Description
IsUserTable	The table is a user table.
DeleteTriggerCount	The number of delete triggers associated with the table.
FullTextBackgroundUpdateIndexOn	Background index updating is active for this table's full-text index.
FulltextCatalogId	The ID of any full-text catalog.
FulltextChangeTrackingOn	Change tracking is active for full-text indexing.
FulltextKeyColumn	The key column for full-text indexing.
HasActiveFulltextIndex	The table has an active full-text index.
HasCheckCnst	The table has check constraints.
HasClustIndex	The table has a clustered index.
HasDefaultCnst	The table has default constraints.
HasForeignKey	The table contains foreign key(s).
HasForeignRef	The table contains foreign key references.
HasIdentity	The table contains an IDENTITY column.
HasIndex	The table has an index.
HasNonclustIndex	The table has a clustered index.
HasPrimaryKey	The table has a primary key.
HasRowGuidCol	The table has a Row GUID column.
HasTextImage	Has TEXT, IMAGE, VARCHAR(MAX), or VARBINARY(MAX) column(s).
HasTimestamp	The table has a Timestamp column.
HasUniqueCnst	The table has unique constraints.
HasVarDecimalStorageFormat	VarDecimal compression is active.
InsertTriggerCount	The number of insert triggers associated with the table.
UpdateTriggerCount	The number of update triggers associated with the table.
HasColumnSet	The table contains column sets.
DataCompression	Data compression is on for this table.

The script uses the @SERVER_NAME and @DATABASE_NAME input parameters to define the server and analyze the database. They default to the current server and database, but you can alter this. It then creates a session-scoped temporary table to hold all the required metadata. In a first pass, it uses the "core" catalog views (sys.tables, sys.data_spaces and sys.schemas) and a series of OBJECTPROPERTY functions to get a fairly full set of metadata. Following this, a series of subprocesses use various system catalog views (sys.columns, sys.sysindexes, and sys.partitions) to return and calculate other metadata elements that are less readily available.

Hints, Tips, and Traps

- I realize that using SELECT * to return the final output from the script in this recipe contravenes all known best practices, but it saves space in a book. You can—and should—only select the columns that you require.

8-7. Analyzing SQL Server Column Metadata

Problem

You need to obtain SQL Server column metadata for analysis.

Solution

Use the SQL Server system catalog views to return full column metadata.

Running the following script will give you extensive information about all the SQL Server columns in a specified database (C:\SQL2012DIRecipes\CH08\SQLServerColumnMetadata.sql):

```
DECLARE @SERVER_NAME NVARCHAR(128) = @@SERVERNAME
DECLARE @DATABASE_NAME NVARCHAR(128) = DB_NAME()


-------------------------------------------

IF OBJECT_ID('tempdb..#Metadata_ColumnTableType') IS NOT NULL
DROP TABLE tempdb..#Metadata_ColumnTableType;

CREATE TABLE #Metadata_ColumnTableType
(
 SERVER_NAME VARCHAR(128) NULL,
 DATABASE_NAME VARCHAR(128) NULL,
 TABLE_SCHEMA VARCHAR(8) NULL,
 TABLE_NAME VARCHAR(8) NULL,
 COLUMN_NAME VARCHAR(8) NULL,
 column_id INT NULL,
 DataType VARCHAR(8) NULL,
 ColLength INT NULL,
 precision TINYINT NULL,
 scale TINYINT NULL,
 CollationName VARCHAR(8) NULL,
 IsNullable BIT NULL,
 IsIdentity BIT NULL,
 IsComputed BIT NULL,
 IsFileStream BIT NULL,
 IsSparse BIT NULL,
 IsColumnSet BIT NULL,
 object_id INT NULL,
 default_object_id INT NULL,
 ColDefinition VARCHAR(max) NULL,
 DefaultName VARCHAR(250) NULL,
 DefaultDefinition VARCHAR(max) NULL,
 IsFulltextIndexed BIT NULL,
```

```
 CalcDefinition VARCHAR(4000) NULL,
 CHARACTER_SET_NAME VARCHAR(250) NULL,
 IsPersisted BIT NULL,
 IsCharCol INT NULL,
 IdentitySeedValue INT NULL,
 IdentityIncrementValue INT NULL,
 IdentityLastValue BIGINT NULL,
 DateCreated DATETIME NULL,
 DateModified DATETIME NULL,
 FullTextTypeColumn INT NULL,
 IsIndexable INT NULL,
 IsRowGuidCol INT NULL,
 IsXmlIndexable INT NULL,
 UsesAnsiTrim INT NULL
)

INSERT INTO #Metadata_ColumnTableType
(
SERVER_NAME
,DATABASE_NAME
,TABLE_SCHEMA
,TABLE_NAME
,COLUMN_NAME
,column_id
,DataType
,ColLength
,precision
,scale
,CollationName
,IsNullable
,IsIdentity
,IsComputed
,IsFileStream
,IsSparse
,IsColumnSet
,object_id
,default_object_id
,ColDefinition
,DefaultName
,DefaultDefinition
,IsFulltextIndexed
,CalcDefinition
,CHARACTER_SET_NAME
,IsPersisted
,IsCharCol
,IdentitySeedValue
,IdentityIncrementValue
,IdentityLastValue
,DateCreated
,DateModified
,FullTextTypeColumn
```

```
    ,IsIndexable
    ,IsRowGuidCol
    ,IsXmlIndexable
    ,UsesAnsiTrim
    )

SELECT DISTINCT

@SERVER_NAME
,@DATABASE_NAME
,SCH.name AS TABLE_SCHEMA
,TBL.name AS TABLE_NAME
,COL.name AS COLUMN_NAME
,COL.column_id
,TYP.name AS DataType
,CASE
WHEN TYP.name IN ('nchar','NVARCHAR') THEN (COL.max_length / 2)
ELSE COL.max_length
END AS ColLength
,COL.precision
,COL.scale
,COL.collation_name AS CollationName
,COL.is_nullable AS IsNullable
,COL.is_identity AS IsIdentity
,COL.is_computed  AS IsComputed
,COL.is_filestream AS IsFileStream
,COL.is_sparse AS IsSparse
,COL.is_column_set AS IsColumnSet
,COL.object_id
,COL.default_object_id
,CAST('' AS VARCHAR(MAX)) AS ColDefinition
,CAST('' AS VARCHAR(250)) AS DefaultName
,CAST('' AS VARCHAR(MAX)) AS DefaultDefinition
,CAST(NULL AS BIT) AS IsFulltextIndexed
,CAST('' AS VARCHAR(4000)) AS CalcDefinition
,CAST('' AS VARCHAR(250)) AS CHARACTER_SET_NAME
,CAST(0 AS BIT) AS IsPersisted
,CASE
WHEN TYP.collation_name IS NOT NULL THEN 1
ELSE 0
END AS IsCharCol
,CAST(0 AS INT) AS IdentitySeedValue
,CAST(0 AS INT) AS IdentityIncrementValue
,CAST(0 AS BIGINT) AS IdentityLastValue
,OBJ.create_date AS DateCreated
,OBJ.modify_date AS DateModified
,COLUMNPROPERTY(TBL.object_id, COL.name, 'FullTextTypeColumn') AS FullTextTypeColumn
,COLUMNPROPERTY(TBL.object_id, COL.name, 'IsIndexable') AS IsIndexable
,COLUMNPROPERTY(TBL.object_id, COL.name, 'IsRowGuidCol') AS IsRowGuidCol
,COLUMNPROPERTY(TBL.object_id, COL.name, 'IsXmlIndexable') AS IsXmlIndexable
,COLUMNPROPERTY(TBL.object_id, COL.name, 'UsesAnsiTrim') AS UsesAnsiTrim
```

```
FROM        sys.types AS TYP
            INNER JOIN sys.columns AS COL ON TYP.user_type_id = COL.user_type_id
            INNER JOIN sys.tables AS TBL
            INNER JOIN sys.schemas AS SCH
            ON TBL.schema_id = SCH.schema_id
            INNER JOIN sys.objects AS OBJ
            ON TBL.object_id = OBJ.object_id
            ON COL.object_id = TBL.object_id

WHERE       TBL.type_desc = 'USER_TABLE'
            AND TBL.is_ms_shipped = 0

ORDER BY TABLE_SCHEMA, TABLE_NAME, COL.column_id

IF OBJECT_ID('tempdb..#Tmp_ColFileStream') IS NOT NULL
DROP TABLE tempdb..#Tmp_ColFileStream;

SELECT
SCH.name AS TABLE_SCHEMA
,TTP.name AS TABLE_NAME
,COL.name AS COLUMN_NAME
,COL.is_filestream AS IsFileStream

INTO        #Tmp_ColFileStream

FROM        sys.columns COL
            INNER JOIN sys.table_types TTP
            ON COL.object_id = TTP.type_table_object_id
            INNER JOIN sys.schemas SCH
            ON TTP.schema_id = SCH.schema_id

IF OBJECT_ID('tempdb..#Tmp_ColCalculated') IS NOT NULL
DROP TABLE tempdb..#Tmp_ColCalculated;

SELECT
SCH.name AS TABLE_SCHEMA
,TTP.name AS TABLE_NAME
,COL.name AS COLUMN_NAME
,COL.is_persisted AS IsPersisted
,COL.definition AS CalcDefinition

INTO        #Tmp_ColCalculated

FROM        sys.table_types TTP
            INNER JOIN sys.schemas AS SCH
            ON TTP.schema_id = SCH.schema_id
            INNER JOIN sys.computed_columns COL
            ON TTP.type_table_object_id = COL.object_id
```

```
-- Column Defaults

IF OBJECT_ID('tempdb..#Tmp_ColDefault') IS NOT NULL
DROP TABLE tempdb..#Tmp_ColDefault;

SELECT
SCH.name AS TABLE_SCHEMA
,TTP.name AS TABLE_NAME
,COL.name AS COLUMN_NAME
,SDC.name AS DefaultName
,SDC.definition AS DefaultDefinition

INTO        #Tmp_ColDefault

FROM        sys.default_constraints SDC
            INNER JOIN sys.columns COL
            ON SDC.parent_object_id = COL.object_id
            AND SDC.parent_column_id = COL.column_id
            INNER JOIN sys.table_types TTP
            ON COL.object_id = TTP.type_table_object_id
            INNER JOIN sys.schemas SCH
            ON SCH.schema_id = TTP.schema_id

-- Identity Details

IF OBJECT_ID('tempdb..#Tmp_IdentityDetails') IS NOT NULL
DROP TABLE tempdb..#Tmp_IdentityDetails;

SELECT
SCH.name AS TABLE_SCHEMA
,TTP.name AS TABLE_NAME
,ICL.name AS COLUMN_NAME
,ICL.column_id
,CAST(ICL.seed_value AS INT ) AS seed_value
,CAST(ICL.increment_value AS INT ) AS increment_value
,CAST(ICL.last_value AS BIGINT ) AS last_value
,ICL.object_id

INTO        #Tmp_IdentityDetails

FROM        sys.table_types TTP
            INNER JOIN sys.schemas SCH
            ON TTP.schema_id = SCH.schema_id
            INNER JOIN sys.identity_columns ICL
            ON TTP.type_table_object_id = ICL.object_id

-- Update with Filestream data

UPDATE   DM

SET         DM.IsFileStream = FS.IsFileStream
```

449

```
FROM            #Metadata_ColumnTableType DM
                INNER JOIN #Tmp_ColFileStream FS
                ON FS.TABLE_SCHEMA = DM.TABLE_SCHEMA
                AND FS.TABLE_NAME = DM.TABLE_NAME
                AND FS.COLUMN_NAME = DM.COLUMN_NAME

-- Update with Calculated data

UPDATE          DM

SET             DM.CalcDefinition = CC.CalcDefinition
                ,DM.IsPersisted = CC.IsPersisted

FROM            #Metadata_ColumnTableType DM
                INNER JOIN #Tmp_ColCalculated CC
                ON DM.TABLE_SCHEMA = CC.TABLE_SCHEMA
                AND DM.TABLE_NAME = CC.TABLE_NAME
                AND DM.COLUMN_NAME = CC.COLUMN_NAME

-- Update with Defaults

UPDATE          DM

SET             DM.DefaultDefinition = CONVERT(VARCHAR(MAX),CD.DefaultDefinition)
                ,DM.DefaultName = CD.DefaultName

FROM            #Metadata_ColumnTableType DM
                INNER JOIN #Tmp_ColDefault CD
                ON DM.TABLE_SCHEMA = CD.TABLE_SCHEMA
                AND DM.TABLE_NAME = CD.TABLE_NAME
                AND DM.COLUMN_NAME = CD.COLUMN_NAME


-- Update FullText indicator

UPDATE          Tmp
SET             Tmp.IsFulltextIndexed = 1
FROM            #Metadata_ColumnTableType Tmp
                INNER JOIN sys.fulltext_index_columns FTI
                ON Tmp.object_id = FTI.object_id
                AND Tmp.Column_id = FTI.Column_id

-- Update Identity Details

UPDATE          DM
SET             DM.IdentitySeedValue = Tmp.seed_value
                ,DM.IdentityIncrementValue = Tmp.increment_value
                ,DM.IdentityLastValue = Tmp.last_value
FROM            #Metadata_ColumnTableType DM
                INNER JOIN #Tmp_IdentityDetails TMP
                ON DM.object_id = Tmp.object_id
                AND DM.column_id = Tmp.column_id

SELECT * from #Metadata_ColumnTableType;  -- Once again I have wickedly used SELECT *
```

The output is shown in Figure 8-4.

	TABLE_CATALOG	TABLE_SCHEMA	TABLE_NAME	COLUMN_NAME	COLUMN_DEFAULT	IS_NULLABLE	DATA_TYPE	CHARACTER_MAXIMUM_LENGTH	CHARACTER_OCTET_LENGTH
61	CarSales_Book	dbo	Stock	Make	NULL	YES	varchar	50	50
62	CarSales_Book	dbo	Stock	Marque	NULL	YES	nvarchar	50	100
63	CarSales_Book	dbo	Stock	Model	NULL	YES	varchar	50	50
64	CarSales_Book	dbo	Stock	Colour	NULL	YES	tinynt	NULL	NULL
65	CarSales_Book	dbo	Stock	Product_Type	NULL	YES	varchar	50	50
66	CarSales_Book	dbo	Stock	Vehicle_Type	NULL	YES	varchar	20	20
67	CarSales_Book	dbo	Stock	Cost_Price	NULL	YES	numeric	NULL	NULL

NUMERIC_PRECISION	NUMERIC_SCALE	CONSTRAINT_TYPE	CHECK_CLAUSE
NULL	NULL	NULL	NULL
NULL	NULL	NULL	NULL
NULL	NULL	NULL	NULL
3	0	FOREIGN KEY	NULL
NULL	NULL	NULL	NULL
NULL	NULL	NULL	NULL
18	2	NULL	NULL
NULL	NULL	NULL	NULL
NULL	NULL	NULL	NULL
NULL	NULL	NULL	NULL
NULL	NULL	NULL	NULL

Figure 8-4. *Column metadata returned by the script in Recipe 8-7*

How It Works

Returning column metadata can be done, quite simply, using this script, which I hope you find suitably exhaustive. The column metadata returned is shown in Table 8-7.

Table 8-7. *Column Metadata*

Field Name	Description
SERVER_NAME	The server name.
DATABASE_NAME	The database name.
TABLE_SCHEMA	The schema of the table.
TABLE_NAME	The table name.
COLUMN_NAME	The column name.
column_id	The internal column ID used by the system metadata.
DataType	The SQL Server data type.
ColLength	The column length.
precision	The column's numeric precision (the total number of digits).
scale	The column's numeric scale (the number of digits after the decimal place).
CollationName	The SQL Server collation.
IsNullable	The column can contain NULL values.
IsIdentity	The column is an IDENTITY column.
IsComputed	The column contains a computed value.
IsFileStream	The column is a FILESTREAM column.

(*continued*)

Table 8-7. (*continued*)

Field Name	Description
IsSparse	The column contains sparse data.
IsColumnSet	The column is part of a column set.
object_id	The internal object ID used by the system metadata.
default_object_id	The ID of any stand-alone default.
ColDefinition	The column definition.
DefaultName	The name of a column default, if there is one.
DefaultDefinition	The column default.
IsFulltextIndexed	The column is indexed using full text indexing.
CalcDefinition	The column calculation for a calculated column.
CHARACTER_SET_NAME	The character set used.
IsPersisted	The column value is persisted in the table.
IsCharCol	The column is a text type.
IdentitySeedValue	The IDENTITY start value.
IdentityIncrementValue	The IDENTITY increment value.
IdentityLastValue	The last IDENTITY value.
DateCreated	The date the column was created.
DateModified	The date the column was modified.
FullTextTypeColumn	The column is part of a full-text index.
IsIndexable	The column can be indexed.
IsRowGuidCol	The column contains a Row GUID.
IsXmlIndexable	The column can support XML indexing.
UsesAnsiTrim	The column uses ANSI TRIMs.

Like the script in the previous recipe, the script takes the @SERVER_NAME and @DATABASE_NAME input parameters to define the server and to analyze the database. The variables default to the current server and database, but you can alter this. It then creates a session-scoped temporary table to hold all the required metadata for column-level information. An initial trawl through the metadata uses sys.tables, sys.types, sys.schemas, and sys.objects—as well as many COLUMNPROPERTY functions to return a core set of column metadata. Then a series of secondary processes returns FILESTREAM information, calculated column metadata, defaults, and IDENTITY metadata, as well as full-text metadata. This data is then used to update the temporary table.

Hints, Tips, and Traps

- The data returned from this script can be output to disk, if you prefer, by using SELECT...INTO instead of a simple SELECT at the end of the script.

- You may find that this script returns data that is too detailed for your requirements. Feel free to reduce the amount of information returned if you do not need it.

- Remember that you can use SSMS to view basic metadata. Well, yes—sort of. To begin with the blindingly obvious, let's remember that if you can connect to an SQL Server database in SSMS (and if you have sufficient rights), you can expand a table to see the column names, data type, and length. You can also expand keys, constraints, triggers, indexes, and statistics.

8-8. Displaying Microsoft Access Metadata
Problem

You want to analyze metadata for an Access database from which you will be extracting data.

Solution

Use the Access Documenter to provide a rich, detailed, and legible report describing the metadata for some or all of the tables in an Access database. The following steps explain how.

1. In Access, click Tools ➤ Analyze ➤ Documenter.

2. In the Documenter dialog, select the table(s) and queries you wish to analyze. The resulting dialog box looks something like Figure 8-5.

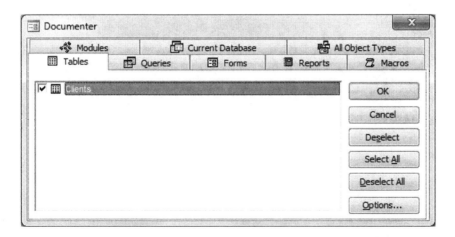

Figure 8-5. *The Access Documenter dialog box*

3. Click OK. After a few seconds, you should get the Documenter output (see Figure 8-6).

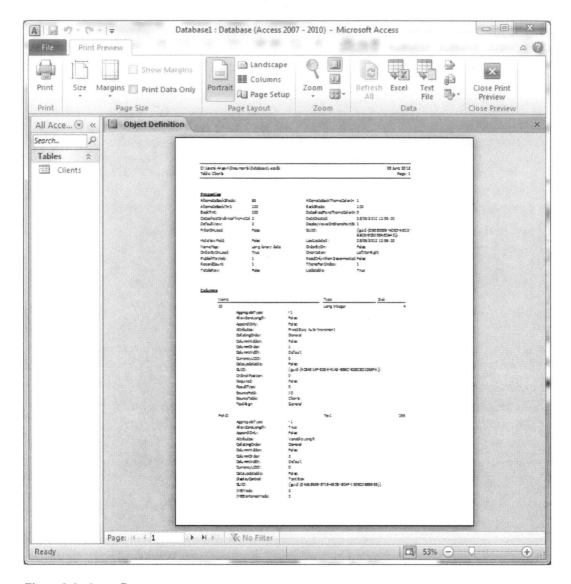

Figure 8-6. *Access Documenter output*

4. If you want to save an electronic copy, click File ➤ Export and select Rich Text Format as the destination format.

You can then open the resulting file with (say) Microsoft Word, and peruse the metadata at your leisure.

How It Works

Although considerably more limited in its range of data types than commercial SQL databases, Access has metadata too, and there are times when it helps to obtain this before—or during—a data load process. You can write complex ADOX code to return Access metadata if you wish, but Access can do this for you quite easily, so I prefer this simpler approach. This presumes that Microsoft Access is installed, and that the database you wish to query is accessible to (linked to or directly opened by) Access.

Hints, Tips, and Traps

- In the Tools ➤ Options menu's View tab, make sure that System Objects is checked. Tables are listed in the MySysObjects table.

8-9. Reading MySQL Metadata

Problem

You want to display metadata from a MySQL database to better understand the source data that you have to import.

Solution

Use the INFORMATION_SCHEMA views in MySQL to obtain a detailed description of the source metadata. Follow this process:

1. In a new or existing SSIS project, create a new SSIS package.

2. Add a Data Flow task on to the Control Flow pane, and double-click to open it.

3. Right-click in the Connection Managers tab. Select New Connection.

4. Select ODBC from the list of connection managers. This is shown in Figure 8-7.

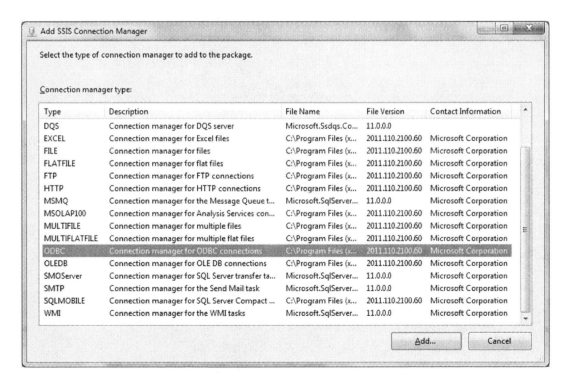

Figure 8-7. *Adding an ODBC connection manager*

5. Click Add.

6. Click New to create a new data connection.

7. Click Use Connection String.

8. Enter a connection string like the following:

```
DRIVER = {MySQL ODBC 5.1 Driver};SERVER = localhost;DATABASE = INFORMATION_SCHEMA;
UID = root
```

9. Of course, you should use your own server and user ID (UID). It is important, however, to specify the INFORMATION_SCHEMA database. Add the current password. The dialog box should look like Figure 8-8.

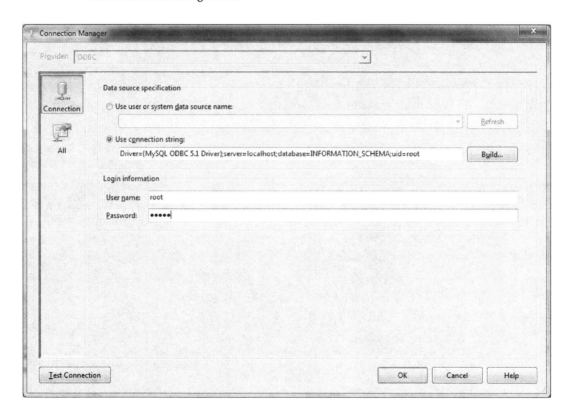

Figure 8-8. *Selecting an existing DSN*

10. Click OK twice.

11. Right-click the Data Flow pane. Select Variables. Add a new variable named **MySQLMetadata**. Ensure that the variable's data type is Object.

12. Add an ODBC source to the Data Flow pane, and double-click to Edit.

13. Select the connection manager that you created in steps 4 to 10.

14. Select SQL Command as the data access mode.

15. Enter or paste the following SQL into the SQL Command text field:

```
SELECT TABLE_NAME FROM INFORMATION_SCHEMA.TABLES;
```

16. The dialog box should look like Figure 8-9. Click OK to confirm the creation of the data source.

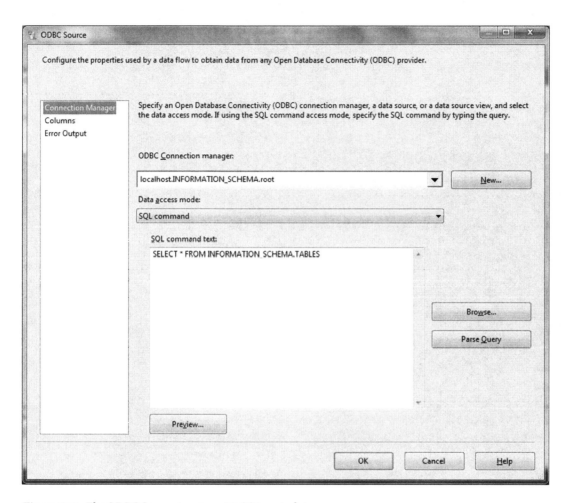

Figure 8-9. *The ODBC Source to return MySQL metadata*

17. Add a Recordset Destination onto the Control Flow pane.

18. Drag a connector from the ODBC source to the Recordset Destination.

19. Double-click to edit the Recordset Destination.

20. Select the variable (MySQLMetadata) that you created in step 11 as the Variable Name.

21. Click the Input Columns tab and select the columns you wish to output.

22. Click Refresh. The dialog box should look like Figure 8-10.

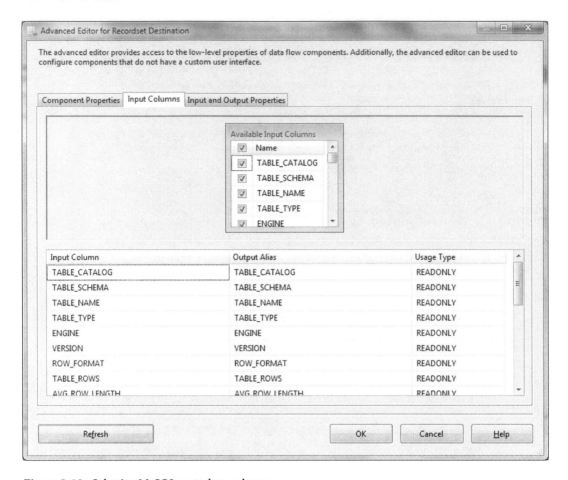

Figure 8-10. *Selecting MySQL metadata columns*

23. Click OK.

24. Right-click the Data Flow path that connects the source to the destination. Select Enable Data Viewer.

Now, when you run the package, the MySQL metadata will appear in the Data Viewer Grid, as shown in Figure 8-11.

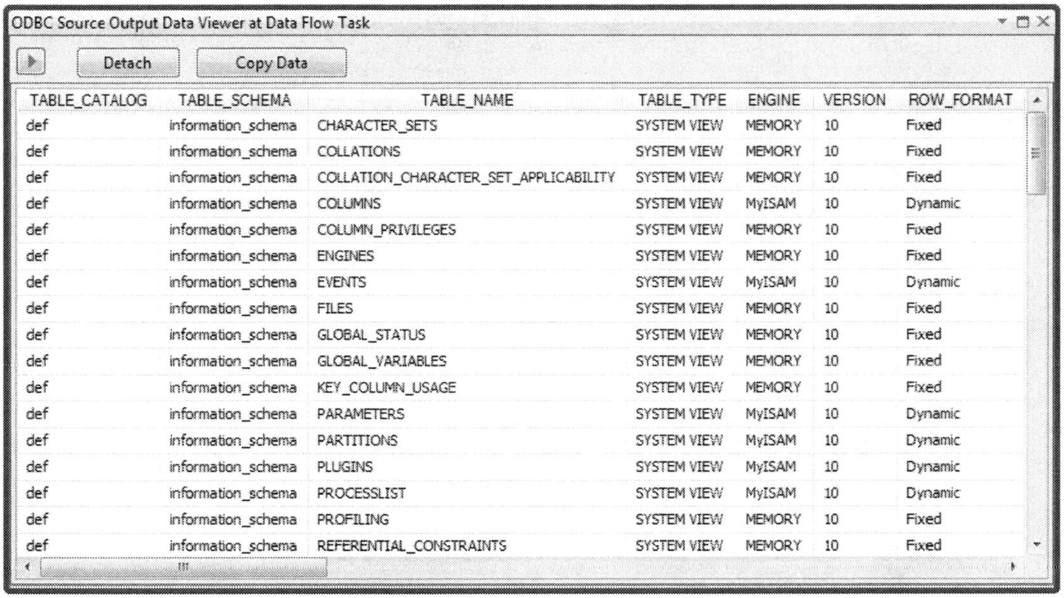

TABLE_CATALOG	TABLE_SCHEMA	TABLE_NAME	TABLE_TYPE	ENGINE	VERSION	ROW_FORMAT
def	information_schema	CHARACTER_SETS	SYSTEM VIEW	MEMORY	10	Fixed
def	information_schema	COLLATIONS	SYSTEM VIEW	MEMORY	10	Fixed
def	information_schema	COLLATION_CHARACTER_SET_APPLICABILITY	SYSTEM VIEW	MEMORY	10	Fixed
def	information_schema	COLUMNS	SYSTEM VIEW	MyISAM	10	Dynamic
def	information_schema	COLUMN_PRIVILEGES	SYSTEM VIEW	MEMORY	10	Fixed
def	information_schema	ENGINES	SYSTEM VIEW	MEMORY	10	Fixed
def	information_schema	EVENTS	SYSTEM VIEW	MyISAM	10	Dynamic
def	information_schema	FILES	SYSTEM VIEW	MEMORY	10	Fixed
def	information_schema	GLOBAL_STATUS	SYSTEM VIEW	MEMORY	10	Fixed
def	information_schema	GLOBAL_VARIABLES	SYSTEM VIEW	MEMORY	10	Fixed
def	information_schema	KEY_COLUMN_USAGE	SYSTEM VIEW	MEMORY	10	Fixed
def	information_schema	PARAMETERS	SYSTEM VIEW	MyISAM	10	Dynamic
def	information_schema	PARTITIONS	SYSTEM VIEW	MyISAM	10	Dynamic
def	information_schema	PLUGINS	SYSTEM VIEW	MyISAM	10	Dynamic
def	information_schema	PROCESSLIST	SYSTEM VIEW	MyISAM	10	Dynamic
def	information_schema	PROFILING	SYSTEM VIEW	MEMORY	10	Fixed
def	information_schema	REFERENTIAL_CONSTRAINTS	SYSTEM VIEW	MEMORY	10	Fixed

Figure 8-11. *MySQL metadata in SSIS*

How It Works

MySQL (from version 5) also has an INFORMATION_SCHEMA that you can query to get. The only difference from the other databases seen so far is that you have to access this metadata over ODBC, in the absence of an OLEDB provider from the supplier (though you may find that third-party providers do the trick). Also, the way that the metadata is obtained is a little more quirky, as you can see.

The following code snippet will return MySQL metadata over an ODBC connection:

```
SELECT    TABLE_NAME
FROM       OPENROWSET('MSDASQL', 'DSN=MySQLMetadata',
                      'SELECT TABLE_NAME FROM INFORMATION_SCHEMA.TABLES')
```

If you are working a lot with MySQL, then it could be worth your while to add a linked server (as described in Recipe 4-9) and use an OPENQUERY to get INFORMATION_SCHEMA data. The following code snippet is an example, and presumes that the linked server name is MYSQL:

```
SELECT    TABLE_NAME
FROM       OPENQUERY(MYSQL,'select TABLE_NAME FROM INFORMATION_SCHEMA.TABLES')
```

The MySQL INFORMATION_SCHEMA data, as stated earlier, only works with MySQL databases from version 5. However, if you are faced with data from a previous version of MySQL, you can use the following SQL to query the metadata, in place of that given earlier:

```
SELECT *
FROM       OPENROWSET('MSDASQL', 'DSN=MySQLMetadata',
                      'SHOW TABLES')
```

Without going into all the arcane details of the MySQL metadata possibilities, Table 8-8 shows a few of the essential tables and fields that you are likely to need when querying MySQL for its metadata.

Table 8-8. MySQL Metadata

Table	Column	Notes
TABLES	TABLE_SCHEMA	The database containing the table.
	TABLE_NAME	The name of the table.
COLUMNS	TABLE_CATALOG	The database containing the table.
	TABLE_SCHEMA	The schema owning the table.
	TABLE_NAME	The name of the table.
	COLUMN_NAME	The column name.
	DATA_TYPE	The data type.
	IS_NULLABLE	Nullable flag.
	COLUMN_DEFAULT	Default (if one exists).
	CHARACTER_MAXIMUM_LENGTH	Maximum length in characters.
	NUMERIC_PRECISION	Numeric precision (numbers only).
	NUMERIC_SCALE	Numeric scale (numbers only).
	CHARACTER_SET_NAME	

The closest that I can get to "generic" SQL for MySQL to return all important metadata is the following (C:\SQL2012DIRecipes\CH08\MySQLMetadata.sql):

```
SELECT
CO.TABLE_CATALOG
,CO.TABLE_SCHEMA
,CO.TABLE_NAME
,CO.COLUMN_NAME
,CO.ORDINAL_POSITION
,CO.COLUMN_DEFAULT
,CO.IS_NULLABLE
,CO.DATA_TYPE
,CO.CHARACTER_MAXIMUM_LENGTH
,CO.CHARACTER_OCTET_LENGTH
,CO.NUMERIC_PRECISION
,CO.NUMERIC_SCALE
,CO.CHARACTER_SET_NAME
,CO.COLUMN_TYPE
,CO.COLUMN_KEY
,KCU.CONSTRAINT_NAME
,KCU.REFERENCED_TABLE_NAME
,KCU.REFERENCED_COLUMN_NAME
```

```
FROM            COLUMNS CO
LEFT JOIN       KEY_COLUMN_USAGE KCU
                ON CO.COLUMN_NAME = KCU.COLUMN_NAME
                AND CO.TABLE_NAME = KCU.TABLE_NAME
                AND CO.TABLE_SCHEMA = KCU.TABLE_SCHEMA;
```

This gives most of the base metadata that you are likely to need for data ingestion, and it can be used either in OPENQUERY or in SSIS. The REFERENCED_TABLE_NAME and REFERENCED_COLUMN_NAME columns let you deduce foreign keys.

Other information that you may require are triggers, which can be obtained from the Triggers INFORMATION_SCHEMA table. A basic query would be:

```
SELECT TRIGGER_SCHEMA, TRIGGER_NAME, EVENT_MANIPULATION, EVENT_OBJECT_SCHEMA,
EVENT_OBJECT_TABLE, ACTION_STATEMENT, ACTION_TIMING
FROM INFORMATION_SCHEMA.TRIGGERS;
```

You might need to use this more than you think because MySQL up to and including version 5 does not support CHECK constraints, and many MySQL developers use triggers to emulate CHECK constraint behavior. So looking into existing triggers can indicate what constraints on data are (or the developer thinks should be) in place.

You can copy the results of the query from the Data Viewer Grid using the Copy Data button. If you require a more permanent capture of the metadata you can replace the Recordset destination with an OLEDB destination and store the output in SQL Server. This approach is described (for DB2) in Recipe 8-13.

Hints, Tips, and Traps

- When using SSIS to return MySQL metadata, you can use an ODBC DSN instead of entering a connection string. However, you must be sure to use a 64-bit DSN if you are working in a 64-bit environment. The ODBC connection manager lists all available DSNs without indicating if they are 64-bit or 32-bit. See Recipes 4-8 and 4-9 for more information on creating 32-bit and 64-bit DSNs for MySQL.

- Setting the SSIS project Properties for Run64BitRuntime to False will not solve the 32-bit DSN problem.

- If you click Build in step 7 and then follow the process to create a System DSN (described in Recipe 4-8), you will not only create the correct connection string, but also create a DSN of the correct "bitness." You will need to run SSIS with administrative privileges to do this.

8-10. Displaying Oracle Metadata from SSIS
Problem

You need to analyze the Oracle metadata for a database that you have to import into SQL Server.

Solution

Use SSIS to query the Oracle metadata contained in the Oracle system dictionary. The steps that follow explain how to do it.

1. Create a new SSIS package.

2. Add a Data Flow task to the Control Flow pane.

3. Click the Data Flow tab.

4. Add an OLEDB source task to the Data Flow pane.

5. Double-click to open it.

6. Select the OLEDB connection manager that you have already created.

7. Select SQL Command as the data access mode.

8. Paste the following code into the Command text box (C:\SQL2012DIRecipes\CH08\ OracleMetadata.sql):

```
SELECT COLUMN_NAME, DATA_TYPE, DATA_LENGTH
     , CAST(DATA_PRECISION AS NUMBER(38,0)) AS DATA_PRECISION, NULLABLE
     , HIGH_VALUE, LOW_VALUE
FROM all_tab_columns
WHERE table_name='SOURCEDATA'
```

9. You should have a dialog box similar to Figure 8-12.

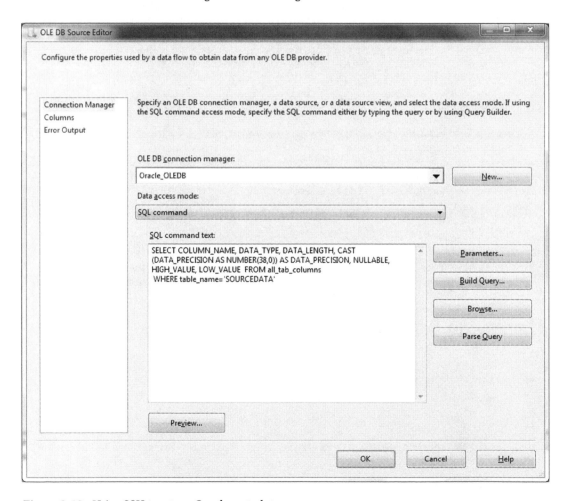

Figure 8-12. *Using SSIS to return Oracle metadata*

10.   Click Preview to display the metadata.

11.   Click OK to close the dialog box.

How It Works

Let us suppose that when trying to import an Oracle table using SSIS and either the Oracle or Microsoft OLEDB providers, you have met a data error when attempting to preview or load data. Yet you know that the OLEDB provider is working because you can see the list of tables. What can you do to get a look at the Oracle metadata? Here you are querying the Oracle catalog to return metadata. It is a standard pass-through query where I am presuming that the source table is named SOURCEDATA.

Using SSIS and an OLEDB data source lets you send a query to the Oracle system views, which then returns metadata about the Oracle source database. To store the metadata that is returned, all you need to do is add an OLEDB destination component, create a destination table, and run the SSIS package.

8-11. Querying Oracle Metadata Using T-SQL

Problem

You need to analyze the Oracle metadata for a database that you have to import into SQL Server.

Solution

Use T-SQL to query the Oracle data dictionary. The following illustrates how to do this.

1.   Execute the following code snippet in a Management Studio query window
     to output metadata about an Oracle database
     (C:\SQL2012DIRecipes\CH08\MoreOracleMetadata.sql):

```
SELECT *
FROM OPENROWSET('ORAOLEDB.Oracle','MyOracleDatabase';'TestOracle';'Me4BOss',
'
SELECT
COLUMN_NAME,
DATA_TYPE,
DATA_LENGTH,
CAST(DATA_PRECISION AS NUMBER(38,0)) AS DATA_PRECISION,
NULLABLE

FROM all_tab_columns
WHERE table_name=''SOURCEDATA''
')
```

Table 8-9 describes the result set from the preceding query.

Table 8-9. *Oracle Metadata*

COLUMN_NAME	DATA_TYPE	DATA_LENGTH	DATA_PRECISION	NULLABLE
ID	NUMBER	22	NULL	Y
THENUMBER	NUMBER	22	NULL	Y
THETEXT	VARCHAR2	4000	NULL	Y

How It Works

The T-SQL OPENROWSET command passes a SELECT query to the Oracle database (MyOracleDatabase in this example). Oracle processes the query and returns the information that has been requested for the source table SOURCEDATA. The Logon is **TestOracle** and the password is **Me4B0ss**. In this example, we are using the Oracle OLEDB provider (ORAOLEDB.Oracle).

Hints, Tips, and Traps

- You will need to analyze the source metadata for all source tables—including those that you are using in joins as part of your SQL SELECT query to get as full a picture as possible of any potential problems.

8-12. Understanding the Oracle Data Dictionary
Problem

You want to drill down into Oracle metadata.

Solution

Learn to appreciate the basics of the Oracle data dictionary. The next few examples take you on a rapid overview of some of the core aspects of the Oracle data dictionary from the viewpoint of the SQL ETL developer.

This extremely rapid overview necessitates the "mini-recipe" approach, so I will take you on a fly-past of six of the core aspects of the Oracle data dictionary. All the following code snippets are in the file (C:\SQL2012DIRecipes\CH08\.ExtendedOracleMetadata.sql).

Core Column Data

To analyze or debug data types, a good look at the ALL_TAB_COLUMNS dictionary table can be invaluable. The SQL is

```
SELECT
TABLE_NAME, COLUMN_NAME, DATA_TYPE, DATA_LENGTH, DATA_PRECISION, DATA_SCALE, NULLABLE,
DATA_DEFAULT, CHARACTER_SET_NAME, CHAR_COL_DECL_LENGTH, CHAR_USED

FROM    ALL_TAB_COLUMNS
```

Keep the following in mind:

- DATA_PRECISION is the length—in decimal digits (for the NUMBER type) or in binary digits (for the FLOAT type).

- DATA_SCALE is the number of digits to the right of decimal point in a number.

- CHAR_USED is C if the maximum length is specified in characters; B if it is specified in bytes.

Constraints

To see the data that is not allowed into the Oracle database, you can look at all the constraints on one or more tables using the following SQL:

```
SELECT    ACC.TABLE_NAME, ACC.COLUMN_NAME, AC.SEARCH_CONDITION

FROM      ALL_CONS_COLUMNS ACC INNER JOIN ALL_CONSTRAINTS AC
          ON ACC.CONSTRAINT_NAME = AC.CONSTRAINT_NAME

WHERE     CONSTRAINT_TYPE = 'C'
```

You can, of course, extend the WHERE clause to limit the output to the table(s) that you wish to analyze.

Primary Keys

If you need to verify the primary keys of the tables that you are importing, try the following:

```
SELECT    A.Table_name, C.Column_name
FROM      ALL_CONSTRAINTS A
          JOIN ALL_CONS_COLUMNS C
          ON A.CONSTRAINT_NAME = C.CONSTRAINT_NAME
WHERE     CONSTRAINT_TYPE = 'P'
```

You can extend the WHERE clause to limit the output to the table(s) that you wish to analyze. You can also tweak the CONSTRAINT_TYPE in the WHERE clause to get the following:

- P: Returns primary key constraints.

- C: Returns NOT NULL or check constraints.

- R: Returns foreign key constraints.

- U: Returns unique key constraints.

Indexes

Without going into the myriad details of Oracle indexing, it can nonetheless be of use to know which columns are indexed in the source data. This is especially appropriate if you are using staging tables to transform data; this information can give you a "heads-up" on which fields to index in order to accelerate data staging processes. The SQL is

```
SELECT ALL_IND_COLUMNS.INDEX_NAME, ALL_IND_COLUMNS.TABLE_OWNER,
       ALL_IND_COLUMNS.TABLE_NAME, ALL_IND_COLUMNS.COLUMN_NAME
```

```
FROM    ALL_INDEXES INNER JOIN ALL_IND_COLUMNS
        ON ALL_INDEXES.INDEX_NAME = ALL_IND_COLUMNS.INDEX_NAME;
```

If an index name appears more than once, it is because you are facing a multicolumn index.

Don't hesitate to look further into the ALL_INDEXES table to see if there is any other metadata that can help you. In general, this is true of all Oracle's data dictionary tables. They provide a wealth of useful information.

Referential Integrity Constraints

To get a simple overview of referential integrity constraints, all you need is to query two tables:

- ALL_CONSTRAINTS

- ALL_CONS_COLUMNS

The trick is how you join them—as the following SQL snippet shows.

```
SELECT
ACR.CONSTRAINT_NAME
,ACR.TABLE_NAME AS PK_TableName
,AC.COLUMN_NAME AS PK_ColumnName
,ACR1.TABLE_NAME AS FK_TableName
,AC1.COLUMN_NAME AS FK_ColumnName

FROM    ALL_CONS_COLUMNS AC1
        INNER JOIN ALL_CONSTRAINTS ACR1
        INNER JOIN ALL_CONSTRAINTS ACR
        INNER JOIN ALL_CONS_COLUMNS AC
        ON ACR.CONSTRAINT_NAME = AC.CONSTRAINT_NAME
        ON ACR1.R_CONSTRAINT_NAME = ACR.CONSTRAINT_NAME
        ON AC1.CONSTRAINT_NAME = ACR1.CONSTRAINT_NAME

WHERE ACR.CONSTRAINT_TYPE= 'P'
```

Triggers

Finally, you can see the triggers that have been used—which can sometimes give an understanding of why the data is the way it is—with the following SQL:

```
SELECT TRIGGER_NAME, TRIGGER_TYPE, TRIGGERING_EVENT, TABLE_NAME, WHEN_CLAUSE,
DESCRIPTION, TRIGGER_BODY
FROM ALL_TRIGGERS
```

How It Works

If I say that the alternative title for this recipe is "the shortest guide ever to the Oracle data dictionary," I hope that the objective of what I am describing here will be clear. Whereas some databases leave you scrambling for enough metadata, with Oracle, it often seems quite the reverse—you feel that you are drowning in the sea of information that Oracle calls the *data dictionary*. So this recipe provides the shortest course you will probably ever get on Oracle metadata. I can only stress that there are many ways of obtaining Oracle metadata. There is so much available, that I am concentrating on an extremely simple subset of the metadata that I have found helpful in the past. I hope that you will find them useful as a starting point that you can expand and build on. Of course, for each of the approaches that follow, there are another dozen ways to get what you are looking for—so go ahead and keep searching the Oracle dictionary (among all the resources available out there), for you will certainly find other ways of obtaining the metadata you seek.

8-13. Displaying DB2 Metadata
Problem

You need to query metadata from a DB2 database from which you will soon be importing data.

Solution

Use SSIS to capture and store DB2 metadata from DB2's INFORMATION_SCHEMA tables. The following steps describe how to do it.

1. Create tables to hold the DB2 metadata in SQL Server using the following DDL:

```
CREATE TABLE dbo.IS_DB2_Views
(
 TABLE_CATALOG NVARCHAR(50) NULL,
 TABLE_SCHEMA NVARCHAR(50) NULL,
 TABLE_NAME NVARCHAR(50) NULL,
 VIEW_DEFINITION NVARCHAR(MAX) NULL,
 CHECK_OPTION NVARCHAR(10) NULL,
 IS_UPDATABLE NVARCHAR(5) NULL
);
GO

CREATE TABLE dbo.IS_DB2_Tables
(
 TABLE_CATALOG NVARCHAR(50) NULL,
 TABLE_SCHEMA NVARCHAR(50) NULL,
 TABLE_NAME NVARCHAR(50) NULL,
 TABLE_TYPE NVARCHAR(26) NULL
);
GO

CREATE TABLE dbo.IS_DB2_TableConstraints
(
 CONSTRAINT_CATALOG NVARCHAR(50) NULL,
 CONSTRAINT_SCHEMA NVARCHAR(50) NULL,
 CONSTRAINT_NAME NVARCHAR(50) NULL,
 TABLE_CATALOG NVARCHAR(50) NULL,
 TABLE_SCHEMA NVARCHAR(50) NULL,
 TABLE_NAME NVARCHAR(50) NULL,
 CONSTRAINT_TYPE NVARCHAR(50) NULL,
 IS_DEFERRABLE NVARCHAR(5) NULL,
 INITIALLY_DEFERRED NVARCHAR(5) NULL
);
GO
```

```
CREATE TABLE dbo.IS_DB2_Schemas
(
 CATALOG_NAME NVARCHAR(50) NULL,
 SCHEMA_NAME NVARCHAR(50) NULL,
 SCHEMA_OWNER NVARCHAR(50) NULL,
 DEFAULT_CHARACTER_SET_CATALOG NVARCHAR(50) NULL,
 DEFAULT_CHARACTER_SET_SCHEMA NVARCHAR(50) NULL,
 DEFAULT_CHARACTER_SET_NAME NVARCHAR(50) NULL,
 SQL_PATH VARCHAR(MAX) NULL
);
GO

CREATE TABLE dbo.IS_DB2_Columns
(
 TABLE_CATALOG NVARCHAR(50) NULL,
 TABLE_SCHEMA NVARCHAR(50) NULL,
 TABLE_NAME NVARCHAR(50) NULL,
 COLUMN_NAME NVARCHAR(50) NULL,
 ORDINAL_POSITION INT NULL,
 COLUMN_DEFAULT NVARCHAR(2002) NULL,
 IS_NULLABLE NVARCHAR(5) NULL,
 DATA_TYPE NVARCHAR(50) NULL,
 CHARACTER_MAXIMUM_LENGTH INT NULL,
 CHARACTER_OCTET_LENGTH INT NULL,
 NUMERIC_PRECISION INT NULL,
 NUMERIC_PRECISION_RADIX INT NULL,
 NUMERIC_SCALE INT NULL,
 DATETIME_PRECISION INT NULL,
 INTERVAL_TYPE NVARCHAR(50) NULL,
 INTERVAL_PRECISION INT NULL,
 CHARACTER_SET_CATALOG NVARCHAR(50) NULL,
 CHARACTER_SET_SCHEMA NVARCHAR(50) NULL,
 CHARACTER_SET_NAME NVARCHAR(50) NULL
);
GO
```

2. Create a new SSIS package. Add a Data Flow task on to the Control Flow tab. Double-click to open this package and switch to the Data Flow tab.

3. Add an OLEDB connection manager to both the destination (SQL Server) database.

4. Add an ADO.NET connection manager in the Providers list. Expand .NET Providers for OleDb. Select ".NET Providers for OleDb \IBM DB2 for i5/OS IBMDA400 OLE DB Provider" (or the provider which you are using). Enter the fully qualified server name, the username, and password. Select the Initial Catalog.

5. Add an Execute SQL task. Configure it to use the destination (SQL Server OLEDB) connection manager. Set the SQL Statement to:

```
TRUNCATE TABLE IS_DB2_Tables;
TRUNCATE TABLE IS_DB2_Columns;
TRUNCATE TABLE IS_DB2_Views;
TRUNCATE TABLE IS_DB2_Schemas;
TRUNCATE TABLE IS_DB2_TableConstraints;
```

6. Add a sequence container, connect the Execute SQL Task to it, and add five Data Flow tasks inside it. Name them **Tables**, **Views**, **Columns**, **Schemas**, and **Table Constraints**. Set each one to use the DB2 connection manager, and set the data access mode to SQL Command. Define the commands as follows:

Data Flow Task	SQL Code
Tables	SELECT TABLE_CATALOG, TABLE_SCHEMA, TABLE_NAME, TABLE_TYPE FROM INFORMATION_SCHEMA.TABLES
Views	SELECT TABLE_CATALOG, TABLE_SCHEMA, TABLE_NAME, VIEW_DEFINITION, CHECK_OPTION,IS_UPDATABLE FROM INFORMATION_SCHEMA.VIEWS
Columns	SELECT TABLE_CATALOG, TABLE_SCHEMA, TABLE_NAME, COLUMN_NAME, ORDINAL_POSITION, COLUMN_DEFAULT, IS_NULLABLE, DATA_TYPE, CHARACTER_MAXIMUM_LENGTH, CHARACTER_OCTET_LENGTH, NUMERIC_PRECISION, NUMERIC_PRECISION_RADIX, NUMERIC_SCALE, DATETIME_PRECISION, INTERVAL_TYPE, INTERVAL_PRECISION, CHARACTER_SET_CATALOG, CHARACTER_SET_SCHEMA, CHARACTER_SET_NAME FROM INFORMATION_SCHEMA.COLUMNS
Schemas	SELECT CATALOG_NAME, SCHEMA_NAME, SCHEMA_OWNER ,DEFAULT_CHARACTER_SET_CATALOG , DEFAULT_CHARACTER_SET_SCHEMA ,DEFAULT_CHARACTER_SET_NAME, SQL_PATH FROM INFORMATION_SCHEMA.SCHEMATA
Table Constraints	SELECT CONSTRAINT_CATALOG, CONSTRAINT_SCHEMA ,CONSTRAINT_NAME, TABLE_CATALOG, TABLE_NAME ,CONSTRAINT_TYPE, IS_DEFERRABLE ,INITIALLY_DEFERRED FROM INFORMATION_SCHEMA.TABLE_CONSTRAINTS

The final package should look something like Figure 8-13.

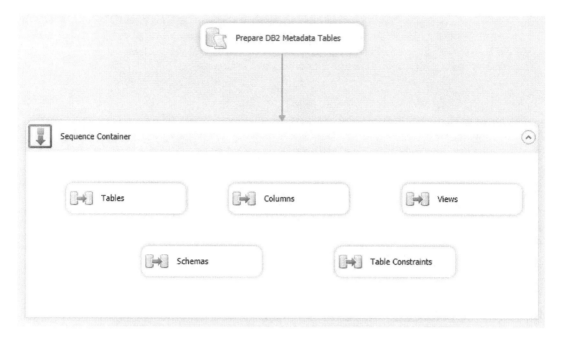

Figure 8-13. *An SSIS package to return DB2 metadata*

7. Run the package.

When you query (and join) the five metadata tables you can get a clearer insight into the DB2 metadata.

How It Works

Being able to take a quick peek at the metadata behind a data source may be edifying (and can frequently help you to debug data flow problems), but in some cases it is not enough. You need to be able to gather and store the metadata for reference on a local system.

This can be useful when you need to

- Analyze the metadata in greater detail.

- Store metadata and validate against future data ingestion in order to discover changes and/or anomalies.

This recipe shows you how to gather a base set of DB2 metadata. Fortunately, this particular database uses INFORMATION_SCHEMA views, and so we can use them to source our metadata. In essence, this is nothing more than a simple data transfer—only the source data is not data, but metadata. This makes DB2 a good example of a technique that you can use for any source database that implements these metadata views. You will need to have a DB2 OLEDB provider installed and working on the destination SQL Server.

▪ **Note**   As the INFORMATION_SCHEMA views for each database can vary—in both the number of views and their contents—this model cannot be used identically for all SQL databases that allow metadata to be discovered using this approach. It is, however, easy to extend and modify for other databases.

8-14. Obtaining SQL Server Metadata Using .NET

Problem

You want to obtain complete metadata, but without using INFORMATION_SCHEMA or system views.

Solution

Use the .NET GetSchema class to query metadata from a variety of data sources.

1. The following destination tables are required, and can be defined using this DDL
(C:\SQL2012DIRecipes\CH08\DotNetMetadataTables.sql):

```
CREATE TABLE dbo.ADOSQLServerMetadataViews
(
 ID INT IDENTITY(1,1) NOT NULL,
 TableCatalog VARCHAR(50) NULL,
 TableName VARCHAR(50) NULL,
 TableSchema VARCHAR(50) NOT NULL,
 CheckOption VARCHAR(50) NULL,
 IsUpdatable VARCHAR(5) NULL
);

CREATE TABLE dbo.ADOSQLServerMetadataViewColumns
(
 ID INT IDENTITY(1,1) NOT NULL,
 ViewCatalog VARCHAR(50) NULL,
 ViewName VARCHAR(50) NULL,
 ViewSchema VARCHAR(50) NOT NULL,
 TableCatalog VARCHAR(50) NULL,
 TableName VARCHAR(50) NULL,
 TableSchema VARCHAR(50) NOT NULL,
 ColumnName VARCHAR(50) NULL
) ;

CREATE TABLE dbo.ADOSQLServerMetadataTables
(
 ID INT IDENTITY(1,1) NOT NULL,
 TableCatalog VARCHAR(50) NULL,
 TableName VARCHAR(50) NULL,
 TableSchema VARCHAR(50) NOT NULL,
 TableType VARCHAR(50) NULL
);

CREATE TABLE dbo.ADOSQLServerMetadataIndexes
(
 ID INT IDENTITY(1,1) NOT NULL,
 ConstraintCatalog VARCHAR(50) NULL,
 ConstraintSchema VARCHAR(50) NULL,
 ConstraintName VARCHAR(50) NULL,
 TableCatalog VARCHAR(50) NULL,
```

471

```
  TableSchema VARCHAR(50) NULL,
  TableName VARCHAR(50) NULL
) ;

CREATE TABLE dbo.ADOSQLServerMetadataIndexColumns
(
  ID INT IDENTITY(1,1) NOT NULL,
  ConstraintCatalog VARCHAR(50) NULL,
  ConstraintSchema VARCHAR(50) NULL,
  ConstraintName VARCHAR(50) NULL,
  TableCatalog VARCHAR(50) NULL,
  TableSchema VARCHAR(50) NULL,
  TableName VARCHAR(50) NULL,
  ColumnName VARCHAR(50) NULL,
  OrdinalPosition VARCHAR(50) NULL,
  KeyType VARCHAR(50) NULL,
  IndexName VARCHAR(50) NULL
);

CREATE TABLE dbo.ADOSQLServerMetadataColumns
(
  ID INT IDENTITY(1,1) NOT NULL,
  TableCatalog VARCHAR(50) NULL,
  TableName VARCHAR(50) NULL,
  TableSchema VARCHAR(50) NOT NULL,
  ColumnName VARCHAR(50) NULL,
  OrdinalPosition INT NULL,
  ColumnDefault VARCHAR(50) NULL,
  IsNullable VARCHAR(5) NULL,
  DataType VARCHAR(50) NULL,
  CharacterMaximumLength VARCHAR(50) NULL,
  CharacterOctetLength VARCHAR(50) NULL,
  NumericPrecision VARCHAR(50) NULL,
  NumericPrecisionRadix VARCHAR(50) NULL,
  NumericScale VARCHAR(50) NULL,
  DateTimePresision VARCHAR(50) NULL,
  CharacterSetCatalog VARCHAR(50) NULL,
  CharacterSetSchema VARCHAR(50) NULL,
  CharacterSetName VARCHAR(50) NULL,
  CollationCatalog VARCHAR(50) NULL,
  IsFilestream VARCHAR(5) NULL,
  IsSparse VARCHAR(5) NULL,
  IsColumnSet VARCHAR(5) NULL
) ;
```

2. Create a new SSIS package, and configure an ADO.NET connection manager that points to the source SQL Server database.

3. Add a Data Flow task, and switch to the Data Flow pane.

4. Add a Script Component onto the Data Flow pane.

5. Select Source as the Data Flow type, and click OK.

6. Double-click the Script Component to edit it. Make sure that Inputs and Outputs is selected in the left-hand pane. Rename Output 0 as **MetadataOutput**. Select Output Columns.

7. Click Add Column to add a new column. In the properties pane on the right of the dialog box, rename the column **TableCatalog**. Set its data type to String, with a length of 0.

8. Add the following columns, with the given data types and lengths:

Column	DataType and Length
TableCatalog	String, 0
TableSchema	String, 0
TableName	String, 0
TableType	String, 0

The dialog box should look something like that in Figure 8-14.

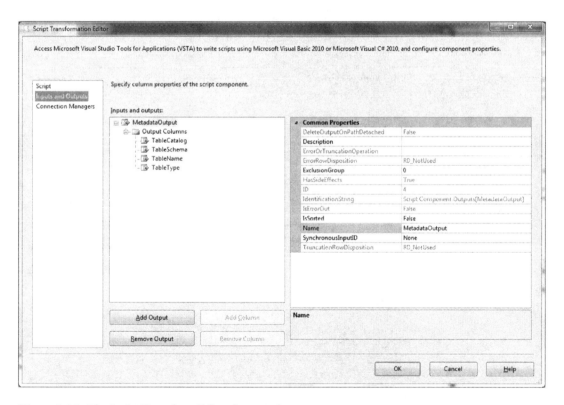

Figure 8-14. *The Script Transform Editor for metadata*

9. Click Connection Managers and add a connection manager named **ADONETSource**. Select the ADO.NET connection manager that you created earlier.

10. Click Script, set the script language to Visual Basic 2010, and then click the Design Script button.

11. Right-click References in the left-hand pane. Select Add Reference. Select System. Data.SQLClient from the available .NET components. Click OK.

12. Add the following code (C:\SQL2012DIRecipes\CH08\GetschemaCode.vb):

```vb
Public Class ScriptMain
    Inherits UserComponent

    Dim ConnMgr As IDTSConnectionManager100
    Dim SQLConn As SqlConnection
    Dim SQLReader As SqlDataReader
    Dim DSTable As DataTable

    Public Overrides Sub AcquireConnections(ByVal Transaction As Object)

        ConnMgr = Me.Connections.ADONETSource
        SQLConn = CType(ConnMgr.AcquireConnection(Nothing), SqlConnection)

    End Sub

    Public Overrides Sub PreExecute()
        MyBase.PreExecute()

        DSTable = SQLConn.GetSchema("Tables")

    End Sub

    Public Overrides Sub PostExecute()
        MyBase.PostExecute()
    End Sub

    Public Overrides Sub CreateNewOutputRows()

        For Each Row In DSTable.Rows

            MetadataOutputBuffer.AddRow()

            MetadataOutputBuffer.TableCatalog = Row("TABLE_CATALOG").ToString
            MetadataOutputBuffer.TableSchema = Row("TABLE_SCHEMA").ToString
            MetadataOutputBuffer.TableName = Row("TABLE_NAME").ToString
            MetadataOutputBuffer.TableType = Row("TABLE_TYPE").ToString

        Next

    End Sub

End Class
```

13. Close the Script screen.

14. Click OK to close the Script Component dialog box.

15. Add an OLEDB destination component to the Data Flow pane. Link the Script Component to the OLEDB destination and configure it to use the ADOSQLServerMetadataTables table, which was created as part of the prerequisites.

16. Map the columns. You will note that the destination table columns correspond to the columns that you added to the Script Component output buffer.

17. Repeat steps 3-16 for the other tables. The column definitions are provided in Table 8-10.

Table 8-10. *Column Definitions for Returning GetSchema Metadata in SSIS*

Table Name	Column	DataType and Length
ADOSQLServerMetadataViews	TableCatalog	String, 50
ADOSQLServerMetadataViews	TableSchema	String, 50
ADOSQLServerMetadataViews	TableName	String, 50
ADOSQLServerMetadataViews	CheckOption	String, 50
ADOSQLServerMetadataViews	IsUpdatable	String, 5
ADOSQLServerMetadataColumns	TableCatalog	String, 50
ADOSQLServerMetadataColumns	TableSchema	String, 50
ADOSQLServerMetadataColumns	TableName	String, 50
ADOSQLServerMetadataColumns	ColumnName	String, 50
ADOSQLServerMetadataColumns	OrdinalPosition	four-byte signed integer [DT_I4]
ADOSQLServerMetadataColumns	ColumnDefault	String, 50
ADOSQLServerMetadataColumns	IsNullable	String, 5
ADOSQLServerMetadataColumns	DataType	String, 50
ADOSQLServerMetadataColumns	CharacterMaximumLength	four-byte signed integer [DT_I4]
ADOSQLServerMetadataColumns	CharacterOctetLength	four-byte signed integer [DT_I4]
ADOSQLServerMetadataColumns	NumericPrecision	four-byte signed integer [DT_I4]
ADOSQLServerMetadataColumns	NumericPrecisionRadix	four-byte signed integer [DT_I4]
ADOSQLServerMetadataColumns	NumericScale	four-byte signed integer [DT_I4]
ADOSQLServerMetadataColumns	DateTimePrecision	String, 50
ADOSQLServerMetadataColumns	CharacterSetCatalog	String, 50
ADOSQLServerMetadataColumns	CharacterSetSchema	String, 50
ADOSQLServerMetadataColumns	CharacterSetName	String, 50
ADOSQLServerMetadataColumns	CollationCatalog	String, 50

(continued)

Table 8-10. (*continued*)

Table Name	Column	DataType and Length
ADOSQLServerMetadataColumns	IsFilestream	String, 5
ADOSQLServerMetadataColumns	IsSparse	String, 5
ADOSQLServerMetadataColumns	IsColumnSet	String, 5
ADOSQLServerMetadataViewColumns	ViewCatalog	String, 50
ADOSQLServerMetadataViewColumns	ViewSchema	String, 50
ADOSQLServerMetadataViewColumns	ViewName	String, 50
ADOSQLServerMetadataViewColumns	TableCatalog	String, 50
ADOSQLServerMetadataViewColumns	TableSchema	String, 50
ADOSQLServerMetadataViewColumns	TableName	String, 50
ADOSQLServerMetadataViewColumns	ColumnName	String, 50
ADOSQLServerMetadataIndexes	ConstraintCatalog	String, 50
ADOSQLServerMetadataIndexes	ConstraintSchema	String, 50
ADOSQLServerMetadataIndexes	ConstraintName	String, 50
ADOSQLServerMetadataIndexes	TableCatalog	String, 50
ADOSQLServerMetadataIndexes	TableSchema	String, 50
ADOSQLServerMetadataIndexes	TableName	String, 50
ADOSQLServerMetadataIndexColumns	ConstraintCatalog	String, 50
ADOSQLServerMetadataIndexColumns	ConstraintSchema	String, 50
ADOSQLServerMetadataIndexColumns	ConstraintName	String, 50
ADOSQLServerMetadataIndexColumns	TableCatalog	String, 50
ADOSQLServerMetadataIndexColumns	TableSchema	String, 50
ADOSQLServerMetadataIndexColumns	TableName	String, 50
ADOSQLServerMetadataIndexColumns	ColumnName	String, 50
ADOSQLServerMetadataIndexColumns	OrdinalPosition	four-byte signed integer [DT_I4]
ADOSQLServerMetadataIndexColumns	KeyType	String, 50
ADOSQLServerMetadataIndexColumns	IndexName	String, 50

You will need to set the appropriate script for each source. The definitions are are as follows (all are in the file C:\SQL2012DIRecipes\CH08\GetSchemaCodeProcessing.vb):

'Views:

```
DSTable = SQLConn.GetSchema("Views")

MetadataOutputBuffer.TableCatalog = Row("TABLE_CATALOG").ToString
MetadataOutputBuffer.TableSchema = Row("TABLE_SCHEMA").ToString
MetadataOutputBuffer.TableName = Row("TABLE_NAME").ToString
MetadataOutputBuffer.IsUpdatable = Row("IS_UPDATABLE").ToString
MetadataOutputBuffer.CheckOption = Row("CHECK_OPTION").ToString
```

'Table Columns:

```
DSTable = SQLConn.GetSchema("Columns")

MetadataOutputBuffer.TableCatalog = Row("TABLE_CATALOG").ToString
MetadataOutputBuffer.TableSchema = Row("TABLE_SCHEMA").ToString
MetadataOutputBuffer.TableName = Row("TABLE_NAME").ToString
MetadataOutputBuffer.ColumnName = Row("COLUMN_NAME").ToString
MetadataOutputBuffer.OrdinalPosition = Row("ORDINAL_POSITION").ToString
MetadataOutputBuffer.ColumnDefault = Row("COLUMN_DEFAULT").ToString
MetadataOutputBuffer.IsNullable = Row("IS_NULLABLE").ToString
MetadataOutputBuffer.DataType = Row("DATA_TYPE").ToString
MetadataOutputBuffer.CharacterMaximumLength = Row("CHARACTER_MAXIMUM_LENGTH").ToString
MetadataOutputBuffer.CharacterOctetLength = Row("CHARACTER_OCTET_LENGTH").ToString
MetadataOutputBuffer.NumericPrecision = Row("NUMERIC_PRECISION").ToString
MetadataOutputBuffer.NumericPrecisionRadix = Row("NUMERIC_PRECISION_RADIX").ToString
MetadataOutputBuffer.NumericScale = Row("NUMERIC_SCALE").ToString
MetadataOutputBuffer.DateTimePresision = Row("DATETIME_PRECISION").ToString
MetadataOutputBuffer.CharacterSetCatalog = Row("CHARACTER_SET_CATALOG").ToString
MetadataOutputBuffer.CharacterSetSchema = Row("CHARACTER_SET_SCHEMA").ToString
MetadataOutputBuffer.CharacterSetName = Row("CHARACTER_SET_NAME").ToString
MetadataOutputBuffer.CollationCatalog = Row("COLLATION_CATALOG").ToString
MetadataOutputBuffer.IsFilestream = Row("IS_FILESTREAM").ToString
MetadataOutputBuffer.IsSparse = Row("IS_SPARSE").ToString
MetadataOutputBuffer.IsColumnSet = Row("IS_COLUMN_SET").ToString
```

'View Columns:

```
DSTable = SQLConn.GetSchema("ViewColumns")

MetadataOutputBuffer.ViewCatalog = Row("VIEW_CATALOG").ToString
MetadataOutputBuffer.ViewSchema = Row("VIEW_SCHEMA").ToString
MetadataOutputBuffer.ViewName = Row("VIEW_NAME").ToString
MetadataOutputBuffer.TableCatalog = Row("TABLE_CATALOG").ToString
MetadataOutputBuffer.TableSchema = Row("TABLE_SCHEMA").ToString
MetadataOutputBuffer.TableName = Row("TABLE_NAME").ToString
MetadataOutputBuffer.ColumnName = Row("COLUMN_NAME").ToString
```

'**Indexes:**

```
DSTable = SQLConn.GetSchema("Indexes")

MetadataOutputBuffer.TableCatalog = Row("TABLE_CATALOG").ToString
MetadataOutputBuffer.TableSchema = Row("TABLE_SCHEMA").ToString
MetadataOutputBuffer.TableName = Row("TABLE_NAME").ToString
MetadataOutputBuffer.ConstraintCatalog = Row("CONSTRAINT_CATALOG").ToString
MetadataOutputBuffer.ConstraintSchema = Row("CONSTRAINT_SCHEMA").ToString
MetadataOutputBuffer.ConstraintName = Row("CONSTRAINT_NAME").ToString
```

'**Index Columns:**

```
DSTable = SQLConn.GetSchema("IndexColumns")

MetadataOutputBuffer.TableCatalog = Row("TABLE_CATALOG").ToString
MetadataOutputBuffer.TableSchema = Row("TABLE_SCHEMA").ToString
MetadataOutputBuffer.TableName = Row("TABLE_NAME").ToString
MetadataOutputBuffer.ConstraintCatalog = Row("CONSTRAINT_CATALOG").ToString
MetadataOutputBuffer.ConstraintSchema = Row("CONSTRAINT_SCHEMA").ToString
MetadataOutputBuffer.ConstraintName = Row("CONSTRAINT_NAME").ToString
MetadataOutputBuffer.ColumnName = Row("COLUMN_NAME").ToString
MetadataOutputBuffer.OrdinalPosition = Row("ORDINAL_POSITION").ToString
MetadataOutputBuffer.KeyType = Row("KEYTYPE").ToString
MetadataOutputBuffer.IndexName = Row("INDEX_NAME").ToString
```

18. The final package will probably look something like Figure 8-15.

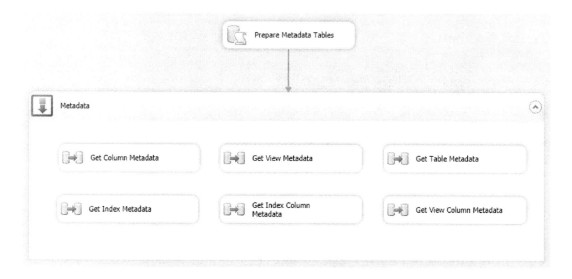

Figure 8-15. *SSIS package to return SQL Server metadata*

Run the package, and the selected metadata will be loaded into to the SQL Server tables.

How It Works

Another way to obtain metadata is to use the .NET GetSchema class. This technique is more complex to implement than the techniques that you have seen so far in this chapter. It is, however, considerably more extensible and powerful than using INFORMATION_SCHEMA views. The example in this recipe returns metadata for the following:

- Tables

- Views

- Table columns

- View columns

- Indexes

- Index columns

Metadata for each of these object types is stored in its own specific output table. These tables can then be joined and queried (a bit like the INFORMATION_SCHEMA views in SQL Server) to get an overview of the source metadata.

The package looks much more complex than it really is, as all it does is use a script to obtain the source data from each of the metadata schemas, and this requires creating multiple output columns for each one. For each of the six metadata sources, you create a Script Component data source that will query a specific set of metadata using the .GetSchema function. Each script task will have the requisite set of output columns that map to the output of the .GetSchema function. The columns added to the data flow will then be sent to an OLEDB destination task—and into a database.

To make the SSIS package slightly more reusable, you may want to set the table name, and/or the connection string as variables. You can also specifically define the columns that you wish to store in SQL Server. The important thing is to ensure that you have defined all the output columns that you need to map metadata source columns to before writing the code to carry out the data mapping. Note that the index numbers of the columns used to map the data table to the output buffer are the index numbers of the source data—not the buffer columns that you created in the SSIS package.

Adding a data viewer to the data flow can also help tremendously. To do this, right-click the connection between the Script Component data source and the OLEDB destination, and select Data Viewers. Now when you run the package, the viewer is displayed for you to see the data as it is processed.

Hints, Tips, and Traps

- The script component can define the source metadata. Notably, you can

  - Specify which type of connection that you wish to use.

  - Specify the schema collection that you wish to store.

  - Add any restrictions that you require.

Summary

This chapter contains many ways to profile source data using SQL Server. To give you a clearer overview, Table 8-11 describes the various methods which we have looked at in this chapter and their advantages and disadvantages.

Table 8-11. *Advantages and Disadvantages of Techniques Used in This Chapter*

Technique	Advantages	Disadvantages
sp_columns_ex / sp_tables_ex	Simple to use.	Only work with linked servers.
		Somewhat limited metadata.
System dictionary	Extremely complete.	Complex to query.
		Requires experience and practice.
		Can require ad hoc query rights.
INFORMATION_SCHEMA views	Simple to access.	Limited metadata.
	Easy to query.	Not available for all databases.
		Can vary between databases.
GetSchema	Requires coding.	Initially complex.
	Easy to use once configured.	

Clearly, the approach that you take to obtain metadata depends on the source data itself, as you cannot gather metadata from Access in the same way that you can from flat files. Even when dealing with relational databases, you may be required to apply very different approaches. Equally, the type of connectivity available can shape your choice. For a linked server, sp_columns_ex may suffice. If you are using other means to connect to the data source, then this approach is simply not available.

Finally, there is the level of detail in the metadata that you want to retrieve can be a deciding factor. For an eminently reasonable amount of metadata, then INFORMATION_SCHEMA views could suffice. For the truly profound levels of detail, you may have to query the system catalog of the source database.

So it is now up to you to decide the level of metadata to return—if any—and which is the most appropriate method of doing this. Hopefully, this chapter has given you some ideas and approaches to try out. I hope even more that they help you to build robust and trouble-free ETL solutions with SQL Server.

CHAPTER 9

■ ■ ■

Data Transformation

As we all know, the "T" in ETL stands for "transformation". Yes, you may be able to connect to a data source, and yes, you may be able to pour data into an SQL Server destination database. Frequently, however, many changes must be applied to the data as it progresses from source to destination. Consequently, this chapter will look at some of the major data transformation challenges that face the ETL developer.

Inevitably, it is impossible to foresee every data transformation requirement and every twist and turn that data can, or must, take as it flows through an ETL process. So, equally inevitably, this chapter cannot foresee every need for data transformation nor provide every solution that could be required. Nonetheless, it will attempt to provide an overview of the classic solutions to standard data transformation problems. These will include the following:

> *Data deduplication*—or the art of removing duplicates.
>
> *Denormalizing data*—or *unpivoting* (also called *transposing*) columns of data into rows.
>
> *Pivoting* data.
>
> *Subsetting* data—from fixed- and variable-length data into multiple columns.
>
> *Concatenating* data.
>
> *Merging* data.
>
> *Character-level data transformation*—to apply the required UPPER, lower, or TitleCase.
>
> A look at the *main types of SCD* (slowly changing dimensions).
>
> Plus a few other tools for your ETL armory.

A few elements have been included that may seem far too elementary. Yet I felt that it was best to be exhaustive (albeit briefly), and use this as an opportunity to provide a rapid overview of the fundamental set of SSIS transforms that give the product its power and versatility. I will also stick to the philosophy of this book and describe parallel T-SQL solutions where appropriate, as I am a firm believer in using the appropriate tool for the job, and not shoehorning everything into SSIS.

Equally, I have steered clear of data cleansing except where Data Quality Services in SQL Server 2012 are concerned. Data cleansing is a heinously complex subject, which frequently goes beyond simple data transformation, and requires, all too often, intensive manual labor, or third-party products—and so really is a stand-alone subject outside the scope of this book.

The examples used in this chapter are available on the book's companion web site, and can be found in the C:\SQL2012DIRecipes\CH09 directory once you have downloaded them. Please note also that I will not be explaining many times over how to use OLEDB connection managers to point to source data in SSIS since this has been explained in detail throughout many of the recipes in Chapters 1–7. Please refer to the recipes in the first part of the book—and specifically Chapters 4 (for SQL Server destinations) and 7 (for SQL Server sources) to revise complete details on SSIS data source and data destination connections and tasks.

9-1. Converting Data Types

Problem

You need to convert between data types as part of an ETL process to ensure that source data types do not cause the process to fail.

Solution

Use the SSIS Data Conversion task to change data types in the data flow and ensure that the destination data types can accept the source data. The procedure is as follows:

1. Create or open an SSIS package and add a Data Flow task. Switch to the Data Flow pane.

2. Add an OLEDB connection manager and configure it to connect to the CarSales database.

3. Add an OLEDB Source task and configure to use the OLEDB connection manager defined in step 2 and the Clients table.

4. Add a Data Conversion task to your SSIS package.

5. Connect the Data Source task to it.

6. Select the column(s) you wish to modify.

7. For each column whose data type needs altering, choose the new data type, and if necessary, its length in the grid in the lower part of the dialog box. It should look like Figure 9-1.

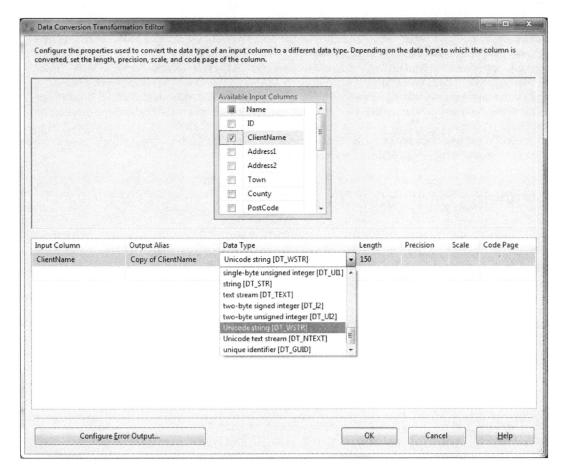

Figure 9-1. *The SSIS Data Conversion task*

8. Add an OLEDB destination task and connect the Data Conversion task to it.

9. Configure the destination task to connect to the requisite database and table and map the columns.

How It Works

In SSIS, inside a Data Flow task you can use the Data Conversion task to change a data type. You will be converting to one of the SSIS internal data types. These are described in Appendix A. Once a Data Conversion task has been implemented as part of a data flow (most often by connecting it to a Data Source), you can select the column(s) whose data you wish to change and then select the destination data type. SSIS will create a second column for each modified data type, so be sure to map the appropriate column in the destination task.

At risk of laboring the blindingly obvious, you can also convert data in T-SQL using two main functions:

- CAST
- CONVERT

The subtleties and limitations (as well as the date and time styles used by CONVERT) of these two functions have been discussed exhaustively since SQL Server was initially released many years ago, so I recommend that you use the function that you are most comfortable with.

You can only convert a data type to another data type if the conversion is supported, which in most cases means that the destination data type is **longer** than the source (a VARCHAR(500) will not fit into a VARCHAR(10), for instance); or that the destination data type **larger** than the source (a BIGINT will not find into a TINYINT, for example); or that the destination is less restrictive (a text cannot be converted into a DATE data type unless it can be read as a date).

As conversion errors will often only appear at runtime, you can avoid painful debugging by ensuring that you anticipate data type conversion errors while developing your packages.

9-2. Removing Duplicates from Data

Problem

You have data loaded into an SQL Server table—possibly a staging table—and you want to remove any duplicate records.

Solution

Use the ROW_NUMBER() windowing function and a CTE (common table expression) to deduplicate records. The following shows how (C:\SQL2012DIRecipes\CH09\DedupeSmallRecordsets.sql):

```
WITH Dedupe_CTE (RowNo, ClientName, Country, Town, County, Address1, Address2,
ClientType, ClientSize)
AS
(
 SELECT ROW_NUMBER() OVER (PARTITION BY ClientNameORDER BY ClientNameDESC) AS RowNo,
 ClientName, Country, Town, County, Address1, Address2, ClientType, ClientSize
 FROM dbo.Client
)
DELETE FROM Dedupe_CTE WHERE RowNo > 1;
```

How It Works

When all the data that you load is already perfect, then you have few, if any, problems. Unfortunately, the real world is not always that simple, and one of the essential—indeed often one of the first—things that must done is to remove duplicates from a set of data. Duplicates can not only cause problems for users further down the line (and cause problems whose cause may be hard to trace back to the source), they can cause ETL processes to fail outright. This can become painfully clear if you are using the T-SQL MERGE command, which will choke on duplicate key data for instance.

For a small to medium-sized dataset (and it is hard to define exactly what that means as it will depend on table width and row sizes. as well as record counts and system resources) using the ROW_NUMBER() windowing function that appeared with SQL Server 2005 is a sure and easy way to deduplicate data. The essential information to provide to the ROW_NUMBER() windowing function is the list of fields to partition by—as this will define the elements that you consider to be duplicated. Although not difficult, removing duplicates (also known as deduplication) has to be done carefully. Excessive zeal (a.k.a. sloppy data analysis) can result in data being removed from a source completely, whereas insufficient precision (that is often a manifestation of poor analysis, too) can lead to duplicates remaining. A secondary concern is process efficiency. Depending on the size of the dataset from that you are removing duplicates, you may find that you need to experiment with different techniques to get the fastest accurate result.

9-3. Deduplicating Large Recordsets

Problem

You want to remove duplicate records from a large table using T-SQL.

Solution

Use temporary tables and ROW_NUMBER() to remove duplicate records.

For a larger table, the following technique could take less time to execute than the method used in Recipe 9-2 to remove duplicates from a data table (C:\SQL2012DIRecipes\CH09\DedupeLargeRecordsets.sql):

```
IF OBJECT_ID('TempDB..#Tmp_Client_DUPS') IS NOT NULL DROP TABLE TempDB..#Tmp_Client_DUPS;
IF OBJECT_ID('TempDB..#Tmp_Client_DUPData') IS NOT NULL DROP TABLE
TempDB..#Tmp_Client_DUPData;

-- get duplicates
SELECT      ClientName,Country,Town,County,Address1,Address2,ClientType,ClientSize
INTO        #Tmp_Client_DUPS
FROM        CarSales_Staging.dbo.ClientWithDuplicates
GROUP BY    ClientName,Country,Town,County,Address1,Address2,ClientType,ClientSize
HAVING      COUNT(*) > 1;

-- get full data on deletes
SELECT
TD.ClientName,TD.Country,TD.Town,TD.County,TD.Address1,TD.Address2,
TD.ClientType,TD.ClientSize,
ROW_NUMBER() OVER (PARTITION BY
TD.ClientName,TD.Country,TD.Town,TD.County,
TD.Address1,TD.Address2,TD.ClientType,TD.ClientSize
ORDER BY TD.ClientName,TD.Country,TD.Town,TD.County,TD.Address1,TD.Address2,
TD.ClientType,TD.ClientSize DESC) AS RowNo

INTO        #Tmp_Client_DUPData

FROM        dbo.Client TD
            INNER JOIN #Tmp_Client_DUPS DUP
            ON TD.ClientName = DUP.ClientName
            AND TD.Country = DUP.Country
            AND TD.Town = DUP.Town
            AND TD.County = DUP.County
            AND TD.Address1 = DUP.Address1
            AND TD.Address2 = DUP.Address2
            AND TD.ClientType = DUP.ClientType
            AND TD.ClientSize = DUP.ClientSize;
-- delete
DELETE  C
FROM        dbo.Client C
INNER JOIN  #Tmp_Client_DUPData TMP
```

```
                ON  C.ClientName = TMP.ClientName
                AND C.Country = TMP.Country
                AND C.Town = TMP.Town
                AND C.County = TMP.County
                AND C.Address1 = TMP.Address1
                AND C.Address2 = TMP.Address2
                AND C.ClientType = TMP.ClientType
                AND C.ClientSize = TMP.ClientSize;

-- reinsert single records
INSERT INTO dbo.Client
(
ClientName
,Country
,Town
,County
,Address1
,Address2
,ClientType
,ClientSize
)
SELECT
ClientName
,Country
,Town
,County
,Address1
,Address2
,ClientType
,ClientSize

FROM    #Tmp_Client_DUPData
WHERE   RowNo = 1;
```

How It Works

For larger record sets, or when using a subset of columns to establish that records are duplicates, then an approach based on temporary tables is often faster, even if it is longer to code. As a rule of thumb, I generally feel happy using the ROW_NUMBER() approach from Recipe 9-2 up to 1,000,000 records. Above that, I tend to test that approach alongside other solutions and see which performs best.

First, the solution script loads all duplicate records into a temporary table named #Tmp_Client_DUPS. It then collates the full data for duplicate records into the #Tmp_Client_DUPDatatemp table. Finally, all records that are duplicates are deleted from the source table, and a single example of each duplicate record is loaded from #Tmp_Client_DUPData back into the source table.

This approach does use ROW_NUMBER() to isolate a single example of each record to keep, but the use of ROW_NUMBER is only applied to a subset of data—those records that are duplicates. In some cases, records are considered duplicates if only a few of the component columns are identical. This process is easy to adapt to such a contingency, as you can define the subset in the #Tmp_Client_DUPStable, and use these columns to join to the source data to transfer the full record set into the #Tmp_Client_DUPDatatable. As this process actually deletes the data in the core table before reinserting duplicates, I strongly advise you to make it part of a transaction. Should you do this, then in the event of a process failure, the source table will be restored to its original state.

An advantage that is frequently overlooked about this approach is that it lets you count the records that were duplicates (or triplicates, etc.) and log the counters easily. You can also add checks and balances, and output the temporary tables to disk if you wish to preserve copies of the duplicate data as it goes through the process.

This recipe's deduplication process can take quite a while to run, so you may want to test for duplicates before branching into a fully operational deduplication routine. Testing for duplicates can be as simple as the following (C:\SQL2012DIRecipes\CH09\TestForDuplicates.sql):

```
DECLARE @DupCount INT = 0;

SELECT @DupCount   = SUM(TotalDups) AS Dups
FROM (
      SELECT COUNT(*) AS TotalDups
      FROM dbo.Client
      GROUP BY ClientName, Country, Town, County, Address1, Address2, ClientType, ClientSize
      HAVING COUNT(*) > 1
 ) A;

IF @DupCount > 0
BEGIN
      -- Main code from Recipe 9-3 here
END;
```

9-4. Deduplicating Data in an ETL Data Flow

Problem

You wish to deduplicate data as it flows through an SSIS load package.

Solution

Use the SSIS Aggregate transform to remove duplicates in a data flow. The following steps describe one way to do this.

1. Create a new SSIS package and add a source and a destination OLEDB connection manager named, respectively, **CarSales_OLEDB** and **CarSales_Staging_OLEDB**. Configure them to point to the CarSales and CarSales_Staging SQL Server databases, respectively.

2. Add a Data Flow task. Double-click to Edit. Add an OLEDB Source task, and configure to use the CarSales_Staging_OLEDB connection manager, and use the dbo.Client table as its source data.

3. Add an Aggregate transform, and connect the data source to it. Double-click to edit.

4. Check the column names for all the columns that you wish to group by, which in this context means to remove duplicates for. Ensure that the Operation column is set to **Group By** for all input columns. The dialog box should look something like Figure 9-2.

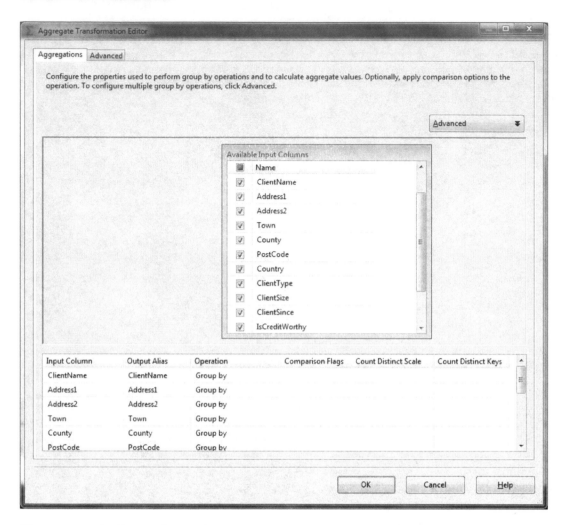

Figure 9-2. *Deduplicating data in SSIS*

5. Click OK to confirm.

6. Add an OLEDB destination task, configure it to use the CarSales_Staging_OLEDB connection manager.

7. Click New to create a destination table, which you can rename if you wish. Click OK to confirm the table creation. Next, click Mappings and map the source to destination columns. Click OK to complete the destination task.

You can now run the package and deduplicate the data.

How It Works

SSIS also allows you to remove duplicates. However, you will look in vain for a task with this name, or anything like it, in the toolbox. Instead, you can do this using the Aggregate transform. Setting the operation to Group By for all columns will deduplicate records.

You can also remove duplicates in SSIS using the Sort transform. Rather than re-describe most of the steps that you just saw, follow all the preceding steps, replacing steps 3 and 4 with the following process:

1. Add a Sort transform and connect the data source to it. Double-click to edit.

2. Check the column names for all the columns that you wish to use as a deduplication key. Leave any that you do not want to use to isolate duplicates as Pass-through. Check "Remove rows with duplicate sort values".

■ **Note** Both of these transforms are "blocking" or synchronous transforms. Therefore, they will have to complete before any other data transformation or output can continue. This can cause memory pressures when running the package.

9-5. Subsetting Column Data Using T-SQL

Problem

You need to break down the contents of a column into smaller, discrete portions.

Solution

Apply SQL's string manipulation functions to cut the data into fixed-length subsets.

Figure 9-3 shows an example of a 25-character string.

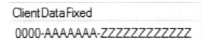

Figure 9-3. *A 25-character fixed-length string to be split*

And here is the T-SQL that will break Figure 9-3's string down into its component parts (C:\SQL2012DIRecipes\CH09\SubsetColumnData.sql):

```
SELECT
LEFT(ClientDataFixed,4)            AS LeftCol
,SUBSTRING(ClientDataFixed,6,7)    AS CentreCol
,RIGHT(ClientDataFixed,12)         AS RightCol

FROM    dbo.ClientSubset;
```

The result is shown in Figure 9-4.

Figure 9-4. *The string after it has been split*

How It Works

A frequent requirement, especially if your data is sourced from an older system, is to break down the contents of a column into smaller, discrete portions. Think of a social security number, where different parts of the data have different significations. Both T-SQL and SSIS can perform this task equally easily—and equally fast. The only difference can be how to overcome the problem of variable-length substrings. Here, as you will see in Recipe 9-6, SSIS reserves you a pleasant surprise.

In T-SQL there are three, core, string manipulation functions that help you separate out the elements of a fixed-length string. As they need little or no explanation, it suffices to say that they are, as follows:

- LEFT
- SUBSTRING
- RIGHT

Breaking down strings into multiple substrings when the strings (and consequently the subsets) are of variable length is only a little harder. It will require judicious use of the following string manipulation functions:

- LEN: Returns the number of characters in a string
- CHARINDEX: Gives the position of one or more characters in a string
- REPLACE: Replaces one or more characters in a string
- REVERSE: Reverse a string of characters

I am assuming that there will always be a specific character that can be used to isolate the substrings, and that this specific character does not appear inside a subset. Fortunately, for these types of columns, it is rare for this not to be the case. The character can vary for each substring, however.

Let's suppose that you have the following source data given in Figure 9-5.

ClientDataVariable

0000-AAAAAAA-ZZZZZZZZZZZZ-XXX

Figure 9-5. *A variable-length string to be split in T-SQL*

The following is the T-SQL that will break it down into its component parts (C:\SQL2012DIRecipes\CH09\VariableLengthSubsetting.sql):

```
SELECT
ID
,CASE -- First Column or entire column, any number of columns
WHEN LEN(ClientDataVariable) - LEN(REPLACE(ClientDataVariable, '-', '')) <> 0 THEN
LEFT(ClientDataVariable, CHARINDEX('-',ClientDataVariable) - 1)
WHEN LEN(ClientDataVariable) - LEN(REPLACE(ClientDataVariable, '-', '')) = 0 THEN
ClientDataVariable
END AS ColLeft

,CASE -- Three or Four columns, second column
WHEN LEN(ClientDataVariable) - LEN(REPLACE(ClientDataVariable, '-', '')) = 3
THEN LEFT(SUBSTRING(ClientDataVariable, CHARINDEX('-',ClientDataVariable) + 1,
LEN(ClientDataVariable) - CHARINDEX('-',ClientDataVariable)
```

```
- CHARINDEX('-',REVERSE(ClientDataVariable))), CHARINDEX('-',SUBSTRING(ClientDataVariable
, CHARINDEX('-',ClientDataVariable) + 1, LEN(ClientDataVariable)
- CHARINDEX('-',ClientDataVariable) - CHARINDEX('-',REVERSE(ClientDataVariable)))) -1)
WHEN LEN(ClientDataVariable) - LEN(REPLACE(ClientDataVariable, '-', '')) = 2
THEN SUBSTRING(ClientDataVariable, CHARINDEX('-',ClientDataVariable) + 1
, CHARINDEX('-',ClientDataVariable, CHARINDEX('-',ClientDataVariable) + 1)
- CHARINDEX('-',ClientDataVariable) - 1)
END AS Col2

,CASE -- Four columns, third column
WHEN LEN(ClientDataVariable) - LEN(REPLACE(ClientDataVariable, '-', '')) = 3
THEN RIGHT(SUBSTRING(ClientDataVariable, CHARINDEX('-',ClientDataVariable) + 1,
LEN(ClientDataVariable) - CHARINDEX('-',ClientDataVariable)
- CHARINDEX('-',REVERSE(ClientDataVariable)))
, CHARINDEX('-',SUBSTRING(REVERSE(ClientDataVariable), CHARINDEX('-',ClientDataVariable)
+ 1, LEN(ClientDataVariable) - CHARINDEX('-',ClientDataVariable)
- CHARINDEX('-',REVERSE(ClientDataVariable)))) -1)
END AS Col3

,CASE  -- Last column, any number of columns
WHEN (LEN(ClientDataVariable) - LEN(REPLACE(ClientDataVariable, '-', ''))) <> 0
THEN REVERSE(LEFT(REVERSE(ClientDataVariable), CHARINDEX('-',REVERSE(ClientDataVariable)) - 1))
END AS ColRight;

FROM    dbo.ClientSubset
```

Figure 9-6 shows the result.

Results | Messages

	ID	ColLeft	Col2	Col3	ColRight
1	1	0000	AAAAAAA	ZZZZZZZZZZZ	XXX

Figure 9-6. *A variable-length string once split*

Hints, Tips, and Traps

- This T-SQL snippet is hard-coded for a specific number of columns. To extend the number of columns, the CASE statement for columns three or four can be copied and adapted to extend the model to handle further columns.
- There must be as many ways of performing this operation as there opinions about beer or wine. So please do not take this as the only way in that it can be done. Experiment until you find a solution that suits your requirements. Defining an SQLCLR function could be another solution, or even a T-SQL function. You need to remember, however, that anything that will cause the data to switch from set-based processing to row-by-row processing will cripple the efficiency of this process.
- This process can be written as dynamic SQL to handle a variable number of columns, but I will not be showing that here. I will leave you to extend it if you need this facility.
- The code which subsets a column can be run as part of a T-SQL UPDATE statement to assign the data to different columns in a table.

9-6. Generating Fixed-Length Column Data Subsets Using SSIS

Problem

You wish to subset the contents of a fixed-length column into multiple columns as part of an SSIS data flow.

Solution

Use the Derived Column transform to subset data during a controlled and regular data flow. The following steps explain how to do this.

1. Create or open an SSIS package with a Data Flow component and a valid data source.

2. In the Data Flow pane, add a Derived Column Data Flow Transformation from the toolbox, and connect to the data source (or to the data flow in a complex package).

3. Double-click to edit.

4. Add the following three elements to the lower part of the dialog box:

Derived Column Name	Expression
LeftCol	SUBSTRING(ClientDataFixed,1,4)
MiddleCol	SUBSTRING(ClientDataFixed,6,7)
RightCol	RIGHT(ClientDataFixed,12)

The dialog box should look something like Figure 9-7.

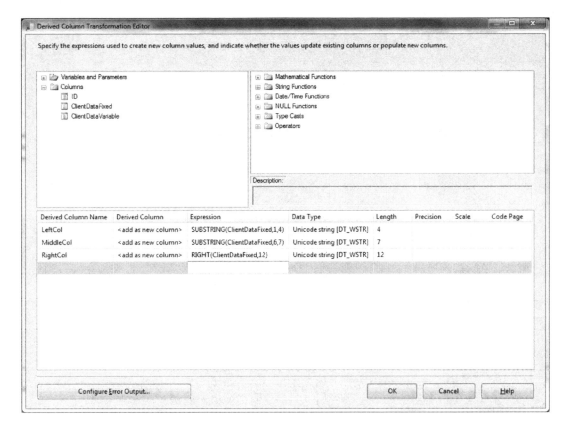

Figure 9-7. *Using a Derived Column transform to split strings*

> 5. Click OK to confirm your modifications. You can then add a Data Flow destination, or further transforms.

How It Works

The Derived Column transform splits the column into multiple elements based on the length of subsets of the source. Each new subset becomes a separate new column. Here, the SUBSTRING function let you define how many characters to extract from the string (given by the second parameter). The first parameter states where inside the string to begin the extraction.

If you add a data viewer, it will show something like Figure 9-8 (depending on the columns that you have selected to view).

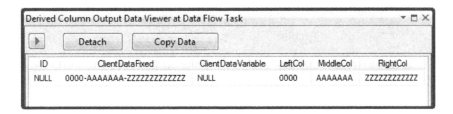

Figure 9-8. *Using a data viewer to view split strings*

Hints, Tips, and Traps

- To avoid typos when using column names in a data flow, you can always expand Columns on the top left, and drag a column name into the Expression field.

- Remember to give a meaningful name to the new derived columns.

9-7. Generating Variable-Length Column Data Subsets
Problem

You wish to subset the contents of a variable-length column into multiple columns as part of an SSIS data flow.

Solution

Use the Derived Column transform's FINDSTRING function to cut up the data into smaller defined chunks.

The process for variable-length strings is virtually identical to that used in Recipe 9-6 for fixed-length strings. The solution for this recipe is to follow Recipe 9-6 and amend step 3 by adding the following four elements to the lower part of the dialog box (C:\SQL2012DIRecipes\CH09\SSISSubset.txt):

Derived Column Name	Expression
LeftCol	FINDSTRING(ClientDataVariable,"-",1) == 0 ? SUBSTRING(Client,1,FINDSTRING(ClientDataVariable,"-",1)) : SUBSTRING(ClientDataVariable,1,FINDSTRING(ClientDataVariable,"-",1) - 1)
Col2	FINDSTRING(ClientDataVariable,"-",2) == 0 ? "" : SUBSTRING(ClientDataVariable,FINDSTRING(ClientDataVariable,"-",1) + 1,FINDSTRING(ClientDataVariable,"-",2) - FINDSTRING(ClientDataVariable,"-",1) - 1)
Col3	FINDSTRING(ClientDataVariable,"-",3) == 0 ? "" : SUBSTRING(ClientDataVariable,FINDSTRING(ClientDataVariable,"-",2) + 1,FINDSTRING(ClientDataVariable,"-",3) - FINDSTRING(ClientDataVariable,"-",2) - 1)
RightCol	FINDSTRING(ClientDataVariable,"-",1) == 0 ? "" : RIGHT(ClientDataVariable, FINDSTRING(REVERSE(ClientDataVariable),"-",1) - 1)

The dialog box should look something like Figure 9-9.

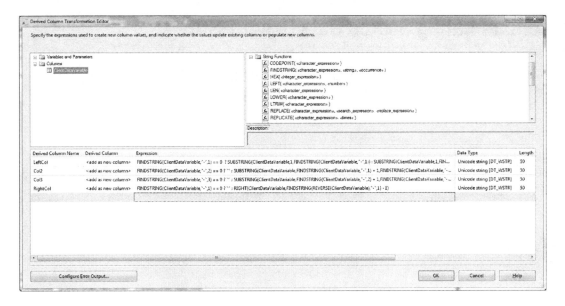

Figure 9-9. *A Derived Column transform used to split strings*

How It Works

Where variable-length strings are concerned, SSIS has a pleasant surprise in store. Unlike T-SQL, you can tell it to find the nth occurrence of a character—thereby skipping the first (few) times that a delimiter appears. This is done using the FINDSTRING function, which allows you to specify that occurrence of a delimiter to look for.

The reason for the apparent repetition of the SUBSTRING function is that SSIS requires us to handle NULLs. One way of doing this is to use the ternary operator (If...Then...Else) and then add the entire string for the first column to return and zero-length strings for the others if the separator is not present. If you don't, and there are fields without subset data for any record, the task will fail.

As this is SSIS, it is quite difficult (though not impossible) to make this process dynamic—that is, detect a variable number of subelements. So I will not be looking at this possibility here. In any case, SSIS is predicated on standardized recurring data structures, so this is par for the course.

If you add a Data Viewer to the data flow after the Derived Column transform, you can see the results of your endeavors. It should look something like Figure 9-10.

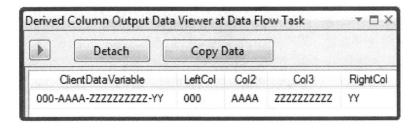

Figure 9-10. *Subsetting variable-length columns using SSIS*

9-8. Concatenating Source Data Using T-SQL

Problem

You wish to concatenate data from several columns into a single column. The data has already been loaded into an SQL Server table.

Solution

Use the FOR XML "black box" technique to concatenate data from two or more columns.

The following code snippet will concatenate all the Invoice IDs from the Invoicetable for each client in the Client table (C:\SQL2012DIRecipes\CH09\Concatenate.sql):

```
SELECT
ID,
LEFT(CA. CnCatLst, LEN(CA. CnCatLst)-1) AS InvoiceIDs
FROM
dbo.Client C
CROSS APPLY
(
SELECT          CAST(InvoiceNumber AS VARCHAR(50)) + ',' AS [text()]
FROM            dbo.Invoice I
WHERE           I.ClientID = C.ID
ORDER BY        I.ID
FOR XML PATH('')
) CA (CnCatLst)
ORDER BY        ID;
```

How It Works

Sometimes you will need to concatenate source data into some form of list—probably delimited. Concatenating data in this way is another of those areas of SQL processing that can create waves of energetic discussion as to the "best" way of performing the operation. Indeed, some brilliant papers have been written on this subject alone, which I can only urge you to consult. I do not wish, here, to continue the discussion, so I will suggest, simply, one technique that I have used since it was originally published on the Internet many years ago: the XML "black box" approach.

This technique seems to be a great trade-off between complexity and efficiency, and providing that the concatenated text does not exceed two gigabytes—but if it does, there will, I suspect, be other problems to handle long before this becomes the blocking issue. There are other ways of removing the final comma in a concatenated text. You can use the STUFF function, if you prefer.

9-9. Concatenating Data Using SSIS

Problem

You wish to concatenate data as part of an SSIS ETL process during the data flow.

Solution

Use a custom SSIS Script task to use .NET to apply concatenation. The following steps cover how it is done.

1. Create a new SSIS package. Add two new OLEDB connection managers—one named **CarSales_OLEDB**, which connects to the CarSalesdatabase, and the other named **CarSales_Staging_OLEDB**, which connects to the CarSales_Staging database. If you prefer, you can reuse the connection managers from Recipe 9-4—or (better still) define them as Package-Level connection managers.

2. Add a new Data Flow task. Double-click to edit.

3. Add a data source and configure it as follows:

OLEDB Connection Manager:	CarSales_OLEDB
Data Access Mode:	SQL Command
SQL Text:	SELECT ClientID, InvoiceNumber
	FROM dbo.Invoice
	ORDER BY ClientID, InvoiceNumber;

4. Preview the data to make sure that all is working, and if it is, click OK.

5. Add a Script Component task, define the type as Transform, and connect the Data Source task to it. Double-click to edit.

6. Click Input Columns on the left and select the ClientID and InvoiceNumber columns. The dialog box should look like Figure 9-11.

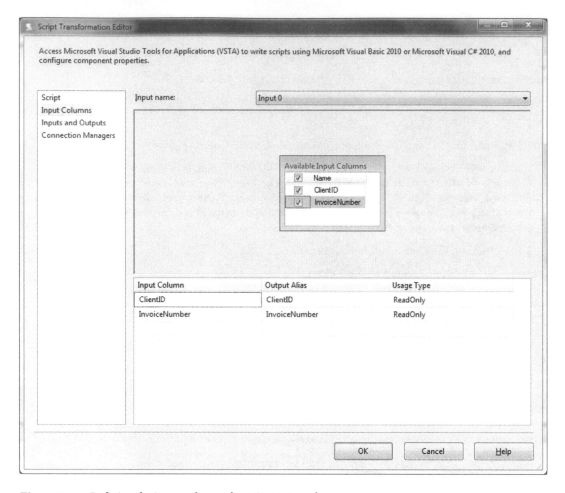

Figure 9-11. *Defining the input columns for a Script transform*

7. Select Output 0.

8. Click Inputs and Outputs on the left, then click Output Columns and add two new columns—**ListOutput** and **GroupOutput**. Set both as DT_STR and of suitable length.

9. Select Output 0 and set the SynchronousInputID to None. This pane should look like Figure 9-12.

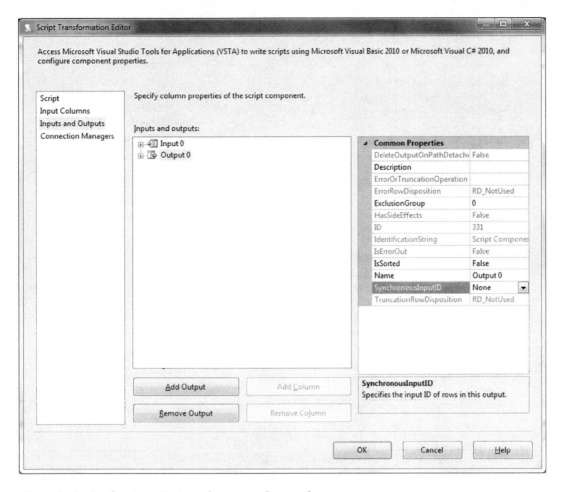

Figure 9-12. *Configuring a Script task output to be asynchronous*

10. Click Script, select Microsoft Visual Basic 2010 as the script language, followed by Edit Script.

11. In the Script window, add the following directive to the Imports region:

```
Imports System.Text
```

12. Replace the ScriptMain code with the following script (C:\SQL2012DIRecipes\CH09\SSISConcatenation.vb):

```
Public Class ScriptMain
    Inherits UserComponent

    Dim InitValue As String = ""
    Dim ControlValue As String = ""
    Dim CurrentElement As String = ""
    Dim ConcatValue As New StringBuilder
    Dim ConcatCharacter As String = ","
```

499

```
        Public Overrides Sub PreExecute()
            MyBase.PreExecute()
        End Sub

        Public Overrides Sub PostExecute()
            MyBase.PostExecute()
        End Sub

        Public Overrides Sub Input0_ProcessInput(ByVal Buffer As Input0Buffer)

            While Buffer.NextRow()
                Input0_ProcessInputRow(Buffer)
            End While

            If Buffer.EndOfRowset Then

                Output0Buffer.AddRow()
                Output0Buffer.GroupOutput = ControlValue
                Output0Buffer.ListOutput = ConcatValue.Remove(ConcatValue.Length - 1, ↵
                                        1).ToString
                Output0Buffer.SetEndOfRowset()

            End If

        End Sub

        Public Overrides Sub Input0_ProcessInputRow(ByVal Row As Input0Buffer)

            ' If first record - initialise variables
            If InitValue = "" Then
                InitValue = Row.ClientID.ToString
                ControlValue = Row.ClientID.ToString
            End If

            CurrentElement = Row.InvoiceNumber.ToString
            ControlValue = Row.ClientID.ToString

            'Process all records
            If InitValue = ControlValue Then

                ConcatValue = ConcatValue.Append(CurrentElement).Append(ConcatCharacter)

            Else
                ' Write grouping element and concatenated string to new outputs
                Output0Buffer.AddRow()
                Output0Buffer.ListOutput = ConcatValue.Remove(ConcatValue.Length - 1, ↵
                                        1).ToString
                Output0Buffer.GroupOutput = InitValue
```

```
                InitValue = Row.ClientID.ToString
                ConcatValue = ConcatValue.Remove(0, ↵
                            ConcatValue.Length).Append(CurrentElement). ↵
                            Append(ConcatCharacter)


            End If
        End Sub

    End Class
```

13. Close the Script window, and click OK to close the Script Task Editor.

14. Add an OLEDB destination task, configure it to use the CarSales_Staging_OLEDB connection manager.

15. Click New to create a destination table, which you can rename if you wish. Click OK to confirm the table creation. Next, click Mappings and map the source to destination columns. Click OK to complete the destination task.

You can now output the data from the Script task directly to a Data Flow destination, or continue to process the data with further transforms.

How It Works

You may also need to concatenate strings in SSIS, as well. This can be done in a few ways, but I will stick to explaining a custom SSIS script task, which achieves the desired result quickly and painlessly.

The script performs essentially one task—it processes every record in the input, and checks whether the "grouping" field (here the ClientID) has changed from the previous record. If this field has not changed, then the field containing the value to be concatenated (InvoiceNumber) is added to the ConcatValue variable. If it has changed, a new record is added to the output buffer, and the two fields (ListOutput containing the concatenated fields, and GroupOutput containing the "grouping" field) are added to the output buffer.

Here I have used a comma as the separator—you may choose the separator used in your source data, and modify the code accordingly. Should the data not be sorted before it is processed by the script task, you will have to add a sort task and ensure that it is ordered by (at the very least) the "grouping" field (ClientID in this example).

The script uses the ProcessInputRow overridden method, which you are probably used to, as it is used to process all the records in the input buffer as they flow through the script task. You might be less familiar with the ProcessInputoverridden method. This is required for an asynchronous function, detects the end of the recordset being processed, and then finalizes any required processing.

You may prefer not to use a StringBuilder (hence the need to reference System.Text) than a string for concatenation. Be warned, however that StringBuilder can be much faster and more efficient. This is because that it will not be destroyed and re-created in memory each time that it is changed, as is the case with a string. However, its efficiency will depend on the number of concatenations and the length of the result. So feel free to compare and test the two possibilities.

▓ **Note** This is an asynchronous transform, and so it will not only block the data flow until it has finished, but it will add considerable memory pressure to the whole SSIS package.

9-10. Duplicating Columns

Problem

You need to create duplicate columns in your data.

Solution

Alias the same column multiple times in T-SQL or use the SSIS Derived Column transform.

In T-SQL, creating a duplicate column can be done using the following code snippet:

```
SELECT
ClientName, ClientName AS EsteemedVisitor
FROM CarSales.dbo.Client;
```

In SSIS, you can add a Derived Column transform to a data flow and connect it to the Source task (or any task in the data flow). Double-click the Derived Column transform and add a new column name to the Derived Column Name field in the grid. Then expand Columns in the top left of the dialog box and drag the appropriate column name to the Expression field. You can then click OK to close the dialog box. The new column will appear in the data flow from this task onward.

How It Works

At the risk of stating the obvious, you can duplicate any input column as part of a data transformation with majestic ease. In T-SQL, all you need to do is alias the column. In SSIS, you use the Derived Column transform as part of a data flow. Remember that in the latter case, you can replace an existing column or add a new column to the data flow. You cannot change the data type, however, and will have to do this using a separate Data Conversion transform.

9-11. Converting Strings to Uppercase or Lowercase

Problem

You wish to convert all or part of a string to uppercase or lowercase as part of a data flow or after data has been loaded into an SQL Server table.

Solution

Use the UPPER and LOWER functions in T-SQL and SSIS to perform character case conversion.

How It Works

The solution is fortunately extremely simple. You convert strings to uppercase or lowercase with the following functions:

	T-SQL	SSIS
Uppercase conversion	UPPER(Column or Column alias)	UPPER(Column name in dataflow)
Lowercase conversion	LOWER(Column or Column alias)	LOWER(Column name in dataflow)

In SSIS, converting text to uppercase or lowercase can be carried out using a Derived Column transform. If you take the example given in Recipe 9-12, you can use the SSIS UPPER or LOWER functions on the column selected as the Expression.

While this may be considered a first step on the primrose path to the everlasting bonfire of data cleansing (a subject that I wish in large part to avoid because it could easily become the subject of a separate tome that I have no intention of attempting to write), it is nonetheless worth a short detour into the arena of simple character transformation—if only to clarify basic techniques. So that is the UPPER and LOWER functions dealt with.

9-12. Converting Strings to Title Case

Problem

You wish to convert all or part of a string to title case, which is where Each First Character Is In Uppercase.

Solution

Title case in SSIS can be generated as part of a script transform. In T-SQL, you are probably best using a CLR function. Next, I explain how to use both of these options. I presume in this recipe that an SSIS package with data source and destination already exist.

Title Case Using SSIS

1. Add a Script component to the Data Flow pane. Select Transformation as the type of operation. Double click to edit.

2. Click Input Columns in the left-hand pane. Select the column(s) to be converted to Proper Case. In this example, it will be the InvoiceNumber column.

3. Click Inputs and Outputs in the left-hand pane. Click Output Columns, and then click Add Column to add a column. Name it **ProperOut**. Ensure that the data type corresponds to the type and length of the input column.

4. Click Script in the left-hand pane. Select Microsoft Visual Basic 2010 as the script language, followed by Edit Script.

5.   Add the following script:

```
Public Overrides Sub Input0_ProcessInputRow(ByVal Row As Input0Buffer)

        Dim cultureInfo As System.Globalization.CultureInfo = ↵
            System.Threading.Thread.CurrentThread.CurrentCulture
        Dim textInfo As TextInfo = cultureInfo.TextInfo

        If Not Row.InvoiceNumber_IsNull Then
            Row.ProperOut = textInfo.ToTitleCase(Row.InvoiceNumber)
        End If
    End Sub
End Sub
```

6.   Compile the script by selecting Build ➤ Build (project reference). Close the Script
     window and click OK to finish creating the script task.

Title Case Using T-SQL

As this solution uses CLR, I refer you to Recipe 10-21 for details on how exactly to create a CLR function. The
code for this function (named, imaginatively "FncProperCase") is (C:\SQL2012DIRecipes\CH09\TitleCase.vb):

```
using System;
using System.Data;
using System.Collections;
using System.Data.SqlTypes;
using System.Data.SqlClient;
using Microsoft.SqlServer.Server;
using System.Globalization;

public partial class UserDefinedFunctions
{
    [Microsoft.SqlServer.Server.SqlFunction(IsDeterministic = true, IsPrecise = true)]
    public static SqlString FncProperCase(string inputData)
    {

        System.Globalization.CultureInfo cultureInfo = ↵
                        System.Threading.Thread.CurrentThread.CurrentCulture;
        TextInfo textInfo = cultureInfo.TextInfo;

        inputData = textInfo.ToTitleCase(inputData);

        return new SqlString(inputData);
    }
};
```

Once your CLR function has been loaded into SQL Server, the T-SQL to call it is:

```
SELECT
dbo.FncProperCase(LOWER(ClientName))
FROM dbo.Clients;
```

How It Works

Proper case in SSIS is not so simple—but is not really difficult either, because the .NET framework has the ToTitleCase function as part of the TextInfo class. So calling this function can solve a host of problems. It is not perfect, and there are a few annoying conversions that it will not handle, but if you can put up with the annoyances, it is remarkably useful.

Proper case in T-SQL function can be achieved using "stringwalking" code, but such an approach is likely to be unbelievably slow in an ETL scenario. The code can be extremely laborious to write, too. So I propose wrapping the .NET TextInfo call in an SQL Server CLR function instead. Doing that can slow down the processing of your data considerably. However, the sheer simplicity and reliability of the solution makes it very tempting, so I have shown it to you despite the unavoidable performance hit due to the row by row processing imposed by a function call.

Hints, Tips, and Traps

- Another option—that still uses a script component—is a regular expression. How to use a regular expression in a script component is explained in Recipe 10-20. Consequently, all you have to do is find a decent piece of Regex code that will apply a good, proper case conversion. There are several available if you type **regex proper case** into your preferred search engine.

- You must first convert the field to LOWER—unless you want it left in UPPER case—as this .NET function will not override uppercase characters and convert them to proper case.

- You can use the function as part of a T-SQL UPDATE clause, of course.

9-13. PIVOTing Data in T-SQL
Problem

You want to pivot data that has already been loaded into an SQL Server database.

Solution

Use the T-SQL PIVOT keyword as part of a data update process.

Pivoting data using T-SQL is not technically difficult, and becomes surprisingly easy with a bit of practice. The following is the T-SQL to pivot and aggregate data for car sales per marque/per month, using the CarSales.dbo.Stock table from the CarSales database (C:\SQL2012DIRecipes\CH09\PivotData.sql):

```
SELECT
Marque AS TotalMonthlySalesPerMarque, [January], [February], [March], [April], [May],
[June], [July], [August], [September], [October], [November], [December]
FROM
        (
          SELECT
          S.Marque
          ,DATENAME(month, I.InvoiceDate) AS SaleMonth
```

```
        ,L.SalePrice
    FROM    dbo.Stock S
            INNER JOIN dbo.Invoice_Lines L
            ON S.ID = L.StockID
            INNER JOIN dbo.Invoice I
            ON L.InvoiceID = I.ID
    ) AS SRC
PIVOT
(
SUM(SalePrice)
FOR SaleMonth IN ([January], [February], [March], [April], [May], [June], [July],
[August], [September], [October], [November], [December])
) AS PVT
;
```

How It Works

Sometimes source data, even perfectly normalized source data, just does not fit the requirements of an import process. While this is more particularly the case when creating reporting systems, it can also occur with more traditional data import requirements. So it helps to be able to pivot source data—and transpose the data from rows into columns. Of course, this is a data denormalization, and worse, it will cause data to be aggregated to a point where it will become impossible to reconstitute the source. However, as long as you are aware of the limitations and risks, it is a valid and useful technique in certain circumstances.

Before proceeding with a more detailed explanation of the code, it is probably worth clarifying the underlying concepts and vocabulary.

Data Type	Comments
Pass-through	Data that is not affected by the transposition and that flows through the process as left-hand column(s) without being modified in any way—or without modifying the data.
Key or Set Key	Grouping data that appears as left-hand column(s).
Pivot Column	Data from a column that will be transposed into column titles.
Pivot Data	Data from the pivot column that will be transposed and aggregated into the relevant pivot column and row intersection.

In this example, the inner SELECT statement returns the three columns that will be used to transpose the data:

> *A **Key column**,* which will be the left-hand column (Marque in this example). There can be as many of these as you wish.
>
> *The **pivot column*** (the SaleMonth derived from the InvoiceDate column).
>
> *The **pivot data*** (or value column) that is aggregated and transposed (SalePrice).

This inline query—that is aliased as SRC—is then PIVOTed. This means specifying:

- Which column is aggregated (SalePrice) and which aggregation function is applied—SUM in this example.

- How the column that will be transposed is extrapolated into multiple columns. This means specifying the column names.

Finally, the outer SELECT specifies the pass-through columns (taken from the inline query) and the transposed columns (taken from the PIVOT statement) that will be returned.

Inevitably, this is a fairly rigid approach since the pivoted columns have to be specified unequivocally for the statement to work. It is also possible if you really wish (and was the approach that was used in the dark days before SQL Server 2005) to use multiple CASE statements to transpose columns. I will leave this approach to the history books. Most examples of pivoted data show the transposed columns as dates (years, years, and months, etc.). This is in no way compulsory, and any source data column can be pivoted.

It is also possible to make the SQL dynamic, and so to allow for variable input data—up to a point. This approach boils down to determining the list of pivoted columns, as a variable, and then using this variable inside the T-SQL that pivots the data—itself defined as a T-SQL variable.

If we take the preceding example, the code for dynamic T-SQ pivoting is (C:\SQL2012DIRecipes\CH09\DynamicPivot.sql):

```
DECLARE @ColumnList VARCHAR(8000)
SELECT
@ColumnList = LEFT(TR.ColList, LEN(TR.ColList)-1)
FROM
            (
              SELECT QUOTENAME(DATENAME(month, InvoiceDate)) + ',' AS [text()]
              FROM    dbo.Invoice
              GROUP BY DATENAME(month, InvoiceDate), MONTH(InvoiceDate)
              ORDER BY MONTH(InvoiceDate)
              FOR XML PATH('')
            ) TR (ColList);


DECLARE @TransposeSQL VARCHAR(MAX) = '
SELECT
Marque AS TotalMonthlySalesPerMarque, '+ @ColumnList + '
FROM
            (
              SELECT
              S.Marque
              ,DATENAME(month, I.InvoiceDate) AS SaleMonth
              ,L.SalePrice
              FROM    dbo.Stock S
                      INNER JOIN dbo.Invoice_Lines L
                      ON S.ID = L.StockID
                      INNER JOIN dbo.Invoice I
                      ON L.InvoiceID = I.ID
            ) AS SRC
PIVOT
(
SUM(SalePrice)
FOR SaleMonth IN ('+ @ColumnList + ')
) AS PVT
;'
EXECUTE CarSales.dbo.sp_executesql @statement = @TransposeSQL;
```

Hints, Tips, and Traps

- Though not inelegant, this approach is not without its problems. Specifically, when outputting the data, you need to be able to analyze the metadata of the destination table, and add new columns if they do not exist when compared to the list of transposed columns in the PIVOT statement. While not difficult, this is a little laborious, and I will not be showing how to do it here.

9-14. Pivoting Data in SSIS with SQL Server 2012
Problem

You need to pivot data as part of an SSIS data flow.

Solution

Use the new, simplified SSIS 2012 pivot task, as follows.

1. Create a new SSIS Package and add an OLEDB connection manager named **CarSales_OLEDB**.

2. Add an OLEDB Source component, and configure as follows:

OLEDB Connection Manager: CarSales_OLEDB

Data Access Mode: SQLCommand

SQL Command Text:
```
SELECT   S.Marque
,DATENAME(month, I.InvoiceDate) AS SaleMonth
,L.SalePrice
FROM        dbo.Stock S
            INNER JOIN dbo.Invoice_Lines L
            ON S.ID = L.StockID
            INNER JOIN dbo.Invoice I
            ON L.InvoiceID = I.ID
            ORDER BY S.Marque, MONTH( I.InvoiceDate);
```

3. Confirm with OK.

4. Add a Pivot task and connect the OLEDB source component to it. Double-click to edit.

5. Click the Pivot Key pop-up list. Select the column that contains the pivot key (or pivot column if you prefer) data. This will become the new column title taken from a source column of data. In this example it is SaleMonth.

6. Click the Set Key pop-up list and select the column that contains the data that will be grouped into the leftmost column of the pivot table. In this example, it is Marque.

7. Click the Pivot Value pop-up list and select the column whose data will be aggregated for each row in the pivot table.

8. Click in the "Generate pivot output columns from values" field and replace [value1],[value2],[value3] with the list of new column headers for the pivot key. These should correspond to the distinct values in the Set Key list.

9. Click Generate Columns Now. Confirm the dialog box that confirms the column list. The dialog box should look like Figure 9-13.

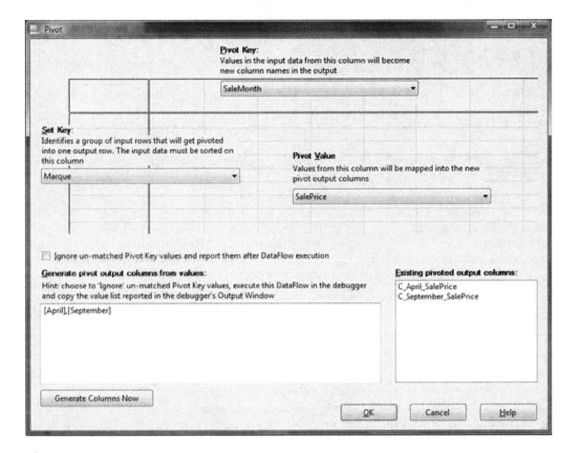

Figure 9-13. *Pivoting data in SSIS 2012*

10. Confirm with OK.

You can now run the package and unpivot the source data.

How It Works

If you have suffered with the trickier aspects of the SSIS pivot task, then you will no doubt be relieved to know that SQL Server 2012 makes this particular process so much easier thanks to a much enhanced user interface that guides you through the pivot process to a large extent.

What is essential to understand are the following four concepts:

Pass-through elements (data that is not affected by the pivot operation).

The key or **Set Key** (the grouping element).

The **pivot column** (transposed into column titles from row elements).

The **pivot data**.

Once you have established that, all you have to do is to select the relevant column in the dialog box shown in Figure 9-15.

Another way to return the list of Pivot Key values is to use SQL to generate a concatenated list of field names using a variation on the concatenation technique described in Recipe 9-8. It could be something like this:

```
SELECT
LEFT(CA. CnCatLst, LEN(CA. CnCatLst)-1)
FROM
            (
            SELECT    '[' + DATENAME(month, I.InvoiceDate) + '],' AS [text()]
            FROM      CarSales.dbo.Invoice I
            GROUP BY  DATENAME(month, I.InvoiceDate)
            FOR XML PATH('')
            ) CA (CnCatLst) ;
```

Hints, Tips, and Traps

- This new SSIS task may not be perfect, admittedly. However, it does make pivoting data in SSIS much easier.

- If you have a long list of pivoted columns, then you can obtain their names by checking the "Ignore unmatched Pivot Key values and report them after execution" box. Then run the package and select View/Output. The missing fields will be listed as information in the Output window. You can copy and paste them from there into the Pivot task editor. You must define at least one pivot column first,however. The PIVOT task will only use the SUM function, no other aggregations (count, average, etc.) are possible.

- You must SORT on the Key column(s) in the source component SQL (if importing using SQL to define the source data) or using a Sort transform (if there is no other way of ensuring sorted data) to ensure that all pivots for an identical key appear on the same row. Otherwise, the results will be more than a little surprising.

- If there are multiple pass-through columns, only the first value is returned—there is no concatenation.

- Duplicate records will cause failure ("duplicate rows" means rows that have the same values in the set Key columns and the Pivot columns, only no other data is analyzed). Use SELECT DISTINCT (if duplicates) or GROUP BY/SUM (to preaggregate) in the source SQL or add an Aggregate transform before the PIVOT transform if you want to avoid an apparently inexplicable (and extremely annoying) apparent failure.

- The limitations described in the last two points can be overcome in many cases by extending the SQL SELECT statement used to source the initial data.

9-15. Pivoting Data in SSIS with SQL Server 2005 and 2008

Problem

You need to pivot data as part of an SSIS ETL process using an older version of SSIS.

Solution

Use the SSIS Pivot task. The following steps explain how to do this.

1. As the first three steps using SQL Server 2012 are identical to those required for previous versions, you need to carry out steps 1 to 3 from Recipe 9-16.

2. Click the Input Columns tab and select the three input columns: Marque, SaleMonth, and SalePrice.

3. Click the Input and Output properties tab and expand Pivot Default Input/Input Columns. Configure the PivotUsage properties of the input columns as follows:

    Marque: 1

    SaleMonth: 2

    SalePrice: 3

4. Expand Pivot Default Output/ Output Columns. Click Add Column three times to add the following three columns: Marque, March, and May.

5. Configure the properties of the input columns as follows:

Marque:	SourceColumn (LineageID of the source column Marque.)
March:	SourceColumn (LineageID of the source column SalePrice.)
	PivotKeyValue (March)
May:	SourceColumn (LineageID of the source column SalePrice.)
	PivotKeyValue (May)

6. Confirm with OK.

How It Works

Pivoting data with SQL Server 2005 and 2008 will require some manual intervention that requires you to understand the concepts and data. This can seem somewhat counterintuitive at first, but hopefully will become clearer as you configure an SSIS Pivot task.

As I have suggested before, this is a fairly rigid approach because the pivoted columns have to be defined individually and completely (with none overlooked) for the transform to work. You can anticipate future columns when configuring the task, however. These will contain NULLs until source data becomes available.

There are four potential column types whose PivotUsage must be set for each input column:

- 0 = Pass-through (data that is not affected by the pivot operation)
- 1 = Key or Set Key (the grouping element)
- 2 = Pivot column (transposed into column titles from row elements)
- 3 = Pivot data

For each column (whatever its type among the four defined), you must specify the LineageID of the source column and place this in the SourceColumn property. For the pivot columns only, add the source lineage ID of the VALUE as SourceColumn, and the element from the pivot column as the PivotKeyValue. Add a column title as the **Name**.

Hints, Tips, and Traps

- All the comments which applied to pivoting records in SSIS 2012 in Recipe 9-14 apply equally to older versions of SQL Server.

9-16. Consolidating Multiple Identical Data Sources in T-SQL
Problem

You need to ensure that data from more than one source flows into a unique destination using T-SQL. Your input sources are identical in that they provide the same columns of data.

Solution

Use UNION, UNION ALL, and INTERSECT. For example, the following code snippet will output all the records from the identical source tables (C:\SQL2012DIRecipes\CH09\ConsolidateDateSources.sql):

```
SELECT ClientName, County, Country FROM dbo.Client
UNION ALL
SELECT ClientName, County, Country FROM dbo.Client1;
```

Should you wish to output only the unique values, then use:

```
SELECT ClientName, County, Country FROM dbo.Client
UNION
SELECT ClientName, County, Country FROM dbo.Client1;
```

To return only the records having distinct values that are present and identical in both queries use:

```
SELECT ClientName, Country, Country FROM dbo.Client
INTERSECT
SELECT ClientName, County, Country FROM dbo.Client1;
```

How It Works

There will be many occasions when you will need to ensure that data from more than one source flows into a unique destination. This will probably involve consolidating data from multiple identically structured sources into a single destination, whose structure is also identical to the source.

There are nonetheless some subtle differences in the ways in that these three functions work:

- `UNION ALL`: Duplicate data is allowed into the destination, if present in multiple sources.

- `UNION`: No duplicate data is allowed into the destination.

- `INTERSECT`: Only data present and identical in all the sources is allowed into the destination.

Hints, Tips, and Traps

- In all T-SQL queries for these operators, the number and the order of the columns must be the same and the data types must be compatible.

- When using T-SQL, you are not restricted to data sources from the same database—you can use three-part notation and refer to data sources from another database. What is probably even more important is that you can use four-part notation to use `UNION`/`UNION ALL`/`INTERSECT` and `EXCEPT` across linked servers—or using `OPENDATASOURCE`.

9-17. Consolidating Multiple Identical Data Sources in SSIS

Problem

You need to ensure that data from more than one source flows into a unique destination as part of an SSIS data flow.

Solution

Use the Union All transform—and optionally the Merge transform. The following steps show you how.

1. In an SSIS package, add a Data Source control for each source—whatever the type—and configure to output the same fields.

2. Add a Union All task to the Data Flow pane and connect the output paths from all your data sources to the Union All task.

3. Double-click the Union All task to map the source fields from all the data sources to each other. Click OK to confirm the changes, and continue with the data flow.

Should you wish to remove any duplicates, then perform the following steps.

1. In an SSIS package, add a Data Source control for each of the two sources—whatever the type—and configure to output the same fields using an SQL query. Ensure that the SQL query sorts the data by all the columns.

2. Right-click each of the two sources. Select Show Advanced Editor, then select the Input and Output Properties, and click Source Output. Set the IsSorted property to True. Then expand the Output Columns for the Source Output and select the sort column(s) used in the SORT statement of the data source control. Set their SortKeyPosition to 1, 2, and so forth—corresponding to the sort statement of the data source control.

3. Add a Merge transform to the Data Flow pane and connect the two sources to it. Either can be either of the merge inputs that you will be prompted for.

As a minor extension, should you wish to obtain the same effect as an INTERSECT in SSIS:

1. In an SSIS package, add a Data Source control for each of the two sources—whatever the type—and configure to output the same fields using an SQL query. Ensure that the SQL query sorts the data by all the columns.

2. Right-click each of the two sources. Select Show Advanced Editor, then select the Input and Output Properties, and click Source Output. Set the IsSorted property to True. Then expand the Output Columns for the Source Output, and select the sort column(s) used in the SORT statement of the data source control. Set their SortKeyPosition to 1, 2, and so forth—corresponding to the sort statement of the data source control.

3. Add a Merge Join transform to the Data Flow pane, and connect the two sources to it. Either can be either of the left or right merge inputs that you will be prompted for.

4. Double-click the Merge Join transform to edit it, and ensure that all the columns are flagged as join keys. Select all the columns from one of the data sources. The dialog box should look something like Figure 9-14.

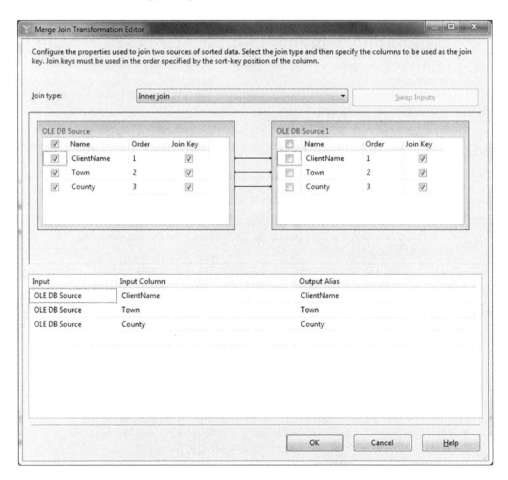

Figure 9-14. *Merge Join key mapping*

5. Click OK to confirm your changes, and continue with the data flow.

How It Works

With a little tweaking, SSIS allows you to do exactly the same thing as T-SQL when it comes to consolidating multiple identical data sources. When amalgamating all the data from multiple sources, SSIS, in effect, allows for two ways of doing this:

- The MERGE transform
- The UNION ALL transform

There are some differences, of course. MERGE is essentially a UNION ALL that requires sorted inputs—and that can only handle two inputs at once. UNION ALL can handle multiple inputs.

To consolidate data and remove duplicates (to imitate a UNION rather than a UNION ALL) in SSIS, simply add a Sort transform downstream of the Merge or Union All transform, and (after defining the sort keys) check "Remove rows with duplicate sort values".

The Union All transform will output all the records from the source tables.

Hints, Tips, and Traps

- To test the output from a Merge Join, Merge, or Union All transform, add a variable (any name, but it must be an integer) and then add a Row Count transform to the output of the transform that will amalgamate the data. Set the Row Count task variable name to the variable that you just created, and once confirmed, add a data viewer on the path from the Merge Join, Merge, or Union All transform to the Row Count transform.

- The Merge Join transform is a blocking join, which can cause considerable memory pressure, and that is reputed to be slower than some other solutions—such as the Lookup transform.

9-18. Normalizing Data Inside a Single Table Using T-SQL

Problem

You need to "unpivot" source data from multiple columns in a single table into a normalized record structure inside the same table.

Solution

Apply the T-SQL UNPIVOT command to create the required extra records inside the data table. The following is an example of how to do this.

1. Create a denormalized data table such as this (C:\SQL2012DIRecipes\CH09\ tblClientList.sql):

```
CREATE TABLE dbo.ClientList
(
 ID INT NULL,
 PrimaryContact NVARCHAR(50) NULL,
 SecondaryContact NVARCHAR(80) NULL,
 ThirdContact NVARCHAR(50) NULL
);
GO
```

2. Apply the following T-SQL snippet to rotate (unpivot) the three columns—
   PrimaryContact, SecondaryContact, and ThirdContact—into one column, CliName. It
   will also add a column named NameType to display the source column for each item of
   data (C:\SQL2012DIRecipes\CH09\Unpivot.sql).

```
SELECT      ID, NameType, UPV.CliName
FROM        CarSales_Staging.dbo.ClientList
UNPIVOT     (CliName FOR NameType in (PrimaryContact, SecondaryContact,
            ThirdContact)) as UPV;
```

How It Works

All too frequently—and probably when importing data from spreadsheets, Access databases, or badly-designed
data sources—you will find that the source data is denormalized. So instead of multiple records, you have data for
the same attribute spread across multiple columns. There are frequent occasions when there is a perfectly valid
reason for this, but when integrating such data into SQL Server, in many cases you will have to normalize it. This
will mean rotating the multiple columns into a single column of data, with an extra (though optional) column
indicating which source column the data came from.

Before SQL Server 2005, this involved hard labor with CASE statements. Fortunately, T-SQL has had the
UNPIVOT clause for several years now, which makes the normalization task much easier. The same functionality is
also available in SSIS, using the UNPIVOT task, as you will see in Recipe 9-19.

Rotating columns of a table-valued expression into column values in T-SQL is as simple as adding an
UNPIVOT clause to the select statement. Essentially you have to select all columns that will not be rotated, and
then add a new column that is aliased in the UNPIVOT statement—and optionally a second column that will
contain the name of the source column.

The only real reproach I can make concerning the UNPIVOT clause is that it is somewhat rigid. I have seen
(and I am sure you have, too) Excel spreadsheets with a variable number of columns containing denormalized
data. Fortunately, a little dynamic SQL can solve this—providing that you are able to specify a common root or
stem to the denormalized column names.

The following T-SQL will unpivot all columns whose names contain the word "contact"—however many
there may be (C:\SQL2012DIRecipes\CH09\DynamicUnpivot.sql):

```
DECLARE @ColList VARCHAR(8000) = '';
DECLARE @SQLCode VARCHAR(8000) = '';
DECLARE @ColFilter VARCHAR(1000) = 'contact';
DECLARE @KeyCol VARCHAR(1000) = 'ID';
DECLARE @TableName VARCHAR(1000) = 'ClientList';

SELECT    @ColList = @ColList + QUOTENAME(COLUMN_NAME) + ','
FROM      INFORMATION_SCHEMA.COLUMNS
WHERE     TABLE_NAME = @TableName
          AND COLUMN_NAME LIKE '%' + @ColFilter + '%';

IF LEN(@ColList) > 1
BEGIN

SET @ColList = LEFT(@ColList, LEN(@ColList) -1 )
```

```
SET @SQLCode =
'
SELECT ' + @KeyCol + ', ContactType, UPV.' + @ColFilter + '
FROM ' + @TableName + '
UNPIVOT (' + @ColFilter + ' FOR ContactType in (' + @ColList + ')) as UPV
';

EXECUTE CarSales_Staging.dbo.sp_executesql @statement =  @SQLCode;

END

ELSE
PRINT 'No Matching columns';
```

The column filter (i.e., the column that specifies the columns to rotate while not including any others) is frequently the hard part of this operation. In a production environment I would advise counting the columns in the source data, counting up any non-pivoted columns, and counting those that are pivoted. Then verifying that all denormalized columns have been unpivoted is easy with a little very basic arithmetic. If you do not want to output the column from that the data was sourced, all you have to do is not add the NameType field to the principal SELECT statement. You must leave it in the PIVOT statement, however. The column aliases for the data column and the source column can be whatever you want (within the limits of SQL Server object naming limitations, of course). Just remember to make them identical between the UNPIVOT clause and the SELECT statement.

Hints, Tips, and Traps

- All the same comments that applied to the standard use of UNPIVOT in Recipe 9-10 apply to the dynamic SQL used here.

9-19. Normalizing Data Inside a Single Table Using SSIS
Problem

You need to "unpivot" source data from multiple columns into normalized records as part of an SSIS data flow.

Solution

Use the SSIS Unpivot Data Flow Transformation to create the required extra records inside the data flow.

To avoid repeating how to connect to a source database in SSIS, I am assuming that you already have an existing SSIS package and that you will be importing data from the CarSales_Staging.dbo.ClientList table. With this assumption, what follows shows how to do it.

1. In the Data Flow pane, add an Unpivot Data Flow Transformation from the toolbox, and connect to the data source (or to the data flow in a complex package).

2. Double-click to edit.

3. Select the left-hand check box for all columns that you want to unpivot.

4. Select the right-hand check box for all columns that you do not want to unpivot.

5.   In the lower part of the dialog box, enter a destination column name for the new column that will hold the unpivoted data. Do this for every input column that will be unpivoted.

6.   At the bottom of the dialog box, enter a "Pivot key value column name". In this example it is **NameType**. This will be the second new column that will contain the title that you will see for the source data column in the denormalized data source. The dialog box should look something like Figure 9-15.

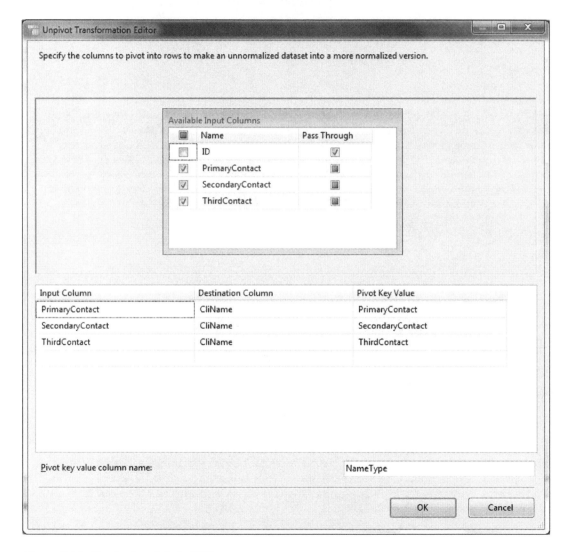

Figure 9-15. *Unpivoting data in SSIS*

7.   Click OK to confirm your modifications. You can then add a Data Flow destination, or further transforms.

How It Works

The SSIS Unpivot task does exactly what its name implies—it unpivots data from a source table. First, you have to specify any fields that will not be pivoted. These are set as Pass Though fields. In this example, there is only one, and it is the ID field. Then you must select all the columns that will be pivoted and preferably give them all the same destination column name. They are the Contact fields here. Finally, you indicate to SSIS the title of the column containing the values to use as data (NameType in this example).

Hints, Tips, and Traps

- If you want to be sure that the normalization has worked, try adding a data grid viewer after the Unpivot transform. It could look something like Figure 9-16.

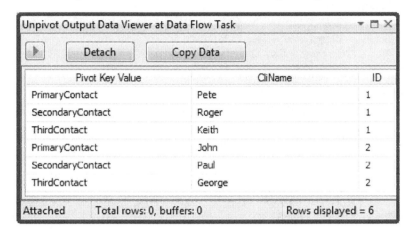

Figure 9-16. *Using a data viewer to examine unpivoted data in SSIS*

- A destination column name is not compulsory—if you will not be using it in the downstream data flow or data load process.

9-20. Normalizing Data into Multiple Relational Tables Using T-SQL

Problem

You have a single source of data that is denormalized and that you have to normalize into a related table set as part of your data transformation.

Solution

Use T-SQL to normalize data. Suppose you have a denormalized data source (one table) that has to be transformed into a relational hierarchy of three tables:

> **Clients:** The top-level table.

> **Invoice:** A second level in the table hierarchy, which has as a foreign key the ClientID that maps to the client level.

> **Invoice_Lines:** The third and final level in the table hierarchy, which has as the InvoiceID foreign key that maps to the Invoice level.

Your data will come from a single source table (CarSales_Staging.dbo.DenormalisedSales) that, incidentally, lends itself to being normalized. You will need to run the following T-SQL (`C:\SQL2012DIRecipes\CH09\NormaliseData.sql`):

```
-- Add Clients
INSERT INTO        dbo.Client (ClientName, Country, Town)

SELECT DISTINCT    ClientName, Country, Town
FROM               CarSales_Staging.dbo.DenormalisedSales DNS
WHERE NOT EXISTS   (
                      SELECT   ID
                      FROM     dbo.Client
                      WHERE    ClientName = DNS.ClientName
                      AND      Country = DNS.Country AND Town = DNS.Town
                   );

-- Add Order Header
INSERT INTO        dbo.Invoice (InvoiceNumber, TotalDiscount, DeliveryCharge, ClientID)

SELECT DISTINCT    DS.InvoiceNumber, DS.TotalDiscount, DS.DeliveryCharge, CL.ID
FROM               dbo.DenormalisedSales DS
                   INNER JOIN dbo.Client CL
                   ON   CL.ClientName = DS.ClientName
                   AND  CL.Country = DS.Country
                   AND  CL.Town = DS.Town;

-- Add order detail
INSERT INTO        dbo.Invoice_Lines (SalePrice, StockID, InvoiceID)

SELECT DISTINCT    DS.SalePrice, DS.StockID, IV.ID
FROM               CarSales_Staging.dbo.DenormalisedSales DS
                   INNER JOIN dbo.Invoice IV
                   ON   IV.InvoiceNumber = DS.InvoiceNumber;
```

How It Works

It is frequent to receive data as a single denormalized source (be it a flat file or a relational table) that has to be "broken down" into a relational structure of multiple tables—or in a word, normalized. What this script does is to parse each level in the table hierarchy. Starting with the highest (client) level it extracts client data into a first table. Then the Invoice data is isolated into an Invoice table, and finally the order detail data is deduced. The essential aspect to retain is that it is a "top to bottom" approach. This means that you must begin with the highest table in the relational hierarchy, and work down to the lowest. Each of the "lower" tables contains a foreign key that contains the primary key of the table "above" in the relational hierarchy. Exactly how this will work in your data context is likely to vary hugely, but here you have an overall approach that you can take and adapt to your specific circumstances.

In this recipe, I am deliberately assuming a minimal level of complexity—notably assuming that the natural IDs in the source data have to be mapped to surrogate IDs in the destination data tables. If this is not the case, then you can simply use the surrogate IDs where they exist as primary and foreign keys. In this example, if the InvoiceNumber were to be kept instead of the InvoiceID as the primary/foreign key relationship between the

Invoice and Invoice_Lines tables, you would not need to lookup the InvoiceID at the OrderDetail stage. One thing to bear in mind is that you may not always be facing denormalized source data, but could have to denormalize data in order to renormalize using a different relational structure. Also remember that this approach will work across databases (three part references) as well as across linked servers (four part references) and using OPENROWSET or OPENDATASOURCE. This example shows how to avoid creating duplicate client records using WHERE NOT EXISTS. This statement can be omitted if you are sure that there cannot be duplicates in the source data, as it will slow the process down. It can also be added and modified for all sublevels of the normalization process.

Hints, Tips, and Traps

- For large tables, you will not only need effective indexes in place on the foreign key columns of the destination tables, but probably judiciously chosen nonclustered covering indexes on the columns used to lookup the foreign keys as well. Here, the INCLUDE statement will have to contain the foreign keys (InvoiceID and ClientID).

- If the data source is a table, given that it will be reused in multiple queries, it is nearly always worthwhile indexing it. The exact indexing structure will depend on the data, and the ratios of records between each normalized table. However it is a good rule of thumb to create a clustered index on the elements that identify the highest level of data (Clients in this example), followed by covering non-clustered indexes on the elements that isolate each sublevel (and that map to a related table). These are InvoiceNumber and InvoiceID in this example.

- If you will be inserting and updating data, then it is probably better—and safer—to carry out the initial normalization to staging tables, cross-reference these to the destination tables to lookup IDs from the destination tables and finally perform any upserts. To speed things up you can use temporary tables as staging tables, and index them if necessary.

- Instead of INSERT INTO, you can use MERGE (although not in SQL Server 2005) so that you not only insert new records but also update old ones. In most cases, this will necessitate a natural ID (or columns that will not be updated) as part of the ON clause. For a fuller example of MERGE, see Recipe 9-24.

9-21. Normalizing Data into Multiple Relational Tables Using SSIS
Problem

You have a single source of data that is denormalized and that you have to normalize as part of your data flow using SSIS.

Solution

Use the SSIS Lookup transform to normalize data. The following steps explain how to do it using the same source and destination tables as in the Recipe 9-20.

1. Create a new package and add two OLEDB connection managers (**CarSales_OLEDB** and **CarSales_Staging_OLEDB**) that are configured to access the CarSales and CarSales_Staging databases, respectively.

2. Delete any data in the tables Clients, Invoice and Invoice_Lines in the database CarSales.

3. Add a Data Flow task, name it **Clients**, and double-click to edit.

4. Add an OLEDB source task and configure it as follows:

Name:	Denormalized Source
OLEDB Connection Manager:	CarSales_Staging_OLEDB
Data Access Mode:	SQL Command
SQL Command Text:	

```
SELECT    ClientName, Country, Town
FROM      dbo.DenormalisedSales
GROUP BY  ClientName, Country, Town
ORDER BY  ClientName, Country, Town;
```

5. Click OK to confirm your modifications.

6. Right-click the OLEDB source task and select Show Advanced Editor. Select Input and Output properties. Set the IsSorted property of the OLEDB Source Output to True. Expand the OLEDB Source Output/Output columns. Set the SortKeyPosition for the columns that make up the unique key (ClientName, Country, Town) to 1, 2, and 3. Confirm your changes with OK.

7. Add a Lookup transform on to the Data Flow pane, and connect the OLEDB source task to it. Configure it as follows:

General

Cache Mode:	Full Cache
Connection Type:	OLEDB Connection
Rows with no matching entries:	Redirect to NoMatch output

Connection

Connection Manager:	CarSales_OLEDB
Use the results of an SQL query:	

```
SELECT    ClientName, Country, Town, ID
FROM      dbo.Client
ORDER BY  ClientName, Country, Town;
```

Columns:	Map the columns ClientName, Country, Town
Available Lookup Columns:	ID

8. Confirm your changes with OK.

9. Add an OLEDB destination task to the Data Flow pane. Connect the Lookup task to it using the NoMatch output. Double-click to edit and configure as follows:

OLEDB Connection Manager:	CarSales_OLEDB
Data Access Mode:	Table or view – Fast Load
Name of Table or View:	dbo.Client

10. Confirm your changes using OK.

11. Return to the Control Flow pane and add a second Data Flow task. Name it **Invoice** and double-click to edit.

12. Repeat steps 3 to 6, but with the following modifications:

OLEDB source task (step 3):

SQL Command Text:	SELECT InvoiceNumber, TotalDiscount, DeliveryCharge, ClientName, Country, Town FROM dbo.DenormalisedSales GROUP BY InvoiceNumber, TotalDiscount, DeliveryCharge, ClientName, Country, Town ORDER BY ClientName, Country, Town;

Lookup task (step 6):

Rows with no matching entries:	Fail Component
Connection:	Use the results of an SQL query: SELECT ClientName, Country, Town, ID FROM dbo.Client ORDER BY ClientName, Country, Town;
Columns:	Map the columnsClientName, Country, Town
Available Lookup Columns:	ID – output aliasClientID

OLEDB destination task (step 8):

Name of Table or View:	dbo.Invoice

13. Return to the Control Flow pane and add a second Data Flow task. Name it **Invoice_Lines** and double-click to edit.

14. Repeat steps 3 to 6, but with the following modifications:

OLEDB source task (step 3):

SQL Command Text:	SELECT InvoiceNumber, SalePrice, StockID FROM dbo.DenormalisedSales ORDER BY InvoiceNumber;

Lookup task (step 6):

Rows with no matching entries:	Fail Component
Connection:	Use the results of an SQL query:

```
SELECT    ID, InvoiceNumber
FROM      dbo.Invoice
ORDER BY  InvoiceNumber;
```

Columns:	Map the columns InvoiceNumber
Available Lookup Columns:	ID – output aliasInvoiceID

OLEDB destination task (step 8):

Name of Table or View:	dbo.Invoice_Lines

The final package should look like Figure 9-17.

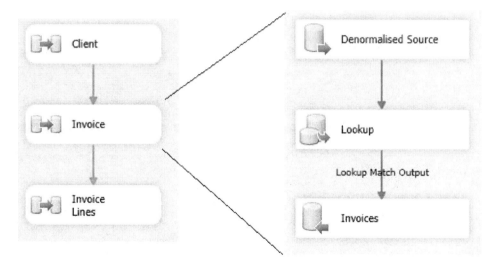

Figure 9-17. *An SSIS data normalization package*

How It Works

SSIS can perform essentially the same sequence of operations as T-SQL can to normalize a denormalized data source. It also means starting from the highest-level entity (client in this example) and working down through the related entities (via InvoicetoInvoice_Lines, here). Normalization always means understanding the way that you will break down the source data into a relational structure and how you will map relationships between the tables. When using SSIS, it is extremely important to have this clear in your mind before starting to create a package, because it underpins the way that you will be using Lookup transforms to find the foreign keys for each table.

At the top (Client table) level we are detecting existing clients by using a Lookup transform to read the existing client data and only add those clients that do not already exist by using the Lookup NoMatch output. If you are only adding new data, then this step is not necessary.

As in the T-SQL solution described previously, this process starts with the highest-level table in the relational hierarchy (Clients) and works down through Invoices to Invoice_Lines. First, the client data is extracted. This is done by selecting unique client data using a GROUP BY clause (step 3). Any *new* clients are added to the destination table (Clients). New records are detected by using a Lookup transform where only records that are not found are allowed through into the destination table. The second Data Flow task isolates any Invoice data and uses a Lookup task to deduce the ClientID. This will be the foreign key in the relational schema. Finally a similar process is applied to Invoice_Lines, only here it is the InvoiceID that is found using the Lookup task.

Hints, Tips, and Traps

- You cannot use a lookup cache for the client IDs when detecting existing clients and looking up client IDs for invoices because the data will change once new clients are added, which makes the cache outdated.

9-22. Denormalizing Data by Referencing Lookup Tables in T-SQL
Problem

You want to ensure that reference (or lookup) tables are used correctly when denormalizing data in a table that has already been loaded into SQL Server.

Solution

Make careful use of basic JOINs to ensure that lookup tables are used properly in the data source.

Here I take Recipe 9-21 as an example. If you look at step 3 and presume that the Country field must be used to obtain the ID of the country from the Countries table, the following T-SQL snippet can be used to replace the "simple" SELECT that looks up only Client information (C:\SQL2012DIRecipes\CH09\LookupNormalisation.sql):

```
SELECT DISTINCT      DNS.ClientName, DNS.Country, DNS.Town, C.ID AS CountryID
FROM                 CarSales_Staging.dbo.DenormalisedSales DNS
                     INNER JOIN CarSales_Staging.dbo.Countries C
                     ON DNS.Country = C.CountryCode
WHERE NOT EXISTS     (
                     SELECT ID
                     FROM dbo.Client
                     WHERE ClientName = DNS.ClientName
                     AND Country = DNS.Country
                     AND Town = DNS.Town
                     );
```

How It Works

Using this T-SQL instead of the original code in Recipe 9-21 will import the relevant country name instead of its ID. This is a fairly "classic" requirement to avoid excessive normalization and the over-use of lookup tables when you consider that the data architecture does not require such a finely-grained level of normalization.

Hints, Tips, and Traps

- Should you need to allow NULLs, then use a LEFT OUTER JOIN instead of an INNER JOIN.

- You can perform multiple lookups in a single T-SQL statement, of course. However, be aware that too many of them will slow down the process.

9-23. Denormalizing Data by Referencing Lookup Tables in SSIS

Problem

You want to ensure that lookup tables are properly referenced during an ETL process using SSIS to avoid excessive normalization of data.

Solution

Use the Lookup component as part of the data flow, and map the data adequately to use the lookup data in place of the reference code in the source. The following is an example.

1. Create a new SSIS package.

2. Add two new OLEDB connection managers. One named **CarSales_OLEDB**, which you configure to connect to the CarSales database, the other named **CarSales_Staging_OLEDB**, which you configure to connect to the CarSales_Staging database.

3. Add a new Flat File connection manager that you configure to connect to the C:\SQL2012DIRecipes\CH09\ClientList.Csvfile. Name it **ClientList**. In the Advanced tab, set the data types for the three columns as follows:

ID:	Four-byte signed integer
ClientName:	string [DT_STR] – length of 50
ClientCountry:	Single-byte unsigned integer

4. Create the following destination table (in the CarSales_Staging database):

    ```
    CREATE TABLE dbo.ClientWithCountry
    (
     ID numeric(20, 0) NULL,
     ClientName VARCHAR(50) NULL,
     CountryName_EN NVARCHAR(50) NULL
    );
    GO
    ```

5.   Add a Data Flow task and switch to the Data Flow pane.

6.   Add a Flat File source component and rename it **ClientList**. Double-click to edit.

7.   Configure it to point to the Flat File connection manager ClientList. Click OK to close the Flat File Source Editor.

8.   Add a Sort task and connect the Flat File source component to it. Name it **Sort Clients**. Double-click to edit. In Available Input Columns, check ID to sort on the ID. Click OK to close the Sort Transformation Editor.

9.   Add a Lookup task and connect the Sort Clients task to it. Name it **Lookup Country Name**. Double-click to edit.

10.   In the General tab, set the following options:

Cache Mode:	Full Cache
Connection Type:	OLEDB Connection Manager
Specify how to handle rows with no matching entries:	Redirect Rows to NoMatch output

11.   In the Connection tab, set the following options:

OLEDB Connection Manager:	CarSales_OLEDB	
Use the results of an SQL Query:	SELECT	CountryID, CountryName_EN
	FROM	Countries
	ORDER BY	CountryID

12.   In the Columns tab, drag ClientCountry from the Available Input Columns to link to CountryID in the available Lookup columns, as shown in Figure 9-18.

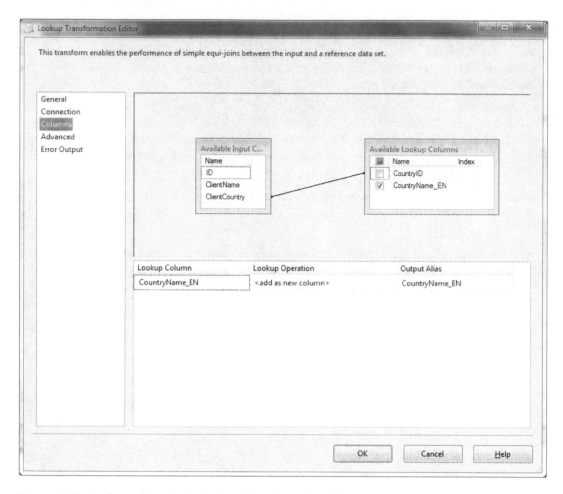

Figure 9-18. Lookup column in the Lookup Transformation Editor

13. Click OK to confirm your modifications.

14. Add a Derived Column task and connect the Lookup task to it. When prompted, select the Lookup NoMatch output. Double-click to edit the Derived Column task.

15. In the grid in the lower half of the Derived Column Transformation Editor dialog box, add a Derived column named **CountryName_EN**. Set its Expression to N/A (in double-quotes). Click OK to confirm your modifications.

16. Add a Merge task to the Data flow pane. Connect the Lookup Country Name task to it. When prompted, ensure that the Input is Merge Input 1 and that the Output is Lookup Match Output. Click OK to confirm this.

17. Connect the Derived Column transform to the Merge task.

18. Add an OLEDB Destination task. Name it **Client With Country**. Double-click to edit and configure as follows:

OLEDB Connection Manager:	CarSales_Staging
Data Access Mode:	Table or View – Fast Load
Name of Table or View:	dbo.ClientWithCountry

19. Click Mappings on the left and ensure that each source field is mapped to the corresponding destination field with the same name. Note that ClientCountry (the source country ID field) is not mapped.

20. Click OK to finish your modifications. The data flow should look like Figure 9-19.

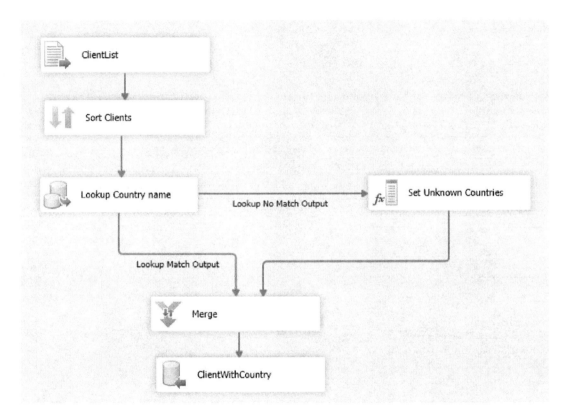

Figure 9-19. *The completed data flow when denormalizing data using a Lookup task*

You can now run the package and import and denormalize the data.

How It Works

This process uses a reference column (ClientCountry in the source file) and uses this to look up the corresponding country in a reference table (CarSales.Dbo.Countries). As this approach will exclude any source records without a corresponding reference element, the NoMatch output is also used, and merged with the "match" output to ensure that all records are sent to the destination. In effect, this process replaces an ID for a country with the country name.

Hints, Tips, and Traps

- When mapping a TINYINT data type in an SQL Server to SSIS, you must set the SSIS data type to a single-byte unsigned integer.

9-24. Processing Type 1 Slowly Changing Dimensions (SCDs) Using T-SQL

Problem

You need to ensure that all the source data in your process is updated in the destination table and any new records added.

Solution

Use the T-SQL MERGE command to both add new records and update existing records. The following steps describe how to do this.

1. Suppose that you have a destination table containing all the values required, a business key (the client ID from the source data), and a surrogate key that will be used for data warehousing. The table's DDL follows (C:\SQL2012DIRecipes\CH09\tblClient_SCD1.sql):

```
CREATE TABLE CarSales_Staging.dbo.Client_SCD1
(
 ClientID INT IDENTITY(1,1) NOT NULL,
 BusinessKey INT NOT NULL,
 ClientName VARCHAR(150) NULL,
 Country VARCHAR(50) NULL,
 Town VARCHAR(50) NULL,
 County VARCHAR(50) NULL,
 Address1 VARCHAR(50) NULL,
 Address2 VARCHAR(50) NULL,
 ClientType VARCHAR(20) NULL,
 ClientSize VARCHAR(10) NULL
) ;
GO
```

2. You can then run this snippet of T-SQL from the CarSales_Staging database (C:\SQL2012DIRecipes\CH09\SCD1.sql):

```
USE CarSales_Staging;
GO

MERGE    CarSales_Staging.dbo.Client_SCD1      AS DST
USING    CarSales.dbo.Client     AS SRC
ON       (SRC.ID = DST.BusinessKey)

WHEN NOT MATCHED THEN
```

```
INSERT (BusinessKey, ClientName, Country, Town, County, Address1, Address2,
ClientType, ClientSize)
VALUES (SRC.ID, SRC.ClientName, SRC.Country, SRC.Town, SRC.County, Address1,
Address2, ClientType, ClientSize)

WHEN MATCHED
AND (
            ISNULL(DST.ClientName,'') <> ISNULL(SRC.ClientName,'')
            OR ISNULL(DST.Country,'') <> ISNULL(SRC.Country,'')
            OR ISNULL(DST.Town,'') <> ISNULL(SRC.Town,'')
            OR ISNULL(DST.Address1,'') <> ISNULL(SRC.Address1,'')
            OR ISNULL(DST.Address2,'') <> ISNULL(SRC.Address2,'')
            OR ISNULL(DST.ClientType,'') <> ISNULL(SRC.ClientType,'')
            OR ISNULL(DST.ClientSize,'') <> ISNULL(SRC.ClientSize,'')
        )

THEN UPDATE

SET
        DST.ClientName = SRC.ClientName
       ,DST.Country = SRC.Country
       ,DST.Town = SRC.Town
       ,DST.Address1 = SRC.Address1
       ,DST.Address2 = SRC.Address2
       ,DST.ClientType = SRC.ClientType
       ,DST.ClientSize = SRC.ClientSize
    ;
```

How It Works

Ever since SQL Server 2008 introduced the MERGE command, it has been possible to carry out UPSERTs—Inserts, Deletes, and Updates—using a single command. It is also worth noting that the upsert techniques used to handle slowly changing dimensions are not restricted to the world of data warehousing. A Type 1 SCD is nothing other than an UPSERT, and so is useful in an unlimited range of scenarios.

Of all the SCD types, a Type 1 slowly changing dimension is by far the easiest to handle, as it consists of a simple in-place update of existing data, with no attempt to track the evolution of the changes.

The SQL snippet used will map the two tables on the business key. It will also do the following:

- Insert a new record into the destination table if the record referenced by the business key if the key is not already present (WHEN NOT MATCHED), as well as adding an auto-incremented surrogate key.

- Update the other fields if any of them are different between the source and destination tables (WHEN MATCHED AND...).

I am taking the dbo.Clienttable as the source data from the CarSales database, and updating the data, suitably transformed, in the CarSales_Staging.dbo.Client table. This example presumes that the business key is a unique primary key. I am presuming that we will not be using WHEN NOT MATCHED to delete dimension data, and will only look at UPSERTing data—that is inserting and updating dimension data.

Hints, Tips, and Traps

- Ensure that all columns used to compare data in the WHEN MATCHED ... AND clause are also present in the THEN UPDATE SET clause.

- In this example, I am applying an upsert across databases residing on the same server. This technique can be applied to tables inside the same database or across linked servers.

9-25. Handling Type 2 Slowly Changing Dimensions in T-SQL

Problem

You need to track the changes over time as source data is added, inserted, and updated in a destination table.

Solution

Use T-SQL's MERGE command to carry out UPSERTS as a Type 2 slowly changing dimension and consequently to track the changes over time, as follows.

1. Create a table to hold Type 2 SCD data using the following DDL
   (C:\SQL2012DIRecipes\CH09\tblClient_SCD2.sql):

```
CREATE TABLE CarSales_Staging.dbo.Client_SCD2
(
 ClientID INT IDENTITY(1,1) NOT NULL,
 BusinessKey INT NOT NULL,
 ClientName VARCHAR(150) NULL,
 Country VARCHAR(50) NULL,
 Town VARCHAR(50) NULL,
 County VARCHAR(50) NULL,
 Address1 VARCHAR(50) NULL,
 Address2 VARCHAR(50) NULL,
 ClientType VARCHAR(20) NULL,
 ClientSize VARCHAR(10) NULL,
 ValidFrom INT NULL,
 ValidTo INT NULL,
 IsCurrent BIT  NULL
) ;
GO
```

2. Run the following code to carry out a Type 2 SCD upsert
   (C:\SQL2012DIRecipes\CH09\SCD2.sql):

```
USE CarSales_Staging;
GO

-- Define the dates used in validity - assume whole 24 hour cycles
DECLARE @Yesterday INT = CAST(CAST(YEAR(DATEADD(dd,-1,GETDATE())) AS CHAR(4))
+ RIGHT('0' + CAST(MONTH(DATEADD(dd,-1,GETDATE())) AS VARCHAR(2)),2)
+ RIGHT('0' + CAST(DAY(DATEADD(dd,-1,GETDATE())) AS VARCHAR(2)),2) AS INT)
```

```
DECLARE @Today INT = CAST(CAST(YEAR(GETDATE()) AS CHAR(4))
+ RIGHT('0' + CAST(MONTH(GETDATE()) AS VARCHAR(2)),2)
+ RIGHT('0' + CAST(DAY(GETDATE()) AS VARCHAR(2)),2) AS INT);

-- Insert statement for the latest, newest update to an existing dimension record

INSERT INTO dbo.Client_SCD2 (BusinessKey, ClientName, Country, Town, Address1,
Address2, ClientType, ClientSize, ValidFrom, IsCurrent)

SELECT ID, ClientName, Country, Town, Address1, Address2, ClientType, ClientSize,
@Today, 1
FROM

(
-- Merge statement
MERGE   CarSales_Staging.dbo.Client_SCD2        AS DST
USING   CarSales.dbo.Client                     AS SRC
ON      (SRC.ID = DST.BusinessKey)

WHEN NOT MATCHED THEN

INSERT (BusinessKey, ClientName, Country, Town, County, Address1, Address2,
ClientType, ClientSize, ValidFrom, IsCurrent)
VALUES (SRC.ID, SRC.ClientName, SRC.Country, SRC.Town, SRC.County, Address1,
Address2, ClientType, ClientSize, @Today, 1)

WHEN MATCHED
AND (
            ISNULL(DST.ClientName,'') <> ISNULL(SRC.ClientName,'')
            OR ISNULL(DST.Country,'') <> ISNULL(SRC.Country,'')
            OR ISNULL(DST.Town,'') <> ISNULL(SRC.Town,'')
            OR ISNULL(DST.Address1,'') <> ISNULL(SRC.Address1,'')
            OR ISNULL(DST.Address2,'') <> ISNULL(SRC.Address2,'')
            OR ISNULL(DST.ClientType,'') <> ISNULL(SRC.ClientType,'')
            OR ISNULL(DST.ClientSize,'') <> ISNULL(SRC.ClientSize,'')
        )

-- Update statement for a changed dimension record, to flag as no longer active
THEN UPDATE

SET DST.IsCurrent = 0, DST.ValidTo = @Yesterday

OUTPUT SRC.ID, SRC.ClientName, SRC.Country, SRC.Town, SRC.Address1, SRC.Address2,
SRC.ClientType, SRC.ClientSize, $Action AS MergeAction
) AS MRG

WHERE MRG.MergeAction = 'UPDATE'
;
```

The destination table will have new records added, and changed records added and flagged as being the latest version.

How It Works

Here we are looking at a technique that can be so powerful when data has to be updated, and a history of the changes maintained in SQL Server tables. As we are dealing with SCDs, I will presume that we will not be using WHEN NOT MATCHED to delete dimension data, and will only look at UPSERTing data—that is inserting and updating dimension data. A Type 2 SCD is a technique for change tracking using historical records in a table, while indicating the valid date ranges and the current data. This also has many uses outside a data warehousing environment.

To illustrate all of this, I am here taking the dbo.Client table as the source data from the CarSales database, and exporting this data, suitably transformed, into the CarSales_Stagingdatabase. This example presumes that the business key is a unique primary key.

Handling a Type 2 SCD is only slightly more complex than a Type 1. What this process does is track changes over time to the dimension attributes by

- Adding a new record every time a dimension attribute (the value in any column containing the descriptive data) changes.

- Logging the date when the change occurs, thus ensuring that the start date for each new record is kept, as well as the date the previous record ceased being valid.

- Flagging the current record for every business key, which can improve reporting performance.

This supposes a destination table containing all the values required, a business key (the client ID from the source data) and a surrogate key that will be used for data warehousing. As well as these "core" fields, the following fields will be required to track the evolution of the dimension over time:

ValidFrom: Logs the date from that this dimension record was valid.

ValidTo: Logs the date to that this dimension record was, or is, valid.

IsCurrent: Indicates that this is the current record (the most recent data) for a dimension element.

The preceding SQL snippet maps the two tables on the business key and inserts a new record into the destination table if the record referenced by the business key is not already present (WHEN NOT MATCHED), as well as adding an auto-incremented surrogate key and setting today's date as the ValidFrom date.

If any differences between the source and destination tables are detected(using the WHEN MATCHED AND...clause) then severel events are triggered. Firstly an auto-incremented surrogate key is updated and today's date is set as as the ValidFrom date. The outcome is that this record is flagged as the current record. Then yesterday's date is set as the ValidTo date for the previous valid record for this business key.

All of this may seem complex, but it is made extremely simple using the OUTPUT clause of the MERGE statement. What the code does is carry out the INSERT and UPDATE as before for new and existing records, and then it selects the UPDATEd records (funneled via the OUTPUT clause) as a separate INSERT. This way, the latest modifications to the source data become a new record—handled as a separate INSERT—and any required tracking data, such as the ValidFrom date and the IsCurrent flag, is added at this stage.

Hints, Tips, and Traps

- The ValidFrom and ValidTo dates are added as INT data types, rather than DATE or DATETIME purely with a view to future loading into Analysis Services, where the choice of data type can not only make dates easier to manipulate, but can also enhance processing times. Feel free to use any of the date data types if you need to.

- I am presuming a 24-hour cycle on dimension date validity, for the sake of simplicity. If your requirements are more complex, then the validity range of the dimension record can be any valid date range.

- You may not need to check for data differences on all columns. If certain columns contain data that is not considered an essential attribute, then do not use it in the WHEN MATCHED ... AND clause.

9-26. Handling Type 2 Slowly Changing Dimensions with SSIS
Problem

You need to track the changes over time as source data is added to a destination table as part of an SSIS data flow process.

Solution

Use SSIS package that uses a conditional split and an Execute SQL task to treat this as a Type 2 SCD. The following shows you how.

1. In the destination database (CarSales_Staging) create a table that for the Client_SCDSSIS2 Type 2 dimension. The DDL for this table is (C:\SQL2012DIRecipes\CH09\tblClientSCDSSIS2.sql):

```
USE CarSales_Staging;
GO

CREATE TABLE CarSales_Staging.dbo.Client_SCDSSIS2
(
 SurrogateID INT IDENTITY(1,1) NOT NULL,
 BusinessKey INT NOT NULL,
 ClientName VARCHAR(150) NULL,
 Country VARCHAR(50) NULL,
 Town VARCHAR(50) NULL,
 County VARCHAR(50) NULL,
 Address1 VARCHAR(50) NULL,
 Address2 VARCHAR(50) NULL,
 ClientType VARCHAR(20) NULL,
 ClientSize VARCHAR(10) NULL,
 ValidFrom INT NULL,
 ValidTo INT NULL,
 IsCurrent BIT NULL
);
GO
```

2. Create a temporary table—in disk while creating and testing the package in the staging database—that will be used to update the dimension table. The DDL for this table is

```
CREATE TABLE CarSales_Staging.dbo.Tmp_Client_SCDSSIS2
(
 SurrogateID INT NOT NULL
);
GO
```

3. Create a new SSIS package named **SCD_Type2**. Add two OLEDB connection managers—one named **CarSales_OLEDB**, connecting to the CarSales database, the other named **CarSales_Staging_OLEDB**, connecting to the CarSales_Staging database. Set the RetainSameConnection property for the latter to True.

4. Add the following two variables:

Name	Scope	DataType	Value	Comments
TempTable	SCD_Type2	String	Tmp_Client_SCD	Used to switch from the database-based table to the temporary table.
ValidFrom	SCD_Type2	Int32		Automatically gets the current date.

5. Set the EvaluateAsExpression property to True for the ValidFromvariable. Set the expression (this will get the current date as an integer) as:

```
YEAR( GETDATE()) * 100000 + MONTH( GETDATE()) * 1000 + DAY( GETDATE())
```

6. In the Control Flow tab, add an Execute SQL task, and configure as follows:

Name	Create Temp Table for Session
Connection:	CarSales_Staging_OLEDB
SQL Statement:	CREATE TABLE ##Tmp_Client_SCDSSIS2
	(SurrogateID INT NOT NULL)

7. Even if you will not be using this temporary table until the package is debugged and functioning, it is just as well to create it now. Click OK to confirm your changes.

8. Add a Data Flow task and name it **Main SCD Type 2 Process**. Connect the previous Execute SQL task (Create Temp Table for Session) to it. Double-click to edit.

9. Add an OLEDB Source connection to the Data Flow pane, name it **Source Data**, and configure as follows:

    OLEDB Connection Manager: CarSales_OLEDB

    Data Access Mode: SQL Command

    SQL Command Text: SELECT   ID, ClientName,

                                         Country, Town, County, Address1,
                                         Address2, ClientType, ClientSize

                               FROM   dbo.Client

                               ORDER BY ID

10. Confirm with OK.

11. Right-click the Source Data OLEDB Source connection and select Show Advanced Editor. Select the Input and Output Properties tab, click the OLEDB Source Output, and set the IsSorted property to True in the right of the dialog box.

12. Expand the OLEDB Source Output and expand the Output columns. Click the column ID and set the SortKeyPosition property to 1.

13. Add a Lookup transformation and connect the source you just created to it. Double-click to edit. In the General tab, set it to use an OLEDB connection manager, the Cache mode to Full Cache, and to redirect rows to NoMatch output. In the Connection pane, set the OLEDB connection manager to CarSales_Staging_OLEDB and to use the results of the following SQL query:

```
SELECT    SurrogateID, BusinessKey, ClientName, Country, Town, County, Address1,
          Address2, ClientType, ClientSize, ValidFrom, ValidTo, IsCurrent
FROM      dbo.Client_SCDSSIS2 WITH (NOLOCK)
ORDER BY  BusinessKey
```

14. In the Columns pane, map the ID column (available input columns) to the BusinessKey column (available lookup columns), and then select all the other columns from the available lookup columns, except ValidFrom, ValidTo, and IsCurrent. Alias all the lookup columns by prefixing them with DIM_. The dialog box should look like Figure 9-20.

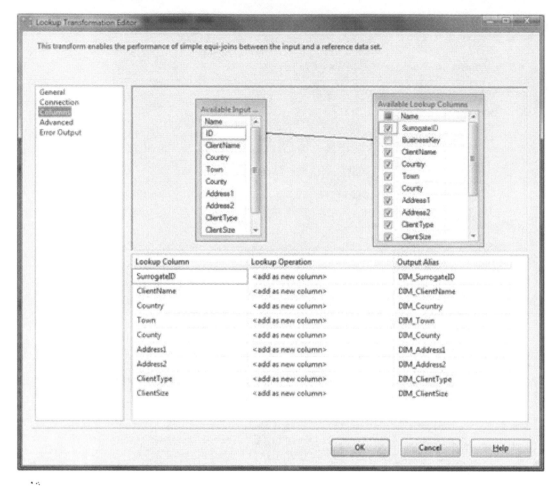

Figure 9-20. Lookup columns for an SSIS Type 2 SCD

15. Click OK to confirm.

16. Add a Conditional Split transform and connect the Lookup transform to it using the Lookup Match Output. Double-click to edit. Create an output named **DataDifference**, with a condition like this:

```
(ClientSize != DIM_ClientSize) || ( ClientName) != ([ClientName])
```

17. Once the comparison for **each field** has been entered (only one is shown here), click OK to finish your modifications.

18. Add a Multicast transform, and connect the Conditional Split transform to it using the DataDifference output.

19. Add a Merge transform and connect the Lookup transform to it. Be sure to select the Lookup NoMatch Output and to map this to the Merge Input 1. Then connect the Multicast transform to the Merge transform. Double-click to edit. Ensure that the columns are correctly mapped, as shown in Figure 9-21.

Output Column Name	Merge Input 1	Merge Input 2
ID (Sort key: 1)	ID (Sort key: 1)	ID (Sort key: 1)
ClientName	ClientName	ClientName
Country	Country	Country
Town	Town	Town
County	County	County
Address1	Address1	Address1
Address2	Address2	Address2
ClientType	ClientType	ClientType
ClientSize	ClientSize	ClientSize

Figure 9-21. Merge column mapping in SSIS

20. Add a Derived Column transform, connect the Merge transform to it, and add two derived columns, like in Figure 9-22.

Derived Column Name	Derived Column	Expression	Data Type
ValidFrom	<add as new column>	@[User::ValidFrom]	four-byte signed integer [...
IsCurrent	<add as new column>	1	four-byte signed integer [...

Figure 9-22. Derived Column transform

21. Confirm with OK.

22. Add an OLEDB destination and connect the Derived Column transform to it. Configure it as follows:

    OLEDB Connection Manager: CarSales_Staging_OLEDB

    Data Access Mode: Table or View – Fast Load

    Name of Table or View: dbo.Client_SCDSSIS2

23. Once you have ensured that the columns are mapped—including mapping the source data ID column to the SCD Type 2 table Business Key, confirm with OK.

24. Add an OLEDB Destination and connect the Multicast transform to it. Configure it as follows:

    OLEDB Connection Manager: CarSales_Staging_OLEDB

    Data Access Mode: Table name or view name variable

    Variable Name: User::TempTable

25. Click Mappings and ensure that the ID column from the source data is mapped to the SurrogateID column of the destination table. Once you have ensured that the column is mapped, confirm with OK. The data flow is finished and looks like Figure 9-22.

26. Return to the Control Flow tab and add an Execute SQL task. Name it **Update SCD Type 2 table**. Connect the previous Data Flow task to it and configure it as follows:

Connection: CarSales_Staging_OLEDB

SQL Statement:	UPDATE	SCDSSIS2
	SET	SCDSSIS2.IsCurrent = 0
		,SCDSSIS2.ValidTo = YEAR(DATEADD(d,-1,GETDATE())) * 100000
		+ MONTH(DATEADD(d,-1,GETDATE())) * 1000
		+ DAY(DATEADD(d,-1,GETDATE()))
	FROM	dbo.Client_SCDSSIS2SCDSSIS2
	INNER JOIN	Tmp_Client_SCDSSIS2 TMP
		ON SCDSSIS2.SurrogateID = TMP.SurrogateID
	WHERE	SCDSSIS2.IsCurrent = 1

How It Works

Unfortunately, efficiently processing slowly changing dimensions in SSIS is not intuitive or as simple as it could be. Yes, there is—and has been since SSIS appeared—a Slowly Changing Dimension transform, but unfortunately it is more a learning tool than a real-world piece of kit. I will not even recommend using it here.

So you are left with the moderately unpalatable solution of writing your own SSIS package to handle slowly changing dimensions. Luckily, a Type 1 SCD is nothing more than an in-place update (or insert for new data). When it comes to Type 2 SCDs, however, the package is fairly complex, so here is an overview of what it does:

- Links to the current dimension table.

- Links to the source data table or view.

- Detects any new dimension records (by mapping the business key between the two data sets and detecting where there are no matches) and load them.

- Analyzes all existing records in the two data sources, and compares attribute fields. Where any of these differ, two things will happen:

  - Add a new record for the latest version of the dimension data (suitably flagged as valid).

  - Updates the previously valid version with the validity set to false, and the date it ceased being valid.

To get this to work, the updates to the existing records will use the session-scoped temporary table to identify the records to update. In this way, a set of record IDs for later update can be stored as part of the core data flow process, and the update command can be run once this "core" process has finished. Initially this temporary table will be persisted on disk. It will be replaced by the session-scoped temporary table ##Tmp_Client_SCDSSIS2once all debugging is completed. The main thing about such an approach is that it avoids using an OLEDB Command transform as part of the data flow, which would fire for every record—yet apply to the entire dimension table, causing massive unnecessary work for the server.

This means that the overall high-level process looks like Figure 9-23.

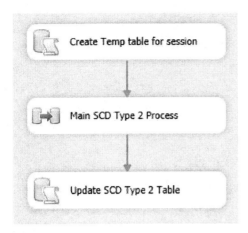

Figure 9-23. *SSIS SCD Type 2 process*

The "core" process—the Data Flow task from Figure 9-23 looks like Figure 9-24.

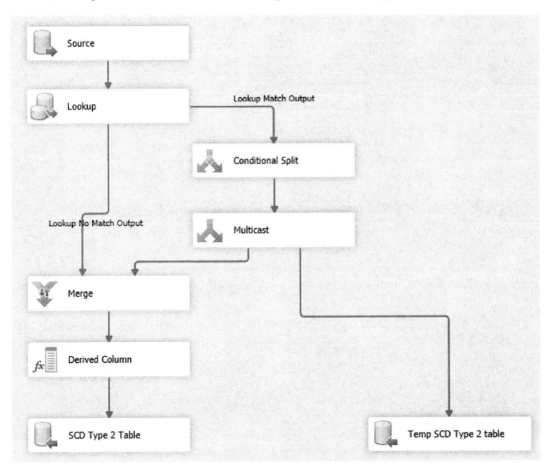

Figure 9-24. *Detail of SSIS SCD Type 2 process*

The temporary table can be deleted—and the session-scoped table used in its place—once everything is working. It is, however, vital to use it during the development phase.

So, once the package has run, and you have debugged it, you can do the following:

1. Change the Variable value for TempTable to ##Tmp_Client_SCDSSIS2.

2. Alter the reference in the task Update SCD Type 2 table so that the temp table used is the session-scoped temporary table. The code needs to be tweaked to use:

```
INNER JOIN ##Tmp_Client_SCDSSIS2 TMP
```

3. Delete the dbo.Tmp_Client_SCDSSIS2 table in the CarSales database.

Your SSIS package will now use the session-scoped temporary table to update the destination table records and avoid the need for an extraneous table to persist in the database.

Hints, Tips, and Traps

- The reason for aliasing the dimension columns in the Lookup transform is that it (a) makes it much easier to track the use of columns with identical names in the package, and (b) it prevents SSIS applying two or three part dotted notation names that can rapidly become extremely hard to manipulate.

- It is important to sort both the source data sets (source and lookup) and to tell SSIS that they are sorted. Otherwise, you will get some very strange results from the Merge transform.

- Be sure to implement NULL handling or the conditional split will fail.

- If you are dealing with large dimensions, then you should place the cache file on the fastest drive array possible—or even a solid-state disk, if you can. Any speed gains here will have a marked effect on the whole package.

9-27. Handling Type 3 Slowly Changing Dimensions Using T-SQL
Problem

You need to track the last version of one or more columns in a denormalized single record in the destination table using T-SQL.

Solution

Use MERGE in T-SQL to carry out a Type 3 SCD. The following describes how to do it.

1. Create a destination table containing the business key and an attribute, as well as previous version columns for the attribute and the data that it is valid to. The DDL for such a destination table is (C:\SQL2012DIRecipes\CH09\tblClient_SCD3.sql):

```
CREATE TABLE CarSales_Staging.dbo.Client_SCD3
(
 ClientID INT IDENTITY(1,1) NOT NULL,
```

```
    BusinessKey INT NOT NULL,
    ClientName VARCHAR(150) NULL,
    Country VARCHAR(50) NULL,
    Country_Prev1 VARCHAR(50) NULL,
    Country_Prev1_ValidTo INT NULL,
    Country_Prev2 VARCHAR(50) NULL,
    Country_Prev2_ValidTo INT NULL,
    ) ;
    GO
```

2. Run the following code snippet(C:\SQL2012DIRecipes\CH09\SCD3.sql):

```
USE CarSales_Staging;
GO

DECLARE @Yesterday INT = CAST(CAST(YEAR(DATEADD(dd,-1,GETDATE())) AS CHAR(4))
+ RIGHT('0' + CAST(MONTH(DATEADD(dd,-1,GETDATE())) AS VARCHAR(2)),2) + RIGHT('0'
+ CAST(DAY(DATEADD(dd,-1,GETDATE())) AS VARCHAR(2)),2) AS INT)

MERGE    CarSales_Staging.dbo.Client_SCD3         AS DST
USING    CarSales.dbo.Client                      AS SRC
ON       (SRC.ID = DST.BusinessKey)

WHEN NOT MATCHED THEN

INSERT (BusinessKey, ClientName, Country)
VALUES (SRC.ID, SRC.ClientName, SRC.Country)

WHEN MATCHED
AND      (DST.Country <> SRC.Country
               OR DST.ClientName <> SRC.ClientName)

THEN UPDATE

SET       DST.Country = SRC.Country
          ,DST.ClientName = SRC.ClientName
          ,DST.Country_Prev1 = DST.Country
          ,DST.Country_Prev1_ValidTo = @Yesterday
          ,DST.Country_Prev2 = DST.Country_Prev1
          ,DST.Country_Prev2_ValidTo = DST.Country_Prev1_ValidTo
;
```

How It Works

Let us be clear, a Type 3 SCD applies denormalization to a table so that multiple column sets are used to provide versioning. I find that it helps to understand Type 3 SCDs as denormalized data. This allows you to concentrate on appreciating the limitations and the drawbacks of this approach. This is another way of saying only use it if you have no other alternative! A Type 3 SCD is a single table with a set of duplicate columns for each value whose evolution you wish to track, as well as the date that the data evolved. This is ungainly, necessitates extremely wide tables, and, at some point, involves losing historical data since it is impossible to have previous column versions for all time—because SQL Server will run out of columns.

However, in the interest of completeness, it is worth seeing how to apply this technique. I have only shown how to track a single attribute column in this example, and only for two previous versions. However, once the principles are established, it is very easy to extend the model to handle multiple columns and many previous versions.

The preceding SQL snippet will map the two tables on the business key, as well as the following:

- Insert a new record if one does not exist for the business key.

- If the business key exists:

  - Move the previous value for the Country to the "Previous - 2", and add the date that the move occurred.

  - Move the value for the Country to the "Previous - 1", and add the date that the move occurred.

- Add the latest country to the Country column.

Once again—and as in Recipes 9-25 and 9-26—I am taking the source data from one database (CarSales) and updating the data in another database (CarSales_Staging). The source and destination objects can be in the same database, or even in different databases across linked servers.

Hints, Tips, and Traps

- Once again, the ValidTo date is added as an INT data type, rather than DATE or DATETIME, purely with a view to future loading into Analysis Services, where the choice of data type can not only make dates easier to manipulate, but can also enhance processing times. Feel free to use any of the date data types if you need to.

- This example does not need an IsCurrent flag because, by definition, the Town column is the current version.

- You can also update data as part of this approach, as I show using the ClientName field.

9-28. Handling Type 4 Slowly Changing Dimensions Using T-SQL
Problem

As part of an ETL flow, you need to store current data in one table and historical data in a second table.

Solution

Use the MERGE command to perform a Type 4 SCD data flow in T-SQL. The following steps go over how to do this.

1. Create the two following tables using this DDL
   (C:\SQL2012DIRecipes\CH09\tblClient_SCD4andHistory.Sql):

```
CREATE TABLE CarSales_Staging.dbo.Client_SCD4_History
(
 ClientID INT IDENTITY(1,1) NOT NULL,
 BusinessKey INT NOT NULL,
 ClientName VARCHAR(150) NULL,
 Country VARCHAR(50) NULL,
```

```
  Town VARCHAR(50) NULL,
  County VARCHAR(50) NULL,
  Address1 VARCHAR(50) NULL,
  Address2 VARCHAR(50) NULL,
  ClientType VARCHAR(20) NULL,
  ClientSize VARCHAR(10) NULL,
  ValidTo INT,
  HistoricalVersion INT
  ) ;
  GO

  CREATE TABLE CarSales_Staging.dbo.Client_SCD4
  (
  ClientID INT IDENTITY(1,1) NOT NULL,
  BusinessKey INT NOT NULL,
  ClientName VARCHAR(150) NULL,
  Country VARCHAR(50) NULL,
  ) ;
  GO
```

2. Run the following code (C:\SQL2012DIRecipes\CH09\SCD4.sql):

```
USE CarSales_Staging;
GO

-- Define the dates used in validity - assume whole 24 hour cycles
DECLARE @Yesterday INT = CAST(CAST(YEAR(DATEADD(dd,-1,GETDATE())) AS CHAR(4))
+ RIGHT('0' + CAST(MONTH(DATEADD(dd,-1,GETDATE())) AS VARCHAR(2)),2)
+ RIGHT('0' + CAST(DAY(DATEADD(dd,-1,GETDATE())) AS VARCHAR(2)),2) AS INT)

DECLARE @Today INT = CAST(CAST(YEAR(GETDATE()) AS CHAR(4))
+ RIGHT('0' + CAST(MONTH(GETDATE()) AS VARCHAR(2)),2)
+ RIGHT('0' + CAST(DAY(GETDATE()) AS VARCHAR(2)),2) AS INT);

-- Drop temp table, if it exists

IF OBJECT_ID('Tempdb..#Tmp_Client') IS NOT NULL DROP TABLE #Tmp_Client;

CREATE TABLE #Tmp_Client
(
 BusinessKey INT NOT NULL,
 ClientName VARCHAR(150) NULL,
 Country VARCHAR(50) NULL,
 Town VARCHAR(50) NULL,
 County VARCHAR(50) NULL,
 Address1 VARCHAR(50) NULL,
 Address2 VARCHAR(50) NULL,
 ClientType VARCHAR(20) NULL,
 ClientSize VARCHAR(10) NULL,
 ) ;
```

```
-- Outer insert for Type 4 records if an existing record changes, using output from
MERGE into temp table
INSERT INTO #Tmp_Client (BusinessKey, ClientName, Country, Town, Address1, Address2,
ClientType, ClientSize)

SELECT BusinessKey, ClientName, Country, Town, Address1, Address2, ClientType,
ClientSize
FROM

(
-- Merge statement
MERGE     CarSales_Staging.dbo.Client_SCD4          AS DST
USING     CarSales.dbo.Client                       AS SRC
ON        (SRC.ID = DST.BusinessKey)

WHEN NOT MATCHED THEN

INSERT (BusinessKey, ClientName, Country, Town, Address1, Address2, ClientType,
ClientSize)
VALUES (SRC.ID, SRC.ClientName, SRC.Country, SRC.Town, SRC.Address1, SRC.Address2,
SRC.ClientType, SRC.ClientSize)

WHEN MATCHED
AND
ISNULL(DST.ClientName,'') <> ISNULL(SRC.ClientName,'')
OR ISNULL(DST.Country,'') <> ISNULL(SRC.Country,'')
OR ISNULL(DST.Town,'') <> ISNULL(SRC.Town,'')
OR ISNULL(DST.Address1,'') <> ISNULL(SRC.Address1,'')
OR ISNULL(DST.Address2,'') <> ISNULL(SRC.Address2,'')
OR ISNULL(DST.ClientType,'') <> ISNULL(SRC.ClientType,'')
OR ISNULL(DST.ClientSize,'') <> ISNULL(SRC.ClientSize,'')

THEN UPDATE

SET
        DST.ClientName = SRC.ClientName
        ,DST.Country = SRC.Country
        ,DST.Town = SRC.Town
        ,DST.Address1 = SRC.Address1
        ,DST.Address2 = SRC.Address2
        ,DST.ClientType = SRC.ClientType
        ,DST.ClientSize = SRC.ClientSize


OUTPUT DELETED.BusinessKey, DELETED.ClientName, DELETED.Country, DELETED.Town,
DELETED.Address1, DELETED.Address2, DELETED.ClientType, DELETED.ClientSize, $Action
AS MergeAction
) AS MRG

WHERE MRG.MergeAction = 'UPDATE'
;
```

```
-- Update history table to set final date, version number

UPDATE     TP4

SET        TP4.ValidFrom = @Yesterday

FROM       CarSales_Staging.dbo.Client_SCD4_History TP4
INNER JOIN #Tmp_Client TMP
           ON TP4.BusinessKey = TMP.BusinessKey

WHERE      TP4.ValidFrom IS NULL;


-- Add latest history records to history table

INSERT INTO CarSales_Staging.dbo.Client_SCD4_History
(
BusinessKey
,ClientName
,Country
,Town
,County
,Address1
,Address2
,ClientType
,ClientSize
,ValidFrom
,HistoricalVersion
)

SELECT
BusinessKey
,ClientName
,Country
,Town
,County
,Address1
,Address2
,ClientType
,ClientSize
,@Today
,(SELECT ISNULL(MAX(HistoricalVersion),0) + 1 AS HistoricalVersion
  FROM dbo.Client_SCD4_History WHERE BusinessKey = Tmp.BusinessKey)

FROM    #Tmp_Client Tmp;
```

How It Works

The final variation on this theme that I have shown you here, is a Type 4 SCD. This is, basically, a Type 2 table with a separate history table for the previous versions of the data. Type 4 is a multitable split, where the most recent data is stored in an "active" table, and older data in a History table.

This recipe requires:

- A destination table containing all the values required, a business key (the client ID from the source data) and a surrogate key that will be used for data warehousing. This is identical in all respects to the Client_SCD1 table described earlier. Here, however, I will duplicate it and name it Client_SCD4 for the sake of clarity. Once again, all the destination tables are in the CarSales_Staging database, but could be in the same database as the source or even on another server.

- A destination table for the historical versions of the dimension data. This table is identical to the dimension table, and contains two additional fields: ValidTo and HistoricalVersion. The former stores the date when the data ceased to be current, the latter provides a version number for the data that can help to track how frequently data evolves.

The SQL snippet maps the source and main destination tables on the business key while taking the source data from the CarSales_Staging database. It also does the following.

- Inserts a new record if one does not exist for the business key.

- If one exists:

  - Moves the old record to the historical table.

  - Adds a new record to the main destination table.

Note the use of the DELETED table to get the previous value of data from the table Client_SCD4, rather than the current value that is returned by default. Also, rather than use the OUTPUT clause to return data from the MERGE command to a session-scoped temporary table, you can insert the data into a table variable, as part of the MERGE statement. However, temporary tables can be more efficient to use (especially if you index them) for larger data sets, so I prefer to use them in ETL processes, unless I can be reasonably sure that there will only be a few hundred records output at most.

9-29. Handling Type 4 Slowly Changing Dimensions with SSIS

Problem

As part of an ETL flow, you need to store current data in one table and historical data in a second table as part of an SSIS data flow.

Solution

Use the SSIS Multicast and conditional split tasks to process a Type 4 SCD. The following steps go over how to do it.

1. Create a temp table on disk (for testing and debugging) that will eventually be replaced by a session-scoped temporary table—as was done in Recipe 9-28. The DDL for this is (C:\SQL2012DIRecipes\CH09\tblTmpSCD4.sql):

```
CREATE TABLE CarSales_Staging.dbo.Tmp_SCD4
(
 ID INT NOT NULL,
 ClientName VARCHAR(150) NULL,
 Country VARCHAR(50) NULL,
```

```
Town VARCHAR(50) NULL,
County VARCHAR(50) NULL,
Address1 VARCHAR(50) NULL,
Address2 VARCHAR(50) NULL,
ClientType VARCHAR(20) NULL,
ClientSize VARCHAR(10) NULL
);
GO
```

2. Create a Type 4 history table, as described in Recipe 9-28, as well as the Client_SCD4 Type 1 table, also described in Recipe 9-28.

3. Carry out steps 1 to 10 in the previous recipe, only the code for the temporary table in step 4 will be as follows (C:\SQL2012DIRecipes\CH09\tblTmpSessionSCD4.sql):

```
CREATE TABLE ##Tmp_SCD4
(
ID INT NOT NULL,
ClientName VARCHAR(150) NULL,
Country VARCHAR(50) NULL,
Town VARCHAR(50) NULL,
County VARCHAR(50) NULL,
Address1 VARCHAR(50) NULL,
Address2 VARCHAR(50) NULL,
ClientType VARCHAR(20) NULL,
ClientSize VARCHAR(10) NULL
);
```

4. Ensure that the variable name for the temp table in step 2 is Tmp_SCD4.

5. Add an OLEDB Destination and connect the Lookup transform to it using the Lookup NoMatch output. Configure it as follows:

OLEDB Connection Manager:	CarSales_Staging_OLEDB
Data Access Mode:	Table or View – Fast Load
Name of Table or View:	dbo.Client_SCD

6. Once you have ensured that the columns are mapped, confirm with OK.

7. Add a Derived Column transform, connect the Multicast transform to it, and add a derived column, like this:

Derived Column Name:	ValidFrom
Expression:	@[User::ValidTo]

8. Add an OLEDB Destination and connect the Derived Column transform to it. Configure it as follows:

OLEDB Connection Manager:	CarSales_Staging_OLEDB
Data Access Mode:	Table or View – Fast Load
Name of Table or View:	dbo.Client_SCD4_History

9. Once you have ensured that the columns are mapped using the columns from the dimension table (this is very important), confirm with OK. The column mapping should look like Figure 9-25 (the source ID is the business key in this example).

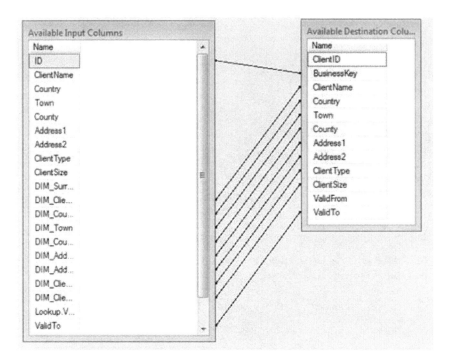

Figure 9-25. *Dimension column mapping*

10. Add an OLEDB Destination and connect the Derived Column transform to it. Configure it as follows:

OLEDB Connection Manager:	CarSales_Staging_OLEDB
Data Access Mode:	Table or View – Fast Load
Name of Table or View:	Tmp_SCD4

11. Once you have ensured that the columns are mapped using the data from the data source (this, too, is extremely important), confirm with OK.

12. Return to the Control Flow pane and add an Execute SQL task. Name it **Update Dimension table**. Connect the previous Data Flow task to it, and configure it as follows:

Connection: CarSales_Staging_OLEDB

```
UPDATE    DIM

SET

SCD2.ValidFrom = YEAR(DATEADD(d,-1,GETDATE())) * 100000

+ MONTH(DATEADD(d,-1,GETDATE())) * 1000

+ DAY(DATEADD(d,-1,GETDATE()))

,DIM.ClientName = TMP.ClientName

,DIM.Country = TMP.Country

,DIM.Town = TMP.Town

,DIM.County = TMP.County

,DIM.Address1 = TMP.Address1

,DIM.Address2 = TMP.Address2

,DIM.ClientType = TMP.ClientType

,DIM.ClientSize = TMP.ClientSize


FROM       dbo.Client_SCD4 DIM

INNER JOIN Tmp_SCD4 TMP

              ON DIM.ClientID = TMP.ID
```

How It Works

As SCDs of types 2 and 4 are tougher, they require some adroit SSIS programming to be both efficient (especially with large dimensions) and maintainable. As you can see, the approaches given in this recipe and the previous one attempt to balance these two conflicting demands. Nonetheless, do not assume that these are the only ways of dealing with the problem of SCDs in SSIS, and feel free to extend and tweak them to suit your specific requirements.

Using SSIS to maintain a Type 4 slowly changing dimension is largely an extension of the techniques described earlier (in Recipe 9-26) to maintain a Type 2 SCD. So I have not described every step, but merely highlighted the differences. Figure 9-26 shows what the finished package looks like.

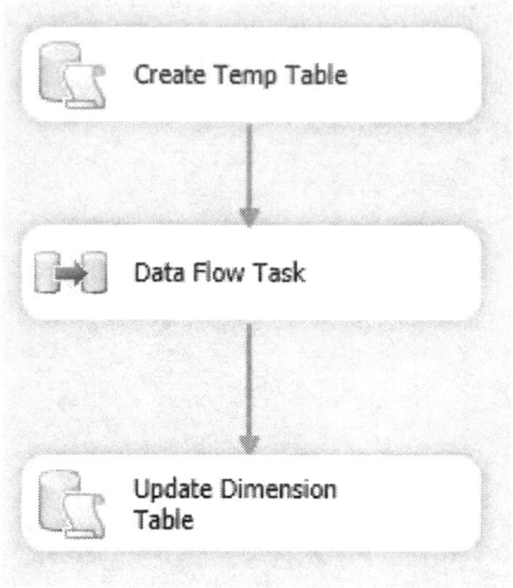
Create Temp Table
Data Flow Task
Update Dimension Table

Figure 9-26. *High-level data flow for an SSIS Type 4 SCD*

And the Data Flow task looks like Figure 9-27.

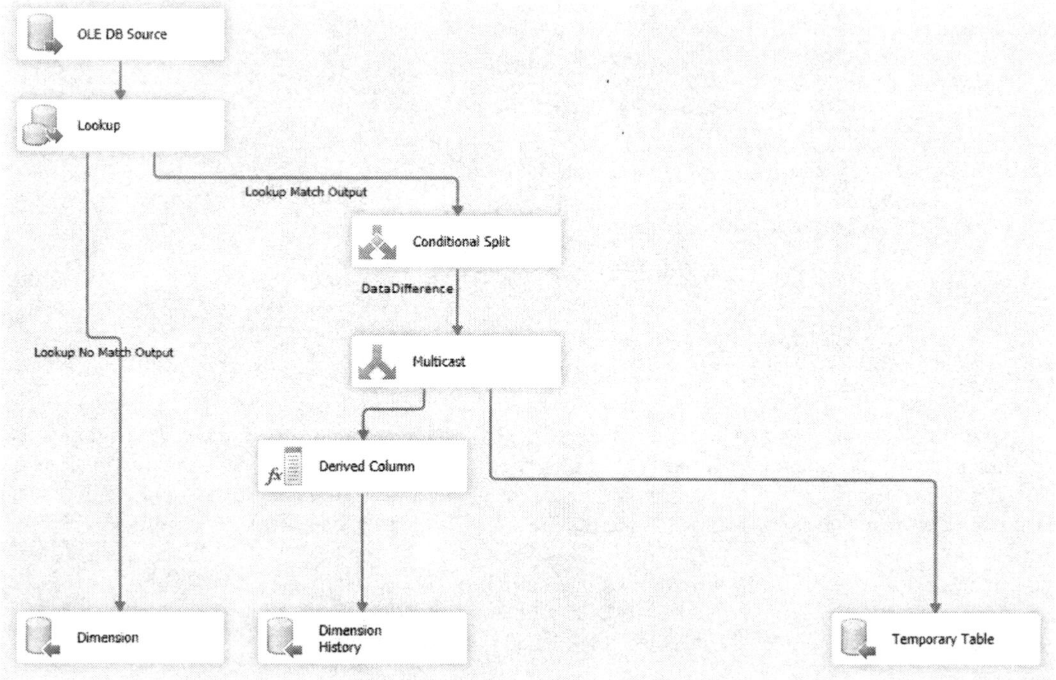
OLE DB Source
Lookup
Lookup Match Output
Conditional Split
DataDifference
Lookup No Match Output
Multicast
Derived Column
Dimension
Dimension History
Temporary Table

Figure 9-27. *Data flow detail for an SSIS Type 4 SCD*

The package does the following:

- Gets the source data, maps to the dimension table using the business key, and sends any non matched (new) records directly to the dimension table.

- Detects any records that already exist in the dimension table that are different from the source records. As both source and existing dimension data are in the data flow, changed (historical) records can be sent directly to the dimension history table.

- New (changed) data for existing dimension records are sent to a temporary table.

- Finally, the dimension table is updated with new data for existing records.

Once the package has run, and you are happy with it, you can do the following:

- Change the variable value for TempTable to ##Tmp_SCD4.

- Alter the reference in the task Update SCD Type 4 table so that the temp table used is the session-scoped temporary table. The code needs to be tweaked to use:

```
INNER JOIN ##Tmp_SCD4 TMP
```

- Delete the dbo.Tmp_SCD4 table in the CarSales database.

9-30. Cleansing Data As Part of an ETL Process
Problem

You wish to cleanse data as part of an ETL process using SSIS.

Solution

Use SQL Server Data Quality Services in SSIS 2012, as follows.

1. Ensure that Data Quality Services is installed and running on an SQL Server 2012 instance.

2. Create a new SSIS package and add the following two connection managers (at project or package level):

Name	Type	Data Source	Comments
CarSales_Staging_OLEDB	OLEDB	CarSales_Staging	The connection for the source data.
CarSales_OLEDB	OLEDB	CarSales	The connection for the destination database.

3. Add a new Data Flow task and switch to the Data Flow pane.

4. Add an OLEDB source and configure as follows:

Name:	Car Sales
Connection Manager:	CarSales_Staging_OLEDB
Data Access Mode:	Table or view
Name of Table or View:	CarColoursForDQSInSSIS

5. Add a DQS Cleansing task, name it **DQS Cleansing**, and connect the data source that you just created to it. Double-click to edit.

6. Click New to create a Data Quality connection manager. Select the DQS server name from the pop-up list of available DQS servers, and then click OK.

7. Select the DQS Knowledge Base containing the domain that you wish to use. The dialog box should look like Figure 9-28.

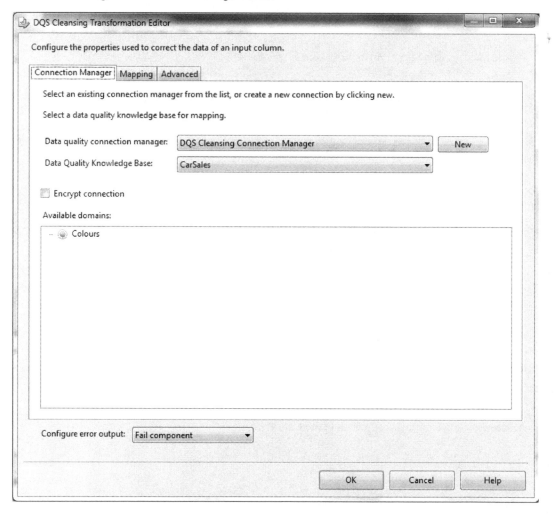

Figure 9-28. *Configuring the DQS connection manager*

8. Click the Mapping tab to switch to the Mapping pane. Select the Color check box in the upper section of the dialog box. This indicates that source column is to be cleansed.

9. In the lower section of the dialog box, select Colors as the DQS cleansing domain to be used for the Color column in the source data. The dialog box should look something like Figure 9-29.

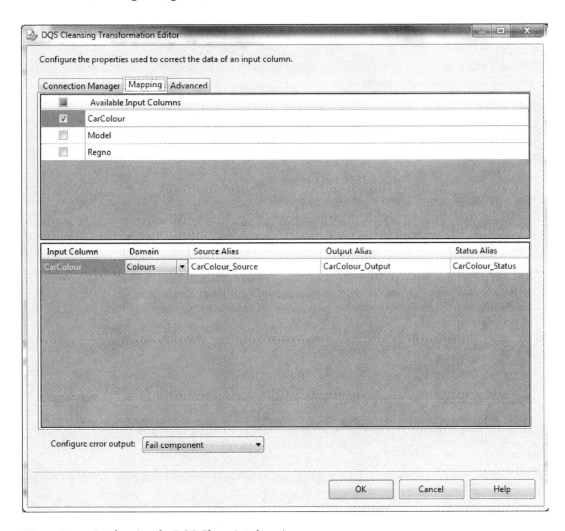

Figure 9-29. *Configuring the DQS Cleansing domain*

10. Confirm your modifications to the DQS Cleansing task.

11. Add a Conditional Split task to the Data Flow pane and connect the DQS Cleansing task to it. Double-click to edit. Add the following three outputs:

Output Name	Condition	Comments
New	[Record Status]=="New"	Creates an output for records where DQS cannot either validate or correct the data being cleansed.
Correct	[Record Status]=="Correct" || [Record Status]=="Corrected"	Creates an output for records where DQS accepts the data as valid.

12. Click OK to confirm your changes.

13. Add an OLEDB destination to the Data Flow pane. Connect this destination to the Correct output from the Conditional Split task, and then configure it as follows. Afterward, map the source to the destination columns. You will not need to map the DQS status column(s).

Name:	Correct Records
OLEDB Connection Manager:	CarSales_OLEDB
Data Access Mode:	Table or view – fast load
Name of Table or View:	Dbo.stock

14. Add an OLEDB destination to the Data Flow pane. Connect this destination to the new output from the Conditional Split task, and then configure it as follows. Afterward, map the source to the destination columns. You will not need to map the DQS status column(s).

Name:	New Records
OLEDB Connection Manager:	CarSales_Staging_OLEDB
Data Access Mode:	Table or view – fast load
Name of Table or View:	Dbo.Stock_FailedCleansing. (Use SSIS to create a "New" table)

The final package should look like that in Figure 9-30.

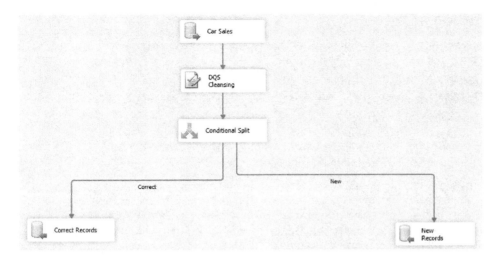

Figure 9-30. *DQS cleansing package overview*

You can now run the package. Assuming that all goes well, it will load validated data directly into the destination table and send any data that requires further intervention to the staging table.

How It Works

As I mentioned in the introduction to this chapter, there is one aspect of data cleansing that I will touch on, and that is SQL Server Data Quality Services. Unfortunately, I cannot give a complete introduction to SQL Server Data Quality Services, as that would require a chapter to itself. However, I can explain how to use it to cleanse data as it flows through an SSIS process using the SSIS DQS Cleansing task.

Should you not yet be familiar with Data Quality Services, then all you need to know for the purposes of this recipe is that it allows you to compare data being loaded into an SQL Server table with a set of reference data (contained in a Knowledge Base). Each Knowledge Base can contain many Domains (think of them as a kind of advanced and cleverly designed lookup table). You can then use a domain to validate and even correct the source data as it flows into the destination table. When DQS analyzes source data and compares it with a domain, it will flag data as New—that is unknown in the Knowledge Base, Correct—data in the source is exactly as it is in the Knowledge Base or Corrected—the Knowledge Base contains a mapping that allows DQS to replace source data with what should be used.

It is worth noting that data cleansing using the DQS Cleansing task can get much more complex than the simple example in this recipe suggests. Each column that is cleansed using a domain in a Knowledge Base will add a _Source and an _Output column, as well as a _Status column. This allows you to add fine-grained logic to your data flows. The corollary of this subtlety is that it can imply extremely intricate decision logic in the data flow.

At least one DQS Knowledge Base must be created and populated with a functioning domain. In this example, I have created a Colours domain to cleanse the color references of new cars being added to the Stock table in the sample database.

Source data to be validated—in this example I am using a source table containing Stock in the CarSales_Staging database. This table is called CarColoursForDQSInSSIS.

A second destination table, Stock_FailedCleansing, is the staging database. This table holds records that failed cleansing for manual correction, and can probably be used to update the DQS Knowledge Base.

Hints, Tips, and Traps

- The data source can be any source that SSIS can import. It does not have to be a database table.

- This example only shows one domain being used to cleanse one source column. You can use the DQS cleansing task to cleanse multiple source columns at once if you so choose.

- This example assumes that "correct" and "corrected" data are identical. You may prefer to separate them into two data paths (to add counters or to output corrected data to a separate staging table for analysis purposes using a Multicast task, for instance). The two paths can then be sorted and merged into a single destination.

- The decision as to how to handle new domain data is a potentially a very big question. Do you keep it out of the destination table and reprocess it manually once the ETL process is finished? Or do you allow the data to be loaded into the destination table, flag any anomalies, and update this data in place (not shown here)? The decision will depend on the subtleties of each particular process.

Summary

This chapter has taken you on a (fairly whirlwind) tour of some of the many available data transformation techniques that you could be called upon to apply in your career as an ETL developer. Hopefully, you have seen that most of the "classic" problems facing the ETL developer (Data Type transformation, pivoting and normalizing data, subsetting columns, and concatenating columns to name but a few) can be resolved either as part of an SSIS pipeline or once data has been imported into staging tables in SQL Server.

I have given a certain weight in this chapter to slowly changing dimensions, as they seem to be becoming more and more a part of the ETL universe. This is possibly due to the increasing importance of business intelligence (BI) in the enterprise. In any case, handling data loads where the destination data can change over time is now a fundamental part of many ETL processes, and so I wanted to ensure that the core techniques for handling such datasets were explained.

I am fully aware that there many challenges for which I have not been able to describe solutions, given space constraints. I am also aware that for each of the techniques described in this chapter, there are many alternative solutions and variations on each theme. Nonetheless, I hope that the recipes provided in this chapter will help you resolve some of the more "classic" ETL problems that you are likely to encounter, and that you can take this information as a starting point that you can use to build your own solid and robust data transformation processes, with both SSIS and T-SQL.

CHAPTER 10

Data Profiling

Every person whose work involves data ingestion and consolidation wants to know exactly what constitutes the source data that they are using. While this does not mean knowing every morsel of data in every table, it can and should mean having a high-level view of what is (and equally important—what is not) in a column of data. This knowledge can often be a valuable first step in deciding on the validity of a data source, and even in choosing whether or not to proceed with an ETL process. Indeed, since introduction of the Data Profiling task in SSIS 2008, the importance of data profiling seems to have been recognized by Microsoft. Self-evidently, then, it seems worth taking an in-depth look at the art and science of data profiling with SQL Server. Consequently, the aim of this chapter is to help you understand what data profiling is and what it can do to help you when working with databases. Indeed, I suspect that many, if not most, SQL Server developers and DBAs have been using some kind of data profiling techniques as part of their job already, even if they were not actually using the term "data profiling" to describe what they were doing.

Data profiling with SQL Server is not limited to the SSIS Data Profiling task. In this chapter, I will show many different approaches to data profiling, in which you "roll your own" profiling techniques using T-SQL and SSIS—and even CLR (Common Language Runtime). This is to show you that data profiling is a varied art form, and that it can be used in many different ways to help out with differing problems. As ever, we will start with the simplest techniques and then progress to more complex ones.

As the terms used in this area can cause confusion, let's start by defining what we mean by data profiling. *Data profiling* is running a process to return metrics from a data set.

The first—and frequently the main type of data profiling that you can perform is ***attribute analysis***. It consists of looking at the data in an individual column and abstracting out a high-level view of the following:

- Null counts and null ratios.

- Domain analysis (the counts and ratios of each element in a column).

- Field length maximum and minimum and frequently the length distribution (dominant length and percentage dominant length).

- Numerical maximum and minimum.

- Value distribution (domain analysis, median, unique/distinct values and outliers).

- Pattern profiles (the format of texts and numbers) and the percentage of pattern compliance.

- Data type profiling.

The second type of data profiling that we look at briefly in this chapter in the context of the SSIS Data Profiling task is ***relational analysis***— how columns and records relate to oneanother (if at all). This includes:

- Orphaned records—and the number and the percentage of orphans

- Childless records—and the number and the percentage of childless records

- Key (join) profile—cardinality (how many map to a join)

Some data profiling can be applied to any data type; some are type-specific. By this, I mean that you may want to look for NULLs in text or numeric fields, whereas you will only look for numerical distribution in numeric fields, and field lengths in text fields.

Clearly the first question to ask is why profile data? In reply, I would suggest that data profiling could—and frequently should—be used in two cases:

- To analyze source data before writing a complex ETL process.

- As part of an ETL process.

To understand the need for profiling better, consider the all-too-frequent ETL scenario that faces a DBA or developer. A file, or a link to some data arrives in your e-mail and you have to "integrate it." There may be some (limited) documentation, and both the documentation and the data might—or just might not—be trustworthy. Profiling the data, both to perform attribute and relational analysis, can save you a lot of time, in that it enables you to

Discover anomalies and contradictions in the data.

Ask more accurate and searching questions of the people who deliver the data.

Explain to the people in your company or department (who are convinced that they have just given you a magic wand to solve all their data needs) how the data can, realistically, be used, and how it can (or not) integrate into your destination databases and data warehouses.

Data profiling as part of an ETL process can be critical for any of the following reasons:

- To maintain a trace of data quality metrics.

- To alert you to breaches of defined thresholds in data quality.

- To allow you to develop more subtle analysis of data quality, where graduations of quality (as opposed to simply pass or fail) can evolve. These analyses can then be sent as alerts during or after a load routine.

Once you have these analyses, then the next question should be "how and why is this important?" Well, the reply will depend on your specific data set. If the column in question contains data that is fundamental to later processing (a customer ID, say), then you might wish to set a threshold for NULLs (either as an absolute value or as a percentage) above which processing is halted. Alternatively, if a NULL in this column is going to cause a process to fail further into the ETL routine, then a single NULL might be enough to invalidate the data flow. The point is that getting the figures now may take a few seconds. Discovering the error after five or six hours of processing is a real waste of time.

If you agree with the preceding premise, you may still be wondering: why should you want to go to the trouble of developing your own profiling routines when a perfectly good SSIS task exists? Well, there are several possible reasons why you might want to prefer a custom approach:

- The Data Profiling task will only work with SQL Server sources (2000 and up), whereas custom profiling can be made to work with many different data sources.

- You may want to perform profiling without necessarily using SSIS.

- The Data Profiling task is only available from SQL Server 2008 onward. You may still be using SQL Server 2005 in some cases.

- To save time, you could want to perform data profiling on an existing data flow during data ingestion, rather than run a task that runs independently of a data flow.

- You want to go beyond the "out of the box" profiling request types that are available in SSIS.

- You want to add further statistical analysis to profiling results.

- The XML output can require some clunky workarounds to read as part of an ETL process.

- You want to test data for sufficient probable accuracy before running a time- and resource-consuming ETL process. This is not easy when using the Profiling task.

- You want records that your profiling captures as statistically questionable to be removed from a data flow, and/or output to a separate data destination for analysis.

- You want to perform targeted subsetting—that is, you have experienced the types of data that tend to cause problems, and you want to profile data that has certain characteristics in order to reduce profiling time.

The techniques described in this chapter will not attempt to automate data cleansing because it is a subject I will not look at in any detail. However, I hope to show that effective use of data profiling techniques can be an extremely useful first step (some might say an essential step) in data cleansing.

The techniques outlined in this chapter are all specific, rather than generic. By this I mean that all the pieces of each profiling or analysis techniques described in this chapter will have to be assembled into a custom process that is adapted to a specific data source. These methods do not attempt to fit any data source or to auto-adapt to data sources.

To test the examples in this chapter, you have to download the sample files from the book's companion web site and install them in the C:\SQL2012DIRecipes\CH10 folder. You will also need the two sample databases, CarSales and CarSales_Staging, which are also on the web site.

10-1. Profiling Data Attributes
Problem

You want to obtain attribute information (counts, NULL records field lengths, and other basic details for a field or fields) from an SQL Server data source.

Solution

Use T-SQL functions to profile and return the attributes of the source data. Here is one example:

```
SELECT COUNT(*) FROM CarSales.dbo.Stock WHERE Marque IS NULL;
```

How It Works

We began by looking at data profiling using T-SQL. This snippet returns the number of records that have NULLs for a specific column.

To explain this concept further, I will assume that you are analyzing data that has already been loaded into SQL Server. In my experience, this is a frequent scenario when you are first loading data into a staging database from which it will eventually be transferred into an ODS (operational data store) or Data Warehouse. In Recipe 10-3, you see how to use them with data that is not yet in SQL Server. Fortunately, this approach only requires you to apply a series of built-in functions that you probably already know. They are shown in Table 10-1.

Table 10-1. *Attribute Profiling Functions in T-SQL*

Function	Use in profiling
NULL	Detect NULL values.
MAX	Get the maximum numeric value—or, combined with LEN, the maximum string length.
MIN	Get the minimum numeric value—or, combined with LEN, the minimum string length.
COUNT	Count the number of records.
LEN	Get the length of a character field.

Along with judicious use of the GROUP BY and DISTINCT keywords, these functions will probably cover most of your basic data attribute profiling requirements. Indeed, given these functions' simplicity and ease of use, it is probably faster to look at all of them at once—and see the core attribute profiling types at the same time—rather than laboriously explain each one individually. I am aware that all this may seem way too simple for many readers. Nevertheless, in the interest of completeness, Table 10-2 gives the code snippets that you might find yourself using. All the examples presume that you are using the CarSales.dbo.Stock table.

Table 10-2. *Attribute Profiling Examples in T-SQL*

Profile task	Code	Comments
NULL Profiling	SELECT COUNT(*) FROM dbo.Stock WHERE Marque IS NULL;	How many records have NULLs in a specific column?
NULL Percentage	SELECT (SELECT CAST(COUNT(*)AS NUMERIC (18,3)) FROM dbo.Stock WHERE Marque IS NULL) / (SELECT COUNT(*) FROM dbo.Stock);	The percentage of the total this represents.
Maximum	SELECT MAX(ID) FROM dbo.Stock;	The maximum value in a numeric column.
Minimum	SELECT MIN(ID) FROM dbo.Stock;	The minimum value in a numeric column.
Maximum Count	SELECT COUNT(*) FROM dbo.Stock WHERE ID = (SELECT MAX(ID) FROM dbo.Stock);	The number of values that are of the maximum value in a numeric column.

(continued)

Table 10-2. (*continued*)

Profile task	Code	Comments
Minimum Count	SELECT COUNT(*) FROM dbo.Stock WHERE ID = (SELECT MIN(ID) FROM dbo.Stock);	The number of values that are of the minimum value in a numeric column.
Maximum Length	SELECT MAX(LEN(Marque)) FROM dbo.Stock;	The maximum length of a character (string) column.
Minimum Length	SELECT MIN(LEN(Marque)) FROM dbo.Stock;	The minimum length of a character (string) column.
Zero-length String Count	SELECT COUNT(*) FROM dbo.Stock2 WHERE LEN(Marque) = 0;	The number of zero-length strings.
Count	SELECT COUNT(*) FROM dbo.Stock;	The number of records.

Hints, Tips, and Traps

- If you are looking for a fast, but not 100 percent accurate record count where a tiny margin of error is acceptable, then you can return row counts using the following code snippet. The accuracy of the result will depend on how recently the table metadata was updated, but any large insert/delete will have caused the statistics to be recalculated:

```
SELECT      OBJECT_NAME(object_id) AS TableName, row_count
FROM        sys.dm_db_partition_stats
WHERE       object_id = OBJECT_ID('Stock');
```

- As the basic data profiling shown in this recipe is standard T-SQL, it will work for other databases on the same server as well as linked servers. All you need to do is use the correct three- or four-part notation to point to the table that you are profiling.

10-2. Profiling Domain and Value Distribution

Problem

You want to obtain domain and value profile distribution data from a SQL Server source table.

Solution

Use T-SQL functions to return domain and value distribution information. Essentially, this means discovering the number of records that contain each value and the percentage of each value in the data set.

The code snippets in Table 10-3 give you a snapshot of the domain distribution in a data table. Both of the code examples profile the CarSales.dbo.Stock table.

Table 10-3. *Domain and Value Distribution in an SQL Server Data Source*

Distribution	Code	Comments
Domain Distribution	`SELECT TOP (100) PERCENT Marque,` `COUNT(Marque) AS NumberOfMarques,`	This code snippet combines analysis of:
	`COUNT(Marque)/`	The domain values;
	`(SELECT CAST(COUNT(*) AS NUMERIC(18,8))`	The number of records that contain each value;
	`FROM CarSales.dbo.Stock)`	
	`* 100 AS DomainPercent`	The percentage of each value in the data set.
	`FROM           CarSales.dbo.Stock`	
	`GROUP BY     Marque`	
	`ORDER BY     Marque DESC;`	
Numeric Value Distribution	`SELECT       ID, COUNT(ID) AS` `             NumberOfValues`	This code snippet combines analysis of:
	`FROM         CarSales.dbo.Stock`	The numeric values;
	`GROUP BY     ID`	
	`ORDER BY     NumberOfValues DESC;`	The number of records that containing each value.

How It Works

Value distribution simply means getting the metrics for

- The number of records containing each of the values (text or numeric) in a specified field.

- The percentages of records containing each of the values (text or numeric) in a specified field.

Applying value distribution analysis to a set containing a vast number of different values might not be particularly useful in itself. I am suggesting that this approach is best suited to the analysis of fields containing a small variety of values—most often lookup or reference values—where the distribution of data is an indicator of data reliability.

Hints, Tips, and Traps

- The solution in this recipe can also be applied to non-SQL server data sources or linked servers.

- Profiling linked server sources is likely to be extremely slow, and while it can be useful for an initial data analysis, it might not be practical as part of a regular ETL process.

- You can see how to store the output from the profile requests in Recipe 10-5.

10-3. Profiling External Data

Problem

You want to profile data not (yet) in SQL Server.

Solution

Use T-SQL and OPENROWSET to access the source data over OLEDB.

Should you be looking at data in a text file—or an OLEDB data source—then you can use OPENROWSET to return the NULL count as follows (using, in this example, the sample file C:\SQL2012DIRecipes\CH10\Stock.Txt):

```
SELECT COUNT(*)
FROM OPENROWSET('MSDASQL', 'Driver={Microsoft Access Text Driver (*.txt, *.csv)};
  DefaultDir= C:\SQL2012DIRecipes\CH10;','select * from Stock.Txt')
WHERE Model IS NULL;
```

Similarly, the percentage of NULLs can be calculated using the following T-SQL:

```
SELECT
(SELECT CAST(COUNT(*) AS NUMERIC (10,3))
FROM OPENROWSET('MSDASQL', 'Driver={Microsoft Access Text Driver (*.txt, *.csv)};
  DefaultDir= C:\SQL2012DIRecipes\CH10;','SELECT * FROM Stock.txt WHERE Model IS NULL'))
/
(SELECT COUNT(*)
FROM OPENROWSET('MSDASQL', 'Driver={Microsoft Access Text Driver (*.txt, *.csv)};
  DefaultDir= C:\SQL2012DIRecipes\CH10;','SELECT * FROM Stock.Txt'));
```

The code snippets are in the file C:\SQL2012DIRecipes\CH10\ProfileExternalData.Sql.

How It Works

All the techniques described in Recipes 10-1 and 10-2 to carry out domain and data analysis can be used with OPENROWSET. The art here is to connect to the "external" (by which I mean non-SQL Server) data source. Once this is done using the requisite driver, you use the appropriate SQL snippet in the pass-through query. The functions that are used to profile the data are identical to those used in the previous two recipes.

OPENROWSET can access much more than text files. However, as the techniques for using this command to read data from Microsoft Access, Excel, and various RDBMSs are explained in Chapters 1 and 4, respectively, I refer you to these chapters for more information on the actual external connection. The profiling code will still be the same as that shown here.

▓ **Note** In this recipe's examples, I am using the ACE driver to read text files because this allows the code to run in both 32-bit and 64-bit environments. You will have to install the ACE driver as described in Recipe 1-1 for this to work. If you are in a 32-bit environment, then you can use the Microsoft Text Driver, and replace "Microsoft Access Text Driver (*.txt, *.csv)" with "Microsoft Text Driver (*.txt; *.csv)" in the code for this recipe.

10-4. Profiling External Data Faster

Problem

You want to profile data from a source other than SQL Server data in the shortest possible time.

Solution

Use T-SQL and OPENROWSET while minimizing the number of times the dataset is read. One way to do so is to use a temporary table, as in the following example (C:\SQL2012DIRecipes\CH10\Stock.Txt):

```
DECLARE @Cost_Price              INT
DECLARE @Registration_Year       INT
DECLARE @ROWCOUNT                 INT
DECLARE @Mileage_MAX             INT
DECLARE @Mileage_MIN             INT
DECLARE @Registration_Year_NULL INT
DECLARE @Cost_Price_NULL         INT

SELECT
CASE
WHEN Registration_Year IS NULL THEN 1 ELSE 0
END AS Registration_Year
,CASE
WHEN Cost_Price IS NULL THEN 1 ELSE 0
END AS Cost_Price
INTO    #NullSourceRecords
FROM    OPENROWSET('MSDASQL', 'Driver={Microsoft Access Text Driver (*.txt, *.csv)};
  DefaultDir= C:\SQL2012DIRecipes\CH10;','select Registration_Year, Cost_Price from Stock.txt')
WHERE Registration_Year IS NULL OR Cost_Price IS NULL

SELECT
@ROWCOUNT = COUNT(*)
,@Mileage_MAX = MAX(Mileage)
,@Mileage_MIN = MIN(Mileage)
FROM OPENROWSET('MSDASQL', 'Driver={Microsoft Access Text Driver (*.txt, *.csv)};
  DefaultDir= C:\SQL2012DIRecipes\CH10;','select Registration_Year, Cost_Price from Stock.txt')

SELECT
 @Registration_Year_NULL = SUM(Registration_Year)
 ,@Cost_Price_NULL = SUM(Cost_Price)
FROM    #NullSourceRecords

PRINT    @ROWCOUNT
PRINT    @Mileage_MAX
PRINT    @Mileage_MIN
PRINT    @Registration_Year_NULL
PRINT    @Cost_Price_NULL
PRINT    CAST(@Registration_Year_NULL AS NUMERIC (12,6))
              / CAST(@ROWCOUNT AS NUMERIC (12,6))
```

How It Works

You have probably guessed after reading Recipe 10-4 (and will soon find out if you are using your own large text file as the data source) that re-reading the entire file every time that you wish to profile one column is a very long-winded way to go about profiling your data. So if you are profiling several columns, I suggest minimizing the number of times that the data is read by grouping the profile data where possible so that as many profile elements as possible can be read each time the source file is read.

The code snippet in the current recipe reads the source text file twice—but twice only. The first trawl through the file is looking for NULL values in two columns (Registration_Year and Cost_Price). It creates a temporary table that isolates a narrow dataset containing only 1 or 0 indicating whether there are NULL values for each column. These columns are then summed to give the total NULL values for the columns in question. The second parse of the source file does not apply a WHERE clause—and returns the record count as well as maximum and minimum values for required columns. Any percentage calculations can then be carried out.

Hints, Tips, and Traps

- See Recipe 2-5 for a more detailed discussion of OPENROWSET when used with text files. Specifically, remember that OPENROWSET is built for ad hoc occasional connections, and that a linked server is the recommended solution for more regular connections.

- For a linked server, you can simplify things somewhat by using SQL similar to the following (where MyOracleDatabase is the linked server name). Remember to use the four-part notation to reference the table correctly:

```
SELECT COUNT(*)
FROM MyOracleDatabase..HR.EMPLOYEES
WHERE LAST_NAME IS NULL
```

- It can be more laborious to profile external data if your source data file does not contain column names. In this situation, you require a Schema.Ini file, as described in Recipe 2-6. Here is the Schema.Ini file (C:\SQL2012DIRecipes\CH10\Schema.Ini) for a data source file (C:\SQL2012DIRecipes\CH10\StockNoHeaders.Txt) that does not contain headers :

```
[StockNoHeaders.txt]
Format=CSVDelimited
ColNameHeader=False
MaxScanRows=0
Col1=MAKE Long
Col2=MARQUE long Width 20
Col3=MODEL Text Width 50
Col4=PRODUCT_TYPE Text Width 15
Col5=REGISTRATION_YEAR Text Width 4
Col6=MILEAGE Long
Col7=COST_PRICE Long
CharacterSet=ANSI
```

Running the code in this recipe—and using the pass-through query 'SELECT * FROM StockNoHeaders.txt'—will profile the source data from a text file that does not contain headers.

10-5. Running and Logging a Complete DataProfile

Problem

You wish to carry out a complete data profile of a source table and store the profile results that you have gathered using the T-SQL-based techniques described in Recipes 10-1 to 10-4.

Solution

Design a T-SQL script to profile all the information that you consider vital, and write the output to an SQL Server table. Then you can run profiling T-SQL and store the profile data that is returned. What follows is one example.

1. Create a profile data log table using the following DDL
    (C:\SQL2012DIRecipes\CH10\tblDataProfiling.Sql):

```
CREATE TABLE CarSales_Staging.dbo.DataProfiling
(
 ID int IDENTITY(1,1) NOT NULL,
 DateExecuted DATETIME NULL CONSTRAINT DF_Log_DataProfiling_DateExecuted
                             DEFAULT (getdate()),
 DataSourceObject varchar(250) NULL,
 DataSourceColumn varchar(250) NULL,
 ProfileName varchar(50) NULL,
 ProfileResult numeric(22, 4) NULL
) ;
GO
```

2. Run the following T-SQL to capture and store the profile data
    (C:\SQL2012DIRecipes\CH10\LogProfileData.Sql):

```
DECLARE @Rowcount               INT;
DECLARE @Model_NULL             INT;
DECLARE @Mileage_NULL           INT
DECLARE @Model_PERCENTNULL      NUMERIC(8,4);
DECLARE @Mileage_PERCENTNULL    NUMERIC(8,4);
DECLARE @Model_MAXLENGTH        INT;
DECLARE @Model_MINLENGTH        INT;
DECLARE @Mileage_MAX            INT;
DECLARE @Mileage_MIN            INT;


SELECT     @Rowcount = COUNT(*),
           @Mileage_MAX = MAX(Mileage),
           @Mileage_MIN = MIN(Mileage),
           @Model_MAXLENGTH = MAX(LEN(Model)),
           @Model_MINLENGTH = MIN(LEN(Model))
FROM       CarSales.dbo.Stock;


SELECT   @Model_NULL = COUNT(*)
FROM     CarSales.dbo.Stock
WHERE    Model IS NULL;
```

```
SELECT    @Mileage_NULL = COUNT(*)
FROM      CarSales.dbo.Stock
WHERE     Mileage IS NULL;

SET       @Model_PERCENTNULL = ↵
              CAST(@Model_NULL AS NUMERIC(5,2)) / CAST(@Rowcount AS NUMERIC(5,2));
SET       @Mileage_PERCENTNULL = ↵
              CAST(@Mileage_NULL AS NUMERIC(5,2)) / CAST(@Rowcount AS NUMERIC(5,2));

INSERT INTO CarSales_Staging.dbo.DataProfiling (DataSourceObject, DataSourceColumn,
ProfileName, ProfileResult)
VALUES ('CarSales_Staging.dbo.Stock', 'ALL', 'NbRows', @Rowcount, 100);
INSERT INTO CarSales_Staging.dbo.DataProfiling (DataSourceObject, DataSourceColumn,
ProfileName, ProfileResult)
VALUES ('CarSales_Staging.dbo.Stock', 'Mileage', 'MaxMileage', @Mileage_MAX, 100);
INSERT INTO CarSales_Staging.dbo.DataProfiling (DataSourceObject, DataSourceColumn,
ProfileName, ProfileResult)
VALUES ('CarSales_Staging.dbo.Stock', 'Mileage', 'MinMileage', @Mileage_MIN, 100);
INSERT INTO CarSales_Staging.dbo.DataProfiling (DataSourceObject, DataSourceColumn,
ProfileName, ProfileResult)
VALUES ('CarSales_Staging.dbo.Stock', 'Model', 'MaxLn_Model', @Model_MAXLENGTH, 100);
INSERT INTO CarSales_Staging.dbo.DataProfiling (DataSourceObject, DataSourceColumn,
ProfileName, ProfileResult)
VALUES ('CarSales_Staging.dbo.Stock', 'Model', 'MinLn_Model', @Model_MINLENGTH, 100);
INSERT INTO CarSales_Staging.dbo.DataProfiling (DataSourceObject, DataSourceColumn,
ProfileName, ProfileResult)
VALUES ('CarSales_Staging.dbo.Stock', 'Model', 'NbNulls_Model', @Model_NULL, 100);
INSERT INTO CarSales_Staging.dbo.DataProfiling (DataSourceObject, DataSourceColumn,
ProfileName, ProfileResult)
VALUES ('CarSales_Staging.dbo.Stock', 'Mileage', 'NbNulls_Mileage',
@Mileage_NULL, 100);
INSERT INTO CarSales_Staging.dbo.DataProfiling (DataSourceObject, DataSourceColumn,
ProfileName, ProfileResult)
VALUES ('CarSales_Staging.dbo.Stock', 'Model', 'PctNulls_Model',
@Model_PERCENTNULL, 100);
INSERT INTO CarSales_Staging.dbo.DataProfiling (DataSourceObject, DataSourceColumn,
ProfileName, ProfileResult)
VALUES ('CarSales_Staging.dbo.Stock', 'Mileage', 'PctNulls_Mileage',
@Mileage_PERCENTNULL, 100);
```

How It Works

Gathering profiling data is only part of the story. You will most probably want to do either or both of the following:

- Store the data in a data table (as to ensure SLAs (Service Level Agreements) are met or to track data profiles over time).

- Use the analysis of the stored profile data to inhibit or allow an ETL process to run.

So here you have a practical example of how to use the data you have gathered. I am presuming that we wish to analyze the data in an SQL Server source table and to store the results in a table of profile data. I am going to use the CarSales_Staging database for this table.

■ **Note** In a production environment, you could be using a separate database to store profile data. Here I am using the same database as the source data purely to make the example simpler.

This script presupposes that you wish to gather the following data:

- Null counts and null ratios for two columns.

- Numerical maximum and minimum for one column.

- Field length maximum and minimum for one column.

So the T-SQL gathers this information and records it to the dbo.DataProfiling table. Once the information is gathered, it can then be used for decision making in an ETL process, as described in Recipe 10-17.

This T-SQL is clearly hard-coded to be used in a highly specific set of circumstances and a specific table. My defense for the rigidity of this code is that you will probably never want to profile every column, but will in most cases want to look at specific columns—and so will code for a specific problem.

To accelerate the procedure, you can try to minimize the number of separate queries in the stored procedure. In any case, it is faster to calculate any values (notably the number of rows) that you will reuse only once, and hold them in a variable, than to recalculate them every time.

10-6. Profiling Data Quickly in SSIS
Problem

You want to profile data using SSIS as quickly as possible.

Solution

Use the SSIS Data Profiling task to run a quick profile in order to spend a minimal amount of time defining the elements to profile in a table or a view. You can carry out this task to analyze the Client table of the CarSales database, as follows:

1. Create a new SSIS package. Add an ADO.NET connection manager to theCarSales source database. Name it **CarSales_ADONET**.

2. Add a Data Profiling task to the Control Flow pane. Double-click to edit. In the General tab, select File Connection as the destination type.

3. Select New File Connection as the destination and configure the File Connection Manager Editor to create a new file named (in this example) **C:\SQL2012DIRecipes\ CH10\SSISProfile.xml**. The dialog box should look like Figure 10-1.

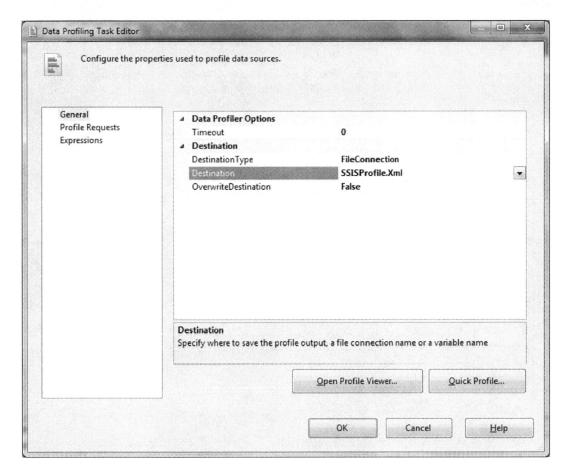

Figure 10-1. *Configuring the Output Destination in an SSIS Data Profiling task*

4. Click Quick Profile and select the CarSales_ADONET connection that you created in step 1 from the ADO.NETConnection pop-up list.

5. Select the table to analyze—in this case it is dbo.Client.

6. Check all the profile types that you wish to analyze. In this example, I am selecting all possible profile types. This dialog box should look like Figure 10-2.

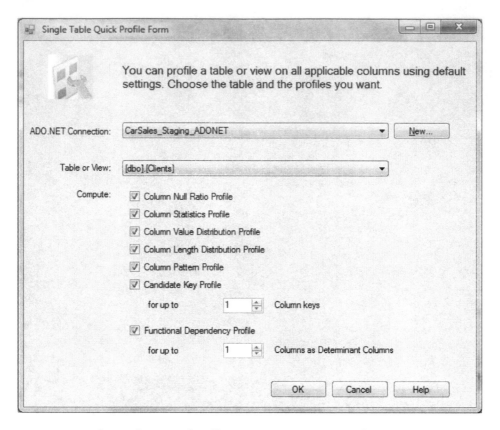

Figure 10-2. Selecting the types of profile to run in an SSIS Data Profiling task

7. Confirm your modifications with OK. You will see the selected profile requests, as shown in Figure 10-3.

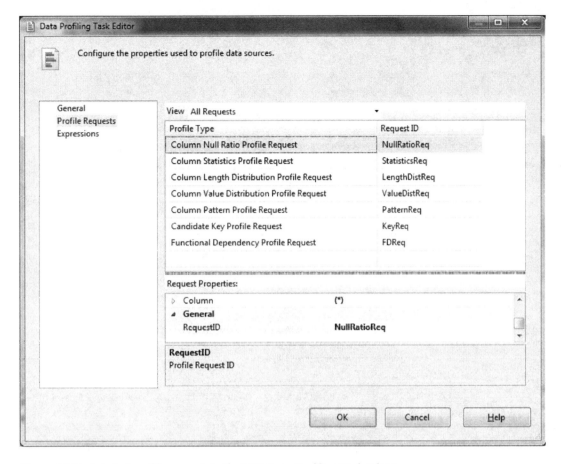

Figure 10-3. *Selected profile requests in the SSIS Data Profiling Task Editor*

8. Click OK in the Data Profiling Task Editor to confirm your profile selection.

You can now run the SSIS package containing the profile task, and, consequently, profile the source data. This will generate the XML output file that you specified in step 3 (C:\SQL2012DIRecipes\CH10\SSISProfile.xml). While it is possible to read this XML file directly in a web browser, you will probably find it easier to read it using the Data Profile Viewer, as described in Recipe 10-9.

How It Works

Since SQL Server 2008, SSIS has provided a task to profile source data. This task is slightly set apart from other SSIS tasks in that (at least in my experience) it is something that tends to be run "interactively" when initially looking at data, rather than as part of a structured ETL process. This said, you could also use it as part of a more comprehensive process if you need to. Once the task has run against a data source, you can then examine the output (most easily with the Data Profile Viewer described in Recipe 10-9) and decide if the source data matches your expectations. This recipe shows you how to obtain a profile using the Quick Profile option of the SSIS Profile task. Once a quick profile has been created, a series of profile requests is generated. These can be tweaked—or deleted—from the Profile Requests pane. Then the Profiling task can be run, and the output viewed in the Profile Viewer, as described in Recipe 10-9.

While ensuring a good overall analysis of data sources, the task does have the following limitations:

- Data sources are limited to tables and views from SQL Server 2000 and up over an ADO.NET connection.

- The account running the task must have read/write permissions, including CREATE TABLE permissions, on the TempDB database.

- The task can only produce an XML output file. Moreover, this file must be viewed using either the supplied Data Profile Viewer, or by loading the XML data using a custom task, as described in Recipe 10-10.

The breadth and depth of the analysis provided by this task are non-negligible, and cover the areas described in Table 10-4. As you can see, the Data Profiling task—even when resorting to the Quick Profile option—can provide you with a remarkably complete set of initial profile data.

Table 10-4. *SSIS Data Profiling Task Options*

Element	Description	Potential Use
Candidate Key	Indicates whether a column or set of columns is a key, or could be a key, for the selected source table.	Determines the potential of a column (or set of columns) to be a unique key.
Column Length Distribution	Returns all the distinct lengths of string values in the selected column and the percentage of rows in the table for each column length.	Determines the range of lengths of data in a column.
Column Null Ratio	Returns the percentage of null values in the selected column.	Determines the percentage of NULLs in the column.
Column Pattern	Returns a set of regular expressions that cover the specified percentage of values in a string column.	Determine the text patterns in a column. This covers the way the text looks and is formatted.
Column Statistics	Indicates statistics such as minimum, maximum, average, and standard deviation for numeric columns, and minimum and maximum for DATETIME columns.	Determines the ranges of values and dates of data in a column.
Column Value Distribution	Indicates all the distinct values in the selected column and the percentage of rows in the table that each value represents.	Determines exactly how many distinct values exist in a column in order to define the distribution of values.
Functional Dependency	Indicates the extent to that the values in one column (the dependent column) depend on the values in another column or set of columns (the determinant column).	Determines if value sets correspond between columns.
Value Inclusion	Indicates the overlap in the values between two columns or sets of columns.	Determines the potential of a column (or set of columns) to be a foreign key.

Hints, Tips, and Traps

- You can create as many quick profiles as you wish, each from a separate table or view. They will all be added to the profile requests.

10-7. Creating Custom Data Profiles with SSIS
Problem

You want to use SSIS to profile data while adjusting the profile specifications to suit your precise requirements.

Solution

Rather than running a quick profile, use the Data Profiling task to configure the available options to return the information that suits you. Once again I will use the CarSales.dbo.Stock table as the data to be profiled.

1. Create a new SSIS package. Add an ADO.NET connection manager to the CarSales source database. Name it **CarSales_ADONET**.

2. Right-click in the Connection Managers tab and select New File Connection. Select the Usage Type Create File and browse to the chosen folder (C:\SQL2012DIRecipes\CH10\CustomProfile.Xml in this example). Click Open to create the file and OK to close the New File Connection dialog box.

3. Add a Data Profiling task to the Control Flow pane. Double-click to edit. In the General tab, select File Connection as the destination type.

4. Select the CustomProfile.xml connection that you created in step 3.

5. Set Overwrite Destination to True.

6. Click Profile Requests on the left to active the Requests pane.

7. Scroll down to the bottom of the available profile requests (if any exist), click in a blank record, and select a profile request from those available in the pop-up list. In this example, I suggest starting with a Column Length Distribution Profile Request.

8. Press Tab or Enter to confirm the request creation. SSIS will give this request a name (LengthDistReq probably).

9. In the lower part of the pane—the Request Properties section—you will now configure the request, starting with the connection to the source database. For the property named Connection Manager, select the CarSales_ADONET Connection manager that you created in step 1.

10. Select dbo.Stock as the TableOrView property.

11. Select Make as the Column Property.

12. Click OK.

You can now run the package and analyze the resulting XML profile data.

How It Works

If you prefer to create and fine-tune profiles directly, then you can do so by configuring the SSIS Data Profiling task manually rather than use the Quick Profile approach. The profiling options are fairly wide-ranging—as seen in Table 10-6. With a little practice, however, they become fairly easy to use.

Defining a profile will always include one of the elements from Table 10-5. This is essentially the core definition of which database, table and columns that you are profiling.

Table 10-5. *Compulsory Elements in an SSIS Data Profiling Task*

Element	Comments
Connection Manager	An existing or newly created ADO.NET connection manager.
Table or View	A table or view available through the selected connection manager.
Column	A single column (or all columns selected by using the asterisk "*") from the table that you wish to profile.
RequestID	A user-defined name for this profile element. Although SSIS will name each profile request, you can overwrite these names with your own.

Once you have specified the database, table and column you have to indicate which type of profile you wish to run. You can also specify certain parameters specific to the type of profile. Each of these configurations forms a separate profile request. The various options that are specific to each type of profile request are explained in Table 10-6.

Table 10-6. *SSIS Profile Task Options*

Element	Description	Potential Use
Candidate Key	Indicates whether a column or set of columns is a key, or an approximate key, for the selected table.	Determine a column (or set of columns) potential as an unique key.
Column Length Distribution	Indicates all the distinct lengths of string values in the selected column and the percentage of rows in the table that each length represents.	Determine the range of column lengths.
Column Null Ratio	Indicates the percentage of null values in the selected column.	Determine the percentage of NULLs.
Column Pattern	Returns a set of regular expressions that cover the specified percentage of values in a string column.	Determine the text patterns in a column.
Column Statistics	Indicates statistics such as minimum, maximum, average, and standard deviation for numeric columns, and minimum and maximum for DATETIME columns.	Determine ranges of values and dates.
Column Value Distribution	Indicates all the distinct values in the selected column and the percentage of rows in the table that each value represents.	Determine how many distinct values exist in a column.

(continued)

Table 10-6. (*continued*)

Element	Description	Potential Use
Functional Dependency	Indicates the extent to which the values in one column (the dependent column) depend on the values in another column or set of columns (the determinant column).	Determine if value sets are accurate between columns.
Value Inclusion	Indicates the overlap in the values between two columns or sets of columns.	Determine a column (or set of columns) potential as a foreign key.

You can only profile one column at a time for each profile request. However, you can create multiple profile requests for the same profile type, and so cover several columns.

Hints, Tips, and Traps

- To delete a profile click it in the Profile Requests pane, and press the Delete key. You can use Ctrl and Shift to select multiple profile requests.

- SSIS will autogenerate a RequestID for each profile type. You can rename it using the RequestID property.

- The various Strength Thresholds (Key Strength for the Candidate Key, InclusionStrengthThreshold and SupersetColumnsKeyThreshold for Value Inclusion, and FDStrengthThreshold for Functional Dependency) are the percentage of unique elements in the dataset. If the corresponding ThresholdSetting is set to Specified, then you will only get a result if the profiling analysis returns this percentage or greater of unique records. Otherwise, you will get an empty dataset returned. To return results whatever the percentage of unique records, set the ThresholdSetting to None. Alternatively, you can set a lower threshold percentage for unique records.

- The MaxNumberOfViolations is a count of duplicate elements in the columns—which can be a potential for problems. You can adjust this figure to suit your requirements.

- By setting SupersetColumnsKeyThreshold is to Exact when analyzing potential foreign keys, you can filter out combinations where the superset column is not an appropriate key for the superset table because of non-unique values.

- You can get around the SSIS limitation on available data sources by using OPENDATASOURCE in a .NET data source. Be warned that this will be incredibly slow.

10-8. Using the SSIS Data Profiling Task on non-SQL Server Data Sources

Problem

You want to use the SSIS Data Profiling task to profile data from non-SQL Server data sources.

Solution

Use a linked server as the source of the data to get around the SSIS limitation of using ADO.NET connection managers only. The following steps explain how to do it.

1. Use a linked server to connect to another data source (be it a CSV file or an Oracle database, for instance).

2. In SSMS, create a view using the linked server as the source of the data.

3. Connect the SSIS Data Profiling task to the view, which becomes the data source (as described in Recipe 10-6, step 4).

4. Continue with Recipe 10-6 (for a quick profile) or 10-7 (for a custom profile) to create the XML profile output.

How It Works

I realize that all the documentation states that the SSIS Data Profiling task will only work with an ADO.NET connection and an SQL Server data source. And, what is more, the documentation is right. However, you can "cheat" to some extent this way.

Be aware that this will probably be the slowest Data Profiling task that you have ever seen. I have tested this on CSV files that took approximately five times longer to profile than the same data stored in SQL Server. So you might not want to do this in production, but may perhaps want to do it as part of an initial data analysis step when faced with a new data source.

■ **Note** As creating linked servers to Microsoft Office sources, text files, and third-party RDBMSs were covered in Chapters 1, 2, and 4, respectively, I refer you to those chapters for the connection specifics.

10-9. Reading Profile Data
Problem

You want to read the XML profile data created using the SSIS Data Profiling task.

Solution

Use the Data Profile Viewer installed with SSIS, as follows.

1. Run the following: "C:\Program Files (x86)\Microsoft SQL Server\110\DTS\ Binn\DataProfileViewer.exe"

2. Click Open in the toolbar. Navigate to—and load—the profile XML file that you created as the output destination when configuring the Profiling task.

3. Select the profile element corresponding to the profile that you want to analyze (see Figure 10-4). The Data Profile Viewer will show all the profile requests in a tree view on the left.

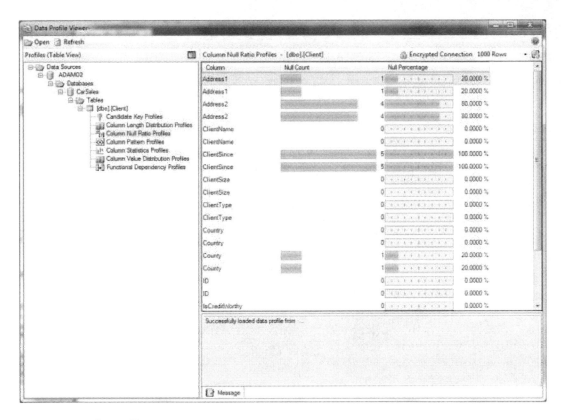

Figure 10-4. *The Profile Viewer*

How It Works

Rather than wading through reams of cryptic XML, you will probably prefer to run the Data Profile Viewer to see the results of the data profiling. You will need to expand the tree and navigate down from Server, via Database, to the table (or view) whose elements you wish to analyze.

Hints, Tips, and Traps

- You can also run the Data Profile Viewer directly from inside an SSIS package by editing the Data Profile task and clicking the Open Profile Viewerbutton. This will automatically open the correct XML file—assuming that you have run the Data Profile task.

- Another way of running the Data Profile Viewer is to click Start ➤ All Programs ➤ Microsoft SQL Server 2012 ➤ Integration Services ➤ Data Profile Viewer.

■ **Note**   The output file might contain sensitive data about your database and the data that it contains. If this is the case, you should consider storing it in a suitably protected folder.

10-10. Storing SSIS Profile Data in a Database
Problem

You want to store the profile data created using the SSIS Profiling task in an SQL Server database.

Solution

Use a custom XML task to read the XML file produced by the SSIS Profiling task and shred the profile data into SQL Server tables. The following explains one way to profile the data from the CarSales sample database and store the results in the CarSales_Staging database.

1. Create the following tablesin the CarSales_Staging database
    (C:\SQL2012DIRecipes\CH10\SSISProfileTables.Sql):

```
USE CarSales_Staging;
GO

CREATE TABLE dbo.DataProfiling_ColumnValueDistribution
(
 ProfileRequestID NVARCHAR(255) NULL,
 NumberOfDistinctValues INT NULL,
 ColumnValueDistributionProfile_Id BIGINT NOT NULL,
 DateAdded DATETIME NOT NULL DEFAULT GETDATE(),
 ID int IDENTITY(1,1) NOT NULL
) ;
GO

CREATE TABLE dbo.DataProfiling_ColumnStatistics
(
 ProfileRequestID NVARCHAR(255) NULL,
 MinValue DECIMAL(28, 10) NULL,
 MaxValue DECIMAL(28, 10) NULL,
 Mean DECIMAL(28, 10) NULL,
 StdDev DECIMAL(28, 10) NULL,
 ID int IDENTITY(1,1) NOT NULL,
 DateAdded DATETIME NOT NULL DEFAULT GETDATE()
) ;
GO

CREATE TABLE dbo.DataProfiling_ColumnNulls
(
 ProfileRequestID NVARCHAR(255) NULL,
 NullCount TINYINT NULL,
 ID int IDENTITY(1,1) NOT NULL,
 DateAdded DATETIME NOT NULL DEFAULT GETDATE()
) ;
GO
```

```
CREATE TABLE dbo.DataProfiling_ColumnLength
(
 ProfileRequestID NVARCHAR(255) NULL,
 ColumnLengthDistributionProfile_ID BIGINT NULL,
 MinLength TINYINT NULL,
 MaxLength TINYINT NULL,
 ID int IDENTITY(1,1) NOT NULL,
 DateAdded DATETIME NOT NULL DEFAULT GETDATE()
) ;
GO

CREATE TABLE dbo.DataProfiling_ValueDistributionItem
(
 Value NVARCHAR(255) NULL,
 Count INT NULL,
 ValueDistribution_Id BIGINT NOT NULL
) ;
GO

CREATE TABLE dbo.DataProfiling_LengthDistributionItem
(
 Length tinyint NOT NULL,
 Count bigINT NULL,
 LengthDistribution_Id BIGINT NOT NULL
) ;
GO

CREATE TABLE dbo.DataProfiling_Join_ValueDistribution
(
 ValueDistribution_Id BIGINT NOT NULL,
 ColumnValueDistributionProfile_Id BIGINT NOT NULL
) ;
GO

CREATE TABLE dbo.DataProfiling_Join_LengthDistribution
(
 LengthDistribution_Id BIGINT NOT NULL,
 ColumnLengthDistributionProfile_Id BIGINT NOT NULL
) ;
GO
```

2. Create a new SSIS package. Add two ADO.NET connection managers, the one named
    CarSales_ADONET should point to the CarSales database; the one named
    CarSales_Staging_ADONET should point to the CarSales_Staging database.

3. Add an Execute SQL task. Configure it to use the connection manager for the profile
    data. Name it **Prepare Tables** and set the SQL Statement to (C:\SQL2012DIRecipes\
    CH10\TruncateSSISProfileTables.Sql):

```
TRUNCATE TABLE dbo.DataProfiling_ColumnLength;
TRUNCATE TABLE dbo.DataProfiling_ColumnNulls;
TRUNCATE TABLE dbo.DataProfiling_ColumnStatistics;
```

```
TRUNCATE TABLE dbo.DataProfiling_ColumnValueDistribution;
TRUNCATE TABLE dbo.DataProfiling_Join_LengthDistribution;
TRUNCATE TABLE dbo.DataProfiling_Join_ValueDistribution;
TRUNCATE TABLE dbo.DataProfiling_LengthDistributionItem;
TRUNCATE TABLE dbo.DataProfiling_ValueDistributionItem;
```

4. Add a Data Profiling task and double-click to edit. Define a new File Destination named **C:\SQL2012DIRecipes\CH10\MyProfile.Xml**—as described in Recipe 10-6, step 3.

5. Create four profile requests, as follows, all using the CarSales_ADONETconnection manager:

Profile Type	Name	TableOrView	Column	Options
Column Null Ratio Profile	ColumnNull_↵ Client_Town	Client	Town	
Column Statistics Profile	ColumnLength_↵ Client_Name	Client	ClientName	IgnoreLeadingSpaces = True IgnoreTrailingSpaces = True
Column Length Distribution Profile	ColumnStatistics_ InvoiceLines_↵ SalePrice	InvoiceLines	SalePrice	
Column Value Distribution Profile	ColumnValue_↵ Client_Country	Client	Country	ValueDistribution↵ Option = AllValues

6. Run the package to create an initial output XML file (By clicking Debug ➤ Start Debugging, for instance).

7. Add a Data Flow task, join the Profile task to it, and double-click to open the Data Flow pane.

8. Add an XML source and configure as follows:

Data Access Mode:	XML File Location
XML Location:	The C:\SQL2012DIRecipes\CH10\MyProfile.Xml file created in step 3
XSD Location:	Generate an XSD from the MyProfile.Xml, named **C:\SQL2012DIRecipes\CH10\MyProfile.Xsd**.

9. Confirm your modifications with OK.

10. Create eight OLEDB destination tasks, all using the connection manager, and configure them to use the following outputs from the XML source to the destination tables. (You should map all the columns that are available in the destination tables that correspond to source columns, as shown.)

XML Data Source Output	Destination Table
ColumnStatisticsProfile	dbo.DataProfiling_ColumnStatistics
ColumnNullRatioProfile	dbo.DataProfiling_ColumnNulls
ColumnLengthDistributionProfile	dbo.DataProfiling_ColumnLength
LengthDistribution	dbo.DataProfiling_Join_LengthDistribution
LengthDistributionItem	dbo.DataProfiling_LengthDistributionItem
ColumnValueDistributionProfile	dbo.DataProfiling_ColumnValueDistribution
ValueDistribution	dbo.DataProfiling_Join_ValueDistribution
ValueDistributionItem	dbo.DataProfiling_ValueDistributionItem

11. The Data Flow pane should look something like Figure 10-5.

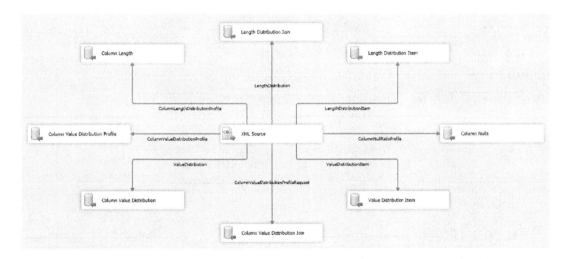

Figure 10-5. *Data Flow for a custom profile output*

You can now run the package. Once it has run the profile data, it will be available in the destination tables for analysis.

How It Works

Profiling data and then analyzing with the Data Profile Viewer is great when you are first getting to know your data, but it can prove limiting when you want to store this information for future use—either once the data loading process has finished, or as part of a business process to test the profile results before allowing a load to continue. So you are likely to want to store the profile data in order to compare it with acceptable thresholds and use some logic to control the data flow. This requires a two-step approach:

First, define the Profiling task, and output the results to a variable.

Second, load a small subset of the XML from the variable into SQL Server tables to capture the essential data.

This technique does imply the following prerequisites:

- A Data Source that you must configure to connect to a suitable data source.

- A Data Flow task that is configured to use the data source that you have defined.

As you can see, some profile types, such as Column Null Ratio profile and Column Statistics profile can be shredded directly into a single output table. Other profile types such as Column Length Distribution Profile and Column Value Distribution Profile require only a single table if all you want is the count of the number of distinct elements, but will require two other tables (a table for all the individual items and a many-to-many table to join the items to the aggregate table) if you want the details of every value and the number of times it appears.

As it would be far too detailed to show how to obtain every possible piece of profile information, this recipe is an overview of four of the four main profile types that I have found useful when applying business rule analysis to an SSIS data load. I will not explain every last detail of how to use an XML data source, as many ways of doing this were covered in Chapter 3. However, you should be able to take this recipe as an example on which you can build to create your own profile output tables. The relationship between the profile type that you are analyzing and the output table(s) is given in Table 10-7.

Table 10-7. *Table Used for Profile Types*

Profile Type	Table(s) Used
Column Null Ratio Profile	Dbo.DataProfiling_ColumnNulls
Column Statistics Profile	Dbo.DataProfiling_ColumnStatistics
Column Length Distribution Profile	Dbo.DataProfiling_ColumnLengthDistribution <= Dbo.DataProfiling_Join_LengthDistribution => Dbo.DataProfiling_LengthDistributionItem
Column Value Distribution Profile	Dbo.DataProfiling_ColumnValueDistribution <= Dbo.DataProfiling_Join_ValueDistribution => Dbo.DataProfiling_ValueDistributionItem

Hints, Tips, and Traps

- There are many, many outputs from the XML file produced by the Data Profiling task. Should you need a better understanding of the file, then I suggest that you open the MyProfile.Xsd file (created in step 8) in Visual Studio, or even read the XML to see how the data is structured.

- If you do not wish to use a file for the XML data, then once the package is tested and debugged, you can define a string variable (at package level) and use this both as the destination for the Profiling task and as the source data for the XML data source. However, any further work on the package will necessitate resetting these as file-based data while the package is modified and debugged. Then the string variable can be reapplied.

- Of course, you can extend this package to handle to other profile types, such as Functional Dependency or Value Inclusion.

10-11. Tailoring Specific Source Data Profiles in SSIS

Problem

You want to profile your data in a way that is tailored to your source data and profiling requirements.

Solution

Use SSIS to create a custom profiling package using standard SSIS tasks and go beyond the standard options available in the SSIS Data Profiling task.

1. Create an SSIS package. Name it **Profiling.Dtsx**.

2. Create the CarSales_Staging.dbo.DataProfiling table whose DDL was given in Recipe 10-5 to store profile data (unless you have already created it, of course).

3. Create an ADO.NET connection for this task that connects to the destination (CarSales_Staging) database. I am naming it **CarSales_Staging_ADONET**.

4. Add a Flat File connection manager and connect to the data source file, C:\SQL2012DIRecipes\CH10\Stock.Txt in this example. Name it **StockFile**. Make sure that you set the data type for the Mileage column to four-byte signed integer [DT_I4] in the Advanced pane.

5. Add the following variables in your package:

Variable Name	Type	Value
Mileage_MAX	Int32	0
Mileage_MIN	Int32	0
RowCount	Int32	0

6. Having clicked on the Data Flow pane, Click the "Click here . . . " prompt to add a Data Flow task.

7. Add a Flat File source, and configure it to use the StockFile connection manager.

8. Add a Row Count task from the toolbox onto the Data Flow pane and connect the Flat file source to it.

9. Double-click to add the RowCount variable from the pop-up list of available variables (Figure 10-6). Confirm with OK.

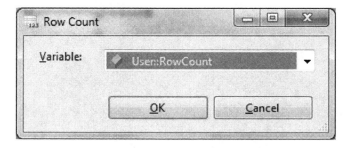

Figure 10-6. *Adding a variable to an SSIS data flow*

10. Add an Aggregate task on to the Data Flow pane. Name it **Attribute Analysis** and connect the Row Count task to it.

11. Double-click the Aggregate task to edit it.

12. Select the column(s) that you wish to analyze in the upper part of the Aggregations tab—or drag the column down to the lower part of the pane. I will use the Mileage column in this example, once for the maximum and once for the minimum.

13. Select the type of analysis that you wish to apply from the pop-up in the Operation column. In this example I am using Maximum first and Minimum second.

14. Rename the output alias appropriately. I suggest **Mileage_MAX** and **Mileage_MIN**, respectively. The Aggregate Transformation dialog box should look something like Figure 10-7.

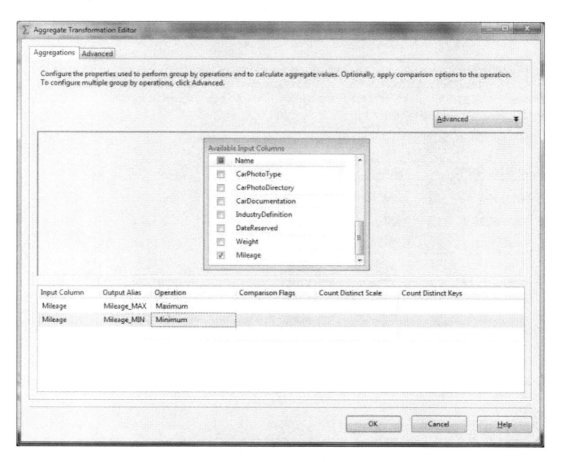

Figure 10-7. *The Aggregate Transformation dialog box in SSIS*

15. Click OK to confirm your modifications. Return to the Data Flow tab.

16. Add an Unpivot transform task onto the Data Flow pane. Connect the Aggregate task to it. Double-click to edit the Unpivot task.

17. In the Unpivot Transformation Editor dialog box, select the columns containing the profiling information that you wish to unpivot. Set the both destination columns to ProfileResult. Set the Pivot Key column name to ProfileName. You should see the dialog box shown in Figure 10-8, or something similar.

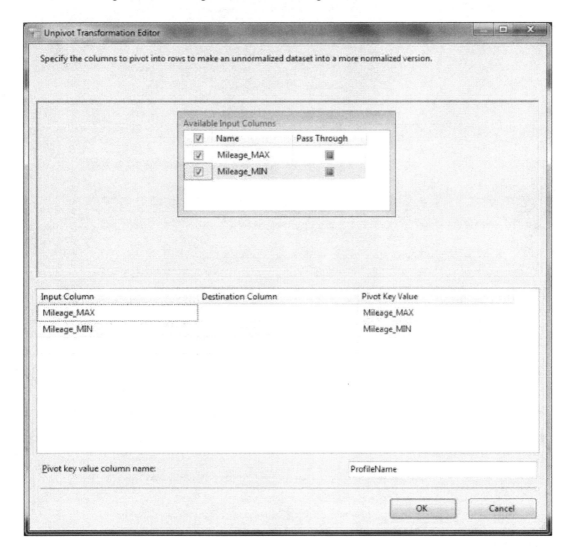

Figure 10-8. *Unpivoting custom profile data in SSIS*

18. Click OK to confirm your changes.

19. Add a Derived Column transformation task to the Data Flow pane. Connect the Unpivot task to it and add the following derived column:

DataSourceColumn: Set the expression as "Mileage"

DataSourceObject: Set the expression as "Invoice.Txt"

The dialog box should resemble Figure 10-9.

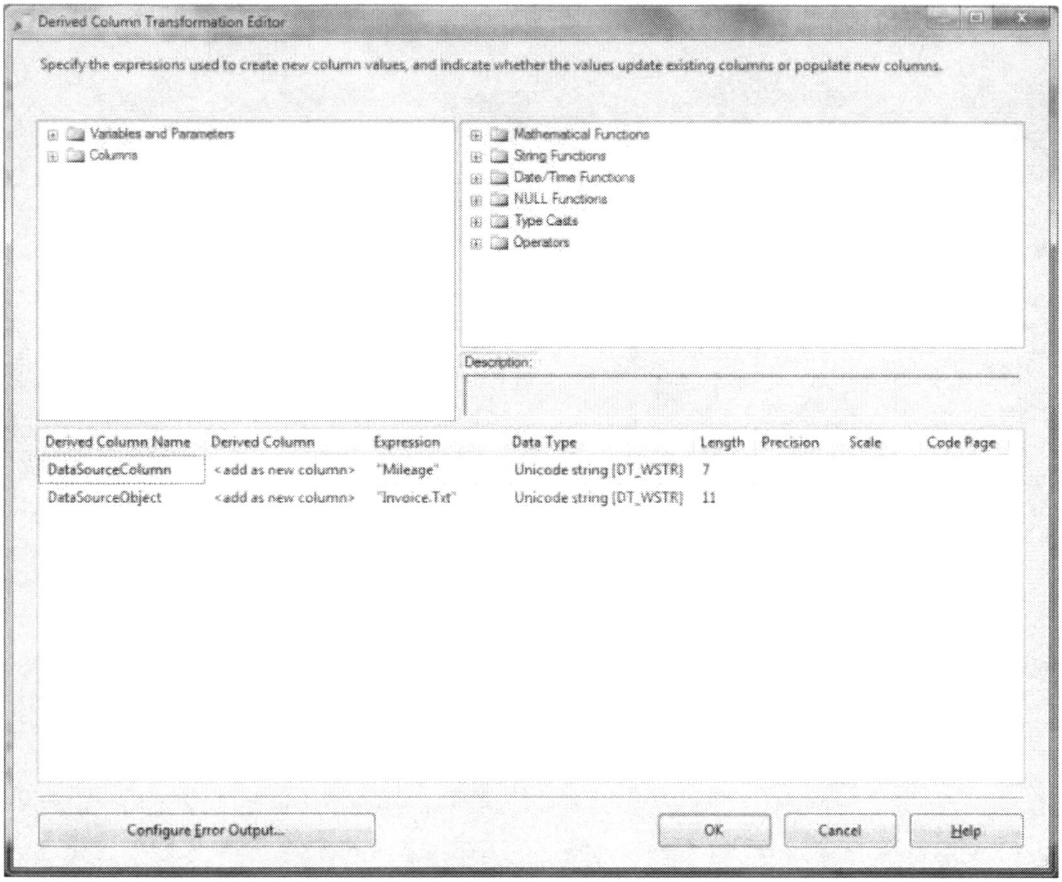

Figure 10-9. Adding derived columns

20. Add an OLEDB destination task to the Data Flow pane. Connect the Derived Column task to it.

21. Double-click the OLEDB destination task and configure it to connect to an SQL Server database. Connect to the DataProfiling table. Map the available input columns to the available output columns in the Mappings pane. The mapping should look like in Figure 10-10.

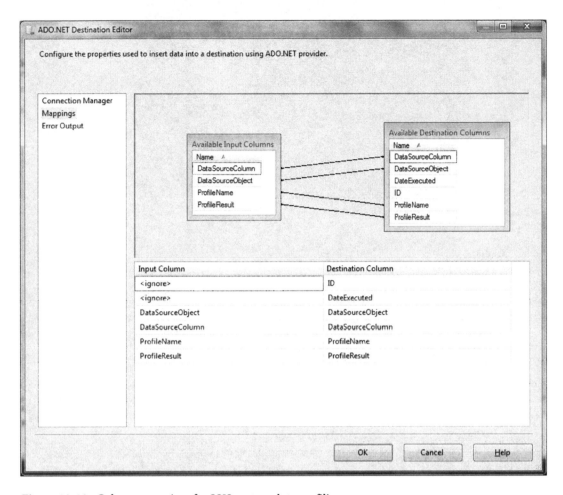

Figure 10-10. *Column mappings for SSIS custom data profiling*

22. Click OK. Your Data Flow pane should look like Figure 10-11.

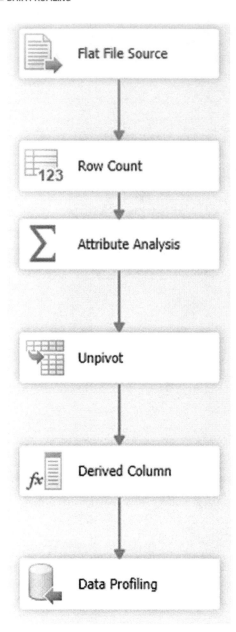

Figure 10-11. *Data flow for a custom Profiling task*

23. Return to the Control Flow pane and add an Execute SQL task. Name it **Add Rowcount**. Connect the Data Flow task to this new task. Double-click to edit.

24. Configure it to use the CarSales_Staging_ADONET connection manager that you created in step 3.

25. Click Parameters on the left. Map the following parameter:

Variable Name	Direction	Data Type	Parameter Name
User::RowCount	Input	Int16	@RowCount

26. Enter the following SQL Statement:

```
INSERT INTO dbo.DataProfiling (DataSourceObject, ProfileName, ProfileResult)
VALUES ('Invoice.Txt', 'RowCount', @Rowcount)
```

The dialog box should look like the one in Figure 10-12.

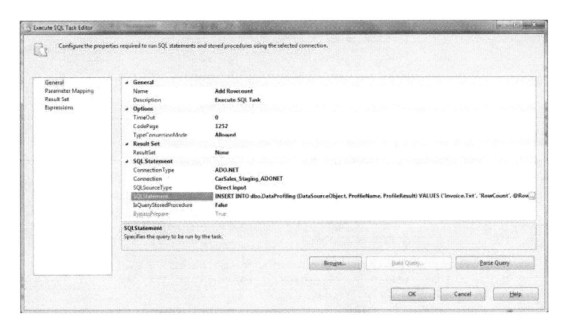

Figure 10-12. *Execute SQL task to run a T-SQL INSERT statement*

27.   Click OK. The final Package should look like Figure 10-13.

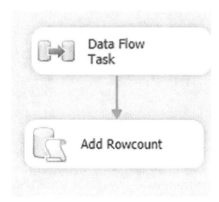

Figure 10-13. *The final Data Flow to return specific profile data from SSIS*

Now when you run the package, the source data will be read and the aggregates will be written to the destination table. The data itself will not be imported.

How It Works

Good as the SSIS Profiling task is, there could well be many occasions when you prefer to go to the trouble of profiling data another way—that probably means using some of the standard Data Flow components. Such a "do-it-yourself" approach to SSIS profiling has things in its favor:

- You can run it **while you are importing data**—so once a data import process has finished you do not need to spend time performing a profile analysis, be this using T-SQL or the SSIS Data Profiling task on the imported data.

- You can profile **any data source that SSIS can connect to**—and not just ADO.NET SQL Server (2000 and up) sources. At least you can without "cheating" (as described in Recipe 10-8)—and the consequent speed hit.

What this package does is to collect a small series of profiling counters. Some—like Mileage_MAX and Mileage_MIN—are added as columns, as was the case in previous recipes. Others (RowCount here) are passed to a package variable an added once the initial profiling has been run. This latter technique is necessary as the rowcount task only allows its variable to be used once a data flow is finished.

Anyhow, most of the basic numeric profiling that you can carry out with T-SQL can also be done using SSIS. As I said previously (but it is important and so bears repetition), the advantage of using SSIS is that data profiling can be part of an existing data flow, which is frequently faster than running T-SQL queries on a staging table after an initial data load.

However, every silver lining has its cloud, and with SSIS and custom data profiling there are several sets of problems. First, SSIS only includes a subset of the statistical functions that are available out of the box in T-SQL:maximum, minimum, count, distinct count, and domain analysis.SSIS does not contain functions to compute field length and domain percentages.

Overcoming these limitations requires some code to be run after the initial processing. This is described in Recipe 10-16. Also, combining all the profiling that you may need (attribute profiling and domain analysis) can require relatively complex SSIS machinations, and outputting the results is somewhat laborious, as this involves capturing the total number of rows processed and capturing maximum and minimum values for a column.

Hints, Tips, and Traps

- Ensure that all variables are scoped at the package level.

- If you are using SQL Server 2005 or 2008, you will have to add the variable name using the Custom Properties dialog box, as shown in Figure 10-14.

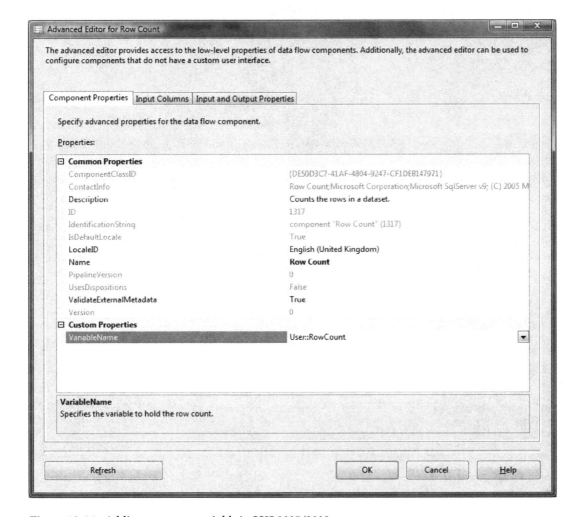

Figure 10-14. *Adding a counter variable in SSIS 2005/2008*

- When setting variables as the source expression for a derived column, remember that you can expand the Variables tree in the upper left-hand pane of the Derived Column Transformation Editor dialog box, and drag the variable to the Expression column.

- SSIS will only allow the appropriate analysis to be applied—you cannot select average, maximum, or minimum for non-numeric data. So if you are using a Flat File source, make sure that you have specified a numeric data type as part of the Advanced column properties, or use a data conversion task to ensure a numeric data type.

- To apply several analyses to the same column, drag the column down from the upper part of the tab to the lower part of the dialog box.

- To delete a column from an aggregate analysis, right-click it in the lower part of the Aggregate Transform Editor and select Delete.

- If the source data is a flat file, and this does not contain column names, be sure to add them in the Advanced pane of the Data Source Editor.

- You can add as many Row Count tasks as you wish to an SSIS task. However, each will require a separate variable to be declared and attributed.

10-12. Domain Analysis in SSIS

Problem

You want to provide custom domain analysis for a data sourceat the same time that you are carrying out the attribute analysis of the data source.

Solution

Use SSIS to create a custom profiling package.

I presume that you want to carry out a domain analysis (that is, looking at the distinct data elements contained in a column and returning counts and percentages of the total) alongside an attribute analysis, as was shown in Recipe 10-11. To avoid repeating much of the same package creation, I will use the package created in Recipe 10-11 as a basis for extending the development to include domain analysis. You can download this package from the book's web site if you have not already created it.

1. Create the following table
   (`C:\SQL2012DIRecipes\CH10\tblDataProfilingDomainAnalysis.Sql`):

   ```
   CREATE TABLE CarSales_Staging.dbo.DataProfilingDomainAnalysis
   (
    ID INT IDENTITY(1,1) NOT NULL,
    DataSourceObject NVARCHAR(150) NULL,
    DataSourceColumn NVARCHAR(150) NULL,
    DataSourceColumnData NVARCHAR(150) NULL,
    DataSourceColumnResult NVARCHAR(150) NULL,
    DateExecuted DATETIME NOT NULL DEFAULT (getdate())
   ) ;
   GO
   ```

2. Open the SSIS package created in Recipe 10-11 (Profiling.Dtsx). Move to the Data Flow pane.

3. Delete the connector between the Row Count task and the Attribute Analysis Aggregate task. Add a Multicast task and connect the Row Count task to it. Connect the Multicast task to the Attribute Analysis Aggregate task.

4. Add an Aggregate task on to the Data Flow pane. Connect the Multicast source to it. The first part of the Data Flow pane should look like Figure 10-15.

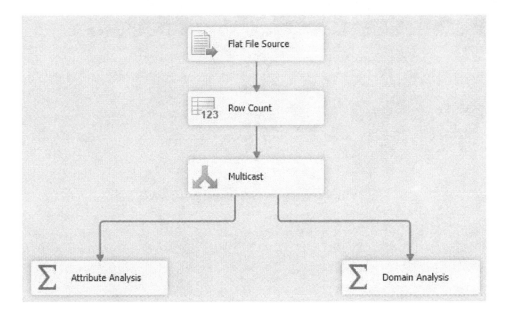

Figure 10-15. *Custom domain analysis in SSIS*

5. Double-click the Aggregate task that you just created. Name it **Domain Analysis**. Drag the column name that you wish to use for domain analysis down to the lower half of the dialog box twice. I am using Product_Type in this example.

6. Select Group By for one operation and Count for the other. Set the Output Alias for the Group By aggregation to Product_Types and the Output Alias for the Count aggregation to Product_Types_COUNT. The Aggregate Transform dialog box should look like Figure 10-16.

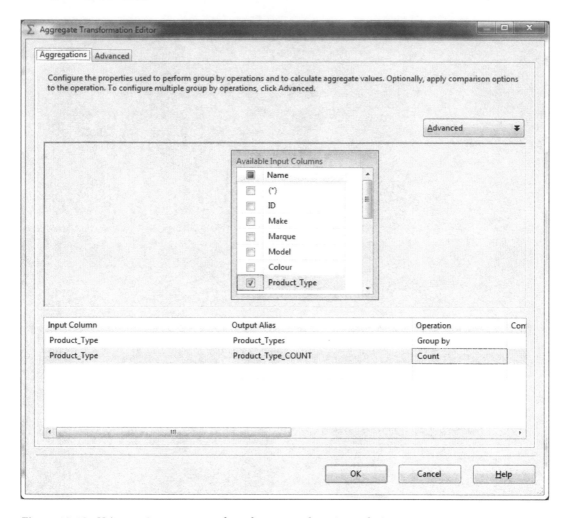

Figure 10-16. Using an Aggregate transform for custom domain analysis

7. Confirm your modifications with OK.

8. Add a new Derived Column task to the Data Flow pane. Add the following columns:

DataSourceColumn: set the expression as (DT_WSTR,260)"PRODUCT_TYPE".

DataSourceObject: set the expression as Stock.Txt

Product_Types: set the expression as (DT_WSTR,260)Product_Types

9. Add an OLEDB destination task to the Data Flow pane. Connect the Derived Columns task you just created to it.

10. Double-click the OLEDB destination task and configure it to use the CarSales_ Staging_ADONET connection manager. Map to the DataProfilingDomainAnalysis table. Map the available input columns to the available output columns in the Mappings pane, as shown in Figure 10-17. Click OK.

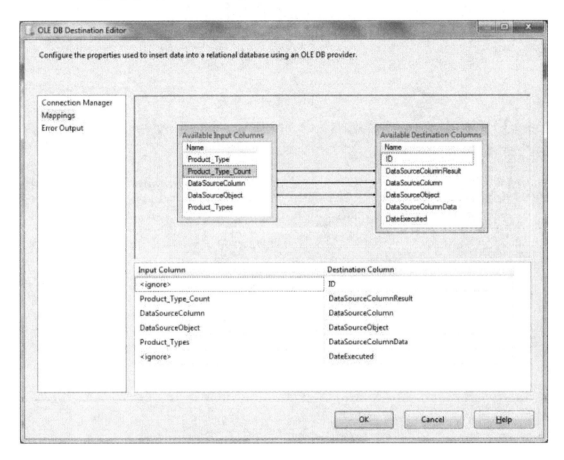

Figure 10-17. *Mapping output columns in an OLEDB data destination for custom profiling*

When you run the SSIS package, your destination table will contain the counts for each distinct element in the selected column.

Hints, Tips, and Traps

- In a "real-world" data profiling scenario, you may find it necessary to carry out data type conversions. To do this, simply use the Data Conversion task, which is described in Recipe 9-1.

10-13. Performing Multiple Domain Analyses

Problem

You want to return multiple domain analyses for a data source in the same SSIS package.

Solution

Use SSIS to create a custom profiling package and use the Multicast transform to create multiple data flow paths that you then profile independently. To avoid repetition, I will extend the package created in Recipe 10-11 and extended in Recipe 10-12. You can download this from the book's web site if you wish.

1. In the Profiling.Dtsx package, double-click the Aggregate task Domain Analysis to edit it. Click the Advanced button.

2. Rename the Aggregation name (currently Aggregate Output 1) to **ProductTypes**.

3. Add a new Aggregation name (in the blank cell under the newly renamed ProductTypes). Call it **Marques**.

4. Drag the column name that you wish to use for domain analysis (Marques in this example) down to the lower half of the dialog box twice.

5. Select Group By for one operation and Count for the other. Set the Output Alias for the Group By aggregation to Marques and the Output Alias for the Count aggregation to Marques_COUNT. The Aggregate Transform dialog box should look like Figure 10-18.

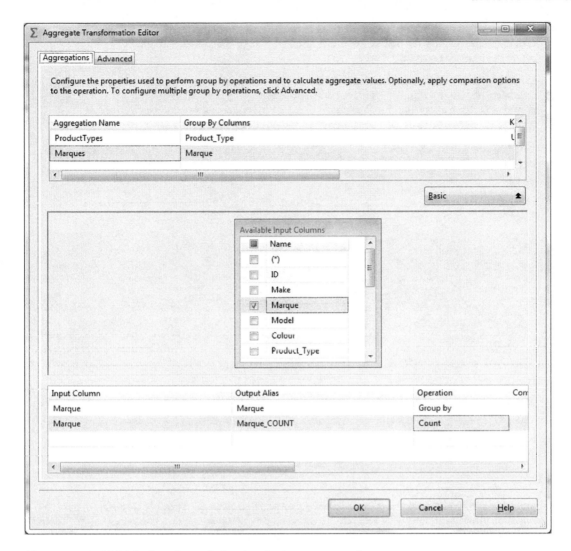

Figure 10-18. *Multiple domain analysis using the Aggregate transform*

6. Confirm with OK.

7. Add a new Derived Column task to the Data Flow pane. Connect this to the Aggregate task. Add the following columns:

DataSourceColumn: Set the expression as Marques

DataSourceObject: Set the expression as Stock.Txt

Product_Types: Set the expression as (DT_WSTR,260)Marques

8. Add an OLEDB destination task to the Data Flow pane. Connect the Derived Columns task you just created to it. If there are multiple outputs suggested, ensure that you select the Marques output.

9. Double-click the OLEDB destination task and configure it to connect to an SQL Server database. Map to the DataProfilingDomainAnalysistable. Map the available input columns to the available output columns in the Mappings pane, as was done previously (but using the Marques derived column rather than Product_Type). Click OK.

Your data flow should look like Figure 10-19.

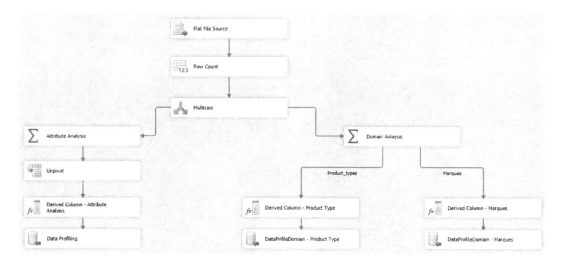

Figure 10-19. *Data flow of multiple domain analyses*

How It Works

There is a slight layer of complication that is imposed when you wish to carry out Multiple Domain Analyses as part of the same data flow. Essentially what you have to do is extend the Aggregate task Domain Analysis, so that it provides multiple outputs—one for each domain for which you wish to return profile data.

Hints, Tips, and Traps

- This way you can add as many domain analyses as you wish to a data flow. All will execute in parallel to the attribute analysis.

- It now becomes incredibly easy to profile data at the same time that you load it—or stage it. As you already have a multicast task in the data flow, all you have to do is use another output from this to load and transform your data.

- In this recipe—and in Recipes 10-11 and 10-12—you can load the data as well as profiling it. All you need to do is add an OLEDB destination task, which you configure to use a destination table that maps to the input data columns, and connects the Multicast transform to it.

10-14. Pattern Profiling in a Data Flow
Problem

You want to produce pattern profiles as part of a data flow.

Solution

Use an SSIS Script task to profile patterns in a data flow to see how the letters and numbers in a field are represented and formatted, without looking at the exact text or numbers used. The following steps explain how.

1.   Create a new SSIS package. Add a Data Flow task to the Control Flow pane.

2.   Add an OLEDB connection manager named **CarSales_OLEDB**, which you configure to connect to the CarSales source database.

3.   Add an OLEDB Connection manager named **CarSales_Staging_OLEDB**, which you configure to connect to the CarSales_Staging destination database.

4.   Double-click to edit (or click the Data Flow tab).

5.   Add a Data Source task. Configure to connect to the CarSales_OLEDB connection manager. Connect to the Stock table.

6.   Add an SSIS Script transformation task to the Data Flow pane of your SSIS task. Connect it to the data source.

7.   Double-click the Script transformation task. Select the column(s) that you will be profiling. I will use Make in this example.

8.   Click Inputs and Outputs in the left-hand column. Expand Output 0 and click Add Column.

9.   Rename the column appropriately (I am calling it Car here). Set its data type to String in the Data Type Properties.

10. Select Script in the left-hand column. Click the Design Script button to enter the Script editor.

11. Add the following line to the Imports Region:

```
Imports System.Text.RegularExpressions
```

12. Replace the Input0_ProcessInputRow method with the following code:

```
Public Overrides Sub Input0_ProcessInputRow(ByVal Row As Input0Buffer)

    Dim CarRow As String

    Dim regexTxt As System.Text.RegularExpressions.Regex = ↵
            New System.Text.RegularExpressions.Regex("[A-Z]", ↵
                            RegexOptions.IgnoreCase)
    Dim regexNum As System.Text.RegularExpressions.Regex = ↵
            New System.Text.RegularExpressions.Regex("[0-9]")
```

```
        CarRow = CStr(Row.Car)
        CarRow = regexTxt.Replace(CarRow, "X")
        CarRow = regexNum.Replace(CarRow, "N")
        Row.CarPattern = CarRow

End Sub
```

13. Close the Script editor. Click OK to close the Script Transformation Editor.

14. Add an Aggregate transform task onto the Data Flow pane. Connect the Script task to it. Double-click the Aggregate transform task to edit it.

15. Select the column you added in step 7. Make sure that Group By is selected as the operation.

16. Click OK to close the Aggregation task.

17. Add a destination task onto the Data Flow pane. Connect the Aggregation task to it. Configure this task to output the profile pattern data using the CarSales_Staging_ OLEDB connection manager. Create a new table named **CarPatternProfile** by clicking New in the OLEDB destination editor, using the suggested columns. The final SSIS data flow should look like Figure 10-20.

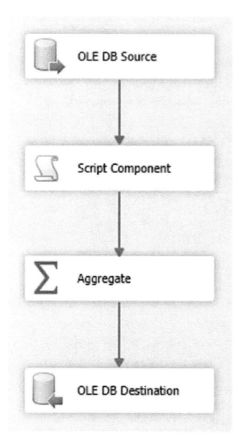

Figure 10-20. *The final SSIS data flow for pattern profiling*

Running this task should produce a series of patterns in the table created in step 17, one for each distinct set of characters in the source data. You can see these patterns using the following T-SQL:

```
SELECT * FROM CarSales_Staging.dbo.CarPatternProfile
```

How It Works

SSIS (or more accurately .NET) comes into its own with pattern profiling. Using regular expressions, patterns can be gathered and analyzed in a fraction of the time that would be required using T-SQL. The glorious simplicity of the .NET code that is required is another reason to suggest this as the only reasonable way of carrying out the task.

What this script does is to use a regular expression to detect in one case alphabetical characters, in another case numbers from an input column, and replace them with "X" and "N" respectively. This is the output from the Script task. This output is then aggregated to show only one example of each pattern.

In this recipe's example, I am assuming that any pattern profiling is carried out as the only aim of the SSIS package, and not as part of a wider profiling or data flow process. As it was described earlier, the pattern Profiling task will not handle NULLs in the source data, so you will have to exclude NULLs at source, or use a conditional split task to isolate NULLs from the data path used for pattern profiling. Also, it can be a good idea to add a Multicast task to the data flow and use one of the outputs from this task as the source for the Script task if you are profiling during a data load, and not using the profiling data to validate or invalidate the process.

Hints, Tips, and Traps

- Do not forget to reference System.Text.RegularExpressions, as this is fundamental for getting regular expressions to function correctly.

- Should you wish to perform pattern profiling on several columns at once, then you will need to add a Multicast task to the data flow immediately after the data source, and then duplicate the other three tasks (Script, Aggregate, and Destination) as many times as you have columns to profile. In this case, you will probably also need a Derived Column task in each data path, simply to add the name of the column that you are profiling (assuming that you are adding all the profiles to the same destination table).

10-15. Pattern Profiling Using T-SQL

Problem

You want to perform pattern profiling using a T-SQL-based solution, but with acceptable performance.

Solution

Create a CLR function to use regular expressions to provide pattern profiling and discover how the letters and numbers in a field are represented and formatted, without examining the exact text or numbers. The following steps explain how you do it.

1. Create the following code, either in a text editor, or, preferably, in Visual Studio. Name it **C:\SQL2012DIRecipes\CH10\CLRRegex.cs**.

   ```
   using System;
   using Microsoft.SqlServer.Server;
   using System.Data.Sql;
   ```

```
using System.Data.SqlTypes;
using System.Text.RegularExpressions;

namespace Adama
{
 public class RegexProfiling
  {

    [SqlFunction(IsDeterministic = true, IsPrecise = true)]
    public static object PatternProfiler(string charInput)
     {

      string patternOutput = null;
      System.Text.RegularExpressions.Regex regexTxt = ↩;
          new System.Text.RegularExpressions.Regex("[A-Z]", RegexOptions.IgnoreCase);
      System.Text.RegularExpressions.Regex regexNum = ↩;
          new System.Text.RegularExpressions.Regex("[0-9]");

      patternOutput = charInput;
      patternOutput = regexTxt.Replace(patternOutput, "X");
      patternOutput = regexNum.Replace(patternOutput, "N");

      return patternOutput;

    }
  }
}
```

2. Compile the DLL from your code. In Visual Studio, or SSDT, this is as simple as
    pressing F5. Otherwise, you will need to enter:

```
csc /target:library /out: C:\SQL2012DIRecipes\CH10\CLRRegex.dll ↩
C:\SQL2012DIRecipes\CH10\CLRRegex.cs
```

Of course, remember to use the path to the .cs file that you have created, and the
output path to the DLL that you want to use.

3. Now add the DLL as an assembly to SQL Server. This presumes that your server is
    enabled for CLR. Enter the following code in a Management Studio query window:

```
CREATE ASSEMBLY RegexPatternProfiling FROM 'C:\SQL2012DIRecipes\CH10\CLRRegex.dll'
```

4. Then create a function with the assembly by using the following code in a
    Management Studio query window:

```
CREATE FUNCTION PatternProfiler
(
 @charInput NVARCHAR(4000)
)
RETURNS NVARCHAR(4000)
AS EXTERNAL NAME [RegexPatternProfiling].[Adama.RegexProfiling].[PatternProfiler];
```

5. You can now use the PatternProfiler function just like any T-SQL function to return the pattern from a column, using the following T-SQL:

```
SELECT Col1, PatternProfiler(Col1) AS Pattern_Profile
FROM DataSource
```

How It Works

If you really want to stick to T-SQL for all your data profiling, then it can be done, but it must be admitted, slowly and laboriously as far as pattern profiling is concerned. Effective pattern profiling requires regular expressions, and these are only accessible to T-SQL using CLR. This implies developing a CLR function, and then loading the .NET assembly containing the function into the database, which is somewhat finicky. Then the analysis can call the CLR-based function. This CLR function is essentially the same code described in Recipe 10-20.

■ **Note** The topic of creating and using CLR-based functions is too huge to be treated in this chapter—or even this book. For a complete description of creating and managing SQL Server CLR-based functions please refer to *Pro SQL Server 2005 Assemblies* by Robin Dewson (Apress, 2006).

It is also possible to generate pattern profiles in T-SQL. The code can be very simple (as you can see in the following code), but, as any T-SQL programmer knows, it will be abysmally slow when used to process large datasets, as it is both function-based and a "stringwalking" function at that. So, in the interests of completeness but with a strong caveat about performance, here is a simple T-SQL function that you can use to profile patterns. It also lets you choose the pattern characters as part of the input parameters. For the sake of simplicity I am creating this function in the database where it will be used.

```
CREATE FUNCTION dbo.fn_PatternProfile
(
 @STRING VARCHAR(4000)
 ,@NUMERICPATTERN CHAR(1)
 ,@TEXTPATTERN CHAR(1)
)

RETURNS VARCHAR(4000)

AS

BEGIN

DECLARE @STRINGPOS INT= 1;
DECLARE @TESTCHAR CHAR(1)= '';
DECLARE @PATTERNCHAR CHAR(1)= '';
DECLARE @PATTERNOUT VARCHAR(4000)= '';

WHILE @STRINGPOS <= LEN(@STRING)
BEGIN

SET @TESTCHAR = SUBSTRING(@STRING,@STRINGPOS,1)
```

```
IF @TESTCHAR
IN('A','B','C','D','E','F','G','H','I','J','K','L','M','N','O','P','Q','R','S','T','U','V','W',
'X','Y','Z')
SET @PATTERNCHAR = @TEXTPATTERN
ELSE IF UPPER(@TESTCHAR) IN('1','2','3','4','5','6','7','8','9')
SET @PATTERNCHAR = @NUMERICPATTERN
ELSE SET @PATTERNCHAR = @TESTCHAR
SET @PATTERNOUT =  @PATTERNOUT + @PATTERNCHAR
SET @STRINGPOS = @STRINGPOS + 1
END;

RETURN(@PATTERNOUT)

END;
```

You can then apply this function in the following way:

```
SELECT dbo.fn_PatternProfile(CountryName_EN,'N','A'), CountryName_EN
FROM dbo.Countries
```

This code is a "stringwalking" function, and simply iterates through every character in a field and replaces alphabetical characters with the character defined for the variable @TEXTPATTERN and numerals with the character defined for the variable @NUMERICPATTERN. It is extremely easy to extend this function to detect other characters, and replace them with yet other pattern markers.

10-16. Profiling Data Types
Problem

You want to profile the data types in your source data and indicate what the smallest data type should be used to contain the data in the column.

Solution

Use an SSIS Script task to return profile information about the source data types. The following steps describe how.

1. Create a new SSIS package. Add a new connection manager corresponding to the data source that you are using. For all but flat files, you can accept the data types suggested by SSIS. For Flat File connection managers, click the Advanced pane and set the OutputColumn Width to a relatively large figure for string columns. Set any columns that you have doubts about to a large string value too—I suggest 4000. Confirm the modifications to the connection manager. In this example, I will use a Flat File connection manager that connects to the C:\SQL2012DIRecipes\CH10\Stock.Txt file.

2. Add a Data Flow task and double-click to edit.

3. In the Data Flow pane. Add a Source task of a type that you configure to use the Configuration Manager that you just created.

4. Add a Script component (defined as a Transformation when prompted) and connect the source task to it. Double-click to edit.

5. Click the Input Columns pane and make sure that all the columns you wish to analyze are selected.

6. Click the Script pane and select the Microsoft Visual Basic 2010 Script Language. Click Edit Script to open the Script editor.

7. Add the following lines to the Imports region:

```
Imports System.IO
Imports System.Text
```

8. Replace the ScriptMain class with the following:

```
Public Class ScriptMain
    Inherits UserComponent

    Dim ColDataType(3) As Integer            ' set to the number of columns ⮠
                                             handled (base 0)
    Dim ColDataLength(3) As Integer          ' set to the number of columns ⮠
                                             handled (base 0)
    Dim ColDecimalPrecision(3) As Integer    ' set to the number of columns ⮠
                                             handled (base 0)
    Dim ColDecimalScale(3) As Integer        ' set to the number of columns ⮠
                                             handled (base 0)

    Dim ProposedDataType(17) As String

    Public Overrides Sub PreExecute()

        ProposedDataType(0) = "unknown"
        ProposedDataType(1) = "bit"
        ProposedDataType(2) = "tinyint"
        ProposedDataType(3) = "smallint"
        ProposedDataType(4) = "int"
        ProposedDataType(5) = "BIGINT"
        ProposedDataType(6) = "smallmoney"
        ProposedDataType(7) = "money"
        ProposedDataType(8) = "decimal"
        ProposedDataType(9) = "single"
        ProposedDataType(10) = "double"
        ProposedDataType(11) = "time"
        ProposedDataType(12) = "date"
        ProposedDataType(13) = "smalldatetime"
        ProposedDataType(14) = "datetime"
        ProposedDataType(15) = "datetime2"
        ProposedDataType(16) = "char"
        ProposedDataType(17) = "varchar"

    End Sub

    Public Overrides Sub PostExecute()
        MyBase.PostExecute()

        Dim outFile As String = "C:\SQL2012DIRecipes\CH10\Output.txt"
        Dim sb As New StringBuilder
```

607

```vb
        For i = 0 To ColDataType.Length - 1

            sb.AppendLine("Col" & i & "," & ProposedDataType(ColDataType(i)) & "," & ↵
              ColDataLength(i) & "," & ColDecimalPrecision(i) & "," & ColDecimalScale(i))

    Next

    Using OutWrite As New StreamWriter(outFile)
        OutWrite.Write(sb.ToString)
    End Using

End Sub

Public Overrides Sub Input0_ProcessInputRow(ByVal Row As Input0Buffer)

    GetDataType(Row.ID, 0)
    GetDataType(Row.InvoiceNumber, 1)
    GetDataType(Row.DeliveryCharge, 2)
    GetDataType(Row.ClientID, 3)
    GetDataType(Row.TotalDiscount, 4)

End Sub

Public Function GetDataType(ByVal InputCol As String, ByVal ColIndex As Integer) As Integer

    Dim IsFound As Boolean = 0
    Dim SuggestedDataType As Integer

    Dim MaxMoney As Decimal = 922337203685477.62 ' should be .5808
    Dim MinMoney As Decimal = -922337203685477.62 ' should be .5807
    Dim MaxSmallMoney As Decimal = 214748.3647
    Dim MinSmallMoney As Decimal = -214748.3648
    Dim MinDateTime As Integer = 1753
    Dim MaxDateTime As Integer = 9999
    Dim MinSmallDateTime As Integer = 1900
    Dim MaxSmallDateTime As Integer = 2079
    Dim MinDateTime2 As Integer = 0

    Dim DecimalPrecision As Integer = 0
    Dim DecimalScale As Integer = 0
    Dim StringLength As Integer = 0

    ' no detection of decimal separator or date/time formats..

    If Boolean.TryParse(InputCol, 0) Then
        IsFound = True
        SuggestedDataType = 1
    End If
```

```
If Not IsFound Then

    If IsNumeric(InputCol) Then  ' Initial test for numeric values

        ' Integer first - straight mapping:

        If Not IsFound Then
            If Byte.TryParse(InputCol, 0) Then ' 0 - 256
                IsFound = True
                SuggestedDataType = 2
            End If
        End If

        If Not IsFound Then
            If Int16.TryParse(InputCol, 0) Then ' - 32768 to 32767
                SuggestedDataType = 3
                IsFound = True
            End If

        End If

        If Not IsFound Then
            If Int32.TryParse(InputCol, 0) Then ' -2147483648 to 2147483647
                IsFound = True
                SuggestedDataType = 4
            End If
        End If

        If Not IsFound Then
            If Int64.TryParse(InputCol, 0) Then ' -9223372036854775808 to
                                                ' 9223372036854775807
                IsFound = True
                SuggestedDataType = 5
            End If
        End If

        ' If not an integer, try the decimal data types

        ' Money first
        If Not IsFound Then
            If Decimal.TryParse(InputCol, 0) Then

                If InputCol.Length - InputCol.IndexOf(".", 0) <= 5 Then

                    If InputCol >= MinSmallMoney And InputCol <= MaxSmallMoney Then
                        IsFound = True
                        SuggestedDataType = 6
                    End If
```

```vbnet
                          If Not IsFound Then
                              If InputCol >= MinMoney And InputCol <= MaxMoney Then
                                  IsFound = True
                                  SuggestedDataType = 7
                              End If
                          End If

                      End If

                      If InputCol.Length - InputCol.IndexOf(".", 0) > 5 Then

                          If Not IsFound Then
                              IsFound = True
                              SuggestedDataType = 8
                              DecimalPrecision = InputCol.Length - 1
                              DecimalScale = InputCol.Length - InputCol.IndexOf(".", 0) - 1
                          End If

                      End If

                  End If
              End If

              ' If not one of the other numeric types - it has to be single or double!
              If Not IsFound Then
                  If Single.TryParse(InputCol, 0) Then
                      IsFound = True
                      SuggestedDataType = 9
                  End If
              End If

              If Not IsFound Then
                  If Double.TryParse(InputCol, 0) Then
                      IsFound = True
                      SuggestedDataType = 10
                  End If
              End If

          End If
      End If

' Date types
If Not IsFound Then

    Dim DV As DateTime

    If DateTime.TryParse(InputCol, DV) Then

        If IsDate(InputCol) Then
```

```
            If Hour(InputCol) = 0 And Minute(InputCol) = 0 ↵
                            And Second(InputCol) = 0 Then
                ' has no time aspect, so is a date

            If Year(InputCol) = 1 And Month(InputCol) = 1 Then

                ' Has no year/month aspect - so is a time
                IsFound = True
                SuggestedDataType = 11
            End If

            If Year(InputCol) >= MinDateTime2 And Year(InputCol) <= MaxDateTime Then
                IsFound = True
                SuggestedDataType = 12
            End If

        End If

        If Not IsFound Then
            If Year(InputCol) >= MinSmallDateTime And Year(InputCol) ↵
                            <= MaxSmallDateTime Then
                IsFound = True
                SuggestedDataType = 13
            End If
        End If

        If Not IsFound Then
            If Year(InputCol) >= MinDateTime And Year(InputCol) <= MaxDateTime Then
                IsFound = True
                SuggestedDataType = 14
            End If
        End If

        If Not IsFound Then
            If Year(InputCol) >= MinDateTime2 And Year(InputCol) <= MaxDateTime Then
                IsFound = True
                SuggestedDataType = 15
            End If
        End If

    End If

    End If

End If

'Then Text

If Not IsFound Then
    SuggestedDataType = 16
    StringLength = InputCol.Length
End If
```

611

```
    ' Apply the most inclusive data type

    'First, if there is a date so far, and it becomes a number (or vice-versa)
    'automatically becomes text

    If ((ColDataType(ColIndex) >= 1 And ColDataType(ColIndex) <= 10) ↵
                                          And (SuggestedDataType >= 11 ↵
                                          And SuggestedDataType <= 15)) ↵
                                          Or ((ColDataType(ColIndex) >= 11 ↵
                                          And ColDataType(ColIndex) <= 15) ↵
                                          And (SuggestedDataType >= 1 ↵
                                          And SuggestedDataType <= 10))
    Then

        SuggestedDataType = 15

    End If


    ' Remember the chosen data type
    If ColDataType(ColIndex) < SuggestedDataType Then
        ColDataType(ColIndex) = SuggestedDataType
    End If

    ' For text types, set the col length
    If SuggestedDataType = 16 Then

        If InputCol.Length > ColDataLength(ColIndex) Then
            ColDataLength(ColIndex) = InputCol.Length
        End If

    End If

    ' For decimal types get precision and scale
    If SuggestedDataType = 7 Then

        If DecimalPrecision > ColDecimalPrecision(ColIndex) Then
            ColDecimalPrecision(ColIndex) = DecimalPrecision
        End If

        If DecimalScale > ColDecimalScale(ColIndex) Then
            ColDecimalScale(ColIndex) = DecimalScale
        End If

    End If

    Return SuggestedDataType

    End Function

End Class
```

6. Tweak the code to use the column names in your data source. Rescope the four arrays (`ColDataType, ColDataLength, ColDecimalPrecision, ColDecimalScale`) to correspond to the number of columns. Define an output file and directory suited to your environment. In this example, it is `C:\SQL2012DIRecipes\CH10\Output.Txt`.

7. Close the Script editor. Click OK to close the Script Transformation Editor. The final package should look like Figure 10-21.

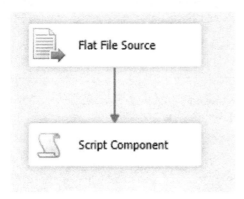

Figure 10-21. *Profiling data types*

You can now run the SSIS package.

How It Works

Data profiling does not only mean looking at the values contained in a data source. It can, and sometimes should, involve looking at the data types too. This can then be used in conjunction with any metadata that you have concerning the source, to highlight discrepancies and eventually allow you to make changes to the destination data table data types. For instance, if you have a range of integers between 10 and 200 in a column, and the type is set to BIGINT, then you may want to consider changing the type of the relevant column in any tables in your destination database, as well as making suggestions to the DBA of the data source.

Let's be clear about this, what we are doing here is saying what the data type should, and could be, given the data currently in a specified column. We are not saying what the data is according to SSIS, OLEDB providers, .NET providers or source metadata. Once again, we are running the source data through a process to analyze it and say what SQL Server data type it should be in an ideal world. Just remember that there may be very good reasons for an apparently inappropriate data type, as the DBA who is in charge of the source may know things about the future directions of the data that you do not. And conversely, he or she may not...

Therefore this SSIS script that attempts to deduce the most suitable data type for each source column in a source file. It is not perfect, but hopefully is an acceptable trade-off between efficiency, reliability, and complexity. Running the package will create a text file (called `C:\SQL2012DIRecipes\CH10\Output.txt` in this example) that contains four columns:

- The suggested data type
- The maximum length for a character field
- The decimal precision for decimal data types
- The decimal scale for decimal data types

The script defines five arrays: Four to hold a column's DataType, DataLength, DecimalPrecision, and Scale, then one to hold the data types it will be attributing. Next the ProposedDataType array is initialized with the 17 possible data types as part of the script's pre-execute phase. The script's post-execute phase is defined to output the text file of the final analysis. Each column that is to be analyzed is passed to the GetDataType function for each row in the source data.

Then to the core of the script—the GetDataType function. This takes the source data for each column and attempts to deduce its data type and length. First it tries various integer types, then other numeric types, then dates, and then if all else fails, a character type. The data types are in an order of preference, so that a type with a more encompassing definition will always be retained over a narrower data type, to ensure that the data can load successfully.

Hints, Tips, and Traps

- The initial length of the columns is a matter of personal preference. The larger it is, the less chance there is of a load failure, but the slower the process will be.

- This script will evaluate all the rows in the data source. If this is too much, then merely insert a Row Sampling task between the data source and the Script task, edit it to set a relevant number of rows to sample, and connect (using the Sampling Selected Output) to the Script task.

- This script could be taken further to use column names instead of numbers, and to automate scoping of variables, and so forth—but I will leave that as a challenge for the reader!

- Data types are explained in Appendix B.

10-17. Controlling Data Flow via Profile Metadata
Problem

You want to use profiling data to add control flow logic to an ETL process.

Solution

Use an SSIS Script task to profile the data and output source data to a RAW file that will be used for future processing if the profiling tests allow the process to continue. The following steps explain how to do it.

1. Create a new SSIS package. Add a connection manager named **Invoice_Source** to the source data (C:\SQL2012DIRecipes\CH10\Invoice.Txt in this example).

2. At package level, add the following variable:

Variable Name	Scope	DataType	Value
IsSafeToProceed	Package	Boolean	True

3. Add a Data Flow task, name it **Profile Load,** and double-click to edit.

4. Add a Flat File source that you configure to use the Invoice_Source connection manager that you created in step 1.

5. Add a Script component that you set as a transform and connect the Flat File source to it. Double-click to edit. Add the IsSafeToProceed variable as a read-write variable. Click InputColumns and select the column to profile (InvoiceNumber in this example). Set the ScriptLanguage to Microsoft Visual Basic 2010 and click Edit Script.

6. Replace ScriptMain with the following code:

```
Public Class ScriptMain
    Inherits UserComponent
    Dim NullCounter As Integer
    Dim RowCounter As Integer

    Public Overrides Sub PreExecute()
        MyBase.PreExecute()
    End Sub

    Public Overrides Sub PostExecute()

        If (NullCounter / RowCounter) >= 0.25 Then

            Me.Variables.IsSafeToProceed = False

        End If

    End Sub

    Public Overrides Sub Input0_ProcessInputRow(ByVal Row As Input0Buffer)

        If Row.InvoiceNumber_IsNull Then
            NullCounter = NullCounter + 1
        End If

        RowCounter = RowCounter + 1

    End Sub

End Class
```

7. Close the Script editor and confirm your modifications with OK.

8. Add a Raw File destination. Name it **Pause Output** and connect the Script task to it. Double-click to edit.

9. Configure the Raw File destination as follows:

Access Mode:	FileName
File Name:	C:\SQL2012DIRecipes\CH10\Invoice.Raw
Write Option:	Create always

10. Ensure that all the columns are selected, and then confirm your modifications with OK.

11. Return to the Control Flow pane and add a second Data Flow task. Name it **Final Load** and connect the first Data Flow task to it. Double-click the connector and set the Precedence Constraint Editor as follows. The dialog box should then look like Figure 10-22.

Evaluation Operation: Expression and Constraint

Value: Success

Expression: @IsSafeToProceed

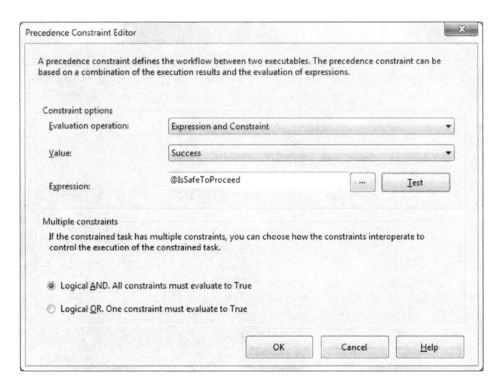

Figure 10-22. *Precedence Constraint Editor in SSIS*

12. Confirm your changes.

13. Double-click the second Data Flow task to edit it.

14. Add a Raw File source named **Continue Load**, which you configure to use the same file that you defined in step 9 (C:\SQL2012DIRecipes\CH10\Invoice.Raw).

15. Add an OLEDB destination named **Final Load**, to which you connect the Raw File source. Configure it to load the data into the CarSales_Staging database, creating a table from the OLEDB destination. The final package should look like Figure 10-23.

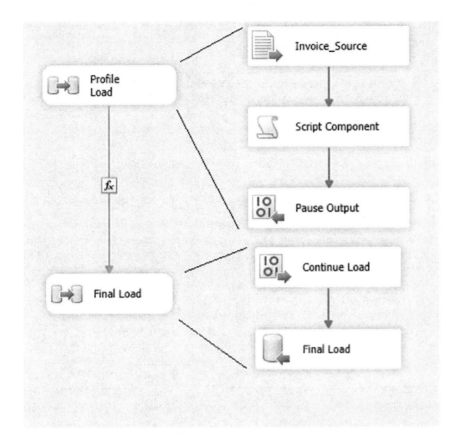

Figure 10-23. *Controlled data flow in SSIS*

How It Works

Profiling data as it is loaded allows you to capture metrics that you specify, which can then be used to halt processing if necessary. Inevitably this means pausing the data flow while counters are finalized and analyzed. So the trick is to find a way to stage the data efficiently while awaiting the results of the profiling. My preferred solution is to use a RAW file destination to hold the data temporarily, and then continue the final load into the destination table(s) if the profiling has found no anomalies. This will slow down the process to some extent, but as it is nearly always the final load that is the slowest part of an SSIS package, it avoids a wasted load and reload if there is a problem. Outputting data into a raw file is extremely fast—and in virtually all cases should prove faster than loading into a staging table. In the best of all possible worlds you should place the RAW file in the SQL Server itself, if you can on a fast disk array.

The code used here is a very simple example to illustrate the principle. During a data load the number of NULLs in a column will be tested, and if it exceeds 25 percent, then the process will halt. This is set in the PostExecute method. If the number of NULLs is below this threshold, then the package will continue into its final phase—loading the data into the destination tables.

There are other solutions, of course. You can profile the data once it has been loaded, for instance. This is probably the easiest solution, as you can use any combination of the T-SQL techniques described in this chapter to produce a data profile that should alert you to any potential issues with the data load. Also any stored procedures or SQL code can be run as Execute SQL tasks at the end of an SSIS package and can output alerts to your logging infrastructure, as described in Chapter 12.

Alternatively you can choose to profile data while it is being loaded. There are two possibilities here:

- Profile any staged data using T-SQL from an Execute SQL task.

- Insert a Multicast task after the data source and profile the data using the some of the various SSIS scripts shown earlier in the chapter. Using a separate data path will avoid slowing down the processing if asynchronous transforms are used.

Hints, Tips, and Traps

- This recipe's script is ridiculously simple, but it is there to give you an idea of how to profile data during a load, and use the results of the profiling to control the package flow.

- You can extend the profiling using any of the SSIS techniques described earlier in this chapter.

Summary

This chapter showed many ways of profiling source data using SQL Server. The question is which method to choose and when. Obviously, the answer will depend on your circumstances and requirements. You can profile data not yet in SQL Server if you can connect to it. This essentially means an OLEDB provider (over ODBC if necessary) to use T-SQL commands on the source. However, in practice, this could be extremely slow. If you are using SSIS, then in any real-world setting the data has to be in SQL Server, or the workarounds to get the SSIS Data Profiling task to read the source can make it unbearably slow.

If your data has already been staged into SQL Server, then the horizons that open to you (at least as far as profiling data is concerned) are considerably wider. You can use SSIS or T-SQL to profile the data, and for a quick data profile, the SSIS Data Profiling task can be set to run virtually instantly. You can also store the profile output as XML or shred it into an SQL Server table.

Once you have profiled your data, you can then use the results to make decisions as to whether or not to continue the data load. This presumes that the source data either is a RAW file on disk or has been loaded into a staging table. In either case, your source data can then proceed to the next stage of the ETL process.

As a schematic overview, Table 10-8 is my take on the various methods and their advantages and disadvantages.

Table 10-8. *Advantages and Disadvantages of the Techniques Described in This Chapter*

Technique	Advantages	Disadvantages
T-SQL Profiling	Relatively simple.	Requires multiple specific code snippets.
SSIS Profile Task	Easy to use.	Limited.
		Requires XML viewer or cumbersome output workaround.
Custom SSIS Profiling	Easy to integrate into an existing SSIS package.	Complex to set up.
T-SQL Profiling Script	Copy and paste.	Can provide too much information.
SSIS Script Task Profiling	Highly adaptable and extensible.	Complex.
SSIS Pattern Profiling	Easy to set up.	
T-SQL Pattern Profiling	Easy to set up.	Very slow.

■ ■ ■

CHAPTER 11

Delta Data Management

Fortunately, much of data integration is a relatively simple case of transferring all the data from a source (whatever it may be) to a destination (hopefully SQL Server). The destination is cleared out before the load process, and the objective is to get the data from A to B accurately, completely, and in the shortest possible time. Yet this basic scenario will inevitably not match everybody's requirements all of the time. When developing ETL solutions you may frequently be called upon to ensure that only changes in data are applied from the source to the destination. Detecting data changes, and only (re)loading a subset of changed data will be the subject of this chapter. In an attempt to give a simple title to a subject that can prove quite complex, I propose calling this *delta data management*.

Preamble: Why Bother with Delta Data?

There are several reasons that spending the time to set up delta data handling can pay big dividends:

> **Time saved:** If the source data contains only a small percentage of inserts, updates, or deletes, then applying only these changes instead of reloading a huge amount of data can prove considerably faster.

> **Reduced network load:** If you are able to isolate modified data at the source, then the quantities of data sent from the source to the destination can be reduced considerably.

> **Less stress on the server(s):** This means reduced processor utilization and less disk activity.

> **Less blocking:** While blocking is hopefully not a major problem in a reporting or analysis environment (especially during overnight processes), it can be an issue in certain circumstances, and so is best if it is kept to a minimum.

In any case, you might find it easier to consider the arguments—both those for managing delta data and those against it; they are provided in Table 11-1.

Table 11-1. *A Brief Overview of the Advantages and Disadvantages of Loading Delta Data*

	Advantages	Disadvantages
Full loads	Simplicity.	Can be much slower.
		Resource consumption.
		Blocking.
Delta data	Can be much faster.	Complexity.
	Less network load.	Time to implement.
	Less server load.	Harder to debug and maintain.

It follows that when faced with an ETL project, you must always ask yourself the question "is it worth the effort required to implement delta data loading techniques?" As is so often the case when faced with these sorts of question, it is largely impossible to say immediately where the thresholds for efficiency gains lie. So be prepared to apply some basic testing to get your answer, unless there is another compelling reason to choose the "truncate and load" technique over the development of a—possibly quite complex—delta data load process.

Delta Data Approaches

At the risk of oversimplification, let's say that there are two main ways of detecting data changes:

> **At source:** A method to flag changed records, including indication of the change type (insert, delete, or update).

> **During the ETL load:** A method to compare source and destination records—and isolating those that differ.

This simple overview quickly requires a little more in-depth analysis.

Detecting Changes at Source

Flagging the data change at source probably comes closest to an ideal solution from the ETL developer's point of view. This is for the following reasons:

- Only changed records need to be moved between systems.

- No full comparison between two data sets is required because the source system maintains its own history of changes.

- Delta information may even be held in separate tables, avoiding expensive scans of large source tables to isolate delta subsets.

- The work is most often done by the source system DBA.

Detecting Changes During the ETL Load

Unfortunately, many source systems are destined to remain closed-off "black boxes" to the ETL developer. This is often because the source system DBAs will not countenance anything perceived as adding system overhead to their databases. Such recalcitrance on the part of DBAs can even extend to low-overhead solutions such as change tracking and change data capture, which are the subject of Chapter 12. Another possible reason for being unable to tweak a source system is that it is a third-party development where any modifications are practically or legally impossible. So, if you are not allowed to touch the source system in any way, you have to compare data sets and deduce changes during the load process.

However, performing data comparisons during (or, as we shall see in some cases, before) a load process can nonetheless allow for faster data loads with less network and server stress. So what we need to consider here is how to compare data.

Put simply, there are two main record comparison approaches:

- Compare columns between source and destination data sets for each important field. This does not necessarily need to be all columns, and can be a subset that reflects the requirements of how the destination data will be used.

- Use an indicator field that is stored in both source and destination data sets. This can be the following:

    - A date added and/or date updated field.

    - A hash field (a checksum).

    - A ROWVERSION field (formerly called a Timestamp field, even if it has nothing to do with the time or the date). Indeed any other counter field that increments if the data changes will do.

In either case, you will look for three kinds of differences:

- Data present in the source and absent from the destination (inserts).

- Data present in the destination and missing in the source (deletes).

- Data present in both the source and the destination, but where the comparison indicates a change (updates).

So, let's start looking at ways of applying this knowledge to data loads in practice. I will begin with the more usual case of data comparison during load, and then look at ways of applying delta flags in source systems. Remember that the recipes in this chapter exist to solve different ETL challenges and circumstances. Each has its advantages and drawbacks. In the real world, you may well find yourself mixing and matching techniques from different recipes in order to solve an ETL challenge.

As is customary in this book, you will have to download the sample data from the book's companion website if you wish to follow the examples. This means creating the sample databases CarSales and CarSales_Staging, which are used in virtually all the examples in this chapter. I will use the CarSales database as the source of data, and the CarSales_Staging database as the destination database in the examples in this chapter.

The sample data you can download will always have a key column and if you alter the examples for your own data then you should also have a key column. As you may already have discovered in your career with SQL Server, loading delta data without key columns varies from extremely difficult to impossible. Remember also that an SQL Server ROWVERSION is also a unique number, which is incremented each time a field is modified, and has nothing to do with date and time.

Before leaping into the recipes in this chapter, you need to be forewarned that some of them are longer than those seen elsewhere in this book. Indeed, at first sight they may seem complex to implement. The best advice that I can give you is to read them through thoroughly a couple of times before applying them to your own ETL challenges. I particularly recommend that you take a good look at the Control Flow and Data Flow figures, where given, to get a clearer understanding of the process in each case. Also when you are creating your own ETL solutions based on these ideas, do not hesitate to look ahead to what is to come, and to skip to the "How It Works" section to ensure that you have understood the whys and wherefores of a process.

Finally, as delta data management has to handle a set of challenges for which there are only a finite set of solutions, some of the recipes in this chapter do have similar phases. Rather than reiterate the same information over and over again, I do occasionally require you to refer to elements in other recipes in the chapter in order to complete a specific step in a process.

11-1. Loading Delta Data as Part of a Structured ETL Process

Problem

You want to load only new data, update any changed records, and remove any deleted records during regular data loads.

Solution

Use SSIS and detect the way in which the source data has changed. Then process the destination data accordingly to apply inserts, updates, and deletes to the destination table. I'll explain how this is done.

1. Create three tables in the destination database (CarSales_Staging) using the following DDL (dropping them first, if you have created them for use with another recipe, of course) (C:\SQL2012DIRecipes\CH11\DeltaInvoiceTables.Sql):

    ```
    CREATE TABLE dbo.Invoice_Lines
    (
     ID INT NOT NULL,
     InvoiceID INT NULL,
     StockID INT NULL,
     SalePrice NUMERIC(18, 2) NULL,
     VersionStamp VARBINARY(8) NULL -- this  field is to hold ROWVERSION data
    );   -- The destination table with no IDENTITY column or referential integrity
    GO

    CREATE TABLE dbo.Invoice_Lines_Updates
    (
     ID INT NOT NULL,
     InvoiceID INT NULL,
     StockID INT NULL,
     SalePrice NUMERIC(18, 2) NULL,
     VersionStamp VARBINARY(8) NULL -- this  field is to hold ROWVERSION data
    ) ;  --The "scratch" table for updated records
    GO

    CREATE TABLE dbo.Invoice_Lines_Deletes
    (
    ID INT NULL
    ) ;  -- The "scratch" table for you to deduce deleted records
    GO
    ```

2. Create an SSIS package (I will name it SSISDeltaLoad.dtsx) and add two OLEDB connection managers: one to the source database (name it **CarSales_OLEDB**) and one to the destination database (name it **CarSales_Staging_OLEDB**).

3. Add a Data Flow task to the Control Flow pane. Name it **Inserts and Updates**. Double-click this to enter the Data Flow pane.

4. Add an OLEDB source adapter. Configure it to use the CarSales_OLEDB connection manager and to select all required rows from the Invoice_Lines source table using the following SQL snippet:

```
SELECT      ID, InvoiceID, StockID, SalePrice
            ,VersionStamp AS VersionStamp_Source
FROM        dbo.Invoice_Lines WITH (NOLOCK)
```

5. Add a Multicast transform to the Data Flow pane. Name it **Split Data**. Connect the Inserts and Updates data source adapter to it.

6. Add a Lookup transform to which you connect the Multicast transform. Name it **Lookup RowVersions**. On the General pane of the Lookup transform, configure it as follows:

Cache Mode:	No Cache
Connection Type:	OLEDB Connection Manager
Specify how to handle rows with NoMatch entries:	Send rows with no matching entries to the No Match output

7. Click Connection on the left. Set the connection manager to CarSales_Staging_OLEDB because as you will be comparing the source data with the destination data that you are looking up with this Lookup transform.

8. Set the Lookup to "Use results of an SQL Query" and enter the following SQL:

```
SELECT      ID, VersionStamp
FROM        dbo.Invoice_Lines WITH (NOLOCK)
```

9. Click Columns on the left. The two tables, source (on the left), and destination (on the right) will appear. Drag the ID column from the Available Lookup Columns (or Destination) table on the right to the ID column of the Available Input Columns (Source) table on the left. This maps the unique IDs of the two data sources to each other.

10. Select the VersionStamp column of the Available Lookup Columns (or destination) table on the right and provide an output alias—I suggest **VersionStamp_Destination**. This allows you to compare the VersionStamps for source and destination for each record. The dialog box should look like Figure 11-1.

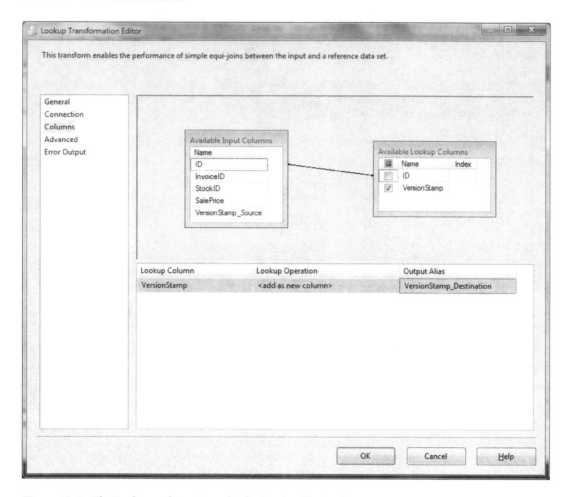

Figure 11-1. The Lookup task to return the destination VersionStamp

11.   Click OK to confirm your modifications. Return to the Data Flow pane.

12.   Add an OLEDB destination transform on to the Data Flow pane and connect the Lookup transform to it. The Input Output Selection dialog box will appear. Select the No Match output and click OK.

13.   Double-click the OLEDB destination adapter to configure it. Ensure that the CarSales_ Staging_OLEDB connection manager is selected and that the destination table is dbo. Invoice_Lines. This inserts any new records directly into the destination table.

14.   Click Mappings on the left. Ensure that all columns that you wish to import are mapped correctly. Click OK to return to the Data Flow pane. So far, you have completed the Insert part of the process.

15.   Now it is time to move to the Update part of the process. Add a Conditional Split transform onto the Data Flow pane. Connect the Lookup transform to it. Name it **Detect Rowversion Difference**. This sends the Lookup Match Output to the Conditional Split.

16. Double-click to edit the Conditional Split. Add a single output condition named **VersionStamp Differences** where the condition is

   [VersionStamp_Source] != (DT_I8) [VersionStamp_Destination]

17. The dialog box should look like Figure 11-2. Note that you have to convert the destination data type from a Varbinary to a BigInt (DT_I8), whereas SSIS does this for you when reading the ROWVERSION field from the source.

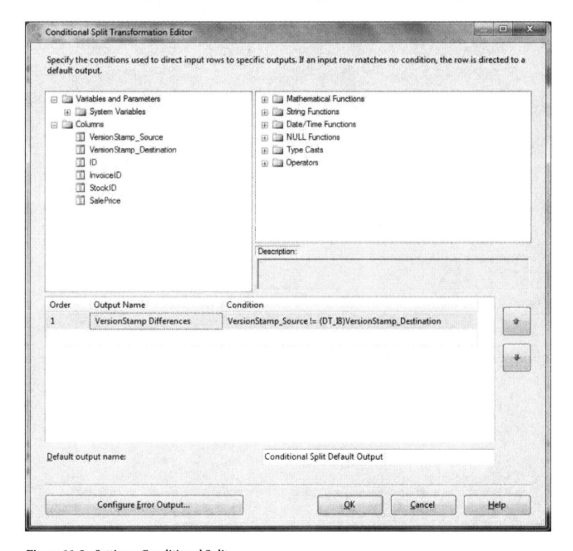

Figure 11-2. Setting a Conditional Split

18. Click OK to confirm, and close the dialog box.

19. Add an OLEDB destination adapter to the data flow and name it **Scratch Table for Updates**. Connect the Conditional Split transform to it. The Input Output dialog box will appear, where you should select the VersionStamp Differences output (which is, in fact, the source for the destination adapter). Set the OLEDB connection manager as CarSales_Staging_OLEDB, the data access mode as Table or View–Fast Load, and the destination table as Invoice_Lines_Updates. Click Mappings. Ensure that all columns are mapped as in Figure 11-3, and then click OK to confirm your modifications. This completes the initial phase of handling updates—storing update data in a scratch table.

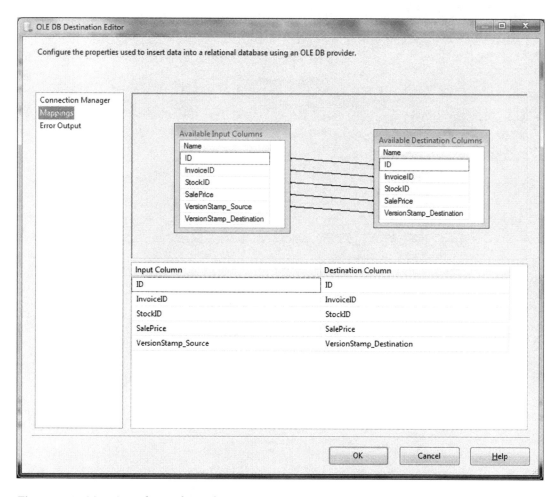

Figure 11-3. *Mapping columns for updates*

20. Now we can move to managing Deletes. Add an OLEDB destination adapter to the data flow and connect the Split Data Multicast transform to it. Name it **Scratch Table for Deletes** and configure it to send rows to the Invoice_Lines_Deletes table as follows:

Connection Manager: OLEDB_Destination

Data Access Mode: Table or View – Fast Load

Name of the Table or the View: Invoice_Lines_Deletes

21. Click Mappings. Ensure that the two ID columns are mapped. The dialog box should look like Figure 11-4.

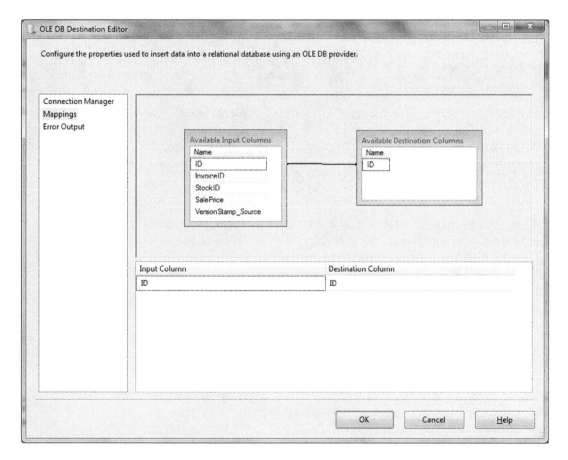

Figure 11-4. *Mapping ID columns for deletes*

22. Click OK to return to the Data Flow pane.

23. Click the Control Flow tab to return to the Control Flow pane. The Data Flow pane should look more or less like Figure 11-5.

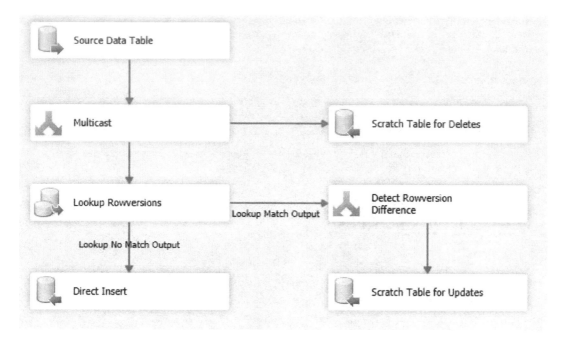

Figure 11-5. *The Data Flow pane for delta data detection in SSIS*

24. To finish, we can apply update and delete logic. Click the Control Flow tab and add an Execute SQL task. Connect this to the Data Flow task. Name it **Update Data**. Configure the Execute SQL task as follows (C:\SQL2012DIRecipes\CH11\11-1_Update.Sql):

Connection: OLEDB_Destination

SQL Statement:
```
UPDATE DST
SET
        DST.InvoiceID = UPD.InvoiceID
        ,DST.SalePrice = UPD.SalePrice
        ,DST.StockID = UPD.StockID
        ,DST.VersionStamp = UPD.VersionStamp
FROM    dbo.Invoice_Lines DST
        INNER JOIN dbo.Invoice_Lines_Updates UPD
        ON DST.ID = UPD.ID
```

25. Click OK to finish editing this task.

26. Add a new Execute SQL task. Connect the Update Data Execute SQL task to it, and name it **Delete Data**. Configure this new task as follows (C:\SQL2012DIRecipes\CH11\11-1_Delete.Sql):

Connection:	OLEDB_Destination
SQL Statement:	DELETE

```
DELETE
FROM dbo.Invoice_Lines
WHERE ID IN
   (SELECT dbo.Invoice_Lines.ID
    FROM    dbo.Invoice_Lines
    LEFT OUTER JOIN dbo.Invoice_Lines_Deletes
    ON dbo.Invoice_Lines.ID = dbo.Invoice_Lines_Deletes.ID
    WHERE (dbo.Invoice_Lines_Deletes.ID IS NULL))
```

27. Click OK to confirm your changes.

28. Add a final Execute SQL Task. Name it **Truncate Scratch Tables**. Connect this to the preceding Execute SQL task (UpdateData). Configure the Execute SQL task as follows:

Name:	Truncate Scratch tables
Connection:	OLEDB_Destination
SQL Statement:	TRUNCATE TABLE dbo.Invoice_Lines_Deletes

```
TRUNCATE TABLE dbo.Invoice_Lines_Deletes
TRUNCATE TABLE dbo.Invoice_Lines_Updates
```

29. Click OK to finish editing. The package is ready. The Data Flow pane should look like Figure 11-6.

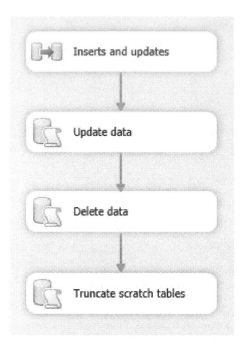

Figure 11-6. *Dataflow for simple delta data updating*

How It Works

This recipe takes a fairly common scenario: you have a table on a source system that you need to load into your staging database. Rather than truncate the entire table and reload it, you wish to insert any new records, delete any that have been removed, and update any changed records. The source table contains a `VersionStamp` column, which you want to use to isolate delta data for updates. It also contains a primary key (or a unique ID), which allows you to identify records uniquely. Consequently you can perform any appropriate inserts and deletes to handle new and removed data, as well as identify records whose data needs updating. Let us also assume that, unfortunately, you have no control over the source data or the server on which it resides; you have only read rights to the source data. So the entire source table or—alternatively, a data set containing all the records modified since the last data load—has been made available.

The trick with this technique is to avoid the OLEDB Command SSIS transform when deleting or updating rows; it will fire for every row and apply the updates potentially hundreds of thousands of times. One solution is to use a couple of tables specifically to hold all required data for deletes and updates, and process all `DELETE` and `UPDATE` operations as T-SQL using these tables. These two tables can be created as part of the package—and dropped afterward—or left in a staging database for auditing purposes.

This process can seem a little daunting at first view. Figure 11-7 provides a schematic overview to clarify the process.

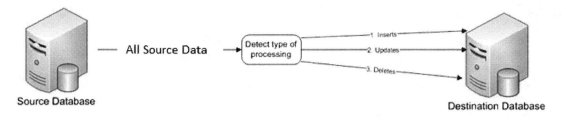

Figure 11-7. *Basic delta detection flow*

This approach is best used when you can be sure that only a small percentage of data has changed, and that you have a primary key (or an unique ID) in the source table, and a column that indicates that a change has happened. It is suitable when you cannot obtain the rights to create and drop persisted scratch tables in the source database.

The prerequisites for the approach to work are as follows:

- A copy of the source table in the destination database, containing all the columns whose data you wish to INSERT, with the VersionStamp column data type altered to VARBINARY(8). This allows you to store the value of the VersionStamp when the record was last loaded. This table contains the final copy of the source dataset after all insert, delete, and update operations have been applied. Any IDENTITY columns in the destination table must be simple INT/BIGINT data types (without the IDENTITY specification) in the destination table.

- A second scratch copy of the source table in the destination database, containing all the columns whose data you wish to load into the final destination table, with the VersionStamp column data type altered to VARBINARY(8). This copy will be used to hold the UPDATEs detected in the source dataset before they are applied to the final table.

- A one-column scratch table to hold the unique IDs of all records that will be DELETEd from the final destination table. This column's data type must match that of the unique ID in the source data table.

The core of this recipe is how it handles inserts and updates—also known as *upserts*. This approach has become classic, and uses the Lookup transform to detect differences between the source and destination data sets. Records that do not exist in the destination table are added directly as part of the data flow. Modified records are added to a scratch table, and then this is used to update the destination data table using a T-SQL UPDATE command. I am also including record deletions in the recipe for the sake of completeness. This could mean physically deleting records, or applying a so-called *soft-delete*, where an extra Boolean field exists in the destination table (called, for instance, IsDeleted), which is set to True when a record has been deleted in the source data. Of course, some scenarios may not require handling deletions at all.

I have to be realistic and admit that this approach has one potential drawback. It will pull all the data from the source across a network to the destination server. If this is a problem for you, then consider looking at the solutions proposed in Recipes 11-4, 11-6, and 11-7.

■ **Note**　When using a Lookup transform, ensure that you are only selecting the columns that you need. Whichever cache mode you are using, returning a minimal set of fields can only make the process faster.

Hints, Tips, and Traps

- The two "scratch" tables that allow you to delete and update records efficiently must (for this recipe, anyway) be persisted to disk for the duration of this operation. They can be in the same database as the destination data table, or in a database where you keep only such "scratch" and staging tables. You may prefer to create them at the start of the process and drop them at the end, instead of leaving them on disk and truncating them at the start of the process. It is entirely your choice.

- In step 9, if your unique key is composed of several columns, then remember to map them all.

- As a VersionStamp is binary, you can be obliged to convert it to BIGINT for comparison purposes. This is true for an SSIS Conditional Split task, which cannot compare binary types. T-SQL can compare binary types, however. Oh, and I am giving the name VersionStamp to the Delta Flag column so that it is clear that even if it is a Timestamp field—it has nothing to do with time!

- Caching can accelerate the use of the MERGE transform, as described in Recipe 13-16.

- Instead of persisted "scratch" tables, you can use session-scoped temporary tables, as described in Recipe 11-4.

- To perform logical deletes (and assuming that there is a IsDeleted BIT column in the Invoice_Lines destination table, replace the SQL in the "Delete Data" Execute SQL task with the following (C:\SQL2012DIRecipes\CH11\12-1_LogicalDelete.Sql):

```
UPDATE  dbo.Invoice_Lines
SET     IsDeleted = 1
WHERE   ID IN (
                SELECT dbo.Invoice_Lines.ID
                FROM   dbo.Invoice_Lines
                LEFT OUTER JOIN dbo.Invoice_Lines_Deletes
                    ON dbo.Invoice_Lines.ID = dbo.Invoice_Lines_Deletes.ID
                WHERE dbo.Invoice_Lines_Deletes.ID IS NULL
              )
```

- If there is no single (VersionStamp or hash) field that allows you to identify that data has changed in a row, you may only have one solution: to compare all, or most, of the columns in a row with those in the other table. This is not only considerably more laborious to set up, it is also slower in most cases. Still, if it is the only alternative to reloading an entire table, it may be your only solution. For an example of multifield comparison, you could look at the MERGE...ON statement in Recipe 11-2.

- Unfortunately, it is not possible to detect new records as we did in this recipe when using SSIS for SQL Server 2005 (as there is not a NoMatch output). If you are stuck using SSIS 2005, then I suggest running a parallel data load of all the source IDs into the Invoice_Lines_Deletes destination table. This is then compared with the final destination table using a T-SQL DELETE statement to delete any records that are no longer in the source system (or perform an UPDATE if you want to perform a soft-delete).

11-2. Loading Data Changes Using a Linked Server

Problem

You have a source database on a linked server connected to the local destination server, and you want to manage delta data changes rather than carry out full data loads.

Solution

Use the T-SQL MERGE function to manage data transfer from the linked server source to the local server destination. This will automatically handle insertion for new records, updates of existing records, and (optionally) deletion of records no longer in the data source. The following steps explain how it is done.

1. Ensure that you have—at least for the purposes of this example—identical source and destination table structures in both the source and destination databases, such as the following, for example (C:\SQL2012DIRecipes\CH11\tbl12-2_Invoice_Lines.Sql):

    ```
    CREATE TABLE CarSales_Staging.dbo.Invoice_Lines
    (
    ID INT NOT NULL,
    InvoiceID INT NULL,
    StockID INT NULL,
    SalePrice NUMERIC(18, 2) NULL
    ) ;
    GO
    ```

2. Ensure that you have a correctly configured linked server, with all necessary permissions for the user running the process on the destination server to read the source data. In this example, the linked server is named ADAMREMOTE. Setting up a linked server to an SQL Server source database is described in Recipe 5-2.

3. Assuming that you have all the prerequisites in place, the following piece of T-SQL will ensure delta-based synchronization of the source and destination tables (C:\SQL2012DIRecipes\CH11\LinkedServerMerge.Sql).

    ```
    --Merge routine

    -- The two data sets
    MERGE   CarSales_Staging.dbo.Invoice_Lines AS DST

    USING   ADAMREMOTE.CarSales.dbo.Invoice_Lines AS SRC
            ON DST.ID = SRC.ID

    -- Deletes
    WHEN NOT MATCHED BY SOURCE

    THEN DELETE

    -- Updates
    WHEN MATCHED AND
    ```

```
                        (
                        ISNULL(SRC.InvoiceID,0) <> ISNULL(DST.InvoiceID,0)
                        OR ISNULL(SRC.StockID,0) <> ISNULL(DST.StockID,0)
                        OR ISNULL(SRC.SalePrice,0) <> ISNULL(DST.SalePrice,0)
                        )

        THEN UPDATE

        SET             DST.InvoiceID = SRC.InvoiceID
                        ,DST.StockID = SRC.StockID
                        ,DST.SalePrice = SRC.SalePrice

        -- Inserts
        WHEN NOT MATCHED THEN

        INSERT
                        (
                         ID
                         ,InvoiceID
                         ,StockID
                         ,SalePrice
                        )

        VALUES

                        (
                         ID
                         ,InvoiceID
                         ,StockID
                         ,SalePrice
                        )

        ;
```

How It Works

Handling inserts, updates, and deletes is also possible using a linked server as the data source. This has become much easier since the arrival of SQL Server 2008, and the T-SQL MERGE function. The point to note is that you can also use MERGE when the destination server has a linked server connection to the source server.

The two data tables are aliased as follows:

- The source (SRC) using four-part notation, including the linked server name (ADAMREMOTE in this example).

- The destination (DST) on the local server.

The unique identifier field(s) are used as the join between the two tables. Deletes are defined using the WHEN NOT MATCHED BY SOURCE clause. Updates are defined using the WHEN MATCHED AND clause—and comparing the field(s) that detect deltas. Inserts are defined using the WHEN NOT MATCHED clause.

One useful technique that you might find useful is to add the following line at the start of the code:

```
DECLARE @OutputIDs TABLE  (AccountID BIGINT, ActionType VARCHAR(40))
```

And the following line at the end, before the semicolon:

```
OUTPUT COALESCE(INSERTED.ID, DELETED.ID), $Action INTO @OutputIDs
```

This will store a list of all record IDs affected by the operation, as well as the type of operation for each one into the @OutputIDs table variable. You can then use this table as a source of logging and/or debugging information.

⬛ **Note**   Using MERGE is only really efficient if a couple of basic conditions are respected. First, you need an index on the columns used in the join (the ON statement) for the source table and a clustered index on the columns used in the join for the destination table. If you do not have these indexes in place, then you may find that MERGE is slower than alternative solutions.

Hints, Tips, and Traps

- Here I am comparing multiple fields; of course, you can use a VersionStamp, hashdata, or a column containing an updated data flag to detect deltas, if one of these column types exists in both the source and the destination databases.

- Remember to end the MERGE routine with a semicolon.

- If the destination table's ID column is an IDENTITY column, you will need to encapsulate the code performing the inserts with SET IDENTITY_INSERT ON – and SET IDENTITY_INSERT OFF.

11-3. Loading Data Changes From a Small Source Table as Part of a Structured ETL Process
Problem

You have a small, source data set and want to manage data changes as part of a regular load process.

Solution

Use the T-SQL MERGE function as part of an SSIS package.

1. Create a new SSIS package and add two OLEDB connection managers: one named **CarSales_OLEDB** (which you connect to the source CarSales database), the other named **CarSales_Staging_OLEDB** (which you connect to the CarSales_Staging destination database).

2. Add an Execute SQL task to the Control Flow pane. Name it **Create staging table**. Configure as follows (C:\SQL2012DIRecipes\CH11\11-3_CreateStagingTable.Sql):

Connection:	CarSales_Staging_OLEDB
SQL Statement:	IF OBJECT_ID('dbo.Invoice_Lines_STG') IS NOT NULL DROP TABLE dbo.Invoice_Lines_STG;

```
GO

CREATE TABLE dbo.Invoice_Lines_STG

(

  ID int NOT NULL,

  InvoiceID INT NULL,

  StockID INT NULL,

  SalePrice NUMERIC(18, 2) NULL,

  VersionStampVARBINARY(8) NULL

);

GO
```

3. Confirm your modifications.

4. Execute the task to create the Invoice_Lines_STG table.

5. Add a Data Flow task. Name it **Get source data**. Double-click to edit.

6. Add an OLEDB source. Name it **CarSales**. Configure as follows:

OLEDB Connection Manager:	CarSales_OLEDB
Data Access Mode:	SQL Command
SQL Command Text:	SELECT ID, InvoiceID, StockID, SalePrice, VersionStamp
	FROM dbo.Invoice_Lines

7. Confirm your changes

8. Add an OLEDB destination. Name it **CarSales_Staging_OLEDB**. Connect to the OLEDB source and configure as follows:

OLEDB Connection Manager:	CarSales_Staging_OLEDB
Data Access Mode:	Table or view- Fast Load
Name of the table or view:	dbo.Invoice_Lines_STG

9. Map the columns and confirm your changes.

10. Return to the Control Flow pane.

11. Add an Execute SQL task to the Control Flow pane. Name it **MERGE Data**. Configure
as follows (C:\SQL2012DIRecipes\CH11\11-3_MergeSSISMerge.Sql):

Connection:	CarSales_Staging_OLEDB
SQL Statement:	--Merge routine

```
--Merge routine
-- The two data sets
MERGE    dbo.Invoice_Lines AS DST

USING    dbo.Invoice_Lines_STG AS SRC
         ON DST.ID = SRC.ID

-- Deletes
WHEN NOT MATCHED BY SOURCE
THEN DELETE

-- Updates
WHEN MATCHED AND
            (
              ISNULL(SRC.VersionStamp,0) <> ISNULL(DST.VersionStamp,0)
            )
THEN UPDATE
SET         DST.InvoiceID = SRC.InvoiceID
           ,DST.StockID = SRC.StockID
           ,DST.SalePrice = SRC.SalePrice
           ,DST.VersionStamp = SRC.VersionStamp

-- Inserts
WHEN NOT MATCHED THEN
INSERT
            (
              ID
             ,InvoiceID
             ,StockID
             ,SalePrice
             ,VersionStamp
            )
```

```
VALUES
            (
            ID
            ,InvoiceID
            ,StockID
            ,SalePrice
            ,VersionStamp
            )
    ;
```

12. Confirm your configuration.

13. Add an Execute SQL task to the Control Flow pane. Name it **Drop Staging Table**.
    Configure as follows:

Connection: CarSales_Staging_OLEDB

SQL Statement: `IF OBJECT_ID('dbo.Invoice_Lines_STG') IS NOT NULL`

                            `DROP TABLE dbo.Invoice_Lines_STG`

This will remove the staging table from the destination database once the rest of the process has run.
The SSIS package should look like Figure 11-8.

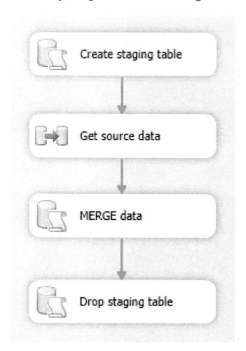

Figure 11-8. *Control flow for SSIS-based MERGE*

How It Works

If the simplicity of the T-SQL MERGE command appeals to you, you can call it from SSIS as well. In this simple example, it pulls all the source data from the source system, and writes it to a staging table. This simplicity is clearly a major attraction. Such an approach is best suited to transferring all the source data to a staging table on the destination server, and you have sufficient disk space for a duplicate table. It requires nearly identical source and destination table structures (which is nearly always a sine qua non for delta data management). Here the MERGE function is virtually identical to that used in the previous recipe, except that because both source and destination are on the same server, four-part notation is not required.

I am using a ROWVERSION column to detect deltas. You may use a hashdata or a Data Updated column if your data has these. If the destination table's ID column is an IDENTITY column, you need to set IDENTITY_INSERT ON and OFF.

Hints, Tips, and Traps

- You may use a session-scoped temporary table instead of a table on disk. This will require you to use variables for the table names and select statements (and initially use persisted tables in the destination database), as well as setting the destination connection manager to retain the same connection, as described in Recipe 11-4.

- For staging tables of any size, you might be advised to create an index (clustered or nonclustered) on the staging table on its primary or unique keys—or whatever column(s) are used in the USING...ON clause. For MERGE to function efficiently, you must add a clustered index to the destination table columns used in the join (ON) clause of the MERGE statement.

- The staging table may be on another (staging) database on the destination server, and, in any case, benefit from being on a separate disk array to the final destination table.

- You may be pleasantly surprised by the speed with which large data sets can be updated using MERGE rather than the SSIS approach outlined in the first recipe of this chapter. However, inevitably, the speed of a process depends on the environment in which you are working.

- As was the case for Recipe 11-1, the drawback to this approach is that all the source data must travel across a network. So it might not suit larger data sets.

11-4. Detecting and Loading Delta Data Only
Problem

You want to isolate changed data at the source before applying changes to the destination table—and avoid transferring nonmodified data across the network.

Solution

Send a hash code for all records from the destination server back to the source server. Use this to detect changes and only return changed records to the destination server. The following explains how you can do this.

1. Create the four ETL metadata tables that will provisionally hold delta data information. For updates in the *source* database, use the following DDL:

    ```
    CREATE TABLE CarSales.dbo.TMP_Updates (ID INT);
    ```

2. For inserts in the *source* database, use the following DDL:

    ```
    CREATE TABLE CarSales.dbo.TMP_Inserts (ID INT);
    ```

3. For updated data in the ***destination*** database, use the following DDL (drop this table first if you have created it for another recipe). The code is in (C:\SQL2012DIRecipes\CH11\tbl11-4_Invoice_Lines_Updates.Sql):

    ```
    CREATE TABLE CarSales_Staging.dbo.Invoice_Lines_Updates
    (
     ID INT  NOT NULL,
     InvoiceID INT  NULL,
     StockID INT  NULL,
     SalePrice NUMERIC(18, 2) NULL,
     DateUpdated DATETIME,
     LineItem SMALLINT,
     VersionStamp VARBINARY(8) NULL,
     HashData VARBINARY(256) NULL
    ) ;
    GO
    ```

4. For deletes in the ***destination*** database use the following DDL:

    ```
    CREATE TABLE CarSales_Staging.dbo.TMP_Deletes (ID INT);
    GO
    ```

5. As a destination table for this recipe, create the following table.). The code is in (C:\SQL2012DIRecipes\CH11\tbl11-4_Invoice_Lines.Sql):

    ```
    CREATE TABLE CarSales_Staging.dbo.Invoice_Lines
    (
     ID INT  NOT NULL,
     InvoiceID INT  NULL,
     StockID INT  NULL,
     SalePrice NUMERIC(18, 2) NULL,
     DateUpdated DATETIME,
     LineItem SMALLINT,
     VersionStamp VARBINARY(8) NULL,
     HashData VARBINARY(256) NULL
    ) ;
    GO
    ```

6. Add three package-scoped variables. The references to the database tables will be replaced later with references to temporary tables. Configure these variables—for the moment—as follows:

Name:	DeleteTable
DataType:	String
Value:	Tmp_Deletes
Name:	UpdateTable
DataType:	String
Value:	Tmp_Updates
Name:	InsertTable
DataType:	String
Value:	Tmp_Inserts

7. Create a new SSIS package and add create two OLEDB connection managers: one correctly configured for the source server (CarSales) and one correctly configured for the destination server (CarSales_Staging), named **CarSales_OLEDB** and **CarSales_Staging_OLEDB**, respectively. Set the RetainSameConnection property to True for both the source and destination connection managers.

8. Add a new Execute SQL task onto the Control Flow pane. Name it **Create Temp tables on Source**. This task creates the session-scoped temporary tables that will hold the IDs of all records to insert and update from the source dataset (in production if not in development). Configure as follows:

Name:	Create Temp tables
Connection:	CarSales_OLEDB
SQL Statement:	`CREATE TABLE ##TMP_INSERTS (ID INT);`
	`CREATE TABLE ##TMP_UPDATES (ID INT);`

9. Confirm with OK to return to the Data Flow pane.

10. Add a new Execute SQL task onto the Control Flow pane. Connect the previous Execute SQL task to it. Name it **Create Temp tables on Destination**. This task creates the session-scoped temporary table that will hold all the IDs in the source data (which will be used to isolate records to delete). Configure as follows:

Name:	Create Temp tables
Connection:	CarSales_Staging_OLEDB
SQL Statement:	`CREATE TABLE ##TMP_DELETES (ID INT);`

11. Confirm with OK to return to the Data Flow pane.

12. Add a Data Flow task to the Control Flow pane. Name it **Delta Detection**. Connect the Execute SQL task "Create Temp Tables on Source" to it. Double-click to enter the Data Flow pane.

13. Add an OLEDB source adapter. Configure it to select the ID and delta detection rows from the source table (Invoice_Lines) using an SQL command, like this:

Name:	Create Temp tables
Connection:	CarSales_OLEDB
SQL Statement:	`SELECT    ID, HashData AS HashData_Source`
	`FROM      dbo.Invoice_Lines WITH (NOLOCK)`

14. Add a Multicast transform to the Data Flow pane. Connect the data source adapter to it.

15. Add a Lookup transform to which you connect the Multicast transform. Name it **Detect Hash Deltas**. On the General pane of the Lookup transform, configure it as follows:

Cache Mode:	No Cache
Connection Type:	OLEDB Connection Manager
Specify how to handle rows with NoMatch entries:	Send rows with no matching entries to the No Match output

16. Click Connection on the left. Set the connection manager to CarSales_Staging_OLEDB because as you will be comparing the source data with the destination data that you are looking up with this Lookup transform.

17. Set the Lookup to "Use results of an SQL Query " and enter the following SQL:

```
SELECT    ID, HashData
FROM      dbo.Invoice_Lines WITH (NOLOCK)
```

18. Click Columns on the left. The two tables, source (on the left), and destination (on the right) will appear. Drag the ID column from the Available Lookup Columns (or Destination) table on the right to the ID column of the Available Input Columns (Source) table on the left. This maps the unique IDs of the two data sources to each other.

19. Select the HashData column of the Available Lookup Columns (or destination) table on the right and provide an output alias—I suggest **HashData_Destination**. This allows you to compare the hashes for source and destination for each record.

20. Click OK to confirm your modifications. Return to the Data Flow pane.

21. Add an OLEDB destination adapter to the Data Flow pane and set its ValidateExternalMetadata property to False. Connect the Lookup transform to this destination, ensuring that you select the Lookup NoMatch output. Configure as follows:

OLEDB Connection Manager:	CarSales_OLEDB
Data Access Mode:	Table name or view name variable
Variable Name:	InsertTable

22. Click Mappings and ensure that the ID columns are connected. Click OK to confirm your modifications. You will be creating a temporary table of all new IDs in the data source, which you will use later to transfer only these records (the inserts) to the destination server.

23. Add an OLEDB destination adapter to the Data Flow pane. Connect the Multicast transform to it. Name it **Records to Delete**, and set its ValidateExternalMetadata property to False. Double-click to edit.

24. Set the connection manager to CarSales_Staging_OLEDB and the data access mode to table name or view name variable. Select DeleteTable as the table variable name.

25. Click Mappings. Ensure that the ID columns are connected. Then click OK to confirm. This way, you create a temporary table of all IDs in the source dataset that you can compare with current IDs in the destination dataset to deduce deleted records.

26. Now it is time to move to the Update part of the process. Add a Conditional Split transform on to the Data Flow pane. Name it **Detect Hash Deltas**. Connect the Lookup transform to it. The Lookup Match output should be applied automatically. This sends the Lookup Match Output to the Conditional Split.

27. Double-click to edit the Conditional Split. Add a single output condition named **HashData Differences**, where the condition is

```
(DT_UI8) HashData_Source != (DT_UI8) HashData_Destination
```

28. Click OK to confirm. Close the dialog box.

29. Add an OLEDB destination adapter to the data flow and connect the Conditional Split transform to it. The Input Output dialog box will appear, where you should select the HashData Differences output (which is, in fact, the source for the destination adapter). Set the following:

OLEDB Connection Manager:	CarSales_OLEDB
Data Access Mode:	Table name or view name variable
Variable Name:	UpdateTable

30. Click Mappings and ensure that the ID columns are mapped correctly, and then click OK to confirm your modifications. This sends a subset of all IDs with different hashes to the session-scoped temporary table. The Data Flow pane should look like Figure 11-9.

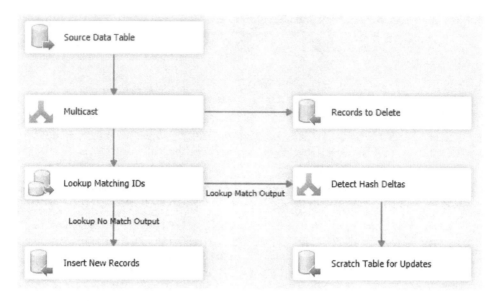

Figure 11-9. *Data flow for hash-based delta detection*

31. Click the Control Flow tab to return to the Control Flow pane.

32. Now we can move on to the second part of the process—using the IDs that identify the Inserts, Deletes, and Updates to perform the data modifications, fetching (in the case of inserts and updates) only the records that are required. Let's begin with Deletes. Click the Control Flow tab and add an Execute SQL Task. Name it **Delete Data**. Connect this to the Delta Detection Data Flow task. Configure the Execute SQL task as follows (C:\SQL2012DIRecipes\CH11\11-4_DeleteData.Sql):

Connection: CarSales_Staging_OLEDB

SQL Statement:

```
DELETE FROM   dbo.Invoice_Lines
WHERE         ID IN (
                  SELECT    DST.ID
                  FROM      dbo.Invoice_Lines DST
                  LEFT OUTER JOIN   ##TMP_Deletes TMP
                                    ON TMP.ID = DST.ID
                  WHERE     TMP.ID IS NULL
              )
```

33. Now on to Inserts. Add a Data Flow task to the Control Flow pane. Add the previous task (DeleteData) to it. Name the task **Insert Data**. Set its DelayValidation property to True.

34. Add a new package-scoped variable named **InsertSQL**. This must be a string containing the SELECT statement corresponding to the source data, joined to the TMP_Inserts temp table. In this example, the following value will be used; it will be tweaked to use the temp table once all is working (C:\SQL2012DIRecipes\CH11\11-4_InsertSQL.Sql):

```
SELECT    SRC.ID, SRC.InvoiceID, SRC.StockID, SRC.SalePrice, SRC.HashData
FROM      dbo.Invoice_Lines SRC
          INNER JOIN  TMP_Inserts TMP
          ON  SRC.ID = TMP.ID
```

35. Edit the "Insert Data" Data Flow task.

36. Add an OLEDB source to the Data Flow pane. Rename it **CarSales_OLEDB**, and configure it as follows:

OLEDB Connection Manager:	CarSales_OLEDB
Data Access Mode:	SQL Command from variable
Variable Name:	InsertSQL

37. Add an OLEDB destination connector to the Data Flow pane. Connect the source to it. Configure as follows:

OLEDB Connection Manager:	CarSales_Staging_OLEDB
Data Access Mode:	Table or view - Fast load
Name of the Table or View:	dbo.Invoice_Lines

38. Click Columns and ensure that all the required columns are selected, and then click OK to confirm your changes. This makes a second trip to the source server, and adds any new records not already in the destination dataset.

39. Return to the Control Flow pane.

40. Finally, we're on to Updates. First, add two package-scoped string variables, as follows (C:\SQL2012DIRecipes\CH11\11-4_UpdateDataTable.Sql):

Name:	UpdateDataTable
Value:	Invoice_Lines_Updates
Name:	UpdateSQL
Value:	

    ```
              SELECT    SRC.ID, SRC.InvoiceID,
                        SRC.StockID, SRC.SalePrice,
                        SRC.LineItem, SRC.DateUpdated
                        SRC.HashData
              FROM      dbo.Invoice_Lines SRC
                        INNER JOIN TMP_Updates TMP
                        ON SRC.ID = TMP.ID
    ```

41. The UpdateSQL variable selects only the records that need to be updated from the source server. UpdateDataTable refers to the temporary table of data containing all the records that require updating. UpdateCode performs the update on the destination server. Name it **Update Data**. Connect the previous Data Flow task (Insert Data) to it. Set its DelayValidation property to True.

42. Double-click to edit. Add an OLEDB source to the Data Flow pane. Rename it **CarSales_OLEDB**. Set its ValidateExternalMetadata property to False. Configure it as follows:

OLEDB Connection Manager:	CarSales_OLEDB
Data Access Mode:	SQL Command from variable
Variable Name:	UpdateSQL

43. Add an OLEDB destination connector to the Data Flow pane. Connect the source to it. Configure as follows:

OLEDB Connection Manager:	CarSales_Staging_OLEDB
Data Access Mode:	SQL Command from variable
Variable Name:	UpdateDataTable

44. Click Mappings and ensure that all the required columns are mapped, and then click OK to confirm your changes. This makes a second trip to the source server and adds any new records not already in the destination dataset to the Invoice_Lines_Updates scratch table, which will end up by being a temporary table soon, too.

45. Return to the Data Flow pane. Add an Execute SQL task, which you rename **Carry out updates**. Connect the "Update Data" Data Flow task to this. Set its DelayValidation property to True.

46. Edit the **Carry out updates** Execute SQL task and set the following (C:\SQL2012DIRecipes\CH11\11-4_CarryOutUpdates.Sql):

Connection: CarSales_Staging_OLEDB

```
SQL Statement:    UPDATE      DST
                  SET         DST.InvoiceID = UPD.InvoiceID
                              ,DST.SalePrice = UPD.SalePrice
                              ,DST.LineItem = UPD.LineItem
                              ,DST.UpdateDate = SRC.UpdateDate
                              ,DST.StockID = UPD.StockID
                              ,DST.HashData = UPD.HashData
                  FROM        dbo.Invoice_Lines DST
                              INNER JOIN   ##Invoice_Lines_Updates UPD
                              ON DST.ID = UPD.ID
```

The Control Flow pane should look like Figure 11-10.

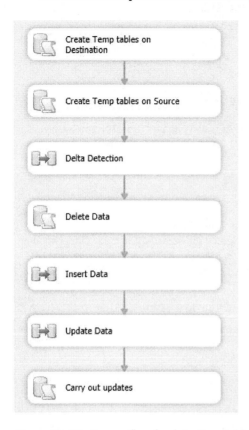

Figure 11-10. *Process flow for detecting and loading only delta data*

That, finally, is it. You have an SSIS package that can detect data differences and only return the full data for any records that are new or need updating. Once the process is debugged and functioning, you can modify the variable values to use temporary tables, as follows (C:\SQL2012DIRecipes\CH11\11-4_VariablesForTempTables.Sql):

DeleteTable:	TempDB..##TMP_Deletes
UpdateTable:	TempDB..##TMP_Updates
InsertTable:	TempDB..##TMP_Inserts
UpdateDataTable:	TempDB..##Invoice_Lines_Updates

```
InsertSQL:    SELECT      SRC.ID, SRC.InvoiceID,
                          SRC.StockID, SRC.SalePrice,
                          SRC.HashData
              FROM        dbo.Invoice_Lines SRC
                          INNER JOIN    TempDB..##TMP_Inserts TMP
                          ON SRC.ID = TMP.ID
```

```
UpdateSQL:      SELECT          SRC.ID, SRC.InvoiceID, SRC.StockID,

                                SRC.SalePrice, SRC.HashData

                FROM            dbo.Invoice_Lines SRC

                                INNER JOIN   TempDB..##TMP_Updates TMP

                                ON SRC.ID = TMP.ID
```

Finally, you can delete the provisional tables, TMP _Updates and TMP_Inserts, in the source database, and TMP_Deletes and Invoice_Lines_Updates in the destination database. The process will now use the temporary tables instead of persisted tables.

How It Works

The downside of Recipes 11-1 and 11-3 is that the entire dataset is transferred from the source server every time that the process runs. An improvement on this approach might be to detect any records which are different, and only send across the records that have changed, which is done in this recipe.

So, assuming that you have extremely limited rights on the source server, how can this be done?

The solution is to use a two-phase process:

- First, bring back only the Key column(s) and the Delta Flag column to the destination server.

- Then, detect the deltas (insert, update, and delete) and request only the appropriate records for each from the source server.

In this example, I am using a hash code to detect deltas —and consequently presume that your source data has a hash code generated for each insert and update. This approach works equally well with TIMESTAMP or ROWVERSION columns or date fields.

It is worth noting that this approach is only productive if you have a Delta Detection column, and will probably not prove much use if you are comparing multiple columns in the source and destination data sets, because you will almost inevitably end up bringing most of the data back from the source server twice. In my tests, using this approach can show real speed improvements with wide tables, but can be slower with very narrow tables. In a 15-column table of mixed data types, a few of them medium-length VARCHARs and a 2 percent data differential, I got a 10 percent reduction in processing time. In a 150-column table containing several tens of very wide columns and the same 2 percent data differential, the process ran nearly four times faster. Of course, your results depend on your source data, network, and destination server configuration.

Figure 11-11 gives perhaps a clearer, illustrated view of the process.

Figure 11-11. *Process flow to detect data modifications at source*

On the technical level, this technique will use session-scoped temporary tables to hold the delta IDs of records that will be updated and deleted. To achieve this in practice, you need to set the `RetainSameConnection` connection property, where the temporary table will be created (source or destination) to True. This ensures that the same connection is used throughout the duration of the SSIS package, and therefore, that any session-scoped temporary tables used are available for all steps that need to use them. Then you have to ensure that any temporary tables that you create must be session-scoped—that is, their names begin with double hashes (##).

This recipe's approach is best used in the following circumstances:

- When you are importing wide tables that have a reliable delta-detection column.

- When the modified data is only a small percentage of the total.

- When you do not want to persist tables to disk for temporary data sets in the destination database.

Please note that there is a little "scaffolding" to set up before creating the package, which you will need to remove afterward. This comment may need explaining, so here goes. In order to use session-scoped temporary tables easily in SSIS, it helps enormously to first create normal tables in the source and development environments that you will use to set up the package—pretty much like you did in Recipe 11-1. When creating the package, you will use SSIS variables to refer to the scratch tables in the source and destination databases. When all is working, alter the SSIS variables to point to the session-scoped temporary tables, and delete the corresponding tables in their respective databases. I call these tables "provisional."

The four ETL metadata tables are used as described in Table 11-2.

Table 11-2. *ETL Metadata Tables Used in This Recipe*

ETL Metadata Table	Description
Source database table for IDs of new records.	Once deltas have been detected on the destination database, their IDs are sent back to the source database so that the corresponding records can be sent for insertion at the destination.
Source database table for IDs of updated records.	Once data changes have been detected on the destination database, their IDs are sent back to the source database so that the corresponding records can be sent for insertion at the destination.
Destination database table to hold modified data.	The IDs of updated records on the destination database.
Destination database table for IDs of deleted records.	The IDs of deleted records on the destination database.

In this recipe, the `VERSIONSTAMP` column used in Recipe 11-1 is replaced by a `VARCHAR` column named `HashData`, which holds the hash calculation used for delta detection.

Hints, Tips, and Traps

- As you are using session-scoped temporary tables, you could have data spill out of memory and into TempDB; so it is well worth ensuring that your TempDB is configured correctly (the correct number of files for the number of processors, etc.; see Books On Line (BOL) for details).

- As for the *scaffolding* (the permanent table(s) that you use to hold delta data), you can test it using the materialized database tables until you are happy that everything is working, and only then replace the variable references to the temporary tables at the end of your first phase of testing.

- There are two main tweaks to remember:

  - ValidateExternalMetadata must be False for all OLEDB source and destination connectors that use a temporary table.

  - DelayValidation must be True for all Data Flow tasks that use a temporary table.

11-5. Performing Delta Data Upserts with Other SQL Databases

Problem

You are using another SQL database as a data source and you want to transfer only modified or new records to the destination, as well as IDs of deleted records.

Solution

Use a delta detection column and use temporary tables as shown in the previous recipe. The following steps detail a simplified approach to this for an Oracle data source.

1. Create an Oracle global temporary table using the following DDL (C:\SQL2012DIRecipes\CH11\tblOracleDelta.Sql):

    ```
    create global temporary table SCOTT.DELTA_DATA
    (
    "EMPNO" NUMBER(4,0)
    ) ;
    on commit preserve rows
    ```

2. Create a destination SQL Server table using the following DDL (C:\SQL2012DIRecipes\CH11\tblOracle_EMP.Sql):

    ```
    CREATE TABLE dbo.Oracle_EMP
    (
     EMPNO NUMERIC(4, 0) NULL,
     LASTUPDATED datetime NULL,
     ENAME VARCHAR(10) NULL,
     JOB VARCHAR(9) NULL,
     MGR NUMERIC(4, 0) NULL,
     HIREDATE datetime NULL,
     SAL NUMERIC(7, 2) NULL,
     COMM NUMERIC(7, 2) NULL,
     DEPTNO NUMERIC(2, 0) NULL
    ) ;
    ```

3. Create a new SSIS package and add two OLEDB connection managers: one (named **CarSales_Staging_OLEDB**) for your destination SQL Server database (CarSales_Staging) and one (named **Source_Oracle_OLEDB**) using the Oracle Provider for OLEDB to connect to your Oracle instance. Set RetainSameConnection as True for both.

4. Add a Data Flow task. Name it Isolate new IDs for Insert. Double-click to edit.

5. Add an OLEDB data source. Name it **Oracle Source**. Edit and configure as follows:

   OLEDB Connection Manager: Source_Oracle_OLEDB

   Data Access Mode: SQL Command

   SQL Command: `SELECT    EMPNO`

         `FROM      SCOTT.EMP`

6. Click OK to confirm.

7. Add a Lookup transform and configure to select the EMPNO from the destination table `Oracle_EMP`. Join on the EMPNO column. Redirect rows that do not match to the NoMatch output, and click OK.

8. Add an OLEDB destination. Name it **Oracle Delta** and configure it as follows:

   OLEDB Connection Manager: Source_Oracle_OLEDB

   Data Access Mode: Table or View

   Table or View Name: Scott.DELTA_DATA

   Your Data Flow pane should look like Figure 11-12.

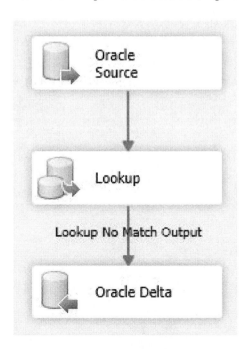

Figure 11-12. *Oracle delta data processing*

651

9. Return to the Control Flow pane and add a new Data Flow task. Name it **Insert new records**. Double-click to edit.

10. Add an OLEDB source. Name it **Delta Records** and configure as follows (C:\SQL2012DIRecipes\CH11\11-5_DeltaRecords.Sql):

OLEDB Connection Manager:	Source_Oracle_OLEDB
Data Access Mode:	SQL Command
SQL Command Text:	SELECT DISTINCT
	S.EMPNO, S.ENAME, S.JOB, S.MGR,
	S.HIREDATE, S.SAL, S.COMM,
	S.DEPTNO, S.LASTUPDATED
	FROM SCOTT.DELTA_DATA D, SCOTT.EMP S
	WHERE D.EMPNO = S.EMPNO

11. Click OK to confirm.

12. Add an OLEDB destination. Name it **Delta Output**. Connect the "Delta Records" OLEDB source to it. Map all the columns and click OK. Return to the Control Flow pane.

13. Add an Execute SQL task and name it **Delete temp table**. Connect the "Insert new records" Data Flow task to it and configure as follows:

Connection:	Source_Oracle_OLEDB
SQL Statement:	DELETE FROM SCOTT.DELTA_DATA

14. Click OK to confirm. The Control Flow pane should look like Figure 11-13.

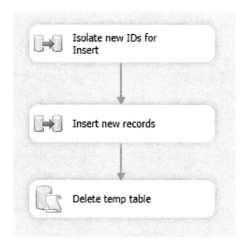

Figure 11-13. *Oracle SQL-based delta data processing*

How It Works

Most of the current commercially available and open-source SQL databases use temporary tables in one way or another. As it would not be feasible to show how they all can be used in this context, I have briefly outlined how they can be used this way with Oracle, as this product is the one that SQL Server DBAs and developers tend to encounter rather often. I can only hope that the techniques described next will be of use as a starting point if you are using another RDBMS. Remember, if all else fails, you can always use a "normal" persisted table if you can convince the source system DBA to allow it.

As this is essentially similar to the process described in Recipe 11-4, I have only given a brief overview, and drawn your attention to any pertinent differences. Specifically, I have only looked at data inserts, and am leaving you to extrapolate how to perform deletes and updates based this approach.

This technique is most appropriate when you wish to get delta data back from an Oracle data source, and have convinced the Oracle DBA to create a global temporary table and give the account that you will use to extract data and the rights to access the table in question. It is also fundamental to have the relevant Oracle client software installed and configured on your server.

Hints, Tips, and Traps

- Here, too, it is essential to set the Oracle OLEDB connection manager RetainSameConnection property to True.

- Equally fundamental is the "on commit preserve rows" when creating the temporary table in the Oracle source database—without this, the process will not work.

- Note that an Oracle temporary table is not like an SQL Server temp table—it physically exists on disk. However, only the user connected during the SSIS session will be able to use the data that they are inserting into the table. The downside to this is that the data must be deleted afterward, or it will remain in the table and cause errors the next time this process is run.

11-6. Handling Data Changes Without Writing to the Source Server

Problem

You want to transfer only changed records from a source database, but you are not allowed to create ETL metadata tables on the source.

Solution

Isolate the IDs of new or changed records, and return them as part of the SELECT query to the source database. If your deltas are very small, the following steps explain how it can be done.

1. On the destination database (CarSales_Staging) create a table type to hold IDs:

    ```
    CREATE TYPE DeltaIDs AS TABLE (ID INT);
    GO
    ```

2. Also on the destination database (CarSales_Staging), create a stored procedure to return the data that corresponds to the set of IDs that will be passed in using a table-valued parameter (C:\SQL2012DIRecipes\CH11\pr_SelectDeltaData.Sql):

```
CREATE PROCEDURE CarSales_Staging.dbo.pr_SelectDeltaData
(
@DeltaSet DeltaIDs READONLY
)

AS

SELECT
S.ID
,S.InvoiceID
,S.StockID
,S.SalePrice
,CAST(S.HashData AS VARCHAR(50)) AS HashData

FROM        dbo.Invoice_Lines S
            INNER JOIN   @DeltaSet D
            ON S.ID = D.ID;
GO
```

3. Create the Invoice_Lines destination table using the following DDL (and remember to drop any previous versions if they exist). The DDL is in C:\SQL2012DIRecipes\CH11\tbl11-5_Invoice_Lines.Sql:

```
CREATE TABLE dbo.Invoice_Lines
(
ID INT NOT NULL,
 InvoiceID INT NULL,
 StockID INT NULL,
 SalePrice NUMERIC(18, 2) NULL,
 HashData VARCHAR(50) NULL
);
GO
```

4. Create a new SSIS package and add two OLEDB connection managers named **CarSales_OLEDB** and **CarSales_Staging_OLEDB**, which you configure to connect to the source and destination servers, respectively. Then add an ADO.NET connection manager named **CarSales_ADONET**, which you configure to connect to the source server. This last connection manager will be used to pass back the Table Valued Parameter (TVP) containing the required IDs and then call the stored procedure to return delta data.

5. Add a new package-scoped variable named **InsertDeltas**, which must be an object type.

6. Add a new Data Flow task named **Get Source delta information**. Double-click to edit.

7. Add an OLEDB source adapter and name it **Source delta**. Configure it to use the CarSales_OLEDB connection manager. Select the ID and delta detection rows from the source table (Invoice_Lines) using an SQL command and the following code:

```
SELECT      ID, Hashdata
FROM        dbo.Invoice_Lines
```

8. Add a Lookup transform, as described in steps 6 to 11 in Recipe 11-1. Here, however, you are using the Hashdata column instead of the VersionStamp column from the Available Lookup Columns. Name the destination column in the Lookup transform **HashData_Destination**.

9. Add a Recordset destination to the Data Flow pane. Connect the Lookup transform to this, ensuring that you select the No Match output. Double-click to edit. Select InsertDeltas as the variable name (to hold the output). The dialog box should look like Figure 11-14.

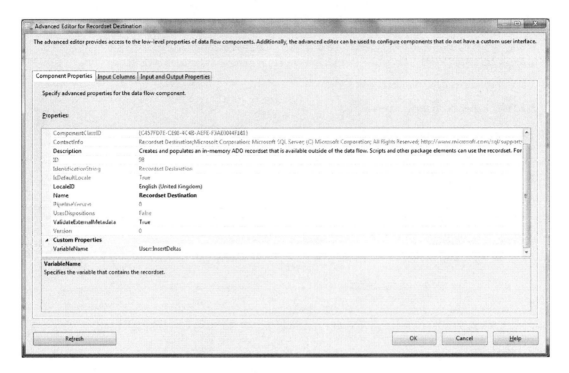

Figure 11-14. *Recordset destination configuration*

10. Click Input Columns and select the ID column. This will pass only new (unmatched) IDs through into the Recordset variable. Click OK to return to the Control Flow tab.

11. Add a new Data Flow task and connect the preceding "Get Source delta information" Data Flow task to it. Name it **Inserts**. Double-click to edit.

12. Add a script component to the Data Flow pane, naming it **Source Data**. Select Source as the Script Component type. Double-click to edit. Set the read-only variables as InsertDeltas and the script language as Microsoft Visual Basic 2010.

13. Click Inputs and Outputs. Expand Output 0 and rename it **MainOutput**. Then add five columns, as follows:

ID	4-byte signed integer
InvoiceID	4-byte signed integer
StockID	4- byte signed integer
SalePrice	Decimal, scale 2
HashData	String, length 50

14. Click connection managers on the left. Click Add. Name the new connection manager **DataBaseConnection**. Select the ADO.NET connection manager CarSales_ADONET.

15. Click Script on the left and then Edit Script.

16. Add the following to the Imports region:

```
Imports System.Data.SqlClient
```

17. Replace the ScriptMain class with the following code (C:\SQL2012DIRecipes\CH11\TVPDeltas.vb):

```vb
Public Class ScriptMain
    Inherits UserComponent

    Dim connMgr As IDTSConnectionManager100
    Dim sqlConn As SqlConnection

    Public Overrides Sub AcquireConnections(ByVal Transaction As Object)

        connMgr = Me.Connections.DataBaseConnection
        sqlConn = CType(connMgr.AcquireConnection(Nothing), SqlConnection)

    End Sub

    Public Overrides Sub PostExecute()
        MyBase.PostExecute()
    End Sub

    Public Overrides Sub CreateNewOutputRows()

        Dim DA As New OleDb.OleDbDataAdapter
        Dim TBL As New DataTable
        Dim Row As DataRow = Nothing

        DA.Fill(TBL, Me.Variables.InsertDeltas)

        Dim cmd As New SqlClient.SqlCommand("dbo.pr_SelectDeltaData", sqlConn)
        cmd.CommandType = CommandType.StoredProcedure
        Dim DeltaPrm As SqlClient.SqlParameter = ↩
                    cmd.Parameters.Add("@DeltaSet", SqlDbType.Structured)
        DeltaPrm.Value = TBL
        Dim RDR As SqlClient.SqlDataReader = cmd.ExecuteReader()
```

```
        If RDR.HasRows = True Then

            Do While RDR.Read()
                With MainOutputBuffer
                    .AddRow()
                    ' Map data
                    .ID = RDR.GetSqlInt32(0)
                    .InvoiceID = RDR.GetSqlInt32(1)
                    .StockID = RDR.GetSqlInt32(2)
                    .SalePrice = RDR.GetDecimal(3)
                    If Not RDR.GetSqlString(4).IsNull Then
                        .HashData = RDR.GetSqlString(4)
                    End If
                End With
            Loop

        End If
    End Sub
End Class
```

18. Click OK to confirm.

19. Add an OLEDB destination component to the Data Flow pane. Name it **Inserts**.
    Connect the Script source component to it. Configure it to connect to the destination
    table as described in previous recipes. Click Columns and ensure that all the required
    columns are selected. Click OK to confirm your changes. This makes a second trip to
    the source server and adds any new records not already in the destination. The final
    package will look like Figure 11-15.

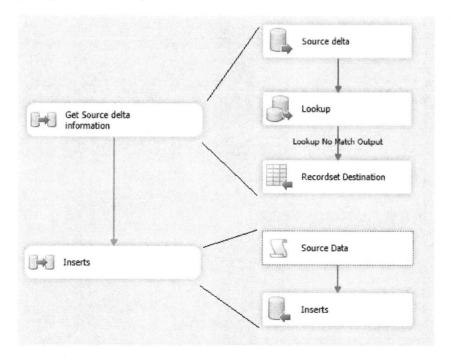

Figure 11-15. *The complete package to query delta data*

How It Works

There are times when session-scoped temporary tables cannot be used on a source database. In most cases, this is because the DBA looking after the source database will not give the account that SSIS is using the necessary rights, and/or because the additional load that this causes for the source server is deemed unacceptable. There is another solution that can prove useful, which is to isolate the IDs of new or changed records, and return them as part of the SELECT query to the source database. You must nonetheless convince the source system's DBA to add a user-defined table type and one or more stored procedures to the source system.

However, a word of caution is required. This approach is designed to handle extremely small deltas. It is definitely not scalable to large data sets, and can cause extreme memory pressure on the destination server. Also, this technique will only work when using SQL Server 2008 and above, as user-defined table types are only available from this version onward.

As the two techniques shown in this recipe are extensions of the approach given in the two previous recipes, I have not explained the entire process, but only the part that allows you to select insert delta data. The rest of the process is nearly identical to that described earlier, and so it will not be repeated here. In these examples, I use hashes to isolate deltas; but of course, you may prefer to use ROWVERSION or date fields.

This recipe does is the following:

> **Detects the delta data**. However, unlike in previous recipes, the IDs to INSERT or UPDATE will be stored in an SSIS object using a Recordset destination component.

> **Returns the SSIS Recordset to the source server** by passing it as a table-valued parameter (TVP) to a stored procedure in the source database.

On a more technical level, what happens is this: first, the SSIS variable object is used to populate an ADO.NET data table. Then, this ADO.NET data table is passed back as the table-valued parameter to the stored procedure that uses the TVP to extract a subset of data. Finally, the data subset is passed to the Script source output buffer. What is so elegant about this approach is that an ADO.NET data table can be passed as a table-valued parameter to an SQL Server stored procedure, with no extra processing, loops, or other work.

Hints, Tips, and Traps

- Remember to add null handling for all nullable columns.

- System.Data.SqlClient must be referenced in the Imports region, as it will be used to call the stored procedure on the source database.

11-7. Detecting Data Changes with Limited Source Database Access

Problem

You need to detect delta data when no permissions are given on the source database, except the right to read the source table(s).

Solution

Detect the delta identifiers at the destination and then pass them back as part of the SELECT clause for the data extraction. The following explains how to go about using this approach.

1. Create a new SSIS package. Add two OLEDB connection managers named **CarSales_ Staging_OLEDB** (which connects to the CarSales_Staging database) and **CarSales_ OLEDB** (which connects to the CarSales database). Set the RetainSameConnection property to True for the CarSales_Staging_OLEDB connection manager.

2. Add the following variables:

Variable Name	Type	Value	
UpdateCounter	INT16		
InsertCounter	INT16		
DeleteTable	String	##TMP_Deletes	
InsertTable	String	##TMP_Inserts	
UpdateTable	String	##TMP_Updates	
DeltaInserts	Object		
DeltaUpdates	Object		
InsertSQL	String	SELECT	ID, InvoiceID, StockID, SalePrice, HashData
		FROM	dbo.Invoice_Lines
UpdateSQL	String	SELECT	SRC.ID, SRC.InvoiceID, SRC.StockID, SRC.SalePrice, SRC.HashData
		FROM	dbo.Invoice_Lines SRC
UpdateDataTable	String	##Invoice_Lines_Updates	

3. Add an Execute SQL task. Name it **Create Temp tables on Destination**. Set the Connection to CarSales_Staging_OLEDB. Set the SQL Statement to the following (C:\SQL2012DIRecipes\CH11\CreateTempTablesOnDestination.Sql):

```
IF OBJECT_ID('TempDB..##TMP_DELETES') IS NULL
CREATE TABLE TempDB..##TMP_DELETES (ID INT);

IF OBJECT_ID('TempDB..##Invoice_Lines_Updates') IS NULL
CREATE TABLE ##Invoice_Lines_Updates
(
 ID INT NOT NULL,
 InvoiceID INT NULL,
 StockID INT NULL,
 SalePrice NUMERIC(18, 2) NULL,
 VersionStamp VARBINARY(8) NULL,
 HashData VARCHAR(50) NULL
);
```

4.   Add a new Data Flow task and connect the previous task (Create Temp tables on Destination) to it. Configure it so that it looks like Figure 11-16. See Recipe 11-1 for details on how to do this.

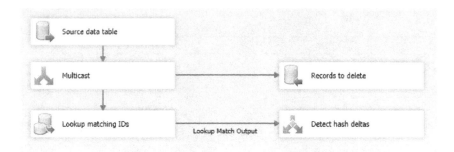

Figure 11-16. *Data flow for detecting changes at the destination database*

5.   Add two Row Count transforms. Connect one to the "Lookup matching IDs" Lookup transform—using the NoMatch output—and name it **Insert Count**. Configure it to use the User::InsertCounter variable. Connect the other to the Detect Hash Deltas Conditional Split transform using the HashData Differences output. Configure it to use the User::UpdateCounter variable. Name it **Update Count**.

6.   Add a Recordset destination to the data flow. Connect the Row Counter Update Count. Double-click to edit and set the variable name to **User::DeltaUpdates**. Click the Input Columns tab and select the ID column. This will direct the IDs to the ADO Recordset.

7.   Add a second Recordset destination to the data flow. Connect the Row Counter Insert Count. Double-click to edit and set the variable name to User::DeltaInserts. Click the Input Columns tab and select the ID column. This will direct the IDs to the ADO Recordset. The Delta Detection Data Flow task should now look like Figure 11-17.

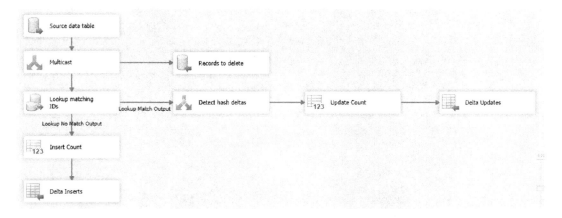

Figure 11-17. *Data flow when returning changes to the source database*

8. The Data Flow task is preparing all three data manipulation processes—Insert, Update, and Delete—by isolating the IDs required in the source data for each of these three operations. We will now see how they are used.

9. Add an Execute SQL task, which you name **Delete Data**, and to which you connect the "Delta Detection" Data Flow task. Configure it to use the CarSales_Staging_OLEDB configuration manager. Set the SQLStatement to the following:

```
DELETE
FROM    dbo.Invoice_Lines
WHERE   ID IN (
                SELECT        DST.ID
                FROM          dbo.Invoice_Lines DST
                              LEFT OUTER JOIN  ##TMP_Deletes TMP
                              ON DST.ID = TMP.ID
                WHERE         TMP.ID IS NULL
              )
```

10. Set the ByPassPrepare property to True.

11. Add a Sequence container. Name it **Inserts** and connect the Delete Data task to it. Inside this container, add a Script task, which you name **Set SELECT for Inserts**. Set the read-only variables to User::DeltaInserts. Set the read-write variables to User::InsertSQL.

12. Click the Edit Script button.

13. Add the following Imports directives:

```
Imports System.Data.OleDb
Imports System.Text
```

14. Replace the Main method with the following script (C:\SQL2012DIRecipes\CH11\11-7_WhereClauseInserts.vb):

```
Public Sub Main()

    Dim SB As New StringBuilder

    Dim DA As New OleDbDataAdapter
    Dim DT As New DataTable
    Dim RW As DataRow
    Dim sMsg As String = ""

    DA.Fill(DT, Dts.Variables("DeltaInserts").Value)

    For Each RW In DT.Rows
        SB.Append(RW(0).ToString & ",")
    Next

    Dts.Variables("InsertSQL").Value = Dts.Variables("InsertSQL").Value.ToString ↵
                        & " WHERE ID IN (" & SB.ToString.TrimEnd(",") & ")"

    Dts.TaskResult = ScriptResults.Success

End Sub
```

15. Close the script and click OK.

16. Add a Data Flow task, name it **Insert Data**, and connect the Script task to it. Double-click the precedence constraint and configure it like Figure 11-18.

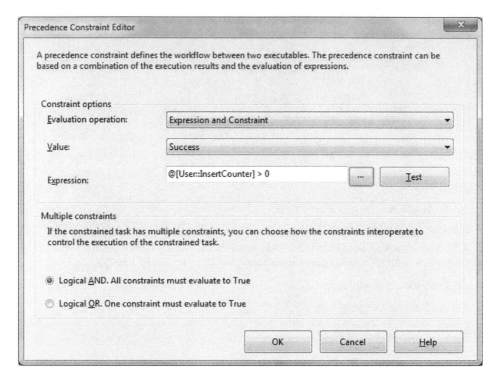

Figure 11-18. *The Precedence Constraint dialog box*

17. Edit the Data Flow task. Add an OLEDB source and configure it like this:

OLEDB Connection Manager:	CarSales_OLEDB
Data Access Mode:	SQL Command from Variable
Variable Name:	InsertSQL

18. Set the ValidateExternalMetadata property to False. Click Columns and select all the source columns.

19. Add an OLEDB destination, configure it to use the CarSales_Staging_OLEDB connection manager and to load data into the dbo.Invoice_Lines table. Map all the columns.

20. Add a Sequence container, name it **Updates** and connect the Inserts Sequence container to it. Inside this container, add a Script task, which you name **Set SELECT for Updates**. Set the read-only variables to User::DeltaUpdates. Set the read-write variables to User::UpdateSQL. Click the Edit Script button.

21. Add the following to the Imports region:

```
Imports System.Data.OleDb
Imports System.Text
```

22. Replace the Main procedure with the following code
(C:\SQL2012DIRecipes\CH11\11-7_WhereClauseDeletes.vb):

```vb
Public Sub Main()

    Dim SB As New StringBuilder

    Dim DA As New OleDbDataAdapter
    Dim DT As New DataTable
    Dim RW As DataRow
    Dim sMsg As String = ""

    DA.Fill(DT, Dts.Variables("DeltaUpdates").Value)

    For Each RW In DT.Rows
        SB.Append(RW(0).ToString & ",")
    Next

    Dts.Variables("UpdateSQL").Value = Dts.Variables("UpdateSQL").Value.ToString ↵
                            & " WHERE ID IN (" & SB.ToString.TrimEnd(",") & ")"

    Dts.TaskResult = ScriptResults.Success

End Sub
```

23. Close the script and click OK.

24. Add a Data Flow task, name it **Insert Data**, and connect the Script task to it. Double-click the precedence constraint and configure it as in step 9, but with the expression as @UpdateCounter > 0.

25. Edit the Data Flow task. Add an OLEDB source and configure it like this:

OLEDB Connection Manager:	CarSales_OLEDB
Data Access Mode:	SQL Command from Variable
Variable Name:	UpdateSQL

26. Set the ValidateExternalMetadata property to False. Click Columns and select all the source columns.

27. Add an OLEDB destination. Configure it as follows:

Connection Manager:	CarSales_Staging_OLEDB
Data Access Mode:	SQL Command from Variable
Variable Name:	UpdateDataTable

28. Click Columns and map all the columns.

29. Return to the Data Flow pane and add an Execute SQL task. Name it **Carry out updates** and configure as follows:

Connection Type:	OLEDB
Connection:	CarSales_Staging_OLEDB
SQL Statement:	UPDATE DST

```
UPDATE DST
SET
DST.InvoiceID = UPD.InvoiceID
,DST.SalePrice = UPD.SalePrice
,DST.StockID = UPD.StockID
,DST.HashData = UPD.HashData
FROM        dbo.Invoice_Lines DST
            INNER JOIN  ##Invoice_Lines_Updates UPD
            ON DST.ID = UPD.ID
```

30. Set the ValidateExternalMetadata property to False. Click OK to finish. The completed package should look like Figure 11-19.

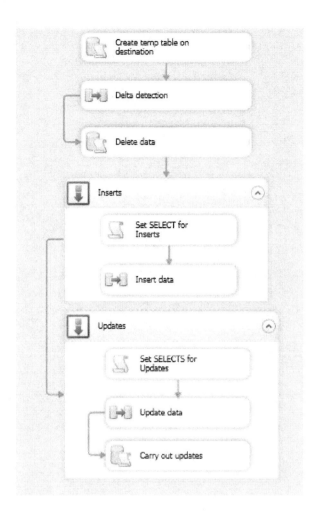

Figure 11-19. *The complete process to isolate deltas at the destination and return queries to the source for delta data*

How It Works

There are times when no permissions are given on the source database except the right to read the source table(s) from which you will be extracting data. This effectively rules out using temporary tables, or probably passing a table-valued parameter to a stored procedure as described in the preceding recipe. So, are there any other valid alternatives to extracting a huge dataset to a staging table and performing delta comparison in a staging database?

Fortunately, there is one viable alternative, but I must stress that it is only of any real use when dealing with relatively small deltas. This technique consists of detecting the delta identifiers, and then passing them back as part of the SELECT clause for the data extraction.

As this is largely an extension of the technique described in the Recipe 11-6, I will attempt to be succinct in the description of techniques that are described more fully in that recipe in order to concentrate here on the different way of passing back the delta IDs to the source database. This take on the problem will use temporary tables on the destination server to hold the IDs for all records that need deleting, and all the data for records that need updating. Delta data will be detected using a hash column. However, at this point, whereas delta IDs for deletes will be used to populate the ##Tmp_Deletes table, IDs for insertions and updates will each populate an ADO recordset. These IDs will then be used as the WHERE clause of the SQL SELECT statement sent back to the source server to get the records for inserts (which will be loaded directly into the destination table), and also for updates, which will be loaded into the temp table ##Tmp_Updates (used to perform updates in the destination table as a single set-based operation).

Figure 11-20 illustrates a process overview.

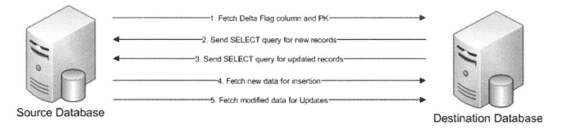

Figure 11-20. *Process to detect delta data at the destination and return selective requests to the source*

The approach described in this recipe is best used in the following circumstances:

- When you have nothing other than SELECT permissions on the source data table.

- When you expect a very small set of delta data.

- When the source data set is large.

The core of the approach is that in both the Insert and Update data processes an SSIS object variable is used to fill an ADO.NET Data Table. Each row in this data table is an ID that must be loaded from the source data, and so each one is added to a stringbuilder to concatenate a list that will become part of the WHERE clause of the SQL statement sent to the source data table.

Hints, Tips, and Traps

- As the package described in this recipe will use temporary tables, you have to use the "scaffolding" approach described in Recipe 11-5. That is, create normal tables in the destination database for the temp tables ##TMP_Deletes, ##TMP_Inserts, ##TMP_Updates, and ##Invoice_Lines_Updates while creating the SSIS package. Then replace the references to the real tables with references to temp tables in the SQL and variables, and delete the tables in the destination database.

- It is important to use the counters for the Insert and Update flows, as otherwise invalid SQL is sent back to the source database, causing the process to fail.

- To repeat, this approach is not suited for enormous deltas. However, fast and efficient as the stringbuilder is (at least compared to string variables), it is slow and heavy in a data flow.

11-8. Detecting and Loading Delta Data Using T-SQL and a Linked Server When MERGE Is Not Practical
Problem

You want to detect delta data at a linked source server and transfer only the delta data to the destination without using MERGE. This could be because using MERGE is slower than a table-based solution.

Solution

Detect delta identifiers at source, compare at destination, and then request only the delta data for upserts. This is how it is done - presuming that you have a linked server named ADAMREMOTE containing the CarSales database and the dbo.Invoice_Lines table. The code is in (C:\SQL2012DIRecipes\CH11\TableMergeReplacement.Sql).

```
IF OBJECT_ID('TempDB..#Upsert') IS NOT NULL DROP TABLE #Upsert

SELECT      ID, VersionStamp
INTO        #Upsert
FROM        ADAMREMOTE.CarSales.dbo.Invoice_Lines

-- Inserts
;
WITH Inserts_CTE
AS
(
SELECT      ID
FROM        #Upsert U
WHERE       ID NOT IN (
                        SELECT ID FROM dbo.Invoice_Lines WITH (NOLOCK))
                      )

INSERT INTO dbo.Invoice_Lines
(
ID
,InvoiceID
,SalePrice
,StockID
,VersionStamp
)

SELECT
SRC_I.ID
,InvoiceID
,SalePrice
,StockID
,VersionStamp

FROM            ADAMREMOTE.CarSales.dbo.Invoice_Lines SRC_I WITH (NOLOCK)
INNER JOIN      Inserts_CTE CTE_I
                ON SRC_I.ID = CTE_I.ID

-- Updates
;
WITH Updates_CTE
AS
```

```
(
SELECT          S_U.ID
FROM            dbo.Invoice_Lines S_U WITH (NOLOCK)
                INNER JOIN   #Upsert U WITH (NOLOCK)
                ON S_U.ID = U.ID
WHERE           S_U.VersionStamp<> U.VersionStamp
)


UPDATE          DST_U
SET             DST_U.InvoiceID = SRC_U.InvoiceID
                ,DST_U.SalePrice = SRC_U.SalePrice
                ,DST_U.StockID = SRC_U.StockID
                ,DST_U.VersionStamp = SRC_U.VersionStamp


FROM            dbo.Invoice_Lines DST_U
                INNER JOIN   ADAMREMOTE.CarSales.dbo.Invoice_Lines SRC_U
                ON SRC_U.ID = DST_U.ID
                INNER JOIN   Updates_CTE CTE_U
                ON DST_U.ID = CTE_U.ID


-- DELETES
DELETE FROM     dbo.Invoice_Lines
WHERE           ID NOT IN (SELECT ID FROM #Upsert)
```

How It Works

It's not just SSIS that can benefit—in certain circumstances—from an initial detection of delta data before actually carrying out the required inserts and updates; if you have a linked server connection to your source data, then you can use this approach using T-SQL too. You can use a similar process to the one described in the previous recipe to

- Collect the primary key and delta-flag columns from the source table.

- Compare this with the destination data table.

- Return to the source to collect new and modified data.

The preceding code snippet applies this logic to detect and upsert/delete delta data only. It is a "pull" process run from the destination server. This method, of course, uses more roundtrips to the source server, but it does give you greater control, and is less of a "black box" than the MERGE function, and may well be easier to understand. Another point in its favor is that only one temporary table is required on the destination server. I must nonetheless emphasize that any potential speed gains depend on the infrastructure (the configurations of the source and destination servers, as well as the network links) and—crucially—the nature of any indexes on the source and destination tables. So you should test this approach and compare with a simple MERGE before assuming that it is right for you. This process works best when your testing shows that the selective transfer of data between the two systems is faster than a simple MERGE.

It works like this: first, the primary key and delta detection flag columns are transferred from the source server to the temporary #Upsert table on the destination server. Then, any new records are identified (by using a plain old WHERE NOT IN or a similar clause) using the primary key column in the source and destination tables. Any updates detected are fetched from the source server and applied at the destination. The delta detection flag column permits this. Finally, any deletes—soft or hard—can be applied using another WHERE NOT IN or similar clause. Remember that you can add indexes to the temporary tables if it accelerates the processing.

■ **Note** If you do not have the indexes in place which make MERGE so efficient then you may find that MERGE is slower than alternative solutions. Inevitably, this will depend on each set of circumstances, and so you have to test any possible solutions in your specific environment.

11-9. Detecting, Logging, and Loading Delta Data
Problem

You want to handle delta data upserts while being able to track the changes and have updates performed as required.

Solution

Use triggers and trigger metadata tables to detect the data changes and SSIS to perform periodic loads into the destination database.

1. Create two tables in the **destination** database (CarSales_Staging)—dropping any previous versions that you have already created—to hold the data used for updates and deletes. For this example, they are as follows (C:\SQL2012DIRecipes\CH11\ TriggerTablesSource.Sql):

```
CREATE TABLE CarSales_Staging.dbo.Invoice_Lines_Updates
(
 ID int NOT NULL,
 InvoiceID INT NULL,
 StockID INT NULL,
 SalePrice NUMERIC(18, 2) NULL,
CONSTRAINT PK_Invoice_Lines_Updates PRIMARY KEY CLUSTERED
(
 ID ASC
) WITH (PAD_INDEX  = OFF, STATISTICS_NORECOMPUTE  = OFF, IGNORE_DUP_KEY = OFF,
ALLOW_ROW_LOCKS  = ON, ALLOW_PAGE_LOCKS  = ON)
) ;
GO

CREATE TABLE CarSales_Staging.dbo.Invoice_Lines_Deletes
(
 ID INT NOT NULL,
CONSTRAINT PK_Invoice_Lines_Deletes PRIMARY KEY CLUSTERED
(
ID ASC
) WITH (PAD_INDEX  = OFF, STATISTICS_NORECOMPUTE  = OFF, IGNORE_DUP_KEY = OFF,
ALLOW_ROW_LOCKS  = ON, ALLOW_PAGE_LOCKS  = ON)
) ;
GO
```

2. Create a tracking table in the **source** database. For the sake of simplicity, I will presume that the source data has a single primary key column, and that this column is an INT data type (C:\SQL2012DIRecipes\CH11\TriggerTablesDestination.Sql).

```
CREATE TABLE CarSales.dbo.DeltaTracking
(
 DeltaID BIGINT IDENTITY(1,1) NOT NULL,
 ObjectName NVARCHAR (128) NULL,
 RecordID BIGINT NULL,
 DeltaOperation CHAR(1) NULL,
 DateAdded DATETIME NULL DEFAULT (getdate()),
CONSTRAINT PK_DeltaTracking PRIMARY KEY CLUSTERED
(
 DeltaID ASC
) WITH (PAD_INDEX  = OFF, STATISTICS_NORECOMPUTE  = OFF, IGNORE_DUP_KEY = OFF,
ALLOW_ROW_LOCKS  = ON, ALLOW_PAGE_LOCKS  = ON)
) ;
GO
```

3. Again, for the sake of simplicity, here is a (fairly) generic tracking trigger that can be added to any table (in the *source* database), which has a single primary key column of an INT data type (C:\SQL2012DIRecipes\CH11\tr_DeltaTracking.Sql):

```
CREATE TRIGGER CarSales.dbo.tr_DeltaTracking
ON dbo.Invoice_Lines FOR INSERT, UPDATE, DELETE
AS

DECLARE @InsertedCount BIGINT
DECLARE @DeletedCount BIGINT
DECLARE @ObjectName    NVARCHAR(128)

SELECT     @InsertedCount = COUNT(*) FROM INSERTED
SELECT     @DeletedCount = COUNT(*) FROM DELETED

SELECT     @ObjectName = OBJECT_NAME(parent_id)
FROM       sys.triggers
WHERE      parent_class_desc = 'OBJECT_OR_COLUMN'
           AND object_id = @PROCID

-- Inserts
IF @InsertedCount > 0 AND @DeletedCount = 0
BEGIN
INSERT INTO dbo.DeltaTracking (RecordID, ObjectName, DeltaOperation)

SELECT
ID
,@ObjectName AS ObjectID
,'I' AS DeltaOperation
FROM INSERTED
END

-- Deletes
IF @InsertedCount = 0 AND @DeletedCount > 0
BEGIN
INSERT INTO dbo.DeltaTracking (RecordID, ObjectName, DeltaOperation)
```

```
SELECT
ID
,@ObjectName AS ObjectID
,'D' AS DeltaOperation
FROM DELETED
END

-- Updates
IF @InsertedCount > 0 AND @DeletedCount > 0
BEGIN
INSERT INTO dbo.DeltaTracking (RecordID, ObjectName, DeltaOperation)

SELECT
ID
,@ObjectName AS ObjectID
,'U' AS DeltaOperation
FROM INSERTED
END
GO
```

4. Synchronize the data between the source and destination tables before allowing any data modifications to the source table. This is as simple as (a) preventing updates to the source data table, (b) loading the source data into a clean destination table, and (c) allowing DML operations on the source data again.

5. Now that the infrastructure is in place, you can proceed to the creation of the actual ETL package itself. Create a new SSIS package and name it **Prepare Scratch tables**. Add two OLEDB connection managers named **CarSales_Staging_OLEDB** and **CarSales_OLEDB**.

6. Add an Execute SQL task to the Control Flow pane. Configure as follows:

Connection Type:	OLEDB
Connection:	CarSales_Staging_OLEDB
SQL Statement:	`TRUNCATE TABLE dbo.Invoice_Lines_Deletes`
	`TRUNCATE TABLE dbo.Invoice_Lines_Updates`

7. Add a Sequence Container to the Control Flow pane. Name it **Upsert and Delete Deltas**. Inside this container, add three Data Flow tasks named **Inserts**, **Deletes**, and **Updates**.

8. Add an Execute SQL task to the Control Flow pane. Name it **Delete Data**. Configure as follows:

Connection Type:	OLEDB
Connection:	CarSales_Staging_OLEDB
SQL Statement:	

```
DELETE      DST
FROM        dbo.Invoice_Lines DST
            INNER JOIN  dbo.Invoice_Lines_Deletes DL
            ON DST.ID = DL.ID
```

9. Add an Execute SQL task to the Control Flow pane. Name it **Update Data**. Configure as follows:

Connection Type:	OLEDB
Connection:	CarSales_Staging_OLEDB
SQL Statement:	

```
UPDATE      DST
SET         DST.InvoiceID = UPD.InvoiceID
            ,DST.StockID = UPD.StockID
            ,DST.SalePrice = UPD.SalePrice
FROM        dbo.Invoice_Lines DST
INNER JOIN  dbo.Invoice_Lines_Updates UPD
            ON DST.ID = UPD.ID
```

10. Add an Execute SQL task to the Control Flow pane. Name it **Delete Tracking Records**. Configure as follows:

Connection Type:	OLEDB
Connection:	CarSales_OLEDB
SQL Statement:	

```
DELETE FROM dbo.DeltaTracking
WHERE ObjectID = OBJECT_ID('dbo.Invoice_Lines')
```

The SSIS package should look like Figure 11-21.

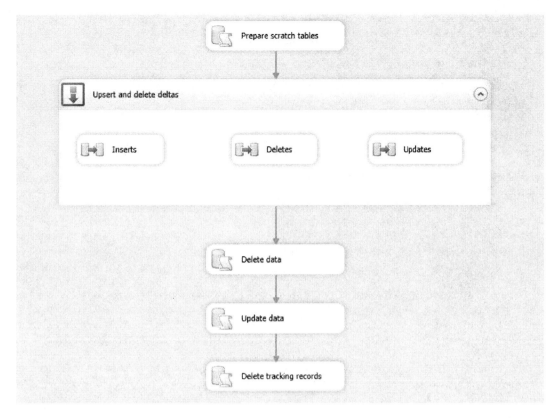

Figure 11-21. *Process flow for trigger-based delta data upserts*

11. Double-click the "Inserts" Data Flow task and add an OLEDB source to the Data Flow pane. Configure it as follows:

OLEDB Connection Manager:	Car_Sales_OLEDB
Data Access Mode:	SQL Command
SQL Command Text:	SELECT SRC.ID

```
                      ,SRC.InvoiceID
                      ,SRC.StockID
                      ,SRC.SalePrice
           FROM       dbo.Invoice_Lines SRC
                      INNER JOIN   dbo.DeltaTracking TRK
                      ON SRC.ID = TRK.RecordID
           WHERE      TRK.DeltaOperation = 'I'
                      AND ObjectID = OBJECT_ID('dbo.Invoice_Lines')
```

12. Add an OLEDB destination to the Data Flow pane. Connect the OLEDB source to it. Configure it as follows:

OLEDB Connection Manager: CarSales_Staging_OLEDB

Data Access Mode: Table or View - Fast Load

Table or View: dbo.Invoice_Lines

13. Click Mappings and ensure that all the columns are mapped between the source and destination.

14. Double-click the "Deletes" Data Flow task and add an OLEDB source to the Data Flow pane. Configure it as follows:

OLEDB Connection Manager: CarSales_OLEDB

Data Access Mode: SQL Command

SQL Command Text:

```
SELECT  TRK.RecordID
FROM    dbo.DeltaTracking TRK
WHERE   TRK.DeltaOperation = 'D'
        AND ObjectID = OBJECT_ID('dbo.Invoice_Lines')
```

15. Add an OLEDB destination to the Data Flow pane. Connect the OLEDB source to it. Configure it as follows:

OLEDB Connection Manager: CarSales_Staging_OLEDB

Data Access Mode: Table or View - Fast Load

Table or View: dbo.Invoice_Lines_Deletes

16. Click Mappings and ensure that the RecordID and ID columns are mapped between the source and destination.

17. Double-click the "Updates" Data Flow task and add an OLEDB source to the Data Flow pane. Configure it as follows:

OLEDB Connection Manager: CarSales_OLEDB

Data Access Mode: SQL Command

SQL Command Text:

```
SELECT SRC.ID
       ,SRC.InvoiceID
       ,SRC.StockID
       ,SRC.SalePrice
       ,SRC.DateUpdated
```

```
FROM          dbo.Invoice_Lines SRC

              INNER JOIN  dbo.DeltaTracking TRK

              ON SRC.ID = TRK.RecordID

WHERE         TRK.DeltaOperation = 'U'

              AND ObjectID = OBJECT_ID('dbo.Invoice_Lines')
```

18.   Add an OLEDB destination to the Data Flow pane. Connect the OLEDB source to it.
      Configure it as follows:

OLEDB Connection Manager: Car_Sales_Staging_OLEDB

Data Access Mode: Table or View - Fast Load

Table or View: dbo.Invoice_Lines_Updates

19.   Click Mappings and ensure that all the columns are mapped between the source and
      destination.

You can now run the package and load any delta data.

How It Works

This approach is essentially in two parts:

- First, detect the changes to the source table using triggers, and then log the changes.

- Second, carry out periodic data loads using the logged changes to indicate the records to
  load and modify.

A long-standing and reliable way of tracking delta data is to use triggers to flag inserts, updates, and deletes.
There are several ways to store the data flags indicating data changes; however, the two classic ways are either to
use extra columns in the source tables or to create and use separate "delta" tables. I will explain the delta table
method, which traditionally means recording the unique ID of the record affected in a table to a table (most
probably on the source data server) either in the source database or in another database. Then these delta IDs
can be used to isolate the data sets needed to perform upserts and deletes in destination data.

The trigger-based process to track changes looks like Figure 11-22.

Figure 11-22. *A trigger-based process to track changes*

Not all DBAs allow their source databases to be encumbered (this word is used from their point of view) with extraneous tables and triggers, so this solution is not always applicable in practice. However, when it is possible, it has many advantages, as well as a few disadvantages.

The advantages are:

- A simple log of data changes and the change type.

- The log (the delta table) is narrow and easy to use.

The major inconveniences and potential problems are:

- The underlying logic that keeps data in sync can be very complex.

- There are performance implications because triggers are fired for every change.

- If there are existing triggers, then trigger sequencing and interaction can be problematic.

- Long-running transactions (unless transactions are correctly handled) can cause problems.

- Data inconsistencies happen if the process is not analyzed thoroughly.

A trigger-based approach is best used when you can count on the agreement and involvement of the source data DBA. It also means getting it accepted can slow down DML operations on the source database, but that the ease and speed of the data transfer to a destination server are a sufficient compensation. You also need to be sure that there are no unforeseen side effects and that the process has been thoroughly tested.

In this example, I used standard tables in a destination database to hold the data used for updates and deletes, simply because it is easier to set up and can persist data for investigation and test purposes. You may prefer to use session-scoped temporary tables (as described in previous recipes).

Once you have set up a delta-tracking process using triggers, it is equally easy to use pure T-SQL to perform inserts, updates, and deletes in a destination database. You can create three separate triggers—one each for update, delete, and insert operations—and you can hard-code the table name and/or object ID if you prefer. I find that a generic trigger makes maintenance of delta tracking much easier.

This approach lets you use the same tracking table for multiple source data tables—assuming that they all have a single-column primary key of the same data type. When things are not this simple, you have several choices:

- Separate tables for multicolumn source tables

- Separate tables for data types

- Widen your table to hold several possible key columns

- Add multiple columns for different key data types

- Use an NVARCHAR column to hold all possible primary keys—and risk the speed hit when reading and writing

- Have one complex trigger to handle multiple primary key columns

- Have a trigger per type of primary key and/or PK data type

Given the multiple possibilities, I can only suggest that you try out some of these approaches to find the one best suited to your environment.

A similar approach is possible with many other SQL databases, providing that they allow triggers to be used. As all requirements (and the syntax for different database) are different, I can only encourage you to consult the relevant product documentation, and to use this recipe as an overall model.

Hints, Tips, and Traps

- This process presumes that the source and destination data will be, and will be kept, in sync. Should the two get out of sync, you need to prevent updates to the source data table while it is loaded into a clean destination table, and delete or truncate all records relative to this table from the delta table before allowing DML operations on the source data again.

- The Deletes and Updates tables may be in another database, of course—or even on another (linked) server, if that suits your infrastructure and operational requirements.

- You can simply load all data in a delta table to a staging table, and then insert/update/delete. This is likely to be slower, but it allows you to keep a trace of all operations.

- It is a very good idea to wrap the whole SSIS package in a transaction, as this will ensure that you do not

  - Lose delta records.

  - Attempt duplicate inserts.

  - Carry out old updates.

- It is possible to create the scratch tables at the start of this stored procedure and drop them at the end, if you prefer. This way, any failures will leave you with the scratch tables intact, which can help with debugging. Of course, you must then remember to drop them manually before re-running the package.

- The particular implementation in this recipe presumes that you have a clear cutoff point in the source database, which allows delta data to be transferred to the destination with no modification of the source during the delta data load. Should the source database be continually active, then you need to use the DateAdded field in the tracking table to define a cutoff point, and then delete (not truncate) operations up to this date and time, which have been duplicated across the databases once the delta load is successfully completed.

11-10. Detecting Differences in Rowcounts, Metadata, and Column Data

Problem

You want to detect differences in rowcounts, metadata, and column data without using SSIS or T-SQL.

Solution

Use the TableDiff utility. From a Command window to detect if there have been any changes made to a source table before running an ETL delta data load.

Once again, I will use a few mini-recipes to describe how to use TableDiff because its various applications are too different to be rolled into one simple example.

Metadata and Rowcounts

The following code, run in a Command window, will return the rowcounts for the two tables and indicate if that the metadata is identical for the two tables.

```
"C:\Program Files\Microsoft SQL Server\110\COM\Tablediff.exe"
 -sourceuser Adam
 -sourcepassword Me4BOss
 -sourceserver ADAMO2
 -sourcedatabase CarSales
 -sourceschema dbo
 -sourcetable Sales
 -destinationuser Adam
 -destinationpassword Me4BOss
 -destinationserver ADAMO2
 -destinationdatabase CarSales_Staging
 -destinationschema dbo
 -destinationtable Sales
 -q
```

It is the -q (quick) parameter that tells TableDiff only to compare record counts and metadata. Should the two tables have differing columns, then TableDiff will return: "have different schemas and cannot be compared."

Row Differences

To get details on any records that differ between the two tables (without the -q parameter and preferably sending the output to an SQL Server table rather than the Command window), add the following:

```
-dt -et DataList
```

DataList is the name of the table (in the destination database) that will hold the list of anomalies.

Column Differences

To see all data differences at column level, add the -c parameter.

The resulting table has the columns listed in Table 11-3.

Table 11-3. *DataDiff Output*

Column Name	Possible values	Comments
ID		Contains the PK, GUID, or unique ID.
Msdifftool-Errorcode	0, 1, or 2	0 for a data mismatch.
		1 for a record in the destination table, but not the source.
		2 for a record in the source table, but not the destination.
MSdifftool_Offendingcolumns		The name of the column where the data differs between the two tables.

Create a T-SQL Script to Make the Destination Table Identical to the Source Table

To make the tables identical, run the script created by the -f [filename] parameter. This is usually where TableDiff comes in useful—when source and destination are out of sync and you want to "reset" them to allow one of the delta data detection techniques to resume.

The SQL that is created is "row by row." To get faster (set-based) synchronization, you can use the data in the output table and dynamic SQL to write a less verbose script.

How It Works

It is difficult to discuss delta data management without at least a passing reference to TableDiff.exe. This is a Microsoft tool that was originally designed to compare tables in a replication scenario, but which can also be useful to

- Very quickly detect whether two tables' metadata are identical or not.

- Get rowcounts from two tables.

- Isolate rows present in either of the two tables, but not in both.

- Isolate all data changes between records in the two tables.

- Create an SQL script to apply the changes to make the tables identical.

TableDiff.exe is a command-line tool, which requires a substantial set of parameters. However, once these are set up as a .cmd file, then it becomes easier to handle and can be run from a scheduler, an SSIS Execute Process task, or an SQL Server Agent job. You will need a primary key, Identity column, and rowguide or unique key column in at least one of the tables, preferably in both. Incidentally, TableDiff is installed by default with SQL Server.

Hints, Tips, and Traps

- If the fast comparison parameter (–q) is used, then no output table will be created.

- The output table will not be not overwritten if the two tables are identical.

- The output table structure varies according to the input parameters—the MSdifftool_ OffendingColumns column only appears if there are column level differences.

- There are other parameters for TableDiff.exe, and I suggest that you consult BOL should you need them.

Summary

This chapter contained many ways of detecting data changes at source and applying them to a destination database using SQL Server. Table 11-4 presents my take on the various methods, including their advantages and disadvantages.

Table 11-4. Advantages and Disadvantages of Delta Data Management Techniques in This Chapter

Technique	Advantages	Disadvantages
Full data transfer with temporary tables used for update and delete management.	Much faster than using the OLEDB task.	Complex to set up.
Linked server and MERGE	Faster than transferring all the data before using MERGE. Easy to set up.	Requires a linked server.
Detecting delta data at source—transferring the Delta Flag column first in SSIS.	Can be considerably faster than transferring all the data before detecting deltas.	Complex to set up. Requires a Delta Flag column in the source data. Needs temporary tables on the source.
Detecting delta data at the source and passing back TVP of IDs.	Can be considerably faster than transferring all the data before detecting deltas.	Complex to set up. Requires a Delta Flag column in the source data. Only suitable for tiny delta sets.
Detecting delta data at the source and passing back custom SELECT statements.	Can be considerably faster than transferring all the data before detecting deltas.	Complex to set up. Requires a Delta Flag column in the source data. Only suitable for tiny delta sets.
Detecting delta data at source—transferring Delta Flag column first using T-SQL.	Can be considerably faster than transferring all the data before detecting deltas.	Complex to set up. Requires a Delta Flag column in the source data. Needs temporary tables on the source. Necessitates a linked server.
Trigger-based delta data tracking.	Can be considerably faster than full data transfer.	Requires source database modification. Necessitates management of tracking tables.
TableDiff	Only suitable in certain circumstances.	Requires learning the utility.

Delta data management is a horrendously complex challenge, and there are few easy solutions. Some readers may find the techniques elaborated in this chapter too complicated to be applied. Others may find them too simple. Yet others may be facing challenges which seem to make any solution impossible. However, with patience and correct analysis, most delta data issues can be resolved. The art and science is to find the correct approach to take. So do not hesitate to test various solutions, and also to "mix and match" techniques taken from the various recipes in this chapter. If you do not have "flag" columns in the source table, try and get them added. If you cannot add such columns, then try and use hashing techniques to identify changed rows. Do not be afraid of using temporary or persisted tables as a staging technique. Above all - take your time when defining the appropriate solution and test it thoroughly.

■ ■ ■

CHAPTER 12

Change Tracking and Change Data Capture

This chapter focuses on two core techniques that allow you to detect modifications to source data and consequently update a destination table with the corresponding changes. Using their most simplistic definitions, these techniques are

- ***Change Tracking***: Detects that a row has changed. Lets a process return the latest version of the data from the source table.

- ***Change Data Capture***: Detects that a row has changed. Stores all the intermediate changes, as well as the final state of a record.

The former uses a tracking table and simple versioning, while the latter reads the SQL Server transaction log and provides sophisticated version tracking. Both techniques are relatively lightweight as far as the overhead that they impose on the source system is concerned, and both are largely self-managing. Either can be implemented as a T-SQL-based solution or using SSIS. Neither requires any schema changes to be made to the source table(s). Both allow you to decide when the updates to the destination table(s) are to be applied, and so can easily be integrated into a regular ETL process. In my experience, both are extremely robust and reliable. So if these are the similarities, what are the differences—at least at a simple level suited to handling data integration challenges?

- Change Tracking is a synchronous process that detects that rows were changed, but not what data was modified. It is available in all versions of SQL Server.

- Change Data Capture is an asynchronous process that reads the SQL Server transaction log to detect changes to the tables that you are tracking. It can also allow you to see the history of all changes to the data in a table. It is only available in the Enterprise version of SQL Server.

While these two approaches are extremely efficient, they can seem, at first, a little complex to implement. After a little time spent using them, I hope you will agree that this is only an impression. To dispel any initial apprehension, I advise you to read a recipe thoroughly before you start to implement a solution, and to take a good look at the process flow diagrams to get a clear view of how the technique can be applied.

The sample files for this chapter are available on the book's companion web site, and once installed, will be in the C:\SQL2012DIRecipes\CH11 folder.

12-1. Detecting Source Table Changes with Little Overhead and No Custom Framework

Problem

You want a low-overhead solution that can detect changes in the source data and apply them to a destination table without using triggers, altering the source table DDL, or any complex processes.

Solution

Activate Change Tracking on the source table, and then isolate the changes and apply them to the destination. The following steps explain how you do this.

1. Activate Change Tracking in the source database (which will be CarSales in this example) using the following T-SQL snippet (C:\SQL2012DIRecipes\CH11\ ActivateChangeTracking.Sql):

    ```
    USE CarSales;
    GO

    ALTER DATABASE CarSales SET ALLOW_SNAPSHOT_ISOLATION ON;
    ALTER DATABASE CarSales SET CHANGE_TRACKING = ON
    (CHANGE_RETENTION = 3 DAYS, AUTO_CLEANUP = ON);
    ```

2. Create the destination table in the destination database (which will be CarSales_Staging in this example). This is the table that will be updated using Change Tracking in this recipe. What follows is the DDL to create the table (C:\SQL2012DIRecipes\CH11\tblClient_CT.Sql):

    ```
    CREATE TABLE CarSales_Staging.dbo.Client_CT
    (
     ID INT IDENTITY(1,1) NOT NULL,
     ClientName NVARCHAR(150) NULL,
     Country TINYINT NULL,
     Town VARCHAR(50) NULL,
     County VARCHAR(50) NULL,
     Address1 VARCHAR(50) NULL,
     Address2 VARCHAR(50) NULL,
     ClientType VARCHAR(20) NULL,
     ClientSize VARCHAR(10) NULL,
    ) ;

    GO
    ```

3. Enable Change Tracking for the table(s) that you wish to track, using the following T-SQL snippet (C:\SQL2012DIRecipes\CH11\ChangeTrackingClient.Sql):

    ```
    USE CarSales;
    GO

    ALTER TABLE CarSales.dbo.Client
    ENABLE CHANGE_TRACKING ;
    GO
    ```

4. Add the extended property, LAST_SYNC_VERSION, to the table that you are tracking (dbo.Client in this example), which will be used to store the number of the last synchronized version of the data. You can do this with the following T-SQL snippet—this can only be added once (C:\SQL2012DIRecipes\CH11\ LastSynchVersionProperty.Sql):

```
USE CarSales;
GO

EXECUTE sys.sp_addextendedproperty
@level0type = N'SCHEMA'
,@level0name = dbo
,@level1type = N'TABLE'
,@level1name = Client
,@name = LAST_SYNC_VERSION
,@value = 0
;
```

5. Run the following T-SQL code to apply the relevant Inserts, Deletes, and Updates to the destination table (C:\SQL2012DIRecipes\CH11\ChangeTrackingProcess.Sql):

```
USE CarSales;
GO

BEGIN TRY

DECLARE @LAST_SYNC_VERSION BIGINT
DECLARE @CURRENT_VERSION BIGINT
SET @CURRENT_VERSION = CHANGE_TRACKING_CURRENT_VERSION()

SELECT    @LAST_SYNC_VERSION = CAST(value AS BIGINT)
FROM      sys.extended_properties
WHERE     major_id = OBJECT_ID('dbo.Client')
          AND name = N'LAST_SYNC_VERSION'

-- need test to ensure that an update will not be missing data..

DECLARE @MIN_VALID_VERSION BIGINT

SELECT @MIN_VALID_VERSION = CHANGE_TRACKING_MIN_VALID_VERSION(OBJECT_ID('dbo.
                                                    Client'));

IF @LAST_SYNC_VERSION >= @MIN_VALID_VERSION
BEGIN

-- Inserts

INSERT INTO    CarSales_Staging.dbo.Client_CT
               (ID,ClientName,Country,Town,County, Address1,Address2,
                ClientType,ClientSize)
```

```
SELECT          SRC.ID,ClientName,Country,Town,County,Address1,Address2,
                ClientType,ClientSize
FROM            dbo.Client SRC
INNER JOIN      CHANGETABLE(CHANGES Client, @LAST_SYNC_VERSION) AS CT
                ON SRC.ID = CT.ID
WHERE           CT.SYS_CHANGE_OPERATION = 'I'

-- Deletes

DELETE FROM     DST
FROM            CarSales_Staging.dbo.Client_CT DST
                INNER JOIN    CHANGETABLE(CHANGES Client, @LAST_SYNC_VERSION) AS CT
                ON CT.ID = DST.ID
WHERE           CT.SYS_CHANGE_OPERATION = 'D'

-- Updates

UPDATE          DST
SET             DST.ClientName = SRC.ClientName
                ,DST.Country = SRC.Country
                ,DST.Town = SRC.Town
                ,DST.County = SRC.County
                ,DST.Address1 = SRC.Address1
                ,DST.Address2 = SRC.Address2
                ,DST.ClientType = SRC.ClientType
                ,DST.ClientSize = SRC.ClientSize
FROM            CarSales_Staging.dbo.Client_CT DST
                INNER JOIN    dbo.Client SRC
                ON DST.ID = SRC.ID
                INNER JOIN    CHANGETABLE(CHANGES Client, @LAST_SYNC_VERSION) AS CT
                ON SRC.ID = CT.ID
WHERE           CT.SYS_CHANGE_OPERATION = 'U'

END

-- after an UPSERT/DELETE

EXECUTE sys.sp_updateextendedproperty
@level0type         = N'SCHEMA'
,@level0name        = dbo
,@level1type        = N'TABLE'
,@level1name        = Client
,@name              = LAST_SYNC_VERSION
,@value             = @CURRENT_VERSION
;

END TRY

BEGIN CATCH

-- Add your error logging here

END CATCH
```

How It Works

Fortunately for SQL Server developers and DBAs alike, in SQL Server 2008 Microsoft introduced a lightweight solution to the problem of delta data management. This solution is called *Change Tracking*, and it does not require any triggers or handcrafted tables. The only requirement is a primary key on the source and destination tables.

Its advantages are as follows:

- It is a lightweight solution, with little extra overhead on the server and minor disk space requirements.

- There are no changes required to the source table.

- It is a nearly real-time solution.

- It is largely self-managing in that you can set a retention period for delta data to be tracked, and SQL Server handles cleansing this historical data. This does not mean, however that data synchronization is automatic, just that managing the Change Tracking objects is largely handled for you.

- It is available in all versions of SQL Server.

There are several limitations, however. The main one is that Change Tracking does not support "pull" data synchronization from a destination—the following error message informs you, if you try:

```
Msg 22106, Level 16, State 1, Line 3
The CHANGETABLE function does not support remote data sources.
```

So this requires some tweaking—and specifically stored procedures on the source server to isolate and supply the data to Insert, Delete, and Update. Other disadvantages include:

- Change Tracking must be disabled before a PRIMARY KEY constraint can be dropped on the source table.

- Data type changes of nonprimary key columns are not tracked.

- The index that enforces the primary key cannot be dropped or disabled.

- Truncating the source table requires re-initialization of Change Tracking. This essentially means that Change Tracking must be disabled, and then re-enabled for the source table.

■ **Note**   Microsoft advises you to enable Snapshot Isolation, which means that TempDB will be used heavily, so you need to ensure that your TempDB is configured correctly. There are alternatives, however, to using Snapshot Isolation. See Books Online (BOL) for full details.

Nonetheless, Change Tracking is a robust solution that is well suited to many delta data situations. It is best used in the following circumstances:

- You wish to avoid triggers or user tables when isolating delta data.

- When the (admittedly low) overhead that it adds to the source system is acceptable.

I will not be providing an exhaustive description of all that can be done using Change Tracking, nor will I detail how it is managed in a production environment. Should you need this information, then BOL does a good job of describing it, and there are many excellent references to this subject online and in print. After all, this book is resolutely ETL-focused.

Setting up Change Tracking is easy. First, Change Tracking must be set up on the source database, and then any tables whose DML you wish to follow must have Change Tracking enabled. Once this is done, SQL Server can detect changed records, as well as the type of change (Insert, Update, or Delete) and carry out any required data integration processes based on these changed records.

Once you have set up Change Tracking, you can start to use it. What you need to know is that you will have to

- Get the last successful version number for a DML operation that was updated in the destination database.

- Check that you have the data, since that version number in your Change Tracking history (using the command CHANGE_TRACKING_MIN_VALID_VERSION).

- Perform the required Insert, Update, and Delete operations on the destination table.

- Log (here to the extended properties of the table) the latest successful version number for the DML operations that have been sent to the destination table.

In this recipe, I am using two databases in the same server. Of course, you may use linked servers to perform this operation. Just remember to use the correct four-part notation if this is how you decide to implement Change Tracking.

There could well be cases where you only wish to add or update data in a destination database when the contents of certain columns changes only. For instance, when dealing with clients in a financial reporting application, changes in address could be irrelevant, but changes in credit rating could be fundamental. So to avoid updating data only when the contents of relevant columns has changed, Change Tracking will also let you detect which columns have been modified. This makes the technique altogether more subtle as thus far *any* change—including potentially irrelevant ones—have been notified by Change Tracking. It follows that if you track only changes to specific columns then Change Tracking becomes less of a blunt instrument. Consequently, the overhead caused by irrelevant updates on a destination server can be avoided because you will only be performing essential DML operations.

So, if you wish to track changes only to certain columns …

1. First, disable Change Tracking if it is enabled, using:

```
ALTER TABLE CarSales.dbo.Client DISABLE CHANGE_TRACKING
```

2. Then, re-enable it using:

```
ALTER TABLE CarSales.dbo.Client
ENABLE CHANGE_TRACKING
WITH (TRACK_COLUMNS_UPDATED = ON)
```

3. Next, alter any Update statements (you could also apply this to Insert and Delete statements, but this is more rare) to include a WHERE clause like the following:

```
AND CHANGE_TRACKING_IS_COLUMN_IN_MASK(COLUMNPROPERTY(OBJECT_ID
('CarSales.dbo.Client'), 'ClientName', 'ColumnId'),
CT.SYS_CHANGE_COLUMNS ) = 1
```

Note that you must define the object ID and column ID for each column to track individually—and using the COLUMNPROPERTY function is the easiest way to obtain these. This code snippet will detect changes to the ClientName column of the tracked table dbo.client. You then run the T-SQL code shown in step 5 of this recipe to port only the changes from source to destination where the Client column has been modified. Indeed, the operation will be even more efficient if you tweak the T-SQL UPDATE so that only the relevant column (Client) is updated.

■ **Note** Although Change Tracking does not add a lot of extra overhead to the source server, just exactly how much this is, and whether it is acceptable, will depend on each set of circumstances. For a server with a very high volume of transactions, even the slight overhead that Change Tracking adds might prove excessive. You have to test Change Tracking in your specific environment to decide if it is the correct solution for your requirements.

Hints, Tips, and Traps

- The reason for storing a property called LAST_SYNC_VERSION is that when detecting deltas, you need to tell SQL Server back to which point in the history of DML modifications you want to perform data upserts/deletes. Since Change Tracking uses sequential numbering to identify every DML operation on the tracked table, you will need to know, for every data extraction operation, what was the last version number used. I suggest storing this as an extended property, although if you wish, you can store it in a logging table.

- Change Tracking version numbering begins with 0.

- The specified retention period must be at least as long as the maximum time between data synchronizations.

- If you set AUTO_CLEANUP to OFF, then you will have to reset it to ON at some point to clear down the change history. Cleaning up Change Tracking cannot be done any other way.

- There is an inevitable trade-off between the retention period for delta tracking (set using CHANGE_RETENTION) and the efficiency of the database. The longer the retention period, the easier it is to go back in time to detect changes—but the database will be the larger and slower.

- I prefer to wrap the DML operations that execute Change Tracking in a transaction, as this will ensure that the Insert, Delete, and Update commands will be carried out automatically and completely—or not at all. Of course, you should add sufficient error trapping and logging to ensure that any errors are bubbled up to the DBA in time to correct any bugs before the change retention period is past. Otherwise, only a complete resynchronization of the source and destination tables will ensure that both data sets are identical. However, transactions that work perfectly across databases on the same server will require MSDTC when implemented using linked servers.

- To resynchronize the source and destination tables, simply truncate the destination table and INSERT.. SELECT the data (or any other table load technique that you prefer) from the source data into it. This will have no effect on the Change Tracking. You must then log (or set the extended property) for the Last_Synch_Version to the Current_Version of the Change Tracking, so that only DML from this point is detected when the two sources are synchronized.

- To disable Change Tracking, simply use the following T-SQL snippets:

  ```
  ALTER TABLE dbo.Client DISABLE CHANGE_TRACKING;
  ```

  and then

  ```
  ALTER DATABASE CarSales SET CHANGE_TRACKING = OFF;
  ```

- Note that you must disable Change Tracking for all tables before you can disable it at the database level.

12-2. Pulling Changes into a Destination Table with Change Tracking

Problem

Using Change Tracking, you want to pull rather than push data changes detected into a destination table.

Solution

Apply "pull" delta data using Change Tracking. The following T-SQL can do this—where the source data is on a linked server, named R2.

1. Run steps 1 through 4 in Recipe 12-1 to enable Change Tracking on the source server (R2) and place the destination table on the local server.

2. Run the following T-SQL to synchronize the data from the remote server to the local server (C:\SQL2012DIRecipes\CH11\PullChangeTracking.Sql):

```
DECLARE @LAST_SYNC_VERSION BIGINT
DECLARE @CURRENT_VERSION BIGINT
DECLARE @MIN_VALID_VERSION BIGINT

-- To get the LAST_SYNC_VERSION
SELECT       @LAST_SYNC_VERSION = CAST(SEP.value AS BIGINT)
FROM         R2.CarSales.sys.tables TBL
             INNER JOIN   R2.CarSales.sys.schemas SCH
             ON TBL.schema_id = SCH.schema_id
             INNER JOIN   R2.CarSales.sys.extended_properties SEP
             ON TBL.object_id = SEP.major_id
WHERE        SCH.name = 'dbo'
AND          TBL.name = 'client'
AND          SEP.name = 'LAST_SYNC_VERSION'

-- Gets maximum version in CHANGETABLE - so available for updating (use instead of
CHANGE_TRACKING_CURRENT_VERSION)

SELECT @CURRENT_VERSION = MaxValidVersion FROM OPENQUERY(R2,
'
SELECT
CASE WHEN MAX(SYS_CHANGE_CREATION_VERSION) > MAX(SYS_CHANGE_VERSION) THEN MAX(SYS_CHANGE_
CREATION_VERSION)
ELSE MAX(SYS_CHANGE_VERSION)
END AS MaxValidVersion
FROM CHANGETABLE(CHANGES Carsales.dbo.Client, 0) AS CT
')

-- Gets minimum version This one works over a linked server!
SELECT Min_Valid_Version FROM R2.CarSales.sys.change_tracking_tables

IF @LAST_SYNC_VERSION >= @MIN_VALID_VERSION
BEGIN
```

```
-- Get all data for INSERTS/UPDATES/DELETES into temp tables
-- Deletes

DECLARE @DeleteSQL VARCHAR(8000) =

'SELECT ID
FROM OPENQUERY(R2, ''SELECT      ID
FROM      CHANGETABLE(CHANGES Carsales.dbo.Client,' + CAST(@LAST_SYNC_VERSION AS VARCHAR(20))+')
AS CT
WHERE     CT.SYS_CHANGE_OPERATION = ''''D''''''')'

IF OBJECT_ID('tempdb..#ClientDeletes') IS NOT NULL
DROP TABLE tempdb..#ClientDeletes

CREATE TABLE #ClientDeletes (ID INT)

INSERT INTO #ClientDeletes EXEC (@DeleteSQL)

-- Inserts
DECLARE @InsertsSQL VARCHAR(8000) =
        'SELECT ID,ClientName,Country,Town,County,Address1,Address2,ClientType,ClientSize
        FROM OPENQUERY(R2,
                    ''SELECT SRC.ID,ClientName,Country,Town,County,Address1,Address2,
                    ClientType,ClientSize
                    FROM      Carsales.dbo.Client SRC
                    INNER JOIN  CHANGETABLE(
                                        CHANGES Carsales.dbo.Client, ' +
                                        CAST(@LAST_SYNC_VERSION
                                        AS VARCHAR(20))+') AS CT
                            ON SRC.ID = CT.ID
                    WHERE     CT.SYS_CHANGE_OPERATION = ''''I''''''')'

IF OBJECT_ID('tempdb..#ClientInserts') IS NOT NULL DROP TABLE tempdb..#ClientInserts
CREATE TABLE #ClientInserts
(
ID INT NOT NULL,
 ClientName VARCHAR(150) NULL,
 Country VARCHAR(50) NULL,
 Town VARCHAR(50) NULL,
 County VARCHAR(50) NULL,
 Address1 VARCHAR(50) NULL,
 Address2 VARCHAR(50) NULL,
 ClientType VARCHAR(20) NULL,
 ClientSize VARCHAR(10) NULL
)
```

```
INSERT INTO #ClientInserts EXEC (@InsertsSQL)

-- Updates

DECLARE @UpdatesSQL VARCHAR(8000) =
                    'SELECT    ID,ClientName,Country,Town,County,Address1,Address2,
                               ClientType,ClientSize
                     FROM      OPENQUERY(R2, ''SELECT         SRC.ID,ClientName,Country,Town,
                                                             County,Address1,Address2,
                                                             ClientType,ClientSize
                                               FROM           Carsales.dbo.Client SRC
                                               INNER JOIN     CHANGETABLE(CHANGES
                                                             Carsales.dbo.Client,'
                                             + CAST(@LAST_SYNC_VERSION AS VARCHAR(20))
                                             + ')  AS CT
                                                        ON SRC.ID = CT.ID
                     WHERE    CT.SYS_CHANGE_OPERATION = ''''U'''''')' ;

IF OBJECT_ID('tempdb..#ClientUpdates') IS NOT NULL DROP TABLE tempdb..#ClientUpdates;

CREATE TABLE #ClientUpdates
(
 ID INT NOT NULL,
 ClientName VARCHAR(150) NULL,
 Country VARCHAR(50) NULL,
 Town VARCHAR(50) NULL,
 County VARCHAR(50) NULL,
 Address1 VARCHAR(50) NULL,
 Address2 VARCHAR(50) NULL,
 ClientType VARCHAR(20) NULL,
 ClientSize VARCHAR(10) NULL
) ;

INSERT INTO    #ClientUpdates
(ID,ClientName,Country,Town,County,Address1,Address2,ClientType,ClientSize) EXEC
(@UpdatesSQL) ;

-- Carry out INSERTS/UPDATES/DELETES

-- Inserts
INSERT INTO      CarSales_Staging.dbo.Client
                 (ID, ClientName, Country, Town, County, Address1, Address2,
                  ClientType, ClientSize)
SELECT           ID, ClientName, Country,Town, County, Address1, Address2,
                 ClientType, ClientSize
FROM              #ClientInserts
```

```
-- Updates

UPDATE          DST
SET             DST.ClientName = UPD.ClientName
                ,DST.Country = UPD.Country
                ,DST.Town = UPD.Town
                ,DST.County = UPD.County
                ,DST.Address1 = UPD.Address1
                ,DST.Address2 = UPD.Address2
                ,DST.ClientType = UPD.ClientType
                ,DST.ClientSize = UPD.ClientSize
FROM            CarSales_Staging.dbo.Client DST
INNER JOIN      #ClientUpdates UPD
                ON DST.ID = UPD.ID


-- Deletes
DELETE FROM  DST
FROM         CarSales_Staging.dbo.Client DST
INNER JOIN   #ClientDeletes DLT
             ONDLT.ID = DST.ID

-- To set the new LAST_SYNC_VERSION
EXEC R2.CarSales.sys.sp_updateextendedproperty
@level0type = N'SCHEMA'
,@level0name = dbo
,@level1type = N'TABLE'
,@level1name = Client
,@name = LAST_SYNC_VERSION
,@value = @CURRENT_VERSION
;
END
```

How It Works

You can perform "push" data synchronization over linked servers using Change Tracking, but can it be done using a "pull" approach? The answer is a guarded "yes." Guarded not because there is any inherent difficulty, but because you will need to apply a series of workarounds to the limitations of the Change Tracking functions, which are supplied out of the box, and which we saw in the Recipe 12-1.

So what are the potential problems?

- The CHANGETABLE function will not work using a linked (four-part notation) server.

- The CHANGE_TRACKING_MIN_VALID_VERSION function will not work over a linked server.

- Wrapping the CHANGETABLE function in a table-valued user-defined function on the source server will not work, because UDFs also are problematic over linked servers.

- Wrapping the CHANGETABLE function in a stored procedure on the source server can work—but extracting the data requires MSDTC (the Distributed Transaction Coordinator) to be running on the source server, because it will create an implicit transaction. Also, you need to configure the linked server for RPC (you will be executing stored procedures against a remote server). These two limitations can be a deal-breaker for some DBAs—as well as a considerable hassle. So for these reasons, we will avoid this approach.

This leaves us with OPENQUERY and dynamic SQL as a solution. It is not perfect, but it allows us to return all the required data (minimum change version, maximum change version, as well as all the data pertaining to Inserts, Updates, and Deletes) without any hassle as far as the server-level configuration is concerned.

Hints, Tips, and Traps

- You can use table variables instead of temporary tables if you prefer. For larger datasets temporary tables may be preferable, as they can be indexed, which can be useful in some situations.

- Here too you can use specific column tracking using the COLUMNPROPERTY function, as described in the "How It Works" section of Recipe 12-1.

12-3. Using Change Tracking as Part of a Structured ETL Process

Problem

You want to use Change Tracking as part of a structured ETL process.

Solution

Use Change Tracking information as part of an SSIS package to ensure that data modifications in a source table are applied to a destination table. Since this package is a little complex, I suggest that before leaping in to create it, you first read it through to get an idea of where it is going. Having said that, the following steps illustrate how it is done.

1. Run steps 1 through 4 in Recipe 12-1 to enable Change Tracking on the source server (R2), and place the destination table on the local server (unless you have already done this, of course).

2. Create a new SSIS package, and add the three following connection managers:

Source_OLEDB:	An OLEDB connection to the source database.
Source_ADONET:	An ADO.NET connection to the source database.
Destination_OLEDB:	An OLEDB connection to the destination database. Set the RetainSameConnection property to False.

3. Add the following package-scoped variables:

VariableName	Type	Value
CurrentVersion	Int64	0
DeleteTable	String	TMP_Deletes
LastSynchVersion	Int64	0
MinValidVersion	Int64	0
SQLDelete	String	`SELECT ID FROM dbo.Client`
SQLInsert	String	`SELECT ID, ClientName, Country, Town, County, Address1, Address2, ClientType, ClientSize` `FROM dbo.Client`
SQLUpdate	String	`SELECT ID, ClientName, Country, Town, County, Address1, Address2, ClientType, ClientSize` `FROM dbo.Client`
UpdateTable	String	TMP_Updates

4. Add an Execute SQL task, configured as follows:

Name:	Get Parameters
Connection Type:	Source_ADONET
SQL Statement:	`SELECT @CurrentVersion = CHANGE_TRACKING_CURRENT_VERSION();`
	`SELECT @MinValidVersion =` `CHANGE_TRACKING_MIN_VALID_VERSION(OBJECT_ID('dbo.Client'));`
	`SELECT @LastSynchVersion = CAST(value AS BIGINT)`
	`FROM      sys.extended_properties`
	`WHERE     major_id = OBJECT_ID('dbo.Client')`
	`AND       name = N'LAST_SYNC_VERSION';`

5. Map the following parameters:

Variable Name	Direction	Data Type	Parameter Name
User::CurrentVersion	Output	Int64	@ CurrentVersion
User::MinValidVersion	Output	Int64	@MinValidVersion
User::LastSynchVersion	Output	Int64	@LastSynchVersion

6. Confirm your alterations.

7. Add a Script task, name it **Define SQL Variables**, and connect the task Get Parameters to it. Double-click the precedence constraint and set to:

Evaluation Operation:	Expression and Constraint
Value:	Success
Expression:	@LastSynchVersion >= @MinValidVersion

8. Add the following variables:

Read-only:	LastSynchVersion
Read-Write:	SQLDelete,SQLInsert,SQLUpdate

9. Add the following script, which will set the SQL SELECT required to return only the delta data (C:\SQL2012DIRecipes\CH11\ChangeTrackingSSIS.vb):

```vb
Public Sub Main()

    Dim SQLInsertText As String = "SELECT SRC. ID, ClientName, Country, Town, County, ↵
                            Address1, Address2, ClientType, ClientSize" _
                            & " FROM dbo.Client SRC" _
                            & " INNER JOIN CHANGETABLE(CHANGES Client, " ↵
                            & Dts.Variables("LastSynchVersion").Value & ") AS CT" _
                            & " ON SRC.ID = CT.ID" _
                            & " WHERE CT.SYS_CHANGE_OPERATION = 'I'"

    Dts.Variables("SQLInsert").Value = SQLInsertText

    Dim SQLDeleteText As String = "SELECT ID FROM CHANGETABLE(CHANGES Client, " ↵
                            & Dts.Variables("LastSynchVersion").Value & ") AS DEL" _
                            & " WHERE SYS_CHANGE_OPERATION = 'D'"

    Dts.Variables("SQLDelete").Value = SQLDeleteText

    Dim SQLUpdateText As String = "SELECT SRC. ID, ClientName, Country, Town, ↵
                            County, Address1, Address2, ClientType, ClientSize " _
                            & " FROM dbo.Client SRC" _
                            & " INNER JOIN CHANGETABLE(CHANGES Client, " ↵
                            & Dts.Variables("LastSynchVersion").Value & ") AS CT" _
                            & " ON SRC.ID = CT.ID" _
                            & " WHERE    CT.SYS_CHANGE_OPERATION = 'U'"

    Dts.Variables("SQLUpdate").Value = SQLUpdateText

    Dts.TaskResult = ScriptResults.Success

End Sub
```

10. Confirm your changes.

11. Add an Execute SQL task, name it **Prepare temporary tables**, connect the Define SQL Variables task to it and configure as follows (C:\SQL2012DIRecipes\CH11\ PrepareTemporaryTables.Sql):

Name:	Get Parameters
Connection Type:	OLEDB
Connection:	Source_OLEDB
SQL Statement:	CREATE TABLE ##Tmp_Deletes (ID INT);
	CREATE TABLE ##Tmp_Updates
	(
	ID INT NOT NULL,
	ClientName VARCHAR(150) NULL,
	Country VARCHAR(50) NULL,
	Town VARCHAR(50) NULL,
	County VARCHAR(50) NULL,
	Address1 VARCHAR(50) NULL,
	Address2 VARCHAR(50) NULL,
	ClientType VARCHAR(20) NULL,
	ClientSize VARCHAR(10) NULL
	)

12. Confirm your alterations.

13. Add a Sequence container, which you name **Upsert and Delete Deltas**, and connect the "Prepare temporary tables" task to it.

14. Inside the Sequence container, add three Data Flow tasks named **Inserts**, **Updates**, and **Deletes**. Set DelayValidation for Deletes and Updates to True. Configure as follows:

Inserts

Source (OLEDB)

OLEDB Connection Manager:	Source_OLEDB
Data Access Mode:	SQLCommandFromVariable
Variable Name:	SQLInsert

Destination (OLEDB)

OLEDB Connection Manager:	Destination_OLEDB
Data Access Mode:	Table or View–Fast Load
Name of Table or View:	dbo.Clients
Keep Identity:	True

Updates

Source (OLEDB)

OLEDB Connection Manager:	Source_OLEDB
Data Access Mode:	SQLCommandFromVariable
Variable Name:	SQLUpdate

Destination (OLEDB)

OLEDB Connection Manager:	Destination_OLEDB
Data Access Mode:	Table or View name from variable
Variable Name:	UpdateTable
Validate External Metadata (property):	False

Deletes

Source (OLEDB)

OLEDB Connection Manager:	Source_OLEDB
Data Access Mode:	SQLCommandFromVariable
Variable Name:	SQLDelete

Destination (OLEDB)

OLEDB Connection Manager:	Destination_OLEDB
Data Access Mode:	Table or View name from variable
Variable Name:	DeleteTable
Validate External Metadata (property):	False

15. Ensure that all source to destination mappings for all three destinations are correct, and confirm your changes.

16. Add an Execute SQL task, name it **Delete Data**, and connect the "Upsert and Delete Deltas" Sequence container to it. Configure as follows:

Connection Type:	OLEDB
Connection:	Destination_OLEDB
SQL Statement:	DELETE DST
	FROM dbo.Client DST
	INNER JOIN Tmp_Deletes DL
	ON DST.ID = DL.ID

17. Confirm your changes.

18. Add an Execute SQL task, name it **Update Data**, and connect the "Delete Data" Execute SQL task to it. Configure as follows (C:\SQL2012DIRecipes\CH11\UpdateData.Sql):

Connection Type:	OLEDB
Connection:	Destination_OLEDB
SQL Statement:	UPDATE DST
	SET
	DST.ClientName = SRC.ClientName
	,DST.Country = SRC.Country
	,DST.Town = SRC.Town
	,DST.County = SRC.County
	,DST.Address1 = SRC.Address1
	,DST.Address2 = SRC.Address2
	,DST.ClientType = SRC.ClientType
	,DST.ClientSize = SRC.ClientSize
	FROM dbo.Client DST
	INNER JOIN Tmp_Updates SRC
	ON DST.ID = SRC.ID

19. Confirm your changes.

20. Add an Execute SQL task, name it **Set latest version number**, and connect the "Update Data" Execute SQL task to it.

21. Configure the Execute SQL task as follows
    (C:\SQL2012DIRecipes\CH11\UpdateExtendedPropertySSIS.Sql):

Connection Type:	ADO.NET
Connection:	Source_ADONET
SQL Statement:	`EXEC sys.sp_updateextendedproperty`
	`@level0type = N'SCHEMA'`
	`,@level0name = dbo`
	`,@level1type = N'TABLE'`
	`,@level1name = Client`
	`,@name = LAST_SYNC_VERSION`
	`,@value = @CurrentVersion`
	`;`

22. Add the following parameter:

Name	Direction	Type	Value
User::CurrentVersion	Input	Int64	@CurrentVersion

23. Confirm your changes with OK. The package should look like Figure 12-1.

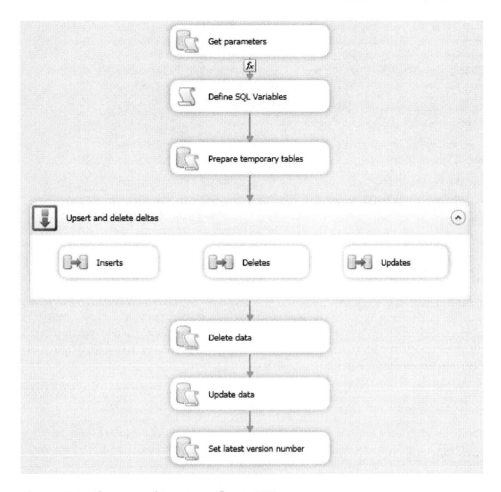

Figure 12-1. *Change Tracking process flow in SSIS*

How It Works

You can also use Change Tracking information in an SSIS package to ensure that only delta data changes are applied to a destination database. This presumes that Change Tracking has been enabled and configured for a source table (or tables). Unfortunately, you have to convince the source system DBA to configure Change Tracking, which might not be easy.

I want to draw your attention to the fact that this recipe uses two "scaffolding" techniques that will help create the package more easily, but which will be altered during (or just before) processing:

- One, I use variables to define the source data that refer directly to the source tables—without using Change Tracking. These variables will be replaced during execution by the code required to select delta data only.

- Two, I start by using permanent "scratch" tables in the destination database for the delta deletes and updates, and finish by switching (once everything is tested and ready for deployment) to temporary tables.

There are a couple of prerequisites for his to work. First (and perhaps self-evidently), Change Tracking must be configured on the source system. Second, both source and destination tables must be synchronized before running the process (here I will use the Client tables described in Recipe 12-1).

Once the package has been tested and works (remember to truncate the Tmp_Deletes and Tmp_Updates tables between each test), you can tweak it to use the session-scoped temporary tables, as follows:

1. First, change the values of the TMP_Updates and TMP_Deletes variables to ##TMP_Updates and ##TMP_Deletes, respectively.

2. Then, change the SQL statement in the Delete Datastep to use the ##Tmp_Deletes table instead of Tmp_Deletes.

3. Next, change the SQL statement in the Update Datastep to use the ##Tmp_Updates table instead of Tmp_Updates.

4. Finally, delete the Tmp_Deletes and Tmp_Updates tables in the destination database.

12-4. Detecting Changes to Source Data Using the SQL Server Transaction Log

Problem

You want to detect net changes to source tables without any extra objects being created in the source database and apply data changes to the destination table at regular intervals.

Solution

Use the Change Data Capture (CDC) feature of SQL Server Enterprise version to track the changes without triggers in a relatively lightweight fashion by reading the SQL Server transaction log. In this example, I am using CarSales as the source database and CarSales_Staging as the destination database.

1. First (if not already done), CDC must be enabled at database level. The following T-SQL snippet will do this (C:\SQL2012DIRecipes\CH11\EnableCDC.Sql):

```
USE CarSales;
GO

sys.sp_cdc_enable_db;
```

2. Create a table to track each ETL load that uses CDC. You will need DDL as follows (C:\SQL2012DIRecipes\CH11\tblCDCLSN.Sql):

```
CREATE TABLE CarSales.dbo.CDCLSN
(
 ID INT IDENTITY NOT NULL
 ,FinalLSN BINARY(10)
 ,TableName VARCHAR(128)
 ,DateAdded DATETIME DEFAULT GETDATE()
```

```
     ,NbInserts INT
     ,NbUpdates INT
     ,NbDeletes INT
    );
    GO
```

3. Enable CDC for the table that you will be tracking, using a T-SQL snippet something
   like this (C:\SQL2012DIRecipes\CH11\EnableCDC.Sql):

```
USE CarSales;
GO

sys.sp_cdc_enable_table
@source_schema = 'dbo',
@source_name = 'Client' ,
@role_name = 'CDCMainRole',
@supports_net_changes = 1 ;
GO
```

4. Run the following code at regular intervals to synchronize the destination table with
   the source table (C:\SQL2012DIRecipes\CH11\RunCDC.Sql):

```
DECLARE @InitialLSN BINARY(10)
DECLARE @FinalLSN BINARY(10)
DECLARE @TmpLSN BINARY(10)
DECLARE @NbInserts INT = 0
DECLARE @NbUpdates INT = 0
DECLARE @NbDeletes INT = 0

-- Get the highest LSN
SELECT     @FinalLSN = sys.fn_cdc_get_max_lsn()
SELECT     @TmpLSN = FinalLSN
FROM       dbo.CDCLSN
WHERE      TableName = 'dbo_Clients'
           AND ID = (SELECT MAX(ID) FROM dbo.CDCLSN WHERE TableName ='dbo_Clients')

-- Get the lowest LSN which will be used and test for changes
IF @FinalLSN = @TmpLSN
RETURN

SELECT @InitialLSN = ISNULL(@TmpLSN,sys.fn_cdc_get_min_lsn('dbo_Clients'))

-- deletes (1=delete), need PK only
DELETE FROM    dbo.Clients_New
WHERE          CustomerNumber IN (
                              SELECT    CustomerNumber
                              FROM      cdc.fn_cdc_get_net_changes_dbo_Clients(
                                                  @InitialLSN, @FinalLSN, 'all')

                              WHERE   __$operation = 1
                          )
```

```
                SET @NbDeletes = @@ROWCOUNT

                -- updates (4=value after update), need field list
                UPDATE        D
                SET           D.CustomerName = S.CustomerName
                FROM          dbo.Clients_New D
                INNER JOIN    (SELECT  CustomerID,CustomerName
                               FROM     cdc.fn_cdc_get_net_changes_dbo_Clients(@InitialLSN, @FinalLSN,
                                                                   'all')
                               WHERE   __$operation = 4) S
                               ON S.CustomerID = D.CustomerID

                SET @NbUpdates = @@ROWCOUNT

                -- Inserts (2=Insert), need field list
                INSERT INTO   dbo.Clients_New (CustomerID,CustomerName)
                SELECT        CustomerID,CustomerName
                FROM          cdc.fn_cdc_get_net_changes_dbo_Clients ( @InitialLSN,
                              @FinalLSN, 'all')
                WHERE         __$operation = 2

                SET @NbInserts = @@ROWCOUNT

                -- once all operations complete, add new highest LSN to history table for next run

                INSERT INTO   dbo.CDCLSN (FinalLSN,TableName, NbInserts, NbUpdates, NbDeletes)
                VALUES        (@FinalLSN,'dbo_Clients', @NbInserts, @NbUpdates, @NbDeletes);
```

How It Works

SQL Server 2008 introduced a major new feature to the area of delta data management in ETL processes, in the form of Change Data Capture. Now, while this technology is not restricted to helping those who have to load data between SQL server databases and instances, it is certainly a great help to data integration practitioners.

CDC (to give it a frequently-used acronym) has many uses and applications, and it is not limited to ETL scenarios. Indeed, it can be fairly complex to use. Consequently, this recipe will not be an exhaustive introduction to CDC, but will be narrowly centered on how CDC can perform Inserts, Updates, and Deletes between SQL Server source and destination databases. These can be staging databases, data warehouses—indeed, it can be used in a multitude of possible scenarios. The focus, as ever in this book, is on ETL processes.

CDC requires you to specify "start" and "end" parameters that allow you to tell it which block of changes to analyze and process. It can let you specify a time range, but here I prefer to use SQL Server *log sequence numbers* (LSNs) because they are the "natural" indicators of operations in the transaction log—which is where CDC sources all the information that it uses. This requires a method of identifying the upper and lower thresholds of the range of LSNs to process. To do this, I prefer to save the last (upper) LSN used to a tracking table, which allows the upper threshold of a previous operation to become the lower threshold of the current operation. As a bonus, this table stores the number of records affected by each Insert, Update, and Delete operation performed during the ETL load.

Here, inevitably, I am showing how this can be done for only one table. You will have to duplicate this operation for each table for which you wish to use CDC. Oh, and make sure that you are using the Enterprise version of SQL Server—this will not work if you are deploying only the Standard or BI versions in production.

The T-SQL does the following:

> *First*, we need to get the highest LSN, which will be used as an upper threshold for all delta modifications. This effectively sets the "upper limit" on operations that will be processed using CDC. OLTP operations may continue in the table, but they will not be picked up for ETL.

> *Second*, we need to get the lowest LSN, which will be used as the lower threshold for all delta modifications—either the last highest from the table where we are logging operations or, if this is the first time that the process is run, the minimal LSN (this was detected when CDC was set up for the table).

However, we must not execute the process if upper and lower ranges are identical. This is because the LSN range function (`cdc.fn_cdc_get_net_changes_<table>`) acts like an SQL BETWEEN clause, and so if the upper and lower LSNs are identical, there will always be one operation that will be processed. So the code tests for this, and exits if the two LSNs are the same.

Otherwise, if there has been at least one new operation, the process will Insert/Update/Delete any new or changed data (in any order) using the `cdc.fn_cdc_get_net_changes_<table>` function.

■ **Note** Although Change Data Capture (like Change Tracking) does not add a lot of extra overhead to the source server, just exactly how much this is, and whether it is acceptable, will depend on each set of circumstances. For a server with a very high volume of transactions, even the slight overhead that CDC adds might prove too much. You will have to test it in your specific environment.

Hints, Tips, and Traps

- Change Data Capture is *only* available with the Enterprise version of SQL Server.

- When CDC-enabling the table(s), the `@supports_net_changes` parameter is fundamental because we are only interested in final "net" changes for ETL delta data, and not the intermediate states between data loads.

- Should you need to disable CDC, you must first disable it at table level:

```
sys.sp_cdc_disable_table
    @source_schema = 'dbo',
    @source_name = 'Clients' ,
    @capture_instance = 'dbo_Client' ;
GO
```

- You can check CDC-enabled tables with

```
SELECT name, type, type_desc FROM sys.tables WHERE is_tracked_by_cdc = 1 ;
```

- And then, once all tables have had CDC disabled, you can disable CDC itself at database level using the following:

```
sys.sp_cdc_disable_db ;
GO
```

- If you really want to see all the changes, by type, for the LSN range (assuming that you have declared and attributed values to the variables @InitialLSN and @FinalLSN):

```
SELECT * FROM cdc.fn_cdc_get_net_changes_dbo_Clients(@InitialLSN,
@FinalLSN, 'all') ;
```

- If your process requires it, then you can "soft-delete" records (by flagging them as no longer active) rather than deleting them in the destination table.

- You can use the update_mask column to deduce the fields to update, and write some clever dynamic SQL, if you prefer. Nonetheless, I think that it is best to stick to a more global approach, as defined in this recipe.

- If you want to use defined time ranges, during which all modified data must be detected, then you need the sys.fn_cdc_map_time_to_lsn function to have SQL Server CDC find the LSNs that correspond to the upper and lower time thresholds.

- The following snippet, if added to the declarations section of the T-SQL code (and replacing the @InitialLSN and @FinalLSN attribution), will get the LSN thresholds for the last six hours. Care should be taken with this approach because you could potentially miss a range, so please be careful when using time thresholds to return LSN thresholds.

```
DECLARE @LowerTimeThreshold DATETIME2 = DATEADD(hh,-6,GETDATE())
DECLARE @UpperTimeThreshold DATETIME2 = GETDATE()

SELECT @InitialLSN = sys.fn_cdc_map_time_to_lsn('smallest greater than',
@LowerTimeThreshold)
SELECT @FinalLSN = sys.fn_cdc_map_time_to_lsn('largest less than or
equal', @UpperTimeThreshold)
```

- Of course, you may prefer to set defined periods for the window of changed data—but I will leave it up to you to tweak the T-SQL to do this.

- If storing LSNs in a table is too convoluted, you can always store just the last (highest) LSN as an extended property of the source table, using sp_AddExtendedProperty. This is similar to the approach described in Recipe 12-1 to store version numbers when applying Change Tracking.

- Defining Change Data Capture requires the user to be a member of the sysadmin fixed server role.

12-5. Applying Change Data Capture with SSIS
Problem

You are running a structured ETL package and want it to use Change Data Capture in a way that is completely integrated with SSIS.

Solution

Use SSIS 2012 and its new Change Data Capture tasks. The following steps show how it can be done using the Client table in the CarSales database as the source and using the CarSales_Staging database as the destination.

1. Implement CDC at the database and table level (unless this has already been done) using the following code (C:\SQL2012DIRecipes\CH11\EnableCDCSSIS.Sql):

```
USE CarSales;
GO

sys.sp_cdc_enable_db;
GO

sys.sp_cdc_enable_table
@source_schema = 'dbo',
@source_name = 'Client' ,
@role_name = 'CDCMainRole',
@supports_net_changes = 1
```

2. Using the following DDL, create a table to hold the IDs of records to be deleted in the destination table (C:\SQL2012DIRecipes\CH11\tblCDC_Client_Deletes.Sql):

```
CREATE TABLE CarSales_Staging.dbo.CDC_Client_Deletes
(
 ID INT NOT NULL
) ;
GO
```

3. Using the following DDL, create a table to hold the data for records to be updated in the destination table (C:\SQL2012DIRecipes\CH11\tblCDC_Client_Updates.Sql):

```
CREATE TABLE CarSales_Staging.dbo.CDC_Client_Updates
(
 ID INT NOT NULL,
 ClientName NVARCHAR(150) NULL,
 Address1 VARCHAR(50) NULL,
 Address2 VARCHAR(50) NULL,
 Town VARCHAR(30) NULL,
 County VARCHAR(30) NULL,
 PostCode VARCHAR(10) NULL,
 Country CHAR(3) NULL,
 ClientType NCHAR(5) NULL,
 ClientSize VARCHAR(10) NULL,
 ClientSince SMALLDATETIME NULL,
 IsCreditWorthy BIT NULL,
 DealerGroup HIERARCHYID NULL,
 MapPosition GEOGRAPHY NULL
) ;
GO
```

4. Create a destination table using the following DDL:

```
CREATE TABLE CarSales_Staging.dbo.Client_CDCSSIS
(
 ID INT IDENTITY(1,1) NOT NULL,
 ClientName NVARCHAR(150) NULL,
 Address1 VARCHAR(50) NULL,
 Address2 VARCHAR(50) NULL,
 Town VARCHAR(50) NULL,
 County VARCHAR(50) NULL,
 PostCode VARCHAR(10) NULL,
 Country TINYINT NULL,
 ClientType VARCHAR(20) NULL,
 ClientSize VARCHAR(10) NULL,
 ClientSince SMALLDATETIME NULL,
 IsCreditWorthy BIT NULL,
 DealerGroup HIERARCHYID NULL,
 MapPosition GEOGRAPHY NULL,
CONSTRAINT PK_Client PRIMARY KEY CLUSTERED
(
ID ASC
) WITH (PAD_INDEX = OFF, STATISTICS_NORECOMPUTE = OFF,
IGNORE_DUP_KEY = OFF, ALLOW_ROW_LOCKS = ON, ALLOW_PAGE_LOCKS = ON)
) ;
GO
```

Creating a table to track the LSN range used in each delta load is also required—as in Recipe 12-4—but as you will see, the CDC Control task can create this for you, and so I will let it do just this.

5. Create a new SSIS package. Add the following three connection managers at project level (by right-clicking the Connection Managers folder in the Solution Explorer and selecting New Connection Manager). All will have the .ConnMgr extension in the Connection Managers folder and will appear without this extension in the Connection Managers tab:

Name	Type	Comments
CarSales_OLEDB	OLEDB	The connection to the CDC-enabled source database.
CarSales_Staging_OLEDB	OLEDB	The connection to the destination (synchronized) database.
CarSales_ADONET	ADO.NET	The connection used for LSN tracking. Here I am placing this in the source database. This **must** be an ADO.NET connection or the CDC task cannot use it.

6. At package level, add a new String variable named **CDCState**.

7. Add a CDC Control task named **CDC LSN Start** to the Control Flow pane. Open it and set the following parameters:

Name	Type	Comments
SQL Server CDC Database/ ADO.NET Connection Manager	CarSales_ADONET	This is the previously-defined connection to the source database that has CDC enabled.
CDC Control Operation	Mark initial load start	This tells the task that this is the start of an initial load.
Variable containing CDC State	CDCState	The variable to store the LSN.
Connection Manager where the database where the state is stored	CarSales_ADONET	

8. Click New for the "table to use for storing state". Confirm the default table DDL (see Figure 12-2).

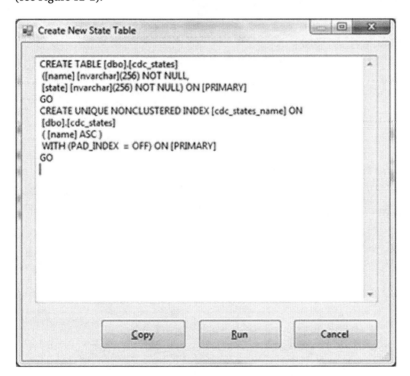

Figure 12-2. Defining the State Storage table in SSIS 2012 CDC

The code is

```
CREATE TABLE dbo.cdc_states
(
 name NVARCHAR(256) NOT NULL,
 state NVARCHAR(256) NOT NULL
) ;
```

```
GO
CREATE UNIQUE NONCLUSTERED INDEX cdc_states_name ON
 dbo.cdc_states
 ( name ASC )
 WITH (PAD_INDEX  = OFF) ;
GO
```

9.   Click Run to create the table.

10.   Set the State name as **CDCState**. The dialog box should look like Figure 12-3.

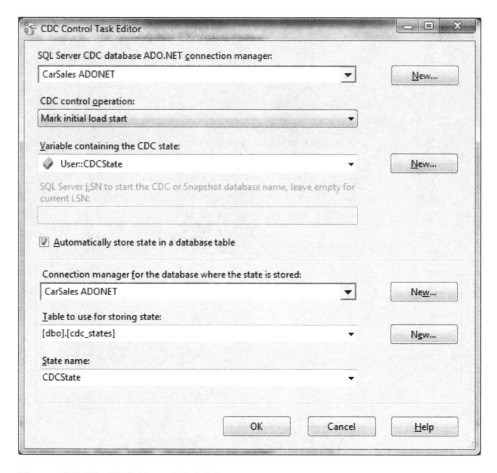

Figure 12-3. *The CDC Control Task Editor*

11.   Click OK to confirm your changes.

12.   Add a Data Flow task to the Control Flow pane, connect the CDC control to it, and
      switch to the Data Flow pane.

13. Add an OLEDB source task, configured as follows:

Name:	CarSales
OLEDB Connection Manager:	CarSales_OLEDB
Data Access Mode:	Table or View
Name of Table or View:	dbo.Client

14. Add an OLEDB destination task, linked to the source task and configured as follows:

Name:	CarSales_Staging
OLEDB Connection Manager:	CarSales_Staging_OLEDB
Data Access Mode:	Table or View - fast load
Name of Table or View:	dbo.Client_CDCSSIS
Keep Identity:	Checked

15. Map all the source columns to the destination columns. The data flow should look like Figure 12-4.

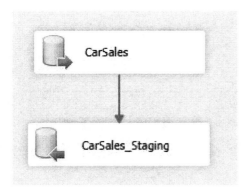

Figure 12-4. *Process flow for SSIS 2012 CDC*

16. Return to the Control Flow tab. Add a CDC Control task. Name it **CDC LSN end**. Connect the Data Flow task to it, and then double-click to edit.

17. Set the same parameters as previously (step 8) but ensure that the CDC Control Operation is now "Mark initial load end". The dialog box should look like Figure 12-5.

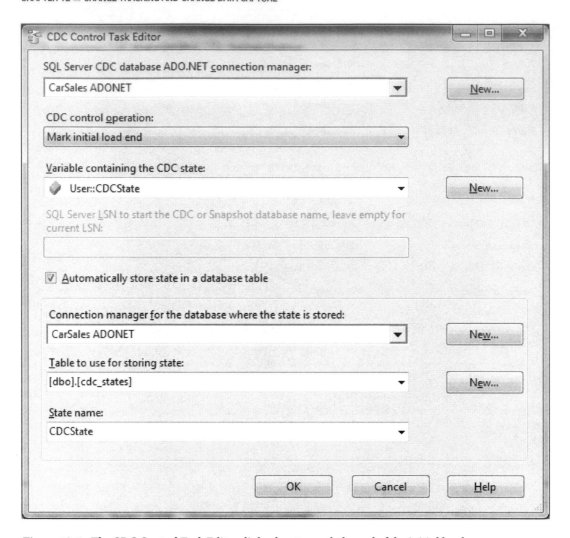

Figure 12-5. *The CDC Control Task Editor dialog box to mark the end of the initial load*

18. Run the package to start Change Data Capture. The entire package should look like Figure 12-6.

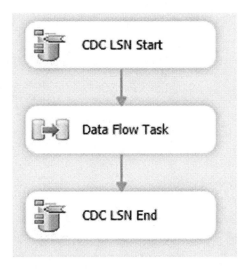

Figure 12-6. *Process flow when instantiating CDC*

19. Create a new SSIS package in the same SSIS project (this will enable you to use the same connection managers that you used in the initial load).

20. At package level, add a new String variable named **CDCState**.

21. Add an Execute SQL task to the Control Flow pane. Configure it as follows:

Name:	Prepare Staging Tables
Connection Type:	OLEDB
Connection:	CarSales_Staging_OLEDB
SQL Statement:	`TRUNCATE TABLE dbo.CDC_Client_Updates`
	`TRUNCATE TABLE dbo.CDC_Client_Deletes`

22. Add a CDC Control task, name it **Get starting LSN**, and connect the previous task (Prepare Staging Tables) to it. Configure it exactly as described in the previous recipe, but set the CDC Control Operation to "Get processing range".

23. Add a Data Flow task. Connect the CDC Control task to it. Switch to the Data Flow pane.

24. Add a CDC Source task. Open it and configure it as follows:

Name:	CDC Source
ADO.NET Connection Manager:	CarSales_ADONET
CDC-enabled Table:	dbo.Client
CDC Processing Mode:	Net
Variable containing CDC State:	CDCState

25. The dialog box should look like Figure 12-7. Click OK to confirm your modifications.

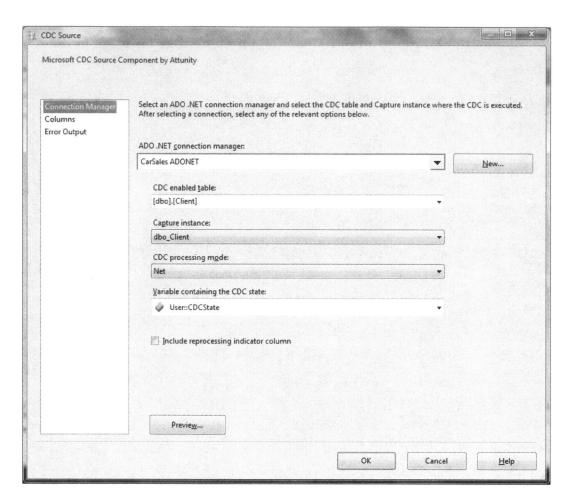

Figure 12-7. *The CDC Source dialog box*

26. Add a CDC splitter task (in the SSIS toolbox, this is with the Other Transforms) and connect the CDC Source task to it.

27. Add an OLEDB destination task and connect the CDC splitter to it. Name it **Inserts** and select the InsertOutput as the output to use from the CDC Splitter task.

28. Configure the OLEDB destination task as follows:

Name:	Inserts
OLEDB Connection Manager:	CarSales_Staging_OLEDB
Data Access Mode:	Table or view – Fast Load
Name of Table or View:	dbo.Client_CDCSSIS

29. Map all the data columns (**not** those used by CDC and which begin with __) and click OK.

30. Add an OLEDB destination task and connect the CDC splitter to it. Name it **Deletes** and select DeleteOutput as the output to use from the CDC Splitter task. Configure the OLEDB destination task as follows:

Name:	Deletes
OLEDB Connection Manager:	CarSales_Staging_OLEDB
Data Access Mode:	Table or view – Fast Load
Name of Table or View:	dbo.CDC_Client_Deletes

31. Map the ID column only and click OK.

32. Add an OLEDB destination task and connect the CDC splitter to it. Select the UpdateOutput as the output to use. Name it **Updates** and configure the OLEDB destination task as follows:

Name:	Updates
OLEDB Connection Manager:	CarSales_Staging_OLEDB
Data Access Mode:	Table or view – Fast Load
Name of Table or View:	dbo.CDC_Client_Updates

33. Map all the data columns (but not the CDC specific columns—those beginning with a double underscore) and click OK. The Data Flow should look like Figure 12-8.

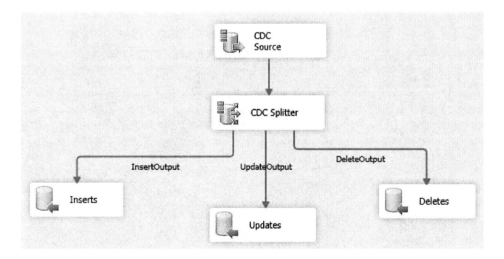

Figure 12-8. *The CDC upsert process*

34. Return to the Control Flow pane. Add a CDC Control task, which you name **Set end LSN**. Connect the Data Flow task to it, and configure as for the "Get starting LSN" CDC Control task, only be sure to select "Mark processed range" as the CDC control operation.

35. Add an Execute SQL task. Connect the "Set end LSN" CDC Control task to it. Configure as follows:

Name:	Updates
Connection Type:	OLEDB
Connection Manager:	CarSales_Staging_OLEDB
SQL Statement	UPDATE D
C:\SQL2012DIRecipes\CH11\SSISCDCUpdates.Sql	SET

```
UPDATE D
SET
     D.ClientName = S.ClientName
    ,D.Address1 = S.Address1
    ,D.Address2 = S.Address2
    ,D.Town = S.Town
    ,D.County = S.County
    ,D.PostCode = S.PostCode
    ,D.Country = S.Country
    ,D.ClientType = S.ClientType
    ,D.ClientSize = S.ClientSize
    ,D.ClientSince = S.ClientSince
    ,D.IsCreditWorthy = S.IsCreditWorthy
    ,D.DealerGroup = S.DealerGroup
    ,D.MapPosition = S.MapPosition

FROM        CarSales.dbo.client D
INNER JOIN  dbo.CDC_Client_Updates S
            ON S.ID = D.ID
```

36. Add an Execute SQL task. Connect the Execute SQL task, which you name **Updates**, to it. Configure as follows:

Name:	Deletes
Connection Type:	OLEDB
Connection Manager:	CarSales_Staging_OLEDB
SQL Statement:	DELETED

```
DELETED
FROM       CarSales.dbo.client D
INNER JOIN dbo.CDC_Client_Deletes S
           ON S.ID = D.ID
```

You can now run the package (which should look like Figure 12-9). Any modifications made to the source data will be reflected in the destination table.

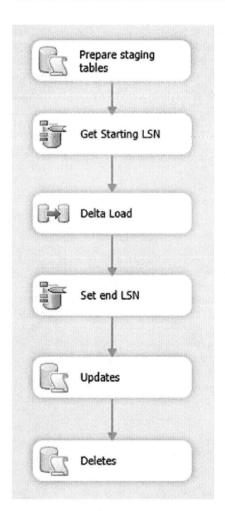

Figure 12-9. *The complete CDC process flow*

How It Works

New in SQL Server 2012 is the possibility of using Change Data Capture from SSIS "directly" (without having to use SSIS as a wrapper to call purely T-SQL-based techniques). This approach uses the three Attunity-developed SSIS tasks shown in Table 12-1.

Table 12-1. *SSIS Tasks for Change Data Capture*

Element	Type	Description
CDC Control Task	Task	Handles the range of data to be processed using LSNs.
CDC Source	Data Source	Connects to a CDC-enabled table.
CDC Splitter	Transform	Splits data output according to the type of data modification (Insert, Update, or Delete).

It is important to understand that a CDC-based process requires an initial "synchronization" load that copies all the data from the source table into the destination table and stores the end LSN used, so that only delta data will then be transferred from source to destination. This is nearly always best handled as a separate SSIS package. Once you have carried out the initial load, you can use SSIS to keep the source and destination tables in sync using CDC. As you can see, SSIS is essentially an interface to the underlying CDC process. As the process itself was described in Recipe 12-4, I will not rehash it here, and instead refer you back a few pages.

The CDC state table contains data something like Figure 12-10.

Figure 12-10. *CDC state table*

I do not advise tweaking this but suggest that you leave it well alone. This table that stores CDC state can be in any available database, and does not have to be in the same database as either the source or the destination. Exactly where you place the CDC_Client_Updates and CDC_Client_Deletes tables is entirely up to you. I prefer to place them in a staging table so as not to clutter a final database—but this will depend on the architecture that you choose (or are constrained) to follow.

The CDC Splitter task is in essence a very cleverly configured—and completely locked—conditional split task. You cannot add outputs or columns to it. However, you can use the CDC-specific columns (__$start_lsn, __$operation and $__update_mask) in the destination tables if you so wish. In this case, you may also want to send the InsertOutput to a staging table for further processing.

Hints, Tips, and Traps

- You can add an Execute SQL task to truncate the destination table to the start of this package if you so wish—in case you need to run it more than once.

- I realize that best practice dictates that we use SQL to SELECT only the columns that will be part of the data flow, but in my experience, CDC nearly always transfers all columns—so I have opted for the simpler source data selection solution and taken the entire table.

- In a production environment, you will doubtless have to drop indexes before the initial load and re-create them afterward.

- If you create the connection managers at package level, then they can be used in both the initial load package and the delta data load—assuming that both packages are in the same project.

12-6. Using Change Data Capture with Oracle Source Data
Problem

You want to detect—with minimal impact—changed data on the Oracle source database, and only apply modifications to an SQL Server destination database.

Solution

Use the Oracle-CDC tools supplied with SQL Server 2012 Enterprise version to mine the Oracle redo log for changes to the data in tracked tables, and then update SQL Server tables with the relevant data modifications. The following explains how to install and use them.

1. Locate the `Tools\AttunityCDCOracle\x64\1033` directory on your SQL Server media, and run the files `AttunityOracleCdcDesigner.msi` and `AttunityOracleCdcService.msi`.

2. Unless the Oracle source has already been set to run in `ARCHIVELOG` mode, run SQL*Plus (having logged in AS SYSDBA) and execute the following commands (`C:\SQL2012DIRecipes\CH11\OracleArchivelog.Sql`):

   ```
   SHUTDOWN IMMEDIATE;
   STARTUP MOUNT;
   ALTER DATABASE ARCHIVELOG;
   ALTER DATABASE OPEN;
   ALTER DATABASE ADD SUPPLEMENTAL LOG DATA;
   ```

3. Click Start ➤ All Programs ➤ Change Data Capture for Oracle by Attunity ➤ Oracle CDC Service configuration. This will run the Oracle Change Data Capture Service Configuration by Attunity MMC snap-in.

4. Click Action ➤ Prepare SQL Server. Enter or select an SQL Server instance and define the authentication mode and any necessary parameters. The dialog box should look like Figure 12-11.

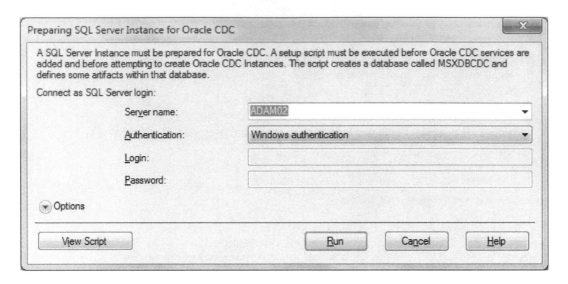

Figure 12-11. *The prepare SQL Server dialog box for the Oracle CDC Service Configuration by Attunity MMC snap-in*

5.   Click Run and confirm with OK. The MSXDBCDC database is created on the selected
     server.

6.   Click Action ➤ New Service and define a new Oracle CDC service. I suggest leaving
     the service name proposed by the creation process, but you must remember to add
     the master password and define the Associated SQL Server instance. The dialog box
     should look like Figure 12-12.

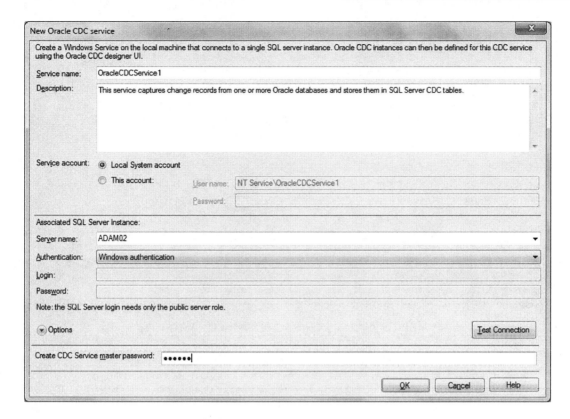

Figure 12-12. *Creating a new Oracle CDC service*

7. Close the Change Data Capture Service Configuration for Oracle by Attunity MMC snap-in.

8. You now need to create a CDC instance. Click Start ➤ All Programs ➤ Change Data Capture for Oracle by Attunity ➤ Oracle CDC designer configuration.

9. The Connect To SQL Server dialog box appears. Enter or select a server name and choose a mode of authentication plus any required parameters (see Figure 12-13).

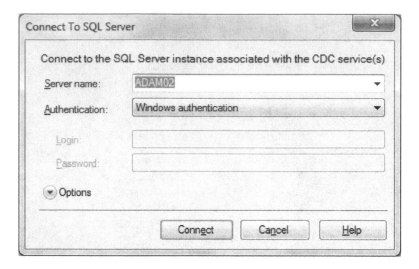

Figure 12-13. *The Connect To SQL Server dialog box in the Oracle CDC designer configuration MMC snap-in*

10. Click Connect. You will now be running the Oracle CDC designer configuration MMC snap-in.

11. Click the service in the left pane, right-click, and choose New Oracle CDC Instance. Enter an Oracle CDC instance name, and then click Create Database. The database will have the same name as the instance by default, but you can change the database name. The dialog box should look like Figure 12-14.

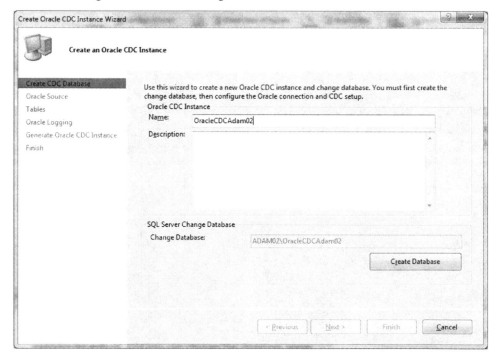

Figure 12-14. *The Create CDC Database pane of the Create Oracle CDC Instance Wizard*

12. Click Next and define the Oracle connection parameters in the Oracle Source pane. Fortunately, the dialog box is friendly and helpful (and can be seen in Figure 12-15).

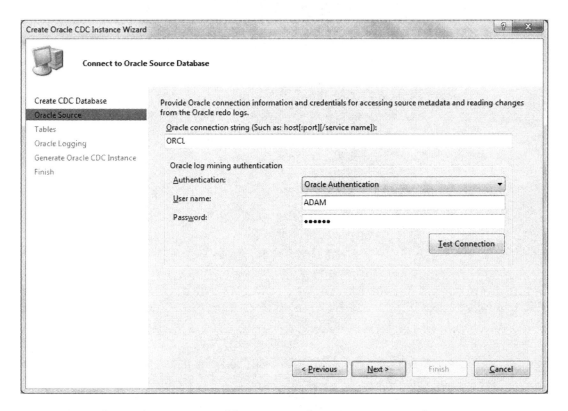

Figure 12-15. *The Oracle Source pane of the Create Oracle CDC Instance Wizard*

13. Click Next. The Tables pane of the wizard appears.

14. Click Add. Enter or select a database schema, and then click Search to display the available tables. Select any tables you wish to use as data sources. The dialog box should look something like Figure 12-16.

Figure 12-16. *Selecting source tables in Oracle*

15. Click Add, followed by OK to confirm each table. Once all the tables have been added, click Close. You will return to the Tables pane of the wizard with the selected tables listed. The dialog box should look like Figure 12-17.

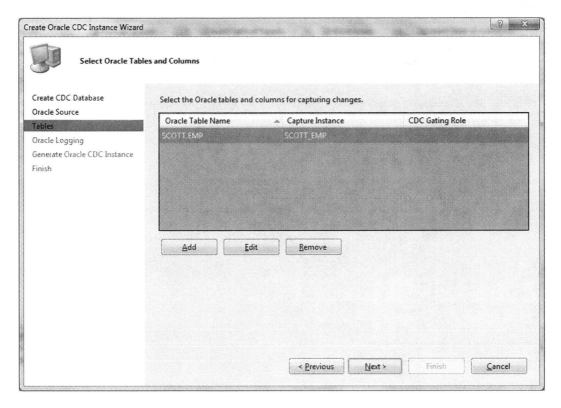

Figure 12-17. *Selected tables for Oracle CDC*

16. Click Next. The Oracle Logging dialog box will appear, rather like in Figure 12-18.

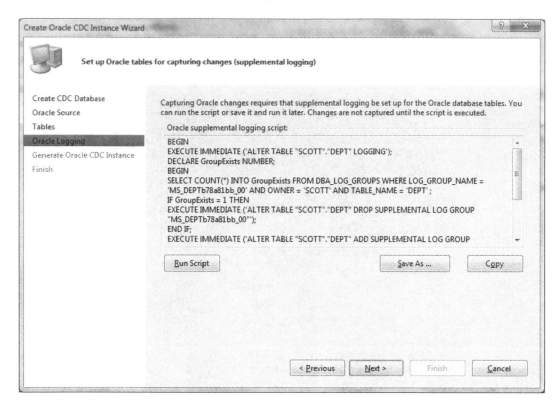

Figure 12-18. *The Oracle Logging pane*

17.   Click Run Script. Confirm (or modify) the connection elements in the dialog box
(see Figure 12-19).

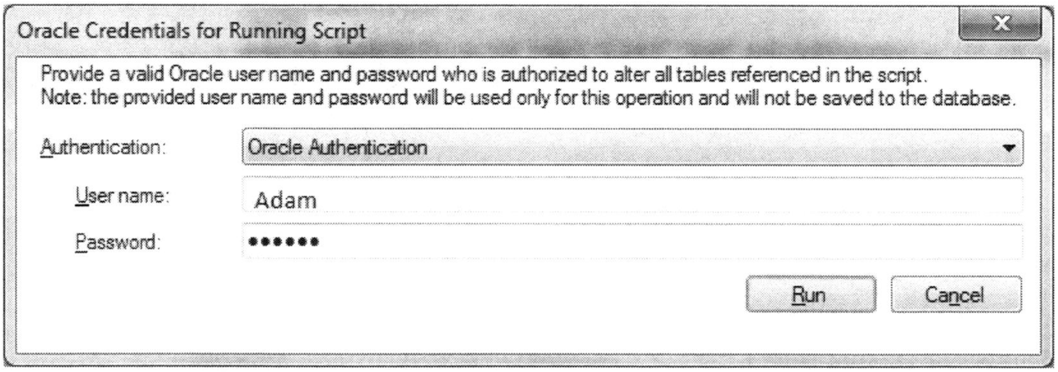

Figure 12-19. *Oracle credentials for running the CDC script*

18. Click Run. You should get a dialog box confirming that the supplemental logging script was run successfully. Click OK to confirm this dialog box, and then click Next.

19. Click Run to generate the destination tables enabled for CDC in the SQL Server database. The dialog box should look like Figure 12-20 after this process has run.

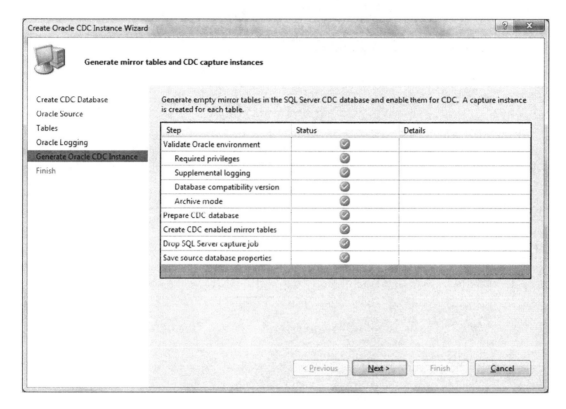

Figure 12-20. *The Generate Oracle CDC Instance pane—after successfully generating "mirror" tables in SQL Server*

20. Click Next, and then Finish in the final dialog box (see Figure 12-21).

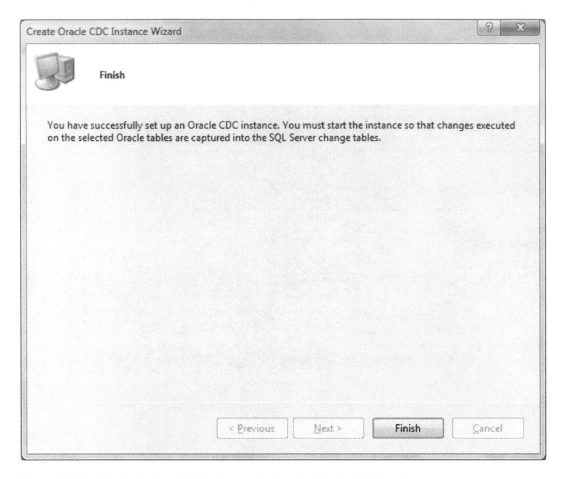

Figure 12-21. The final wizard dialog box confirming that Oracle CDC is set up

21. You now need to synchronize the source and destination databases—as in previous recipes dealing with Change Data Capture. Ensure that you have prevented any changes to the Oracle source table(s), and then copy the data from them into the "mirror" destination tables (as Attunity calls them) in SQL Server. You can see these tables by expanding Tables in the destination SQL Server database that you created as part of the CDC configuration (see Figure 12-22).

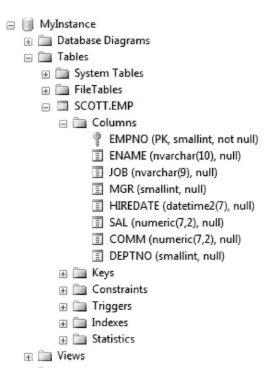

- MyInstance
  - ⊞ Database Diagrams
  - ⊟ Tables
    - ⊞ System Tables
    - ⊞ FileTables
    - ⊟ SCOTT.EMP
      - ⊟ Columns
        - 🔑 EMPNO (PK, smallint, not null)
        - ▦ ENAME (nvarchar(10), null)
        - ▦ JOB (nvarchar(9), null)
        - ▦ MGR (smallint, null)
        - ▦ HIREDATE (datetime2(7), null)
        - ▦ SAL (numeric(7,2), null)
        - ▦ COMM (numeric(7,2), null)
        - ▦ DEPTNO (smallint, null)
      - ⊞ Keys
      - ⊞ Constraints
      - ⊞ Triggers
      - ⊞ Indexes
      - ⊞ Statistics
  - ⊞ Views

Figure 12-22. Mirror tables in SQL Server

22. You are now ready to instantiate Change Data Control. To do this, right-click the instance name in the Change Data Capture MMC, and select Start. This is shown in Figure 12-23.

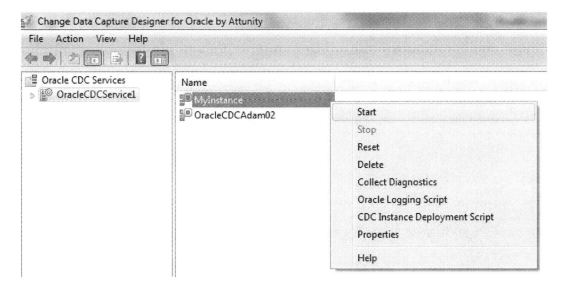

Figure 12-23. Starting CDC for Oracle

This will synchronize the data in the destination Table in SQL Server with the source table in Oracle. You can then run step 22 every time that you wish to synchronize the data.

How It Works

In essence, the Attunity tools for Oracle CDC are a very clever imitation of the Microsoft approach for SQL Server. As is the case for the pure Microsoft CDC technique, the source database log is read to detect changes, and these changes are then written to the destination database, in a format identical to that used in MS CDC.

You can monitor the changes handled by the Change Data Capture process by clicking an instance in the Change Data Capture designer. It will show you useful data concerning the number and state of transactions (see Figure 12-24).

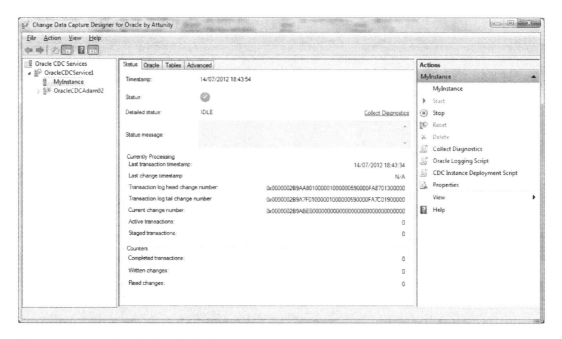

Figure 12-24. *Monitoring Oracle CDC*

The table that stores the history of changes data is a system table named `cdc.<Schema>_<TableName>_CT`. It looks like Figure 12-25.

	__$start_lsn	__$end_lsn	__$seqval	__$operation	__$update_mask	EMPNO	ENAME	JOB	MGR	HIREDATE	SAL	COMM	DEPTNO
1	0x0000002B9F5801000001	0x00000000000000000000	0x0000002B9F580000000	3	0x02	7902	FORD	ANALYST	7566	1981-12-03 00:00:00.0000000	3000.00	NULL	20
2	0x0000002B9F5801000001	0x00000000000000000000	0x0000002B9F580000001	4	0x02	7902	ADAM	ANALYST	7566	1981-12-03 00:00:00.0000000	3000.00	NULL	20

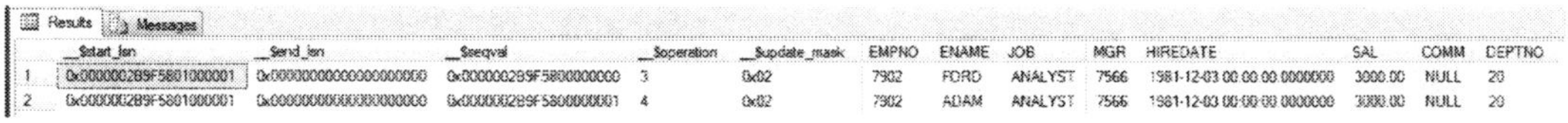

Figure 12-25. *The Oracle CDC system table of changes*

Hints, Tips, and Traps

- These Attunity tools are only available with the Enterprise version of SQL Server.

- When you install the two Attunity .msi packages, you may have with the impression that nothing has happened. Click Start ➤ All Programs to make certain that you can see Change Data Capture for Oracle by Attunity, which should contain Oracle CDC designer configuration (this should also be in the Start menu) and Oracle CDC service configuration.

- Of course, you can install the 32-bit version of these tools if you are running the Enterprise version of SQL Server in 32 bits. I am merely presuming that this is likely to be unlikely.

- At step 14, you can enter all or part of the table name to restrict the list of tables returned when searching for source tables.

Summary

In this chapter, you have seen two techniques that allow you to synchronize data between source and destination databases while only applying required Inserts, Updates, and Deletes to the destination. The first technique, Change Tracking is available in all versions of SQL Server. It is a synchronous process that tracks only the fact that a record has changed. The second technique, Change Data Capture, reads the SQL Server transaction log (or even the Oracle redo log) and can track the finest grain of sequential data changes—although such a level of detail is not required for the ETL-based focus of this book. However, Change Data Capture is only available in the Enterprise version of SQL Server.

The one that you choose to implement will depend on your requirements and SQL Server licensing. Both are robust and efficient. I can only urge you to test both and consequently add two extremely powerful tools to your ETL armory.

CHAPTER 13

▓ ▓ ▓

Organising And Optimizing Data Loads

Once you have succeeded in getting a set of data into SQL Server the next challenge is how to load it automatically, faster, more smoothly and more easily. Over and above this, you want your processes to run as reliably as is feasible with as little manual intervention as possible. This can involve many techniques, such as:

- Handling multiple identical source files for serial loading.

- Loading multiple files from one or more directories.

- Ordering file loads (to load files by size, for instance).

- Setting up parallel file loads—and dispatching files to multiple processes, with load balancing if possible.

- Loading data in parallel from a single OLEDB or ADO.NET data source.

- Reducing load times with parallel `Bulk Insert`.

- Creating efficient parallel read and write loads (a.k.a. writing to the same table from multiple simultaneous sources).

- Dealing with batch loads.

Many of these techniques have interchangeable aspects, so I encourage you to consider them all before deciding what is the best way to make your ETL challenge less of a problem and more of a satisfying solution. Then you can mix and match any relevant parts of these recipes to produce a solution that suits your needs.

This chapter only looks at these purely "structural" techniques. In the real world, you will also have to deal with indexes, and how and when to use them in ETL processes; how best to handle constraints and locks when loading data; and, of course, logging and recovery. These elements are handled separately in the next chapter.

This chapter will not go into the details of configuring source and destination connection managers. Nor will it describe exhaustively how to set up Data Flow tasks, data sources, and destinations. These—and other basic aspects of SSIS data loads—were handled in previous chapters, specifically Chapter 2 for Flat File sources, and Chapters 4 and 5 for SQL Server and other RDBMS sources. Should you need this information, please consult the appropriate chapter.

To avoid pointless repetition, I do not specify all the intricacies of a "classic" multifile load other than in Recipe 13-1. Consequently, I would advise you to cast an eye over this recipe before attempting Recipes 13-2 to 13-6, which are varied extensions of some of the ways in which you can load multiple source files.

As ever, the samples used in this chapter are available on the book's companion web site. Once downloaded, they will be found in the `C:\SQL2012DIRecipes\CH13` directory.

13-1. Loading Multiple Files

Problem

You have a directory of flat files in CSV format that need loading into SQL Server.

Solution

Use SSIS and a Foreach Loop container, as follows.

1. Open SSIS and create a new package. I suggest naming it **MultipleFileLoad**, as that is what it will do.

2. Add a variable at package level. Call the variable **FileName**. Make it of type String.

3. Right-click in the Connection Managers tab and select New Flat File Connection.

4. Name the connection manager (I will be naming it **Stock Files**).

5. Click the Browse ... button, and navigate to the directory containing the files to load (C:\SQL2012DIRecipes\CH13\MultipleFlatFiles). Select one of the files (Stock01.Csv in this example). Ensure that all the relevant configuration information is entered (in this example, SSIS will guess all of this correctly). Click Columns on the left to ensure correct column mapping and click OK.

6. Add an OLEDB connection manager at project level that connects to the CarSales database (unless you have one already).

7. Add a Foreach Loop container on to the Control Flow pane. Name it **Load Files** and double-click to edit it.

8. Select Collection on the left, and choose Foreach File Enumerator as the enumerator type.

9. Click the Browse ... button and navigate to the directory containing the files to load (C:\SQL2012DIRecipes\CH13\MultipleFlatFiles).

10. In the Files field, enter the file and/or extension filter to limit the files that will be enumerated (*.Csv in this example). Click the Fully Qualified radio button to return the full path and file name. The resulting dialog box should look like Figure 13-1.

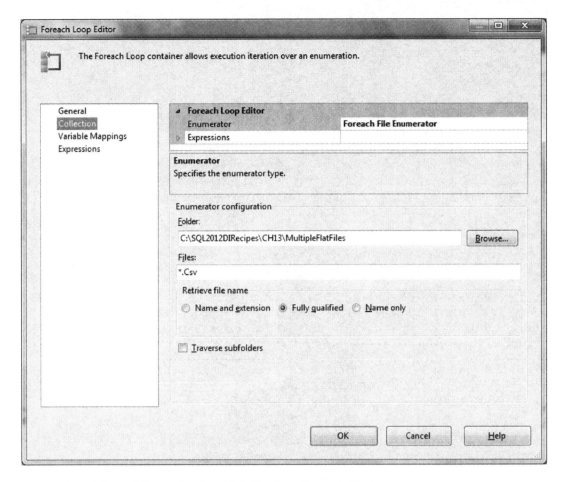

Figure 13-1. *A Foreach loop to load multiple files from the same directory*

11. Select Variable Mappings on the left. Select FileName as the variable to use (see Figure 13-2).

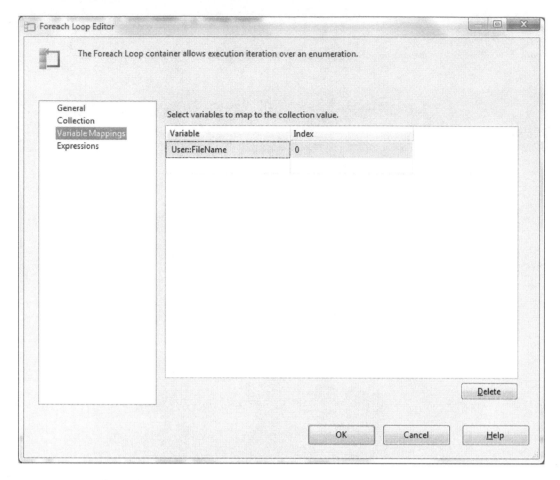

Figure 13-2. *Defining the variable to use for the file to load*

12. Click OK to close the dialog box.

13. Add a Data Flow task inside the Foreach Loop container, and configure it to load from the Flat File source to a destination table (CarSales.dbo.Stock in this example). This is described in detail in Recipe 2-2, but you will use the Stock01.Csv file as the source in this recipe.

14. Click the Flat File connection manager named Stock Files that you created in step 4, and display the Properties window (by pressing F4), unless it is already visible.

15. In the Expressions property, click the Ellipses button to display the Expressions dialog box.

16. In the Property Column, select Connection String.

17. Click the Ellipses button for the Connection String property to display the Expression Builder dialog box.

18. Expand the variables list, and drag the User::FileName variable down into the Expression Field. Your dialog box should look like Figure 13-3.

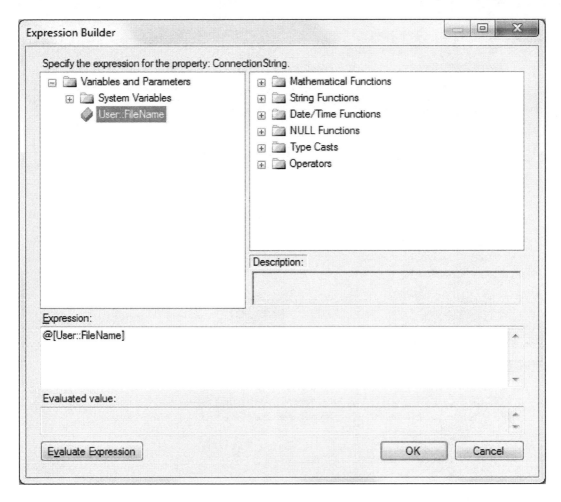

Figure 13-3. *Setting the file name as an expression for multiple file loads*

19. Click OK to close the dialog box. You will return to the Property Expressions Editor dialog box, which should look like Figure 13-4.

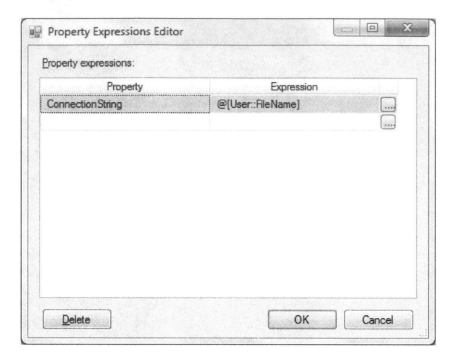

Figure 13-4. *Setting the connection string as an expression*

20. Click OK to close the dialog box. You have now told SSIS to use the file name found in the FileName variable instead of the hard-coded file name that you originally used when setting up the connection manager. Your task should look like Figure 13-5.

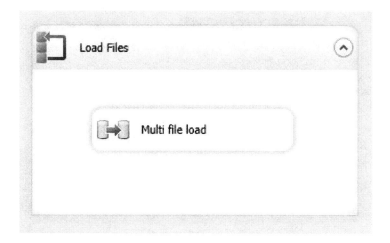

Figure 13-5. *The final multiple file load package*

21. Run the package.

Assuming that all was set up correctly, then all the files in the source directory should load into the destination table.

How It Works

Although the solution is more an answer to the problem of removing any manual intervention in a data load (rather than a pure acceleration technique), there could be occasions when you are presented with dozens—or hundreds—of files in the same source directory that have an identical structure and need to be loaded into an SQL Server table. Fortunately, SSIS can handle this easily, and here you can see how it is done. I realize that this was covered in the chapter on XML data sources, but it is just different enough (and so frequently needed) that I prefer to cover this with a recipe specifically devoted to text files.

The process is essentially a loop through all or a selection of the files in a directory. You will need a string variable that is used to hold the name of each file that is loaded and that is used (once the process is running) to replace the actual file that you defined when creating the SSIS task. In all other respects, this process is nearly identical to a single file load. This technique presumes that all the files that will be loaded are the same format, and will be loaded into the same table. This recipe does not dwell on the intricacies of mapping a text file to an SQL Server table using the Flat File connection manager and the Data Flow task. That information is covered in Recipe 2-2.

Hints, Tips, and Traps

- The file and/or extension filter is just as you would use it in a search operation or a good, old-fashioned DOS/Command window. Indeed, you can test the filter that you intend to use in a Command window (remember DIR *.CSV?).

- The variable that will be used to hold the file name in step 11 will always be the variable 0, so there is no need to change this.

- At step 18, you can evaluate the expression to test if it will work—but do not be surprised if nothing is displayed. The contents of the variable will only appear if you have entered a value for the FileName variable in the Variables pane.

- You are limited to one search pattern (for example, *.Csv) when loading all the files in a directory. If you need to use multiple search patterns—read on because this is explained in Recipe 13-2.

13-2. Selecting Multiple Text Files to Import
Problem

You wish to select a specific selection of identically-structured flat files to import into SQL Server in a single operation.

Solution

Use the MULTIFLATFILE connection manager to choose a set of flat files from one or more different folders and load them in a single operation. The following steps explain how to do it.

1. Create a new SSIS package and add a Data Flow task. Double-click to activate the Data Flow pane.

2. Create an OLEDB connection manager named **CarSales_OLEDB** that connects to the CarSales database.

3. Right-click in the Connection Managers tab and select New Connection. From the list of possible connections, choose MULTIFLATFILE and click add (or double-click MULTIFLATFILE). The Multiple Flat Files Connection Manager Editor appears. As you will see, it bears an uncanny resemblance to the Flat File Connection Manager Editor.

4. Give the connection manager a name (I will call it **MultiFileSelection**), and then click Browse. In the standard Windows Open dialog box, you can Ctrl-click (or use a combination of Shift-click and Ctrl-click) to select multiple files. In this example you need to navigate to the directory C:\SQL2012DIRecipes\CH13\MoreMultipleFlatFiles.

5. Click Open to confirm your selection. Complete the other options for flat file definition, as described in Recipe 13-1, step 5.

6. Add a Flat File source. Use the MultiFile Flat File connection manager (named **MultiFileSelection**) that you created in step 2 as its connection manager.

7. Add a destination task. Connect the source task to the destination. Complete the package by configuring the task to use the CarSales_OLEDB connection manager to connect to the dbo.Stock destination table. Map the source and destination columns.

You can now run the package and load the files you selected in step 3 into the destination table.

How It Works

There are many ways of importing multiple files (text or otherwise), and the "classic" approach of using a Foreach Loop container is described in Recipe 12-1. Where the Foreach Loop approach falls down is in a situation where you want to load some—but not all—of the files in a source directory, and there is no possibility of filtering using wildcards. However, there is another approach that is both simple and efficient that can be used with text files and which allows you to specify the *exact files* to be loaded. It involves using the MULTIFLATFILE connection manager, and can be configured to load a selected subset of files, or a subset of files based on one or more wildcard definitions (if this does not include the very files that you do *not* wish to load). This technique presumes that all the source files have an identical format.

■ **Note**   You can only browse to one source folder from the Multiple Flat Files connection manager. To extend the selection, you have to enter—or copy and paste—multiple folders in the FileName field of the Multiple Flat Files Connection Manager Editor dialog box. Each file or path must be separated by a pipe (|) character.

Hints, Tips and Traps

- To use wildcards for file selection, you need to set up the connection manager as described earlier, then select it and press F4 (or View ➤ Properties Window) to display the properties for the connection manager. You can then edit the ConnectionString property to use wildcards in the file names.

- Using the ConnectionString property, you can also extend the file source information to handle multiple directories—with or without wildcards by typing or pasting in the required path and file name. Merely separate each source path/wildcard element with a pipe character (|).

- If you have created a complex path to multiple directories, then avoid clicking the Browse button (or the ellipsis), or you will lose your path since it will be replaced (not added to) by the new path.

- If you replace an existing set of files to load with another set, SSIS will ask you to confirm that you wish to keep the existing metadata that describes the flat file structure. Assuming that the file format is the same, you can confirm this dialog box if it appears.

13-3. Loading Multiple Files Using Complex Selection Criteria
Problem

You have many directories containing flat files in the same format that need loading into SQL Server. To further complicate matters, those files have differing extensions. You want to be able to modify these parameters easily.

Solution

Use SSIS and script arrays to define the source folders and file extensions. Then iterate over the arrays to specify the files to load. These next steps cover the process to follow.

1. Create an SSIS package and name it **MultipleFilesFromVariousDirectories**.

2. Add the following variables:

Variable Name	Type	Value	Comments
FileName	String		Holds the name of the file that will be loaded.
FileExtension	String		Holds the extension of the file that will be loaded.
FolderName	String		Holds the folder/directory of the file that will be loaded.
MultipleFileExtensions	Object		The array that will hold all the various extensions be used to filter files.
MultipleFolderNames	Object		The array that will hold all the various folders be used to filter files.

3. Add a Script task on to the Control Flow pane, and double-click to edit. Give it the name **Set Arrays of source folders and File extensions** and set the Script Language to Microsoft Visual Basic 2010.

4. Add the following read/write variables:

MultipleFileExtensions

MultipleFolderNames

The easiest way to do this is to click the Ellipse button to the right of the read/write variables, and select the required variables. This will give you the following dialog box (see Figure 13-6).

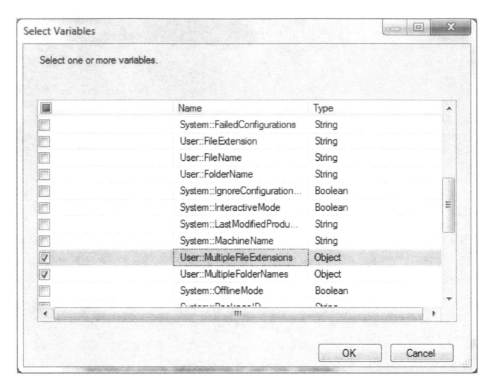

Figure 13-6. *Selecting read/write variables for a Script task*

5. Confirm with OK.

6. Click the Edit Script button.

7. Replace the Main method with the following code. This script is explained at the end
    of the recipe (C:\SQL2012DIRecipes\CH13\SSISComplexSelection.Vb):

```
Public Sub Main()

' Declare and populate an array with folder names
        Dim MultipleFolderNames As New System.Collections.ArrayList()

        MultipleFolderNames.Add("C:\SQL2012DIRecipes\CH13\MultipleFlatFiles")
        MultipleFolderNames.Add("C:\SQL2012DIRecipes\CH13\MoreMultipleFlatFiles")


        ' Declare and populate an array with file extensions
        Dim MultipleFileExtensions As New System.Collections.ArrayList()

        MultipleFileExtensions.Add("*.Csv")
        MultipleFileExtensions.Add("*.txt")
```

```
        ' Pass the arrays to SSIS variables
        Dts.Variables("MultipleFileExtensions").Value = CObj(MultipleFileExtensions)
        Dts.Variables("MultipleFolderNames").Value = CObj(MultipleFolderNames)

        Dts.TaskResult = ScriptResults.Success
End Sub
```

Of course, you will have to enter the folder names and file filters and/or extensions that correspond to your environment.

8. Close the SSIS Script window and click OK to close the Script Task Editor.

9. Add a Foreach Loop container on to the Control Flow pane, name it **Loop through all folders**, connect the "Set Arrays of source folders and File extensions" script task to this, and double-click to edit the Foreach Loop container.

10. Click Collection in the left pane. Select the Foreach From Variable Enumerator as the enumerator type.

11. In the lower part of the dialog box (Enumerator Configuration), select the MultipleFolderNames variable. The dialog box should look like Figure 13-7.

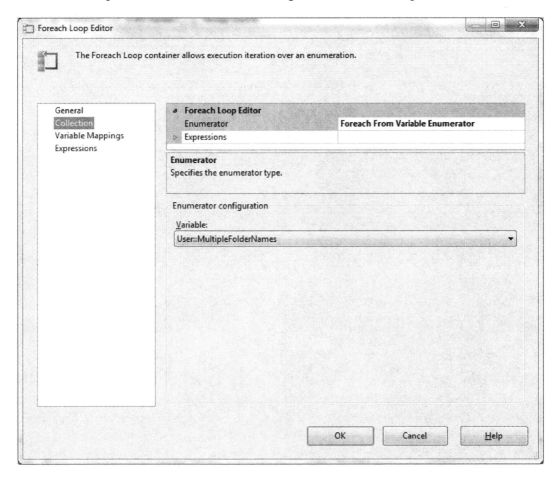

Figure 13-7. *Using a Foreach task to iterate over an object variable*

12. Click Variable Mappings in the left-hand pane, and then select the FolderName SSIS variable from the list. The dialog box should look like Figure 13-8.

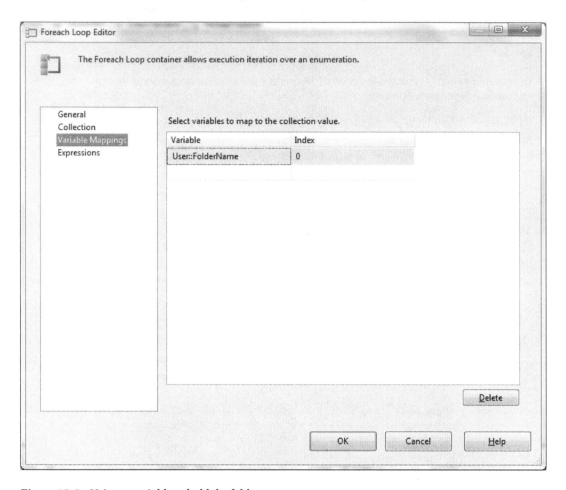

Figure 13-8. Using a variable to hold the folder to use

13. Confirm with OK.

14. Add another Foreach Loop container onto the Control Flow pane, but this time inside the Foreach Loop container (Loop through all folders) that you just created, name it **Loop through multiple file extensions**. Double-click to edit.

15. Repeat steps 10-14, to define how a Foreach Loop Container will iterate over a collection, but this time using the MultipleFileExtensions enumerator and the FileExtension variable.

16. Add a Foreach Loop Container inside the Foreach Loop Container (Loop through multiple file extensions) that you just created, name it **Load Files**, and configure it just as you did to load all the files from a single directory (described in Recipe 12-1). Double-click to edit this container.

17. Click Collection in the left-hand pane, then on the Ellipse button for the Expressions. Select the following properties and set them as follows:

Directory: User::FolderName

FileSpec: User::FileExtension

The Property Expressions Editor should look more or less like Figure 13-9.

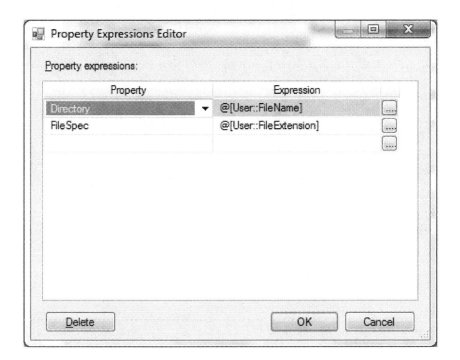

Figure 13-9. *The property expressions editor used to get the folder and extension from SSIS variables*

18. Click OK to close the dialog box. The Foreach Loop Editor should look like Figure 13-10.

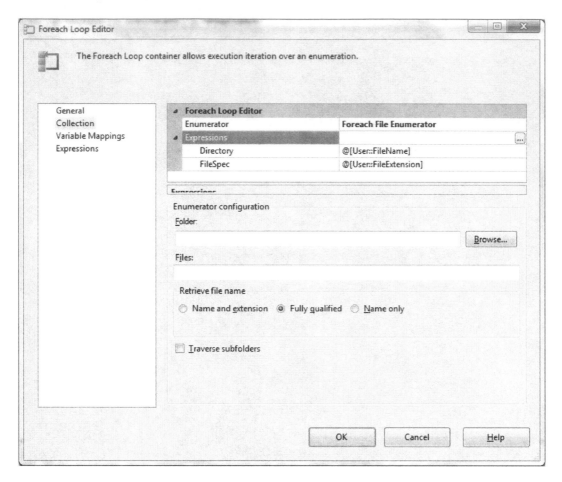

Figure 13-10. *Using expressions in a Foreach task*

19. Click OK to close the dialog box.

20. Add a Data Flow task (again as in Recipe 13-1) and configure it to load from Flat File source (C:\SQL2012DIRecipes\CH13\MultipleFlatFiles\Stock01.Csv) into the CarSales.dbo.Stock destination table, as described in Recipe 13-1, step 13. The SSIS package Control Flow pane should look like Figure 13-11.

Figure 13-11. *The complete package for multiple file loads from multiple directories*

You can now run the package and load all the .Txt and .Csv files from the
C:\SQL2012DIRecipes\CH13\MultipleFlatFiles and C:\SQL2012DIRecipes\CH13\MoreMultipleFlatFiles
directories.

How It Works

SSIS can load all the files in a directory "out of the box." Nine times out of ten, this will solve all of your
file-loading needs. For simple selection of multiple files, you also have the Multiple Flat Files Connection
manager, described in Recipe 13-2. However, there could well be other cases where the source files are in *several
different directories* (possibly on different servers); or have *different file extensions* (for instance, text files,
but from processes or people who name them either .CSV or .TXT) or certain specific types of file names, but
not others, and where multiple file filters are needed to ensure that you are only including the files that you can
handle.

Fortunately, multiple source files can be handled with a little tweaking and minimal effort in SSIS. In this
recipe, I suggest using arrays as the repository for hard-coded lists of items such as directory names and file
extension names. It is here that the interesting part of this approach lies. After this, it is simply a question of
nesting the file load loop inside two other loops—one to cycle through the file paths, and the other to cycle
through the file filter criteria. While this may seem complicated, it is a simple way of extending the multiple file
load technique to handle a multitude of possible requirements. Indeed, I would suggest the approach described
here as a basis for most complex file selection processes.

I created and used several SSIS variables to allow SSIS to iterate over a set of folders and file extensions. First,
you must have two string variables: one to hold the directory (that SSIS calls a "folder") name and another to hold

the file extension name. You will also need a string variable to hold the file name of the actual file that is being loaded. Finally, you will need two object variables: one to hold the list of directory names and another to contain the list of file extensions.

There are only a couple of things to note about the script code. First, you are using standard .NET arrays, and populating them using .Add. Second, once the arrays are created, you need to pass them to SSIS variables so that they can be used outside the Script task. While it is not strictly necessary to cast them as objects, I feel that it is better practice to remind oneself—in code—what is actually happening.

■ **Note**   The one fundamental common point to the files that you want to load is that they *must* have the same format. If the source files do not have identical structures, then you will have to set up a source and destination component pair for each type of source file format.

Hints, Tips, and Traps

- Inevitably, there are many ways of loading files from multiple folders and where there are several possible file extensions. Indeed, there are probably as many approaches as there are coders. So tweak and test until you find a solution that you are happy with. Purists may object to hard-coding values in a Script component, for instance. A more flexible approach (but one that is a little more work) is to have a tab-delimited reference file (database table or XML file) of folders and file extensions. This reference file or table is then loaded into an SSIS object (recordset), and a single Foreach Loop container can then read through the elements, assign them to the folder, and filter variables at the same time. Such an approach also removes the need for nested loops. Anyway, you choose and adapt the method that you feel happiest with.

- As you have set variables for the path and file filter, you will see a warning for the Load Files task. This is nothing to worry about.

- Remember to use a UNC (Universal Naming Convention) path for server and directory names, to ensure portability.

- One thing that can be disconcerting is that you can access SSIS expressions in two ways for the Foreach Loop container—and each way gives a different set of variables. To use variables for the file path and file filter, you need to use the variables in the Collection pane of the Foreach Loop Editor dialog box—and not the Expressions pane that you select by clicking Expressions on the left of the dialog box.

- This recipe's approach ends up with a similar result to the MULTIFLATFILE connection manager explained in Recipe 12-2. However, the current recipe's approach is infinitely more supple and extensible.

13-4. Ordering and Filtering File Loads
Problem

You need to select a specific set of files and load them in a defined order based on their properties.

Solution

Use ADO.NET datasets and SSIS script tasks.

In this example, I will presume that you have a directory of flat files in CSV format that need loading into SQL Server, and that it is important to load the oldest files first. The follow steps explain the way to do this.

1. Open SSIS and create a new package. I suggest naming it **OrderAndFilterFileLoad**, as that is what it will do.

2. Add the following variables at package level:

Variable Name	Type	Value	Comments
ADOFilteredAndSortedTable	Object		The SSIS object that holds the result list of sorted files.
FileName	String		The variable used by the Foreach Loop container that loads the files (in the correct, sorted order).
FileFilter	String		The variable used to hold the file name to obtain file system attributes for source files, which can be used to order the final list.
SortColumn	String		The column that acts as a sort key.
FileSource	String		The source directory.
ADOTable	Object		The SSIS object that holds the initial unsorted list of files.

3. Add a Script task on to the Control Flow pane. Name it **PopulateRecordset** and double-click to edit. Add the following read/write variables:

    ADOFilteredAndSortedTable

    ADOTable

4. Click the Edit Script button.

5. In the SSIS Script window, add the following directive in the Imports region:

    `Imports System.IO`

6. Replace the `Main` method with the following code. This script is explained at the end of the recipe (`C:\SQL2012DIRecipes\CH13\OrderedFilteredFileLoad.Vb`):

```
Public Sub Main()

    'Declare all variables

    Dim FileSource As String = Dts.Variables("FileSource").Value.ToString
    Dim FileFilter As String = Dts.Variables("FileFilter").Value.ToString
    Dim SortColumn As String = Dts.Variables("SortColumn").Value.ToString
```

```vbnet
Dim MainDS As New System.Data.DataSet
Dim MainTable As New System.Data.DataTable
Dim MainRow As System.Data.DataRow
Dim MainCol As New System.Data.DataColumn

Dim dirInfo As New System.IO.DirectoryInfo(FileSource)
Dim fileSystemInfo As System.IO.FileSystemInfo
Dim FileCounter As Int16 = 0
Dim FileName As String
Dim FileFullName As String
Dim FileSize As Long
Dim FileExtension As String
Dim CreationTime As Date
Dim DirectoryName As String
Dim LastWriteTime As Date

' Define table structure

MainDS.Tables.Add(MainTable)
MainTable.Columns.Add("FileName", System.Type.GetType("System.String"))        ' 0
MainTable.Columns.Add("DateAdded", System.Type.GetType("System.DateTime"))      ' 1
MainTable.Columns.Add("DateLoaded", System.Type.GetType("System.DateTime"))     ' 2
MainTable.Columns.Add("FileSize", System.Type.GetType("System.Int32"))          ' 3
MainTable.Columns.Add("CreationTime", System.Type.GetType("System.DateTime"))   ' 4
MainTable.Columns.Add("FileExtension", System.Type.GetType("System.String"))    ' 5
MainTable.Columns.Add("DirectoryName", System.Type.GetType("System.String"))    ' 6
MainTable.Columns.Add("LastWriteTime", System.Type.GetType("System.DateTime"))  ' 7

' Loop through directory, and add records to the ADO table

For Each fileSystemInfo In dirInfo.GetFileSystemInfos(FileFilter)

    FileName = fileSystemInfo.Name
    FileFullName = fileSystemInfo.FullName

    Dim fileDetail As New FileInfo(FileFullName)

    FileSize = fileDetail.Length
    CreationTime = fileDetail.CreationTime
    FileExtension = fileDetail.Extension
    DirectoryName = fileDetail.DirectoryName
    LastWriteTime = fileDetail.LastWriteTime

    MainRow = MainTable.NewRow()

    MainRow(0) = FileName
    MainRow(1) = Now()
    MainRow(2) = CDate("01-01-1900")
    MainRow(3) = FileSize
    MainRow(4) = CreationTime
```

```
        MainRow(5) = FileExtension
        MainRow(6) = DirectoryName
        MainRow(7) = LastWriteTime

        MainTable.Rows.Add(MainRow)

        FileCounter = CShort(FileCounter + 1)

    Next

    ' Create ADOLoopTable - used for the actual batch loop

    Dim SortedFilteredDS As System.Data.DataSet = MainDS.Clone
    Dim SortedFilteredRows As DataRow() = ↵
        MainDS.Tables(0).[Select]("FileSize > 1", & SortColumn & " ASC")
    Dim SortedFilteredTable As DataTable = SortedFilteredDS.Tables(0)

    For Each ClonedFilteredRow As DataRow In SortedFilteredRows
        SortedFilteredTable.ImportRow(ClonedFilteredRow)
    Next

    ' Convert the tables into SSIS objects:

    Dts.Variables("ADOFilteredAndSortedTable").Value = CType(SortedFilteredDS, Object)

    Dts.TaskResult = ScriptResults.Success

End Sub
```

7. Close the SSIS Script window and click OK to close the Script task editor.

8. Add a Foreach Loop container on to the Control Flow pane and name it **Load Files**. Connect the Populate Recordset script task to this and double-click to edit the Foreach Loop container.

9. Select Collection on the left, and choose For Each ADO Enumerator as the enumerator type. The resulting dialog box should look like Figure 13-12.

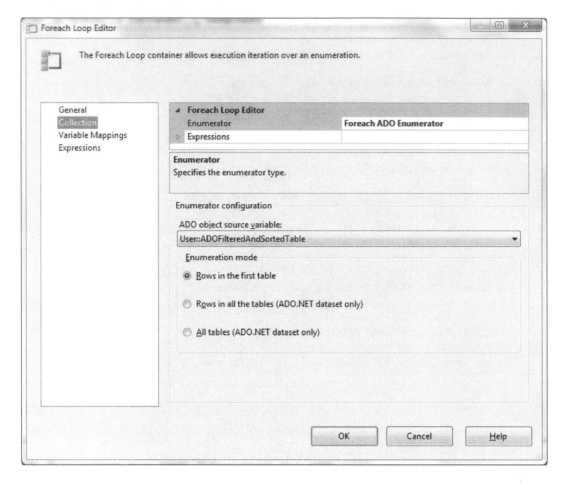

Figure 13-12. *Looping over an ADO.NET object*

10. Select Variable Mappings on the left. Select User::FileName as the variable to use.

11. Click OK.

12. Add a Data Flow task into the Foreach Loop container, and configure it just as you did for Recipe 12-1 (not forgetting to set the Flat File connection manager connection string as an expression). The final package should look like Figure 13-13.

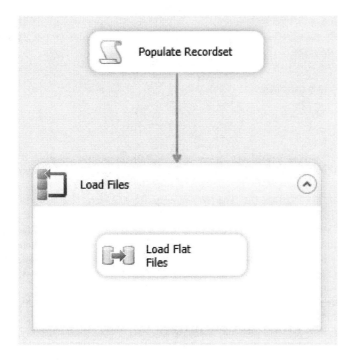

Figure 13-13. *The completed package to filter and sort file loads*

You can now run the package. However, before running this package, remember to add the actual data for the Directory to be processed, the file filter, and the sort column in the Variables window. In this case, it would be as follows.

FileSource: C:\SQL2012DIRecipes\CH13\MultipleFlatFiles

FileFilter: Stock*.Csv

SortColumn: CreationTime

Alternatively, if you are running the package from the command line, an SQL Server agent job, or the SSIS catalog, then remember to add the references to the variables as appropriate.

How It Works

There will be many occasions where you are required to load data from files in a directory. These files could be flat file data (comma separated files, for instance), XML files or even Image files.

Now, loading all the files in a directory is a standard technique, and was explained previously in Recipe 12-1. However, as many commentators have noted, the standard Foreach Loop container does not allow you to do anything other than specify the file name and extension patterns, and nothing more. There are occasions when you might need to specify the load order or filter the files in a directory based on the properties that they expose to the file system, such as creation date or file size, among others.

Although there are several ways of ordering and filtering the source files (whatever type of data they contain), I prefer to use SSIS and the Script task for this. Such an approach relies on ADO.NET datasets to perform sorting and filtering. This method is both resilient and easy to maintain. It will require creating and using two .NET datasets. One holds the names and attributes of the files in the directory you are using to store the files to be loaded. A clone of this .NET dataset is then created—the clone that is filtered and sorted. This cloned dataset is used to iterate through the files to load.

To make this process a little more flexible, I am suggesting passing in as variables:

- The **name** of the directory to be processed.

- The file **filter**.

- The **sort** column.

Passing these items is, of course, not strictly necessary, but it makes the package more easily reusable. You also need a string variable to hold the file name of the actual file that is being loaded and an object variable to hold the sorted datatable.

Following is how the script code works: To make the script more dynamic, two variables are declared and their contents passed in from SSIS variables. These (FileSource and FileFilter) will pass in the directory to be parsed, and the file filter to be applied. Variables are declared to hold all the required attributes of the files. Of course, if you are only sorting and/or filtering on one or two attributes, then you need only use the corresponding variables to make the code easier to maintain. Initially a Main dataset is created. This in turn holds the Main table, which will be populated with the list of files from the selected directory. The Main table is defined, with columns for each file attribute that you are likely to use. The next part of the script loops through the directory (passed in as a variable), gets the file name, and attributes according to the file filter (passed in as a variable). Each attribute is passed to the corresponding script variable. A new row in the table is added, and each column is populated with the attribute from the script variable. As it is not possible to sort or filter an ADO dataset directly, a cloned datatable is created (SortedFilteredDS), which is sorted and/or filtered, using the pseudo-code:

```
[Select]("Selection criteria as text", "Sort Column as text ASC/DESC")
```

Each source row from the Main table is copied into the cloned SortedFilteredTable table. The cloned datatable is passed out as an SSIS variable that will be used in the Foreach Loop task. I have added a file counter that you can pass out of the SSIS task if you wish for auditing and logging.

Hints, Tips, and Traps

- Remember to use a UNC path for server and directory names, to ensure portability.

- You do not need to refer to the columns in the datatable by their zero-based index (as I did in the code for this recipe). You can use the column name, for example:

```
MainRow("FileName") = FileName
```

- The variable names that you choose do not have to be identical to the column names—I merely find this simpler to both code and debug.

- When (or indeed if) sorting—as this is not compulsory—remember to use the column name that you defined as part of the ADO.NET table to sort on.

- Passing in the sort column as a variable means that you have to be careful about the quoted strings. If you are hard-coding the sort column, then merely entering **FileSize ASC** (to sort by the FileSize column in the ado.NET datatable) will suffice.

- The filter criteria can be more complex, and can include multiple columns and standard comparison operators. A more complex example could be:

```
"FileSize > 10000 AND LastWriteTime <= '2010-12-25'"
```

- Note that all text strings used in the filter criteria must be in single quotes, and that there are several possible date formats. I prefer to use YYYY-MM-DD.

- If you want to sort without filtering, then you need to apply some cunning. The .NET Select method requires a filter before you can sort; that is, there is not an overload that allows you merely to enter the sort argument. So a good way to cheat is to use code as in the following:

```
[Select]("FileSize >= 1", "CreationTime ASC")
```

This filters on all files of one byte or more (which means all files of any use in most circumstances), but it sorts by file creation date.

- If you are using SSIS 2005 or 2008, you need to add a reference to System.Xml in the Imports directive.

13-5. Loading Multiple Flat Files in Parallel
Problem

You want to load data from identically-structured multiple flat files, from a single directory, faster than you could by loading the files in strict sequence.

Solution

Load the data in parallel, as follows.

1. Create a table in SQL Server to hold the file names using the following DDL (C:\SQL2012DIRecipes\CH13\tblSimpleParallelLoad.Sql):

```
CREATE TABLE CarSales_Staging.dbo.SimpleParallelLoad
(
 ID INT IDENTITY(1,1) NOT NULL,
 FileName VARCHAR (250) NULL,
 ProcessNumber  AS (ID%(4))
) ;
GO
```

2. Create a table in SQL Server to hold the data, once loaded, using the following DDL (C:\SQL2012DIRecipes\CH13\tblParallelStock.Sql):

```
CREATE TABLE CarSales_Staging.dbo.ParallelStock
(
 ID bigint IDENTITY(1,1) NOT NULL,
 Make VARCHAR (50) NULL,
 Marque NVARCHAR(50) NULL,
 Model VARCHAR (50) NULL,
 Colour TINYINT NULL,
 Product_Type VARCHAR (50) NULL,
 Vehicle_Type VARCHAR (20) NULL,
 Cost_Price NUMERIC(18, 2) NULL
)
```

3. Enter the list of source files into the table (SimpleParallelLoad) that you created in step 1. The DDL for this—in the current recipe—is (C:\SQL2012DIRecipes\CH13\ PrepSimpleParallelLoad.Sql):

```
USE CarSales_Staging
GO
SET IDENTITY_INSERT dbo.SimpleParallelLoad ON
GO
INSERT dbo.SimpleParallelLoad (ID, FileName)
VALUES (1, N'C:\SQL2012DIRecipes\CH13\MultipleFlatFiles\Stock01.Csv')
GO
INSERT dbo.SimpleParallelLoad (ID, FileName)
VALUES (2, N'C:\SQL2012DIRecipes\CH13\MultipleFlatFiles\Stock02.Csv')
GO
INSERT dbo.SimpleParallelLoad (ID, FileName)
VALUES (3, N'C:\SQL2012DIRecipes\CH13\MultipleFlatFiles\Stock03.Csv')
GO
INSERT dbo.SimpleParallelLoad (ID, FileName)
VALUES (4, N'C:\SQL2012DIRecipes\CH13\MultipleFlatFiles\Stock04.Csv')
GO
SET IDENTITY_INSERT dbo.SimpleParallelLoad OFF
GO
```

4. Create a new SSIS package and name it **SimpleParallelProcessing**. Add two connection managers—one OLEDB, the other ADO.NET—that connect to the database you will use to load the data and metadata (CarSales_Staging in this example). I will name them **CarSales_Staging_OLEDB** and **CarSales_Staging_ADONET**, respectively.

5. Add the following variables at the task level, as well as the initial values given:

Variable Name	Type	Value	Comments
CreateList	Boolean	String	A flag indicating that the list is to be deleted and re-created.
FileFilter	String	*.CSV	Allows you to specify the file extension to use.
FileSource	String	C:\SQL2012DIRecipes\CH13	Allows you to specify the file directory to use.

Of course, you should use your own file filter and source directory if you are not following this example exactly.

6. Add a Sequence container onto the Data Flow pane, and name it **Create table of files to process**.

7. Add an Execute SQL task into the Sequence container, and name it **Prepare Table**.
   Double-click to edit. Set the following elements:

   Connection Type: OLEDB

   Connection: CarSales_Staging_OLEDB

   SQL Statement: TRUNCATE TABLE dbo.SimpleParallelLoad

   The Execute SQL Task Editor dialog box should look like it does in Figure 13-14.

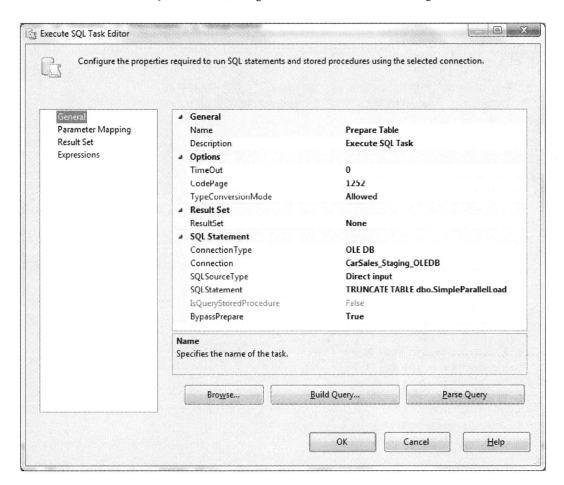

Figure 13-14. *Execute SQL task to truncate tables*

8. Click OK to confirm.

9. Add a Script component into the Sequence container under the Execute SQL task that
   you just created. Name it **Loop Through Files and Write to table** and connect the
   Execute SQL task Prepare Table to it.

10. Double-click to edit, set the Script Language to Microsoft Visual Basic 2010 and add the following read-only variables:

    User::FileFilter
    User::FileSource

11. Click Edit Script.

12. Replace the Main method with the following (C:\SQL2012DIRecipes\CH13\ SimpleParallelLoad.Vb):

```vb
Public Sub Main()

        Dim sqlConn As SqlConnection
        Dim sqlCommand As SqlCommand

        sqlConn = DirectCast(Dts.Connections("CarSales_Staging_ADONET"). ↩
                        AcquireConnection(Dts.Transaction), SqlConnection)

        Dim FileSource As String = Dts.Variables("FileSource").Value.ToString
        Dim FileFilter As String = Dts.Variables("FileFilter").Value.ToString
        Dim dirInfo As New System.IO.DirectoryInfo(FileSource)
        Dim fileSystemInfo As System.IO.FileSystemInfo
        Dim FileName As String

        Dim sqlText As String

        For Each fileSystemInfo In dirInfo.GetFileSystemInfos(FileFilter)

            FileName = fileSystemInfo.Name

            sqlText = "INSERT INTO dbo.SimpleParallelLoad (FileName) VALUES('" & FileName & "')"

            sqlCommand = New SqlCommand(sqlText, sqlConn)
            sqlCommand.CommandType = CommandType.Text
            sqlCommand.ExecuteNonQuery()

        Next

        Dts.TaskResult = ScriptResults.Success

End Sub
```

13. Close the SSIS Script task window and click OK to confirm your modifications to the Script component.

14. Add a Script Component into the Sequence container under the Script task that you just created. Name it **Reset variable** and connect the "Loop Through Files and Write to table" Script component to it. Double-click to edit this second Script component, and add the CreateList read/write variable.

15. Click Edit Script and replace the Main method with the following:

```
Public Sub Main()

        Dts.Variables("CreateList").Value = False

        Dts.TaskResult = ScriptResults.Success

End Sub
```

16. Close the SSIS Script Task window and click OK to confirm your modifications. The first part of the package is now complete, and this will (re-)create the list of files to process, as required. The SSIS package should look like Figure 13-15.

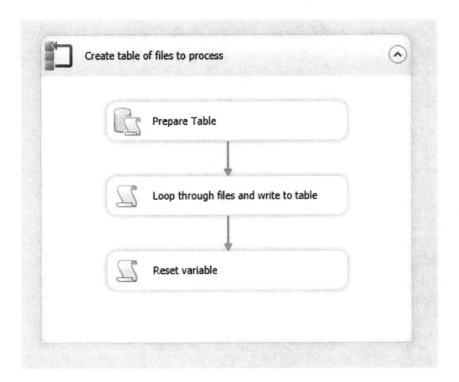

Figure 13-15. *The initial section of the parallel load package*

17. Now to move on to the actual parallel processing. Add the following variables at package level:

Variable Name	Type	Value	Comments
Batch_0	Object		The first of the four batches.
Batch_1	Object		The second of the four batches.
Batch_2	Object		The third of the four batches.

(continued)

Variable Name	Type	Value	Comments
Batch_3	Object		The fourth of the four batches.
FileName_Batch_0	String		The name of the file that will be loaded by batch one.
FileName_Batch_1	String		The name of the file that will be loaded by batch two.
FileName_Batch_2	String		The name of the file that will be loaded by batch three.
FileName_Batch_3	String		The name of the file that will be loaded by batch four.

18. Add an Execute SQL task under the Sequence container, connect the latter to the new task, and rename it **Prepare destination table**. Double-click to edit. Set the following elements:

Connection Type: OLEDB

Connection: CarSales_Staging_OLEDB

SQL Statement: `TRUNCATE TABLE dbo.ParallelStock`

19. Click OK to confirm.

20. Add a new Flat File connection manager, name it **Process0**, and configure it to connect to any of the source files. In the properties for this connection manager, set the expression for its ConnectionString to be @[User::FileName_Batch_0] (as explained in Recipe 13-1, steps 14 to 20).

21. Add an Execute SQL task under the "Prepare destination table" task, connect the latter to the new task, and rename it **Get Batch 0**. Double-click to edit. Set the following elements:

Connection Type: ADO.NET

Connection: CarSales_Staging_ADONET

SQL Statement:
```
SELECT    FileName
FROM      dbo.SimpleParallelLoad
          WITH (NOLOCK)
WHERE     ProcessNumber = 0
```

22. Click OK to confirm.

23. Add a Process Loop container under the "Prepare destination table" task, connect the latter to the new task, and rename it Load all files in Batch 0. Double-click to edit. Set the following elements :

Enumerator: Foreach ADO Enumerator

ADO Object Source Variable: Batch_0

Variable: FileName_Batch_0

24. Click OK to confirm.

25. Add a Data Flow task inside the Foreach Loop container, and configure it to connect the Flat File connection manager Process0 to the destination table (ParallelStock) using the CarSales_Staging_OLEDB connection manager. Ensure that Tablock is checked.

26. Repeat steps 22 through 24 three times (once for each additional parallel load). Be sure to name the Flat File connection managers **Process1**, **Process2**, and **Process3**. Name the Process Loop containers **Load all files in Batch 1**, **Load all files in Batch 2**, and **Load all files in Batch 3**. The final package should look like Figure 13-16.

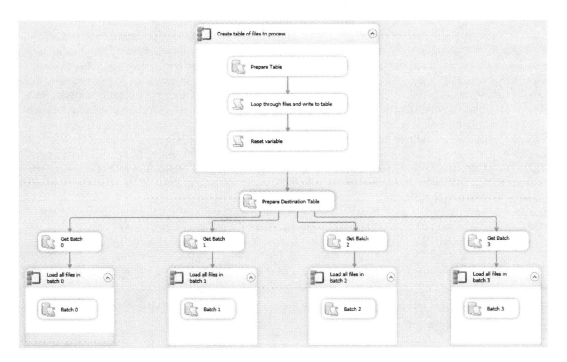

Figure 13-16. *The complete parallel load package*

You can now run the package.

How It Works

This recipe is based on the scenario where you receive many flat files, all having the same format, and all need to be loaded into the same table. Clearly you can process them sequentially, as was shown in previous recipes, but parallel processing should prove to be faster in most cases. The speed gain is generally worth the extra effort required to create a more complex SSIS package.

In this recipe, we perform the load operation in two distinct parts:

- First, cycle through the files in a directory and store the file paths in an SQL Server table.

- Second, load the files using this table as the source of the file names, where each separate file load tasks iterates through the files it has been allocated independently of the other files that will be loaded.

It is important to separate out the two parts, and first to attribute process numbers to the source files so that each branch of the process flow only loads its own set of files, as each process is separate from every other process. You can think of it as giving "flags" to each file to tell it which path to follow.

You can use an ADO.NET recordset as part of this technique, as was described previously in the Recipe 13-4, but I prefer to introduce another method which is to use a persisted database table. This seems preferable because using a table allows you to store the list on disk, and can provide a basis for logging and batch processing, as will be described in Recipe 13-12.

We have to be clear about exactly what this package will achieve. It will simply divide all the source files into batches (here I will use four, each one of which will be a separate parallel process) and process them all. It will not attempt to perform any load balancing or process ordering. This approach therefore works well when all the files are much the same size, and you are not looking for optimal sequencing. It is, however, alluring in its simplicity—both conceptually and practically. The technique used to define which file is attributed to which process is to use an SQL Server Identity column, and then apply "% 4" to create the numbers 0 to 3 (the remainder when the modulo operator is applied) as a separate ProcessNumber column to each file in turn. In this example, the process thread attribution is defined as a calculated column, to avoid extra steps. The table of file names and batch numbers is then used as the source list for the parallel load. Of course, you do not need to use four parallel processes—you can use more or less. Just how many processes are required for an optimal data load could require considerable testing on your part in a configuration identical to your production environment.

By way of extending the functionality, I will add a tweak to reuse—or truncate—the list of files to process, which will allow reprocessing a defined list of files, if the source data changes. This is what the `CreateList` variable is used for. When the package is loaded, this variable is set to True, so the initial list is truncated in the `SimpleParallelLoad` SQL Server table, then repopulated. After the table is populated, the variable is set to False, so the table is persisted, unless you need to re-create it. This allows you to pass in the variable from the command line or from an SQL Server Agent job, and control re-processing.

If this process seems rather complex, then I suggest that you take a good look at the screen capture of the whole job that you will find in Figure 13-16. This will hopefully make things somewhat clearer.

■ **Note**   It is essential to check the Tablock check box in the OLEDB destination task, as this will allow parallel bulk loads to take place. Failing to do this will slow down the load considerably. Generally, the destination database must not be in FULL recovery mode for efficient parallel loads. Also, there should not be any nonlustered indexes in place. This is discussed in greater depth in Recipe 14-10.

Hints, Tips, and Traps

- Always test the time taken to perform parallel processing, and never presume that it will automatically be faster. Test, test, and re-test!

- The Sequence container that contains the tasks to isolate the list of files to process is not strictly necessary, but it helps to visually isolate this initial part of the process.

- You can use a stored procedure rather than SQL text in the Script task. Although this is slightly more complex, it is considered better coding practice. In this case, use `sqlCommand.CommandType = CommandType.StoredProcedure`, add the name of the stored procedure as the `SqlCommand`, and define any parameters in the Parameters pane.

- For simplicity's sake, in this recipe I have placed the `SimpleParallelLoad` control table in the same database as the one in which the data is loaded. In a production environment, you might want to place it in a separate logging and monitoring database.

- What is the optimal number of parallel load tasks? This is a good question, and one that necessitates judicious use of the hallowed answer, "It depends." Generally, "no more than there are free processor cores, and not so many that you are choking the I/O subsystem," is a more accurate answer. So once again, it is best to test and measure on a test system that is identical to your production environment before attempting a production run.

13-6. Loading Source Files with Load Balancing

Problem

You want to load multiple identically-structured files in parallel using the available processors to optimum effect.

Solution

Load the files in parallel using load balancing. Now I'll show you how to carry out to a multiple parallel file load while optimizing time by balancing the load across the available processor cores:

1. Create a table to log the files once they have been loaded. The code to create this is (C:\SQL2012DIRecipes\CH13\tblBulkFilesLoaded.Sql):

```
CREATE TABLE CarSales_Staging.dbo.BulkFilesLoaded
(
 ID int IDENTITY(1,1) NOT NULL,
 DateAdded DATETIME NULL DEFAULT GETDATE(),
 FileName NVARCHAR(250) NULL,
 Source TINYINT NULL
) ;
GO
```

2. Create a new SSIS task. Add an OLEDB connection manager to the destination database (CarSales_Staging in this example) named **CarSales_Staging_OLEDB**. Create an ADO.NET connection manager to the CarSales_Staging database named **CarSales_Staging_ADONET**. This will be used to write to the BulkFilesLoaded table.

3. Add the following variables:

Variable Name	Type	Value	Comments
FilePath	String	C:\SQL2012DIRecipes\CH13\ MultipleFlatFiles	The path to the source files.
FileType	String	.CSV	The source file extension.
MaxFiles	Int32	1000	The maximum possible number of files to process.
RecordSet	Object		The ADO recordset that holds the list of files to process.
Counter0	Int32		The lowest counter value corresponding to the processor affinity of available processors.

(continued)

Variable Name	Type	Value	Comments
FileName0	String		The file name variable mapping to the lowest processor affinity.
...			
Counter'n'			The highest counter value corresponding to the highest processor affinity.
FileName'n'			The file name variable mapping to the highest processor affinity.

4. Add an Execute SQL task named **Prepare Log Table**, and double-click to edit. Configure as follows:

Connection Type: ADO.NET

Connection: CarSales_Staging_ADONET

SQL Statement: `TRUNCATE TABLE dbo.BulkFilesLoaded`

5. Add a Script task and connect the previous task to it. Set the following variables as read/write: User::FilePath, User::FileType, User::MaxFiles, User::RecordSet.

6. Set the script language to Microsoft Visual C# 2010, and click Edit Script.

7. Add the following references to the namespaces region:

```
using System.IO;
```

8. Replace the `Main` method with the following code (`C:\SQL2012DIRecipes\CH13\LoadBalancing1.cs`):

```
public void Main()
    {

        // Create dataset to hold file names
        DataSet ds = new DataSet("ds");
        DataTable dt = ds.Tables.Add("FileList");

        DataColumn IndexID = new DataColumn("IndexID", typeof(System.Int32));
        dt.Columns.Add(IndexID);
        DataColumn FileName = new DataColumn("FileName", typeof(string));
        dt.Columns.Add(FileName);
        DataColumn IsProcessed = new DataColumn("IsProcessed", typeof(Boolean));
        dt.Columns.Add(IsProcessed);


        // create primary key on IndexID field
        IndexID.Unique = true;
        DataColumn[] pK = new DataColumn[1];
```

```
        pK[0] = IndexID;
        dt.PrimaryKey = pK;

        DirectoryInfo di = new DirectoryInfo(Dts.Variables["FilePath"].Value.ToString());
        FileInfo[] filesToLoad = di.GetFiles(Dts.Variables["FileType"].Value.ToString());

        DataRow rw = null;

        Int32 MaxFiles = 0;

        foreach (FileInfo fi in filesToLoad)
        {
            rw = dt.NewRow();
            rw["IndexID"] = MaxFiles + 1;
            rw["FileName"] = fi.Name;
            rw["IsProcessed"] = 0;
            dt.Rows.Add(rw);
            MaxFiles += 1;
        }

        Dts.Variables["User::MaxFiles"].Value = MaxFiles;

        Dts.Variables["User::RecordSet"].Value = dt;

        Dts.TaskResult = (int)ScriptResults.Success;
    }
```

9. Close the Script window. Confirm your changes to the Script task with OK.

10. Add a For Loop container to the Control Flow pane and connect the Script task to it.
    Name it **Container 0**. Double-click to edit and set the For Loop properties as follows:

    InitExpression: @Counter0 = 0

    EvalExpression: @Counter0 <= @MaxFiles

    AssignExpression: @Counter0 = @Counter0 + 1

11. Add a Script component inside the For Loop container, name it **Get next available file
    name**, and set the following variables as read/write: User::FileName0,User::Counter0.

12. Set the Script language as Microsoft Visual C# 2010, and click Edit Script.

13. Add the following references to the namespaces region:

    ```
    using System.Data.OleDb;
    using System.Xml;
    using System.Threading;
    ```

14. Set the Main method as follows:

```
public void Main()
    {

        DataTable dT = new DataTable();
        DataRow[] matchingRows;
        String fileName = "";
        Variables vars = null;
        Variables varsMax = null;

        PollLabel:

        try
        {

            Dts.VariableDispenser.LockOneForWrite("User::RecordSet", ref vars);

            dT = (DataTable)vars[0].Value;

            matchingRows = dT.Select("IsProcessed  = 0", "IndexID ASC");

            int numberOfRows = matchingRows.GetLength(0);

            if (numberOfRows != 0)
            {
                fileName = matchingRows[0][1].ToString();
                matchingRows[0]["IsProcessed"] = true;

                Dts.Variables["FileName0"].Value = fileName;
                vars[0].Value = dT;
            }
            else
            {
                Dts.VariableDispenser.LockOneForRead("User::MaxFiles", ref varsMax);
                Dts.Variables["Counter0"].Value = varsMax[0].Value;
            }

            vars.Unlock();
        }

        catch
        {
            System.Random RandomNumber = new System.Random();
            Thread.Sleep(RandomNumber.Next(200, 800));
            goto PollLabel;
        }
        Dts.TaskResult = (int)ScriptResults.Success;
    }
```

15. Add a Data Flow task in the Foreach Loop container, and connect the Script component to it. Double-click the precedence constraint (the green arrow), and set the constraint options as follows:

Evaluation Operation:	Expression and Constraint
Value:	Success
Expression:	@Counter0 != @MaxFiles
Logical And:	All constraints must evaluate to True

16. Confirm your modifications with OK, and configure the actual file load using the Data Flow task. I will not describe this here, as it has been covered exhaustively in other recipes, particularly in Recipe 13-1.

17. Add an Execute SQL task in the Foreach Loop container, and connect the Data Flow task to it. Configure as follows:

Connection Type:	ADO.NET
Connection:	CarSales_Staging_ADONET
SQL Statement:	INSERT INTO dbo.BulkFilesLoaded
	(Filename, Source)
	VALUES (@FileName0, 0)

18. Click ParameterMapping on the left, and add the following parameter:

Variable Name	Direction	Data Type	Parameter Name
User::FileName0	Input	String	@FileName0

19. Confirm your modifications with OK.

20. Repeat steps 10 through 19 for each parallel load that you wish to add. You will have to alter every reference to FileName0 to become FileName'n' (the number of the process). Do the same for Counter0. Remember that this means not just in the script code, but also variable names and the variables used in the For Loop parameters in step 10 and in the precedence constraint in step 15. Your package should look like that in Figure 13-17.

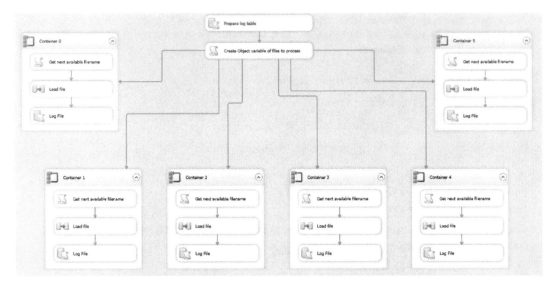

Figure 13-17. *The process flow for the load balancing package*

How It Works

The previous recipe loaded multiple sets of files in parallel, but it made no attempt to balance the load process. It presumed that all the files are of roughly similar sizes, and that all the processing cores to which they are assigned are able to work to their full potential, without being required to switch to other processes—and consequently slow down the file load.

While such an approach can solve many load requirements, there will inevitably be cases where you will need to implement an approach that can balance the load. This means that each processing core will be able to take the next file to process when it becomes available, without pre-assigning files to a specific SSIS path—and consequently pre-assigning them to a processor or core.

Balancing a load across the available processors (or processing cores) is somewhat more complex, but it has the advantage of processing all source files as fast as the hardware will allow. Indeed, the only tricky part of this process is to isolate the list of files to load, and then to ensure that (a) there are no conflicts when file names are taken from the list, (b) that no file is loaded twice, and (c) that there are no deadlocks when file names in the list are updated as having been loaded. My preferred solution to this problem is to use an ADO DataTable to hold the list of files, and to let SSIS handle this as an object variable. The fact that this is in memory is as near a guarantee as you can get that there will not be simultaneous read/write access to the list of files (and consequently locking issues)—as can be the case if you store it in an SQL Server table.

As with most approaches to parallel processing, I advise you only to set up a load path when there is an available processor core. In this recipe, therefore, when defining the variables to use, you should set up eight Counter variables and eight Filename variables, numbered 0 through 7 if your server has eight cores that SSIS can use for the process.

Oh, and just for once, I have scripted this one in C#. I am conscious of the fact that many SQL Server developers seem to tend toward using VB.NET, but do not want to exclude those who prefer C#. After all, it has been around for scripting in SSIS since SQL Server 2008 appeared.

The code works like this:

First, as far as the "Create object variable of files to process" Script task is concerned. This task does two things:

- First, it creates a dataset and datatable to hold the list of files to process.

- Second, it populates this datatable with the names of the files to process.

This first half of the code creates a dataset, and then creates a datatable containing the required columns (IndexID, FileName, IsProcessed). Then, using the file path and extension, it loops through the names of all the requisite files in the source directory and adds them to the FileName column of the datatable. Finally, the datatable is passed out to the RecordSet SSIS variable.

The Script component inside the Foreach loop (which is duplicated for every parallel load) reads the datatable from the RecordSet SSIS object variable. To do this it first locks the variable—very briefly—and filters the datatable to return only files that have not been processed. It then takes the first available file name, sets the IsProcessed flag to True and unlocks the variable. There is also a simple conflict-detection process that causes the process to sleep for a random number of milliseconds should the variable be locked by another of the load processes. It is worth noting that the datatable has to be converted from the SSIS object variable to be used when it is passed into the Script component—but not to when it is returned back to the SSIS object variable.

Hints, Tips, and Traps

- It is possible to use an SQL Server table to store the list of files to load, and to update each one once it has been loaded, but handling read/write conflicts—and ensuring that no table is loaded twice—can be a little tricky, in my experience. Using an in-memory object allows for such read and write speeds that conflict can be avoided. At least this has been the case in the systems in which I have used this particular approach.

- It is important to use the LockOneForWrite approach with certain variables in the scripts. This is because if you lock certain variables that require frequent virtually simultaneous access at the script level (using read/write variables) you will inevitably cause contention at some point during package execution, and this will cause the whole package to fail.

- The MaxFiles variable is used as a safeguard to prevent infinite loops when processing files from the in-memory dataset. If there are no available files in the datatable, the process iterates until the maximum number of files is reached.

13-7. Loading Data to Parallel Destinations

Problem

You want to quickly load data from a single source table on a multiprocessor server.

Solution

Read the data from the source table then split the source into two separate data flows. Use parallel destination loading to accelerate the load part of the process. To load an SQL Server table using parallel loading:

1. Create a new SSIS package, and name it **SingleSourceParallelProcessing**. Add two connection managers, both OLEDB. The first will connect to the source database that you will be using to load the data from (CarSales in this example). The second will connect to the destination database (CarSales_Staging, here). I will name them **CarSales _OLEDB** and **CarSales_Staging_OLEDB**, respectively.

2. Add a Data Flow task onto the Control Flow pane. Name it **Parallel Table Import**. Double-click to edit.

3. Add an OLEDB source task that you name **Stock**. Double-click to edit and set the OLEDB connection manager to CarSales _OLEDB. Set the data access mode as SQL Command, and enter or build the following query (C:\SQL2012DIRecipes\CH13\StockToParallel.Sql):

```
SELECT
ID
,Make
,Marque
,Model
,Registration_Date
,Mileage
,ID % 2 AS ProcessNumber

FROM    dbo.Stock
```

4. Click OK to confirm.

5. Add a Conditional Split task onto the Data Flow pane. Name it **Separate out according to process number**. Connect the data source task to this new task. Double-click to edit.

6. Add two outputs named **Process0** and **Process1**. Set the conditions as follows:

ProcessNumber == 0

ProcessNumber == 1

This way, the contents of the ProcessNumber column that you created as part of the source SQL will be used to direct the data to an appropriate destination. The dialog box should look like Figure 13-18.

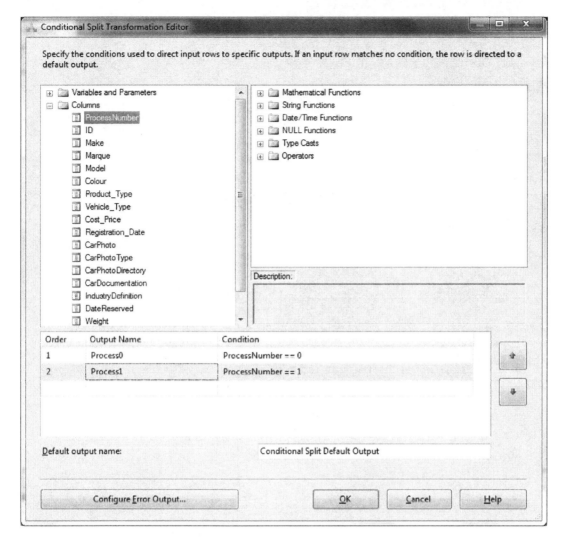

Figure 13-18. *Defining outputs from a Conditional Split task*

7. Add two OLEDB destinations to the Data Flow pane. Name them **Process0** and **Process1**.

8. Connect the Conditional Split task to the Process0 destination. Select Process0 as the output from the Input Output Selection dialog box (see Figure 13-19).

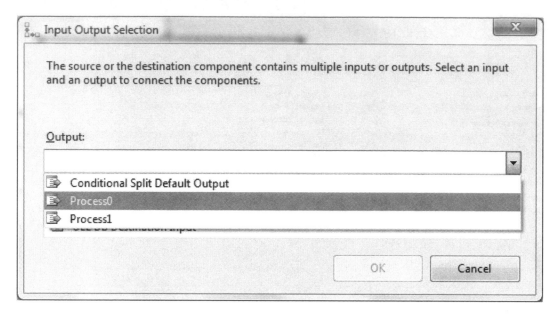

Figure 13-19. Selecting an output from a Conditional Split task

9.   Double-click the Process0 OLEDB destination task, and configure it as follows:

OLEDB Connection Manager:	CarSales_Staging_OLEDB
Name of Table or View:	ParallelTableLoad
Keep Identity:	Checked
Table Lock:	Checked

10.   Click OK to confirm.

11.   Repeat steps 7 through 9 for each destination task.

12.   You can now run the package, which should look like Figure 13-20.

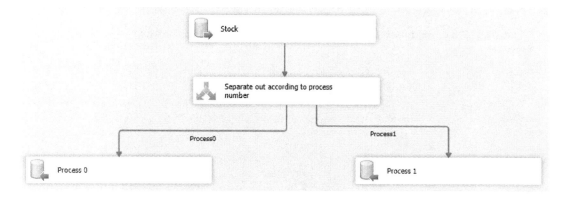

Figure 13-20. The final package for parallel destination loads

How It Works

This recipe takes a simple look at loading data in parallel from a single data source. This source can be any database table that can be read using an OLEDB or an ADO.NET data source. As there are a few minor variations on this idea, I show the core method first, and then explain a couple of extensions to this technique in the next couple of recipes.

In all these examples I am only be creating two parallel loads. Of course, you can extend this to handle the number best suited to your requirements—and your system. As ever, there are no hard and fast rules as to how many parallel loads to run for optimal performance. You will have to test and tweak for the best results.

Let us start with a source datatable. It can be an SQL Server source—or indeed any data source that SSIS can connect to. The classic sources other than SQL Server are the main relational databases on the market. I presume that you are faced with a single datatable and a single destination table. As part of the initial SELECT clause, a "process path" identifier is generated. In this case, it is deduced from the ID using the SQL Server modulo operator (%). This guarantees that each source record will be attributed either a 0 or a 1 as a flag to be used by the Conditional Split task. This allows the load to be split into two—even for a single destination table. However, you must be using the Bulk Insert API (table or view—fast load) and have to select Table Lock for parallel inserts to be sure to work.

Hints, Tips, and Traps

- When using SQL to generate the ProcessNumber, it can be a good idea to preview the results before running a vast import.

- Remember that you can always perform a simple load of the batch number column only, and then count the number of rows for each batch to check that you are getting a reasonably balanced distribution.

- There may be times when you need to calculate the ProcessNumber field without having a nice, simple unique ID field as a starting point, as was the case in this example. So, try using code like the following as part of the SELECT statement:

```
,ABS(CAST(HashBytes('SHA1', CAST(Make AS VARCHAR(20))+ Marque) AS INT)) % 2 AS ProcessNumber
```

  This code will create a hash from one or more fields, which is then used to derive the ProcessNumber field.

- There are similar ways for generating the process number from the pass-through SQL, which you can use if you are connecting to a database other than SQL Server. This will depend on the flavor of the SQL used by the database, however, and so I can only refer you to the documentation for the particular database that you are using.

13-8. Using a Single Data File As a Multiple Data Source for Parallel Destination Loads
Problem

You want to load data quickly from a single flat file and have multiple processors available.

Solution

Enable the source file to be read by multiple source tasks, and consequently allow efficient parallel loading into the destination table, as follows.

1. Create a new SSIS package, and add an OLEDB connection manager to the destination database (CarSales_Staging in this example), named **CarSales_Staging_OLEDB**.

2. Right-click in the Connection Managers tab and select New Flat File Connection. Name the connection manager **Stock**.

3. Click the Browse ... button, and navigate to the directory containing the file to load (C:\SQL2012DIRecipes\CH13\MultipleFlatFiles). Select Stock01.Csv (in this example). Ensure that all the relevant configuration information is entered (SSIS should guess all of this correctly).

4. Add a new Data Flow task and double-click to edit.

5. Add a Flat FileSource task and configure it to use the Flat File Connection named Stock that you created in step 2.

6. Add a Script component to the Data Flow pane, and set it as a transformation command type. Connect the Flat File source task Stock to this Script task, which I suggest naming Generate Hash.

7. Edit the Script component, select input Columns on the left pane, and select:

   - Make

   - Marque

   Or the columns that you wish to use to generate a hash key. The dialog box should look like Figure 13-21.

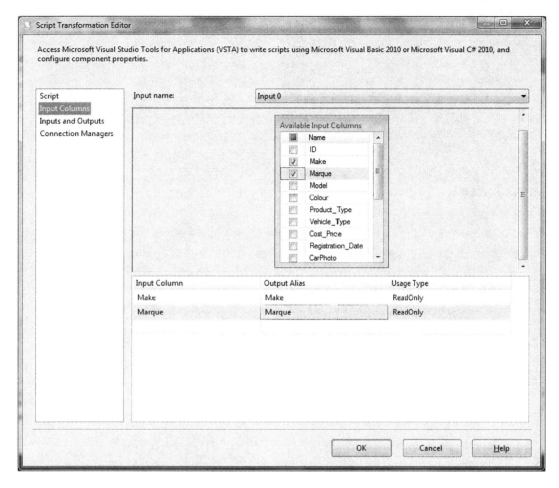

Figure 13-21. *Selecting input columns for a Script task*

8. Select Inputs and Outputs in the left pane, and add an output column (expand Output 0 select Output Columns and click the Add Columns button). Name the Output column **ProcessNumber**. It should preferably be of DataType 4-byte signed or unsigned integer. The dialog box will look like Figure 13-22.

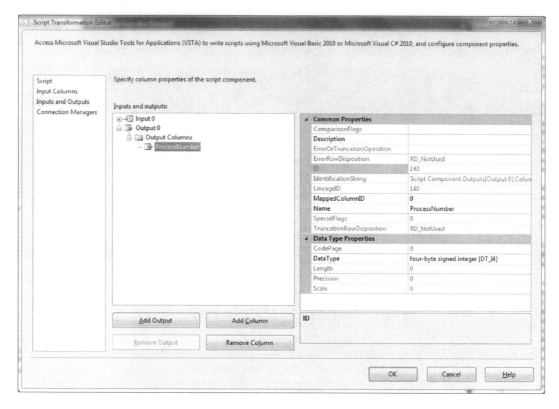

Figure 13-22. *Creating an output column for a Script task*

9. Select Script in the left pane. Set the script language to Microsoft Visual Basic 2010 and click Edit Script. Start by adding the following two directives to the Imports region of the script file:

```
Imports System.Security.Cryptography
Imports System.Text
```

10. Replace the method Input0_ProcessInputRow with the following code:

```
Public Overrides Sub Input0_ProcessInputRow(ByVal Row As InputOBuffer)

        Row.ProcessNumber = GetHashValue(Row.Marque & Row.Make) Mod 2

    End Sub
```

11. Add the following function in the ScriptMain class:

```
Private Function GetHashValue(ByVal SourceData As String) As Object

    Dim dataToHash As [Byte]() = New UnicodeEncoding().GetBytes(SourceData)
    Dim SHA  As datatype = New SHA256Managed
    Dim hashedData As [Byte]() = SHA.ComputeHash(dataToHash)
```

```
RNGCryptoServiceProvider.Create().GetBytes(dataToHash)
Dim hashedDataInt As Int64 = BitConverter.ToInt64(hashedData, 0)
Return Abs(hashedDataInt)

End Function
```

12. Close the SSIS Script window and click OK.

13. Add an OLEDB destination task and connect the Script task to it.

14. Double-click to edit the destination task, configure it to use the CarSales_Staging_OLEDB connection manager and the Stock destination table. Click Columns on the left to map the columns.

15. Click OK to finish.

You can now run the package and load the data.

How It Works

This recipe attempts to answer the question, "How do I derive a process thread column from a flat file to enable multiple data destinations?" The answer is fairly straightforward and consists of using a Script task to generate the hash and corresponding ProcessNumber field. To avoid reiterating everything that was described in the previous recipe, I will merely explain the differences, and use previous the example as a basis for extension.

There are a few things to note about the script code. First, the procedure Input0_ProcessInputRow will fire for every row that this SSIS package processes. So what you are doing is to add a new column to the row—and then add the process number to this. Note that you have to create the new output column before you can create the script (at least if you want to avoid annoying alerts and errors). Second the GetHashValue function takes the concatenated input columns, and creates an SHA hash, which it then converts (well, the first Byte, anyway) to an integer. This integer is then used to derive the process number using the MOD function (not unlike the T-SQL % function used in the previous recipe).

Hints, Tips, and Traps

- The hash value does not need to be based on all the fields in the source table, as it is not necessary to ensure uniqueness given that we are not using this hash for comparison purposes, but merely for an approximate balance in the data batch definition. So use any combination of fields that you feel gives an equitable distribution.

- If you have an integer field in the source data, and do not need to generate a hash to deduce a flow ID, then you can simply use the following single line of code to define the process flow number: Row.ProcessNumber = (CType(Row.ID % 2, Int32) + 1;

13-9. Reading and Writing Data from a Database Source in Parallel

Problem

You want to load data efficiently from a source database into SQL Server using all available processor cores.

Solution

Create an SSIS package with multiple data flow tasks that will read and write the data in parallel, as follows.

1. Create a new SSIS package. Add two OLEDB connection managers—one to the source database CarSales (**CarSales_OLEDB**) and one to the destination database CarSales_Staging (**CarSales_Staging_OLEDB**).

2. Create a destination table in the destination database (CarSales_Staging) using the following DDL (C:\SQL2012DIRecipes\CH13\tblExportStock.Sql):

```
CREATE TABLE CarSales_Staging.dbo.ExportStock
(
 ID BIGINT NOT NULL,
 Make VARCHAR (50) NULL,
 Marque NVARCHAR(50) NULL,
 Model NVARCHAR(50) NULL,
) ;
GO
```

3. Add a Data Flow task and double-click to edit.

4. Add an OLEDB source and configure as follows:

OLEDB Connection Manager:	CarSales_OLEDB
Data Access Mode:	SQL Command
SQL Text:	SELECT ID, Make, Marque, Model
	FROM dbo.Stock WITH (NOLOCK)
	WHERE (AccountID % 4) = 0
	OPTION (MAXDOP 1)

5. Add an OLEDB destination, connect the previous task to it, and configure as follows:

OLEDB Connection Manager:	CarSales_Staging_OLEDB
Data Access Mode:	Table or View – Fast Load
Name of the Table or View:	dbo.ExportStock
Table Lock:	Checked

6. Click Mapping and map the columns (all have the same names in both source and destination, so SSIS should do his for you).

7. Repeat steps 5 through 6 for each available processor core in your server, only be careful to increment the modulo factor by one each time. It should read for the second source to destination task pair: WHERE (AccountID % 4) = 1; for the third source to destination task pair: WHERE (AccountID % 4) = 2; and so forth.

How It Works

Another solution that can prove extremely efficient (if the source and destination database disk installation and network setup allow for it), is to perform multiple parallel reads and writes, where the source data is segmented into multiple paths using modulo to return a value that is used as a data path identifier. This will give you multiple source components that can then connect to multiple destination components, and thus process parallel data loads.

Given that this recipe is essentially an amalgam of techniques used in previous recipes, I will not explain all the details of the process here. For all the gory details, please refer to Recipes 13-7 and 13-8.

As before, be sure to test the efficiency of the process on your data and equipment before assuming that it will bring real benefits. Once again, remember only to add as many flow processes as you have available and free processor cores.

This technique will not deliver linear improvements in processing time as you add more parallel processes. However, it should shorten the data load time nonetheless. If the source data does not have an integer field to use to set the data segmentation, then consider using a data hash on one or more fields as the basis for the modulo function, as described previously.

Hints, Tips, and Traps

- Do not be afraid to experiment with the various available parameters. You may not need the MAXDOP option (which is only available for SQL Server sources, in any case). You may find that multiple connection managers may or may not bring benefits.

- Should you be switching to ODBC data connections, it is worth noting that there is no limitation on the number of ODBC destination components that can run in parallel against the same table or different tables. BOL states, however, that the limitations of the ODBC provider being used may restrict the number of concurrent connections through the provider. These limitations limit the number of supported parallel instances possible for the ODBC destination.

13-10. Inserting Records in Parallel and in Bulk

Problem

You want to load data efficiently from a source file into SQL Server.

Solution

Read the data in multiple contiguous ranges from the single source file and write the data in parallel using SSIS and multiple BULK INSERT tasks. The following explains how it is done.

1. Create a new SSIS task. Create the following package-scoped variable. This will be the range of records processed by each Bulk Insert task:

Variable Name	Type	Value
RecordRange	Int16	1,000,000 (or the approximate number of records in the source file divided by the number of processing cores)

2.   Add an OLEDB Configuration Manager, configured to connect to the destination database named **CarSales_Staging_OLEDB**.

3.   Add a Flat File connection manager named **BulkLoad** and configure it to read the source file (`C:\SQL2012DIRecipes\CH13\BulkStock.Csv`).

4.   Create the CarSales_Staging.dbo.BulkStock destination table using the following DDL (`C:\SQL2012DIRecipes\CH13\tblBulkStock.Sql`):

```
CREATE TABLE CarSales_Staging.dbo.BulkStock
(
 ID BIGINT NULL,
 Make VARCHAR(50) NULL,
 Marque NVARCHAR(50) NULL,
 Model VARCHAR(50) NULL
) ;

GO
```

5.   Assuming that you are loading data into a staging table, add an Execute SQL task to the data flow pane, name it **Prepare destination table**, and configure as follows:

Connection Type:	OLEDB
Connection:	CarSales_Staging_OLEDB
SQL Statement:	`TRUNCATE TABLE dbo.BulkStock`

6.   Add a Sequence container to the Data Flow pane. Connect the previous task—"Prepare destination table"—to it.

7.   Add as many Bulk Insert tasks inside the Sequence container as you have available processor cores in your server. Configure each one (using the Connection pane) to read data using the BulkLoad source Configuration Manager and to write to the appropriate destination table, as shown in Figure 13-23.

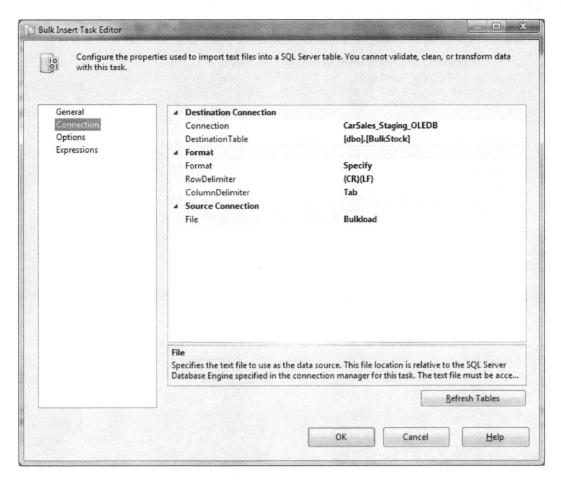

Figure 13-23. *The Bulk Insert task*

8. Double-click the first of the Bulk Insert tasks, and click Expressions. Expand
    Expressions in the right-hand pane, and click the Ellipse button. Select the LastRow
    property and set it to the User::RecordRange variable. Confirm the expression with
    OK, and then confirm all your modifications for the Bulk Insert task with OK.

9. Double-click the second of the Bulk Insert tasks, and click Expressions. Expand
    Expressions in the right-hand pane, and click the Ellipse button. Set the following two
    expressions:

    FirstRow: @[User::RecordRange] + 1

    LastRow: (@[User::RecordRange] * 2)

10. Double-click the third of the Bulk Insert tasks, and click Expressions. Expand Expressions
    in the right-hand pane, and click the Ellipse button. Set the following two expressions:

    FirstRow: (@[User::RecordRange] * 2) + 1

    LastRow: (@[User::RecordRange] * 3)

11. Do the same thing for all the Bulk Insert tasks *except the last one*—ensuring that you increment the multipliers (the *2 and *3 in the preceding step) by one for each task.

12. Double-click the *last* of the Bulk Insert tasks, and click Expressions. Expand Expressions in the right-hand pane, and click the Ellipse button. Select the FirstRow property and set it to (@[User::RecordRange] * n) + 1—where n is the multiplier. Do not set the last Row property, as this will default to the last row in the source file. Confirm the expression with OK, and then confirm all your modifications for the Bulk Insert task with OK.

The final package should look like Figure 13-24.

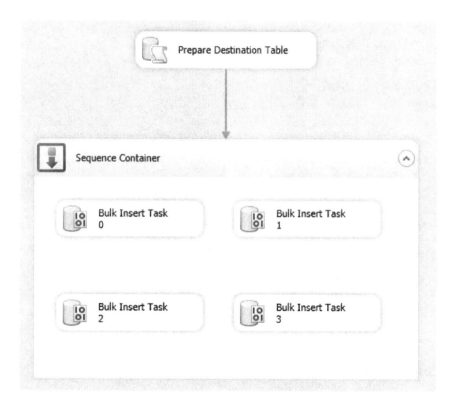

Figure 13-24. The parallel bulk load package

Now, when you run the package, the source file will be loaded in parallel using as many processor cores as there are available, and for which there is a corresponding Bulk Insert task. Each Bulk Insert task will load a separate set of records.

How It Works

There are occasions when you will have a single, extremely large source file, and a very restricted time window in which to load the data. This is when you need to be able to load batches of data from the same file in parallel. Fortunately, the Bulk Insert task can do exactly this, as it allows you to specify both the initial record to load from a source file as well as the final record to load. So if you know (approximately) how many records there are likely to be in a source file, as well as how many parallel processes you are running, then you can use SSIS expressions to define these parameters for each parallel load, and perform a parallel bulk insert from a single source file.

You can count the records in the source file to get an exact figure to use for the definition of the subsets of records to load, but the time taken to get an exact figure is likely to render the operation pointless in most cases, and so an approximate figure should suffice. Should the file sizes vary considerably, then you may have no choice but to get the real row count. To do this, merely create a data flow task, using a Flat File source. Select one column only from those available, and connect to a Row Count transform, configured with the FileCounter variable as the rowcount variable. As you test your package, you will be able to get an approximate record count from the source file, and place this figure in the FileCounter variable.

■ **Note** When I refer to "available" processor cores, I mean those that can be used for the ETL process that you are building. If you have the luxury of a server dedicated to SSIS and the process that you are designing will have exclusive access to the server resources then defining the cores that you can use is easy—it is all of them. If the server will be used for other process at the same time as your load process is running, then you will have to decide just how many cores you want SSIS to use.

Hints, Tips, and Traps

- Creating more Bulk Insert tasks than there are available processor cores can be counterproductive, since switching between cores—and the associated waits—can slow the process down considerably.

- You can adjust the various configuration options available for Bulk Inserts as you see fit—they are explained in Recipe 5-3.

- Unfortunately, the Bulk Insert task offers few logging, counter, or error trapping options.

13-11. Creating Self-Optimizing Parallel Bulk Inserts
Problem

You want load balancing for parallel bulk inserts. You want the process to adjust to the number of records to load based on the last load job.

Solution

Extend the package created in Recipe 13-10 to count and store the record count for a data load. This then becomes the basis for the record counter used to calculate a balanced load in subsequent loads. The package from Recipe 13-10 is available at C:\SQL2012DIRecipes\CH13\13_10.Dtsx.

Taking the package as a basis, perform the following steps.

1. Create the SSISVariables SQL Server table—used to store SSIS variables—using the following DDL (C:\SQL2012DIRecipes\CH13\tblSSISVariables.Sql):

    ```
    CREATE TABLE CarSales_Staging.dbo.SSISVariables
    (
     ID INT IDENTITY(1,1) NOT NULL,
     SSISPackageName NVARCHAR (50) NULL,
    ```

```
SSISVarName NVARCHAR (50) NULL,
SSISVarValue NVARCHAR (50) NULL,
LastUpdated DATETIME NULL,
CONSTRAINT PK_SSISVariables PRIMARY KEY CLUSTERED
  (
   ID ASC
  )
) ;
GO
```

2. Add one record to the SSISVariables table, using T-SQL like the following:

    ```
    INSERT INTO dbo.SSISVariables (SSISPackageName, SSISVarName, SSISVarValue)
    VALUES ('ParallelBulkInsertFile.dtsx', 'RecordRange', '1000000')
    ```

3. Create an ADO.NET connection manager named **CarSales_Staging_ADONET** and configured to connect to the database where the dbo.SSISVariables table is located (CarSales_Staging).

4. Add a new Execute SQL task named **Get Range of Records**. Configure it as follows:

Connection Type:	ADO.NET
Connection:	CarSales_Staging_ADONET
SQL Statement:	SELECT @RecordRange = CAST(SSISVarValue AS INT)
	FROM dbo.SSISVariables
	WHERE SSISVarName = 'RecordRange'

5. Click ParameterMapping and add a parameter, as follows:

Variable Name:	User::RecordRange
Direction:	Output
Type:	Int64
Parameter Name:	@RecordRange

    Confirm all your modifications.

6. Connect the new task to the existing task, "Prepare destination table".

7. Add a new Execute SQL task named **Redefine Data Ranges**. Connect the Sequence container to it. Configure it as follows:

Connection Type:	ADO.NET
Connection:	CarSales_Staging_ADONET
SQL Statement:	UPDATE dbo.SSISVariables
	SET SSISVarValue =
	FLOOR(@RecordRange / @FileCounter)
	WHERE SSISVarName = 'RecordRange'

8. Click ParameterMapping and add a parameter, as follows:

> Variable Name: User::RecordRange
>
> Direction: Input
>
> Type: Int64
>
> Parameter Name: @RecordRange

9. Confirm all of your modifications.

The final package should look like Figure 13-25.

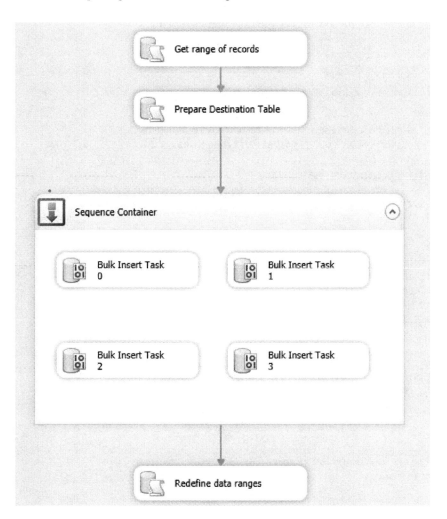

Figure 13-25. *Bulk loading data with dynamic ranges of records*

How It Works

Should you face source files that can vary slightly or even moderately in size, you can calculate and store the most recent load counter and use it as the basis for calculating the range of records to be loaded by each Bulk Insert task. This is done, of course, in an attempt to produce the nirvana of all software development—a self-managing program! The range of records to load is nothing more than the row count for the most recent load divided by the number of load threads.

13-12. Loading Files in Controlled Batches
Problem

You want to load multiple varying files in specified batches within a defined time frame.

Solution

Use SSIS to create a batch control framework to load data in batches, and parameterize the input directory and extension, as follows.

1. Create an SQL Server table (BatchFileLoad) to store the batch metadata using the following DDL (C:\SQL2012DIRecipes\CH13\tblBatchFileLoad.Sql):

```
CREATE TABLE CarSales_Staging.dbo.BatchFileLoad
(
 ID int IDENTITY(1,1) NOT NULL,
 FileName VARCHAR (250) NULL,
 IsToload BIT NULL,
 IsLoaded BIT NULL,
 FileSize BIGINT NULL,
 CreationTime DATETIME NULL,
 FileExtension VARCHAR (5) NULL,
 DirectoryName VARCHAR (250) NULL,
 LastWriteTime DATETIME NULL
) ;
GO
```

2. Create a new SSIS task and name it **BatchFileLoad**. Add two Connection managers—an ADO.NET connection manager named **CarSales_Staging_ADONET** and an OLEDB connection manager named **CarSales_Staging_OLEDB**, both of which connect to the database where you will be both loading the data and persisting the metadata.

3. Add a new Flat File connection named **Data Source File**. Configure it to use any of the files in the source directory.

4. Create the following variables:

Variable Name	Scope	Type	Value/Comments
ADOTable	Package	object	n/a
			The object variable that will contain the list of files to process.
BatchQuantity	Package	Int32	50
			The quantity of files to process per batch.
CreateList	Package	Boolean	True
			A flag to indicate whether the list of files is to be dropped and re-created or not.
FileFilter	Package	String	*.CSV
			The file extension for all the files to be processed.
FileSource	Package	String	C:\SQL2012DIRecipes\CH13
			The source directory for the source files.
IsFinished	Package	Boolean	False
			The flag used to indicate that the process has finished.
ListConn	Package	String	CarSales_StagingADONET
			The connection manager name
MaxFilesToProcess	Package	Int64	5000
			The upper threshold for the maximum number of files to process per batch.
MaxProcessDuration	Package	Int32	7200
			The upper threshold for the maximum number of seconds to run the batch before ceasing processing.
ProcessFile	Package	String	n/a
			The file currently being processed.
SortElement	Package	String	FileSize.
			The indicator of how the list is sorted.
TotalFilesLoaded	Package	Int64	0
			The process counter for the number of files processed in the batch.

5. Add a For Loop container to the Control Flow pane. Name it **Create table of files to process**.

6. Inside, add an Execute SQL task named **Prepare Table**.

7. Then add two Script components named **Loop Through Files and Write to table** and **Reset Variable**.

8. Next, connect the Components in the order shown in Figure 13-26.

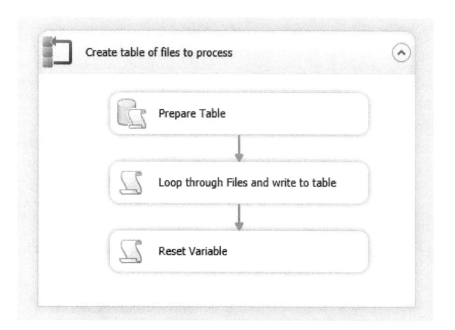

Figure 13-26. *Defining the list of files to process for a controlled file load*

9. Set the EvalExpression for the "Create table of files to process" task to:

   @CreateList == True

10. Configure the Prepare Table task so that:

    Connection Type: ADO.NET

    Connection: CarSales_Staging_ADONET

    SQL Statement: TRUNCATE TABLE dbo.BatchFileLoad

11. Configure the "Loop Through Files and Write to table" Script component, as follows:

    ReadOnly Variables: User::FileFilter,User::FileSource,User::ListConn

12. Set the language of the Script component to Microsoft Visual Basic 2010 and click Edit Script.

13. Add the following to the Imports region:

```
Imports System.Data.SqlClient
Imports System.IO
```

14. Use the following to replace the Main method (C:\SQL2012DIRecipes\CH13\
ControlBatchLoad.Vb):

```
Public Sub Main()

        Dim sqlConn As SqlConnection
        Dim sqlCommand As SqlCommand

        sqlConn = DirectCast(Dts.Connections(Dts.Variables("ListConn").Value.ToString). ↵
                    AcquireConnection(Dts.Transaction), SqlConnection)

        Dim FileSource As String = Dts.Variables("FileSource").Value.ToString
        Dim FileFilter As String = Dts.Variables("FileFilter").Value.ToString

        Dim dirInfo As New System.IO.DirectoryInfo(FileSource)
        Dim fileSystemInfo As System.IO.FileSystemInfo
        Dim FileName As String
        Dim FileFullName As String
        Dim FileSize As Long
        Dim FileExtension As String
        Dim CreationTime As Date
        Dim DirectoryName As String
        Dim LastWriteTime As Date

        Dim sqlText As String

        For Each fileSystemInfo In dirInfo.GetFileSystemInfos(FileFilter)

            FileName = fileSystemInfo.Name
            FileFullName = fileSystemInfo.FullName

            Dim fileDetail As New FileInfo(FileFullName)

            FileSize = fileDetail.Length
            CreationTime = fileDetail.CreationTime
            FileExtension = fileDetail.Extension
            DirectoryName = fileDetail.DirectoryName
            LastWriteTime = fileDetail.LastWriteTime
```

```
        sqlText = "INSERT INTO dbo.BatchFileLoad " _
                & "(FileName, IsToload, IsLoaded, FileSize, CreationTime, " _
                & "FileExtension, DirectoryName, LastWriteTime) " _
                & "VALUES('" & FileName & "', 1, 0, " & FileSize & ", '" _
                & String.Format("{0:s}", CreationTime) & "', '" & FileExtension & "', '" _
                & DirectoryName & "', '" & String.Format("{0:s}", LastWriteTime) & "')"

        sqlCommand = New SqlCommand(sqlText, sqlConn)
        sqlCommand.CommandType = CommandType.Text
        sqlCommand.ExecuteNonQuery()

    Next

    Dts.TaskResult = ScriptResults.Success

End Sub
```

15. Close the Script window and confirm with OK.

16. Configure the Reset Variable task with the following variable:

    ReadWrite Variables: CreateList

17. Add the following script to the Script task once you have set the language to Microsoft
    Visual Basic 2010:

```
Public Sub Main()
      Dts.Variables("CreateList").Value = False

      Dts.TaskResult = ScriptResults.Success
End Sub
```

18. Close the Script window and confirm with OK.

    This completes the first part of the package—the process to iterate through all the files to process,
    and store their data in the BatchFileLoad table, as well as the possibility of restarting the process, and
    regenerating the list of files.

19. Add a Script task to the Control Flow pane. Name it **Initialize file counter** and set the
    following variable:

    ReadWrite Variables: User::TotalFilesLoaded

20. Add the following script to the Script task once you have set the language to Microsoft Visual Basic 2010:

```
Public Sub Main()

        Dts.Variables("TotalFilesLoaded").Value = 0
        Dts.TaskResult = ScriptResults.Success

End Sub
```

21. Close the Script window and confirm with OK.

22. Add a For Loop container to the Control Flow pane. Name it **Batch Process**. Set its EvalExpression to:

```
@IsFinished == False || @TotalFilesLoaded < @MaxFilesToProcess || ↵
DATEADD( "ss", @MaxProcessDuration, @[System::ContainerStartTime] ) > GETDATE()
```

23. Inside this For Loop container, add the following, connected in this order:

   • An Execute SQL task named **Get Batch**.

   • A Foreach Loop container named **Process Files while there are files to Process**.

   • An Execute SQL task named **Count remaining files to process**.

24. Inside the Each Loop container, named Load Batch, add the following, connected in this order:

   • A Data Flow task named **Data Load**.

   • An Execute SQL task named **Log file is loaded**.

   • A Script task named **Increment file counter**.

This part of the package should look like Figure 13-27.

Figure 13-27. *Processing a controlled bulk load*

25. Configure the "Get Batch" Execute SQL task so that its attributes are as follows:

Connection:

Connection Type:	ADO.NET
Connection:	CarSales_Staging_ADONET
SQL Statement:	SELECT TOP (@BatchQuantity) [FileName]
	FROM dbo.BatchFileLoad
	WHERE IsToload = 1
	AND IsLoaded = 0
	ORDER BY FileSize

ResultSet:	Full Result Set
ResultSet:	Variable Name: User::ADOTable
Result Name:	0

Parameter Mapping:

Variable Name:	User::BatchQuantity
Direction:	Input
Data Type:	Int32
Parameter Name:	@BatchQuantity

26. Configure the Data Load task so that the data flow source is the Flat File connection named Data Source File, and the data flow destination is an OLEDB destination using the CarSales_Staging_OLEDB connection. Ensure that you have mapped the columns.

27. Configure the "Log file is loaded" task with the following attributes:

Connection Pane:

Connection Type:	ADO.NET
Connection:	CarSales_Staging_ADONET
SQL Statement:	UPDATE BatchFileLoad
	SET IsLoaded = 1
	,DateLoaded = GETDATE()
	WHERE FileName = @ProcessFile

Parameter Mapping Pane:

Variable Name:	User::ProcessFile
Direction:	Input
Data Type:	String
Parameter Name:	@ProcessFile

28. Configure the Script task named Increment File counter, adding the following variable:

ReadWrite Variables: User::TotalFilesLoaded

29. Add the following script to the Script task once you have set the language to Microsoft Visual Basic 2010:

```
Public Sub Main()
        Dts.Variables("TotalFilesLoaded").Value  = Dts.Variables("TotalFilesLoaded").Value + 1
        Dts.TaskResult = ScriptResults.Success
End Sub
```

30. Close the Script window and confirm with OK.

31. Configure the "Count remaining files to process" Execute SQL task so that it is as follows:

Connection Pane:

Connection Type:	ADO.NET
Connection:	CarSales_Staging_ADONET
SQL Statement:	DECLARE @FileCountToProcess INT
	SELECT @FileCountToProcess = COUNT(*) FROM BatchFileLoad
	WHERE IsLoaded = 0
	IF @FileCountToProcess = 0
	BEGIN
	SET @IsFinished = 1
	END
	ELSE
	BEGIN
	SET @IsFinished = 0
	END

Parameter Mapping Pane:

Variable Name:	User::IsFinished
Direction:	Output
Data Type:	String
Parameter Name:	@IsFinished

You can now run the process.

How It Works

Another frequent requirement in my experience is to load data from multiple files, and to load them in batches. There are several possible reasons for wanting to do this:

- You cannot guarantee that the data load will finish in a required (or reasonable) time, and you need to be able to stop the load at any time, and continue the load later.

- You want to load files for a specified period, and have the process cease after the last complete file load once the specified period has elapsed.

- You need to perform intermediate processing once batches of data have been loaded.

- Your ETL process is more efficient if the data is loaded in optimized batches (shredding XML files or due to indexing constraints for instance).

Of course, a batch process that can handle these requirements must also be able to sort source files, and log which file is loaded. Inevitable it must be sufficiently resilient to allow graceful recovery and restart from the point of failure.

So here you have an SSIS package that fulfils these requirements. To make it more flexible, it allows you to pass in the parameters in Table 13-1 as SSIS variables.

Table 13-1. *The SSIS Parameters Used in a Parallel Load*

Parameter	Description
Batch size	The number of source files processed per batch.
Total process size	The number of source files processed before the SSIS package stops.
Maximum process duration	The number of seconds the process will run—plus the time needed to finish the current file load.
The directory to process	The directory where source files are stored.
The file filter	This is the file extension most of the time.

This package is in two parts. First, a loop container is processed that gathers the data for all the files to process, and writes this data to an SQL Server table. A table is used to ensure that all metadata is persisted to a data store that can be guaranteed reliable. Second, another loop container processes the files, as long as files remain to process—and time remains and the maximum number of files is not reached. Inside this "logic" loop container is another that provides the batch loading.

The process needs to know if it is a completely new load, or if it is continuing an existing load. To this end, the @CreateList variable is passed in as False if the process is to continue where it left off. The default is True, assuming (optimistically) that the process will always finish in time, without error, and that there will never be too many files to process. As there are three Blocking thresholds, these must be passed in when running the process—or the defaults accepted:

- Maximum time (detected by comparing the container start time to the number of seconds added to the system date).

- Maximum number of files (incremented each time a file is loaded).

- All files loaded (flagged when the final batch contains no files).

The initial part of the process—the "Create table of files to process" For Loop container—defines the list of files to be loaded in the BatchFileLoad table, and flags them initially as not yet loaded. The counter variable that tracks the actual number of files loaded is set to 0. The outer (control) For Loop container checks that

- Not all the files have been loaded.

- The allotted time has not been exceeded.

- The total number of files to process has not been exceeded.

Assuming that none of these is true, then control passes to the load process. First, the specified number of files to load are selected from the BatchFileLoad table (or as many as remain if this is a lesser number), and passed to an ADOTable ADO.NET object. Then, the inner (load) For Loop container processes the files in ADOTable. This consists of

- Loading the file.

- Logging the successful load to the BatchFileLoad control table.

- Incrementing the total files loaded counter.

The "Loop Through Files and Write to table" task loops through all the files in the specified directory, and writes the file names and relevant attributes to the Control table. It uses an existing ADO.NET connection manager. In this example, the SQL is sent as text, but you could use a stored procedure and send in the values as parameters.

The SQL in "Count remaining files to process" counts the number of files in the "control" table that remain to be processed. It then sets the IsFinished "stop" variable to True if this is the case, which is picked up by the Foreach Loop container as the indicator to pass control on to the next task.

■ **Note**   This process, as it has been described, has no error handling to simplify the explanations and code. However, in a production environment, you should definitely add error trapping and handling, and at a minimum, you should detect file load failure and log a failed file load. You should also define the `MaximumErrorCount` at the level of the Load Batch container to indicate the number of errors allowed before failing the package.

Hints, Tips, and Traps

- In a real-world environment, you may prefer to store the metadata (the BatchFileLoad table) in a different database. It is entirely up to you.

- Of course, you must set the variable values and connection managers to meet your requirements.

- You can extend this process to handle files from multiple folders and file filters using the techniques described in Recipe 13-3.

13-13. Executing SQL Statements and Procedures in Parallel Using SSIS

Problem

You want to accelerate an SSIS ETL process that contains several T-SQL stored procedures.

Solution

Execute the SQL using multiple concurrent tasks. This is as easy as setting up two or more Execute SQL tasks in parallel.

1. Add an Execute SQL task on to the Control Flow pane, under the preceding task (if there is one) for each process to be executed in parallel.

2. Connect the preceding task (if there is one) to all the new Execute SQL tasks.

3. Connect all the new Execute SQL tasks to the following task (if there is one).

4. Define the SQL (as a stored procedure call or as T-SQL code) for each of the tasks. Create or use any connection managers you require.

A purely theoretical package could look like Figure 13-28.

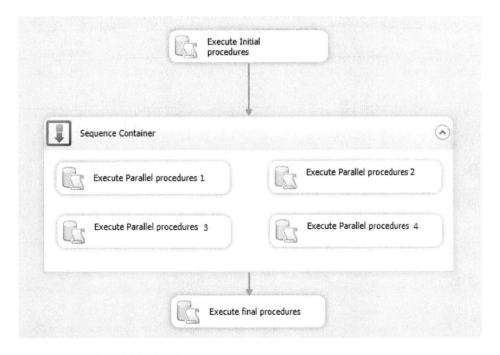

Figure 13-28. *Parallel SQL tasks*

How It Works

There may be times when you prefer to avoid the purely sequential nature of T-SQL, and want to execute a series of T-SQL statements or stored procedures in parallel. While the two classic technical solutions to this are simple to implement, the practice can be a minefield. If you are going to do this, you have to be absolutely certain that:

- Any processes run in parallel will not block each other, and paralyze your system. This could mean that they will not be writing to the same tables at the same time, for instance. In an ETL scenario this means ensuring that NOLOCK hints are used appropriately for data reads. And of course, the I/O subsystem has to be able to handle the increased contention.

- Such processes are not competing for the same resources (disk, memory, etc.), which could lead to a situation where your system will slow down to a crawl as SQL Server attempts to handle all the conflicting requirements.

- Your system has multiple processors, that are unused or little used when you run the parallel process.

- The process flow logic allows for parallel execution. That is you can run process A and process B simultaneously because process B does not depend on process A. In the real world, this means designing the package from the start to handle parallel processing.

In any case, I would advise erring on the side of caution. So in any case always test the parallel processes many, many times—you never know when a conflict or lock will occur in these circumstances. Then baseline the timings for the sequential process and use this to compare with the parallel process. If you are obtaining significantly faster results, then ask the question, "What are the risks?" Never assume that parallel will automatically be faster.

Of course, there can be no hard and fast list of when to process in parallel and when not to, so all I can do is suggest a few circumstances when I have found it useful. Of course, there could be hundreds of other possibilities:

- You wish to update indexes, or re-index tables, where the tables and indexes are on separate filegroups on separate disk arrays, so there will be little or no I/O contention. Having said this, (re)indexing in parallel even when indexes and data are on the same disks can prove faster in parallel, in my experience—just beware of clogging up your system I/O with the parallel indexing!

- The processes are completely separate—one is aggregating data in one database while another is loading data from a linked server into a separate database.

13-14. Executing SQL Statements and Procedures in Parallel Without SSIS

Problem

You want to accelerate an ETL process that contains several T-SQL stored procedures. You do not want to use SSIS.

Solution

Shell out to the operating system to call T-SQL stored procedures using SQLCMD. The code that follows is a purely hypothetical example to illustrate the principle.

1. Using a text editor, create a command file like this (I am calling it
   C:\SQL2012DIRecipes\CH13\runinparallel.cmd):

   ```
   START SQLCMD -E -dCarSales_Staging -Q"EXEC dbo.pr_AA_1_Par" -b
   START SQLCMD -E -dCarSales_Staging -Q"EXEC dbo.pr_AA_2_Par" -b
   ```

2. Save the file.

3. Call the command file from inside T-SQL, like this, for instance:

```
DECLARE @CmdResult INT
EXEC        @CmdResult = master..xp_CmdShell 'C:\SQL2012DIRecipes\CH13\runinparallel.cmd'
IF (@result <> 0)
    RETURN
```

How It Works

This technique uses xp_cmdshell to run an operating system command file. The file runs SQLCMD calls and uses the uppercase -Q option to quit after running, and -b to quit on error. -E specifies a trusted connection. The START command will run each SQLCMD in a separate window—and separate process.

Calling parallel processes from T-SQL requires either:

- Shelling out to the operating system

- Creating a CLR process to handle multithreading.

Here I am only looking, briefly, at the former because I have never used the latter in a production environment, yet. However, as we are "going against the grain" of T-SQL, be warned that this is potentially fraught with issues in a production environment, and will require:

- Permissions (and possibly the xp_cmdshell Proxy Account)—consult Books Online (BOL) for this.

- Enabling xp_cmdshell. Many DBAs will not allow this—so be warned!

Hints, Tips, and Traps

- Of course, the database and the stored procedure names must correspond to those that you want to run in parallel.

- You can use -vnn (for example -v16) to set the severity level that will cause an error and quit the process.

- This approach presumes that you have implemented error trapping and logging in the stored procedure.

- You can send multiple (sequential) stored procedures as part of a parallel process call. In this case, separate each stored procedure with a semicolon as part of the START line.

- I strongly suggest adding error trapping when using xp_cmdshell.

13-15. Executing SQL Statements and Procedures in Parallel Using SQL Server Agent

Problem

You want to accelerate an ETL process that contains several T-SQL stored procedures. You do not want to use SSIS.

Solution

Use SQL Server Agent. Although it is an extremely simplistic solution, it is possible nonetheless to use SQL Server Agent to run T-SQL processes (be they stored procedures or code snippets) in parallel. All you have to do is to create as many SQL Server agent jobs as there are processes to run, and set each one's schedule to start at exactly the same time.

Hints, Tips, and Traps

- Although you can use SQL Server Agent to launch parallel SSIS packages, it is probably easier to use a single SSIS package that, in turn, then invokes other subpackages.

- Things get stickier when you require further processes to run after the initial parallel processes. In this case, my preferred solution is to have the parallel processes log their outcomes to a table, and the successive process polls this table. Once all the parallel processes have finished, the secondary process can start.

Summary

This chapter illustrates many ways of accelerating data loads. I hope that they will either be of immediate use in your quest to optimize your ETL processes, or alternatively, will inspire you to find optimal ways of loading data.

Many of the recipes in this chapter are based on using parallel loads. I am presuming that you will be using multiprocessor servers to run your processes, but in today's world, it is rare for this not to be the case. Remember nonetheless that splitting source reads and destination loads will not automatically give better results, and that you must test every method that you are evaluating before you deploy it into production.

To give a clearer overview, Table 13-2 shows my take on the various methods.

Table 13-2. *Advantages and Disadvantages of the Approaches Used in This Chapter*

Technique	Advantages	Disadvantages
Multiple sequential file loads	Easy to set up.	Slow.
Multiple sequential file loads from multiple directories	Avoids copying files to a single source directory. Can be extended to provide many advantages.	Slow. Trickier to set up.
MULTIFLATFILE connection manager	Easy to set up. Avoids copying files to a single source directory.	Slow.

(continued)

Table 13-2. (*continued*)

Technique	Advantages	Disadvantages
Ordering and filtering file loads	Impossible with standard or MULTIFLATFILE connection managers.	Trickier to set up.
Parallel file loads	Relatively easy to set up.	Files must be identical in format.
	Considerable increase in throughput.	Only efficient on multiprocessor servers.
Parallel file loads with load balancing	Considerable increase in throughput.	Hard to set up.
		Only efficient on multiprocessor servers.
Parallel loading from a single data source	Relatively easy to set up.	Only efficient on multiprocessor servers.
	Some increase in throughput.	
Parallel reads and parallel writes for SQL databases	Relatively easy to set up.	Only efficient on mulbrocessor servers.
	Considerable increase in throughput.	
Controlled batch file loads	Allows timed loads and controlled numbers of files to be loaded.	Hard to set up.
Parallel SQL statements	Requires SSIS or xp_cmdshell.	No dependencies between the procedures.

■ ■ ■

ETL Process Acceleration

Sometimes, getting source data to load fast into SQL Server requires a good look at the whole process. Certainly, if you can take full of advantage of all available processor cores and attempt to parallelize the load, you could shorten load times—as we saw in Chapter 13. Yet here are other aspects of ETL loads that also need to be taken into consideration if you are trying to optimize a load and ensure that the entire time taken by a job (and not just the data load) is reduced to fit into an acceptable timeframe.

In this chapter, we take a look at some of these other aspects of ETL loads, and how they can be tweaked to ensure optimal load times. They include:

- Using the SSIS Lookup Cache efficiently.

- Index management for destination tables.

- Ensuring minimal logging.

- Ensuring bulk loads rather than row-by-row inserts.

As ever, any sample files are available on thee-book's companion web site. Once downloaded and installed, they are found in the C:\SQL2012DIRecipes\CH14 folder. I advise you to drop and re-create any tables or other objects for each recipe.

As a precursor to examining some of these more "advanced" ideas, there are a handful of basic techniques that bear repetition. So, before embarking on complex solutions to challenging load times, just remember to look at the following as a first step:

- When defining source data in a Lookup task, use a SELECT T-SQL query and not a table source. This is because any unused source columns will take up SSIS pipeline bandwidth unnecessarily.

- Using NOLOCK (or any equivalent for non-SQL Server databases) when reading external data sources can improve data reads.

- If you are using flat file sources, only select the columns (in the Columns pane) that you need to send through the SSIS pipeline. As is the case with database sources, this narrows the row width, and thus allows for a greater number of rows in the SSIS pipeline.

- For flat files you can also select the FastParse option if the data and time fields are not locale-sensitive.

- If you need to sort source data from a database source, it is frequently better to use ORDER BY in the source database.

- Performing datatype conversions in the source database can improve SSIS throughput.

- Transferring flat files in a compressed format and then uncompressing them on a local server disk (especially a fast one) can be more efficient than reading flat files across a network.

- Inevitably, you are loading data into SQL Server—so an optimized server can make a tremendous difference. It is always worth ensuring that TempDB is configured optimally (as many files as processors, files on a separate disk array, etc.). Of course, separating data from log files from indexes is equally fundamental.

- Check out the allocated SQL Server memory on your servers. Numerous times, I have seen an artificially low threshold applied for no reason. Nothing will slow down your queries like lack of memory.

- As SQL Server and SSIS love memory—can you get any more added? This can be the simplest remedy for slow ETL processes.

- Is the default network packet size suited to your environment? This is a complex subject, but increasing the packet size (using the network packet size configuration option) from the default of 4096 to 32767 – or to 16Kb in Secure Socket Layer (SSL) and Transport Layer Security (TLS) environments can allow for increased throughput. In SSIS this is the Packet Size option in the All pane of an OLEDB connection manager.

- If you can avoid asynchronous transformations (sort and aggregate transforms, for instance) – then do so. This can mean sorting data in the source database or convincing flat file providers to deliver pre-sorted datasets.

In any case, ensuring that the basic optimization techniques are respected will never harm your load process. So with the foundations in place, it could be time to turn to some of the more advanced possibilities.

As ETL optimization can never be attained by applying a single technique, there is, perhaps inevitably, a certain overlap between the recipes in this chapter. This is specifically the case for the final recipe, which amalgamates several of the techniques that are seen in many of the other recipes in this chapter. This is in an attempt to give a final "holistic" overview to end with.

14-1. Accelerating SSIS Lookups
Problem

You want to build SSIS packages that use the Lookup task as efficiently as possible.

Solution

"Warm" the Lookup transform data cache so that a lookup requires little or no disk access.

1. Create a destination table using the following DDL:

```
CREATE TABLE dbo.CarSales_Staging.CachedCountry
(
 ID INT,
 ClientName NVARCHAR(150),
 CountryName_EN NVARCHAR(50)
)
```

2. Create a new SSIS package.

3. Add two OLEDB connection managers. The first named **CarSales_OLEDB** that connects to the CarSales database, the second named **CarSales_Staging_OLEDB** that connects to the CarSales_Staging database.

4. Add a Data Flow task and name it **Prepare Cache**. Double-click to edit.

5. Add an OLEDB source connection and configure as follows:

OLEDB Connection Manager:	CarSales_OLEDB
Data Access Mode:	SQL Command
SQL Command Text:	SELECT CountryID, CountryName_EN
	FROM dbo. Countries WITH (NOLOCK)

6. Confirm with OK.

7. Add a Cache transform and connect the OLEDB source to it. Double-click to edit.

8. Click New to create a new Cache connection manager. Name it **ClientDimensionCache**, check Use File Cache, and enter the path to where the cache file will be stored (**C:\SQL2012DIRecipes\CH14\CachePreLoad.caw** in this example). The dialog box should look roughly like Figure 14-1.

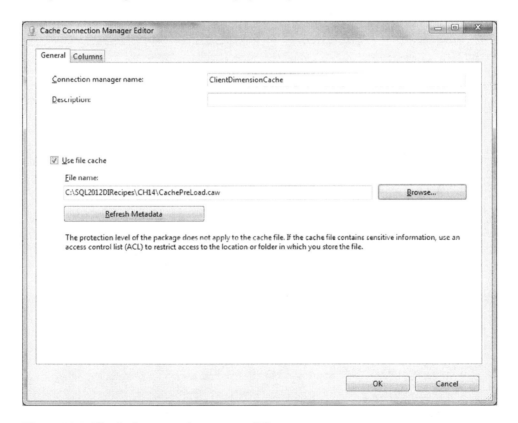

Figure 14-1. *The Cache connection manager Editor*

9. Click the Columns tab and set the Index Position to 1 for the ID (in this example). The dialog box should look like Figure 14-2.

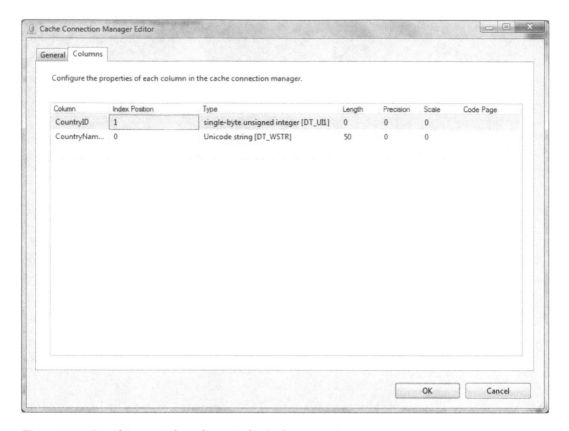

Figure 14-2. Specifying an index column in the Cache connection manager

10. Click OK to confirm the Cache connection manager specification. Return to the OLEDB source editor.

11. Click Columns on the left and ensure that the columns are mapped between the source and destination.

12. Click OK to finish modifications of the OLEDB source editor.

13. Return to the Control Flow pane by clicking Control Flow.

14. Add a new Data Flow task named Data Load, and connect the "Prepare Cache" Data Flow task to it. Double-click to edit.

15. Add an OLEDB source task. Configure it as follows:

OLEDB Connection Manager:	CarSales_OLEDB
Data Access Mode:	SQL Command
SQL Command Text:	SELECT ID, ClientName, Country
	FROM Client

16. Add a Lookup task. Connect the OLEDB source task to it. Configure the Lookup task as follows:

Pane	Option	Setting
General	Cache Mode	Full Cache
	Connection Type	Cache Connection Manager
	No matching Entries	Fail Component
Connection	Cache Connection Manager	ClientDimensionCache
Columns		Map the Country and CountryID columns. Select the CountryName_EN column from the Available Lookup Columns.

The Lookup Transformation Editor dialog box will look like Figure 14-3.

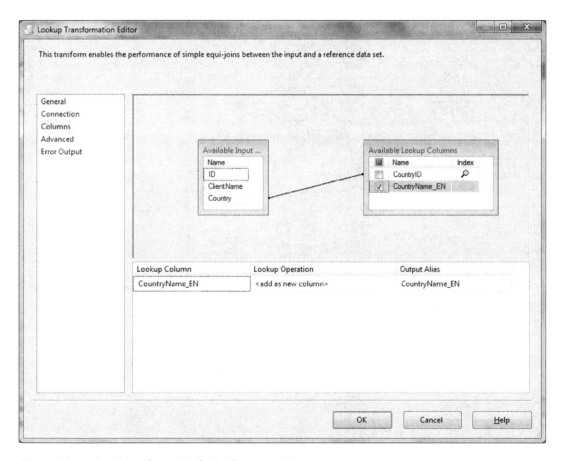

Figure 14-3. *Mapping columns in the Cache connection manager*

17. Click OK to confirm your changes.

18. Add an OLEDB destination task. Connect it to the Lookup transform and use the Lookup Match Output. Double-click to edit.

19. Configure the OLEDB destination like this:

OLEDB Connection Manager:	CarSales_Staging_OLEDB
Data Access Mode:	Table or view – Fast load
Name of Table or View:	CachedCountry

20. Click Mapping on the left and verify that the columns are mapped.

21. Click OK to confirm your changes.

You can now run the package and use the preloaded cache in the Lookup task.

How It Works

The Lookup transform has been part of SSIS since the product was released, and complaints about its performance began at about that time. An efficient solution to the speed-hit a Lookup transform can cause arrived with SQL Server 2008 and the Lookup transform data cache. Essentially, it is a way of pre-loading and/or reusing the cache data in an SSIS project. So, assuming that your ETL job allows for it, this recipe shows how to preload the Lookup cache.

The advantage of a file cache is that it can be used several times in a process, and from multiple packages. If you are warming a cache for use in a single package—the same one that the cache is being prepared—then you are probably better off only preloading the cache into memory.

A few SSIS Lookup Cache options need further explanation, as given in Table 14-1.

Table 14-1. *SSIS Cache Options*

Option	Definition	Comments
Full cache	The results of the query (or table) are loaded entirely. The query to fill the cache is executed nearly at the start of the SSIS package execution.	This is extremely resource-intensive because sufficient memory must be available to load the required data. Also, a full load can take some considerable time if a large table is queried, as well as adding strain to the I/O subsystem.
Partial cache	Matching rows are loaded, and the least recently-used rows are removed from the cache.	The query is only executed when the lookup is requested.
No cache	No records are loaded into the cache.	Requires no memory—but usually the slowest lookup option. Can be I/O intensive because each lookup is a separate query.
Enable cache for rows with no matching entries	Stores rows that do not match to avoid costly further lookups.	Ensures that pointless I/O does not occur. If a record is not in the reference dataset, then the SSIS cache will "remember" this and not look for it a second time.
Cache size	You can specify the cache size to allocate.	Different for 32-bit and 64-bit environments. It can take some practice to get this optimal.

> **Note** For the most efficient cache warming, you should have an index on the columns used in the lookup (`CountryID` and `CountryName_EN` in this example). This could be a covering index using `INCLUDE CountryName_EN`.

Hints, Tips, and Traps

- Preloading a data cache can nonetheless take a long time, and is not a magic bullet that will solve all speed issues when using the Lookup transform. However, it can allow for useful parallel processing if you are able to preload the cache early in a process ready for later use. Equally, if the cache is persisted to disk it can be reused by other packages.

- Columns must have matching data types for them to be mapped correctly.

- The Lookup cache does not use disk spooling in the case of memory overflow. There must be enough memory for a full cache load or the memory that you specify for a partial cache.

- If storing cache data on disk, the faster the disk array, the better the performance will be.

- You can only preload the cache data if it will not change during the ETL process.

14-2. Disabling and Rebuilding Nonclustered Indexes in a Destination Table

Problem

You want to disable indexes on a table (or tables) to speed up data loading.

Solution

Store a list of all the current nonclustered indexes on the destination table. Then disable all the nonclustered indexes before performing the data load. Finally, rebuild all the indexes in the table. The following steps explain how to do this in an SSIS package.

1. Create the following table to hold the persisted list of indexes to disable (`C:\SQL2012DIRecipes\CH14\tblIndexList.Sql`):

    ```
    CREATE TABLE CarSales_Staging.dbo.IndexList
    (
     TableName VARCHAR(128)
     ,SchemaName VARCHAR(128)
     ,IndexScript VARCHAR(4000)
    );
    GO
    ```

2. Run the following script to create a stored procedure that collates and stores the list of indexes to disable (`C:\SQL2012DIRecipes\CH14\pr_IndexesToDisable.Sql`):

    ```
    USE CarSales_Staging;
    GO
    ```

```
CREATE PROCEDURE   dbo.pr_IndexesToDisable
AS

TRUNCATE TABLE dbo.IndexList;

INSERT INTO     dbo.IndexList (TableName, SchemaName , IndexScript)

SELECT
                ,SSC.name
                ,SOB.name
                ,'ALTER INDEX ' + SIX.name + ' ON ' + SSC.name + '.' + SOB.name + '
DISABLE'

FROM            sys.indexes SIX
                INNER JOIN sys.objects SOB
                ON SIX.object_id = SOB.object_id
                INNER JOIN sys.schemas AS SSC
                ON SOB.schema_id = SSC.schema_id

WHERE           SOB.is_ms_shipped = 0
                AND SIX.type_desc = 'NONCLUSTERED'
                AND SOB.name = 'Clients' -- Enter the table name here

ORDER BY        SIX.type_desc, SOB.name, SIX.name ;
GO
```

3. Execute the following code to create a stored procedure that will disable the indexes
    in the selected database (C:\SQL2012DIRecipes\CH14\pr_DisableIndexes.Sql):

```
USE CarSales_Staging;
GO

CREATE PROCEDURE dbo.pr_DisableIndexes
AS

DECLARE @TableName NVARCHAR(128), @SchemaName NVARCHAR(128), @DisableIndex NVARCHAR(4000)

DECLARE   DisableIndex_CUR CURSOR

FOR
SELECT DISTINCT TableName, SchemaName FROM dbo.IndexList

OPEN DisableIndex_CUR

FETCH NEXT FROM DisableIndex_CUR INTO @TableName, @SchemaName

WHILE @@FETCH_STATUS <> -1
BEGIN

SET @DisableIndex = 'ALTER INDEX ALL ON' + @SchemaName + '.' + @TableName + 'DISABLE'
```

```
    EXEC (@DisableIndex)

    FETCH NEXT FROM DisableIndex_CUR INTO @TableName, @SchemaName

    END;

    CLOSE DisableIndex_CUR;
    DEALLOCATE DisableIndex_CUR;
```

4. Run the following script to create a stored procedure that rebuilds all disabled indexes (C:\SQL2012DIRecipes\CH14\pr_RebuildIndexes.Sql):

```
USE CarSales_Staging;
GO

CREATE PROCEDURE dbo.pr_RebuildIndexes
AS

DECLARE @TableName NVARCHAR(128), @SchemaName NVARCHAR(128), @RebuildIndex NVARCHAR(4000)

DECLARE  RebuildIndex_CUR CURSOR

FOR
SELECT DISTINCT TableName, SchemaName FROM dbo.IndexList

OPEN RebuildIndex_CUR

FETCH NEXT FROM RebuildIndex_CUR INTO @TableName, @SchemaName

WHILE @@FETCH_STATUS <> -1
BEGIN

SET @RebuildIndex = 'ALTER INDEX ALL ON ' + @SchemaName + '.' + @TableName + ' REBUILD'

EXEC (@RebuildIndex)

FETCH NEXT FROM RebuildIndex_CUR INTO @TableName, @SchemaName

END;

CLOSE RebuildIndex_CUR;
DEALLOCATE RebuildIndex_CUR;
```

5. Create a new SSIS package.

6. Add two OLEDB connection managers. The first, named **CarSales_OLEDB**, connects to the CarSales database; and the second, named **CarSales_Staging_OLEDB**, connects to the CarSales_Staging database.

7. Add a new ADO.NET connection manager named **CarSales_Staging_ADONET** that you configure to connect to the CarSales_Staging database.

8.   Add an Execute SQL task named **Create Index Metadata**. Double-click to edit.

9.   Configure the Execute SQL task to use the ADO.NET connection manager CarSales_Staging_ADONET. Set IsQueryStoredProcedure to True, and the SQL Statement to dbo.pr_IndexesToDisable.

10.   Add an Execute SQL task named **Disable Indexes**. Connect the preceding Execute SQL task to it. Double-click to edit.

11.   Configure the Execute SQL task to use the ADO.NET connection manager CarSales_Staging_ADONET. Set "IsQueryStoredProcedure" to True, and the SQL Statement to dbo.pr_DisableIndexes.

12.   Add a dataflow task. Connect the preceding Execute SQL task to it. Double-click to edit.

13.   Add an OLEDB source task. Configure it to use CarSales_OLEDB the connection manager and the Clients source table.

14.   Add an OLEDB destination task. Configure it to use the CarSales_OLEDB_Staging connection manager and the Clients destination table.

15.   Click Columns and ensure that the columns are mapped correctly.

16.   Click OK to finish configuring the data flow. Return to the Data Flow pane.

17.   Add an Execute SQL task named **Rebuild Indexes**. Connect the preceding Data Flow task to it. Double-click to edit.

18.   Configure the Execute SQL task to use the CarSales_Staging_ADONET connection manager. Set IsQueryStoredProcedure to True, and the SQL Statement to dbo.pr_RebuildIndexes. The data flow should look like Figure 14-4.

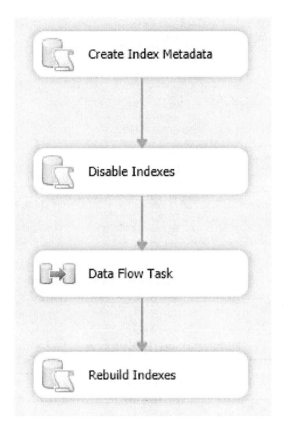

Figure 14-4. *The data flow when disabling and rebuilding nonclustered indexes*

Having disabled any nonclustered indexes first, you can now run the package to load the data, and rebuild them after the load.

How It Works

When loading large amounts of data, it is frequently much faster to disable any nonclustered indexes (especially if there are several of them) and rebuild them after the data load. This is due to the following:

- The overhead required to maintain multiple indexes is considerable.

- SQL Server cannot use the Bulk Load API if there are nonclustered indexes on a table (in most cases anyway, but more of that in Recipe 14-10).

Consequently, you could find yourself needing a technique that detects and disables any nonclustered indexes before running a data load, and then rebuilds the indexes on the tables once the load phase has completed. This is what happens in the current recipe. We use a persisted table to store the code required to disable any indexes, as well as the table(s) and schema(s) to which they belong. This is what the dbo.pr_IndexesToDisable stored procedure does. After that, a simple cursor in the dbo.pr_DisableIndexes stored procedure loops over the code that disables indexes and applies it. Once the load has finished, the same table provides the information (table(s) and schema(s)) needed to REBUILD the indexes—using the stored procedure dbo.pr_RebuildIndexes.

This technique is ideal when you wish to keep clustered indexes (which means that your data will have to be loaded presorted according to the index key)—or there are no clustered indexes. I realize that this approach may seem convoluted, but it avoids hard-coding index names into an SSIS package, and so allows the package to manage changes to indexes without any input from the developer.

Hints, Tips, and Traps

- Never disable a clustered index! You will render the table inaccessible.

- Remember that the stored procedure sp_foreachtable can be used as a quick way to rebuild all the indexes in a database, too.

- By judicious extension of the WHERE clause, you can perform this operation for multiple tables. You will have to alter the ALTER INDEX...REBUILD statement to take account of this.

- You can REORGANIZE instead of REBUILD indexes if the table fragmentation is minimal, and you are adding or replacing very small amounts of data. However, you cannot REORGANIZE indexes where ALLOW_PAGE_LOCKS is set to OFF.

- You must disable ColumnStore indexes before modifying the data in the underlying table. You can identify ColumnStore indexes in the sys.indexes system view since they have the type_desc 'NONCLUSTERED COLUMNSTORE'.

14-3. Persisting Destination Database Index Metadata

Problem

You want to gather relevant index metadata about your destination database and store it independent of the SQL Server system tables. This way, you can drop indexes with impunity and re-create them after a data load.

Solution

Query SQL Server metadata to gather the index metadata and store it in a database table. The following script shows one way of doing this.

1. Create a table in the destination database to store the index metadata using the following DDL (C:\SQL2012DIRecipes\CH14\tblMetaData_Indexes.Sql):

```
IF OBJECT_ID('dbo.MetaData_Indexes') IS NOT NULL
DROP TABLE dbo.MetaData_Indexes;

CREATE TABLE CarSales_Staging.dbo.MetaData_Indexes
(
 SERVER_NAME NVARCHAR(128) NULL,
 DATABASE_NAME NVARCHAR(128) NULL,
 SCHEMA_NAME NVARCHAR(128) NULL,
 TABLE_NAME NVARCHAR(128) NULL,
 INDEX_NAME NVARCHAR(128) NULL,
 name NVARCHAR(128) NULL,
 index_column_id INT NULL,
 key_ordinal INT NULL,
 type_desc NVARCHAR(60) NULL,
 is_unique BIT NULL,
 ignore_dup_key BIT NULL,
```

```
    is_primary_key BIT NULL,
    is_unique_constraint BIT NULL,
    fill_factor tinyINT NULL,
    is_padded BIT NULL,
    is_disabled BIT NULL,
    allow_row_locks BIT NULL,
    allow_page_locks BIT NULL,
    has_filter BIT NULL,
    filter_definition NVARCHAR(max) NULL,
    is_included_column BIT NULL,
    is_descending_key BIT NULL,
    FileGroup NVARCHAR(128) NULL,
    TableObjectID INT NULL,
    IsNoRecompute BIT NULL,
    IndexDepth INT NULL,
    IsAutoStatistics BIT NULL,
    IsClustered BIT NULL,
    IsFulltextKey BIT NULL,
    DataSpace NVARCHAR(128) NULL
) ;
GO
```

2.   Run the following code to gather the index metadata (C:\SQL2012DIRecipes\CH14\
GatherIndexMetadata.Sql):

```
DECLARE @SERVER_NAME NVARCHAR(128) = @@SERVERNAME
DECLARE @DATABASE_NAME NVARCHAR(128) = DB_NAME()

INSERT INTO MetaData_Indexes
(
SERVER_NAME
,DATABASE_NAME
,SCHEMA_NAME
,TABLE_NAME
,INDEX_NAME
,name
,index_column_id
,key_ordinal
,type_desc
,is_unique
,ignore_dup_key
,is_primary_key
,is_unique_constraint
,fill_factor
,is_padded
,is_disabled
,allow_row_locks
,allow_page_locks
,has_filter
,filter_definition
,is_included_column
,is_descending_key
```

```
            ,FileGroup
            ,TableObjectID
            ,IsNoRecompute
            ,IndexDepth
            ,IsAutoStatistics
            ,IsClustered
            ,IsFulltextKey
            ,DataSpace
            )

            SELECT DISTINCT TOP (100) PERCENT
            @SERVER_NAME
            ,@DATABASE_NAME
            ,SCH.name AS SCHEMA_NAME
            ,TBL.name AS TABLE_NAME
            ,SIX.name AS INDEX_NAME
            ,COL.name
            ,SIC.index_column_id
            ,SIC.key_ordinal
            ,SIX.type_desc
            ,SIX.is_unique
            ,SIX.ignore_dup_key
            ,SIX.is_primary_key
            ,SIX.is_unique_constraint
            ,SIX.fill_factor
            ,SIX.is_padded
            ,SIX.is_disabled
            ,SIX.allow_row_locks
            ,SIX.allow_page_locks
            ,SIX.has_filter
            ,SIX.filter_definition
            ,SIC.is_included_column
            ,SIC.is_descending_key
            ,CAST(NULL AS VARCHAR(128))
            ,TBL.object_id
            ,CAST(NULL AS BIT)
            ,INDEXPROPERTY(TBL.object_id,  SIX.name,'IndexDepth') AS IndexDepth
            ,INDEXPROPERTY(TBL.object_id,  SIX.name,'IsAutoStatistics') AS IsAutoStatistics
            ,INDEXPROPERTY(TBL.object_id,  SIX.name,'IsClustered') AS IsClustered
            ,INDEXPROPERTY(TBL.object_id,  SIX.name,'IsFulltextKey') AS IsFulltextKey
            ,DSP.name AS DataSpace

            FROM      sys.data_spaces DSP
                      INNER JOIN sys.indexes SIX
                      ON DSP.data_space_id = SIX.data_space_id
                      INNER JOIN sys.tables TBL
                      ON SIX.object_id = TBL.object_id
                      INNER JOIN sys.schemas SCH
                      ON TBL.schema_id = SCH.schema_id
                      INNER JOIN sys.index_columns SIC
                      ON SIX.index_id = SIC.index_id
```

```
                AND SIX.object_id = SIC.object_id
                INNER JOIN sys.columns COL
                ON SIC.column_id = COL.column_id
                AND TBL.object_id = COL.object_id
                LEFT OUTER JOIN   sys.xml_indexes XMI
                ON SIX.name = XMI.name
                AND SIX.object_id = XMI.object_id

WHERE       TBL.is_ms_shipped = 0
                AND XMI.name IS NULL

ORDER BY  SCHEMA_NAME, TABLE_NAME, INDEX_NAME, SIC.key_ordinal

-- Add FileGroup, NoRecompute, note that online & drop existing are not stored in
-- metadata

IF OBJECT_ID('tempdb..#Tmp_IndexFileGroups') IS NOT NULL
DROP TABLE tempdb..#Tmp_IndexFileGroups;

SELECT DISTINCT
DSP.name AS DataSpace
,TBL.name AS TABLE_NAME
,TBL.object_id AS TableObjectID
,SIX.name
,SIX.type_desc
,STT.no_recompute

INTO #Tmp_IndexFileGroups

FROM        sys.data_spaces DSP
                INNER JOIN sys.indexes SIX
                ON DSP.data_space_id = SIX.data_space_id
                INNER JOIN sys.tables TBL
                ON SIX.object_id = TBL.object_id
                INNER JOIN sys.stats STT
                ON STT.object_id = TBL.object_id
                AND STT.name = SIX.name

WHERE       SIX.name IS NOT NULL

-- Update Filegroup


UPDATE    D
SET       D.FileGroup = Tmp.DataSpace
          ,D.IsNoRecompute = TMP.no_recompute
FROM      MetaData_Indexes D
          INNER JOIN #Tmp_IndexFileGroups TMP
          ON D.TableObjectID = Tmp.TableObjectID
```

How It Works

Dropping and re-creating indexes—as opposed to disabling and rebuilding them, which we saw in Recipe 14-2—requires you to be able to store DROP and CREATE index scripts. One way to obtain these is to use SQL Server Management Studio to extract index scripts either individually or for a selection of tables. These can then be stored in text files or stored procedures that you call. However, it can become very wearing to maintain a script-based solution like this, and so I have another suggestion, which is to gather and store, independently, the index metadata from the system views in a denormalized form, which then allows you to drop and create any of your indexes whenever you want. Although more work, this solution does have several advantages:

- It is easy to regenerate the metadata as indexes are added, deleted, and updated in the database.

- You do not have to handle a parallel set of scripts.

- It suits ETL tasks where your tests show that it is faster to load the data into heaps and add clustered indexes after the data load—possibly because the source data is not sorted and adding sort transforms in SSIS creates too much memory pressure.

In this recipe, then, is a script that gathers and stores the metadata needed to drop and create (nearly) all the indexes in a staging database and store the index metadata in persisted tables on disk.

Once you have learned how to use this script, it becomes part of a more dynamic ETL process. This is done by

- Creating and executing the DROP script before the data load.

- Creating and executing the CREATE after the data load.

However, these extensions of the process are the subject of Recipes 14-4 and 14-5, respectively.

The fields that are stored and used to drop and re-create the indexes need some explaining, as provided in Table 14-2.

Table 14-2. *Fields Used to Store Index Metadata*

Field Name	Source Table	Description
SERVER_NAME		Gets the server name from the current environment.
DATABASE_NAME		Gets the database name from the current environment.
SCHEMA_NAME	sys.tables	The schema name.
TABLE_NAME	sys.tables	The table name.
INDEX_NAME	sys.indexes	The index name.
name	sys.columns	The column name.
index_column_id	sys.index_columns	The internal ID of the index column.
key_ordinal	sys.index_columns	The position of the index column.
type_desc	sys.indexes	Full description of the type of index.
is_unique	sys.indexes	Is the index unique?
ignore_dup_key	sys.indexes	Is a duplicate key to be ignored?
is_primary_key	sys.indexes	Is this column part of a primary key?

(*continued*)

Table 14-2. (*continued*)

Field Name	Source Table	Description
is_unique_constraint	sys.indexes	Is this column part of a unique constraint?
fill_factor	sys.indexes	The fill factor for the index.
is_padded	sys.indexes	Is the index padded?
is_disabled	sys.indexes	Is the index disabled?
allow_row_locks	sys.indexes	Does the index allow row locking?
allow_page_locks	sys.indexes	Does the index allow page locking?
has_filter	sys.indexes	Does the index have a filter (i.e., is it a filtered index)?
filter_definition	sys.indexes	The definition of any filter, if there is one.
is_included_column	sys.indexes	The column is part of a covering index.
is_descending_key	sys.indexes	The sort key is DESC.
FileGroup	sys.tables	The file group used for storage.
TableObjectID	sys.stats	The internal object ID.
IsNoRecompute	sys.stats	Indicates that a computed column is not to be recalculated.
IndexDepth	sys.stats	The index level.
IsAutoStatistics	sys.stats	Index statistics are created automatically.
IsClustered	sys.stats	The index is a clustered index.
IsFulltextKey	sys.stats	This is the key for a full text index.
DataSpace	sys.dataspaces	The dataspace for storage.

■ **Note**   Stored index metadata can become a core element in ETL process index maintenance. Instead of truncating the MetaData_Indexes table at the start of each process, you can merely update the table with new index metadata—and delete unused index metadata. You can then add a flag column to indicate index priority and sequencing. This allows you to classify essential indexes as priority one, for example, and process them early in the ETL cycle. You continue in this way until any remaining indexes are processed at the end of the cycle.

Hints, Tips, and Traps

- Always script your staging database and make a backup copy before dropping indexes.
- The script assumes no need for quoted identifiers in the metadata. If this is not the case with your database naming convention, then you need to handle quoted identifiers.
- You can tweak the script to select all the tables that follow a specific naming convention, or all the objects in a specific schema by judicious tweaks of the WHERE clause of the initial SELECT statement.

- No spatial index management is handled in this script.

- No full-text index management is handledin this script—this approach is designed for staging databases.

- No column indexes are managed in this script—these have to be dropped and re-created in any case.

- The scripts used to store the index metadata DROP and subsequently CREATE the indexes can be turned into stored procedures and called from SSIS Execute SQL tasks in an SSIS package. Recipe 14-2 is an example of this.

- The index metadata can be stored in a separate database or a separate schema, if you prefer.

- No IF EXISTS trapping has been added to the script since we are dealing with staging databases, where indexes are regularly dropped. You may prefer to add this to the script.

- I have no qualms about using cursors in these kinds of script. The overhead is minimal given the small number of records processed. In any case the cursor overhead is infinitesimal compared to that used by an indexing process.

14-4. Scripting and Executing DROP Statements for Destination Database Indexes

Problem

You want to drop all existing indexes in a staging database before running a data load.

Solution

To remove all the existing indexes, use the index metadata that you obtained using the technique described in Recipe 14-3 to generate and run the DROP scripts. The following is the script to do this (C:\SQL2012DIRecipes\CH14\DropIndexes.Sql):

```
-- Create table to hold script elements

IF OBJECT_ID('tempdb..#ScriptElements') IS NOT NULL
DROP TABLE tempdb..#ScriptElements;

CREATE TABLE #ScriptElements (ID INT IDENTITY(1,1), ScriptElement NVARCHAR(MAX))

-- Non-Clustered Indexes

INSERT INTO #ScriptElements (ScriptElement)

SELECT DISTINCT
'DROP INDEX '
+ INDEX_NAME
+ ' ON '
+ DATABASE_NAME + '.' + SCHEMA_NAME + '.' + TABLE_NAME

FROM    MetaData_Indexes
```

```
WHERE   type_desc = 'NONCLUSTERED'
        AND is_primary_key = 0
        AND is_unique_constraint = 0

-- Unique constraints

INSERT INTO #ScriptElements (ScriptElement)

SELECT DISTINCT
'ALTER TABLE '
+ DATABASE_NAME + '.' + SCHEMA_NAME + '.' + TABLE_NAME
+ ' DROP CONSTRAINT '
+ INDEX_NAME

FROM    MetaData_Indexes
WHERE   is_unique_constraint = 1


-- Clustered Indexes

INSERT INTO #ScriptElements (ScriptElement)

SELECT DISTINCT
'DROP INDEX '
+ INDEX_NAME
+ ' ON '
+ DATABASE_NAME + '.' + SCHEMA_NAME + '.' + TABLE_NAME

FROM    MetaData_Indexes
WHERE   type_desc = 'CLUSTERED'
        AND is_primary_key = 0

-- Primary Key Indexes

INSERT INTO #ScriptElements (ScriptElement)

SELECT DISTINCT
'ALTER TABLE '
+ DATABASE_NAME + '.' + SCHEMA_NAME + '.' + TABLE_NAME
+ ' DROP CONSTRAINT '
+ INDEX_NAME

FROM    MetaData_Indexes
WHERE   is_primary_key = 1

-- Create and execute DROP scripts

DECLARE @DropIndex NVARCHAR(MAX)

DECLARE  DropIndex_CUR CURSOR
```

819

```
FOR
SELECT ScriptElement FROM #ScriptElements ORDER BY ID

OPEN DropIndex_CUR

FETCH NEXT FROM DropIndex_CUR INTO @DropIndex

WHILE @@FETCH_STATUS <> -1
BEGIN

EXEC (@DropIndex)

FETCH NEXT FROM DropIndex_CUR INTO @DropIndex

END ;

CLOSE DropIndex_CUR ;
DEALLOCATE DropIndex_CUR ;
```

How It Works

The code defined here is reasonably simple, fortunately. First, it gathers all the information required to DROP any nonclusteredindexes, then any unique constraints, any clustered indexes, and finally, any primary key indexes. Then the DROP scripts are created and executed for these indexes in that order (thanks to the ID column).

It is important to drop any nonclustered indexes first, as dropping clustered indexes on a table before dropping the nonclustered indexes will cause the nonclustered indexes to be updated, and consequently slow the process down considerably.

Hints, Tips, and Traps

- When adding indexes at various stages in an ETL process, you can use the index creation script and filter it using relevant table names and index types to create specific indexes as required.

14-5. Scripting and Executing CREATE Statements for Destination Database Indexes

Problem

You want to re-create the indexes that you dropped before a data load.

Solution

Generate CREATE scripts using the metadata for indexes that you persisted to a database table in Recipe 14-3. This way, the destination database will be fully optimized. The following is the script to do it (C:\SQL2012DIRecipes\CH14\CreateIndexes.Sql):

```
DECLARE @SORT_IN_TEMPDB BIT = 1
DECLARE @DROP_EXISTING BIT = 0
```

```
DECLARE @ONLINE BIT = O
DECLARE @MAX_DEGREE_OF_PARALLELISM TINYINT = O

-- Create table to hold script elements

IF OBJECT_ID('tempdb..#ScriptElements') IS NOT NULL
DROP TABLE tempdb..#ScriptElements;

CREATE TABLE #ScriptElements (ID INT IDENTITY(1,1), ScriptElement NVARCHAR(MAX))

-- Non-Clustered Indexes

IF OBJECT_ID('tempdb..#Tmp_IndexedFields') IS NOT NULL
DROP TABLE tempdb..#Tmp_IndexedFields;

-- IndexedFields
;
WITH Core_CTE ( INDEX_NAME, Rank, Name )
AS
(
SELECT    INDEX_NAME,ROW_NUMBER()
          OVER( PARTITION BY INDEX_NAME ORDER BY INDEX_NAME, key_ordinal)
          ,CAST(name AS VARCHAR(MAX))
FROM      MctaData_Indexes
WHERE     is_included_column = O),

   Root_CTE ( INDEX_NAME, Rank, Name )
            AS ( SELECT INDEX_NAME, Rank, name
                   FROM Core_CTE
                 WHERE Rank = 1 ),

Recursion_CTE ( INDEX_NAME, Rank, Name )
            AS ( SELECT INDEX_NAME, Rank, name
                   FROM Root_CTE

                 UNION ALL

                 SELECT Core_CTE.INDEX_NAME, Core_CTE.Rank,
                        Recursion_CTE.name + ', ' + Core_CTE.name
                   FROM Core_CTE

                 INNER JOIN Recursion_CTE
                   ON Core_CTE.INDEX_NAME = Recursion_CTE.INDEX_NAME
                  AND Core_CTE.Rank = Recursion_CTE.Rank + 1 )

SELECT INDEX_NAME, MAX( Name ) AS IndexFields_Main
INTO #Tmp_IndexedFields
FROM Recursion_CTE
GROUP BY INDEX_NAME;

-- Included fields
```

```
IF OBJECT_ID('tempdb..#Tmp_IncludedFields') IS NOT NULL
DROP TABLE tempdb..#Tmp_IncludedFields;


WITH Core_CTE ( INDEX_NAME, Rank, Name )
            AS ( SELECT INDEX_NAME,
                        ROW_NUMBER() OVER( PARTITION BY INDEX_NAME ORDER BY INDEX_NAME ),
                        CAST( name AS VARCHAR(MAX) )

                    FROM MetaData_Indexes WHERE is_included_column = 1 ),

    Root_CTE ( INDEX_NAME, Rank, Name )
            AS ( SELECT INDEX_NAME, Rank, name
                    FROM Core_CTE
                  WHERE Rank = 1 ),

Recursion_CTE ( INDEX_NAME, Rank, Name )
            AS ( SELECT INDEX_NAME, Rank, name
                    FROM Root_CTE

                  UNION ALL

                  SELECT Core_CTE.INDEX_NAME, Core_CTE.Rank,
                         Recursion_CTE.name + ', ' + Core_CTE.name
                    FROM Core_CTE

                  INNER JOIN Recursion_CTE
                     ON Core_CTE.INDEX_NAME = Recursion_CTE.INDEX_NAME
                    AND Core_CTE.Rank = Recursion_CTE.Rank + 1 )

SELECT      INDEX_NAME, MAX( Name ) AS IndexFields_Included
INTO        #Tmp_IncludedFields
FROM        Recursion_CTE
GROUP BY    INDEX_NAME;

-- Create Index Script

-- First, metadata for core indexes

IF OBJECT_ID('tempdb..#Tmp_IndexData') IS NOT NULL
DROP TABLE tempdb..#Tmp_IndexData;

SELECT DISTINCT
MetaData_Indexes.SCHEMA_NAME
,MetaData_Indexes.TABLE_NAME
,MetaData_Indexes.INDEX_NAME
,#Tmp_IndexedFields.IndexFields_Main
,#Tmp_IncludedFields.IndexFields_Included
,MetaData_Indexes.type_desc
,MetaData_Indexes.is_unique
,MetaData_Indexes.has_filter
```

```
,MetaData_Indexes.filter_definition
,MetaData_Indexes.is_padded
,MetaData_Indexes.IsNoRecompute
,MetaData_Indexes.[ignore_dup_key]
,MetaData_Indexes.[allow_page_locks]
,MetaData_Indexes.[allow_row_locks]
,MetaData_Indexes.fill_factor
,MetaData_Indexes.DataSpace
,MetaData_Indexes.is_primary_key
,MetaData_Indexes.is_unique_constraint

INTO        #Tmp_IndexData

FROM        MetaData_Indexes
            INNER JOIN #Tmp_IndexedFields
            ON MetaData_Indexes.INDEX_NAME = #Tmp_IndexedFields.INDEX_NAME
            LEFT OUTER JOIN #Tmp_IncludedFields
            ON MetaData_Indexes.INDEX_NAME = #Tmp_IncludedFields.INDEX_NAME

-- Create primary keys

INSERT INTO #ScriptElements (ScriptElement)

SELECT DISTINCT
' ALTER TABLE '
+ SCHEMA_NAME + '.' + TABLE_NAME
+ ' ADD CONSTRAINT '
+ INDEX_NAME
+ ' PRIMARY KEY '
+ CASE
WHEN type_desc = 'CLUSTERED' THEN 'CLUSTERED '
ELSE
'NONCLUSTERED   '
END
+ ' (' + IndexFields_Main + ')'
+ ' ON [' + DataSpace + ']'

FROM            #Tmp_IndexData

WHERE           #Tmp_IndexData.is_primary_key = 1

-- Create clustered indexes

INSERT INTO    #ScriptElements (ScriptElement)

SELECT DISTINCT
'CREATE '
+ CASE
WHEN is_unique = 1 THEN 'UNIQUE '
ELSE ''
END
```

823

```
+ 'CLUSTERED INDEX '
+ INDEX_NAME + ' ON ' + SCHEMA_NAME + '.' + TABLE_NAME + ' (' + IndexFields_Main + ')'
+ ' WITH ('
+ CASE
WHEN is_padded = 1 THEN ' PAD_INDEX  = OFF, '
ELSE ' PAD_INDEX  = ON, '
END
+ CASE
WHEN IsNoRecompute = 1 THEN ' STATISTICS_NORECOMPUTE  = OFF, '
ELSE  'STATISTICS_NORECOMPUTE  = ON, '
END
+ CASE
WHEN [ignore_dup_key] = 1 THEN ' IGNORE_DUP_KEY  = ON, '
ELSE ' IGNORE_DUP_KEY  = OFF, '
END
+ CASE
WHEN [allow_page_locks] = 1 THEN ' ALLOW_PAGE_LOCKS  = ON, '
ELSE 'ALLOW_PAGE_LOCKS  = OFF, '
END
+ CASE
WHEN fill_factor IS NOT NULL THEN ' FILLFACTOR  = ' + CAST(fill_factor AS VARCHAR(5)) + ','
ELSE ''
END
+ CASE
WHEN [allow_row_locks] = 1 THEN ' ALLOW_ROW_LOCKS  = ON, '
ELSE ' ALLOW_ROW_LOCKS  = OFF, '
END
+ CASE
WHEN @SORT_IN_TEMPDB = 1 THEN ' SORT_IN_TEMPDB  = ON, '
ELSE ' SORT_IN_TEMPDB  = OFF, '
END
+ CASE
WHEN @DROP_EXISTING = 1 THEN ' DROP_EXISTING  = ON, '
ELSE ' DROP_EXISTING  = OFF, '
END
+ CASE
WHEN @ONLINE = 1 THEN ' ONLINE  = ON '
ELSE ' ONLINE  = OFF '
END
+ CASE
WHEN @MAX_DEGREE_OF_PARALLELISM = 0 THEN ''
ELSE ' MAXDOP = ' + CAST(@MAX_DEGREE_OF_PARALLELISM AS NVARCHAR(2))
END
+ ')'
+ ' ON [' + DataSpace + ']'

FROM       #Tmp_IndexData

WHERE      #Tmp_IndexData.is_primary_key = 0
           AND #Tmp_IndexData.is_unique_constraint = 0
           AND type_desc = 'CLUSTERED'
```

```
-- Create Unique Indexes

INSERT INTO #ScriptElements (ScriptElement)

SELECT DISTINCT
' ALTER TABLE '
+ SCHEMA_NAME + '.' + TABLE_NAME
+ ' ADD CONSTRAINT '
+ INDEX_NAME
+ ' UNIQUE '
+ CASE
WHEN type_desc = 'CLUSTERED' THEN 'CLUSTERED '
ELSE
'NONCLUSTERED  '
END
+ ' (' + IndexFields_Main + ')'
+ ' ON [' + DataSpace + ']'

FROM        #Tmp_IndexData

WHERE       #Tmp_IndexData.is_unique_constraint = 1 ;

-- Create non-clustered indexes

INSERT INTO #ScriptElements (ScriptElement)

SELECT DISTINCT
'CREATE '
+ CASE
WHEN is_unique = 1 THEN 'UNIQUE '
ELSE ''
END
+ 'NONCLUSTERED INDEX '
+ INDEX_NAME + ' ON ' + SCHEMA_NAME + '.' + TABLE_NAME + ' (' + IndexFields_Main + ')'
+ CASE
WHEN IndexFields_Included IS NOT NULL THEN ' INCLUDE ' + ' (' + IndexFields_Included + ')'
ELSE ''
END
+ CASE
WHEN has_filter = 1 THEN ' WHERE ' + filter_definition
ELSE ''
END
+ ' WITH ('
+ CASE
WHEN is_padded = 1 THEN ' PAD_INDEX  = OFF, '
ELSE ' PAD_INDEX  = ON, '
END
+ CASE
WHEN IsNoRecompute = 1 THEN ' STATISTICS_NORECOMPUTE  = OFF, ' -- CHECK LOGIC
ELSE  'STATISTICS_NORECOMPUTE  = ON, '
END
```

```sql
+ CASE
WHEN [ignore_dup_key] = 1 THEN ' IGNORE_DUP_KEY  = ON, '
ELSE ' IGNORE_DUP_KEY  = OFF, '
END
+ CASE
WHEN [allow_page_locks] = 1 THEN ' ALLOW_PAGE_LOCKS  = ON, '
ELSE 'ALLOW_PAGE_LOCKS  = OFF, '
END
+ CASE
WHEN fill_factor IS NOT NULL THEN ' FILLFACTOR  = ' + CAST(fill_factor AS VARCHAR(5)) + ','
ELSE ''
END
+ CASE
WHEN [allow_row_locks] = 1 THEN ' ALLOW_ROW_LOCKS  = ON, '
ELSE ' ALLOW_ROW_LOCKS  = OFF, '
END
+ CASE
WHEN @SORT_IN_TEMPDB = 1 THEN ' SORT_IN_TEMPDB  = ON, '
ELSE ' SORT_IN_TEMPDB  = OFF, '
END
+ CASE
WHEN @DROP_EXISTING = 1 THEN ' DROP_EXISTING  = ON, '
ELSE ' DROP_EXISTING  = OFF, '
END
+ CASE
WHEN @ONLINE = 1 THEN ' ONLINE  = ON '
ELSE ' ONLINE  = OFF '
END
+ CASE
WHEN @MAX_DEGREE_OF_PARALLELISM = 0 THEN ''
ELSE ' MAXDOP = ' + CAST(@MAX_DEGREE_OF_PARALLELISM AS NVARCHAR(2))
END
+ ')'
+ ' ON [' + DataSpace + ']'

FROM        #Tmp_IndexData

WHERE       #Tmp_IndexData.is_primary_key = 0
            AND #Tmp_IndexData.is_unique_constraint = 0
            AND type_desc = 'NONCLUSTERED'
 ;
-- Create and execute CREATE scripts

DECLARE @CreateIndex NVARCHAR(MAX)

DECLARE  CreateIndex_CUR CURSOR

FOR
SELECT ScriptElement FROM #ScriptElements ORDER BY ID
```

```
OPEN CreateIndex_CUR

FETCH NEXT FROM CreateIndex_CUR INTO @CreateIndex

WHILE @@FETCH_STATUS <> -1
BEGIN

EXEC (@CreateIndex)

FETCH NEXT FROM CreateIndex_CUR INTO @CreateIndex

END ;

CLOSE CreateIndex_CUR ;
DEALLOCATE CreateIndex_CUR ;
```

How It Works

I realize that this is a very long script, but it is interesting to see how the index metadata can be used to re-create indexes in a destination database. When re-creating indexes, remember that

- If you are dropping all the indexes, drop the nonclustered indexes first, followed by the clustered index.

- If you are creating a clustered index as well as nonclustered indexes, remember to create the clustered index first.

This script uses the data in the MetaData_Indexes table to re-create all the scripts required to re-create the indexes as they were before they were dropped. This is not a simple process because complex key columns and covering indexes have to be managed, and so a judicious use of temporary tables is required.

The script assembles, in this order, the scripts to

- Create primary keys.

- Create clustered indexes.

- Create unique indexes.

- Create nonclustered indexes.

All the requisite scripts are stored in the temporary table #ScriptElements. This table is then iterated over by a cursor that executes the statements—and consequently generates the indexes.

Hints, Tips, and Traps

- This script can become part of an ETL process, as described in Recipe 14-2.

- You can always change the EXEC to PRINT inside the final cursor loop if you want to script out the CREATE INDEX statements and store them as text files.

- If time is of the essence (and you are using the Enterprise version of SQL Server), you can create some or all of your indexes offline. This has the advantage of allowing users to access your finalized data faster, even if some indexes are not immediately available.

14-6. Storing Metadata, and Then Scripting and Executing DROP and CREATE Statements for Destination Database XML Indexes

Problem

You are using XML indexes in a table that will be the destination for a large ETL update and you need to drop and re-create these indexes as part of the ETL process.

Solution

Store the metadata required to create DROP and CREATE statements for XML indexes. Then use this information to manage the indexes themselves.

1. Create the following table to hold the persisted metadata for XML indexes (C:\SQL2012DIRecipes\CH14\tblMetadata_XMLIndexes.Sql):

```
IF OBJECT_ID('dbo.Metadata_XMLIndexes') IS NOT NULL
DROP TABLE dbo.Metadata_XMLIndexes;

CREATE TABLE CarSales_Staging.dbo.Metadata_XMLIndexes
(
 SERVER_NAME NVARCHAR(128) NULL,
 DATABASE_NAME NVARCHAR(128) NULL,
 SCHEMA_NAME NVARCHAR(128)  NULL,
 TABLE_NAME NVARCHAR(128)  NULL,
 PrimaryIndexName NVARCHAR(128) NULL,
 TableID INT  NULL,
 XMLPrimaryIndexID INT  NULL,
 XMLSecondaryaryIndexID INT  NULL,
 INDEX_NAME NVARCHAR(128)  NULL,
 SecondaryTypeDescription NVARCHAR(60)  NULL,
 DataSpace NVARCHAR(128)  NULL,
 Allow_Page_Locks BIT NULL,
 Allow_Row_Locks BIT NULL,
 Is_Padded BIT NULL,
 IsPrimaryXMLIndex BIT NULL,
 XMLColumnNameNVARCHAR (128) NULL
 ) ;
GO
```

2. Run the following script to collate and store XML index metadata (C:\SQL2012DIRecipes\CH14\GatherXMLIndexMetadata.Sql):

```
INSERT INTO Metadata_XMLIndexes
(
SERVER_NAME
,DATABASE_NAME
,SCHEMA_NAME
,TABLE_NAME
```

```
,PrimaryIndexName
,XMLPrimaryIndexID
,DataSpace
,TableID
,[Allow_Page_Locks]
,[Allow_Row_Locks]
,Is_Padded
,IsPrimaryXMLIndex
,XMLColumnName
)

SELECT
@SERVER_NAME
,@DATABASE_NAME
,SCH.name AS SCHEMA_NAME
,TBL.name AS TABLE_NAME
,XIN.name AS INDEX_NAME
,XIN.index_id AS IndexID
,DSP.name AS DataSpace
,TBL.object_id AS TableID
,XIN.allow_page_locks
,XIN.allow_row_locks
,XIN.is_padded
,1
,COL.name

FROM    sys.tables TBL
        INNER JOIN sys.xml_indexes XIN
        ON TBL.object_id = XIN.object_id
        INNER JOIN sys.schemas SCH
        ON TBL.schema_id = SCH.schema_id
        INNER JOIN sys.data_spaces DSP
        ON XIN.data_space_id = DSP.data_space_id
        INNER JOIN sys.index_columns SIC
        ON XIN.index_id = SIC.index_id
        AND XIN.object_id = SIC.object_id
        INNER JOIN sys.columns COL
        ON SIC.object_id = COL.object_id
        AND SIC.column_id = COL.column_id

WHERE   XIN.secondary_type_desc IS NULL ;

-- Secondary XML indexes

INSERT INTO #Metadata_XMLIndexes
(
SERVER_NAME
,DATABASE_NAME
,SCHEMA_NAME
,TABLE_NAME
,PrimaryIndexName
```

```
            ,TableID
            ,XMLPrimaryIndexID
            ,XMLSecondaryaryIndexID
            ,INDEX_NAME
            ,SecondaryTypeDescription
            ,DataSpace
            ,Allow_Page_Locks
            ,Allow_Row_Locks
            ,Is_Padded
            ,IsPrimaryXMLIndex
            ,XMLColumnName
            )


        SELECT
        @SERVER_NAME AS SERVER_NAME
        ,@DATABASE_NAME AS DATABASE_NAME
        ,SCH.name AS SCHEMA_NAME
        ,TBL.name AS TABLE_NAME
        ,SIX.name AS PrimaryIndexName
        ,TBL.object_id AS TableID
        ,SIX.index_id AS XMLPrimaryIndexID
        ,XIN.index_id AS XMLSecondaryaryIndexID
        ,XIN.name AS INDEX_NAME
        ,XIN.secondary_type_desc AS SecondaryTypeDescription
        ,DSP.name AS DataSpace
        ,XIN.allow_page_locks AS AllowPageLocks
        ,XIN.allow_row_locks AS AllowRowLocks
        ,XIN.is_padded AS IsPadded
        ,0
        ,COL.name

        FROM    sys.indexes SIX
                INNER JOIN sys.tables TBL
                ON SIX.object_id = TBL.object_id
                INNER JOIN sys.xml_indexes  XIN
                ON SIX.object_id = XIN.object_id
                AND SIX.index_id = XIN.using_xml_index_id
                INNER JOIN sys.schemas SCH
                ON TBL.schema_id = SCH.schema_id
                INNER JOIN sys.data_spaces DSP
                ON XIN.data_space_id = DSP.data_space_id
                INNER JOIN sys.index_columns SIC
                ON XIN.index_id = SIC.index_id
                AND XIN.object_id = SIC.object_id
                INNER JOIN sys.columns COL
                ON SIC.object_id = COL.object_id
                AND SIC.column_id = COL.column_id
        ;
```

3. Execute the following code to DROP XML indexes in the selected database
(C:\SQL2012DIRecipes\CH14\DropXMLIndexes.Sql):

```sql
-- Drop table to hold script elements

IF OBJECT_ID('tempdb..#ScriptElements') IS NOT NULL
DROP TABLE tempdb..#ScriptElements;

CREATE TABLE #ScriptElements (ID INT IDENTITY(1,1), ScriptElement NVARCHAR(MAX))

-- Non-Clustered Indexes

IF OBJECT_ID('tempdb..#Tmp_IndexedFields') IS NOT NULL
DROP TABLE tempdb..#Tmp_IndexedFields;

-- Secondary XML index

INSERT INTO #ScriptElements

SELECT DISTINCT
'DROP INDEX '
+ INDEX_NAME
+ ' ON '
+ DATABASE_NAME + '.' + SCHEMA_NAME + '.' + TABLE_NAME

FROM        Metadata_XMLIndexes

WHERE       IsPrimaryXMLIndex = 0 ;

-- Primary XML index

INSERT INTO #ScriptElements

SELECT DISTINCT
'DROP INDEX '
+ PrimaryIndexName
+ ' ON '
+ DATABASE_NAME + '.' + SCHEMA_NAME + '.' + TABLE_NAME

FROM        Metadata_XMLIndexes

WHERE       IsPrimaryXMLIndex = 1 ;

-- Drop and execute DROP scripts

DECLARE     @DropIndex NVARCHAR(MAX)

DECLARE     DropIndex_CUR CURSOR

FOR
SELECT ScriptElement FROM #ScriptElements ORDER BY ID
```

```
OPEN DropIndex_CUR

FETCH NEXT FROM DropIndex_CUR INTO @DropIndex

WHILE @@FETCH_STATUS <> -1
BEGIN

EXEC (@DropIndex)

FETCH NEXT FROM DropIndex_CUR INTO @DropIndex

END ;

CLOSE DropIndex_CUR;
DEALLOCATE DropIndex_CUR;
```

4. Now you can run your ETL package that loads the source data into the
    destination—or staging—database.

5. Run the following T-SQL to re-create XML indexes in the staging database
    (C:\SQL2012DIRecipes\CH14\CreateXMLIndexes.Sql):

```
DECLARE @SORT_IN_TEMPDB BIT = 1
DECLARE @DROP_EXISTING BIT = 0

-- Create table to hold script elements

IF OBJECT_ID('tempdb..#ScriptElements') IS NOT NULL
DROP TABLE tempdb..#ScriptElements;

CREATE TABLE #ScriptElements (ID INT IDENTITY(1,1), ScriptElement NVARCHAR(MAX))

-- Non-Clustered Indexes

IF OBJECT_ID('tempdb..#Tmp_IndexedFields') IS NOT NULL
DROP TABLE tempdb..#Tmp_IndexedFields;

INSERT INTO #ScriptElements

SELECT DISTINCT
'CREATE PRIMARY XML INDEX '
+ PrimaryIndexName
+ ' ON '
+ DATABASE_NAME + '.' + SCHEMA_NAME + '.' + TABLE_NAME
+ ' (' + XMLColumnName  + ') '
+ ' WITH ('
+ CASE
WHEN is_padded = 1 THEN ' PAD_INDEX  = OFF, '
ELSE ' PAD_INDEX  = ON, '
END
```

```
+ CASE
WHEN [allow_page_locks] = 1 THEN ' ALLOW_PAGE_LOCKS  = ON, '
ELSE 'ALLOW_PAGE_LOCKS  = OFF, '
END
+ CASE
WHEN [allow_row_locks] = 1 THEN ' ALLOW_ROW_LOCKS  = ON, '
ELSE ' ALLOW_ROW_LOCKS  = OFF, '
END
+ CASE
WHEN @SORT_IN_TEMPDB = 1 THEN ' SORT_IN_TEMPDB  = ON, '
ELSE ' SORT_IN_TEMPDB  = OFF, '
END
+ CASE
WHEN @DROP_EXISTING = 1 THEN ' DROP_EXISTING  = ON, '
ELSE ' DROP_EXISTING  = OFF '
END
+ ')'

FROMMetadata_XMLIndexes

WHEREIsPrimaryXMLIndex = 1 ;

-- Secondary XML index

INSERT INTO #ScriptElements

SELECT
'CREATE XML INDEX '
+ INDEX_NAME
+ ' ON '
+ DATABASE_NAME + '.' + SCHEMA_NAME + '.' + TABLE_NAME
+ ' (' + XMLColumnName  + ') '
+ ' USING XML INDEX '
+ PrimaryIndexName
+ ' FOR ' + secondarytypedescription
+ ' WITH ('
+ CASE
WHEN is_padded = 1 THEN ' PAD_INDEX  = OFF, '
ELSE ' PAD_INDEX  = ON, '
END
+ CASE
WHEN [allow_page_locks] = 1 THEN ' ALLOW_PAGE_LOCKS  = ON, '
ELSE 'ALLOW_PAGE_LOCKS  = OFF, '
END
+ CASE
WHEN [allow_row_locks] = 1 THEN ' ALLOW_ROW_LOCKS  = ON, '
ELSE ' ALLOW_ROW_LOCKS  = OFF, '
END
+ CASE
WHEN @SORT_IN_TEMPDB = 1 THEN ' SORT_IN_TEMPDB  = ON, '
ELSE ' SORT_IN_TEMPDB  = OFF, '
END
```

833

```
+ CASE
WHEN @DROP_EXISTING = 1 THEN ' DROP_EXISTING  = ON, '
ELSE ' DROP_EXISTING  = OFF '
END
+ ')'

FROM      Metadata_XMLIndexes
WHERE     IsPrimaryXMLIndex = 0
ORDER BY  SERVER_NAME, DATABASE_NAME, SCHEMA_NAME, TABLE_NAME ;

-- Create and execute CREATE scripts

DECLARE  @CreateIndex NVARCHAR(MAX)

DECLARE  CreateIndex_CUR CURSOR

FOR
SELECT ScriptElement FROM #ScriptElements ORDER BY ID

OPEN CreateIndex_CUR

FETCH NEXT FROM CreateIndex_CUR INTO @CreateIndex

WHILE @@FETCH_STATUS <> -1
BEGIN

EXEC (@CreateIndex)

FETCH NEXT FROM CreateIndex_CUR INTO @CreateIndex

END ;

CLOSE CreateIndex_CUR;
DEALLOCATE CreateIndex_CUR;
```

How It Works

This recipe is rather like the sum of Recipes 14-3, 14-4, and 14-5—but with all the parts of the process rolled into one. It does the following (and it will only work if you already generated the "core" index metadata—specifically the primary key):

- First, it stores the metadata required to DROP and CREATE XML indexes in the table Metadata_XMLIndexes.

- Second, it uses this information to generate and execute DROP scripts.

- Finally, it uses this information to generate and execute CREATE scripts.

These scripts can be placed in an ETL process at appropriate stages in the process, as demonstrated in Recipe 14-2. The fields created by the script are described in Table 14-3.

Table 14-3. *Fields Used to Store XML Index Metadata*

Field Name	Source Table	Description
SERVER_NAME		Gets the server name from the current environment.
DATABASE_NAME		Gets the database name from the current environment.
SCHEMA_NAME	sys.schemas	The schema name.
TABLE_NAME	sys.tables	The table name.
PrimaryIndexName	sys.indexes	The index name for the primary key.
TableID	sys.tables	The internal table id in the system tables.
INDEX_NAME	sys.xml_indexes	The primary XML index name.
XMLSecondaryaryIndexID	sys.xml_indexes	The secondary XML index internal ID.
XMLPrimaryIndexID	sys.xml_indexes	The primary XML index internal ID.
SecondaryTypeDescription	sys.xml_indexes	The type of secondary index.
DataSpace	sys.dataspaces	The index storage.
Allow_Page_Locks	sys.xml_indexes	Are page locks allowed?
Allow_Row_Locks	sys.xml_indexes	Are row locks allowed?
Is_Padded	sys.xml_indexes	Are the indexes padded?
IsPrimaryXMLIndex	sys.xml_indexes	Is this the primary XML index.
XMLColumnName	sys.xml_indexes	The name of the column in the table storing XML data.

■ **Note** You cannot re-create XML indexes unless the table's primary key has been created first.

Hints, Tips, and Traps

- The scripts used to store the XML index metadataDROP and subsequently CREATE the indexes can be turned into stored procedures and called from SSIS Execute SQL tasks in an SSIS package.

- The XML index metadata can be stored in a separate database or a separate schema, if you prefer.

14-7. Finding Missing Indexes
Problem

You suspect that indexes are missing in your destination database and want to deduce and create them.

Solution

Use the missing index DMVs. This requires you to run the following T-SQL snippet:

```
SELECT     TOP (100) PERCENT
sys.objects.name AS TableName
,COALESCE(sys.dm_db_missing_index_details.equality_columns
,sys.dm_db_missing_index_details.inequality_columns) AS IndexCols
,sys.dm_db_missing_index_details.included_columns
,user_seeks
,user_scans

FROM       sys.dm_db_missing_index_details
           INNER JOIN sys.objects
           ON sys.dm_db_missing_index_details.object_id = sys.objects.object_id
           INNER JOIN sys.dm_db_missing_index_groups
           ON sys.dm_db_missing_index_details.index_handle =
               sys.dm_db_missing_index_groups.index_handle
           INNER JOIN sys.dm_db_missing_index_group_stats
           ON sys.dm_db_missing_index_groups.index_group_handle =
               sys.dm_db_missing_index_group_stats.group_handle
ORDER BY   TableName, IndexCols ;
```

How It Works

Use SQL Server's Missing Index DMVs to determine if there are any missing indexes—and if these indexes are useful. The Missing Index DMVs will not only give you the core columns and tables that you can use to script out any necessary CREATE INDEX statements, but also give you an indication (in the user_seeks and user_scans columns) of the number of times an index is used by your process. An index that is used only once might not be worth creating. If it is used more than once, then it should probably be given serious consideration.

My advice here is—assuming that you are running an ETL process on a development server with no one but you connected—is to restart the SQL Server instance, and then run your ETL process from end to end. That way, only you (the developer) can decide whether an index needs to be used in an ETL process. SQL Server has many tools to suggest indexes; you can decide whether to apply them or not.

I will not attempt any exhaustive description of indexing requirements here—there are so many thousands of pages published on paper and on the Web that this is not necessary. So I hope that a succinct overview from an ETL perspective will suffice.

Should you wish to get SQL Server's opinion on any missing indexes for a particular query, then using the STATISTICS XML option is often the fastest and simplest route. All you have to do is encase your query in SET STATISTICS XML ON and SET STATISTICS XML OFF like this:

```
SET STATISTICS XML ON

SELECT ...
FROM ...
WHERE ...

SET STATISTICS XML OFF
GO
```

You will then see (if there are potentially missing indexes) an XML snippet at the top of the XML showplan, which indicates any missing indexes. This is not particularly hard to read; for each table, any equality, inequality, and included columns are indicated. You can "nest" a series of SQL statements, or even lists of stored procedures, between the SHOWPLAN statements, and get a series of XML results that you can then analyze independently.

Another way to see potentially missing indexes—and as well, the script to create the indexes—is to display the actual or estimated execution plan in SSMS/SSDT. In addition to the execution plan, you get (in a fetching shade of green) the missing index(es). Right-clicking the missing index gives you the Missing Index Details... option. Clicking it scripts out the CREATE INDEX statement.

You need to be aware that SSMS/SSDT will not output an execution plan and the XML showplan, if you ask for both. Moreover, apart from the toolbar buttons, you can also use Query/Display Estimated Execution Plan and Include Actual Execution Plan to display execution plans. When all is said and done, this is the same output as entering the SHOWPLAN statements.

If you prefer a more robust approach to tuning your queries, then you may prefer to use the Database Tuning Advisor. This gives more information than you could need, but most of it is useful—the estimated query size, for example. To use the Database Tuning Advisor, perform the following steps.

1. Right-click and select Analyze Query in Database Tuning Advisor.

2. Connect to the Database Tuning Advisor. Query should be selected in the General tab.

3. Select the database that you will use for the query.

4. Click Start Analysis in the toolbar.

5. In the Recommendations tab, right-click in the Definition column for every suggestion where the Target of Recommendation column contains the word "Index" to get a CREATE INDEX script.

Hints, Tips, and Traps

- Remember—once again—that you do not have to use the indexes that are suggested.

- As the multiple options of the Database Tuning Advisor are explained in detail in Books Online and in many excellent articles on the Web, I will not go through them here.

14-8. Managing Check Constraints
Problem

You want to drop check constraints before loading data and re-enable them after the data load.

Solution

Use SQL Server metadata to create the required DROP and CREATE scripts. The following process gathers the metadata for check constraints. Then it executes the DROP statements. After a data load, you can run the script to re-create the check constraints.

1. Create the table to hold the persisted metadata for the check constraints, using DDL like the following (C:\SQL2012DIRecipes\CH14\tblMetaData_CheckConstraints.Sql):

```
IF OBJECT_ID('dbo.MetaData_CheckConstraints') IS NOT NULL
DROP TABLE dbo.MetaData_CheckConstraints;
```

```
CREATE TABLE CarSales_Staging.dbo.MetaData_CheckConstraints
(
 SCHEMA_NAME NVARCHAR (128) NOT NULL,
 TABLE_NAME NVARCHAR (128) NOT NULL,
 COLUMN_NAME NVARCHAR (128) NOT NULL,
 CheckConstraintName NVARCHAR (128) NOT NULL,
 definition NVARCHAR(max) NULL,
) ;
GO
```

2. Populate the metadata table for the foreign key constraints using the following code
    snippet (C:\SQL2012DIRecipes\CH14\CheckConstraintMetadata.Sql):

```
INSERT INTO MetaData_CheckConstraints
(
SCHEMA_NAME
,TABLE_NAME
,COLUMN_NAME
,CheckConstraintName
,definition
)

SELECT
SCH.name AS SCHEMA_NAME
,TBL.name AS TABLE_NAME
,COL.name
,CHK.name AS CheckConstraintName
,CHK.definition

FROM        sys.schemas AS SCH
            INNER JOIN sys.tables AS TBL
            ON SCH.schema_id = TBL.schema_id
            INNER JOIN sys.check_constraints CHK
            ON TBL.object_id = CHK.parent_object_id
            INNER JOIN sys.columns COL
            ON CHK.parent_object_id = COL.object_id
            AND CHK.parent_column_id = COL.column_id

WHERE       CHK.is_disabled = 0 ;
```

3. DROP the check constraints in the destination database by running the following piece
    of T-SQL (C:\SQL2012DIRecipes\CH14\DropCheckConstraints.Sql):

```
-- Create DROP statements

-- Drop table to hold script elements

IF OBJECT_ID('tempdb..#ScriptElements') IS NOT NULL
DROP TABLE tempdb..#ScriptElements;

CREATE TABLE #ScriptElements (ID INT IDENTITY(1,1), ScriptElement NVARCHAR(MAX))
```

```
INSERT INTO #ScriptElements

SELECT DISTINCT
'ALTER TABLE '
+ SCHEMA_NAME
+ '.'
+ TABLE_NAME
+ ' DROP CONSTRAINT '
+ CheckConstraintName

FROM        MetaData_CheckConstraints ;

-- Execute DROP scripts

DECLARE @DropFK NVARCHAR(MAX)

DECLARE  DropFK_CUR CURSOR

FOR
SELECT ScriptElement FROM #ScriptElements ORDER BY ID

OPEN DropFK_CUR

FETCH NEXT FROM DropFK_CUR INTO @DropFK

WHILE @@FETCH_STATUS <> -1
BEGIN

EXEC (@DropFK)

FETCH NEXT FROM DropFK_CUR INTO @DropFK

END ;

CLOSE DropFK_CUR;
DEALLOCATE DropFK_CUR;
```

4. Carry out the data load process to update the destination database.

5. Using code like the following, re-create the foreign keys from the persisted metadata
    (C:\SQL2012DIRecipes\CH14\CreateCheckConstraints.Sql):

```
-- Drop table to hold script elements

IF OBJECT_ID('tempdb..#ScriptElements') IS NOT NULL
DROP TABLE tempdb..#ScriptElements;

CREATE TABLE #ScriptElements (ID INT IDENTITY(1,1), ScriptElement NVARCHAR(MAX));

INSERT INTO #ScriptElements
```

```
SELECT DISTINCT
'ALTER TABLE '
+ SCHEMA_NAME
+ '.'
+ TABLE_NAME
+ ' ADD CONSTRAINT '
+ CheckConstraintName
+ ' CHECK '
+ [definition]

FROM          MetaData_CheckConstraints ;

-- Execute CREATE scripts

DECLARE @CreateFK NVARCHAR(MAX)

DECLARE  CreateFK_CUR CURSOR

FOR
SELECT ScriptElement FROM #ScriptElements ORDER BY ID

OPEN CreateFK_CUR

FETCH NEXT FROM CreateFK_CUR INTO @CreateFK

WHILE @@FETCH_STATUS <> -1
BEGIN

EXEC (@CreateFK)

FETCH NEXT FROM CreateFK_CUR INTO @CreateFK

END ;

CLOSE CreateFK_CUR;
DEALLOCATE CreateFK_CUR;
```

How It Works

When discussing constraint management, I am not including all constraints. As for the purposes of ETL, I am suggesting that primary keyand unique constraints are treated as indexes. Nonetheless, you might want or need to drop and re-create check constraints as you do indexes. So here we have the scripts to get the constraint metadata, and produce DROP and ADD scripts, which you can use in a staging process.

It does the following:

- First, it stores the metadata required to DROP and ADD check constraints in the table MetaData_CheckConstraints.

- Second, it uses this information to generate and execute DROP scripts.

- Finally, it uses this information to generate and execute ADD scripts.

These scripts can be placed in an ETL process at appropriate stages in the process, as demonstrated in Recipe 14-2.

The check_constraints table is used to obtain metadata—along with (inevitably) data from sys.tables, sys.schemas, and sys.columns. This metadata is then molded into the DROP and CREATE scripts used to manage check constraints.

14-9. Managing Foreign Key Constraints

Problem

You want to drop foreign key constraints before loading data and re-enable them after the data load.

Solution

Use SQL Server metadata to create the required DROP and CREATE scripts. The following script gathers and stores the metadata for foreign key constraints. The DROP scripts are then run before a data load. Following the load, the foreign key constraints are reapplied.

1. Create the table to hold the persisted metadata for the foreign key constraints, using DDL like the following (C:\SQL2012DIRecipes\CH14\tblTmp_Metadata_ForeignKeys.Sql):

```
IF OBJECT_ID('dbo.Tmp_Metadata_ForeignKeys') IS NOT NULLTmp_Metadata_ForeignKeys
DROP TABLE dbo.Tmp_Metadata_ForeignKeys

CREATE TABLE CarSales_Staging.dbo.Tmp_Metadata_ForeignKeys
(
 SCHEMA_NAME SYSNAME NOT NULL,
 TABLE_NAME SYSNAME NOT NULL,
 FOREIGN_KEY_NAME SYSNAME NOT NULL,
 COLUMN_NAME SYSNAME NULL,
 REFERENCED_TABLE_SCHEMA_NAME SYSNAME NOT NULL,
 REFERENCED_TABLE_NAME SYSNAME NOT NULL,
 REFERENCED_COLUMN_NAME SYSNAME NULL,
 ColumnList NVARCHAR(300) NULL
);
GO
```

2. Populate the metadata table for the foreign key constraints, using the following code snippet (C:\SQL2012DIRecipes\CH14\ForeignKeyMetadata.Sql):

```
INSERT INTO Tmp_Metadata_ForeignKeys

SELECT
SCH.name AS SCHEMA_NAME
,OBJ.name AS TABLE_NAME
,FRK.name AS FOREIGN_KEY_NAME
,COL.name AS COLUMN_NAME
,RefSCH.name AS REFERENCED_TABLE_SCHEMA_NAME
,RefTBL.name AS REFERENCED_TABLE_NAME
```

```
          ,RefCOL.name AS REFERENCED_COLUMN_NAME
          ,CAST(NULL AS NVARCHAR(300)) AS ColumnList

FROM        sys.foreign_keys FRK
            INNER JOIN sys.objects OBJ
            ON FRK.parent_object_id = OBJ.object_id
            AND FRK.schema_id = OBJ.schema_id
            INNER JOIN sys.schemas SCH
            ON OBJ.schema_id = SCH.schema_id
            INNER JOIN sys.foreign_key_columns FKC
            ON FRK.object_id = FKC.constraint_object_id
            AND FRK.parent_object_id = FKC.parent_object_id
            INNER JOIN sys.columns COL
            ON FKC.constraint_column_id = COL.column_id
            AND FKC.parent_object_id = COL.object_id
            INNER JOIN sys.columns AS RefCOL
            ON FKC.referenced_object_id = RefCOL.object_id
            AND FKC.referenced_column_id = RefCOL.column_id
            INNER JOIN sys.objects AS RefTBL
            ON FKC.referenced_object_id = RefTBL.object_id
            INNER JOIN sys.schemas AS RefSCH
            ON RefTBL.schema_id = RefSCH.schema_id

WHERE       FRK.is_ms_shipped = 0
            AND FRK.is_not_trusted = 0 ;

-- Define (concatenate) list of key columns

IF OBJECT_ID('TempDB..#Tmp_IndexedFields') IS NOT NULL
DROP TABLE TempDB..#Tmp_IndexedFields

;
WITH Core_CTE ( FOREIGN_KEY_NAME, Rank, COLUMN_NAME )
              AS ( SELECT FOREIGN_KEY_NAME,
ROW_NUMBER() OVER( PARTITION BY FOREIGN_KEY_NAME ORDER BY
FOREIGN_KEY_NAME),
CAST( COLUMN_NAME AS VARCHAR(MAX) )
FROM Tmp_Metadata_ForeignKeys),

Root_CTE ( FOREIGN_KEY_NAME, Rank, COLUMN_NAME )
AS ( SELECT FOREIGN_KEY_NAME, Rank, COLUMN_NAME
FROM    Core_CTE
WHERE   Rank = 1 ),

Recursion_CTE ( FOREIGN_KEY_NAME, Rank, COLUMN_NAME )
AS
    ( SELECT FOREIGN_KEY_NAME, Rank, COLUMN_NAME
      FROM Root_CTE

      UNION ALL
```

```
        SELECT Core_CTE.FOREIGN_KEY_NAME, Core_CTE.Rank,
        Recursion_CTE.COLUMN_NAME + ', ' + Core_CTE.COLUMN_NAME
        FROM Core_CTE
        INNER JOIN Recursion_CTE
        ON Core_CTE.FOREIGN_KEY_NAME = Recursion_CTE.FOREIGN_KEY_NAME
        AND Core_CTE.Rank = Recursion_CTE.Rank + 1
)

SELECT    FOREIGN_KEY_NAME, MAX( COLUMN_NAME ) AS ColumnList
INTO      #Tmp_IndexedFields
FROM      Recursion_CTE
GROUP BY  FOREIGN_KEY_NAME;

UPDATET

SET       T.ColumnList = Tmp.ColumnList

FROM      Tmp_Metadata_ForeignKeys T
          INNER JOIN   #Tmp_IndexedFields Tmp
          ON T.FOREIGN_KEY_NAME = Tmp.FOREIGN_KEY_NAME;
```

3. DROP the foreign keys in the destination database by running the following piece of
    T-SQL (C:\SQL2012DIRecipes\CH14\DropForeignKeys.Sql):

```
-- Drop table to hold script elements

IF OBJECT_ID('tempdb..#ScriptElements') IS NOT NULL
DROP TABLE tempdb..#ScriptElements;

CREATE TABLE #ScriptElements (ID INT IDENTITY(1,1), ScriptElement NVARCHAR(MAX));

INSERT INTO #ScriptElements

SELECT DISTINCT
'ALTER TABLE '
+ SCHEMA_NAME
+ '.'
+ TABLE_NAME
+ ' ADD CONSTRAINT '
+ FOREIGN_KEY_NAME
+ ' FOREIGN KEY ('
+ ColumnList
+ ') REFERENCES '
+ REFERENCED_TABLE_SCHEMA_NAME
+ '.'
+ REFERENCED_TABLE_NAME
+ ' ('
+ ColumnList
+ ')'
```

```
FROM      Tmp_Metadata_ForeignKeys

-- Execute DROP scripts

DECLARE @DropFK NVARCHAR(MAX)

DECLARE  DropIndex_CUR CURSOR

FOR
SELECT ScriptElement FROM #ScriptElements ORDER BY ID

OPEN DropIndex_CUR

FETCH NEXT FROM DropIndex_CUR INTO @DropFK

WHILE @@FETCH_STATUS <> -1
BEGIN

EXEC (@DropFK)

FETCH NEXT FROM DropIndex_CUR INTO @DropFK

END;

CLOSE DropIndex_CUR;
DEALLOCATE DropIndex_CUR;
```

4. Carry out the data load process to update the destination database.

5. Using code like the following, re-create the foreign keys from the persisted metadata
    (C:\SQL2012DIRecipes\CH14\CreateForeignKeys.Sql):

```
-- Drop table to hold script elements

IF OBJECT_ID('tempdb..#ScriptElements') IS NOT NULL
DROP TABLE tempdb..#ScriptElements;

CREATE TABLE #ScriptElements (ID INT IDENTITY(1,1), ScriptElement NVARCHAR(MAX));

INSERT INTO  #ScriptElements

SELECT DISTINCT
'ALTER TABLE '
+ SCHEMA_NAME
+ '.'
+ TABLE_NAME
+ ' ADD CONSTRAINT '
+ FOREIGN_KEY_NAME
+ ' FOREIGN KEY ('
+ ColumnList
```

```
+ ') REFERENCES '
+ REFERENCED_TABLE_SCHEMA_NAME
+ '.'
+ REFERENCED_TABLE_NAME
+ ' ('
+ ColumnList
+ ')'

FROM       Tmp_Metadata_ForeignKeys;

-- Execute CREATE scripts

DECLARE @CreateFK NVARCHAR(MAX)

DECLARE  DropIndex_CUR CURSOR

FOR
SELECT ScriptElement FROM #ScriptElements ORDER BY ID

OPEN DropIndex_CUR

FETCH NEXT FROM DropIndex_CUR INTO @CreateFK

WHILE @@FETCH_STATUS <> -1
BEGIN

EXEC (@CreateFK)

FETCH NEXT FROM DropIndex_CUR INTO @CreateFK

END;

CLOSE DropIndex_CUR;
DEALLOCATE DropIndex_CUR;
```

How It Works

The sys.objects, sys.foreign_keys, sys.schemas, sys.foreign_key_columns, and sys.columns tables are used to get the metadata. It is a little more complex than the metadata required for check constraints, but it works! Then the DROP and CREATE scripts are written based on this metadata. All you have to do is copy and execute the scripts that are produced. It does the following (very much like Recipe 14-8):

- First, it stores the metadata required to DROP and ADD foreign keys in the Tmp_Metadata_ForeignKeys table.

- Second, it uses this information to generate and execute DROP scripts.

- Finally, it uses this information to generate and execute ADD scripts

These scripts can be placed in an ETL process at appropriate stages in the process, as demonstrated in Recipe 14-2.

Hints, Tips, and Traps

- Always script out your staging database and make a backup copy before dropping constraints.

- When adding foreign key constraints at various stages in an ETL process, you can use the constraints creation script and filter it using relevant table names to create specific foreign key constraints, as required.

- This script assumes no need for quoted identifiers in the metadata. If this is not the case with your database naming convention, then you need to handle quoted identifiers.

- You may prefer to test that foreign key work (using a piece of T-SQL to isolate nonconforming records) first.

14-10. Optimizing Bulk Loads
Problem

You want to make a bulk load run as fast as possible.

Solution

Ensure that the BulkLoad API is used to perform the load. Then verify that only minimal logging is used during the data load, and that any indexes and constraints are handled appropriately. The following is an example using SSIS.

1. Create a destination table using the following DDL (C:\SQL2012DIRecipes\CH14\tblFastLoadClients.Sql):

    ```
    CREATE TABLE CarSales_Staging.dbo.FastLoadClients
    (
     ID INT,
     ClientName NVARCHAR (150),
     Address1 VARCHAR (50),
     Address2 VARCHAR (50),
     Town VARCHAR (50),
     County VARCHAR (50),
     PostCode VARCHAR (10),
     ClientType VARCHAR (20),
     ClientSize VARCHAR(10),
     ClientSince DATETIME,
     IsCreditWorthy BIT,
     DealerGroup BINARY(892)
    ) ;
    GO
    ```

2. Create a new SSIS package.

3. Add two OLEDB connection managers, the first named **CarSales_OLEDB**, which connects to the CarSales database, the second named **CarSales_Staging_OLEDB**, which connects to the CarSales_Staging database.

4. Create the following metadata tables:CarSales_Staging.dbo.IndexList (Recipe 14-3, step 1), CarSales_Staging.dbo.Metadata_XMLIndexes (Recipe 14-6, step 1), CarSales_Staging.dbo.MetaData_CheckConstraints (Recipe 14-8, step 1), and CarSales_Staging.dbo.Tmp_Metadata_ForeignKeys (Recipe 14-9, step 1).

5. Add an Execute SQL task named **GatherIndexMetadata**. Configure it to use the CarSales_Staging_OLEDB connection manager. Set the SQL source type as Direct Input, and the SQL Statement as the code given in Recipe 14-3, step 2.

6. Add an Execute SQL task named **GatherXMLIndexMetadata**. Connect it to the task created previously (GatherIndexMetadata). Configure it to use the CarSales_Staging_OLEDB connection manager. Set the SQL source type as Direct Input, and the SQL Statement as the code given in Recipe 14-6, step 2.

7. Add an Execute SQL task named **GatherCheckConstraintMetadata**. Connect it to the task created previously (GatherXMLIndexMetadata). Configure it to use the CarSales_Staging_OLEDB connection manager. Set the SQL source type as Direct Input, and the SQL Statement as the code given in Recipe 14-8, step 2.

8. Add an Execute SQL task named **GatherForeignKeyMetadata**. Configure it to use the CarSales_Staging_OLEDB connection manager. Connect it to the task created previously (GatherCheckConstraintMetadata). Set the SQL source type as Direct Input, and the SQL Statement as the code given in Recipe 14-9, step 2.

9. Add an Execute SQL task named **DropForeignKeys**. Configure it to use the CarSales_Staging_OLEDB connection manager. Connect it to the task created previously (GatherForeignKeyMetadata). Set the SQL source type as Direct Input, and the SQL Statement as the code given in Recipe 14-9, step 3.

10. Add an Execute SQL task named **DropCheckConstraints**. Configure it to use the CarSales_Staging_OLEDB connection manager. Connect it to the task created previously (DropForeignKeys). Set the SQL source type as Direct Input, and the SQL Statement as the code given in Recipe 14-8, step 3.

11. Add an Execute SQL task named **DropXMLIndexes**. Configure it to use the CarSales_Staging_OLEDB connection manager. Connect it to the task created previously (DropCheckConstraints). Set the SQL source type as Direct Input, and the SQL Statement as the code given in Recipe 14-6, step 3.

12. Add an Execute SQL task named **DropIndexes**. Configure it to use the CarSales_Staging_OLEDB connection manager. Connect it to the task created previously (DropXMLIndexes). Set the SQL source type as Direct Input, and the SQL Statement as the code given in Recipe 14-4.

13. Add an Execute SQL task named **Set BulkLogged Recovery**. Configure it to use the CarSales_Staging_OLEDB connection manager. Connect it to the task created previously (DropIndexes). Set the SQL source type as Direct Input, and the SQL Statement as the code shown here:

```
ALTER DATABASE CarSales
SET RECOVERY BULK_LOGGED;
```

14. Add a Data flow task, which you connect to the Execute SQL task named Set BulkLogged Recovery. Double-click to edit.

15. Add an OLEDB source, which you configure to use the CarSales_OLEDB connection manager and the source query:

```
SELECT      ID, ClientName, Address1, Address2, Town, County, PostCode, ClientType
            ,ClientSize, ClientSince, IsCreditWorthy, DealerGroup
FROM        Client
```

16. Add an OLEDB destination,which you connect to the OLEDB source. Double-click to edit.

17. Select the CarSales_Staging_OLEDB connection manager and the dbo.FastLoadClients table using the Table or View—Fast Load data access mode.

18. Ensure that Table Lock is checked.

19. Click OK to finish your configuration.

20. Return to the Data Flow pane.

21. Add an Execute SQL task named **CreateIndexes**. Configure it to use the CarSales_Staging_OLEDB connection manager. Connect it to the Data Flow task created previously. Set the SQL source type as Direct Input, and the SQL Statement as the code given in Recipe 14-5.

22. Add an Execute SQL task named **CreateXMLIndexes**. Configure it to use the CarSales_Staging_OLEDB connection manager. Connect it to the task created previously (CreateIndexes). Set the SQL source type as Direct Input, and the SQL Statement as the code given in Recipe 14-6, step 5.

23. Add an Execute SQL task named **CreateCheckConstraints**. Configure it to use the CarSales_Staging_OLEDB connection manager. Connect it to the task created previously (CreateXMLIndexes). Set the SQL source type as Direct Input, and the SQL Statement as the code given in Recipe 14-8, step 5.

24. Add an Execute SQL task named **CreateForeignKeys**. Configure it to use the CarSales_Staging_OLEDB connection manager. Connect it to the task created previously (CreateCheckConstraints). Set the SQL source type as Direct Input, and the SQL Statement as the code given in Recipe 14-9, step 5.

25. Add an Execute SQL task named **Set BulkLogged Recovery**. Configure it to use the CarSales_Staging_OLEDB connection manager. Connect it to the task created previously (CreateForeignKeys). Set the SQL source type as Direct Input, and the SQL Statement as the following code:

```
ALTER DATABASE CarSales
SET RECOVERY FULL;
```

You can now run the load process. Once it has finished, you should *immediately* back up the database.

How It Works

In this recipe, we are aiming for two, somewhat interdependent, objectives:bulk loading and minimal logging. The reasons for trying to attain these objectives are simple:

- Using the **SQL Server BulkLoad API** during a data load will write data in batches, and not row by row. This will inevitably result in considerably shorter process duration, because using the bulkload API will always be faster than a "normal" row-by-row write to a table. It always requires table locking.

- **Minimal logged operations** are nearly always faster than logged operations because of the reduced overhead they imply. This is because minimally logged operations only track extent allocations and metadata changes. This means lower memory requirements, less disk I/O, and reduced processor load. Minimally logged operations also reduce one potential area of risk, which is log space. Even if your log is optimized to perfection, a large data load can fill the log—or disk—and thus stop the load process. If the log has to be resized during a load, this will cause the load to slow down considerably while more log space is added.

However, many bulkload operations require the database to be in SIMPLE or BULK_LOGGED recovery mode to use the bulkload API. An operation can be a bulk load operation without being minimally logged, but ensuring that the two are combined should always be the preferred outcome if load speed is the main aim.

However, attaining the nirvana of ultimate speed in data loads is not just as simple as setting a recovery mode and ensuring that the TABLOCK hint is set. There are two other fundamental aspects to consider:replication and indexes.

The first of these is simple: if replication is enabled on a table, then minimal logging is—by definition—impossiblebecause the transaction log is used by the replication process.

Indexing is much more complicated because the outcome can depend onthe type of index (clustered or nonclustered) and whether the table is empty or not.

Let's look at these possibilities in more detail.

- **Heap table**(no indexes): This is the simplest case, where data pages are minimally logged.

- **Heap table** (with nonclustered indexes): Data pages are minimally logged. Index pages, however, are minimally logged when the table is empty, but logged if there is data in the table. There is an exception to this rule—the first batch that is loaded into an empty table. For this first batch, both data and indexes are minimally logged. For the second and all further batches, only the data is minimally logged—index pages are fully logged.

- **Clustered index**: If the table is empty, data and index pages are minimally logged. If the table contains data, both data and index pages are fully logged.

You will note that in this recipe, I switched to the Bulk-Logged recovery model for the duration of the load. I also backed up the database once the load finished. This is an admittedly simplistic case where the destination database is clearly a staging area and there are no transactions running during the load process. I am aware that this might not be the case in many other situations, which could render this approach impracticable.

■ **Note**   Efficient bulk loading can get more complex than it seems since there are many ways in which the core requirements can mesh. All this is described exhaustively in the Microsoft whitepaper *The Data Loading Performance Guide* (http://msdn.microsoft.com/en-us/library/dd425070(v=sql.100).aspx). This whitepaper may have been written for SQL Server 2008, but its insights apply equally well to SQL Server 2012. It can take many months of experience, however, to appreciate all the subtleties and interactions of high-performance data loading using SQL Server.

One aspect of bulk inserts that was not covered in this recipe (it was covered exhaustively in many of the recipes in Chapter 13) was parallel loading of data. In my experience, parallel loads will always be faster than single loads. However, this means being able to perform parallel loads, which implies:

- **The destination table is not indexed**—as in this case, parallel data importing is supported by all three bulk import commands: BCP, BULK INSERT, and INSERT... SELECT * FROM OPENROWSET(BULK...). This is because when indexes exist on a table, it is impossible to carry out a parallel load operation simply by applying the TABLOCK hint. Consequently, before a bulk-import operation, you must drop indexes.

- **The TABLOCK hint must be specified**. This is because concurrent threads block each other if TABLOCK is not specified.

- **Parallelization works best for nonoverlapping data sources**—files where any "key" fields are completely separated in each source file.

If you are using BULK INSERT, BCP, or INSERT ... SELECT * FROM OPENROWSET(BULK...), and the table is empty and has a clustered index (and the data in the data file is ordered in the same way as the clustered index key columns), you must also carry out the following:

- Bulk import the data with the clustered index already in place.

- Specify the ORDER hint, as well as the TABLOCK hint.

If the destination table is empty, this should be faster than dropping the clustered index, loading the data, and then regenerating the clustered index, since a sort step is not required.

Hints, Tips, and Traps

- Creating indexes can take considerable time and (especially creating clustered indexes) can prove exhausting for system resources. So the obvious approach is to try and run indexing operations in parallel. This is handled easily from SSIS by using a sequence container with a series of Execute SQL tasks, each of which handles one or more indexing operations. My only advice is not to go overboard on this, and certainly do not set up too many parallel tasks since the disk subsystem will probably saturate long before you get any shorter processing. My advice is to try a couple parallel tasks, extend one at a time, and then time the results. Indeed, when rebuilding or reorganizing indexes in parallel, I also advise you to handle all the indexes for a single table inside the same process, and not reprocess indexes from the same table using multiple threads.

- If you drop secondary indexes, you can try re-creating them in parallel by running the creation of each secondary index from a separate client. This can be tricky to set up, however.

- If you are importing a **small** amount of new data relative to the amount of existing data, dropping and rebuilding the indexes may be counterproductive. The time required to rebuild the indexes could be longer than the time saved during the bulk operation.

- You can avoid Lock Escalation by using:

  ```
  ALTER TABLE CarSales SET (LOCK_ESCALATION = DISABLE)
  ```

- If trace flag 610 is enabled, inserts into a table with indexes are generally a minimally logged operation. Tables with clustered indexes support multiple bulk load streams inserting data concurrently, provided that these streams contain nonoverlapping data. If data overlap is detected, data streams will block—but not deadlock.

- `BATCHSIZE = 0` should be not used for tables that have indexes—set a batch size as bulk import operations tend to perform much better with large batch sizes. The only caveats are that if there are multiple indexes on a destination, this could increase memory pressure due to the sort requirement. Also, in parallel loads (without the `TABLOCK` hint being used), a large batch size can lead to blocking.

Summary

It is my hope that this chapter has given you insight into some of the many techniques used to reduce the time for an ETL process to load data. The search for efficiency centered on using the SQL Server Bulk Insert API efficiently, and consequently learning to manage destination table indexes and constraints in an optimal fashion to ensure that minimal logging is applied.

However, there are as many optimization techniques as there are different challenges to overcome and issues to resolve. I can only advise you to take a step back when faced with a tight SLA to attain and assess the problem in its entirety. Always aim for bulk loads, try to ensure that minimal logging is in place, and use the most efficient drivers/providers that you can find. Narrow the source data down to the essential, and avoid any superfluous columns. You can even narrow data types if you are sure that you will not be truncating source data. Generally, it is more efficient to sort data in source databases, and ask for source files to be presorted (then indicate this to SSIS, BCP, or BULK INSERT).

Above all, take nothing as a given—and test, test, and re-test.

When tailoring an ETL process, it is always worth thinking through your indexing strategy. This chapter has shown you the following approaches:

- Inhibit (disable) all but the clustered indexes. Then rebuild all the indexes on the destination and/or staging tables.

- Drop all indexes (clustered, unclustered, and any other). Then,load the data and finally re-create all indexes—in the correct order to avoid wasting time and server resources.

Other potential strategies can include:

- Disable all but the clustered indexes. Then drop any clustered indexes and load the data. Finally, create any clustered indexes and rebuild other indexes.

- Disable all but the clustered indexes. Then drop any clustered indexes and load the data. Next, create any clusteredindexes. Potentially much later, rebuild any other indexes that are essential for the ETL package to function optimally, leaving user indexes to be rebuilt offline.

CHAPTER 15

■ ■ ■

Logging and Auditing

Designing, developing, and implementing sophisticated data integration systems is always a test of your knowledge and ingenuity. The challenge does not stop, however, when the system seems ready for production. As no ETL system can ever be perfect, any industrial-strength process needs to be able to handle errors gracefully. Not only that, but it must also be able to tell you that an error has occurred and be able to decide whether it can continue with a data load or not. It also has to be able to track the progress of a process as it runs, and return all the information and metrics that you need proactively to monitor the process as it runs and (more likely) after it has run. This means gathering data on

- What has run, and when.

- What has succeeded, and when.

- What has failed, including when and why, which most of the time includes error source, error messages, error codes, and the severity of the error.

Equally important is the requirement to keep metrics (counters)—at every important stage of the process—for both error rows and rows successfully processed.

On top of this, you will need another fundamental metric—time elapsed—for all important parts of the process. There are three main reasons for wanting this data:

- To find and correct errors as fast as possible if a process should fail.

- To get an easily accessible, high-level overview of the process once it has run, and to keep an eye on any potential warning signs.

- To build comparisons over time of the essential metrics gathered during a process. These comparisons will allow you to see—in the cold hard light of accumulated data—which parts of the process take more time or resources. Consequently, you can be proactive about resolving any potential issues.

Yet merely running the process from end to end is not enough in many cases. You then need to verify the results, and for the finalized datasets, produce counters of (among other things) the following:

- New records

- Updated records

- NULLS in essential final data sets

- Counters for core data

As well as any or all of the following:

- Counters of the number of records added, deleted, or updated in staging tables to cross-reference with process counters and ensure that there is nothing missing or superfluous.

- Metadata comparison elements (if you are getting data from an outside supplier, they may send information on the amount and types of data sent, which you should compare with the actual data received).

- Unit tests (for want of a better term) on key data items to verify acceptable levels of data counts and essential domain counters and percentages.

These metrics, as well as error-detection indicators, can be used to control process flow and enhance the data integration with decision-making steps. But before leaping in to the technical solutions, I propose stepping back a little, and taking a high-level view of the logging process. So far in this chapter, we have defined "why" we log data. I now want to look at the global "where" and "how."

Assuming that you are convinced that logging is a good idea, the next question is—where do I log all this information? There are three main possibilities—although you may know or prefer others:

- Log the information to an SQL Server table.

- Log the information to a file (text or XML).

- Log the information to a system log.

Each has its advantages and disadvantages, which are reviewed in Tables 15-1, 15-2, and 15-3.

Table 15-1. *Logging to an SQL Server Table*

Advantages	Disadvantages
Easy to add to stored procedures and SSIS packages.	Unforgiving of data type mismatches and length overflows.
Easy to query.	Can compete for database resources.
Available for comparison and baselining.	

Table 15-2. *Logging to a File*

Advantages	Disadvantages
Easy to add to SSIS.	Can compete for server resources.
Relatively easy to add to T-SQL.	Harder to read, query, and subset.
Handles heavy-duty logging during a process without adding extra strain to the database.	Can grow excessively and be hard to prune selectively.

Table 15-3. *Logging to a System Log*

Advantages	Disadvantages
Easy to add to SSIS.	Harder to query from T-SQL.
Easy to view with Windows tools.	Can add excessive clutter to system logs.
Very easy to query with LogParser.	

At the risk of being simplistic, I am not even going to suggest that metrics (record counts) and audit data (counters, timers, and unit tests) be stored anywhere else than in database tables. My reasoning is as follows.

- The data stored is ideal for data tables, as it is clearly typed (INT/BIGINT, DATETIME, BOOLEAN).

- There is virtually no long-winded text data, as is the case when error-logging. So the data tables are narrow and the system overhead is minimal.

- Auditing data is a T-SQL process for the most part, so storing the metrics in a database makes analyzing metrics incredibly easy.

- The metrics exist for baselining and comparison—so having them available in data tables allows monitoring systems to be built directly on top of the data.

In the end, deciding on which type of logging or even which mixture of log types to use will depend on your system requirements. You also need to ask where these logs will be placed. Here again, the choices are simple:

- Place the logs on the SQL Server and/or SSIS servers.

- Place the logs on a separate database server or file server.

Here, too, the final decision may not be as obvious as it may first seem. Tables 15-4 and 15-5 outline the pros and cons of each.

Table 15-4. *Placing Logs on the SQL Server*

Advantages	Disadvantages
No network latency.	Competition for system resources.
Local accessibility.	Can "crowd out" disk space.

Table 15-5. *Placing Logs on a Distributed Server*

Advantages	Disadvantages
Little competition for local system resources.	Network latency.
	Risk of network problems.

You may find that a mixture of log destinations and log systems best suits your project. All I wish to do is raise your awareness of the possibilities. The only suggestion that I will make—and one that I will follow in the examples in this chapter—is that you use a separate Logging and Auditing database when using SQL Server tables as the log destination. The reasons for this are fairly obvious:

- You are not cluttering up a staging or ODS (operational data store) database with non-relevant data.

- You may be able to place the database files for the logging database on separate spindles to avoid contention.

- You are creating the basis for a scalable solution should the logging eventually move to a separate server—or indeed should your enterprise centralize all ETL and processing logs and counters to facilitate reporting.

Also, to keep this database clearer, I will use the Log and Audit schemas for different aspects of the logging and auditing process.

Whatever the type of logging, you will always be faced with finding a correct balance between slowing down a process through logging everything that happens and being unable to quickly find the reason for errors. Logging is less a science than an art, and every system has different requirements. Too many counters, and you cannot see the woods for the trees; too few, and you cannot see accidents waiting to happen. The only real way to know if you are right is when your process runs smoothly and you can track down errors or counters easily and quickly.

So, given that there is no one solution—because there in no one single requirement—this chapter will show how to log at three levels of process:

- Simple logging using T-SQL or built-in SSIS logging to tables and files.

- Simple logging to a centralized log database from both T-SQLand SSIS.

- Complex event and counter logging to a centralized custom log database from T-SQL or SSIS.

All of these techniques are examined in this chapter to give you some ideas on how to enhance your processes to make them more robust and resilient in the unforgiving environment that is real-world data integration.

All the examples in this chapter are available on the book's companion web site. Once installed, they can be found in `C:\SQL2012DIRecipes\CH15`. You will also need to create the `CarSales_Logging` database as described in Appendix B.

15-1. Logging Events from T-SQL
Problem

You want to apply a simple but robust means to log events—both success and failure—from T-SQL-based ETL routines.

Solution

Create a logging table and a stored procedure that writes events and event details (including error information) to this table. You can then call this stored procedure from your ETL stored procedures or scripts.

1. Create the table to store logged events using the following DDL (`C:\SQL2012DIRecipes\CH15\tblEventDetail_Simple.Sql`):

```
CREATE TABLE CarSales_Logging.log.EventDetail_Simple
(
 EventDetailID INT IDENTITY(1,1) NOT NULL,
 Event VARCHAR(150) NULL,
 Comments VARCHAR(MAX) NULL,
 ErrorNo INT NULL,
 ErrorDescription VARCHAR(MAX) NULL,
 ErrorLineNo INT NULL,
 ErrorSeverity INT NULL,
 ErrorState INT NULL,
 StartTime DATETIME NULL,
 Logtime DATETIME DEFAULT GETDATE()
) ;
GO
```

2. Create the stored procedure that is required to perform logging using the following DDL (C:\SQL2012DIRecipes\CH15\pr_Logging_Simple.Sql):

```
CREATE PROCEDURE CarSales_Logging.log.pr_Logging_Simple
(
@Event VARCHAR(150)
,@Comments VARCHAR(MAX) = NULL
,@ErrorNo INT = NULL
,@ErrorDescription VARCHAR(MAX) = NULL
,@ErrorLineNo INT = NULL
,@ErrorSeverity INT = NULL
,@ErrorState INT  = NULL
,@StartTime DATETIME
)

AS

INSERT INTO CarSales_Logging.log.EventDetail_Simple
(
Event
,StartTime
,Comments
,ErrorNo
,ErrorDescription
,ErrorLineNo
,ErrorSeverity
,ErrorState
)

VALUES
(
@Event
,@StartTime
,@Comments
,@ErrorNo
,@ErrorDescription
,@ErrorLineNo
,@ErrorSeverity
,@ErrorState
) ;
GO
```

3. You can then call this stored procedure from inside other procedures or scripts, as shown in the following code:

```
BEGIN TRY
DECLARE @StartTime DATETIME = GETDATE()

--  your processing here
```

```
--  Here we log successful processing
EXECUTE Log.pr_Logging_Simple 'Load sales data', @StartTime, 'The sales data loaded successfully'
END TRY
BEGIN CATCH

--  Here we log unsuccessful processing
DECLARE @ErrorNo_TMP INT
DECLARE @ErrorDescription_TMP VARCHAR(MAX)
DECLARE @ErrorLineNo_TMP INT
DECLARE @ErrorSeverity_TMP INT
DECLARE @ErrorState_TMP INT

SELECT @ErrorNo_TMP = ERROR_NUMBER()
SELECT @ErrorDescription_TMP = ERROR_MESSAGE()
SELECT @ErrorLineNo_TMP = ERROR_LINE()
SELECT @ErrorSeverity_TMP = ERROR_SEVERITY()
SELECT @ErrorState_TMP = ERROR_STATE()

 EXECUTE Log.pr_Logging_Simple
'Load sales data'
,@Comments = 'Error loading sales data'
,@StartTime = @STARTTIME
,@ErrorNo = @ErrorNo_TMP
,@ErrorDescription = @ErrorDescription_TMP
,@ErrorLineNo = @ErrorNo_TMP
,@ErrorSeverity = @ErrorSeverity_TMP
,@ErrorState = @ErrorState_TMP
END CATCH
```

How It Works

ETL processes can be large and complex, and consequently require large and complex logging systems. However, before launching into an all-singing, all-dancing logging infrastructure, it is probably easiest to start with a simple stored procedure to log the following:

- Success/failure

- The time of the event

- Any error details

For the sake of brevity, I will refer to all these as "process status" elements.

The approach in this recipe requires a simple table structure to store the logged events and a stored procedure to log events. The 'sproc to log' events can be called anywhere from inside another stored procedure, or from an SSIS Execute SQL task. Also, it presumes that any stored procedure or T-SQL that logs results will use a T-SQL TRY...CATCH pattern so that both successes and failures can be logged. This is explained in Recipe 15-8.

The logging routine works like this: first, each successful step in a stored procedure is logged using the Log.pr_Logging_Simple stored procedure once it has completed. Any errors are passed to the CATCH block, which uses the same procedure to log the failure and all available error information that is returned by the CATCH block.

No one could claim that this approach is all-embracing, but provided that you run the Log.pr_Logging_Simple stored procedure after every major step in your stored procedures (and reset the variable @STARTTIME before each step), you will have a simple yet reliable logging process.

Hints, Tips, and Traps

- This recipe's approach does not explicitly flag errors, but lets you query the columns containing error data to isolate error records. Of course, you can create views over the logging table to isolate errors, as shown in Recipe 15-19.

- Remember to set a variable with the time that the process started. Instantiate it with the time that the process (or part of a process) begins—not the time that you log the outcome—or you will not be able to deduce the runtime by subtracting the start time from the time the process ended and the logging took place. This moment can also be the time an error occurred.

- The call to log an event can be repeated several times in the course of a stored procedure. It could be when the stored procedure starts or when a unit of work inside a stored procedure has run.

15-2. Logging Data from SSIS

Problem

You have built an SSIS package and you want to add logging to it.

Solution

Configure SSIS logging from inside your SSIS package.

1. Select Logging from the SSIS menu—or right-click the Control Flow pane and click Logging. The Configure SSIS Logs:Logging dialog box will appear.

2. When the logging screen is displayed, select the provider type from the list of Provider types, and click Add for each one that you wish to use.

3. Ensure that the checkbox for each log provider is checked.

4. For each log provider, select or add a connection to the log destination by clicking the pop-up in the Configuration column.

5. In the left-hand Containers pane of the dialog box, check each container that you wish to log events for (these are the various tasks that make up your SSIS package). The dialog box should look something like Figure 15-1.

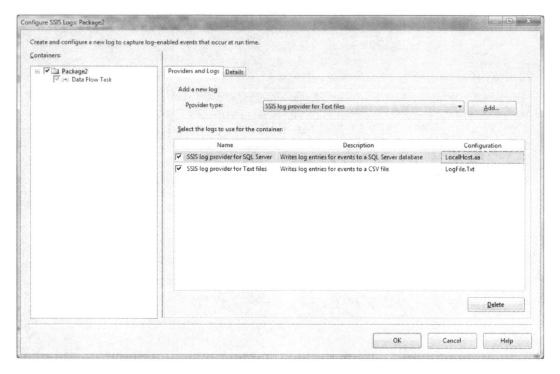

Figure 15-1. *Selecting log destinations*

6. Click the Details tab of the dialog box, and then the task for which you want to select logged events.

7. Check the Events checkbox to select all events.

8. Click OK.

When you run your SSIS package, all the events that you selected will be logged to the providers that you added.

How It Works

SSIS comes with advanced and complete logging facilities that allow you to track the progress and status of an SSIS package as it executes. Indeed, you have seen SSIS logging if you have viewed the Progressor Execution Resultstab in BIDS/SSDT—for you are seeing much of the same log information here as you will see in your custom logging.

Using this built-in logging infrastructure requires you to answer three basic questions:

- How are you going to log events?

- Which steps in the SSIS package do you want to log?

- What events do you want to log for each package step?

The "how" part means where you want to store logged information—or which log provider you wish to use, in SSIS terms. These include the following:

- An SQL Server table
- An XML file
- A text file
- An SQL Server Profiler Trace file
- The Windows event log

Any combination or all of these can be used concurrently. Each, of course, must be read using an appropriate tool. Indeed, most can be converted to another type of log using tools such as LogParser—described in Recipe 2-21. SSIS logging is, in essence, a simple set of options to be enabled.

■ **Note** While describing how to log events from SSIS, I want to add a quick comment. This approach, while not exactly deprecated in SQL Server 2012, has been largely superseded by the SSIS catalog in the SSIS server. You can still use this approach in SQL Server 2012 (and have no other real alternative in previous versions), but you need to be aware that there is now another solution available. This new technique is explained in Recipes 15-16 to 15-18.

Once you know where you want to save logging information, you can decide what information to save and for which package step. This information is the Logged Event in SSIS-speak, and is described in Table 15-6.

Table 15-6. *Logged Events in SSIS*

Event	Description
BufferSizeTuning	The reasons and resulting sizes of changes in buffer sizes (In the Data Flow task only).
Diagnostic	Returns package diagnostics information.
Error	Displays Error events.
ExecStatusChanged	Displays changes in task execution status.
FileSystemOperation	The file system operation that was performed (In the File System task only).
Information	Displays Information events. These are task-specific and vary according to the task selected for logging.
PipelineBufferLeak	Outstanding (memory-hogging) buffers consuming memory (In the Data Flow task only).
PipelineComponentTime	Information on the validation and execution of each Data Flow component (In the Data Flow task only).
PipelineExecutionPlan	The execution plan for a data flow (In the Data Flow task only).
PipelineExecutionTrees	The scheduler input when the execution plan is being created (Data Flow task only).
PipelineInitialization	Information from Pipeline Initialization (In the Data Flow task only).

(continued)

Table 15-6. (*continued*)

Event	Description
PipelinePostEndOfRowset	A component is given an end-of-rowset signal.
PipelinePostPrimeOutput	A component has returned from its Prime Output call.
PipelinePreEndOfRowset	A component is given a pre-end-of-rowset signal.
PipelinePrePrimeOutput	A component is given its pre-Prime Output call.
PipelineRowsSent	Rows were provided as input to a dataflow component.
PostExecute	Displays events occurring during the post-execute phase. PostExecute events.
PostValidate	Displays events occurring during the post-validation phase. PostValidate events.
PreExecute	Displays pre-execution events occurring during the pre-execute phase.
PreValidate	Displays events occurring during the pre-validation phase.
Progress	Handles progress notifications.
QueryCancel	Handles Cancel events. Polled at intervals to determine whether to cancel package execution.
TaskFailed	Handles task failures. Indicates that a task has failed.
Warning	Displays Warning events. These vary according to the task selected for logging. They are task-specific.

Once again, any or all of these events can be logged to all selected log providers.

A word of warning: it is easy to go overboard when logging SSIS packages, and to consequently end up with massive files (or tables) of log data, where it is impossible to see the woods for the trees. So be cautious when selecting the events you wish to log, given that judicious selection is as important as logging itself. Equally, logging events to all the log providers is usually complete overkill and normally one log provider will suffice.

Hints, Tips, and Traps

- To add, remove, or reconfigure a logging provider, click Logging in the left-hand pane first. Otherwise, however hard and often you click a log to use, you will not be able to select it.

- Log provider configuration uses standard SSIS connection managers. These can be edited directly from the Connection Managers pane.

- Configuring the log provider for SQL Server logging will create the sysssislog table in the destination database (this will be sysdtslog90 for SQL Server 2005). SSIS will also create the sp_ssis_addlogentry (sp_dts_addlogentry stored procedure in SQL Server 2005) in the destination database, which is used by SSIS to write log information to the destination table. Both can be tweaked if you prefer, as described in Recipe 15-4.

- Only experience will teach you which pieces of logging information you really need in each different set of circumstances. Generally, it pays to begin testing with as much logging information as you can digest, and then to reduce the number of events logged as you move into production. The sheer quantity of information made available can result in a counter productive flood of data that is never used, unless a modicum of moderation is applied in practice.

15-3. Customizing SSIS Logging

Problem

You need to select the SSIS events to log with greater precision and subtlety than the Recipe 15-2 solution provides.

Solution

Choose the events to log and the details to be logged for each event.

1. Follow steps 1 through 5 of Recipe 15-2 to configure SSIS logging.

2. In the Configure SSIS Logging dialog box, click the Details tab, and then click the Advanced button.

3. Select (or deselect) the event details you wish to log for each logged event. You should end up with something like Figure 15-2.

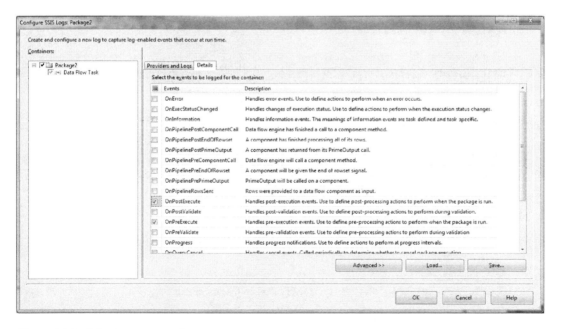

Figure 15-2. *Selecting events to log*

4. Click OK to confirm and close the dialog box.

How It Works

As simple as SSIS logging is, there are nonetheless a few available tweaks to allow developers to

- Select logged details.
- Load and save logging details.
- Reapply logging details.
- Modify the logging details file.

Choosing an event to trigger logging is only part of the story. All events can log the

- Computer (the name of the computer).
- Operator (the user executing the package).
- Source (the package).
- Sourceid (the package identifier).
- ExecutionID (the GUID of the execution context—the parent or child package).
- MessageText (any message returned).
- Databytes (currently unused).

As well as the

- Event (the name of the event).
- StartTime (the exact date and time the event began).
- EndTime (the exact date and time the event ended).

15-4. Saving and Applying Complex SSIS Logging Details

Problem

Redefining the same set of logging details for SSIS tasks is too time-consuming.

Solution

Save the set of log details to an XML file, and then re-apply them.

1. In the left pane, select the task whose logging details you wish to save.

2. In the Configure SSIS Loggingdialog box, click the Details tab, and then click the Save button.

3. Choose a path and enter a file name.
   (C:\SQL2012DIRecipes\CH15\MyTaskLogDetails.Xml in this example).

4. Click Save.

5. Click OK.

Then SSIS lets you save the details of task logging, and then re-apply them to multiple packages quickly and easily, like this:

1. Select the task whose logging details you wish to modify.

2. In the Configure SSIS Logging dialog box, click the Details tab, and then click the Load button.

3. Select the previously saved logging details file (C:\SQL2012DIRecipes\CH15\MyTaskLogDetails.Xml).

4. Click Open.

5. Click OK.

How It Works

If you have defined a complex set of logged details for a task (a Data Flow task, for instance), it can be extremely laborious and time-consuming to redefine the same logged events, individually, for multiple similar tasks. If you have saved a set of details to log, they can be applied to another SSIS package.

As logging details are saved as XML, you can edit the resulting XML in any text editor or any XML editor (such as XML Notepad from Microsoft). You will need to reapply any saved packages to existing tasks should you wish for these changes to be applied to your tasks. An abbreviated example of a saved file follows:

```
<?xml version="1.0" encoding="utf-8"?>
<DTSLoggingTemplate xmlns:xsi="http://www.w3.org/2001/XMLSchema-instance"
xmlns:xsd="http://www.w3.org/2001/XMLSchema" Name="TaskHost"
xmlns="www.microsoft.com/SqlServer/Dts">
<EventsFilter Name="OnError">
<Filter>
<Computer>true</Computer>
<Operator>true</Operator>
<SourceName>false</SourceName>
<SourceID>true</SourceID>
<ExecutionID>true</ExecutionID>
<MessageText>true</MessageText>
<DataBytes>true</DataBytes>
</Filter>
</EventsFilter>
...
</DTSLoggingTemplate>
```

As you can see, the structure is mercifully simple, and so it is easy to edit the XML file to add or remove EventsFilters and Filters.

Hints, Tips, and Traps

- You cannot load logging details for multiple tasks simultaneously.

- To apply all the logging details for a type of task, you are better loading the logging details file saved from a similar type of task. For instance, a File System task contains logging details for FileSystemOperation. So to apply your selections for this type of logging detail, you must first save logging details from a File System task.

- SSIS is very forgiving if you load a saved logging details file from one type of task into another type of task (let's say you save logging details for a Script task and load the details into a Data Flow task). Only details common to both tasks will be loaded, and any details not specific to the destination task will be ignored.

15-5. Extending SSIS Logging to an SQL Server Destination

Problem

You want to take advantage of the ability to log information to an SQL Server table when using SSIS, but you would like to adapt and extend this process to add your own elements to the log table.

Solution

Extend the built-in log table and stored procedure to suit your needs.

1. Click the table named `dbo.sysssislog` in the database you chose to hold the logging information. This will be in the System Tables folder.

2. Right-click, and choose Design.

3. Enter a column name (in this example, `ProcessID`) and a data type (here, for instance `INT`).

4. Save and close the table.

5. In SQL Server Management Studio, expand the Programmability ➤ Stored Procedures node.

6. Expand System Stored Procedures and right-click `sp_ssis_addlogentry`. Choose Modify.

7. Modify the procedure T-SQL as follows (C:\SQL2012DIRecipes\CH15\Modifiedsp_ssis_addlogentry.Sql):

```
ALTER PROCEDURE dbo.sp_ssis_addlogentry
@event sysname,
@computer NVARCHAR(128),
@operator NVARCHAR(128),
@source NVARCHAR(1024),
@sourceid UNIQUEIDENTIFIER,
@executionid UNIQUEIDENTIFIER,
@starttime DATETIME,
@endtime DATETIME,
@datacode int,
@databytes image,
@message NVARCHAR(2048),
@PROCESSID INT = 1 -- NOTE: The added field

AS
```

```
INSERT INTO sysssislog
(
event,
computer,
operator,
source,
sourceid,
executionid,
starttime,
endtime,
datacode,
databytes,
message,
ProcessID -- NOTE: This has been added to extend the logging capability
)

VALUES
(
@event,
@computer,
@operator,
@source,
@sourceid,
@executionid,
@starttime,
@endtime,
@datacode,
@databytes,
@message,
@ProcessID --NOTE: This has been added to extend the logging capability
)

RETURN 0 ;

GO
```

8. Press F5 or click Execute to recompile the stored procedure.

How It Works

If you have saved logging data using the SSIS log provider for SQL Server, you may have noticed the stored procedure (sp_ssis_addlogentry) and the table that it creates (sysssislog). These are not completely set in stone, and you can make minor changes to the logging default element if you wish. You can do the following, for instance:

- Add or remove columns.

- Extend the sp_ssis_addlogentry stored procedure (in SSIS 2012 and 2008, and 2008R2) and sp_dts_addlogentry (in SSIS 2005) to add further elements to the logging.

- Modify the table name and/or schema.

You can add further columns to the log table structure as you wish, and then extend the sp_ssis_addlogentry logging procedure to enter any new data. You might wonder why or when this could be necessary, so here is a plausible scenario. Let's say that you have an extremely complex ETL procedure that runs daily and numbers each daily process. Eventually, you will want to store a process identifier. You want to prepare the ground for this now using a hard-coded identifier. This is exactly what we did in the recipe. It involved modifying the logging table and the logging stored procedure.

I am presuming in this example that you are using the default object names created by SQL Server. There are a few points to note:

- You will have to find the table corresponding to the version of SQL Server that you are using.

- You are perfectly free to script any table changes rather than use SSMS if you prefer.

If you have altered the structure of the table to which SSIS logs data, you will have to alter the sp_ssis_addlogentry stored procedure if you want to take advantage of your changes to the table. This is a standard stored procedure, and consequently, modifying it is extremely simple. In the real world, you probably have a table with a process identifier from which you wish to extract the latest process run ID and add it to the logged data, rather than hard-coding it as I did here.

The table that SSIS creates for SQL Server logging—dbo.sysssislog—contains the fields shown in Table 15-7.

Table 15-7. *Fields in the dbo.sysssislog Table*

Field Name	Description
event	The event that triggered the logging (OnError, etc.)
computer	The computer where the process ran.
operator	The operator who ran the process.
source	The task that triggered the logging.
sourceid	The GUID of the task that caused logging to take place.
executionid	The execution GUID.
starttime	The date and time the process started.
endtime	The date and time the process ended.
datacode	The internal code.
databytes	The number of bytes processed.
message	The message sent from the event.

You can rename this table if you need to, without any untoward consequences. The only thing to watch for is that if you change the table name, then you must remember to alter the logging query (sp_dts_addlogentry) so that it points to the renamed table. Should you need to do this, the following is one way:

1. Click the table named dbo.sysssislog in the database you chose to hold the logging information.

2. Right-click, and choose Rename.

3. Replace the old table name with the new name.

4. In SQL Server Management Studio, expand the Programmability ➤ Stored Procedures node, and then expand System Stored Procedures.

5. Right-click sp_ssis_addlogentry and select Modify.

6. Replace the table name dbo.sysssislog with the new table name from step 3 at the INSERT INTO statement.

7. Press F5 or click Execute to recompile the stored procedure.

Hints, Tips, and Traps

- You can also place the log table in a different schema if you wish—just remember to indicate the correct schema in the stored procedure instead of "dbo".

- Remember that on SQL Server 2008 and 2012, the table is dbo.sysssislog, and on the 2005 version, it is dbo.sysdtslog90.

- In SSIS 2005, the stored procedure is called sp_dts_addlogentry and is in the Stored Procedures folder.

- Of course, you may use T-SQL DDL to add any new columns.

- Note that you are not modifying any of the built-in parameters passed to the stored procedure—these must remain as initially defined.

15-6. Logging Information from an SSIS Script Task
Problem

You have a Script task in an SSIS package and you want to write information to the standard log providers from it.

Solution

Use the Dts.Log method to write to any of the usual log providers.

1. As part of the Script task, enter the following code (here in Microsoft Visual Basic 2010) to log an event:

```
Dim nullBytes(0) As Byte
Dts.Log("My script task has done something",0, nullBytes)
```

2. Include this snippet in the Try … Catch error trapping blocks of your script code, as in the following example (C:\SQL2012DIRecipes\CH15\SCriptTaskLogging.vb):

```
Public Sub Main()
        Try

                'Some code here

                Dim nullByte() As Byte
                Dts.Log("Write to log that all has worked", 0, nullByte)
```

```
        Catch ex As Exception
            Dts.Log(ex.Message, 0, nullByte) 'Log the error message
        End Try

        Dts.TaskResult = ScriptResults.Success
    End Sub
```

How It Works

There is a specific way of writing user-defined log information to all enabled log providers that can be called from an SSIS Script task. You will need to do the following:

- Ensure that the Script task is selected in the Container spane of the Configure SSIS Logsdialog box.

- In the Detail stab of the Configure SSIS Logs dialog box, ensure that Script Task Log Entry is checked.

This script will now log process error information to all the log providers that have been enabled for the package.

15-7. Logging from T-SQL to the SSIS Log Table
Problem

You have a complex SSIS package that frequently uses stored procedures, and you want to log process and error information from both SSIS and T-SQL to a centralized table. You would prefer to use the built-in log table.

Solution

Create a stored procedure to write log data to the built-in the dbo.sysssislog table from T-SQL code and stored procedures.

1. Create a stored procedure to perform logging from your T-SQL procedures, using the following code (C:\SQL2012DIRecipes\CH15\pr_SQLtoSSISLogging.Sql):

```
CREATE PROCEDURE dbo.pr_SQLtoSSISLogging
@event sysname,
@message NVARCHAR(2048),
@datacode int,
@starttime DATETIME,
@source NVARCHAR(1024),
@operator NVARCHAR(128)

AS

DECLARE @computer NVARCHAR(128)
DECLARE @sourceid UNIQUEIDENTIFIER
DECLARE @endtime DATETIME
DECLARE @executionid UNIQUEIDENTIFIER
DECLARE @databytes VARBINARY(MAX)
```

```
SET @computer = @@SERVERNAME
SELECT @operator = USER_NAME()
SET @sourceid = NEWID()
SET @endtime = GETDATE()
SET @executionid = NEWID()
SET @databytes = CONVERT(VARBINARY(MAX),'x')

INSERT INTO dbo.sysssislog
(
event,
computer,
operator,
source,
sourceid,
executionid,
starttime,
endtime,
datacode,
databytes,
message
)

VALUES
(
@event,
@computer,
@operator,
@source,
@sourceid,
@executionid,
@starttime,
@endtime,
@datacode,
@databytes,
@message
)

RETURN 0 ;

GO
```

2. At the start of your stored procedure, place the following code:

```
DECLARE @source NVARCHAR(1024)
DECLARE @starttime DATETIME
DECLARE @operator NVARCHAR(128)
SELECT @source = OBJECT_NAME(@@PROCID)
SELECT @operator = USER_NAME()
```

Before each part of the process that you wish to log place the following code in your T-SQL:

```
SET @StartTime = GETDATE()
-- Your code here
EXECUTE pr_SQLtoSSISLogging 'Success', 'Log to SSIS Table', 0, @StartTime, @source, @operator
```

3. Configure logging to an SQL Server table as described in Recipe 15-2.

How It Works

You may prefer to centralize log data to a single table and to use the SSIS log provider table. This means that all your logging data is in one place, whether it was triggered by an SSIS task or an SQL stored procedure. If you do this, however, you might find that the dbo.sysssislog standard SSIS table is a little restrictive and perhaps not ideal for logging information from T-SQL stored procedures. But as a quick and efficient solution, this approach certainly has its merits—all the more so as you have nothing to do to log information from SSIS other than configure logging as described in Recipe 15-2. When performing this operation, I prefer to leave the stored procedure that writes to the dbo.sysssislog table in the same database as the dbo.sysssislog table itself.

Hints, Tips, and Traps

*   If you do not want to insert dummy data (GUIDs for sourceId and executionID), you may prefer to alter the table types to VARCHAR, which will allow you to store other information.

*   Equally, allowing NULLs for some—if not most—of the columns in the dbo.sysssislog table will give you greater flexibility, as this means that you can tweak the stored procedure to write to the table so it does not need to include superfluous data.

*   If you are using this approach as part of an error-trapping TRY...CATCH block, (as described previously) you can replace the "datacode" with the error code returned from @@ERROR.

*   Of course, you may add further elements to the stored procedure (and the corresponding columns to the table it logs to) if you wish.

*   While I say that this is normally run from a stored procedure, it can be run from most T-SQL snippets, such as code in SSIS Execute SQL tasks or T-SQL code called from an SQL Server Agent. It might require a little tweaking, however—such as replacing OBJECT_NAME(@@PROCID) with a hard-coded reference.

15-8. Handling Errors in T-SQL
Problem

You want your stored procedures (and T-SQL snippets) to be resilient and handle errors gracefully.

Solution

Use TRY...CATCH blocks in stored procedures and T-SQL snippets to catch and process errors. The following is the "wrapper" code to handle error trapping in a stored procedure:

```
DECLARE @StartTime DATETIME
DECLARE @ProcName VARCHAR(150) -- The calling procedure
DECLARE @ProcStep VARCHAR(150) -- The step in the procedure
SET @ProcName = OBJECT_NAME(@@PROCID)

BEGIN TRY
SET @ProcStep = 'My test'

--Your code here --

END TRY
BEGIN CATCH

DECLARE @Error_Number int
DECLARE @ ErrorDescription VARCHAR(MAX)
DECLARE @ErrorLine INT
DECLARE @ErrorSeverity INT
DECLARE @ErrorState INT
DECLARE @Message VARCHAR(150)

SET @Error_Number = ERROR_NUMBER()
SET @ErrorDescription = ERROR_MESSAGE()
SET @ErrorLine = ERROR_LINE()
SET @ErrorSeverity = ERROR_SEVERITY()
SET @ErrorState = ERROR_STATE()
SET @Message = 'Error in procedure: ' +  @ProcName + ' - ' + @ErrorDescription

RAISERROR(@Message ,16,1)

END CATCH
```

How It Works

Logging has to track both success and failure. Consequently, you need to be able to develop ETL packages and routines that handle failure gracefully (rather than merely blocking and stopping) and which can pass details of the failure to the chosen type of logging. Here then are the principal methods of capturing errors and returning error data to a log.

Many chapters in many tomes have been written about error trapping in T-SQL. So, rather than discuss all the possibilities, this is the tried and tested way to handle errors in your ETL stored procedures—the TRY...CATCH block to collect any error details. As you probably know, the CATCH block can return the following for an error:

- The error number

- The error description

- The line number where the error occurred

- The error severity (in SQL Server terms)
- The error state

It can be as simple as this, really. Of course, there are many subtleties in error trapping, and for those I can only refer you to the many excellent commentators who have described it so thoroughly. As a basic principle, you should always add at least elementary error handling to T-SQL routines. Also, wrapping essential parts (or indeed all) of your stored procedure in a transaction will allow data modifications to be rolled back in case of a failure. If copying and pasting this boilerplate text becomes a little repetitive, then please see Recipe 15-12 for a technique to add it to the SSMS template collection.

15-9. Handling Errors in SSIS

Problem

You want your SSIS packages to be resilient and to be able to deal with errors gracefully when executing.

Solution

Apply SSIS's built-in error handling. The following is a high-level example.

1. Create a new SSIS package. Add the following OLEDB Source connection managers (unless they are already available in the package or at project level):

Type	Name	Database
OLEDB	Car_Sales_OLEDB	Car_Sales
OLEDB	Car_Sales_Staging_OLEDB	Car_Sales_Staging

2. Create the following variables:

Name	Scope	DataType	Value
ErrorRowsDestination	Package	Integer	
ErrorRowsSource	Package	Integer	

3. Add a Data Flow task. Double-click to edit.

4. Add an OLEDB source component, edit it, and select the Car_Sales_OLEDB connection manager. Choose the Clients table.

5. Click Error Output on the left. Select all the cells in the main pane, and then select Redirect Row from the Set this value to selected cells pop-up. Click Apply. The dialog box should look like Figure 15-3.

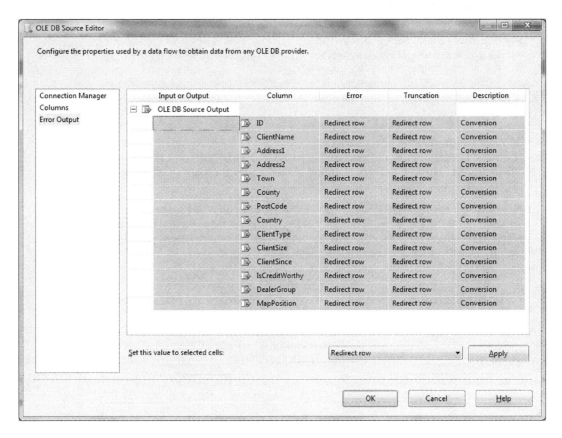

Figure 15-3. *Redirecting error rows in a Data Flow task*

6. Confirm with OK. For the moment, disregard the warning.

7. Add an OLEDB destination to which you connect the OLEDB source component. Double-click and select the Car_Sales_Staging_OLEDB connection manager. Create a new table named **Clients** and map the columns. Set the Error Output for the task to Redirect Row.

8. Add two Row Count tasks to the Data Flow pane. Name them **RowCountSource** and **RowCountDestination**. Connect the former to the OLEDB source task and the latter to the OLEDB destination task. As you connect the Row Counter (using the red precedence constraint), the Configure Error Output dialog box will appear. Just click OK.

9. Add the ErrorRowsSource variable to the Row Count task named RowCountSource, and the ErrorRowsDestination variable to the Row Count task named RowCountDestination.

10. Add a Script component—choose the Transform option. Connect the Row Count task named RowCountSource to it. Double-click to edit.

11.   Click Inputs and Outputs and add a new output column to Output 0. Name the
column **ErrorColumn**. Click Script on the left, and then Edit Script. Add the following
(assuming that the script language is set to Microsoft Visual Basic 2010):

```
Public Overrides Sub Input0_ProcessInputRow(ByVal Row As Input0Buffer)
  Row.ErrorDescription = ComponentMetaData.GetErrorDescription(Row.ErrorCode)
End Sub
```

12.   Add a Flat File destination task. Connect the Script task to it and configure it with
a delimited file destination. I suggest calling it **C:\SQL2012DIRecipes\CH15\
SSISErrors.Txt**.Map all the source columns to it (including the three columns added
by SSIS—ErrorCode, ErrorColumn, and ErrorDescription).

13.   Add an OLEDB destination. Connect the RowCountDestination task to it and double-
click to edit. Use the Car_Sales_Staging_OLEDB connection manager and create a
new table to contain error records. This, too, will contain the fields ErrorCode and
ErrorColumn. The data flow should look like Figure 15-4.

Figure 15-4. *Data flow with error redirection*

You can now run the import process. Any errors in the OLEDB source will be sent to the flat file
SSISErrors.Txt. Any errors in the destination task will be captured to the destination database.

How It Works

SSIS also has its own error handling, of course. The essential place where graceful error handling is required is as
part of a data flow, when data cannot be passed through the SSIS pipeline correctly.

SSIS offers three options when a data row contains an error (which tend to be data type errors or data
length errors):

- ***Continue*** (which might not always succeed).
- ***Discard*** the row.
- ***Redirect*** the row to a file or data table.

As merely avoiding a row with an error will result in an incomplete load and no tracking of the missing
records, I only look at the redirect option here. This way you get to isolate any erroneous records. In the real
world, you can send error records to a flat file, the normal destination database—or indeed any database. I find
it much easier to output the source errors to a flat file, as it can handle nearly everything that you throw at it. If
you want to use a destination table here, you must ensure that it has columns that are wide enough to handle
overflow due to truncation—assuming that you are handling truncation errors. In practice, this nearly always
means setting all columns to a very wide NVARCHAR type.

Hints, Tips, and Traps

- A Flat File destination cannot handle certain source column types, such as image columns. You will need to remove these from the column mapping.

- The Script component to add the error description is not absolutely necessary—but it helps to have fuller error descriptions when debugging!

- You can also redirect error information from the data conversion task and the derived column task.

15-10. Creating a Centralized Logging Framework

Problem

You have developed a fairly complex SSIS package with many calls to T-SQL stored procedures, and you want to log events to a single repository.

Solution

Develop a custom logging framework to handle logging events from both T-SQL and SSIS. Here is one such framework:

1. Create the table (using the following DDL) to hold logged information (C:\SQL2012DIRecipes\CH15\tblEventDetail.Sql):

```
CREATE TABLE CarSales_Logging.log.EventDetail
(
EventDetailID INT IDENTITY(1,1) NOT NULL,
Process VARCHAR(255) NULL,
Step VARCHAR(255) NULL,
Comments VARCHAR(MAX) NULL,
ErrorNo INT NULL,
ErrorDescription VARCHAR(MAX) NULL,
ErrorLineNo INT NULL,
ErrorSeverity INT NULL,
ErrorState INT NULL,
StartTime DATETIME NULL,
Logtime DATETIME NULL
);
GO
```

2. Using the following DDL, create the stored procedure that logs any outcome (C:\SQL2012DIRecipes\CH15\pr_LogEvents.Sql):

```
CREATE PROCEDURE CarSales_Logging.log.pr_LogEvents
(
@Process VARCHAR(150)
,@Step VARCHAR(150)
,@StartTime DATETIME
,@Comments VARCHAR(MAX) = NULL
,@ErrorNo INT = NULL
```

```
,@ErrorDescription VARCHAR(MAX) = NULL
,@ErrorLineNo INT = NULL
,@ErrorSeverity INT = NULL
,@ErrorState INT = NULL
)

AS

INSERT INTO CarSales_Logging.log.EventDetail
(
Process
,Step
,StartTime
,Comments
,ErrorNo
,ErrorDescription
,ErrorLineNo
,ErrorSeverity
,ErrorState
)

VALUES
(
@Process
,@Step
,@StartTime
,@Comments
,@ErrorNo
,@ErrorDescription
,@ErrorLineNo
,@ErrorSeverity
,@ErrorState
) ;
GO
```

3.   Add logging for all your T-SQL-based processes, like this:

```
-- Start Header ---------------------------------------------------------
DECLARE @StartTime DATETIME
DECLARE @ ProcName VARCHAR(150) --- The calling procedure
DECLARE @ProcStep VARCHAR(150) -- The step in the procedure
SET @ProcName = OBJECT_NAME(@@PROCID)

BEGIN TRY
---- End Header ---------------------------------------------------------

SET @ProcStep = 'My test'

--Your code here --
```

```
        EXECUTE CarSales_Logging.log.pr_Logging_Simple @ProcName, @ProcStep, @StartTime,
        'Part of the process OK'

        -- Start Footer -------------------------------------------------

        END TRY
        BEGIN CATCH

        IF @@trancount > 0 ROLLBACK TRAN
        SET XACT_ABORT OFF;

        DECLARE @Error_Number int
        DECLARE @ ErrorDescription VARCHAR(MAX)
        DECLARE @ErrorLine INT
        DECLARE @ErrorSeverity INT
        DECLARE @ErrorState INT
        DECLARE @Message VARCHAR(150)

        SET @ERROR_NUMBER = ERROR_NUMBER()
        SET @ErrorDescription = ERROR_MESSAGE()
        SET @ErrorLine = ERROR_LINE()
        SET @ErrorSeverity = ERROR_SEVERITY()
        SET @ErrorState = ERROR_STATE()

        EXECUTE CarSales_Logging.log.pr_Logging_Simple @ProcName, @ProcStep, @StartTime,
        'Error - Stored Procedure', @ERROR_NUMBER, @ErrorDescription, @ErrorLineNo,
        @ErrorSeverity, @ErrorState

        SET @Message = 'Error in procedure: ' +  @ProcName
        RAISERROR(@Message ,16,1)

        END CATCH
        -- End footer ----------------------------------------------
```

4. Create an ADO.NET connection manager named **CarSales_Logging_ADONET**,
    which connects to the CarSales_Logging database.

5. Add Logging to SSIS tasks as follows. For a task or container whose outcome you wish
    to log (in this example it will be a Data Flow task).

6. Add the following two variables at the scope of the task (the safest way to do this is to
    select the task before creating the variables):

Variable Name	Type	Value
IsError	Boolean	False
StartTime	DateTime	

7. With the task selected, click the Event Handlers tab, and select OnPreExecute from the list of available event handlers.

8. Click "Click here to select ... " and then add an Execute SQL task onto the Event Handlers pane. Name it **Get StartTime**. Configure it to use the ADO.NET connection CarSales_Logging_ADONET.

9. Add the following parameter to the Parameter Mapping pane:

Variable	Direction	Type	ParameterName
User::TaskStartTime	Output	DateTime	@TaskStartTime

10. Add the following SQL as the SQL Statement:

```
SELECT @TaskStartTime = GETDATE()
```

11. Close and confirm the task. This will pass the task start time to an SSIS variable scoped at task level.

12. Select OnError from the list of event handlers and click "Click here to select ... ". Add an Execute SQL task onto the Event Handlers pane. Name it **Log Failure**. Add the ADO.NET connection to the database used for logging.

13. For the Log Failure Execute SQL task, add the following parameters:

VariableName	Direction	DataType	ParameterName
User::ErrorCode	Input	Int32	@ErrorNo
User::ErrorDescription	Input	String	@ErrorDescription
System::PackageName	Input	String	@Process
System::SourceName	Input	String	@Step
User::StartTime	Input	DateTime	@StartTime
User::IsError	Input	Boolean	@IsError

14. In the Log Failure SQL task, add the following SQL as the SQL Statement to execute:

```
SET @IsError = 1
EXECUTE dbo.pr_LogEvents@Process, @Step, @StartTime, 'SSIS Error', @ErrorNo,
@ErrorDescription
```

15. Select OnPostExecute from the list of event handlers, and click "Click here to select ... ". Add an Execute SQL task onto the Event Handlers pane. Name it **Log Success**. Add the ADO.NET connection to the database used for logging.

16. Add the following parameters:

VariableName	Direction	DataType	ParameterName
User::TaskStartTime	Input	DateTime	@TaskStartTime
System::PackageName	Input	String	@Process
User::IsError	Input	Boolean	@IsError

17. In the Log Success SQL task, add the following SQL as the SQL Statement to execute:

```
IF @IsError = 0
BEGIN
EXECUTE dbo.pr_LogEvents @Process, @Step, @StartTime
END
```

18. Return to the Control Flow pane.

How It Works

If you have built—or are building—a moderately complex SSIS package to load data, then you probably also want to be able to log all relevant information to a central repository. Equally probably, this could be an SQL Server table rather than a text file. The reasons for this are that

- A central point of focus avoids having to search through multiple sources of information.

- A T-SQL table can be searched and filtered very rapidly.

So what are the advantages and disadvantages of logging to T-SQL using "roll your own" logging rather than using and extending the built-in solutions proposed by SSIS? Table 15-8 provides a succinct overview.

Table 15-8. *Advantages and Disadvantages of Creating a Custom Logging Framework*

Advantages	Disadvantages
Extremely useful to store a centralized record of process flow—or to put it simply, a list of what worked and what did not.	More effort to implement.
Highly customizable.	Tricky to debug.
Logging highly targeted and specific information does not cause resource contention.	Easy to forget to add a log call to tasks and code.
Only required events and information are logged.	Can itself be a source of package errors and cause package failure.
Easy-to-specify duration of data storage. Keeps only recent information.	
Simple to extract high-level data for baselining.	
Can help in debugging.	

Nevertheless, I am firmly convinced that logging to a central table is very well suited to production ETL jobs, and I have been applying it for years. If anything, it becomes a habit and a valuable assistance, not only after packages have gone into production, but also when debugging them.

You may want to suggest that building custom logging frameworks is a thing of the past now that SQL Server 2012 has the SSIS catalog to provide logging. My response is that while the SSIS catalog is a wonderful tool for logging SSIS tasks and packages, it is not (at least not yet) a centralized repository for logging all events, including those generated by stored procedures. However, if SSIS handles your entire ETL process without any calls to stored procedures, then SSIS catalog logging is certainly the way to go. The SSIS catalog is described in Recipes 15-16 to 15-18.

The approach that I am suggesting here is to have a single SQL Server table to log event data generated when an SSIS task or T-SQL code fragment succeeds or fails. A single stored procedure logs the outcome. This stored procedure is called from T-SQL or from SSIS. In any case, for the reasons outlined at the start of this chapter, I also strongly advise that any logging use its own database.

The DDL for the log table explains its use. As the terminology is different between T-SQL and SSIS, some choices of vocabulary have been made for the table field names, but I hope that they are self-explanatory. The only fields that might need further explanation are Step and Process. I have added these because a package can potentially log many events, and these events are nested (stored procedures call other 'sprocs, SSIS packages call SSIS packages, which in turn have tasks). These two fields allow you to track which process calls what sub element, and consequently creates a simple hierarchy to track this nesting of calls. It means always containing the reference to the

- *Process*: The container (the SSIS package or stored procedure).

- *Step*: The element or task to log.

I would suggest that this approach is useful for small- to medium-sized SSIS processes, where essential—but not over-detailed logging—is required. For very complex ETL systems, you will need to extend these tables and procedures to suit your specific requirements.

A centralized approach like this is going to need to store three types of elements:

- Data common to SSIS and T-SQL.

- Data specific to either SSIS or T-SQL.

- Error details (which can also be common to both SSIS and T-SQL or specific to one or the other).

So, as the assumptions underlying this approach are that you want fairly minimal logging, let us assume that the following basic principles need to be logged for each step:

- The package process

- The package step

- A description of what is logged

- Start time

- End time (the time that the event is logged)

- Error details if an error is caught

You will need the following:

- A table to store success.

- A stored procedure to log event outcomes.

- An ADO.NET connection manager to the database used for logging. I suggest ADO.NET over OLEDB purely for the ease with which it can handle parameter passing, especially when there are multiple parameters. You can use an OLEDB connection manager if you wish.

Logging from T-SQL becomes a combination of straight logging (as described in Recipe 15-7) and error handling (described in Recipe 15-8). Here is an example of a stored procedure template where I have wrapped the error handling in a standard header and footer, and used the same stored procedure to log successful steps as well as any failures. This stored procedure outline can even become the model for all your stored procedures in an ETL process.

Logging from SSIS to a centralized table (the same one that you use when logging from stored procedures) necessitates judicious use of event handlers to work cleanly and efficiently. What you can do for most tasks is use the following:

- The OnPreExecute event handler to set the time at which the task began.

- The OnPostExecute event handler to log the task completion.

- The OnError event handler to log the fact that the task has failed, along with any error messages.

Also, you will need to set two task-scoped variables (the scope is important) so that the start time can be initialized, and an error flag set (which will prevent both the OnPostExecute event handler from logging the event as well as the OnError event handler, should an error occur). In other words, flagging the IsError variable to True as part of the OnError event allows the error state to be picked up by the log process which occurs when the OnPostExecute event fires. As the Log Success task also tests this variable when it fires, it will only call the stored procedure to log an event when an error has **not** occurred.

The use of Getdate() while pointing at the server that performs the logging can be important, but you cannot be sure that all your servers will be synchronized to return the exact same date and time. So if you are using a script package and the Now() function on a server hosting SSIS, while logging takes place on another server, you could end up with incoherent timestamps.

Hints, Tips, and Traps

- If your SSIS package is so simple that it contains only one step, then you can use the System::StartTime system variable to record the start time, and you will not need to use—or set—the TaskStartTime variable.

- Do not be tempted to use the ContainerStartTime system variable to record package start time—this will give the start time of the Execute SQL task performing the logging— **not** the task you are trying to monitor.

- When logging from T-SQL, the order of the input parameters for the stored procedure is important, as any noncompulsory (NULL) parameters must follow compulsory ones.

15-11. Logging to a Centralized Framework When Using SSIS Containers

Problem

When using SSIS containers and a custom logging framework based on event handlers, you find that the same events are logged many times over.

Solution

Apply your custom logging framework in a specific way to SSIS containers so that only one log entry is made. Here is how it can be done:

1. Create an SSIS package.

2. Create an ADO.NET connection manager named **CarSales_Logging_ADONET** that connects to the CarSales_Logging database—unless it exists already, of course.

3. Create the following variables:

Name	Scope	DataType
ContainerStart	Package	DateTime

4. Add an Execute SQL task. Name it **SetStartTime**. Double-click to edit and configure it as follows:

ConnectionType:	ADO.NET
Connection:	CarSales_ADONET
SQLSourceType:	Direct Input
SQLStatement:	`SELECT @ContainerStart = GETDATE()`
IsQueryStoredProcedure:	False

5. Click ParameterMapping on the left, and add the following parameter:

VariableName	Direction	DataType	ParameterName
ContainerStart	Output	DateTime	@ContainerStart

6. Click OK to complete your modifications

7. Connect this Execute SQL task to the container you wish to log.

8. Add two Execute SQL Tasks. Connect both to the container you wish to log. Double-click one of the precedence constraints and set it to Failure. Name one **Log Success** and the other (connected via the precedence constraint set to Failure) **Log Failure**.

9. For both of these tasks, add the ContainerStart parameter as described in step 3, but with the direction set to Input.

10. For both of these tasks, double-click to edit and set the following:

ConnectionType:	ADO.NET
Connection:	CarSales_Staging_ADONET
SQLSourceType:	Direct Input
IsQueryStoredProcedure:	False

11. For the Log Success task, set the SQLStatement as:

```
EXECUTE pr_Logging @Process, @Step, @StartTime
```

12. For the Log Failure task, set the SQLStatement as:

```
EXECUTE pr_Logging @Process, @Step, @StartTime, 'SSIS Error', 5000,'Failure to Load
Staging Tables'
```

The package should look something like in Figure 15-5.

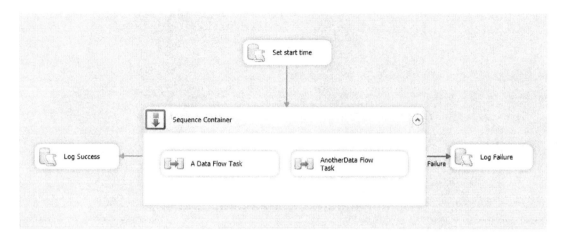

Figure 15-5. *Logging events for a container object*

How It Works

Unfortunately, containers require a slightly different approach to logging—assuming that you wish make a single log entry for the entire container. This is because if you use the event handlers for the container in Recipe 15-10, they will all fire repeatedly as the tasks in the container fire, which causes multiple identical log entries. So the easy solution is to add three Execute SQL tasks:

- One before the container, and connecting to the contained, to set the start time.

- One connected to the container using a Success precedence constraint to log success.

- One connected to the container using a Failure precedence constraint to log failure.

This way, the container is logged once and with any error messages for eventual failure.

15-12. Logging to a Centralized Framework When Using SSIS Script Tasks and Components
Problem

You want to write to a custom logging framework from inside the script code that you have written.

Solution

Use .NET from inside the Script task or Component to call the stored procedure that carries out logging.

1. Create an SSIS package.

2. Create an ADO.NET connection manager named CarSales_Logging_ADONET that connects to the database CarSales_Logging—unless it exists already, of course.

3. Add a Script task. Double-click to Edit.

4. Set the script language to Microsoft Visual Basic 2010 and click the Edit Script button.

5. At the appropriate point(s) in your script add the following code to write to the log table (C:\SQL2012DIRecipes\CH15\CentralisedSSISLogging.vb):

```
Dim StartTime As Date = Now()
Dim cnMgr As SqlClient.SqlConnection

cnMgr = DirectCast(Dts.Connections("CarSales_ADONET") ↩
    .AcquireConnection(Dts.Transaction), SqlClient.SqlConnection)

Dim cmd As New SqlClient.SqlCommand

cmd.CommandText = "Log.pr_LogEvents"
cmd.CommandType = CommandType.StoredProcedure
cmd.Parameters.AddWithValue("Process", DbType.String).Value = ↩
    Dts.Variables("PackageName").Value
cmd.Parameters.AddWithValue("Step", DbType.String).Value = ↩
    Dts.Variables("TaskName").Value
cmd.Parameters.AddWithValue("StartTime", DbType.DateTime).Value = StartTime
cmd.Parameters.AddWithValue("Comments", DbType.String).Value = ↩
    "This seems to have worked!"

cmd.ExecuteNonQuery()

Dts.Connections("CarSales_Logging_ADONET").ReleaseConnection(Nothing)

Dts.TaskResult = ScriptResults.Success
```

6. Close the script window and click OK to complete your modifications.

How It Works

One slightly specific requirement in logging SSIS packages is detailed logging from Script tasks. Certainly, if the task is simple, then merely adding the three event handlers (OnPreExecute, OnPostExecute, and OnError) will suffice. However, a few tweaks may be required to push this a little further and to track events—and errors—more fully.

Should your Script task be complex or iterative, you may want to log process events as part of the task execution. You will need the following:

- An ADO.NET connection manager to the logging database.

- The logging stored procedure (Log.pr_LogEvents), as given in Recipe 15-10.

- The logging table (log.EventDetail), as defined in Recipe 15-10.

Of course, if you are logging multiple events from inside the Script task, then for all subsequent events you will only need to reset the Comments parameter and add cmd.ExecuteNonQuery(). You will need to add ImportsSystem.Data.SqlClient to the script file. You will also need to add the most accurate and descriptive comment for the event that you can, as you may need to understand it in a log table one day.

There are a few differences if you wish to write to the central log table from an SSIS Script component. Specifically the connection manager is defined for the task, and then "acquired" inside the script.

You will again need an ADO.NET connection manager to the logging database, the logging stored procedure (Log.pr_LogEvents), and the logging table (log.EventDetail).

Assuming that these are in place, carry out the following steps:

1. Double-click to edit the Script component.

2. Click Connection Managers and then click Add.

3. Select the ADO.NET connection manager that you are using for logging from the list. The dialog box should look like Figure 15-6.

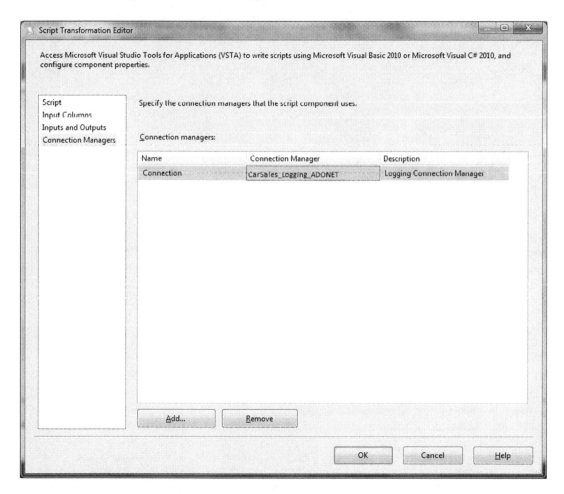

Figure 15-6. *Logging from a Script task*

887

4. Click Script and then Edit Script.

5. Add the following to the body of the code:

```
Public Overrides Sub AcquireConnections(ByVal Transaction As Object)

        SQLMgr = Me.Connections.LogConnection

        cnMgr = CType(SQLMgr.AcquireConnections(Nothing), ⏎
                        SqlClient.SqlConnection)

End Sub
```

6. Add the logging code (as just described) for the Script task.

If you have added an OnError event handler to the SSIS script task, it would be particularly useful to ensure that any error messages raised during script execution were logged accurately. This can be done by trapping any errors, and then firing an error event—which passes the error message to the task error handler. It could be something like this:

```
Try

  'Your code here

Catch ex As Exception

' Error code and description passed to handler
Dts.Events.FireError(20, "", ex.Message, "", False)

End Try
```

This way, if an error is encountered, the OnError SSIS event is triggered and the specific error message is logged to the central error table—without having to write complex logging code as part of the Script component.

■ **Note** Even if it is easy enough to copy and paste the Execute SQL tasks that comprise the logging infrastructure triggered by the event handlers, it can rapidly become a little wearing. Another valid approach is to define the three Execute SQL logging tasks for the OnPreExecute, OnPostExecute, and OnError tasks—but at package level—that is, click anywhere inside the Control Flow pane before clicking the Event Handler tab. This means that any event handler set here will fire for **every** task in the package. However, you then add a degree of control by setting the DisableEventHandler property for the package to False, and set it to True **only** for the tasks that you want to log. You will, however, still have to define task-scoped variables for each of the tasks that will be logged.

As a final point, copying and pasting T-SQL logging and error-handling code into dozens of stored procedures can rapidly become as frustrating as it is tedious. So it is probably worth reminding ourselves that SSMS allows you to use stored procedure templates when creating sprocs. The trick is to locate the directory where these are stored.

On 32-bit Windows, it is (on my 32-bit workstation, at least):

```
C:\Program Files\Microsoft SQL
Server\110\Tools\Binn\VSShell\Common7\IDE\SqlWorkbenchProjectItems\Sql\
```

On 64-bit Windows, it is (on my 64-bit workstation, at least):

```
C:\Program Files (x86)\Microsoft SQL
Server\110\Tools\Binn\VSShell\Common7\IDE\SqlWorkbenchProjectItems\Sql\
```

In either case, you can use one of the existing directories or create your own alongside those that you find there. You can then copy an SQL file containing your template structure (with a suitable name) into the directory.

Once this is done, all you have to do is to press Ctrl+Alt+T or click View Template Explorer to display the template window, and then open the template you previously created as a model for your new procedure.

If you really want to go overboard, you can set the template as the default New Stored Procedure template by pasting the contents of your logging template into the following file:

```
C:\Program Files\Microsoft SQL Server\110\Tools\Binn\VSShell\Common7\IDE\ ↵
SqlWorkbenchProjectItems\Sql\Stored Procedure\ Create Stored Procedure (New Menu).sql
```

In SSMS, expand Programmability/Stored Procedures for a database. Right-click and select New Stored Procedure. You will have your template loaded ready to be extended.

15-13. Logging to a Text or XML File from T-SQL
Problem

You want to log process information to a text or XML file rather than to an SQL Server table.

Solution

Create a CLR-based stored procedure to log information to disk, as follows.

1. First, you need a simple CLR routine to output the log data to disk. This is done by creating a CLR stored procedure named **WriteToDisk**, using the following C# code (for an overview of how to create and load a CLR routine, see Recipe 10-21):

```csharp
using System;
using System.Diagnostics;
using System.IO;

public class DiskWriter
{
Microsoft.SqlServer.Server.SqlProcedure()
public static void WriteToDisk(string theData, string theFile)
{
File.WriteAllText(theFile, theData);
}
}
```

2. Once you have deployed and installed the CLR stored procedure, you can use it to write to a text file. This is as then easy as stringing together the elements you wish to log and passing them to the CLR stored procedure, as the following T-SQL snippet shows:

```
DECLARE @OUTPUT NVARCHAR(MAX)
DECLARE @PackageName VARCHAR(150)
DECLARE @StepName VARCHAR(150)
DECLARE @StartTime DATETIME
DECLARE,@MachineName VARCHAR(150)

SET PackageName = 'MyPackage'
SET StepName = 'FirstStep'
SET StartTime = CONVERT(VARCHAR(20), @StartTime, 112)
SET MachineName = 'MyPC'

SET @OUTPUT = @PackageName + ',' + @StepName + ',' + @StartTime + ',' + @MachineName

EXECUTE  dbo.WriteToDisk @OUTPUT,'C:\SQL2012DIRecipes\CH13\AA_log.Csv'
```

How It Works

Should you prefer to write status information to a file outside SQL Server (as text or XML), then it can be done using fairly "classic" techniques. There could be several reasons for you wanting to do this:

- Logging to a file reduces database overhead—at the slight cost of running a CLR function.

- You can log data to a different server easily, further reducing load on a main SQL Server.

- You prefer log data to be kept outside a database.

- Should there be a fatal database problem, you still have log data.

First, you will need a CLR-based stored procedure that takes two input parameters:

- The row of data to be written to the file.

- The full path of the file to which data will be written.

This procedure consists of just one line that uses the WriteAllText function to add a line to the file that is specified. Once this CLR assembly is compiled and deployed to SQL Server and the assembly created, it is called just like any other stored procedure.

Writing an XML log can require some preparation of the XML. Here I will format data taken from a log table and export to XML using the same format as that used by SSIS:

```
DECLARE @OUTPUT NVARCHAR(MAX)

;
WITH XML_CTE (XMLOUTPUT) AS
(
SELECT
ERROR_LOG_ID AS 'record/event',
CREATEDATE AS 'record/message',
CREATEUSERNAME AS 'record/computer'
```

```
FROM CarSales_Logging.Log.EventDetail

FOR XML PATH('dtslog'), ROOT('dtslogs')
)

SELECT @OUTPUT = XMLOUTPUT FROM XML_CTE

EXECUTE  dbo.WriteToDisk @OUTPUT,'D:\AdamProject\Test\AA_XML.XML'
```

Hints, Tips, and Traps

- You can either write each event to disk as it occurs, or perform a single write operation at the end of you process. The text output in the first example presumes the former approach; the XML example presumes the latter choice. Writing every line ensures that in case of a massive failure, you still have your logging; whereas writing out the data at the end of the process can be considered more of an optional extra to complement database logging.

15-14. Logging Counters in T-SQL
Problem

You want to log counters (record counts) to track the quantities of records processed by each phase of a T-SQL-based procedure.

Solution

Create a custom counter logging framework.

1. At a minimum, you will need a repository to store the counters that you are logging. The simplest storage medium is an SQL table, so here is the DDL for the Log_ProcessCounters table (C:\SQL2012DIRecipes\CH15\tblLog_ProcessCounters.Sql):

```
CREATE TABLE CarSales_Logging.log.Log_ProcessCounters
(
 ID INT IDENTITY(1,1) NOT NULL,
 PROCESSID INT NULL,
 CounterType NVARCHAR(250) NULL,
 CounterDescription NVARCHAR(250) NULL,
 CounterResult BIGINT NULL,
 ProcessName VARCHAR(150) NULL,
 ProcessStep VARCHAR(150) NULL,
 UserName VARCHAR(150) NULL,
 ComputerName VARCHAR(150) NULL,
 DateCreated DATETIME NULL DEFAULT GETDATE()
)
```

2. As you are unlikely to want to write SQL to use this table repeatedly to store counters, create a stored procedure to carry out this repetitive task using the following DDL (C:\SQL2012DIRecipes\CH15\pr_LogCounters.Sql):

```
CREATE PROCEDURE CarSales_Logging.log.pr_LogCounters
(
@CounterType NVARCHAR(250)
,@CounterDescription  NVARCHAR(250)
,@CounterResult BIGINT
,@ProcessName NVARCHAR(150) = NULL
,@ProcessStep NVARCHAR(150) = NULL
,@UserName NVARCHAR(150) = NULL
,@ComputerName NVARCHAR(150) =  NULL
)

AS

DECLARE @PROCESSID INT
SELECT @PROCESSID = MAX(ID) FROM dbo.ProcessHistory

INSERT INTO dbo.Log_ProcessCounters
(
ProcessID
,CounterType
,CounterDescription
,CounterResult
,ProcessName
,ProcessStep
,UserName
,ComputerName
)

VALUES
(
@PROCESSID
,@CounterType
,@CounterDescription
,@CounterResult
,@ProcessName
,@ProcessStep
,@UserName
,@ComputerName
)
```

3. Once the log counter table and the stored procedure are in place, logging any event that can set the built-in @@ROWCOUNT global variable is simple if you use the following code. At the start of the stored procedure, ensure that the following lines are present:

```
DECLARE @ProcName VARCHAR(128)
DECLARE @UserName VARCHAR(128)
SET @ProcName = OBJECT_NAME(@@PROCID)
SELECT @UserName = USER_NAME()
```

4. At each event to log, add the following code snippet:

```
EXECUTE CarSales_Logging.log.pr_LogCounters
'SourceData'
,'Rows Truncated from myTable'
,@@ROWCOUNT
,@ProcName
,'Truncate table'
,@UserName
,@@SERVERNAME
```

How It Works

Logging counters is an extension to the logging techniques described in Recipe 15-8. My advice here is not to skip implementing counter logging, as it can be incredibly useful if you want to track, baseline, and improve any data load process. I am presuming that all counters are generated by a process step, and therefore I am including the references to the process name and process step to allow you to link the two. The @CounterType parameter is to allow later analysis and classification of counters. Of course, you can remove it if you feel that it is not useful for your logging requirements.

Hints, Tips, and Traps

- Logging all counters at the end of a process (as opposed to after each step) is slightly faster, but the difference is usually so tiny compared to the overall processing time that this should not influence your design decisions. Also, the effort involved in passing multiple counter variables to a single Execute SQL task should not be underestimated. Indeed, given the potential for error in this approach, I feel that it is best avoided.

- Remember that @@ROWCOUNT will be updated by SQL Server at virtually each event in a stored procedure. This means that you must capture the result and pass it to a user-defined variable, which you then use in the call to the pr_LogCounters sproc if you are worried that the figure captured by @@ROWCOUNT might not be the one that you are looking for.

- The reason for defining all but the three essential parameters in the pr_LogCounters stored procedure as having a default of NULL is because this way you can always use a shortened procedure call if you are not interested in the other logging elements.

15-15. Logging Counters from SSIS
Problem

You want to log counters (record counts) to track the quantities of records processed at all the important stages in an SSIS package.

Solution

Use the SSIS Row Count task to capture the record counts, then write them to your custom counter logging framework.

1. Create the Log_ProcessCounters table and the pr_LogCounters stored procedure described in Recipe 15-14.

2. Open the Variables pane by right-clicking in the Control Flow pane and selecting Variables.

3. Click the Add Variable button and give the variable a name. Ensure that it is an integer of sufficient size. For the purposes of this recipe, I will use the name **NumberOfRecordsHandled**.

4. Add a Data Flow task, and double-click to edit.

5. Add a Source component, configured to connect to any valid source. I will use the CarSales database and the Clients table.

6. Add a Row Count task to the Data Flow pane. Connect the source component to it.

7. Double-click the Row Count task to edit it.

8. Select the variable you just created from the list of variables in the Variable property. You should end up with something like that shown in Figure 15-7.

Figure 15-7. *Selecting a variable for a Row Count task*

9. Click OK.

10. Add a destination component, configured to use any valid SQL Server destination database. I suggest the CarSales_Staging database and the Client stable, as given in Appendix B.

11. Connect the Rowcount task to the destination component. Double-click the destination component and map the columns.

12. Select the Control Flow pane, and add an Execute SQL task onto the Control Flow after the last task to execute (the Data Flow task in this example). Connect the preceding task to this new task.

13. Double-click to edit the Execute SQL task, and add or create an ADO.NET connection. Name it **LogCounters**. Connect to the server and database where you will be logging the counter.

14. Click Parameter Mapping in the left-hand pane of the dialog box, and set the following parameters:

Variable Name	Direction	Data Type	Parameter Name
System::MachineName	Input	String	@MachineName
System::PackageName	Input	String	@PackageName
System::UserName	Input	String	@UserName
User::NumberOfRecordsHandled	Input	Int32	@Counter

15. Set the following as the SQL statement:

```
EXECUTE CarSales_Logging.log.pr_LogCounters 'SourceData', 'Rows added to myTable',
@Counter, @PackageName, 'Insert Data', @UserName, @MachineName
```

16. Click OK to confirm your modifications.

When you run this package, the counter that stored the number of rows recorded by the SSIS user variable is written to the log table.

How It Works

When running an SSIS task, you will probably need to log essential counters, which could include input rows, output rows, and errorrows.

Counters can be logged to an SQL Server table, a text file, or an XML file. They can be logged either as the process executes or at the end of the package. This approach captured row counts during process execution and then wrote them to a destination table.

Counter logging is as simple as adding a Row Counter task inside an SSIS Data Flow task—be it a Data Flow source, Data Flow transformation, and so forth. The Row Counter will record the number of rows that pass through the data pipeline at the point where the Row Counter task is situated.

Hints, Tips, and Traps

- If you wish to record several counters, then each must be defined as a separate variable. You can, however, write all your counters to the log table as part of a single Execute SQL task in which you call the pr_LogCounters stored procedure many times. In this case, you must remember to set all the "counter" variables as parameters in this task.

- Remember that SSIS variable scope can trap the tired or unwary programmer. It is probably better to set all the user-defined variables at package-level (by clicking the Control Flow pane before defining them) if you wish to avoid wasting plenty of time on particularly annoying debugging.

- You can use an OLEDB connection manager if you prefer, but this requires the use of positional parameters that I personally find very wearing, and so I can only encourage you to use ADO.NET connection managers. As you will be writing at most only a few records to SQL Server, any speed differences between the two connection managers are simply not an issue.

- If all the parameters that you are passing to the stored procedure are SSIS variables, then you can set IsQueryStoredProcedure to True in the Execute SQL task named LogCounters. You then use only the stored procedure name (log.pr_LogCounters) as the SQL Statement.

15-16. Creating an SSIS Catalog

Problem

You want to take advantage of the possibilities made available in SQL Server 2012 to store and run SSIS packages from an SQL Server database.

Solution

Create an SSIS catalog and deploy an SSIS project to it.

1. In SSMS, right-click Integration Services Catalogs, and select Create Catalog.
2. Add a password for the encryption key that protects the database.
3. Click OK.
4. Expand Integration Services Catalogs, Right-click SSISDB and choose Create Folder.
5. Enter a folder name and click OK.

You have now created an SSIS catalog, so you can deploy an SSIS project to it. This is done as follows:

6. In SSDT, open a project. Select Project ➤ <Project name> Properties. The property Pages dialog box for your project appears as in Figure 15-8.

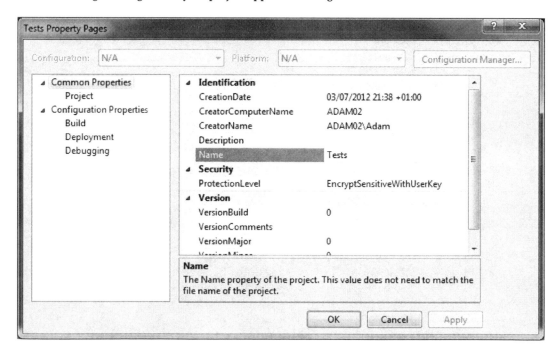

Figure 15-8. SSIS project properties

7. Expand Configuration Properties in the left-hand pane and click Deployment. Add the server to which you will be deploying the project and the Server Project Path. The dialog box should look like Figure 15-9.

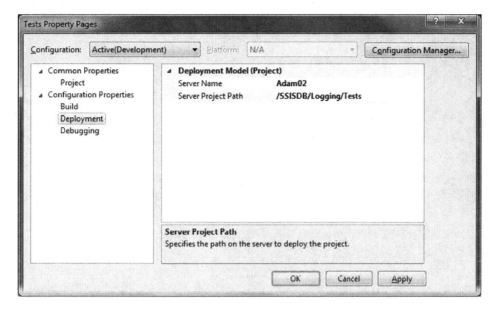

Figure 15-9. SSIS project properties for deployment

8. Click OK to finish configuring the project properties.

9. Deploy your SSIS package by right-clicking project in the Solution Explorer and choose Deploy.

10. Click Next if you see the start page.

11. In the Select Source pane, confirm that the project is the one that you wish to deploy. The dialog box should look like Figure 15-10.

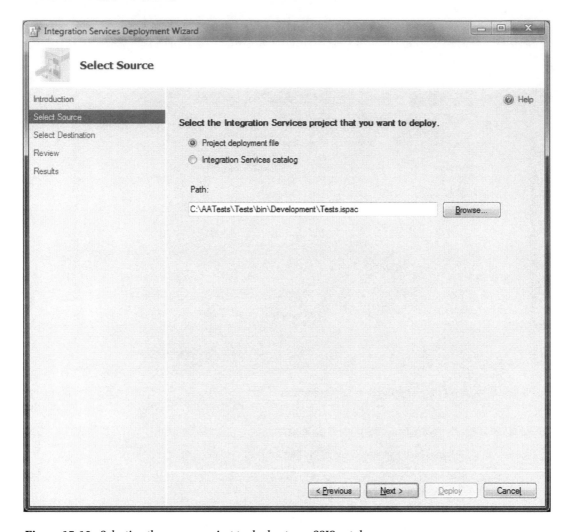

Figure 15-10. Selecting the source project to deploy to an SSIS catalog

12. Click Next.

13. In the Select Destination pane enter or browse for the server and path to which you wish to deploy the project. The dialog box should look like Figure 15-11.

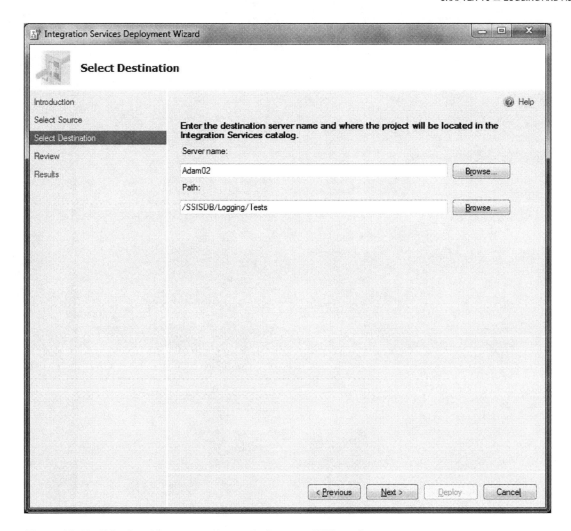

Figure 15-11. *Selecting the source project to deploy to an SSIS catalog*

14. Click Next. The dialog box should look like Figure 15-12.

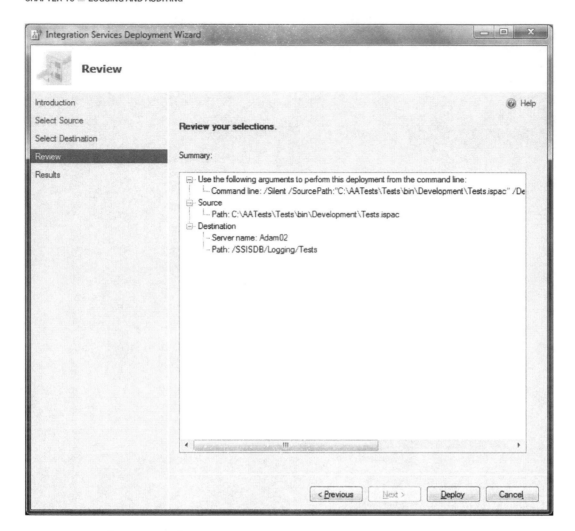

Figure 15-12. *The project deployment review pane*

15. Click Deploy. The results pane of the Deployment wizard will appear once the project has been deployed. It will be similar to Figure 15-13.

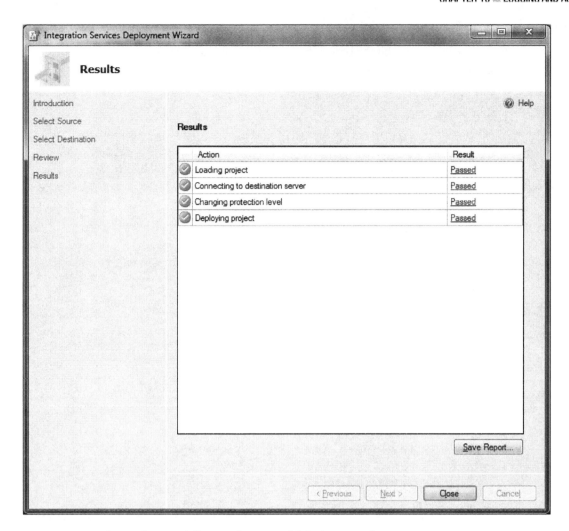

Figure 15-13. *The results pane following the successful deployment of an SSIS project*

16. Click Close.

How It Works

In essence, the SSIS catalog is an SQL Server database that allows you to store SSIS projects. Once a project is deployed into this database—or Catalog as it is called—you can run packages from a centralized location. You can also request different levels of logging for events and counters without making any modifications to the packages that have been deployed to the catalog.

The process that we used consists of the following four steps:

- Create the SSISDB database that SQLServer uses to manage SSIS projects.
- Create any folder(s) into which you want to deploy your project.
- Prepare the project.
- Deploy the project.

It is, quite simply, as easy as that. You can then see any projects that you have deployed by expanding the Integration Services Catalogs folder for the server to which you deployed the project. You will see the folder that you created, the project, and all the packages in the project—something like the completely trivial example shown in Figure 15-14.

Figure 15-14. *The Integration Services Catalog in SSMS*

Hints, Tips, and Traps

- The SSIS catalog database is called SSISDB and this name cannot be changed.
- When redeploying a project, you get an alert warning you that you are about to overwrite an existing project.
- You can run any packed stored in the catalog by right-clicking it in SSMS and selecting Execute … followed by OK.
- CLR Integration must be enabled for an SSIS catalog to be created. If this is not the case in your environment, the following is the T-SQL snippet to enable it:

```
sp_configure 'show advanced options', 1;
GO
RECONFIGURE;
GO
sp_configure 'clr enabled', 1;
GO
RECONFIGURE;
GO
```

15-17. Reading Logged Events and Counters from the SSIS Catalog

Problem

You want to look quickly at the events and counters made available in the SSIS catalog using SQL Server 2012.

Solution

Display the prebuilt reports made available from SSMS. Here is how:

1. Expand Integration Services Catalogs ➤ SSISDB ➤ <FolderName> ➤ Projects ➤ <ProjectName> ➤ Packages.

2. Right-click the package to execute and choose Execute.

3. Select the Advanced pane and set the logging level to Performance.

4. Click OK. The package will run. The following dialog box will appear as in Figure 15-15.

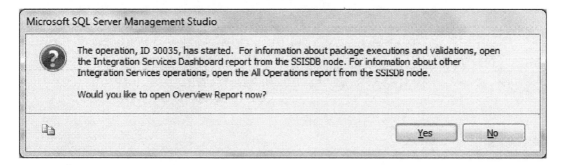

Figure 15-15. *Opening an Overview report in SSMS*

5. Click Yes to show Overview report. You will see something like Figure 15-16.

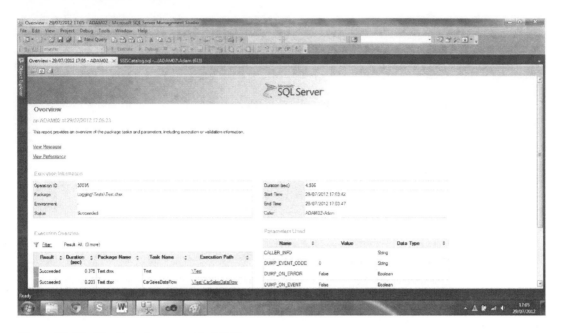

Figure 15-16. *The Overview report in SSMS*

6. You can refresh a report while the underlying package is still running. Indeed, you should always ensure that a package has finished before using any data provided by the catalog reports.

How It Works

Now that you have deployed a project to the SSIS catalog, you can view events and metrics every time that you run a package. Indeed, this option is available by default when you use SSMS to run a package from the catalog.

The following are the three basic reports that are available:

- The Overview report

- The Performance report

- The Messages report

You can switch from one to another by clicking the hyperlinks in each report. You can also see the execution details for each task in a package by clicking the Execution Path elements in the Overview report. In Figure 15-16, these are \Test and \Test\CarSalesDataFlow.

The SSIS catalog lets you choose a logging level; however, it must be chosen before executing a package. The four available levels are shown in Table 15-9.

■ **Note** Table 15-9 is taken with permission from Matt Masson's blog entry at
www.mattmasson.com/index.php/2011/12/what-events-are-included-in-the-ssis-catalog-log-levels/.
Matt is coauthor of *SQL Server 2012 Integration Services Design Patterns* (Apress, 2012).

Table 15-9. *Verbosity Levels for SSIS Catalog Logging*

Level	Events Included	Comments
None	Logging is turned off. Only the package execution status is logged.	Captures enough information to say whether the package succeeded or failed, and does not log any messages to the [operation_messages] view.
Basic	All events are logged, except custom and diagnostic events. This is the default value. The events include: OnPreValidate OnPostValidate OnPreExecute OnPostExecute OnInformation OnWarning OnError	Captures similar information to what is displayed on the console by the default when a package is run with dtexec.
Performance	Only performance statistics and OnErrorOnWarning events are logged.	This log level is required to track the performance information for the run (how long it took to run each task/component, etc.) but does not log all the events captured by the Basic log level.
Verbose	All events are logged, including custom and diagnostic events.Custom events include those events that are logged by Integration Services tasks.	The Verbose log level captures all log events (including performance and diagnostic events). This logging level can introduce some overhead on performance.

Hints, Tips, and Traps

- The Catalog reports are only available for SSIS packages that have been deployed as part of SSIS projects to the Integration Services Catalog.

- Remember to deploy any changes before rerunning a package.

- The catalog is definitely not a debugging tool. Always debug your packages thoroughly before deploying them.

- The Overview report gives you the ExecutionID, which is a unique reference to a package's execution.

15-18. Analyzing Events and Counters In-Depth via the SSIS Catalog

Problem

Using SQL Server 2012, you want to do an in-depth review of selected events and counters in the SSIS catalog.

Solution

Query the catalog views of the SSISDB database.

1. Use T-SQL to run the SSIS package, which is stored in the Catalog, using the following code snippet—using your own folder name, project name, and package name, of course—(C:\SQL2012DIRecipes\CH15\CatalogExecution.Sql):

```
DECLARE @execution_id bigint
EXECUTE SSISDB.catalog.create_execution
@package_name=N'Test.dtsx'
,@execution_id=@execution_id OUTPUT
,@folder_name=N'Logging'
,@project_name=N'Tests'
,@use32bitruntime=False
,@reference_id=Null

EXECUTE SSISDB.catalog.set_execution_parameter_value  @execution_id, 50,
'LOGGING_LEVEL', 3 -- Verbose

EXECUTE SSISDB.catalog.start_execution @execution_id

SELECT @execution_id  -- Returns the execution ID for later querying
```

2. Query information concerning the package and the tasks it runs using the following T-SQL (C:\SQL2012DIRecipes\CH15\CatalogPackageAndTasks.Sql):

```
SELECT
project_name
,package_name
,CASE status
 WHEN 1 THEN 'Created'
 WHEN 2 THEN 'Running'
 WHEN 3 THEN 'Cancelled'
 WHEN 4 THEN 'Failed'
 WHEN 5 THEN 'Pending'
 WHEN 6 THEN 'Ended unexpectedly'
 WHEN 7 THEN 'Succeeded'
 WHEN 8 THEN 'Stopping'
 WHEN 9 THEN 'Completed'
 END AS StatusFullDescription
,CONVERT(VARCHAR(25),start_time,103) AS RunDate
,CONVERT(VARCHAR(25),start_time,108) AS RunTime
,DATEDIFF(ss, start_time, end_time) AS ExecutionDurationInSeconds
,available_physical_memory_kb
,total_physical_memory_kb

FROM            SSISDB.catalog.executions
WHERE           execution_id = @execution_id
```

The output could be something like Figure 15-17.

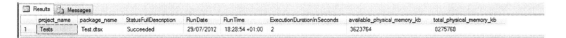

Figure 15-17. *Catalog information about packages*

> 3. Get list of the executables (tasks) inside the package using the following snippet
>   (C:\SQL2012DIRecipes\CH15\CatalogExecutables.Sql):

```
SELECT
 executable_id
,execution_id
,executable_name
,package_name
,package_path

FROM SSISDB.catalog.executables

WHERE    execution_id = @execution_id
```

The output will appear something like Figure 15-18.

	executable_id	execution_id	executable_name	package_name	package_path
1	10002	30043	Test	Test.dtsx	\Package
2	10003	30043	CarSalesDataFlow	Test.dtsx	\Package\CarSalesDataFlow

Figure 15-18. *Catalog information about tasks*

> 4. Now look at the finer details of the executables inside the package using the following
>   T-SQL (C:\SQL2012DIRecipes\CH15\CatalogExecutionDetail.Sql):

```
SELECT
EX.executable_name
,EX.package_name
,EX.package_path
,CONVERT(VARCHAR(25),ES.start_time,100) AS StartTime
,CONVERT(VARCHAR(25),ES.end_time,100) AS EndTime
,ES.execution_duration
,CASE ES.execution_result
WHEN 0 THEN 'Success'
WHEN 1 THEN 'Failure'
WHEN 2 THEN 'Completion'
WHEN 3 THEN 'Cancelled'
END AS ExecutionResultFullDescription
,ES.execution_path

FROM  SSISDB.catalog.executables EX
INNER JOIN SSISDB.catalog.executable_statistics ES
```

```
ON EX.executable_id = ES.executable_id
AND EX.execution_id = ES.execution_id

WHERE ES.execution_id = @execution_id

ORDER BY ES.start_time
```

The output will appear similar to that in Figure 15-19.

	executable_name	package_name	package_path	Start Time	End Time	execution_duration	Execution Result Full Description	execution_path
1	Test	Test.dtsx	\Package	Jul 29 2012 6:28PM +01:0	Jul 29 2012 6:28PM +01:0	374	Success	\Test
2	CarSalesDataFlow	Test.dtsx	\Package\CarSalesDataFlow	Jul 29 2012 6:28PM +01:0	Jul 29 2012 6:28PM +01:0	328	Success	\Test\CarSalesDataFlow

***Figure 15-19.** Output from the SSIS catalog showing executables*

5. Return the number of rows sent down each data path using the following T-SQL code snippet (C:\SQL2012DIRecipes\CH15\CatalogRowCounts.Sql):

```
SELECT
 package_name
,task_name
,dataflow_path_id_string
,dataflow_path_name
,source_component_name
,destination_component_name
,SUM(rows_sent) AS RowsSent
,execution_path

FROM SSISDB.catalog.execution_data_statistics

WHERE execution_id = @execution_id

GROUP BY
 execution_id
,package_name
,task_name
,dataflow_path_id_string
,dataflow_path_name
,source_component_name
,destination_component_name
,execution_path
```

The output will be something like that in Figure 15-20.

	package_name	task_name	dataflow_path_id_string	dataflow_path_name	source_component_name	destination_component_name	RowsSent	execution_path
1	Test.dtsx	CarSalesDataFlow	Paths[CarSales.OLE DB Source Output]	OLE DB Source Output	CarSales	CarSales_Staging	5	\Test\CarSalesDataFlow

***Figure 15-20.** Returning the number of rows sent down each data path from the SSIS catalog*

6. You can now get the detail of the execution phases using T-SQL like this
(C:\SQL2012DIRecipes\CH15\CatalogExecutionPhases.Sql):

```
SELECT
package_name
,task_name
,subcomponent_name
,execution_path
,phase
,start_time
,end_time
,DATEDIFF(ms, start_time, end_time) AS ExecutionDurationInMilliSeconds

FROM SSISDB.catalog.execution_component_phases

WHERE execution_id = @ExecutionID

ORDER BY phase_stats_id
```

The output could be something like Figure 15-21.

	package_name	task_name	subcomponent_name	execution_path	phase	start_time	end_time	ExecutionDurationInMilliSeconds
1	Test.dtsx	CarSalesDataFlow	CarSales	\Test\CarSalesDataFlow	AcquireConnections	2012-07-29 18:28:55.4480110 +01:00	2012-07-29 18:28:55.4642111 +01:00	16
2	Test.dtsx	CarSalesDataFlow	CarSales	\Test\CarSalesDataFlow	Validate	2012-07-29 18:28:55.4642111 +01:00	2012-07-29 18:28:55.5422112 +01:00	78
3	Test.dtsx	CarSalesDataFlow	CarSales	\Test\CarSalesDataFlow	ReleaseConnectio...	2012-07-29 18:28:55.5422112 +01:00	2012-07-29 18:28:55.5422112 +01:00	0
4	Test.dtsx	CarSalesDataFlow	CarSales_Staging	\Test\CarSalesDataFlow	AcquireConnections	2012-07-29 18:28:55.5422112 +01:00	2012-07-29 18:28:55.5578112 +01:00	15
5	Test.dtsx	CarSalesDataFlow	CarSales_Staging	\Test\CarSalesDataFlow	Validate	2012-07-29 18:28:55.5578112 +01:00	2012-07-29 18:28:55.5890113 +01:00	32
6	Test.dtsx	CarSalesDataFlow	CarSales_Staging	\Test\CarSalesDataFlow	ReleaseConnectio	2012-07-29 18:28:55.5890113 +01:00	2012-07-29 18:28:55.5890113 +01:00	0
7	Test.dtsx	CarSalesDataFlow	CarSales	\Test\CarSalesDataFlow	AcquireConnections	2012-07-29 18:28:55.6358114 +01:00	2012-07-29 18:28:55.6514114 +01:00	16
8	Test.dtsx	CarSalesDataFlow	CarSales	\Test\CarSalesDataFlow	Validate	2012-07-29 18:28:55.6514114 +01:00	2012-07-29 18:28:55.7294115 +01:00	78

Figure 15-21. *Detail of the execution phases returned from the SSIS catalog*

7. Finally, you can return any messages captured during the package's execution, using
code like this (C:\SQL2012DIRecipes\CH15\CatalogMessages.Sql):

```
SELECT
 message_time
,CASE message_type
WHEN -1 THEN 'Unknown'
WHEN 10 THEN 'Pre-validate'
WHEN 20 THEN 'Post-validate'
WHEN 30 THEN 'Pre-execute'
WHEN 40 THEN 'Post-execute'
WHEN 50 THEN 'StatusChange'
WHEN 60 THEN 'Progress'
WHEN 70 THEN 'Information'
WHEN 80 THEN 'VariableValueChanged'
WHEN 90 THEN 'Diagnostic'
WHEN 100 THEN 'QueryCancel'
WHEN 110 THEN 'Warning'
WHEN 120 THEN 'Error'
WHEN 130 THEN 'TaskFailed'
WHEN 140 THEN 'DiagnosticEx'
```

```
WHEN 200 THEN 'Custom'
WHEN 400 THEN 'NonDiagnostic'
END AS   MessageType
,CASE message_source_type
WHEN 10 THEN 'Entry APIs, such as T-SQL and CLR Stored procedures'
WHEN 20 THEN 'External process used to run package'
WHEN 30 THEN 'Package-level objects'
WHEN 40 THEN 'Control Flow tasks'
WHEN 60 THEN 'Control Flow containers'
WHEN 50 THEN 'Data Flow task'
END AS MessageSourceType
,message
,extended_info_id

FROM SSISDB.catalog.operation_messages

WHERE operation_id = @ExecutionID

ORDER BY operation_message_id
```

The output could be something like Figure 15-22.

	message_time	MessageType	MessageSourceType	message	extended_info_id
1	2012-07-29 18:28:55.4018109 +01:00	Pre-validate	Package-level objects	Test:Validation has started.	NULL
2	2012-07-29 18:28:55.4018109 +01:00	Pre-validate	Control Flow tasks	CarSalesDataFlow:Validation has started.	NULL
3	2012-07-29 18:28:55.4174119 +01:00	Information	Control Flow tasks	CarSalesDataFlow:Information: Validation phase is beginning.	NULL
4	2012-07-29 18:28:55.4174119 +01:00	Progress	Control Flow tasks	CarSalesDataFlow:Progress: Validating - 0% complete.	NULL
5	2012-07-29 18:28:55.4174119 +01:00	Custom	Control Flow tasks	CarSalesDataFlow:Data flow engine will call a component method	NULL
6	2012-07-29 18:28:55.4486119 +01:00	Diagnostic	Package-level objects	ExternalRequest_pre: The object is ready to make the following external request: 'IDataInitialize::GetDataSource(NULL, CLSCTX_INPROC_SERVER, Conne	NULL
7	2012-07-29 18:28:55.4486119 +01:00	Diagnostic	Package-level objects	ExternalRequest_post: 'IDataInitialize::GetDataSource succeeded'. The external request has completed.	NULL

Figure 15-22. *Messages in the SSIS catalog captured during package execution*

How It Works

The seven steps in this recipe performed the following queries on the SSIS catalog views:

- **Step 1** sets the logging level of verbosity and runs the package. It then returns the unique ID that you will use to query all events and metrics associated with this specific package execution. It uses the @ExecutionID variable, which is used by all the following queries.

- **Step 2** gives information about the package itself—specifically, if it was successful.

- **Step3** lists all the tasks that are called by the package.

- **Step 4** gives details—especially success or failure—for each task inside the package.

- **Step 5** gives you the number of rows sent down each data path in each task in the package.

- **Step 6** gives you all the steps—or phases—in each task. It specifically gives you each execution duration in milliseconds, which is invaluable for debugging and profiling.

- **Step 7** gives you the detailed messages that SSIS returns during execution.

▓ **Note**   You will only get information returned in step 5, and the quantity of information returned in step 7, if the logging level is set to Verbose, as was done in step 1 of this recipe.

The values for the logging level (that you set using the stored procedure SSISDB.catalog.set_execution_parameter_value) are given in Table 15-10.

Table 15-10. *Logging levels*

Level	Value
None	0
Basic	1
Performance	2
Verbose	3

Of course, these are only examples of some ways in which you can query the catalog views in the SSISDB database. This database is extremely complete and merits deep examination. However, there is just not enough space here to do it justice, so I will leave you to examine in greater depth the views (and their many associated stored procedures and functions). Figure 15-23 gives you an overview.

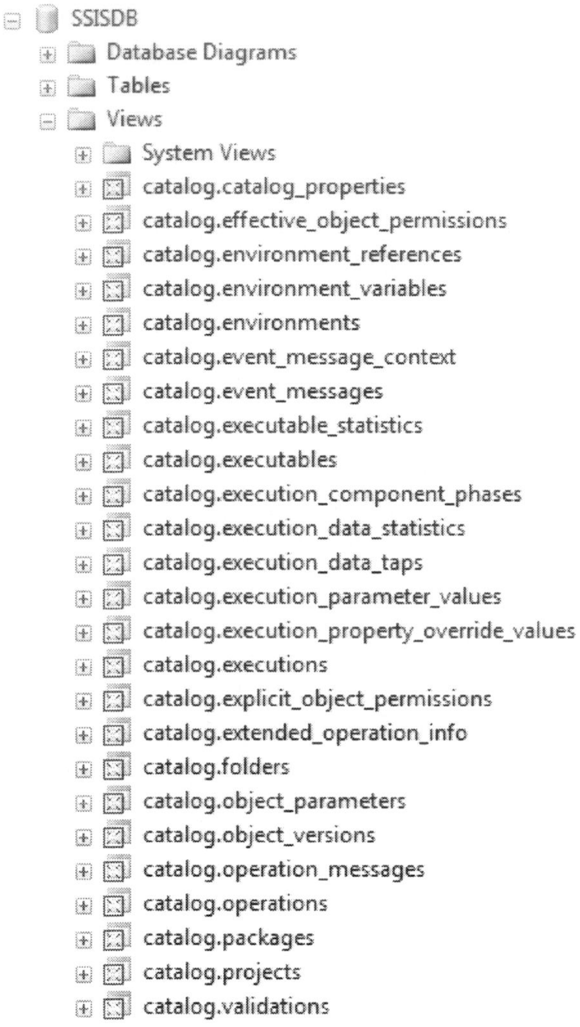

- SSISDB
  - Database Diagrams
  - Tables
  - Views
    - System Views
    - catalog.catalog_properties
    - catalog.effective_object_permissions
    - catalog.environment_references
    - catalog.environment_variables
    - catalog.environments
    - catalog.event_message_context
    - catalog.event_messages
    - catalog.executable_statistics
    - catalog.executables
    - catalog.execution_component_phases
    - catalog.execution_data_statistics
    - catalog.execution_data_taps
    - catalog.execution_parameter_values
    - catalog.execution_property_override_values
    - catalog.executions
    - catalog.explicit_object_permissions
    - catalog.extended_operation_info
    - catalog.folders
    - catalog.object_parameters
    - catalog.object_versions
    - catalog.operation_messages
    - catalog.operations
    - catalog.packages
    - catalog.projects
    - catalog.validations

Figure 15-23. *The SSISDB catalog views*

■ **Note** A superb set of reports by Jamie Thomson that allow you to visualize the data held in the SSIS catalog is available at http://ssisreportingpack.codeplex.com/.

Hints, Tips, and Traps

- You do not have to execute the preceding T-SQL snippets in any specific order. The only compulsory one is step 1, which returns the ExecutionID that you then use in all queries.

- You can also get the latest execution_id by using:

```
SELECT      MAX(execution_id)
FROM        catalog.executions
WHERE       package_name = 'Test.dtsx'
            AND folder_name = 'Tests'
```

- This data is persisted in the SSISDB tables, so you do not have to query it immediately after the package has run.

- The preceding queries can be extended to output the selected data to your own high-level log tables.

15-19. Creating a Process Control Framework

Problem

You want to enable your custom logging framework to become a fully-fledged process tracking system.

Solution

Extend your custom logging framework to add elements allowing you to track the sequence and hierarchy of events as well as identifying load details.

1. First, you need to add a **Calling Process** and a **Calling Step** to the EventDetail table. Alter the structure of the event logging table to look like this:

```
DROP TABLE CarSales_Logging.log.EventDetail
GO
CREATE TABLE CarSales_Logging.log.EventDetail(
 EventDetailID INT IDENTITY(1,1) NOT NULL,
 Process VARCHAR(255) NULL,
 Step VARCHAR(255) NULL,
 CallingProcess VARCHAR(255) NULL,
 CallingStep VARCHAR(255) NULL,
 Comments VARCHAR(MAX) NULL,
 ErrorNo INT NULL,
 ErrorDescription VARCHAR(MAX) NULL,
 ErrorLineNo INT NULL,
 ErrorSeverity INT NULL,
 ErrorState INT NULL,
 StartTime DATETIME NULL,
 Logtime DATETIME NULL
)
GO
```

2. Alter the stored procedure (now extended to handle the process hierarchy to log any outcome) to be:

```
DROP PROCEDURE CarSales_Logging.log.pr_LogEvents
GO
CREATE PROCEDURE CarSales_Logging.log.pr_LogEvents
(
@Process VARCHAR(150)
,@Step VARCHAR(150)
,@CallingProcess VARCHAR(150)
,@CallingStep VARCHAR(150)
,@StartTime DATETIME
,@Comments VARCHAR(MAX) = NULL
,@ErrorNo INT = NULL
,@ErrorDescription VARCHAR(MAX) = NULL
,@ErrorLineNo INT = NULL
,@ErrorSeverity INT = NULL
,@ErrorState INT = NULL
)

AS

INSERT INTO EventDetail
(
Process
,Step
,CallingProcess
,CallingStep
,StartTime
,Comments
,ErrorNo
,ErrorDescription
,ErrorLineNo
,ErrorSeverity
,ErrorState
)

VALUES
(
@Process
,@Step
,@CallingProcess
,@CallingStep
,@StartTime
,@Comments
,@ErrorNo
,@ErrorDescription
,@ErrorLineNo
,@ErrorSeverity
,@ErrorState
)
```

3. Now you need to identify and track each process. So create a table to contain process data:

```
CREATE TABLE CarSales.CarSales_Logging.log.RunHistory
(
 RunID INT NULL,
 RunStartDate DATETIME NULL,
 Notes NVARCHAR(MAX) NULL,
 IsSuccess BIT NULL,
 RunEndTime DATETIME NULL,
 RunDuration  AS (DATEDIFF(second,RunStartDate,RunEndTime))
)
```

4. Create the following stored procedure to log when a process starts:

```
CREATE PROCEDURE CarSales_Logging.log.dbo.pr_InitiateProcess
AS
-- need to add start time
DECLARE @StartDate DATETIME
DECLARE @RunID INT

SET @StartDate = GETDATE()
SELECT @RunID - ISNULL(MAX(RunID),1) + 1 FROM CarSales_Logging.log.RunHistory

INSERT INTO  CarSales_Logging.log.RunHistory (RunID)
VALUES           (@RunID)
```

You must add this stored procedure as an Execute SQL Task at the start of an SSIS package.

5. Create the following stored procedure to log when a process ends:

```
CREATE PROCEDURE CarSales.Log.pr_FinaliseProcess
(
@IsProcessSuccess BIT
)
AS

DECLARE @RunID INT
SELECT @RunID = MAX(RunID) FROM BI_Logging.CarSales_Logging.log.RunHistory

DECLARE @NoteComment VARCHAR(250)

IF @IsProcessSuccess = 1
BEGIN
SET            @NoteComment = 'Automated data load successfull'
END
ELSE
BEGIN
SET            @NoteComment = 'Automated data load FAILED!!'
END
```

```
UPDATE          CarSales_Logging.log.RunHistory
SET             IsSuccess = @IsProcessSuccess
                ,RunEndTime = GETDATE()
                ,Notes = @NoteComment
WHERE           RunID = @RunID

-- Truncate logs and counters over 3 months old

DELETE  FROM CarSales_Logging.Log.EventDetail
WHERE DATEDIFF(dd, DateCreated, GETDATE())  > 180

DELETE  FROM CarSales_Logging.Log.ProcessCounters
WHERE DATEDIFF(dd, DateCreated, GETDATE())  > 180
```

You must add this stored procedure as an Execute SQL Task at the end of an SSIS package.

To pass the calling package and step from a "parent" package to a "child" package, carry out the following:

6. In the parent package edit the Execute Package task, and ensure that the Reference Type is Project Reference. The dialog will look like Figure 15-24.

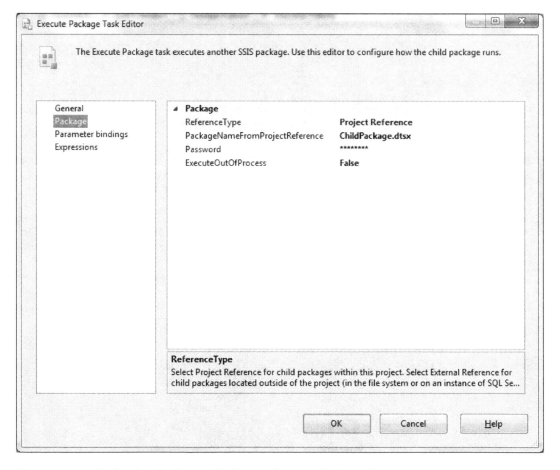

Figure 15-24. *Configuring the Execute Package task to use a Project reference*

7. Click on Parameter bindings on the left, and click Add twice.

8. Add the two following parameters:

    CallingPackage   System::PackageName

    CallingStep   System::TaskName

The dialog will look like Figure 15-25.

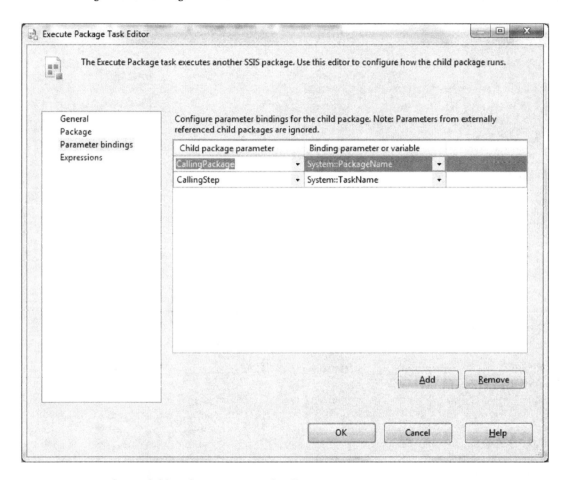

Figure 15-25. *Defining child package parameter bindings*

9. Click OK to finish the parent package

10. In the child package, click inside the Control Flow pane then click the Parameters tab.

11. Click the Add Parameter icon twice (this is the icon on the left above the column title "name").

12. Add The following two parameters:

Name	Data type	Sensitive	Required
CallingPackage	String	False	True
CallingStep	String	False	True

The pane will look like Figure 15-26.

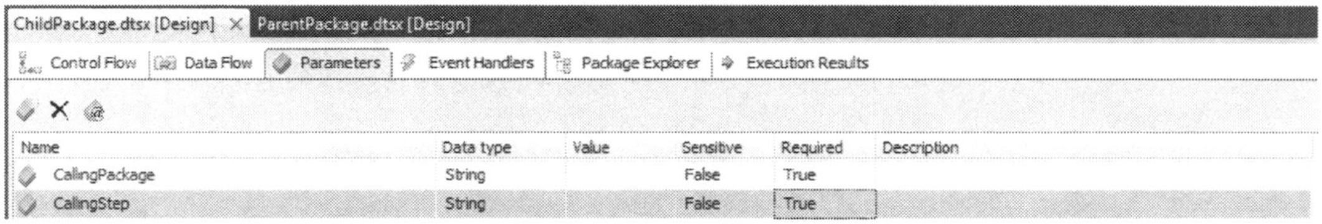

Figure 15-26. *Defining package parameters*

13. Deploy the project.

You can now run the package (from the catalog, as described in Recipe 15-17). This technique will only work with SSIS projects which use the project deployment model and where the child package is contained in the same project that contains the parent package.

How It Works

Every developer who spends any amount of time with SQL Server and SSIS for ETL will probably end up developing a logging framework. So far, this chapter has outlined a simple set of tables and stored procedures that allow basic to intermediate logging, but for more advanced ETL processes, this may not be enough. So here are a handful of ideas that you can use—in whole or in part—to extend a simple logging framework. As describing a truly complex logging framework would require a book by itself (and which I have absolutely no intention of writing), I have shown some ideas in the hope that you will pick and choose the ones that you find useful when developing your own complex data load processes.

If you have a more complex ETL package, you may want to add the process and step from which a stored procedure was called (as well as the current procedure/package and batch/task) to both the table in which you are logging events, and of course, the stored procedure that logs events. The point of this is that it enables you to see a clearly defined hierarchy describing which process/step combination called each consequent process and step. This will allow you to create views or stored procedures—or even an interface in Reporting Services or .NET (for instance)—which will allow you to drill down through a process log from the highest level to the lowest.

In T-SQL, passing the calling process and step between stored procedures means adding two (more) parameters to the "child"sproc, and passing the @ProcName and @ProcStep variables from the "parent" stored procedure to the "child" stored procedure. Using the preceding stored procedure will do the trick.

In SSIS, passing the calling process and step is more complex, and involves using package parameters as part of a package configuration. However, it is an extremely robust technique and well worth the effort. These parameters can then be referenced using a Derived Column transform, for instance, or passed to a logging stored procedure.

If you are using an older version of SQL Server then the way to pass the calling package and task is to define two configuration variables and reference the system::TaskId and System::PackageID variables.

The final element for a simple process flow control framework is to track every occasion on which it runs, as well as logging its eventual success or failure. This is extremely easy, and merely requires a single table to track the history of process execution. The DDL for such a table was given in step 14.

Clearly, you will have to detect success or failure in some fashion (such as an SSIS variable that is set to False should a package task fail, or perhaps detecting any NOT NULL error columns in the log table—or indeed, any way that suits your overallprocess) and pass the information to the @IsProcessSuccess input variable.

Finally, you need to be aware of the following:

- The duration of any process is determined by calculating the number of seconds between the start and end times.

- The two stored procedures that log start and end times can be called from SSIS, SQL Server Agent, or another stored procedure.

The tables used in this slightly more developed framework will look something like that shown in Figure 15-27.

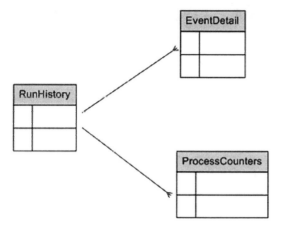

Figure 15-27. *The tables used in a basic process control framework*

Creating a logging framework that is capable of storing all the data that you may one day deem necessary while remaining modular and accessible is not easy. The final challenge is to be able to analyze the key data. To this particular end, I suggest adding the following two views:

- vw_LatestEvents: Isolates only the events that occurred during the latest process run.

- vw_LatestErrorEvents: Identifies any errors that occurred during the latest process run.

The code to create these views is mercifully simple(C:\SQL2012DIRecipes\CH15\ProcessViews.Sql):

```
CREATE VIEW      CarSales_Logging.Log.vw_LatestEvents
AS
SELECT           EventDetailID, Process, Step, Comments, ErrorNo, ErrorDescription
FROM             CarSales_Logging.Log.EventDetail
WHERE            RunID = (SELECT    MAX(RunID) AS RunID
                                    FROM            CarSales_Logging.log.RunHistory)
GO
```

```
CREATE VIEW     CarSales_Logging.Log.vw_LatestErrorEvents
AS
SELECT          EventDetailID, Process, Step, Comments, ErrorNo, ErrorDescription
FROM            CarSales_Logging.Log.EventDetail
WHERE           RunID = (SELECT     MAX(RunID) AS RunID
                         FROM       CarSales_Logging.log.RunHistory)
                         AND        (ErrorNo IS NOT NULL
                                     OR ErrorDescription IS NOT NULL
                                     OR ErrorSeverity IS NOT NULL)
GO
```

Taken together, these three elements (tracking the hierarchy of events, a process run table, and views) add a basic process control layer to your custom logging framework. I accept that this is a very simplistic framework, but it is one that you can take as a starting point to extend and adapt.

15-20. Linking the SSIS Catalog to T-SQL Logging
Problem

You want to centralize logging from both the SSIS catalog and T-SQL stored procedures into a single coherent logging framework. Unfortunately, there is no way of writing from T-SQL into the SSIS catalog.

Solution

You can't centralize logging—but you can get very close by passing into T-SQL log tables the executionID and the task GUID for each ExecuteSQL task that calls a stored procedure. This allows you to join the two log sources (SSIS catalog and custom log table) and maintain a single view over the separate logs.

1. Pass in the parameter System::TaskID (string)—the GUID for the task. This will be the executable_guid in SSISDB.catalog.executables.

2. Pass in the parameter System::ServerExecutionID—this is the [execution_id] from the same table.

3. Capture these input parameters in the header of every sproc called from SSIS using T-SQL similar to the following:

```
CREATE PROCEDURE CarSales_Logging.log.pr_TestCatalog

(
@SSISTaskGuid NVARCHAR(50)
,@SSISExecutionID INT
)

AS
-- Your code here
```

4. Ensure that these elements are added to the tables used for logging T-SQL events, and passed into the stored procedures that carry out logging as used in previous recipes.

How It Works

Unfortunately, there does not seem to be a way to write to the SSIS catalog tables—and thus to centralize logging when using stored procedures called from SSIS. However, if you log the steps and other information from sprocs (as described in previous recipes), and pass in the two essential variables that allow you to link the stored procedure to the SSIS logging (@SSISTaskGuid and @ExecutionID), you can then reconstitute the whole process from a logging perspective, because your custom logging table(s) can then map back to SSISDB.catalog. executables.

15-21. Baselining ETL Processes
Problem

You want to track the evolution of key metrics for a regular ETL process.

Solution

Extend your custom logging framework to include tables and stored procedures to enable baselining. The following shows how to create and use the objects that you will need:

1. Create the RunHistory table described previously, to provide a RunID.

2. Create the following three reference tables using DDL(C:\SQL2012DIRecipes\CH15\ ReferenceTables.Sql):

```
CREATE TABLE CarSales_Logging.Log.RefTables
(
ID INT IDENTITY(1,1) NOT NULL,
DatabaseName VARCHAR(150) NULL,
SchemaName VARCHAR(150) NULL,
TableName VARCHAR(150) NULL,
TableMaxThreshold BIGINT NULL,
TableMinThreshold BIGINT NULL,
TablePercentAcceptableVariation NUMERIC(8, 4) NULL
)
CREATE TABLE CarSales_Logging.Log.RefBaselineProcessess
(
ID INT IDENTITY(1,1) NOT NULL,
ProcessName VARCHAR(150) NULL,
ProcessMaxThreshold BIGINT NULL,
ProcessMinThreshold BIGINT NULL,
ProcessPercentAcceptableVariation NUMERIC(8, 4) NULL
)
CREATE TABLE CarSales_Logging.Log.RefBaselineCounters
(
ID INT IDENTITY(1,1) NOT NULL,
CounterName VARCHAR(150) NULL,
CounterComments VARCHAR(4000) NULL,
CounterMinThreshold INT NULL,
CounterMaxThreshold INT NULL,
CounterPercentAcceptableVariance INT NULL
)
```

3. Add the three baseline tables using the following DDL
(C:\SQL2012DIRecipes\CH15\BaselineTables.Sql):

```
CREATE TABLE CarSales_Logging.Log.TableSize
(
 ID INT IDENTITY(1,1) NOT NULL,
 TableSchema VARCHAR(50) NULL,
 TableName VARCHAR(50) NULL,
 SpaceUsedKB BIGINT NULL,
 SpaceReservedKB BIGINT NULL,
 Rowcounts BIGINT NULL,
 RunID INT NULL,
 DateUpdated DATE NULL
)
CREATE TABLE CarSales_Logging.Log.ProcessCounterBaseline
(
 ID INT IDENTITY(1,1) NOT NULL,
 RunID INT NULL,
 CounterName VARCHAR(150) NULL,
 CounterNumber BIGINT NULL
)
CREATE TABLE CarSales_Logging.Log.ProcessBaseline
(
 ID INT IDENTITY(1,1) NOT NULL,
 RunID INT NULL,
 ProcessName VARCHAR(150) NULL,
 ProcessDuration INT NULL
)
```

4. Create the three stored procedures that update the baseline tables using the following
DDL(C:\SQL2012DIRecipes\CH15\BaselineSprocs.Sql):

```
-- pr_AuditCounters
CREATE PROCEDURE CarSales_Logging.Log.pr_AuditCounters

AS

DECLARE @RunID INT
SELECT @RunID=MAX(RunID) FROM CarSales_Logging.log.RunHistory

INSERT INTO CarSales.Log.ProcessCounterHistory (RunID, CounterName, CounterNumber)

SELECT TOP 1000
@RunID
,CounterName
,CounterNumber

FROM        CarSales_Logging.Log.ProcessCounterBaseline AS D
            INNER JOIN CarSales_Logging.Log.RefBaselineProcessessAS S
            ON D.CounterName = S.CounterName
WHERE       D.RunID = (SELECT MAX(RunID) FROM CarSales_Logging.log.RunHistory)
```

```
-- pr_AuditEvents
CREATE PROCEDURE CarSales_Logging.Log.pr_AuditEvents

AS

DECLARE @RunID INT
SELECT @RunID=MAX(RunID) FROM CarSales_Logging.log.RunHistory

INSERT INTO CarSales_Logging.Log.ProcessHistory (RunID, StageName, StageDuration)

SELECT TOP 1000
@RunID
,StageName
,DurationInSeconds

FROM        CarSales_Logging.Log.EventDetail D
            INNER JOIN CarSales_Logging.Log.RefBaselineprocesses S
            ON D.Step = S.StageName

WHERE       D.RunID = (SELECT MAX(RunID) FROM CarSales_Logging.log.RunHistory)

-- pr_AuditTableSize
CREATE PROCEDURE CarSales_Logging.Log.pr_AuditTableSize

AS

DECLARE @RunID INT
SELECT @RunID=MAX(RunID) FROM CarSales_Logging.log.RunHistory

DELETE FROM CarSales_Logging.Log.TableSize WHERE RunID = @RunID

INSERT INTO CarSales_Logging.Log.TableSize
(TableName, SpaceUsedKB, SpaceReservedKB, Rowcounts, RunID)

SELECT DISTINCT
SO.name AS TableName
,DPS.used_page_count * 8 AS SpaceUsedKB
,DPS.reserved_page_count * 8 AS SpaceReservedKB
,DPS.row_count AS RowCounts
,@RunID

FROM      CarSales.sys.dm_db_partition_stats DPS
          INNER JOIN CarSales.sys.indexes SIX
          ON DPS.object_id = SIX.object_id
          AND DPS.index_id = SIX.index_id
          INNER JOIN CarSales.sys.objects SO
          ON DPS.object_id = SO.object_id
WHERE     SIX.type_desc = N'CLUSTERED'
          AND SO.name IN (
                        SELECT TableName FROM CarSales_Logging.Log.RefTables
                    )
```

How It Works

If you have patiently set up a logging infrastructure and captured a multitude of events that occur during an ETL process, you have certainly given yourself a useful toolkit to check that your process runs and finds the source of any errors, should they occur. Yet this mountain of data can quickly and easily become a source of useful information for tracking the evolution of regular processes. With relatively little effort, you can extract the key metrics from your log tables, store them separately (which allows you to prune the main log tables frequently to avoid excessive growth), and then track the evolution of the main process timings and row counts that make up your ETL process. This helps you foresee which parts of a data load and transformation could be potential problems that make your ETL job extend beyond the agreed time window.

Once again, I am suggesting a simple framework of a few tables, views, and stored procedures that allow you to extract the main information from your log tables. Feel free to extend this and use the front-end tool of your choice to present the results. I am the first to admit that none of this is difficult, but I still prefer to include this extension to the logging infrastructure to provide a starter kit for baselining and to prove that logging is worth while beyond mere error tracking.

I suggest storing three main elements:

- Timings for core processes

- Counters for key steps

- Table sizes for essential tables

Now, as this baselining infrastructure needs to be simple but easy to extend, I am going to avoid any hard-coding of the processes, counters, and tables that you will be tracking. So as well as the "baselining" tables that will store the essential data culled from the log tables, I suggest three "reference" tables that will hold the names of the processes, counters, and tables whose key data will be stored independently of the logs and will become the basis for the baselining and tracking.

As you can see in the `ref_BaselineCounters` table, I have included fields for threshold levels and percentages so that you can define limits to the acceptable counters, time (in seconds), or table sizes, respectively, and set up alerts if you wish.

Once the DDL is run, you need to add any of the following to the reference tables:

- Table names

- Process names (the name used inside the stored procedure that will be logged, or the name of the SSIS task that will be executed)

- Core counter names

So, nothing very complicated here. Yet this simple structure can be extremely useful because it lets you obtain a high-level view of process evolution over time. All you have to do is ensure that you have addedto the reference tables the names of all the processes (or process steps), counters, and tables you wish to track, and then ensure that the three stored procedures run at the end of your ETL process. Then you can (for instance) link Excel to the baseline tables, and produce a simple dashboard of how long your processes take and how the main counters evolve while you see the increase in table sizes. To add a final flourish, you can set thresholds for all the timings, counters, and table sizes, and use these to set up proactive alerts should ever a threshold be breached.

15-22. Auditing an ETL Process

Problem

You want to check that an ETL process has run not only successfully, but also with no overruns or indicators of potential future problems.

Solution

Audit the log data and isolate key metrics that you define.

1. In all your T-SQL stored procedures, remember to add the following code snippet to all data flows in T-SQL, which are INSERTS (both SELECT...INTO and INSERT INTO).

    ```
    ...
    ,GETDATE() AS DATE_PROCESSED
    ...
    ```

2. For all T-SQL updates, simply remember to add:

    ```
    ...
    ,DATE_PROCESSED = GETDATE()
    ...
    ```

To add the processing date and time inside an SSIS data flow you will need to add a Derived Column task on to the Data Flow pane between the Data Source and destination tasks.

3. Join the Derived Column task to preceding an following tasks.

4. Double-click the Derived Column task to edit it, add a name (how about **Last_Processed**), and set the expression as GETDATE()—SSIS will set the datatype to DT_DBTIMESTAMP automatically.

5. Map the derived column to the LAST_PROCESSED column in the destination table in the Destination task.

6. You will need a table to store the most recent audit data. Suggested DDL is (C:\SQL2012DIRecipes\CH15\tblTableAuditData.Sql):

    ```
    CREATE TABLE dbo.TableAuditData
    (
    ID INT IDENTITY(1,1) NOT NULL,
    QualifiedTableName VARCHAR(500) NULL,
    LastUpdatedDate DATETIME NULL,
    LastRunID INT,
    LastRecordCount BIGINT
    )
    ```

7. The DDL for the stored procedure that captures the audit data is (C:\SQL2012DIRecipes\CH15\pr_AuditETL.Sql):

    ```
    CREATE PROCEDURE pr_AuditETL

    AS

    DECLARE @SQL AS VARCHAR(MAX)
    DECLARE @TableToAudit AS VARCHAR(150)
    DECLARE @SchemaToAudit AS VARCHAR(150)
    DECLARE @DatabaseToAudit AS VARCHAR(150)
    ```

```
DECLARE Tables_CUR CURSOR
FOR
SELECT SchemaName, TableName, DatabaseName FROM dbo.RefTables

OPEN Tables_CUR

FETCH NEXT FROM Tables_CUR INTO @SchemaToAudit, @TableToAudit, @DatabaseToAudit

WHILE @@FETCH_STATUS =0
BEGIN

SET @SQL = 'INSERT INTO dbo.TableAuditData (LastUpdatedDate, LastRunID,
QualifiedTableName, LastRecordCount) SELECT MAX(LastRunDate), MAX(RunID),''' +
@DatabaseToAudit + '.' + @SchemaToAudit + '.' + @TableToAudit + ''',COUNT(RunID)
FROM '+ @DatabaseToAudit + '.' + @SchemaToAudit + '.' + @TableToAudit

EXECUTE (@SQL)

FETCH NEXT FROM Tables_CUR INTO @SchemaToAudit, @TableToAudit, @DatabaseToAudit
END

CLOSE Tables_CUR
DEALLOCATE Tables_CUR
```

How It Works

Once you have logged all that has happened while an ETL process was running, you might wish to carry out some cross-checks at the end of the process to ensure that certain essential elements are in place. This boils down to a few simple checks on key tables—or even all the tables—that you have created or updated.

These checks can include verifying:

- The last processed date(s) for table data
- Cube last processed date
- Row counters (total rows in a table and rows last updated)

This is not difficult and rarely takes long. However, it can be well worth the effort as a cross-check on the counters logged by your processes. For this technique, I use the tables used in previous recipes for logging.

One field is fundamental to auditing staging and data tables—DATE_PROCESSED. This must be a DATETIME field, inevitably. I suggest not setting this as a default of GETDATE(), as it is too easy to forget that a default will only fire when a row is created, not updated. I equally suggest avoiding triggers to set the last processed date and time in ETL processes, since they can slow down the process significantly.

Once all important tables have a LAST_PROCESSSED date field, you can set up a short stored procedure to count the numbers of rows per table and return the last processed date. For certain tables, you may want to return the number of rows inserted or updated, as well as the total number of rows, to get an idea of the percentage of rows modified.

Hints, Tips, and Traps

- Once you have the selected data, you can store it in an audit table (with the process ID for instance) to track process metrics over time.

- If you are looking at a large collection of tables, you may want to store the list of tables in a table and convert the preceding code to dynamic SQL to collect the counters for a varying group of ETL tables.

- Counting the rows in large tables can take an extremely long time, so you may prefer to use the old sys.sysindexes table to get record counts. However, cross-database use of this system view is extremely turgid to say the least, and may prove unusable in practice.

15-23. Logging Audit Data

Problem

You want to be able to carry out in-depth verification of audit data to track key events such as inserts, updates, and deletes.

Solution

Add metadata columns to ETL tables and extend your ETL process to update these columns during the ETL job. The following are ways of tracking each of these events.

Auditing Inserts

Probably the simplest way of logging inserts to set the IsInserted column to 0 before running a process, and then ensure that you add 1 (True) to this column as part of your INSERT statement.

If you are using SSIS, then add an IsInserted derived column and enter 1 as the expression.

Auditing Updates

As for inserts, ensure that the IsUpdated column is set to 1 (True) as part of an UPDATE.

If you are using SSIS and have a separate update path, use a separate or temporary tables as described in Chapter 11. Then, add an IsUpdated column to the table holding updated records. Enter 1 as the value.

Auditing Deletes

By definition, deleted rows will no longer be present in a table, so this leaves you with two choices:

- Logical deletions (flag records as deleted, and exclude in further processing).

- Store deleted records in a _Deleted table.

You can even combine the two. Initially flag records as deletedand then output those records into a _Deleted table after primary (and presumably time-sensitive) processing has completed.

For the sake of completeness, logical deletion is as easy as setting an IsDeleted flag to 1 (True).

Storing deleted records in a _Deleted table during processing can use a T-SQL trigger—something like the following:

- A copy of the table (imaginatively called `Clients_DELETED`, for instance, if it is to be based on the `Clients` table).

- One extra column in the `_DELETED` table named `DATETIMEDELETED`—which is a `DATETIME` datatype.

- A delete trigger, something like:

```
CREATE TRIGGER Trg_Del_Clients ON dbo.Clients
AFTER DELETE
AS
IF @@ROWCOUNT = 0 RETURN
INSERT INTO dbo.Clients_Deleted (ID, ClientName, DeleteDate)
SELECT ID, ClientName, GETDATE() FROM DELETED
```

How It Works

Verifying that the number of records added or updated, or that staging tables were processed on the date of a batch job are not enough for in-depth auditing. You need to be able to check resulting data tables for the following:

- Inserts

- Updates

- Deletes

- Number of times updated

While the techniques for these are well-known, it is probably worth recapitulating the best ways of carrying out these requirements. I am not going to give a crash course in SQL Server's built-in auditing capabilities, as these have been documented superbly elsewhere (www.bradmcgehee.com/2010/03/an-introduction-to-sql-server-2008-audit springs to mind). Moreover, in an ETL context, I feel that full-fledged auditing is overkill. So here we have just taken a cursory glance at basic auditing of ETL tables. You are free, inevitably, to extend these techniques to better meet any requirements that you have.

There are a couple of reasons for implementing key event auditing:

- As a sanity check to ensure that reasonable percentages of rows of a data table are being inserted, updated, or deleted.

- Running counts of the number of records affected by the type of operation allows you to track these percentages over time and compare each run to a baseline.

For each table that you will be logging, you need to ensure that the following columns are present:

```
IsInserted BIT NULL
IsUpdated BIT NULL
IsDeleted BIT NULL
DATE_PROCESSED DATETIME
```

Hints, Tips, and Traps

- You may, if you prefer, use a Change_Type column (probably a CHAR(1)) and store I, D, or U if you prefer, instead of using separate columns for the type of operation.

- Remember to save the state of all the important columns of the source table! If you are copying a large percentage of the columns and rows, consider copying the table with a simple INSERT INTO—if time, table size, and disk space permit!

Summary

In this chapter, you saw the various ways in which you can log both the steps events in an ETL process and the metrics associated with these steps. You also saw how to write them to both SQL Server tables and to files on disk.

I hope that you have come to appreciate the power of the built-in logging available in SSIS, especially the wealth of information available in the SSIS 2012 catalog. However, as you have also seen, there will be times when you need to extend these capabilities. This can range from minor tweaks to the built-in objects that allow you to log events from SSIS, to the creation of a completely customized process flow control framework.

However, the main thing to appreciate is the enormous range and subtlety of the logging and monitoring capacities of SQLServer. You can choose the approach and techniques that best suit your specific requirements.

I hope that this chapter has assisted you in making your choice.

APPENDIX A

■ ■ ■

Data Types

Data types are simultaneously the lifeblood and bane of data migration. They can literally make or break your ETL process. The first, and indeed the fundamental, aspect of a successful data load process is data type mapping. Quite simply, if any source data is a type that SQL Server cannot understand, then an import is likely to fail.

Therefore (and as a quick refresher course), this appendix presents the data types that you need to understand, first in SQL Server, and then in SSIS.

SQL Server Data Types

Table A-1 is a quick overview of SQL Server data types. I realize that data types are not exactly the most exciting thing on the planet, but they are fundamental to data ingestion and data type validation. So even if you never learn this stuff by heart, at least you have it here as an easily available reference.

Table A-1. *SQL Server Data Type Ranges and Storage*

Data Type	Description	Range	Storage
Bigint	Large integer—exact numeric	−9,223,372,036,854,775,808 to 9,223,372,036,854,775,807	8 bytes
Int	Integer	−2,147,483,648 to 2,147,483,647	4 bytes
Smallint	Small integer—exact numeric	−32,768 to 32,767	2 bytes
Tinyint	Tiny integer—exact numeric	0 to 255	1 byte
Bit	Binary digit	0 or 1	1 byte
Decimal	(p[, s])—precision and scale		Precision of 1–9: 5 bytes
			Precision of 10–19: 9 bytes
			Precision of 20–28: 13 bytes
			Precision of 29–38: 17 bytes
Numeric	Same as numeric		
Money	Accurate to 4 decimal places	−922,337,203,685,477.5808 to 922,337,203,685,477.5807	8 bytes
Smallmoney	Accurate to 4 decimal places	− 214,748.3648 to 214,748.3647	4 bytes

(continued)

Table A-1. (*continued*)

Data Type	Description	Range	Storage
Float	Approximate number typefor use with floating point numeric data	− 1.79E+308 to −2.23E−308, 0 and 2.23E−308 to 1.79E+308	Depends on the value being stored
Real	Approximate number typefor use with floating point numeric data	− 3.40E + 38 to −1.18E − 38, 0 and 1.18E − 38 to 3.40E + 38	4 bytes
Datetime		January 1, 1753 toDecember 31, 9999	
Datetime2		01/01/0001to13/12/9999	
DateTimeOffset			
Smalldatetime		January 1, 1900 toJune 6, 2079	
Char (n)	Fixed-length, single-byte character	8000 characters	N bytes
Varchar (n)	Variable-length, single-byte character	8000 characters	N bytes
Varchar(MAX)	Variable-length, single-byte character	(2^31) -1	Actual data + 2 bytes
nChar (n)	Fixed-length, double-byte character	4000 characters	N bytes times 2
nVarchar (n)	Variable-length, double-byte character	4000 characters	2 times number of characters entered + 2 bytes
nVarchar(MAX)	Variable-length, double-byte character	(2^31) -1 characters	2 times number of characters entered + 2 bytes
Binary (n)	Fixed-length binary data	8000 binary characters	N bytes
Varbinary (n)	Variable-length binary data	8000 binary characters	N bytes
Varbinary(MAX)		(2^31) -1 binary characters	Actual data + 2 bytes
Uniqueidentifier	Uniqueidentifier data type		16-byte
Timestamp	Automatically generated, unique binary number		8 bytes
XML	XML data	2 GB	Actual data
HierarchyID			Avariable-length, system data type
Geography	Geographic and geodesic data		CLR data type
Geometry			CLR data type

SSIS Data Types

Table A-2 provides a quick refresher course on the available SSIS data types.

Table A-2. *SSIS Data Types*

Data Type	Description
DT_BOOL	A Boolean value.
DT_BYTES	A binary variable-length data value. Its maximum length is 8000 bytes.
DT_CY	A currency value. This is an eight-byte signed integer with a scale of 4 digits and a maximum precision of 19 digits.
DT_DATE	A date type consisting of year, month, day, hour, minute, seconds, and fractional seconds. The fractional seconds have a fixed scale of 7 digits.
	It is implemented using an 8-byte floating-point number.
DT_DBDATE	A date type consisting of year, month, and day.
DT_DBTIME	A time type consisting of hour, minute, and second.
DT_DBTIME2	A time type consisting of hour, minute, second, and fractional seconds. Fractional seconds have a maximum scale of 7 digits.
DT_DBTIMESTAMP	A timestamp structure that consists of year, month, day, hour, minute, second, and fractional seconds. The fractional seconds have a fixed scale of 3 digits.
DT_DBTIMESTAMP2	A timestamp structure that consists of year, month, day, hour, minute, second, and fractional seconds. Fractional seconds have a maximum scale of 7 digits.
DT_DBTIMESTAMPOFFSET	A timestamp structure that consists of year, month, day, hour, minute, second, and fractional seconds. The fractional seconds have a maximum scale of 7 digits.
DT_DECIMAL	An exact numeric value having a fixed precision and a fixed scale. A 12-byte unsigned integer data type with a separate sign, a scale of 0 to 28, and a maximum precision of 29.
DT_FILETIME	A 64-bit value that represents the number of 100-nanosecond intervals since January 1, 1601. The fractional seconds have a maximum scale of 3 digits.
DT_GUID	A GUID.
DT_I1	A one-byte, signed integer.
DT_I2	A two-byte, signed integer.
DT_I4	A four-byte, signed integer.
DT_I8	An eight-byte, signed integer.
DT_NUMERIC	An exact numeric value with a fixed precision and scale. This data type is a 16-byte unsigned integer with a separate sign, a scale of 0 to 38, and a maximum precision of 38.
DT_R4	A single-precision floating-point value.
DT_R8	A double-precision floating-point value.

(*continued*)

Table A-2. (*continued*)

Data Type	Description
DT_STR	A null-terminated ANSI/MBCS character string with a maximum length of 8000 characters.
DT_UI1	A one-byte, unsigned integer.
DT_UI2	A two-byte, unsigned integer.
DT_UI4	A four-byte, unsigned integer.
DT_UI8	An eight-byte, unsigned integer.
DT_WSTR	A null-terminated Unicode character string with a maximum length of 4000 characters.
DT_IMAGE	A binary value with a maximum size of 2^311 (2,147,483,647) bytes.
DT_NTEXT	A Unicode character string with a maximum length of 230 to 1 characters.
DT_TEXT	An ANSI/MBCS character string with a maximum length of 231 to 1 characters.

Default Data Mapping in the Import/Export Wizard

The Import/Export Wizard bases data conversion on a set of XML files that you can find in the following directories: `C:\Program Files (x86)\Microsoft SQL Server\110\DTS\MappingFiles` and/or `C:\Program Files\Microsoft SQL Server\110\DTS\MappingFiles`.

There are three good reasons for knowing that these exist:

- They provide a baseline reference of data type mapping, which although are perhaps not definitive, can be a valuable guide.

- The files can be modified to suit the data type mappings that you prefer to use.

- You can write your own data type mapping files for use with the Import/Export Wizard—although I do not show you how to do this.

Tables A-3 to A-35 provide a tabular view on the mapping data from some of these files, so you can see what the Import/Export Wizard suggests as basic data type mapping, and then possibly use it as a basis for your own conversion processes.

MSSQL9 to MSSQL8

Table A-3. *MSSQL9 to MSSQL8 Data Mapping*

Source Data Type	Destination Data Type	Length	Precision	Scale
smallint	smallint			
int	int			
real	real			
float	FLOAT			
smallmoney	smallmoney			
money	money			
bit	bit			
tinyint	tinyint			
bigint	bigint			
uniqueidentifier	uniqueidentifier			
varbinary	varbinary			
varbinarymax	image			
timestamp	timestamp			
binary	binary			
image	image			
text	text			
char	CHAR			
varchar	VARCHAR			
varcharmax	TEXT			
nchar	NCHAR			
nvarchar	nvarchar			
nvarcharmax	ntext			
XML	ntext			
ntext	ntext			
decimal	decimal			
numeric	numeric			
datetime	datetime			
datetime2	datetime			
datetimeoffset	datetime			

(continued)

Table A-3. (*continued*)

Source Data Type	Destination Data Type	Length	Precision	Scale
time	datetime			
date	datetime			
smalldatetime	smalldatetime			
sql_variant	sql_variant			

MSSQL to DB2

Table A-4. *MSSQL to DB2 Data Mapping*

Source Data Type	Destination Data Type	Length	Precision	Scale
smallint	SMALLINT			
int	INTEGER			
real	REAL			
float	DOUBLE			
smallmoney	DECIMAL		10	4
money	DECIMAL		19	4
bit	SMALLINT			
tinyint	SMALLINT			
bigint	BIGINT			
uniqueidentifier	CHAR	38		
varbinary	VARCHAR(8000) FOR BIT DATA			
timestamp	CHAR(8) FOR BIT DATA			
binary	CHAR(8000) FOR BIT DATA			
xml	LONG VARGRAPHIC			
image	VARCHAR(32672) FOR BIT DATA			
sql_Variant	VARCHAR(32672) FOR BIT DATA			
text	LONG VARCHAR			
char	CHAR			
varchar	VARCHAR			
nchar	GRAPHIC			
nvarchar	VARGRAPHIC			
ntext	LONG VARGRAPHIC			

(*continued*)

Table A-4. (*continued*)

Source Data Type	Destination Data Type	Length	Precision	Scale
decimal	DECIMAL			
numeric	DECIMAL			
datetime	TIMESTAMP			
datetime2	TIMESTAMP			
datetimeoffset	TIMESTAMP			
date	DATE			
time	TIMESTAMP			
smalldatetime	TIMESTAMP			
sysname	VARGRAPHIC	128		

MSSQL to IBMDB2

Table A-5. *MSSQL to IBMDB2 Data Mapping*

Source Data Type	Destination Data Type	Length	Precision	Scale
smallint	SMALLINT			
int	INTEGER			
real	REAL			
float	DOUBLE			
smallmoney	DECIMAL		10	4
money	DECIMAL		19	4
bit	SMALLINT			
tinyint	SMALLINT			
bigint	BIGINT			
uniqueidentifier	CHAR	38		
varbinary	BLOB			
timestamp	TIMESTAMP			
binary	BLOB			
xml	LONG VARGRAPHIC			
image	BLOB			
sql_Variant	BLOB			
text	CLOB			

(*continued*)

Table A-5. (*continued*)

Source Data Type	Destination Data Type	Length	Precision	Scale
char	CHAR			
varchar	VARCHAR			
nchar	GRAPHIC			
nvarchar	VARGRAPHIC			
ntext	DBCLOB			
decimal	DECIMAL			
numeric	DECIMAL			
datetime	TIMESTAMP			
datetime2	TIMESTAMP			
datetimeoffset	TIMESTAMP			
date	DATE			
time	TIME			
smalldatetime	TIMESTAMP			
sysname	VARGRAPHIC	128		

MSSQL to Jet4

Table A-6. *MSSQL to Jet4 Data Mapping*

Source Data Type	Destination Data Type	Length	Precision	Scale
smallint	Short			
int	Long			
real	Single			
float	Double			
smallmoney	Currency			
money	Currency			
bit	Short			
sql_variant	LongBinary			
tinyint	Byte			
bigint	Decimal		19	0
uniqueidentifier	GUID			
varbinary	VarBinary			

(*continued*)

Table A-6. (*continued*)

Source Data Type	Destination Data Type	Length	Precision	Scale
varbinarymax	LongBinary			
timestamp	VarBinary	8		
binary	VarBinary			
image	LongBinary			
text	LongText			
xml	LongText			
char	VarChar			
varchar	LongText			
varcharmax	LongText			
nchar	VarChar			
ntext	LongText			
nvarchar	LongText			
nvarcharmax	LongText			
decimal	Decimal			
numeric	Decimal			
datetime	DateTime			
datetime2	VarChar	29		
datetimeoffset	VarChar	36		
time	VarChar	18		
date	VarChar	10		
smalldatetime	DateTime			

MSSQL to SSIS11

Table A-7. *MSSQL to SSIS11 Data Mapping*

Source Data Type	Destination Data Type	Length	Precision	Scale
smallint	DT_I2	6		
int	DT_I4	11		
real	DT_R4	24		
float	DT_R8	24		
smallmoney	DT_CY	22		

(*continued*)

Table A-7. (*continued*)

Source Data Type	Destination Data Type	Length	Precision	Scale
money	DT_CY	22		
bit	DT_BOOL	10		
tinyint	DT_UI1	3		
bigint	DT_I8	20		
uniqueidentifier	DT_GUID	39		
varbinary	DT_BYTES			
varbinarymax	DT_IMAGE			
timestamp	DT_BYTES	8		
binary	DT_BYTES			
xml	DT_WSTR			
image	DT_IMAGE	255		
sql_Variant	DT_WSTR	255		
text	DT_TEXT	255		
char	DT_STR			
varchar	DT_STR			
varcharmax	DT_TEXT			
nchar	DT_WSTR			
nvarchar	DT_WSTR			
nvarcharmax	DT_NTEXT			
ntext	DT_NTEXT	255		
decimal	DT_NUMERIC	31		
numeric	DT_NUMERIC	31		
datetime	DT_DBTIMESTAMP	30		
datetime2	DT_DBTIMESTAMP2			
date	DT_DBDATE	30		
time	DT_DBTIME2			
datetimeoffset	DT_DBTIMESTAMPOFFSET			
smalldatetime	DT_DBTIMESTAMP	30		

OracleClient to MSSQL

Table A-8. *OracleClient to MSSQL Data Mapping*

Source Data Type	Destination Data Type	Length	Precision	Scale
NUMBER	NUMERIC			
FLOAT	float			
REAL	FLOAT			
INT	NUMERIC		38	
RAW	varbinary			
LONG RAW	image			
BLOB	image			
LOBLOCATOR	image			
BFILE	image			
VARGRAPHIC	image			
LONG VARGRAPHIC	image			
timestamp	datetime			
CLOB	ntext			
char	nchar			
ROWID	nchar	18		
VARCHAR2	nvarchar			
NVARCHAR2	nvarchar			
LONG	ntext			
NCHAR	NCHAR			
NCLOB	ntext			
DATE	datetime			
INTERVAL	datetime			

OracleClient to MSSQL11

Table A-9. *OracleClient to MSSQL11 Data Mapping*

Source Data Type	Destination Data Type	Length	Precision	Scale
NUMBER	NUMERIC			
FLOAT	float			
REAL	FLOAT			
INT	NUMERIC		38	
RAW	varbinary			
LONG RAW	image			
BLOB	image			
LOBLOCATOR	image			
BFILE	image			
VARGRAPHIC	image			
LONG VARGRAPHIC	image			
timestamp	datetime2			
TIMESTAMP WITH TIME ZONE	datetimeoffset			
CLOB	ntext			
char	nchar			
ROWID	nchar	18		
VARCHAR2	nvarchar			
NVARCHAR2	nvarchar			
LONG	ntext			
NCHAR	NCHAR			
NCLOB	ntext			
DATE	date			
INTERVAL	datetime			

OracleClient to SSIS11

Table A-10. *OracleClient to SSIS11 Data Mapping*

Source Data Type	Destination Data Type	Length	Precision	Scale
NUMBER	DT_NUMERIC	31		
FLOAT	DT_R8	24		
REAL	DT_R8	24		
INT	DT_NUMERIC		38	
RAW	DT_BYTES	255		
LONG RAW	DT_IMAGE	255		
BLOB	DT_IMAGE	255		
LOBLOCATOR	DT_IMAGE	255		
BFILE	DT_IMAGE	255		
VARGRAPHIC	DT_IMAGE	255		
LONG VARGRAPHIC	DT_IMAGE	255		
timestamp	DT_DBTIMESTAMP2			
TIMESTAMP WITH TIME ZONE	DT_DBTIMESTAMPOFFSET			
CLOB	DT_NTEXT	255		
char	DT_WSTR			
ROWID	DT_WSTR	18		
VARCHAR2	DT_WSTR			
NVARCHAR2	DT_WSTR			
LONG	DT_NTEXT	255		
NCHAR	DT_WSTR			
NCLOB	DT_NTEXT	255		
DATE	DT_DBDATE			
INTERVAL	DT_DBTIMESTAMP	30		

Oracle to MSSQL

Table A-11. *Oracle to MSSQL Data Mapping*

Source Data Type	Destination Data Type	Length	Precision	Scale
NUMBER	NUMERIC			
FLOAT	float			
REAL	FLOAT			
INT	NUMERIC		38	
RAW	varbinary			
LONG RAW	image			
BLOB	image			
LOBLOCATOR	image			
BFILE	image			
VARGRAPHIC	image			
LONG VARGRAPHIC	image			
timestamp	datetime			
CLOB	text			
char	CHAR			
ROWID	CHAR	18		
VARCHAR2	varchar			
NVARCHAR2	nvarchar			
LONG	text			
NCHAR	NCHAR			
NCLOB	ntext			
DATE	datetime			
INTERVAL	datetime			

Oracle to MSSQL11

Table A-12. *Oracle to MSSQL11 Data Mapping*

Source Data Type	Destination Data Type	Length	Precision	Scale
NUMBER	NUMERIC			
FLOAT	float			
REAL	FLOAT			
INT	NUMERIC		38	
RAW	varbinary			
LONG RAW	image			
BLOB	image			
LOBLOCATOR	image			
BFILE	image			
VARGRAPHIC	image			
LONG VARGRAPHIC	image			
timestamp	datetime2			
TIMESTAMP WITH TIME ZONE	datetimeoffset			
CLOB	text			
char	CHAR			
ROWID	CHAR	18		
VARCHAR2	varchar			
NVARCHAR2	nvarchar			
LONG	text			
NCHAR	NCHAR			
NCLOB	ntext			
DATE	date			
INTERVAL	datetime			

Oracle to SSIS11

Table A-13. *Oracle to SSIS11 Data Mapping*

Source Data Type	Destination Data Type	Length	Precision	Scale
NUMBER	DT_NUMERIC	31		
FLOAT	DT_R8	24		
REAL	DT_R8	24		
INT	DT_NUMERIC		38	
RAW	DT_BYTES	255		
LONG RAW	DT_IMAGE	255		
BLOB	DT_IMAGE	255		
LOBLOCATOR	DT_IMAGE	255		
BFILE	DT_IMAGE	255		
VARGRAPHIC	DT_IMAGE	255		
LONG VARGRAPHIC	DT_IMAGE	255		
timestamp	DT_DBTIMESTAMP2			
TIMESTAMP WITH TIME ZONE	DT_DBTIMESTAMPOFFSET			
CLOB	DT_TEXT	255		
char	DT_STR			
ROWID	DT_STR	18		
VARCHAR2	DT_STR			
NVARCHAR2	DT_WSTR			
LONG	DT_TEXT	255		
NCHAR	DT_WSTR			
NCLOB	DT_NTEXT	255		
DATE	DT_DBDATE			
INTERVAL	DT_DBTIMESTAMP	30		

SQLClient9 to MSSQL8

Table A-14. *SQLClient9 to MSSQL8 Data Mapping*

Source Data Type	Destination Data Type	Length	Precision	Scale
smallint	smallint			
int	int			
real	real			
float	FLOAT			
smallmoney	smallmoney			
money	money			
bit	bit			
tinyint	tinyint			
bigint	bigint			
uniqueidentifier	uniqueidentifier			
varbinary	varbinary			
varbinarymax	image			
timestamp	timestamp			
binary	binary			
image	image			
text	ntext			
char	nchar			
varchar	nvarchar			
varcharmax	ntext			
nchar	nchar			
nvarchar	nvarchar			
nvarcharmax	ntext			
XML	ntext			
ntext	ntext			
decimal	decimal			
numeric	numeric			
datetime	datetime			
smalldatetime	smalldatetime			
sql_variant	sql_variant			

(continued)

Table A-14. (*continued*)

Source Data Type	Destination Data Type	Length	Precision	Scale
smallint	smallint			
int	int			
real	real			
float	FLOAT			
smallmoney	smallmoney			
money	money			
bit	bit			
tinyint	tinyint			
bigint	bigint			
uniqueidentifier	uniqueidentifier			
varbinary	varbinary			
varbinarymax	varbinary			
timestamp	timestamp			
binary	binary			
image	image			
text	ntext			
char	nchar			
varchar	nvarchar			
varcharmax	nvarchar			
nchar	nchar			
nvarchar	nvarchar			
nvarcharmax	nvarchar			
xml	xml			
ntext	ntext			
decimal	decimal			
numeric	numeric			
datetime	datetime			
smalldatetime	smalldatetime			
sql_variant	sql_variant			

SQLClient to DB2

Table A-15. *SQLClient to DB2 Data Mapping*

Source Data Type	Destination Data Type	Length	Precision	Scale
smallint	SMALLINT			
int	INTEGER			
real	REAL			
float	DOUBLE			
smallmoney	DECIMAL		10	4
money	DECIMAL		19	4
bit	SMALLINT			
tinyint	SMALLINT			
bigint	BIGINT			
uniqueidentifier	CHAR	38		
varbinary	VARCHAR(8000) FOR BIT DATA			
timestamp	CHAR(8) FOR BIT DATA			
binary	CHAR(8000) FOR BIT DATA			
xml	LONG VARGRAPHIC			
image	VARCHAR(32672) FOR BIT DATA			
sql_Variant	VARCHAR(32672) FOR BIT DATA			
text	LONG VARGRAPHIC			
char	GRAPHIC			
varchar	VARGRAPHIC			
nchar	GRAPHIC			
nvarchar	VARGRAPHIC			
ntext	LONG VARGRAPHIC			
decimal	DECIMAL			
numeric	DECIMAL			
datetime	TIMESTAMP			
datetime2	TIMESTAMP			
datetimeoffset	TIMESTAMP			

(continued)

949

Table A-15. (*continued*)

Source Data Type	Destination Data Type	Length	Precision	Scale
date	DATE			
time	TIME			
smalldatetime	TIMESTAMP			
sysname	VARGRAPHIC	128		

SQLClient to IBMDB2

Table A-16. *SQLClient to IBMDB2 Data Mapping*

Source Data Type	Destination Data Type	Length	Precision	Scale
smallint	SMALLINT			
int	INTEGER			
real	REAL			
float	DOUBLE			
smallmoney	DECIMAL		10	4
money	DECIMAL		19	4
bit	SMALLINT			
tinyint	SMALLINT			
bigint	BIGINT			
uniqueidentifier	CHAR	38		
varbinary	BLOB			
timestamp	CHAR(8) FOR BIT DATA			
binary	BLOB			
xml	LONG VARGRAPHIC			
image	BLOB			
sql_Variant	BLOB			
text	DBCLOB			
char	GRAPHIC			
varchar	VARGRAPHIC			
nchar	GRAPHIC			
nvarchar	VARGRAPHIC			
ntext	DBCLOB			

(continued)

Table A-16. (*continued*)

Source Data Type	Destination Data Type	Length	Precision	Scale
decimal	DECIMAL			
numeric	DECIMAL			
datetime	TIMESTAMP			
datetime2	TIMESTAMP			
datetimeoffset	TIMESTAMP			
date	DATE			
time	TIME			
smalldatetime	TIMESTAMP			
sysname	VARGRAPHIC	128		

SQLClient to MSSQL11

Table A-17. *SQLClient to MSSQL11 Data Mapping*

Source Data Type	Destination Data Type	Length	Precision	Scale
smallint	smallint			
int	int			
real	real			
float	FLOAT			
smallmoney	smallmoney			
money	money			
bit	bit			
tinyint	tinyint			
bigint	bigint			
uniqueidentifier	uniqueidentifier			
varbinary	varbinary			
varbinarymax	varbinary			
timestamp	timestamp			
binary	binary			
image	image			
text	ntext			
char	nchar			

(*continued*)

Table A-17. (*continued*)

Source Data Type	Destination Data Type	Length	Precision	Scale
varchar	nvarchar			
varcharmax	nvarchar			
nchar	nchar			
nvarchar	nvarchar			
nvarcharmax	nvarchar			
xml	xml			
ntext	ntext			
decimal	decimal			
numeric	numeric			
datetime	datetime			
smalldatetime	smalldatetime			
sql_variant	sql_variant			
datetime2	datetime2			
time	time			
date	date			
datetimeoffset	datetimeoffset			

SQLClient to Oracle

Table A-18. *SQLClient to Oracle Data Mapping*

Source Data Type	Destination Data Type	Length	Precision	Scale
smallint	INTEGER			
int	INTEGER			
real	FLOAT			
float	FLOAT			
smallmoney	NUMBER		10	4
money	NUMBER		19	4
bit	NUMBER		1	
tinyint	NUMBER		5	
bigint	NUMBER			
uniqueidentifier	RAW	16		

(continued)

Table A-18. (*continued*)

Source Data Type	Destination Data Type	Length	Precision	Scale
varbinary	BLOB			
timestamp	RAW		8	
binary	BLOB			
image	BLOB			
text	NCLOB			
char	NCHAR			
varchar	NVARCHAR2			
nchar	NCHAR			
nvarchar	NVARCHAR2			
XML	NVARCHAR2			
ntext	NCLOB			
decimal	NUMBER			
numeric	NUMBER			
datetime	DATE			
datetime2	TIMESTAMP			
date	DATE			
time	TIMESTAMP			
datetimeoffset	TIMESTAMP WITH TIME ZONE			
smalldatetime	DATE			
sql_variant	BLOB			

SQLClient to SSIS

Table A-19. *SQLClient to SSIS Data Mapping*

Source Data Type	Destination Data Type	Length	Precision	Scale
smallint	DT_I2	6		
int	DT_I4	11		
real	DT_R4	24		
float	DT_R8	24		
smallmoney	DT_CY	22		
money	DT_CY	22		

(*continued*)

Table A-19. (*continued*)

Source Data Type	Destination Data Type	Length	Precision	Scale
bit	DT_BOOL	10		
tinyint	DT_UI1	3		
bigint	DT_I8	20		
uniqueidentifier	DT_GUID	39		
varbinary	DT_BYTES			
timestamp	DT_BYTES	8		
binary	DT_BYTES			
xml	DT_WSTR			
image	DT_IMAGE	255		
sql_Variant	DT_WSTR	255		
text	DT_NTEXT	255		
char	DT_WSTR			
varchar	DT_WSTR			
nchar	DT_WSTR			
nvarchar	DT_WSTR			
nvarcharmax	DT_NTEXT			
varcharmax	DT_NTEXT			
ntext	DT_NTEXT	255		
decimal	DT_NUMERIC	31		
numeric	DT_NUMERIC	31		
datetime	DT_DBTIMESTAMP	30		
datetime2	DT_DBTIMESTAMP2			
date	DT_DBDATE	30		
time	DT_DBTIME2			
datetimeoffset	DT_DBTIMESTAMPOFFSET			
smalldatetime	DT_DBTIMESTAMP	30		

SSIS11 to DB2

Table A-20. *SSIS11 to DB2 Data Mapping*

Source Data Type	Destination Data Type	Length	Precision	Scale
DT_I1	SMALLINT			
DT_I2	SMALLINT			
DT_I4	INTEGER			
DT_I8	BIGINT			
DT_UI1	SMALLINT			
DT_UI2	INTEGER			
DT_UI4	BIGINT			
DT_UI8	DECIMAL		20	
DT_R4	REAL			
DT_R8	DOUBLE			
DT_CY	DECIMAL		19	4
DT_BOOL	SMALLINT			
DT_GUID	CHAR	38		
DT_BYTES	VARCHAR(8000) FOR BIT DATA			
DT_IMAGE	VARCHAR(32672) FOR BIT DATA			
DT_TEXT	LONG VARCHAR			
DT_NTEXT	LONG VARGRAPHIC			
DT_STR	VARCHAR			
DT_WSTR	VARGRAPHIC			
DT_DECIMAL	DECIMAL		28	
DT_NUMERIC	DECIMAL			
DT_DBTIMESTAMP	TIMESTAMP			
DT_DBTIMESTAMP2	TIMESTAMP			
DT_DBTIMESTAMPOFFSET	TIMESTAMP			
DT_DATE	TIMESTAMP			
DT_DBDATE	DATE			
DT_DBTIME	TIMESTAMP			
DT_DBTIME2	TIMESTAMP			
DT_FILETIME	TIMESTAMP			

SSIS11 to IBMDB2

Table A-21. *SSIS11 to IBMDB2 Data Mapping*

Source Data Type	Destination Data Type	Length	Precision	Scale
DT_I1	SMALLINT			
DT_I2	SMALLINT			
DT_I4	INTEGER			
DT_I8	BIGINT			
DT_UI1	SMALLINT			
DT_UI2	INTEGER			
DT_UI4	BIGINT			
DT_UI8	DECIMAL		20	
DT_R4	REAL			
DT_R8	DOUBLE			
DT_CY	DECIMAL		19	4
DT_BOOL	SMALLINT			
DT_GUID	CHAR	38		
DT_BYTES	BLOB			
DT_IMAGE	BLOB			
DT_TEXT	CLOB			
DT_NTEXT	DBCLOB			
DT_STR	VARCHAR			
DT_WSTR	VARGRAPHIC			
DT_DECIMAL	DECIMAL		28	
DT_NUMERIC	DECIMAL			
DT_DBTIMESTAMP	TIMESTAMP			
DT_DBTIMESTAMP2	TIMESTAMP			
DT_DBTIMESTAMPOFFSET	TIMESTAMP			
DT_DATE	TIMESTAMP			
DT_DBDATE	DATE			
DT_DBTIME	TIMESTAMP			
DT_DBTIME2	TIME			
DT_FILETIME	TIMESTAMP			

SSIS11 to MSSQL

Table A-22. *SSIS11 to MSSQL Data Mapping*

Source Data Type	Destination Data Type	Length	Precision	Scale
DT_I1	smallint			
DT_I2	smallint			
DT_I4	int			
DT_I8	bigint			
DT_UI1	tinyint			
DT_UI2	int			
DT_UI4	bigint			
DT_UI8	numeric		20	
DT_R4	real			
DT_R8	float			
DT_CY	money			
DT_BOOL	bit			
DT_GUID	uniqueidentifier			
DT_BYTES	binary			
DT_IMAGE	image			
DT_TEXT	text			
DT_NTEXT	ntext			
DT_STR	varchar			
DT_WSTR	nvarchar			
DT_DECIMAL	decimal		28	
DT_NUMERIC	numeric			
DT_DBTIMESTAMP	datetime			
DT_DBTIMESTAMP2	datetime2			
DT_DBTIME2	time			
DT_DBTIMESTAMPOFFSET	datetimeoffset			
DT_DATE	datetime			
DT_DBDATE	date			
DT_DBTIME	datetime			
DT_FILETIME	datetime			

DB2 to MSSQL

Table A-23. *DB2 to MSSQL Data Mapping*

Source Data Type	Destination Data Type	Length	Precision	Scale
TIME	DATETIME			
TIMESTAMP	datetime			
DATE	DATETIME			
CHAR	CHAR			
CHAR () FOR BIT DATA	BINARY			
VARCHAR	VARCHAR			
VARCHAR () FOR BIT DATA	VARBINARY			
LONG VARCHAR FOR BIT DATA	image			
LONG VARCHAR	text			
GRAPHIC	NCHAR			
VARGRAPHIC	NVARCHAR			
SMALLINT	SMALLINT			
INT	INT			
INTEGER	INT			
BIGINT	BIGINT			
DECIMAL	NUMERIC			
NUMERIC	NUMERIC			
REAL	REAL			
FLOAT	FLOAT			
DOUBLE	FLOAT			

SSIS to Jet

Table A-24. *SSIS to Jet Data Mapping*

Source Data Type	Destination Data Type	Length	Precision	Scale
DT_I1	Short			
DT_I2	Short			
DT_I4	Long			
DT_I8	Decimal		19	0
DT_UI1	Byte			
DT_UI2	Long			
DT_UI4	Decimal		19	0
DT_UI8	Decimal		19	0
DT_R4	Single			
DT_R8	Double			
DT_CY	Currency			
DT_BOOL	Byte			
DT_GUID	GUID			
DT_BYTES	LongBinary			
DT_IMAGE	LongBinary			
DT_TEXT	LongText			
DT_NTEXT	LongText			
DT_STR	LongText			
DT_WSTR	LongText			
DT_DECIMAL	Decimal			
DT_NUMERIC	Decimal			
DT_DBTIMESTAMP	DateTime			
DT_DATE	DateTime			
DT_DBDATE	DateTime			
DT_DBTIME	DateTime			
DT_FILETIME	DateTime			

DB2 to MSSQL11

Table A-25. *DB2 to MSSQL11 Data Mapping*

Source Data Type	Destination Data Type	Length	Precision	Scale
TIME	time			
TIMESTAMP	datetime2			
DATE	DATE			
CHAR	CHAR			
CHAR () FOR BIT DATA	BINARY			
VARCHAR	VARCHAR			
VARCHAR () FOR BIT DATA	VARBINARY			
LONG VARCHAR FOR BIT DATA	image			
LONG VARCHAR	text			
GRAPHIC	NCHAR			
VARGRAPHIC	NVARCHAR			
SMALLINT	SMALLINT			
INT	INT			
INTEGER	INT			
BIGINT	BIGINT			
DECIMAL	NUMERIC			
NUMERIC	NUMERIC			
REAL	REAL			
FLOAT	FLOAT			
DOUBLE	FLOAT			

SSIS to Oracle

Table A-26. *SSIS to Oracle Data Mapping*

Source Data Type	Destination Data Type	Length	Precision	Scale
DT_I1	INTEGER			
DT_I2	INTEGER			
DT_I4	INTEGER			
DT_I8	NUMBER		20	
DT_UI1	NUMBER		5	
DT_UI2	INTEGER			
DT_UI4	NUMBER		20	
DT_UI8	NUMBER		20	
DT_R4	FLOAT			
DT_R8	FLOAT			
DT_CY	NUMBER		19	4
DT_BOOL	NUMBER		1	
DT_GUID	RAW	16		
DT_BYTES	BLOB			
DT_IMAGE	BLOB			
DT_TEXT	CLOB			
DT_NTEXT	NCLOB			
DT_STR	VARCHAR2			
DT_WSTR	NVARCHAR2			
DT_DECIMAL	NUMBER		28	
DT_NUMERIC	NUMBER			
DT_DBTIMESTAMP	TIMESTAMP			
DT_DBTIMESTAMP2	TIMESTAMP			
DT_DATE	DATE			
DT_DBDATE	DATE			
DT_DBTIME	DATE			
DT_DBTIME2	TIMESTAMP			
DT_DBTIMESTAMPOFFSET	TIMESTAMP WITH TIME ZONE			
DT_FILETIME	DATE			

DB2 to SSIS11

Table A-27. *DB2 to SSIS11 Data Mapping*

Source Data Type	Destination Data Type	Length	Precision	Scale
TIME	DT_DBTIME			
TIMESTAMP	DT_DBTIMESTAMP2			
DATE	DT_DBDATE	30		
CHAR	DT_STR			
CHAR () FOR BIT DATA	DT_BYTES			
VARCHAR	DT_STR			
VARCHAR () FOR BIT DATA	DT_BYTES			
LONG VARCHAR FOR BIT DATA	DT_IMAGE	255		
LONG VARCHAR	DT_TEXT	255		
GRAPHIC	DT_WSTR			
VARGRAPHIC	DT_WSTR			
SMALLINT	DT_I2	6		
INT	DT_I4	11		
INTEGER	DT_I4	11		
BIGINT	DT_I8	20		
DECIMAL	DT_NUMERIC	31		
NUMERIC	DT_NUMERIC	31		
REAL	DT_R4	24		
FLOAT	DT_R8	24		
DOUBLE	DT_R8	24		

IBMDB2 to MSSQL

Table A-28. *IBMDB2 to MSSQL Data Mapping*

Source Data Type	Destination Data Type	Length	Precision	Scale
TIME	DATETIME			
TIMESTAMP	datetime			
DATE	DATETIME			
CHAR	CHAR			
CHAR () FOR BIT DATA	BINARY			
VARCHAR	VARCHAR			
VARCHAR () FOR BIT DATA	VARBINARY			
LONG VARCHAR FOR BIT DATA	image			
LONG VARCHAR	text			
GRAPHIC	NCHAR			
VARGRAPHIC	NVARCHAR			
SMALLINT	SMALLINT			
INTEGER	INTEGER			
BIGINT	BIGINT			
DECIMAL	NUMERIC			
NUMERIC	NUMERIC			
REAL	REAL			
FLOAT	FLOAT			
DOUBLE	DOUBLE			
BLOB	image			
CLOB	text			
DBCLOB	ntext			

IBMDB2 to MSSQL11

Table A-29. *IBMDB2 to MSSQL11 Data Mapping*

Source Data Type	Destination Data Type	Length	Precision	Scale
TIME	time			
TIMESTAMP	datetime2			
DATE	date			
CHAR	CHAR			
CHAR () FOR BIT DATA	BINARY			
VARCHAR	VARCHAR			
VARCHAR () FOR BIT DATA	VARBINARY			
LONG VARCHAR FOR BIT DATA	image			
LONG VARCHAR	text			
GRAPHIC	NCHAR			
VARGRAPHIC	NVARCHAR			
SMALLINT	SMALLINT			
INTEGER	INTEGER			
BIGINT	BIGINT			
DECIMAL	NUMERIC			
NUMERIC	NUMERIC			
REAL	REAL			
FLOAT	FLOAT			
DOUBLE	DOUBLE			
BLOB	image			
CLOB	text			
DBCLOB	ntext			

IBMDB2 to SSIS11

Table A-30. *IBMDB2 to SSIS11 Data Mapping*

Source Data Type	Destination Data Type	Length	Precision	Scale
TIME	DT_DBTIME2			
TIMESTAMP	DT_DBTIMESTAMP2			
DATE	DT_DBDATE	30		
CHAR	DT_STR			
CHAR () FOR BIT DATA	DT_BYTES			
VARCHAR	DT_STR			
VARCHAR () FOR BIT DATA	DT_BYTES			
LONG VARCHAR FOR BIT DATA	DT_IMAGE	255		
LONG VARCHAR	DT_TEXT	255		
GRAPHIC	DT_WSTR			
VARGRAPHIC	DT_WSTR			
SMALLINT	DT_I2	6		
INTEGER	DT_I4	11		
BIGINT	DT_I8	20		
DECIMAL	DT_NUMERIC	31		
NUMERIC	DT_NUMERIC	31		
REAL	DT_R4	24		
FLOAT	DT_R8	24		
DOUBLE	DT_R8	24		
BLOB	DT_IMAGE	255		
CLOB	DT_TEXT	255		
DBCLOB	DT_NTEXT	255		

Jet to MSSQL8

Table A-31. *Jet to MSSQL8 Data Mapping*

Source Data Type	Destination Data Type	Length	Precision	Scale
Short	smallint			
Long	int			
Single	real			
Double	float			
Currency	money			
Bit	bit			
Byte	tinyint			
GUID	uniqueidentifier			
BigBinary	binary			
LongBinary	image			
VarBinary	varbinary			
LongText	ntext			
VarChar	nvarchar			
Decimal	decimal			
DateTime	datetime			
Short	smallint			
Long	int			
Single	real			
Double	float			
Currency	money			
Bit	bit			
Byte	tinyint			
GUID	uniqueidentifier			
BigBinary	binary			
LongBinary	image			
VarBinary	varbinary			
LongText	nvarchar			
VarChar	nvarchar			
Decimal	decimal			
DateTime	datetime			

Jet to SSIS

Table A-32. *Jet to SSIS Data Mapping*

Source Data Type	Destination Data Type	Length	Precision	Scale
Short	DT_I2	6		
Long	DT_I4	11		
Single	DT_R4	24		
Double	DT_R8	24		
Currency	DT_CY	22		
Bit	DT_BOOL	10		
Byte	DT_UI1	3		
GUID	DT_GUID	39		
BigBinary	DT_BYTES			
LongBinary	DT_IMAGE	255		
VarBinary	DT_BYTES			
LongText	DT_NTEXT	255		
VarChar	DT_WSTR			
Decimal	DT_NUMERIC	31		
DateTime	DT_DBTIMESTAMP	30		

ACE to SSIS

Table A-33. *ACE to SSIS Data Mapping*

Source Data Type	Destination Data Type	Length	Precision	Scale
Short	DT_I2	6		
Long	DT_I4	11		
Single	DT_R4	24		
Double	DT_R8	24		
Currency	DT_CY	22		
Bit	DT_BOOL	10		
Byte	DT_UI1	3		
GUID	DT_GUID	39		
BigBinary	DT_BYTES			
LongBinary	DT_IMAGE	255		
VarBinary	DT_BYTES			
LongText	DT_NTEXT	255		
VarChar	DT_WSTR			
Decimal	DT_NUMERIC	31		
DateTime	DT_DBTIMESTAMP	30		

Excel to SQL Server and SSIS Data Mapping

Table A-34 presents the default data type mapping for importing data from Excel.

Table A-34. *Excel to SQL Server and SSIS Data Mapping*

Excel	SQL Server	SSIS
Numeric	FLOAT(53)	DT_R8
Currency	MONEY	DT_CY
Boolean	BIT	DT_BOOL
Date/Time	DATETIME	DT_DATE
String	NVARCHAR(255)	DT_WSTR
Memo	NVARCHAR(MAX)	DT_NTEXT

Access to SQL Server and SSIS Data Mapping

Table A-35 gives the default data type mapping for importing data from Access.

Table A-35. *Access to SQL Server and SSIS Data Mapping*

Access	SQL Server	SSIS
Text	NVARCHAR(255)	DT_WSTR
Memo	NVARCHAR(MAX)	DT_NTEXT
Number	FLOAT(53)	DT_R8
DateTime	DATETIME	DT_DATE
Currency	MONEY	DT_CY
Yes/No	BIT	DT_BOOL
OLEObject	Varbinary (MAX)	DT_IMAGE
Hyperlink	NVARCHAR(255)	DT_WSTR

Oracle to SQL Server and SSIS Data Mapping

This collection of data types includes data types that are deprecated, but that you can still find in older Oracle databases and need to import into SQL Server. They are given in Table A-36.

Table A-36. *Oracle to SQL Server and SSIS Data Mapping*

Oracle	SQL Server	SSIS	Comments
BFILE	VARBINARY(MAX)		An Oracle BFILE can be up to 4GB.
BLOB	VARBINARY(MAX)	DT_IMAGE	An Oracle BLOB can be > 2GB.
CHAR(n)	CHAR(n)	DT_STR	
CLOB	VARCHAR(MAX)	DT_NTEXT / DT_TEXT	An Oracle CLOB can be > 2GB.
DATE	DATETIME		
FLOAT	FLOAT	DT_R8	
FLOAT([1–53])	FLOAT([1–53])	DT_R8	
BINARY_FLOAT			
BINARY_DOUBLE	FLOAT(53)		
INT	NUMERIC(38)	DT_NUMERIC	
INTERVAL	DATETIME		
LONG	VARCHAR(MAX)	DT_NTEXT / DT_TEXT	2GB limit in both databases.
LONG RAW	VARBINARY(MAX)	DT_IMAGE	2GB limit in both databases.

(continued)

Table A-36. (*continued*)

Oracle	SQL Server	SSIS	Comments
NCHAR	NCHAR	DT_WSTR	
NCLOB	NVARCHAR(MAX)	DT_NTEXT	An Oracle NCLOB can be > 2GB.
NUMBER	NUMERIC	DT_R8 ??	
NUMBER([1–38])	NUMERIC([1–38])	DT_NUMERIC	
NUMBER(3)	TINYINT	DT_UI1	If the greatest value is 255 or less; else use TINYINT.
NUMBER(5)	SMALLINT	DT_I2	If the data range is between –32768 and 32767; else use INT.
NUMBER(10)	INT	DT_I4	If the data range is between–2,147,483,648 and 2,147,483,647; else use BIGINT.
NVARCHAR2	NVARCHAR	DT_WSTR	Both databases have a 4000-byte limit.
RAW	VARBINARY	DT_BYTES	
REAL	FLOAT		
ROWID	CHAR(18)	DT_STR	
TIMESTAMP	DATETIME	DT_DBTIMESTAMP	If the data range is between January 1, 1753 and December 31, 9999; else VARCHAR(n)—the actual length will depend on the fractional seconds' precision.
UROWID	CHAR(18)	DT_STR	
VARCHAR2	VARCHAR	DT_STR	Both databases have a 4000-byte limit.

If you know that the range of dates or numbers used will map to a specific SQL Server data type, then you can map a NUMBER(3) to a TINYINT, for example. If you are not sure, then always map to a larger data type to avoid load failure.

Oracle to SQL Server Replication Data Type Mapping

A very slightly different data mapping is used by the Oracle to SQL Server process. You might find it useful. It's provided in Table A-37.

Table A-37. *Oracle to SQL Server Replication Data Mapping*

Oracle Data Type	SQL Server Data Type
BFILE	VARBINARY(MAX)
BLOB	VARBINARY(MAX)
CHAR([1–2000])	CHAR([1–2000])
CLOB	VARCHAR(MAX)
DATE	DATETIME
FLOAT	FLOAT
FLOAT([1–53])	FLOAT([1–53])
FLOAT([54–126])	FLOAT
INT	NUMERIC(38)
INTERVAL	DATETIME
LONG	VARCHAR(MAX)
LONG RAW	IMAGE
NCHAR([1–1000])	NCHAR([1–1000])
NCLOB	NVARCHAR(MAX)
NUMBER	FLOAT
NUMBER([1–38])	NUMERIC([1–38])
NUMBER([0–38],[1–38])	NUMERIC([0–38],[1–38])
NVARCHAR2([1–2000])	NVARCHAR([1–2000])
RAW([1–2000])	VARBINARY([1–2000])
REAL	FLOAT
ROWID	CHAR(18)
TIMESTAMP	DATETIME
TIMESTAMP(0–7)	DATETIME
TIMESTAMP(8–9)	DATETIME
TIMESTAMP(0–7) WITH TIME ZONE	VARCHAR(37)
TIMESTAMP(8–9) WITH TIME ZONE	VARCHAR(37)
TIMESTAMP(0–7) WITH LOCAL TIME ZONE	VARCHAR(37)
TIMESTAMP(8–9) WITH LOCAL TIME ZONE	VARCHAR(37)
UROWID	CHAR(18)
VARCHAR2([1–4000])	VARCHAR([1–4000])

MySQL Data Types

The best guide to MySQL to SQL Server data type mapping is the Microsoftwhitepaper *Guide to Migrating from MySQL to SQL Server 2008* (www.microsoft.com/en-us/download/details.aspx?id=24662). Although not (yet) updated for SQL Server2012, it is an invaluable resource.

Sybase to SQL Server Data Type Conversion

The best guide to Sybase to SQL Server data type mapping is in the Microsoft whitepaper *Guide to Migrating from Sybase ASE to SQL Server 2008* (www.microsoft.com/en-us/download/details.aspx?id=24662). Although not (yet) updated for SQL Server2012, it is avitalresource.

■ ■ ■

Sample Databases and Scripts

Sample Databases and Files

As I stated in the introduction, I prefer to use a different set of sample databases than the evergreen AdventureWorks, as the latter is possibly too complex to illustrate data integration processes simply and clearly. The database schema that I propose is extremely simple and very lightweight. Indeed, it will result in the tiniest data loads that you have ever met. However, as reality is likely to compensate for this in your day job, I hope that no one minds too much.

The sample data consists of five databases:

Database	Description
CarSales	The main database. Sometimes used as source data.
CarSales_Staging	The database used for staging processes and as a source for SQL Server data.
CarSales_DW	A dimensional database for loading data into an SSAS cube.
CarSales_Logging	A separate database for logging and auditing ETL processes.
CarSales_Cube	An SSAS database that is a source of dimensional data.

These databases—along with all other sample files used in this book—are in the SQL2012DIRecipes.Zip file, which is available at www.apress.com/9781430247913. Simply click the tab labeled "Source Code/Downloads" about midway down the page to download the file. Then uncompress it with your preferred utility. Make sure that you keep the underlying directory structure.

CarSales

The main database used is the CarSales database. It consists of six tables:

- Client
- Colors
- Countries
- Invoice
- Invoice_Lines
- Stock

The design was chosen because it covers just about every SQL Server data type and has a minimum of referential integrity to simulate a real-world environment.

The C:\SQLDIRecipes\Backups folder (assuming that you have downloaded the examples from the book's web site) contains the following files:

CarSales.Bak   The CarSales database backup file.

CarSales_Staging.Bak   The CarSales_Staging database backup file.

CarSales_DW.Bak   The CarSales_DW database backup file.

CarSales_Cube.abf   The CarSales_Cube SSAS database backup file.

CarSales_Logging.Bak   The CarSales_Logging database backup file.

Creating the CarSales Database

The CarSales database can be created using the following script
(C:\SQLDIRecipes\Databases\CarSalesDatabaseCreation.Sql):

```
USE master
GO
CREATE DATABASE CarSales
 CONTAINMENT = NONE
 ON  PRIMARY
     (NAME = N'CarSales', FILENAME = N'C:\SQLDIRecipes\Databases\CarSales.mdf',
      SIZE = 33792KB , MAXSIZE = UNLIMITED, FILEGROWTH = 1024KB )
LOG ON
     (NAME = N'CarSales_log', FILENAME = N'C:\SQLDIRecipes\Databases\CarSales_log.ldf',
      SIZE = 4224KB , MAXSIZE = 2048GB , FILEGROWTH = 10%)
GO

ALTER DATABASE CarSales SET COMPATIBILITY_LEVEL = 110
GO
ALTER DATABASE CarSales SET QUOTED_IDENTIFIER OFF
GO
ALTER DATABASE CarSales SET RECOVERY SIMPLE
GO
ALTER DATABASE CarSales SET  READ_WRITE
GO
```

If the database exists, it can be dropped using the following script:
(C:\SQLDIRecipes\Databases\DropDatabase.Sql)

```
IF db_id('CarSales') IS NOT NULL
DROP DATABASE CarSales;
GO
```

■ **Note**   You can use this script for any of the supplied relational databases simply by changing the database name to that of the database that you wish to drop.

The CarSales tables can be created using the following script. Remember to begin with USE DATABASE and the name of the required database, which should be either CarSales or CarSales_Staging (C:\SQLDIRecipes\Databases\.Sql):

```
USE CarSales;
GO

If OBJECT_ID('dbo.Client') IS NOT NULL DROP TABLE dbo.Client

CREATE TABLE dbo.Client
(
 ID int IDENTITY(1,1) NOT NULL,
 ClientName NVARCHAR(150) NULL,
 Address1 VARCHAR(50) NULL,
 Address2 VARCHAR(50) NULL,
 Town VARCHAR(50) NULL,
 County VARCHAR(50) NULL,
 PostCode VARCHAR(10) NULL,
 Country TINYINT NULL,
 ClientType VARCHAR(20) NULL,
 ClientSize VARCHAR(10) NULL,
 ClientSince SMALLDATETIME NULL,
 IsCreditWorthy BIT NULL,
 DealerGroup HIERARCHYID NULL,
 MapPosition GEOGRAPHY NULL
) ;
GO

If OBJECT_ID('dbo.Colours ') IS NOT NULL DROP TABLE dbo.Colours

CREATE TABLE dbo.Colours
(
 ColourID TINYINT NOT NULL,
 Colour NVARCHAR(50) NULL
) ;
GO

CREATE TABLE dbo.Countries
(
 CountryID TINYINT NOT NULL,
 CountryName_EN NVARCHAR(50) NULL,
 CountryName_Local NVARCHAR(50) NULL
) ;
GO

If OBJECT_ID('dbo.Invoice ') IS NOT NULL DROP TABLE dbo.Invoice

CREATE TABLE dbo.Invoice
(
 ID int IDENTITY(1,1) NOT NULL,
 InvoiceNumber NVARCHAR(50) NOT NULL CONSTRAINT DF_Invoice_InvoiceNumber  DEFAULT (newid()),
 ClientID INT NULL,
```

```
 InvoiceDate DATETIME NULL,
 TotalDiscount NUMERIC(18, 2) NULL,
 DeliveryCharge SMALLMONEY NULL
) ;
GO


If OBJECT_ID('dbo.Invoice_Lines ') IS NOT NULL DROP TABLE dbo.Invoice_Lines

CREATE TABLE dbo.Invoice_Lines
(
 ID int IDENTITY(1,1) NOT NULL,
 InvoiceID INT NULL,
 StockID BIGINT NULL,
 SalePrice MONEY NULL,
 Timestamp TIMESTAMP NULL,
 HashData  AS
     (hashbytes('SHA1',((((CONVERT(varchar(20),InvoiceID)+CONVERT(varchar(20),StockID))
     +CONVERT(varchar(20),isnull(SalePrice,(0))))
     +CONVERT(varchar(20),isnull(DateUpdated,'2000-01-01')))
     +CONVERT(varchar(20),isnull(LineItem,(0))))))),
 DateUpdated DATETIME2(0) NULL,
 LineItem SMALLINT NULL
)
GO


If OBJECT_ID('dbo.Stock ') IS NOT NULL DROP TABLE dbo.Stock

CREATE TABLE dbo.Stock
(
 ID bigint IDENTITY(1,1) NOT NULL,
 Make VARCHAR(50) NULL,
 Marque NVARCHAR(50) NULL,
 Model VARCHAR(50) NULL,
 Colour TINYINT NULL,
 Product_Type VARCHAR(50) NULL,
 Vehicle_Type VARCHAR(20) NULL,
 Cost_Price NUMERIC(18, 2) NULL,
 Registration_Date DATE NULL,
 CarPhoto VARBINARY(max) NULL,
 CarPhotoType VARCHAR(5) NULL,
 CarPhotoDirectory VARCHAR(150) NULL,
 CarDocumentation NVARCHAR(max) NULL,
 IndustryDefinition XML NULL,
 DateReserved DATETIME2(7) NULL,
 Weight float NULL,
 Mileage NUMERIC(32, 4) NULL,
 Chassis UNIQUEIDENTIFIER NULL CONSTRAINT DF_Stock_Chassis  DEFAULT (newid())
) ;
GO
```

Here is the script that you can use to create primary keys in the CarSales database
(C:\SQLDIRecipes\Databases\CarSalesCreatePrimaryKeys.Sql):

```
USE CarSales;
GO

If OBJECT_ID('PK_Client') IS NULL
BEGIN
ALTER TABLE dbo.Client ADD CONSTRAINT PK_Client PRIMARY KEY CLUSTERED
(ID ASC) WITH (PAD_INDEX = OFF, STATISTICS_NORECOMPUTE = OFF, IGNORE_DUP_KEY = OFF,
ALLOW_ROW_LOCKS = ON, ALLOW_PAGE_LOCKS = ON) ;
END

If OBJECT_ID('PK_Colours') IS NULL
BEGIN
ALTER TABLE dbo.Colours ADD CONSTRAINT PK_Colours PRIMARY KEY CLUSTERED
(ColourID ASC) WITH (PAD_INDEX = OFF, STATISTICS_NORECOMPUTE = OFF, IGNORE_DUP_KEY = OFF,
ALLOW_ROW_LOCKS = ON, ALLOW_PAGE_LOCKS = ON) ;
END

If OBJECT_ID('PK_Countries') IS NULL
BEGIN
ALTER TABLE dbo.Countries ADD CONSTRAINT PK_Countries PRIMARY KEY CLUSTERED
(CountryID ASC) WITH (PAD_INDEX = OFF, STATISTICS_NORECOMPUTE = OFF, IGNORE_DUP_KEY = OFF,
ALLOW_ROW_LOCKS = ON, ALLOW_PAGE_LOCKS = ON) ;
END

If OBJECT_ID('PK_Invoice') IS NULL
BEGIN
ALTER TABLE dbo.Invoice ADD CONSTRAINT PK_Invoice PRIMARY KEY CLUSTERED
(ID ASC) WITH (PAD_INDEX = OFF, STATISTICS_NORECOMPUTE = OFF, IGNORE_DUP_KEY = OFF,
ALLOW_ROW_LOCKS = ON, ALLOW_PAGE_LOCKS = ON) ;
END

If OBJECT_ID('PK_Invoice_Lines') IS NULL
BEGIN
ALTER TABLE dbo.Invoice_Lines ADD CONSTRAINT PK_Invoice_Lines PRIMARY KEY CLUSTERED
(ID ASC) WITH (PAD_INDEX = OFF, STATISTICS_NORECOMPUTE = OFF, IGNORE_DUP_KEY = OFF,
ALLOW_ROW_LOCKS = ON, ALLOW_PAGE_LOCKS = ON) ;
END

If OBJECT_ID('PK_Stock') IS NULL
BEGIN
ALTER TABLE dbo.Stock ADD CONSTRAINT PK_Stock PRIMARY KEY CLUSTERED
(ID ASC) WITH (PAD_INDEX = OFF, STATISTICS_NORECOMPUTE = OFF, IGNORE_DUP_KEY = OFF,
ALLOW_ROW_LOCKS = ON, ALLOW_PAGE_LOCKS = ON) ;
END

GO
```

You also have the following script to create foreign keys in the CarSales database
(C:\SQLDIRecipes\Databases\CarSalesCreateForeignKeys.Sql):

```
USE CarSales;
GO

If OBJECT_ID('FK_Client_Countries') IS NULL
ALTER TABLE dbo.Client  WITH CHECK ADD CONSTRAINT FK_Client_Countries FOREIGN KEY(Country)
REFERENCES dbo.Countries (CountryID);
ALTER TABLE dbo.Client CHECK CONSTRAINT FK_Client_Countries;

If OBJECT_ID('FK_Invoice_Client') IS NULL
ALTER TABLE dbo.Invoice  WITH CHECK ADD CONSTRAINT FK_Invoice_Client FOREIGN KEY(ClientID)
REFERENCES dbo.Client (ID);
ALTER TABLE dbo.Invoice CHECK CONSTRAINT FK_Invoice_Client;

If OBJECT_ID('FK_Invoice_Lines_Invoice') IS NULL
ALTER TABLE dbo.Invoice_Lines  WITH NOCHECK ADD CONSTRAINT FK_Invoice_Lines_Invoice FOREIGN
KEY(InvoiceID) REFERENCES dbo.Invoice (ID);
ALTER TABLE dbo.Invoice_Lines CHECK CONSTRAINT FK_Invoice_Lines_Invoice;

If OBJECT_ID('FK_Invoice_Lines_Stock') IS NULL
ALTER TABLE dbo.Invoice_Lines  WITH NOCHECK ADD CONSTRAINT FK_Invoice_Lines_Stock FOREIGN
KEY(StockID) REFERENCES dbo.Stock (ID);
ALTER TABLE dbo.Invoice_Lines CHECK CONSTRAINT FK_Invoice_Lines_Stock;

If OBJECT_ID('FK_Stock_Colours') IS NULL
ALTER TABLE dbo.Stock  WITH CHECK ADD  CONSTRAINT FK_Stock_Colours FOREIGN KEY(Colour)
REFERENCES dbo.Colours (ColourID);
ALTER TABLE dbo.Stock CHECK CONSTRAINT FK_Stock_Colours;

GO
```

The following is the script to drop all primary keys (C:\SQLDIRecipes\Databases\DropPrimaryKeys.Sql):

```
USE CarSales;
GO

If OBJECT_ID('PK_Client') IS NOT NULL ALTER TABLE dbo.Client
DROP CONSTRAINT PK_Client;
If OBJECT_ID('PK_Colours') IS NOT NULL ALTER TABLE dbo.Colours
DROP CONSTRAINT PK_Colours;
If OBJECT_ID('PK_Countries') IS NOT NULL ALTER TABLE dbo.Countries
DROP CONSTRAINT PK_Countries;
```

```
If OBJECT_ID('PK_Invoice') IS NOT NULL ALTER TABLE dbo.Invoice
DROP CONSTRAINT PK_Invoice;
If OBJECT_ID('PK_Invoice_Lines') IS NOT NULL ALTER TABLE dbo.Invoice_Lines
DROP CONSTRAINT PK_Invoice_Lines;
If OBJECT_ID('PK_Stock') IS NOT NULL ALTER TABLE dbo.Stock
DROP CONSTRAINT PK_Stock;
GO
```

Should you need it, here is the script to drop foreign keys from the CarSales database (C:\SQLDIRecipes\Databases\DropForeignKeys.Sql):

```
USE CarSales;
GO


If OBJECT_ID('FK_Client_Countries') IS NOT NULL
ALTER TABLE dbo.Client DROP CONSTRAINT FK_Client_Countries;
If OBJECT_ID('FK_Invoice_Client') IS NOT NULL
ALTER TABLE dbo.Invoice DROP CONSTRAINT FK_Invoice_Client;
If OBJECT_ID('FK_Invoice_Lines_Invoice') IS NOT NULL
ALTER TABLE dbo.Invoice_Lines DROP CONSTRAINT FK_Invoice_Lines_Invoice;
If OBJECT_ID('FK_Invoice_Lines_Stock') IS NOT NULL
ALTER TABLE dbo.Invoice_Lines DROP CONSTRAINT FK_Invoice_Lines_Stock;
If OBJECT_ID('FK_Stock_Colours') IS NOT NULL
ALTER TABLE dbo.Stock DROP CONSTRAINT FK_Stock_Colours;
GO
```

Here too is a script to remove data from the CarSales database (C:\SQLDIRecipes\Databases\RemoveCarSalesData.Sql):

```
USE CarSales;
GO


DELETE FROM CarSales.dbo.Invoice_Lines;
DELETE FROM CarSales.dbo.Stock;
DELETE FROM CarSales.dbo.Colours;
DELETE FROM CarSales.dbo.Invoice;
DELETE FROM CarSales.dbo.Client;
DELETE FROM CarSales.dbo.Countries;

GO
```

The CarSales database schema looks like Figure B-1.

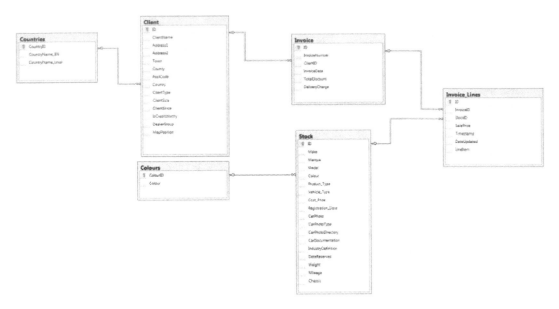

Figure B-1. *The CarSales database*

CarSales_Staging

This database is essentially a "scratchpad" for testing loading techniques as well as database-to-database loads. The core tables are the same as those in the CarSales database—but without any primary or foreign keys. Other tables can be created as required by a recipe. This database can be created using the following script (C:\SQLDIRecipes\Databases\CarSales_StagingDatabaseCreation.Sql):

```
USE master
GO

IF db_id('CarSales_Staging') IS NOT NULL
DROP DATABASE CarSales_Staging';
GO

CREATE DATABASE CarSales_Staging
 CONTAINMENT = NONE
 ON  PRIMARY
( NAME = N'CarSales_Staging', FILENAME = N'C:\SQLDIRecipes\Databases\CarSales_Staging.mdf' ,
SIZE = 33792KB , MAXSIZE = UNLIMITED, FILEGROWTH = 1024KB )
 LOG ON
( NAME = N'CarSales_Staging_log', FILENAME =
N'C:\SQLDIRecipes\Databases\CarSales_Staging_log.ldf' , SIZE = 4224KB , MAXSIZE = 2048GB ,
FILEGROWTH = 10%)
GO
ALTER DATABASE CarSales_Staging SET COMPATIBILITY_LEVEL = 110
GO
ALTER DATABASE CarSales_Staging SET QUOTED_IDENTIFIER OFF
GO
```

```
ALTER DATABASE CarSales_Staging SET RECOVERY SIMPLE
GO
ALTER DATABASE CarSales_Staging SET  READ_WRITE
GO
```

CarSales_DW

The CarSales_DW database is a dimensional structure based on the CarSales database, which feeds into the CarSales cube. It contains the following tables:

- Dim_Clients

- Dim_Geography

- Dim_Products

- Fact_Sales

The database looks like Figure B-2.

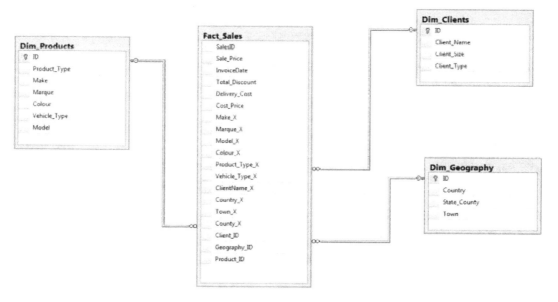

Figure B-2. *The CarSales_DW database*

The code to create the CarSales_DW database is:
(C:\SQLDIRecipes\Databases\CarSales_DWDatabaseCreation.Sql)

```
USE master
GO

IF db_id('CarSales_DW') IS NOT NULL
DROP DATABASE CarSales_DW';
GO
```

```
CREATE DATABASE CarSales_DW
 CONTAINMENT = NONE
 ON  PRIMARY
( NAME = N'CarSales_DW', FILENAME = N'C:\SQLDIRecipes\Databases\CarSales_DW.mdf' , SIZE =
33792KB , MAXSIZE = UNLIMITED, FILEGROWTH = 1024KB )
 LOG ON
( NAME = N'CarSales_DW_log', FILENAME = N'C:\SQLDIRecipes\Databases\CarSales_DW_log.ldf' , SIZE
= 4224KB , MAXSIZE = 2048GB , FILEGROWTH = 10%)
GO
ALTER DATABASE CarSales_DW SET COMPATIBILITY_LEVEL = 110
GO
ALTER DATABASE CarSales_DW SET QUOTED_IDENTIFIER OFF
GO
ALTER DATABASE CarSales_DW SET RECOVERY SIMPLE
GO
ALTER DATABASE CarSales_DW SET  READ_WRITE
GO
USE CarSales_DW
GO

CREATE TABLE dbo.Fact_Sales
(
 SalesID int IDENTITY(1,1) NOT NULL,
 Sale_Price numeric(18, 2) NULL,
 InvoiceDate datetime NULL,
 Total_Discount numeric(18, 2) NULL,
 Delivery_Cost numeric(18, 2) NULL,
 Cost_Price decimal(18, 2) NULL,
 Make_X nvarchar(50) NULL,
 Marque_X nvarchar(50) NULL,
 Model_X nvarchar(50) NULL,
 Colour_X nvarchar(50) NULL,
 Product_Type_X nvarchar(50) NULL,
 Vehicle_Type_X nvarchar(50) NULL,
 ClientName_X nvarchar(150) NULL,
 Country_X varchar(50) NULL,
 Town_X nvarchar(50) NULL,
 County_X nvarchar(50) NULL,
 Client_ID int NULL,
 Geography_ID int NULL,
 Product_ID int NULL
) ;
GO

CREATE TABLE dbo.Dim_Products
(
 ID int IDENTITY(1,1) NOT NULL,
 Product_Type nvarchar(50) NULL,
 Make nvarchar(50) NULL,
 Marque nvarchar(50) NULL,
 Colour nvarchar(50) NULL,
```

982

```
 Vehicle_Type nvarchar(50) NULL,
 Model nvarchar(50) NULL,
 CONSTRAINT PK_Dim_Products PRIMARY KEY CLUSTERED
(
        ID ASC
)WITH (PAD_INDEX  = OFF, STATISTICS_NORECOMPUTE  = OFF, IGNORE_DUP_KEY = OFF, ALLOW_ROW_LOCKS  =
ON, ALLOW_PAGE_LOCKS  = ON) ON PRIMARY
) ;
GO


CREATE TABLE dbo.Dim_Geography
(
 ID int IDENTITY(1,1) NOT NULL,
 Country nvarchar(50) NULL,
 State_County nvarchar(50) NULL,
 Town nvarchar(50) NULL,
 CONSTRAINT PK_Dim_Geography PRIMARY KEY CLUSTERED
(
        ID ASC
)WITH (PAD_INDEX  = OFF, STATISTICS_NORECOMPUTE  = OFF, IGNORE_DUP_KEY = OFF, ALLOW_ROW_LOCKS  =
ON, ALLOW_PAGE_LOCKS  = ON) ON PRIMARY
) ;
GO


CREATE TABLE dbo.Dim_Clients
(
 ID int IDENTITY(1,1) NOT NULL,
 Client_Name nvarchar(150) NULL,
 Client_Size varchar(10) NULL,
 Client_Type varchar(10) NULL,
 CONSTRAINT PK_Dim_Clients PRIMARY KEY CLUSTERED
(
        ID ASC
)WITH (PAD_INDEX  = OFF, STATISTICS_NORECOMPUTE  = OFF, IGNORE_DUP_KEY = OFF, ALLOW_ROW_LOCKS  =
ON, ALLOW_PAGE_LOCKS  = ON) ON PRIMARY
) ;
GO
```

This database has a stored procedure (dbo. pr_FillDW), which takes data from the CarSales database and uses it to populate the CarSales_DW database (C:\SQLDIRecipes\Databases\CarSales_FillDW.Sql).

```
CREATE procedure dbo.pr_FillDW

AS


-- Geography

TRUNCATE TABLE dbo.Dim_Geography
```

```
INSERT INTO dbo.Dim_Geography
(
Country
,State_County
,Town
)

SELECT DISTINCT
C.CountryName_EN
,L.County
,L.Town

FROM              CarSales_Book.dbo.Countries C
                  INNER JOIN   CarSales_Book.dbo.Client L
                  ON           C.CountryID = L.Country

-- Clients

TRUNCATE TABLE dbo.Dim_Clients

INSERT INTO dbo.Dim_Clients
(
Client_Name
,Client_Size
,Client_Type
)

SELECT DISTINCT   ClientName, ClientSize, ClientType
FROM              CarSales_Book.dbo.Client


-- Products

TRUNCATE TABLE dbo.Dim_Products

INSERT INTO dbo.Dim_Products
(
Product_Type
,Make
,Marque
,Model
,Colour
,Vehicle_Type
)

SELECT DISTINCT   S.Product_Type, S.Make, S.Marque, S.Model, C.Colour, S.Vehicle_Type
FROM              CarSales_Book.dbo.Colours C
                  INNER JOIN   CarSales_Book.dbo.Stock S
                  ON           C.ColourID = S.Colour
-- Fact table
```

```
TRUNCATE TABLE dbo.Fact_Sales

INSERT INTO dbo.Fact_Sales
(
Sale_Price
,InvoiceDate
,Total_Discount
,Delivery_Cost
,Cost_Price
,Make_X
,Marque_X
,Model_X
,Colour_X
,Product_Type_X
,Vehicle_Type_X
,ClientName_X
,Country_X
,Town_X
,County_X
)

SELECT DISTINCT
L.SalePrice, I.InvoiceDate, I.TotalDiscount, I.DeliveryCharge, S.Cost_Price, S.Make,
S.Marque, S.Model, C.Colour, S.Product_Type, S.Vehicle_Type, CL.ClientName, CR.CountryName_EN,
CL.Town, CL.County

FROM        CarSales_Book.dbo.Colours C
            INNER JOIN    CarSales_Book.dbo.Stock S
            ON            C.ColourID = S.Colour
            INNER JOIN    CarSales_Book.dbo.Invoice_Lines L
            ON            S.ID = L.StockID
            INNER JOIN    CarSales_Book.dbo.Invoice I
            ON            L.InvoiceID = I.ID
            INNER JOIN    CarSales_Book.dbo.Client CL
            ON            I.ClientID = CL.ID
            INNER JOIN    CarSales_Book.dbo.Countries CR
            ON            CL.Country = CR.CountryID


-- Set GeographyID

UPDATE      F

SET         F.Geography_ID = G.ID

FROM        dbo.Fact_Sales F
            INNER JOIN    dbo.Dim_Geography G
            ON            F.Country_X = G.Country
            AND           F.County_X = G.State_County
            AND           F.Town_X = G.Town
```

985

```
-- Set ProductID

UPDATE          F

SET             F.Product_ID = P.ID

FROM            dbo.Fact_Sales F
                INNER JOIN    dbo.Dim_Products P
                ON            F.Product_Type_X = P.Product_Type
                AND           F.Make_X = P.Make
                AND           F.Marque_X = P.Marque
                AND           F.Model_X = P.Model
                AND           F.Vehicle_Type_X = P.Vehicle_Type


-- Set Client ID

UPDATE          F

SET             F.Client_ID = C.ID

FROM            dbo.Fact_Sales F
                INNER JOIN    dbo.Dim_Clients C
                ON            F.ClientName_X = C.Client_Name
GO
```

The CarSales SSAS Cube

This is, to all intents and purposes, identical to the CarSales_DW database in structure. It consists of:

Sales: The core (and only) fact table.

Products: The Products dimension.

Clients: The Clients dimension.

Geography: The Geography dimension.

There is no time dimension, as the objective here is to allow data export, not to explain cubed development.

Restoring the CarSales_Cube SSAS Database

The CarSales_Cube database can be restored using the script
(C:\SQLDIRecipes\Databases\CarSales_CubeDatabaseRestore.Mdx). The XMLA for restoring this Analysis
Services database is truly too long to be reproduced here—but you will find it on the book's web site.

CarSales_Logging

The CarSales_Logging database is a very simple database that holds the logging and auditing tables used in
Chapter 15. It contains no tables initially—the tables that you choose to use depend on the recipe(s) that you
choose to follow. The code to create the database is
(C:\SQLDIRecipes\Databases\CarSales_LoggingDatabaseCreation.Sql):

```
USE master
GO

IF db_id('CarSales_Logging') IS NOT NULL
DROP DATABASE CarSales_Logging';
GO

CREATE DATABASE CarSales_Logging
 CONTAINMENT = NONE
 ON  PRIMARY
( NAME = N'CarSales_Logging', FILENAME = N'C:\SQLDIRecipes\Databases\CarSales_Logging.mdf' ,
SIZE = 33792KB , MAXSIZE = UNLIMITED, FILEGROWTH = 1024KB )
 LOG ON
( NAME = N'CarSales_Logging_log', FILENAME =
N'C:\SQLDIRecipes\Databases\CarSales_Logging_log.ldf' , SIZE = 4224KB , MAXSIZE = 2048GB ,
FILEGROWTH = 10%)
GO
ALTER DATABASE CarSales_Logging SET COMPATIBILITY_LEVEL = 110
GO
ALTER DATABASE CarSales_Logging SET QUOTED_IDENTIFIER OFF
GO
ALTER DATABASE CarSales_Logging SET RECOVERY SIMPLE
GO
ALTER DATABASE CarSales_Logging SET  READ_WRITE
GO
```

Directory Structure for the Sample Files

The directory structure of the files in the SQL2012DIRecipes.Zip file is provided in Table B-1.

Table B-1. *The Directory Structure for the Sample Files*

Folder	Description
C:\SQL2012DIRecipes\CH01	Sample files for Chapter 1.
C:\SQL2012DIRecipes\CH02	Sample files for Chapter 2.
C:\SQL2012DIRecipes\CH03	Sample files for Chapter 3.
C:\SQL2012DIRecipes\CH04	Sample files for Chapter 4.
C:\SQL2012DIRecipes\CH05	Sample files for Chapter 5.
C:\SQL2012DIRecipes\CH06	Sample files for Chapter 6.
C:\SQL2012DIRecipes\CH07	Sample files for Chapter 7.
C:\SQL2012DIRecipes\CH08	Sample files for Chapter 8.
C:\SQL2012DIRecipes\CH09	Sample files for Chapter 9.
C:\SQL2012DIRecipes\CH10	Sample files for Chapter 10.
C:\SQL2012DIRecipes\CH11	Sample files for Chapter 11.
C:\SQL2012DIRecipes\CH12	Sample files for Chapter 12
C:\SQL2012DIRecipes\CH13	Sample files for Chapter 13.
C:\SQL2012DIRecipes\CH13\MoreMultipleFlatFiles	Sample files for Chapter 13.
C:\SQL2012DIRecipes\CH13\MultipleFlatFiles	Sample files for Chapter 13.
C:\SQL2012DIRecipes\CH14	Sample files for Chapter 14.
C:\SQL2012DIRecipes\CH15	Sample files for Chapter 15.
C:\SQL2012DIRecipes\Databases	Where the database files (.mdf and .ldf) are stored.
C:\SQL2012DIRecipes\DatabaseScripts	Scripts to create the databases and SSAS cube.

Index

▨ F, G, H, I, J, K

■ O, P, Q, R

■ S

CPSIA information can be obtained at www.ICGtesting.com
Printed in the USA
LVOW052048221112

308396LV00001B/1/P